BF 3   2013

Fifth Edition

A HISTORY OF PSYCHOLOGY

IDEAS AND CONTEXT

D. Brett King
University of Colorado at Boulder

William Douglas Woody
University of Northern Colorado

Wayne Viney
Colorado State University

PEARSON

Boston   Columbus   Indianapolis   New York   San Francisco   Upper Saddle River
Amsterdam   Cape Town   Dubai   London   Madrid   Milan   Munich   Paris   Montréal   Toronto
Delhi   Mexico City   São Paulo   Sydney   Hong Kong   Seoul   Singapore   Taipei   Tokyo

Editor in Chief: Ashley Dodge
Acquisitions Editor: Susan Hartman
Editorial Assistant: Amandria Guadalupe
Director of Marketing: Brandy Dawson
Executive Marketing Manager: Kelly May
Marketing Coordinator: Courtney Stewart
Managing Editor: Denise Forlow
Program Manager: Reena Dalal
Project Manager: Alyssa Guarino
Senior Operations Supervisor: Mary Fischer
Operations Specialist: Diane Peirano

Art Director: Jayne Conte
Cover Designer: Suzanne Behnke
Cover Image: Shutterstock
Director of Digital Media: Brian Hyland
Digital Media Editor: Learning Mate Solutions, Ltd.
Digital Media Project Manager: Tina Gagliostro
Full-Service Project Management and Composition:
  Anju Joshi, PreMediaGlobal
Printer/Binder: STP Courier
Cover Printer: STP Courier
Text Font: 10/12 Times LT Std

Credits and acknowledgments borrowed from other sources and reproduced, with permission, in this textbook appear on page 536.

Library of Congress Cataloging-in-Publication Data
Viney, Wayne.
  A history of psychology : ideas and context / D. Brett King, University of Colorado at Boulder, William Douglas Woody, University of Northern Colorado, Wayne Viney, Colorado State University.—Fifth edition.
    pages cm
  Includes bibliographical references and index.
  ISBN-13: 978-0-205-96304-1
  ISBN-10: 0-205-96304-8
  1. Psychology—Philosophy—History. 2. Psychology—History. I. King, D. Brett. II. Woody, William Douglas. III. Title.
  BF38.V56 2014
  150.9—dc23   2013023112

10 9 8 7 6 5 4 3 2 1

ISBN 10: 0-205-96304-8
ISBN 13: 978-0-205-96304-1

Dedication

To Michael Wertheimer—a mentor for the three of us who has served as a continuing inspiration

To Donald A. Crosby—a consummate scholar and authority on William James who has deeply influenced our work

And to

Cheri King who has been active in every phase of this work from the first to the fifth edition

Lisa Woody for her enthusiasm, support, and encouragement

Finally

In loving memory of Wynona Rose Viney

CONTENTS

PREFACE

A History of Psychology: Ideas and Context, first published by Allyn & Bacon in 1993, was written for all who are interested in psychology and its history. The first four editions included numerous distinctive features preserved and amplified in this fifth edition. However, a number of substantial revisions have been necessary as a means of updating the book to include recent historical scholarship and enhanced pedagogical techniques.

As with previous editions, this text strives for comprehensive examples of psychological thought from ancient Eastern and Western cultures, the Roman Empire, the Middle Ages, and the Renaissance. In the modern world, from about 1600, the focus is on intellectual traditions that contributed to the formal founding of psychology as an independent discipline. These traditions include rational and empirical philosophies, advances in physiology, new quantitative techniques, evolutionary theory, naturalistic approaches to emotional problems, and significant humanitarian reform movements in the nineteenth century. The text provides in-depth coverage of the intellectual trends that followed psychology's formal founding in the late 1870s, based on an analysis of the major systems of thought and key developments in basic and applied psychology. The final chapter focuses on major trends in scientific and professional psychology from the latter half of the twentieth century to the early twenty-first century.

The book opens with a brief chapter on historiography that explores selected philosophical issues pertinent to disciplinary histories: What are the origins of historical consciousness? What is history? Why study history? Is there a pattern in history? Can history be objective? We believe that discussions of such questions result in more critical, appreciative, and informed readers who think not only about historical content, but also about the complex methodological tasks confronting the historian.

Chapter 2 introduces and explains enduring philosophical problems encountered throughout the history of psychology: Do humans have free will? What are the methods by which we make truth claims? What is an explanation? What is science? What is the subject matter of psychology? We have found that the history of psychology is more meaningful to students who have a working knowledge of the classic positions on

fundamental philosophical problems. A careful reading of the materials in Chapter 2 will clarify and lend richness to topics encountered in subsequent chapters.

Like many texts, this book presents examples of psychological thought encountered in documents from ancient cultures. Typically, the Greek and Roman periods are covered, but this book adds two critical features to the section on ancient thought: First, psychological contributions of important early women such as Theana, Myia, Aesara, and Hypatia are included. Second, in addition to reviewing the usual materials from the Greek and Roman periods, this text provides overviews of psychological thought from ancient Chinese, Indian, Babylonian, Persian, Egyptian, and Hebraic cultures. This emphasis on the broad scope of psychological thought is continued in later chapters that include contributions of Arab scholars such as Avicenna and Rhazes, Spanish scholars such as Juan Luis Vives and Juan Huarte, and neglected scholars such as Oliva Sabuco and Héloise.

The chapter on the Renaissance includes a consideration of medical, economic, and geographic contexts that contributed to intellectual developments in this remarkable period. The plague, geographic discoveries, new inventions such as the telescope, the breakdown of authority, and the rediscovery of Greek classics had enormous influence on the development of thought. The works of important thinkers such as Galileo Galilei, Niccoló Machiavelli, and Michel de Montaigne are highlighted. Montaigne, a neglected figure in the history of psychology, is presented as a pivotal figure because of his powerful influence on subsequent thinkers such as Francis Bacon and René Descartes. The Renaissance period was regressive in some arenas. It was certainly no Renaissance for women! On the contrary, the Inquisition and the witch hunts amounted to a holocaust for women.

This text devotes extensive space to the intellectual contexts that contributed to the development of psychology. Most texts show how psychology grew out of developments in empiricism, rationalism, physiology, and evolutionary theory. We trace these developments in traditional detail and highlight the changing fortunes of curiosity in the works of the empiricists and rationalists. Curiosity, once regarded as a mark of vanity, was increasingly regarded as a virtue. We also include an emphasis on the key roles played by the growth of quantitative techniques, particularly those developed by Jacques Quételet and elaborated by Francis Galton. Early applications of statistics by Florence Nightingale and Dorothea Dix are highlighted as well. We call attention to the fact that psychology, as a formal discipline, was founded in an age of humanitarian reform movements (e.g., suffrage, abolition of slavery, new prison standards, universal education and education for women, and agitation by reformers for better treatment conditions for people with mental impairments and emotional disorders). We believe that extensive humanitarian reforms created a climate of opinion that helped legitimize the new discipline.

The second half of the text outlines the major classic schools or systems of psychology, emphasizing the basic and applied contributions of each school. A description of the formal founding of psychology begins with nineteenth-century advances in psychophysics and voluntarism, an early school of psychology founded by the German scientist Wilhelm Wundt. Additional consideration is given to scholars who shaped the new discipline of psychology in Europe and the United States, including Edward Bradford Titchener, Franz Brentano, Carl Stumpf, Oswald Külpe, and Hermann Ebbinghaus.

The seminal works of William James and his American contemporaries figure strongly in the chapter on functionalism. The chapter on behaviorism reviews Russian reflexology, Edward Lee Thorndike's learning theory, and John B. Watson's radical school of behaviorism. The neobehaviorism chapter describes the work of diverse researchers working in the behaviorist tradition and culminates with an overview of B. F. Skinner's experimental analysis of behavior. The next chapter focuses on Gestalt psychology, an innovative school that challenged conventional mechanistic and elementaristic approaches to psychology.

The advent of the psychodynamic school is detailed in the evolution of Sigmund Freud's psychoanalytic theory as well as resourceful challenges to his work from Alfred Adler, Carl Jung, and Karen Horney. The philosophical underpinnings of humanistic psychologies are traced in the works of scholars such as Unamuno, Kierkegaard, and Heidegger. These materials are followed by overviews of the works of Abraham Maslow, Gordon Allport, Carl Rogers, and Viktor Frankl.

The final chapter has been revised and updated, providing scholarship that better reflects psychology from the late twentieth century and the early twenty-first century. The chapter explores the cognitive emphasis and major trends in content areas such as clinical psychology, biopsychology, behavioral genetics, psychopharmacology, psychoneuroimmunology, social psychology, industrial-organizational psychology, and psychology and the law. The chapter closes with a brief discussion of the problem of unity and disunity in the sciences including psychology. Conceptual and methodological pluralism is a major characteristic of many academic disciplines at the outset of the twenty-first century. The quest for unification as well as discussions about the advantages of pluralism will likely continue for some time to come.

More than 450 new references have been included. Study questions and a glossary of terms appear at the end of each chapter. Major sections of the text are introduced with a timeline. Moreover, numerous luminaries are covered in this text that were not included in previous editions.

Some final words are in order regarding some of the historiographic and philosophical biases of the authors. Disciplinary histories, such as those about art, music, philosophy, or psychology, are commonly *internal* histories that focus on historical developments within a discipline. Although emphasis on internal developments may be the primary goal in disciplinary histories, these works are nevertheless richer if attention is also directed to *external* history—that is, to contextual political, economic, religious, philosophical, scientific, and social forces that help shape the flow of events within a discipline. In this spirit, we identify some external forces that helped shape psychology. The complex, multidimensional characteristics of the task, however, guarantee that it cannot be carried out successfully. The historian who may be versed in economic context for a given period of time may not be so well versed, for example, in religious history and context. The complicated rich texture of the past is beyond the grasp of most of us. Nevertheless, an awareness that our discipline did not develop in a vacuum is itself valuable.

Another historiographic bias is illustrated in the organization of this text. We believe that nature and history are filled with real discontinuities, disjunctions, and surprises. Events, especially in the intellectual arena, seldom flow with measured, uniform, unvarying regularity. But even if the flow of events had been linear and logical, it would be impossible to present the story in such a fashion because the historian has little choice but to be selective with respect to the materials to be presented. The past is marked by a burly, robust accumulation of materials, some apparently more relevant and some less relevant to our interests. To present the story in all its thick detail would require more time than most of us could devote to the subject; hence, we must resort to the thinness of concepts. If the historian could function more as a photographer than as an artist, the product would still be based on many arbitrary decisions. In the main, we attempt to allow chronology to dictate the flow of ideas and we hope, from time to time, to capture some of the rich detail of the past. At other times, we will break with strict chronology to follow a single idea forward in time and then backtrack to follow another idea forward in time. Thus, the interests of coherence sometimes trump the dictates of chronology.

Study aids are provided in each chapter to help students focus on important materials and concepts. Key words in the text are presented in boldface to help the reader focus on major ideas. A phonic pronunciation guide for difficult names (e.g., Xenophanes [*zeh NAH fuh neez*]) is included to assist students in feeling more "at home" with the materials.

NEW TO THIS EDITION

This edition of the text retains all the unique features that appealed to students in previous editions but also includes numerous distinctive additions as follows:

- We have reviewed and incorporated over 450 new references. This text remains as one of the most heavily referenced texts in the field.
- New materials have been included on the nature of historical consciousness to highlight research into an area with important pedagogical and substantive consequences for historical studies in general and the history of science and psychology in particular. Additionally, we have incorporated new scholarship on the historical, present, and future unity and diversity of psychology.
- There is now an outpouring of new work in biological psychology, and our text reflects this explosion. We evaluate possible neurophysiological determinants of intention and implications for free will and determinism, an issue that occupies increasing attention of historians and philosophers of science and psychology. We also address the recent history of these and related research areas such as psychoneuroimmunology, psychopharmacology, and recent technological advances in neuroscience.
- We added a section on the significance of evolution in the development of psychology. There are now growing numbers of new books and courses

on behavioral genetics, evolutionary psychology, and evolutionary interpretations of such topics as the determinants of mate selection and mate guarding.
- Beginning with the first edition, we have focused on the significance of humanitarian reform movements in shaping the development of psychology. That emphasis has been expanded in this edition by reference to the work of Alice Paul in the women's suffrage movement. We also call attention to likely changes in the historiography of the Inquisition based on the opening of the Vatican archives.
- There are numerous updates in this edition on the philosophy and psychology of William James. The addition of recent scholarship on James compliments a section of the text that has been recognized as a strength.

This text is available in a variety of formats—digital and print. To learn more about our programs, pricing options, and customization, visit www.pearsonhighered.com.

SUPPLEMENTS

Pearson Education is pleased to offer the following supplements to qualified adopters:

Instructor's Manual and Test Bank

This Instructor's Manual and Test Bank provides instructors with support material, classroom enrichment information, and wealth of assessment questions. Corresponding to the chapters in the text, each of the manual's chapters contains discussion questions, lecture outlines, and a test bank.

MyTest Test Bank

This test bank is available in computerized format, which allows instructors to easily create and print quizzes and exams. Questions and tests can be authored online, allowing instructors ultimate flexibility and the ability to efficiently manage assessments anytime, anywhere. Instructors can easily access existing questions, edit, create, and store using simple drag and drop Word-like controls. For more information, go to www. PearsonMyTest.com.

PowerPoint Presentation

The PowerPoint Presentation is an exciting interactive tool for use in the classroom. Each chapter pairs key concepts with images from the textbook to reinforce student learning.

ACKNOWLEDGMENTS

We express appreciation to the literally thousands of students at the University of Colorado at Boulder, Colorado State University, and the University of Northern Colorado who have studied previous editions of this text and have provided helpful, critical, and appreciative commentary. Their enthusiasm, generosity, and insights have played a major role in shaping this fifth edition.

We also express appreciation to the many scholars who have offered suggestions for each of the editions of this book. A considerable list of reviewers who have helped us over the years include Thomas M. Atkinson, Steve Coleman, Edward Crossman, Robert Dippner, David Edwards, Matthew Fanetti, Laurel Furumoto, Allan M. Hartman, Mary Henle, Howard Markowitz, Michelle Merwin John Mueller, Robert Presbie, Elizabeth Scarborough, David Schneider, Margaret Thomas, Michael Wertheimer, and William Woodward. The intellectual resources of our reviewers have made an immeasurable contribution to this book.

It has been a pleasure to work with the publication and production teams at Pearson through each of the five editions of this book. We are especially grateful to Executive Editor Susan Hartman for her encouragement, strong support, and early suggestion that we begin work on a fifth edition. Program Manager Reena Dalal and Project Manager Alyssa Guarino have been extremely patient and supportive going well beyond the call of duty by conveying an intrinsic interest in the project and our work. We have been impressed with the competent assistance of Project Vendor Anju Joshi as we worked through our proofreading of the copyedited chapters of this book. The entire team has been admirably personable and professional throughout the entire process.

We are indebted to Cheri King for her careful editorial eye and her painstaking help in securing archival permissions. We express our gratitude to several archivists and historians for their help in providing archival materials including David Baker, Robert Harper, Mott Linn, Carlos and Mai Parada, Lizette Royer, and Nanci Young.

A few additional individuals merit a special word of thanks. We would like to share our appreciation to our wives Cheri King and Lisa Woody for their enduring good humor, patience, support, and wisdom. We have each benefited immeasurably from our association with Donald A. Crosby, philosopher and Professor Emeritus from Colorado State University. Crosby's extensive expertise in the history of philosophy and his authoritative work on William James have contributed to the scope and to many of the details of this work. We express deep gratitude to Professor Emeritus Michael Wertheimer of the University of Colorado at Boulder. The three of us have been influenced by his love of history, energy, generosity, wisdom, and wit. This edition, along with the previous four editions, reflects his continuing influence.

We also express our appreciation to our children: philosopher Donald Wayne Viney for his many contributions, especially to the first half of this work; biologist Michael David Viney for helpful and thoughtful discussions on philosophy of science and evolution; and our younger children Brady, Devin, and Tylyn King and Nate and Ian Woody for generously sharing their parents with the very demanding requirements of a project such as this.

Finally, in loving memory of Wynona Rose Viney (1934–2009).

D.B.K., W.D.W., W.V.

Historiographic and Philosophical Issues

1

■ ■ ■

Critical Issues in Historical Studies

If we cling to our ignorance of history, error crushed to earth,
will rise again, and we will have to go on solving the same
old problems again and again.

—MARY HENLE (1976)

The story of psychology begins in ancient times. As a self-conscious formal discipline, psychology is little more than a century old, but the subject matter captured the human imagination long before psychology became a science. In our journey, we will travel back thousands of years to visit the epic work of philosophers and scientists who wrestled with issues that continue to fascinate modern psychologists. Examining the work of early scholars on topics such as memory, emotions, dreams, perception, brain activity, learning, and mental disorders adds scope and richness to our understanding of psychology.

Our story will be more compelling if we examine problems associated with the study of history. A number of questions come to mind. What is history? Can the historian offer anything more than opinion? Why study history at all? Developing sensitivity to such philosophical questions makes for a more stimulating intellectual journey.

WHY STUDY HISTORY?

The study of history is an important pursuit and numerous arguments have been proposed about why we should investigate it (see Wertheimer, 1980a). Let's take a look at a handful of the more compelling arguments.

History as a Key to Understanding the Future

In his book *The Future of an Illusion,* Sigmund Freud (1927/1961c) observed that "the less [we know] about the past and the present the more insecure must prove [our] judgment of the future" (p. 5). Freud's sentiment reflects an earlier statement by Thomas Jefferson (1782/1904) who argued that "history, by apprizing [*sic*] [people] of the past, will enable them to judge of the future; it will avail them of the experience of other times and other nations" (p. 207). History offers patterns that, when properly viewed, may prove consequential to our understanding and possible control of the present and the future. In other words, psychologists who appreciate their history may be in a better position to understand the discipline while anticipating future trends.

History as a Way to Enrich the Present

We live in a world of spatial, cultural, and temporal dimensions. We can travel to distant countries. We can study geography and different languages and cultures. We can communicate through the Internet with a friend halfway across the world. In short, we can overcome our spatial and cultural limitations. Unfortunately, we can be just as narrow with respect to our time frame as we are with our knowledge of the physical world and other cultures. Imagine how it would restrict your view of yourself if you only had memories about the last few years of your life. All those early experiences helped shape and define who you are today. It turns out that we can be as "lost" historically as when we cannot find our way in the physical world or when we travel in a culture that is foreign to everything we understand.

In a way, history is memory. Just as there is a freedom that comes with a healthy and functional memory, so there is an intellectual freedom that comes with a broad historical perspective. In a later chapter on humanistic psychology, we'll explore the value of living in the present moment. But an extreme emphasis on the present would leave us naïve and uninformed in an isolated temporal prison. We live more fully in the here and now if we have a rich knowledge and memory for events that contributed to the present. To neglect the past is to impoverish the present.

History as a Contribution to Liberal Education

In a real sense, the study of history serves to nourish a liberal and informed perspective. Robert I. Watson (1966), a prominent historian of psychology, once remarked that history helps us

overcome "narrow provincial, class, and regional prejudices" (p. 64). In his view, psychologists, of all people, should seek to avoid "subjugation to influences of which one is unaware" (p. 64). History helps an individual achieve perspective and integration that might not be possible by other means. Particularly given the increasing specialization in psychology, history can serve to provide context and a broader perspective within psychology (Benjamin & Baker, 2009). Knowledge of the history of a discipline accentuates the understanding of influences, developments, and relations and contributes to a more informed and integrated perspective. This achievement alone can be so satisfying that the study of history needs no other justification.

History Teaches Humility

We enjoy an advantage over previous generations because we can build on knowledge and discoveries of the past and avoid unnecessary duplication of earlier mistakes. A perspective from past knowledge is larger and more informed than perspectives from the present alone. When we study history, we are humbled by the genius, the effort, and the creative insight of previous thinkers. Helson (1972) reminds us that in history "student[s] may meet better minds in the literature than any [they] may have contact with in person" (p. 116). We may also encounter minds that have worked through problems that we assumed were fresh or original. History all too often reveals that our innovative idea is a rediscovery of something known long ago. History can teach humility.

History Teaches a Healthy Skepticism

When we have an understanding of history, we are less likely to fall prey to grandiose notions, utopian dreams, and schemes that promise more than they deliver. Psychology has suffered its share of counterfeit ideas, including mesmerism, phrenology, craniometry (the measurement of the skull to determine intelligence and personality), and even some modern therapies. History teaches us to be wary of the big claim, the single method to end all methods, and the one and only definition. Helson (1972) cautioned against easy acceptance that our future lies with a solitary panacea, such as "computer models of brain function, or that there is only one psychophysical law, or that trend analysis is the last answer to statistical treatments" (p. 116). Historical knowledge counsels against the glib acceptance of the latest fad or inflated idea. Jaynes (1973a) pointed out that history may help us "liberate ourselves from the persuasions of fashions" (p. xi). At the very least, we can hope that historical knowledge will make us less gullible and help us think critically about history and other topics (Goodwin, 2005).

History Influences Human Thought Processes

Henle (1976) pointed out that most of us find it difficult to see our errors or question our assumptions. She argued that human cognition is often resistant to criticism and prone to a degree of inertia or self-preservation. For her, knowledge of history "gives us distance not only from our immediate objective, but from our own thinking" (p. 16). History heightens awareness of the errors of others, but also keeps us thinking straight. As Henle warned in the quotation that opened this chapter, if we are blind to the lessons of history, then we will be doomed to solve the same old problems.

SOME PROBLEMS IN HISTORIOGRAPHY

A number of questions are important here. What makes history? Can history be objective? Does history have a discernable pattern or direction? Such questions form the subject matter of historiography. The term **historiography** has multiple meanings. In a narrow and literal sense, it refers to the writing of history, including techniques and strategies for investigating specific content areas. The term also encompasses philosophical questions about history and historical method (later, we will review some philosophical questions encountered in historical studies). A third meaning of *historiography* refers to the characteristics of a body of historical writings. For

example, historical accounts of psychology have sometimes neglected the contributions of women and other cultural minorities. Fortunately, critical awareness of our biases has led to research that addresses how psychology has profited from the contributions of women (see Bohan, 1992a, 1992b; Gavin, 1987; O'Connell & Russo, 1983, 1988, 1990; Scarborough & Furumoto, 1987), African-American psychologists (see Guthrie, 2003; Phillips, 2000; Sawyer, 2000), and Hispanic psychologists (see Martinez & Mendoza, 1984).

Working on the idea that history can be more meaningful if we address historiographic questions, we will now examine questions and issues about history and historical method. We'll find that the positions we take can influence our view of the history of psychology or any other history for that matter.

The Development of Historical Consciousness

Gilderhus (1992) suggests that primitive peoples often lacked historical consciousness because immediate survival was their primary concern. Even so, survival depends on memory along with an awareness of time-based events. This temporal awareness has survival value and contributes to the development of historical consciousness. Knowledge of the historical significance of events benefits both individuals and society.

Historical consciousness grows from the belief that important events carry real significance in the pursuit of religion, politics, or science. In Hebraic literature, for example, people are encouraged to remember events associated with their delivery from Egyptian bondage. In more recent history, phrases such as *never again, lest we forget, 9/11,* and *united we stand* serve as reminders of the horrors of the Holocaust or the sacrifices of war and terrorism. On certain occasions, political or religious holidays heighten historical consciousness. Christians regard the crucifixion of Jesus as the most central event in history—an event that ushered in a new theological epoch. Indeed, the Christian community measures time itself in terms of this critical incident.

Gilderhus (1992) observed that historical consciousness in Greek times grew out of attempts to separate history from mythology. The legendary Greek historian **Herodotus** (*hi RAH duh tuhs*) (c. 484–c. 425 BCE) became the first to attempt a comprehensive history of the world. Documenting contemporary episodes as well as past events, he traveled widely, made extensive notes, and gained access to eyewitness testimony whenever possible. Herodotus wrote history with an emphasis on natural rather than supernatural causes.

The naturalistic approach to history was extended in the work of **Thucydides** (*thoo SIHD ih deez*) (c. 460–c. 401 BCE). Remembered for his classic *History of the Peloponnesian War,* Thucydides documented the war between Athens and Sparta from 431 to 404 BCE. Thucydides had a passion for accuracy and for naturalistic explanations stripped of theological overtones. Aware of previous attempts to write history in terms of miracles, mysteries, and divine purposes, Thucydides insisted on discovering positive facts and presenting them in a naturalistic context. Faith in the accuracy of historical writings creates respect for written histories and may foster historical consciousness. We turn now to one of the most fundamental and challenging issues in historiography—the problem of defining history.

Historical consciousness is more than knowledge of specific histories such as the history of the American Civil War, the history of a country, or the history of an academic discipline such as psychology. At a minimum, historical consciousness includes a sensitivity to the great range of philosophical problems associated with the writing of history, an endeavor to approach history with both critical and appreciative orientations, awareness of the dynamic ever-changing nature of historical inquiry, and an attempt to approach every subject historically (Viney, 2010). American philosopher and psychologist William James (1911) argued that "we give humanistic value to almost anything when we teach it historically. Geology, economics, [and] mechanics are humanities when taught with reference to the successive achievements of the geniuses to which these sciences owe their being. When not taught in this way, literature remains grammar, art a catalogue, history a list of dates, and natural science a sheet of formulas and weights and measures" (pp. 312–313).

What Is History?

In popular usage, the term **history** sometimes denotes the chronology of events that provides a raw material for the historian. The term also refers to stories we tell about our past. Dictionary definitions typically emphasize both meanings (i.e., history as a chronology of previous events and history as a narrative or interpretive study of the past). History has both empirical and explanatory components. The *empirical* component includes data such as unpublished letters; newspaper and Internet accounts; audio, video, or digital recordings; and official documents. The *explanatory* component refers to the efforts of historians to make sense of data. Additional perspectives on the nature of history are provided in Table 1.1.

So, how are we to define *history*? Let's begin with the idea that history has an empirical component. That is, real events that took place in the past can enter our present experiences through records. The empirical component can also include eyewitness accounts or personal experiences for more recent events. For instance, where were you on September 11, 2001? If you remember, chances are the episode is vivid in your memory. Events such as the terrorist attack on the World Trade Center resonate, in part, because they provide a way of aligning ourselves with the yardstick of history.

The task of the historian is to become acquainted with as much data as possible. Data collection may include interviews, traveling to archives to examine unpublished letters and documents, and reading old newspapers. After collecting data, the historian must engage in an interpretive study. Such study includes examining contradictions, discriminating between what is relevant and what is not, and assigning weights to different bits of evidence. In a way, the process is like working a complicated jigsaw puzzle when we know in advance that there will always be missing pieces.

The working definition of *history* suggested here is as follows: History is the interpretive study

Table 1.1 Some Perspectives on the Nature of History

History as Subjective Study

We read history through our prejudices. —Wendell Phillips

What is history but a fable agreed upon. —Napoleon I (Bonaparte)

History as a Record of the Past

History is not history unless it is the truth. —Abraham Lincoln

History as Cyclical

History repeats itself; that's just one of the things that's wrong with history. —Clarence Darrow

The Importance of History

Who cannot give an account of three thousand years remains in the darkness of inexperience. —Wolfgang Goethe

The less we know of the past, the more unreliable our judgment of the present and future. —Sigmund Freud

The Value of History

If I have seen farther than others, it is because I have stood on the shoulders of giants. —Isaac Newton

History is the witness that testifies to the passing of time; it illumines reality, vitalizes memory, provides guidance in daily life, and brings us tidings of antiquity. —Cicero

[W]ithout history there can be no psychology. —Carl Jung

A Presentist View of History

Let the past serve the present. —Mao Tse-tung

A Historicist View of History

We cannot escape history. We…will be remembered in spite of ourselves…. The fiery trial through which we pass will light us down, in honor or dishonor, to the last generation. —Abraham Lincoln

---

of the events of the human past. The definition assumes empirical and explanatory components in the work of a historian.

Can History Be Objective?

If we agree that history is the interpretive study of the human past, we nevertheless encounter the problem of the faithfulness or truthfulness of our interpretations. Abraham Lincoln (1856/1950) said, "History is not history unless it is the truth" (p. 149). People have a kind of commonsense faith that historical research—whether it deals with religious, political, scientific, or social topics—is an accurate reflection of the landscape of the past. Even the historian embarking on a new project may believe it possible to provide a narrative truer to the chronology of events than did previous works.

The question of objectivity is a critical issue in the philosophy of history. Thousands of pages are devoted to the importance of this problem in historical journals and texts. Historians do not usually make direct observations. Even if they did, we have no guarantee of objectivity. Historians must be selective with respect to available data, sometimes in the absence of well-established criteria for selection. Finally, historians are creatures of the present and, as such, may write history in the light of present personal and cultural perspectives.

We can't easily close the case against objectivity for several reasons. Objectivity is a desirable ideal in any scientific investigation. If we reject objectivity, we run into the assumption that one person's opinion is as good as another's. Finally, objectivity offers the hope that historical narratives can rise above the prevailing climate of opinion. If achieved, history can be used to repudiate, disagree with, or tell an unpopular story. Chinese leader Mao Tse-tung (1893–1976) believed that history should serve the Communist revolution (Lifton, 1968, p. 144). Such an extreme position fuels the debate over the merits of objectivity because it reveals that history is not necessarily bound to political, religious, or philosophical ideologies.

Before proceeding, we should explore possible meanings of **objectivity in history**. The term *objective* could refer to a correspondence between a historical narrative and the events of the past it describes. If objectivity refers to such a correspondence, then the work of the historian would be judged as deficient. For one thing, a historical narrative can never recapture the fullness of lived experience. Objectivity then, as correspondence, is suspect. Perhaps historians are more like painters than photographers. Even if they were like photographers, historical events would always offer another angle for a shot, a different way to frame it, a new magnification, or different films with varying sensitivity to color.

Another meaning of *objectivity* involves the attempt to portray all sides of an issue in a fair manner, even if something disagrees with the author's perspective. Objectivity, viewed in this way, is an attitude, one we may expect of a historian. In this context, the historian is reminded to be aware of ulterior motives and to hold them in check.

Before leaving the question of objectivity, let's return to Abraham Lincoln's contention that "history is not history unless it is the truth." Most historians might agree if we could add that, for any event, there is more than one possible true history. For example, the Civil War can be regarded not as one war but as many wars. It was a different war for the South than for the North. The two sides could not even agree on the causes of the war. It was also a different war for each of the various states. From this line of reasoning, there can be multiple "true" histories of the American Civil War, each disagreeing on countless details.

The Tyranny of the Present

Historians are creatures of the present, but can they free themselves from natural biases imposed by their world view? Historians, like psychotherapists, must have a well-developed empathy for their subject. If such empathy is possible, then historians may be capable of suspending or neutralizing present biases; that is, they may literally "feel" their way back into the past so that deep and authentic understandings become a possibility. In short, we follow a commitment of "understanding the past for its own sake" (Stocking, 1965, p. 212). Stocking adds that a past-minded approach places emphasis on *understanding* the past rather than *judging* it; this perspective also avoids the temptation to use the past to glorify the present. As noted earlier, an adequate history can tell an unpopular story that is damaging to present interests. But is this ideal of past-mindedness possible? Can a historian suspend the present frame of reference with its possible distortions and prejudices? Put another way, can the historian capture an earlier era or frame of mind in all its intricacy, richness, and context? As noted, the problem resembles a common issue debated among clinical psychologists. Can we empathically "crawl into the mind" of another person or do individual differences prohibit genuine congruence of thought and feeling?

Related to this idea, **presentism** emphasizes the difficulty in divorcing historical facts from current perspectives. The presentist questions whether the historian can recapture the past with true objectivity. Buss (1977) wrote, "There is no such thing as hard-core, indubitable facts that are invariant across different theoretical explanations" (p. 254). The presentist is tuned to the effects of inevitable selective, judgmental, and contextual forces in historical scholarship. Scholars with a more past-minded orientation might counter that *because* we are aware of such forces, we can neutralize their effects.

Issues surrounding presentism and past-mindedness have stimulated discussion in the historiography of the behavioral sciences (see Ash & Woodward, 1987, pp. 1–11, 295–309; Dewsbury, 1990; Furumoto, 1989; Harrison, 1987; Henle, 1989; Young, 1966). As with most issues, extremes of past-mindedness and presentism create difficulties. William James (1890/1981) once referred to absolutism as "the great disease of philosophic thought" (p. 334).

Sounding a similar theme, Dewsbury (1990) raised doubts about the superiority of either approach and argued for a moderate and tolerant approach to historiography with room for past-minded and presentist orientations. Such an approach would be sensitive to the role of present beliefs in our understanding and writing of history but also insist that authentic history will often challenge and shape our present beliefs.

Is There a Pattern or Direction in History?

To ask whether history has a pattern or direction is to ask something about the meaning of history. Patterns offer information and the discovery of a pattern can be useful. We'll take a look at a few hypotheses about the direction of history that are applicable to the history of psychology.

CYCLICAL HYPOTHESIS   As the name suggests, the **cyclical hypothesis** claims that history repeats itself. We find an ebb and flow to events marked by endless repetition. Kingdoms rise and fall, only to rise again; freedom is gained and lost, only to be regained once more. Cycles of poverty and plenty play out along with war and peace, discovery and intellectual stagnation, innocence and corruption, and revolution and stability. Even our ways of understanding, according to this view, are cyclical. A rational and scientific era may arise in one era before falling to arbitrary political or religious authority, only to see the rational-scientific method return to prominence at a later time.

Cycles exist in every science, and psychology has seen its share. For example, neuroscientists in the twentieth century wondered if the right and left hemispheres of the brain mediate different emotional and intellectual processes, or do the hemispheres function in a more integrated fashion? Interest in lateralization of function in the cerebral hemispheres is not new. Long before modern neuroscience took an interest, Brown-Sequard (1890) wrote an article titled "Have We Two Brains or One?" The article is only one of many from that period to struggle with the problem of the lateralization of function. Another

example from the history of psychology came in the early emphasis on conscious and experiential processes, only to face later rejection with the advent of behaviorism before an interest in consciousness and experience reemerged in the closing decades of the twentieth century.

LINEAR-PROGRESSIVE HYPOTHESIS   A linear hypothesis can be either progressive or regressive, but let us assume optimism and consider only a linear-progressive view. According to the **linear-progressive hypothesis**, each generation builds upon discoveries from previous generations. Each new generation works up from a stronger base, giving rise to growth and progress in human knowledge and among human institutions. Brief regressions and setbacks may ensue, but the overall victory belongs to progress and growth. The German mathematician Gottfried Wilhelm Leibniz was the best-known modern champion of progress theory. His theory of history was born in an age of optimism about the promise of scientific discovery. The theory achieved widespread popularity, inspiring some supporters to promote progress as a law of nature (Gawronski, 1975). In this tradition, Karl Marx advanced one of the better-known progress theories.

Progress theory may have a persuasive influence on those who study the living conditions of the past. In a book entitled *The Good Old Days—They Were Terrible*, Bettmann (1974) recounts the hardships of American life from the end of the Civil War to the early 1900s. It was an era made almost unbearable with filth and pollution in major cities from factories, coal-fired steam engines, city streets teeming with horse manure, insects, and poor sewage. In a time before air-conditioning, poorly ventilated houses and apartments claimed many lives during summer and winter months. Crime flourished, often beyond control, in major cities and on the frontier. "Dominating the record was, of course, the West, where the gun-happy barbarity was damned by observers both foreign and native for producing a 'great dismal swamp of civilization' " (Bettmann, 1974, p. 87). Education for women was little more than a faint hope, and school conditions remained deplorable for all but wealthy men. In the absence of refrigeration, food was spoiled, and diets were lean and inadequate. Epidemics of yellow fever, tuberculosis, smallpox, whooping cough, and measles raged throughout the country. Child labor laws had not yet been enacted, and unsafe factories took an enormous toll in injuries and death, with little recourse for victims or their families. The problems, of course, intensified for Southern slaves. Given the adversity, most today would probably rather not return to the "good old days."

CHAOS HYPOTHESIS   The coming of the nuclear age dampened earlier optimism about the inevitability of human progress. It became clear that the entire structure of human achievement could be brought to ruin by a chance technological accident or by the design of political systems deficient in world perspective. The Nazi genocide of European Jews during the Holocaust tested the hypothesis that progress is inevitable.

According to the **chaos hypothesis**, history itself has no overall identifiable and universal meaning. History is, as noted by Fisher (1936), simply "the play of the contingent and the unforeseen" (p. v). The meanings found in history are the meanings we impose, not meanings that inhere in history itself. This idea was captured in a letter from Jean-Paul Sartre to Albert Camus. Sartre (1965) observed, "History, apart from the man who makes it, is only an abstract and static concept, of which it can neither be said that it has an objective, nor that it has not.... The problem is not to *know* its objective, but to *give* it one" (p. 103). In the same spirit, Becker (1932) regarded human beings as "little more than a chance deposit on the surface of the world, carelessly thrown up between two ice ages by the same forces that rust iron and ripen corn" (p. 14).

For some, psychology is the product of a chaotic history. In an article titled "Psychology Cannot Be a Coherent Science," Koch (1969) charged that a century's worth of research in psychology generated a wealth of pseudoknowledge and trivial thinking. Koch argued that psychology's history is "a succession of changing doctrines about what to emulate in the natural sciences—especially

physics" (p. 64). In his mind, psychology failed to discover an adequate methodology and never reached the standard of a cumulative and progressive science.

Critics maintain that chaos theory discourages any attempt to take responsibility for our future. If what happens in the future is independent of individual human belief and action, what incentive exists to shape our future?

In addition to the theories outlined earlier, providential theories claim that a deity plays a role in shaping history. Others embrace a more pluralistic approach, suggesting that many histories exist rather than one absolute history. A pluralistic approach counsels suspicion of any sweeping attempt to characterize all history as fitting one convenient hypothesis.

What Makes History?

We turn now to an issue of controversy among historians, one that holds special relevance for students of psychology. The central question here asks whether history is fashioned through the bold actions of exceptional people or the "spirit of the times" in which they live. The **great-person theory** suggests that uncommon individuals transcend the conditions of their day and shape history through their courage or wisdom or some other virtue. In contrast, the German terms **Zeitgeist** (spirit of a time) and **Ortgeist** (spirit of a place) argue that prevailing conditions, not individuals, forge historical events. The idea is that no person is greater than his or her time.

American philosopher Ralph Waldo Emerson's optimistic work titled *Self-Reliance* makes a compelling case for the great-person theory. For Emerson (1841/1981), history "resolves itself very easily into the biography of a few stout and earnest persons" (p. 138). He tells us that with Caesar, we have a Roman Empire; with Luther, the Reformation; with Fox, Quakerism; and with Wesley, Methodism. Following his lead, it is with Wundt that we have the formal discipline of psychology; with Freud, psychoanalysis; with Rorschach, the inkblot test; and so on. The great-person theory emphasizes the causal role of particular persons in particular circumstances and the ability of the individual to control or to change the direction of events.

Critics argue that the great-person theory results from an unsophisticated view of forces at work in the world; late in his life, E. G. Boring (1966) noted that the sudden insights of great people may serve as memory aids for students rather than accurate depictions of history (Rosenzweig, 1987). Causation in history is complex, so we must be tuned to multiple forces that create an idea, event, or institution. Seldom can a critical occurrence or invention be credited to the labor of a single individual. As an example, powered flight could never have developed from individual effort prior to invention of the internal combustion engine. A relevant background of invention, material, culture, education, and social support must be present to nurture a significant historical happening. In addition to promoting hero worship, the idea that one person alone is responsible for any substantial contribution ignores the complexities of life and history. The place (*Ortgeist*) and time (*Zeitgeist*) must be conducive before advances can be made.

English philosopher Herbert Spencer (1873) believed in the possibility of a "science of history" where context played a central role in historical causation. Likewise, the Canadian naturalist Grant Allen (1878a, 1878b) argued that the great intellectual achievements in ancient Greece were due to geography and other external forces and had nothing to do with specific individuals. Herman Melville's *Moby-Dick* captures this philosophy of history when a crewmember advises Captain Ahab to call off the chase for the albino whale. Ahab replies, "This whole act's immutably decreed. 'Twas rehearsed by thee and me a billion years before this ocean rolled. Fool! I am the Fates' lieutenant; I act under orders" (Melville, 1851/1976, pp. 548–549). Such fatalism may, of course, have its origin in a theological or naturalistic context. We should note that an extreme emphasis on environmental context may overlook the importance of individual actions in the stream of historical causation.

William James (1880) provides a different approach to the problem of historical causality. He argued that historical development is a causal interplay between people and their environment. He agreed that our environment sets boundaries, but added that human effort changes our world. According to James, any account of history that neglects the individual dissolves into vagary and incoherence (see Viney, 2001). James proposes a balanced approach where an individual's idea cannot achieve fruition without social and material support. On the other hand, some ideas might never make an historical impact if not borne in the mind of a unique and creative individual.

Disagreements over the forces that make history continue as a topic in historical scholarship. In an article titled "Genius without the 'Great Man,'" Ball (2012) suggests ways to engage with eminent figures without resorting to *hagiography* (a term originally meaning the worshipful and celebratory descriptions of the lives of saints). In this context, hagiography refers to a tendency to pedistalize individuals by giving them excessive credit for new historical developments. Continuing efforts to explore more comprehensive understandings of historical causation can be found in the ways psychology has been understood in a variety of countries (see Pickren, 2012). Let's consider another historiographic issue that is the subject of current debate in both the history of science and the history of psychology.

The New History or the Old?

In the late 1980s, a bold movement challenged the way disciplinary histories (e.g., history of science, history of philosophy, history of psychology) had been written. The claim was that older disciplinary histories amounted to little more than celebrations of the succession of achievements of "great men" (women and minorities were often ignored). A related claim was that older histories were *internalist*, meaning that ideas and developments were presented within each discipline while ignoring important cultural, social, economical, philosophical, and religious contexts that shape ideas. The older histories were also accused of being presentist and "whiggish." A whiggish interpretation of science, according to Harrison (1987), is a way of selecting and organizing historical materials so that they converge with and glorify the current worldview. The resulting historical account is too clean or even naïve as it ignores the messy false leads, blind alleys, cul-de-sacs, and missteps that characterize day-to-day science. The claim was made that older histories had relied too much on secondary sources, leading to a perpetuation of inaccuracies or outright mistakes. The new history promised a corrective for the superficial scholarship of the old history through greater use of archival sources and original works.

Still another difference between the old history and the new is that the former has been written by practicing scientists with an interest in the history of their disciplines. The new history more often comes from professional historians trained in history of science programs. An emphasis on educational differences between old and new historians may be problematic for the simple reason that some scientists have advanced historical training while some professional historians have a considerable background in science. We should counsel caution about placing too much emphasis on the relationship between scholarly degrees and one's area of personal competence. Still, we can find value in studying the lives of prominent scientific figures. Sokal (2006) observed that

> an individual's character and temperament, and the specific circumstances of his or her early life and upbringing, can help shape (and perhaps determine) the course of that person's career and, quite possibly, even the content of his or her scientific ideas. To be sure, some philosophically aware historians of science argue that such claims derive from a focus on the "accidentals" of the past and that they downplay the real significance of an individual's scientific work. But biographers and psychologists interested in life histories know better. (p. 19)

In a pivotal article, Furumoto (1989) stimulated a strong interest in problems of historiography and promoted discussion among psychologists about how the history of the field should be written. Subsequent attempts to write histories are responsive to values of the new history. At the same time, Lovett (2006) believes the new history has been accepted uncritically despite few actual differences between works from the two camps. Indeed, Lovett cited works from scholars who embrace the new histories as little more than accounts of a succession of achievements of past luminaries. Further, he demonstrated that some older histories draw heavily from primary sources and archival materials. Based on Lovett's analysis, any catalog of differences between the new and old histories, in many cases, is a distinction without a distinction. Arguably, intellectual history is better served with multiple vantage points rather than conformity to any dominant ideological, educational, or methodological prescriptive structure.

What Is the History of Psychology, the History Of?

In a thoughtful article on the ideological roots of modern science, Dear (2005) asks the interesting question "What is the history of science, the history of?" The question can be expanded beyond the scope of Dear's paper and applied to any disciplinary history including the history of psychology. Some early histories of psychology were histories of experimental psychology (Boring, 1950). Other histories focused on great systems of psychology such as behaviorism, psychoanalysis, and functionalism (Heidbreder, 1933). Other texts outlined major theories or systems along with historical developments in specific areas such as emotion, learning, and motivation (Chaplin & Krawiec, 1979). With the exponential growth of applied psychology, some scholars have argued for the inclusion of major historical developments in fields such as clinical psychology, industrial-organizational psychology, and psychology and the law.

A related question has to do with what counts as psychology. As we will see in future chapters, many early philosophers discussed topics relevant to psychology, but should their discoveries count as a part of our history? Some scholars (Brock, 2006; Richards, 1987; Smith, 1988) find it problematic to write about the history of psychology before it existed as a separate discipline. Others, including the authors of this text, believe modern psychology is best understood in the context of early scientists and philosophers who often obsessed over topics such as emotion and the nature of mental illness, association and learning, memory and motivation. A larger question revolves around the discontinuities and continuities between recent scientific investigations and the work of early pioneers. An exclusive emphasis on modern history runs the risk of missing legitimate and productive connections with the past that enrich our understanding of the present, whereas a comprehensive approach runs the risk of minimizing real differences between older and newer perspectives and methods.

If we hold in mind the issues of historiography, the study of psychology's history becomes more meaningful. Persistent questions should play in the background of historical study: Is there a pattern? What would the discipline be like without this or that person and his or her contributions? How has my current perspective changed as a result of my knowledge of history? To what extent can we suspend our current biases? Awareness of such questions lends depth and richness in our quest to understand the history of psychology.

THE HISTORY OF THE HISTORY OF PSYCHOLOGY

Interest in the history of psychology is as old as the discipline itself. Early textbook writers such as Wilhelm Wundt and William James acknowledged earlier contributions from disciplines such as physics, physiology, and philosophy. As noted, people discussed psychological topics centuries before psychology became a formal discipline. So it's no surprise that early psychologists were interested in the history of psychological ideas even while the formal discipline was in its infancy.

In addition to earlier and modern texts, numerous books of readings in the history of psychology have been published (Benjamin, 1997; Dennis, 1948; Diamond, 1974b; Fancher, 1996; Henle, Jaynes, & Sullivan, 1973; Herrnstein & Boring, 1966; Pickren & Dewsbury, 2002; Sahakian, 1968; Sexton & Misiak, 1971). Some helpful books trace the development of psychology in various countries (Hiroshi, 2002; Misiak & Sexton, 1966; Sexton & Misiak, 1976). With the growth of interest in the history of psychology, other resources have appeared that are useful to students writing term papers and to scholars conducting research. Select bibliographies show how to find biographical information on various psychologists (Benjamin, 1974; Benjamin & Heider, 1976; Zusne, 1984), and numerous guides and sourcebooks outline how to discover other kinds of information on the history of psychology. For example, Viney, Wertheimer, and Wertheimer (1979) produced a large bibliography of sources in English on the history of psychology; Watson (1974/1976, 1978) compiled three volumes that provide lists of major works from the world's great psychologists (Volume 1, 1974), a bibliography of sources about these same psychologists (Volume 2, 1976), and resources for the study of the history of psychology (1978). Benjamin and colleagues (1989) prepared a bibliography of sources in the history of psychology compiled from notes and news sections from major journals. Sokal and Rafail (1982) published a guide to manuscript collections in the history of psychology for scholars interested in archival materials. From 1927 to December 2006, the *Psychological Abstracts* was the primary guide to world literature in psychology, but the electronic search tool PsycINFO has replaced it (see Benjamin & VandenBos, 2006). In addition to PsycINFO, a wealth of source materials is available to students interested in the history of psychology. Selected examples are presented in Table 1.2.

Prior to the 1960s, scholarly work on the history of psychology was disjointed and restricted to a few isolated researchers. Only a handful of journals accepted historical articles and only a few textbooks and books of readings

Table 1.2 Selected Source Materials for Students Interested in the History of Psychology

Source	Brief Description
PsycINFO	Primary electronic search tool and guide to world literature in psychology. Includes extensive references on historical materials.
History of Psychology	Flagship journal for the Society for the History of Psychology.
Journal of the History of the Behavioral Sciences	Includes articles on the history of psychology as well as histories of other behavioral sciences.
History of the Human Sciences	Interdisciplinary journal with historical articles in fields such as anthropology, political science, psychology, and sociology.
Theory and Psychology	Bimonthly journal with articles on the conceptual foundations of psychology including historical underpinnings.
Journal of the History of the Neurosciences	Organ of the International Society for the History of the Neurosciences. Includes historical articles on basic, clinical, and behavioral neurosciences.
American Psychologist	Flagship journal of the American Psychological Association. Includes archival documents, obituaries of well-known psychologists, and occasional historical articles.
American Journal of Psychology	Founded by G. Stanley Hall in 1887, explores the basic science of psychology. Often includes articles on the history of psychology.
Classics in the History of Psychology	A website containing hundreds of full-text classic articles in the history of psychology (http://psychclassics.yorku.ca/).
This Week in the History of Psychology	Podcasts consisting of twenty-five-minute interviews with experts on landmark events in the history of psychology (www.yorku.ca/christo /podcasts/).

hit the market. Informal meetings of interested individuals occurred at the annual conventions of the American Psychological Association, but opportunities were scarce.

The mid-1960s ushered in a dramatic change. During this period, the *Journal of the History of the Behavioral Sciences* was first published in January 1965 and, ten months later, the Archives of the History of American Psychology were established in Ohio at the University of Akron. That same year, the American Psychological Association approved the formation of Division 26, the Division of the History of Psychology, later renamed the Society for the History of Psychology. Psychologists interested in history quickly established physical, organizational, and social support for scholarly activities. In 1967, the first graduate program offering

a Ph.D. in the history of psychology was established at the University of New Hampshire. A year later, another important society was launched—Cheiron, the International Society for the History of Behavioral and Social Sciences (the inspiration for the society's name came from Cheiron, a centaur in Greek mythology known for wisdom, knowledge, and immortality).

In the twenty-first century, the history of psychology remains an invaluable topic of study. A survey of more than seven hundred psychology departments in American colleges and universities revealed that over 80 percent offer undergraduate courses in the history of psychology (Fuchs & Viney, 2002). Such courses are typically taught during the junior or senior year and sometimes serve as capstone courses for psychology majors. Further, accredited graduate programs in counseling and clinical psychology include instruction on the history of psychology as a core part of graduate education. Most departments of psychology offer a history course as a component of undergraduate and graduate education. Though professional organizations such as Cheiron and Division 26 (History of Psychology) of the American Psychological Association have weathered ups and downs in membership, researchers remain interested in the area. Because of the growth of scholarly work, the American Psychological Association approved a journal, *History of Psychology,* launched in 1998 under the initial editorship of Michael M. Sokal, a prominent historian of science who also served as president of the History of Science Society. Today, the history of psychology is considered an important facet of the history of science.

The history of psychology is an intrinsically interesting subject, covering groundbreaking thinkers and a wealth of ideas about human and animal nature. From the ideas of the earliest Greeks about mental illness, to concepts of childhood in the Middle Ages, to the nineteenth-century vision of a new discipline called psychology—the story is a fascinating and worthwhile adventure. Finally, and perhaps more urgently, the historical study of psychology provides an invigorating perspective on the present scene that would be difficult if not impossible to achieve in any other way.

Review Questions

1. List and briefly describe five reasons for the study of history.
2. What is historiography? What issues are typically studied in historiography?
3. What is history? Do you agree that history has an empirical component?
4. In what sense can the historian be objective?
5. List and describe three hypotheses regarding the pattern or direction of history.
6. Describe specific developments in the latter part of the twentieth century that contributed to the advance of scholarly work in the history of psychology.

Glossary

chaos hypothesis   The belief that there is no pattern or direction in history; history has no meaning except that attributed to it by humans.

cyclical hypothesis   The belief that history can be understood in terms of repetitive patterns or cycles. For example, it might be argued that freedom is lost, only to be regained and lost again; thus, there is endless repetition.

great-person theory   The view that unique individuals play a causal role in history. Contrast with *Zeitgeist* and *Ortgeist.*

Herodotus (c. 484–c. 425 BCE)   First great Greek historian to write history with an emphasis on natural rather than supernatural causes.

historiography   The writing of history along with the study of the methodological and philosophical issues that are pertinent to the work of the historian.

history   The interpretive study of the events of the human past.

linear-progressive hypothesis   A view of history marked by belief in the inevitable growth and progress of human knowledge and institutions.

objectivity in history   An attitude of the historical researcher marked by an attempt to present fairly all sides of an issue.

Ortgeist   The spirit of the place. Contrasts with the great-person theory of history and emphasizes the importance of place and time (*Zeitgeist*) as conditions for the production and acceptance of new ideas.

presentism   An orientation toward history emphasizing the pervasive influence of current prejudices on the interpretation of past events.

Thucydides (c. 460–c. 401 BCE)   Greek historian and author of the *History of the Peloponnesian War.* He worked to achieve accurate naturalistic accounts of historical events.

Zeitgeist   The spirit of the time. Contrasts with the great-person theory of history and emphasizes the importance of time and place (*Ortgeist*) as conditions for the production and acceptance of new ideas.

2

■ ■ ■

Philosophical Issues

But man, proud man, Drest in a little briefe authoritie, Most ignorant of what he's most assur'd (His glassie Essence) like an angry Ape Plaies such phantastique tricks before high heauen, As makes the Angels weepe.

—WILLIAM SHAKESPEARE (1604–1605/1964)

In the 1870s, the new science of psychology developed its own identity, but continued to be haunted by many of the same problems that successive generations of scholars had explored. We think a study of the history of psychology is more meaningful if you are aware of the perennial themes and issues that challenged the discipline. In this chapter, we'll examine critical philosophical problems that shaped psychology's development.

EPISTEMOLOGY

The term **epistemology** is derived from the Greek *episteme,* which means to understand or to know. Epistemology is a branch of philosophy concerned with theories of knowledge. As you might guess, psychologists have had a long-standing curiosity about epistemological issues. For example, Jean Piaget (1896–1980) was trained in zoology and gained fame for his studies of human cognitive development, but he didn't consider himself a biologist or a psychologist. Instead, Piaget viewed himself as a student of **genetic epistemology**, the study of the ways we solve problems as a function of our cognitive level. As a genetic epistemologist, Piaget demonstrated that our understanding of the world and our ways of solving problems evolve as we mature. Let's take a look at epistemological issues that hold special relevance for psychologists.

A Priori and A Posteriori Knowledge

As you read the history of psychology, you'll encounter the idea that certain truths are presumed to be known a priori. What does that mean? The philosophical term **a priori** comes from the Latin meaning "from what is prior" or "from what comes before." By contrast, the term

a posteriori means "from what comes later." Since the time of Immanuel Kant (1724–1804), *a posteriori* refers to that which is derived from or comes after experience and *a priori* refers to self-evident truths that come before experience. For example, let's look at the following proposition: If *A* is larger than *B* and *B* is larger than *C,* then *A* is larger than *C.* The claim can be made that the truth of the proposition is known a priori. No one would deny that the proposition itself is known through experience. That is, without experience, we would not even know about the proposition. But we can still claim to know the truth of the relationships among *A, B,* and *C* through intellectual insight alone. In other words, we can grasp certain relationships without learning or benefit of prior experience. According to the theory of a priori knowledge, it can be argued, for example, that one could immediately grasp the truth of a statement such as "We cannot both exist and not exist at the same time."

Philosophers and psychologists have struggled with the role of the a priori in human knowledge. Extreme claims contribute to the problem. For instance, some thinkers argue that knowledge of good and evil is known a priori. On the other extreme, we encounter the argument that all knowledge is dependent on experience. Psychologists emphasize the centrality of experience as the basis of knowledge. But like philosophers, we wrestle with evidence that some relationships are discerned without learning or previous experience.

Nativism versus Empiricism

This issue is a close relative to the issue of a priori and a posteriori knowledge. **Nativism** holds that some perceptions are operational from birth, built in as a natural outcome of the structural and functional properties of the nervous system. By contrast, **empiricism** holds that all perceptions are learned or developed from experience. The problem of depth perception illustrates the dispute between nativists and empiricists. We have the ability to see our world in three dimensions, but

do we learn to see in depth or is depth perception a natural or unlearned ability? Classic research suggests that newborns have perceptual abilities that may not be learned. Gibson and Walk (1960) constructed a visual cliff, a platform that ended in a steep drop, but was covered by a bridge of transparent glass. Although it was safe to cross the transparent bridge, baby goats and chicks only a few hours old avoided the visual cliff. Wertheimer (1961) demonstrated that newborn human infants, only minutes old, will turn their heads in the direction of a sound. It would seem difficult to attribute such findings to learning or experience. The empiricist must resort to intra-uterine learning to explain avoidance of a visual cliff or sound localization. This possibility seems remote. Later in the text, we will see philosophers such as George Berkeley and Immanuel Kant contributing to empiricist and nativist arguments.

Instinct versus Learning

The problem of **instinct** versus **learning** has had a turbulent history during psychology's modern era (see Diamond, 1971, 1974a). Many early psychologists stressed the role of instincts in human and animal psychology. William McDougall (1871–1938) was perhaps the best example of an early theorist who believed that instincts play a central role in human life. McDougall (1908/1960) claimed that instincts operate in diverse behaviors such as curiosity, fighting, and maternal behavior. After a time, a group of psychologists called the behaviorists replaced instinct theories with an emphasis on learning. Behaviorism assumed that we learn to be aggressive, we learn to be inquisitive, and we learn to be good parents. Behaviorist research showed that some behaviors assumed to be instinctual were subject to learning. In early studies, Zing-Yang Kuo (1898–1970) demonstrated that rat killing by cats is more subject to learning than anybody of the time had believed (1921, 1924). Depending on rearing conditions, baby kittens may grow to become rat killers but may also grow up fearful of rats or may grow tolerant or even cooperative, living peacefully in the same cages with rats and eating and drinking from the same dishes. Kuo showed that the conditioning history of the individual kitten is the key to understanding that kitten's later interaction with rats. Kuo's enthusiasm led him to title one of his articles "A Psychology without Heredity" (1924).

Although behaviorism demonstrated the importance of learning, it did not banish instinct theory from psychology. Interest in the topic accelerated after World War II. Ethologists such as Konrad Lorenz (1903–1989) and Nikolaas "Niko" Tinbergen (1907–1988) and sociobiologists such as Edward O. Wilson (b. 1929) contributed new insights to the area. Desmond Morris's 1967 best-selling book *The Naked Ape* also stimulated public awareness of instinct theory.

Terms such as *a priori, nativism,* and *instinct* refer to abilities or capacities built into living systems. Important differences appear in the capacities denoted by these terms. For example, a priori knowledge is more cognitive than an instinct, which appears with a high degree of automaticity. A native ability such as the innate capacity to see in depth also seems less cognitive than a priori knowledge, which refers to real intellectual insight or the capacity to discern certain fundamental relationships. Terms such as *a posteriori, empiricism,* and *learning* are somewhat comparable because they stress the importance of experience.

What Are the Criteria by Which We Claim to Know Truth?

As human beings, we live our lives and make decisions based on epistemological categories that serve as guides to knowledge. On what grounds can we claim to have knowledge? On the grounds of authority? What about reason? Faith? Personal observation? Science? A clash of epistemologies provides the essential ingredient in disputes between science and law, between science and religion, and even between scientists and other scientists. Let's take a look at common epistemological criteria used as a basis for knowledge.

AUTHORITY   Reference to **authority** is the most common method of assessing truth. During childhood, we incorporate the values, beliefs, and judgments of our parents. They serve as the original authorities during our formative years of development. As we mature, we find a wealth of authority in modern culture. Authorities can be found in caregivers, teachers, books, the media, institutions, the Internet, religious teachings, and legal codes. Often we seek no independent verification or substantiation—the word of the authority is sufficient.

In his 1947 book *Man for Himself,* psychologist Erich Fromm (1900–1980) provided a thoughtful analysis of the problem of authority. For Fromm, the great sin in authoritarian epistemology is to become too much like the authority. If we become as knowledgeable as the authority, we no longer need its information and direction. As a means of survival, some authorities discourage questions and restrict information so followers will not discover contradictory opinions. Authorities may encourage study, but only if it is sanctioned and determined to be "safe." Abuse often begins when an authority claims to be the exclusive and sufficient basis of knowledge.

The history of ideas reveals countless episodes where authoritarian abuse produced tragic results. The Spanish theologian Michael Servetus (1511–1553) was branded a heretic for not conforming to accepted scriptural doctrines. He was burned at the stake. Almost a half-century later, Giordano Bruno (1548–1600) was condemned to the same fate for his unorthodox religious, scientific, and political opinions. The executions of Bruno and Servetus exemplify how commitment to authority can crush threatening ideas. Shakespeare's quotation at the beginning of this chapter may have been rooted in outrage at the abuse of authority.

Unfortunately, authoritarian abuse is not a historical relic. Abusive authoritarian forces steal into art, literature, science, religion, politics, and people themselves. The 1978 mass suicide of over 900 Americans in Jonestown, Guyana (see *Time,* 1978), is a tragic example of abusive authoritarian control (pp. 16–21). The balance between necessary and abusive authority is a critical problem confronting every human group. The irony of abusive authority is that people are easily led to rationalize or even idealize authority.

Within the history of psychology, we will encounter the problem of authority over and over again. Despite potential for abuse, authority has utilitarian value. The scientist, for example, may rely on other scientists and experiments for fresh insights. Authority is not the problem, but rather the way we use it.

EMPIRICISM   The term *empiricism* is derived from Greek and Latin terms that were close in meaning to our word *experience*. In contemporary usage, empiricism refers to a theory of knowledge where experience plays a central role. Experience of the world depends on sensory information. According to empiricism, knowledge is based on observable facts represented in experience. As the story of the history of psychology unfolds, we will see that empiricism is often contrasted with rationalism (discussed in the following text). Empiricists can be discovered in most historical periods and places, but Great Britain boasted a line of thinkers who gave priority to experience. John Locke (1632–1704) argued that there is nothing in the intellect that was not previously in the senses. An earlier British empiricist, Francis Bacon (1561–1626) has been called the Great Herald of the Empirical Spirit because of his campaign to encourage observation and data collection. For Bacon, we should rely less on authority and more on the empirical method.

From an uncritical standpoint, empiricism seems an obvious alternative to authority, tradition, and legalism as a way of obtaining knowledge. But empiricism as a way of knowing is not free of problems. First, as discussed with a priori and a posteriori knowledge, certain forms of knowledge may not depend on sensory information. We also know that sensory information can be unreliable. The senses are easily conditioned by emotion, social context, learning, and motivation. It is little wonder that philosophers and psychologists raised questions about the adequacy of empiricism as a way of knowing.

RATIONALISM   The term **rationalism** comes from the same Latin root as the term *reason*. Rationalists argue that the mind has innate organizing principles so information from the senses is filtered and patterned in ways that are built into the organism. Rationalists believe sensory information alone is not an adequate basis for knowledge. They emphasize the activity of mind, the capacity to reason, and the ability to discern some meanings on an intuitive basis. Early philosophers and scientists such as Descartes, Galileo, Leibniz, and Kant advocated rationalism.

Early psychologists and philosophers debated whether the new psychology should be based on empiricism or rationalism. As early as 1732, Christian von Wolff wrote a book titled *Empirical Psychology;* two years later, he wrote a complementary book titled *Rational Psychology.* In the United States, Laurens Hickok also wrote separate books under the titles of *Rational Psychology* (1849) and *Empirical Psychology* (1854). Early writers believed rationalism and empiricism offered useful but different methods. As we will see in Chapters 6 and 7, the tensions between rational and empirical psychology remain with us.

AESTHETICISM   **Aestheticism** is a doctrine that the principles of beauty apply to other arenas of thought. In this sense, aestheticism is an epistemology or way of knowing; for aestheticists, inquiry itself is a search for truth and beauty. This perspective is well illustrated in the book *The Double Helix* by Watson (1968). After Watson and Crick constructed the DNA model, the comment was made that the model was "too pretty not to be true" (Watson, 1968, p. 134). The aesthetic test has been of historical importance in the humanities—especially in art and music—but scientists also seem to delight in a beautiful model or a "pretty theory." Physicist Paul Dirac, as quoted by Brush (1974b), "stated that a theorist should prefer beautiful equations to uglier ones that yield closer agreement with experimental data" (p. 1167).

PRAGMATISM   Pragmatic philosophy offers still another perspective on epistemology. The term **pragmatism** is derived from a Greek root, translated as *pragma,* which refers to "things accomplished" or "things done." In this tradition, Francis Bacon believed we should emphasize theories and propositions that can be tested. Immanuel Kant used the term *pragmatic* to refer to that which is prudent. Under the late nineteenth-century leadership of Charles Sanders Peirce (*purse*) and William James, pragmatism became a major philosophical movement. Peirce and James emphasized the practical consequences of theories, definitions, ideas, and concepts. In typical American fashion, James talked about the "cash value" of an idea. Does the idea produce real productive work that makes a difference in the world of experience? Or does it lead to dead ends and muddled thinking? James believed that viable ideas produce sustained intellectual and physical work. He argued that a definition does not close our intellectual quest; on the contrary, a good definition raises questions and invigorates additional work (see James, 1907/1975b, pp. 31–32).

For the pragmatist, the world is in flux, and concepts must be altered and updated to be responsive to new discoveries. Concepts can outlive their usefulness and may need to be discarded. As methods improve and cultural biases shift, truth itself changes. Pragmatism judges truth in terms of utility or workability, but this is not the whole story. Rather, pragmatism calls for a deep awareness of change and a suspicion of big claims that cover too much territory. James (1876b) revealed his pragmatic side when he defined philosophy as the "habit of always seeing an alternative" p. 178).

One problem with pragmatism is that an idea or concept may appear sterile or unworkable in the present intellectual context, but may yield important truths at a later time. The Copernican model of the solar system appeared unworkable at first, but later revolutionized our knowledge of astrophysics. A naïve, extreme, or corrupted dose of pragmatism may discourage inquiry. William James and other pragmatists, however, would never permit such a consequence. James was more interested in opening than in closing doors (see James, 1909/1977, p. 19).

SKEPTICISM   According to **skepticism**, all truth claims are suspect and must be questioned. So it might appear counterintuitive to include skepticism as a way of knowing, but in the words of Rauch (1993), "all of your conclusions, every single one of them, may need to be corrected" (p. 45). Rauch argues for an epistemic humility that encourages skeptical analysis as an essential part of science and honest inquiry. We need not surrender provisional knowledge, but we must be suspicious of certitude because there is always a new perspective or a fresh discovery that challenges old conclusions. Skepticism, as a method of discovering problems, can offer a potent source of progress and knowledge. A society that discourages critical analysis and skepticism risks freezing the knowledge industry. In contrast, a society that encourages a skeptical ethic along with an evolutionary epistemology will be dynamic and open to the discovery mission (see Harrison, 2006). A productive and progressive science thrives on adversarial positions, conflicting theories, healthy curiosity, and a sincere skeptical attitude. Later in the text, we'll see how curiosity was considered a sin for centuries and how such a view resulted in intellectual stagnation. We will also find that skepticism in the late Renaissance period stimulated the development of modern science.

The Role of Emotions in Knowledge

Emotions play in our belief structures, complicating the problem of human knowledge. It can be challenging to sort out our competing beliefs when we are dispassionate. When emotions such as hate, fear, love, and anger enter the picture, our knowledge problems are compounded. Throughout this text, we will visit tensions between authority and reason. You might notice that the problem of emotion gives rise to these tensions. Though emotions may attach to either authority *or* reason, strong emotions "condition to" authority more than to reason. The expression *condition to* is important because emotions may be attached by any number of means to the claims of reason or to the claims of authority. For example, the dissonance associated with the violation of reason may be a source of emotion.

Let us return, however, to a consideration of emotion and its relation to authority. Authority is visible in our most vulnerable moments such as birth, marriage or other long-term commitments, illness, tragedy, and death. We sing to authority songs of praise, gratitude, thanksgiving, worship, and allegiance. Though protest music attacks authority, it is rare to encounter music inspired by claims of reason, but it is common to encounter music inspired by claims of authority. We create symbols inspired by authority and then idolize those symbols and pledge our allegiance to them. We set aside special holidays to celebrate authority, and we participate in self-denial and in rituals that underscore our loyalty and commitment. Failure to observe a ritual is often a source of the most intense anxiety and self-criticism. Our personal identity is seldom tied to reason like the character of Mr. Spock on the classic *Star Trek* movies and television series. Personal identities of the overwhelming majority, even in matters such as dress and food, are tied to authority. Deviance may trigger legitimate fears of social ostracism. For example, people who undergo a dramatic conversion from one belief to another may be disowned by parents or other authorities. Though science values openness, a scientific community may ostracize a scientist who deviates from standard practice.

Emotional problems are compounded when we believe that authority is absolute and immune from questioning. When reason and authority clash, the problem is both intellectual and emotional. The emotional power of authority is reflected in memory. Memorization is a valued activity in authority systems, and those who can recite the words of authority from memory are held up as role models. Children, especially, are encouraged to commit the words of authority to memory. A mechanical recitation is often more valued than a reflective and creative analysis.

Few topics are as important to human welfare and survival as epistemology, yet the subject is avoided or neglected because of its vexing questions. Unfortunately, emotion coupled with ignorance and the inevitable blind spots encountered in all belief systems undermine the critical reflection necessary to understand belief structures. The problem of knowledge is not a trivial or irrelevant metaphysical issue. It is a practical problem relevant to daily life and should thus be confronted in a vigorous and honest fashion. The Shakespeare quotation is a poetic reminder of the certitude that often accompanies ignorance and its consequences.

We come full circle to our original question. On what grounds can we lay claim to knowledge? We turn now to the interplay between science and epistemology.

Science and Epistemology

Conceived as a way of knowing, science represents an epistemology that blends empirical, rational, pragmatic, and aesthetic dimensions. From the beginning of the modern period, philosophers of science have studied scientific methodology, but they could not agree on what science is or how it operates. Later, we will observe disagreements, particularly between Francis Bacon and René Descartes, about the nature of science. Because of long-standing disagreements about the nature of science, we must caution against assuming *one* traditional view of science. In what follows, we will examine three critical thinkers to gain insight into their philosophies about science and epistemology.

KARL RAIMOND POPPER   Sir **Karl Raimond Popper (1902–1994)** was born in Vienna, where he studied mathematics, physics, and philosophy at the University of Vienna. His 1935 book *The Logic of Scientific Discovery* is a classic in the philosophy of science. After a lengthy and distinguished career at a variety of institutions, Popper died in 1994, in London.

Arguably, Popper's most original and noteworthy assertion is that observational evidence and induction cannot verify scientific theories. Regardless of the number of positive instances of an observation, one cannot justify drawing a universal conclusion. Though every observed swan may have been white, there is no basis for declaring that *all* swans are white. There is an inherent limitation in the method of induction so it cannot serve as a conclusive foundation for scientific procedure. Indeed, nothing in the inductive method per se serves as an adequate basis for distinguishing between legitimate science and a pseudoscience such as astrology. A pseudoscience may garner positive observations in support of its theories, but, according to Popper, such observations do not serve as a definitive verification principle.

In place of inductive methods, Popper argues that science should be guided by a hypothetico-deductive system that serves as the basis for the falsification of theories. The scientist must construct theories and deduce testable consequences from them. Such consequences may be consistent with the predictions of the theory or at variance with such predictions. A theory that is falsifiable is a successful scientific theory. A theory that is not falsifiable is not, by Popper's estimate, a scientific theory.

According to Popper, the integrity of science hinges on an honest quest for negative instances. One mark of nonscientific or pseudoscientific theories is that they tend to live forever because they are not falsifiable. Survivability is not the first task of a good theory; rather, a good theory possesses the virtues of simplicity and clarity. After scientists construct theories with such virtues, the next task is to search for empirical materials that are inconsistent with predictions of the theory.

Popper (1959) argued that there is no such thing as neutral observation; rather, "observation is always *observation in the light of theories....* It is only the inductivist prejudice that leads people to think that there could be a phenomenal language free of theories" (p. 59, italics in original). Popper admitted that he is offering a "theory of theories" (p. 59). His larger vision of the scientific enterprise is that it is by no means a basis for certitude. What Popper offers is an evolutionary epistemology that recognizes the crucial but tentative role of theory in human thought. Popper (1959) likens theories to "nets cast to catch what we call 'the world': to rationalize, to explain, and to master it. We endeavor to make the mesh ever

finer and finer" (p. 59). There is the hope of progress, but no grounds for certainty. Popper was concerned with the distinction between science and pseudoscience. According to Popper, genuine scientific theory is not invulnerable, and a major characteristic of science is that it does evolve.

Popper's philosophy of science has been criticized because it ignores the history of science and ignores what scientists actually do (see Toulmin, 1972, pp. 478–503). According to the criticism, Popper's theory is not empirical. That is, the theory is driven by abstractions of the intellect, by the method of reason, rather than by careful studies of how scientists actually conduct their work. The result is that we have prescriptions about how scientists ought to work rather than illumination about how they do work.

A stronger criticism comes from scientists and philosophers who have challenged the doctrine of *falsifiability*. In his book *Abusing Science,* Kitcher (1982) noted that one problem with falsifiability, at least in its naïve applications, is that it may discourage legitimate auxiliary hypotheses when a theory is threatened with empirical consequences it cannot predict. Kitcher gave the example of the failure of Uranus to follow an orbit predicted by Newtonian mechanics. The "behavior" of Uranus could have been taken as a falsification of Newtonian theory, but astronomers tried a different alternative. They plotted the course of a hypothetical planet whose existence would exert the necessary forces to account for the strange behavior of Uranus. Later, the discovery of Neptune resolved the difficulties because the orbit of Neptune was consistent with calculations worked out in advance for the hypothetical planet. Many scientists and philosophers would argue for falsifiability in scientific procedure, but others would suggest Popper overextends the concept. Its role may be clear enough in some scientific activity, but in other types (e.g., the descriptive mapping of a molecule or the naturalistic observations of the predatory behavior of the cheetah) the role of falsifiability is not so clear. A negative consequence of Popper's theory is that it may restrict the range of what counts as legitimate science.

THOMAS S. KUHN   As the author of *The Structure of Scientific Revolutions*, **Thomas S. Kuhn (1922–1996)** wrote one of the most influential books in the history and philosophy of science. Kuhn was initially interested in theoretical physics, but after assisting with an elementary science course for nonscientists, his interests shifted to the history and philosophy of science. Specifically, he shared that historical scientific studies "radically undermined some of [his] basic conceptions about the nature of science and the reasons for its special success" (Kuhn, 1970, p. v).

After extensive and broad-based liberal studies at Harvard and a year at Stanford University's Center for Advanced Studies in the Behavioral Sciences, Kuhn devoted himself almost exclusively to the development of the ideas later set forth in his book. Kuhn's first interest was in the nature or development of scientific advances. He addressed a different central problem than did Popper, but the two theories cover common territory, though in different ways.

Kuhn's work emphasized the importance of understanding science in terms of community structures and historical development. The scientific community shares an intellectual background, standard reference sources, textbooks, ways of solving problems, and values. The community exerts pressures on the individual, especially during student years and in early scientific-professional years when the young scientist is establishing a reputation. Kuhn did not mean that the scientific community is a closed club. Such an interpretation is an unfortunate "popular caricature of Kuhn's position" (Kitcher, 1982, p. 168). Kuhn recognized the diversities that exist in the scientific community. Nevertheless, there is much that community members share in common.

Kuhn was interested in the evolution of science over time. Competing schools of thought mark early prescientific development and are prone to quarrel over basic definitions, methods, and assumptions. He noted that the early stages of electrical research gave rise to competing views about the nature of electricity. The same is true in our field as early psychologists engaged in vigorous debates over subject matter and appropriate methods.

Kuhn (1970) notes that the early search for research consensus is difficult because "all of the facts that could possibly pertain to the development of a given science are likely to seem equally relevant. As a result, early fact-gathering is a far more nearly random activity than the one that subsequent scientific development makes familiar" (p. 15). In time, one competing school will prevail over the others. The dominant school attracts a loyal following while promising a set of problems worthy of sustained study. The leading school now dictates the intellectual agenda, ushering in a transition to what Kuhn called **normal science**.

Normal science has a record of past achievement; it defines problem areas and provides methods of practice. Most scientists work in this tradition. When the time is right, Kuhn tells us, a **paradigm** emerges as an elaboration on the meaning of normal science. In a sociological sense, paradigm refers to "the entire constellation of beliefs, values, techniques, and so on, shared by members of a given community" (Kuhn, 1970, p. 175). The term also refers to conventional ways of approaching and solving problems. Paradigms define boundaries within which scientists do their work and clarify the legitimate methods of analysis and ways of looking at problems.

Normal science is comparable to solving puzzles. Scientists find puzzle pieces and fit them into their appropriate places. Kuhn used the expression *mopping up* to describe the work of scientists during the normal science phase. During this phase, there is little focus on novel events. Indeed, mopping-up operations aim at forcing "nature into the preformed and relatively inflexible box that the paradigm supplies" (Kuhn, 1970, p. 24). According to Kuhn, three classes of problems engage scientists as they proceed with the business of normal science. First, scientists search for facts that the paradigm designates as significant; second, facts are matched with theory; and third, scientists elaborate and extend the theory. The paradigm drives many rewarding problems, but there is little motivation for exploring anomalies or ideas that do not conform to the large picture.

In the course of normal science, serendipitous findings and anomalies cannot be ignored. Sometimes discoveries occur through accidents and at other times are theory driven. Kuhn (1970) noted that X-rays are "a classic case of discovery through accident, a type that occurs more frequently than the impersonal standards of scientific reporting allow us easily to realize" (p. 57). He described events that led German physicist Wilhelm Conrad Röntgen (1845–1923) to discover X-rays and how even a notable scientist such as Lord Kelvin (1824–1907) believed they were a hoax. The prevailing paradigm had not predicted or anticipated Röntgen's X-ray discovery, but it was a finding that could not be ignored.

In most cases, efforts are made to assimilate new discoveries or anomalies into the prevailing paradigm. Such efforts are understandable because the scientific community has a vested interest in the traditional paradigm. It has commanded loyalties and lifetimes of hard work. However, a succession of anomalous findings are so compelling they cannot be ignored. Such a turn of events creates a crisis that causes some members of the community to lose faith. The community response is predictable: Some try to find ad hoc hypotheses to rescue the paradigm, whereas others search for new ways to organize the larger picture.

According to Kuhn, scientific revolutions are marked by new and more successful organizations of the world. With a paradigm shift, a new vision replaces the old way of seeing things. Kuhn (1970) noted that his "book portrays scientific development as a succession of tradition-bound periods punctuated by noncumulative breaks" (p. 208). Following a revolution, the old paradigm is rejected and scientists return to a normal science that operates within the new paradigm.

Both Kuhn and Popper advanced evolutionary epistemologies, and both challenged absolutistic approaches to science. Kuhn has a broader interpretation of what counts as legitimate science than does Popper. Mopping-up activities, accidental discoveries, and descriptive studies all comprise the business of science. Kuhn has been criticized for covering too much ground with the term *paradigm.* He acknowledged the criticism and attempted to correct it. Kuhn's model of science was subjected to the same criticism leveled against Popper—namely, that it does not do justice to the extreme diversity in the history of science. We turn now to a third orientation that offers a radical difference from Popper and Kuhn.

PAUL K. FEYERABEND In his book *Science in the Making,* Joel Hildebrand, a chemist and former president of the American Chemical Association, challenged the idea that there is *one* scientific method. Hildebrand (1957) argued that "to be successful in unlocking doors concealing nature's secrets, a person must have ingenuity. If [we do] not have the key for the lock, [we] must not hesitate to pick it, to climb in a window, or even kick in a panel" (p. 26). Hildebrand argues that scientific success values ingenuity and determination more than method.

Hildebrand's statement is by no means esoteric. In *Reflections of a Physicist,* Percy W. Bridgman (1955) said, "there is no scientific method as such" (p. 416). In that same source, he pointed out that scientists do not follow "any prescribed course of action…[;] science is what scientists do, and there are as many scientific methods as there are individual scientists" (p. 83). Zoologist P. B. Medawar (1984) shared the same sentiment in his book *The Limits of Science*: "There is indeed no such thing as 'the' scientific method. A scientist uses a very great variety of stratagems… [and] no procedure of discovery can be logically scripted" (p. 51).

Medawar challenged the idea that breakthroughs follow a calculus of discovery. Perhaps some discoveries arrive in such a neat fashion, but he argued for the role of serendipity in science. Consider again the discovery of X-rays. Medawar (1984, p. 46) asks us to imagine a scientist prior to 1900 approaching a funding agency with a proposal "to discover a means of making human flesh transparent." The idea would be greeted with scorn. Still, the discovery of X-rays didn't follow any preplanned logical pathway connected to scientific goal setting.

Hildebrand, Bridgman, and Medawar do not wish to undermine respect for science. Quite the contrary, they have a keen interest in scientific advancement. What they are saying is that science is not as tidy, objective, and coherent as we have been led to believe. A similar theme is sounded by Brush (1974b) in a thoughtful article titled "Should the History of Science Be Rated X?" He shows that what we learn in the history of science may "not be a good model for students" because it challenges our idealized image of science.

In a 1975 book titled *Against Method,* **Paul K. Feyerabend (1924–1994)** outlined an anarchistic theory of knowledge. Although acknowledging the negative implications of anarchism, especially for political science, he finds appropriate and healthy implications for anarchism in epistemology and science. His analysis of the history of science offers a vigorous disagreement with Popper and Kuhn. Feyerabend (1975) contended,

> The idea of a method that contains firm, unchanging, and absolutely binding principles for conducting the business of science meets considerable difficulty when confronted with the results of historical research—there is not a single rule, however plausible, and however firmly grounded in epistemology, that is not violated at some time or other. It becomes evident that such violations are not accidental events; they are not results of insufficient knowledge or of inattention which might have been avoided. On the contrary, we see that they are necessary for progress. (p. 23)

Feyerabend went on to say that conscious decisions to break from conventional wisdom and method are not only facts in the history of science but necessary to the progress of science. In his thinking, successful and creative scientists break or reverse rules, defend ad hoc hypotheses, work inductively and then deductively, and work sometimes for unity and sometimes for plurality. The rule, he tells us, is *anything goes.*

Feyerabend (1975) argued that "even a law-and-order science will succeed only if anarchistic moves are occasionally allowed to take place" (p. 26). Drawing on examples from the history of science as evidence, he suggested that "the idea of a fixed method, or of a fixed theory of rationality, rests on too naive a view of [human beings and their] social surroundings" (Feyerabend, 1975, p. 27, 1988).

Feyerabend's position should not be viewed as a debunking or skepticism of science. However, his position calls for closer scrutiny of the history of scientific discovery. He also encourages more detailed empirical analysis of what scientists actually do. For example, is the hands-on lab work of the chemist the same method as the astronomer calculating the trajectory of a comet? Does the abstract algebraist use the same method as the marine biologist who studies the feeding habits of sharks? Is there one scientific method adapted for various fields of science or is there a diversity of methods within specific disciplines? If there is no *one* scientific method, are there at least features (e.g., the importance of quantification) that all methods share?

Relevance of Epistemology to Psychology

Early psychologists disagreed about the appropriate methodology for the new psychology. Should there be one method or many? If there is but one, which should it be? The philosophy of science dictates such questions. From some points of view, the scientific status of psychology hinges on methodological purity. Other philosophy-of-science considerations dictate psychology's status among the sciences. Within Kuhn's scheme, psychology could be regarded as a pre-paradigmatic science. It enjoys higher status in Feyerabend's schemes if for no other reason than that the methodological purity of all the sciences is called into question. Further, there is wider latitude of acceptance in Feyerabend's scheme about what constitutes "normal science."

The issues raised here are of historical interest, but they also command the attention of contemporary scientists and philosophers. As we proceed through the history of psychology, we will encounter questions about the nature of science and the scientific status of psychology.

THE PROBLEM OF CAUSALITY

From the time of Aristotle to the present, philosophers and scientists have debated the nature and meaning of causation. Contributing to the richness of the problem are questions concerning the possible influence of unconscious processes in human life, the role of intention or purpose in determining behavior, and the question of whether the individual can be an agent of change (i.e., a cause). In what follows, we will review classic and modern approaches to the problem of causation.

Aristotle struggled with the meaning of causation, paving the way for centuries of debate and speculation on the issue. He believed that causation is not a simple one-dimensional affair. To know the cause of anything, we must understand several things. First, we must understand what conditions led up to the event. Aristotle referred to antecedent conditions as the **efficient cause**, essentially that which sets a thing in motion. When domino *B* falls after being hit by *A*, we can say that the movement of *A* is the efficient cause of the fall of *B*. Aristotle also believed we need to understand the material structure of a thing to understand causation. When a physician takes a hammer and strikes the patellar tendon, the knee reflex will cause the patient's leg to kick. If the physician's hammer is the efficient cause of the reflex, there must also be a material cause. In this case, we would not observe the reflex if there had been nerve or muscle damage. So part of the cause of the reflex is the material structure of the knee including the nerves, tendons, and muscles. In other words, the reflex depends on a physical substrate, which Aristotle called the **material cause**. Domino *A* (an efficient cause) impacting domino *B* could knock *B* over if both were made of the same material. But if *B* were made of lead and *A* of light wood, then *B* would not fall when impacted by *A*. The so-called causal

sequence depends on a material structure as well as antecedent conditions.

Aristotle described a third kind of cause known as the **formal cause**. This refers to the form, shape, or identifying properties of a thing. A sculptor may chisel away at two pieces of granite, using one to create a bust of Beethoven and the other to shape a likeness of Mozart. For both busts, the material is the same but the form is different. The formal cause carries information value. The functional or causal properties of a thing depend on form. Domino *B* would not fall when impacted by *A* if it were too short or different in form than *A*. So form may also be essential to an understanding of a causal sequence. An airplane could be constructed of appropriate material (material cause) and have an excellent propulsion system (efficient cause), but if the wing were damaged or poorly designed (formal cause), the plane would not fly.

According to Aristotle, if you want to understand a sequence of events, you need to know the goal and purpose that caused it. Let's return to the knee reflex example. The physician was conducting a neurological exam, so she used a hammer to strike the patient's knee. That was her purpose. Aristotle called this the **final cause**, the end or purpose for which a change was produced. Aristotle might say you cannot understand the knee reflex, or rather the cause of the knee reflex, until you understand the physician's intention or purpose.

For Aristotle, knowledge of causation rests on understanding form, material, antecedent conditions, and the purpose for which a thing was intended. Aristotle believed in a balance of all four dimensions of causation. His student, Theophrastus, believed science should concern itself primarily with material and efficient causation and not with final causation.

The Aristotelian notion of final causation should not be confused with teleological interpretations of the world encountered in numerous theological beliefs. The term **teleology** refers to purpose or design. Technically, *teleology* can be defined as the investigation of evidence that there is design or purpose in nature. The assumption of design leads to the next question: What was the origin of the design or purpose? There are two types of teleological answers to that question. **Intrinsic teleology** is the position that design, order, and purpose are immanent in nature—simple manifestations or characteristics of nature. But **extrinsic teleology** makes the claim that any design in nature reflects the work of a designer and that the designer has imbued the design with the designer's own purpose. Though Aristotle believed in an unmoved mover (God), it is problematic as to whether he would subscribe to the kind of teleology encountered in some theologies.

Intrinsic teleology has become archaic in physics and chemistry. Psychologists can't dismiss intrinsic teleology as easily. Despite attempts by behaviorists to build a psychological science like physics based on material and efficient causation, teleology has constituted a persistent problem for psychologists. Many psychologists have found it difficult, if not impossible, to resist expressions such as *goal directed, intention, plans, purposive behavior, anticipation*, and *expectancy*. Such terms, unless defined in unusual ways, suggest intrinsic teleology or final causation. But can human behavior be explained with the same material and efficient causation used to explain the movement of a billiard ball, the trajectory of a comet, or the changes in the metabolism of a cell? Or must we invoke some form of final causation to account for the complexity of human behavior? We will encounter opposition to teleological explanations in the works of theorists such as Jacques Loeb, John B. Watson, Clark Hull, and B. F. Skinner while theorists such as William McDougall, Edward Chace Tolman, and Gordon Allport favor teleological explanations. Rychlak and Rychlak (1990) and Rychlak (1994) insist that teleological assumptions play a critical role in psychology.

You may have heard the familiar warning that correlation does not imply causation. But neither does correlation imply that there is not a causal relationship between two events. Correlation is neutral with respect to the question of causation. Perhaps causation is not a scientific construct. Maybe it is simply a historical

and philosophical curiosity. To be sure, there are those who are content to study correlations or functional relationships. But the idea of causality is so entrenched in common sense that it refuses to vanish. Some still argue that science entails a search for fundamental processes that underlie and explain correlational data.

In psychology, questions associated with the problem of causality will show themselves time after time. Some of the questions are as follows: To what extent do events influence us that are not a part of our consciousness? If unconscious processes influence us, then can we claim to be rational or free? Is it possible to build an adequate science of human experience and behavior on the basis of material and efficient causes? Can we rise above cause-and-effect relations and exercise freedom of choice? We'll address these questions throughout the book, beginning with the last issue.

FREE WILL AND DETERMINISM

This must have happened to you. A boss or supervisor (or even a professor) seems to go out of his or her way to make your life difficult. No matter how hard you try at work or in class, you can't succeed. Times like this make us feel as if we have little or no control over our lives. But at other times, we experience an overwhelming sense of control, where things in our life work because we make them work.

Do we have power over our lives or are the causes of everything beyond our reach? This is at the heart of one of philosophy's oldest problems. Several of psychology's greatest figures have dedicated serious consideration to this issue (James, 1884/1979a; Skinner, 1971). Sigmund Freud, John Watson, Ivan Pavlov, and B. F. Skinner stand in the determinist camp, whereas William James, Carl Jung, Gordon Allport, and Carl Rogers are committed to a belief in freedom of choice. The issue of free will and determinism represents a source of controversy between humanistic and behaviorist psychologies. It is an issue with far-reaching implications for psychology. If humans have some degree of freedom, then a psychology based on strict determinism cannot do justice to its subject matter. On the other hand, if causality exists in nature—including human nature—then belief in freedom of choice is unwarranted and may work against psychology. This issue is more alive now than a half century ago. It has been the subject of numerous books and articles in psychology (see Churchland, 2006; Harris, 2012; Rychlak, 1988; Rychlak & Rychlak, 1990; Vedral, 2006; Viney, 1990; Lequyer, 1856/1998).

The doctrine of **free will** assumes that people make choices that are to some degree independent of antecedent conditions. It assumes we can rise above genetic, chemical, physical, and social influences. We can anticipate alternatives in the decision-making process and weigh their possible outcomes. Behavior may be predictable, but there's an element of unpredictability in our actions. If we feel we can rise above causal forces, we're more likely to view ourselves as rational or responsible creatures. By the way, most advocates of free will do not attribute this quality to animals.

Most **libertarians** (people who believe in free will) agree that environmental and genetic forces impose limitations on us, but they still believe in at least some freedom of choice. Although libertarians may disagree about the power of the causes that affect our lives, they are likely to believe that the person or the self is not simply passive or reactive. Instead, the self acts on the environment with awareness and purpose. Let's take a look at arguments in support of the libertarian position.

1. *Argument for an adequate explanation of human experience.* Psychologists have never been able to make perfect predictions of simple, let alone complex, behavior. For example, there's no way we can write biographies in advance. Such predictive failure challenges the adequacy of strict determinism. The determinist position struggles with the spontaneity and unpredictability in human behavior. Libertarians claim that their position offers a better fit with our observations and theories about experience and behavior. The libertarian perspective is embarrassed by neither our regularities nor our irregularities, uncertainties, and novelties.

2. *Logical contradictions in determinism.* Libertarians argue that if determinism is true, a determinist cannot logically declare that he or she *believes* in determinism. Why? Because the determinist is not the real believer. Belief is a mere consequence of antecedents. According to determinism, the very words *I believe in determinism* are conditioned by more fundamental forces. It is not that one believes in determinism, but that consequences have transpired to result in the statement *I believe in determinism.* Strict determinism implies a passive nature about the self that is well illustrated in B. F. Skinner's (1983a) statement, "If I am right about human behavior, I have written the autobiography of a nonperson" (p. 32).

3. *Argument from morality.* Libertarians argue that determinism makes a mess of morality. According to determinism, any immoral behavior can be explained in terms of causes that had no prevision of the ends they were achieving. In other words, individuals are not responsible for their actions. Indeed, the term *responsibility* is a hollow term—it means little more than ability to respond.

4. *Argument from indeterminism.* Libertarians argue that strict determinism is a pre-twentieth-century concept that is no longer applicable in the physical sciences. Following quantum theory and Heisenberg's uncertainty principle, the physical world must now be viewed from a probabilistic rather than a strictly causal framework. The doctrine of **indeterminism** holds that it is not possible to apply strict cause-and-effect explanations in the world of subatomic particles. This well-known doctrine has led some individuals to argue that indeterminism applies to psychology. Although indeterminism is not identical with purposive free will, an indeterminist would tell us that human nature is characterized by an inherent uncertainty.

As you can guess, the libertarian perspective has not gone unchallenged. **Determinism** states that there are causes, both known and unknown, for every behavior or experience. Taylor (1967b) defined *determinism* as the philosophical doctrine that "states that for everything that ever happens there are conditions such that, given them, nothing else could happen" (p. 359).

The great physicist Albert Einstein (1879–1955) proclaimed, "God doesn't play dice with the universe" (Michelmore, 1962, p. 128). As a determinist, Einstein believed that the law of cause and effect operates at every level of reality. He once remarked that "God is clever, but…not malicious" (Michelmore, 1962, p. 111). He's suggesting that the world, because of its lawfulness, is knowable. It may be difficult to discover causes and laws, but with persistence we *can* make discoveries—nature is not vicious or unknowable. This is the optimistic side of determinism: Nature is knowable, and problems can be solved when cause-and-effect relations are discovered.

Belief in freedom of the will may discourage inquiry (such a belief may have delayed the development of a scientific psychology). In this respect, the determinist offers the following rebuttal to indeterminism: Even if indeterminism applies to the world of fundamental particles, it is not applicable in larger physical systems. A system as complicated, say, as a basketball remains as a reliable and determinate system, even if the behavior of the smallest physical units sustaining it are indeterminate. Historically, science has always proceeded on the assumption of the lawfulness or statistical regularity of its subject matter. But now let us turn to a few major arguments in defense of determinism.

1. *Historical argument.* The history of the free will–determinism controversy is a history of victories for determinism and retreats for the theory of free will. With increasing knowledge of brain structure and function, lawful explanations are extended to an ever-widening spectrum of behaviors. The term *will* once occupied a great amount of space in psychology textbooks, but as knowledge has progressed, we have less need for the term. In the history of neuroscience, for example, mechanistic explanations have replaced explanations based on the will on countless occasions.

2. *Argument from morality.* The determinist can counter the libertarian by stating that belief in free will can also make a mess of morality.

Many of history's most barbaric practices were justified on the grounds that the victim had made a free choice and now deserved punishment. From medieval times, aggressive witch hunts made a sport of persecuting people who allegedly used free will to make a pact with the devil.

3. *Argument from reasonable expectancy.* As we think about our world, we develop reasonable expectations that things are lawful. The world is not capricious; given a specific set of weather conditions, we can have a reasonable expectation that a Chinook wind will hit Boulder, Colorado, within a specified period of time. In a similar manner, we may reasonably expect stress and other circumstances to contribute to an emotional breakdown. We don't need to attribute the breakdown to an act of free choice. Most of us live our lives on the basis of reasonable expectations. If an expectation is not confirmed, we assume we neglected to take some variable into consideration. Without determinism, we have no grounds for reasonable expectations about the world.

The free will–determinism debate is a defining issue for psychology. Throughout the book, we will outline where various psychologists stand on this issue. As noted, the issue is alive and well in contemporary psychology. With the advance of the neurosciences, the debates over free will and determinism have, if anything, intensified and grown more technical (see Baer, Kaufman, & Baumeister, 2008; Libet, 1985; Schlosser, 2012; Wegner, 2002). Many of the recent debates have centered around research on neurophysiological precursors of intentions. If intentions lack automaticity and some degree of causal efficacy, do we have free will? If the conclusion is negative, we are still haunted by vexing existential questions raised by William James (1979a). Am I the author of nothing? What does it mean to face a world foredone?

THE MIND–BODY PROBLEM

The mind–body problem belongs to a subdisciplinary area of philosophy known as *ontology.* Philosophers have used the term **ontology** in diverse ways. For our purposes, we can define it as the study of the nature and relations of being. When we ask, "what is real?" we are asking an ontological question. Is the mind real? Is there a mind that is somehow independent from the brain? What is the relationship between the mind and the brain? Is there one fundamental reality (monism), two (dualism), or perhaps many (pluralism)? If there is more than one reality, how do the various types of reality coexist—and do they influence each other? Do psychologists study the mind or do they study only behavior? All of these are ontological questions because they ask the essential question: What is real? Let's explore some traditional solutions to ontological problems.

Monism

According to monistic philosophy, everything belongs in some intimate way to everything else. As an elegant solution to the problem of ontology, **monism** suggests that reality, whatever it is, is all of one piece. If everything belongs in an intimate way to every other thing, then nothing is alien or foreign because all things are part of one thing. What appears as foreign or alien is only a product of the present gaps in our knowledge. Monism offers hope for a unity of knowledge because we all study the same thing, but at different levels and from diverse perspectives. One form of monism nurtures the belief that psychology is reducible to the field of physics. Although monism appeals to simplicity, a major problem arises because monists can't agree about what the one and only reality is. Monism, in fact, comes in oppositional forms. Let's consider them and their implications for the mind–brain problem.

MATERIALISM **Materialism** is a monistic ontology characterized by the belief that matter is the fundamental constituent of all things. A material monist might argue that the body exists, but not the mind. Terms such as *mind, spirit*, and *consciousness* are understood in terms of the material, efficient, and formal operations of brain activity. It follows that there is no mind–brain problem as such because all so-called mental activity is

reducible to physical, chemical, or physiological processes. Many key figures such as Democritus, Thomas Hobbes, Julien Offray de la Mettrie, Herman von Helmholtz, Ivan Pavlov, and John B. Watson have been materialists.

IDEALISM As an alternative to materialism, **idealism** emphasizes mind or spirit as the pre-eminent feature of life. It represents a radical departure from materialism and a different emphasis with respect to the mind–body problem. According to idealism, as the term is employed in philosophy, the mental world of experience is foundational to all science and, for that matter, all knowledge. It would be impossible to know anything apart from consciousness or experience. Thus, the mental world (experience, awareness, consciousness) has priority—it is the only world to which we have immediate access. The material world is regarded as derivative—an intellectual or philosophical product that has its origin in the world of experience. For the idealist, psychology is the science that studies mental processes and experience. Further, an idealist would argue that all science begins with experience and is about experience. Thus, it is the mind or the mental world that has ontological status. The material world is a construction—a mere by-product of a more important reality. Several key figures, including Plato, Gottfried Wilhelm Leibniz, George Berkeley, and Gustav Fechner, have identified with idealism.

DOUBLE-ASPECT MONISM This variety of monism displays sensitivity to the claims of materialism and idealism. **Double-aspect monism** emphasizes the idea that there is a language for mental processes and a language for underlying physical processes, but both languages refer to the same reality. We use words such as *mind, experience, consciousness, awareness*, and *thinking*. We also have a rich and growing language that refers to fundamental physical structures and processes such as neurons, neurotransmitters, cell assemblies, and synaptic transmission. According to double-aspect monism, both languages are legitimate but both refer to the same underlying reality approached from two perspectives. Benedict Spinoza, an early advocate of double-aspect theory, argued that human beings may be described in mentalistic terms or in the language of the physical sciences. The two languages provide different perspectives just as one may describe a coin from the perspective of the obverse or the reverse. According to double-aspect theory, the mind–body problem is a problem of language. The ontological problem, however, remains. What is real? Is reality reduced to words? Despite its problems, double-aspect theory can embrace a tolerant and robust approach to psychology that includes legitimate roles for descriptions that refer to mental and to physical processes.

EPIPHENOMENALISM   A final version of monism known as **epiphenomenalism** is often classified as a dualistic position, but for reasons that shall soon be apparent, it is more accurately classified as a monistic position. An *epiphenomenon* is an appearance or a kind of "overflow" resulting from the operation of something that is more basic or fundamental. According to epiphenomenalism, mental processes (e.g., thought, consciousness, cognitions) are a kind of "overflow" or by-product of brain activity. The mental world has no independent status; it is a mere epiphenomenon or appearance. Plato employed the analogy of a guitar; the physical strings produce the epiphenomenal sound much like the physical brain produces the epiphenomenal mind (Plato, *The Phaedo*, 1961). According to epiphenomenalism, causality always runs one way, from the physical to the mental. There is no mental causation because the mind has no independent status apart from its physical substrate. Epiphenomenalism is clearly a variation of materialism.

Dualism

In contrast with monism, **dualism** asserts that there are two fundamental orders of reality—mind and body. Each has ontic (i.e., real) status. Naïvely, most of us experience the reality of mental processes; we also experience the reality of the physical world. According to the dualistic position, we are assured that neither the mental nor the physical world is a mere appearance. For all of its popular appeal, at least to the Westerner, dualism presents a major problem. If there are two orders of reality, how do they get along with each other? Can one influence the other? Or can each influence the other, and if so, how? Most dualistic mind–body positions address the issue of how mind and body collaborate. Let's examine the better-known positions.

INTERACTIONISM   According to **interactionism**, sometimes called the *commonsense* position, mental events are real—they influence each other and they influence bodily events. Bodily events also influence each other, and they influence mental events. Although interactionism sometimes appeals to common sense, it is not without problems. First, interactionists have difficulty specifying how an immaterial mental system can be causal with respect to a physical system (or, for that matter, how a material system can be causal with respect to an immaterial one). Second, a major problem centers around the locus of interaction. Where do mind and body influence each other? René Descartes, history's most famous interactionist, addressed this problem with considerable courage and suggested that the pineal gland, located in the center of the head, is the seat of interaction. Centuries later, we have found that people can function fairly well following a pinealectomy. In this sense, Descartes's theory of the locus of interaction was testable, but was demonstrated to be wrong. Descartes also failed to show how a mental event can influence physical events and vice versa. His followers' subsequent attempts also proved unsuccessful. For all its commonsense appeal, interactionism leaves us with more questions than answers.

PSYCHOPHYSICAL   PARALLELISM According to **psychophysical parallelism**, mental events are real, and they influence other mental events. Bodily events are also real, and they influence other bodily events. Mental events cannot, however, influence bodily events, and bodily events cannot influence mental events. The two orders of reality are nevertheless, by definition, parallel with each other. That is, whatever is happening in one order is, by definition, happening simultaneously in the other order. The philosopher Gottfried Wilhelm Leibniz, the best-known advocate of this position, provides an intriguing allegory. Imagine that mind and body are like two clocks on a wall, each displaying the same time. They are synchronized but independent. One clock has no causal influence over the other, yet they function in agreement with each other. According to Leibniz, mind and body are by definition parallel, but there is no causal influence between these two independent orders of reality.

Parallelism avoids the problems encountered in the interactionist position, but at a considerable expense—it flies in the face of common sense. Most of us, for example, assume that the experience of pain is connected to the chance encounter with the hot stove top and the resulting burn. The burn is mental and physical, and there is a causal connection between them. A more difficult problem is that parallelism implies a kind of preestablished harmony between mind and body. Explaining how preestablished harmony works might prove more difficult than explaining an interaction.

EMERGENTISM The philosophical position known as **emergentism**, in at least one of its variations, argues that mental processes are produced by brain processes, but are qualitatively different. For example, the experience of a toothache emerges out of complex neurological activity that may have been activated by decay or some kind of damage. The experience itself, though emerging out of bodily activity, is not captured by descriptions of bodily activity. The experience seems to have a career of its own and a reality that is qualitatively set apart. To clarify, let's take an analogy from chemistry. Salt is a product of sodium and chloride, yet the compound salt has unique properties that differ from sodium and chloride. Sodium alone or chloride alone can be lethal to the living organism, yet when combined in the form of salt, they can prove vital to life. The compound seems to have "emergent" properties of its

own that are not a simple summation of separate elements. In a similar manner, mental processes, though produced by brain processes, are radically and qualitatively different. The experience of a sunrise, a poem, or a symphonic passage emerges from brain activity, but the global mental experience with its inspirational, affective, and associative meanings appears to be a reality unto itself quite different qualitatively from the underlying firing of neurons or the neurochemical activities in the synapse.

Emergentism is by no means a unified or consistent philosophical orientation. There are varieties of emergentism such as epiphenomenalism that are more consistent with monism (Crick, 1994), but other varieties that are more consistent with dualism. Thus, an emergentist might argue that causal forces work from the parts to the whole and from the whole to the parts. Such an argument is consistent with a functional or pragmatic dualism, if not a metaphysical dualism. Let us turn now to another approach to the problem of ontology.

Pluralism

A final commonsense belief is that we live in a "multiverse" of separate orders of things. Ontological **pluralism** embraces the reality of mind and body but also insists that these two orders do not exhaust the possibilities. In a discussion of ontological pluralism, MacCormac (1990) pointed out that concepts arise "from physical brain processes…but they do not always find their origin solely in brain activity" (p. 417). A concept may have its origin in any of a great number of cultural sources, but because it depends on the physical system for its expression, its causal sources can be diverse. An ontological pluralist may believe that there are many separate real things, including different types of conscious experience and other orders of reality that do not obey rules that we know. Pluralism raises even more problems than interactionism. For each separate reality we posit, we must now struggle with the problem of the interaction of that reality with others. For example, as the mind–body theorist must struggle with how mind and body influence each other, the classical theist must struggle with the problem of theodicy (the relation of God to the world). It is little wonder that those with unity-loving natures are repulsed by pluralism—it is a messy philosophy. But the pluralist would insist that the world is not simple. Pluralism has been a continuing subject of interest in philosophy and science throughout the twentieth century (see Ford, 1990; James, 1909/1977; Reck, 1990).

A major variation on pluralism could be labeled **attributive pluralism**. This position emphasizes the relationship between an object and the words used to describe the object. People, as users of words, may attribute various qualities to an object. For example, let's take the question, *what is a sunset?* A plurality of possible descriptions exists as an answer. Now imagine that we pose this question to a sample of different professionals. If we called on a physicist, a musician, a neuroscientist, an artist, a psychologist, and a poet, we would find a delightful array of explanations. The musician might invite us to listen to a new composition, "The Sunset Symphony," capturing the sunset as an auditory experience. Not to be outdone, the artist shows us a canvas depicting a sun fading above a seascape, revealed in vivid oil paint. Both are aesthetic representations, but we may ask, what is the real sunset? Does the physicist have the answer with all his or her elegant mathematical formulas? What about the neuroscientist who shares impressive monitoring of retinal images and occipital activity? Does the psychologist's analysis of the perceptual process offer the answer? Or even his normative testing on what sunsets mean to different people. Or shall we give the poet the final word? To adjudicate the claims of our scholars, we might convene a panel of philosophers consisting of two monists and two pluralists. The monists agree that the true sunset is one thing but disagree on what that one thing is—for one it is physical, for the other, experiential. One of the pluralists argues that there are many objective sunsets. The other contends that there are many legitimate descriptive modes: Sunsets are, after all, what we describe them to be. The most fundamental reality is, therefore,

our words. But the other pluralist insists that realities exist beyond our words.

Let us now leave the mind–body problem, with the comment that the various schools and systems of psychology we encounter will disagree with each other on this issue. We will encounter materialists, double-aspect theorists, pluralists, interactionists, and others. A major key to understanding a given school or system will be to assess that school's or system's position on the mind–body problem.

Psychogeny

A close relative of the study of mind–body relations is encountered in the problem of psychogeny (*sy KAW gin ee*). The term **psychogeny** is derived from the Greek term **psyche** (*sy kee*), which has been translated as "spirit," "soul," or "mind." Each of these terms has different connotations, but they also share something in common in that they each refer to a principle of existence that embodies mentalistic concepts such as awareness, consciousness, sentience, or experience. Psychogeny may be defined as the study of the origin of psyche or the study of theories of the origin of psyche. Two very broad theories are briefly reviewed in the materials that follow, but more detailed discussion is available (see Viney & Woody, 1995).

PSYCHOGENIC IDENTITY THEORY   Two key features of **psychogenic identity theory** are that (1) psyche is instilled in the primitive biological substratum of the organism at a given point in time, and (2) there is continuity or identity between the psychically endowed biological substratum and the later mature, self-reflective, fully conscious adult. Psychogenic identity theorists have never been able to agree with each other about the time of infusion of psyche into the body. For centuries, theologians argued that an embryo becomes human at forty days if it is male and eighty days if it is female (see De Rosa, 1988, p. 347). More recently, a popular belief claimed that psyche is instilled at fertilization. Kuhse and Singer (1993), in their work on embryo experimentation, note, "what this claim amounts to is that the newly fertilized egg, the early embryo, and I are in some sense of the term, the same individual" (p. 66). Because of its emphasis on the independence of psyche, psychogenic identity theory is consistent with idealism and some forms of dualism. Although identity theory has popular appeal, it is not without a host of problems, many of which surfaced from recent work in embryo experimentation.

An example of a major problem with psychogenic identity theory is encountered in research on microsurgical sectioning of fertilized eggs. According to some forms of psychogenic identity theory, conception (the fertilization of an egg) marks the entry point of psyche into its material substrate. A colony of cells (a morula or blastocyst) develops following conception and results, according to psychogenic identity theory, in one body and one psyche. But we now know that following conception the morula can be surgically divided resulting in two, three, four, or more individuals. Each piece can be transplanted into a host, and we can artificially create twins, triplets, or quadruplets. Such procedures have long been used in the production of dairy cattle (see Seidel & Elsden, 1989) and are in theory, if not practice, available to humans (see Elmer-DeWitt, 1993). At conception, according to psychogenic identity theory, there was one psyche and one body. But assume now that the developing blastocyst or morula is cut in half and there are now two bodies. If both bodies possess a psyche, the second psyche must have been instilled *after* conception. Thus, the theory of the entry of psyche exclusively at the time of conception is severely compromised.

There are other problems for psychogenic identity theory. For example, in the early days of pregnancy, two separate colonies of cells (twins) developing in the uterus may float together and now form one individual—a chimera (see Austin, 1989). If both bodies possessed a psyche prior to floating together, what happened to the second psyche after the two came together? Clearly, for all of its popular appeal, psychogenic identity theory is not without serious problems. We now consider a second theory of psychogeny.

PSYCHOGENIC EMERGENTISM Emergentism, as a mind–body position, contains an implicit theory of the origin of psyche. Psyche, according to this position, has no independent origin of its own, but rather develops with the developing body. Further, the complexity and the functional properties of the mental arena are dependent on the health and well-being of the organism. **Psychogenic emergentism** avoids the problems of identity theory, but comes with a set of problems of its own.

One of the major problems associated with psychogenic emergentism has to do with the arbitrary time of emergence. According to the theory, psyche is associated with some arbitrary level of neural complexity, but how much complexity is required? Is there some remote sense in which a single cell is conscious? Is a colony of cells, without a nervous system and without a circulatory system, conscious? At the other end of the scale, one might insist that consciousness is not consciousness until it is aware of itself. But how do we know when an organism has the capacity for reflective self-awareness? Psychogenic emergentism suffers the same problem as identity theory. Neither theory provides a satisfactory scientific answer regarding the time of infusion or emergence of psyche into a material substrate.

Another problem for psychogenic emergentism has to do with the experienced continuity of consciousness. It is the same *I* or *me* today as it was many years ago. Although my world may have been unstable resulting in experiences I could never have imagined, and although I may not believe the same things I once did, it is nevertheless the same me who has done the changing. The persistent and obstinate nature of experienced continuity challenges psychogenic emergentism. We live in a constantly changing world that should result in major personality shifts, yet most of us experience ourselves to be remarkably consistent over time.

The emergentist might argue that pathological discontinuities and disassociations exist in personality, often resulting from environmental changes or neurological damage, just as an emergentist might predict. Such a rebuttal appears appropriate. Discontinuities in personality may well present a challenge to identity theory with its emphasis on a somewhat autonomous psyche. But it is also true that continuity of personality, especially in the face of change or even crisis, presents a challenge to emergentism with its emphasis on a more fragile and dependent psyche. There are many other problems and issues, including some interesting moral issues, associated with both theories (see Viney & Woody, 1995).

The relationship of mind and brain, like the problem of free will and determinism, is neither a relic of the past nor exclusively a philosophical problem. Indeed, there may be a greater outpouring of scholarly work on this problem at the dawn of the twenty-first century than at any other time in history. Contemporary philosophers, biologists, neuroscientists, computer scientists, and psychologists have produced a wealth of thoughtful approaches to the problem (see Buncombe, 1995; Crick, 1994; Dennett, 1991; Edelman, 1992; Searle, 1992, 1995a, 1995b; Tye, 1995). The mystery of the mental arena remains as elusive as ever, but contemporary advances in the neurosciences, the computing sciences, biology, psychology, and philosophy may provide additional pieces for a puzzle that is of unparalleled complexity.

THE PROBLEM OF EXPLANATION

The word *explain* comes from the Latin *explanare,* which means to make plain, flatten, or spread out. As we use it, the word *explain* refers to our attempts to interpret or understand events or relationships. If you've worked with small children, you know a single word can satisfy as a nominal explanation. For example, a child may be content to learn that "this dog is a collie, but that one is a golden retriever." Before long, we learn that words are arbitrary, so deeper understandings and more nuanced interpretations are needed. We'll see the same thing play out in the pages of this book. For example, throughout history and in the present, free will is offered as an explanation for desirable and undesirable behaviors (legal and religious systems draw on this explanation). However, scientists hold nagging and legitimate concerns about

whether free will can explain anything (see Viney, 1990). Explanations based on authority, though problematic, are common in most cultural settings. Aristotle's laws of causation, covered earlier in this chapter, can be regarded as the "four be-causes" in that they explain why things happen. For example, the billiard ball rolls into the pocket because external forces and their directional vectors propelled it. This explanation is based on material and efficient causation. Now consider a different example: Wynona decided to go for lunch because she was hungry. This is a teleological explanation based on intention or purpose. Four additional explanatory modes encountered in science and in psychology are covered in the following section. Whether there is any explanatory mode free of problems is arguable.

Explanation by Analogies and Comparisons

The term *analogy* comes from the Greek *analogia,* referring to proportion or equality of ratios. In everyday use, *analogy* refers to the idea that one thing is somewhat like another thing even though the two are also different. For example, in an attempt to explain how the eye works, scientific texts often draw an analogy between the eye and the camera. The film (or card in digital cameras) is like the retina as it registers or codes images, the aperture is like the pupil, and the diaphragm is like the iris. The camera lens is compared to the lens of the eye (when the latter has a cataract, it is compared to a smudged camera lens). A partially detached retina may be compared to a wrinkled film surface or a faulty card. The history of science finds insight in analogous explanations. Scientists have drawn analogies between the structure of atoms and the structure of our solar system. René Descartes compared nerves to water pipes. Physicists compared the travel of light through a vacuum to bullets (the particle theory) or to waves in an ether (the wave theory). In medical circles, cholesterol is compared to deposits that clog pipes.

Explanations by comparisons are central to the development of human cognitive processes. Small children use comparisons to form concepts. A kitten is to a cat as a puppy is to a dog or a car is to a driver as an airplane is to a pilot. In politics, comparisons are used in pejorative ways when Democrats are compared to Communists and Republicans to Fascists. Such comparisons underscore the danger of thinking in terms of comparisons and analogies. An emphasis on the similarities between one thing and another can lead to overgeneralization, faulty thinking, or outright error.

Let's consider a greater problem that happens when we overemphasize the explanatory legitimacy of presumed similarities. A judge, while sentencing a teenager, acknowledged that the juvenile came from a disadvantaged home. The judge added that scores of other teenagers come from disadvantaged backgrounds, but don't commit crimes. What are the problems with the comparison made by the judge? Further careful analysis will reveal all kinds of differences between the subject and the comparison target. One purpose of science (and all critical and responsible thinking) is to "chase variance," meaning a relentless pursuit of the hidden and visible differences that make a real difference in the world. Superficial and shallow comparisons based on presumed likenesses are unworthy of serious thinkers. Analogies may be helpful, but they should evoke deep suspicions (see Simanek, n.d.). At best, analogies and comparisons offer programs for more intellectual work. At worst, they promote intellectual laziness.

MODELS AS EXPLANATIONS Models in science are comparable to analogies (see Eacker, 1975; Hesse, 1967), but more sophisticated. The term *model* in scientific literature refers to a conceptual framework marked by attempts to find logical, structural, or functional similarities between one thing and another. An engineer or meteorologist may explain the dynamics of a tornado by building a miniature replica in a laboratory where temperature, humidity, circulating winds, and targets can be manipulated in controlled and systematic ways. In recent years, computer models of the brain have provided insights into human cognition. Earlier, psychologists used steam boiler models to explain emotional expression. The greater the pressure generated in a steam boiler, the greater the need for a release of energy. If energy is not released in a controlled fashion, an explosion will occur. The

model suggests that the pressures of living generate energy. If such energy is "bottled up" or not released through healthy exercise and verbal expression, then a nervous breakdown may result. The same cautions that apply to simple analogies apply to models. A model may be helpful, but it may fail to do justice to the target it seeks to explain. Later, we will encounter a school of humanistic psychology that rejects all models in favor of a direct study of human beings.

NUMERICAL EXPLANATIONS Science has made remarkable progress in quantifying an increasing range of natural phenomena. This development is so critical that a later section is devoted to early and often surprising quantitative breakthroughs that influenced the emerging science of psychology. An early pioneer in the area named Francis Galton believed that every bodily and mental attribute could be quantified and summarized in a mathematical formula. In this tradition, formulae have been written to describe sensory thresholds, intellectual ability, mortality expectations, the relative contributions of heredity and environment to specific behaviors, and a host of other areas. Such formulae provide descriptive and predictive tools for the scientist, but can a mathematical formula unpack the deeper nature of the target it seeks to explain? Is intelligence the same as an intelligence quotient? In a way, we return to the same problem we encountered with analogies. When can we be sure we have a real identity between one thing and another? Quantitative explanations are integral to science, but may leave us grasping for more nuanced truths.

NEUROLOGICAL AND PHYSIOLOGICAL EXPLANATIONS The advent of brain sciences brought a growing faith that human experience and behavior can be explained in terms of underlying neurophysiological processes. Recent history has witnessed unprecedented advances in our understanding of the relationship between the nervous system and psychological processes. But can we believe that underlying neural processes offer adequate explanations for psychological events? There's no question we benefit from knowing that deposits of amyloidal plaques in nerve structures are associated with Alzheimer's disease. The discovery of such plaques may uncover a piece of the puzzle and even suggest intervention techniques, but we may still lack an adequate explanation for the disease's role in experience and behavior. We must still struggle with the possible roles of heredity, diet, exercise, a more penetrating analysis of the chemistry of amyloidal proteins, immune reactions to such proteins, and so forth. Biochemical explanations, though useful, may leave us without a satisfactory explanation of the ultimate causes and characteristics of the disease. The virtue of neuroscience centers on its practical and heuristic values. A concept or a theory with heuristic value is one that leads to productive new ideas and hypotheses. Neurological and physiological explanations lead to questions of a biochemical, chemical, or physical nature. Each level of analysis presents new mysteries, but may fail to provide an adequate explanatory framework relevant to all the dimensions of a problem. As noted earlier, no explanation is free of problems. As we explore how scholars throughout history have explained psychological phenomena, it is helpful to think critically about the problem of explanation. In what sense are analogies and models helpful and in what sense are they misleading? Does the identification of a physiological or neurological correlate of a psychological event do justice to the complexity of that event? Or are emergent properties in psychological events not reducible to their physical underpinnings (see Dupré, 1993)? Later in the text, we will encounter schools of thought (e.g., the Gestalt school and the psychology of William James) that question whether one level of explanation (e.g., the neurological level) can ever do justice to another level (e.g., the psychological level). We will revisit the problem of explanation in new and interesting ways.

In addition to the philosophical problems mentioned in this chapter, additional problems hold special interest for psychologists. Do human beings have an essential built-in moral nature (i.e., are we morally good, evil, or simply neutral at birth?)? What is the appropriate unit of study in psychology? Should we focus on part processes such as reflex activity or should we focus on the whole organism in its natural environment? Such issues and others like them will surface as we consider the various systems of psychology. If you are interested, several resources focus on philosophical issues in psychology (Eacker, 1972, 1975; Rubenstein & Slife, 1988; Wertheimer, 1972).

Review Questions

1. Define the term *epistemology*.
2. Distinguish between a priori and a posteriori knowledge.
3. Differentiate between nativist and empiricist accounts of depth perception.
4. Briefly explain at least five different ways of assessing truth.
5. According to Karl Popper, what is the key distinguishing feature between a legitimate science and pseudoscience?
6. Trace Kuhn's view on the development of science. What does Kuhn mean by terms such as *normal science* and *paradigm*?
7. If you were arguing for Feyerabend's philosophy of science, what evidence would you employ?
8. List and briefly describe Aristotle's four kinds of causation.
9. Distinguish between intrinsic and extrinsic teleology.
10. Advance three arguments in support of determinism and three arguments in defense of free will.
11. Outline two monistic and two dualistic approaches to mind and brain.
12. Which of the various mind–brain positions seems most adequate to you? What are some of the problems with this position?
13. Outline two major problems for identity theory encountered in recent research on embryo experimentation.

Glossary

aestheticism   The belief that the principles of beauty are applicable to other arenas of thought. In epistemology, aestheticism attempts to integrate truth and beauty.

a posteriori   Literally, *from what is later*. Generally refers to the belief that knowledge is dependent on experience and past learning. Contrast with *a priori*.

a priori   Literally, *from what is prior.* Generally refers to the presumed capacity to discern truths through intellectual insights with minimal dependence on past experience and past learning. Contrast with *a posteriori.*

attributive pluralism   Emphasizes the varieties of descriptive modes applicable for most phenomena. For example, a sunset may be described in the language of physics, anthropology, psychology, or any of a variety of other disciplinary languages. Events can also be described poetically or musically.

authority   One of the most common tests of truth. Reference to books, institutions, legal codes, or other people as appropriate and adequate repositories of knowledge.

determinism   The belief in universal causation. Implies that whatever happens is based on antecedents such that, given them, nothing else could happen. Contrast with *free will.*

double-aspect monism   A mind–brain position emphasizing the availability of two languages to describe the same phenomena. In this case, there is the language of physiology versus language that employs mentalistic concepts. The position assumes that both refer to the same underlying reality.

dualism   The belief that there are two fundamentally different realities. For example, mental processes are considered by the dualist to be largely independent and qualitatively different from brain processes.

efficient cause   According to Aristotle, the force that sets a thing in motion. Thus, domino *A,* impacting domino *B,* is the efficient cause of the fall of *B.*

emergentism   A mind–brain position embracing the idea that mental processes are produced by brain processes. Some emergentists believe that mental processes, though produced by brain processes, are qualitatively different from the physical system from which they emerge.

empiricism   A philosophical position that emphasizes the importance of experience, observation, and learning in the acquisition of knowledge.

epiphenomenalism   A mind–body position marked by the belief that physical events are causal with respect to mental events. Mental events are viewed as completely dependent on physical functions and, as such, have no independent existence or causal efficacy.

epistemology   A branch of philosophy concerned with problems of knowledge such as what can we know or how can we know?

extrinsic teleology   The view that design or order in nature reflects the work of a designer.

Feyerabend, Paul K. (1924–1994)   Philosopher of science who has argued for an anarchistic epistemology marked by belief that there is no such thing as a single unified and unchanging scientific method.

final cause   According to Aristotle, the goals or purposes for which an action was intended.

formal cause   The form or shape that contributes to a causal sequence. Thus, an airplane could not fly if critical components were not shaped properly.

free will   The assumption that human beings make choices that are to some degree independent of antecedent conditions. Contrast with *determinism.*

genetic epistemology   The study of ways of knowing and ways of solving problems as a function of developmental level.

idealism   A philosophical orientation emphasizing mind or spirit as the preeminent feature of life. Contrast with *materialism.*

indeterminism   The doctrine that it is impossible to apply strict cause-and-effect explanations to events at the subatomic level.

instinct   An organized sequence of behaviors characteristic of a given species. It is assumed that instinctive behaviors are not learned.

interactionism   A commonsense belief in the interdependence of the mental and the physical realms. According to this position, mental events may be causal with respect to physical events and vice versa.

intrinsic teleology   The position that design, order, and purpose are immanent in nature.

Kuhn, Thomas S. (1922–1996)   A philosopher of science who emphasized the importance of understanding science in terms of its community structures and evolutionary processes. His book *The*

Structure of Scientific Revolutions is one of the most influential works in its field in the twentieth century.

learning   Any change in performance or behavior that is attributable to the effects of practice or experience.

libertarian   In philosophy, one who believes in free will. Contrast with *determinism.*

material cause   Aristotle's contention that things behave as they do partly because of their material structure. For example, a billiard ball could not function properly if it were made of cork or rubber.

materialism   A monistic ontology characterized by the belief that all real things are composed exclusively of matter. Implies that all being can be understood in terms of the principles of material structure.

monism   The position that reality is one thing. Thus, everything relates to everything else in a completely interconnected world. Contrast with *pluralism.*

nativism   The position that there are perceptions that are built in or operational from birth and that are informative about the world. For example, the nativist argues that we have an innate capacity to see in depth. Contrast with *empiricism.*

normal science   A notion introduced by Thomas Kuhn that refers to conventional ways of solving problems in science at a given time or during the reign of a particular paradigm.

ontology   A branch of philosophy that studies the nature and relations of being. Considers the question, "what is real?"

paradigm   According to Thomas Kuhn, the beliefs, attitudes, values, methods, and assumptions that guide the intellectual community at a given time.

pluralism   The belief that there are many real things and many different orders of reality. Contrast with *monism.*

Popper, Karl Raimond (1902–1994)
Mathematician and philosopher noted for a hypothetico-deductive approach to science. His book *The Logic of Scientific Discovery* is one of the classics in the philosophy of science.

pragmatism   A U.S. philosophical movement associated with the work of Charles S. Pierce and William James. James emphasized the close connections between empiricism, pluralism, and pragmatism. According to pragmatism, concepts must be judged in terms of their cash value or the practical work they do in the world. Thus, truth is judged by utility and the practical consequences achieved by an idea.

psyche   The Greek term for soul or mind. Includes mental processes such as thought, memory, sensation, and perception.

psychogenic emergentism   The idea that mental processes develop or emerge with the development of the body.

psychogenic identity theory   A theory of the origin of psyche that stresses the continuity or identity of the psychically endowed biological substratum of the organism and the later mature, self-reflective, fully conscious adult.

psychogeny   Literally, the origin of psyche. Theories of the origin of psyche.

psychophysical parallelism   A mind–brain doctrine that assumes the independent existence of mental and physical events. According to parallelism, the mental and the physical are, by definition, congruent. They do not interact with each other; rather, they are like two clocks that always agree on the time, but are nevertheless independent systems.

rationalism   A philosophical orientation deriving from the Latin *ratio,* meaning to reason or think. Rationalist philosophers emphasize a priori knowledge, deduction, and an active mind that selectively organizes sensory data.

skepticism   The philosophical position that all truth claims are suspect and must be questioned.

teleology   Refers to purpose or design. According to Aristotle, design or purpose is an intrinsic part of the natural order. Thus, it is the purpose of a seed to sprout under the proper conditions and grow into a plant. Such a teleology can be thought of as intrinsic and is in contrast with the extrinsic teleology encountered in certain religions. Extrinsic teleology implies that things do what they do because they fulfill purposes imposed by deity.

2

Early Psychological Thought

Chapters 3 through 5 provide an overview of psychological thought from ancient times through the late Renaissance period, ending about 1600. Psychology developed as a formal academic and professional discipline in the late nineteenth century, but a deep interest in psychological topics developed long before that time. Though our methods and tools of inquiry have expanded, we'll find surprising continuities across time with respect to questions about psychology. What is an emotion and how can we control our emotions? How do we learn and how can we improve learning? Is there one motive (maybe the will to power or sexuality) that dominates all other motives? What is the mind and how can two minds know the same thing? What is the relation of the brain to mental processes? Who can best investigate the problems of psychology and what methods should be employed? The thoughts and discoveries of past thinkers enrich the history of science, revealing that we do not live in complete temporal isolation. The following timeline highlights important developments in early psychological thought.

Timeline

c. 600 BCE to AD 1600	
600–470 BCE	Era of the Greek cosmologists and early Greek medics
470–322 BCE	Golden Age of Greece—philosophy features the work of Socrates, Plato, and Aristotle
c. 175	*On the Diagnosis and Cure of the Soul's Passions* by Galen
354	Birth of Augustine
c. 380	Christianity becomes official religion of Rome
415	Martyrdom of Hypatia of Alexandria
570	Birth of Muhammad
711	Muslims invade Spain
732	Charles Martel defeats Muslims near Tours (stops northern expansion)
965	Birth of Alhazen (his *Book of Optics* later becomes a classic)
980	Birth of Avicenna
c. 1095	*The Incoherence of the Philosophers* by Al-Ghazali
1095	Beginning of Crusades
1215	Magna Carta is issued
1225	Birth of Thomas Aquinas
1232	Inquisition is established by Pope Gregory IX
1252	Innocent IV allows torture as part of inquisition interrogations
1304	Birth of Petrarch (one of the founders of Renaissance humanism)
1347	Beginning of great plague (contributes to growth of skepticism)
1354	Mechanical clock installed at Strasbourg Cathedral
c. 1400	Aristotle's works translated into Latin, bringing philosophy to a wider audience
1409	Founding of University of Leipzig, later to become birthplace of psychology
1431	Joan of Arc burned as a witch
1456	Gutenberg prints the first Bible, feeding the development of a larger reading public
1486	*The Malleus Maleficarum* by Kramer and Sprenger (Bible of the witch hunts)
1492	Columbus sails to America
1500	Leonardo da Vinci draws a model of musket, a precursor of guns
1513	*The Prince* by Machiavelli (a classic in political theory and social psychology)
1517	*Ninety-Five Theses against Indulgences* by Martin Luther challenges church authority
1519	Ferdinand Magellan starts voyage that results in first circumnavigation
1543	*On the Revolutions of the Celestial Spheres* by Nicolaus Copernicus
	On the Structure of the Human Body by Andreas Vesalius
1561	Birth of Francis Bacon

c. 1576	*Apology for Raimond Sebond* by Michel de Montaigne helps initiate a skeptical crisis
1583	University of Edinburgh (an early secular university)
1587	*New Philosophy on the Nature of Man* by Oliva Sabuco
1588	Birth of Thomas Hobbes
	Francis Drake defeats Spanish Armada
1596	Birth of René Descartes
1600	Beginning of Modern period
	Giordano Bruno argues for a sun-centered cosmos and is burned at the stake

3

■ ■ ■

Ancient Psychological Thought

We must not be too sure of the ignorance of our ancestors.

—WILL DURANT (1954)

The story of psychology is told in ancient manuscripts and documents such as the Vedas of the Hindus, the Talmud of the Hebrews, the Avesta of the Zoroastrians, and early Greek epic narratives and poems such as the *Iliad*. Ancient writings are rich in speculative as well as practical psychology. Because early cultures existed in physical and intellectual isolation, their psychology doesn't always appear as coherent or linear as in later periods. Even if it seems disjointed at times, it is important to explore the story of ancient psychology.

EARLY CHINESE PSYCHOLOGIES

In a survey of the social history of Chinese psychology, Petzold (1987) called attention to "the special sensitivity of psychology to political and ideological influences" (p. 213). Early psychological thought in China was tied to a larger worldview organized around the number 5. The Chinese believed in five basic elements of wood, fire, metal, earth, and water. In early work on sensation, they explored the powers of five basic organs, including the ear, the eye, the nose, the mouth, and the body. They believed the sense organs corresponded with sensations of hearing, vision, smell, taste, and touch. Ancient Asian scholars also organized colors, smells, sounds, tastes, and tissues around the number 5. For example, they identified the five tastes as sweet, sour, salt, bitter, and acid. Basic colors were thought to consist of green, red, yellow, black, and white. Basic smells were identified as burning, fragrant, goatish, rank, and rotten. Later developments included attempts to identify the basic emotions, parts of the body, and virtues. Based on one early classification, the basic emotions were designated as anger, joy, desire, sorrow, and fear (Fernberger, 1935, p. 547).

The number 5 also guided an analysis of human relationships. The brilliant thinker **Confucius (551–479 BCE)** proposed that different types of human relations include "ruler and minister, father and son, elder brother and younger brother, husband and wife, and one friend and another" (Chan, 1967, p. 189). The five, in this case, illustrate the paternal emphasis in Chinese culture. Confucius was interested in the moral life and harmony among people. Although a great humanist, his teachings were counterproductive for the development of some sciences. For example, his belief that the body is sacred discouraged the practice of dissection for centuries.

One of the greatest Chinese philosophers, **Hsün Tzu (c. 298–c. 212 BCE)**, is sometimes compared with the Greek philosopher Aristotle. Like Aristotle, Hsün Tzu was a naturalist who emphasized the regularity and orderliness of nature. He argued for rational and empirical methods and opposed superstition. For Hsün Tzu, we cannot count on divine intervention because nature goes its own way. Given his thinking, it makes no sense to pray for rain because natural phenomena cannot be controlled. Hsün Tzu was a strong advocate of learning and self-advancement. He believed basic human nature is evil, but we can attain goodness through education.

The concepts of **yin** and **yang** dominated ancient Chinese philosophy and psychology. At first, yin and yang were viewed as antagonistic cosmic forces, but later thinkers recognized them as both opposite and complementary. Yang is associated with qualities such as force, hardness, masculinity, heat, and dryness. Yin is related to qualities such as weakness, softness, femininity, hearing, coldness, and moistness. Physical and psychological well-being and social balance depended on equilibrium between yin and yang. Early Chinese medicine worked toward restoring and maintaining this essential balance. For example, acupuncture, dating from the third millennium BCE, was designed to stimulate or drain energy flow or *chi*, necessary to maintain balance and health. Other therapies, including diet, herbs, and disciplined activity such as *Tai Chi* (Tong, 2003), focused on restoring a balance of yin and yang forces. Castiglioni (1941), for example, noted the importance of organ therapy by pointing out that warriors "drank blood or ate the liver of tiger" (p. 103). Consuming the tiger's blood or

liver was thought to intensify yang in the warrior, leading to greater courage.

Early Chinese scholars stressed the importance of cognitive processes. In Chinese thought, the mind plays a dominant role, whereas the body acts as its servant. This doesn't imply a radical separation of mind and body because mental processes are nurtured inside the body. Mind and body are integrated and inseparable. Chinese thought opened the door to a physiological psychology where the mind is as significant as the body.

BABYLONIA

Babylonia was regarded as one of antiquity's greatest civilizations. For centuries, their culture wielded a far-reaching influence on other nations in the Mediterranean basin. The authority of Babylonian ideas colored the intellectual traditions of the Greeks, Egyptians, Jews, and Arabs. Close to the old riverbeds of the Tigris and Euphrates, the ruins of Babylon are situated about sixty miles south of the present city of Baghdad.

The Babylonians studied mathematics, geography, astronomy, law, medicine, and language. Writing was an important art among their elite and skilled citizens. During the last century, scholars deciphered many of their cuneiform writings on clay tablets including two famous Babylonian works—the *Epic of Gilgamesh* and the *Code of Hammurabi*.

Thousands of major and minor gods populated their belief system. Deities were thought to rule over everything from astronomical events to taxation. Only human imagination, it seemed, could limit the gods of Babylon. Sometimes friendly and other times hostile, Babylonian deities were anthropomorphic and engaged in human affairs. Help from the gods was invoked through magic rites, prayers, incantations, and the special powers and methods of priests and physicians.

A universe of demons challenged the power of Babylonian gods and threatened humanity. Alexander and Selesnick (1966) mention that "each disease had its specific demon. Insanity was caused by the demon Idta" (p. 20). Demons were exorcised through special medicines (e.g., certain plants were thought to have the power to kill demons), confessions, magic rites, and other procedures designed to restore harmony with divine forces. The Babylonians encouraged prevention as well as treatment. Charms, religious symbols, and virtuous behavior could ward off demons. In keeping with prevailing opinions of the day, it was wise to avoid women because they were said to have the power to inspire demonic possession.

The Babylonians offered accurate descriptions of diseases, including epilepsy (Magiorkinis et al., 2010), and their astronomy was sufficiently advanced to permit predictions of eclipses. They were interested in human and animal anatomy and showed mathematical sophistication. As with other early cultures, the Babylonians offered a curious blend of empirical and superstitious explanations of their world.

EGYPT

In many ancient civilizations, science cannot be easily separated from religion. In ancient Egypt, prevailing religious perspectives influenced many ideas about psychology. When it came to religion, the polytheistic Egyptians had no trouble finding things to worship. A variety of plants and animals, the sun, the moon, the stars, rivers, mountains, and people served as objects of worship. A belief in immortality was a centerpiece of Egyptian religions, guiding the art of mummification and elaborate burial customs. The quality of bodily preservation was thought to enhance the soul's ability to survive after death and weather the transition to immortality.

Many ancient thinkers saw a link between cognition and the activity of the heart. It was apparent with the naked eye that blood vessels connected the heart to the entire body. As a result, considerable evidence suggests that Egyptians viewed the heart as the seat of cognitive activity (see Laver, 1972). In spite of their belief that the brain was subservient to the heart, the ancients did observe correlations between head injuries

and disorders of speech, memory, and movement (Rose, 2009). In fact, Egyptians were apparently the first to provide a description of the brain. In his classic book *A History of Medicine*, Castiglioni (1941) suggested that some Egyptians recognized the brain as the source of mental activity.

Laver (1972) noted that the Egyptians emphasized the importance of names. An object and its name shared a close identity so that the cursing of a name or the destruction of a name could hold great psychological importance. The Egyptian emphasis on the importance of names may have carried over into later Jewish culture.

Egyptian women achieved higher social status than their counterparts in most ancient and modern cultures. Women held political offices, took the initiative in courtship if they wished, owned property, made formal proposals for marriage, and in general, wielded considerable power in their homes. Although pharaohs and some wealthy citizens had harems, women enjoyed unparalleled status and power in the majority of monogamous families.

A hallmark of Egyptian civilization was its superior engineering. Even in the twenty-first century, we marvel at their construction of canals and pyramids. Egyptian science—with the possible exception of geometry—was less impressive. The Egyptians' medicine was a blend of superstition and observation. They believed that insects, filth, and devils spread disease. They treated disease with rituals, incantations, rest, surgery, enemas, and medications designed for ingestion or external applications. Medications were created from plants, honey, animal dung, oil, blood, and animal organs. The Egyptians placed considerable emphasis on hygiene and regularly practiced circumcision and fumigation of the vagina. Alexander and Selesnick (1966) noted that the Egyptians "recognized the emotional disorder that the Greeks later called 'hysteria'" (p. 21). A woman's emotional disorder was believed to result from a uterus that had wandered to another part of her body. Egyptian doctors fumigated the vagina in an attempt to return the uterus to its normal resting location. This explanation for hysteria (named after the Greek word for uterus, *hysteron*) persevered for centuries, even into the late Middle Ages.

OTHER ANCIENT EASTERN PSYCHOLOGIES

Some of the oldest civilizations, dating from the fourth millennium BCE, existed in what is now India and Pakistan. Some early cultures enjoyed well-constructed houses connected to sewers, streets, shops, and baths. Anthropologists have discovered a variety of bronze and copper utensils and pottery along with jewelry and copper weapons.

During this time, psychological thought flourished in the area now India and Pakistan. We can find pronounced psychological themes in the ancient **Vedas**, the oldest sacred books of India. The term *Veda* means "knowledge." Although orthodox Hindus date the books from the beginning of time, historians are more likely to date them from earlier than 1000 BCE. The *Vedic* treatises contain a philosophic knowledge known as the **Upanishads**.

Selected verses from the Vedas and Upanishads offer a glimpse of early Indian beliefs about psychology. A major theme centers on the problems of knowledge and desire. As we will see, the Greeks debated the relative merits of the senses versus the intellect. In ancient Indian philosophy, neither is to be trusted. The ancient Indians emphasized respect for the mystery of life and encouraged intuition and the development of spiritual sensitivities. People who became too involved with their world developed false consciousness, inordinate desire, and an undisciplined nature. They advocated austerity, self-denial, and cleansing of excessive desires of the senses through fasting and meditation.

Early Indian thinkers showed little interest in studying sensory phenomena, owing perhaps to their distrust of the senses. Anatomical studies were also rare. The Indians were, however, careful observers of pregnancy. They believed an infant's personality could be traced to maternal characteristics during pregnancy. For example, an ill-tempered mother might give birth to an epileptic child, while an alcoholic mother might deliver an infant with a weak memory. An immoral mother could give birth to an effeminate son. Women were subjected to stringent controls, perhaps because of their potential for influence. The *Code of Manu* illustrates the point: "No act is to be done according to her own will by a young girl, a young woman, or even by an old woman. . . . The good wife of a husband. . .must never do anything disagreeable to him" (see Welles, 1957, p. 33). In contrast to Egyptian culture, Indian women were subjected to the will of their father, husband, or sons.

Indians believed that diseases resulted from devils, filth, or imbalance of humors. Excessive emotional expression could produce mental disorders. The Indians used charms, incantations, meditation, and exorcism to combat disease. They emphasized personal hygiene and, following the teachings of Siddhartha Gautama (the Buddha or Enlightened One), they engaged in psychotherapeutic yoga and meditation exercises designed to induce a quiet spirit and resignation. Knowledge of yoga was slow to come to Western psychology, although one finds early discussions of yoga not as a practice but as a religion in the work of Leuba (1925).

THE HEBREWS

Jewish philosophy and psychology developed in the context of radical monotheism. Their belief in a single god contrasted with the polytheisms of the Babylonians, Egyptians, and Greeks. Jewish life and thought were conditioned by one of the most famous religious expressions in history, "Hear, O Israel, the Lord our God, the Lord is One." The task of every Jew was to know the one God by understanding the word of Jehovah as set forth in the Torah. Scholarly activity was held in high regard and has remained so for several millennia.

The Hebrews viewed Jehovah as an all-powerful source of reward and punishment. At the same time, they stressed human responsibility and freedom of choice. People were viewed as victims of a natural duplicity. On the one hand, we are creatures of the flesh, but we are also spiritual creatures with a spark of the divine and are capable of self-renunciation for community benefit. On occasion, the Hebrews embraced a kind of fatalism, but the stronger tradition might be characterized in terms of an if–then belief system. *If* the people obey God's commandments, *then* beneficial consequences follow. Failure to obey, however, results in punishment. The future is open and rewards or punishments depend on human behavior. This basic perspective has shaped much of Western thought.

Ben-Noun (2004) claimed that the roots of psychiatry are traced to ancient Israel. Likewise, Rotenberg and Diamond (1971) found evidence that the Hebrews advanced a concept of moral insanity. Hebraic thinkers also considered disorganized behavior as illustrated in Daniel 4:33 where Nebuchadnezzar was isolated from people and fostered a delusion that he was an animal. According to the Hebrews, the anger of Jehovah might cause mental illness (Deut. 28:28), but human disobedience was thought to produce such vengeance. Demonological explanations of mental and physical ailments can be found in Hebrew thought and in later Christianity, but such perspectives conflict with Hebraic concepts of the absolute oneness of God. We come across this tension in the later philosophy of Spinoza (discussed in Chapter 7) and other Jewish mystical traditions (Bakan, 1958).

The Hebrews gave the leading role to the man in marriage but the Talmud admonished men to honor their wives above themselves. The Hebrew people were unique in their regard for children. The "fruit of the womb" was viewed as a gift from God (Psalms 127:3) and children's children as "the crown of old men" (Proverbs 17:6). At the same time, extensive duties were imposed on children. "Honor thy father and thy mother: that thy days may be long upon the land" was literally true, because the actions of wayward or rebellious children were tantamount to a capital crime.

Most ancient cultures practiced infanticide. Influenced by Egyptian and Babylonian beliefs, the Hebrews may have performed child sacrifice in a limited fashion. In most countries of the Mediterranean basin, unwanted children were abandoned on hillsides, sacrificed to the gods, thrown into rivers, or sold to strangers (see DeMause, 1974). Children were sacrificed because of real or imagined defects, sometimes at the direction of religious beliefs. Consistent with prevailing views about women, girls were victims of infanticide far more than boys.

PERSIA

At one time, the great Persian Empire was as large as the continental United States. It encompassed the countries surrounding the eastern Mediterranean and extended east to the Indus River in India, including much of what is now Iran and Afghanistan. The Persian Empire had its beginnings about 900 BCE and thrived from about 600 BCE until Alexander the Great's conquest in 331 BCE. For nearly two centuries, the Persians existed as contemporaries and rivals with the Greeks.

Persia was the birthplace of the Zoroastrian religion, which originated in the teachings of a prophet named **Zarathustra**. According to legend, the god Ahura-Mazda revealed his teachings to Zarathustra, resulting in the Zoroastrian holy book called the **Avesta** (sometimes called the **Zend-Avesta**). This work includes rules for medical practice and divides physicians into three groups, including those who used holy words to treat people; the Avesta also describes the use of a stimulant to induce euphoria as a treatment for depression, which Zargaran et al. (2012) describe as early psychiatry. Although Zarathustra taught that there is one God, his followers saw the world in terms of a struggle between Ahura-Mazda and Angro-Mainyus, the prince of devils. Persian culture drew considerable influence from this theological dualism. Diseases and emotional disorders were viewed as the work of the devil, giving rise to predictable treatments involving exorcism, incantations, and magical and religious rites. Humans were viewed as the testing ground for the forces of good and evil. According to Zarathustra, people have free will, giving them the liberty to follow Ahura-Mazda or Angro-Mainyus.

Crimes were viewed as offenses against Ahura-Mazda and punishments could be severe.

Public whippings, crucifixion, mutilations, and stonings were commonplace. As you can guess, the intellectual climate in Persia was not friendly to the growth of philosophy or science.

GREECE

MacLeod (1975) is one of many historians who suggested that the period from 600 to 300 BCE in Greece represents one of the great creative periods in human history. Although early Mediterranean cultures had a profound impact, we can trace many intellectual Western traditions to the Greeks.

The earliest Greeks evidently occupied the isle of Crete and other smaller islands off the coast of the mainland as early as 3000 BCE. As with other cultures, the distinction between legend and history is blurred. For centuries, the legendary figure of Agamemnon and the city of Troy were thought to exist only in Homer's epic tales. That view was shattered when treasure hunter and amateur archeologist Heinrich Schliemann (1822–1890) made the greatest archaeological discovery of the nineteenth century. At the age of eight, Schliemann had claimed that one day he would excavate Troy. In 1871, his prophecy came true when he uncovered the ruins of the ancient city (see Schliemann, 1875/1968; Schuchhardt, 1891/1971). His discovery underscores the difficulties of assessing legendary stories from the past. Our incredulity can be unwarranted as often as our credulity.

Ancient Greece produced an explosion of intellectual curiosity, but we're not really sure how it happened. From a geographical standpoint, it was neither the best nor the worst of locations to support civilization. Whereas only about a quarter of the rocky peninsula was fit for growing crops, fishing and hunting provided food and forests supplied fuel. As in other parts of the ancient world, the institution of slavery provided leisure time for the elite classes. For a variety of reasons, the Greeks produced remarkable accomplishments in science, literature, philosophy, political theory, and the arts. In addition, the earliest hints of naturalistic psychology are found in the Greek mind.

The Cosmologists

The earliest Greek philosophers were interested in the nature of the universe (cosmology) and the origin of the universe (cosmogony). In addition to introducing concepts such as evolution and atomic theory, Greek cosmologists speculated about many topics that address psychology.

THALES Thales (*THAY leez*) of Miletus was probably born a few years before 625 BCE. He was a pivotal figure who insisted on scientific interpretations of the world over mystical ones. Possibly influenced by Egyptian cosmology, he believed the earth resembled a flat-rimmed saucer floating on the sea. But another question haunted him: Is there a single element from which everything is derived? Many ancient Greek thinkers obsessed over finding the fundamental stuff of the universe. In this tradition, Thales believed that water was the primal substance (Green & Groff, 2003). It made sense. Plants and animals depend on water for survival. It appears in a diversity of forms from rain to snow to steam. In its three forms (solid, liquid, and vapor or steam), water seemed to imitate or characterize the world.

Thales also developed an interest in the problem of movement. He wanted to know what makes it possible for a creature to move. His fascination with movement evolved from his curiosity about magnets. Writing later, Aristotle suggested that Thales believed a magnetic stone possessed a soul (Kirk & Raven, 1957, pp. 93–95). Apparently, he believed that a soul has kinetic and motive force that makes movement possible. So far as we know, Thales did not speculate about how water—the primal physical substrate of the world—interacts with soul. Lost in thought, the story is told, Thales met his death after plummeting into a well. A cautionary tale, it seems, to keep in mind for the brooding philosopher.

ANAXIMANDER Thales's successor and pupil was **Anaximander of Miletus (610–c. 547 BCE)**. Like his mentor, Anaximander (*an Ack suh man der*) wondered about a basic element in nature, but he rejected water as the primary substance. He questioned, for example, how water could be the basic substrate of fire. If water was not the basic substance, neither could it be any other thing that we observe. When we look at nature, we see water, trees, and rocks. We're actually seeing a manifestation of something basic, but not something the senses can understand. As a result, Anaximander claimed the basic stuff of the universe was infinite and formless, so he named it *apeiron* (meaning "without boundary").

Anaximander believed in a succession of worlds, each evolving through a cyclical process of beginning, maturation, and decay. In the beginning, oceans dry up and form land, giving home to creatures to inhabit its surface. In this process, life develops out of the interaction of opposites—moisture and fire, coolness and heat. Anaximander claimed that the first creatures were encased in a protective hard surface. As they aged, the creatures crawled out of the waters onto dry land, producing a gradual change in their protective body surface. Often viewed as the first recorded evolutionary theorist, Anaximander believed that the first humans came from fish-like creatures (see Kirk & Raven, 1957, p. 141). He observed that, unlike many other creatures, humans have a long period of dependency after birth. Because human infants are so dependent, he believed that the first humans could not have survived by themselves. So how did they endure? Anaximander concluded that another creature must have nurtured the first human infants.

He is often credited with constructing the first world map. He may also have been the first Greek to construct a sundial. Although only fragments of his writings exist, Anaximander's interests ranged over all the sciences in his culture, from astronomy to biology.

ANAXIMENES   Like Thales and Anaximander, the early Greek philosopher **Anaximenes (c. 588–c. 524 BCE)** was a member of the Milesian school. Anaximenes (*uh NAHK suh meh neez*) also shared their interest in cosmological problems. He taught that air is the primal substance of the universe and

can be transformed through rarefaction and condensation. Following condensation, air becomes clouds. Through further condensation, clouds become rain. Rain becomes hail. With subsequent condensation, water becomes land and condensed land becomes rocks. Through rarefaction, heavy, windy air becomes lighter air, and very light air becomes fire. Condensation is associated with coldness and rarefaction with heat. He concluded that earthquakes could result from disturbances of air, the result of too much moisture or extensive drought.

Anaximenes taught that the soul is rarefied air and that air is the principle of living things. In his mind, the soul holds the body together (Kirk & Raven, 1957). Maybe he believed this because of how the body decomposes when the breath of life or soul leaves the body. He also claimed that cosmic air holds the world together and even suggested that air is a god.

PYTHAGORAS   Born on the island of Samos, **Pythagoras (c. 580–c. 500 BCE)** is remembered as a legendary figure in mathematics and philosophy. In fact, Pythagoras likely coined the term **philosophy**, constructed from *philo* (meaning love) and *sophia* (meaning wisdom). As a philosopher—one who loves knowledge—Pythagoras was known for pure and applied interests. He had a deep love for the search for abstract and universal principles. As the founder of a religious society, he also applied philosophy and science to ethical conduct and the good life.

Pythagoras and his followers shifted the perspective from cosmology to an interest in human problems. Formal mathematical explanations replaced an emphasis on primordial substances. The Pythagoreans believed that all things in the universe have numerical qualities. Pythagoras claimed that numbers are absolute and unchanging and can affect the existence of objects on earth. For example, Pythagoras argued that although humans cannot draw a perfect triangle, the lengths of the sides of a drawn triangle relate to each other in ways that depend on the perfect relations of sides in an abstract triangle. The unchanging, perfect world of numbers affects the changing temporal world here on earth. For Pythagoras, even psyche was a "mathematical entity" (Green & Groff, 2003, p. 22). Unlike some other scholars of their day, the Pythagoreans viewed the brain as the seat of mental life. They also count among the first Westerners to use music as therapy.

In terms of religious assumptions, the Pythagoreans believed in immortality and the transmigration of souls. For this reason, they advised against eating animals; killing an animal might mean that you are invading the habitat of an ancestor's soul. They encouraged discipline and balance and avoided excessive laughter. Presumably, the expression of strong emotions undermined dignity and character. The Pythagoreans valued study, especially before speaking on matters pertaining to their beliefs. They imposed prohibitions on their followers that may have resulted in compulsive behavior. The Pythagoreans warned against putting the left shoe on first, wearing rings, looking in mirrors beside lamps, eating beans, or allowing swallows to nest under your roof.

The Pythagoreans assumed important stands on civil rights. Despite unreliable estimates, we know slavery was a common practice in ancient Greece. Although critical to the Greek economy, Pythagoras condemned slave labor. And at a time when women were often prohibited from studying science and mathematics, he invited them to his school. According to Waithe (1987b), numerous women were associated with Pythagorean societies from the sixth to the second century BCE. Fortunately, the tradition carried on after his death. In fact, several women joined neo-Pythagorean schools as late as the third century CE.

Unlike their sisters in Egypt, most Grecian women did not enjoy social status in antiquity. Perhaps Pythagoras appreciated the education of women because his wife and daughter were both accomplished thinkers. Pythagoras's wife **Theana** was a philosopher who played a key role in the society's educational activities. Their daughter **Myia** was one of the earliest Pythagoreans and her work focused on moderation and balance (see Waithe, 1987b, pp. 15–16). She provided some of the earliest advice on the care of infants. Myia emphasized the importance of milk and bland foods, moderation in temperature, good ventilation, and soft clothing. A later Pythagorean scholar named **Aesara** also discussed balance. In a fragment of her writing, she argued that physical and mental health result from harmony, making her one of the first to emphasize a balance theory of health.

XENOPHANES   Based in Elea, a town in southern Italy, another group of philosophers called the Eleatics contemplated different questions related to epistemology. The first of the Eleatics was **Xenophanes** (*zeh NAH fuh neez*), born about 560 BCE in Colophon. Known for his epistemological skepticism, he distinguished between knowledge and opinion, insisting that humans do not have certain knowledge, only opinion. A strict monotheist, Xenophanes attacked Homer's portrayal of anthropomorphic gods in epic poems such as the *Iliad* and the *Odyssey*. It troubled him how the gods of Homeric polytheism indulged in corrupt human actions and emotions including jealousy, deceit, and adultery. In an early work on psychology and religion, Xenophanes noted that Ethiopians view their gods as Ethiopian while Thracians view their gods as Thracian. He thought it strange that people conceptualize their gods as wearing clothes. He argued that if animals could draw, they would draw their gods to look like themselves. The one god above all gods, according to Xenophanes, was in no way—physically or mentally—similar to mortals.

Although known for epistemology, Xenophanes also studied meteorological and astronomical problems. He taught that a new sun, made of ignited clouds, arises each morning and proceeds in a straight line forever. Xenophanes's anti-polytheistic views may have fueled his concept of multiple suns.

PARMENIDES   Born around 515 BCE, **Parmenides** (*pahr MEHN ih deez*) of Elea influenced several later philosophers, especially Plato. In a poem likely titled "On Nature," Parmenides shares a message from a goddess on "the way of truth" and "the way of seeming." The way of seeming is the way mortals view their world. The way of truth is the way an immortal might see the world. Although controversy surrounds the appropriate interpretation of Parmenides's poem, he teaches that reason and the senses provide contrasting information about the world. Through the senses, we are aware of plurality, division, and change. In contrast, reason can show that "every attribute of reality can be deduced from every other" (Kirk & Raven, 1957, p. 268). Parmenides believed unity and permanence exist in the real world. Reason provides the means through which we move beyond the realm of appearance, an idea that marks him as an early rationalist.

Parmenides was also one of the first to emphasize a philosophy of *being* as opposed to a philosophy of *becoming*. A philosophy of becoming emphasizes process, change, variety, and transition. Few things are more *apparent* than the inevitability of change. The word *apparent*, however, is well chosen, especially to those who embrace a philosophy of being. For such a philosophy, the change that we observe with the senses may be an illusion. A philosophy of being emphasizes unity, permanence, and a perfect reality that forms the backdrop of transient things. Philosophies of being and becoming offer different implications for psychology. In a statement that could almost have been written by an early Greek, the American psychologist Abraham Maslow (1962) contrasted being-psychology with becoming-psychology as "the perfect with the imperfect, the ideal with the actual. . .the timeless with the temporal, end-psychology with means-psychology" (p. iv).

Parmenides also studied the mechanisms of perception. He apparently believed that "like" perceives "like," whereas some early philosophers taught that we perceive by virtue of opposites. For example, the theory of opposites holds that we experience the heat of hot water by virtue of the contrast between the temperature of the water and the temperature of the skin. However, Parmenides argued that we perceive light because we have fire or light within us. The light in the pupil of the eye responds to "its own kind." A corpse could not perceive light because the light or

fire is deficient in the corpse. But the corpse could know coldness, silence, and so on (see Kirk & Raven, 1957, p. 283).

ZENO   **Zeno of Elea** and Melissus of Samos were students and followers of Parmenides. They both devoted themselves to a defense of Parmenides's philosophy of being. Melissus, also known for defeating an Athenian fleet in a sea battle, wrote a book titled *On Nature or What Exists.* In his book, Melissus argued that what exists is infinite and homogeneous (Green & Groff, 2003). He noted that most theories of becoming or change imply that something can come from nothing. Melissus believed that there is a true reality that is one in nature and that undergirds the plurality of things we know with our senses. In this assertion, he is a forerunner of later Greek atomists.

Zeno is best known for his paradoxes of motion. None of the remaining fragments of Zeno's teachings contains all of his arguments about motion, but the essential idea is illustrated as follows. Suppose an archer releases an arrow at point A and the arrow is aimed at a target at point B. To get to point B, the arrow must first traverse half the distance. Once it has gone halfway, it must travel half of the remaining distance, and so forth. Because we can continue dividing the remaining distance by two indefinitely, there is a logical problem about whether the arrow can ever reach its goal. By infinitely dividing the distance into progressively smaller pieces, Zeno approached the foundations of differential calculus over two thousand years before Leibniz and Newton. Now, how does such a paradox relate to Parmenides?

Although motion is apparent to the senses, it violates logic and reason. Zeno's paradoxes also cast doubt on all of experience, particularly experience of change. When the senses conflict with reason, which should we choose? Reason, according to Parmenides, is superior to the senses; therefore, motion must be an illusion like other forms of change and becoming. Vlastos (1967) argues that "commonplaces may conceal absurdities and hence [we have] the need of reexamining even the best entrenched and most plausible assumptions" (p. 378).

HERACLITUS Whereas Parmenides was the best-known early philosopher of being, **Heraclitus** (*hehr uh KLY tuhs*) was the best-known philosopher of becoming. Most biographical information about Heraclitus is suspect. His dates are unknown, but he was probably active around 480 BCE. Known as the "Dark Philosopher," he is often portrayed in sculptures and paintings as weeping in anguish over the folly of human nature (Lurie, 1979). Possibly blind, he apparently lived in Ephesus and was an elitist who had little respect or liking for other philosophers. The feeling was mutual. Other philosophers often disparaged his work. Heraclitus proved unpopular because of his arrogance, his attacks on fellow philosophers and their works, and a philosophy that countered prevailing opinion. Although later philosophers such as Plato and Aristotle belittled his work and characterized him as morose, Heraclitus was treated with greater respect in recent centuries.

Heraclitus is most famous for his statement, "Upon those that step into the same rivers different and different waters flow" (Kirk & Raven, 1957, p. 146). In his thinking, constancy is illusory; experienced change is real, and his empiricism focuses on a world that is becoming. Even the most immutable element is subject to change over long periods of time. If you were looking for a metaphor for his views in an element of nature capable of change—something that could transform nearly everything it came into contact with—what would you choose? Heraclitus decided on fire. It is a natural choice because fire is ever changing. Fire can transform one thing into another, causing something to burn or melt or rise in steam. Like Xenophanes, Heraclitus believed that a new sun appears in the sky at the beginning of every day.

Heraclitus believed that the soul could be wet or dry and that wetness is harmful; in fact, complete wetness means death. Partial wetness interferes with normal functioning. For example, drunkenness wets the soul and interferes with judgment. A dry soul is wise. Heraclitus seems to be arguing against excessive emotions in one of his fragments that asserted, "It is hard to fight with anger; for what it wants it buys at the price of soul" (Kirk & Raven, 1957, p. 211). Heraclitus trusted the senses more than his contemporaries or successors, but he found some senses to be more trustworthy than others. For example, he believed vision to be more accurate than audition. Heraclitus believed that the senses become clogged in sleep leading to memory loss. Memory, however, returns with the reactivation of the senses when we awaken.

Heraclitus had little respect for the knowledge and opinions of others. He accused people of being deaf to what they hear and, in anticipation of later books and films, he saw humans as apes when compared with a god. The moralistic Heraclitus had contempt for the masses that lack discipline as evidenced by overeating. He mocked conventional religion. Blood sacrifices and prayers to idols offended him, and he likened the practice to talking with houses. It is little wonder Heraclitus lived in semi-isolation and, according to one account, committed suicide at age sixty (Kirk & Raven, 1957, p. 182). Although disliked in his times, Heraclitus's influence in later science, philosophy, and even theology has been extensive, with continued influence on the study of theory (Ajit, 2008), people who dissociate (Mendelowitz, 2008), and the study of self-identity (Skolnick, 2008).

LEUCIPPUS AND DEMOCRITUS The story of early Greek philosophy, science, and psychology takes a modern flavor with the early atomists **Leucippus** (*loo KIHP uhs*) and Democritus (*duh MAHK rih tuhs*). Leucippus, who lived around 500 BCE, was the founder of atomic theory, but **Democritus (c. 460–c. 370 BCE)** refined the theory. Although we know little about the life of Leucippus, it is known that Democritus was a citizen of Abdera in Thrace. He apparently traveled around the Mediterranean world and had diverse interests including science, religion, and ethics. Whereas Heraclitus was characterized as weeping over the misery and foolishness of the human condition, Democritus is often portrayed as laughing at it. Lurie (1979) claimed, "To ancient writers, the two philosophers personified two contrasting approaches to *vita humana*, the contemplation of which evoked weeping in the one and laughter in the other" (p. 279).

According to Leucippus and Democritus, reality is composed of both the void and atoms. The void is empty space, and Leucippus noted that movement would be impossible without the void. Atoms were thought to be so small as to elude human perception. If any tangible object could be divided again and again, one would finally arrive at the atom, a unit that could not be divided (*atom* comes from the Greek word *atemmein*, meaning *a* or "not" and *temmein* or "divide"). Leucippus and Democritus taught that atoms vary in arrangement, position, and shape. There were hooked atoms, rough atoms, smooth atoms, and so on. The sensible qualities one experiences result from the arrangement and shapes of atoms. For example, a dense and heavy object is more compact, possibly consisting of many atoms hooked together. Fire consists of smooth atoms, and the soul, according to Democritus, is material and consists of smooth atoms that disperse at death (Katona, 2002).

The atomists taught that all things come into existence out of a great whirl of atoms. Atoms in the whirl begin to separate, like being attracted to like, and in time worlds are generated. They believed in many worlds, some moist, some dry, some supporting plants and animals, and others devoid of life.

Democritus argued for a strict determinism. He believed that randomness was an appearance. Behind the appearance of randomness was reason and a strict mechanical necessity. When he spoke on psychological topics, he employed the language of causation. For example, small spherical atoms cause a bitter taste while large jagged atoms create a salty taste. In an early statement on the psychology of religion, Democritus argued that fear motivated a belief in popular Greek gods.

Democritus believed all objects give off images of themselves, consisting of thin layers of atoms shaped like the object (Wade, 2005).

As these thin layers move through the void and impact our senses, we develop a perception of the object, provided we have like atoms that can respond to the layer of projected atoms—like responds to like. Democritus's ethical system consisted of a sophisticated pleasure theory. Pleasure is desirable but may be attained through discipline rather than indulgence and through austerity rather than possession of things.

Early Greek Concepts of Illness

In early Greek thought, human strengths and weaknesses were often attributed to the gods. Legendary stories about the Trojan War offer examples of such divine intervention. Following encouragement from the goddess Athena, the warrior Diomedes fought the Trojans with improbable strength and courage, but madness befell Ajax when Achilles's armor was awarded to Odysseus. Both mental and physical calamities could be visited upon those who, for whatever reason, fell on the wrong side of a deity. People found themselves in a near-constant quest to appease their gods, attempting to invoke their pleasure and praying for divine assistance.

Scholars disagree about the autonomy of the individual in Homeric thought. Simon and Weiner (1966) represent traditional views when they pointed out that in Homeric thought "the tendency is to ascribe origins of mental states to forces or agencies outside the person. . . . If Achilles forbears and does not slay Agamemnon on the spot, it is because Athena comes down, pulls Achilles by his hair, and says 'wait'" (p. 307). Smith (1974), however, argued that "Homeric man was not a puppet of the gods as has often been charged" (p. 315). In defense of his contention, Smith quoted lines from the *Odyssey* in which Zeus declares that humans blame the gods too readily and that they bring sorrows on themselves in addition to ordained sorrows.

Even if there were some room for individual initiative in Greek thought, it is clear that fate and divine ordination played a role in human problems. Indeed, early Greek concepts of health and illness were comparable in some respects to

Babylonian concepts. The transition to more naturalistic approaches was slow.

AESCULAPIUS   The earliest mythic figure in Greek medicine was **Aesculapius** (*EHS kuh lop ee uhs*) (or Asclepius), the son of Apollo, the god of Greek medicine. Homer described Aesculapius as the father of Machaon and Podaleirius, two surgeons who served with the Achaean forces in their war with the Trojans. Aesculapius is also reputed to be the father of Hygieia, regarded by Greeks and Romans as the goddess of health.

Over three hundred temples were built in Greece and Rome to carry on the healing traditions associated with Aesculapian mythology. The temples, always located in places of beauty, were designed to fill people with expectations of imminent recovery from their ills. Therapy consisted of sleep, suggestion, diet control, drugs, massage, and baths. Suggestion likely played a role and remission of symptoms was common. The Aesculapian physicians encouraged their patients to dream about Aesculapius, making their dreams prophetic of actual cures.

Like many ancients, the Aesculapians used the snake in their healing rites (the snake was a symbol of mystery, power, and knowledge). A statue in the Vatican museum depicts Aesculapius with a serpent coiled around a rod—a symbol of medicine persisting into modern times. The Aesculapians practiced both rational and supernatural techniques, but focused more on mystical procedures that bring to mind the methods of contemporary faith healers.

ALCMAEON   The work of **Alcmaeon** (*ALK mee on*) of Crotona offers a major milestone in Greek medicine. His exact dates are uncertain, but his work is believed to originate around 500 BCE. He practiced dissection, making him one of the first to use an empirical approach to anatomy and physiology. Although only fragments remain of his work, it appears he attempted to trace sensory channels to the brain. Unlike many scholars of the time, he understood that the brain was involved in thinking and intelligence (Celesia, 2012; Rose, 2009). He believed that sleep occurs when blood

travels from the brain to large blood vessels. Juhasz (1971) noted that this is the first known theory of sleep. Alcmaeon also believed that many sensory defects result when the channels to the brain become clogged.

In addition to anatomical work, Alcmaeon advanced a homeostatic-equilibrium theory of health. He believed that health prevails so long as there is balance between coldness and warmth, wetness and dryness, and sweetness and bitterness. His ideas make empirical sense. A common illness can bring dehydration or excessive moisture. Sickness can also produce a fever and shivering as well as bitterness or a bad taste in the mouth. According to Alcmaeon, death results when any of the paired opposites is too strong. He also emphasized the lack of moderation (e.g., eating too much or too little) as a cause of disease.

EMPEDOCLES   **Empedocles** (ehm PEHD uh kleez) **(c. 490–c. 430 BCE)** was another early homeostatic theorist influenced by Parmenides and Pythagoras. Empedocles taught that four basic elements (fire, earth, air, and water) are born out of two first principles (love and strife). The idea of four basic elements may have been borrowed from earlier Mediterranean cultures, but the principles of love and strife are original with Empedocles. According to Empedocles, the principles of love and strife act as forces of attraction and repulsion that interact with the four basic elements. If all things are composed of fire, earth, air, and water, we still need principles to account for the organizations and combinations. Love, or the force of attraction, accounts for organic unity, whereas strife or repulsion accounts for disintegration and the breakdown of objects or events. Empedocles believed that thought and reason have their substrate in the blood because, according to this theory, the four elements are perfectly blended in blood. Blood represents a near equal mix of fire, earth, air, and water. This opens the possibility that an imbalance of elements in the blood can cause a thought disorder.

Because he believed in the transmigration of the soul, Empedocles was a vegetarian. He taught that there is a "greatest god" that is not anthropomorphic. He believed that the principles of love and strife operate in the cosmos as well as within the individual life. Thus, principles of attraction and harmony are responsible for the birth and organization of the world.

Empedocles, like Anaximander, also believed in a form of evolutionary theory. He argued that creatures survive who are "accidentally compounded in a suitable way; but where this did not happen, the creatures perished and are perishing still" (Kirk & Raven, 1957, p. 337). Empedocles believed that nature had experimented with grotesque creatures without necks, partly male and partly female, with eyes "strayed alone" and with animal-like features. As the result of strife and improper mixtures of the elements, these creatures perished. But when like chanced to meet like, appropriately, and when there was harmony in the process of organization, then creatures were produced that survived. Despite later rejection of these ideas by Aristotle (Smith, 2010), Empedocles proposed an early variation of natural selection, even if he did not apply survival of the fittest in the manner Darwin would over two thousand years later.

Empedocles spoke against animal and human sacrifice as the primal sin. The following condemnation is but one of several expressing Empedocles's outrage: "Father lifts up his own dear son, his form changed, and, praying, slays him—witless fool; and the people are distracted as they sacrifice the imploring victim" (Kirk & Raven, 1957, p. 350). Some accounts suggest that he hanged himself or drowned after falling overboard from a ship. In the best-known legend, he jumped into an active volcano to prove his immortality, a deed memorialized in Matthew Arnold's 1852 poem, *Empedocles on Etna*.

HIPPOCRATES **Hippocrates** (hih PAHK ruh teez) **(c. 460–c. 377 BCE)** was the most famous physician of antiquity. Born on the island of Cos, he practiced medicine there and in Athens. He helped establish an empirical approach in the medical school of Cos. The body of writings attributed to Hippocrates (*Corpus Hippocraticum*) covers a breadth of medical subjects. Scholars are torn about the degree to which his work

Hippocrates

was written by Hippocrates or by his colleagues (Green & Groff, 2003). We'll discuss his work at the school of Cos with the understanding that other physicians contributed some of the ideas.

Sometimes called the founder of medicine, Hippocrates devised a naturalistic account of all disease, both physical and mental. Like Empedocles, he taught that disease results from a disturbance of balance in the elements that make up our bodies. To treat a patient, you must restore balance (Maher & Maher, 2003). He believed that intelligence results from a proper blend of fire and water. However, an excess of water causes stupidity, as revealed in symptoms such as slowness, weeping without reason, and suggestibility. An excess of fire could result in an impulsive person who rushes from one thing to another without focus or concentration. Hippocrates believed this condition could turn into madness without proper treatment. Treatment for an excess of fire included eating fish in place of meat, moderate (natural) exercise, induction of vomiting after surfeits, eating barley bread rather than wheat, and reduction of sexual intercourse.

For Hippocrates, dreams represent the activity of the soul. "When the body is awake the soul is its servant. . .but when the body is at rest, the soul, being set in motion and awake, administers her own household" (Goshen, 1967,

p. 12). He saw dreams as indicators of illness. The greater the contrast between dream and reality, the greater the illness. The sleeping soul can, through dreams, reveal a host of important messages about the body. For example, dreams of abnormal rivers may signify blood disorders, trees barren of fruit may foretell reproductive problems, and troubled seas may indicate disorders of the stomach.

The Cos school accepted Empedocles's four-element theory of fire, earth, air, and water. They believed these elements were manifest in four bodily humors: black bile, yellow bile, blood, and phlegm. In turn, the four elements and humors were associated with four qualities of cold, hot, dry, and wet. Differences of opinion emerged about how the humors were associated with various qualities. According to one classification (Castiglioni, 1941), blood is associated with heat, phlegm with coldness, yellow bile with dryness, and black bile with wetness (p. 162). Health was thought to result from an organic balance of the four humors and disease from an imbalance. The empirical basis for Hippocratic thought is evident. High body temperatures, sweating, jaundiced conditions, pallor, discoloration of urine, and excess of phlegm—conditions associated with illness—can be related to the four-humor theory. Some theorists continue to argue for a four-factor personality theory rooted in the psychological qualities that Hippocrates associated with the four humors (Merenda, 1987).

After careful observation of symptoms (Nutton, 2006), Hippocrates employed many treatments to restore balance. He was a strong believer in diet control, honey being a favorite prescription. He advocated therapies such as exercises, fresh air, rest, laughter, baths, and bleeding. Hippocrates also employed a variety of surgical techniques, including trephining to relieve pressure from brain tumors. He taught that the brain is the seat of intellectual activities and he was the first to classify emotional disorders. His classification included mania, melancholia, paranoia, and epilepsy. Hippocrates challenged popular supernatural assumptions of the time that epilepsy was a "sacred disease" (Todman, 2008)

and instead concluded that it was a natural disorder of the brain. Hippocrates and the school at Cos arrived at a medicine without gods and demons, one that rejected the mysticism and superstition for holistic treatment. In addition to the development of terminology for spinal structures (Panourias et al., 2011), he treated psychological problems within the framework of a thorough naturalism (Green & Groff, 2003). Hippocrates argued that if physicians could do no good, they should do no harm. Accordingly, his treatments undoubtedly offered beneficial and pleasant consequences, making the Hippocratic period a brief era of enlightenment.

Relativism

Ancient Greek thinkers explored another issue in epistemology that centered on the status of truth. The question here asks: Is truth relative or are there independent and enduring truths that reason can discern? In this section, we will discuss the relativistic doctrine of Protagoras, and in the materials that follow, we will consider the arguments against **relativism** offered by Socrates.

PROTAGORAS   Born in Abdera, **Protagoras (c. 485–c. 410 BCE)** lived most of his adult life in Athens. He was a famous **sophist** or teacher remembered for a relativistic doctrine summarized in the belief that the human being is the measure of all things. What is the meaning of such a statement? Does it describe the way things are or does it represent an unjustified deification of the individual—an anthropocentric view of the world?

Let us examine arguments for Protagoras's relativistic doctrine. These arguments are related to the problem of subjectivism and objectivism discussed in Chapter 2. Protagoras argued that senses condition our world. For example, if pizza tastes good to one person but not to another, then it is true that pizza is good and it is also true that it is bad. Truth is relative. If a painting appears ugly to one person but beautiful to another, then it is true that the painting is both ugly and beautiful. Protagorean relativism, extended to groups, contributed to democratic notions of majority rule.

If a group votes for a given legislation, then that legislation has truth value for that group.

The philosophical basis of Protagorean relativism had major implications for psychology. Psychologists have always had an interest in how people see their world. Techniques such as projective tests, free association, introspection, and phenomenological descriptions are a few ways we have attempted to understand the world of the individual—a world that has a face value and legitimacy all its own.

The Golden Age of Greece

As the work of early cosmologists and physicians diminished, a more comprehensive philosophy emerged in the work of Plato and Aristotle. The range of their interests covered topics in the physical and biological sciences, psychology, political science, and sociology along with traditional philosophical issues such as logic, metaphysics, and ethics.

SOCRATES   The pivotal work of **Socrates (c. 470– c. 399 BCE)** is like a saber slashing through the history of philosophy, dividing all Greek thinkers before him as pre-Socratic philosophers and all those who followed as post-Socratics. Despite his remarkable fame, little is known about the man himself. At various times, this brilliant but polarizing figure has been described as a saint and a martyr, as well as grotesque, degenerate, independent, ugly, courageous, dignified, and deranged. What is known about the historical Socrates comes from differing sources that often contradict each other. His best-known student, Plato, provides the most reliable source of information, although his philosophy might influence the portrait of his mentor.

Socrates was born about 470 BCE in Athens and died in 399 BCE in the same city. His mother was a midwife and his father was possibly a sculptor. A young female philosopher named Aspasia had a profound influence on Socrates. He regards her as his teacher and she appears throughout his dialogues. In an early work on women in science, Mozans (1913) suggested that Aspasia's emphasis on equality and the rights of women influenced both Socrates and Plato.

Socrates served time in the Athenian army during the Peloponnesian War and won distinction for his courage (he modeled the same courage later during imprisonment and execution). His passion for philosophy was so great; he was almost a victim of it. Socrates loved philosophy more than his wife and children and craved it more than material comfort or social success. He was so wholly dedicated to the pursuit of truth and ideas that he devoted little thought to ordinary needs such as food and clothing. He was disciplined, independent, simple in his tastes, and an engaging conversationalist. The picture emerges of a person with a powerful social presence complemented by a discriminating ability to entertain other viewpoints.

Socrates enticed people into conversation on topics such as the nature of justice, virtue, or prudence. He asked simple questions about how a person defined terms, and then listened with care to his or her answers. After the person offered a definition, Socrates asked questions about how the definition covered a variety of situations. Often his probing questions proved embarrassing, revealing the individual's untenable grasp of the concept. But the nature of the dialogue was so captivating that curious listeners surrounded Socrates. Like many young people of any era, the youth of Athens were attracted to ideals, integrity, intellectual excitement, and inspiration. Socrates provided that and more for his disciples.

Although an inspiration to Athens's younger minds, Socrates was a nuisance and a threat to the political and religious establishment. Wielding his merciless and biting intellect, Socrates criticized powerful Athenian political and military leaders, exposing their incompetence. Because most conservative Athenians preferred answers to questions, his constant probing into established wisdom proved an unbearable irritation. As a consequence, he was brought to trial on three trumped-up charges: (1) corrupting the youth of Athens, (2) denying Greek gods, and (3) attempting to establish new gods. Historians have argued that the indefensible charges concealed the true reason for Socrates's trial; namely, he had incurred too many personal enemies.

In characteristic style, Socrates turned his trial into a condemnation of his judges and accusers. He refused to compromise on any point as he steadfastly maintained his innocence. Had Socrates made a gesture of appeasement, he might have been rewarded with a light sentence and the whole affair would have been forgotten. His uncompromising integrity would never permit that kind of concession. He found no grounds for yielding on any point, even at the expense of his life. As a result, his accusers sentenced him to die. Upon receiving the death sentence, Socrates faced his enemies and stated, "For my part I bear no grudge at all against those who condemned me and accused me" (*Apology*, 41d). He argued "that the difficulty is not so much to escape death; the real difficulty is to escape from doing wrong" (*Apology*, 39a). The long thirty days that followed his sentence offered countless opportunities for escape, but, as emphasized in *The Crito*, he refused to break the law in any manner (Silverman, 2010). In *The Phaedo,* Plato provided a moving account of the execution. When several of Socrates's disciples wept bitterly, he reprimanded them for their weakness. When it was his time to die, the seventy-year-old philosopher drank the hemlock poison without drama. He walked around the room, making observations about the poison's effects before it claimed his life.

During his life, Socrates had rebelled against the teachings of the sophists. As professional teachers, the sophists received money for their instruction. Although disagreements persist about the range of topics included in sophist instruction, their teachings undoubtedly included rhetoric and argument. The range of their activities may have been considerably greater. In an article on the beginnings of psychotherapy, Pivnicki (1969) pointed out that Antiphon, a sophist, had a doorplate advertising his qualifications to heal grief and melancholia by means of words. Guthrie (1960) noted, "the Sophists were not a particular philosophical school, but rather a profession. They were itinerant teachers, who made a living out of the new hunger for guidance in practical affairs" (p. 66). Socrates believed the sophists' practical concerns with winning arguments and making money from teaching overshadowed their love of wisdom. He also took issue with their emphasis on sensation and relativism. This point deserves elaboration.

As we saw in the previous section, the sophist Protagoras argued that individual perception is the source of knowledge. Socrates claimed that we obtain knowledge through analysis of concepts. For example, we may ask someone to define a triangle. Individual triangles may be small or large, and they may come in a variety of colors or materials. Although color or size may be qualities associated with a particular triangle, they are not associated with triangles in general. In defining an appropriate concept of triangles, we must abstract only those qualities that all triangles have in common. For Socrates, there are objective and universal qualities that participate in a correctly framed concept, and following the appropriate conceptual work, we can assess whether a specific shape is or is not a triangle. As noted by Stace (1962), "It is no longer open to anyone to declare that whatever he chooses to call a triangle is a triangle. . . . The Sophist can no longer say 'whatever seems to me right, is right for me'" (p. 145). Socrates emphasized the power of reason; he believed that through the rational process, we can discern objective truths. This orientation exerted an enormous influence on Plato and Aristotle and later thinkers.

Socrates found little interest in physics, astronomy, or the biological sciences. For this reason, some scholars charge that he had a detrimental effect on these disciplines. His major object of inquiry was psychological and philosophical rather than physical or biological. Whereas most of Socrates's thought was directed inward, his quest for truth was in keeping with the scientific spirit.

Socrates believed that self-knowledge is vital to virtue. He believed that human beings do not knowingly engage in evil but rather that evil results from ignorance. It follows that the role of the good teacher is crucial. The teacher assists the student in the quest for knowledge. As knowledge increases, virtue increases. Because virtue includes a host of socially desirable behaviors, knowledge is the means by which the individual and society may advance. But true knowledge is elusive. Socrates believed himself to be ignorant but still wiser than those who were blind to their ignorance. The tensions between Socrates's personal admission of ignorance and any claims he might have made to be a virtuous man are still topical in philosophy (Brickhouse & Smith, 1990). He believed that most people are informed by half-truths, misinformation, and false concepts. Smith (1974) argues that Socrates was among the first to formulate a scientific approach to psychology that emphasized multiple (moral, social, anatomical, and physiological) causes of behavior. In explaining his reasons for choosing death by poison, Socrates insisted that his decision was not based on any one simple set of factors. In other words, the cause was not simply mental, physical, or social but rather a combination of all these factors. Smith insists that Socrates would have opposed twentieth-century reductionism.

One of the students present at Socrates's death was **Aristippus**, head of a school of philosophy at Cyrene. Following the death of Aristippus, his daughter **Arete** headed the school. Waithe (1987a) noted that we know nothing about Arete's personal views, but we do know something about the teachings of her school at Cyrene (p. 198). It was one of the first to advance a systematic treatment of the roles of pleasure and pain in human life. The Cyrenaics advanced a sophisticated approach to pleasure, arguing that discipline, knowledge, and virtuous actions are more likely to result in pleasure, whereas negative emotions such as anger, fear, and remorse should be avoided because they multiply pain. In her thirty-five years as a teacher, Arete was thought to have "written forty books, and to have counted among her pupils one hundred and ten philosophers" (Waithe, 1987a, p. 198). The school at Cyrene provided one of the first approaches to psychological hedonism—a doctrine that would surface again as a systematic philosophical position in the eighteenth and nineteenth centuries under the leadership of Jeremy Bentham. Richardson (1990) notes, "Towards the end of the *Protagoras*, Socrates suggests that the 'salvation of our life' depends upon applying to pleasures and pains a

science of measurement" (p. 7). The meaning of hedonism (or the pursuit of pleasure) in the works of Socrates and Plato continues to provide lively discussion (see Richardson, 1990; Weiss, 1989).

PLATO   Unlike most philosophers of his time, many of Plato's writings have survived to the present day. **Plato (c. 428–c. 347 BCE)** typically presented his ideas in the literary form of the *dialogue* often set on the streets of Athens or at a gathering of friends. Participants in the dialogue argued the various facets of concepts such as justice or virtue. Some dialogues turned into monologues as one participant held forth on a topic for a lengthy period. The collected works of Plato include a few letters as well as the numerous dialogues, including well-known works such as *The Apology*, *The Crito*, *The Laws*, *The Meno*, *The Phaedo*, *The Republic*, *The Sophist*, *The Symposium*, *The Theaetetus*, and *The Timaeus*. In addition to his recognition as a Western philosopher and teacher, Plato is regarded as a significant literary figure.

Plato was born to a wealthy family in Athens between 429 and 427 BCE. He came of age in a turbulent period marked by the hardships of warfare. The Peloponnesian War waged between Athens and Sparta had started in 431 BCE and persisted until 404 BCE. At the same time, a plague ravaged Greece. Few details are known about Plato's youth, but he doubtless received an excellent early education befitting a member of an aristocratic family. As a young man, he served in the war effort against Sparta, but little is known about his military activities. Everything changed for Plato when Socrates entered his life. As a young man, Plato was present at Socrates's trial (*Apology*, 34a) and witnessed his teacher's death. Afterward, Plato was embittered and disillusioned, especially with politics. Members of his own family had been part of a corrupt ruling party following the war. Though his family's status guaranteed a political future, Plato rejected it in favor of travel to numerous Mediterranean countries. Upon his return to Athens, he founded what can be regarded as the first European university, a remarkable school known as the **Academy**. The exact date of his university's founding remains in dispute, but it was here that Plato spent the remaining forty years of his life. At the Academy, he produced important philosophical works and taught students without charging tuition (a tradition inherited from Socrates). Plato died at age eighty-one, probably in 347 BCE. His nephew, Speusippus, succeeded him as head of the Academy.

Plato's early dialogues reveal the stamp of Socrates's influence. Plato's originality doesn't assert itself until his later works. His transformation from student and recorder to an established philosopher remains difficult to discern. In his mature philosophy, we encounter discussions of ethics, politics, law, art, religion, epistemology, and psychology. He is critical to the history of psychology because he introduced an early conflict model of psychological disorders.

Method   It's often said that Plato rejected empirical knowledge or knowledge based on sensory information. Such a point doesn't misrepresent Plato, yet the claim is too strong without qualification. Plato's *The Timaeus* included materials on astronomy based on observation and materials on anatomy based on dissection. Additionally, descriptive sciences were taught in the Academy. It seems Plato accorded a more important role to the senses in practice than in theory. Nevertheless, he believed rational processes provide true knowledge, whereas sensory information alone offers only appearance and opinion. But opinion and appearance are not without value. For example, a person may have a correct opinion about tomorrow's weather or the stock market. The correct opinion, though not certain knowledge (i.e., justified, true belief), may still offer practical value.

Theory of Forms   According to Plato, sense objects always have a particular or individual quality. Furthermore, objects of sense are always changing. They are in the process of becoming—either growing or decaying. In contrast with the world of sense is the world of forms, known through intuition or rational processes. The **theory of forms**, according to Plato, points to the true world, a world of absolute being, perfect, unchanging, and independent of individuals

and particulars and known only through reason. If there were no individual triangles available to the world of sense, that would not undermine the principles of triangularity or the form of the triangle, which, for Plato, has absolute being. Sense objects (e.g., particular triangles) may participate in or partially represent the real world of forms, but individual objects of sense are always incomplete, temporal, spatial, and changeable. The form is timeless, immutable, and unextended. In this way, Plato bridges the seemingly irreconcilable gap between the empirical justification for a world of becoming, as argued by Heraclitus, and rational justification for a world of being, as argued by Parmenides and Zeno. Even if the world as we know it ceased to exist, the principles of triangularity and the formal nature of the triangle would continue as part of the very fiber of the absolute world of forms. If the world of forms is not known through the senses, how is it known?

Whereas it is the body, via the senses, that reveals the changing, illusory, temporal world, it is the soul that reveals the world of forms through reason (Leahey, 2005). Plato believed that the soul of human beings is immortal. Plato also believed that the soul may be reincarnated into another body. In its new incarnation, the soul may have dim recollections of the real world of forms that it once knew. Now, chained to the body and the senses, it is a difficult task for the soul to comprehend true forms. Juhasz (1971) noted, "the metaphor 'eye of the soul' was originated by Plato in the *Republic*" (p. 51). The **eye of the soul** perceives the real world of forms through memories, images, and higher cognitive functions. The soul's vision of true reality is diminished when it concentrates on the welter of sensory information. The qualitative division between the permanent and perfect world of forms and being known only through reason and the temporal and changing world of becoming known through experience remains a strong theme in Western philosophy.

Nature of the Soul   Plato's thoughts on the nature of the soul are complex and often appear contradictory. Reasons for the apparent contradictions are readily identified. First,

Plato's writings cover several decades, and, like the changing degree of influence that Socrates had on his views, his thought on the nature of the soul evolved over time. Because scholars cannot always agree on the chronological order of Plato's writings, we can't be certain how his thought developed. To complicate matters, Plato enjoyed speaking in metaphors. He used different metaphors during different periods in his career. At one point, he compared the soul to a scribe. At another time, it was compared to a charioteer (reason) trying to reign in two powerful horses (appetite and spirit) in competition against each other. We'll consider the problem of the definition of *soul* in Plato before looking at the functional and structural properties of the soul.

Plato's term **psyche** is typically translated as soul. But scholars disagree about the exact meaning of *psyche*. Soul is a reasonable translation in the sense that Plato believed that psyche was immortal. But Plato also ascribed mental properties to psyche so that the term *mind* could serve as a reasonable translation. Unfortunately, Plato did not provide an unambiguous definition, so analysts attempt to understand the functional and structural properties of psyche. To further complicate matters, translations have been influenced by the temporal and cultural contexts of the translators. In the Middle Ages, for example, church scholars consistently translated *psyche* as soul.

We encounter many functional qualities of the soul in platonic literature. The soul is active; it compares, discriminates, organizes, exercises control, and masters. In a helpful article on the Platonic model of the mind and mental illness, Simon (1972) enumerated the soul's mental processes, characterized in terms of higher and lower activities. Sleeping is a lower activity, whereas waking is higher. Childishness, conflict, and appetite are lower. Adulthood, harmony, and rational processes are higher activities. Plato conceptualized the soul as engaged in psychological activities, including memory, ideation, knowing, feeling, and willing.

Plato divided the psyche into three major functions (Smith, 2010). The rational soul is highest among the three and the appetitive soul is lowest. Intermediate between the other two is the affective soul. In this structural arrangement, the rational soul is located in the head. Appetite resides in the gut. The affective soul can be found in the chest. The tripartite division was illustrated with the famous example of the charioteer and the two horses mentioned earlier. Plato favored metaphors that emphasize the entrapment of the soul in the body, such as in his famous allegory of the cave in *The Republic*. For Plato, we are all chained like prisoners in a darkened cave, unable to see the real world. Relying only on sensory experience, we glimpse little about our world beyond flickering shadows cast on a cave wall. Reason, however, can liberate us. Although chained as a prisoner of the senses, our soul can overcome its limitations and escape captivity through reason. Only with reason, can we know the real world of forms outside the cave.

Memory   Plato believed that prior to birth, the soul dwells in perfection in the world of forms. His views about memory are built around the idea that the rational soul can recall material from this perfect world. He draws upon the technology of his day to conceptualize memory. In his time, people would write on a wooden surface coated in a layer of wax. Likewise, Plato proposed the metaphor of the soul as a wax slate. Juhasz (1971) pointed out that "in different persons the quality of the wax as well as the quality of the pattern varies" in our memories (p. 52). The metaphor of the scribe in Plato's *Philebus* implies processes of storage and retrieval as well as comparison. Plato offers an early model of memory that bridges the world of sensation with the world of forms.

Learning and Education   Plato believed that education was central to good political leadership. In the ideal Platonic state, only accomplished philosophers could serve as leaders. Learning was also critical for the attainment of individual virtue. He accepted the Socratic notion that ignorance is the major culprit in wrongdoing. For Plato, learning and education are important in their own right but they also serve utilitarian ends. Virtue, harmony in society, harmony within the individual, and knowledge of universal forms are all products of learning.

Perception   For Plato, perception provides, at best, an approximation to reality and, at worst, outright illusion. He was not concerned with sensation and perception, but *The Timaeus* contains passages devoted to how the senses operate. Vision takes place, for example, when fire in the eye communicates with fire in the world. In other words, we see by virtue of the correspondence of like elements (Wade, 2005). In vision, fire from the eye proceeds outward, but in audition, shock propagated by the air impacts the ear. Plato believed that small passages from the tongue to the heart are responsible for tastes. He believed we see through the eyes, but not with them. The eyes, as the other senses, provide a chaos of sights, sounds, tastes, and so on. But seeing also involves comparisons, organization, memory, and other activities of the rational soul.

Motivation   Plato recognized the roles of pleasure and pain in human life (see Weiss, 1989). Although these belonged to the lower appetitive realm, he nevertheless believed that pleasure in moderation represents harmony and balance, whereas pain signifies discord. A particular motive might involve a complex interaction of appetite, spirit, and reason. For example, fear might be present in the appetitive dimension, but depending on spirit and reason might or might not manifest itself in behavior. Spirit and reason might complement fear with courage and with a rationale to stand one's ground. But if courage is deficient in the affective division of the soul, then cowardly behavior might be associated with fear. Plato believed that human beings seek pleasure, but the source of pleasure may change with growth. With maturity, the greatest pleasure results from the highest activities of philosophy—the comprehension of the ideal world of forms.

Mental Disorders   From the time of Homer to the time of Plato, thinking about mental disorders evolved from supernatural to more natural models of psychopathology—a development that would repeat itself as the Middle Ages gave way to the modern era. Moving beyond earlier ideas about supernatural forces and imbalances of humors, Socrates and Plato focused on psychological forces involved in mental disorders. Simon (1972) outlined several important contributions of Plato's work: (1) the recognition that powerful irrational and asocial forces may dominate the mind; (2) the view that mental disorder results from discord among the rational, appetitive, and affective components of the psyche; and (3) the belief that mental problems result from ignorance.

Plato believed that irrational and primal forces exist within all people. As evidence, he suggested that dreams reveal bizarre instincts such as incest with a parent or unnatural unions with gods or beasts. As an aside, the Greeks had sexual fantasies about their beautiful and often anthropomorphic gods. As with some other ancient cultures, the Greeks were sexually attracted to statues, a curious fetish known as *agalmatophilia* (see Scobie & Taylor, 1975).

In *The Timaeus,* Plato spoke of mental disease as a lack of intellectual function. Madness results when the appetitive psyche dominates a weak rational psyche. The impulsive and unbridled appetitive psyche was viewed as asocial. It is of a lower order, being tied to the selfish aims of the body. It is the rational soul, capable of participating in the real world of forms that brings sanity into the system. Plato spoke of justice in the soul, apparently referring to the importance of an appropriate relationship between the divisions of the soul (Seeskin, 2008). Lack of justice results in madness for the individual just as lack of justice produces a troubled social order.

Simon (1972) outlined two kinds of ignorance that, for Plato, play a role in mental disorder. The first is the ignorance associated with deficiencies in self-knowledge. Socrates also condemned this brand of ignorance, reportedly telling the jury at his trial that "the unexamined life is not worth living." A second type involves ignorance of the ideal and of the world of forms. Reliance on the sensual, the temporary, the illusory world of the senses is a form of ignorance, one that may ultimately promote the ascendance of the appetitive soul—an unfortunate consequence for emotional health.

Plato saw philosophy, especially dialectics, as an ideal basis for changing cognitions about the world. In this sense, philosophy becomes a kind of therapy, or talking cure, for dysfunctional thinking. Plato also recognized the role of learning in mental disturbance, warning that many children's stories and fairy tales offer contaminating influences; he also believed that other aspects of family life hold negative effects on children. In *The Republic,* Plato saw a role for the professional in the care and rearing of children. He was not impressed with the qualifications of the typical parent.

Love   The Platonic vision of love and its significance remains a dominant theme in Western thought. Plato advocated higher and lower forms of love, an approach that follows a hierarchical arrangement consistent with his entire philosophical system (Perper, 2010). Eros, or erotic love, is bound to the body or the senses and can enslave people to their passions (Soble, 2009), but the soul can progress in its capacity to love (*The Symposium*). Stace (1962) noted that in all love, Plato believed we are searching for beauty. We may find beauty first in eros, but then in people, then in knowledge, and finally in philosophy.

Plato's impact on Western thought has been extensive. Although Alfred North Whitehead (1979) may have overstated his claim that Western philosophy "consists of a series of footnotes to Plato" (p. 39), Plato's emphasis on the conflict between rational and irrational forces foreshadowed the work of Sigmund Freud. Plato's lasting influence on Western thought is illustrated by the terms *Platonism* and *neo-Platonism,* referring to the philosophies of individuals or groups who emulate Plato. Though some contemporary scholars find much to criticize in Plato (Rauch, 1993), others argue that the ancient sage has much to teach us about contemporary topics such as ecology, ethics, and virtuous behavior (see Ali, 2012; Lane, 2012; Ophuls, 2011).

ARISTOTLE   This brilliant philosopher was born in Stagirus in 384 BCE. After his physician father died when **Aristotle** was a small boy, he lived under the care of a guardian. At age seventeen, he joined Plato's Academy in Athens where he remained until age thirty-seven. Following Plato's death in 347 BCE, Aristotle left the Academy and resided for brief periods in Atarneus in Asia Minor and in Mytilene (located on the island of Lesbos in the eastern Aegean Sea). At the invitation of Philip of Macedonia, Aristotle tutored a young prince named Alexander III (356–323 BCE), later to gain infamy as the conqueror Alexander the Great.

Following a five-year period as Alexander's mentor, Aristotle returned to Athens and founded a school known as the **Lyceum** (the name honors a wolf deity known as Apollo Lyceus, the god of shepherds). As the former teacher of a prince, Aristotle enjoyed many benefits and opportunities, including political protection and an abundance of supplies. During his most productive years, he established a library and scientific laboratories at the Lyceum. This prolific period inspired many of his four hundred books, most rather modest in length.

Aristotle taught at the Lyceum for thirteen years, but was forced to leave Athens when the political climate turned volatile. Following Alexander the Great's death in 323 BCE, the pro-Macedonian party was overthrown and replaced by a party that expressed hostility to Macedonia. Because Aristotle had once tutored Alexander, the Athenians viewed him as pro-Macedonian. In order to escape persecution and the possible fate of his intellectual grandfather Socrates, Aristotle fled Athens and took up residence in Chalcis. He died shortly thereafter, in 322 BCE, at sixty-three years of age. Unlike his teacher Plato, Aristotle was much more a creature of this world. As such, he focused attention on the immediate world more than any abstract world of forms. Although sympathetic to select features of Platonic rationalism, he was an unapologetic empiricist. The comprehensive nature of Aristotle's thought is revealed in his work. He was educated in the mathematics, astronomy, and physics of his day and made many original contributions in the physical sciences. As a founder of zoology, he was the first known collector and classifier of zoological specimens. Single-handedly, he founded formal logic. He was also creative in political philosophy, metaphysics, and axiology, and was acquainted with the medical wisdom of his day. Aristotle's intellectual activities and achievements—impossible in an age of specialization such as our own—remain impressive. He stands among the leading scholars of all time, perhaps the last person to know all or at least most of the available scholarship in his or her culture at a given time.

Earlier, in Chapter 2, we discussed Aristotle's notions of material, efficient, formal, and final causation. The concept of final causation, for which Aristotle has been severely criticized, attempted to establish reasons, purposes, or ends for which things in the world exist. Aristotle rejected the idea that the universe is irrational or chaotic. Development is also a key feature in Aristotle's thinking; for example, he proposed three separate seven-year periods of development prior to adulthood (Lerner, 2009). Additionally, he emphasized the idea that there is direction in nature and that this direction is toward reason. Let us now turn to a consideration of some of Aristotle's psychological concepts.

Soul and Body   Robinson (1989a) noted, "It is a mark of Aristotle's intellectual independence that, after no less than twenty years of instruction in the Academy, he would arrive at a conception of soul so radically different from the Socratic one passed down in Plato's dialogues" (p. 44). Guthrie (1960) pointed out that for Aristotle "we cannot understand the soul if we neglect the body. . .so, with a particular sense; we cannot understand sight unless we examine the structure and workings of the eye" (p. 147). In an early model of physiological psychology, Aristotle claimed that soul and body are as interdependent as matter and form (Leahey, 2005). Jager and VanHoorn (1972) noted that in the natural philosophy of Aristotle, there is material and form and "in the phenomenal world there can be no real separation between the two; no shape without some solid material; no solid material without some shape" (p. 321); Aristotle's views are sometimes called **hylomorphism**, a term from *hule* meaning matter and *morphe* meaning form. Aristotle applied the matter–form interdependence to the soul–body

question. In *De Anima,* Aristotle affirmed that "we can wholly dismiss as unnecessary the question whether the soul and the body are one: it is as meaningless as to ask whether the wax and the shape given to it by the stamp are one" (412b, 5). So that which is mental is not separable from that which is physical. Aristotle's hylomorphism, applied to the mind–body problem, establishes the legitimacy of both domains, but at the same time, sounds a cautionary note to those who flirt with extreme materialism or idealism. Either extreme can result only in a strained and fragmentary psychology. Whereas mind, according to Aristotle, is closely tied to the body, it is more than a set of organizational properties operating in a physical substrate (see Green, 1998). Indeed, mental processes are more than a mere addition of their physical elements. Formal processes depend on a physical structure, but also enjoy some degree of independence and causal efficacy.

Aristotle proposed a hierarchy of the psyche. At the most elementary level, all life forms have a nutritive function. Even in plants, the basic processes of growth and reproduction are necessary for survival. Beyond the nutritive function, animals have sensitive (sensing or perception) and movement (locomotion) functions (Smith, 2010). Over and above these there is the function of reason, which is divided into passive and active components. Passive reason is closely associated with the senses and with the function of common sense, which ties one sense to another through the ability to compare or make judgments. Aristotle argued that the passive mind is "related to what is thinkable, as sense is to what is sensible" (*De Anima,* 429a, 15).

We must come to grips with ambiguities in Aristotle's writings, especially ones pertaining to the relationship of soul to body. Numerous passages in *De Anima* present his hylomorphic or unified approach to soul and body. But some of Aristotle's writings introduce an apparent qualitative split between soul and body. One attempt to resolve the contradiction is that the early Aristotle, still under the influence of Plato, embraces the qualitative split while the more seasoned Aristotle embraces hylomorphism. For the present, we may regard Aristotle's hylomorphism as an extremely useful approach to the mind–body problem, one with important implications for psychology. We leave unanswered the nature of those dimensions of soul that for Aristotle appear to be transcendent and immortal.

Memory   In his work *On Memory and Reminiscence,* Aristotle reminds his audience that the object of memory remains in the past, whereas the object of perception stands in the present and the object of expectation waits in the future (in this context, Aristotle noted the possibility, one day, of a science of expectation). He argued that memory must be based on something within us like an impression or a picture. If the receiving surface is too soft, too hard, frayed, or decaying, memory will be defective. Aristotle believed that elderly people have poor memories because of decay and the very young have poor memories because of rapid growth. He noted that defects of memory point to symptoms of mental derangement. A common symptom is the inability to discriminate a mere phantasm or picture in the head from a real memory. Aristotle argued that memory is a faculty of sense perception—a faculty that perceives time. Aristotle makes a distinction between memory and recollection. For him, recollection is a "searching for an 'image' in a corporeal substrate" (*On Memory and Reminiscence,* 453a, 15–16). Recollection involves effort and an active process of searching. Aristotle pointed out that memory can occur without recollection (i.e., there can be a spontaneous quality about memory). Recollection, however, cannot take place without memory; Aristotle probably meant that recollection is successful only when the so-called imprint, or picture, is found. He pointed out that failures of recollection imply a need for relearning.

In his discussion of the pragmatics of recollection, Aristotle outlined important laws of association that are still with us today. How are we to proceed most efficiently with the task of recollection? He noted that an ordered event is easy to remember, but "badly arranged subjects are remembered with difficulty" (*On Memory and Reminiscence,* 452a, 3). Recollection is facilitated

by similarity, contrast, contiguity (*On Memory and Reminiscence,* 451b, 15), and frequency (*On Memory and Reminiscence,* 452a, 30). Aristotle also pointed out that recollection is more efficient if we begin with the first item in a series, but failing that, we may be successful if we recover a middle item. Mistakes in memory result from the numbers of associations that can be made for any event. In the recollection of a name, for example, the mind can be deflected from the right direction so we may mispronounce or even make a mistake.

Sensing   Aristotle noted that sensation depends partly on sense objects. Some sense objects, such as color or timbre, are of such a nature that they can be detected by only one sense. Aristotle said that, "such objects are what we propose to call the special objects of this or that sense" (*De Anima,* 418a, 15). In addition to special objects, Aristotle argued that there are "common sensibles" or activities that are common to all the senses. Robinson (1989a) pointed out that common sense "is not a separate and distinct sense in itself but a mode of perceptual integration" (p. 75). The "common sensibles" were thought to be figure, number, magnitude, movement, and rest. If the term *figure* refers to a sensory pattern, then one could well imagine that patterns of various sorts could be detected within any sensory domain. Aristotle was not specific about how each "common sensible" operates in each sensory domain. Jager and VanHoorn (1972) pointed out that Aristotle's general theory of sensing must be understood in terms of his theory of actuality and potentiality. Potential sensing is present, for example, when one listens for the chime of the clock while actual sensing happens when hearing and chiming occur together. Smith (1971) stated that Aristotle's theory "requires an object–organism interaction through a medium of contact" (p. 375). Aristotle was not always clear about the nature of that medium. For sound, the medium was air; for smell, he said, the medium had no name (*De Anima,* 419a, 30). He found evidence for a medium in the fact that the object of sense "sets in movement only what lies between, and this in turn sets the organ in movement: If what sounds or smells is brought into immediate contact with the organ, no sensation will be produced" (*De Anima*, 419a, 28–30). But if there is a medium for sight, smell, and sound, what are the media for taste and touch? Aristotle argued that these latter two do have media, "for we do perceive everything through a medium" (*De Anima*, 423b, 5).

He argued that the skin and tongue are merely related to the real organs of touch and taste. Thus, the skin is the medium of touch, but not the organ of touch. Presumably, the same is true for the tongue—it is simply a medium. Aristotle found evidence for this conclusion in the fact that direct contact with the skin produces a sensation of touch. The skin must therefore be the medium rather than the organ of touch (Green & Groff, 2003). Recall that Aristotle believed that direct contact with the sense organ itself results in no sensation. It is noteworthy that Aristotle was troubled over whether touch is a single sense or a group of senses (*De Anima*, 422b, 15). As for gustation, he believed that there are two contrary simple tastes, sweet and bitter. Secondary tastes include saline on the side of bitter and succulent on the side of sweet. Between the extremes are other secondary tastes such as harsh, pungent, astringent, and acid. He believed that smells follow the same patterns as tastes: sweet, bitter, pungent, and so on.

Aristotle was one of the first to study perceptual illusions and his writings include several examples (see Johannsen, 1971). The first, possibly discovered by Aristotle, is obtained by crossing the second finger over the first. With the eyes closed, the adjacent sides of the fingers are then stimulated by a common object, creating a tactile illusion of two objects. Aristotle believed that the illusion possibly results from the fact that, in natural finger position, the same object seldom stimulates the two outer sides of the fingers simultaneously. Another illusion reported by Aristotle was one of movement, described in his work on dreams. It is illustrated when we turn away from a moving object and fix our eyes on something steady, we may continue to perceive motion.

Imagination and Thought   In Aristotle's writings, the term *phantasia* can be translated as "imagination" (Juhasz, 1971), so we may use *phantasia* as a synonym for "mental image." Aristotle

drew a sharp distinction between imagination and perception or sensation. Unlike the way the latter two terms are used today, they are equivalent for Aristotle. He argued that "perception of the special objects of sense is always free from error" (*De Anima*, 427b, 10). But imagination, which we can employ anytime, can lead to falsehoods. Juhasz (1971) pointed out that imagination in Aristotle's theory "is pure appearance without the subject of the perception. As such it is at once highly susceptible to error" (p. 54). Perception, according to Aristotle, cannot be called up anytime because it is dependent on the correspondence between the sense object and the sense organ. Because thinking often happens in the absence of the objects of perception and because it is impossible to think without mental images, thinking is also susceptible to error. Thus, perceiving, as a correspondence between external and internal movements, is accurate, but imagination does not have the corrective influence of the external world; so additions, deletions, and distortions are possible in thought. Thinking that is dependent on images or imagination can easily go astray.

The relationship among sensing, imagination, and thinking clarifies Aristotle's empiricism. It is important to remain close to empirical observables because, in so doing, we minimize the risk of error. But we must now point to a difficulty in the interpretation of Aristotle's theory of thought. It appears that Aristotle also believed in the existence of a form of thought independent of sensing and that is active in nature, a form that is perhaps a manifestation of a higher order of the soul. Thus, for Aristotle, one kind of thinking may be conditioned by imagination, but he seems also to have believed in a higher reason closer in nature to platonic beliefs about reason.

Dreams   In many ancient cultures, dreams were explained as prophecies or signs from a deity, but Aristotle argued that dreams are not divine messages. He suggested that lower animals also dream and that persons of the most inferior type claim to foresee the future in dreams sent by God. Such persons, he said, are "garrulous and excitable" and given to so many prophetic experiences that they, like gamblers, find occasional luck. But it is only chance when a vision predicts some event in the world.

Aristotle called attention to the persistence of movement observed in nature. Waves from a pebble thrown into a pond persist across the pond; something heated by a fire loses its heat only gradually. Aristotle believed that the same principle holds for the senses. Thus, if we look at a bright light, and "we close the eyes, then, if we watch carefully, it appears in a right line with the direction of vision (whatever this may be), at first in its own colour; then it changes to crimson, next to purple, until it becomes black and disappears" (*On Dreams*, 459b, 10). Aristotle also called attention to the persistence of the perception of movement and strong odors. He concluded that "the dream proper is a presentation based on the movement of sense impressions, when such presentation occurs during sleep" (*On Dreams*, 462a, 25).

But do dreams have significance beyond the fact that they represent complicated afterimages? The answer is yes. If they fail to convey divine messages in a theological sense, they nevertheless have biological significance. The dream may be a message of the development of pathology. When large movements of the body (e.g., walking) have subsided, we have in sleep and in the dream a special sensitivity to small movements. Aristotle noted that the smallest residual light image may register in the dream as lightning or the smallest sound as thunder. By extension, small changes in the body may be represented in the dream—so he agrees with the popular medical thought of his day that physicians as well as speculative philosophers "should pay diligent attention to dreams" (*On Prophesying by Dreams*, 463a, 5).

Motivation and Values   The subject of motivation concerns why people do what they do. Aristotle believed that we are motivated to seek pleasure and happiness, but in so doing we should also seek the good. Stace (1962) observed, "For Aristotle an action is not good because it yields enjoyment. On the contrary, it yields enjoyment because it is good" (p. 315). But what is the good? Unlike other animals, we have a unique capacity for reason. One manifestation of the good is the

development of our rational capacity. Goodness and virtue also consist partly of subordinating the appetites and passions to rational control (Sobel, 2009). Sometimes, he believed, our failure to achieve goodness is rooted in excess or lack of moderation. We should seek a golden mean between extremes. As Guthrie (1960) adds, "Courage is a mean between cowardice and foolhardiness, temperance a mean between abstinence and self-indulgence, generosity between meanness and extravagance, proper pride between abjectness and arrogance" (p. 155). Aristotle recognized the importance of at least four sets of contributing factors in achieving the good: individual differences, habit, social supports, and freedom of choice. Individual differences are manifested in his idea that the mean between extremes may vary from person to person. Thus, what is courage for one person would be foolhardiness for another. For Aristotle, learning and habit are keys to good or ethical behavior. In his discussion of ethics, he refers to the importance of habit (*Nicontachean Ethics*, 1095b, 1–9) and to the close correspondence between happiness and virtuous actions (*Nicomachean Ethics*, 1100b, 10). Aristotle believed that social supports and good fortune (e.g., friends, riches, power, good children, beauty, good family) help us to find happiness; those who are childless, solitary, or physically unattractive will have greater difficulty attaining happiness. But even in the face of misfortune, we can find redemption in effortful and habitual virtuous activity. We can attain happiness in spite of circumstance and "bear the chances of life most nobly and altogether decorously if [we are] 'truly good' and 'four-square beyond reproach' " (*Nicomachean Ethics*, 1100b, 20). Aristotle's emphasis on habit would be echoed over two thousand years later in the work of American psychologist William James. Critical and appreciative work on Aristotle's views on character formation continues to find its way into contemporary literature in psychology (see Lewis, 2012).

Psychological Thought Following Aristotle

After Aristotle departed Athens, his student **Theophrastus (c. 372–c. 287 BCE)** assumed leadership of the Lyceum. Like his teacher, Theophrastus had great breadth of interest and he continued the school's scientific and philosophical traditions. In philosophy, he extended some of Aristotle's work on logic. He produced two botanical works that contained the first system for classifying plants, granting him status as the founder of botany. His psychological interests are revealed in a book titled *Characters,* which provides descriptions of negative character traits such as boorishness and tactlessness. Theophrastus reviewed a wide corpus of Greek work on sensation (Stratton, 1917; Wade, 2000) and argued for the central role of the brain in sensation. He was more of an empiricist than Aristotle, believing that science should emphasize material and efficient causation rather than final causation.

Although Theophrastus continued the Aristotelian tradition, it did not survive as a dominant force in Greek thought. After Aristotle's death, Stace (1962) noted, "the rest of the story of Greek philosophy is soon told, for it is the story of decay" (p. 339). The decay was illustrated by a loss of interest in the pursuit of wisdom for its own sake and a growing demand for the achievement of immediate gratification. Investigation of great questions in science and metaphysics was replaced by narrow self-centered concerns such as how to be happy and how to maximize personal gains. New ideas diminished. Long after the Golden Age of Greece, philosophy was largely derivative.

The schools of stoicism, epicureanism, and neo-Platonism took center stage after the passing of the Golden Age. As Stace (1962) noted, each school shared a focus on individuals and their concerns (p. 340). On occasion, a figure emerged who addressed great issues, but such pursuits counted as secondary concerns for them.

Review Questions

1. Discuss psychological thought as it is encountered in documents and manuscripts from ancient cultures such as China, Egypt, and India.
2. Many of the early Greeks were interested in the primal substance of the world. Contrast Thales,

Democritus, Anaximander, and Anaximenes with respect to their views on the primal substance.
3. Myia of the Pythagorean school provided some of the earliest advice on the care of infants. Briefly summarize her advice.
4. Contrast the philosophy of becoming as advanced by Heraclitus with the philosophy of being as advanced by Parmenides.
5. Trace the development of Greek medical thought from Aesculapius to Hippocrates.
6. How did Socrates argue against the relativism of Protagoras?
7. Briefly outline the contributions of Socrates to psychology.
8. Outline Plato's conflict model of mental disorders.
9. Discuss Plato's methodology. Include in your discussion a statement about Plato's theory of forms and explain the meaning of his metaphor "eye of the soul."
10. Briefly state Plato's position on memory, perception, and motivation.
11. Contrast Plato with Aristotle with respect to their approaches to knowledge.
12. What was Aristotle's approach to the soul–body question?
13. Outline Aristotle's positions on memory, sensing, and motivation.
14. Briefly discuss Aristotle's approach to dreaming.
15. What are the essential features of psychological and philosophical thought following Aristotle?

Glossary

Academy   A facility purchased by Plato by a park named Academeca in Athens. Plato taught students at this facility, which became known as the Academy. The Academy flourished during Plato's life and for hundreds of years after his death.

Aesara   One of the first Greek philosophers to emphasize the importance of balance to health.

Aesculapius   Possibly a historical figure, but the name comes from the Greek mythical God Asclepius, son of Apollo. Asclepius was a great physician who, in Greek mythology, was killed by Zeus because he sinned by raising a man from the dead. Many temples were built in honor of Asclepius.

Alcmaeon   Early Greek physician who worked around 500 BCE. He advocated an empirical, rational, and naturalistic approach to medicine. One of the first to practice dissection.

Anaximander of Miletus(610–c. 547 BCE)
Greek scientist and philosopher and one of the first to advance a theory of organic evolution.

Anaximenes (c. 588–c. 524 BCE)   A cosmologist who taught that air is the primal substance and that this substance is transformed into other things through condensation and rarefaction.

Arete   Daughter of Aristippus and head of the school of philosophy at Cyrene following the death of Aristippus.

Aristippus   Student of Socrates who headed the school of Cyrene following the death of Socrates.

Aristotle (384–322 BCE)   The pupil of Plato and one of the great philosophers who is especially noteworthy for his work in physics, biology, and psychology. Aristotle also founded logic and set forth an original and comprehensive view of causality.

Avesta   Holy book of the Zoroastrian religion.

Confucius (551–479 BCE)   Well-known early Chinese philosopher interested primarily in the moral life with a focus on methods that promote personal and interpersonal harmony.

Democritus (c. 460–c. 370 BCE)   Refined the atomic theory set forth earlier by the philosopher Leucippus. Taught that reality was based on atoms and the void. Atoms were thought to be indivisible and invisible. Their basic structures accounted for the nature of the observable material world.

Empedocles (c. 490–c. 430 BCE)   Early homeostatic theorist who taught that four basic elements (air, earth, fire, and water) combine with two first principles (love and strife). Love unites and organizes, whereas strife results in disintegration and disorganization.

eye of the soul   A metaphor employed by Plato to convey the idea that the soul can sometimes apprehend true reality.

Heraclitus   Probably active around 480 BCE, Heraclitus was the first process philosopher. Emphasized the idea that only change is real.

Hippocrates (c. 460–c. 377 BCE)   Sometimes regarded as the Father of Greek Medicine, Hippocrates advanced a thoroughgoing naturalistic account of all illness, both physical and mental. Advanced the first classification system of mental disorders.

Hsün Tzu (c. 298–c. 212 BCE)   An early Chinese philosopher who advanced a thoroughgoing naturalistic philosophy. He is sometimes viewed as the Chinese Aristotle.

hylomorphism   A mind–body position advanced by Aristotle, comes from *hule* meaning matter and *morphe* meaning form. Aristotle stressed the interdependence of matter and form. Thus, seeing as a mental process cannot be separated from the physical structure of the eye.

Leucippus   Greek philosopher who lived around 500 BCE. He was the founder of atomic theory later refined by Democritus.

Lyceum   A school near Athens founded by Aristotle.

Myia   Daughter of Pythagoras and Theana. One of the first to give advice on child rearing.

Parmenides   Early philosopher who did his work shortly after 500 BCE. He was one of the first to attempt to distinguish between appearance and reality. According to Parmenides, the senses reveal only appearances, whereas reason leads to real truths. In contrast with Heraclitus, Parmenides emphasized a philosophy of being as opposed to a philosophy of becoming.

philosophy   A term likely coined by Pythagoras from *philo* (meaning love) and *sophia* (meaning knowledge or wisdom). Hence, the love of wisdom.

Plato (c. 428–c. 347 BCE)   The student of Socrates and the teacher of Aristotle. One of the great philosophers of all time remembered, among other things, for his emphasis on the importance of reason as a means of discerning the formal abstract nature of truth. Advanced an early conflict model of mental illness and speculated on numerous psychological topics such as memory and sensation.

Protagoras (c. 485–c. 410 BCE)   A sophist (teacher) who emphasized the doctrine of relativism. Protagoras argued that the world is conditioned by our senses and hence truth is relative.

psyche   The Greek term for soul or mind. Includes mental processes such as thought, memory, sensation, and perception.

Pythagoras (c. 580–c. 500 BCE)   An enduring figure in Western intellectual history who did his work around 570 BCE. He is remembered for his emphasis on the importance of quantification and for specific contributions such as the famous Pythagorean theorem. His beliefs in the primacy of reason and the nature of the soul were influential later in the work of Socrates and Plato.

relativism   The doctrine that knowledge is not absolute; rather, it is a product of human mental processes with all their inherent limitations. Thus, according to the position, truths change as a function of time, place, and circumstance.

Socrates (c. 470–c. 399 BCE)   Teacher of Plato and so important in Greek thought that all philosophy before him is called pre-Socratic. He reacted against the relativism of Protagoras and taught that reason is the basis of true knowledge. He emphasized the importance of self-knowledge and is thus an important figure in the history of psychological thought.

sophist   A type of teacher in ancient Greece. The sophists often emphasized relativism and how to live successfully. They often offered plausible but fallacious arguments. Hence, terms such as *sophistry* and *sophistic* refer to arguments that appear to be sound but are later found to be superficial or fallacious.

Thales   An early Greek cosmologist active around 600 BCE. Thales was known for his contention that water is the primordial substance. He was also interested in the problem of movement and the nature of motive forces that make movement possible.

Theana   An accomplished philosopher and wife of Pythagoras who played a key role in the educational activities of the Pythagorean school.

Theophrastus (c. 372–c. 287 BCE)   Succeeded Aristotle at the Lyceum. Extended many of Aristotle's ideas but emphasized material and efficient causes. He is sometimes regarded as the Father of Botany.

theory of forms   According to Plato, there are universal and true principles comprehended through reason. For example, the senses reveal only particular triangles, but reason reveals the principles of triangularity. A goal of education is to uncover the true formal properties of things.

Upanishads   Vedic treatises dealing with philosophical and psychological matters. See *Vedas*.

Vedas   Oldest sacred books of India setting forth many early ideas on psychological matters.

Xenophanes (c. 560–c. 478 BCE)   An early Greek philosopher remembered for his epistemological skepticism. He argued that human beings do not have certain knowledge and he scoffed at anthropomorphic concepts of deity.

yang   Ancient Chinese concept representing qualities such as force, hardness, masculinity, and heat. Contrasts with but also complements the concept of yin.

yin   Ancient Chinese concept representing qualities such as softness, coldness, passivity, and moistness. Contrasts with but also complements the concept of yang.

Zarathustra   Major prophet of the Zoroastrian religion.

Zend-Avesta   See *Avesta*.

Zeno of Elea   Active around 450 BCE, Zeno was a follower of Parmenides. He is remembered for paradoxes that supposedly revealed contradictions between reason and the senses. His paradoxes of motion are particularly noteworthy. For example, an arrow on its way toward a target presents a certain paradox. It must first travel half the distance, but then it must travel half the remaining distance. Because Zeno thought it is possible to divide forever, the arrow should never reach its target.

4

■ ■ ■

The Roman Period and the Middle Ages

But soul is not in the universe, on the contrary the
universe is in the soul.

—Plotinus, *Enneads*, V, p. 411

In ancient times, the Roman Empire held a great deal of the world in its iron grip. Its period of dominance spanned more than ten centuries, beginning in obscurity in the seventh century BCE and ending with the unseating of Rome's last emperor in 476 CE. At the height of its power in 100 CE, the Roman Empire occupied the countries surrounding the Mediterranean Sea and ran to the western shores of Spain. Its border stretched as far east as the Persian Gulf and, to the north, it encompassed the British Isles. Its southern command stretched to Africa, reaching well past the pyramids of Egypt.

As early as the second century BCE, one million people lived in Rome, but the population of the greater empire boasted fifty to one hundred million people. Early in its history, Roman society was grounded in superstition and polytheism. Citizens were expected to uphold the qualities of conformity, duty, order, loyalty, and perseverance. In this paternalistic society, the father of a family enjoyed complete legal power. An unfaithful wife could be sentenced to death. A disobedient child could be brutally punished or sold into slavery.

By the first century CE, the Roman way of life embraced material comfort and amusement. The Romans indulged in baths and swimming and exercise facilities as well as soaps, cosmetics, exotic clothing, jewelry, and music imported from Greece. A proliferation of holidays offered citizens the chance to attend games and circuses. For the delight of bloodthirsty crowds, exhibitions pitted wild animals imported from Africa and the North against slaves and professional gladiators. A handful of citizens protested the slaughter of humans and animals, but their voices were drowned in the cry for greater spectacle.

The scientific spirit didn't flourish in a population addicted to games and bloodlust. The Romans adored technology, but had little use for science. Geology held some interest, probably because Italy was prone to earthquakes and volcanic eruptions. The Romans used geometry in their architecture, but did little to extend the discipline beyond the pioneering discoveries of Euclid (325–265 BCE) and Pythagoras (c. 580–c. 500 BCE). Astrology motivated some attention to the stars. The Romans had an interest in medicine, mostly because of its practical applications. The study of medicine also fueled some curiosity about psychological questions.

ROMAN MEDICINE

Medicine flourished during this period, owing to the practical need for sustaining Rome's formidable armies. Despite it all, medicine in the early Roman Period was primitive. Barbers conducted surgery along with captives from other countries. Superstition and miracle cures triumphed over scientific inquiry. As with other sciences, Roman medicine borrowed from earlier Greek advances.

An influential Greek physician named **Asclepiades (c. 124 BCE)** was an early figure in the study of mental disorders. His practice in Rome attracted numerous patients and students. Asclepiades distinguished between delusions and hallucinations and argued that therapy for mental disorders should be pleasant and expedient. Like Hippocrates, he relied heavily on diet, music, massage, baths, and exercise. An Aesculapian temple erected in the third century BCE proved popular with the Romans, who basked in its gentle and relaxed atmosphere.

The Greeks contributed to Roman medicine, but the relationship was turbulent. Although Greek physicians were better trained, Romans became suspicious when their surgeries or medicines failed. Greek doctors were viewed with a mixture of admiration and paranoia. In that context, the work of Rome's best-known physician flourished.

Galen

In the history of Western medicine, Claudius **Galenus (c. 129–c. 199 CE)** stands as second in importance only to Hippocrates. Galen studied philosophy in Pergamum and anatomy in Alexandria, Egypt. He studied and commented on earlier philosophical and medical works while developing his own ideas (Green & Groff, 2003). Roman law prohibited dissection of human cadavers, so Galen conducted anatomical studies on pigs, apes, and other animals, even dissecting the eyes of oxen (Wade, 2005). When he became physician and surgeon for the gladiators, Galen was allowed to conduct limited studies on human anatomy. He wrote nearly four hundred treatises covering numerous medical issues and conditions. Today, unfortunately, only eighty-three of his works exist. From his remaining work, we can conclude that he was a dedicated student of psychology.

Galen subscribed to the Greek four-humor theory of black bile, blood, phlegm, and yellow bile. In addition to humors, he argued that four qualities (cold, warm, dry, and moist) play a role in sickness and wellness. When one is in good health, he believed, humors and qualities remain in balance. An imbalance produces illness.

But what affects the balance? Galen claimed that various foods could increase or decrease the humors and qualities. Geography, occupation, and age could also play a role. Even seasonal changes might make a difference. For example, Galen associated the springtime with blood, warmth, and moistness. The winter months brought phlegm, coldness, and moistness.

Drawing on his studies of the humors and qualities, Galen proposed an early personality theory. The four cardinal humors could be associated with four personality traits or temperaments (a word derived from the Latin verb *temperare*, meaning "to mix"). An individual with a *choleric* temperament would be quick tempered and fiery. The *phlegmatic* type would be described as sluggish and unemotional. A sunny person who is cheerful and optimistic would possess a *sanguine* temperament. The *melancholic* person would be sad with a tendency toward depression.

As with physical illness, Galen believed most mental disorders result from an imbalance in humors and qualities. For example, an imbalance of black bile may produce melancholia. Mania (frenzied excitement) was thought to be a "hot disease" related to an excess of yellow bile and heat. How do you treat an excessive humor? He proposed treatments that relied on the opposite of the excess. A physician might counteract a "hot dry disease" by wrapping the patient in cold wet towels. A "cold wet disease" might be treated with warm and dry remedies.

Galen believed in a physiological basis for mental disorders, but also thought that our minds can influence our bodies. As an example, Jackson (1969) cites the case in which Galen treated a woman for insomnia. During his examination, Galen was ready to conclude that the woman had an excess of black bile resulting from melancholia. At that moment, another person in the examining room mentioned seeing the famed dancer Pylades at the theater. Galen noted that the woman's expression changed and her heart rate became irregular. In subsequent examinations, he mentioned other dancers, but found no jump in her heart rate. Whenever Pylades was mentioned, however, Galen documented a reliable physiological reaction. He concluded the woman was in love with the dancer. In his mind, it served as proof that mental states have important physiological consequences.

Galen's book *On the Diagnosis and Cure of the Soul's Passions* contains advice on seeking another person's counsel for emotional problems. The other person, as noted by Jackson (1969), should be "an older man—mature, respected, free from passions—who would point out the person's faults in regard to his passions" (p. 380). Galen seems to advocate an early psychotherapy. Although authoritarian and direct, his therapy stressed a confrontation of passions. Galen believed that passions (powerful experiences such as greed, anger, and jealousy) burned with greater intensity than typical emotions (Maher & Maher, 2003) and were the root of psychological problems.

As a vitalist, Galen believed the universe was dynamic and alive. His vitalism is apparent in his ideas about the **pneuma**. In his time, *pneuma* referred to air drawn in as breath that is distributed to bodily tissue. However, Galen studied it in a different way. Largely derived from the tripartite theory of Erasistratus (Smith, 2010), Galen used pneuma to describe three vital principles of life. The first, known as **natural spirit**, is found in all plant and animal life. Largely unconscious, natural spirit is involved in simple, day-to-day processes of vegetative maintenance and survival. Pneuma also functioned in the **vital spirit**, a process that regulated body heat. Galen also spoke of the *psychic pneuma*, usually translated as **animal spirit**. Whereas the vital spirit was in the heart, the animal spirit had its seat in the brain. Not surprisingly, this type of pneuma controlled higher cognitive functions. Although Galen believed that the substance of the brain was involved in mental activity, his emphasis on the actions of the pneuma in the ventricles (brain cavities) may have influenced the later medieval notion that the mental faculties were located in the ventricles of the brain (Green, 2003; Rose, 2009).

For the time, Galen was a rigorous scientist. He conducted empirical studies on animals and traveled to search for medications and new ideas. He thoroughly studied his patients' physical symptoms, and he was a "tireless interrogator of his patients" to better understand their histories and symptoms (Mattern, 2011, p. 479). Galen was a flexible thinker, but subsequent generations pressed his work into the confines of narrow dogma.

Early Christian leaders interpreted Galen's concept of the pneuma (especially animal spirit) as consistent with church doctrine that the body is subservient to the soul. As a result, Galen's ideas were assimilated into Christian doctrine. For centuries, his teachings were praised and became the basis of dogmatism in a climate that forbade medical research and dissection. In the absence of experimentation, errors in Galen's work went unnoticed. For 1,500 years, major psychological topics such as thought, movement, and perception were explained in terms of vital principles or animal spirits. Galen's pneuma theory remained unchallenged until the discoveries of the seventeenth- and eighteenth-century physiologists.

ROMAN PHILOSOPHY

The Roman Period featured several schools of philosophy including stoicism, Epicureanism, skepticism, and neo-Platonism. All were derivative and practical (Henley & Thorne, 2005). Unlike their Greek predecessors, Roman philosophers were not known for original contributions or for great world questions. The individual became the primary focus, especially how one could escape the ills of the world and live a good life.

Stoicism

The school of **stoicism**, founded by **Zeno of Cyprus (c. 335–c. 263 BCE)**, thrived for over five hundred years. The early leaders of the stoic school were not interested in the physical sciences. Instead, they focused on discipline, self-control, and the absolute lawfulness of nature. The stoics advocated suppression of self-will and appetite. Virtue was found in duty, reason, principle, and the elimination of all passions. Rather than seeking outright pleasure, happiness was supposed to be found in a life of austerity and discipline. According to Diogenes Laertius (1972), Zeno injured a toe while walking, interpreted this as a sign that his life was to end, and willingly took his own life as a meaningful gesture of acquiescence to duty (see Kaplan et al., 2007).

The stoics disliked the idea of arbitrary boundaries that divide geographical regions into states. People should identify with each other rather than identifying with nations. True wisdom can never come from subordinating oneself to a state. With resignation, however, they noted that the number of the wise in the world is a mere trifle. Most human beings, the stoics believed, are fools.

EPICTETUS A slave by birth, **Epictetus** (*EHP ihk TEE tuhs*) **(c. 50–c. 135)** taught stoic principles that appealed to poor Romans and possibly to early Christians who identified with the plight of slaves. His birth is estimated to have been between the years 50 and 55 and he died about 130 CE. He was lame, possibly due to mistreatment as a slave. After finding freedom around his late

teen years, he was permitted to attend lectures. He devoted himself to philosophy, which he viewed as a cure for the soul. According to Meredith (1986), Epictetus conceived the lecture room of the philosopher as a kind of hospital, a place offering restoration and healing.

As a slave, Epictetus developed deep sensitivities to things beyond human influence and control. There is wisdom, he believed, in resigning ourselves to events we cannot change. All we can do is place faith in larger forces, even if we don't understand their purpose. Rather than rage against unalterable forces, we must trust that events unfold according to some critical design. His stoicism echoes today whenever someone says, "things happen for a reason."

The early Christian writer Paul also hints at a stoic message in his prison epistles, such as Philippians 4:11, where he writes, "I have learned in whatever state I am, *in this* to be content." Despite parallels between stoicism and Paul's teachings, there are major differences (see Wilson, 1997). After Paul, most Christians expressed hostility toward beliefs that deviated from rigidly defined views of Christianity. In practice, however, many were stoic. Yet below the surface, the differences may be far greater than any similarities (see James, 1902/1985, p. 45).

Epictetus loved simplicity, order, moral courage, self-control, and discipline. Hallie (1967) noted that he demanded daily self-examination as a means of promoting self-knowledge. He insisted that people take responsibility for the things they can control. Though we often find ourselves in circumstances we cannot change, we can control our attitude toward such events and avoid complaining. James (1902/1985), for example, cited stoic resignation and acceptance of life's events as an optimistic approach to spiritual experience.

Epictetus had a strong influence on the Roman emperor **Marcus Aurelius (121–180 CE)**, who argued that we should accept disagreeable events beyond our control. We must recognize that such things are a significant part of a larger whole. If we could but see the whole picture with clarity of mind and careful evaluation (Suibhne, 2009), we would discover the selfishness of a grumbling and critical attitude.

Stoic philosophy—if conscientiously followed—may foster an admirable tranquility in the face of difficulties. On the other hand, could stoicism lead to passivity? Or perhaps even a tendency to underestimate our ability to make changes that would benefit ourselves and others? Could stoicism have provided an adequate philosophical base for later scientists, scholars, and humanitarian reformers, outraged at suffering and injustice and eager to understand and control natural forces?

Epicureanism

Named after **Epicurus of Samos (341–270 BCE)**, **Epicureanism** arose around the same time as stoicism, approximately three hundred years prior to Christianity. The Epicureans believed pleasure is good and pain is an evil to be avoided (Bergsma et al., 2008). They warned against excesses such as gluttony that may produce temporary pleasure but long-term discomfort. Other things that interfere with pleasure include false opinions, fear of death, and excessive fear of the gods. The Epicureans advised against heavy social responsibility. Instead, one should strive for an uncomplicated existence. The school of Epicureanism survived until at least 200 CE.

LUCRETIUS   The philosophy of **Lucretius (c. 96–c. 55 BCE)** is expressed poetically in his work *De Rerum Natura* ("On the Nature of Things" or "On the Nature of the Universe"). The work is composed of six books that cover matter and space, movements and shapes of atoms, life and mind, sensation and sex, cosmology and sociology, and meteorology and geology.

Lucretius argued that if body and mind were independent, why do they parallel each other? He insisted that mind cannot exist apart from body: "Mind and body as a living force derive their vigour and vitality from their conjunction" (Lucretius, *On the Nature of the Universe*, p. 113). He insists that the mind comes into existence with the birth of the body and grows

with the body. For those who believe that spirits are slipped into the body from outside, he points out that, "it is surely ludicrous to suppose that spirits are standing by at the mating and birth of animals—a numberless number of immortals on the look-out for mortal frames, jostling and squabbling to get in first. . .or is there perhaps an established compact that first come shall be first served?" (*On the Nature of the Universe*, p. 119).

Like Leucippus and Democritus of old, Lucretius believed all things are composed of different sizes and shapes of atoms. However, he wasn't a conventional determinist. He argued that as atoms fall through space, they swerve from their path; these swerves interfere with a determinist order of things and serve as a theoretical basis for free will. Latham (1967) claims Lucretius wanted to demonstrate that "voluntary action arises from within and ultimately from the unpredictable movement of a single atom" (p. 101).

Lucretius believed that sensation was the basis of knowledge. Senses provide information about the material world, so the senses and their functions are keys to understanding the mind. He concluded that vision is activated when we see thin atomic films emanating from objects. Latham (1959) believed Lucretius would likely say, "psychologists are wrong in thinking that the mind is anything other than an assemblage of very mobile particles that easily group themselves into patterns or images in conformity with other images that impinge upon them from outside objects" (p. 11). Lucretius also described epilepsy, sleep, and vision in epic poetry (York, 2011), and he described the neurology of movement in surprisingly contemporary terms (Hyam et al., 2011).

Taste results "when we squeeze it out by chewing food, just as if someone were to grasp a sponge full of water in his hand and begin to squeeze it dry. Next, all that we squeeze out is diffused through the pores of the palate and the winding channels of the spongy tongue" (Lucretius, *On the Nature of the Universe*, p. 149). Different tastes result from blending food atoms with the interatomic atoms found in sensory channels. As a result, a food that excites the taste of one person may disgust another.

As an Epicurean, Lucretius was interested in ethics and a way of life that maximizes pleasure and minimizes pain. He argued against immediate gratification and for the value of discipline. He valued true piety, which for him was the capacity to philosophize with an undisturbed mind. Lucretius lamented the superstition that parades as piety, the "oft repeated show of bowing a veiled head before a graven image; this bustling to every altar; this kowtowing and prostration on the ground with palms outspread before the shrines of the gods; this deluging of altars with the blood of beasts; this heaping of vow on vow" (Lucretius, *On the Nature of the Universe*, p. 208). He taught that fear of death and fear of hell are great evils to overcome.

In his book on cosmology and sociology, Lucretius proposed a theory of the evolution of social groups, religion, and language. Early human groups evolved because of a necessary contract to protect defenseless offspring and others who were weak. Any group breaking the contract failed to survive. As for religious beliefs, Lucretius argued that many are born in fear of the forces of nature. He proposed that language evolved gradually; we first imitated the sounds of animals and gradually recognized the convenience of communication through verbal symbols.

As an empiricist, a materialist, and an Epicurean, Lucretius was a creature of this world. His philosophy conveys his love of nature and his preference for simple explanation. His ideas are clearly derived from earlier Greek thought, but some scholars suggest we underestimate his originality (Latham, 1967, p. 99).

Neo-Platonism

In terms of lasting influence, **neo-Platonism** was the most important school of philosophy following Aristotle. It married early Greek traditions with Jewish and Christian mysticism. For good or ill, it was a participant in the wedding of philosophy and religion that characterized thinking in the Middle Ages. Neo-Platonism fueled theological

discussions on the activities of the soul, the corruption and transience of the material world, the problem of evil, and the illusory nature of sense perception.

PLOTINUS Considered the founder of neo-Platonism, **Plotinus (205–270 CE)** was probably born an Egyptian, but received a Greek education in Alexandria. His extensive travels cultivated knowledge of Indian and Persian philosophies. About 245, he settled in Rome and befriended the emperor Gallienus. During two productive decades there, Plotinus attracted numerous students. With his student Porphyry, he produced six volumes titled *Enneads* (Green & Groff, 2003). Plotinus probably left Rome following the assassination of Gallienus in 268 CE.

Inspired by Plato, Plotinus argued that the "Soul is not in the universe, on the contrary the universe is in the Soul; bodily substance is not a place to the Soul; Soul is contained in Intellectual-Principle and is the container of the body" (*Enneads*, V, p. 411). According to Moore (1946), Plotinus is arguing that "knowables cannot be external to mind." Mental processes, or activities of the soul, therefore have a certain primacy; they are not to be regarded as derivative.

Plotinus merged Platonic thought and religion (Leahey, 2005). For him, a world of matter is a world of multiplicity and divisibility. Three unextended or nonmaterial things are above matter. The first was an abstract notion of God, the highest order of reality. The second was an abstract notion of intellectual principle. This order of reality was comparable to Plato's realm of forms containing principles, such as the principle of triangularity, that rise above particulars. The third order of incorporal things was that of the soul. Souls were instantiated in bodies that were temporary carriers. The highest of all things, God, was pure being, and being emanated from God and gave meaning to *nous*, the intellectual principle. Levels of being derived their existence and meaning from God and emanated downward to the world soul, individual souls, and then bodies. These levels of reality formed a hierarchy with pure being, God, as the source and cause of this arrangement. The body could be a burden to the soul and weigh it down or alienate it. In time, the soul transcended the body and would be re-incarnated in a later body. Plotinus also believed in direct communication between souls through extrasensory means.

Moore (1946) pointed out that Plotinus recognized an active quality in perception. She called attention to the fact that "for Plotinus, the perceiving mind has and is a unity. It is not a sub-ordinate of the external object, nor of any physi-cal reality" (p. 48). She quoted Plotinus on this topic: "There can be no perception without a uni-tary percipient whose identity enables it to grasp an object as an entirety" (Plotinus, *Enneads*, IV, p. 346). For Plotinus, perception is not just a matter of imprints or impressions; there must be something more that provides organization and unity. He argued for similar action in memory: "Sensation and memory, then, are not passivity, but power" (*Enneads*, IV, p. 341).

Plotinus also addressed the interplay of happiness and self-understanding. Happiness is attained in knowing the "true-self" through self-knowledge. Merlan (1967) notes, "the concept of the unconscious plays a decisive role in the system of Plotinus" (p. 358). Self-knowledge is elusive; it is attained through contemplation and in the consistency of action and thought. We do not have self-knowledge when we are torn by multiplicity or when we fail to be guided by intelligence.

In a brief essay, Plotinus speculated about "how distant objects appear small" (*Enneads*, II, p. 8). He also noted that as an object recedes, its color or brightness fades, and details grow fuzzy. With distance, we lose perspective on individual parts and respond to the thing as a whole. Plotinus believed that when details are seen, perception becomes more accurate.

Finally, Plotinus argued for freedom of choice and against astrology. He admitted small influences from the stars, but believed that much of astrology was not rational. Plotinus influenced the emerging religion of Christianity and, in turn, shaped psychology and philosophy during the Middle Ages (Kemp, 1996).

HYPATIA OF ALEXANDRIA   The celebrated philosopher–mathematician **Hypatia (c. 370–415 CE)** was the most important leader of the neo-Platonic school in the fourth century. She was the daughter of Theon, a mathematician–astrono-mer who worked at the legendary Royal Library of Alexandria. Though little is known about Hypatia's education, she likely benefited from her father's instruction and the cultural opportu-nities afforded by the library. By her late twen-ties, Hypatia was the leader of the neo-Platonic school at Alexandria. She lectured to students from all parts of the world and mentored several prominent philosophers of her era.

Hypatia is remembered for her expertise in geometry and astronomy, but she probably ac-cepted most of the teachings of the neo-Platonic tradition. Indeed, Hypatia's use of music therapy in the treatment of mental disorders may have been one of several heresies that led to her mur-der (see Richeson, 1940). Music therapy was associated with various forms of non-Christian thought. Hypatia lived in a time of tension be-tween the Christian Church and other religions. Following complications both ideological and political, Hypatia came under the suspicion of Cyril, the Bishop of Alexandria. During Lent in 415, she was a victim of a grisly assassination plot. A group of monks dragged Hypatia into a church, dismembered her body at the altar, and then burned her corpse. Hypatia's tragic story has been the subject of commentary (Viney, 1989; Waithe, 1987a) and offers a reminder of the all-too-human reluctance to allow philosophical free-dom. Her story, told in the motion picture *Agora*, continues to inspire and captivate the imagination (see Bovaira & Augustin, 2010).

Skepticism

Skepticism is rooted in the works of pre-Socratic philosophers such as Anaximander, Xenophanes, and Heraclitus, all of whom emphasized the changing nature of things. It was **Pyrrho (c. 360–c. 270 BCE)**, however, who introduced a systematic philosophy of skepticism that attacked philosophical certitude. Pyrrho believed we must live our lives on the basis of opinion, appearance, and probability. The skeptics noted that every argument has a counterargument. Authorities disagree with each other and, furthermore, our sensory impressions are not consistent. Skeptics also called attention to the fact that different animals have different sensory systems. How do we know that our sensory system is superior to all others? If we cannot trust our senses, neither can we trust reason, because reason is based on initial propositions that are plain assumptions. The skeptics also called attention to the fact that circumstances condition our reactions to the world.

SEXTUS EMPIRICUS   The birth and death dates for the Greek physician **Sextus Empiricus** are uncertain, but he became the leader of the skeptical school in the late second and early third centuries. Sextus argued that human beings should suspend judgment on most matters and live on the basis of probable truths. Skepticism does not have to deny an immutable truth, but even if there is one, how do we know with certainty that we possess it? In contrast with Greek skepticism that challenged the basis of knowledge, Roman Skepticism presented followers with a way to live such that conflicts and disappointments would be minimized. Dogmatic certainty could lead to anxiety, frustration, unhappiness, and disillusionment if confronted with overwhelming contrary evidence. The role of human certainty in war, terror, and genocide provides powerful evidence for these concerns. On the other hand, the openness that goes with suspended judgment can lead to contentment, happiness, and tranquility, and these views may have helped people cope with danger, uncertainty, and sometimes rapid changes that were common in their cultures. According to Sextus, the skeptic is free to consider all sides of an argument and to weigh everything as probable in an open and honest fashion. One can even live life on the basis of a probability, always aware, however, that one may be wrong.

The skeptics tried to avoid the pretension, presumption, and rash personal qualities found in popular philosophies of their day. They admired the humility associated with the admission of human frailties in matters of knowledge. In later historical periods, skeptics argued that pretension is the original human malady, one that leads to personal and social strife including war. The rise of Christianity and Islam diminished the influence of skepticism. We will see that in the sixteenth century, an outraged French humanist named Montaigne resurrected Pyrrhonian skepticism to challenge religious certitude during the Protestant–Catholic wars.

THE FALL OF ROME

At the height of its power, the Roman Empire seemed invulnerable. It is a curiosity that such an awesome political, economic, and military experiment could falter. Ironically, Rome's success contributed to its downfall. For centuries, its crushing military success had won vast territories, but at a price. The empire reached far distances, making the defense of its borders an unbearable economic burden. The conquering forces drained economic and human resources and contributed to its collapse.

In the midst of the need for economic growth, Rome experienced a staggering decline in population and, consequently, in the tax base. As early as the second century, masses of people enjoyed the luxury of smaller families. In the third century, the plague decimated the Roman population. It is also likely that infanticide checked population growth; female infants especially were killed in large numbers. Extensive military campaigns and emasculation of slaves also reduced the population. Rome's downfall was the result of a complex pattern of crumbling economic, moral, social, and political institutions. In addition, Roman authority faced new challenges. Judeo-Christian monotheism defied the worship of multiple gods and polytheism began to fade. In addition to Christianity and Judaism, other competing influences came from the Greeks, Ethiopians, and northern tribes. In fact, the growing tension between Rome and Christianity would produce a later unification, one that would transform the Catholic Church into a dominant force during the Middle Ages.

THE EARLY CHRISTIAN FAITH

The early Christian faith was never a single system of thought (Ehrman, 2003; Pagels, 2003), but rather a movement beset with internal strife during its first three centuries of life. Rival Christian faiths and "heresies" such as Gnosticism, Marcionism, and Montanism competed for disciples. Prominent leaders such as Iranaeus, Tertullian, and Origen differed on matters of doctrine.

During the fourth and fifth centuries, church councils made progress toward a unified theology. However, the early church was embroiled not only with internal conflict, but in conflict with secular powers in Rome. Widespread persecutions began with the burning of Rome in 64 CE. These persecutions had far-reaching implications for the development of doctrine. It is unknown whether the doctrines that became ascendant in the face of injustice and persecution would have prevailed in a more hospitable environment. In any case, church leaders emphasized otherworldliness where existence in the material world was viewed as without value. Life was but a temporary testing ground for human souls on their journey to other worlds that would compensate for the injustice of this world. It was taught that peace and happiness await the righteous in heaven, whereas torment awaits the wicked in hell. With the value of this life and world called into question, science was viewed as trivial. One was advised to attend to the affairs of the soul rather than engage in such frivolities.

On occasion, church doctrine in the Roman era departed from teachings attributed to Jesus of Nazareth. For example, scholars point to discrepancies between attitudes toward women in the patristic church and attitudes displayed by Jesus (Christen, 1984; Daly, 1968; Southard, 1927). Customs of the day forbade speaking to women or even looking at them. Ignoring the prohibition, Jesus spoke to women—even foreign women—in public (see Jeremias, 1975, p. 363). He also accepted women as travel companions and included them in instructional activities. Both practices were violations of existing gender barriers. Jesus also struck at existing divorce standards that favored men. His parables sometimes accorded greater moral status to women and other socially devalued groups than to the conventionally religious and powerful. The patristic church was obsessed with blaming woman for the "fall," but in no instance does Jesus indulge in this practice. The original teachings of Jesus regarding women are not recognizable in the later male-dominated church.

In the fourth century, the Roman emperor Constantine converted to Christianity, issuing a declaration of religious freedom and restoration of church property. At the same time, "barbarians" pushed against the borders as the Roman Empire lapsed into ruins. Authority shifted from state to church. Gradually, the church defined the legitimate boundaries of the intellectual arena. Now, church leaders such as Augustine and Aquinas in the Christian faith, Maimonides in the Jewish faith, and Avicenna in the Islamic faith established the intellectual agenda. Before turning to their teachings, we will discuss general characteristics of the **medieval period**.

THE MEDIEVAL PERIOD

The term *medieval* is derived from the Latin terms *medius* (middle) and *aevium* (age). The Middle Ages refer to a period of European history between the fall of Rome and the rise of the Renaissance. The dates are arbitrary because no one historical event marks the Middle Ages. For our purposes, we may regard the Middle Ages as a period from about 400 CE to about 1300 CE.

The Middle Ages cover a vast expanse of time and space—over a thousand years of history, a geographic region extending from the western shores of Spain to kingdoms in the Northern and Baltic Seas, to Islamic territories (after the seventh century) in the south and east, to what some people regard as "holy land." Three major religious traditions (Christian, Islamic, and Jewish) as well as variations in the economic, social, physical, and political dimensions of cultures contributed to a diversity among peoples. Scholars and historians in psychology often dismiss or overlook this period thoughts about fornication were subdued while awake, but such fantasies held greater power in sleep. Indeed, some of his dreams about sexual intercourse were as real as the act itself. Such dreams depend on memory, and in his discussion, he alluded to deeply buried or hidden memories. He doubted that such hidden memories could be controlled by reason during sleep. Augustine was also aware of self-deception. For example, he pointed out that the soul prepares an excuse as a defense; we may say we need a certain portion of food for our health when it is really for our plea-sure (see *Confessions*, p. 227).

Augustine's psychology must be under-stood in the context of his theocentric vision of the world, a view set forth in his classic work, *City of God*. In part, he wrote the book to chal-lenge the popular idea that Rome was God's city. Augustine saw both people and history as caught between the earthly city and the city of God. The earthly city is temporary and corrupt. Within it, we are caught up in lust, greed, selfishness, ha-tred, ambition, and petty concerns. The city of God, by contrast, is permanent and is ruled by love, order, and beauty. We can participate in the city of God, even as residents of this temporary and corrupt world. Or we may revel in the folly of the earthly city and its hatred for God. Love will hold the key to either the earthly city or the city of God. Self-love and carnal pleasure that Augustine knew so well might persuade the will to embrace the earthly city. But a purer love would compel the will to embrace eternal values in the city of God.

Augustine's works are rich in psychological insights and he has been celebrated as one of the great psychologists (see Brett, 1912–1921/1965, p. 225). He nevertheless promoted ideas that took root in medieval thought while working against the development of science. Harrison (2001) re-minds us that Augustine viewed worldly curios-ity as a spiritually dangerous vice dating back to the sin of Adam and Eve. Consequently, Harrison notes that medieval curiosity was associated with sins of pride, vanity, conceit, and lust. Humility, submission, meekness, and self-abasement were promoted as more noble virtues than curiosity.

A few thinkers embraced doubt and curiosity, but wider acceptance of the scientific spirit waited in the distant future.

Boethius

Along with Augustine, a Roman statesman and philosopher, Anicius Manlius Severinus **Boethius** (*bo EE thee uhs*) **(c. 480–524)**, helped influence Western thought. Knowles (1967) con-tended that "Boethius may rightly be called an eminent founder of the Middle Ages" (p. 329). His personal experiences reflected a kind of mi-crocosm of the larger tensions between reason and faith so characteristic of the period. Inspired by Greek writings, Boethius used reason to sup-port and defend Christian doctrine. Among his numerous treatises on philosophy, science, and theology, his most influential work was *The Consolation of Philosophy*. This book was writ-ten while Boethius was in prison awaiting execu-tion for treason. The grounds for his conviction are obscure, but he was executed by means of strangulation and bludgeoning in 524.

Boethius took a measured approach to rec-oncile faith and reason. He believed that reason might never grasp certain dimensions of faith, but he was convinced that the worlds of Athens and Jerusalem offered insight and wisdom. For hundreds of years, such exploration was a central problem for Jews, Christians, and Muslims who strived for enlightenment from Greek philosophy while maintaining obedience to Moses, Jesus, or Muhammad. Rubenstein (2003) notes, "Fifteen centuries later [*The Consolation of Philosophy*] remains an astonishing performance: A brave and learned Christian man using the tools of classical philosophy to think his way out of a deep depres-sion" (p. 67).

In *The Consolation*, he tackles critical issues including the nature of evil, the attempted recon-ciliation of divine foreknowledge with human free will, and the nature of God. While struggling with his death sentence, Boethius described his nega-tive emotional experience (Nicholson, 1995), and he pondered the source of true happiness and dis-covered it in oneness with God. His writings on his encounter with adversity comforted others for centuries. In his attempts to combine reason, authority, and revelation, Boethius influenced scholastics of the later Middle Ages who employed reason to defend faith.

Islam

The seventh century witnessed the rise of a powerful new religion on the Arabian Peninsula. In middle age, the prophet Mohammed was said to have received a revelation from God. He founded a religion named Islam, meaning "surrender to God." Islam united the Arab peoples (at least until Mohammed's death in 632) and posed a serious challenge to the Jewish and Christian traditions. Within a century of the birth of Mohammed in 570, the Islamic faith had a holy book (the Koran), three holy sites (Mecca, Jerusalem, and Madinat an-Nabi), and hundreds of military victories that claimed vast territories including the entire Arabian Peninsula, Syria, the northern coast of Africa, most of Spain, part of southern France, and the Persian Empire (including what is now Iran, Afghanistan, and Pakistan). Islam's military momentum was finally checked by the Franks under the leadership of Charles Martel (686–741) in the north near Tours, France, in 732, in one of history's most pivotal battles. Had the Islamic armies won the battle of Tours and conquered France, the distribution of Muslims, Jews, and Christians in Europe would have changed dramatically. Aside from military victories, Islam produced notable contributions in medicine and philosophy.

RHAZES   Abu Bakr al-Razi (**c. 854–c. 925**), better known as **Rhazes** (*RAH zees*), was a physician and author of medical textbooks who had wide-ranging interests in psychology, philosophy, and religion. In Baghdad's religious culture, he spoke out against demonological concepts of disease and the arbitrary use of authority in science. Ronan (1982) noted that Rhazes was "quite prepared to criticize ancient authorities, whoever they were, and even wrote a book with the title *Doubts Concerning Galen*" (p. 236). Rhazes attacked superstitious religious beliefs and the concept of miracles. He argued for scientific rationalism and against fanaticism and arbitrary authority.

Rhazes followed in the tradition of Democritus, Empedocles, and Hippocrates. He subscribed to the atomic theory, the four-element (fire, earth, air, and water) theory, and the humor theory. He stressed the importance of distractions, music, diet, bathing, and chemical remedies in treating illnesses. Gordon (1959) noted that Rhazes advocated games such as chess playing and music as diversions for melancholia (p. 158).

Rhazes wrote about social influences on therapy and offered explanations for why some place faith in impostors rather than legitimate healers. He claimed that quacks sometimes produce visible results in treating a medical complaint. People then overgeneralize and credit the dubious healers with greater medical knowledge than they deserve. He noted that legitimate healing is often slow and without immediate visible results.

Rhazes was an empiricist, but religious constraints on freedom of inquiry limited his medical investigations. Religious conservatives believed all questions worth asking were already answered by the Koran. As in previous times, dissection was forbidden. Despite the restrictive conditions, Rhazes described the reflex action of the pupil in response to light (Riese, 1959) and was renowned for his accurate descriptions of many diseases, including facial palsy (Sajadi et al., 2011), and for his studies on the relationship between hygiene and pathology. According to Gordon (1959), he was the first person to apply chemistry to medical research (p. 163).

As Gordon points out, Rhazes's chemical writings had an unfortunate consequence. He presented one of his chemistry books to Prince Al-Mansur. The prince was delighted and even asked Rhazes to demonstrate one of the chemical experiments described in the book. The experiment failed and the prince was furious. In a rage, he bashed Rhazes over the head. The beating produced blindness from which Rhazes never recovered. He died in poverty around 925.

AVICENNA The most influential Arabian philosopher and physician of the Middle Ages was **Avicenna** (*AH vuh SEEN uh*) **(980–1037)**, a mercifully shortened Western version of Abū 'Alī al-Husayn ibn 'Abd Allāh ibn Sīnā. Avicenna's interests ranged over medicine, metaphysics, cosmology, logic, political and religious philosophy, and psychology. Ronan (1982) pointed out that Avicenna has been called "the 'Galen of Islam' partly because of his encyclopedic book entitled *Canon of medicine*" (p. 236). *The Canon* reflected the ideas of Galen and others (Dols, 2006) and, according to Gordon (1959), became the medical textbook of choice in European universities (p. 178). Avicenna is remembered less for originality than for his ability to integrate and systematize past knowledge.

Avicenna, the son of a tax collector, was born near Bokhara. He was a child prodigy with an unusual memory and a great appetite for learning. By age ten, he memorized the Koran and displayed considerable skill in literature and science. In his late teens, he was well studied in the medical arts and was already practicing medicine. He was also an avid reader of Greek and Roman literature and philosophy. The political strife of tenth- and eleventh-century Persia complicated Avicenna's life. For a brief time, he lived close to the Caspian Sea near Teheran. He moved to

Hamadan, but political unrest interfered with his work and Avicenna was forced to move to Isfahan. A later shift in the political climate made it possible for him to return to Hamadan. In spite of the turmoil of his times, Avicenna practiced medicine and wrote nearly one hundred books on science, medicine, and philosophy.

Avicenna's greatest intellectual contribution may be his attempt to reconcile faith and reason. Afnan (1958) stated that "nowhere in Islamic philosophy are the problems of reason and revelation better contrasted, and an agreement in essentials more consistently attempted, than in the system of Avicenna. . . . He was deeply animated by the desire to see [philosophy and theology] brought into harmony" (p. 168). Temperamentally, Avicenna was both a rationalist and a mystic. As a rationalist, he was interested in a subject for its own sake and believed reason should guide human nature. As a mystic, he had a love of mystery and used symbolism and allegory in his work. For Avicenna, people find truth through reason and intuitive or mystical processes. He believed the two are not necessarily contradictory.

As a physician, Avicenna encountered many psychological problems in his patients. Like Galen, he observed a relationship between emotions and physiological states such as heart rate. He also accepted humoral explanations of the mind. According to Gordon (1959), Avicenna believed that "unconsumed bile and black bile will cause melancholia. . .abundance of yellow bile leads to irritability, confusion, and violence. An increase of putrefied phlegm causes a morose and serious mood" (p. 175). He also identified a "disorder of love" that appeared to include facets of depression, anxiety, and obsession (Shoja & Tubbs, 2007).

Despite his limited knowledge of anatomy, Avicenna speculated on the brain's role in psychological disorders. He concluded that disturbances in the middle ventricles produce a diminished intellect such as in feebleminded patients. Frontal regions of the brain governed perception and common sense, whereas the brain's posterior regions process memory. Avicenna believed that mental representation of external objects occurred in the ventricles (Kemp, 1998).

Avicenna

Avicenna understood the role of psychology in treating patients. According to Gordon (1959), he tried to cheer melancholic patients by reading to them or using music as therapy (p. 176). Alexander and Selesnick (1966) share a story that reveals he wasn't afraid to use unconventional treatments. One of Avicenna's patients believed he was a cow. As part of his psychotic delusion, the man even bellowed like one. Playing along, Avicenna told the patient a butcher was coming over to slaughter him. The man's hands and feet were bound in preparation for the butcher's visit. At the last minute, Avicenna declared the patient too thin and unfit for slaughter. After Avicenna untied him, the man abandoned his delusion and recovered (see also Aggarwal, 2011).

Avicenna's view of the soul echoes Aristotelian faculty psychology. Afnan (1958) pointed out that Avicenna believed in soul as a single genus divided into three species (p. 136). Different faculties of functions exist within each species. The *vegetative soul* manages the functions of nourishment, growth, and reproduction. The *animal soul* guides receptive and motor functions of perception and movement. The *human soul* governs powers unique to human beings such as intellectual and rational powers and the ability to comprehend universals. Avicenna believed that faculties serve and sustain each other. For example, nutrition serves growth and reproduction, whereas perception serves imagination. His hierarchical arrangement of faculties hints at the influence of Plato, although Avicenna rejected the Platonic notion of the transmigration of the soul.

In all, Avicenna preserved elements of Aristotelian and Platonic thought on the soul and integrated these older ideas with Islamic thought. He believed in the oneness of the soul, although multiple faculties exist within that oneness. Consistent with Islamic teaching, he argued for the separation of soul and body at death and the immortality of the soul.

ALHAZEN   The Islamic scientist and physician, Ibn Al Haitam **(965–1039)** is one of the most critical figures in the study of optics and vision. Known in the West as **Alhazen** (*AL haze uhn*),

few details are available concerning his life. He was apparently born in Basra (located in what is now eastern Iraq), but lived most of his life in Egypt. Alhazen's *Book of Optics* describes many important advances in visual science (Aaen-Stockdale, 2008) and marks him as one of Islam's great scientists. He is important because of his originality and his influence on later science.

Crombie (1961) noted that Alhazen rejected the idea that the transmission of light is instantaneous and also refuted the Platonic theory of extramission (the notion that the eye emits light rays) (p. 102). Gordon (1959) credited Alhazen with being the first to show that light comes to the eye from external objects (p. 179). Alhazen conducted original experiments on angles of refraction and the perception of objects. For example, he determined that objects appear larger on the horizon than at the zenith because of differences in the density of the atmosphere.

Alhazen's *Book of Optics* was a major source of inspiration to later European scientists. Roger Bacon's work on optics (e.g., see his *Opus Majus*) clearly built on the foundations established by Alhazen (Wade, 2005). Time and time again, Bacon quoted Alhazen on topics such as binocular vision, apparent size, double vision, and color perception. Alhazen is, unfortunately, a neglected figure in the history of visual perception.

AL-GHAZALI   One of the most influential philosophers in Islamic intellectual history confronted the problem of knowledge while departing from predecessors such as Alhazen and Avicenna. **Al-Ghazali** (*AL gah zel i*) **(1058–1111)**, a respected mystic and legal scholar, was a prominent teacher in Baghdad, lecturing to hundreds of students on legal, philosophical, and religious issues; additionally, themes of education and moral education run through his writings (Alavi, 2007). Disillusioned by personal religious uncertainties and concerns over legal corruption, Al-Ghazali abandoned teaching to seek solitude and meditation. We know little about this period of his life, but he did devote himself to solitude and spiritual exercises, writing, and teaching to select audiences. Al-Ghazali's prodigious scholarship covered many subjects, but arguably his most important work was known as *The Incoherence of the Philosophers*. Completed about 1095, this work reinforced conservative suspicions about Greek works and Islamic scholars such as Avicenna who attempted to reconcile Greek thought with religious doctrine.

Rubenstein (2003) notes that Al-Ghazali argued that "the very idea of cause and effect is a manmade illusion, since God, not nature, produces every effect" (p. 85). Al-Ghazali was specific on this matter: "Take for instance any two things, such as the quenching of thirst and drinking; satisfaction of hunger and eating; burning and contact with fire. . . . They are connected as the result of the Decree of God (holy be his name), which preceded their existence" (c. 1095/1963, p. 185). He challenged the idea of any kind of connection *in itself*. It follows that one can conclude little about the natural order by studying the regularities of the world. Further, because God's nature is inscrutable, empirical and rational structures are also limited and suspect. Watt (1965) notes that following Al-Ghazali's criticism of the philosophers, "there are no further great names in the philosophical movement in the Islamic east" (p. 1041). Al-Ghazali's book was one of several forces that fueled hardcore fundamentalist movements to silence the voices of rationalist philosophers in the Arab east. Fifteen years after the death of Al-Ghazali, however, another great Islamic scholar made a profound impact on intellectual development in Western Europe.

AVERROËS The last Arabian philosopher–physician of the Middle Ages whom, we will consider is ibn Rushd **(1126–1198)**, known in the West as **Averroës** (*uh VEHR oh eez*). Tsanoff (1964) called Averroës "the greatest Arabian philosopher" (p. 186). In terms of his influence on Western thought, he may be the greatest among many important Arab philosophers.

Averroës was born in Cordoba, Spain. Little is known of his personal life, but apparently he spent most of his years in Spain and in Marrakesh, Morocco. He served as chief justice in Seville and also as court physician for the caliph of Marrakesh. He wrote extensive commentaries on the works of Aristotle that became a major intellectual force in Europe. Averroës worked in the Aristotelian tradition, especially in his attempts to reconcile faith and reason. Arguably, Averroës's most important philosophical work was *Tahafut Al-Tahafat (The Incoherence of the Incoherence)*, written to refute many of the claims to Al-Ghazali's *The Incoherence of the Philosophers*. Averroës elevated the role of reason and the importance of the discovery of compatibilities between the claims of reason and the claims of faith (see c. 1180/2008). Perhaps, more than any other, he was responsible for introducing Aristotle to the West, but his work was met with continuing criticism and rejection in much of the Islamic world.

Aside from his celebrated commentaries, Averroës made substantive scientific contributions. Crombie (1961) credited him with being the first to discover that "the retina rather than the lens is the sensitive organ of the eye" (p. 102). He wrote a major treatise on medicine that was translated into Latin and used in European universities. He was one of the first to observe that patients become immune to smallpox if they survive an attack of the disease.

Toward the end of Averroës's life, hardheaded fundamentalist "know-so" religious authority was prevailing over reason. Philosophical types such as Averroës were persecuted and their books were burned. The intellectual traditions of the Greeks were rediscovered in Europe even as the Muslim world discarded them. The age-old cycle between authority and reason was repeated with predictable consequences for both Arab and European cultures.

Judaism in the Middle Ages

Jerusalem in the Middle Ages, as it is today, hosted a battleground for conflicting religious claims between Christians, Jews, and Muslims. Deprived of a peaceful home of their own, Jewish emigrants settled in other countries of the Mediterranean basin. By the seventh century,

Jewish settlements were established in major cities of northern and southern Europe.

For brief periods, Jewish citizens lived in peaceful and friendly surroundings in isolated regions in Christian and Muslim countries. Unfortunately, such times proved rare. More often than not, Jews found themselves in the crossfire of social, political, and religious hostilities. They typically paid more than their fair share of taxes and were often blamed for natural disasters and social ills. During periods of tension, they were sometimes forced to either convert to the socially dominant religion (Islam or Christianity) or find a new home. Converted Jews faced constant suspicion and were seldom treated well. Outright pogroms against Jews were commonplace in the Middle Ages. In spite of the hardship, Jewish culture was rich in depth and variety with a powerful emphasis on education, the family, cleanliness, and faith.

Like Christians and Muslims, the Jewish community was often torn between rival claims of faith and reason:

> The medieval Jews, like the Moslems and the Christians, covered reality with a thousand superstitions, dramatized history with miracles and portents, crowded the air with angels and demons, practiced magical incantations and charms, frightened their children and themselves with talk of witches and ghouls, lightened the mystery of sleep with interpretations of dreams, and read esoteric secrets into ancient tomes. (Durant, 1950, p. 416)

In this context, our next figure struggled to reconcile faith and reason and became a critical philosopher of the Middle Ages.

MAIMONIDES   Rabbi Moses ben Maimuni (1135–1204) stands as the greatest Jewish philosopher–physician of his time. Known in Europe as Moses **Maimonides** (*my MAHN ih deez*), he was born in Cordoba, Spain. Maimonides was well versed in Hebrew literature and tradition, but

also excelled in secular education provided by his Arab teachers.

When Maimonides was thirteen, Cordoba's moderate political leadership was overthrown. New fanatic leaders gave heretics a choice of conversion to Islam or exile. This was the first of many occasions when Maimonides felt the sting of religious bigotry. He chose exile in Morocco and even pretended to be a convert to Islam for a time. During this period in the early 1160s, he began studying medicine, including psychological disorders, and these interests continued through the end of his life (Gesundheit et al., 2008). He became well known as a scholar during his exile in Morocco, but understood the danger of pretending to be Islamic. Maimonides moved to Palestine, then to Alexandria, and later to Cairo. While in Egypt, he distinguished himself as an author of medical texts, a commentary on Jewish laws and traditions, and a systematic treatise on Jewish religious beliefs. However, his best-known work was *Guide for the Perplexed*, a book destined to create storms of protest in Christian, Jewish, and Muslim cultures.

The *Guide* was written for knowledgeable Jews caught in the intellectual bind between Greek rationalism and religious traditions based on authority and revelation. Although written for Jews, the book was relevant for Muslims and Christians torn between rival epistemologies. The *Guide* was widely read and used in European universities where it was praised or burned depending on the local temper.

In the *Guide*, Maimonides argued that ancient scriptural texts were written to enlighten simple and unlearned people. Great truths were presented as symbolic or fictional stories and parables to ensure their meaning as spiritual messages. Jehovah was even presented in anthropomorphic terms. Maimonides believed conflict between reason and faith results when people interpret scripture in a literal manner. But a marriage of faith and reason is possible for intelligent people who discern the essential spiritual truths behind concrete picture-like representations in scripture. The "perplexed" had experienced the dissonance between faith and reason and needed a workable resolution.

Maimonides was an intellectual elitist who believed that many people had little need for his book and little need for reason. He thought it best for such people to live their lives under the authority of a primitive childlike faith. Although elitist, Maimonides's work legitimized reason and helped pave the way for the coming scientific revolution.

The Rise of the European Universities

European universities began to emerge in the tenth and eleventh centuries. The term *university* was derived from the Latin *universitas*, referring to a whole or a group organized around a common goal. Students who attended early universities sometimes met in European cathedrals or in small gatherings with self-appointed masters who taught in marketplaces or rented rooms. Initially, there were no diplomas, no entrance requirements, and no set curriculum. In most cases, the reputation and eloquence of the teacher attracted students.

By the twelfth century, universities gained momentum throughout Europe. Formal curricula were established, degrees were conferred, guilds were formed to protect both teachers and students, and campus buildings were founded. Students often traveled great distances to witness a debate or hear an inspired teacher. William of Champeaux, Peter Abelard, and Robert Grosseteste were known as legendary teachers.

The rise of the European university was one of the most critical intellectual developments of the Middle Ages. Theology, law, and medicine were soon complemented by liberal arts. Learning became important in its own right. In isolated quarters, students again heard the fragile but persistent voice of reason.

PETER ABELARD   Born at Pallet in France, **Peter Abelard** (*AB uh lahrd*) (**1079–1142**) was the most renowned teacher and scholar of the early twelfth century. He is remembered for his original work in the fields of ethics, logic, and theology. He lectured at well-known centers such as St. Geneviève and Notre Dame and founded an important convent for women.

Abelard wrote about his life in a brief autobiography titled *Historia Calamitatum* (*Story of My Calamities*), translated under the title *The Story of Abelard's Adversities* (see Muckle, 1992). Abelard was known for his eloquence and polemic style in the lecture hall, and he was charged with heresy on several occasions. In his inflammatory style, he attacked "the shortcomings of the clergy, the immorality of priests and monks, the sale of indulgences, [and] the invention of bogus miracles" (Durant, 1950, p. 946). After a brief study with a teacher named Anselm, Abelard claimed that Anselm's name "rested on long practice rather than on ability or learning. . .[and that Anselm] was a wonder in the minds of his listeners, but a nobody in the estimate of his questioners" (Muckle, 1992, p. 21). In the midst of an ultraconservative age, it seemed inevitable that calamity would fall upon such a fierce and uncompromising scholar.

That calamity began when Peter Abelard was introduced to Héloise, a striking woman with unusual intellectual gifts and an insatiable love of learning. Héloise was the delight and pride of her uncle, a man named Fulbert. As a canon of the church, Fulbert valued religious education and he wanted Europe's most renowned teacher to educate his niece. He hired Abelard to tutor her in philosophy and theology. What Fulbert didn't realize is that Abelard had fallen desperately in love with Héloise.

Any attraction between the two seemed unlikely to Fulbert. Abelard was almost two decades older than his beautiful student. And as a teacher of sacred theology, he had taken the vow of celibacy. When Abelard suggested he move into Fulbert's home, it must have seemed like a safe and appropriate arrangement. Before long, Abelard's tutoring sessions with Héloise became intense romantic interludes. Up to this point in his life, Abelard had dedicated himself to the life of the mind. But now? He compared himself to a ravenous wolf consumed with love.

Héloise's uncle was furious when he learned about their affair. He separated them, but that did nothing to quiet their romance. After a time, it was impossible to conceal their relationship. Héloise was pregnant. Abelard proposed to her, but Héloise found she couldn't accept his offer of marriage. She placed Abelard's career above her own desires, knowing that an official marriage would cripple his career.

Héloise gave birth to a son whom they named Astralabe (after an instrument used for charting the heavens). In time, Héloise consented to marry Abelard. To no one's surprise, Fulbert's anger against Abelard was unrequited. Not only had he been deceived but as legal guardian of Héloise, he could have enjoyed a substantial profit if she had married a wealthy suitor.

Fulbert couldn't allow this indignity to pass. In his lust for a reckoning, he hired a gang of thugs to hunt down Abelard. The men attacked the scholar and castrated him. Humiliated, Abelard blamed himself for his calamity and withdrew into the monastic life. He prevailed on Héloise, against her wishes, to become a nun. In time, she agreed. Their son, Astralabe, was raised by Abelard's sister.

Abelard's work as a monk was no less controversial than his work as a teacher. He alienated church authorities and they, in turn, accused him of treating God as an object that could be sliced apart with the scalpel of cold reason. Though such an accusation was not entirely true, Abelard's methods must have seemed harsh to those who preferred an uncritical, faith-based theology. Finally, the hierarchy had had enough. Pope Innocent II ordered a burning of Abelard's books and demanded that Abelard be placed under house arrest and forced to accept the imposition of perpetual silence. Although he had been castrated, his enemies accused him of continuing to lust after Héloise. Abelard was condemned as a heretic but his reputation as a theologian and his works survived despite the book burnings.

Although tragic, the story of Abelard and Héloise is considered one of the great love stories of all time. The novel *Stealing Heaven* (Meade, 1979) captures the details of their celebrated relationship and inspired a motion picture with the same title (see George & Donner, 1988). Abelard and Héloise are buried side by side in the celebrated Père Lachaise cemetery in Paris, a site still visited by thousands every year.

Abelard's Work   The battle between faith and reason reached a new intensity in the work of Abelard and his followers. Abelard believed reason was no less a gift from God than the scriptures. We know truth through reason, and we know truth through scriptures. Both truths come from God, and God cannot be self-contradictory. Nor can truth contradict itself. What are we to do when scripture and reason contradict each other? Abelard took the position that revelation and scripture must be interpreted by reason and that reason will always undergird an adequate faith. His work established a declaration of independence for logic and philosophy. For much of the Middle Ages, products of the Greek mind served as handmaidens of theology, but Abelard insisted that scripture and revelation must be exposed to the light of reason.

If reason is a gift of God and if reason is conveyed through Greek thinkers such as Socrates, Plato, and Aristotle, then it follows that truth and God's wisdom are not the exclusive property of the Hebrews or Christians. Abelard's message was that the God of conventional theology was too small. Such liberal thoughts guaranteed retaliation from those who placed scripture and revelation in higher priority than reason.

Abelard approached theological problems through an early variation of the dialectical method. One of his best-known works, titled *Sic et Non (Yes and No)*, employed the method of opposition to explore theological and philosophical questions. A given question, scripture, or issue was stated in a simple way. Contrasting and supporting arguments and authorities were then set forth. Abelard pitted scripture against scripture and authority against authority. Famous church leaders were contrasted on their positions on various issues. Abelard made little attempt at synthesis; that was the task of the reader. The effect of the work was to create doubt and uncertainty. The church had taken the position that doubt, especially in theological matters, was a sin. Abelard, however, saw doubt in positive terms as a motive for inquiry. He believed that doubt followed by inquiry and reason leads to a more informed faith. Abelard argued that we should not believe a thing because we think God said it. Rather our beliefs should be based on the solid rock of reason, which was also a gift of God.

According to Clanchy (1997), "Abelard was the first modern 'theologian' in the sense that he was the first teacher to promote the word 'theology' and to use it to mean the reconciliation of human reason with Christian revelation" (p. 5). Abelard had an intellectual thirst for religious and philosophical issues. He criticized the chants, prayers, and rituals of his day as little more than mindless, parrotlike repetition. Abelard raised embarrassing questions that were troublesome to those who placed authority and revelation in higher priority than reason. Why would those who had never had a chance to hear the Christian message be condemned to hell? How could subsequent generations inherit the sin of Adam and Eve? If God knows everything in advance, what is the meaning of confession? His detractors believed that Abelard raised too many questions, including ones that best should remain buried. Church officials believed that vain curiosity had been the original sin of Adam and Eve. Ignorance and humility were preferred to the pompous faith in human reason manifested in the works of Abelard.

Abelard was one of the first to imbue his listeners with a spirit of independence and the courage to use reason in the quest for knowledge. He paid dearly for his epistemological bravery and his earlier affair with Héloise, but he is remembered as a bold spirit who integrated Greek and Christian thought.

HÉLOISE   Héloise (*EL uh weese*) (**c. 1098–1164**) is typically known only for her relationship to Abelard. In truth, she was a gifted scholar with knowledge of Latin, Greek, and Hebrew. She had extensive knowledge of Greek and Roman philosophy and Christian theology. In his brief autobiography, Abelard notes that in terms of literary

excellence, Héloise was "the most renowned woman in the whole kingdom" (Muckle, 1992, p. 26). Although the authenticity of Héloise's writings has been disputed, scholarship suggests she did write the works attributed to her (Waithe, 1989, pp. 68–72). She may have even made substantive contributions to Abelard's writings.

Some of Héloise's intellectual concerns grew out of her love affair with Abelard. In letters exchanged with Abelard, she explored social, psychological, and ethical issues (Radice, 1974). She was a precursor of modern psychologists who study love and attraction. In letters to Abelard, Héloise discusses tensions between love as a means to an end (e.g., satisfaction of sexual appetites) and what she called *indifferent love*. This latter term refers to love in its own right or love for the sake of love and not mere physical gratification. Indifferent love transcends society's limitations and regulations. For example, a marriage certificate in the Middle Ages granted conjugal rights to the man. The woman was expected to "perform her wifely duties." Héloise understood the necessity of contracts and social conventions, but believed they distort our understanding of love.

Héloise's psychology and philosophy of love played out in an interesting way. Under pressure from Abelard, she acquiesced to marriage but did not approve of it. Héloise understood that marriage would interfere with Abelard's desire to conform to the religious constraints of the time. As noted by Waithe (1989), "she prefers prostitution, as she calls it, to marriage because marriage would not be for Abelard's good" (p. 79). Abelard preferred a secret marriage that would permit him to work as a teacher, but also sustain physical access to Héloise.

Like Abelard, Héloise embraced a teleological psychology where human action must be understood in terms of intention. Abelard had argued that actions, even one that might result in the tragic death of another, are not necessarily immoral. Héloise believed immoral actions result from a purposeful violation of conscience. According to such a view, a psychology based on material, efficient, and formal causes is inadequate to adjudicate moral issues. The issue remains as critical today as it was in the Middle Ages (see Rychlak & Rychlak, 1990).

Although Abelard believed the "hand of God" guided his calamities, Héloise did not subscribe to such intervention. If the castration of Abelard was divine chastisement, then she did not wish to know or serve this God. Nevertheless, she became a nun to please Abelard. Héloise played the part to perfection. In the shadow of this façade, she thought herself a hypocrite because she loved Abelard, but not God.

ROGER BACON Like Abelard and Héloise, controversy and brilliance marked the life and work of **Roger Bacon (c. 1220–c. 1292)**. Only fragments of information survive about his early life. Evidence is inconclusive about his family background or the exact location of his birth in England. It is known that he studied at Oxford and the University of Paris. He was an independent scholar until age forty when, for unknown reasons, Bacon joined the Franciscan order. It was a troubled union.

Bacon took a radical stand in supporting mathematics and science as keys to understanding theology and God. He was indiscreet in condemning the educational backgrounds of fellow members in the order. Aside from wild speculations, Bacon's alchemy experiments and his belief in astrology offended his superiors. In 1278, the General of the Franciscan order imprisoned Bacon for "certain suspected novelties" (Bridges, 1976, p. 32). The "suspected novelties" may have been Bacon's beliefs that Providence had guided the Greeks and Jews, that the stoics showed a personal morality superior to many Christians, that ethical values can be found in Islamic literature, and that changes in religious faith follow conjunctions of the planets Jupiter and Mercury (Bridges, 1976).

Completed around 1267, Bacon's *Opus Majus* covers topics such as optics, philology, mathematics, experimental science, and moral philosophy. Wade (2005) pointed out that Bacon understood the magnifying powers of convex lenses. Bridges (1976) argued that Bacon "imagined, and was within measurable distance of effecting, the combination of lenses which was to bring far things near, but which was not to be realized till the time of Galileo" (p. 39). Christopher Columbus (c. 1451–1506) discovered a passage from Bacon's *Opus Majus* quoted in Pierre d'Ailly's *Imago Mundi*. Bridges (1976) claims that Bacon's words may have inspired Columbus to make his famous voyage.

In Part One of the *Opus Majus*, Bacon offers important contributions to epistemology (see Burke, 1962) with a discussion of four general causes of human ignorance and error (pp. 3–35). The first involved an unjustified reliance on authority. Another cause can be found in the human tendency to remain a slave to habit, tradition, and custom. In addition, popular prejudices blind people and contribute to ignorance. A final cause springs from conceit about our knowledge or wisdom. On this latter topic, Bacon championed breadth of experience and advocated the importance of learning from common people and the humbling advances of technology. To combat smug preconceptions about our knowledge, he also encouraged a broad curriculum including languages, mathematics, science, and philosophy.

The ideas of Bacon form an intellectual bridge between the Middle Ages and modern thought. Like other influential thinkers of his time, he hoped to reconcile faith and reason. For centuries, the Christian church had vacillated between tolerating and condemning Aristotle's psychology and philosophy. Bacon dreamed of reforming the church on this matter. In his mind, the Greeks did not pose a threat. In fact, their ideas could only strengthen Christian theology. Although a few church authorities tolerated Bacon's radical thought, many in his time considered him a misfit. Like other historical rebels, his voice would find acceptance only after the passing of many years.

THOMAS AQUINAS Another stellar figure from the University of Paris became the greatest church doctor since St. Augustine. Born into an influential family, **Thomas Aquinas** (*uh Kwy nuhs*) **(1225–1274)** received an impressive education at a Benedictine abbey before study-ing liberal arts at the University of Naples. At age twenty, Aquinas joined the Dominican order with the expectation of becoming a scholar who would teach and serve God in absolute poverty.

His decision came as a bitter disappoint-ment for his family. In fact, they kidnapped Aquinas. For one year, his family imprisoned him in an effort to steer him toward a more acceptable profession. He was unmoved. After their failed attempt at persuasion, the family released their captive son. Undeterred, Thomas Aquinas earned a doctorate in theology at the University of Paris in 1256.

He enjoyed the bulk of his teaching and writing career at Paris and in several Italian mon-asteries. Though he lived a mere fifty years, his writings are extensive. Without question, his most famous work is the *Summa Theologica*. In 1323, Pope John XXII canonized Aquinas as a saint of the Catholic Church a century after his birth.

Like Bacon, Maimonides, and Avicenna, Aquinas was committed to a reconciliation of faith and reason. He believed that revealed truths are not discernible from reason. On the other hand, he urged that the voice of reason be given an open and sympathetic audience. Aquinas was the foremost Aristotelian of his time, but he was also a moderate who constructed a system of thought that accommodates reason and faith. He encour-aged an open consideration of rival positions on intellectual issues. Like Aristotle, Aquinas was fascinated with psychology.

Thomas Aquinas studied topics that today would fall under headings such as philosophi-cal psychology and philosophy of science. His psychological interests ranged from intelligence, emotion, the senses, sex and gender (Soble, 2009), and motivation to the study of social influences on human beings, consciousness, and habit. His frequent comparisons between humans and ani-mals reveal his interest in comparative psychol-ogy. He reestablished the scientific approach to nature found in Aristotle's empiricism. Although his psychology follows Aristotle, Aquinas's re-flective philosophical work is a continuing source of inspiration (see McCool, 1990).

Body and Soul Copleston (1962) claimed that Thomas Aquinas accepted Aristotle's soul–body hylomorphism (García-Valdecasas, 2005). You might recall from Chapter 3 that *hylomorphism* refers to the complete interdepen-dence of form and matter. In Aquinas's view, the "name 'man' applies neither to the soul alone nor to the body alone, but to soul and body to-gether, to the composite substance" (Copleston, 1962, p. 94). He rejected the Platonic idea that the soul is imprisoned inside the body. Instead, he saw the union of body and soul as natural and desirable. His Aristotelian emphasis on the unity of soul and body informed his psychology. Emotion must be understood in terms of physio-logical and psychological qualities—the two are inseparable. Likewise, Copleston (1962) notes that sensation "is an act not of the soul using a body, but of the *compositum*; we have no innate ideas, but the mind is dependent on sense-expe-rience for its knowledge" (p. 102). Although he did not advance a system in the modern sense, his psychology assumed a relationship between the material substrate and experience or mental activity. For example, he argued that emotions disturbed thought (Mandler, 2003). Aquinas stressed that personality meant wholeness or completeness.

All of this raised an important question: How could Thomas Aquinas believe in the unity of body and soul while, at the same time, believ-ing in the survival of the soul following death? It is debatable whether he provided a satisfac-tory answer to the question. He did argue that the soul is immortal and that its mode of knowing is conditioned by the state in which it finds itself. While the soul is united with the body, cognition results from the interdependence of physiological and psychological processes. The soul is inher-ently rational (García-Valdecasas, 2005); in the body, the soul knows via the senses, but in another state it has other modes of cognition. Therefore when separated from the body, the soul could still have cognitive capacity. While united with the body, cognition results from the interdependence of physiological and psychological processes (Kemp, 1990).

Theory of Knowledge Gerard (1966) noted that Thomistic psychology is based more on empiricism than authority (p. 318). For Thomas Aquinas, the sensory image was a key building block in knowledge, but he also emphasized intellectual activity in organizing sensory information. McInerny (1990) argued that "Thomism is solidly based on the assumption that we know the world first through our senses and then via concepts formed on the basis of our sense experience" (p. ix). Aquinas sought a middle road between the extremes of empiricism and rationalism.

For Aquinas, scientific activity begins with simple sensory components and practical conceptual processes that organize sensory information. He accepted a moderate form of realism, contending that it is reasonable to believe in a conformity between the mental and physical worlds. He understood, however, that human accounts of the world are variable and may contradict each other. But disagreements, in his view, stimulate further study. In matters of science, Aquinas believed each serious viewpoint should receive a fair hearing along with a search for new data pertinent to disagreements. As a leading theologian, he argued that an adequate theology has little to fear from science and reason. At the time, his position was controversial and dangerous, but made a significant contribution to the reconciliation of faith and reason.

Scholars disagree about the work and influence of Thomas Aquinas. Russell (1959) offered both an appreciative and a critical analysis (pp. 156–160). He agreed that the Thomistic version of Aristotle dominated the Renaissance, but unlike his predecessors, Aquinas was at least a "thorough and intelligent student" of Aristotle. Russell contended that the conclusions in Aquinas's philosophy "are inexorably imposed beforehand by Christian dogma. We do not find the disinterested detachment of Socrates and Plato, where the argument is allowed to take us whither it will. On the other hand. . .opposing points of view are always stated clearly and fairly" (p. 156).

We should note that Aristotle's work was often forbidden prior to Thomas Aquinas. Papal edicts banned the teaching of Aristotle even in cosmopolitan centers such as the University of Paris. In this historical context, Aquinas's work is notable. Ronan (1982) shared, "Almost alone he was able to make the theological faculty [at the University of Paris] change course and come to terms with Aristotelian teaching" (p. 260). Aquinas elevated the role of reason and broadened the concept of revelation. God could be revealed in nature and through reason. Although Thomistic teachings became the stuff of dogma after his death, he should not be held accountable.

Gerard (1966) noted that Thomas Aquinas "reveals an approach to behavior which would seem to be described more accurately as an observational empiricism than as a blind Aristotelianism or a religious dogmatism" (p. 327). As a leading theologian, Aquinas took the position that an adequate theology has little to fear from science and reason. He made contributions to the reconciliation of faith and reason, yet was surprisingly empirical for his times. Thomas Aquinas represents a challenge to those who treat the medieval period as a void without psychological contributions.

WILLIAM OF OCKHAM Before concluding the medieval period, we should mention another Franciscan, **William of Ockham (c. 1285–1349)**. Born near London around 1285, he studied at Oxford University. Like Roger Bacon, William was suspected of embracing heretical ideas. After a time, he was excommunicated because of repeated conflicts with the church over questions of papal authority and succession.

William carried on the empirical tradition set forth in the work of Thomas Aquinas, and his interests included cognition, memory, and mental representation (Kemp, 1998). However, he is best remembered for proposing the law of parsimony or **Ockham's Razor**. William argued that an explanation containing fewer assumptions is preferable to one containing more assumptions. Other things being equal, simplicity is superior to complexity. Plurality, then, should never be posed without necessity. As if wielding a razor, William of Ockham was notorious for shaving away unnecessary assumptions to find the simplest explanation.

Ockham's Razor holds a potent lesson for science and is especially relevant for psychology. For example, psychologists have sometimes attributed human traits to animals, thus violating the law of parsimony. We shall return to this issue again during the course of this book.

Conclusion

Gerard (1966) noted that even historians once wrote off the medieval period as a time dominated by theological preoccupation, blind allegiance to authority, superstition, and ignorance. It is true that if the historian is looking for such qualities in medieval thought, they are easily found. In recent years, however, scholars have come to view the Middle Ages in a different light (e.g., Henley & Thorne, 2005). In an insightful book, Bjornsson (2004) traced critical achievements in antiquity and the Middle Ages that set the stage for the coming scientific revolution. We can no longer dismiss this period of history. Its proper rediscovery is an important task for historians of science.

Review Questions

1. List and briefly define (in a word or two) Galen's constitutional types.
2. Explain Galen's pneuma concept of the soul.
3. Describe the basic teachings of Epicurus, Zeno, and Pyrrho. In what sense are their teachings comparable?
4. What did Plotinus mean when he argued that the "soul is not in the world, rather the world is in the soul"?
5. What is the significance of Augustine's *Confessions* for psychology? Explain Augustine's thought on infant motivation, grief, dreams, and habit breaking.
6. Why, according to Rhazes, do people trust quacks rather than legitimate healers?
7. List and describe major substantive contributions coming out of the works of Avicenna, Averroës, and Alhazen.
8. What is the essential message contained in Maimonides's book *Guide for the Perplexed?*
9. Outline Abelard's position with respect to the roles of faith and reason.
10. What did Héloise mean by indifferent love?
11. According to Roger Bacon, there are four causes for human ignorance and error. What are they?
12. Briefly outline the views of Thomas Aquinas on methodology.
13. Outline some of the general intellectual characteristics of the Middle Ages and the Roman Period.

Glossary

Abelard, Peter (1079–1142)   One of the best-known university teachers in the twelfth century. His book *Yes and No* illustrated contradictions in the positions of past authorities. He argued for a stronger role for reason in Christian epistemology.

Al-Ghazali (1058–1111)   Author of *The Incoherence of the Philosophers*. Attacked the rationality of the Greeks and the concept of causality. Worked against scientific progress in Islam.

Alhazen (965–1039)   One of the greatest Islamic scientists whose *Book of Optics* is one of the most influential classic works on vision. He made many original contributions on topics such as depth perception, apparent size, and binocular vision.

animal spirits   A concept that has enjoyed wide usage, especially in premodern times. In Galen's pneuma concept of the soul, the expression *animal spirits* was used to account for a vital psychological function, namely, the operation of higher cognitive functions. Animal spirits contrasted with *natural spirits,* which account for vegetative functions. See *vital spirits.*

Aquinas, Thomas (1225–1274)   One of the greatest doctors of the church, remembered for his heroic efforts to reconcile faith and reason. He is also remembered for advancing an empirically based system of psychological thought.

Asclepiades   A popular Greek physician who practiced in Rome around 124 BCE. He distinguished between delusions and hallucinations and argued that therapy for emotional problems should be pleasant.

Augustine, Aurelius (354–430) One of the great doctors of the church who wrote extensively about a number of psychological topics including memory, grief, speech, and dreams.

Aurelius, Marcus (121–180 CE) Roman emperor and stoic philosopher who emphasized the importance of enduring hardships that undoubtedly serve a larger purpose. The expression *stoic resignation* characterizes an important dimension of his thought.

Averroës (1126–1198) An Islamic scholar very influential in Europe because of his commentaries on the works of Aristotle. Known also for many substantive scientific discoveries. He discovered that patients once infected with smallpox become immune if they survive the initial infection. He also discovered that the retina is the part of the eye sensitive to light.

Avicenna (980–1037) An influential philosopher of the Islamic world who attempted to reconcile the tensions between revelation and reason. Also remembered for his Aristotelian approach to psychological problems.

Bacon, Roger (c. 1220–c. 1292) One of the first to write on the sources of error in human thought. His catalog of errors included things such as being a slave to habit, relying too much on authority, giving in to popular prejudices, conceit about one's own knowledge.

Boethius (c. 480–524) Attempted to use reason that he learned from Greek thought as a defense of Christianity. Some have regarded him as a kind of founder of the intellectual agenda that was to dominate medieval thought.

Empiricus, Sextus Roman physician and skeptic who criticized dogmatic certainty and argued for the virtues associated with an attitude of suspended judgment.

Epictetus (c. 50–c. 135) A Roman stoic philosopher, popular in his day, who emphasized the stoic virtues of order, discipline, and resignation in those matters beyond our control.

Epicureanism A philosophy based on the goodness of pleasure and the evil of pain. Epicureanism emphasized moderation and the capacity to forego immediate pleasures for long-term gains.

Epicurus of Samos (341–270 BCE) An important post-Aristotelian philosopher who founded a school of thought that focused largely on how to live the good life by maximizing pleasure and minimizing pain.

Galenus (c. 129–c. 199 CE) Rome's greatest physician, remembered for his early anatomical theories and his speculation on a host of medical problems including the problems of emotional illness.

Héloise (c. 1098–1164) A gifted scholar known primarily for her tragic love affair with Peter Abelard. Her letters illustrated a deep philosophy and psychology of the nature of loving relationships.

Hypatia (c. 370–415 CE) Neo-Platonic philosopher noted for her expertise in astronomy and geometry. Possibly one of the first to recommend music therapy for emotional disorders.

Lucretius (c. 96–c. 55 BCE) Roman epicurean philosopher who wrote on a variety of psychological topics, often from the vantage point of the atomic theory of Democritus.

Maimonides (1135–1204) Influential Jewish philosopher who attempted to reconcile the conflicting claims of reason and revelation. His book *Guide for the Perplexed* was widely read and highly controversial.

medieval period The historical period from approximately 400 to 1300. Though it was a period marked by reliance on tradition, revelation, and authority, scholars attempted to find an acceptable role for reason and for observational studies.

natural spirit In Galen's pneuma concept of the soul, natural spirit refers to those vital principles responsible for vegetative functions of the body.

neo-Platonism A school of philosophy founded in the third century that combined selected features of Platonic philosophy with Jewish and Christian mysticism.

Ockham's Razor   The contention of William of Ockham that explanations containing fewer assumptions are to be preferred to those containing more assumptions.

Plotinus (205–270 CE)   Founder of neo-Platonic philosophy and author of a six-volume series entitled *Enneads.* The works of Plotinus are a rich source of psychological thought on topics such as perception, sensation, memory, and thinking.

pneuma   Refers to the air we draw in as we breathe, but also refers to those vital principles that make life possible.

Pyrrho (c. 360–c. 270 BCE)   Founder of a systematic philosophy of skepticism. Also emphasized the importance of finding means to live a calm and untroubled existence.

Rhazes (c. 854–c. 925)   Physician and author of medical texts. Argued against demonology, superstitious religious beliefs, and the arbitrary use of authority in science. He advocated a rational and empirical approach to the problems of medicine and psychology.

skepticism   One of the major systematic approaches to philosophy following the death of Aristotle. The concerns of the skeptics were largely focused on the problems of epistemology and the good life.

stoicism   A major post-Aristotelian philosophy emphasizing discipline and suppression of desire as means to the greatest happiness and virtue.

vital spirit   In Galen's pneuma concept of the soul, vital spirit refers to activities located in the heart that regulate or control body heat.

Tertullian (c. 155–230)   An early Christian scholar remembered for his attacks on child sacrifice, the persecution of Christians, and the brutality of the Roman games. Also remembered for his attacks on Greek philosophy and his emphasis on faith as opposed to reason.

William of Ockham (c. 1285–1349)   An early philosopher friendly to empirical methods and strongly influenced by Thomas Aquinas. See *Ockham's Razor.*

Zeno of Cyprus (c. 335–c. 263 BCE)   Founder of the post-Aristotelian school of stoicism, which emphasized self-control, austerity, and suppression as guides to virtue and happiness.

5

■ ■ ■

The Renaissance

No truth [is] so sublime but it may be trivial tomorrow in the light of new thoughts.

—Ralph Waldo Emerson (1841/1969)

In the twilight of the Middle Ages, European culture witnessed the emergence of a dramatic scientific and philosophical revolution. Beginning in the fourteenth century and stretching to the sixteenth, the **Renaissance** (meaning "the rebirth") inspired an almost unprecedented growth and shift in perspective. Whether the period in question deserves such an extravagant title is debatable. Still, MacLeod (1975) noted, "The metaphor of the Rebirth suggests that freedom had been born and had flourished during the time of the Greeks, that it had subsequently died, and that it was now being reborn" (p. 87).

Any sketch of the Renaissance would have to mention the revolutionary trends in art and architecture. The new aesthetic stressed naturalism in portraying classical and Biblical themes. The High Renaissance in Italian art boasted works by remarkable artisans such as Donato Bramante (1444–1514), Leonardo da Vinci (1452–1519), Michelangelo Buonarroti (1475–1564), and Raphael Sanzio (1483–1520).

When German goldsmith Johannes Gutenberg (1398–1468) invented the printing press around 1440, it proved to be an innovation that forever changed communication. The new technology lowered the expense of publishing and encouraged new intellectual vistas for readers. No longer the exclusive possession of the elite, books found their way into the hands of a broader population. Renaissance literature evolved from tales about God and the afterlife to the interplay of human beings and their lives.

Renaissance music also escaped religious bonds and took greater liberties than in the past. In addition to the religious masses and motets heard in cathedrals, more secular forms emerged, including folk music, art songs, madrigals, court music, and street music. New developments in music theory accompanied a growth in the number of music schools and an increasing demand for musical instruments.

New geographic discoveries expanded intellectual boundaries along with the rediscovery of Greek classics. Another major development during the Renaissance was the powerful revolt against authority as a way of discerning truth. Despite the intellectual rebirth, the Renaissance was stagnant and even regressive in certain ways. And new challenges emerged as Europe faced a devastating pandemic.

THE BLACK DEATH

One of the most destructive calamities in human history ushered in the Renaissance. Throughout history, the plague (sometimes called the "Black Death") has struck with ruinous consequences, but the brief period from 1347 to 1350 witnessed a biological and medical holocaust that decimated the European population. Hundreds of communities were destroyed or deserted. The toll in human numbers is difficult to calculate because population statistics were not well established. Even reliable counts of the dead in some localities did not provide a basis for estimating mortality statistics in other regions. We do know that the fatalities across Europe during this tragic period numbered in the millions. Evidence suggests that one-third of the European population was lost between 1347 and 1350. For some communities, the death rate ran far higher.

The plague brought economic and social consequences that scarred Europe's intellectual landscape (see Herlihy, 1997). Following the loss of one-third of the population, the number of workers diminished, disrupting the equilibrium between supply and demand. Wealth was redistributed with the loss of entire families (Cantor, 2001). As with natural disasters such as earthquakes and floods, law and order crumbled in the wake of theft and violent crime. The soaring death rate pushed community services beyond capacity. Although severe under the best of circumstances, the problems of sanitation in many communities were exacerbated by inadequate burial services and the resulting accumulation of corpses. European streets were cluttered with decomposing victims of the Black Death.

What was the human reaction to the Black Death? One encounters examples of stoic resignation, self-sacrificing heroism, opportunism, and reckless abandon to short-term pleasure in the face of inevitable death. The wealthy could

flee from cities and communities to take isolated shelter in remote estates. Angry and desperate, some searched for a scapegoat to blame. As in other times, Jewish citizens became the target of choice. According to Ziegler (1969/1991), "The massacre [of Jews] was exceptional in its extent and its ferocity; in both, indeed, it probably had no equal until the twentieth century set new standards for man's inhumanity to man" (p. 80).

European Jews provided a familiar scapegoat. Christian teachings had denigrated Jews and they were also resented for their financial success. For centuries, the church followed a strict literal approach to scripture that opposed loans of interest. Based on passages such as Deuteronomy 23:1 and Luke 6:35, church leaders viewed it as a sin to make money on money. St. Ambrose even suggested that money lending for interest was in the same league as murder (see White, 1910). However, Jewish businessmen who were not literalists were free to lend money for interest. This advantage contributed to their financial success, which in turn fostered resentment and jealousy. In 1349, the men, women, and children in the Jewish community of Strasbourg were executed in a mass burning. In addition, the city canceled all debts owed to Jews and confiscated all property belonging to Jewish citizens (Friedrich, 1982). For a host of theological, social, and economic reasons, Jews were blamed for the plague. They were tortured, imprisoned, and massacred sometimes at "the mere news that the plague was approaching" (Ziegler, 1969/1991, p. 77). According to Kelly (2005), Jews sometimes avoided brutality and torture by killing themselves and their children before the angry mobs arrived.

When hostility was not directed at others, it was sometimes turned inward. As in other tragedies, people searched for an explanation for their misfortune. Many believed God had sent the plague as a punishment for the sins of people. If you accept that line of thinking, what would be the next step? For some, self-punishment seemed a solution. Perhaps an act of a sincere, self-inflicted flogging could appease God's wrath. Earlier catastrophes had inspired a similar reaction, but during the plague years it achieved new levels of zealotry among the brotherhood of the flagellants. Vast numbers of flagellants marched through towns beating themselves with sharpened pieces of metal attached to leather thongs. In the words of Ziegler (1969/1991) , "Each man tried to outdo his neighbor in pious suffering, literally whipping himself into a frenzy in which pain had no reality. Around them the townsfolk quaked, sobbed and groaned in sympathy, encouraging the brethren to still greater excesses" (p. 66).

At best, flagellation may have salved a guilty conscience, but open wounds and crowds of people would only favor the spread of the Black Death. Tragically, an understanding of the cause of the epidemic disease waited far in the future. A later generation of scientists determined that the plague was caused by *Yersinia pestis*, a vector-born enterobacteria transmitted from "Oriental rat fleas" (*Xenopsylla cheopis*) carried on the backs of infected black rats (see Biddle, 1995).

An interesting outcome of the plague is that it contributed to doubts about authorities and institutions. People were told that the Black Death was God's punishment for sin. But no one could ignore that even the most godly in their midst—including priests and other church officials—were stricken with the same ferocity as the general population. Trusted institutions, especially the church, seemed helpless to protect people against a nightmare of terrifying proportions. The resulting doubts and resentment directed at authorities formed the intellectual backdrop of the Renaissance. We will now consider other characteristics that contributed to Renaissance science in general and psychology in particular.

A NEW WORLDVIEW: EXPANDING GEOGRAPHIC KNOWLEDGE

Imagine that the year is 1522 and you are living in Europe. You believe the earth is the center of the universe. You believe the sun is red in the evening because it reflects the fires of hell (see White, 1896/1978, p. 97). Now imagine hearing that Ferdinand Magellan's ship has returned after a grueling sea voyage that claimed his life. Magellan's voyage, completed under the leadership of Juan Sebastian del Cano, has become the first to circumnavigate the globe. Although sailing with a crew of more than two hundred and fifty in 1519, a remnant of only thirty-five sailors has returned on the *Vittoria*.

Hearing the news about the first-known voyage around the earth changed the lives of countless Renaissance people overnight. The world was now a different place, better known than before. Magellan's expedition and the stories of other explorations had an unprecedented impact on the European mind. These journeys exposed Europeans to groups of humans for whom the existing Western theological and political worldviews could not account. If it became necessary to expand geographic boundaries, perhaps it was also necessary to expand intellectual boundaries. Some people could enlarge one without expanding the other, but in many cases geographic discoveries contributed to a new curiosity and openness to revolutionary ideas. In that context, the Renaissance flourished.

INFLUENCE OF THE GREEK CLASSICS

By the fifteenth century, Greek texts were commonplace in European centers of learning and in private libraries. A handful of wealthy bibliophiles went to great trouble and expense to acquire private collections of old manuscripts. When Constantinople fell in 1453, Byzantine scientists were forced to leave, and many brought Greek manuscripts to Italy (Delaunay, 1958). Other texts found their way to Europe in the hands of traders who profited from the expeditions of the Crusaders.

However they arrived, the writings of the ancient Greeks influenced the Renaissance imagination. The classics stimulated an interest in the Greek language and in editing and translation. They also invigorated new ways of thinking. It was refreshing to witness the Greek courage to allow speculation to run its course without having to affirm conclusions in a dogmatic fashion that had been imposed beforehand. The classics quickened the reemergence of a naturalistic approach to psychology. Delaunay (1958) offered the opinion that the birth of Renaissance humanism echoed the return of Hellenic values. Whatever their precise role, the rediscovery of the classics kindled interest in human problems and reduced the appeal of theological matters.

DIFFUSION OF AUTHORITY

During the medieval period, the Roman Catholic Church dominated the political, intellectual, and religious life of Europe. During the Renaissance, the church saw its power and authority diminish. Forces at work within the church and external cultural developments contributed to its declining influence.

Emerging nation-states likely posed the single most important challenge to church authority. The leaders of the new nation-states viewed the church as a foreign competitor and jealously protected their territory and assets. People felt widespread resentment about sending money to support a church with a base of power in a distant land.

As noted previously, Johannes Gutenberg invented the printing press around 1440. This invention stimulated a growing number of readers and made available new translations of the Bible, and provided an important underpinning for the development of the sciences. Translations of the Bible prepared by Martin Luther and others were sometimes condemned and placed on the **Index of Forbidden Books** (see Haight, 1978), but nevertheless found their way to the public. The increased availability of the Bible may have contributed to the idea that human beings have direct access to God without need for a church-based intermediary. The concept of the "individual priesthood of the believer" carried the assumption that all persons could read and interpret scripture for themselves. Even so, Protestants who were allowed to read scripture were often not free to read Catholic literature. Censorship, it turns out, was rampant in both Protestant and Catholic countries (see Grendler, 1988).

As mentioned, forces within the church contributed to the demise of its influence and power base. As a large institution, the church struggled with enormous financial demands. To satisfy those needs, religious leaders raised money through the sale of political or religious offices and the abuse of indulgences. An **indulgence** involved an exchange of money for a spiritual favor. After committing a personal sin, an individual might beg for forgiveness by paying a sum so the church would grant a remission. Another person, worried about the soul of a deceased relative, might pay for intercession to change the relative's status in the afterlife. It's no surprise that the practice of granting indulgences offended some faithful Europeans.

During the fourteenth and fifteenth centuries, church leaders wrestled with debilitating power struggles. Important questions were raised as to whether authority should be vested in a single leader or in church councils. Such conflict contributed to the rupture that inspired the Reformation.

A succession of earlier dissidents had called attention to problems within the church, but none had the impact of **Martin Luther (1483–1546)**, an Augustinian monk and theologian. In 1517, Luther nailed ninety-five theses on a church door in Wittenberg, Germany. His bold gesture ushered in a protest movement known as the **Reformation**. Luther hoped to reform Catholic doctrine and practice rather than start a new church. However, authorities within the church interpreted his actions as anti-Catholic. Despite such condemnation, Luther's reform movement found support from emerging Germanic nations struggling for political and economic freedom from Rome (Manchester, 1992) as well as from an emerging group of women who wrote in favor of the Reformation (Zitzlsperger, 2006). After ongoing conflicts with the church, Luther was excommunicated and then exiled to Saxony. Following his excommunication, he spearheaded the Protestant movement until his death in 1546.

How great was the Reformation's influence on the development of science? Scholars hold legitimate differences of opinion. Watson and Evans (1991) concluded that Renaissance science and philosophy gained nothing from the Reformation.

They point to the Protestant John Calvin and his well-known justification for burning Michael Servetus at the stake. Servetus had "described the Holy Land as a barren wilderness (which it was), thus contradicting the scriptural description of it as a land of 'milk and honey'" (Watson & Evans, 1991 p. 151). Many Reformation leaders were as intoxicated with authority as those against whom they rebelled. MacLeod (1975) argued, however, that "just as Luther. . .could exhort his followers to read the Bible and draw their own conclusions, so could other Protestants exhort their followers to look at nature (as Aristotle had done) and draw their own conclusions" (p. 91). In this way, the Reformation may have contributed to the growing importance of the individual in Renaissance humanism (Jansz, 2004). The role of the Reformation in Renaissance science remains subject to interpretation and debate.

GROWTH OF EMPIRICAL STUDIES

A host of empirical discoveries were introduced during the Renaissance period (Bjornsson, 2004). During this time, mapmaking was reestablished as a scientific activity. Based on the careful observations of explorers, descriptions and drawings of coastlines, harbors, and peninsulas were created with a fair amount of accuracy.

Freed from the prohibitions of earlier times, the study of human anatomy flourished during the Renaissance. In 1543, the Belgian scientist **Andreas Vesalius (1514–1564)** published his classic *The Fabric of the Human Body*, an anatomy text based on his painstaking dissections. Other researchers such as Gabriello Fallopio (1523–1562), Bartolommeo Eustachio (1520–1574), and Michael Servetus (1511–1553) also made significant contributions to anatomical knowledge. And, as we'll see later, Leonardo da Vinci (1452–1519) and others used art to complement traditional studies on anatomy (Ginn & Loruso, 2008).

During the late Renaissance, empirical work in botany and zoology made numerous advances. Descriptions of plants and many animal species were more detailed and accurate than in previous generations. The Greeks of antiquity

and medieval scholars such as Roger Bacon and Moses Maimonides had articulated a robust empirical spirit. It was now being realized on a scale they could have never imagined.

QUANTIFICATION

Commenting on a debate about whether there really was a Renaissance, Bochner (1973) declared that "there was indeed a mathematics of the Renaissance that was original and distinctive in its drives and characteristics" (p. 178).

Interest in Renaissance mathematics was fueled by practical demands of navigation along with business, banking, and commercial activities. Ronan (1982) noted that "between the years 1472 and 1500 no less than 214 mathematical books had been published to feed the increasing demand for mathematics by banking houses, merchants, workshops, public administrators, astrologers and scholars" (p. 322). Public contests were even staged where participants competed against each other to solve mathematical problems (Ronan, 1982).

Major schools in Germany, Italy, and France valued mathematics in its own right, independent of practical application. Mathematicians had a strong interest in the discipline for its own sake, leading to original contributions, especially in algebra and geometry. The Renaissance witnessed the development of new mathematical symbols and the solution of numerous equations. The rediscovery of Pythagoras and Euclid, along with new mathematical discoveries, offered new optimism about quantitative methods. Such optimism later served as a decisive force in psychology's development.

CHANGING VISIONS OF THE WORLD

As with mathematics, the late Renaissance witnessed revolutionary changes in cosmology. The term **cosmology** refers to theories about the nature of the universe, including earth's relation to the rest of the solar system. Changing beliefs about the universe provide an important intellectual backdrop for the history of the social sciences because our world visions have far-reaching consequences for how we view ourselves (see Berenda, 1965).

For centuries, the prevailing view was that earth was positioned in the center of the universe. According to this model, the earth was encircled by the sun, the moon, and the other planets. The **geocentric** (earth-centered) cosmology was a dominant intellectual feature of the Middle Ages and early Renaissance. The model was a curious combination of theology wedded to the work of Aristotle and an Egyptian astronomer, geographer, and mathematician named **Ptolemy (c. 100–c. 165)**.

Working in Alexandria during the second century, Ptolemy (*TAHL eh mee*) argued that earth sits motionless in the center of the cosmos. The stars beyond the immediate planetary system were regarded as fixed points of light. If one assumes that such bodies follow strict circular pathways around earth, then we should be able to predict the motion of heavenly bodies. But such predictions fail to match observations. Following the thinking of earlier Greeks, Ptolemy constructed an elaborate though awkward theory to account for locations and movements of celestial bodies (see Thurston, 1994). Although Ptolemy was aware of the possibility of visual illusions, having devoted much of his *Optics* to the topic (Coren, 2003), he argued that human impressions of astronomy were accurate.

One of Ptolemy's proofs for the immovability of earth centers on the following argument: If our planet moves, then an object tossed up should fall in a different location from where it was tossed. Ptolemy's proof fails to account for one fact. If earth is moving, then the thrown object is moving at the same speed as earth at the time of the toss. Hence, even with a moving earth, the object should fall in the same relative location from which it was tossed.

Ptolemy's arguments for a stationary earth located in the center of the universe squared beautifully with many theological beliefs of the Middle Ages. Such beliefs were grounded in scripture and church tradition. Some raised questions about the shape of earth (e.g., was it disc-like, or spherical?), but most agreed it was stationary and central in the scheme of things. By the later Middle Ages, the prevailing belief was in a central, stationary, and spherical earth.

Although popular and accepted, geocentric cosmology was not without nagging biblical perplexities. Does the earth hang on nothing as mentioned in Job 26:7, does it rest on foundations as implied in Job 38:4, Psalms 102:25, and Psalms 104:5, or is it founded on the seas as implied in Psalms 24:2? Would the earth abide forever as proclaimed in Ecclesiastes 1:4, or would it someday be burned as prophesized in II Peter 3:10? If some biblical texts were taken literally, others must be taken metaphorically.

The geocentric worldview was integral to the larger philosophical and theological picture of the world. The model was an abiding source of emotional and intellectual comfort. A stationary earth was fixed at the center of the universe, and Jerusalem was the central point on earth. People were confident in the belief they were the key players in a lawful universe designed for their benefit. The heavens, literally *up there* (not *out there*), radiated the perfection of God. In the Medieval conception of hell, Dante took over from Ptolemy. Despite a lack of physical description in the Bible, the complicated architecture of hell was described in graphic detail in the pages of Dante's *Divine Comedy*.

Questions about the structure of the universe were not just questions about astronomy or physics, but questions about human destiny, theology, philosophy, and the purpose of life on earth. The task of disentangling science from theology in this period was not only vexing from an intellectual standpoint, it was fraught with danger to the well-being of scientists who dared raise questions.

The Heliocentric Theory

The Greek astronomer Aristarchus of Samos (310–230 BCE) was one of the first to advance the idea of a sun-centered cosmos. The idea, however, was not taken seriously until the sixteenth century. **Nicolaus Copernicus**

(1473–1543), a Polish astronomer and canon of the church, is sometimes regarded as the founder of modern astronomy. His book *On the Revolution of the Celestial Spheres*, published days before his death in 1543, proposed that earth turned once daily on its axis and traveled in an annual path around the sun. As a challenge to the old geocentric universe, Copernicus had advanced a new **heliocentric** (sun-centered) cosmology.

In terms of calendar predictions, Copernican theory represented little improvement over Ptolemy's geocentric model. Like Ptolemy, Copernicus believed that the circle is the most perfect geometric figure. It seemed inconceivable to both men that a lawful universe would be based on anything other than perfect circular motion. **Johannes Kepler (1571–1630)**, a German astronomer and mathematician, later proved that they were wrong. He discovered that planets travel in elliptical or oval-shaped motions around the sun. Kepler's calculations were instrumental in delivering a deathblow to the aging geocentric theory. Clinging to the old theory, religious supporters did not give up without a fight. The stage was set for a battle between theology and science, and one man was caught in the crossfire.

Galileo Galilei

The Italian astronomer and physicist **Galileo Galilei (1564–1642)** is one of the most celebrated figures in the history of science. Born in Pisa, Galileo (*Gal uh LAY oh*) received his early education near Florence. In 1581, he returned to the University of Pisa to study medicine. Because of shifting interests and shortage of funds, Galileo withdrew from medical training before receiving a degree. After 1585, he studied mathematics and physics. In 1586, he achieved widespread recognition for his work on a hydrostatic balance, an instrument designed to measure the specific gravity of objects. Galileo held a professorial position in mathematics at Pisa from 1589 to 1592. In 1592, he was awarded a chair in mathematics at the University of Padua.

Early in his career, Galileo believed in Copernican theory, but he was afraid of going public with his convictions. By 1609, he had built an excellent thirty-two-power telescope and was the first to use this instrument in a systematic study of astronomy. After collecting data with his telescope, Galileo developed greater confidence in Copernican theory. The old geocentric theory had predicted that the moon's surface would appear perfect and unblemished. Instead, Galileo found an irregular lunar surface pocked with craters and littered with rocks and mountains. The old theory had taught that all objects in the heavens were visible to the naked eye. But gazing through his telescope, Galileo discovered sunspots along with the moons of Jupiter and the rings of Saturn. One of his students had predicted that, if the heliocentric model is correct, the planet Venus should exhibit phases that resemble lunar phases. Galileo confirmed his student's predictions (Gribben, 2006, p. 97). Galileo's observations proved a daunting challenge to geocentric theory as well as to the prevailing worldview. He pioneered the idea that raw experience can be productively amplified through the use of tools such as the telescope and quantitative descriptions. Galileo's views helped set the stage for the development of other sciences including scientific psychology.

In 1610, Galileo returned to Florence as philosopher and mathematician in the employment of the Grand Duke of Tuscany. Already, his observations were generating acclaim. A year later, he visited the pontifical court in Rome where he demonstrated his telescope. The friendly atmosphere in Rome emboldened Galileo to take a stand in supporting Copernican theory.

Subsequently, academic enemies greeted Galileo's support of Copernicus with fierce criticism and personal attacks. Five years after demonstrating his telescope in the pontifical court, he was summoned back to Rome. In 1616, he faced official charges of possible heresy. Although he was not found guilty, he was ordered to refrain from *holding* or *defending* Copernican doctrine. Select members of the church hierarchy defended Galileo, but a larger and more influential conservative group dominated the proceedings.

In 1624, Pope Urban VIII denied Galileo's request to reverse the prohibition of 1616.

However, the Pope granted Galileo the right to publish a work comparing geocentric and heliocentric theories. Galileo was instructed to treat the heliocentric view as a mere hypothesis while keeping his conclusions consistent with prevailing theological truths. With the Pope's permission, Galileo devoted years of research and writing to creating a masterpiece in cosmology. His book *Dialogue Concerning the Two Chief World Systems—Ptolemaic and Copernican* was published in 1632. The story of how the book survived church censors and obstacles on its way to publication is a lengthy and contradictory tale of intrigue (see Shea, 1986).

Although hailed as a literary and scientific achievement, the *Dialogue* generated a storm of controversy. Within a year of *Dialogue's* publication, Galileo was forced to travel to Rome to stand trial before the Inquisition. In open defiance of the Pope, Galileo had used his book to support Copernican cosmology. He was found guilty of believing and teaching the hated doctrine. The Roman Inquisition ordered him to recant.

At the age of seventy, Galileo was forced to his knees as he faced the holy cardinals. Before his accusers, he placed his hands on the Bible and was coerced into abjuring and cursing his errors. Galileo was made to swear he would never again do anything to arouse suspicion regarding his orthodoxy.

Because of his advanced age, Galileo avoided imprisonment. Removed from family and friends, he was placed under house arrest in a remote country estate. There, he spent the final eight years of his life before dying in 1642. Though he avoided a physical prison, Galileo was placed in a cruel intellectual prison as he was forbidden to continue his work on the problems that had captured his imagination for so many years.

To no one's surprise, Galileo's *Dialogue* and Copernicus's *On the Revolution* were placed on the Roman church's *Index of Forbidden Books*. The controversy over rival cosmologies went beyond a dispute about the nature of the universe. The scope of a larger controversy centered on matters of authority. Under the guise of competing epistemologies, the authority of literal scripture

was pitted against the authority of the new observational sciences. As noted by White (1896/1978), the dominant theological position was "that the divinely appointed way of arriving at the truth in astronomy was by theological reasoning on texts of scripture" (p. 131). Many Protestant and Catholic authorities championed the idea "that the church alone is empowered to promulgate scientific truth" (White, 1896/1978, p. 133).

The complexity of the debate becomes clear in the arguments against Galileo and the Copernican system. Conventional wisdom assumed that the moon generated its own light. However, the heliocentric view claimed that the moon reflects light from the sun. Religious authorities countered with the Genesis 1:16 passage that refers to a lesser light that rules by night. Galileo's discovery of the moons of Jupiter was denounced as an illusion caused by the telescope or perhaps Satan himself. Some authorities raised doubts about telescopic observations on the grounds that the telescope itself possibly added to or distorted the objects in its field of view. In response, Galileo observed hundreds of items close up with the naked eye and at a distance with the telescope (see Gribben, 2006, p. 97). Galileo could find no evidence that the telescope added anything to objects as revealed to the naked eye.

Galileo's observations coupled with his powerful arguments for the Copernican system brought him into conflict not only with the Roman Catholic Church but with Protestant reformers as well. The Protestant response to heliocentrism was mixed and less organized than the Catholic reaction (see Westman, 1986). Martin Luther (1539/1967) complained that "whoever wants to be clever must agree with nothing that others esteem. . . . This is what the fellow does who wishes to turn the whole of astronomy upside down. . . . I believe the holy scripture, for Joshua commanded the sun to stand still and not the earth" (pp. 358–359). But just as some devout Catholics opposed biblical literalism and favored Galileo's beliefs, some liberal Protestant reformers found no incompatibility between the new cosmology and the essential Christian message.

The Larger Meaning of the Copernican Revolution

Prior to the Copernican revolution, people had little appreciation for natural causes. As Deason (1986) tells us, Reformation theologians Luther and Calvin, who echoed the earlier claims of Al-Ghazali, believed that nothing in nature happens through natural inherent forces. For example, Luther "chided physicians and philosophers for ascribing procreation to 'a matching mixture of qualities, which are active in predisposed matter'" (Deason, 1986, p. 176). According to Catholic and Protestant theologies, active causal power resides in God alone, not in natural forces.

Copernican cosmology, however, described inherent, lawful, predictable, and quantifiable natural forces that exist independently. Such forces can be studied without reference to any extrinsic causal force. Geographic discoveries, rather than the new astronomy, fed a growing belief that the dominant theology had been wrong about cosmology. Was it not also possible that it had been wrong about the philosophy that was so closely connected to that cosmology?

Such questions and doubts promoted a new openness, first to physical sciences and later to life sciences. Copernicus and Galileo brought us one step closer to understanding the grand mysteries of the universe, including the mysteries of human experience and behavior.

PSYCHOLOGICAL THOUGHT IN THE RENAISSANCE

Along with discoveries in other sciences and a new emphasis on humanistic studies, several figures prepared the intellectual groundwork for Renaissance psychology. The period also witnessed the first treatise on individual differences. In addition, a trend deemphasized what was called the "will" in favor of broader influences such as intelligence, aptitude, social influence, temperament, and learning. A flood of original ideas contributed to an optimism about a science of human nature.

Petrarch

Francesco Petrarch (1304–1374), an Italian poet, scholar, and moralist, was an early leader in **Renaissance humanism**. From his earliest years as a student, Petrarch (*PEH trark*) obsessed with the recovery and study of ancient Roman and Greek manuscripts. In his mind, intellectual Christianity had epistemological limitations. Medieval scholasticism used hairsplitting logic to study remote theological problems that shed little insight into human nature. Hellenistic philosophy, science, literature, and poetry offered a refreshing contrast. Petrarch embraced Roman and Greek concerns with this world and with the immediate and practical problems of life. Although a loyal Christian, he hoped to widen the horizons of the faithful, focusing attention on the importance of the present and the compatibilities between Christian and classic thought.

In the tradition of Thomas Aquinas, Catholic theology had praised the work of Aristotle. Petrarch, however, preferred Plato to Aristotle. Following Petrarch, heated arguments flared between scholars who preferred Aristotle and those who favored Plato. The debates encouraged deeper studies of the classics, serving to widen Greek influence in the Renaissance. Kristeller (1967) points out that "Petrarch assigned second place to Aristotle, but he was far from holding him in contempt. . . . He repeatedly suggested that the original Aristotle may be superior to his medieval translators and commentators" (p. 127). Petrarch encouraged students to study Aristotle and other Greeks in original form rather than rely on the filters of scholastic writers.

Petrarch set the stage for the expansion of humanistic studies in the Renaissance. Human beings should be understood not just in the context of theology, but also in the context of their natural setting. Petrarch found joy in nature, society, secular studies, and travel. He believed we have the right to be creatures of this world. Such a claim is foundational to the development of a science of human nature.

Niccolò Machiavelli

The Italian civil servant **Niccolò Machiavelli** *(MAK ee uh VEHL ee)* **(1469–1527)** is often regarded as the founder of modern political science. He also was a founder of modern military science. So why is he important for the social and behavioral sciences? Machiavelli established descriptive and objective methodologies that rejected moralistic approaches to human behavior. His views on the malleability of human behavior suggested new possibilities for understanding and control—key elements in any science. He was one of the first to recognize the role of social influence in human life. In many respects, he was an intellectual ancestor to modern social psychology.

Machiavelli was born to a poor family in Florence, Italy. Little is known about his early life, but he acquired a considerable education, especially in the humanities. At age twenty-nine, he was selected for a minor bureaucratic government position in Florence. An effective administrator, he was given greater authority and responsibility and sent on diplomatic missions. He traveled and came into contact with powerful political figures.

In 1502, Machiavelli served as the Florentine secretary for Cesare Borgia (c. 1475–1507). Imposing and ruthless, Borgia was the duke of Valentinois and the captain general of the Papal army. He was also the son of Pope Alexander VI (despite a vow of celibacy, the Pope made no secret that he had fathered several children). Machiavelli had a firsthand look at Borgia's leadership style. Cunning and self-reliant, Borgia could also be cruel and manipulative in running political and military affairs. During this time, Machiavelli developed a fascination with the social psychology of power, leadership, and authority. His fascination would result in major treatises on these topics.

During Machiavelli's lifetime, the political climate was unstable. In Italy, a host of city-states competed for power. At the same time, France, Germany, and Spain tried to influence political developments in Italy. Some Italian city-states formed an alliance with foreign powers, whereas others allied with the Vatican. In the early sixteenth century, Florence was allied with France, but forces loyal to the papacy tried to drive the French from Italy. Machiavelli trained and led a small Florentine army to defend Florence. Despite a hard-fought battle, superior papal forces crushed his army and the French were driven from Italy. A new political order was established in Florence. Machiavelli was imprisoned and then tortured. He managed to avoid being burned at the stake.

After his release, he moved to a rural estate near Florence where he lived in poverty. During a fourteen-year exile, Machiavelli wrote books that earned him a place in history. He wrote his best-known works, *The Prince* and *The Discourses*, in 1513. *The Prince* (1532/1977) offered a monarchical ruler advice on how to stay in power based on methods Machiavelli doubtless saw while working with Cesare Borgia. His other books included *History of Florence* and *The Art of War*. He also wrote comedies, plays, biographies, and short stories, and these works as well as his letters reveal his interests in love and sex (Ruggiero, 2007).

During his exile, Machiavelli tried to regain a civil service position in Florence. He enjoyed a brief return to public service in 1525, but an unstable political situation prevented him from regaining his former position. He died in 1527.

Cesare Borgia and Niccolò Machiavelli

Machiavelli's works aroused indignation and controversy. Thorne (1969) shared that Pope Clement VIII condemned *The Prince*. Gilbert (1967) noted that Machiavelli's works were placed on the *Index of Forbidden Books* in 1559 and that "Cardinal Reginald Pole said that Machiavelli 'wrote with the finger of the devil'" (p. 121). The indignation against Machiavelli's works may lie partly in their objectivity. For example, Machiavelli observed that religion may be employed to invoke obedience and control. A successful leader can use religion to call people back to their roots and founding principles. Such action serves to unite and to weed out corruption. For Machiavelli, religious values are subordinate to political values. The clever leader can manipulate religious people to achieve desired ends. Some leaders who condemned Machiavelli nevertheless used his principles without hesitation.

We noted that Machiavelli emphasized the malleability of human nature. If he held a somewhat cynical view about human nature, he was nevertheless optimistic about attaining a good social order. The suggestibility of the masses could work for the good of humankind. So could the proper use of political and social influence. Machiavelli was interested in the larger social good. He believed that an ideal society was within reach.

As mentioned, Machiavelli contributed to the belief that human behavior can be understood in a naturalistic–scientific context. His views on human nature contained an interesting blend of pessimism and hope. On the pessimistic side, basic human nature was regarded as brutish, selfish, shortsighted, vain, and imitative. Machiavelli believed that self-preservation is the strongest motive. Self-preservation can induce violence and destruction or, under proper leadership, great industry and accomplishment. He taught that the human tendency to imitate others is inconsistent with creative thought, but it can make the masses malleable for shaping. Thus, astute leaders and institutions can enhance virtue and constructive social effort.

Wood (1968) addressed the common misconception that Machiavelli advocated immoral acts. Such acts are sometimes excused if a larger good is attained. For example, deception in Machiavelli's treatment is never an end in itself, but its use is acceptable if a larger good can be achieved. In some degree, most of us are Machiavellian when we use mild deception to avoid a "hard truth" (e.g., that hat looks good on you) because we believe the former will do no harm, whereas the latter may result in unnecessary pain.

In psychological literature, the term **Machiavellianism** refers to "an amoral, manipulative attitude toward other individuals" (Gutterman, 1970, p. 3). When used in such a manner, the term is a corruption. Machiavelli was not, strictly speaking, amoral. At one level, he simply advanced a descriptive science of human social and political behavior without regard to the morality or immorality of such behavior. He attempted to describe what people actually do. Thus, he worked much as today's social scientists who describe what people do. Machiavelli went a step further to show what we *can* do. In this regard, he served as an intellectual forerunner to later psychologists, including behaviorists such as John B. Watson and B. F. Skinner, who strived to predict and control human behavior. For Machiavelli, efficiency, practicality, and the common good take precedence over all moral principles as ends in themselves.

Machiavelli placed strong emphasis on development, socialization, and suggestibility. These processes could be exploited to mold a desirable character and to ward off evils that result from unbridled human nature. His emphasis on socialization would be reflected in the later works of philosophers, sociologists, educators, and psychologists. Let us now turn from Machiavelli's social psychology to a Renaissance thinker with a broader range of psychological interests.

Juan Luis Vives

Watson (1915) has argued that the Spanish humanist **Juan Luis Vives (1492–1540)** should be viewed as the true originator of modern psychology. Vives was born in Valencia, Spain, in 1492 when Columbus launched his fateful voyage. That same year, Jews were expelled from several Spanish cities. Although of Jewish ancestry, Vives was given a Christian education, likely due to his mother's conversion to Christianity a year before his birth. Vives attended school in Valencia where he studied Latin grammar, rhetoric, poetry, and the Greek classics. At age seventeen, he left Valencia to continue his studies at the University of Paris.

Tragically, his parents were later victims of the Spanish Inquisition, a tribunal dealing with religious heresy. A Dominican monk named Tomás de Torquemada (1420–1498) served as First Grand Inquisitor. As an unapologetic anti-Semite, his oppressive and cruel tactics guided the Inquisition long after he stepped down. Though records are incomplete, Vives's father was likely burned at the stake. Years after her death, his mother's body was removed from a Christian cemetery and burned. In her posthumous Inquisition trial, witnesses testified seeing her enter a Jewish synagogue after her conversion, casting doubt on her status as a Christian (Norena, 1970, p. 20). So far as we know, Juan Luis Vives never returned to Valencia.

His education at the University of Paris was a disappointment. At the time, secular and religious forces wrestled for control of the university, undermining the institution and the quality of its programs. He completed only the three-year arts course before leaving with few pleasant memories. In 1512, Vives worked in the Netherlands, first as a student and later as a teacher. In 1520, he was granted a license to give public lectures at the University of Louvain. Vives earned a reputation as a sought-after teacher and scholar. The intellectual climate in the Netherlands was a haven of freedom compared with much of Europe. During this period, Vives established a friendship with Desiderius Erasmus (1466–1536), the most respected scholar of his day.

In 1523, Vives moved to England where he received an appointment at Oxford University. He hoped to settle into teaching and scholarly activities, but a thorny political situation with the king of England interfered with his plans. Vives had established a close friendship with Henry VIII and his first wife, a Spanish princess named Catherine of Aragon. After twenty years of marriage, Catherine had given birth to only one child, a daughter named Mary (later known as "Bloody Mary"). Henry needed a son to succeed him as heir to the throne and demanded a divorce.

Vives befriended Sir Thomas More (1478–1535), a respected English scholar who opposed the king's plans for a divorce. More insisted that Henry could not legally become head of the Church of England if he divorced Catherine. The king disagreed and More was executed as a traitor. No such misfortune befell Vives, but he lost the friendship of both Henry and Catherine during their divorce proceedings. Catherine had asked Vives to be one of her advocates. Vives advised that she forego any defense, leaving the queen disappointed and even enraged. In 1528, Vives left England to return to the Netherlands.

His final years were spent in relative seclusion, but were highly productive, resulting in the publication of *De Anima et Vita (On the Soul and Life)* among other works. According to Norena (1970), this book "inaugurated in European thought the study of man based on reflection and observation without any metaphysical scheme" (p. 117). Vives died in 1540, just two years after the publication of *De Anima*.

Most scholars agree that the title of Vives's work *De Anima et Vita* is misleading. Vives had little interest in the nature of the soul per se; rather, his interest was in the operation of the soul. Brett (1912–1921/1965) argued that with Vives "the high *a priori* road is abandoned and the variety of the soul's manifestations begins to take rank above the formal deduction of its powers" (p. 326). Clements (1967) added that sometimes Vives's "writings seem to show brief but almost brilliant flashes of physiological and psychological insights, e.g., his insistence that medication first be tried on rats and guinea pigs, and his casual observations of the conditioned responses of animals" (p. 234). Clements noted, however, that at other times Vives's writings seem unfocused because of his tendency to pursue moral, religious, or poetic tangents. Let us now explore Vives's psychological work.

EMOTIONS   Vives's interest in human emotion was based on empirical studies (Mandler, 2003). He believed there are inherent temperamental differences that influence emotions, but he also emphasized the effects of environmental or social influences. For example, he suggested emotions are influenced by climate, material culture (including our houses and belongings), and our relationships with other people. Vives believed emotional processes may influence the state of the body and the state of the body may influence emotions. For example, he thought that "sadness causes black bile and black bile increases sadness" (Norena, 1970, p. 273). Vives believed we must learn to control emotion because unbridled emotions interfere with perception, judgment, and reason. Clements (1967) stated that Vives was also sensitive to the beneficial consequences of emotion. Even emotions such as pride, so often judged in a negative light, have their origin in the quest for good. Clements claimed that Vives's physiological emphasis and his work on emotions had a substantial impact on Descartes.

MEMORY   Vives's work on association and memory is a neglected chapter in the history of psychology. Zilboorg (1941) pointed out that Vives "cites example after example of associations through similarity, contiguity, and opposites. The first in the history of psychology, he recognizes the emotional origin of certain associations" (p. 192). Vives recalled that as a youth, he had eaten cherries while ill with a fever. Years later, the taste of cherries resulted in such vivid recall of the fever, it was as if he experienced it again (see Zilboorg, 1941). Vives is among those philosophers dating back to Aristotle who stress the roles of association and emotion in cognitive processes.

Vives's work on memory was characterized less by an interest in what memory is than in how it works. Anything that disturbs the spirits of the brain may have an impact on memory. Illness, alcohol, age, and intelligence are but a few of the factors associated with our ability to remember. Vives believed a memory image can be erased, in which case relearning is necessary to reinstate the image. In most cases, memory images are not completely lost but simply weakened. In these cases,

recollection is facilitated when we recover any image strongly associated with the to-be-recalled image.

LEARNING   Vives was a pioneer in pedagogy, education, and educational psychology (Weinstein & Way, 2003). Unique in his time, Vives supported education for women and the poor, despite his culturally typical views about women's inferiority (Ljungqvist, 2012). He believed in secular education and emphasized the importance of individual instruction. Vives's thoughts on education came from his conviction that knowledge and education were necessary to create social reforms.

Vives's significance in the history of psychology should not be underestimated. He influenced a large number of later scholars, including René Descartes, and the British associationists. His book remained popular even a century after his death.

Leonardo da Vinci

The contemporary expression *Renaissance person* describes a versatile individual with proficiency in multiple disciplines. Such polymaths are rare in our age of specialization. The intellectual breadth of **Leonardo da Vinci (1452–1519)**

Leonardo da Vinci

embodied the true ideal of a Renaissance person. Remembered for world-famous paintings such as *The Mona Lisa* and *The Last Supper*, he was also a mechanic, architect, engineer, inventor, and man of science. His extensive notes (see Richter, 1970) testify to Leonardo's originality and to the breadth of his scientific and engineering interests. His notebooks are filled with sketches of flying machines (including an early conception of a helicopter), numerous drawings of physical geography (da Vinci had advised Columbus to navigate the globe), detailed anatomical drawings based on over thirty dissections he had conducted, sketches of irrigation systems and various military weapons, and architectural drawings that included plans for towns, canals, streets, churches, and palaces. In the history of psychology, Leonardo's contributions center on his studies of the senses, especially vision.

Leonardo was born in the vicinity of Vinci, between Florence and Pisa. He was the illegitimate son of Pietro da Vinci, a notary. His father and members of his father's family raised Leonardo. Little is known about his natural mother. He showed early signs of artistic talent and was apprenticed to a well-known Florentine artist, Andrea de Verrocchio. Da Vinci received most of his education from Verrocchio.

In 1483, Leonardo moved to Milan where he enjoyed a sixteen-year period of creative activity. Following his years in Milan, he moved back to Florence for six years. During this period, Cesare Borgia hired da Vinci as an architect and military engineer. Machiavelli was also working for Borgia at this time, and he befriended the artist. Leonardo made military maps and offered suggestions for the military defense of Florence. Although a pacifist, da Vinci designed a host of deadly weapons and machines. He drew up plans for armored tanks, catapults, submarines, rapid-firing crossbows, cannons, and bottles of poison gas. One of his most notorious weapons was a horse-drawn chariot with revolving scythes that could shred enemy soldiers like a field of grain.

Continuing his anatomical studies, Leonardo conducted autopsies at the Hospital of Santa Maria Nuova. Leonardo's six-year stay in Florence was followed by a second Milan period from 1506 to 1513. He then moved to Rome for three years where he painted *The Mona Lisa*. Da Vinci's last years were spent in France where he enjoyed status as a recognized artist in the court of Francis I. Leonardo worked with enthusiasm and energy until his death on May 2, 1519.

For all of his accomplishments, da Vinci did not leave the world with a major published book. His extensive notes were subsequently published, although many of his notebooks are missing. Despite his vast achievements, he suffered countless failures. He started artistic and engineering projects that were never finished because of the slow pace of his work and his tendency to deviate from initial plans. Leonardo the artist was undoubtedly compromised by Leonardo the scientist and vice versa. He regretted the encroachment of one interest on another, but with his characteristic breadth of appetite, seemed helpless to do anything about it. Let us turn now to da Vinci's psychological contributions.

For Leonardo, vision was sovereign among all the senses. The eye was the premier instrument of human knowledge. He struggled with the ancient notion that "vision is power" or that the eye emits rays, but rejected this in favor of the idea that the eye is simply responsive to light energy. Although apparently unsatisfied with his own accounts of the processing of images (Wade, 2005), Leonardo believed that images are inverted prior to reaching the lens and reinverted by the lens so they are right side up on the retina (we now know he was wrong and that images on the retina are inverted). He made many anatomical drawings of the visual system (see Calder, 1970), including cross sections of the human eye and illustrations of the optic chiasma. Da Vinci was interested in comparative vision and dissected the eyes of animals including a lion, dogs, and an owl in an attempt to understand their visual capacities.

Boring (1942) pointed out that Leonardo da Vinci made many contributions to our understanding of visual perception. As an example, Leonardo illustrated contrast effects by showing that white can appear whiter when contrasted with a darker color. Interestingly, Leonardo also argued that "beauty and ugliness seem more effective through one another" (Zubov, 1968, p. 137). Boring (1942) stated that Leonardo also contributed to our understanding of *aerial perspective*, the effects of atmosphere on distance perception (p. 266). Leonardo understood that colors fade with distance. He also noted that objects lose clarity with distance. There are disputes (see Boring, 1942) about whether da Vinci understood the possible role of retinal disparity in space perception. He wrote many rules for painters pertaining to contrast effects and aerial perspective, but although he was interested in the practical applications of his rules, his interests were more scientific. He was interested in perception in its own right as a guide to understanding nature.

Leonardo also wrote about the other senses and had a strong interest in human emotional expression. In his work *Leonardo da Vinci and a Memory of His Childhood,* Sigmund Freud (1910/1957b) pointed out that Leonardo sometimes accompanied "condemned criminals on their way to execution in order to study their features distorted by fear and to sketch them in his notebook" (p. 69). Leonardo often infused emotional and moral characteristics into his medical illustrations (Lorusso, 2008).

Some of da Vinci's other psychological interests are represented in scattered maxims. For example, he pointed out that "the part always has a tendency to reunite with its whole in order to escape from its imperfection" (Richter, 1970, vol. 2, p. 238). He emphasized the unity of body and spirit by pointing out that "the spirit desires to remain with its body, because, without the organic instruments of that body, it can neither act nor feel anything" (p. 238).

In many respects, Leonardo was an important forerunner of Francis Bacon and René Descartes. Long after da Vinci, both philosophers struggled with the problem of human knowledge and the nature of the scientific method. In a set of maxims, Leonardo outlined a method closer to Bacon's later ideas than to those advocated by Descartes. Leonardo argued that we should first consult experience and then reason. He believed that reason and judgment are more likely to err than experience. More in line with Cartesian thought, he argued that there can be no certainty without mathematics. He also maintained that practice without science is like a sailor without a compass (see Richter, 1970, vol. 2, pp. 239–241).

Leonardo da Vinci was an artist and a man of science. In both capacities, his interests turned to matters that would fascinate later psychologists. His influence in psychology may not have been extensive, because many of his contributions were discovered long after his death in unpublished notes. He does, however, illustrate important psychological discoveries during the Renaissance.

Paracelsus

One of the most enigmatic figures of the Renaissance was the physician–alchemist–astrologer–scientist Philippus Aureolus Theophrastus Bombastus von Hohenheim, who mercifully went by the nickname **Paracelsus (1493–1541)**. Paracelsus was born in Switzerland and it appears he studied at several European universities before completing a doctorate in medicine. He argued against demonology but accepted the possibility that stars influence personality. On psychological matters, he believed that mental processes impact the health of the body and vice versa. He taught that harmony with nature is the key to human happiness. Thus, "if nature takes its proper course, we are happy [but] if nature follows the wrong course we are unhappy" (Jacobi, 1958, p. 203). Paracelsus believed in the role of external physical forces in human health. This part of his theory, and his astrology, had an impact later on Franz Anton Mesmer.

Paracelsus is also known for his radical or even fanatic comments on epistemology. He presented the strongest polemics against the ancients and appealed for a new science based on experience rather than the rational schemes of antiquity. The term *bombastic* is possibly derived from Paracelsus's name Bombastus. If so, the term characterizes his style as he denounced older authorities in a near rage. On one occasion, he publicly burned the books of Avicenna. As Ronan (1982) pointed out, Paracelsus insisted "that knowledge comes not from books in the old scholastic sense but from a study of nature" (p. 310).

His major contribution may have resided in his agitation for mastery over nature. Such mastery was achieved through wisdom based on observation. Rogers (1912) stated, "Paracelsus is the type of a host of men who sprang up all over Europe—men of enthusiasm for nature, and to some extent of original and high ideal, but men whose undisciplined imaginations led them beyond the bounds of sober thinking" (p. 231). People such as Paracelsus represent an important bridge from medieval scholasticism to modern science.

Michel de Montaigne

We mentioned earlier that many Renaissance scholars placed an emphasis on human beings in this world rather than on God and the afterlife. This new emphasis defined the writings of the French skeptic **Michel Eyquem de Montaigne** *(mahn TAYN)* **(1533–1592)**. According to Bloom (1987), "Montaigne, until the advent of Shakespeare, is the great figure of the European Renaissance, comparable in cognitive power

Michel de Montaigne

and in influence to Freud in our century" (p. 1). Groethuysen (1963) pointed out that he attempted to "comprehend life in its own immediate terms without recourse to religious or metaphysical postulates" (p. 634). Many of the world's scholars, including Shakespeare, Burton, Byron, Emerson, and Aldous Huxley, have expressed their debt to Montaigne.

He was born near Bordeaux in the southwest region of France. Montaigne received his formal education at the Collège du Guyenne and then at the University of Toulouse. He practiced law in Bordeaux, but decided to retire from public life in 1571. After his retirement, he began work that would secure for him a place in intellectual history. Montaigne expressed his views in the form of *Essais (Essays)*, a new literary form of his invention. His essays are masterful introspective studies, each projecting a spontaneous and informed opinion on a variety of topics. As we'll see, many probe the depths of psychology and philosophy.

MONTAIGNE'S SKEPTICISM Montaigne's most important philosophical essay was titled "Apology for Raimond Sebond." This essay resurrected earlier Greek and Roman skepticism about the possibility of attaining genuine knowledge. The "Apology" was motivated in part by Montaigne's attempts to work through his own bitterness over the religious wars between Protestants and Catholics. In the summer of 1572, tens of thousands of French Protestants or Huguenots were slaughtered, and Huguenot homes and shops were pillaged during the St. Bartholomew's Day Massacre. Like other religious atrocities of the time, the massacre fed increasing bitterness and hatred between Catholics and Protestants. The intense rivalry troubled Montaigne. Although Catholic, he was friendly to some Protestant ideas and maintained a keen intellectual interest in all religions. His moderate theology aroused suspicion on both sides.

The "Apology" was also motivated by attacks on Raimond Sebond's *Theologia Naturalis (Natural Theology)*, a work that Montaigne had earlier translated from Latin. Sebond, like many theologians of the time, argued that reason can be used in support of the Christian faith. His work, however, was subject to criticism and arguments that his reasoning was unsound. Montaigne, who grounded his religion in faith alone, disagreed with Sebond's contention about reason in support of faith. Nevertheless, he believed Sebond's arguments were as good as those of his critics. Frame (1960, vol. 2, p. 113) noted that the "Apology" is misnamed. Montaigne used "Apology" from the Greek to mean "defense." He did not apologize for Sebond's mistakes. Instead, he wrote a limited defense of Sebond, arguing his errors are no greater than the errors of his critics. The "Apology" itself turns into a trenchant attack on the arrogance of human beings who claim knowledge even when such knowledge is supposedly based on experience or reason.

Montaigne was fearful of those who believed their faith was buttressed by reason. He found too many people who, out of religious zeal, are willing to march in armies. He lamented that "there is no hostility that excels Christian hostility" and contended that "our religion was made to extirpate vices; [but] it covers them, fosters them, incites them" (Apology, p. 120). Montaigne believed virtue is the real product of truth. Given his beliefs, we may view the "Apology" as an attack both on the arrogance of reason and on the impotence of reason.

Montaigne opened his attack by pointing to presumption as the original human malady. Humans are arrogant and filled with unjustified vanity. He devoted over thirty pages to anecdotes and demonstrations showing that animal virtue and intelligence are superior to such qualities in humans. He concluded we have no grounds to believe we are superior to animals. According to Montaigne, humans are, in many respects, not as good or as knowledgeable as animals. Following his comparison of humans with animals, Montaigne moved to arguments relevant to his skeptical thesis.

After examining the ideas of countless thinkers, Montaigne listed the most blatant contradictions in the work of over two dozen famous scholars and philosophers. Next, he mentioned contradictions in philosophies of government, the variability of customs, and the defects of language that render it difficult to convey clearly a single thought

to another person. Indeed, Montaigne argued that most of the troubles of the world are grammatical; lawsuits, wars, and interpersonal difficulties stem from doubts about meanings. Montaigne pointed out that it is with the "mad arrogance of speech [that humans seek] to bring God down to their measure" (Apology, p. 217), and asked the reader to consider the sheer nonsense of early religious beliefs and practices. Montaigne quoted, with approval, St. Paul's contention that those who profess to be wise become fools (Romans 1:22).

Montaigne outlined the effects of emotions and motives on beliefs. Pay a lawyer a bit more, he contended, and that lawyer will find new interest in your case, declaring it more believable. Ministers who preach with emotion become more convinced of their doctrines. A proposition defended in anger may thereby be made more memorable and convincing. Montaigne found that the cognitive-rational apparatus is weakened by wishful thinking.

He declared that change overtakes even science. Truth in one era will find a replacement in another. How can we be sure what is now taken for scientific truth will not be replaced tomorrow? Montaigne attacked claims about the accuracy of sensory information: There may be realities for which we have no sense; we are subject to illusions and do not always recognize them as such; bodily conditions and emotions bias sensory information; and our upbringing affects our opinions. We are always changing and that metamorphosis governs the way we see our world.

Montaigne embraced a kind of epistemological humility—the ability to admit that in matters of knowledge we are all beggars. In her biography of Montaigne, Bakewell (2010) notes that the qualities he embraced included curiosity, the capacity to entertain a variety of perspectives, and adaptability. The arrogance of certitude was, for Montaigne, the underpinning of violence, terrorism, war, unjustified feelings of religious and political superiority, and ignorance.

Montaigne's attack on human knowledge was influential. Popkin (1967) characterized the "Apology" as a pivotal essay that structured seventeenth-century thought by serving as a foil for the work of René Descartes and Francis Bacon. Indeed, according to Durant and Durant (1961), Montaigne's "influence pervaded three centuries and four continents" (p. 413). Winter (1976) observed that the essays were especially well received "in Holland and in England, where at the time a less restrictive political and religious climate prevailed" (p. 106). Popkin (1967) pointed out that Montaigne "succeeded in intensifying the doubts already produced by the religious crisis of the Reformation, the humanistic crisis of the Renaissance, and the philosophical–scientific crisis of revived Pyrrhonism. . . . Bacon, Herbert of Cherbury, and Descartes were to seek new philosophical systems to provide for human knowledge a basis impervious to Montaigne's doubts" (p. 368).

MONTAIGNE'S PSYCHOLOGY Aside from skepticism, Montaigne explored psychological topics such as thought, emotion, motivation, and conflict. His essays use a fresh introspective analysis that is remarkable in contrast with St. Augustine's introspective technique. Augustine's introspections took the reader to the innermost parts of the troubled soul. By contrast, Montaigne's lighter approach, though introspective, was not morbidly introverted. The reader does not just observe, but actively participates with him in the psychological analysis of topics such as anger, fear, happiness, and folly. Though Montaigne did not pretend to develop a coherent psychology, he did consider topics of psychological interest. We will briefly examine Montaigne's views on child rearing and education, the impossibility of pure experience, and the inconsistency of human action.

CHILD REARING AND EDUCATION In Montaigne's time, children were often disciplined in a violent manner (DeMause, 1974). He lamented cruel child-rearing practices and questioned why the courts ignored the physical abuse of children. He believed many parents use brutal punishment not for correction, but for revenge. He also condemned the schools of his day for their strict discipline. Such schools, he argued, were like prisons where wrathful teachers tortured the inmates. Montaigne believed children should find pleasure in learning. Punishment, by contrast, turned children into dullards. He believed the cruelty begins with parents who laugh when their child torments a pet or bullies a peer. After surveying seventy children living prior to the eighteenth century, DeMause (1974) concluded that "all were beaten except one: Montaigne's daughter" (p. 40).

EXPERIENCE IS NEVER PURE Several of Montaigne's essays raise an issue of concern for many early psychologists. The issue is whether there are pure experiences of simple or elementary things, or whether experience is always composed of a mixture of elementary things. For example, is there a pure feeling of joy or is there a pure sense of sweetness? Are there elements in our experience that are not mixed with other elements or that present themselves in an undiluted form? Montaigne's answer, based on his self-observations, is an unqualified "no."

In his essay "We Taste Nothing Pure," he compared human experience to metals such as gold that serve best when they are debased or combined with other materials. Similarly, Montaigne declared that on close examination, experiences always reveal an admixture of a combination. Thus, "our utmost sensual pleasure has an air of groaning and lament about it" (see Frame, 1960, vol. 2, p. 381). Indeed, we are so constituted, according to Montaigne, that we cannot endure intense or sustained pleasure; we escape to more neutral, safe ground. He quoted, with approval, Socrates's contention that some god must have become confused during the creation of pain and pleasure, and, after botching the job, tied the two together by the tail. As we cannot sustain intense pleasure, pain also has its accompanying satisfactions. Over three hundred years later, Sigmund Freud pointed to the tensions and confusions between pleasure and pain. Both men would have been keenly interested in late-twentieth-century research demonstrating the release of endorphins (opiatelike neurotransmitters) that apparently stimulate feelings of well-being or even pleasure following hard work or painful experiences.

The thoroughness with which Montaigne rejected pure experience is illustrated by his confession that his "best goodness. . .has some tincture of vice" (Frame, 1960, vol. 2, p. 383). Throughout his essays, we find evidence of Montaigne's suspicion that a manifest behavior or experience serves as a cover for its opposite counterpart. He was close to an awareness of what would later be called a *reaction formation*. Though such awareness was evident in this writings, Montaigne did not bring himself to the analysis of the human psyche that Freud would later undertake.

INCONSISTENCIES OF HUMAN ACTIONS As a close observer of human behavior, Montaigne found that consistency of actions within individuals is rare, whereas inconsistency is almost a rule of action. Few of us demonstrate stability of conduct or opinion and that irresolution is "the most common and apparent defect of our nature" (Frame, 1960, vol. 2, p. 1). Montaigne finds several reasons for human inconsistency; the first is the result of the variations and vicissitudes of appetite. We follow our appetites, but our appetites constantly change.

Changes in situation or circumstance bring about inconsistency. Montaigne observed that an individual may be bold and adventurous in one context, but fearful or cowardly in another. Context and circumstance play powerful roles in courage, fear, valor, and other human virtues and vices. His emphasis on circumstance and context would be verified by later social psychological experiments.

Though Montaigne saw conduct as a product of circumstance, he also argued our inconsistencies result from different roles we play and different masks we wear. Montaigne's work on inconsistency went beyond earlier work in that he identified some of the sources (e.g., variability of appetite, context, role-playing, influence of authority) that contribute to the problem. Growth toward consistency and integrity was, in his view, one of the greatest challenges confronting human beings. He believed that most of us are unable to bridle appetite, or resist flattery, or avoid prostituting ourselves in the marketplace to whatever advantages might be offered. Montaigne valued the integrity associated with self-directedness.

Montaigne introduced important psychological insights in the late Renaissance period. However, his major contributions consisted of his attitudes about people and life and his recognition of the individual as part of the growing humanism that characterized the Renaissance (Jansz, 2004). As we noted, his skepticism stimulated other scholars to give serious consideration to the problem of human knowledge. His ability to describe behavior and experience opened the door to more naturalistic studies of human beings. For that reason, he is a key figure in the history of the cognitive and behavioral sciences.

Bakewell (2010) captures a central feature in Montaigne's pragmatic psychology—he teaches us how to live! It's okay to be imperfect, reflect on a wider range of phenomena and question everything, be temperate and humble, live in the moment, read voraciously, avoid being a control freak, and work to overcome the blindness and the sleep of habit and traditionalism. Montaigne would also counsel us to question authority and to live appreciatively and critically in the stream of experience.

Oliva Sabuco

Work attributed to **Oliva Sabuco** *(SUH bu ko)* **de Nantes Barrera (1562–1590)** has been the subject of a long-standing and difficult historiographical problem. An influential book dedicated to Phillip II titled *New Philosophy on the Nature of Man* was first published in 1587 in Madrid under her authorship. Shortly after the original publication, Oliva's father Miguel Sabuco issued a legal statement claiming that he was the sole author of the work, and that he had allowed the book to be published under his daughter's name as a way of honoring her. Miguel's subsequent attempts to gain recognition as author, including an attempt to publish an edition of the book in Portugal, met with no success. In fact, the book went through four editions, including one that was edited extensively (with deletions and interpretive commentary) by the Spanish Inquisition. All editions were published under the authorship of Oliva Sabuco.

The question of authorship is still subject to debate, and there are scholars who believe Miguel Sabuco is the author (see Norena, 1975). There are, however, compelling reasons to believe the book was indeed authored by Oliva Sabuco (see Waithe, 1989). In the context of the times, with existing gender inequalities, it seems unlikely the legitimate claims of a man would have been ignored.

Little is known about the personal lives or the educational backgrounds of Miguel or Oliva Sabuco. Most of Oliva's education may have been of an informal nature. She was apparently one of the eight children of Miguel Sabuco and Francisca de Cozar. Oliva was married when she was eighteen, and *New Philosophy on the Nature of Man* was published when she was twenty-five.

Oliva Sabuco was one of the first to write on the subject of the passions and their effects. She had a deep sensitivity to the physical and psychological consequences of emotions such as anger, fear, jealousy, hatred, and depression. She pointed out that such emotions, unchecked, lead to physical and emotional imbalance and even death. She also addressed the salutary consequences of love, hope, happiness, and moderation. Sabuco understood the wisdom of avoiding emotional extremes and the importance of environmental context as a means of maintaining balance and harmony. She believed extremes in sounds, colors, tastes, and odors contribute to illness, whereas moderate and harmonious surroundings promote health.

Oliva Sabuco understood the close connection between physiology and psychology. According to Waithe (1989), Sabuco also viewed "human nature as a microcosm of nature itself" (p. 268). It follows that psychology must be based on a broad epistemological foundation. Sabuco stressed introspection as a way of knowing, but also emphasized close observation of the physical causes of psychological states. She underscored the importance of intellectual processes and the imagination, but she placed equal, if not greater, emphasis on the central role of emotions in human life. Above all, she emphasized the wisdom of moderation in all things and a broad-based approach to knowledge.

Juan Huarte

A significant breakthrough in late Renaissance psychology came from the pen of **Juan Huarte (c. 1530–c. 1592)**, a contemporary of Montaigne. Huarte (*WAHR tae*) can properly be regarded as a pioneer in the study of aptitude, temperament, and individual differences. His book *Examen de Ingenios para las Sciencias* (*The Examination of Men's Wits*) (1594/1959) stands as a classic in differential psychology as well as educational psychology, neuropsychology, and psychiatry (Virués-Ortega et al., 2011).

Like others in this chapter, little is known of Huarte's personal life. He was apparently born in San Juan de Pie del Puerto in Navarre, but spent most of his life in Baeza, Spain. He earned a medical degree at the University of Alcala and enjoyed a successful practice. Throughout his medical career, he was interested in psychological topics set forth in the *Examen*. The book was translated into many languages and went through dozens of printings. Some printings were placed on local indexes of forbidden books during the Inquisition because they offended religious authorities. An example, as noted by Rogers (1959), was Huarte's contention that poetic skill has a natural rather than a divine origin.

In the *Examen*, Huarte states that some children are capable of one kind of knowledge or aptitude but not another. Given such differences, he argues that we should study children at an early age to discover the nature of their abilities and to determine what studies fit their natural capacities. Huarte was sensitive to the importance of introducing subjects at appropriate developmental levels. For example, language (which Juarte viewed largely as a memory task) may be introduced early because small children have excellent memories. Logic requires the development of understanding and should be introduced later in the curriculum.

Huarte believed that humoral temperaments influence individual differences. Heat, cold, moistness, and dryness were thought to produce all individual differences. Humoral temperaments were used to account for differences in age, ethnicity, and intellect. For example, Huarte used his theory to tackle age differences in memory and understanding. Memory was dependent on moistness and understanding was dependent on dryness. He believed the brain of an old person is dry and filled with understanding, but such a brain is poor when it comes to memory. By contrast, children whose brains are endowed with moisture have excellent memory, but poor understanding. Huarte insisted that for all of us, memory is superior in the morning because moisture accrues during sleep. Through the day, the brain dries and hardens. As a result, memory becomes less facile.

Diamond (1974b) pointed out that Huarte emphasized "somatic determinants of behavior" that have their origin in the brain (p. 368). Although Huarte quoted Galen, Aristotle, and Hippocrates, he had the courage to refute them. His final product represented a curious blend of Greek philosophy with emphasis on the natural determinants of behavior and Christian theology that emphasized miraculous enlightenment. Huarte's orientation toward natural determinants of behavior marks him as an important pioneer of differential psychology.

Huarte, as a product of the sixteenth century, perpetuated prevailing views on gender differences. He counseled that women are not to be blamed for their dullness, for they can do nothing about the coldness and moistness that characterize their gender. Huarte's efforts to understand individual differences, coupled with his paternalistic biases, underscore the importance of raising gender-differentiated questions as one reads history.

Conclusion

Huarte's views on women and men were consistent with the contention of Kelly-Gadol (1977) that there was no Renaissance for women. If anything, their social status declined during the three hundred years that are so often viewed as a period of intellectual rebirth. We thus come back to the question about whether the period deserves the extravagant title of *Renaissance*. The reasoned response must surely be "yes and no." There was a Renaissance in some areas, but in others, human beings remained in darkness.

On the positive side, the Renaissance ushered in new geographic and technical advancements that contributed to an expansion of intellectual boundaries. The era witnessed a rediscovery of Greek classics and a strong rebellion against existing authority. Such rebellion may have reinforced the growth of empirical studies and a new confidence in individual judgment. The resurrection of Greek skepticism, particularly as set forth in Montaigne's widely distributed essay "Apology for Raimond Sebond," stimulated interest in the problem of human knowledge. Pioneers in both empirical (e.g., Francis Bacon) and rational (e.g., René Descartes) traditions created a basis for knowledge that challenged the criticisms of the skeptic. In an indirect way, Renaissance skepticism contributed to the epistemological foundations of contemporary science.

The Renaissance produced noteworthy contributions to psychological thought, though such thought occurred as a few isolated islands in a sea of ignorance. As we move to the modern period (from 1600), we will discover more clearly discernible threads of thought marked by ideas building on each other. Such threads of thought will be evident in the chapters that follow on empiricism, rationalism, and the growth of the mechanistic perspective. Returning to the discussion on patterns in history in Chapter 1, history may indeed be sometimes chaotic and sometimes linear.

Review Questions

1. Describe five general characteristics of the Renaissance period.
2. How did the plague contribute to the changing climate of opinion in the Renaissance?
3. Contrast geocentric and heliocentric worldviews and their implications for a science of human nature.
4. Discuss Machiavelli's importance to the history of the social and behavioral sciences.
5. Outline at least three of Vives's contributions to psychological thought.
6. Discuss Leonardo da Vinci's contributions to perception. What are some specific ways in which Leonardo contributed to the growth of empirical studies?
7. In what way does the thought of Paracelsus serve as a bridge from scholasticism to modern science?

8. Outline some of Montaigne's skeptical arguments. Why was Montaigne's skepticism important to the development of modern science?
9. Briefly describe Montaigne's position on child rearing.
10. In what way does Juan Huarte serve as an important pioneer in the study of individual differences?

Glossary

Copernicus, Nicolaus (1473–1543)   Polish astronomer, physician, and minister remembered as the founder of a scientific revolution marked by the belief that the sun, rather than the earth, is the center of the solar system.

cosmology   The study of theories of the nature of the universe including the relation of earth to the rest of the solar system.

da Vinci, Leonardo (1452–1519)   Broad-ranging Renaissance scholar who was an artistic genius, engineer, sculptor, and architect. He is also remembered for his careful studies of human anatomy and his artistic skill in capturing human emotions.

Galilei, Galileo (1564–1642)   Italian astronomer and physicist remembered for improving the telescope and using it systematically in the observation of the solar system.

geocentric   Literally, *earth centered*. Generally refers to the ancient view of Ptolemy that the earth is the center of the solar system.

heliocentric   Literally, *sun centered*. Typically refers to the work of Nicolaus Copernicus who taught that the sun is the center of the solar system.

Huarte, Juan (c. 1530–c. 1592)   One of the first to write on the subjects of individual differences, aptitude, and temperament.

Index of Forbidden Books   Generally refers to books forbidden by the Catholic church because they were regarded as dangerous to faith and morality. Though censorship was practiced from the early days of the church, the *Index* started in the sixteenth century and continued until 1966.

indulgence   Refers to various means of raising money practiced by the Catholic church prior to the Reformation. Generally involved payment of money in exchange for a spiritual favor.

Kepler, Johannes (1571–1630)   German astronomer and mathematician who discovered the elliptical or oval-shaped motions of the planets.

Luther, Martin (1483–1546)   The founder of the Reformation and leader of the Protestant movement. Arguably, Luther contributed to the growth of the empirical spirit by advancing the doctrine of the individual priesthood of the believer, in which people have the right to read and interpret scriptures for themselves.

Machiavellianism   Refers to the application of the principles set forth by Niccolò Machiavelli. Sometimes implies amoral, manipulative attitudes, but, strictly speaking, such an implication is a corruption of the teachings of Machiavelli.

Machiavelli, Niccolò (1469–1527)   Founder of modern political science and modern military science. One of the first to emphasize the importance of socialization and the techniques for molding public opinion. He advocated the utility of a descriptive social science.

Montaigne, Michel de (1533–1592)   Late Renaissance scholar who launched a powerful and influential attack on human knowledge. His skepticism was to have a strong influence on Francis Bacon and René Descartes. Montaigne also speculated on a number of psychological topics such as how to rear children, education, motivation, and emotion.

Paracelsus (1493–1541)   Radical Renaissance epistemologist who argued that observational studies should replace old scholastic techniques and blind allegiance to authority.

Petrarch, Francesco (1304–1374)   Italian poet, scholar, and moralist who was a founder of Renaissance humanism.

Ptolemy (c. 100–c. 165)   Egyptian astronomer, geographer, and mathematician known for an early geocentric cosmology that was widely accepted for over 1,400 years.

Reformation   A sixteenth-century religious movement founded by Martin Luther and motivated by an attempt to reform the Catholic church. Luther's failure to bring about the changes he desired ultimately led to a major split in the church and the beginnings of Protestantism.

Renaissance   Literally, *rebirth*. That period in history from approximately 1300 to 1600 marked by the rediscovery of Greek classics, a new interest in mathematics, expanding geographic knowledge, and a wider epistemology.

Renaissance humanism   Refers to a new interest in human affairs. It was manifested in art as the subject shifted from theological figures to human figures and in music as the subject shifted from the sacred to the secular. In science, there was a new interest in physiological and anatomical studies and a general new focus on topics of human concern.

Sabuco, Oliva (1562–1590)   Late Renaissance writer who emphasized the wisdom of moderation. Sabuco was among the first to understand the role of emotions in physical and psychological health.

Vesalius, Andreas (1514–1564)   Physician and anatomist known for his empirical approach to anatomy based on actual dissections. He revolutionized the study of the human body much as Renaissance explorers such as Columbus and Magellan revolutionized knowledge of geography.

Vives, Juan Luis (1492–1540)   Spanish humanist who advocated an empirical approach to psychology. His book *De Anima et Vita* is a rich source of Renaissance thought on psychological topics.

Modern Intellectual Developments That Contributed to the Birth of Psychology

Chapters 6 through 9 will explore specific developments in the modern period (from 1600) that contributed to the birth of psychology as a science and a profession. Each development created a social and intellectual context that nurtured and promoted the need for a scientific psychology. As you proceed through the following chapters, try to identify ideas and issues that captured the imaginations of scientists and philosophers, resulting in the later subject matter of psychology. We will cover developments in empiricism, rationalism, advances in neurology and physiology, evolution, the discovery of new measurement techniques, and humanitarian reforms.

Timeline

1600 to 1879

1609	Invention of telescope in Holland
c. 1610	Emergence of work of Galileo, Bacon, Descartes—scientific revolution
1620	*Mayflower* lands in New England
	Novum Organum by Francis Bacon
1632	*Dialogue on the Two Chief Systems* by Galileo
1633	Galileo condemned in Inquisition
1636	Founding of Harvard College
1642	Death of Galileo
1651	*Leviathan* by Thomas Hobbes
1662	Royal Society founded in London
1664	*Treatise on Man* by René Descartes
1690	*An Essay Concerning Human Understanding* by John Locke
1701	Founding of Yale University
1705	*Observations on Man* by David Hartley
1709	*Essays on the Mind* by Claude-Adrien Helvétius (emphasizes sensation in mental life)
1710	*An Essay Towards a New Theory of Vision* by George Berkeley
1739	*A Treatise of Human Nature* by David Hume (links experimental method to psychology)
1752	Benjamin Franklin conducts his "kite experiment"
1775	Beginning of American Revolution
1776	Declaration of Independence signed in the United States
1781	*Critique of Pure Reason* by Immanuel Kant
1784	Mesmerism condemned
1789	Beginning of French Revolution
1792	*A Vindication of the Rights of Woman* by Mary Wollstonecraft
1796	Edward Jenner develops smallpox vaccine
1798	*Essay on the Principle of Population* by Thomas Malthus
1806	*A Treatise on Insanity* by Philippe Pinel
1809	Charles Darwin and Abraham Lincoln are born on February 12
	Diseases of the Mind by Benjamin Rush
1821	Catholic Church lifts its ban on teaching Copernican physics
1830	Lyell begins his work on geological evolution
1841	Beginning of Dorothea Dix's humanitarian reform movement
1842	Birth of William James

1843	After testimony from psychological experts, Daniel M'Naughton is found not guilty by reason of insanity
1845	Founding of the journal *Scientific American*
1856	Birth of Sigmund Freud
1859	*Origin of Species* by Charles Darwin
1860	*Elements of Psychophysics* by Gustav Fechner
1861	Beginning of American Civil War
1863	Founding of the National Academy of the Sciences in the United States
1874	Franz Brentano's *Psychology from an Empirical Standpoint*
1875	William James offers first American psychology course at Harvard University
1879	Wundt founds psychology laboratory at Leipzig, Germany

6

■ ■ ■

Empiricism, Associationism, and Utilitarianism

I admit nothing but on the faith of eyes.

—Francis Bacon (in Anderson, 1960, p. 26)

In this chapter, we will begin with the empirical-inductive philosophy of Francis Bacon and conclude with the radical empiricism of David Hume. We will then examine associationism and utilitarianism, two intellectual traditions inspired by empiricism. In Chapter 7, we will explore rationalism, beginning with Descartes and ending with Immanuel Kant. We will then examine commonsense philosophies that are close intellectual relatives of rationalism. We will find that both empirical and rational traditions made unique and clearly identifiable contributions to psychology's development.

EMPIRICISM

The English term *experience* is roughly equivalent to the term **empiricism**, which was derived from the Greek *empeirikos* and its Latin equivalent *empiricus*. Empirical philosophy elevates the roles of observation and experience in human knowledge. Empiricists also reject the idea that the mind at birth is already furnished with knowledge. Modern empiricism, beginning with Francis Bacon, was conceived partly as a promising method for the new inductive sciences and partly as an alternative to the traditions and authorities of the past.

Francis Bacon

Few figures in intellectual history have evoked as much controversy among scholars as **Francis Bacon (1561–1626)**. Mathews (1996) has provided a historical overview of the disagreements over Bacon's contributions. On the appreciative side, Bacon has been regarded as the "Great Herald of the Empirical Spirit," the first to emphasize the methodological unity of the sciences, the first to advocate social support for scientific education, and the first to appreciate the human benefits derived from scientific discovery. Philosophers and scientists such as Charles Darwin, René Descartes, John Locke, and Sir Isaac Newton have acknowledged their intellectual debt to Bacon. And despite vast philosophical differences, Immanuel Kant dedicated his book *Critique of Pure Reason* to Francis Bacon.

Bacon has also been the subject of criticism. For example, he was not a scientist and had little appreciation for the mathematical foundations of science. He also failed to appreciate or acknowledge major scientific breakthroughs of his day, such as John Napier's logarithms or William Harvey's work on blood circulation. Bacon failed to accept Copernican theory and Galileo's contributions. At the same time, Bacon's emphasis on induction charted an intellectual path for the development of science. He clearly stands at the crossroads between Renaissance ideas and emerging modern notions of inductive science (MacDonald, 2007).

Francis Bacon was born on January 22, 1561, in London. Following two years of study at Cambridge University, Bacon worked in Paris

Francis Bacon

on the staff of Sir Amias Paulet, ambassador to France. By 1582, Bacon was back in England practicing law with a firm in London. In 1584, he was elected to Parliament. Bacon's best-known work, *Novum Organum*, meaning "new instrument of the mind," was published in 1620. The triumph of *Novum Organum* was followed, however, by a major reversal. Bacon was convicted of participating in bribery and was forced to resign his office, pay a heavy fine, and serve a brief prison sentence. At age sixty, Bacon turned his attention from legal and legislative matters to science and philosophy. In his remaining years, he published three major works, including *History of the Winds* (1622), *History of Life and Death* (1623), and a Latin translation of his earlier book *The Advancement of Learning*, first published in 1605. At age sixty-five, Bacon was conducting research on the preservation of flesh while stuffing a chicken with snow. He caught a chill that brought on pneumonia. Bacon never recovered. He died on April 9, 1626.

During his life, Bacon dedicated himself to the problem of human knowledge. He was dismayed that centuries of intellectual activity had produced such a paucity of useful knowledge. The problem, according to Bacon, was that prevailing methods of inquiry were flawed. Authority held the human intellect in bondage and the scholastic and philosophical traditions were insufficiently wedded to experience. Bacon even joined ranks with the skeptics in calling attention to sources of error that fostered ignorance. At the same time, Bacon believed the skeptics overextended their claims. He believed that if we use proper methods, there is room for optimism regarding human knowledge.

Bacon is often remembered for his list of **Idols**, or phantoms of the human mind. The Idols are common sources of error that lead us astray in our quest for knowledge. Some Idols reflect weaknesses in the human intellect, whereas others illustrate the unfortunate consequences of social forces. On this latter topic, Bacon recognized that a supportive social and economic structure is required for science to flourish. But let us now turn to an examination of the Idols.

Bacon used the term **Idols of the Tribe** to refer to limitations or impediments to knowledge based on weaknesses in human nature. For example, sensory processes may distort external objects when their images are transported to the brain. What exists in nature may not make its way to our brain without some distortion. Another Idol of the Tribe is illustrated by intellectual inertia, which manifests itself when human beings are satisfied with limited information. This is seen when we impose more simplicity than exists in nature. We are prone to error when we lump too much information into a single category. Bacon believed people are too quick to embrace the "all" and too lazy to respond to the "each."

A second type of error, called the **Idols of the Cave**, include prejudices along with preferred theories and explanations that may blind us to alternative interpretations. Bacon believed that data should be the investigator's first concern. Individuals should be more interested in truth and less interested in confirming a favored hypothesis or theory. Bacon argued that generalizations should be developed only after much data collection. We should be flexible in our investigations and consider alternative interpretations of data.

The **Idols of the Marketplace** include the so-called nominal fallacy: the temptation to take words too seriously or to believe that the mere naming of a thing explains it. Too often, the common usage of terms and definitions misleads us. Bacon would approve the constant reexamination of definitions and classification systems. He recommended vigilance to how we use words and how we allow ourselves to be used by words.

Bacon called the final set of errors the **Idols of the Theatre**. He was referring to "the mischievous authorities of systems, which are founded either on common notions, or on a few experiments, or on superstition" (1620/1960, p. 63). Bacon cautioned against the easy acceptance of faddish systems or paradigms. He cared little whether such paradigms had rational or empirical basis (pp. 60–61) or whether "superstition and an admixture of theology" had corrupted them (p. 62). Bacon's Idols of the Theatre challenged the individual to avoid the easy acceptance of authority.

Bacon (1620/1960) found it understandable that in the quest for knowledge the human mind at "first distrusts and then despises itself" (p. 103). There are, however, many grounds for hope and for transcending the despair and skepticism that can hinder our quest for knowledge. He was an optimist despite the forces that work against human knowledge, the lack of progress, and the inadequacy of past methods. He envisioned a positive science that would benefit human life. Bacon realized that his work was outside the mainstream of such a science; he was a prophet who had a vision of the possibilities of science.

Bacon believed that skepticism was flawed, leading the skeptic to commit the same intellectual errors as others. For example, skeptics often demonstrated how sensory illusions deceive our perceptions. Bacon granted that illusions exist, but the careful selection of materials makes possible the illusions. However, illusions do not justify an attack on *all* sensory information. Bacon was correct in pointing out that skeptics were guilty of overgeneralization. In fact, his defense of sensory information represented little more than a commonsense faith in the validity of sensory data. Bacon pointed out that instruments can serve as aids to the senses and can correct information revealed to the unaided senses. Furthermore, one type of sensory information can be used to cross-check another type. He might have added that even the skeptic must place faith in some form of sensory information in order to call attention to the truth of an illusion.

Bacon did not formulate an explicit and coherent statement of scientific methodology. Nonetheless, he provides sufficient commentary to construct an outline of his beliefs. Bacon realized he was making a provisional statement regarding scientific method. He anticipated that methodology would further evolve as illustrated in his statement that "the art of discovery may advance as discoveries advance" (1620/1960, p. 120).

Bacon's positive approach to science is illustrated in his metaphor characterizing the work of researchers. Some, he said, are like ants who collect and use materials. Others are like spiders, busy spinning webs from their own substance. Between the extremes is the bee who gathers a variety of materials and transforms and digests them in community activity (Bacon, 1620/1960, p. 93). Bacon advocated the latter perspective, the way of the bee. He understood the limitations of mere collection, and cautioned that empirical philosophy can give rise to misinformation as much as rational philosophy, especially when empirical philosophers leap to hasty generalizations based on inadequate experiments (p. 61). Bacon reserved his most vigorous attacks for the rationalists, whose methods divorced them from the data of experience. Bacon's middle road is best described as a new inductivism that rejects the big leap, the temptation to entertain, or the temptation to place excessive trust in the intellect. The new inductivism demands the "reform of human understanding by grounding it solidly in experience" (Stephens, 1975, p. 60). He was accused of advancing a naïve empirical inductivism that entails the mere collection of facts. Such an accusation, however, is inaccurate. Bacon emphasized assimilation and generalization, but cautioned that such activities should not be premature; they should follow massive data collection from many sources.

Bacon cautioned against hastiness when claiming to have attained knowledge. Thus, Bacon's conservatism regarding scientific claims tempered his optimism regarding the possibilities of knowledge. He recommended that investigators commit to two rules before conducting an inquiry: "first, to lay aside received opinions and notions; and second, to refrain the mind for a time from the highest generalizations" (1620/1960, p. 119). Bacon's emphasis was first and foremost on extensive data collection. A massive number of observations should be collected and, if possible, organized for presentation in tabular form. Due attention should be given to negative instances. The second step in Bacon's method was the search for generalizations or higher principles, but, again, the researcher should enter into this step with caution.

Bacon was also interested in the communication of scientific results. With a long-standing interest in rhetoric, he cautioned against the "grand style" and argued for a subdued approach emphasizing objective data based on observation. He recognized that style may seduce human beings. Accordingly, the researcher should forego style for substance.

The Baconian inductive method, with its emphasis on observation, occupies a niche in the evolution of modern science. For example, his emphasis on data and his hesitancy to suggest grand theories inspired the atheoretical psychology of B. F. Skinner (Moore, 2005). The deficiencies of the method—the failure to appreciate hypotheses and mathematics—are now well understood, but the new emphasis on observation was crucial in a time marked by the tendency to rush toward first principles, those things we think we know beforehand. Bacon also helped restore confidence in human knowledge. His optimism influenced several succeeding generations of philosophers and scientists.

Francis Bacon found his way into the history of psychology via another route. In his classification of the sciences, he included topics that still interest contemporary psychologists. He believed society should support empirical studies of sleep and dreaming; development from infancy to old age; the senses; affections such as anger, love, and fear; and cognitive abilities such as imagination, thinking, and memory. Bacon called for the construction of complete natural histories of each of these areas. He believed that understanding the natural history of an area provides scientists with the foundation to erect new knowledge structures. Bacon believed that well-researched and well-written natural histories would provide the background necessary to initiate his great plan for the restoration or renewal of the sciences. At the same time, natural history without the new empirical instruments would grow sterile.

The legacy of Bacon's extreme emphasis on observation can be debated. His emphasis was, at least, an understandable rebellion against extreme rationalism. Bacon's vision for a natural history and an empirical science that studies psychological topics is less debatable. Brett (1912–1921/1965) points out that "the ideas which he expressed ruled the progress of inductive or experimental psychology all through its development" (p. 351). Let us now consider the work of one of Bacon's successors, a man who is easily the equal of Bacon in terms of his influence on Western intellectual history.

John Locke

A number of seventeenth- and eighteenth-century philosophers tackled the possibilities and limitations of empiricism as a way of knowing. Bacon's followers, who were regarded as empiricists, deemphasized his methodological focus. Instead, they explored the larger metaphysical dimensions of empiricism. Bacon's most important immediate successor, **John Locke (1632–1704)** has been described as "the most widely influential philosopher of English speech" (Tsanoff, 1964, p. 329). If Bacon can be viewed as the Great Herald of the Empirical Spirit, it is Locke who launched a serious inquiry into an empirical theory of knowledge.

John Locke was born in Wrington, Somerset, on August 29, 1632. At age fourteen, Locke pursued classical studies at Westminster School. In 1652, he entered Oxford University, where his interests shifted from classical studies to the natural sciences. His bachelor's degree was conferred in 1656 and his master's degree

John Locke

two years later. Following the death of his father and younger brother, Locke inherited most of the family estate. The small inheritance provided independence.

After completing his master's degree, Locke studied natural sciences and medicine. Though he did not extensively practice medicine, he did accept a few patients, including his close friend Lord Ashley, the Earl of Shaftesbury. In addition to serving as Shaftesbury's personal physician, Locke accepted administrative and political responsibilities and tutored Shaftesbury's grandson. Locke also served as an adviser to the government on coinage and as Commissioner of Appeal. These positions left time for Locke to devote himself to philosophy. In the period from 1689 to 1704, he produced an outpouring of scholarship including psychological works such as *An Essay Concerning Human Understanding* (1690/1959) and *Some Thoughts Concerning Education* (1693/1989).

Locke's philosophical interests were occupied with the problem of epistemology. He saw himself as an early "philosopher of science with the self-appointed task of providing epistemological foundations for the emerging empirical sciences" (Soles, 1985, p. 339). His work on education may also be viewed as an extension of his epistemological interests. Though he never married, he had a deep interest in children, especially in how they acquire knowledge. He argued for the improvement of the teaching–learning process. Politically and religiously, Locke was a liberal who argued for natural rights to life, liberty, and property for all individuals (Tigiripalli & Kadarla, 2009). He advocated public education for all people as well as majority rule and the right of all individuals to study religion and hold opinions that are not imposed by religious or political authority.

One of the most celebrated and controversial ideas in Locke's work centers on his belief that, at birth, the mind is as "white paper, void of all characters, without any ideas" (1690/1959, p. 121). Fraser (1959) suggested that Locke did not mean the mind is without latent capacities; he simply meant that the newborn's mind is not furnished with knowledge or ideas (p. 121). Locke's position, though not new, was set forth in a persuasive way. The *Zeitgeist* of the seventeenth century was ripe to entertain the "white paper" hypothesis. If the hypothesis is true, experience in human knowledge becomes preeminent and poses a radical alternative to rationalism. Recall from Chapter 4 that the poet Dante claimed we have innate knowledge of good and evil. It is the kind of claim that inspired Locke to launch a vigorous attack on belief in innate ideas.

In *An Essay,* Locke argued that there are no innate moral ideas, no innate ideas of God (though he believed that the wise of all nations have come to believe in God), no innate speculative principles, and no innate practical principles. Locke insisted that we cannot find universal agreement on any topic, but even if we could, such agreement would not necessarily prove innate ideas. Universal agreement, if it did exist, might indicate little more than common experience. The belief in innate ideas discourages inquiry into possible exterior sources of ideas and, consequently, produces intellectual laziness.

If ideas are not innate, what is their origin? Locke contended that some ideas come to the mind via only one sense. Two events in the same sensory domain in close temporal or spatial conjunction may be associated. Locke called this result an idea. Other ideas result from the operation of two or more senses. He believed that some ideas result from reflection, which is based on extrapolations from previous sensory information. A given idea may also originate from a complicated combination of sensation and reflection.

Locke's strong empirical position on the origin of knowledge placed importance on learning and education as well as their social and environmental context. Ward (2010) argues that with John Locke we encounter a democratization of mind (p. 17). Under Locke's treatment, the individual does not shoulder full responsibility for deficits in knowledge—the requisite information may never have been provided. If individual responsibility is somewhat diminished in Locke's system, social responsibility for others—especially children—is enhanced.

Locke's search for the origin of ideas led him to consider the relationship between ideas and stimulus objects that produce ideas. The relationship between the physical world and the psychological world (the world of ideas) was a necessary step for Locke. The validity of human knowledge concerned him. *Validity* here refers to the correspondence between ideas and objects. Locke hoped to demonstrate that ideas can correspond to the physical world; otherwise, in his words, "The visions of an enthusiast and the reasonings of a sober man will be equally certain" (1690/1959, p. 227). Locke believed that our brains are crammed with imaginations, dreams, chimeras, and illusions, but may also possess real knowledge. Otherwise, Locke argued, "our most serious thoughts will be of little more use than the reveries of a crazy brain" (p. 228). What then are the grounds for believing in a correspondence between ideas and stimulus objects?

Locke believed that the senses furnish certain simple ideas that accurately reflect the external nature of things. For example, we have a simple idea of solidity, and Locke said, "If anyone asks me *what this solidity is,* I send him to his senses to inform him" (1690/1959, p. 156). Solid objects are known by the sense of touch. The idea of solidity is not a fiction but the inevitable result of conformity between psychological and physical realities. Two solid objects struck together produce a real effect, and we are so constituted as to be able to have knowledge of that effect. Locke also argued that our knowledge of mathematical truths represents real knowledge.

Though Locke may be the first to present a formal empirical philosophy, he found it impossible to be a consistent empiricist. Just as he took a commonsense approach to the existence of certain qualities of physical objects, he took an intuitive approach to the certainty of his own existence. Like Descartes, he believed that to think, we must exist. Locke was also open to rationalist ideas on the question of God's existence. Although we have no innate idea of God, we can nevertheless demonstrate God's existence through reason (Locke, 1690/1959, Book 4, Chap. 10). Though Locke was not a consistent empiricist, some of his followers made concerted efforts along this path.

Locke's interest in the problem of knowledge led him to agree with earlier scientists such as Galileo and Boyle that two kinds of qualities characterize stimulus objects in the physical world. **Primary qualities** reside or inhere in an object and are independent of perception. Although there were disagreements about primary qualities, some examples include extension, figure, mobility, and solidity. **Secondary qualities** are hidden powers of an object that result in specific sensations; these are dependent upon the perceptions of the observer. Thus, color, sound, warmth, and taste are examples of secondary qualities. If we examine a red cube, its shape and solidity may be taken as primary qualities, but the redness is a secondary quality. The redness does not reside in the cube in the same manner as does figure and solidity. To illustrate, if we lower the lights in a room, the color of the object seems to change, but the solidity and shape of the object do not change. Color, as a secondary quality, seems to emerge as a result of the interaction among light conditions, the object, and the perceiving subject. The characteristics of the perceiver contribute in a substantial way to the perception of secondary qualities, but such is not the case for primary qualities. For example, back to our red cube: Certain color-blind animals would not see the color red; they would see only shades of gray. Thus, the redness resides in the perceiver and not as an inherent quality of an object, though the object has the power to evoke the perception of redness in some perceptual systems.

The foregoing example from comparative psychology might clarify the nature of secondary qualities. Many people may delight in the taste of vine-ripened tomatoes or fresh cucumbers or radishes, but most dogs would not find them appealing. Similarly, humans avoid odors that appeal to dogs. To summarize, secondary qualities seem to be separable from an object; they result from the interactions of sensory systems and external objects. Primary qualities, by contrast, reside or inhere in an object and are independent of the perceiver.

In other words, it would be difficult to separate a primary quality from an object without destroying the object. Indeed, Galileo suggested a subtraction test as a means of distinguishing between primary and secondary qualities. If a quality can be subtracted from an object without destroying its identity, then that quality is secondary. We could subtract the color orange from a triangle and the triangle would retain its identity as a triangle. The subtraction of figure, however, a primary quality, cannot be accomplished without destroying the object's identity. The distinction between primary and secondary qualities raises all kinds of problems, and as we will see, this distinction captured the attention of Locke's successors.

Sahakian and Sahakian (1975) claimed that Locke's book *Some Thoughts Concerning Education* (1693/1989) "was destined to have a profound influence during the course of two centuries upon the education of children in all classes of society throughout the [W]estern world" (p. 86). The ideas for the book had originally been set forth in Locke's letters to his friend, Edward Clarke, who had asked the philosopher for advice on raising Clarke's eight-year-old son. Garforth (1964) pointed out that we know little about the sources of inspiration for Locke's thoughts on education, but we can be certain he drew from his experiences at Oxford. The writers François Rabelais, John Milton, and John Drury influenced Locke. The Spanish humanist Juan Luis Vives may have also influenced his educational writings. Locke discussed subjects including the relations between parents and children, methods of training, the role of reward and punishment in discipline, curriculum, and the personality characteristics of the tutor.

Locke's ideas on education were generally consistent with his empirical philosophy. He argued that, for the majority of human beings, education contributes more to character than does nature. Locke recognized that there are natural abilities and biases and that these are sometimes difficult to overcome. Nevertheless, it is the environment that largely determines what we will become. For this reason, it is important to attend to a range of environmental influences from the food we eat, to parental influences, to pedagogical technique.

According to Locke, children should have plenty of sleep, fresh air, and exercise. The educator should scrutinize the child's diet: He discouraged eating between meals and consuming too much sugar. Locke clearly understood the relationship between learning and good health. He adopted older notions of **hardening**, a rigorous conditioning where the child endures pain, hardship, and fatigue. Thus, a bed should be hard because feathers may contribute to physical weakness. Forcing the child to endure reasonable amounts of coldness or wetness also accomplished hardening. Consistent with his views on hardening, Locke believed crying is a fault that should not be tolerated. If crying cannot be abated with harsh or disapproving looks, then blows are acceptable if applied in a rational, dispassionate manner (van Drunen & Jansz, 2004). Persuasion, however, is preferable to physical punishment.

Although Locke believed in the judicious use of physical punishment, he emphasized reward and a positive, affectionate relationship between children and adults. He believed that unwarranted punishment works against learning and good character development. Locke argued that excessive punishment may undermine confidence and interfere with vigor and industry. Punishment in educational situations may result in an aversion to learning. Locke also counseled against reward that is not genuine, but he viewed credit for real accomplishment as a cardinal rule of education. Locke recognized that excessive and rigorous assignments result in avoidance of the lesson. A good teacher will be sensitive to the pace of the assignments and make learning enjoyable.

Many of Locke's educational views, especially his ideas on hardening and physical punishment, have been discounted by later scholars. He nevertheless represents an important turning point in the history of educational psychology. In *Letters Concerning the English Nation* (1733/1980), Voltaire extolled Locke's systematic approach to education. Voltaire credited Locke for advocating step-by-step

progress in the development of a child's understanding. He praised Locke for examining what humans have in common with animals and how we differ. In Locke's work, we have an emphasis on topical areas that will later form an important part of the new discipline of psychology. We also encounter an early emphasis on the idea that the environment shapes personality and behavior.

George Berkeley

As founders of modern empirical philosophy, both Bacon and Locke emphasized observation, data collection, and the role of the environment as central means for attaining knowledge. In this tradition, **George Berkeley (1685–1753)** extended Locke's empirical philosophy. Berkeley emphasized the primacy of experience in human knowledge, giving a vision of an untrammeled empiricism. His radical empiricism, and the still more radical work of his successor, David Hume, produced shock waves in philosophy. Indeed, the empiricism of Berkeley and Hume served as a foil for subsequent philosophies. Following their empiricism, the compelling task of philosophy was to elevate faith in common sense and reason.

Although regarded as an Irish philosopher, George Berkeley identified more with his British ancestry. Born in Kilkenny, Ireland, in 1685, he enrolled in Trinity College, Dublin, at age fifteen where he earned his B.A. in 1704 and M.A. in 1707. By 1709, Berkeley had written the classic psychological treatise *An Essay Towards a New Theory of Vision* (1709/1948). In his essay, he argued against Descartes's contention that there are geometric principles known innately that contribute to depth perception. Within a year, Berkeley had written another more important work, *Treatise Concerning the Principles of Human Knowledge* (1710/1957). This book set forth the empirical philosophy that made Berkeley famous.

Berkeley's philosophy frustrated its author. On one hand, his contemporaries either could not refute it or did not bother trying to refute it. On the other hand, they did not believe it or could not find it in themselves to take it seriously. As a consequence, Berkeley drew upon his background in Greek philosophy, particularly Platonic dialogues, to write the classic *Three Dialogues between Hylas and Philonous* (1713/1935), in which he argued his case through Philonous (i.e., love of the mind) against materialist philosophy as voiced by Hylas (i.e., matter).

After formal schooling at Trinity College, Berkeley held several university posts, but he was drawn to the New World. Inspired by his missionary-religious views, he had a long-standing interest in converting American slaves and so-called savages. Before 1700, the legal justification of slavery in England and the American colonies rested in part on the non-Christian status of the slaves; therefore, a baptized slave could no longer be enslaved. Not surprisingly, slave owners challenged the few radical reformers who tried to free slaves through baptism. Berkeley successfully argued before the king's legal officers to change English law so that baptizing slaves would not threaten owners' property rights (Scherer, 1975). Although Berkeley may have been driven by humanitarian motivations to bring religion to people who were enslaved, he closed the door on one method of escape from slavery, playing a small but critical role in perpetuating slavery within the confines of Christianity and the British colonies.

Berkeley wanted to spread the Protestant faith and educate colonists. Finally, in 1728, he was ready to sail for America. One month prior to departing, Berkeley married Anne Forster, the daughter of an Irish magistrate.

He and his wife resided in America for three years. During that time, he lived on his farm in Rhode Island. He preached sermons in the Episcopal Church and organized a philosophical society. He was interested in founding a college in the New World, but promised grant funding from Parliament never materialized. As a result, his stay in America was brief. In 1731, Berkeley and his wife and their infant son Henry set sail for London. Another child—a daughter born in America—died shortly after birth. Berkeley donated his farm to Yale University and contributed books to the Yale and Harvard libraries. A major California city and university would later adopt Berkeley's name. Berkeley died in January of

1753. Biographers describe him as a vigorous and handsome man with the rare combination of humility and genius.

Berkeley battled with the materialistic and skeptical dimensions of the so-called new philosophy. He wanted to restore faith in spiritual interpretations of the world. Interestingly, Locke's empiricism revealed to Berkeley an opening for an attack on the prevailing materialistic interpretations of the world. Recall that Locke's primary qualities reside in objects and are independent of the observer. To be sure, primary qualities are observed by the senses, but Locke's assumption was that such qualities reside in an object whether we discover them or not. With Berkeley, this distinction between primary and secondary qualities became untenable. He shared with his readers that it is absurd to ask what the world is like, independent of experience. The shape of the triangle must be experienced just as the color must be experienced. Furthermore, a figure or shape changes, depending on the angle of perspective, just as color changes, depending on illumination. In *Three Dialogues*, Berkeley placed in the mouth of Hylas, his adversary, the idea that real things "have a fixed and real nature, which remains the same notwithstanding any change in our senses, or in the posture and motion of our bodies" (1713/1935, pp. 55–56). Such, of course, was the materialistic assumption about primary qualities; they were assumed to reside in a material substance independent of the perceiver. But in *Three Dialogues*, we find Philonous responding to Hylas by declaring that *all* sensible qualities, including size, shape, and color, are continually changing and are conditioned by the context or the medium through which we make our observations. So-called primary qualities vary as much as secondary qualities; this distinction could not be established through experience.

Berkeley challenged more than the distinction between primary and secondary qualities. He also called into question the existence of primary qualities independent of experience. Extension, figure, and motion, the so-called primary qualities, exist in experience, as do color, taste, sound, or temperature. In an earlier, more innocent time, people could take refuge in a host of absolutes. Primary qualities were among the absolutes. But the absolutes, one by one, were challenged. At one time, people could believe that Jerusalem was the absolute center of the universe, but following the Copernican revolution, there was no absolute location; location was relative and changing as the earth spins on its axis and follows its orbit around the sun. How many miles do you suppose you have traveled since you started reading this chapter, or, for that matter, how far have you traveled just in the past five minutes? If there were no absolute location, we could still hold on to the idea of absolutes that exist in objects around us. But with Berkeley, these absolutes were challenged. An object viewed one way is a square, but viewed another way, it is a trapezoid. Another object viewed one way is a circle, but viewed from another perspective, it is an ellipse. From one perspective an object is large, but from another it is quite small. Berkeley thus contributed to the demise of absolutes, but it is the absolutes of materialism that he attacked. He left his readers with spiritual absolutes, which remained for Hume to attack.

Berkeley argued that there are no legitimate grounds for assuming that some ideas represent real properties of an object. How can an idea (that which is mental) in any way represent the property of an object (that which is physical)? Thus, for Berkeley, there was no empirical evidence for the world-in-itself that is separate and distinct from the lived world of experience! In fact, the *only* real world *is* the world of experience or the world of the mind. Berkeley is remembered for his famous dictum *esse est percipi*: "to be is to be perceived." Such was the case even for Locke regarding secondary qualities such as color, taste, and odor, which had no absolute being in themselves. Rather, they depend for their existence on a perceiver. But for Berkeley, the expression "to be is to be perceived" applied also to the rest of the world.

Following the conclusions of Berkelean empiricism, we encounter a new skepticism regarding claims for the materialist interpretation of the world. In his dialogues between Hylas and Philonous, Berkeley, speaking through Philonous, declared that he was convinced "that there is no such thing as what philosophers call *material substance*" (1713/1935, p. 11) and later added that "all that we know or conceive are our own ideas" (p. 61). Subjective experience becomes the centerpiece of empiricism pushed to the extreme. The real world is not a nonperceptible world of material substance; rather, the real world is the world as we know it in our own experience. There is an elegant simplicity in this philosophy, just as there is in materialism or any other monistic orientation. But simplicity comes with a price. A philosophy that meets our needs for simplicity sometimes falls short of meeting our equally valid demands for adequacy.

A major problem in Berkelean empiricism centers on the consistency and coherence of experience. There is no principle in experience per se that explains the orderliness of our subjective world. Yet, the world of experience does hold together in an orderly way. When I finish this cup of coffee, I will leave this restaurant, get in my car, drive one mile south, turn right into the faculty parking lot, find a parking space (if I'm lucky), get out of the car, walk to the office, and meet my 9 A.M. appointment. I do not now perceive the car or any of its parts, the street, the stoplights, the parking lot, my office, or desk, but I am convinced all these things exist and the world of my immediate future experience will be reasonably coherent and orderly. How can I account for such order and coherence if my experiences are not driven by the orderly world as such, out there, that makes its step-by-step contributions to the content of my subjective experience? Surely, the orderly content of the mental realm must be tied to the world of objects and such objects contribute to the coherent succession of experiences that will attend my getting from the restaurant to my first appointment.

Berkeley anticipated this criticism. Before we consider his reply, let's caution against the popular misconception that Berkeley denied the existence of the real world. What Berkeley denied was the objective and independent status of primary qualities. If secondary qualities are known only in experience, so also are primary qualities known only in experience. In taking such a step, Berkeley also denied that primary qualities represent a material substance that has objective and independent status. John Locke believed that material substance forms the world of objects. The qualities of objects to which we respond (i.e., the attributes, manifestations, or properties) are either primary or secondary. A secondary quality resides in subjective experience, but a primary quality is supported by a material substance that is not directly perceived. What is perceived is an attribute (e.g., a figure or solidity of an underlying material substance). Asked what this material substance is, Locke declared that it is "something, he knew not what."

Berkeley denied the existence of any mysterious metaphysical material substance that has objective or independent status. Berkeley did not deny the existence of the real world; rather, he gave us a new vision of the real world. It is the materialist account of the world that is rejected, an account that paradoxically uses experience to declare that experience is derivative, and that accords primacy to a mysterious metaphysical material substance that is not directly perceived. The real world for Berkeley was the intimate world of ideas and experience, whereas the material world is derivative.

How did Berkeley respond to the criticism mentioned earlier concerning orderliness of experience? First, Berkeley did not discount the existence of other perceiving minds. Second, as a religious individual in the early 1700s, Berkeley believed in an omnipotent and omniscient God whose apprehension of the world extends throughout space and time. The world operates in an intelligible and orderly way through God's perceptions of the world. Therefore, all of the things that exist are perceived at all times. The glue for Berkeley's empiricism is found in his theism, which is itself supported on rational rather than empirical grounds. It will remain for David Hume to provide us with an empirical philosophy that is stripped of theistic and rational support.

The accusation is made that Berkelean empiricism leads to solipsism. **Solipsism** refers to the philosophical position of extreme subjectivism, which holds that only knowledge of one's own mind is possible. It is understandable that Berkelean empiricism is associated with solipsism because few of us can resist the temptation to view ourselves as *the perceivers* when we hear the dictum "to be is to be perceived." But Berkeley recognized other minds or other perceivers and was explicit in his recognition of God as the permanent perceiver. Thus, we participate in a wider reality and are not necessarily consigned to solipsism. The problem, however, is how we participate. The reader who takes a leap of faith with Berkeley that we live in a wider reality tied to God's perception is rescued from solipsism. Others may find it difficult to reject the contention that Berkelean empiricism leads to solipsism.

Earlier we referred to Berkeley's theory of space or depth perception and we must now return to that topic. Space, like all else according to Berkeley, is reduced to the status of a secondary quality. If space is not a primary quality, why is it such a compelling feature in perception? Furthermore, how can we learn to see in depth, given that all objects in the visual field are represented on the relatively flat surface of the retina?

Berkeley's approach to depth perception as set forth in his book *An Essay Towards a New Theory of Vision* is now counted as a classic psychological treatise. Although Berkeley was not experimental in his visual research and did not cite the experimental studies of his day (Wade, 2009), he argued that there is a close relationship between sight and touch (see Pastore, 1965) and that a vivid visual sensation will be associated with a tactile sensation of closeness, whereas a less vivid visual sensation may be associated with a sensation of reaching. We thus learn to interpret sensations of nearness or distance through the medium of touch. The implications of Berkeley's theory are that distance in and of itself cannot be seen and that cues for distance must be learned (Wade, 2005). Berkeley believed that one who was born blind and who later gained sight would not be able to immediately perceive depth. Berkeley also believed that associations between visual and auditory sensations provide clues to depth perception.

Berkeley's work on depth perception anticipated later psychological investigations of the senses. Though most psychologists and philosophers rejected Berkeley's metaphysical scheme, his questions stimulated their work. Like other empiricists, he also encouraged the importance of human learning and association. As noted before, his extreme emphasis on empiricism also stimulated further work on the problem of knowledge.

David Hume

David Hume (1711–1776) offers one of the most complete and radical statements of empirical philosophy. More than any other, Hume provided an untempered empiricism. We also find in Hume a real concern with psychological topics.

Born near Edinburgh, Scotland, in 1711, David Hume was the second of the three children of Joseph Hume and Catherine Falconer. When David was three years old, his father died, leaving the resolute and devoted Catherine to raise and educate her children. David matriculated in the University of Edinburgh when he was twelve. Despite family pressure to pursue law, Hume displayed an unusual interest in literary and philosophical studies. After leaving the university at about age fifteen, Hume suffered a nervous breakdown. The treatment suggested to him included fresh air and exercise with attention to a balanced diet. Within two years, Hume regained his health and was engrossed in reading literature and philosophy. In 1734, he went to France, where he wrote his first philosophical work, *A Treatise of Human Nature. A Treatise* was divided into three parts, with Part 1 devoted to the problem of human knowledge, Part 2 to the passions, and Part 3 to morals. The first two parts were published in 1739, but their reception was a disaster. Reviews were hostile, the book did not sell, and Hume later claimed the book fell dead born from the press. If the book was an initial failure, history rescued it so that we now view it as a classic. In 1740, Hume published Part 3 of *A Treatise*, dealing with moral subjects such as justice, virtue, and objects of allegiance.

Although Hume's first publication was a disappointment, his later works enjoyed success. In 1748, he published a revision of Part 1 of *A Treatise* under the title *Philosophical Essays Concerning Human Understanding,* and in the same year published *Three Essays, Moral and Political.* Hume died in 1776, the year of the American Declaration of Independence, a cause he supported.

David Hume supported many unpopular causes and was reviled for his unorthodox religious views. All of his books were placed on the *Index of Forbidden Books.* He was the victim of harsh and unfair criticism that prevented him from obtaining university positions because of his religious beliefs. However, friends viewed him as energetic, enthusiastic, cheerful, good-natured, generous, and amiable. His sense of humor is illustrated in his reply to a colleague who was complaining about the spitefulness of the world. Hume jokingly insisted that things were not so bad, for he had written on all sorts of subjects—moral, political, religious—that could excite hostility, and yet he "had not made a single enemy; unless, indeed, all the Whigs, and all the Tories, and all the Christians" (Burton, 1846/1967, p. 443). Hume's self-appraisal is illustrated in the following letter. Hume was apparently asking a friend to find him lodging for a forthcoming visit to London, suggesting "a room in a sober discreet family, who would not be averse to admit a sober,

David Hume

discreet, virtuous, regular, quiet, goodnatured man of a bad character—such a room, I say, would suit me extremely" (Huxley, 1898, p. 40).

Following Berkeley's lead, Hume agreed that experience constitutes the primary subject matter of philosophy. But the events of experience, according to Hume, are not held together by any "necessary connection" that can be established through reason. Neither can it be established that a meaningful sequence of events in experience is driven by an external succession of events that reflect cause–effect relations. Thus, causality, in Hume's treatment, reduces to a psychological problem. Causality cannot be viewed as a primary quality. If domino *A* impacts domino *B*, and domino *B* falls, Hume finds nothing in *A* per se that could be labeled as a cause. Causality does not inhere in an object; rather, causality is more like one of Berkeley's secondary qualities. Causality is what *we* see and what *we* attribute to things, but it does not reside in objects as a substantial quality. Thus, there are no necessary connections "out there," but only our ways of making sense of succession or sequence. All we know is that when *A* hits *B*, then *B* falls over. What we take to be objective causality reduces to our habitual ways of seeing things. Hume noted that our notions of causal connections are based on temporal priority (*A* precedes *B*), spatial contiguity (*A* and *B* are close together), and constant conjunction (*B* regularly falls when impacted by *A*). We form the idea of objective necessary connection only from the regularity of our impressions. We'll return to causality as we explore other dimensions of Hume's views on psychology.

Mental life for Hume could not be verified through reason. Following his radical empirical approach to knowledge, Hume found only impressions and ideas. *Impressions* present themselves directly with considerable force. They include sensations, passions (motives), and emotions. A taste, a color, a hunger pang, a sound, a startling stimulus that results in fear, or an odor could each produce an impression. *Ideas* are fainter images of impressions. The recollection of a taste thirty minutes after eating would constitute an idea, which in this case is a weaker recollection of the original impression. Impressions or ideas may be simple, such as a single clear tone, or compound, such as we might encounter as we respond simultaneously to the color, taste, odor, and feel of a food object such as an apple.

His views on causality, coupled with his position on the sources of knowledge, led to an interesting psychological question. What, according to Hume, is the nature of the self? Most of us experience a sense of personal identity and a causal connection between one idea and another and between our ideas and our actions. According to Hume, this sense of personal identity cannot be based on any mysterious mental substance; neither can it be based on objective causality. How, then, do we explain personal identity?

First, Hume believed the sense of personal identity may be exaggerated. Tsanoff (1964) summarized Hume's position: "All that we find in inspecting our so-called 'selves' is a bundle of sensations, a collection of different perceptions. As in a kind of theatre, they pass, re-pass, glide away, and mingle in boundless variety" (p. 361). Hume is not describing a stream of consciousness but a parade of impressions and ideas that present themselves in no logical order. The parade is ongoing with a mixture of entertaining, sad, vivid, and dull entries of which we are hardly conscious. Thrown into the mix, the parade may include an intense emotional and ecstatic entry followed by a sobering entry that we watch with resentment. In some entries, we may perceive ourselves as active observers, as if we were in the parade being observed by others, whereas in other entries, we may perceive ourselves as passive observers. There is no necessary or logical connection between one entry and another. We do not know from where the parade begins or where it will end. Happily, some seem to enjoy the whole nonsensical succession, but others are not so blessed.

Most of us can muster the intellectual empathy to feel our way into this radical empirical Humean world. If you reflect on your day, you might remember punctuated bits and pieces. They succeed each other without meaningful connections, flickering on and off like tiny flashbulbs. Maybe you're jostled from sleep by a new ringtone on your cell phone alarm. You drag yourself out of bed to get ready before grabbing a protein shake and a bagel on the run as you rush out the door to a brutal biochem class at eight. Abruptly, you're riding the bus to campus, listening to a new download on your iPhone while discreetly sizing up the other students. After class, you head to a Starbucks, ordering a venti iced chai while telling the barista about your sleep deprivation. Quite illogically, the next major awareness seems to be sitting in a classroom where twenty people are critiquing your thesis statement. Between classes, you run the usual online routine, switching between email, class notes, and your bank account while texting a friend. Your electronic addiction takes over, and you're trapped in limbo between updating your Facebook profile and commenting on a funny YouTube video. Time disappears until you leave your MCAT prep class, heading for the bus stop as you contemplate whether or not medical school is the right choice. You collapse on the sofa, thinking about how you should work out tonight. Before long, you're sucked into some awful reality TV show downstairs while ignoring the massive amounts of homework waiting upstairs.

Who knows what the next focal point will be in this disjointed parade? It would seem like an accident if the next entry had even the appearance of being causally related to the current entry. But if you perceive a causal connection, it reflects your attempt to pay attention to the transitions in your day-to-day experiences.

Let's go back to Hume's account of self-identity. As we said, he rejected any notion of a substantial self. He failed to find a single impression or idea that can account for our sense of continuity or identity. In Hume's system, we encounter a succession of selves. But in normal experience, these selves are one and the same. It is the same *you* who enjoys dinner tonight and later enjoys watching a movie this weekend, even if there are gaps between your two experiences and the fact that they are unrelated to each other. In the final analysis, continuity or personal identity is, according to Hume, a product of the imagination, and one cannot make an objective claim on

behalf of such an imagination. We perceive causal connections among the entries in our parade of impressions and ideas when the entries appear to be similar, when one entry regularly follows another, or when entries are close in space or time. The sense of personal identity is a product of the peculiar way we attend to the succession of impressions and ideas. In the end, personal identity is a construction that grows out of the ways we organize the entries and gaps in our experiences.

Hume devotes the second volume of *A Treatise* to a study of what was commonly called the passions. He discusses emotions such as pride, humility, love, hate, respect, and contempt. He emphasized comparative studies in his work on emotion. Hume notes that studies of animals have been useful to anatomists and physiologists and that comparisons of the "anatomy of the mind" may also be useful (see 1739–1740/1978, Book 11, Sec. 12). He argued that some emotions in animals have the same origins as comparable emotions in humans (see pp. 326, 363, 398, 448). Generalizations from one species to another may not always be permissible, but he was ahead of his time in recommending comparative psychological studies.

Another important feature of Hume's approach was his assumption that all emotions "are founded on pain and pleasure" (1739–1740/1978, p. 438). Hume believed emotions such as joy, desire, and hope are derived from pleasure, whereas sorrow, aversion, and fear are derived from pain. He believed that values had their basis in desires (Curry, 2006) and that emotions could drive humans to moral actions even at personal cost (Frank, 2011). Hume provided what he called experimental demonstrations. In a subtitle to his treatise, he declared that the book is "an attempt to introduce the experimental method of reasoning into moral subjects." Hume's so-called experiments consisted of anecdotes or demonstrations, but even so, he attempted to tie his propositions to observable events. In discussing the transfer of an emotion from one object to another, he gives the example that a quarrel with one family member may produce hatred for other family members even though they have done nothing to deserve it.

Hume's originality, intellectual courage, and integrity contributed to his greatness as a philosopher. His work on the problem of causation was the most original work on that topic since Aristotle. Hume exuded courage and integrity in his uncompromising efforts to construct a philosophy of experience.

He is a central figure in the history of psychology for several reasons. More than any empiricist since Bacon, Hume focused on emotion. He hoped to understand the origins of emotions and their role in intellectual life as well as establish a nomenclature for them. The problems of self and self-identity may have been elevated in importance because subsequent scholars considered Hume's treatment of these topics a disaster. Hume's emphases on habit and association as well as his scientific approach to human minds (Froese, 2009) marked him as a contributor to topics of lasting psychological interest. Finally, Hume's work on the problem of causation left a mark on scientific metatheory. Following Hume, the debate over what scientists study would never be the same.

Hume's legacy created an intellectual crisis in the eighteenth and early nineteenth centuries, comparable to the crisis Montaigne's skepticism had created a century before. Bozeman (1977) pointed out that Hume demonstrated "with an awful cogency, that 'the common Lockean philosophy,' when driven to an ultimate conclusion, supplied a sandy foundation for such crucial premises of inductive science as the actual 'existence' of an external world of objects or the operation of causes in that world" (p. 9). Philosophy's compelling task was to reconstruct the conceptual foundations of science. Chapter 7 will examine reactions to Hume's thought.

EMPIRICISM ON THE CONTINENT

The British are credited with founding modern empirical philosophy, but thinkers on the continent also made contributions. The French philosopher **François-Marie Arouet de Voltaire (1694–1778)** praised British empiricism and was instrumental in importing it to the continent. In

the works of Bacon and Newton, Voltaire found a means to challenge the oppression and dogmatic philosophies that had dominated European thought. Voltaire's literary and philosophical works conveyed suspicion of untestable theories and theological dogma. Instead, he supported a philosophy established on observation and experimentation. His vocal support of British thought, especially his praise for John Locke, resulted in a warrant for his arrest and a lengthy exile from Paris. Voltaire's enthusiasm for the new empirical philosophy influenced two French empiricists, **Étienne Bonnot de Condillac (1715–1780)** and **Claude-Adrien Helvétius (1715–1771)**.

Étienne Bonnot de Condillac

Étienne Bonnot de Condillac (*Kohn de YAHK*) was born in Grenoble, France, on September 30, 1715. He studied theology, philosophy, and science at a Catholic seminary at Saint-Sulpice and at the Sorbonne. For a time, he was in the company of Rousseau and Diderot and enjoyed acquaintance with Voltaire, Helvétius, d'Holbach, and Cabanis. He was appointed to the French Academy and the Royal Academy of Berlin. Condillac's writings on education were in demand, adding to his esteem as tutor for the children of royalty. He devoted his later years almost exclusively to writing. He died in 1780 after completing a major treatise on logic.

Condillac rode the crest of a growing criticism of the rational philosophies of Descartes and his followers. The task of philosophy, according to Condillac, is not to discover the nature of the mind but to find out how the mind works. In this emphasis, he can be viewed as a forerunner of functional psychologies (see Chapter 12). Condillac, like John Locke and René Descartes (see Leary, 1980), attempted to establish a moral basis for the new psychology. He wanted a mental science that could make a difference in people's lives.

A practical psychology dominated Condillac's thought. He avoided lengthy consideration of metaphysical problems of causality and the nature of the real world that had so captivated

Berkeley and Hume. Instead, he studied the genetic basis of knowledge. With a thoroughness unequaled even by Locke, Condillac sought to analyze the origins of knowledge.

Condillac asked us to imagine a marble statue that represents a human. Imagine further that the statue's intellect includes no innate ideas. He proposed we chart intellectual growth by opening one sensory channel at a time. He began with the sense of smell and presented one stimulus event (the smell of a rose) to the statue. Condillac argued that with one stimulus, his statue displays intellectual functions such as attention and a sense of existence. When the smell of a rose is followed by the smell of a sweet pea, the statue is now capable of discrimination and a sense of contrast. Condillac proceeded by opening other sensory channels one at a time to demonstrate the emergence of all cognitive functions. If a given stimulus is too intense or painful, the statue is motivated to minimize the pain. Likewise, if a given stimulus yields pleasure, the statue is motivated to maximize the pleasure. He believed we understand the external world through the sense of touch, which produces compelling sensitivities to resistance, solidity, motion, hardness, softness, and so on. As noted, Condillac did not trouble over whether this awareness is subjective or objective. As a practical philosopher, his sensationist theory was focused on learning and education, and his ideas about language and mind influenced eighteenth-century philosophers as well as contemporary thinkers (Hardcastle, 2009).

Condillac is also remembered for his studies on the origin and meaning of human language. He argued that language provides symbols that represent sensations, needs, or desired actions. Through language, discrimination, memory, and thought help communicate experiences and secure advantages. Condillac argued that the excellence of science was based partly on the excellence of scientific language. Scientists must work to avoid common language with its many errors. Instead, scientific concepts should be grounded in the precise language of mathematics. Condillac also emphasized the importance of accurate classification systems and taxonomies in science.

Condillac's focus on the language of science influenced thinkers in the late eighteenth and early nineteenth centuries. It pointed in the direction of positivism, which developed later in the nineteenth century. Under his guidance, empiricism became more practical and psychological, and that may be his greatest legacy within the history of psychology. Condillac demonstrated practical uses of empiricism in the investigation of problems such as the development of language and the learning process.

Claude-Adrien Helvétius

In the work of Claude-Adrien Helvétius (*ehl VA shus*) (1715–1771), we encounter an early version of a radical behaviorism (see Chapter 13) that emphasized the Lockean white paper hypothesis carried to the extreme of denying all inborn capacities. In his essays on the history of materialism, Plekhanov (1967) suggested that Helvétius was so consistent in his materialist philosophy that he "horrified other materialists" (p. 92). Perhaps other materialists were horrified by Helvétius's candid approach to the moral implications of his psychology. Under his treatment, our most treasured virtues are the simple product of education. Human vice and corruption result from poor legislation and a failure to educate the masses. Helvétius gives us an environmental psychology that challenges freedom of choice and autonomy. Such extreme perspectives are seldom popular, even today.

Possibly through family connections, Claude-Adrien Helvétius secured a government post in 1738. Over the next decade, he earned enough money to purchase an estate and retire. Following his retirement in 1748, he turned to philosophy and completed the book *De l'esprit* (*On the Mind*) in 1757. After religious authorities condemned it, Helvétius felt compelled to recant some opinions. Nonetheless, his book became a major influence on the continent and in the British Isles.

Helvétius argued that humans are controlled by society's system of rewards and punishments. At the root of all behaviors are self-interest, the pursuit of pleasure, and the avoidance or the threat of pain. As noted, Helvétius denied hereditary influences, much like the behaviorist John Watson in the early twentieth century (Jahoda, 1992; Roback, 1937). He even suggested that genius resulted from environmental influence. Either we learn to learn or we develop a negative attitude toward learning and remain ignorant. How, then, is it possible that two people given excellent educations should turn out differently, with one being brilliant and productive and the other mediocre? Helvétius argued that chance (an encounter with the right teacher or just the right experience) plays a role in producing such differences. Under his treatment, we all have the potential to be geniuses.

Although not original, Helvétius was influential. His environmentalism and hedonism had a profound effect on the development of utilitarianism (to be discussed next) and his emphasis on the malleability of human beings elevated the importance of learning and education.

ASSOCIATIONISM AND UTILITARIANISM

The practical implications emerging from the thought of empiricists such as Locke, Berkeley, and Hume inspired the associationists and utilitarians of the eighteenth and nineteenth centuries. If knowledge is acquired through experience, then the means of its acquisition is elevated as a topic of study. Knowledge can no longer be taken for granted as a mere given, a gratuity bestowed by God or the benevolent forces of nature. The specifics of how we acquire knowledge now becomes a central focus in any science of human nature.

David Hartley

David Hartley (1705–1757) is regarded as the founder of modern **associationism**. He also studied motivation and the structural and functional characteristics of the nervous system.

Hartley was born in Armley, Yorkshire, England, and was educated at Cambridge.

Originally, he planned to pursue theology, but doctrinal questions drove him away from the ministry and into medicine. His most noteworthy treatise was titled *Observations on Man, His Frame, His Duty and His Expectations* (1749/1966). This work drew inspiration from Locke's work on sensation. Hartley elaborated on the doctrine of association and speculated about how it worked. He also set forth an early classification system of pleasures and pains. He practiced medicine, but had interests in history, music, philosophy, poetry, and religion. Hartley's son, also named David (1732–1813), described his father as a gentle, caring physician who treated both mind and body. Hartley was a liberal who argued in favor of inoculation at a time when it was regarded with suspicion. His son carried on Hartley's liberal perspectives with his opposition to the slave trade and England's war with America. Hartley died in Bath, England, in 1757.

Hartley was one of the first to classify the varieties of pleasure and pain. He identified seven sources of pain and pleasure from (1) the external senses, (2) imagination, (3) opinions of us held by other people, (4) our possessions of the means of happiness, (5) sympathy or empathy with the status (joy or suffering) of other people, (6) the sense of our relationship with God, and (7) our moral sensitivities toward goodness and beauty or evil and deformity. Hartley thought the greatest pleasures derive from the latter three categories. As a religious man, he downplayed the pleasures associated with the first four categories and encouraged the cultivation of the so-called higher pleasures.

Newtonian physics inspired Hartley's views on neurophysiology and these views complemented his associationism (Buckingham & Finger, 1997). Newton had argued that vibrations in nerve fibers transmit sensory information to the brain. Hartley extended Newton's idea. Hartley contended that vibrations from the senses trigger miniature vibrations, or *vibratiuncles*, that persist for brief periods following the initial stimulus. Smith (1987) noted that Hartley thought "the vibrations set up by external energies gradually die away leaving only miniature vibrations or vibratiuncles" (p. 127). According to Hartley, memory is based on vibrations that fade unless appropriate conditions reactivate the vibration. Vibrations in one region may be associated with vibrations in another region resulting in extensive sources of reactivation. And these numerous sources support learned connections and memories. Smith (1987) pointed out that Hartley's associationism echoes concepts included in Ivan Pavlov's *Conditioned Reflexes* (though there is no evidence Hartley influenced Pavlov). Hartley did, however, have a major influence on later utilitarians and empiricists such as Jeremy Bentham, James Mill, and John Stuart Mill.

Jeremy Bentham

British empiricists doubted the validity of innate knowledge. Later associationists and utilitarians joined in this suspicion. In this tradition, **Jeremy Bentham (1748–1832)** called for massive reform in jurisprudence and legal philosophy. Lawmakers and court officials in Bentham's day prided themselves on their intuitive grasp of absolute moral principles. Bentham challenged this belief with the same zeal John Locke displayed when attacking the concept of innate ideas.

In Bentham's day, punishments bore little relationship to the social consequences associated with specific crimes. Instead, as Bentham points out, punishments were based on revulsion at the particular crime under litigation. Thus, a sex crime without known widespread consequences, such as same-sex interaction between consenting adults, might be punished with great severity, whereas a crime with major social consequences might receive a mild reprimand. Bentham advocated a more empirical and objective basis for legal decisions. Therefore, punishment would be based on the measured social consequences of the crime.

Jeremy Bentham was born in Houndsditch, London, on February 15, 1748. He was a precocious child who learned Greek and Latin by age four. He entered Queens College at Oxford in 1760 and graduated with a B.A. when he was sixteen. In 1766, he was awarded an M.A. from

Oxford and went into legal practice in 1767. Bentham disliked practical law because, with minimum effort, most cases could be settled out of court. Despite Bentham's distaste for practical law, he pursued abstract problems of jurisprudence, including questions of interrogation and confession as well as other evidence (Weiss, 2012). In 1789, he published a major theoretical work titled *Introduction to the Principles of Morals and Legislation*. Friends published most of Bentham's work after his death. Some of his most thoughtful work focused on utilitarian approaches to reward and punishment. Bentham exemplified his own philosophy. Even in old age, he exuded a buoyant and optimistic spirit. He died on June 6, 1832, and, in characteristic altruism, donated his body to science.

Bentham argued that the intuitive approach to jurisprudence results in subjectivity and inequality. He contended that there are objective grounds for political, social, and legal theory. He summed up these objective grounds in a single principle of **utilitarianism** sometimes called the *hedonic calculus*. The basic idea is that actions should be judged in terms of their social consequences for pleasure and pain. We should maximize pleasure and minimize pain. At the same time, we must seek the greatest pleasure for the greatest number of people. Punishment should be administered in terms of utilitarian principles. For example, a leader who conspires illegally with a political enemy deserves more punishment than another leader who, for instance, engages in a consensual same-sex relationship with another consenting adult (Soble, 2009), even though same-sex relationships were generally not accepted during Bentham's lifetime. A wealthy person caught embezzling a large sum of money from a financial institution should receive more severe punishment than a person who steals to provide food for his or her children.

Bentham's utilitarian approach to punishment conflicted with intuitionism and retribution theory. Though there are varieties of retribution (see Cottingham, 1979), the purpose of retribution is generally to inflict a penalty on an individual as punishment or vengeance. For Bentham, the goal of punishment is to protect society and reform the offender. The merits of the two theories are open to debate (see Benn, 1967), but Bentham provided a new perspective on punishment and his theory served to correct extreme retribution. His work contributed to the curbing of cruel and unusual punishments (Foucault, 1979). It also produced varying standards regarding the idea that punishment for children should differ from adults.

Bentham also believed in **psychological hedonism**, the idea that people seek pleasure and avoid pain. Although later psychologists embraced this principle, none stated it more eloquently than Sigmund Freud (1930/1961a), who noted that "the purpose of life is simply the programme of the pleasure principle. This principle dominates the operation of the mental apparatus from the start" (p. 76).

Can we quantify pleasure and pain? Can a theoretical and practical balance of pleasure and pain guide our justice system? Bentham and his followers debated such issues. His critics were not optimistic; not until the twentieth century would social psychologists engage in systematic assessment of happiness (Veehoven, 2011). Such debates are of less historical significance than Bentham's attack on intuitionism. Following Bentham, one could conceive that closer scrutiny could benefit social systems and lead to more objective standards of punishment. With his work, a psychological analysis of human motivation is also elevated in importance.

Mary Wollstonecraft

The empirical vision of a world that can be improved through proper education served as a challenge and inspiration to **Mary Wollstonecraft (1759–1797)**, the most visible early pioneer in the battle for the emancipation of women. Though Wollstonecraft did not identify with any single philosophical system, she grasped the value of empiricism. If the mind at birth is as "white paper," as Locke contended, then the role of education in shaping character is paramount. Further, the white paper hypothesis suggested that perceived differences between men and women

may be attributed to differences in educational opportunities.

Gender differences had long been explained in terms of **essentialism**. The term *essence* refers to "the intrinsic nature or character of something; that which makes it what it is" (Brown, 1993, p. 852). As noted by Braaten and Viney (2000), "An essentialist philosophy applied to gender emphasizes natural differences neatly boxed and separated by clear boundaries" (p. 576). Women were regarded as essentially more emotional than men, deficient in judgment and in scientific and mathematical skills, and unconcerned about politics. The essentialist philosophy was used to argue against educational opportunities for women and against the right of women to vote or own property. Empirical philosophy could provide a plausible alternative for gender differences. Perhaps the differences could be explained in terms of the scarce opportunities for women. Wollstonecraft, in her classic book, *A Vindication of the Rights of Woman*, seized on this alternative explanation and challenged the assumed hierarchy of men and women (Taylor, 2003). Botting (2006) argues that despite the difficulties Wollstonecraft faced in her lifetime, she contributed to twenty-first century views of a more egalitarian family.

Mary Wollstonecraft was the second of the seven children of Edward John Wollstonecraft

Mary Wollstonecraft

and Elizabeth Dixon. Edward, a weaver, inherited a large sum of money from his father, but squandered it on gambling, alcohol, and inept business ventures. Some of Mary Wollstonecraft's earliest memories, in the words of Jacobs (2001), were of "her parents as unequal warriors, her mother weak and pretty, her father a sentimental tyrant who fawned over his family one moment, then beat them the next because he was drunk or out of sorts" (p. 18). She resented her father's tyranny and her mother's martyrdom. They displayed favoritism toward her oldest brother and made him sole heir to their estate (he had already inherited money from his grandfather). Under English law, women had no property rights and only limited educational opportunities. Mary Wollstonecraft sensed her intellectual superiority to her older brother and was offended that her brothers enjoyed a classic education while she and her sisters toiled on cooking and sewing.

Despite social barriers, Wollstonecraft acquired an informal education through extensive reading and friendship with progressive thinkers. Fighting career limitations, she served as a teacher before beginning her writing career. Regrettably, her new career provided insufficient funds to cover debts and to provide for her younger sisters. Writing, however, allowed her to unleash her rage over the presumptions, ignorance, and injustices of her day.

A Vindication of the Rights of Woman was written in only six weeks. According to one biographer, "It is ill arranged and full of repetitions, yet its directness, its sincerity and the terse militant strength of some passages make it one of the creative books of its age" (Brailsford, 1963). In her introduction, Wollstonecraft (1792/1929) points to her "wish to persuade women to endeavor to acquire strength, both of mind and body, and to convince them that the soft phrases [of the day such as], susceptibility of heart, delicacy of sentiment, and refinement of taste, are almost synonymous with epithets of weakness, and that those beings who are only the objects of pity. . .will soon become objects of contempt" (p. 5). Her book condemned those who keep women in a state of ignorance,

stupid acquiescence, and "childhood" as a means of preserving their innocence. According to Wollstonecraft, "Ignorance is a frail base for virtue!" (p. 69). She warned that passive women who serve as toys to please their husbands will find little fulfillment after their charms evaporate and the honeymoon ends. Wollstonecraft detested that women had been trained to be deceitful, coquettish, delicate, and docile pets.

Her book pleads for fierce honesty on the part of men and women to confront silly but ruinous social conventions. Such practices rob women of genuine personhood and rob men of rich and meaningful companionship. She insisted that social conventions must change to reach a just and equitable system. Despite technical faults, insights roll off every page of this hastily written but original book. In the words of Jacobs (2001), it is the first "feminist manifesto in the history of human rights" (p. 99). Wollstonecraft demanded educational equality in coeducational systems and economic independence for women through wider employment opportunities. She observed that beyond domestic duties, women of her day did little in society except loiter in a graceful fashion. The antidote was to train women in fields such as medicine, business, government, and politics. She believed that social change would benefit everyone. She believed that good men would find a more satisfying relationship with a competent woman than with an obedient one.

Wollstonecraft spoke with power and passion about parent–child relations. She observed that "meek wives are, in general, foolish mothers; wanting their children to love them best, and take their part, in secret, against the father, who is held up as a scarecrow" (1792/1929, p. 166). She notes that, in such cases, the wife seldom disciplined the child, leaving it to the husband. She lamented the fact that, in many cases, parental affection "is but a pretext to tyrannize." Children are rational creatures in their own right and must not be subjected to selfish and demanding authority, but too often this is the case, especially for girls. She argued that the subjection of a person to "the mere will of another. . .is a most cruel and undue stretch of power, and perhaps as injurious to morality as those religious systems which do not allow right and wrong to have any existence, but in the Divine will" (p. 168). Wollstonecraft believed that love should be merited, not coerced!

Both *A Vindication of the Rights of Woman* and its author faced severe criticism. Wollstonecraft was disparaged for being overly sentimental, impulsive, and indelicate in her love affairs (Stephen, 1993). Most criticisms were *ad hominem* attacks on the drama of her troubled life rather than on the substance of her work. She was, for a time, the common-law wife of Gilbert Imlay, an American traveler and merchant. Her first child, Fanny, resulted from this relationship. When Imlay deserted her, Wollstonecraft attempted suicide. After recovering from her despondency over Imlay, she married the philosopher William Godwin. Their short-lived but happy relationship resulted in the birth of a daughter, also named Mary. Tragically, medical attempts to recover the undescended placenta caused an infection that ended Mary Wollstonecraft's life at the age of thirty-eight. Her first daughter, Fanny, committed suicide. Her second daughter, Mary Wollstonecraft Godwin (1797–1851), married the Romantic poet Percy Bysshe Shelley in 1814 (Seymore, 2001). As Mary Shelley, she referenced her mother's work in a celebrated Gothic novel *Frankenstein; or, The Modern Prometheus,* first published anonymously in 1818.

James Mill

James Mill (1773–1836), a close disciple, trusted colleague, and friend of Jeremy Bentham, played a key role in popularizing and expanding Hartley's associationism and Bentham's utilitarianism. Mill was born the eldest son of James Mill, a cobbler, and Isabel Fenton on April 6, 1773. Though Mill studied for the ministry and was licensed to preach, he had no enthusiasm or success in this work. In 1802, Mill moved to London, where he embarked on a career as an editor and a writer. In 1805, he married Harriet Burrow. The first of their nine children, John Stuart Mill, was born in 1806.

James Mill's meager income came from his writing. His best-known literary work was *History of India*, published in 1818. Because of his extensive knowledge of India, Mill received an appointment as an official in the India House. He educated his own children in a stern, businesslike atmosphere with an emphasis on cognitive learning and a repression of feeling. Though he was a disciple who amplified the ideas of others, his work heightened visibility of the new philosophy's emphasis on education. Mill died on June 23, 1836.

James Mill's best-known psychological work, *Analysis of the Phenomena of the Human Mind* (1829), presents an uncompromising mechanistic approach to mental processes. Beliefs, memories, and expectancies—even purposes and aesthetic preferences—are grounded in association or conditioning. Character and cognitive ability are the products of proper educational procedures, and Mill rigorously educated his son in accordance with these beliefs. In his autobiography, John Stuart Mill (1873/1969) credited his father for adding "greater length and depth" to David Hartley's associationism (p. 43). Inspired by the implications of associationism, Mill became a staunch advocate for education for the masses.

John Stuart Mill

According to Robinson (1982), **John Stuart Mill (1806–1873)** "contributed directly and indirectly to any number of turns psychology would take toward the end of the nineteenth century. His philosophy of science put the older empiricism of Bacon and Locke on modern footing and lent plausibility to the claim that an *experimental* science of mind was within reach" (p. 75). Mill was one of the great liberal thinkers of the nineteenth century. He argued for freedom of expression, representative government, and the importance of the individual. Mill defied popular opinion in his support of the emancipation of women. His interests ranged from epistemology and logic to history, political theory, literature, and psychology. He ranks as one of the great British philosophers.

John Stuart Mill

John Stuart Mill was born on May 20, 1806. The story of young Mill's early life is well known. He was a precocious child, who, in the words of Bertrand Russell (1959), "had his father's educational doctrines ruthlessly inflicted on him. 'I never was a boy,' he complained later in life" (p. 266). Mill, educated by his father, started Greek at age three. At age eight, he was learning Latin and reading the Greek classics. The pace of learning was strained, even for a gifted child. "I was continually incurring his displeasure by my inability to solve difficult problems for which he did not see that I had not the necessary previous knowledge" (Mill, 1873/1969, p. 9). Harsh by twentieth-century standards, young Mill benefited from individual instruction and an erudite teacher. He viewed his education as a mixture of praise and criticism. Mill lamented the absence of holidays, the neglect of manual arts and skills, and the failure to recognize the role of feeling. At the same time, he appreciated his father's interest, diligence, and knowledge.

The Examiners Office of the India House hired Mill where he labored, once again, under his father's supervision. He wrote for the press, commenting that "the writings by which one can live, are not the writings which themselves live" (1873/1969, p. 51). He was nevertheless able to earn a living and to find ample time

for philosophy. Several early articles tackled freedom of speech. Together with his father, Mill was a member of a small fraternity of influential thinkers known as "Benthamites," who supported utilitarian ideas promoted by Jeremy Bentham. Later, John Stuart Mill coined the term *utilitarian* to describe nineteenth-century liberal thought representing Hartleian metaphysics, complete freedom of discussion, representative government, universal education, full employment, and voluntary birth control. In supporting his ideals, John Stuart Mill was once jailed overnight for distributing birth control information.

In the autumn of 1826, Mill suffered a severe depression, declaring later that "the whole foundation on which my life was constructed fell down. . .for some months the cloud seemed to grow thicker and thicker" (1873/1969, p. 81). He lamented having no one to talk with, no one who would understand, least of all his father. In the midst of depression, he concluded that the cultivation of feeling had been lacking in his education. He then explored his feelings by turning to art, poetry, and music. One day, he experienced an epiphany. He was reading a passage from Marmontel's *Memoirs* describing his father's death and the subsequent inspiration of a son to replace the father. Mill said, "A vivid conception of the scene and its feelings came over me, and I was moved to tears. From this moment my burden grew lighter" (1873/1969, p. 85).

In 1830, Mill met **Harriet Taylor (1807–1858)**, a woman unhappily married but unable to divorce due to strict laws. Their friendship deepened over a twenty-year period. Taylor's first husband died in 1849 and she married Mill two years later. In his autobiography, Mill claimed his companionship with Taylor enhanced his intellectual and emotional development. She served as a sounding board and often as a foil for Mill's intellectual work. Speaking in glowing terms, he regarded her as a genius, "a woman of deep and strong feeling, of penetrating and intuitive intelligence, and of an eminently meditative and poetic nature" (Mill, 1873/1969, pp. 111–112). Tragically, Harriet Taylor lived a mere seven years after her marriage to Mill. Devastated but still productive, Mill lived another fifteen years in a house he built to overlook Harriet Taylor's grave. One of Taylor's children by her first husband attended to Mill in his final years. Mill died on May 8, 1873.

Robinson (1982) argued that "Mill anticipated and encouraged the sort of research ordinarily identified as 'behavioristic'. . .he avoided the temptation to rush psychology into scientific status by biologizing it" (p. 75). Instead, the central organizing themes in Mill's conception of psychology are association and the pleasure principle. Mill accepted his father's and Hartley's principles of association, joining the belief that scientific methods can demonstrate elementary laws of the mind. But Mill raised doubts about whether the mechanical approach to association could do justice to the more complex mental phenomena. He observed that "the phenomena of mind are sometimes analogous to mechanical, but sometimes also to chemical laws" (1843/1974, p. 853). By this, he conveyed the idea that elements are not necessarily identifiable in complex ideas. He noted, for example, that we may see white when prismatic colors are properly mixed. We do not see each of the elements. According to Mill, this is an example of "mental chemistry: in which it is proper to say that the simple ideas generate, rather than that they compose, the complex ones" (p. 854). Mill warned, however, that psychological chemistry does not relieve us of the responsibility of identifying the basic properties of complex ideas any more than the chemist is relieved of the responsibility of identifying the elements of a chemical compound.

Mill's optimism about the possibility of a scientific psychology was illustrated in his belief that laws about which we have little or no knowledge govern us. He compared human nature with meteorology. The laws of heat, pressure, and electricity govern the weather. When we understand these laws, we can better understand the weather. By the same rule, biological and sociological laws govern human nature. According to Mill, it is no disparagement against certain sciences such as meteorology or a science of human

nature that predictions must be couched in terms of probabilities or approximations.

Mill raised a question about the reality of a scientific psychology. He answered, "All states of mind are immediately caused either by other states of mind, or by states of body" (1843/1974, p. 849). There is not only a science of psychology that studies successive states of mind or bodily influences on mind, but there is also a science of character formation, which Mill called *ethology*. Ethology, like psychology, can be studied by observational and experimental methods. Mill embraced the concept of an applied psychology (ethology) and a basic psychology.

As noted, Victorian attitudes toward women deeply concerned Mill. His book *The Subjection of Women* (1869/1988) called for radical change and generated predictable hostility by men who wished to conserve the status quo. He argued that "the principle which regulates the existing social relations between the two sexes—the legal subordination of one sex to the other—is wrong in itself, and now one of the chief hindrances to human improvement; and that it ought to be replaced by a principle of perfect equality, admitting no power or privilege on the one side, nor disability on the other" (p. 1). Mill believed that male chauvinism parades in the sciences as natural law or in religion as true theology based on divine ordinance. He had faith, however, that sexism would yield "before a sound psychology, laying bare the real root of much that is bowed down to as the intention of Nature and the ordinance of God" (p. 2).

The origin of Mill's feminist perspective is grounded in his empiricism and utilitarianism (Soble, 2009). In Mill's day, inequality was justified by citing presumed deficiencies in the nature of women. As a staunch empiricist, Mill argued that we cannot claim adequate knowledge about the nature of women so long as they live in political and social circumstances that undermine their abilities. Speculating on the origin of Mill's feminism, Okin (1988) pointed out that "it is certain that, from the time they met, Harriet Taylor was a major influence on the development of Mill's feminism" (p. ix). Mill also credited Taylor for sharpening his sensitivities to the practical, day-to-day consequences of sexism.

Mill's philosophical work and his interest in sexism are vital for a science of human nature. His views on the subjection of women suggest the possibility of a social psychology that could enlighten us on the benefits of gender equality. His philosophical work and social interests are intellectual forerunners of basic and applied psychology. Like many philosophers included in this chapter, Mill was interested in a new science of human nature that would enable us to "understand in order to improve human behavior" (Leary, 1980, p. 292).

Mill influenced a British colleague named **Alexander Bain (1818–1903)** who founded the journal *Mind* in 1876. This journal, initially edited by George Croom Robertson (1842–1892), is recognized as the first psychological journal (King, 2000). *Mind* served as an important outlet for early scholars in psychology and furthered the professionalization of psychology in Great Britain (Neary, 2001) but shifted focus toward a more philosophical journal. Bain not only founded the first psychological journal, but also wrote early critical psychology texts. His books *The Senses and the Intellect* (1855) and *The Emotions and the Will* (1859) influenced the early generation of psychologists.

CONTRIBUTIONS OF EMPIRICISM

Under Bacon, empiricism started in part as a reaction to Montaigne's skepticism. Empirical philosophy's emphasis on personal experience and observation influenced all sciences including psychology. A summary of the influences of empiricism includes, at a minimum, the following:

1. Empiricism provided a new methodology (in Bacon's words, *Novum Organum*) that corrected years of intellectual stagnation and challenged scholasticism, authority, revelation, and tradition.
2. With empiricism came a new emphasis on learning and universal education. If the mind at birth is as "white paper" as Locke

contended, then mental content depends on environment and social structures friendly to education.
3. John Locke's philosophy helped open the door to the study of children and their learning processes.
4. The work of empiricists such as Berkeley and Condillac emphasized the scientific study of the senses. If knowledge is acquired through the senses, we had best understand the capacities of these "windows to the mind."
5. Early empiricists were important pioneers in the study of motivation and emotion. David Hartley provided a classification of pleasures, and Jeremy Bentham was a critical figure in the study of punishment. David Hume was important in the study of the emotions.
6. John Stuart Mill and Harriet Taylor, following the tradition of Mary Wollstonecraft, challenged stereotypes about the abilities of women. Empiricism established an intellectual context that encouraged the liberation of women.
7. Hume's work on causality might properly be regarded as the most creative work on that subject since Aristotle.

Many intellectual components necessary for psychology to develop as a formal science were in place following the work of early empiricists and utilitarians.

Review Questions

1. Briefly describe Bacon's four Idols. What are some of the Idols in our day?
2. What is the Baconian approach to scientific methodology?
3. Distinguish between Locke's primary qualities and secondary qualities. Give examples of each.
4. Discuss some of the implications of Locke's contention that there is nothing in the intellect that was not previously in the senses.
5. What was Berkeley's objection to primary qualities? Briefly argue in defense of Berkeley's position.

6. Outline Hume's general approach to the problem of causality.
7. Show how empiricism evolved from a method (epistemology) under Bacon's treatment to a position on the nature of being (ontology) in the work of Berkeley and Hume.
8. Outline contributions to empiricism made by continental philosophers Condillac and Helvétius.
9. Briefly discuss the nature of the legal problems that contributed to the development of utilitarianism. What were the implications of utilitarianism for a science of human nature?
10. Review Hartley's seven varieties of pleasure.
11. Briefly outline Hartley's contributions to associationism.
12. Distinguish between the concepts of mental mechanics (James Mill) and mental chemistry (John Stuart Mill).
13. In what ways did John Stuart Mill contribute to the development of applied psychology?
14. Outline some of the ways empiricism contributed to an intellectual climate friendly to the development of psychology as a discipline.

Glossary

associationism   Systematic emphasis on the idea that human knowledge is not innate but grows inevitably out of the gradual buildup of associations from sensory data.

Bacon, Francis (1561–1626)   Early modern philosopher of science who called for a close examination of the problem of knowledge and increased sensitivity to sources of error. A powerful advocate of a critical empirical-inductive method.

Bain, Alexander (1818–1903)   Founded *Mind*, the first journal devoted extensively to psychological topics. Also the author of some of the first psychological texts.

Bentham, Jeremy (1748–1832)   Founder of utilitarianism. Argued against intuitive approaches to jurisprudence that resulted in punishments that do not fit the crime and argued for a rational system of punishments and rewards and the need to maximize pleasure for the greatest possible number of people.

Berkeley, George (1685–1753)   British philosopher who argued that the real world is not the world of matter but the world of experience. His dictum *esse est percipi* (to be is to be perceived) marks him as one of the most radical of the early empiricists. Advanced an early empirical approach to depth perception, attempting to demonstrate that we learn to see in depth.

Condillac, Étienne Bonnot de (1715–1780)   French radical empiricist who attempted to show specifically how all knowledge could derive from associations that start with simple sensations.

empiricism   A philosophical position that emphasizes the importance of experience, observation, and learning in the acquisition of knowledge.

essentialism   Belief in the possibility of discerning the fundamental character or intrinsic nature of something.

hardening   An early concept that emphasized the beneficial role of self-imposed hardships (e.g., sleeping on an uncomfortable bed, exposure to cold weather) as means of preparing for subsequent tasks. Hardening is not quite the same as conditioning in that it involved practices that were more likely to be damaging.

Hartley, David (1705–1757)   Founder of modern associationism and one of the first to establish a classification system of pleasures and pains.

Helvétius, Claude-Adrien (1715–1771)   French materialist who argued that human actions can be explained on the basis of rewards and punishments. His views were considered radical in his day and he was forced to recant his position.

Hume, David (1711–1776)   British empiricist who advanced the view that causality is not a property of objects, and therefore, there are no necessary connections. Causality is thus reduced to a psychological problem and is based on consistent conjunction and our ways of making sense of the successive events in the world.

Idols   A term employed by Francis Bacon referring to "phantoms of the mind." Idols are sources of error, such as excessive reliance on authority, that blind us in our quest for truth.

Idols of the Cave   Local prejudices or strongly preferred hypotheses or theories that interfere with objective responses to data.

Idols of the Marketplace   The temptation to take words too seriously so that naming is confused with explaining. To guard against the Idols of the Marketplace, one must constantly reexamine definitions and understand the deceptive dimensions of language.

Idols of the Theatre   Errors of thought based on the easy acceptance of authority or the naïve acceptance of a popular paradigm.

Idols of the Tribe   Errors of thought resulting from inherent human limitations such as sensory distortions and the tendency to overgeneralize.

Locke, John (1632–1704)   One of the greatest philosophers of English speech who insisted that the mind at birth is like a blank slate devoid of characters or ideas. His emphasis on the centrality of experience and learning elevated the importance of universal education.

Mill, James (1773–1836)   British philosopher who advanced an uncompromising mechanistic approach to association. Argued strongly for the education of the masses.

Mill, John Stuart (1806–1873)   One of the great philosophers of English speech who envisioned a science of human nature based on probabilistic notions. Also one of the first to deplore the subjugation of women.

primary qualities   Qualities such as figure, extension, and solidity that are presumed to inhere in objects.

psychological hedonism   Belief that human beings seek in all things to gain pleasure and avoid pain.

secondary qualities   Powers of objects that contribute to specific sensations such as colors, tastes, and sounds.

solipsism   A subjective philosophical position that makes the claim that the only possible knowledge is self-knowledge.

Taylor, Harriet (1807–1858)   Wife of John Stuart Mill. Collaborated with Mill and likely influenced his thought on feminism.

utilitarianism   A philosophy advanced by Jeremy Bentham emphasizing the idea that the moral basis of action should be the greatest good for the greatest number.

Voltaire, François-Marie Arouet de (1694–1778)   French philosopher who advanced the cause of new philosophies based on observation and experiment. His sharp attacks on untestable theories and theological dogma continually placed him at risk.

Wollstonecraft, Mary (1759–1797)   The most visible early pioneer in the battle for the rights of women. Author of *A Vindication of the Rights of Woman*.

7

■ ■ ■

Rationalism

A desire which springs from reason can never be in excess.

—Benedict Spinoza (in Gutmann, 1949, p. 233)

As discussed in Chapter 6, seventeenth-century philosophy confronted the task of combating skepticism and restoring faith in human knowledge. Empirical philosophy, under the leadership of Francis Bacon and John Locke, argued that we attain knowledge through experience and the association of sensory data. As we will see in this chapter, rational philosophy turned to axiomatic first principles and reason as the guides to knowledge. The term **rationalism** was derived from the Latin *ratio*, which means to reason, to think, or to reckon. Major differences separate rationalism and empiricism. First, rational philosophy emphasizes a priori knowledge, whereas empiricism claims that all knowledge is derived from experience. We'll discuss this in a moment. Second, rationalists regard the mind as active in the sense of its capacity to select, organize, and discriminate, whereas empiricists argue for a more passive mind dependent on the laws of association and conditioning. Finally, deductive reasoning is emphasized in rationalism, whereas inductive reasoning is emphasized in empiricism. Let's take a look at these contrasting perspectives.

EMPHASIS ON A PRIORI KNOWLEDGE

According to rationalism, certain essential truths are apprehended in an a priori manner. For example, statements such as *All bachelors are unmarried* or *A line cannot be perpendicular to itself* are grasped as necessarily true once we understand the terms. Granted, we have had experience with language and with specific terms such as *bachelor* and *unmarried* or *line* and *perpendicular*, but according to rationalism, the self-evident nature of the proposition itself is grasped on an a priori basis and such a priori knowledge can form the basis of knowledge (Hatfield, 2009). In the first example about bachelors, we understand that the predicate completely unpacks the subject. In a similar manner, we may grasp more complex relationships. Thus, if *A* is larger than *B* and *B* is larger than *C*, we know also that *A* is larger than *C*. Rationalists also emphasize certain innate capacities and preferences such as the capacity to see in depth or the preference for sweet rather than bitter tastes.

THEORY OF THE ACTIVE MIND

According to empiricism, our senses bring information to the mind. Knowledge about the world is built up through associations based on external influences such as contiguity, similarity, contrast, and reinforcement. Rationalists would not disagree, but they would also argue that the mind is more than a passive repository of sensory information. Instead, the mind organizes, selects, rejects, discriminates, and acts on sensory data. The theory of an **active mind** is tied to rationalism's emphasis on a priori truths. Such truths would hold little significance if they did not translate into action.

DEDUCTION VERSUS INDUCTION

It is incorrect to state that rationalism relies exclusively on reason but empiricism relies exclusively on experience. Reason and experience play a role in both philosophies. Nevertheless, rationalism stresses deductive reason, whereas empiricism is more concerned with the rules of induction. In a **deductive argument**, the premises are claimed to provide definitive grounds for the conclusion. If a deductive argument is valid, then it is impossible for the premises to be true while the conclusion is false. An **inductive argument**, by contrast, intends to show that the conclusion is more likely than not, given the premises. If an inductive argument is strong, then the conclusion is shown to be more probable than not, given the premises. It is characteristic of induction to reason from samples to populations. Conclusions are given in the language of probability in induction, whereas conclusions can be offered as "proved," in a strict sense, in deductive reasoning.

Rationalism and empiricism result in contrasting views of human beings and in different philosophies of science. This chapter will examine the leading rationalists of the seventeenth, eighteenth, and nineteenth centuries. We'll also take a look at the implications of rational philosophy for psychology.

RENÉ DESCARTES

Born on March 31, 1596, **René Descartes (1596–1650)** was the fourth child of Joachim Descartes and Jeanne Brochard. Tragically, his mother died fourteen months later while giving birth to her fifth child. We know little about Descartes's early years, but his childhood was marked by continued illness. Because of his frail condition, he was pampered and his formal education delayed. Joachim Descartes, a practicing lawyer and judge, recognized an unusual curiosity and intellect in his son. In 1604, when Descartes was eight years old, his father enrolled him in a Jesuit School at La Flèche, north of Touraine. Still in frail health, he was excused from morning activities and allowed to sleep in, giving rise to a lifelong habit of sleeping ten hours a day (Rodis-Lewis, 1999). Descartes was a brilliant student with unusual skills in mathematics. He discovered his deepest satisfaction in this area because it offered greater certainty than other subjects.

The period from 1612 to 1628 held no hint that Descartes would one day secure fame as the founder of modern philosophy. In 1616, he earned a law degree from the University of Poiters, but the legal profession did not captivate him. Filled with self-doubt, he turned from academic life to the "book of the world" and to careful introspection into his own life. During this period, he experimented with military life, volunteering for duty in Holland under the Prince of Orange. Following that assignment, he served in the Bavarian Army and, still later, in the Imperial

René Descartes

Army of Hungary. Descartes traveled throughout Western Europe, all the while engrossed with the problems of human knowledge. By the late 1620s, Descartes's proficiency in mathematics gained attention. A renowned cardinal named Pierre de Berulle encouraged Descartes to immerse himself in scholarly activity.

After moving from France to Holland, Descartes began work on his book *The World* (Gaukroger, 1997). Written from 1629 to 1633, this treatise was in essential agreement with Galileo's conclusions in *Dialogue on the Two Chief Systems*. Like Galileo and Copernicus, he did not believe that the earth is immovable or that it rests at the center of the universe. In 1633, he learned that the Inquisition had imprisoned Galileo and burned his book. The disturbing news ensnared Descartes between his loyalty to Catholic authority and his passion for truth. Vrooman (1970) believed it unlikely that Descartes would have suffered his "Italian contemporary's fate, which was first strict confinement and later, while still under surveillance, weekly recitation of the seven penitential psalms for a period of three years" (p. 84). Descartes's letters reveal his intense anxieties in the aftermath of the Galileo affair as well as his identification with the ideas presented in Galileo's *Dialogue* (see Grayling, 2005, pp. 143–147). His worries might have been compounded through inappropriate comparisons with the work of Giulio Cesare Vanini (1585–1619) who had proposed a naturalistic philosophy in his book, *The Secrets of Nature*. Vanini, like Descartes, had a deep interest in natural causation. Unlike Descartes, he did not hesitate to trample on sacred ground by denying the immortality of the soul and raising doubts about miracles. A victim of the Inquisition, Vanini was burned at the stake in 1619.

The fates of Galileo, Vanini, and other scholars underscore the danger in challenging religious authority during the early seventeenth century. In the end, authority conquered reason when Descartes decided against publishing his treatise *The World*. His decision was, in all likelihood, based on intense loyalty to the church rather than on a lack of courage. In a letter to his friend Marin Mersenne, Descartes declared that his argument for the movement of the earth was based on clear proofs. Nevertheless, he said, "I would not wish, for anything in the world, to maintain them against the authority of the church" (see Kenny, 1970, p. 26). Despite four years of work, Descartes made the fateful decision to suppress his treatise. Fortunately, it would not remain so. *The World* was finally published in 1664, fourteen years after his death. Shorto (2008) notes that "Reason vs. faith may be the chronic fever of modernity" (p. 79). It was a fever that has remained virulent well into the twenty-first century.

In 1635, Descartes had a brief relationship with a Dutch servant that resulted in the birth of a daughter named Francine. Although he decided against marriage, Descartes became a dedicated father. Unfortunately, Francine suffered an illness at age five and, according to one account, died in Descartes's arms (Rodis-Lewis, 1999).

Crushed with grief, Descartes withdrew from intimate relationships to immerse himself in work. Between 1628 and 1649, he produced the major works that secured his place in history. During this prolific period, he wrote *Rules for the Direction of the Mind*, probably completed around 1628, but published posthumously in 1684; *Discourse on the Method of Rightly Conducting One's Reason and Seeking the Truth in the Sciences, and in Addition the Optics, the Meteorology and the Geometry, Which Are Essays in This Method*, first published anonymously in 1637; *Principles of Philosophy*, 1644; *Description of the Human Body*, published posthumously in 1664; *The Passions of the Soul*, 1649; and Descartes's most celebrated work, *Meditations on First Philosophy*, 1641. These and other works are published in a two-volume collection titled *The Philosophical Writings of Descartes* (Cottingham, Stoothoff, & Murdoch, 1984–1985).

By the late 1640s, Queen Christina of Sweden (1626–1689) had developed an interest in Descartes's work. In 1649, she invited him to Stockholm to become her personal tutor. Descartes was filled with reservations about the northern climate, the voyage itself, and the demands of courtly life. As a Catholic, he was also apprehensive about living in a Protestant country. His greatest concern centered on whether his need for privacy and solitude would be compromised in the queen's court. Despite reservations, he accepted the invitation and landed in Stockholm in October 1649.

It proved a greater challenge than he had imagined. The queen insisted Descartes conduct her tutorials at 5 A.M. Although never a morning person, he agreed to her demand and awakened early to tutor her for almost five months. The inconvenient schedule and a harsh Stockholm winter took their toll. In January, Descartes admitted in a letter, "I am not in my element here" (Rodis-Lewis, 1999, p. 188). Less than a month later, he contracted pneumonia. René Descartes died in the early hours of February 11, 1650.

In his work, Descartes managed to shape modern science and philosophy with an integrated system of thought. From his earliest years, he was interested in the problem of knowledge. He was troubled about the threat to science and philosophy posed by skeptics such as Charron and Montaigne. As noted by Popkin (1979), Descartes hoped to establish an "intellectual fortress capable of withstanding the assaults of the skeptics" (p. 173). In part, his "intellectual fortress" was built from the labors of his unusual mathematical gifts (unlike Bacon, he appreciated the unique role that math plays in science). Descartes was also well versed in the discoveries of the empirical sciences of his day. In terms of both interest and intellect, he was well qualified to construct a philosophy that would influence the new sciences.

Descartes's Method

Descartes is regarded as a rationalist because he promoted reason as the means of attaining scientific knowledge. His major works emphasize innate ideas, a priori truths, and a preference for deduction. In this philosophical context, his method is grounded in a rebellion against skepticism.

Descartes's search for an intellectual edifice that could withstand the assaults of skepticism began with the method of skepticism itself.

He agreed with Montaigne that it is possible, as an intellectual exercise, to doubt many things—the existence of God, the past, the world, one's own body, and the existence of other people. Descartes's real goal was to push skepticism to its limit, to engage in a kind of hyperbolic doubt to see if he could discover something that was immune to doubt. In the course of his work, he found something he could not doubt—namely, the fact that he was doubting. But in order to doubt, one must think. In order to think, one must exist. On the basis of this reason, Descartes arrived at his celebrated axiom *cogito ergo sum* (I think, therefore I am). He believed this deductive proof of his conscious existence was a distinct idea that constitutes a central feature in the Cartesian method.

Like Bacon, Descartes believed we should lay aside old prejudices and opinions. He was, however, quick to separate science and faith. As noted by Mahaffy (1969), "In the first he is a sweeping reformer; in the second a strict conservative" (p. 24). Our concern here is with Descartes the reformer who, in his *Discourse on Method*, established procedural rules for the intellect and a "strong and unswerving resolution never to fail to observe them" (Cottingham et al., 1984–1985, vol. 1, p. 120). The four rules, also emphasized in his *Meditations*, are as follows:

1. Never accept anything as true unless it is so clear and distinct as to be immune from doubt.
2. Divide all difficulties into as many parts as possible.
3. Start with the easiest and best-known elements and proceed step by step to knowledge of the more complex.
4. Make complete enumerations and comprehensive reviews to ensure that nothing is left out.

Descartes declared that his method was modeled on mathematicians who alone provided "certain and evident reasonings" (Cottingham et al., 1984–1985, p. 120). He believed that his method could be extended to a great range of problems and usher in a new era of discovery of certain knowledge. The results of his inquiry led him to argue that qualitative differences exist between mind and body, humans and animals, and God and the world. The remaining questions about the nature of the interactions between qualitatively different substances plagued and inspired his contemporaries and continue to challenge scholars today.

Although Descartes's system betrays a preference for deduction from self-evident truths, he nevertheless reserves a role for experience in scientific procedure. To be sure, he was conservative in his views of experiments because he realized that an experiment is only a special form of observation that can be poorly conceived and thus result in misinformation. Clarke (1982) pointed out that Descartes is quick to reject the results of experiments that defy reason (p. 18). At the same time, Clarke insists that Descartes "commends the appropriateness of ordinary experience as a foundation for physical science" (p. 23). Mahaffy (1969) calls attention to one of Descartes's letters to the philosopher Marin Mersenne where Descartes expresses his wish "that some patient person would write down an exact description of the actual state of the heavens, without hypotheses or conjecture, after the manner of Bacon. This would be the greatest help to the theorist" (p. 55; see also Kenny, 1970, p. 24). Shorto (2008) notes that Descartes was "foundational to *both* the rationalists and the empiricist traditions" (p. 78).

The Cartesian method includes a place for ordinary experience and simple day-to-day observation. Indeed, Descartes trusted ordinary experience more than experiments and believed that the foundation for science is grounded in simple observation of natural events followed by critical reflection. Descartes noted that at the beginning of an investigation "it is better to resort only to those [observations] which, presenting themselves spontaneously to our senses, cannot be unknown to us if we reflect even a little. The reason for this is that the more unusual observations are apt to mislead us" (Cottingham et al., 1984–1985, vol. 1, p. 143). Clarke called attention to Descartes's simple anatomical observations on beasts killed in butcher houses and to his claim that in unambiguous situations "reasoning is useless without

experience" (Clarke, 1982, p. 205). The role of experience in Descartes's method provides material for reflection. It is reflection based on sensory information that is the source of scientific procedure. Sensory information alone cannot be trusted; it leads only to superficial and existential appearances (see Green, 1985, pp. 53–87). Descartes applied his methods to many topics; some argue that he was the first to systematically investigate consciousness (Frith & Rees, 2007).

Descartes did not deny that discoveries may result from chance observations or blind trial and error. However, such discoveries are not, in a formal sense, part of the scientific method. For Descartes, scientific knowledge presupposes a conceptual or theoretical framework. Clarke (1982) called attention to Descartes's dismay that "the telescope was discovered by experimental manipulation of lenses without a theory to explain the result: 'To the shame of our sciences, this discovery, which is so useful and admirable, was initially made only by experimenting and by chance'" (p. 37).

To summarize, Descartes's emphasis on deduction, mathematical proofs, and self-evident truths betrays a rationalist approach to the philosophy of science. Nevertheless, for Descartes, simple experiences play a key role in the initial stages of inquiry. If one wants to initiate geographic inquiry, Descartes would undoubtedly counsel that one should begin by making observations of coastlines, mountain ranges, the courses of rivers, and so on. Just as a map of the heavens would be helpful to the science of astronomy, so would a well-constructed map benefit a science of geography. Descartes reserves a role for simple experience; what he opposes is premature, poorly conceived, or meaningless experiments that lack an adequate conceptual base. With his emphasis on the role of common experience, Descartes does not fit the role of Bacon's "rationalist spider," that according to Bacon, spins webs out of its own substance.

Descartes provided conclusions that emphasized the role of the individual (Jansz, 2004), and it's no surprise that he influenced later philosophers who studied the problem of knowledge and the new sciences. His immediate successor, Benedict Spinoza, drew inspiration from Descartes's philosophy of science and views of mind and body, forging an important conceptual basis for a science of human nature.

BARUCH SPINOZA

Intense religious persecution prompted a mass exodus of Jews from Spain and Portugal during the late sixteenth century. One of the greatest philosophers of the seventeenth century came from a Jewish family who had fled the cruelty of the Inquisition to find a new home in Holland, known at the time as a haven of religious freedom. **Baruch Spinoza (1632–1677)** was born in Amsterdam on November 24, 1632. He later changed his Jewish name, Baruch, to its Latin equivalent, Benedict.

The young Spinoza was an outstanding student, making him the subject of admiration for the orthodox Jewish community. In time, he became a source of consternation. An unabashed radical, Spinoza raised penetrating questions about fundamental beliefs and criticized ideas based on authority and tradition (Meymandi, 2010). In desperation, the rabbis offered Spinoza a sizable scholarship for his education, but added the condition that he abandon his unorthodox views and conceal his doubts. But Spinoza, as much as any figure we have encountered, was caught in the grip of an irresistible urge to take ideas seriously. The life of the mind could not be compromised. In a bold move, he refused the scholarship.

Brutal consequences followed Spinoza's decision, leading to aggressive public ridicule. On one occasion, a knife-wielding fanatic attacked him. In 1656, he was excommunicated from the synagogue. In the wake of this censure, the faithful Jewish community was prohibited from speaking with Spinoza or reading his works. Goldstein (2006) argues that the persecution of the anti-Semitic Inquisition and of Spinoza himself shaped his philosophical views.

Spinoza's uncompromising dedication to truth was tested on other occasions by offers of financial support. He refused most offers because they held stipulations that compromised his intellectual integrity. As a consequence, he was forced to earn a meager living as a lens grinder. In his remaining free time, he worked on philosophy. By 1663, he had published his *Principles of the Philosophy of René Descartes* (see Curley, 1985, pp. 221–346). He also wrote two controversial works published after his death, *Treatise on the Emendation of the Intellect* (see pp. 3–45), and his best-known work, *Ethics* (see pp. 401–617). A central theme is the denial that an epistemology based on revelation has special status as a means of attaining truth. In contrast, rigorous rational inquiry held promise as a way of ascertaining truth and offering a way to know God. *Ethics* employed methods of inquiry perceived as the most advanced in his day, and therefore it proceeded in step-by-step geometric proofs of the nature of God and existence. By the 1660s, Spinoza's fame spread, and he corresponded with numerous intellectual figures including the philosopher Gottfried Wilhelm Leibniz. However, few of Spinoza's contemporaries appreciated his arguments, so it is little wonder his works were banned.

In 1672, he became enraged when a mob assassinated Jan De Witt (1625–1672), a politician Spinoza admired. Damasio (2003) wrote, "Assailants clubbed and knifed [De Witt and his brother] as they dragged them on the way to the gallows, and by the time they arrived there was no need to hang them anymore. They proceeded to undress the corpses, suspend them upside down, butcher-shop style, and quarter them. The fragments were sold as souvenirs, eaten raw, or eaten cooked, amid the most sickening merriment" (pp. 20–21). Although the riot troubled Leibniz, Damasio (2003) called it "probably Spinoza's darkest hour" (p. 21). His landlord, a man named Van der Spijk, worried when the philosopher planned to march to the site of the execution to protest the mob's savagery. Realizing that his friend would be no match for the bloodthirsty mob, Van der Spijk locked Spinoza in a room in their canal townhouse and prevented him from staging a protest. His friend no doubt saved Spinoza from certain death.

In 1673, Spinoza was offered a chair in philosophy at Heidelberg University with a promise of limited academic freedom. The offer was accompanied, as usual, with an expression of trust that Spinoza would refrain from controversial action that might upset the religious establishment. In characteristic fashion, Spinoza refused. In 1673, a representative from the court of Louis XIV promised a pension if Spinoza would dedicate a new work to the king. As yet another testimony to his unflinching integrity, Spinoza declined.

In 1675, Spinoza completed his greatest work, *Ethics*. However, his efforts to publish resulted in such a storm of protest from the clergy that he abandoned the project. *Ethics* was published posthumously and was promptly banned. During his lifetime, he became accomplished at cutting, grinding, and polishing glass for the construction of microscopes and telescopes. Legend has it that Spinoza worked with glass as a means of earning a living, but Gullan-Whur (1998, p. 90) suggests that scientific interests motivated his work in optics. Tragically, his profession shortened his life as the fine particles and dust associated with grinding and polishing contributed to a disease of the lungs. Consequently, Spinoza died at the age of forty-four on February 21, 1677. During his life and for a century thereafter, his name was anathema to orthodox Catholics, Protestants, and Jews. Though he was not a resident of Spain, his name was placed on the "wanted list" in the Spanish Inquisition. He was accused of atheism and of denying revelation. Strictly speaking, neither charge was true; Spinoza simply gave the world a new vision of God and of revelation.

In Descartes's philosophy, we encounter a dualism of soul and body, at least where humans are concerned. Such a radical separation of soul and body leaves room for free will in humans, but animals may be viewed as automata. Such a split between humans and animals contributes to a polarization of the free will–determinism issue. There was still another split between the sacred realm that includes a transcendent God and the secular world. What is most evident in Spinoza is an unrelenting quest for unity, a quest that results in a denial of the legitimacy of distinctions between sacred and secular, mind and body, and free will and determinism. Let us begin with Spinoza's vision of the union of the sacred and the secular.

During his life, people with mental disorders were thought to be possessed by demons. Spinoza, however, denied the metaphysical basis of demonology in mental illness. He argued that there is only one ultimate reality and that reality is God. There are not separate spiritual powers that control natural events such as the weather, earthquakes, or mental illness. Rather, God is the only spiritual power, and God is imminent in nature and inseparable from truth. What is true is of God, indeed *is* God. When we discover a natural truth, we are thereby discovering something about the infinite substance that is God. With Spinoza, it is not God *or* nature or God *in* nature; rather, God *is* nature. Spinoza believed that the common view that God is separate from nature was a product not of rational reason but of imagination. It was also imagination that projected the popular anthropomorphic God with human needs and a human form, including a sexual identity. Spinoza's view is essentially pantheistic; it argues that God is all things. Thus, any distinction between sacred and secular is false. The scientist or the rationalist can discover as much or more about God as the theologian.

Such radical ideas made Spinoza the subject of ridicule and contributed to his excommunication. Due to his denial of a God separate from the world, Delahunty (1985) noted, "To his immediate successors, his 'hideous hypothesis' seemed a ruseful version of atheistic materialism, honeyed words coating poisoned messages" (p. 125). But Spinoza was neither an atheist nor a materialist, and within a century of his death, he was viewed as a "God-intoxicated man, the last magnificent blaze of the Hebrew religious imagination" (p. 125).

Spinoza also challenged Cartesian notions about separate substances, both mind and body, and their independent interaction in the pineal gland. How, he asked, can a nonphysical mind be causal with respect to a physical substance and how does causal interaction take place in the pineal gland? According to Spinoza, mind and body are not radically separate; rather, they are two aspects of the same fundamental reality. Thus, psychological and neurophysiological processes coexist, and the world of experience (the psychological world) and the world of behavior (the physiological world) are but two expressions of the same thing. Such a position assigns a role to psychology as a scientific discipline. Mental processes are a part of the natural order—the human mind is a part of nature and is subject to nature's laws.

If the human mind is subject to nature's laws, there is no absolute or unconditioned free will. There is, however, a kind of freedom associated with knowledge of the laws of nature. For example, knowledge of the cause of a disease greatly enhances our freedom to deal with the disease, so we need no longer be victimized by it. Spinoza also believed we are freer when not dominated by our passions. Spinoza's book, *Ethics*, deals with ways in which freedom has meaning within a deterministic context. We will encounter this approach later in the thought of Sigmund Freud who, like Spinoza, believed in the lawfulness of the mind, but also embraced the possibility of a hard-won but weak form of freedom that emerges when the ego is not dominated by irrational forces.

Spinoza's psychological thought as set forth in his *Ethics* is rich in insight and worthy of detailed study. For example, he claimed, "anything may be accidentally the cause of either hope or fear" (Gutmann, 1949, p. 163). He connected this proposition with the development of superstition. Spinoza contended that the strength of an emotion is a function of the number of simultaneous causes (p. 259). In a discussion of the origin and nature of emotions, he noted that if we develop hatred for a thing once loved, we hate with greater intensity than had we never loved it in the first place. Why? It is because the greater hatred is fueled by sorrow over the loss of love (p. 156).

Spinoza's rationalism is evident in his use of the geometric method. His ideas were often set forth in terms of axioms, numbered propositions, and demonstrations. Like Descartes, he emphasized the capacity to grasp certain essential truths intuitively. Spinoza also insisted on careful examination of definitions and a procedure that begins with what is self-evident or grasped. He was as suspicious of unexamined sense data as he was of authority or tradition. Spinoza romanticized rationalism, claiming that people who are governed by reason wish no advantage for themselves that they do not wish for others and that reason produces "just, faithful and honorable" people (Gutmann, 1949, p. 203). Also he declared, "a desire which springs from reason can never be in excess" (p. 233).

It can be argued that Spinoza contributed more to the philosophical and intellectual spadework necessary for the development of modern psychology than any thinker we have encountered. His philosophy challenges the separate status of mental processes implied in earlier dualistic theories. Though reviled in his day, Spinoza inspired many later scholars whom we'll study including Johannes Müller and Gustav Fechner (Bernard, 1972) as well as von Helmholtz and Wundt. Alexander and Selesnick (1966) suggest that Spinoza understood ideas such as repression, overcompensation, reaction formation, and the role of pleasure that materialized in later Freudian psychology. Spinoza's influence extended beyond psychology and philosophy, inspiring Albert Einstein to assert, "I believe in Spinoza's God who reveals himself in the harmony of all being" (Brian, 1997, p. 127).

GOTTFRIED WILHELM LEIBNIZ

A contemporary of John Locke and Sir Isaac Newton, **Gottfried Wilhelm Leibniz (1646–1716)** was a genius who shaped European thought in diverse areas such as mathematics, law, history, politics, religion, philosophy, and psychology. Leibniz and Newton are remembered as independent inventors of the differential calculus. Leibniz is also remembered as one of the first to develop a calculating machine. His work can be characterized as a quest for the world's unity. Unlike Spinoza, his philosophy allows a stronger role for diversity within unity.

Leibniz's concern for unity extended to practical problems. For example, he sought to reconcile Protestants and Catholics and to unite medicine and science. He also envisioned a universal language. Leibniz saw the possibility of a united world ruled by reason, science, and an essentially Christian ethic. His practical quests for unity were, of course, frustrated. His metaphysical quest for unity, anchored as it was in theology, fared no better.

Leibniz was born in Leipzig, Germany, in 1646. His father, a professor of moral philosophy at the University of Leipzig, died when his son was six years old. When Leibniz was eight, he was allowed to explore his father's library. It opened a new world for the young man, bringing him into contact with his father's work and values. Leibniz was a precocious student with a broad appetite for studies in language, mathematics, history, religion, and philosophy. At age fifteen, he enrolled in the University of Leipzig, where he earned a doctorate of law in five years. However, university authorities were reluctant to award the doctoral degree to a man of only twenty years. Consequently, Leibniz immediately withdrew and enrolled at the University of Altdorf. Within months of his enrollment, he presented a dissertation and successfully defended it. His doctorate was awarded on February 22, 1667, when he was only twenty-one years of age (Fancher & Schmidt, 2003).

Leibniz refused university positions, believing he could accomplish more goals and live in comfort if he worked for ruling princes and political authorities. Though courtly routine often compromised his intellectual interests, he enjoyed a productive career. He worked four years for the archbishop of Mainz, but most of his time was spent in Hanover where he served under a succession of three rulers. The lives of Leibniz and Spinoza were as dissimilar as the public perceptions of their work; these differences are captured in the title of Stewart's (2007) account of their lives, *The Courtier and the Heretic*.

Leibniz enjoyed countless honors in his lifetime. To name a few, he was elected to the Royal Society, the Paris Academy of Sciences, and the Accademia Fisico-Matematica in Rome. He was nominated president of the Paris Academy of Sciences, the Society of Sciences in Vienna, and the Berlin Society. On one occasion, he was offered the position of custodian of the Vatican library (Aiton, 1985, p. 159). Leibniz died in 1716 at the age of seventy. Later, the town of Hanover erected a marble bust to Leibniz's memory to commemorate his forty years of work in their community.

Monadology

As we noted in the previous section, Spinoza's solution to the mind–brain problem avoided the difficulties of Cartesian interactionism but introduced new problems. In Spinoza's system, diversity was never an equal partner with unity; the former was mere appearance, the latter was reality. Thus, the only possible differences between mind and brain were of an attributional nature. Leibniz was critical of Cartesian interactionism, but neither could he accept the singular vision of Spinoza. Though both shared a belief in reason, Leibniz disagreed with Spinoza's contention that all things are part of one fundamental substance. Leibniz sought to give equal status to the claims of the mental and physical realms and at the same time preserve the world's unity—no small task. He also rejected Spinoza's determinism and the idea that plurality is nothing but appearance.

Leibniz's approach to mind and brain must be understood in the context of his concept of the monad. Leibniz probably adopted the term **monad** (*monas*) from the philosophers Anne Conway and F. M. Von Helmont (see Merchant, 1979). Lady Anne Conway (1631–1679), an influential philosopher in her day, found middle ground between the extreme dualism of Descartes and the extreme monism of Spinoza. She most likely had a strong influence on Leibniz. The term *monad* itself refers to a principle of existence or an ultimate unit of being. For Leibniz, a monad is a unity or an entity harmonious with the entire universe.

Leibniz believed that the universe was created with a **preestablished harmony** of its individual parts. Leibniz chose the analogy of independent synchronized clocks to illustrate his idea of preestablished harmony. Imagine that mind and body are like two clocks set for the same time. Although synchronized, neither clock depends on the other to function. Both are individual and independent while existing in parallel harmony. Following the analogy, both mind and body are accorded a place in the scheme of things and the two orders are perfectly synchronized. The mental is truly individual, yet it corresponds perfectly with the physical. Our cry of pain is parallel with a searing physical burn, and the burn is parallel with the cry of pain. In his psychophysical parallelism, every individual monad brings the sum of the universe along with it.

Unlike Descartes, Leibniz avoids the problems of interactionism. His brand of psychophysical parallelism leaves us with real diversity or individuality within unity. But, we now encounter violence to causality. In Leibniz's system, no monad is causal with respect to any other monad. Monads do not interact in any way, and all monads are simply in harmonious accord by virtue of preestablished harmony. But how are we to account for preestablished harmony? Leibniz's answer is found in theology. The synchronicity of monads reflects a divine order. Somewhat like Newton's notion of a "clockwork universe," God is the great clockmaker, now responsible for setting preestablished harmony in motion.

Poma (2013, p. 3) notes that Leibniz coined the term *theodicy*. Broadly conceived, theodicy refers to the relationship of God to the world and often focuses on the problem of evil. If God is omnibenevolent (i.e., all-loving), omniscient, and omnipotent, then God wants the best of all possible worlds, knows what the best possible world is, and can create the best of all worlds. Therefore, the currently existing world, arranged in a preestablished harmony by a perfect God, must be the best of all worlds despite widespread suffering and evil. In his novel *Candide*, Voltaire (1759/1991) mocked Leibniz's optimism in the guise of Candide's tutor, a character named Professor Pangloss. Throughout *Candide*, after each fresh disaster in an ongoing series of

tragedies, with people suffering and dying all around him, Pangloss remains convinced that all things are for the best and that this is the best of all possible worlds. Additional problems with Liebniz's position are explored by Poma (2013).

It is testimony to Leibniz's influence that some early psychologists rejected preestablished harmony, but still embraced psychophysical parallelism. It offers a practical solution to the mind–brain problem that avoids the tangled difficulties of interactionism, yet enfranchises both mental and physical realms.

Leibniz advanced the position that monads vary with respect to degrees of consciousness. Although all monads have goal-directed qualities, some were viewed as being more aware than others. Leibniz believed that some monads are conscious, whereas others possess higher self-conscious qualities and some are unconscious. Aiton (1985) pointed out that Leibniz "distinguishes between perception, which consists in being conscious of something, and apperception, which consists in being aware of a distinct perception" (p. 283). On the other end of the scale, Leibniz believed that there are **petites perceptions**, French for "small perceptions," of which we are not aware. But many small perceptions in concert form the basis of perception. We may not hear a single drop of water or even a few drops of water at a waterfall, but thousands of drops in chorus form a mighty roar. The idea of petites perceptions suggests the importance of unconscious processes, absolute thresholds, and difference thresholds—all concepts that would serve important roles in the early development of psychology (Rand, 2004).

Leibniz quarreled with the Aristotelian and Lockean emphasis on the role of the senses in knowledge. To Locke's famous dictum "Nothing is in the intellect that was not previously in the senses," Leibniz quipped, "Nothing save the intellect itself." Leibniz's emphasis on the activity of the intellect was driven by the importance he gave to energy. All monads were viewed as being invested with energy. Accordingly, the mind could not be a passive receptacle; rather, it is active, and its nature is to be involved in cognitive activities. One cannot pour knowledge into the mind through the senses as one pours water into a bowl. Thinking activity has its own career; it is not dependent on something external. This is not to argue that sensory activity is unimportant, but it is not *all* important. The active thinking process itself is not the result of something poured in from outside; rather, it is an inherent part of the mental monad. In Leibniz's view, sensory input is not causal (recall that he denied interactionism); instead, it is parallel with thinking processes. Leibniz would find no accident in the fact that sensory enrichment is correlated with certain mental advantages and that sensory deprivation is correlated with certain mental deficits. But neither the sensory nor the mental side must bear the whole brunt of causal explanation. Rather, sensory enrichment and sensory deprivation illustrate the harmony or the parallelism of the monads.

In an idea that has important implications for psychology, Leibniz argued that "nature never takes leaps" (see Aiton, 1985, p. 283); rather, natural processes are characterized by a law of continuity. This same principle later guided Sir Charles Lyell (1797–1875) in his classic *Principles of Geology* as he struggled with tensions between **uniformitarianism** (i.e., the concept that change is gradual and occurs over long periods of time) and special creation with its emphasis on abrupt change or radical discontinuity. In psychology, Leibniz's view emphasized lawful and gradual gradations from unconscious processes to conscious processes. It also underscored the importance of growth and development, but emphasized the maintenance of identity in change. You are the same individual today as yesterday as last week and last year. There is continuity of identity within an evolution that emphasizes the importance of the past to the present and the present to the future. Needless to say, there was a deemphasis on miracles in a system that emphasized preestablished harmony and continuity. At the same time, such a system provides a rich intellectual framework that preserves the uniqueness of psychological processes, yet brings them within the province of

science. Such a view nourished the development of a science of psychology.

Christian von Wolff

Christian von Wolff (1679–1754) was a painstaking rationalist who elaborated on the Leibnizian model. Wolff was a graduate of Leipzig University and later taught mathematics and philosophy at Halle. In 1723, he was exiled because he embraced beliefs offensive to the theological faculty and King Frederick I. He was in exile in Marburg, where he taught mathematics and philosophy for seventeen years. When Frederick I died in 1740, his son and successor, Frederick the Great, invited Wolff to return to Halle. He taught and held administrative posts until his death in 1754.

Wolff was one of the first to use the term *psychology* in a major publication, and he discussed the measurement of mental and emotional experiences (Konstantin, 1960). In 1732, he published a book titled *Empirical Psychology* and complemented it with a publication titled *Rational Psychology* in 1734. According to Wolff, empirical psychology studies the facts associated with the powers of the soul. It includes events in the senses, feelings of pain and pleasure, and so forth (Klempe, 2011). Rational psychology, clearly superior to empirical psychology, according to Wolff, involves the use of reason in the metaphysical study of the soul. Through rational psychology, one might hope to discover principles and laws. Wolff accepted the Leibnizian concept of preestablished harmony. He also advanced an early faculty psychology that influenced subsequent thinkers such as Immanuel Kant and Franz Joseph Gall (see Chapter 8).

IMMANUEL KANT

Based on criteria such as originality and lasting influence, **Immanuel Kant (1724–1804)** takes his place among the great philosophers of all time. Though we include him here as a rationalist, he was a consolidating figure between the extremes of empiricism and rationalism. He rejected the radical empiricism of David Hume, recognizing that it leaves us with nothing but an incoherent parade of sensations. At the same time, in his *Critique of Pure Reason*, he accepts the idea that "all our knowledge begins with experience" (1781/1965, p. 41). Even so, he believed that sensory information is not pure; rather, it is shaped or filtered by a priori considerations. Kant's major work is of an epistemological nature, but like Descartes, his contributions reach far beyond psychology.

The story of Kant's life is an uncomplicated one. He never married. On the rare occasions when he traveled, he seldom journeyed far from Königsberg, the East Prussian city where he was born on April 22, 1724. He attended the University of Königsberg and lived in poverty as a student, often interrupting his studies to gain a meager income as a tutor. After taking the doctorate in 1755, Kant taught a variety of subjects as a private instructor. Only in later years did he secure a professorial position with a decent income.

Kant's early years were defined by rigorous routine, privation, and an absence of individual freedom. Religious instruction was extensive and aversive, dwelling on heaven and hell rather than the value of life. In a biographical sketch, Cassirer (1981), quoting from Kant, pointed out that "the sum of pleasure is 'less than nothing' and the goal of life is not 'happiness' but self sufficiency and independence of will" (pp. 15–16). If we may believe his student Johann Gottfried Herder, Kant as a teacher had overcome his somber youth. Herder described Kant as having "at his service, jest, witticism, and humorous fancy, and his lectures were at once instructive and most entertaining" (cited in Durant & Durant, 1967, p. 532). Perhaps reacting to the religious dogmatism of his past, Kant appeared to Herder as a tolerant objective thinker. "No cabal or sect, no prejudice or reverence for a name, had the slightest influence with him in opposition to the extension and promotion of truth. He encouraged and gently compelled his hearers to think for themselves; despotism was foreign to his nature" (p. 532).

After years as a private instructor, he was offered a professorship in 1770. The following decades witnessed an outpouring of work including *Critique of Pure Reason* (1781/1965); *Critique of Practical Reason* (1788/1956); *The Critique of Judgment* (1790/1952); and *Religion Within the Limits of Reason Alone* (1793/1960). This latter work aroused the ire of Frederick the Great, who accused Kant of undercutting the authority of scripture. Not possessing the fiery spirit of Spinoza, Kant assured the king he would refrain from talking or writing about religion.

After living the whole of his life in Königsberg, Immanuel Kant struggled with dementia (Miranda et al., 2010) and then died on February 12, 1804. Cassirer (1981) illustrated the philosopher's fame: "His funeral turned into a great public ceremony, in which the whole city and the inhabitants of all quarters of it took part. . . . Amid the tolling of every bell in Königsberg, young students came to Kant's house to take up his body, from whence the innumerable procession, accompanied by thousands, wound to the university cathedral" (pp. 414–415). An inscription on Kant's grave reads "The starry heavens above me, the moral law within me."

Sense Experience and Reason

The goal of Kant's epistemological work can be understood partly on the basis of a distinction between analytic a priori knowledge and synthetic a priori knowledge. **Analytic a priori** knowledge refers to formal truths in which a predicate completely unpacks a subject. An example might include a statement such as *All bachelors are unmarried.* Such formal statements play important roles in deductive logic, but taken alone can be trivial or tautological. A *tautology* is an expression that contains a redundancy or pleonasm—that is, a word and its synonym are placed in close conjunction. Examples include statements such as *She was a sophomore in her second year* or *It is a true fact.*

Kant hoped to establish **synthetic a priori** truths that are not trivial but informative. Descartes's statement *I think therefore I am* may be regarded as an example of a synthetic a priori truth in that it is informative. It is not tautological in the same sense as a statement such as *If

A *is larger than* B, *then* B *is smaller than* A. Kant believed that many basic propositions in mathematics are synthetic a priori and are genuinely informative about the world instead of limited to definitions of words (Otte, 2009). An example might include a statement such as *A line is the shortest distance between two points.*

Kant believed knowledge begins with sensory experience. However, sensory experience by itself would not be intelligible apart from certain a priori considerations. For example, we grasp in an a priori way that one object succeeds another in time or that there are spatial differences between objects. Kant also believed there is an intuitive or a priori sense of causality so that the mind itself imposes an if–then judgment. In other words, there are ordering principles of the mind that are yoked with sense experience, and the two together—sense experience and ordering principles—contribute to knowledge. Kant referred to a priori ordering principles such as the intuition of time, space, and causality as **categories of understanding**. The ordering principles envisioned by Kant can be viewed as filters that compromise any kind of one-to-one direct access to the world (Worburton, 2011, pp. 110–114). Kant differentiated between the **noumenal** world and the **phenomenal** world. The noumenal refers to "a thing in itself" or the world as it is, independent of perception. The phenomenal world is the world as it appears to us in experience. According to Kant, the world we know is the phenomenal world. He rejected the idea that we have direct access to the noumenal world.

In contrast with John Locke, Kant regarded the mind as an active agency rather than a passive receptacle. In Kant's view, the mind as an active agency transforms sensory materials into meaningful configurations, connections, and structures. For Kant, reason and experience alone are suspect as sources of knowledge; rather, knowledge results from the interaction of reason and experience.

Social Psychology

Kant kept a watchful eye on both the American and French Revolutions. In particular, the formation of an America federation of states fascinated him. It is well known, of course, that the American experiment succeeded over the protests of people who demanded sovereignty for individual states. The fear was that diversity would be impossible within unity and that a remote and insensitive federal government would undermine basic freedoms. America represented a microcosm of what Kant envisioned for Europe and the world. If the American experiment could work, then perhaps the same could emerge on a larger scale (see his 1795 essay titled *To Perpetual Peace: A Philosophical Sketch* [in Humphrey, 1983, p. 341]). Kant's vision called for a world order that could intervene during a war between states but would nevertheless be constituted to permit sovereignty for states to pursue nonhostile activities. He envisioned plans for international conflict resolution that would not be attempted until the twentieth century.

Kant extended his categorical thought to people. His views of non-Europeans were typical of the negative views of his time and culture; more broadly, he contributed to the development of typical eighteenth-century social views of race (Larrimore, 2008). Kant looked with disdain on any nationalism that undermines humane values. Human beings should work for educational, historical, and humane perspectives that transcend local biases. He was optimistic that, through good education, people could widen their context and enjoy the moral progress that comes from a broader identity.

Kant was one of the first to advance a theory of moral development. He believed that human beings are caught in tensions between heteronomy and autonomy. **Heteronomy**, or government from the outside, is manifested by goodness based on authority, rules or threats, or rewards and punishments. The task of the individual is to grow into moral autonomy manifested in sensitivity to moral maxims or imperatives. **Autonomy** refers to self-government, will, and the ability to act in a moral manner, not just to please an authority or not just because such action is rewarding but because of an intrinsic moral requirement in a given situation (Häyry, 2005). Kant's theory of moral action is related to his belief in the possibility of individual freedom even given the role of cause in the world and in perception (Slife, 2005). Kant also believed that moral actions are based on our regard of other human beings as ends rather than as means. To regard someone as a means carries the risk that we will use them for our own purposes, whether it be economic, sexual, or political. By contrast, when we view another human being as an end, we're placing emphasis on the person's intrinsic worth.

Kant is remembered as one of the great philosophers of all time, but he is also important in the history of science. Along with Descartes and Laplace, he believed in the evolution of the solar system. Kant believed in geological and biological evolution, though he failed to pursue these topics. He made contributions to meteorology, geology, and geography. His most important legacy, however, is that he found a center between the poles of empiricism and pure reason. Kant's middle ground offered the grounding for generations of psychologists and philosophers to build the intellectual foundation for contemporary philosophies of science.

JOHANN FRIEDRICH HERBART

Imagine the challenge of succeeding Immanuel Kant. That daunting task fell to **Johann Friedrich Herbart (1776–1841)**, a mathematician, philosopher, and psychologist. Herbart's interests in psychology ranged from its applications to clinical and educational problems to the quantification of mental functions. He was also interested in the unconscious. Herbart was born in Oldenburg on May 4, 1776. He studied at the University of Jena and later earned his Ph.D. in philosophy at the University of Göttingen. The bulk of Herbart's academic career (1809–1832) was at the University of Königsberg where he became Kant's successor. His final appointment was at Göttingen where he died in 1841.

Herbart was a critical pioneer in educational psychology and mathematical psychology (Huemer & Landerer, 2010), and in Germany he is viewed as an originator of social psychology (Jahoda, 2006). His educational psychology is set forth in a book titled *The Science of Education*

(1902/1977), first published in English in 1902. Herbart outlined pedagogical techniques designed to facilitate learning and retention. He believed that good teachers must help students review familiar material and then relate new materials to older, more familiar material. He also advocated the importance of demonstrating practical applications whenever possible.

One goal of education, according to Herbart, involved building what he called the **apperceptive mass** (Jahoda, 2009). The term **apperception** typically referred to mental operations more complex than those involved in perception. According to Herbart, apperception sets humans apart from the rest of the animal kingdom. He regarded apperception as more than passive awareness and more than a mere set of complex associations. It implies an active capacity to assimilate ideas from one arena and apply them to another. It also involves the ability to apply lessons learned from old problem situations to new problems. Mental illness or a head injury might interfere with apperception because the individual would be capable only of operating effectively in concrete problem situations. For Herbart, apperception implies a capacity to operate at higher levels of abstraction or at a metalevel.

Herbart also saw moral development as the central goal of education. By this he meant that education should instill a capacity for effort, the ability to forego present pleasure for future gain, the development of sensitivities to moral issues, the capability to see things from a variety of vantage points, and the evolution of goodwill. The latter involves the capacity for empathy and a willingness to abide by laws for the larger good.

Herbart's mathematical psychology attempted to account for the fusion of concepts. For Herbart, mathematical formulae played the same role in psychology as in Newton's view of the solar system (Boudewijnse, Murray, & Bandomir, 1999). Although his mathematical approach was initially positive, criticism of his approach emerged after experimental methods entered psychology in the mid-1800s with the work of Fechner, Wundt, and others (Boudewijnse, Murray, & Bandomir, 2001). Herbart's mathematical formulae hold little interest today, but the problems that occupied his thought impacted psychology's early development. For example, he believed that concepts or components of concepts lie beneath the surface of awareness or in the unconscious. He believed that concepts strive to break into consciousness and that more-or-less permeable barriers separate the conscious and unconscious. In his work, we encounter concepts of suppression, repression, threshold, and unconscious processes. All of these were, of course, part of the stock-in-trade for later psychologists like Freud. Herbart did not have a clear grasp of the possibility of a truly experimental psychology that manipulates variables. However, his work invigorated the founding of psychology.

THOMAS REID AND COMMONSENSE PHILOSOPHY

Thomas Reid (1710–1796) bridged the extremes of empiricism and rationalism with a **commonsense philosophy**. The expression *common sense* has multiple meanings, and it is likely that most philosophers and scientists believe their systems appeal, in one way or another, to common sense. The expression sometimes refers to the unreflective or naïve opinions of ordinary people or to collective opinion. These meanings do not, however, resonate with how philosophers use the term. In philosophy, common sense often refers to an opposition to beliefs that are counterintuitive or that do violence to our experience of the world. Robinson (1982) used the term *necessity* to refer to Thomas Reid's concept of common sense. According to Robinson, "When Reid spoke of the principles of common sense he was referring neither to opinion nor [even] to judgment. Rather, he was proposing those very activities of mind and laws of conduct by which life becomes possible" (p. 48). For example, beliefs in an external world, in causation, and in the self as an active manipulator make life possible and contribute to successful adaptation. According to Reid and his followers, the radical empiricism of Berkeley and Hume had left us with a world that was unnatural and that violates common sense at every turn.

Thomas Reid grew up in rural Scotland and enrolled at age twelve in Marischal College in Aberdeen. After graduating at age sixteen, he turned his attention to theological studies. For a number of years, Reid had a pastorate in New Machar, but in 1751 he accepted a position at King's College in Aberdeen. In 1758, he helped form the Aberdeen Philosophical Society, a group of scholars that met regularly over a period of fifteen years. In 1764, Reid succeeded Adam Smith (1723–1790) in the chair of moral philosophy at Glasgow. He remained at Glasgow until his death in 1796. Reid's best-known works include *An Inquiry into the Human Mind* (1764/1970), *Essays on the Intellectual Powers of Man* (1786), and *Essays on the Active Powers of Man* (1790).

According to Reid, an adequate empiricism would not arrive at the skeptical crisis that we find in Hume's work. Indeed, an adequate empiricism will discover important truths in experience that Hume failed to envision. Such truths uncover a different picture of the world than that encountered in Hume's philosophy. What Reid discovered in experience, according to Lehrer (1989), "are innate principles of our constitution yielding conceptions and convictions of the operations of our own minds, of the minds of others, of the qualities of external objects, and of the laws of nature" (p. 8). Thus, according to Reid, there are innate principles of the mind leading to convictions that we find as a natural part of experience and common sense. In other words, there are natural necessities. Robinson (1982) concluded, "even skeptical Hume took for granted that he had sensations and this not out of choice or opinion but because of a natural *necessity*. He could not think otherwise" (p. 48).

Reid believed that a truly empirical philosophy, one that resonates to what is found in human experience, will discover natural necessities that are more complicated than mere sensations. For example, it is experience itself that contributes to belief in the external world. Reid (1764/1970) asked why the smell of a rose is more vivid in the presence of the rose than it is in memory (p. 24). He pointed out that the same question can be asked of any sensation. Why is the taste of an apple more vivid during the act of eating than in memory a few hours later? Experience itself contributes to the belief that we are not the causes of those vivid sensations that occur when we are, for example, smelling or tasting. Reid (1764/1970) argued, "I could as easily doubt of my own existence, as of the existence of my sensations" (p. 24). He went on to say that sensation compels "our belief of the present existence of the thing, [and] memory a belief of its past existence" (p. 25).

Reid argued for a number of propositions that he referred to as "first principles." Examples (see Lehrer, 1989, pp. 160–161) are as follows:

1. "The thoughts of which I am conscious, are the thoughts of a being which I call MYSELF, my MIND, my PERSON."
2. "Those things do really exist which we distinctly perceive by our senses."
3. "We have some degree of power over our actions."

Thus, through experience itself and common sense, Reid attempted to restore faith in the external world (Wade, 2010), a self with real continuity and a belief in causality.

Reid's views elicited some interesting biases. For example, psychologist and historian E. G. Boring appeared surprised that such influential philosophy could emerge from a minister (Robinson, 1989b). Reid's influence was extensive in Europe and America. His admirer, Dugald Stewart (1753–1828), believed that Reid had restored the Baconian vision, clearing the way for an intelligible science of human nature. Stewart's influential book *Elements of the Philosophy of the Human Mind* (1792/1802) extended Reid's thought and applied it to psychological topics such as attention, memory, association, and imagination. Reid and Stewart believed that the mind can be divided into faculties or powers. We'll see in Chapter 8 that Franz Joseph Gall (1758–1828) developed this concept in an attempt to associate each faculty with a specific brain region.

Enfranchising Curiosity

In earlier chapters, we explored the issues of curiosity and forbidden knowledge. For centuries, curiosity about the natural world had been regarded as an intellectual vice, a mark of foolish pride, and an affront to God. Numerous scriptures were taken as warnings against those who probed the secrets and mysteries of the world. As Paul had warned in I Corinthians 1:20, "The wisdom of this world is foolishness with God." This assertion, at a high level of abstraction, would not serve as an impediment to curiosity, but such scriptures were interpreted in a literal and concrete fashion. Such a literal approach foreclosed the possibility of discovering richer meanings that might surface in alternative interpretations.

The empiricists and rationalists disagreed on many things, but they shared in a new interpretation of the role of human curiosity. To be sure, the climate of opinion had shifted. The public hungered for a fresh perspective on old questions. Empiricists and rationalists were eager to outline such an approach. Harrison (2001) pointed out that Francis Bacon linked curiosity to charity, softening attitudes regarding worldly wisdom. Bacon opened his defense of curiosity by agreeing with those who had spoken against it. Curiosity could indeed motivate investigations and produce knowledge that results in pride, conceit, and arrogance, but that is only half the story. God, after all, had made the world. Further, the benefits from studying the world could be used for charitable purposes to aid the poor, the sick, and the disadvantaged. Surely charity was among the most valued of religious virtues. Of course, some doubted the sincerity of Bacon's theological justification of curiosity. It seems probable that in his private thoughts, Bacon would have valued curiosity in its own right. For whatever reasons, he did resort to theological justifications and these no doubt appealed to many quarters.

Other philosophers such as John Locke, David Hume, René Descartes, and Benedict Spinoza defended curiosity as a natural human quality, one that demands nurturing and discipline. In time, the virtues of curiosity and wonder were celebrated as a hallmark of modern thought (see Keen, 1973). Relentless curiosity seems now firmly and legitimately attached to all categories of human thought. Indeed, the reversal in attitudes toward curiosity is so complete that it now seems possible that older attitudes could slip from the grasp of our comprehension.

CONTRIBUTIONS OF RATIONALISM

Born in the late Renaissance, the skeptical crisis of Montaigne stimulated a response from rationalists and empiricists. They hoped to restore faith in human knowledge and construct a philosophical base for the new sciences. In the process, they constructed intellectual foundations that would ultimately support the new discipline of psychology. Though the rationalists concentrated on the problem of knowledge, they also wrote thoughtful works dealing with theoretical and practical questions of psychology. Their pervasive influence was illustrated in extensive references to their work by early pioneers in psychology such as William James and Wilhelm Wundt. At a minimum, the specific contributions of the rationalists to an intellectual atmosphere friendly to the development of the human sciences should include the following:

1. René Descartes, like Francis Bacon, sought to overcome the extreme skepticism of Montaigne by advancing a new method designed to restore faith in human knowledge. Thus, modern rationalism, like empiricism, begins as a new methodology supportive of a scientific approach to the world.
2. Philosophers such as Leibniz and Herbart were among the first to investigate concepts of the threshold, a topic later to become a preoccupation of some of the early psychologists.
3. The concept of thresholds also supported the idea that there is real mental activity not currently in consciousness. The investigation of subconscious and unconscious processes took root in later systems of psychology.
4. By emphasizing the lawfulness of psychological processes, Spinoza laid the conceptual groundwork for a science of psychology. His attacks on demonology

contributed to naturalistic approaches to the study of emotional disorders.

5. Some of the earliest treatises with specific psychological content came from the pens of the rationalists. For example, Christian von Wolff's *Empirical Psychology* (1732) and *Rational Psychology* (1734) were among the early modern attempts to elevate the study of mental powers as a foundational part of philosophy.
6. Some of the rationalists were pioneers in educational and mathematical psychology. Herbart's book *The Science of Education* was an early attempt to explore pedagogical techniques designed to foster learning and improve memory.
7. Rationalists provided a broad vision of the world of experience. They did not deny that observation and association are important in the acquisition of knowledge, but argued that some connections are grasped intuitively or in an a priori fashion.

Like the empiricists, the rationalists contributed to the intellectual and cultural context from which psychology as a formal discipline was born. We'll revisit their influence in later chapters.

Review Questions

1. Identify three ways in which rationalism differs from empiricism.
2. Briefly list four procedural rules for the intellect set forth by Descartes in his *Discourse on Method*.
3. Outline Spinoza's contributions to the intellectual spadework necessary to the development of psychology.
4. What do you see as the advantages and disadvantages of Leibniz's approach to the mind–body problem?
5. Outline Kant's distinction between analytic a priori and synthetic a priori knowledge. What is the significance of the distinction?
6. Briefly describe Kant's theory of moral development.
7. Distinguish between the terms *apperception* and *perception*.

8. Explain what Thomas Reid meant by common sense and explain how Reid argued against Hume's skepticism.

Glossary

active mind   Refers to intelligent, self-organizing properties of mental processes. Contrasts with the "blank slate" hypothesis encountered in empirical philosophies.

analytic a priori   Refers to formal truths in which a predicate completely unpacks a subject. A statement such as *All bachelors are unmarried* is an example.

apperception   Historically a term with many meanings, but it commonly refers to mental processes that are more complex than those involved in perception. It implies a high level of awareness and activity of the mind so that relationships are clearly understood. Contrasts with mere passive awareness.

apperceptive mass   A term employed by Johann Friedrich Herbart (1776–1841) to refer to the goal of education to produce not only knowledge of facts but also a higher level of awareness of relationships.

autonomy   A term employed by Immanuel Kant (1724–1804) that refers to self-government or the ability to act in a moral and responsible manner, not to please an authority but because the individual recognizes the inherent or intrinsic worth of certain actions.

categories of understanding   An expression employed by Kant to refer to inherent ordering principles of the mind that contribute to knowledge. For example, Kant believed that human beings have intuitive understandings of causality and temporal and spatial relationships.

commonsense philosophy   A term referring to the philosophical orientation of philosophers such as Thomas Reid (1710–1796) and his followers. The expression refers to a deeply held opposition to beliefs that are counterintuitive or that do violence to our experience of the world.

deductive argument   Any argument in which the conclusion is claimed to follow necessarily from the premises. A deductive argument is valid if, and only if, it is not possible for the premises to be true and the conclusion false. Otherwise, the argument is invalid.

Descartes, René (1596–1650)   French philosopher who is often regarded as the founder of modern philosophy. Descartes made extensive original contributions in a great variety of areas. He helped elaborate early scientific methodology, provided rich and often testable hypotheses about the relationships between behavior and physiology, and is regarded as one of the key figures in modern rationalism.

Herbart, Johann Friedrich (1776–1841)   German mathematician, philosopher, and psychologist. Herbart was among the first to attempt to quantify mental functions. He was also interested in the role of unconscious processes in human life and in the application of psychological studies to clinical and educational problems.

heteronomy   A term employed by Kant to refer to the varieties of forces outside the organism (e.g., rewards, punishments, authority) that often regulate behavior.

inductive argument   Any argument in which the conclusion is claimed to be more probable than not given the truth of the premises. Inductive arguments are said to be strong or weak, depending on whether the conclusion is or is not made probable according to the truth of the premises.

Kant, Immanuel (1724–1804)   One of the great German philosophers, remembered for his attempts to reconcile empirical and rational approaches to knowledge. Kant believed that knowledge begins with experience, but in his view, there are meaningful connections in experience itself. Kant also advanced an early theory of moral development and was interested in problems associated with nationalism.

Leibniz, Gottfried Wilhelm (1646–1716)   German rational philosopher and mathematician who sought ways to reconcile the legitimate claims of monism and pluralism. Leibniz advocated a universal language and a world united by reason and international government. Leibniz and Isaac Newton independently discovered the differential calculus.

monad   A term employed by Leibniz to refer to a principle of existence. Leibniz believed that the world consisted of many independent monads, but all monads are harmonious with all other monads. Thus, for him, there is a real mental world and that world is completely harmonious with a real physical or physiological world. Hence, mind and body are both real but completely harmonious and independent.

noumenal   In Kant's philosophy, the term *noumenal* refers to a "thing in itself," an object or event independent of experience or perception.

petites perceptions   French term meaning *small perceptions* used by Leibniz to refer to small perceptions below the level of awareness. Leibniz believed that small perceptions in concert form the basis of perception. His concept of petites perceptions represents an early concept of unconscious processes.

phenomenal   The term *phenomenon* is similar to the term *appearance*. In Kant's philosophy, the term *phenomenal* refers to the world as it appears in experience.

preestablished harmony   A concept employed by Leibniz to account for the congruence or harmony of different orders of reality. He believed, for example, that mind and body do not influence each other but they are always congruent. Leibniz believed that God had ordered the world in such a fashion as to permit the simultaneous and harmonious operation of many independent principles of existence.

rationalism   A philosophical orientation deriving from the Latin *ratio*, meaning to reason or think. Rationalist philosophers typically emphasize a priori knowledge, deduction, and the concept of an active mind that selectively organizes sensory data.

Reid, Thomas (1710–1796)   Leader of Scottish commonsense philosophy that sought to reconcile the conflicting claims of empiricism and rationalism.

Spinoza, Baruch (Benedict) (1632–1677)   A key figure in the rationalist tradition, Spinoza sought to demonstrate the artificiality of many of the dualisms introduced by Descartes. For Spinoza, there is no gulf between God and the world or mind and body. He believed that most dualities result from problems of language, but different language systems may simply represent different ways of looking at the same reality.

synthetic a priori   According to Kant, a synthetic a priori truth is known intuitively and is informative about the world. Descartes's statement "I think, therefore I am" may be regarded as a synthetic a priori truth. The truth of the statement is grasped intuitively, but the statement is not a mere tautology; rather, it is informative about the world.

uniformitarianism   The belief that evolutionary changes on earth occur gradually over vast stretches of time.

Wolff, Christian von (1679–1754)   German philosopher and author of early books titled *Empirical Psychology* (1732) and *Rational Psychology* (1734). Wolff believed in both empirical and rational approaches to psychology, but argued that rational approaches would be more fruitful and lead to the discovery of principles by which the mind operates.

8

■ ■ ■

Mechanization and Quantification

There is no bodily or mental attribute. . .which cannot be gripped and consolidated into an ogive with a smooth outline.

—FRANCIS GALTON (1883/1907)

Going back to earliest times, human beings have been interested in the measurement of things. Innovations in measurement provided answers for countless questions, both simple and complex. For example, practical questions motivated an interest in knowing how many days would be spent on a trip. And how far and how fast will I need to travel? How much of this product in exchange for that product? How many pieces of wood of what sizes and shapes will I need to build a house? How many of our soldiers will be needed to battle their soldiers? Measurement plays a critical role because errors can prove devastating to economic, social, and physical well-being.

Breakthroughs in measurement had a profound impact on science, on technology, and even on how we view ourselves. For example, in the nineteenth century, **Hermann Ludwig Ferdinand von Helmholtz (1821–1894)** measured the speed of conduction of a nervous impulse. Boring (1950) wrote that this accomplishment laid the groundwork "for all later work of experimental psychology on the chronometry of mental acts and reaction times. . . . It brought the soul to time, as it were, measured what had been ineffable, actually captured the essential agent of mind in the toils of natural science" (p. 42). The claim that Helmholtz "captured the essential agent of mind" may be excessive, but his work stimulated optimism about the possibility of a science of human nature.

This chapter examines the measurement of physiological and behavioral events that were regarded for centuries as ineffable and, hence, resistant to quantitative studies. The mechanistic perspective inspired new quantitative studies in physiology and behavior, a philosophy that begins with Thomas Hobbes.

THOMAS HOBBES

Thomas Hobbes (1588–1679) argued that the goal of philosophy should involve numerical comparisons to assess magnitudes, distances, motions, and proportions. Hobbes adored the mechanical model. For him, "The heart is a spring, the nerves are strings, the joints are wheels giving motion to the whole body" (Peach, 1982, p. 840). A mechanical model holds promise for psychologists to discover material and efficient causes.

At the time of Hobbes's birth on April 5, 1588, rumors swirled that the Spanish Armada was approaching British shores. Known as the "Invincible Armada," the Spanish fleet of more than one hundred and thirty warships had earned a fierce reputation that posed a legitimate threat to the English people. Rogow (1986) added that Hobbes's mother may also have been troubled because biblical numerologists had predicted earth-shattering catastrophes exactly 1,588 years after the virgin birth. The young Hobbes was sensitive to the anxieties of his times. Mintz (1962) claimed he was afraid of the dark, terrified of death, and feared persecution at the hands of his enemies. Yet for all his dread, Hobbes was a fearless intellectual adventurer who was given the extravagant title of the "Great Columbus of the

Golden Lands of New Philosophies" (see Reik, 1977).

Hobbes was educated at Oxford, but had little interest in the scholastic curriculum. He earned his bachelor's degree when he was twenty and accepted a position as tutor to Baron Hardwick, son of William Cavendish. As a tutor in a well-to-do family, Hobbes enjoyed good pay, access to libraries, travel, and considerable leisure. Aside from brief positions as Francis Bacon's secretary and tutor in the family of Sir Gervase Clinton, Hobbes was associated with the Cavendish family throughout his life. Published in 1651, his masterpiece, *Leviathan*, was an important psychological and political work.

Hobbes was a contemporary of many great minds of the seventeenth century. Around 1635, he visited with Galileo, who may have inspired Hobbes to extend the concept of motion to all natural philosophy. He quarreled with Descartes about which of them had first conceived of color as a secondary quality (in truth, Galileo had discussed the subjective nature of color prior to both men).

Hobbes invited controversy during his life. He was regarded as a corrupter of morals because he spoke against biblical literalism, the authority of the Pope, and excessive reliance on authority. Despite charges against him, people who knew Hobbes held him in high regard and defended him even when disagreeing with his philosophy. He died in 1679 at the age of ninety-one, still a controversial figure.

Like his contemporaries, Hobbes was fascinated with the puzzle of human knowledge. He argued that knowledge has its origin in sensory impressions. Such impressions result from external physical movements that activate the sense organs. The sense organs in turn activate the brain via the nerves. Thus, bodies in motion in the external world set off motions in the sensory channels, and these set off motions in the brain. Ideas, or what Hobbes called "phantasms," result from motions in the brain. Superficially, the emphasis on the sensorial origins of knowledge places him in the empirical tradition. However, Hobbes defies this easy classification because he argued

Thomas Hobbes

that experience alone is incapable of establishing anything of a universal nature (1650/1962a, p. 18). Through experience, we can have knowledge only of specific events, and such knowledge can hardly serve as an adequate basis for science. Thus, it is a mistake to classify Hobbes as an unqualified empiricist.

As mentioned, Hobbes once worked for Francis Bacon, but he did not like the man and he rejected Baconian science. According to Martinich (1999), "Bacon's radical empiricism in science is at the opposite pole of Hobbes's rationalism" (p. 66). Tsanoff (1964) noted that "Hobbes, like Bacon, demanded the fullest survey of the facts in order to apprehend their basic characteristics, but he sought demonstrative conclusions by strict deductions from evident principles" (p. 264). Matson (1982) commented that the Hobbesian view of science is that it "is a body of organized knowledge, for which geometry provides both the model and the starting point" (p. 852). Hobbes's deep admiration for the method of geometry with its emphasis on axioms and deduction places him in the rationalist tradition. In fact, Hobbes loved geometry as a way of reasoning and believed its method was crucial to understanding all sciences including a science of human nature (see Jesseph, 2004). In tearing apart his complicated epistemology, Mintz (1962) contended that Hobbes also represents a nominalist approach to knowledge. According to Hobbes, we begin with knowledge from the senses from which we get information about singular things such as houses, animals, and vehicles. Through reason, we establish all-inclusive names and classification systems that provide order for specific experiences. According to Mintz (1962), "The truth which reason yields for Hobbes is the truth about words, not things; it is a hard truth to find because words are such notorious snares" (p. 25). Epistemologically, Hobbes's work represents a complicated mix of rationalism, nominalism, and empiricism. Fortunately, his ontology is more straightforward than his views on knowledge.

As noted, Hobbes was a dedicated materialist. Whatever exists must have a material nature, including God. A material God could, of course, serve as a first or efficient cause. For example, God might set in motion the rest of material reality. But after serving as first cause, a deity has few remaining duties in Hobbes's mechanistic and materialistic philosophy. Hobbes may have reserved room for humans to honor God, but there is little real work left for the deity. For understandable reasons, Hobbes's theism troubles people who believe in an active God continuously interacting with the world.

Although some would question Hobbes's theism, there could be no question about the seriousness of his views on human nature. Set forth with characteristic vigor and clarity, his views sent shock waves through the intellectual world. Cambridge Platonists joined Catholics and Protestants in a constant assault on Hobbes's works. Zagorin (1968) noted, "In 1683 the University of Oxford condemned a number of his works to the flames" (p. 485).

Hobbes's views of human nature were derived from his materialist metaphysics and buttressed by his friend William Harvey's work on the circulation of the blood. Hobbes took the centrality of motion in Galilean and Keplerian physics and Harvey's physiology and extended them to psychology. As noted, sensations and thoughts are understood in terms of motions in the sense organs and brain. But Hobbes assumed other psychological processes are also based on movements that, in theory, are quantifiable. For example, "Feelings of pleasure and pain result from alterations in the vital motion of the body" (Watkins, 1965, p. 115). For Hobbes, psychological processes depend on a physical substrate; thus, the same quantitative science that Galileo used to study the physical world can be used to study the behavior of human beings.

Hobbes also assumed that powerful drives toward self-interest and self-preservation governed human nature. Our fear and awe of collective power restrains us from inflicting our selfish interests on others. In *Leviathan*, Hobbes (1651/1962b) warns that without a civil state there is the danger of war of everyone against everyone. But with a powerful state that holds us in awe, egoism is held in check. Because of the civil state, we can have invention, industry, culture, navigation, the arts, and knowledge. Without the civil state, we have "continual fear, and danger of violent death; and the life of man [is] solitary, poor, nasty, brutish, and short" (p. 113). Hobbes chides readers who are shocked by his pessimism and asks them to consider whether they lock their doors when they sleep. He also reminds them that they probably secure their valuables and protect their children. He then argues that such actions betray the same accusations against humankind as do the words in his manuscript.

Hobbes's reduction of philosophy to the study of bodies in motion marks him as an important figure in the history of psychology. Matson (1982) pointed out that "Philosophy to Hobbes, is simply science" (p. 851). Hobbes's work offers a psychology uncompromised by dualistic or theological considerations. He is a key figure in the intellectual genealogy of behavioral psychologies and classic psychoanalysis. In a broader sense, Hobbes suggests the importance of studying physiological and social influences with the same quantitative methods that proved so successful in the physical sciences.

RENÉ DESCARTES REVISITED

Like his contemporary Thomas Hobbes, **René Descartes** was obsessed with the problem of movement. But unlike Hobbes, Descartes did not restrict himself to philosophic inquiry. In Chapter 7, we covered his epistemological work, but he also devoted time to groundbreaking research on anatomy and physiology. In a telling story, Huxley (1874) shared how a friend of Descartes, "once calling upon him in Holland begged to be shown his library. Descartes led him into a sort of shed, and, drawing aside a curtain, displayed a dissecting-room full of the bodies of animals in the course of dissection, and said, 'There is my library'" (p. 725). Based on his investigations, Descartes advanced provocative and testable theories about the mechanisms responsible for movement in living organisms. As we will see, most of his theories were wrong, but they stimulated other researchers and contributed

to physiological knowledge that was relevant to psychological questions.

Although familiar with Galen's concept of pneuma, Descartes was not satisfied with its explanations about movement. Perhaps his dissatisfaction can be traced to the technology of his day. Popular mechanical inventions included toys, clocks, and windmills that dazzled the public with their intricate movements. Strandh (1979) describes a fourteenth-century clock that was once on the Cathedral at Lund in Sweden: "Two medieval knights on the dome of the clock hourly exchange blows to the number of the hour. At twelve o'clock, after the twelfth blow, a hymn resounds from a mechanical trombone, a little door beside an image of the madonna opens, and the three kings from the East come out, followed by servants, and file, bowing, past the virgin Mary" (p. 51). If such elaborate movement could be accomplished on a mechanical basis—and understandable in terms of material and efficient causation—could animal and human movements be better explained from a natural or mechanistic perspective rather than a vitalistic one? If so, the pneuma concept of movement was wrong. Descartes looked for a simpler explanation.

He found inspiration while visiting the royal gardens at Saint-Germain-en-Laye, a western suburb of Paris. For the queen's amusement, the Francini brothers had designed elaborate mechanical statues throughout the gardens, making it a kind of seventeenth-century Disneyland. When Descartes stepped on a hidden plate, it triggered the release of water into a complex network of hydraulic pipes that caused the statues to move. In his *Treatise on Man*, Descartes describes a statue of Diana bathing at the water's edge. Move too close and the shy Roman goddess would hide in the surrounding reeds. Move closer still, and an intimidating statue of Neptune charged at you, poised to strike with his trident.

Powered by hydraulic forces, the statues served as a model for Descartes's theory of bodily movement (Jaynes, 1973b). Although the details of the model are difficult to decipher (see Popplestone, 1995), Descartes drew specific comparisons between nervous action and the water pipes that caused movement in the statues.

The discovery of the nerve cell would not come until the nineteenth century, but large nerve fibers (consisting of bundles of axons in a kind of conduit) were visible to the naked eye and had been identified since early times. Descartes believed that nerve fibers, like the water pipes in the statues, were filled with fluids that activate muscles and tendons, the basic machinery of movement. In the case of the nerves, however, the fluids were refined and distilled from the finest elements of the blood. In turn, the blood had been distilled from the finest elements of the digestive juices. He referred to the fluids in the nerves as "spirits" or "animal spirits." Descartes (1637/1985a) argued that the spirits were composed of minute fast-moving particles, which he likened to fine wind or a pure and lively flame.

As noted by Jaynes (1973b), Descartes believed "the nerve pipe fed into the muscle, and when the fluid came down, it billowed the muscle out like a balloon, and so made the limb move" (p. 171). In addition to fluids inside the nerves, Descartes believed small threads ran through the length of the nerves. The threads, when activated by a stimulus, triggered valves in the endings of the nerves in the ventricles of the brain. When the valves opened, the spirits stored in the ventricles were released to move through the nerves to the muscles. The statues at St. Germaine, which moved by both mechanical and hydraulic action, may have encouraged Descartes's belief in the threads and animal spirits.

In his *Treatise on Man*, Descartes provided a specific example of how the machinery of the body functions in response to a simple stimulus. The sequence of events is illustrated in Figure 8.1. A flame (A) touches the skin (B) and then activates the tiny fiber or string (c, d). The string simultaneously opens a valve in the ventricle of the brain. Animal spirits stored in the ventricle (F) rush back to the foot, providing the force for its removal from the fire. Simultaneously, other animal spirits travel other routes to the eyes, hands, and trunk to contribute to the total response pattern of moving away from the flame. All of this

FIGURE 8.1   Descartes's Model of the Reflex

happens with great speed. Indeed, the mechanical action of the thread is instantaneous. Descartes (1664/1985c) likened it to the pulling a rope that rings a bell.

Descartes believed that many human movements and all animal movements are mechanical or nonreflective (Leiber, 2011; Steiner, 2006). Thus, many movements have their origin in the senses that activate the so-called spirits in the ventricles of the brain and these, in turn, result in automatic actions. The automatic actions may include sighing, yawning, startle patterns, or more complex activities such as walking or eating. All such activities are shared in common with the beasts and follow from the actions of nerves, muscles, and senses "in the same way as the movement of a watch is produced merely by the strength of its spring and the configuration of its wheels" (Descartes, 1649/1985b, p. 335).

Descartes envisioned the body as a machine, comparing body parts such as nerves, ventricles, muscles, and tendons to pipes, storage tanks, springs, and wheels. He applied the mechanical-hydraulic explanation to all animal movement and to involuntary human movement. In his view, there was only a quantitative difference between animals and the moving stat-ues. To be sure, animals, as God's creation, were better machines than those machines made by hu-mans, and the superiority of animals to moving statues was manifested in smooth and complex movements. But there were not qualitative differ-ences between machines and animals. As noted by Jaynes (1973b), "Animals were mere water stat-ues, not conscious, not really living—machines without will or purpose or any feeling whatever. He dissected them alive (anesthetics were far off in the nineteenth century), amused at their cries and yelps since these were nothing but the hy-draulic hisses and vibrations of machines" (p. 170). But if a mechanical-hydraulic model could explain animal motion, why couldn't the same model account for human motion? Descartes was unable to take that step.

Descartes (1664/1985c) argued that, in the case of humans, God had united a rational soul with the bodily machine. Caught in the ir-resistible grip of curiosity about the mechanics of soul–body interaction, Descartes (1649/1985b) declared that "there is a little gland (the pineal gland) in the brain where the soul exercises its functions more particularly than in other parts of the body" (p. 340). He believed the soul is joined to the whole body, but specific soul–body interac-tions take place in the pineal gland, which is not divided into halves like other regions of the brain. Descartes also believed, erroneously, that animals do not have pineal glands.

For Descartes, the pineal gland is supplied with nerves that permit it to influence the body even as the body influences the pineal gland. He claimed, for example, "When the soul wants to remember something, this volition makes the gland lean first to one side and then to another, thus driving the spirits toward different regions of the brain until they come upon the one containing traces left by the object we want to remember" (1649/1985b, p. 344). When the spirits find the traces, the informed gland recognizes the stored information. The soul can also exercise will via the gland, but cannot in all cases possess full con-trol over the passions. The reason is that strong passions affect the heart and blood and animal spirits in such a violent way that the soul cannot prevent some movements. The soul is tied to the body and cannot exercise complete autonomy.

Let's say you stub your toe. You might use willpower to divert attention from the pain. But if you fracture your ankle, the pain so arouses the body that no amount of willpower can divert attention from it. Only when the body returns to quiescence can the will again seize control. In some instances, self-control is best assured by finding a circumstance that permits time for re-covery from excess arousal. Thus, the soul can exercise will, but the power of will is limited. In his treatise *The Passions of the Soul*, Descartes applied his model to an analysis of conflict situa-tions and to the control of the passions.

Empirical studies, as much as his origi-nal work on epistemology, secured Descartes's fame as founder of modern philosophy. His legacy was set forth in provocative and testable theories about the mechanics of movement. He influenced the course of neurology and physi-ology long after his death. What were some of his testable theories? First, he argued that ani-mal spirits inflate muscles; second, he tied the muscular system to the ventricles of the brain via the tiny threads or strings that he thought he observed in nerves; third, he ascribed both sensory and motor functions to the same nerve; fourth, he spoke of some nervous transmission as being instantaneous or extremely fast; and fifth, an early concept of the reflex is clearly evi-dent in his work. Finally, his speculations about the beast-machine, in the words of Rosenfield (1968), "became a fountainhead of inspiration for many years" (p. 64). Rosenfield's book *From Beast-Machine to Man-Machine* documents the war of ideas about animals and animal rights in the years following Descartes's death (see also Leiber, 2011). Descartes envisioned a gulf be-tween humans and animals that produced an un-witting but intense range of intellectual activity from poetic celebration of animals to investiga-tions in comparative anatomy, physiology, and psychology (see King & Viney, 1992). His pro-vocative theories inspired many studies to which we now turn.

JAN SWAMMERDAM

A Dutch physician named **Jan Swammerdam (1637–1680)** conducted one of the first tests of Descartes's theory of movement. Remembered for his expertise in entomology and respiration (Cobb, 2006), Swammerdam devised brilliant demonstrations that proved embarrassing to Descartes's notion that a flow of animal spirits from the brain inflates muscles. In his classic work *The Book of Nature* (1758), Swammerdam showed that a muscle with an attached nerve from a frog's leg will continue to contract even when separated from the body. This demonstration alone rules out the ventricles of the brain as a source of animal spirits. He also proved that the muscle contracts even after small cuts sever some of the fibers. Swammerdam (1758) comments that "Tho' the muscle be cut, and its moving fibers separated from each other, all these parts move again, as it were naturally, as soon as the nerve which belongs to them is irritated" (p. 124). If Descartes's theory were correct, animal spirits would escape through the cuts and thus fail to inflate the muscle. These works established Swammerdam's place as one of the most influential seventeenth-century scholars of the nervous system (Pubols, 1959).

The most conclusive evidence against the idea that animal spirits literally inflate a muscle comes from a more complicated demonstration. Swammerdam prepared a cylinder that opened at the top into a narrow pipette. A piston with an attached brass wire with an eyehook was prepared so it could be inserted into the bottom of the cylinder. A silver wire, also with an eyehook, was then passed through the eye of the brass wire. A frog's muscle with attached nerve was placed in the cylinder and the nerve was carefully passed through the eye of the silver wire. The other end of the silver wire passed along the side of the piston and out through the bottom of the cylinder. A drop of water is placed in the pipette and the silver wire is pulled to activate the nerve and the muscle. If the muscle grows in size when contracted, as predicted by Descartes's theory,

the drop of water should be forced upward. The water did not move upward; indeed, if anything, it dropped a bit. These results were clearly inconsistent with Descartes's prediction that a muscle is inflated by animal spirits.

Swammerdam (1758) concluded that at least no "sensible or comprehensive bulk flows through the nerves to the muscles. . . . From these experiments therefore, it may, I think be fairly concluded, that a simple and natural motion or irritation of the nerve alone is necessary to produce muscular motion whether it has origin in the brain, or in the marrow, or elsewhere" (p. 125).

Pubols (1959) pointed out that Swammerdam anticipated the distinction between sensory and motor nerves and challenged the distinction between voluntary and involuntary activity that had been central to Descartes's theory (p. 134). In fairness, Descartes may also have recognized the distinction between sensory and motor nerves, but he also believed individual nerves have both sensory and motor functions. Pubols pointed out that Swammerdam was far ahead of his time, both conceptually and methodologically. His work demonstrated the importance of well-conceived experiments and paved the way for naturalistic studies on the measurement and mechanics of physiological and behavioral events.

NIELS STENSEN

Further work on Descartes's speculations about the pineal gland came from Jan Swammerdam's friend **Niels Stensen (1638–1682)**, sometimes called Nicolaus Steno. Though Stensen respected Descartes's philosophical method, he exposed the great philosopher's anatomical errors. Descartes had said that the pineal gland leans from one side to another and by such action drives the spirits toward various parts of the brain. Stensen argued that the pineal gland could not possibly lean from side to side. He also understood that the pineal gland is not richly supplied with nerves and, therefore, could not be implicated in complex cognitive functions. Finally, Stensen was aware of the fact that animals have pineal glands. His anatomical critique destroyed another building block in the Cartesian system.

Stensen took no delight in attacking Descartes. Even in his criticisms, he was careful to protect the philosopher's memory. In a lecture delivered in Paris and published eighteen years after Descartes's death, Stensen mentioned that all anatomists make mistakes. Though Descartes had committed errors, he had moved beyond all his predecessors in giving a complete account of human and animal actions (see Fearing, 1970, p. 40). However, the anatomical errors of Descartes and others disturbed Stensen. Scherez (1976) quoted from correspondence from Stensen to Leibniz: "If these gentlemen have been so mistaken with material things which are accessible to the senses, what warranty can they offer that they are not mistaken when they talk about God and the Soul?" (p. 33). That question was undoubtedly on the lips of many people following geographic and scientific discoveries that ushered in the modern era.

Because of past errors in anatomy, Stensen called for a new program of anatomical studies that included less extravagant terminology (terms such as *animal spirits* were vague and unacceptable), a more careful and detailed cataloging of anatomical parts, and greater conservatism with respect to assigning functions to anatomical structures. Though open to the rationalism and geometric method of Descartes and Spinoza, Stensen called for a more empirical science of anatomy that looked for structures and efficient causes. Stensen also struggled with tensions between science and religion, and he sought a different resolution than others; he eventually abandoned science and became a bishop, despite remaining in contact with scholars, including Leibniz, who encouraged him to return to scientific pursuits (Cobb, 2006).

STEPHEN HALES

McHenry (1969) pointed out that English physiologist **Stephen Hales (1677–1761)** first demonstrated a spinal reflex. Unfortunately, he did not publish his experiment, but, according to McHenry, "Hales decapitated a frog and found

that reflex movements of the hind leg could still be obtained by pricking the skin, and that the frog would hop about" (p. 112). Such a finding would hardly surprise anybody who has observed decapitation of animals. Reflex activity remains for periods of time, depending on the ambient temperature and the species of animal (spinal reflexes remain for hours or even days in some creatures such as snakes or turtles). But Hales took another step and found that such activity vanishes if the spinal cord is destroyed. Hales's research demonstrated that reflexes could be carried on without the brain but not without the spinal cord.

ROBERT WHYTT

Probably the most accomplished neurophysiologist of his day, **Robert Whytt (1714–1766)** replicated Hales's experiment and subjected it to closer scrutiny. Whytt (*white*) studied medicine at Edinburgh, London, Paris, and Leiden and earned medical degrees from Rheims and St. Andrews. Revered as one of the foremost experimental physiologists of the time (Rocca, 2007), he practiced and taught medicine in Edinburgh and was named fellow of the college in 1737. In addition to his physiological work, Whytt appears to have conducted early observational studies of people with anorexia nervosa and bulimia nervosa (Silverman, 1976) and to have been the first to systematically describe a person with multiple sclerosis (Lincoln & Ebers, 2012).

When Whytt repeated Hales's experiment, he ran a red-hot wire lengthwise through the spine of a decapitated frog. He noted that following this procedure "there is no sympathy between the different muscles or other parts of the body as was observed when the spinal marrow was entire" (McHenry, 1969, p. 114). Whytt also observed some reflex actions remain if small segments of the spinal cord are left intact. Many motions persist after removal of the brain and some persist if small segments of the spinal cord are left intact following decapitation, but all motion stops when the entire spinal cord is destroyed. Based on his research, Whytt emphasized the idea that movement has its origin in the action of a stimulus that

PIERRE JEA[...]

La Mettrie's me[...]
work of the infl[...]
**Jean Georges [...]
1808)**. Physicia[...]
Cabanis was a f[...]
tuals of his day [...]
and deTracy. [...]
Benjamin Frank[...]
La Mettrie, Cab[...]
between psycho[...]
mic and enviro[...]
to Cabanis, psyc[...]
naturalistic cont[...]
cesses such as m[...]
tion are products [...]
also stressed the [...]
environmental e[...]
Cabanis's specifi[...]
phosphorus as cri[...]
1998) or his clain[...]
brain (Turgeon &[...]
sisted in neurosci[...]
Cabanis, research[...]
for its own sake [...]
psychological pro[...]

MAPPING TH[...]
PERIPHERAL [...]

The early ninetee[...]
optimism about dis[...]
mental and physica[...]
cal tools of science[...]
the search for the s[...]
scientific discover[...]
optimism, although[...]

Localization of [...]

A major breakthrou[...]
vous system came [...]
sory and motor trac[...]
series of independe[...]
Bell (1774–1842)[...]
Magendie (1783–[...]
strated that the ver[...]

excites nervous activity. Herrnstein and Boring (1966), commenting on Whytt's work, remarked, "One can now perceive the essentials of the chain of events that ultimately established the reflex as a fundamental concept: a stimulus acts on nervous tissue, leading to a muscle movement whose magnitude is in some way proportional to the strength of the stimulus" (p. 283). In a lasting contribution, Watson and Evans (1991) credited Whytt with introducing "the terms 'stimulus' and 'response'" (p. 248).

Whytt drew distinctions between voluntary and involuntary actions and actions based on habits, which he viewed as being somewhere between voluntary and involuntary actions. Among involuntary actions, he included digestive processes, coughing and sneezing, blushing, salivation, heart action, respiration, and pupillary reactions to changes in light. Because of his extensive research on pupillary dilation and contraction, the pupillary reflex is called *Whytt's reflex* (McHenry, 1969, p. 116). He emphasized the protective or adaptive nature of reflexes and anticipated the empirical findings that formed the foundation of nineteenth-century work on classical conditioning. Whytt, as quoted by Fearing (1970), noted that "The sight or even the recalled idea of grateful food, causes an uncommon flow of spittle into the mouth of a hungry person; and the seeing of a lemon cut produces the same effect in many people" (p. 80).

JOHANN AUGUST UNZER

Though Whytt researched the concept of the reflex, it was **Johann August Unzer (1727–1799)** who popularized the concept. Though Unzer's work was not original, it was systematic. According to Fearing (1970), "The concept of reflection seems firmly established in Unzer, and implies an element of necessity. The conversion of an afferent impulse into an efferent impulse by a mechanism of reflexion gives us a concept of reflex action which is adequate even in the modern sense" (p. 92). McHenry (1969) credited Unzer as "the first to employ the word *reflex* in connection with sensory-motor reactions"

(p. 119). Clarke and O'Malley (1968) also noted that Unzer introduced the terms **afferent**, meaning to move inward toward the central nervous system, and **efferent**, meaning to move outward toward the muscles or glands.

Unzer earned his M.D. degree from the University of Halle in 1748. He is best remembered for his 1771 book *Principles of Physiology*. Aside from his medical research, Unzer indulged in philosophical interests, particularly on the nature of mind and consciousness. His work on reflex action led him to study the relationship between consciousness and nervous activity. He wondered if consciousness was involved in all nervous activity or a product only of high-level, integrated activities mediated by the brain.

The relevance of such questions emerged from a social interest in capital punishment. In 1792, a thief named Nicholas-Jacques Pelletier became the first victim of the guillotine. Before long, the public took a morbid interest in France's notorious beheading machine, named after its advocate, Dr. **Joseph Ignace Guillotin (1738–1814)**. During the French Revolution, record crowds flocked to see a criminal's appointment with "Madame Guillotine." People even brought their children to witness the grisly spectacle. Despite its widespread use, the deadly machine inspired controversy. One question stood out from the others: Was death by guillotine really painless? This question was based on the idea that movement, regardless of its location, may represent some degree of consciousness. After the blade dropped from inside its tall wooden frame, a curious thing happened. Newly severed from its head, the criminal's body would sometimes go into a violent convulsion. Finding both curiosity and fear in the moment, spectators wondered if such thrashing revealed a consciousness of pain. Walker (1973) noted that "there were suggestions that the victims' heads responded after severance—Charlotte Corday's face was slapped [following decapitation] and [reportedly] showed annoyance" (p. 103). Popular curiosity about the sensitivity to pain and consciousness undoubtedly stimulated scientific inquiry. Unzer was one of the first to address the issue.

Unzer conc
tical in decapitate
He reasoned that
the brain cannot
decapitation, it m
an efferent path t
the animal been i
reflexes in decap
and, therefore, pr
the conscious ex
brain activity. Th
decapitation are p

The pioneer
Unzer opened dis
understanding of tl
ive activity playe
research, including
American behavio
was a central buil
viewpoint becaus
between voluntary
and more, early ph
plays an influence
turn to an eightee
that extends the pi

JULIEN OFFR/

The French phys
Offray de La Mc
1751) was one of
of the eighteenth
and medicine at
earned his medic
studied under the
physiologist Herr
La Mettrie's mc
Machine (1747/19
a mechanistic pro
to Descartes. His
tic, evolutionary,
that created an ou
As a result, La M
he obtained securit
and where he was
of Sciences. After
brought a virulent

division—immediately the parts were convulsed.

Experiment 2.   I now destroyed the posterior part of the spinal marrow by the point of a needle—no convulsive movements followed. I injured the anterior part and the animal was convulsed. (p. 183)

In 1811, Bell published his views on neural transmission in a pamphlet that he shared with friends. One hundred copies were printed, but all remained inside the network of Bell's friends and associates. A little more than a decade later, François Magendie began work on nerve physiology, unaware of Bell's research.

FRANÇOIS MAGENDIE   Born in Bordeaux, France, François Magendie (*muh zhon DEE*) was the son of a surgeon. He was raised according to the liberal precepts outlined by Rousseau in his famous book *Émile*. Though he did not start school until age ten, he progressed so rapidly that by age sixteen he was hired to conduct anatomical dissections in a Paris hospital. At age twenty, he was accepted as a medical student and he received his medical degree at age twenty-five. Magendie worked briefly on the medical faculty of Paris. After interpersonal difficulties, he founded a private practice while also providing private instruction in anatomy and physiology. In 1821, he was honored with elections to the Royal Academy of Medicine and the Academy of Sciences.

Magendie was a pioneer in modern experimental physiology. He founded a publication outlet called *Journal of Experimental Physiology* and argued for well-controlled experiments. In addition to his neurological work, Magendie contributed to the physiology of digestion, to the measurement of blood pressure in animals, and to early attempts to measure mechanically the cerebrospinal fluid pressure (Stahnisch, 2008). Grmek (1974) noted that "Magendie introduced into medical practice a series of recently discovered alkaloids: strychnine, morphine, brucine, codeine, quinine, and veratrine. He also generalized the therapeutic use of iodine and bromine salts" (p. 9).

Animal rights activists may have hampered Bell's research in England. Magendie did not face as much scrutiny in his native France (although later scientists such as Charles Darwin and T. H. Huxley criticized his practices and the vivisection reformer Albert Leffingwell blamed Magendie for animal abuse). In his vivisection experiments, Magendie developed techniques that permitted him to sever the anterior roots of the spinal column without disturbing the posterior roots. Operating on several species of animals, he severed anterior and posterior roots one at a time and in combination. The results revealed that severing the anterior roots interferes with movement and severing the posterior roots interferes with sensation. Severing both results in loss of sensation and movement.

The discovery of separate sensory and motor functions of the spinal roots suggested the possibility that other nerve channels are specialized. Indeed, Sir Charles Bell set forth a statement on specific energies of nerves in 1811, but the doctrine of specific energies, implying radical separation of various senses, became a centerpiece in the work of our next figure.

JOHANNES MÜLLER   The legendary physiologist **Johannes Müller (1801–1858)** was born on July 14, 1801, in Coblenz, Germany. A gifted student, he possessed excellent work

Johannes Müller

habits combined with unusual curiosity and ambition. In 1818, he enrolled as a student at the University of Bonn and earned his medical degree in 1822. Following further studies in anatomy in Berlin, Müller returned to Bonn where he taught comparative anatomy, physiology, and pathology. By 1830, Müller was full professor with a comfortable salary. In 1833, he moved to Berlin University as professor of anatomy and physiology. Müller is best remembered for his massive *Handbuch der Physiologie des Menschen* (1833–1840), which, according to MacLeod (1968a), became "the standard reference work for physiologists throughout Europe" (p. 525). Though Müller was highly productive and acclaimed, he suffered incapacitating bouts of depression. His excessive work pace and exacting self-demands no doubt aggravated the disorder. As testimony to Müller's influence, Steudel (1974), claimed that "almost all German scientists who achieved fame after the middle of the nineteenth century considered themselves his students" (p. 568).

Müller had broad interests in anatomy and physiology as well as the psychology of visual hallucinations (Berrios, 2005), but we'll focus on his work on the neurophysiology of the senses. Influenced by Sir Charles Bell, Müller elaborated on the doctrine of **specific energies of nerves** in his *Handbuch*, where he argued that, for each of the five senses, there is a "specific nerve energy" such that the nerve itself imposes the quality of sensation on mental processes (Finger & Wade, 2002). According to Müller, a nerve is capable of transmitting one and only one kind of sensation. No matter how the nerve is stimulated, it will transmit *only* its quality of sensation (Cassedy, 2008). For example, pressure on the eye will result in a visual sensation, whereas a blow to the ear will produce an auditory sensation such as ringing. It follows that one nerve could not substitute for another. Indeed, Boring (1950) noted that Emil du Bois-Reymond, one of Müller's students, "went so far as to say that, were it possible to cross-connect the auditory and optic nerves, we ought to see sounds with our ears and hear light with our eyes" (p. 93).

The influence of the doctrine of specific energies was not limited to physiology. The philosophical implication was that the sense organs conditioned knowledge. Elaborating on the point, Boring (1950) wrote: "The central and fundamental principle of the doctrine is that we are directly aware, not of objects, but of our nerves themselves; that is to say, the nerves are intermediates between perceived objects and the mind and thus impose their own characteristics upon the mind" (p. 82). Such a doctrine represents another important step in the transition from vitalism to mechanism because it ties the mind to the machinery of the body.

Müller's doctrine was one of the most widely accepted physiological notions of the early nineteenth century. As such, it shaped the direction of many later physiological and psychological theories. The doctrine was extended to the idea that specific nerve fiber energies correspond to various psychological qualities (Cassedy, 2008). Thus, Thomas Young and Hermann von Helmholtz suggested that the primary colors possess three different optical fibers (see Herrnstein & Boring, 1966, pp. 40–44). Helmholtz also suggested that thousands of specific auditory energies correspond to each discriminable tone. Other investigators extended the idea of specific energies to other sensory modalities, resulting in the belief that each elementary sense quality was associated with specific nerve fibers. By 1896, a youthful psychologist named Edward Bradford Titchener calculated a kind of psychological table of elements that included thousands of visual and auditory qualities. Titchener found far fewer qualities associated with the other senses (e.g., four taste qualities and four skin qualities), but his total number of elementary qualities for all senses was formidable.

The doctrine of specific energies shaped early psychological thought in other ways. For example, it suggested a radical isolation of the senses from each other. According to Helmholtz, the sense qualities were so heterogeneous that there were no meaningful transitions from one to another. Thus, questions such as whether "sweet is more like blue or red, can simply not be asked"

(Helmholtz, 1896, p. 584). Despite later challenges to the idea that sense qualities have nothing in common with each other (see Hartshorne, 1934; Köhler, 1947; Viney, 1991), such a view prevailed in mainstream psychology for a long time. The doctrine of specific energies was also consistent with nineteenth-century faculty psychologies, including phrenology.

GALL AND SPURZHEIM: A PRODUCTIVE FALSE START

A German anatomist, physiologist, and physician, **Franz Joseph Gall (1758–1828)**, gave psychology its most extreme theory of *localization of function*, the idea that different regions of the brain carry out different functions. Imagine that only one region of your brain controls your sense of self-esteem. Now imagine that it is confined to a small area on the top of your head, toward the back. Another region, say just above your left ear, controls your tendency toward self-destructiveness. Your ability to keep a secret is concentrated in the area above it. A region toward the back of your head controls your talent at forming and maintaining friendships.

Gall was convinced that *faculties* (personality and intelligence traits) are localized in specific regions of the brain (Sizer & Drayton, 1892). A person's faculties could be evaluated by examining the corresponding part of the brain that lies immediately beneath that location. Are you a spiritual person? If so, that region of your brain would swell during infancy, leaving a bump in the skull topography. Awful at math? The cortical area around your left eye would shrink, producing a concave dent. Gall's "doctrine of the skull" insisted that skull indentations and protrusions reveal our greatest strengths and weaknesses, and this information could be used for academic or career counseling (Hershenson, 2008).

Gall and his student, **Johann Kaspar Spurzheim (1776–1832)**, mapped out elaborate charts to guide the assessment of intellectual abilities and personality characteristics based on the shape of the head. Originally, Gall referred to his techniques for measuring the skull as cranioscopy and later as *faculty psychology*. Under Spurzheim's leadership, however, the name changed to **phrenology**, from the literal Greek roots *phrenos* ("the mind") and *logos* ("the study of a thing"). Between 1810 and 1819, Gall and Spurzheim published a four-volume work titled *The Anatomy and Physiology of the Nervous System in General and the Brain in Particular, with Observations on the Possibility of Discovering the Number of Intellectual and Moral Dispositions of Men and Animals through the Configurations of Their Heads*. Brevity, it seems, was not among their collective faculties.

From the outset, phrenology was controversial among scientists and some physicians while proving offensive to many religious and political leaders. Indeed, Gall was forced out of Vienna and his works were banned shortly after the turn of the nineteenth century. Scientists were suspicious of Gall's methodology, whereas religious and political officials were concerned with the moral implications of a theory that emphasized the role of natural causes in human experience. Despite inspiring controversy, phrenology enjoyed great popularity in much of Western Europe and the United States, and many enthusiastic promoters, including George Combe (Wright, 2005) and Nelson Sizer (Sizer & Drayton, 1892), added their own scholarship. The public attended phrenology lectures and read journals devoted to the topic. Voters interested in the campaign leading to the 1852 American presidential election could consult the phrenological *Journal of Man* for an analysis of each candidate. Countless people, rich and poor, consulted practitioners who provided diagnostic services and advice on personal growth and development (giving rise to the taunt, "you ought to have your head examined"). In short, phrenology became a cultural phenomenon.

Many notable Victorians, including Jane Addams, Louisa May Alcott, Susan B. Anthony, Clara Barton, Henry Ward Beecher, Thomas A. Edison, Nathaniel Hawthorne, Andrew Jackson, Helen Keller, Abraham Lincoln, Henry Wadsworth Longfellow, Horace Mann, Karl Marx, Samuel F. B. Morse, Edgar Allan Poe, Theodore Roosevelt, and Booker T. Washington, visited phrenological parlors for readings (Bryan, Bair, & DeAngury, 2003). Conan

Doyle's character Sherlock Holmes interacted with phrenologists (Wagner, 2006). The poet Walt Whitman solicited American phrenologists Lorenzo Fowler (1811–1896) and Orson Fowler (1809–1887) to examine his head. Whitman was so delighted with the glowing results that he published them five times as a means of announcing himself as the "Poet of America" (later, the Fowlers and their brother-in-law, Samuel Wells, published Whitman's seminal *Leaves of Grass* in 1855). American writer and humorist Mark Twain was more skeptical. No stranger to pranks, he paid multiple visits to phrenologists including Lorenzo Fowler. Following his informal single-blind test of phrenology, Twain found it wanting. In a delicious bit of irony, Fowler discovered a cavity on Twain's head that "represented a total absence of the sense of humor" (Neider, 1959, p. 116).

Before long, phrenology became the stuff of quacks, hucksters, and crass moneymaking. The craze began to fade as the world moved into the twentieth century. With a reputation built on noble intentions, greed, and a few outright lies, phrenology was branded a pseudoscience. It was condemned to join other questionable folk sciences such as palmistry, astrology, physiognomy, alchemy, mesmerism, and craniometry. Ironically, phrenology as the "study of the mind" is a better name for the discipline than psychology, meaning the "study of the soul." Perhaps if the phrenologists had been rigorous in their work, we would today have a world populated with the likes of clinical phrenologists and forensic phrenologists and cognitive phrenologists.

Phrenology is an example of a productive false start in the modern quest for an understanding of the relationship between the mental and physical worlds. There can be little question that the work of Gall and Spurzheim mobilized other scientists to investigate localization of function. Further, and equally important, phrenology helped shape public opinion regarding the central role of the brain in intellect and personality. Leading educators and reformers of the day embraced phrenology as a foundation for progressive reform (Tomlinson, 2005). Although flawed methodologically and substantively, phrenology contributed to

the growing climate of opinion that there could be a science of human nature (Sokal, 2001).

PIERRE FLOURENS French physiologist **Pierre Jean Marie Flourens** (*flew RAHNS*) **(1794–1867)** delivered some of the most credible scientific evidence against phrenology. Although trained in medicine, Flourens devoted himself to neurophysiology research. His distinguished career resulted in numerous honors, including election to the French Academy of Sciences.

In his neurological research, Flourens used the surgical method of *ablation*, which involved removing a specific brain structure to determine its function. Through this method, he discovered that respiratory functions are located in the medulla oblongata. He learned that the cerebellum mediates muscular coordination and that the cerebrum governs perceptual and cognitive functions. At first glance, Flourens seems to be advocating localization of function. Although recognizing some localization, he found no reason to agree with phrenologists (Price, 2012). Instead, Flourens argued that the brain functions as a whole. As a sort of action commune, the brain is an interconnected network of activity. He even determined that the brain shows plasticity so that—within limits—select regions of the brain could take over for other injured parts in a recovery of function.

Flourens is also remembered for many other scientific achievements. He discovered the anesthetic properties of chloroform after such properties had been demonstrated for ether and nitrous oxide. His research led to an understanding of the role of the semicircular canals in equilibrium. He was also well known as a biographer of renowned scientists. His studies with the method of ablation had a lasting influence on neurophysiology.

PAUL BROCA Flourens challenged the phrenological claim that intellectual and personality abilities are localized in specific regions of the brain. Now it remained for another French physician to demonstrate that the brain shows localized function. **Paul Broca (1824–1880)**, like Flourens, was an eminent physician–scientist with versatile interests. Indeed, he is often considered one of the founders of modern physical anthropology. He was also elected to the French Senate as a representative for science. Broca published in many fields of medicine, including anatomy, pathology, and surgery.

In 1861, Broca met a mental patient who had been locked in the Bicêtre psychiatric hospital for some thirty years. Although not psychotic, the man was unable to speak except for sputtering the word *tan*. He didn't seem to have a problem comprehending what was said to him; he simply could not speak. Broca checked the patient's speech apparatus and larynx, but didn't find a problem. Less than a week after coming into Broca's surgical unit, the man died. Broca performed an autopsy on the patient, later named "Tan" in neuroscience literature. Broca's autopsy revealed a fluid-filled cavity in the left frontal lobe of Tan's brain. After researching cases with similar lesions, Broca concluded that this region of the brain played a vital role in the production of speech (LaPointe, 2013). He discussed his work at the early 1861 meetings of the Paris Society of Anthropology, even though much of these meetings were devoted to the study of craniometry and race (Lorch, 2011). Although there is evidence that Marc Dax preceded Broca in identifying the left hemisphere as the area of speech localization (Buckingham, 2006; Manning & Thomas-Antérion, 2011), this region of the brain was later named *Broca's area* in his honor. Damage to Broca's area produces *expressive aphasia* or a loss of articulate speech.

By 1874, the German neurologist and psychiatrist **Carl Wernicke (1848–1905)** showed that damage to the superior portion of the left temporal lobe interferes with speech comprehension (the region was later named *Wernicke's area*). Unlike Broca's patients, Wernicke's patients had no trouble speaking. They did, however, have difficulty comprehending language, essentially the opposite problem of Broca's patients. Although not rigorous by scientific standards, Broca's work is viewed as the birth of neuropsychology (Cubelli & De Bastiani, 2011), and his clinical method was clearly more credible than the methods of the phrenologists.

Broca's discovery embarrassed phrenology on two counts—the methodology was superior and the speech area was not located in the front of the head as phrenologists had claimed. However, Broca's discovery challenged the claims of Flourens by demonstrating that when it comes to language, specific regions of the brain are localized, and this finding was embraced by later phrenologists (Sizer & Drayton, 1892).

Extending the Powers of Observation

Progress in understanding nature inevitably follows new ways of seeing the world. For example, new instruments such as the telescope, X-rays, and microscope broadened human powers of observation. Much of our progress in mapping the nervous system has depended on developing new observational techniques.

FRITSCH AND HITZIG   In 1870, German researchers **Gustav Theodor Fritsch (1838–1927)** and **Julius Eduard Hitzig (1838–1907)** collaborated on the electrical stimulation of the cortex. Their classic paper established the field of electrophysiology and, inspired by the work of Broca and others (Gross, 2007), provided a breakthrough in our understanding of the localization of function. Fritsch and Hitzig applied small electrical currents to specific regions of a dog's cortex, producing reliable movements on the side of the body opposite the source of stimulation (Hagner, 2012). It is now well understood that damage to the right side of the brain results in loss of motor functions on the left side of the body, and vice versa. Fritsch and Hitzig provided additional evidence in favor of localization of function (Gross, 2007), though their findings did not support the phrenologists. More importantly, electrical stimulation of the brain, pioneered by Fritsch and Hitzig, has been refined and remains a powerful methodological tool in the neurosciences. According to Clark (1972), Hitzig influenced psychology in another way. He demanded a more scientific approach to the study of emotional disorders and called for more humane treatment for psychiatric patients.

CAMILLO GOLGI AND SANTIAGO RAMÓN Y CAJAL   The Italian pathologist and histologist **Camillo Golgi** (*GOHL gee*) **(1843–1926)** offered another example of how new observational techniques influence our study of nature. Because of their fine structure and embeddedness in other tissue, nerve elements are extremely difficult to observe, even with a microscope. Golgi provided an original approach to the problem. He developed a staining procedure that enhances the features of nerve elements. Bearing his name, the Golgi stain revealed for the first time central features of the fine anatomy of nerve cells (Kruger et al., 2011).

   Santiago Ramón y Cajal (1852–1934), a Spanish physician, histologist, and anatomist, was one of the first to use and refine Golgi's staining methods in the study of the fine structure of the nervous system. Ramón y Cajal (*ro MOHN ee ka HALL*) discovered the anatomical gap between nerve cells, and he understood that transmission proceeds from the synapse to the axon. His extensive productive research and his prolific publication record establish him as the central figure in the discovery of the modern theory of the neuron (Rapport, 2005). In 1906, the Nobel Prize was shared by Golgi and Ramón y Cajal for their extensive contributions to our understanding of the anatomy of the nervous system (López-Muñoz et al., 2006).

SIR CHARLES SHERRINGTON   The work of pioneers such as Flourens, Fritsch, Hitzig, Golgi, and Ramón y Cajal had provided important new study methods and substantive knowledge about the nervous system, but the knowledge was highly fragmented and disjointed. The most comprehensive and integrative research on nervous system properties came from the English neurophysiologist **Sir Charles Sherrington (1857–1952)**. In 1906, Sherrington published a monumental work titled *The Integrative Action of the Nervous System*. His work did for neuroscience what Newton's *Principia* did for classical physics. Indeed, Sherrington's book has been called the "Principia of Physiology" because it defined the field and set the stage for future work. He is remembered, among other things, for coining terms that are still used in the language of neuroscience

(e.g., *synapse, proprioceptive, neuron pool, neuron threshold, nociceptive*), for mapping a variety of neural pathways, and for his investigations on the integrative work of the reflexes (Molnár & Brown, 2010).

   Even a simple task such as standing upright involves a complicated network of reflex activities carried on without conscious awareness. Reflexes are not necessarily isolated or discrete events, but are integrated in an adaptive fashion with ongoing routine activities. Sherrington identified a new type of receptor that detects information in the interior of the muscles and the joints. He referred to information from receptors such as *proprioception*. He showed that the role of proprioception in complex motor activities involves a kind of reciprocity. For example, when one set of muscles is stimulated, another antagonistic set may be automatically inhibited. Following Sherrington, there was a greater appreciation for the complexity and the integrative activity of reflexes. His work also deepened appreciation for the role of reflexes in "higher nervous functions" though, as noted by Swazey (1975), Sherrington resisted reductionism. Thus, "the physical is never anything but physical, or the psychical anything but psychical" (p. 401). Nevertheless, Sherrington believed that the two domains are integrative, and he received many

Sir Charles Sherrington

honors throughout his long and productive career, including the 1932 Nobel Prize in recognition of his pioneering work on the nervous system.

Speed of a Nervous Impulse

As mentioned, Descartes believed the pulling of a thread running the length of a nerve resulted in the release of animal spirits. Following Descartes, it was assumed that the rate of nervous transmission was comparable to the speed of light. Johannes Müller believed that nervous transmission was so fast as to be unmeasurable, but Müller's student, Hermann von Helmholtz, initiated a laboratory investigation that laid to rest still another Cartesian doctrine. Helmholtz's method was fairly simple. He had invented a device called a myograph that consisted of a rolling chart recorder. Moving at a known rate, the recorder registered the action of a stimulus and a response. Using the myograph, Helmholtz recorded the time lag between stimulation of a nerve and muscle contraction. Next, he stimulated the nerve at a point far from the muscle and then at a point near the muscle. The difference in contraction time between the far and near points divided by the distance between points yielded a measure of velocity. The rate of transmission calculated by this method was surprisingly slow. Times ranged from fifty to one hundred meters per second, so the velocity that was supposed to have approximated the speed of light was not even as fast as the speed of sound. What is important about Helmholtz's work is not only the speed of the nervous impulse per se, but that scientific technology had quantified another important physiological process.

By the mid-nineteenth century, there was a heady optimism in scientific circles about the ascendance of materialistic philosophy and the appropriateness of that philosophy to a science of human nature. Several of Johannes Müller's students captured the new optimism, even going so far as to take an oath that there were no forces in the living organism except those of a physical–chemical nature (Wertheimer, 1987, pp. 46–47).

Faith in the quantitative methods of science was complete, at least in the minds of nineteenth-century luminaries such as Hermann von Helmholtz, Emil DuBois-Reymond, Karl Ludwig, and Ernst Brücke. Specific quantitative methods, so successful in physiology, were now needed in the science of psychology. Such methods had already surfaced in the work of scientists who studied probability theory.

Measuring Behavior

What has sometimes been labeled the *origin myth* is nowhere better illustrated than in probability theory and statistics. What was the origin of the science of **statistics**? The term itself comes from a Latin root meaning "state." Political facts and figures, including population and census data, have always been associated with the term *statistics*, but its origins probably lie in dicing and gaming more than census activities.

Games of chance date to early times. People who studied the laws of chance made an important step in developing modern statistics. Among the best-known pioneers in modern probability theory were Blaise Pascal (1623–1662), a French scientist–philosopher, and Galileo Galilei (1564–1642), the Italian astronomer–physicist. Galileo worked on the probabilities of obtaining given numbers associated with throws of dice. For example, in the throw of two dice, the number 12 is less likely than, say, the number 8. The reason is that there is only one way to obtain 12; both dice must fall to display the number 6. But the number 8 can come about in a number of ways: 4 and 4, 3 and 5, and 2 and 6. Galileo was one of the first to calculate probabilities in games involving dice.

Pascal also made many contributions to the formalization of probability theory. His work, along with the work of other early probability theorists, provided a means for making educated predictions under conditions of uncertainty. Such thinking makes it possible to discover law-like principles behind irregularities and uncertainties.

The bell-shaped curve proved to be a critical development in statistics. The French mathematician Abraham DeMoivre (1667–1754) set forth the original derivations in 1733. Pierre Simon de Laplace (1749–1827) and Carl Friedrich Gauss

(1777–1855) also contributed to the development of the curve that is typically called the *Gaussian curve* or sometimes the *normal curve*.

JACQUES QUÉTELET Gauss and Laplace worked on human errors of observation, but it remained for a Belgian mathematician and astronomer to see the wider applications of the Gaussian curve. Lambert Adolphe **Jacques Quételet** (*kat LUH*) **(1796–1874)** is one of the most underestimated figures in the history of psychology. Tylor (1872) claimed that two broad contributions to "physiological and mental science" can be attributed to Quételet. First, according to Tylor (1872), Quételet

> has been for many years the prime mover in introducing the doctrine that human actions, even those usually considered most arbitrary, are in fact subordinate to general laws of human nature . . . ; second, he has succeeded in bringing the idea of a biological type or specific form, whether in bodily structure or mental faculty, to a distinct calculable conception, which is likely to impress on future arguments a definiteness not previously approached. (p. 45)

If individual behavior appears arbitrary or even capricious, such behavior could nevertheless be shown to display amazing regularity. Quételet found interest in the orderliness between variables such as age and criminal activity. He determined that people in the twenty-one to twenty-five age group commit far more thefts than those between the ages thirty-five and forty. Such a relationship between biological and ethical dimensions of behavior suggested important hidden causal links. Quételet also found lawful relationships between literacy level and crime, age of offender and type of crime, time of day and frequency of suicide attempts, and type of crime and sex of offender. On the issue of literacy level and crime, Quételet showed in one study that 61 percent of people accused of various crimes in France in 1828–1829 could not read or write, 27 percent could read or write imperfectly, and 12 percent could read or

write well or had superior education (1842/1968, p. 85). He believed that such a finding implicates society and suggested a causal link between illiteracy and criminal activity.

Quételet conducted studies on the physical characteristics of human beings. He collected data on chest measurements, height, weight, grip strength (measured with a hand dynamometer), heart rate (relative to age peers), respiration, and length of leap. He also investigated mortality statistics and medical epidemiology. He found not only that many physical qualities are distributed in the familiar bell-shaped curve but also that moral or psychological qualities are distributed in exactly the same way. He found regularities in nature that were heretofore unsuspected, suggesting the possibility of a new science. Tylor (1872) pointed out that with Quételet's work, we have "the introduction of scientific evidence into problems over which theologians and moralists have long claimed jurisdiction" (p. 49).

One of Quételet's more celebrated concepts is that of the *homme moyen*, typically translated as the "average man." He tells us that there is a central type in every population and that variation around that central type is lawful. Most people tend to cluster close to the average and departures on either side of the average occur with decreasing frequency. Quételet's quantitative work offered practical benefits. For example, accurate mortality statistics prove useful to the insurance industry. And the knowledge that more people wear a size medium shirt than other sizes holds value for the mass production of clothes.

The practical consequences of Quételet's work were important, but the theoretical consequences were more so. Quételet (1842/1968) spoke of determining "the period at which memory, imagination, and judgments commence, and the stages through which they successively pass in their progress to maturity; then, having established the maximum point, we may extend our inquiries to the law of their decline" (p. 74). Quételet proposed that scientists research memory, and asserted his belief in its lawfulness and its relationship to age. He also proposed a scientific study of reason and imagination, cautioning that "we can only appreciate faculties by their effects; in other words, by the actions or works which they produce" (pp. 74–75). His importance in statistics is undisputed, but he occupies an equally relevant position in psychology's intellectual ancestry. As much as any other, he advanced the idea that behavior can be measured.

SIR FRANCIS GALTON Gould (1981) remarked, "No man expressed his era's fascination with numbers so well as Darwin's celebrated cousin, Francis Galton" (p. 75). His fascination bordered on obsession, fueled by the belief that "there is no bodily or mental attribute . . . which cannot be gripped and consolidated into an ogive with a smooth outline" (Galton, 1883/1907, p. 36). At times, Galton's enthusiasm for measurement ran ahead of his better judgment. For example, his views on racial and gender attributes were based on inadequate data and reflected prejudices of the day. He nevertheless made significant contributions to the psychological study of individual differences and to the theory and practice of measurement; he is considered the founder of educational and behavioral statistics (Clauser, 2007).

Sir Francis Galton (1822–1911) was born in England, in the vicinity of Birmingham. His legendary intellect showed itself at an early age. He learned to read at age two-and-a-half and could read any book in the English language at age five. Growing up in a family of considerable wealth, he was given a sizable inheritance that allowed him to pursue any interest of his choice. He studied medicine, but interrupted his training in favor of a liberal arts degree. Although American psychologist Lewis Terman (1917) estimated that Galton possessed an IQ of 200, he struggled in his studies at Cambridge University and found it a challenge passing his mathematics examinations. He suffered an emotional breakdown while in his third year at Cambridge. Health problems prevented him from taking an honors degree in mathematics, but Galton eventually completed a degree at Cambridge. Afterward, he returned to medical school in London, but experienced a renewed ambivalence about medicine. Once again, he failed to complete his medical training. It didn't matter. A different education was to follow.

After his formal schooling, Galton traveled throughout Africa and the Middle East. He led an exploration into the interior of Africa and produced some of the first accurate maps of central southwest Africa. In recognition of his contributions, the Royal Geographical Society awarded him a gold medal and later made him a Fellow.

In 1853, Galton married Louisa Butler, who came from a family distinguished for academic and intellectual achievements. Galton enjoyed relations with his scholarly in-laws and maintained contacts in London with leading scientists of his day. He corresponded with his cousin Charles Darwin and often visited with Admiral Fitzroy, who had been Darwin's captain on the HMS (Her Majesty's Service) *Beagle*. Galton settled into an enthusiastic work routine that resulted in a bibliography of over three hundred popular and scholarly publications on a wide range of topics. His restless curiosity always pushed him toward intellectual exploration.

Galton developed a keen interest in the weather, inspired in part by his travels. As a pioneer meteorologist, he drew some of the first weather maps and discovered the importance of low- and high-pressure gradients in weather prediction. His skill as an inventor complemented his interest in scientific instrumentation. He developed an improved heliostat for flashing signals on sunny days, proposed a printing telegraph, and improved several meteorological instruments (see Forrest, 1974, p. 294). Galton also was a pioneer in the use of fingerprinting as a means of identification. Drawing on his statistical analysis, he estimated that the odds of two individual fingerprints being identical were one in sixty-four billion. He consulted with his friend Edward Henry, leading to the development of the Galton–Henry system of fingerprint identification. Their work influenced Scotland Yard's criminal investigations and Sir Arthur Conan Doyle's detective fiction featuring Sherlock Holmes. All of this is part of Galton's larger interest in developing new statistical techniques. Before turning to his measurement theory, let's discuss Galton's obsession with counting.

No matter where he found himself, Galton could be counted on to count. In 1885, he attended a crowded public meeting with a tiresome speaker. He wrote that the "communication proved tedious, and I could not hear much of it, so from my position at the back of the platform I studied the expressions and gestures of the bored audience" (1885, p. 174). In an early work of non-verbal social behavior, he observed the crowd, cataloging fidgeting (such as swaying from side to side) as a measure of boredom. Galton (1885) concluded with a word of advice: "Let me suggest to observant philosophers when the meetings they attend may prove dull, to occupy themselves in estimating the frequency, amplitude, and duration of the fidgets of their fellow-sufferers" (p. 174).

Like his cousin Darwin, Galton (1872) had a flair for controversy as seen in his work "Statistical Inquiries into the Efficacy of Prayer." Galton observed that length of life is not related to the amount of prayer offered on a person's behalf. He noted that missionaries often die early, even though they are the subject of considerable prayer. He also found no differences in the life spans of clergy, lawyers, and physicians and argued that public prayers for state leaders are ineffective because such leaders had shorter than average life spans.

Galton's paper was part of a larger debate in the early 1870s that raged over experiments (see Brush, 1974a) proposed by well-known scientists such as the physicist John Tyndall. The proposed experiments, designed to test the efficacy of prayer, triggered an emotional debate among some scientists and the clergy. The clergy were quick to point out that all outcomes of the proposed experiments would be subject to a hopeless array of interpretations. The debate illustrated an unbounded Victorian optimism about the application of measurement techniques to human problems. Such optimism would, of course, accommodate or even mandate a science of psychology. Galton was a chief representative of that optimism.

His contributions to measurement theory and practice had implications for experimental design and the kinds of problems psychologists could investigate. Diamond (1977) stated that without Galton's contributions, "it would have been a far more difficult task to give psychology its new directions, that is, to change it from a normative science, which had been conceived as the propaedeutic basis for philosophy, into a functional science of behavior, independent of

philosophy" (p. 47). His most important discoveries were in the areas of regression and correlation, both concepts growing out his interests in heredity. He used scattergrams to characterize the relationship between the heights of parents and the heights of the adult children. In a scattergram, values of one variable (height of a parent) could be laid out along an x axis and values of another variable (height of an adult child) could be displayed on the y axis. Points in the field of the scattergram could show simultaneous values for a large number of parents and their children. Galton was the first to use the term *co-relation* (later changed to *correlation*) and he contributed to the technical-mathematical characterization of correlations. In his early work, he was interested in correlations of physical traits (e.g., height, weight, circumference of head), but later realized that correlation had wider significance, with implications for a host of sociological and psychological problems. In addition to his contributions to the development of correlation techniques, Galton was the first to use the term *median*, an important contemporary measure of central tendency. Galton also made extensive use of percentiles, and indeed introduced the term *percentile*, although the concept itself was not new with him.

Applications of the New Measurement Techniques

The emerging nineteenth-century faith in new measurement techniques and new methods of analysis shaped psychology. Furthermore, early discoveries of the lawful distribution of physical and behavioral measures of human beings contributed to optimism about the extension of science into the human arena. Of course, occasional abuses tempered the benefits associated with advances in measurement. In his book *The Mismeasure of Man,* Gould (1981) traced abuses of psychological measures of intelligence. He documented the unfortunate results of early craniometry, which attempted to relate intelligence to cranial capacity. Gould showed that carelessness and poor sampling techniques resulted in beliefs that whites possessed larger brains than other racial groups. Therefore, craniometry was used in the service of racial and sexual prejudices.

Racism also found its way into intelligence testing. As discussed in Chapter 12, Binet viewed intelligence scores as assessments of learning and therefore as changeable. H. H. Goddard and others, however, reified IQ. Intelligence as measured by an IQ test was now viewed as something real, genetic, and unchangeable (Gould, 1981). Many prominent psychologists, including Lewis Terman, Robert M. Yerkes, and E. G. Boring, promoted this view of intelligence and intelligence tests. Their interpretations and findings both promoted and reflected the virulent racism spreading through the United States during the early 1900s (Loewen, 2005).

Despite widespread and systematic abuse, measurement techniques did serve as new scientific research tools. Simple descriptive social statistics paved the way for a public awareness that many events, when seen in numerical context, are best conceived in terms of the operation of natural causes. We'll illustrate this point with examples of the early use of social statistics.

One of Quételet's admirers was the famous nurse Florence Nightingale (1820–1910), who is remembered for her efforts to improve sanitary conditions in hospitals and in battlefield emergency hospitals designed to care for sick and wounded soldiers and for her successes as a woman employed outside the home in nineteenth-century United States (Mak & Waaldijk, 2009). Nightingale was fascinated with Quételet's efforts to quantify human behavior and saw an application of statistical techniques in the field of nursing. Nightingale deplored the failure of hospitals to keep uniform statistical records on births, deaths, and number of days for convalescence. As a consequence of her concerns, she agitated for reforms in medical recordkeeping. She demonstrated that during war, disease and poor sanitary conditions produced more deaths among British soldiers than did the enemy. She was among the first to illustrate her arguments with graphs. Because of Florence Nightingale's contributions to descriptive social statistics, she was elected to fellowship in the Royal Statistical Society and as an honorary member of the American Statistical Association. Nightingale saw a role for statistics in moral and political reform efforts. She also saw that statistics could explore questions of social and psychological significance.

Drawing on her admiration of Florence Nightingale, the American reformer Dorothea Lynde Dix (see Chapter 9) used descriptive social statistics in her campaign to improve the treatment environment for mental patients. In her memorials to state legislatures, Dix presented tabular information on admissions, mortality, cure rates, age of onset of illness, and hospital costs. In her reports to legislative bodies, Dix sometimes included frequency data from hospitals on presumed causes of mental illness, including factors such as loss of property, domestic difficulties, grief, unemployment, head injuries, and extravagant religious excitement.

The increasing use of social statistics in the nineteenth century was an important development. Events that had been viewed as capricious, or as acts of the will, or as acts of God, could now be seen in a naturalistic context. Discovery of such regularities in human behavior contributed to the acceptance of the possibility of a science of psychology.

Review Questions

1. Briefly discuss Hobbes's position on epistemology.
2. In what way did Hobbes's work encourage naturalistic and quantitative studies?
3. Briefly describe Hobbes's beliefs about basic human nature.
4. Outline Descartes's views on reflex activity.
5. List and describe four testable hypotheses found in Descartes's views on the physical basis of movement.
6. Briefly describe why Swammerdam's experiment on the nerve-muscle preparation was embarrassing to Descartes's theory.
7. List three arguments advanced by Niels Stensen against Descartes's views on the role of the pineal gland.
8. Briefly characterize Hales's and Whytt's contributions to reflex theory.
9. According to Unzer, the guillotine provided a painless death. What was Unzer's rationale?
10. Why is the work of La Mettrie and Cabanis important to the development of scientific psychology?
11. Briefly describe the Bell–Magendie Law and how it was discovered.

12. What is the doctrine of specific energies and who was its chief advocate?
13. Briefly outline Helmholtz's technique for measuring the speed of conduction of a nervous impulse. Approximately what was the speed?
14. Why is the work of Jacques Quételet so important in the history of psychology?
15. Briefly outline Francis Galton's contributions to the development of quantitative techniques.

Glossary

afferent   In neurology, the term *afferent* refers to movement inward toward the central nervous system.

Bell, Charles (1774–1842)   Codiscoverer with François Magendie that spinal nerves are specialized. The ventral root handles motor functions and the dorsal root handles sensory functions.

Bell–Magendie Law   The discovery by Sir Charles Bell in England and by François Magendie in France that motor functions are localized in the ventral root of the spinal cord, whereas sensory functions are localized in the dorsal root.

Broca, Paul (1824–1880)   A French physician who is remembered, among other things, for his discovery that the anatomical locus for articulate or spoken speech is in a small region of the left frontal lobe—the inferior frontal gyrus, subsequently named *Broca's area.*

Cabanis, Pierre Jean Georges (1757–1808)   Argued for a naturalistic approach to psychological processes such as memory, intelligence, and sensation.

Descartes, René (1596–1650)   French philosopher who is often regarded as the founder of modern philosophy. Descartes made extensive original contributions in a great variety of areas. He helped elaborate early scientific methodology, provided rich and often testable hypotheses about the relationships between behavior and physiology, and is regarded as one of the key figures in modern rationalism.

efferent   Refers to neurological activity that moves outward from the central nervous system toward the muscles and glands.

Flourens, Pierre Jean Marie (1794–1867)   French physician and neurophysiologist who employed the method of ablation (surgical removal or isolation of specific structures) as a means of establishing the functions performed by various parts of the brain.

Fritsch, Gustav Theodor (1838–1927)   German physician and physiologist who, together with Eduard Hitzig, established the field of electrophysiology. Fritsch and Hitzig were pioneers in the use of direct electrical stimulation as a means of establishing brain functions.

Gall, Franz Joseph (1758–1828)   German anatomist, physician, and pioneer in faculty psychology. Gall believed that faculties of the mind were localized in specific regions of the brain and that well-developed or deficient regions were manifested in protrusions or indentations on the skull. Gall was the founder of phrenology, the attempt to assess character by examining the shape of the head.

Galton, Francis (1822–1911)   A key figure in the discovery of new quantitative techniques for the study of behavior. He pioneered many early concepts in statistics including the concept of correlation.

Golgi, Camillo (1843–1926)   Italian physician and histologist famous, among other things, for developing a staining technique that made it possible to distinguish fine nervous structures from surrounding tissue. His methods made a singular contribution to the advance of knowledge in neurophysiology.

Guillotin, Joseph Ignace (1738–1814)   Famous French physician who invented the instrument named after him and used for decapitation.

Hales, Stephen (1677–1761)   One of the first to demonstrate clearly a spinal reflex and the dependence of that reflex on the integrity of the spinal cord.

Helmholtz, Hermann Ludwig Ferdinand von (1821–1894)   One of the great German scientists of the nineteenth century. Among other contributions, he was the first to measure the speed of conduction of the nervous impulse.

Hitzig, Julius Eduard (1838–1907)   German psychiatrist and neurophysiologist who collaborated with Gustav Theodor Fritsch to establish the field of electrophysiology. Fritsch and Hitzig were pioneers in the use of direct electrical stimulation to study brain functions.

Hobbes, Thomas (1588–1679)   One of the first of the modern philosophers to advance a thoroughgoing mechanistic account of human behavior. He also argued that self-interest serves as the primary basis for motivation.

La Mettrie, Julien Offray de (1709–1751) French physician whose famous book *Man a Machine* advanced a deterministic, evolutionary, and mechanistic approach to human mental processes.

Magendie, François (1783–1855) Demonstrated that motor functions are handled by the ventral root of the spinal cord and that sensory functions are handled by the dorsal root. Sir Charles Bell made the same discovery, now referred to as the Bell–Magendie Law.

Müller, Johannes (1801–1858)   Great pioneer in experimental physiology. Remembered, among other things, for his doctrine of specific energies, which argues that each nerve is highly specialized to carry out one kind of function.

phrenology   Literally, *science of the mind.* A theory developed by Franz Joseph Gall and Johann Kaspar Spurzheim that character and personality traits are related to specific regions of the brain. It was also believed that the surface features of the skull (e.g., protrusions and indentations) can be used as a means of assessing character.

Quételet, Jacques (1796–1874)   Early pioneer in statistics who was one of the first to realize that there were quantitative procedures applicable to human behavior. He understood that there are lawful regularities operating in moral and psychological arenas earlier regarded as capricious.

Ramón y Cajal, Santiago (1852–1934)   Spanish physician, histologist, and anatomist who discovered the synapse and developed the modern theory of the neuron.

Sherrington, Charles (1857–1952)   Sherrington was awarded the Nobel Prize in 1932 for his monumental work on the integrative action of the nervous system. He laid the foundations for modern work in neurophysiology and coined many of the terms that are common in the field today.

specific energies of nerves   Early belief that nerves are highly specialized so that they can carry out only one kind of function.

Spurzheim, Johann Kaspar (1776–1832)   A student and disciple of Franz Joseph Gall, Spurzheim helped develop and popularize the theory of personality and character known as *phrenology.* Spurzheim developed elaborate charts designed to assess personality via analysis of the shape of the skull.

statistics   Literally, *characteristics of the state.* A branch of mathematics devoted to the study of appropriate means of collecting and interpreting data. A common focus is on establishing the probability of occurrence of a given event.

Stensen, Niels (1638–1682)   Sometimes known as Nicolaus Steno. He exposed the anatomical errors of Descartes by demonstrating that animals have pineal glands and that the pineal body is not richly supplied with nerves. He further argued that, contrary to the predictions of Descartes, the pineal gland could not possibly move from side to side. Such findings dealt a severe blow to Descartes's theory of nervous action.

Swammerdam, Jan (1637–1680)   With a nerve-muscle preparation, Swammerdam performed a series of classic experiments demonstrating that a flexed muscle could not possibly grow larger because of the inflow of animal spirits. Swammerdam's demonstrations were contrary to predictions derived from the theory of nervous action advanced by Descartes.

Unzer, Johann August (1727–1799)   First to apply the word *reflex* to simple sensorimotor functions. Also introduced the terms *afferent* and *efferent.*

Wernicke, Carl (1848–1905)   German neurologist and psychiatrist who discovered the speech comprehension area in the left temporal lobe of the brain.

Whytt, Robert (1714–1766)   First to identify clearly the components of a reflex in terms of the action of a stimulus on nervous tissue, resulting in a response.

9

■ ■ ■

Naturalism and Humanitarian Reform

In no case may we interpret an action as the outcome of the exercise of a higher psychical faculty, if it can be interpreted as the outcome of the exercise of one which stands lower in the psychological scale.

—Conwy Lloyd Morgan (1894/1977)

Naturalism, as a philosophical perspective, states that scientific procedures and laws apply to all phenomena. Naturalism assumes that all events have a history that is understandable in terms of identifiable forces. In contrast with older beliefs about supernatural phenomena, the modern period approached the world in a more naturalistic way (see Lindberg & Numbers, 1986; White, 1896/1910). The early modern period and late Renaissance witnessed new naturalistic accounts of the histories of the earth and solar system. Later in the modern period, the naturalistic perspective accounted for the origin of life, the origin of physical diseases, and the causes of emotional disorders. As we will see, evolutionary theory and naturalistic accounts of mental disorders play a crucial role in the background of psychology.

The appeal of naturalism in the sciences is based partly on its heuristic value. A **heuristic theory** is one that fosters discovery, learning, and predictive efficiency. Rogers (1960) illustrates the value of naturalism along with the deceptive appeal of non-natural approaches to the world. Imagine you are talking to a medieval scholar named Faustus who believes that invisible demons cause friction. "Really? Demons?" you ask. "Well, what if I push a brick over a rough surface? How would you explain that?" Faustus answers that the number of demons pushing against you as you move the brick over the surface determines the amount of friction. "But wait a minute," you say, trying to trap him. "What if I pour oil over the surface? That would decrease friction." "Of course," Faustus answers, "oil drowns demons so now there are fewer demons to push against the brick."

In all likelihood, the "oil drowns demons" notion was not in the original theory; Faustus came up with it as an ad hoc explanation to rescue his theory. Faustus can explain everything with invisible demons that you can explain using standard naturalistic concepts with identifiable components.

Now ask yourself the following questions: Which theory will have the greatest heuristic value? Which theory will generate more believable, workable, and quantifiable hypotheses regarding the operation of friction? Consider another example. For centuries, demons were used to explain weather phenomena such as destructive hail, lightning, and windstorms (see Kramer & Sprenger, 1486/1971, p. 147). Gradually, with the advent of the scientific revolution, demonological explanations were replaced by naturalistic explanations based on measurable low-pressure centers, high-pressure centers, jet streams, pressure gradients, humidity, sea temperatures, and ambient temperatures. Although observers may perceive supernatural forces as causes of major weather events, heuristic values have led to productive hypotheses about how the weather works and to accuracy in predicting hurricanes, tornados, and droughts. We turn now to a consideration of naturalistic accounts of human origins and emotional disorders and how they have influenced the development of psychology.

EVOLUTIONARY THEORY

As we have seen, evolutionary thinking can be traced back to ancient Greece. As early as the fifth century BCE, Anaximander proposed a protoevolutionary theory that anticipated later models of evolution. Goudge (1973) noted that the roots of protoevolution can be found in early Buddhism, Taoism, and the teachings of Confucius. We will consider the development of evolutionary theory in modern times.

Despite a precedent from earlier cultures, modern theories of organic evolution were a relatively late development. In fact, the idea of evolution is a part of the broader discipline of **cosmogony**—the study of the origin of the cosmos or the universe. We'll examine modern theories of the evolution of the solar system, geological evolution, and organic evolution.

Evolution of the Solar System

By the mid-seventeenth century, scholars attacked the Aristotelian view of the immutability and permanence of the sun and stars. Bold and imaginative new cosmogonies accompanied the new Copernican cosmology, including theories proposed by **René Descartes (1596–1650)**, **Immanuel Kant (1724–1804)**, and **Pierre Simon de Laplace (1749–1827)**. Each theorist believed that our solar system had a natural history. Descartes, perhaps fearful of the Inquisition and the fate of Galileo, denied any intention of contradicting the Genesis account of creation.

Kant and Laplace supported the **nebular hypothesis.** According to this cosmogony, matter in the form of gaseous clouds was once distributed throughout the solar system. In conformity with known laws of motion, attraction, and repulsion, it was assumed that denser regions attract lighter ones and that at some point a series of concentric rings became well elaborated. Forces of attraction within each ring formed spheres corresponding to our planets. The material in the center of the field formed the sun. It was assumed that all planets should exist more or less on the same plane and that denser planets should be closer to the sun. The same laws responsible for our solar system were assumed to operate in other systems as well. The idea that the solar system evolved according to natural laws was an important first step in modern evolutionary thought. The next step was a natural evolutionary account of the history of the earth itself.

Geological Evolution

George-Louis Leclerc (**1707–1788**) enjoyed a life of unusual wealth and is better known by his title, **Comte de Buffon**. Along with Diderot, Voltaire, and Rousseau, Buffon is regarded as a premiere critical thinker in eighteenth-century French history. He published on vision and its development (Wade, 2008), and, drawing on his encyclopedic knowledge, he produced the massive *Histoire Naturelle,* a forty-four-volume effort that covered topics in zoology, botany, geology, meteorology, theology, philosophy, and psychology (see Buffon, 1780–1785/1977). Buffon was one of the first modern figures to propose an evolutionary model.

Buffon claimed that during the course of natural history, the earth evolved through a series of epochs. At one time, it existed in a molten stage. A universal sea came later and then a volcanic stage. In time, continents formed and were later populated with animals and finally human beings. Buffon realized it would take a great deal of time for such a large mass to cool from a molten stage. To estimate the cooling time, he heated spheres of different sizes and then calculated the time for them to cool. Based on an extrapolation from the differential cooling times of the spheres to his estimate of the size of the earth, Buffon concluded it would take the earth just under 43,000 years to cool from a molten stage.

More than fifty years before Buffon's birth, Archbishop James Ussher (1581–1656) studied biblical chronology to calculate the date of creation. Ussher estimated that the world had been born around October 23, 4004, BCE. Many scholars and religious authorities accepted his estimate as an irrefutable fact. Buffon did not. He determined that the total age of the earth was almost 75,000 years, far older than Ussher's estimate.

Troubled by Buffon's geological heresies, ecclesiastical authorities investigated his work. Theologians at the University of Paris condemned his estimate of the earth's history. In response, Buffon published a retraction: "I abandon whatever in my book concerns the formation of the earth, and in general all that might be contrary to the narration of Moses" (see Fellows & Milliken, 1972, p. 82). The King of France may have saved Buffon from further harassment. When the theology faculty denounced Buffon's *Époques,* the king urged a special investigative "committee to proceed with circumspection, an admonition that so impressed the assembled doctors that their committee never reported, some few taking covert revenge in dropping hints that

the work had been judged the harmless product of senility" (p. 83).

Buffon demonstrated anatomical similarities among animals and speculated about common ancestries. Yet, Goudge (1973) pointed out that Buffon "publicly denied that species are mutable" (p. 177). So organic evolution remained, for him, a weak hypothesis. Had he made a stronger statement, it would have led to undesirable repercussions with ecclesiastic authorities. Clodd (1897/1972) insisted that we must read between the lines to understand that Buffon offered modern ideas before the world was prepared to hear them, making him "the most stimulating and suggestive naturalist of the eighteenth century" (p. 111).

The period following Buffon's death nurtured bold new theories about geological evolution. French biologist **Georges Cuvier (1769–1832)** proposed in his **catastrophe theory** that earth-wrenching catastrophes had annihilated entire species and transformed the earth's topography. A challenge to this idea came with the landmark publication of the *Principles of Geology* (1830–1833) by Sir **Charles Lyell (1797–1875)**. He argued for **uniformitarianism**— the belief that evolutionary changes on earth occur gradually over vast stretches of time. Uniformitarianism replaced catastrophe theory and became the orthodox position for well over a century, establishing Lyell as the founder of modern geology. In time, his theory played a central role in Charles Darwin's work.

Evolution in Other Arenas of Intellectual Discourse

The idea of evolution as a process of natural change is applicable to many intellectual arenas. On many occasions, the history of ideas has embraced evolutionary thought, sometimes leading to fierce intellectual battles. For example, a naturalistic perspective was evident in debates about the origin of language. For many cultures, it was considered a divine gift, where "each people naturally held that language was given directly or indirectly by some special or national deity of

French biologist **Jean-Baptiste Lamarck (1744–1829)** is remembered for an early theory of organic evolution and as a pioneer in invertebrate paleontology. His personal life was riddled with tragedy. Ronan (1982) shared that Lamarck "married three or (possibly) four times, but death overtook each wife—Lamarck lived on the poverty line; his personal effects, books and biological collections had to be auctioned to pay for his funeral and he left his large family unprovided for. It included one son who was deaf and another who was insane. Added to all this, he went blind eleven years before his death" (p. 421). Lamarck's professional reputation didn't fare much better. His scientific contributions, though of immense importance in nineteenth-century thought, were the subject of continuous ridicule.

Lamarck's name is associated with *progressionism,* the idea that there is a steady linear advance in nature from simple to more complex forms of life. Taylor (1983) wrote that, in later developments of his thought, Lamarck believed in a "branching evolution and the vanishing of many forms" (this was a bolder claim than it looks; the orthodox claimed God could not make mistakes, and therefore, there could be no vanishing forms) (p. 39). No thinker before Lamarck so well appreciated the importance of extinction of species and adaptation.

Lamarck argued that species are human constructions based on our need for convenient classificatory schemes; individual plants or animals in nature are simply steps in an ongoing process. Each individual may differ from its ancestors, and its offspring may acquire still different characteristics that better fit their environment.

The most controversial aspect of Lamarck's theory was the proposed mechanism of evolution. Like Erasmus Darwin, Lamarck believed that environmental changes (e.g., changes in climate or food supply or in predator populations) had an obvious and profound impact on the needs of living organisms. Once a need is created, such as a behavior pattern to avoid a new predator, adaptive mechanisms are set in motion. The adaptations that are acquired are then transmitted genetically to the offspring. Traits such as a rough

skin or armor, a longer coat for warmth, or avoidance behaviors are passed on to subsequent generations. The sequence, according to Lamarck, is that changes in the environment impact the animal's needs. Changing needs alter the animal's behavior and new behaviors impact biological organization and structure. The new organizations and structures are then passed along.

Taylor (1983) pointed out that Lamarck did *not* say that environmental conditions per se affect heredity (pp. 39–40). Nevertheless, Lamarck's proposed mechanism was not and is not accepted by mainstream biologists, though the idea of the inheritance of acquired characteristics has been, for some reason, quite compelling and slow to die. We will encounter it again and again. It appeared later in the work of William McDougall, and for many years, it had strong appeal in Soviet science because of its perceived consistency with Marxist–Leninist thought. It survives today in unorthodox fringes of biology, but supporting and compelling experimental evidence has not been forthcoming (see the discussion in Taylor, 1983, pp. 48–54).

Charles Darwin

As we have seen, theories of cosmological, geological, and organic evolution were well entrenched in scientific literature prior to Darwin. The missing pieces in the puzzle involved a theoretical mechanism of evolution along with adequate supporting biological evidence. Darwin provided it and, simultaneously with **Alfred Russel Wallace (1823–1913)**, proposed a mechanism for evolution that appealed to the scientific community. Their independent work gave foundation to one of the great epochs in the history of science.

Charles Darwin (1809–1882) was born on February 12, 1809, the same day and year as Abraham Lincoln, another figure with a bold legacy. Darwin was the fifth of the six children of Robert Waring Darwin and Susannah Wedgwood. Charles's mother came from a family with an international reputation for excellence in pottery, fine china, and ceramics. Charles was eight years old when his mother died in 1817. Robert Waring Darwin was the third son of Erasmus Darwin and his first wife, Mary Howard. Robert was a successful physician known for treating patients with sympathy and understanding. Indeed, Wichler (1961) claimed that "his greatest success was a new method of treatment that is today called psychotherapy" (p. 153). Robert Darwin had a forceful personality, and he played a strong role in his son's life.

There is little evidence in Charles Darwin's educational life to suggest he would later achieve eminence in the scientific world. He had no love for primary school, and most of his work was perfunctory at best. At age sixteen, he entered Edinburgh University to pursue a medical degree. It didn't last. Darwin grew bored with classroom experiences and developed a profound aversion to observing surgical procedures. After two years of mediocre work, Charles abandoned his studies at Edinburgh. He enrolled as a theological student at Cambridge University, but discovered he disliked theology as much as medicine. He managed to complete a theology degree in 1831 but never found use for it.

From his early years, Darwin had a keen interest in natural science, driven by a special fondness for organization and collection. He cultivated an extensive knowledge of birds, insects, plant life, and sea fauna. During his time at Cambridge, Darwin suffered through lectures before escaping to study nature. He labored long hours collecting and identifying beetles, a curious hobby for a theology student. He soon commanded respect in the natural sciences. In 1831, Captain Robert FitzRoy (1805–1865) of the Royal Navy wrote to a botany professor named Henslow, asking for a naturalist to accompany him on a South American voyage. Henslow recommended Charles Darwin. Although his father considered it a waste of time, Darwin signed on as an unpaid crewmember on the second survey voyage of the HMS *Beagle*.

He was a few months shy of age twenty-three when the survey voyage began. In the opening lines of his account of the voyage of the HMS *Beagle*, Darwin (1897) described the demanding beginning and purpose of the expedition:

> After having been twice driven back by heavy south-western gales, her Majesty's ship *Beagle*, a ten-gun brig, under the command of Captain Fitz-Roy, R.N., sailed from Devonport on the 27th of December, 1831. The object of the expedition was to complete the survey of Patagonia and Tierra del Fuego, commenced under Captain King in 1826 to 1830—to survey the shores of Chile, Peru, and of some islands in the Pacific—and to carry a chain of chronometrical measurements around the world. (p. 1)

The *Beagle* sailed southwest past the Canary Islands to the coasts of Brazil and Argentina and further south to the Falkland Islands and Tierra del Fuego, the southern tip of South America. The voyage proceeded up the west coast of South America to the Galapagos Islands, the most important natural laboratory for Darwin's theory. As the *Beagle* sailed westward, Darwin visited many islands of the Pacific before reaching New Zealand and Australia. By early May 1836, the Cape of Good Hope was in sight, but unfavorable winds carried the two-masted brig-sloop back to

Charles Darwin

the coast of Brazil instead of the more northern goal of the Cape de Verd Islands. On the last day of August 1836, the *Beagle* made port in the Cape de Verd archipelago. On October 2, the shores of England were in sight. Darwin suffered seasickness throughout much of the journey, but the rewards of his excursions on land more than compensated for his misery at sea.

Darwin's account of the voyage of the *Beagle* reveals his keen ability to observe along with his geological, botanical, and zoological knowledge. Anthropological interests punctuate many passages and reflect his scientific and humane interests. For example, he noted that the people of Tierra del Fuego faced scarce food supplies during the winter months. To Darwin's dismay, the Fuegians cannibalized their elderly women before resorting to eat their dogs. Darwin dwelled on the miserable life of the Fuegians, whom he regarded as the most wretched of people. He was interested in how they arrived at Tierra del Fuego, how they survived, and what they could know of pleasure. Commenting on the Fuegians, Darwin (1897) observed,

> The different tribes have no government or chief, yet each is surrounded by other hostile tribes, speaking different dialects, and separated from each other only by a deserted border or neutral territory: the cause of their warfare appears to be the means of subsistence. Their country is a broken mass of wild rocks, lofty hills, and useless forests: and these are viewed through mists and endless storms. The habitable land is reduced to the stones on the beach; in search of food they are compelled unceasingly to wander from spot to spot, and so steep is the coast, that they can only move about in their wretched canoes. They cannot know the feeling of having a home, and still less that of domestic affection; for the husband is to the wife a brutal master to a laborious slave. Was a more horrid deed ever perpetrated, than that witnessed on the west coast by Byron, who saw a wretched mother pick up her bleeding dying infant-boy, whom her husband had mercilessly dashed on the stones for dropping a basket of sea-eggs! (pp. 215–216)

Darwin's evolutionary approach to life was based on extensive field experience and masses of geological, botanical, zoological, and anthropological data. One can see his new perspective taking shape in his recorded thoughts. At every turn, the importance of the environment in shaping life forced itself on his thinking. But how does evolution work? What is the mechanism? In Tierra del Fuego, Darwin (1897) speculated, "Nature by making habit omnipotent, and its effects hereditary, has fitted the Fuegian to the climate and the productions of his miserable country" (p. 216). The conclusion that the effects of habit are hereditary would have to be modified at a later date.

In the Galapagos Islands, Darwin encountered one of the world's finest natural laboratories for the study of species variation. The Galapagos are located about five hundred miles west of Ecuador. The equator cuts through the northern part of the largest island, but most of the archipelago lies south of the equator. There are ten major islands, with neighboring islands often less than ten miles away and visible from a given island. Climate, altitude, and soil conditions are comparable throughout the archipelago, yet Darwin found surprising and unexplained differences in plant and animal life from island to island. For example, finches on one island had developed a heavy parrot-like beak, whereas their relatives on a nearby island possessed a long and graceful beak. Darwin found plant and animal species that were unique to given islands or groups of islands and other species that were common to all the islands, but that varied from one island to the next. Strong currents probably prevented most animals from traveling from island to island. Darwin (1897) stated, "Most of the organic productions are aboriginal creations, found nowhere else" (p. 377). He speculated that with these islands, "We seem to be brought somewhat near to that great fact—that mystery of mysteries—the first appearance of new beings on this earth" (p. 378).

Nevertheless, for the time, the mechanisms of change and adaptation eluded him.

Darwin's account of his voyage sensitizes us to his emphasis on environmental setting, adaptation, and the sheer indifference and brutality of nature and people. At times, Darwin as the detached observer–naturalist surrendered to Darwin, the empathic human being. After witnessing numerous beatings of slaves and the separation of slave families at auctions, Darwin (1897) bitterly remarked, "I thank God, I shall never again visit a slave country.… These deeds [atrocities against slaves] are done and palliated by men who profess to love their neighbours as themselves, who believe in God, and pray that his will be done on earth!" (p. 499).

On his return to England, Darwin prepared and classified numerous plant and animal collections from his voyage. During this time, he began writing the results of his voyage in scientific papers and books. Published years before his *The Origin of Species,* Darwin's early works were admired in scientific circles and established him as a promising new voice.

His personal life was evolving as well. Darwin considered proposing to his older cousin, Emma Wedgwood. He debated it on scraps of paper under the columns of "Marry" or "Not Marry." Darwin (1958) concluded that one advantage of marriage would be a "constant companion and a friend in old age. . .better than a dog anyhow" (pp. 232–233). Disadvantages included "less money for books" and a "terrible loss of time." He finally decided in favor of marriage and proposed to Emma.

After marriage in 1839, the couple moved south of London and settled into the rural Down House on a small acreage with greenhouses for botanical work and facilities for his biological studies. The Darwins had ten children, although two died in infancy and his daughter, Annie, died at age ten. Throughout Darwin's time at Down, the condition of his health dictated the pace of his life and work. Plagued by nausea, headaches, insomnia, and dizziness, Darwin retreated from conventional social activities into the routine of scientific work. His strict work-oriented schedule

was no doubt a source of therapy, but it also formed the basis of a productive career.

After returning to England, he couldn't fit together several pieces of the evolutionary puzzle. A breakthrough of sorts came in 1838, when Darwin read *An Essay on the Principle of Population* by English economist **Thomas Robert Malthus (1766–1834)**. In his book, Malthus argued that population increases geometrically while food supply tends to increase (in the best of situations) in a slower arithmetic progression. In other words, without proper checks, populations outgrow their food resources. The result is an inevitable struggle for survival that may lead to catastrophe. Although Malthus anticipated the catastrophic effects of unlimited population growth, he nevertheless rejected birth control, regarding it as a mortal sin. Darwin, long an observer of the struggle for existence in plant and animal populations, felt an immediate debt to Malthus. As deBeer (1964) pointed out, "Darwin had already grasped the importance both of variation and of selection; the effect [of Malthus's work] was to suggest to him the inexorable pressure exerted by selection in favour of the better adapted and against the less well adapted" (p. 99).

Even with the impetus from Malthus's essay, Darwin's work moved at a slow pace. In 1844, he shared his ideas with botanist Joseph Hooker. Concerned about his friend's reaction, Darwin admitted it felt like he was "confessing a murder" (cited in Colp, 1986, p. 9). More than twenty years after returning from the Galapagos, he still had not published his ideas.

In 1858, English biologist Alfred Russel Wallace sent a manuscript, asking for critical comments. Darwin was shocked when he read it. Based on his work in the Amazon basin and other regions, Wallace's manuscript spelled out a model of evolution that paralleled Darwin's ideas in remarkable detail. Like Darwin, Wallace had found inspiration in Malthus's essay on population. Eiseley (1957) claimed that Darwin, though shaken, was tempted to let credit for the theory go to Wallace (p. 206). But Charles Lyell and Joseph Hooker were determined to announce the work of Darwin and Wallace and their new approach to evolution. In July 1858, Hooker and Lyell presented essays by Darwin and Wallace at a conference of the Linnean Society of London. Distraught over the death of his infant son, Darwin did not attend. Their work was published in the *Journal of Proceedings* of the Linnean Society on August 20. Like the conference presentation, the joint publication attracted little attention.

Now under great pressure and in delicate health, Darwin dedicated the next thirteen months to summarizing his extensive work. When his now famous *On the Origin of Species by Means of Natural Selection* was published in 1859, the entire stock of 1,250 copies sold out. Scholars continue to ask questions about priority in the discovery of the Darwin–Wallace evolutionary theory as well as the historical treatment of Alfred Russel Wallace (see Brackman, 1980).

A dozen years after the publication of *The Origin of Species*, Darwin came out with a second book on evolutionary theory titled *The Descent of Man* in 1871. Additional publications followed, several outlining the promise of an evolutionary psychology. More and more, nagging health concerns cut into his productivity. After struggling through months of illness, Charles Darwin died on April 19, 1882. One day later, his remains were interred in Westminster Abbey, close to the final resting place of Isaac Newton.

Darwin's *The Origin of Species* ignited a firestorm of controversy that burns to the present day, but it also advanced a revolutionary new way of thinking about evolution. In the first edition, he described the mechanism as *descent with modification* and did not use the phrase *evolution* until the concluding paragraph. As a rich heuristic theory, Darwin's model is built on a foundation of four essential technical features. One might regard the following as a family of theories, each subject to empirical testing.

First, populations of all species tend to produce more members than can possibly survive.

Second, variation appears in all populations.

Third, a struggle for survival ensues, but in specific environmental niches some variations are, by chance, better adapted to survive than others.

Fourth, those variants that are better adapted will tend to endow their offspring with genetic advantages. The outcome is a **natural selection** both for survival and for extinction.

Taylor (1983) pointed out that Darwin said "(1) that *all* changes which become fixed did so in this way, (2) that all changes occurred by *imperceptible gradations,* and (3) that all changes arose in the first instance by *chance*" (p. 17). Darwin assumed that species are always in more or less tension with their environments, making evolution an ongoing affair. He found much evidence in support of the theory—the extinction of entire species, the fact that offspring are similar to their parents but also depart from their parents, and the production of variations through selective breeding. Given sufficient time, Darwin assumed that such variations may result in new species. We should note that some of the original technical features have been called to question, most notably the assumption that all change is gradual. Nevertheless, the broader outlines of the Darwin–Wallace theory formed an integral part of biology since the publication of *The Origin.* The heritage of Darwin had a profound impact on many other intellectual contexts including philosophy, religion, history, morals, and science (see Kohn, 1985; Richards, 1987).

After more than a century and a half, Darwinian evolution is canonical (in the sense of being an accepted theoretical and unifying standard) for the overwhelming majority of scientists. Despite scientific acceptance, large segments of the population—especially in the United States—regard the theory with disdain. Ideologists clash in landmark legal cases, bitter school board meetings, the creation of special schools, and attempts to control textbook content. The National Science Teachers Association (2007) addresses how the evolution controversy intimidates K–12 science teachers and how public opposition to teaching evolution threatens the scientific literacy of students. Despite the difficulty in teasing out facts among the claims and counterclaims, the fact surfaces that evolution has shaped and continues to shape psychology and other scientific disciplines.

SIGNIFICANCE OF EVOLUTIONARY THEORY FOR PSYCHOLOGY

In an early paper titled "The Influence of Darwin on Psychology," Angell (1909) related that in Darwin's time there was already "a disposition to view mental life as intimately connected with physiological processes, as capable of investigation along experimental and physiological lines, and finally as susceptible of explanation in an evolutionary manner" (p. 152). Angell went on to state that with Darwinian thought, new emphasis was given to functional, developmental, and comparative processes as opposed to the simple analysis of the normal adult mind that had interested some early psychologists. The influence of Darwin and evolutionary ideas on psychology may be even greater than Angell could have imagined, particularly given the growing emphasis on application and pragmatism in the United States (Green, 2009).

During the present day, evolutionary theory remains vital in organizations such as the Center for Evolutionary Psychology (CEP) located at the University of California at Santa Barbara. An open-access, peer-reviewed journal titled *Evolutionary Psychology* has enjoyed success along with a wealth of books (see Buss, 2012; Crawford & Krebs, 2008; Ray, 2013; Workman & Reader, 2008) and encyclopedia entries on the topic. Buss (2012) observes that "evolutionary psychology has become a prominent theoretical perspective within psychology over the past two decades" (p. 49). Evolution has grown to become a productive organizing feature in all the biological sciences. Such growth is due in part to a balanced treatment of genetic and environmental influences and a strong emphasis on the centrality of adaptation in a world that is anything but static.

Buss (2012) notes that evolutionary psychology challenges the blank slate hypothesis originating in the modern period with John Locke and embraced by many of the behavioral psychologies. He also acknowledged that evolutionary psychology often focuses attention on the dark sides of human behavior. Evolution also emphasizes the continuities between humans and other animal groups. For example, mate guarding is evident throughout much of the animal kingdom where steps are taken to isolate females from male competitors (see Thornhill & Alcock, 1983). Buss (2002) and Buss and Shackelford (1997) note that mate guarding strategies are evident in humans when potential competitors are denigrated, threatened, or even killed. Mate guarding is also a factor in the isolation of females as when they are forced to remain indoors unless accompanied by a male or when they are forced to thoroughly cover themselves so as to be nearly invisible to potential male poachers. The influence of evolution on psychology is further manifested in the importance of topical areas summarized in the following materials.

Comparative Psychology

Darwin's *The Origin* triggered an explosion of interest in comparisons between animals and humans (Wasserman, 2013). A decade before his death, Darwin (1872/1998) published a captivating book on *The Expression of Emotions in Man and Animals*. In this comparative work, he concluded that human and animal emotions are universal and innate and offer real survival value. In collaboration with a psychiatrist named James C. Browne (1840–1938), Darwin even analyzed the facial expressions of psychotic patients to better understand emotion.

Inspired by this and other works in Darwin's legacy, comparative psychology had widespread popular appeal and was the subject of many articles in popular or cultural magazines, often written by well-known psychologists. The articles investigated an impressive range of subjects: the mental capacity of the elephant (Hornday, 1883), the intelligence of ants (Romanes, 1881), queen ants and queen bees (Wheeler, 1906), the formation of habits in the turtle (Yerkes, 1900), babies and monkeys (Buckman, 1895), and morality in animals (Leuba, 1928). Important theoretical issues surfaced in the early literature of comparative psychology. However, much of the early work was anecdotal in nature, consisting of interesting stories about an individual animal told by an owner or a hunter or naturalist. The stories typically revolved around the animal finding its way home or "solving" some other kind of problem. Based on the anecdote, enthusiastic observers made hasty inferences about the animal's psychological traits. Too often, the same writers indulged in *anthropomorphism*, attributing human characteristics to animals.

Many scientists were interested in comparative psychology (see Dewsbury, 1989), but arguably the most visible was English biologist **George John Romanes (1848–1894)**. For his *Mental Evolution in Animals* (1883), he used some of Darwin's notes and published a chapter from *The Origin* as part of an appendix (Smith, 2010). Romanes's books *Animal Intelligence* (1882) and *Mental Evolution in Man* (1888) were enthusiastic attempts to found a science of animal behavior and reason built on a continuum between humans and animals. Romanes's work called attention to the possibility of a comparative psychology, but was criticized for focusing on anecdotal evidence of remarkable animal feats. The American psychologist Joseph Jastrow (see Cadwallader, 1987) and German physiologist Wilhelm Wundt (1894/1977) were among his most aggressive critics. Romanes was aware of a need to establish definite principles and to avoid anecdotes. Still, he couldn't avoid the charge that anecdotalism and anthropomorphism—if not sensationalism—contaminated his work.

The English scientist **Conwy Lloyd Morgan (1852–1936)** advanced a more disciplined comparative perspective. Morgan (1894/1977) contended that "in no case may we interpret an action as the outcome of the exercise of a higher psychical faculty, if it can be interpreted as the outcome of the exercise of one that stands lower in the psychological scale" (p. 53). Thomas (2001) points out that Morgan initially described this idea as a "basal principle," but later referred to it as a "canon of interpretation." Subsequently, it has come to be known as *Morgan's canon*, but it has been the subject of widespread misinterpretation. Morgan was not advocating simplicity *for its own sake*, and he understood that interpretive efforts must, of

necessity, have a human face. He was arguing for cautious interpretations of data and for the development of deep sensitivities to the adequacy of explanations offered for natural events. The tensions between what Wertheimer (1972) discussed as richness versus precision have been salient from the earliest days of comparative psychology. In the *precision orientation,* we run the risk of oversimplification and of thus doing violence to our subject matter. In the *richness orientation,* we run the risk of reverting to constructs that have no scientific basis. In the final analysis, we agree with Alfred North Whitehead (1920/1971) who reminds us that the "aim of science is to seek the simplest explanations of the facts. We are apt to fall into the error of thinking that the facts are simple because simplicity is the goal of our quest. The guiding motto in the life of every natural philosopher should be Seek simplicity and distrust it" (p. 163).

Developmental Psychology

As we have seen, philosophers such as Rousseau and Locke were interested in the development and care of children. As with comparative psychology, an interest in developmental issues grew out of the Darwinian model of evolution. In addition to his work on naturalism, Darwin also gained a reputation as a pioneer in the study of individual development. His 1877 article "A Biographical Sketch of an Infant," first published in the British journal *Mind*, was based on careful observations of his infant son's sensory acuity, reflexes, moral sense, emotions, and associations. This classic in developmental psychology set the stage for later studies that provided normative data on the physical and psychological development of children. Following Darwin, a child study movement emerged with leaders often acknowledging their debt to evolutionary theory.

German zoologist **Ernst Heinrich Haeckel (1834–1919)** proposed an early attempt to tie evolutionism and psychology that had implications for the study of development and comparative psychology. As one of the first to embrace and promote Darwin's theory, Haeckel (1905) noted,

The greatest progress which psychology has made, with the assistance of evolution, in the latter half of the century culminates in the recognition of *the psychological unity of the organic world.* Comparative psychology, in co-operation with the ontogeny and phylogeny of the *psyche,* has enforced the conviction that organic life in all its stages, from the simplest unicellular protozoon up to man, springs from the same elementary forces of nature, from the physiological functions of sensation and movement. The future task of scientific psychology, therefore, is not, as it once was, the exclusively subjective and introspective analysis of the highly developed mind of a philosopher, but the objective, comparative study of the long gradation by which man has slowly arisen through a vast series of lower animal conditions. (p. 108)

Haeckel had proposed that **ontogeny** (the origin and history of the individual) **recapitulates phylogeny** (the origin and history of the species). In other words, the development of the individual of every species repeats the evolutionary development of that species. In *The Evolution of Man*, Haeckel (1905) demonstrated the difficulty of differentiating between human embryos at various stages of development and the embryos of other animals. Although Haeckel's recapitulation theory is not completely true, it nevertheless contributed to a growing awareness of studies of individual development.

Although Haeckel argued for racial differences in the evolution of language (Alter, 2007), he also argued that the difference in the consciousness of human beings and the consciousness of animals is a matter not of quality but only of degree. Such a position, derived from evolutionary thinking, carries with it a justification for comparative studies as a way of building a science of the mind. Haeckel argued strongly for a scientific psychology based on physiology and the assumed lawfulness of mental processes and evolution.

German physiologist **William Thierry Preyer (1841–1897)** was a colleague of Haeckel

at the University of Jena. He extended Haeckel's ideas to child psychology in his classic textbook *Die Seele des Kindes* (1882), later translated into English as *The Mind of the Child.* Similar to Darwin, Preyer observed the mental growth and language development of his son over a four-year period (Dennis, 1985). Zusne (1975) contended that "Preyer's book provided the greatest single impetus to the development of modern ontogenetic psychology" (p. 161).

The study of infant and child development, like comparative psychology, held popular appeal. Psychological works on infancy and childhood found their way into popular and cultural magazines, with titles such as "The Imitative Faculty of Infants" (Preyer, 1888), "Lingual Development in Babyhood" (Taine, 1876), "Children's Vocabularies" (Gale & Gale, 1902), "The Origin of Right-Handedness" (Baldwin, 1894), "Helen Keller: A Psychological Autobiography" (Jastrow, 1903), and "Development of the Moral Faculty" (Sully, 1886). In addition to popular articles, other psychologists informed the public about the child-development movement. In *Harper's Magazine,* American psychologist G. Stanley Hall (1910) outlined the history of the systematic study of development and discussed specific content areas such as growth norms, language development, and moral development. Sully (1894, 1895, 1896) wrote a series of articles for *Popular Science Monthly* that conveyed the need for a science of childhood and also discussed research areas on imagination, play, childhood art, and childhood fears. The world of the child became a major interest for pioneers such as G. Stanley Hall and William Preyer, who acknowledged their debt to Darwin.

Emphasis on Adaptation

Darwin's emphasis on survival, adaptation, and the shaping forces of the environment played a major role in defining the directions of the new psychology. Following Darwin, the frontiers of psychology were expanded. The detailed study of sensory processes that occupied much of the attention of the earliest psychologists was complemented by a more worldly psychology interested in education, the workplace, the home, and all those institutions and circumstances that influence adaptation. Darwin had a profound influence on the early leaders of American psychology, including William James, John Dewey, James McKeen Cattell, and G. Stanley Hall. As we will see later, each acknowledges a debt to Darwin.

Individual Differences

Sir **Francis Galton (1822–1911)** was not immediately affected by his cousin's book, *The Origin of Species*. In time, however, Darwin's continued scholarship on biological variation inspired Galton to emphasize individual differences in inherited intellectual abilities (Fancher, 2009). Prior to the publication of Darwin's *The Origin,* differences among individuals were often attributed to differences in the will. Older psychologies had stressed the importance of training the will, and expressions such as *diseases of the will* and *defects of the will* were common. Even Darwin, prior to reading Galton's work, had emphasized passion and a rigorous work ethic as the major determinants of individual differences. But after considering Galton's ideas, Darwin wrote to his cousin, "You have made a convert of an opponent in one sense, for I have always maintained that excepting fools, men did not differ much in intellect, only in zeal and hard work" (quoted in Pearson, 1914, p. 6).

Galton believed that differences among individuals are enormous and many are innate. In his classic *Hereditary Genius,* a work he later wished he had called *Hereditary Talent* (see Forrest, 1974, p. 88), he showed that exceptional accomplishment runs in families, suggesting the operation of a powerful hereditary influence. Galton demonstrated that musicians tend to come from families of musicians, judges from families of judges, poets from poets, commanders from commanders, and so on. From these studies, he promoted *eugenics*, the selective breeding of humans to improve the species (Gould, 1981), even though Darwin did not support eugenic ideas

(Shields & Bhatia, 2009). Galton did not, however, control for possible effects of environmental influence. Still, he introduced an important arena of psychological inquiry. Differences in memory, mathematical ability, musical ability, literary ability, and the like were regarded less as matters of willpower and individual responsibility and more as matters amenable to scientific investigation. His radical emphasis on the hereditary basis of individual differences would later be challenged with a radical emphasis on environment in shaping individuals.

It should be noted that Galton's work, a product of the late nineteenth century, had strong sexist and racist biases that can offend contemporary sensitivities. Galton's biases were assimilated into a Victorian public attitude that attributed white male accomplishments to innate superiority rather than to the educational opportunities enjoyed by white males.

Though Galton left unfortunate legacies about race that have continued to reemerge in psychology (Gould, 1981; Winston, 2003), he also opened the door to methods that were used to challenge his biases. As noted in Chapter 8, he introduced correlation methods and, following Quételet, sensitized us to the importance of statistical measures of variability as scientific tools. He also pioneered in the study of identical twins as a method for the investigation of the differential effects of heredity and environment.

Herbert Spencer

Prior to the publication of Darwin's *The Origin*, English philosopher **Herbert Spencer (1820–1903)** advanced his own evolutionary theory based on Lamarckian thought. His theory created little public interest, in part because it was largely speculative. The publication of Darwin's *The Origin* in 1859 sharpened Spencer's enthusiasm for evolution as a unifying principle and he embarked on applying the theory to all branches of human knowledge. He wrote on psychology, sociology, biology, ethics, and other topics, always stressing growth from simplicity to complexity. In his 1864 *Principles of Biology*, Spencer coined

Herbert Spencer

to the biological sciences and to psychology has been enormous. Darwin's work placed human experience and behavior in an uncompromising naturalistic context. It is probably no accident that the first laboratory in psychology opened within twenty years of the publication of *The Origin of Species.*

Though Darwinism places mind and behavior in a naturalistic context, the resulting image of human beings need not be pessimistic. Indeed, numerous scholars (Richards, 1987; Teilhard de Chardin, 1961) have argued that evolutionary theory need not result in moral and ethical nihilism (see Richards, 1987, pp. 595–627). In fact, moral concerns shaped much of Darwin's thinking. He was distressed by human suffering, animal suffering, the seeming indifference and brutality of nature, and the selling and owning of slaves even by those who were members of recognized religious organizations.

the expression *survival of the fittest,* giving rise to arguably the most popular catchphrase in the evolutionary literature. As with Darwin, the themes of species adaptation, survival, and continuity ran through his writings, including his work on brain size and race, which he used to argue for racial superiority of Europeans (Gondermann, 2007).

Spencer, often regarded as a forerunner of functionalism (see Chapter 12), came from the British utilitarian tradition. He believed that goodness gives long-term pleasure. He also believed we tend to repeat activities that result in pleasurable circumstances, an idea rediscovered in later research on learning, and he anticipated many principles of behavior analysis (Leslie, 2006). Like Darwin, Spencer believed that chance mutations produce many evolutionary changes. Spencer's two-volume *Principles of Psychology,* first published in 1855, was standard reading for many early psychologists.

Goudge (1973) pointed out that "evolutionism is a family of conceptions having great vitality and viability" (p. 188). One part of that family is Darwin's technical biological theory. But evolution is more than a technical theory; it is an attitude, an intellectual paradigm. As we have seen, it opened doors to the study of developmental psychology, comparative psychology, individual differences, and adaptation. Its contribution

NATURALISTIC APPROACHES TO EMOTIONAL DISORDERS

The naturalistic perspective gave depth and scope to many intellectual arenas including astronomy, geology, meteorology, and biology. Before it could exert influence, however, naturalism had to dislodge prevailing explanations based on the presumed operation of mysterious, paranormal, or supernatural forces. It wasn't a quiet cultural war. People held deeply entrenched beliefs that spiritual forces caused both physical and emotional problems. Literal interpretation of sacred books and institutional authority encouraged such beliefs. Consequently, naturalism faced unusual resistance. To appreciate naturalistic accounts of psychopathology, let's explore how older beliefs about demons and various spirit forces accounted for emotional disorders.

Demonology

When we think of explanations of mental illness based on demonic possession, we tend to think of people in early times and the Middle Ages.

However, Kirsch (1978) contended that demonological beliefs were more widespread during the Renaissance than in earlier times. He argued that **demonology** reached its apogee in the mid-seventeenth century. For example, in 1609, the year Kepler published his accounts of the elliptical motion of planets, *pricking* was announced as a method of diagnosing demonic possession (Kirsch, 1978). The method of pricking consisted of sticking a witch with a pin until a spot was found that proved insensitive to pain or did not bleed. Such a spot was regarded as the point through which a devil had gained access to a witch's body. This method was added to an arsenal of earlier diagnostic techniques set forth in an influential "bible" on demonology known as *The Witches' Hammer.*

The Witches' Hammer

In 1484, Pope Innocent VIII became troubled that many people in northern Germany had "abandoned themselves to devils" (see Summers, 1971, p. xiii). In response to this threat, the Pope commissioned two Dominican friars and professors of theology to serve as inquisitors. Based on their inquisitorial work, Heinrich Kramer and James Sprenger wrote the **Malleus Maleficarum**, translated as *The Witches' Hammer* or *The Hammer against Witches.* First published in 1486, the *Malleus* was one of the most influential books of the fifteenth and sixteenth centuries. It went through fourteen editions by 1520 and was translated into several European languages. Motivated by paranoia and a fear of anarchy, the *Malleus* was a response to individuals and groups who were perceived as revolutionary and corrupt. In this context, witches were viewed as conspirators against civilization. In his introduction to the *Malleus,* Summers (1971) cited examples of witchcraft techniques that inspired fear. One involved the age-old method of creating an image of someone the witch wished to destroy and then thrusting pins into the image or melting it. That the techniques of witchcraft "worked" should come as no surprise in view of widespread beliefs about magical and supernatural techniques.

Nearly all European countries passed laws against witchcraft, lending it credibility as a perceived threat. Laws were deemed necessary because common people could be moved to panic at the mere suggestion that a witch could manipulate their lives. The credulity and fear of the people made it possible to use witchcraft as a form of blackmail. It is little wonder that forceful action was taken to combat the so-called black arts.

The *Malleus* itself was divided into three parts, devoted to (1) a classification of devils and witches and how their influence in the world can be reconciled with God's omnipotence; (2) methods by which devils and witches accomplish their work, along with defenses and remedies against these methods; and (3) interrogation, judicial, and ecclesiastical procedures for bringing witches to justice. In Part II of the *Malleus,* Kramer and Sprenger suggested that devils can enter the heads of people to manipulate their mental images. Such entry may come about at the request of a witch. It was suggested that demonic possession may be the price one pays for a life of sin. Entry may also result from the light or heavy sin of another person. For example, a devil may possess a child if the parent has engaged in a sin. Some possessions, according to the *Malleus,* are for an individual's greater advantage. For example, Kramer and Sprenger told the story of one priest who had a gift for expelling devils. Because of his ability, he became famous and fell victim to the vice of vanity. Overcome with guilt, he prayed that, as punishment for his sin, he might be possessed by a devil for a period of five months. According to the *Malleus,* "He was at once possessed and had to be put in chains, and everything had to be applied to him which is customary in the case of demoniacs. But at the end of the fifth month he was immediately delivered both from all vainglory and from the devil" (Kramer & Sprenger, 1486/1971, p. 130).

The *Malleus* warned that demonic possession could result in symptoms such as sterility, impotence, loss of sensory functions, loss of motor functions, mental disorganization, pain, somnambulism, epilepsy, mania, and death. In practicing her mischief, it was said that a witch could cast a spell with a mere look or glance. Charms, incantations, poison, or a hex all served as imagined weapons in her arsenal. In addition to causing bodily harm, a witch could conspire with a devil to create emotional disorders. For individuals with sufficient credulity, the verbal threat of a witch could induce intense anxiety and stress. Based on the will to believe, numerous early records reported the gradual or speedy death of a threatened victim.

To battle this sinister influence, prescribed treatments were designed to cast out demons. Such treatments included exorcisms with sacred words, confessions, prayers, visits to holy shrines, repetitions of approved scriptures, and reverent participation in church ceremonies. The pages of the *Malleus* are filled with admonitions against the use of superstitious practices in combating devils and witchcraft. In general, one could be assured that a practice was not superstitious if it was in good accord with church doctrine. Not surprisingly, the same methods used to fight demonic possession were also employed to counter hailstorms, illness in animals, tempests, and other events perceived as works of witches or devils. The sprinkling of holy water, the ringing of church bells at an approaching storm, the making of the sign of the cross, or the utterance of prescribed prayers were encouraged as interventions.

Not all physical and psychological disturbances were viewed as the work of demons or witches. The *Malleus* recommends treatments for disorders caused by something other than witchcraft. For example, a man made sick by inordinate love for a woman may be treated in several ways. "He may be married to her, and so be cured by yielding to nature. . .his love [may be directed] to a more worthy object. . . . He may be directed to someone who. . .will vilify the body and disposition of his love, and so blacken her character that she may appear to him altogether base and deformed. Or, finally, he is to be set to arduous duties which may distract his thoughts" (Kramer & Sprenger, 1486/1971, p. 171).

In many cases, witches were viewed as enemies of civilization and were accused of visiting natural calamities and great suffering upon the world. Authorities felt an urgent need to identify witches, expose their work, and bring them to justice. As a result, witch trials spread across Europe during the sixteenth and seventeenth centuries. Virtually all European countries were caught in a frenzied campaign to stamp out witchcraft. In its various incarnations, the Inquisition targeted members of vilified outgroups, including heretics, witches, intellectuals, and people who were not heterosexual (Murphy, 2012). Consistent with that tradition, the witch trials besieged many of the same individuals, particularly Jews and women, who suffered disproportionately (Burns, 2003; Friedrich, 1982).

Fueled with paranoia and hostile retribution, witch hunts stand among the great crimes in the history of civilization. The true scale of the barbarism remains a mystery. Historians have tried to estimate the number of women who were executed in the name of witchcraft. The numbers prove elusive. Kieckhefer (1976) listed over five hundred European witch trials during the relatively inactive period between 1300 and 1500. Many trials included multiple defendants, but the court records are often piecemeal and incomplete, failing to specify the exact charge or verdict of a case.

Summers (1965) pointed to another reason why the numbers are elusive: "The people, frantic with superstitious fears, may often have taken the law into their own hands" (p. 359). Despite the obstacles, we have compelling evidence that European witch hunts, especially at their height during the sixteenth and seventeenth centuries, amounted to a holocaust that resulted in tens of thousands or even hundreds of thousands of executions. Many towns throughout Europe were decimated. Summers (1965), quoting the commissary Claude de Musici of Treves, pointed out that "from 18 January, 1587, to the 18 November, 1593, there were executed for witchcraft in the diocese of Treves three hundred and sixty-eight persons of both sexes; this does not include the number of sorcerers who were burned at Treves itself" (pp. 486–487). Bromberg (1954) tells of a French judge who "boasted that he had burned eight hundred women in 16 years on the bench" (p. 52). Documentary evidence of large numbers of executions can be found in the legal records of town after town throughout Europe. Several women at a time were burned at the stake in public executions. No country, it seems, was immune. Fortunately, scholars may gradually be able to provide more accurate data on many facets of the Inquisition including executions. The Vatican archives, closed for more than four centuries, were opened to researchers in 1998. It houses a vast collection of records that, according to Murphy (2012), fills about twenty rooms located in a large underground bunker.

Unfortunately, legal codes were written with little thought of protecting innocent people. It was hardly necessary given the prevailing theological view that God protects the innocent. Although comforting in its time, this belief contributed to a judicial inquisition that would bring condemnation from later generations. Let's take a look at some procedures used to prosecute witchcraft.

Part III of the *Malleus* outlined the typical procedure for initiating a trial where one party accused another and then offered evidence in court that supported the accusation. If the accusing party was irresponsible or if that party initiated a frivolous charge, it was liable to a countersuit. In the search for witches, however, this procedure could prove dangerous. Why? The *Malleus* tells us that an individual who accused a witch and served as witness might be vulnerable to the witch's retaliatory powers. From this perspective, Pope Boniface VIII decreed that in heresy trials, including witch trials, the inquisitor may withhold names if there was reason to believe that such witnesses or accusers faced danger.

A second procedure used in witch trials was for an individual simply to serve as an informer. Such an individual provided evidence to the court but did not serve as a witness, thereby enjoying protection from the suspected witch. The third procedure, most common in witch trials, was to initiate a process without an accuser or an informer. This procedure began when there was a suspicion that witches were active in a given region. Based on a suspicion, a judge could bring charges and proceed with a trial. The citizens were given warnings that an inquisition was beginning when a general citation was posted on parish churches or town halls. Any person, under any kind of suspicion, could be placed on trial. For example, if a person touched or cradled a baby—and that baby later became ill—the individual could be tried on grounds of witchcraft.

Deceptive techniques were advocated in the questioning of suspected witches. In advising interrogators, Kramer and Sprenger (1486/1971) suggested, "Let her [a suspected witch] be asked why she persists in a state of adultery or concubinage; for although this is beside the point [in a particular trial], yet such questions engender more suspicion than would be the case with a chaste and honest woman who stood accused" (p. 213). Inquisitors employed many forms of deception and placed great weight on an individual's reactions to questions. Denials were interpreted as cover-ups. On the other hand, if the witch gave an impassioned defense, that could also be taken as a sign of guilt.

In addition to interrogation procedures, certain signs or tests were taken as evidence of demonic possession and witchcraft. For instance, suspected witches were sometimes thrown into water. Floating was taken as evidence of guilt or demonic possession, whereas sinking revealed the witch's innocence. Another test was to determine whether a suspect could weep. It was believed that witches had an inability to shed real tears. The judge nevertheless had to use the weeping test with caution and with close supervision of attendants, because it was said that witches were capable of false tears or of assuming a weeping posture and then smearing spittle on their faces. Still other signs of possession or witchcraft included birthmarks, unusual growths, scars, or moles.

Even sober courtrooms at times deteriorated into theater, the drama coming when witnesses fell into hysterics, denouncing others as witches. Inquisitors often demanded that witches make confession before facing sentence for their crimes. To this end, and despite their grave concerns about the possibility of false confessions, torture was employed and with such efficiency that many accused confessed to the point of giving the inquisitors what they wanted to hear. Russell (1980) suggested that, in Lorraine, "only 10% persisted in denying their guilt to the moment of death" (pp. 79–80). Inquisitors tortured witches using thumbscrews, toe screws, leg vices, racks, whippings, and sustained imprisonment. The confessions often went into lurid detail about how the victim had sworn allegiance to the devil, attended witches' sabbats and other diabolical assemblies, engaged in intercourse with Satan, or eaten the flesh of infants. Such confessions were often made with the expectation that they would sway the court to impose a more humane death sentence. In most cases, confessions served only to reinforce popular stereotypes about the power of witches. Many confessions included lists of accomplices, often enemies of the defendant. Such accomplices were then, of course, also subject to trial. Russell (1980) told of one defendant who named all the court officials as being secretly involved in witchcraft.

Fear of the power of witches was so extensive that unusual precautions surrounded most legal proceedings. Jailers were cautioned against letting a witch touch or stare at them. If they touched the witches' bare hand, they were advised to immediately apply a remedy such as salt that had been consecrated on Palm Sunday or a "blessed disc of wax" stamped with a lamb and blessed by the Holy Father. Witches were led into the courtroom backward so that their eyes might not fall on the judge before his eyes fell on them. Otherwise, the judge might succumb to the witches' power and offer a lighter sentence. Witches were sometimes carried in a basket, under the assumption that their power was diminished so long as their feet did not touch the ground. Many suspects were stripped of all their clothes and all hair was shaved from their bodies. This humiliating exercise was enforced under the assumption that devils or evil spirits might hide or lurk in hair, especially pubic hair.

Most of those convicted of witchcraft were executed, although the sentence might be lighter for those accused of using magic or witchcraft to accomplish a good purpose, such as healing. Executions were often by burning, although other techniques were also employed. Most of the witch hunts and executions had ceased by the close of the eighteenth century.

The vast literature on witchcraft includes much discussion on the causes of such a belief system. Harris (1974) suggested that "the best way to understand the witch mania is to examine its earthly results rather than its heavenly intentions" (p. 237). It is true there was a theological backdrop that supported demonological views, but in addition, any problem—a death, a natural calamity, a financial failure, a physical or emotional illness—could be blamed on demons. Harris also noted that there was an economic basis for the witch hunts. Property was confiscated and sold and profits were made from the legal proceedings. Whatever the causes, the ideological basis of witchcraft was stubborn and died a slow death.

The Demise of Witchcraft

Russell (1980) wrote that as early as 1563, the physician Johann Weyer (1515–1588) wrote a treatise *On Magic* arguing that witches were harmless old women suffering from mental disorders and that natural causes could explain most alleged cases of witchcraft (p. 84). Because of such a bold claim, Weyer was himself accused of being a witch.

Two rationalist philosophers presented a stronger challenge to witchcraft. Baruch Spinoza denied any intermediate forces between human beings and God (Lea, 1957, p. 1361). If God is infinite, then God occupies all points in space and in time, and there can be no forces at work in the world other than God. Therefore, Spinoza viewed belief in demons as nonsense. In an attempt to undermine biblical authority on demonology, he suggested that Jesus acquiesced to popular superstitions when he referred to demons.

Spinoza transformed the radical monotheism of his Jewish heritage into a monistic naturalism. There was a unity between God and nature and an emphasis on natural causality. Spinoza wished to understand all things, including human actions, in terms of natural forces. There were no other forces with which to contend. In his emphasis on causality and on the unity of nature, Spinoza constituted a challenge to the kind of dualism, animism, and vitalism inherent in demonology. His perspective was similar to later scientific thought.

René Descartes provided another major challenge to demonological viewpoints. His emphasis was on the relationship between the activities of the soul, presumably seated in the pineal gland, and the soul's interactions with other parts of the body. Lea (1957) concluded that Descartes's beliefs about the relationship between brain activity and psychological processes (e.g., dreams, images, memory) left no room for other agencies such as demons.

HUMANITARIAN REFORM

Numerous intellectual traditions provided a friendly context for the birth of psychology in the late nineteenth century. Empiricism, rationalism, advances in physiology, the development of new quantitative tools (especially statistics), evolutionary theory, and the naturalistic approach to mental and emotional disturbances all contributed to an intellectual climate supportive of a new science and profession. In addition to these intellectual developments, psychology arose and was nourished in an age of social agitation. Known as the Progressive Era in the United States, it was a time of vigorous social activism with a variety of agendas (Gendzel, 2011). Teeming with optimism, progressive causes inspired dramatic reform on issues such as universal education, improved sanitation, equality for women, birth control, animal rights, prison reform, work conditions in factories, the treatment of the mentally ill, and child protection.

Each reform movement raised questions that called for the development of new knowledge and for scientific investigation into new kinds of problems. For example, labor movements were a response to deplorable eighteenth- and nineteenth-century factory conditions, but there were legitimate concerns on the part of both management and labor about how to balance their respective interests. A growing need emerged for studies on workplace environments, work behavior, work motivation, efficient organizational structures, and equitable distribution of profits. The naturalistic approach to mental and emotional problems opened the door to studies on etiology and the effects of various treatment environments. The reformers themselves realized the need for controlled studies and sometimes collected informal data pertinent to their reform agendas. For example, Dorothea Dix observed that loss of employment and unusual religious excitement often preceded emotional breakdowns.

It is no accident that psychology was born in an age of humanitarian and progressive reform. Once established, though, concerns arose about whether the new discipline was prepared to assist with practical problems. We'll see in subsequent chapters that some psychologists believed the first step should be to build a fund of basic knowledge. Others were impatient to apply psychology to problems in education, mental disorders, industry, and the law. The United States provided fertile soil for attempts by the new discipline to answer the problems of daily life. In particular, a reform agenda built around the humane treatment of mental disorders played a critical role in the social and cultural background of the new psychology.

Reform in the Treatment of People with Emotional Disorders

The metaphysical challenge to witchcraft and demonology paralleled a challenge of a different sort in a reform movement designed to provide humane care for people with mental illness. Revolutionary in its scope, the idea was to treat patients not as witches or demons or animals, but as human beings. Although beliefs and practices varied, the humanitarian reformers brought sweeping changes both in psychiatric treatment and in the public perception of people with mental disorders. As we will see, Europe and the United States played host to some of the more dramatic advances in humanitarian care. Such treatment grew partly out of a naturalistic approach to people with emotional disorders, as illustrated in the work of Franz Anton Mesmer.

FRANZ ANTON MESMER   The son of a forester, **Franz Anton Mesmer (1734–1815)** (*MEZ mur*) was born on May 23, 1734, in Iznang in the German province of Swabia. His mother, Maria Mesmer, encouraged several of her nine children to enter the priesthood but only one son, Johann, fulfilled her dream. Franz Anton began preparing for the ministry at age nine, but music and other interests distracted him. In 1759, Mesmer journeyed to Vienna where he earned a medical degree seven years later. At age thirty-two, Mesmer had earned an M.D. as well as a Ph.D. with his doctoral dissertation titled "The Influence of the Planets on the Human Body" (Buranelli, 1975). In the tradition of the Renaissance alchemist Paracelsus, Mesmer proposed a theory of "animal gravitation" in which celestial bodies affect the health of our minds and bodies.

Brimming with charisma, Mesmer enjoyed friendships with many celebrated figures in European society. In 1768, he married a rich widow named Anna Maria von Bosch and they moved into a mansion in the affluent suburb of Landstrasse. The lavish garden at his Vienna home featured a theater where Mesmer's friend Wolfgang Amadeus Mozart (1756–1791) gave the first performance of his short opera, *Bastien and Bastienne* (Landon, 1990). A patron of the arts, Mesmer was an amateur musician who excelled at the piano, cello, and glass armonica—an instrument of musical glasses designed by Benjamin Franklin in 1761 (Gallo & Finger, 2000).

Like many scholars of his day, Mesmer had a long-standing interest in electricity and magnetism. In the 1770s, he consulted a professor of astronomy named Maximillian Hell (an ironic last name given that Hell was also a Jesuit priest). Mesmer was entranced as Hell described his use of magnets in healing the sick. Curious, the young physician conducted his own investigations on restoring the magnetic balance inside the body to eliminate sickness. Mesmer's magnetic therapy would soon bring fame beyond his

wildest dreams. To no avail, Hell protested that Mesmer unfairly borrowed the idea from him.

Mesmer believed that the magnetism of iron, like the planetary bodies, affected a magnetic fluid in the body that controlled health and disease. He ran magnets across the bodies of his patients and found that some drifted into a trance. Bolstered by his findings on "animal magnetism," he treated patients with a variety of physiological symptoms including deafness, paralysis, blindness, rheumatism, headaches, and chronic pain. He even claimed to cure epilepsy and hysteria.

Although popular with Viennese society, the scientific community greeted Mesmer's animal magnetism with skepticism and scorn. In a celebrated case, he treated a blind concert pianist named Maria Theresia von Paradis, who happened to be a friend of Mozart. After Mesmer claimed he had restored her sight, several eminent physicians challenged his results and branded him a charlatan. In 1777, he was expelled from the medical faculty of the University of Vienna and barred from the practice of medicine. With his gift for controversy, it would not be the last time Mesmer clashed with medical authority (Oon, 2008).

Abandoning his family in 1778, Mesmer took exile in Paris where he caused an immediate sensation. His flair for grandiosity seemed perfectly suited to the extravagance of pre-Revolutionary Parisian society (Hoffeld, 1980). Nestled in a suite at the *Place Vendôme* and later at the fashionable *Hôtel Bullion*, his clinic introduced the idea of psychotherapy as theater. In a dimly lit salon, patients gathered around a *baquet,* a large wooden tub filled with chemicals that Mesmer described—with a Cartesian flourish—as "animal spirits" (the tub contained nothing more than water and bits of metal, stone, and ground glass).

In one of the earliest attempts at group therapy, patients were instructed to take an afflicted part of their body, a paralyzed arm, say, and press it against iron rods rising from the sides of the baquet. As music from a glass armonica soothed in the background, Mesmer made his grand entrance dressed in a lilac robe and brandishing a long iron wand, looking more like a sorcerer than a physician. He wandered from person to person, touching them with the wand and staring deep into their eyes. When he gave the command *Dormez* ("sleep"), his patients would slip into a trance. In the spell of this "crisis," some would tremble or twitch as if in the throes of a seizure. Others would groan or laugh or scream. A few would spin in a frenzied dance or collapse in a cold faint. But after the crisis had passed, most appeared to be free of their affliction.

Before long, Mesmer and his therapy were celebrated in both rich and poor circles. Among the wealthy and titled, Marie Antoinette and the Marquis de Lafayette joined the thousands who flocked to the clinic for the privilege of being mesmerized. As Mesmer's popularity soared, Mozart made mesmerism the stuff of friendly satire in his comic opera, *Così Fan Tutte* (Landon, 1990).

As in Vienna, however, the French medical community came to detest the practice of animal magnetism. Armed with a keen wit and the sort of bombast that might have impressed Paracelsus, Mesmer did not concede defeat. With characteristic audacity, he challenged the French Academy of Medicine to select twenty patients at random; Mesmer would treat ten and academy members would assume care for the remaining patients. Confident of his healing powers, perhaps because his own self-interest biased his evaluation of his methods (Hooley et al., 2013), Mesmer believed the clinical results would demonstrate the validity of his therapy. The academy declined to participate in his contest. For Mesmer, their reluctance must have seemed a small victory in itself.

In its day, Mesmer's controversial magnetic theory was debated with the same intensity that would later surround the work of Sigmund Freud. Like Freud, Mesmer recognized the advantage of spreading his message to an American audience. With support from the Marquis de Lafayette, Mesmer corresponded with George Washington about the possibility of introducing mesmerism to the United States (Buranelli, 1975). Out of respect for Lafayette's distinguished service during the Revolutionary War, Washington was polite but noncommittal.

By 1784, the rift between Mesmer and his medical colleagues swelled into a heated confrontation that traveled all the way to the court of King Louis XVI. Sympathetic to Mesmer's cause, a group calling itself the "Society of Harmony" called on the monarchy to investigate. In our world of congressional hearings, it is not uncommon to have government investigate a medical practice, but it was a rarity in Mesmer's time. The king convened a panel of experts to determine if mesmerism was a legitimate medical practice or little more than a dangerous magic trick. The blue-ribbon panel boasted intellectuals such as the American diplomat and scientist Benjamin Franklin (an ambassador to France at the time), the chemist Antoine-Laurent Lavoisier, the astronomer Jean-Sylvain Bailly, and Joseph Guillotin, a physician and proponent of the beheading machine (both Lavoisier and Bailly would be guillotined during the French Revolution). After examining the evidence, a verdict was issued on August 11, 1784:

> The commissioners have ascertained that the animal magnetic fluid is not perceptible by any of the senses; that it has no action, either on themselves or on the patients subjected to it. . . . Finally, [the commissioners] have demonstrated by decisive experiments that imagination apart from magnetism produces convulsions, and that magnetism without imagination produces nothing. (Binet & Féré, 1887/1891, pp. 16–17)

Unable to find support for mesmerism, the commission insisted that any positive effects of the treatment were the product of deception or the power of suggestion (Bromberg, 1959).

The commission's decision shattered Mesmer's reputation and career. Denounced as an impostor, Mesmer closed his notorious practice and left Paris in disgrace. After a move to London and later Germany, he practiced animal magnetism, but never regained the fame and fortune he had enjoyed in Paris. Mesmer died in obscurity in 1815, but his legacy is well preserved in the modern use of hypnotherapy (Gezundhajt, 2007).

Did Mesmer practice hypnosis? In the formal sense, no. But the practice of mesmerism relied on methods of suggestion that would be refined and investigated by a number of later hypnotherapists including the Marquis de Puységur (1751–1825), James Braid (1795–1860), and Jean-Martin Charcot (1825–1893). Outside of psychology, Mesmer's ideas remained a source of fascination for the public and notable intellectuals of the nineteenth century. The novelist Charles Dickens (1812–1870) dabbled with mesmerical experiments, as did Ada Lovelace (1815–1852), a British mathematician and daughter of Lord Byron (Woolley, 1999).

PHILIPPE PINEL   After Mesmer, the face of humanitarian reform shifted to the work of a bold physician named **Philippe Pinel (1745–1826)** (*pe NEL*), who spearheaded widespread reform in French asylums. A scientist more than a performer, Pinel enjoyed a medical respectability that forever eluded Mesmer.

Born near Castres, France, in 1745, Pinel was the first of seven children and the product of a rich medical heritage—Pinel's father was a surgeon and his mother's family included several physicians. Following an early literary education, Pinel studied theology at Toulouse in 1767 and then switched to medical studies and earned his medical degree in 1773. Condillac's analytic method had a profound impact on Pinel's thinking (Riese, 1951), as did the ideas of Locke, Hippocrates, Rousseau, and Voltaire. A new way of thinking was taking shape with an emphasis on equality, freedom, education, and the improvement of all societal institutions. People with disadvantages were no longer regarded as possessed or evil, but rather as sick or as victims of cruel and uncaring social institutions.

In this climate of optimism about human perfectibility, Pinel introduced legendary reforms at the hospital of the Bicêtre and later at the Salpêtrière. Prior to his arrival in 1792, inmates at the Bicêtre hospital were confined in cramped, poorly ventilated, foul-smelling quarters where they lived in accumulations of filth. Disturbed by the horrible conditions, Pinel petitioned the

French government about a plan to experiment with new methods of treatment. At last, an official visited the Bicêtre hospital and witnessed firsthand the spectacle of patients chained in cells and shouting obscenities. The government official granted the freedom to experiment, but warned that Pinel would likely become the victim of his own show of mercy.

The time had come for dramatic reform. Slowly and cautiously, Pinel liberated fifty patients. The poignant release of one man is illustrated in a memoir from Pinel's son as translated and abridged by Dix (1845/1971):

The experiments commenced with an English captain, whose history was unknown; he had been in chains forty years! As he was thought to be one of the most dangerous, having killed, at one time, an attendant with a blow from his manacles, the keepers approached him with caution; but first Pinel entered his cell unattended. "Ah, well captain, I will cause your chains to be taken off; you shall have liberty to walk in the court, if you will promise to behave like a gentleman, and offer no assault to those you will meet." "I would promise," said the maniac; "but you deride me, you are amusing yourself at my expense; you all fear me, once free." "I have six men," replied Pinel, "ready to obey my orders; believe me, therefore, I will set you free from this duress, if you will put on this jacket." The captain assented; the chains were removed, and the jacket laced;—the keepers withdrew, without closing the door. He raised himself, but fell: this effort was repeated again and again; the use of his limbs, so long constrained, nearly failed: at length, trembling, and with tottering steps, he emerged from his dark dungeon. His first look was the sky! "Ah," cried he, "how beautiful!" The remainder of the day he was constantly moving to and fro, uttering continually exclamations of pleasure;—he heeded no one: the flowers, the trees, above all the sky, engrossed him. At night he voluntarily returned to his cell, which had been cleansed, and furnished with a better bed: his sleep was tranquil and profound. For the two remaining years which he spent in the hospital, he had no recurrence of violent paroxysms, and often rendered good service to the keepers, in conducting the affairs of the establishment. (pp. 30–31)

In dealing with patients, Pinel emphasized logical consequences. For example, on being released from confinement or chains, patients were informed that continued freedom would depend on their behavior. Patient after patient responded to his humane treatment. In time, the fame of the reformer was ensured and his techniques were sometimes revered as an original discovery. In truth, Pinel's methods signaled a return to the psychological medicine of the ancient Greeks.

Based on clinical observation, Pinel's classic book *A Treatise on Insanity* (1806/1977) outlined a simplified and improved classification of mental disorders. Influential in its time, his classification system distinguished five major clinical categories that he called "species." The first was *melancholia,* a disorder that includes depression and/or delusions, especially delusions of persecution or involving suspicion. The second species was *mania without delirium,* a disorder characterized by poor impulse control or acts of fury. Pinel's third species involved *mania with delirium,* characterized by continuous or intermittent nervous excitement and intellectual deterioration. He called the fourth species *dementia* and described it as "marked by ideas unconnected amongst themselves and without relation to external objects" (p. 161). The final category, *idiotisme,* involved a general reduction of intellectual capacity.

With regard to etiology, Pinel rejected the popular belief of his day that all mental disorders have an anatomical or physiological basis. Although he believed that some disorders are associated with malformed skulls, his own research revealed that many mental patients have no identifiable physiological or anatomical abnormality. An individual's environment and lifestyle, Pinel

Philippe Pinel in the courtyard of the Salpêtrière

argued, play powerful roles in the creation of mental illness.

Because the home environment might contribute to mental disorders, he encouraged the admission of patients to mental hospitals. In a 1794 address before the Society for Natural History, Pinel appealed to the Revolutionary French government to construct institutions designed for humane care (Weiner, 1992), a cause later taken up by the American reformer Dorothea Dix. Pinel concluded that hospitals should group patients according to the nature and severity of their disorders. Hospital management and treatment should be interrelated so that patients live in clean and uncrowded quarters with a chance to enjoy fresh air and sunlight as well as opportunities to engage in work. Physical restraint should be used only when necessary.

As one of the founders of *moral therapy* (a precursor to psychotherapy), Pinel dedicated a major section of his *Treatise* to "The Moral Treatment of Insanity." Moral therapy consisted of *talk treatment* in a supportive atmosphere with a therapist who respected the patient's dignity and responsibility. In several respects, Pinel's therapeutic philosophy foreshadowed the modern school of humanistic psychology discussed in Chapter 17.

BENJAMIN RUSH Robinson (1977) noted striking parallels in the lives of Philippe Pinel and **Benjamin Rush (1745–1813)**. Both were born in 1745 and raised during periods of violent revolution. They each developed an interest in the work of the famous Scottish physiologist William Cullen (1710–1790). Both men considered the ministry before deciding on medical careers, and each served in post-Revolutionary positions in their respective governments. Of course, both are remembered as great reformers.

Benjamin Rush was born on the outskirts of Philadelphia, the fourth of seven children. His father, John Rush, died when Benjamin was only five. During the next three years, he lived with his mother, Susanna Hall Harvey Rush, before joining a boarding school run by his uncle, Samuel Finley.

Benjamin Rush

After boarding school, Rush entered the College of New Jersey (now Princeton University), where he earned his bachelor's degree in 1760. He served in a medical apprenticeship from 1761 to 1766 and took courses at the College of Philadelphia. In the fall of 1766, he enrolled at the University of Edinburgh, where he received his medical degree two years later. In 1776, Rush returned to Philadelphia and practiced medicine, primarily among the poor. That same year, he married Julia Stockton (1759–1848). He was appointed chair of chemistry at the College of Pennsylvania, where he established a national reputation as a medical educator. One of his students, Nathaniel Chapman (1780–1853), became the first president of the American Medical Association in 1848. Rush briefly served as surgeon general of the army under George Washington. Disagreements with Washington over the quality of medical service, however, led to Rush's resignation.

As a member of the Continental Congress, Rush was an original signer of the Declaration of Independence. One of his closest friends, Thomas Jefferson (1743–1826), valued Rush's medical knowledge. As president, he sent American explorer Meriwether Lewis (1774–1809) to Philadelphia where Rush educated him about frontier illnesses and bloodletting methods before Lewis began his famous expedition with William

Clark (1770–1838) to the western United States. Rush provided Lewis and Clark with a medical kit including Turkish opium for nervousness and laxatives, which the explorers nicknamed "thunderclappers."

Rush enjoyed friendships with key figures of the day including Jefferson and John Adams (1735–1826). He was instrumental in reconciling the former American presidents who had stopped speaking after bitter political quarrels in the 1790s (McCullough, 2001). Rush had a long-standing interest in dreams (Binger, 1969) and he shared a prophetic one with Adams that involved a reunion with Jefferson. With subtle manipulation, Rush edited disparaging comments in a letter from Jefferson and sent Adams the more laudatory remarks (Ellis, 1993). After further prodding by Rush, Adams and Jefferson resumed their friendship in 1812, and a remarkable correspondence followed that now stands as one of the greatest literary exchanges in the English language. In a curious side note, Jefferson and Adams died on the same day, July 4, 1826, the fiftieth anniversary of the signing of the Declaration of Independence.

During his lifetime, Rush pursued many social causes and wrote articles for the popular press in support of his reform interests. Whereas Jefferson struggled silently with the slavery issue, Rush was active in the abolition movement (Plummer, 1970) even though he owned slaves until the 1790s (Horton & Horton, 2005). He also advocated improved education for women, a national university system, flexibility in school curricula, and a stronger emphasis on practical subjects. He questioned the utility of Greek and Latin and encouraged the teaching of modern languages.

Rush (1806) protested the use of punishment as a means of controlling behavior. He called for reform of inhumane prison conditions and opposed public and capital punishment. He also disliked corporal punishment in schools because it interfered with learning and seemed contrary to the best ideals of a free people. Rush thought disruptive classroom behavior could be better handled through a private conversation with the student or a period of detention after school.

British empiricism, especially David Hartley's physiological psychology, influenced Rush. At the same time, he embraced traditional Christianity though he was not affiliated with any church (theologically, he may have been most comfortable in the community of Christian Unitarians). He emphasized universal salvation with its strong emphasis on social reforms and once remarked, "It is possible to convert men into republican machines. This must be done, if we expect them to perform their parts properly, in the great machine of the government of the state. . . . The wills of the people. . .must be fitted to each other by means of education before they can be made to produce regularity and unison in government" (Rush, 1806, pp. 14–15).

Benjamin Rush remained active in government, medicine, and social activism until his death in 1813. He was buried at Christ Church in Philadelphia. On hearing of his death, Adams wrote to Jefferson, "I know of no character living or dead who has done more real good for his country" (McCullough, 2001, p. 612). Rush's wife mourned his death for more than thirty years, and as a side note, Julia Rush's diary entries have been analyzed as a case study in the psychology of coping with loss (Thielman & Melges, 1986). Two of Benjamin and Julia Rush's thirteen children became prominent professionals: James Rush (1786–1869) was a physician–psychologist, and Richard Rush (1780–1859) was a lawyer and diplomat.

Although dedicated to political and social issues, Rush was also a visible leader in the care and treatment of mental patients. In 1812, he wrote *Medical Inquiries and Observations upon the Diseases of the Mind,* the first psychopathology textbook in America. He is recognized as the first American psychiatrist, and his image is immortalized in the official logo of the American Psychiatric Association.

In contrast with Pinel, Rush's approach to mental disorders is a curious blend of conservative Christianity and scientific materialism. On one hand, he believed in a theocentric universe and in a doctrine of original sin (see Carlson, 1977, pp. 74–104; Carlson & Simpson,

1964, pp. 290–214). On the other hand, Rush (1812/1818) claimed that all psychopathology was the product of physiological processes. As suggested in the title of his classic 1812 book, Rush viewed psychopathology as the study of "diseases of the mind." Mental disorders were thought to have their origin in the blood vessels of the brain. In his opinion, disturbances of circulation were the cause of all disease including mental disorders. As evidence for his theory, he compared the symptomatology of mental disorders with disorders such as strokes that have a known blood vessel pathology. When Rush observed abnormalities of pulse in mental patients, he took it as further proof for his circulation theory.

Rush sometimes departed from his circulation model when studying certain types of mental disease, although he seldom strayed from organic explanations. He also conducted early studies on multiple personality disorder, today called "dissociative identity disorder." The 1811 diagnosis of an American woman named Mary Reynolds (1793–1854) is often regarded as the first case study of someone with multiple personalities. In fact, Rush had described three earlier cases of dissociation in which he accounted for this "doubling" as the product of an abnormal brain (Carlson, 1981).

He also conducted the first medical studies on alcohol and described them in a treatise called "An Inquiry into the Effects of Ardent Spirits upon the Human Body and Mind" (Keller, 1943). At a time when physicians believed drunkenness was neither a disease nor a compulsive condition, Rush became the first to claim that alcoholism was both an addiction and a progressive disease (Levine, 1978).

Rush was open to a variety of treatments and even considered ones his colleagues had discredited. Years after his friend Benjamin Franklin had failed to find value in Mesmer's work, Rush researched animal magnetism in 1789 and 1812 (Schneck, 1978). Although he rejected Mesmer's theory, he believed in the validity of suggestion and imagination and incorporated them into his clinical practice.

Like many physicians of his day, Rush practiced bloodletting, a method dating to Hippocrates. An excess of blood was thought to be responsible for both mental and physical disease, and Rush used bloodletting extensively to treat patients during the Yellow Fever outbreak in 1793. After George Washington developed a throat infection, his physicians drained almost two-thirds of his blood. Washington died hours later at Mount Vernon (Morens, 1999). Ironically, Rush was on trial in Philadelphia at the time for malpractice charges relating to his use of bleeding.

Some of Rush's more notorious and unorthodox treatments were inspired by his circulation theory. He invented a device known as the *gyrator,* a machine that whirled the patient in a circle to stimulate blood flow in the brain. Not surprisingly, many patients passed out after taking a spin in the gyrator. Rush also designed a *tranquilizing chair,* a large wooden chair used to restrain maniacal patients until they regained composure. As shown in Figure 9.1, a patient's arms and legs were strapped to the chair. A headpiece attached

FIGURE 9.1

Benjamin Rush's Tranquilizing Chair

to the chair's back held the patient's head in a rigid upright position. In case the patient was restrained for long periods, an opening in the seat contained a pail that caught urine and fecal matter. Rush believed his tranquilizing chair was more humane than binding people in straitjackets.

Although Rush's methods appear inhumane, he was motivated by sincere humanitarian concern. Rush had a genuine regard for his patients' dignity and demanded they receive adequate heating, baths, and employment. His treatments were not always physical; Rush recognized the importance of a supportive social and psychological environment (Mackler & Hamilton, 1967).

Despite attention to his views on mental disease, Rush's work on psychology has been unduly neglected. His lectures on the mind reveal far-reaching psychological interests (Carlson, Wollock, & Noel, 1981). His syllabus for a course on "physiology, pathology, hygiene, and the practice of medicine" covered topics such as the history of the nature of mind, instinct, memory, imagination, perception, association, hunger, thirst, dreams, sleep, somnambulism, reason, and volition.

Although not generally recognized, Rush coined the word *phrenology* (Noel & Carlson, 1970). He believed that phrenology need not refer to spirits or to an abstract philosophy of being; instead, he saw it as an intelligible and useful science of the mind (Carlson et al., 1981). Rush argued that phrenology was useful to the physician because disorders of the mind influence diseases of the body (Noel & Carlson, 1973).

As with his circulation theory, Rush's ideas about phrenology and psychology were grounded in physiology. He observed that physiological states influence moods. For example, a person may be irritable prior to breakfast, but affable afterward. Diet was important to mental outlook. Rush claimed that vegetables rather than meat had beneficial consequences for our moods. Climate also played a role in human emotional life, with foggy and rainy seasons triggering negative emotions and sunshine producing happiness. Rush believed that light and darkness, music, cleanliness,

and pain influenced human emotions. So did idleness, which he considered the parent of all vice.

Like Philippe Pinel, Benjamin Rush's work shaped the development of psychiatry and humanitarian reform. Despite their influence, the reforms of both men did not translate into a social movement. For a time, reform was restricted to select medical circles. Before long, the call for humanitarian reform began to challenge abusive treatment of psychiatric patients.

Reform in Other Places

From the seventeenth through the nineteenth century, a number of mental hospitals became notorious for their treatment of patients. Although founded in 1247, the General Hospital of St. Mary of Bethlehem didn't become England's first royal hospital to specialize in treating the mentally ill until 1403. In 1547, King Henry VIII granted Bethlehem Hospital to London for the exclusive care of the insane provided the city fund an expansion of the facilities. Better known by its nickname "Bedlam" (now meaning a place of uproar and confusion), the hospital degenerated into a place where patients were treated like savages. In a climate of squalid and inhumane standards, patients were whipped and chained to walls. The hospital's indignities made their way into cultural awareness as evidenced in William Shakespeare's references to Bedlam in *King Lear* and other plays. Still, the public seemed unmoved by the inhumane and squalid conditions. In 1675, Bedlam moved to Moorfields, London, where it became a popular tourist attraction with visitors paying to observe and even taunt the patients. Bedlam was not alone in its mistreatment of mental patients. Later in the United States, violent or hysterical patients at the New York State Lunatic Asylum were locked inside the "Utica Crib," a wooden cagelike box that resembled a coffin but with a little more breathing room.

In 1790, a Quaker widow named Hannah Mills struggled with melancholy and was confined to the York Asylum in Leeds, England (Digby, 1983). Her Quaker friends were not allowed to visit her and the young woman died a short time after her admission. Distraught over Hannah's improper care, the Quaker merchant and philanthropist **William Tuke (1732–1822)** resolved to create an alternative to "madhouses" like Bedlam and the York Asylum.

Tuke appealed to the Society of Friends to help establish the York Retreat in 1796. Without benefit of a medical background, he designed it as a place of moral and humane treatment that resembled the methods of Pinel (at the time, Tuke was unfamiliar with the French reformer's work) but was more personal and individual (Charland, 2002). In contrast with other European asylums, the York Retreat resided on a sprawling, picturesque country estate where patients enjoyed fresh air, rest, and the tranquility of nature. Tuke opposed the use of manacles and chains, and he did away with the widespread practice of bloodletting. Gentle supportive treatment and meaningful occupations were encouraged, along with education programs for attendants.

Later, Tuke's great-grandson, **Daniel Hack Tuke (1827–1895)**, ran the York Retreat. Daniel Hack Tuke earned a medical degree from Heidelberg University in 1853. He distinguished himself as a leading authority on mental disorders and served as an editor of the *Journal of Mental Science*. He wrote numerous papers and wrote or edited several classic books including *A Dictionary of Psychological Medicine* (1892), *Illustrations of the Influence of the Mind upon the Body in Health and Disease* (1872), and *Insanity in Ancient and Modern Life, with Chapters on Prevention* (1878).

New models of humane care began to spread throughout Europe. In Italy, **Vincenzo Chiarugi (1759–c. 1820)** instituted humanitarian reform while working at Bonifazio Hospital and was one of the first to employ psychodrama as a clinical tool. Chiarugi's classification system and studies on etiology and treatment were similar to (and in many cases more advanced than) Pinel's work. Because Chiarugi's views were published prior to Pinel's, we are left to wonder why history has not given greater recognition to this Italian pioneer. One possibility is that Pinel, who was the subject of much public and scientific recognition,

was harsh in his judgment of Chiarugi's work (see Harms, 1967). As a result of Pinel's criticism, which was perhaps unjustified, Chiarugi's work lost prestige and fell into obscurity.

At about the same time, Germany played host to several reform movements as well as a few important theoretical works. Some of the most influential ideas flowed from the pen of **Johann Christian Reil (1759–1813)**, considered one of the founders of modern psychotherapy. Harms (1967) described Reil as a "psychological phenomenologist for whom the modern concepts of *Ganzheit*, totality, unity, centricity are basic elements of scientific interpretation" (p. 86).

Reil viewed mental illness in terms of a failure of the basic unity of psychological processes. The failure of unity or centricity may result from either physical or social–psychological disturbances. Reil's approach to therapeutic intervention included psychodrama, occupational therapy, music therapy, and the encouragement of socially acceptable means of expressing emotion.

Although it would not arrive until a half-century later, Reil anticipated a time when worthwhile experiments would be conducted on the senses. He felt that such research would aid in understanding mental processes and psychopathology (see Harms, 1967). He saw a practical role for scientific psychology in the study of mental disorder.

Reform Becomes a Social Movement: Dorothea Dix

Reform in the care and treatment of mental disorders was, for a time, restricted to local settings. But by the mid-nineteenth century, humanitarian reform became a social movement throughout the United States and Europe. More than any other figure, an American named **Dorothea Lynde Dix (1802–1887)** was the catalyst for making the enlightened techniques of Pinel and Tuke available on a large scale. Prior to Dix, only the upper classes could afford the best treatment. If the "insane poor" were given treatment at all, it was usually of the brutal variety offered at inhumane asylums.

Dorothea Dix

Dorothea Dix, the first of three children of Joseph Dix and Mary Bigelow Dix, was born on April 4, 1802. Her father, unsuccessful in several business ventures, underwent a climacteric religious conversion to become an itinerant Methodist preacher. He was moody, high strung, filled with evangelistic zeal, and often absent from the home. Dorothea's mother was an invalid who had little energy for normal household chores or for the care of Dorothea or her two younger brothers. Dorothea felt no love from her parents and once remarked that she never knew childhood. Gollaher (1995) suggests that Dix, like so many children in the early nineteenth century, was very likely subjected to considerable "physical and emotional mistreatment" (p. 20).

For reasons that are not entirely clear, Dorothea Dix left home at age twelve to live with her widowed paternal grandmother Dix in Boston. Dorothea left no record of her early years and refused in later years to talk about her early childhood. In her new setting, Dix was exposed to a demanding discipline that required long hours of rigorous work. Whatever the task (stitching a quilt or cleaning a room), the demand was for compulsive attention to detail, and perfection was

always the goal. If she hoped for a more loving relationship in her new setting, she was severely disappointed.

In 1816, Dix traveled to Worcester to live with an aunt. Dix proved to be a brilliant student with a voracious appetite for knowledge. Indeed, at the young age of fourteen, she was allowed to start a private school for small children. She attempted to hide her youth with adult dress and mannerisms. As a teacher, she adopted the stern techniques of her time, demanding strict obedience, punctuality, respect, extensive drills, and memory work. Discipline was enforced with a birch rod. After three successful years as a teacher in Worcester, Dorothea Dix returned to her grandmother's home. In Boston, Dix continued her studies, seizing every possible educational opportunity. She took private instruction and enrolled in public lecture courses offered by Harvard professors. She made extensive use of public libraries and enjoyed the intellectual and spiritual stimulation provided by the preaching of the well-known Unitarian preacher William Ellery Channing. Dix developed a special fondness for history, science, and literature and established considerable expertise in botany and astronomy.

By 1821, Dix had opened a "dame" school at her grandmother's home in Orange Court. This school was one of many that prepared students for public grammar schools. Students were expected to read prior to entering the public schools, hence there was great demand for private preparatory schools. In addition to her dame school responsibilities, Dix opened a free evening school for poor children who could not afford the usual private schools. She was a devoted teacher who sought to expand her knowledge so that she might be more effective in the classroom. In spare hours, she worked on a book designed to provide parents and teachers with useful, well-researched information on how to answer children's questions on common natural topics. Her book featured over three hundred questions that children ask: What causes a rainbow? What are clouds? Where do diamonds come from? Her little book was perfect for parents and teachers of the day who struggled to find answers for such questions. First published under the title *Conversations on Common Things,* Dix's book went through sixty editions.

By 1841, it appeared that Dix's career was over. A chronic pulmonary disorder had forced her to take leave of teaching activities for enforced periods of bed rest. In March, she was recovering from an extended illness but had nevertheless agreed to substitute for a Unitarian ministry student who was unable to teach his Sunday School class at the East Cambridge jailhouse.

What Dorothea Dix observed at the jail on that cold New England morning in 1841 changed her life.

In that day, hardened criminals were crammed into the same cell with alcoholics and people with mental illnesses, as well as people who had been diagnosed "feebleminded" (a then-popular classification used to describe individuals with cognitive deficits). The stench of human waste arose from overcrowded cells filled with filth. Shivering from the cold, prisoners huddled together to stay warm in the unheated cells. The stench and misery shocked Dix. She pleaded with the jailer to heat the cells. He refused, declaring that these inmates were incapable of feeling heat or cold and the criminals deserved to freeze. The inhumane conditions compelled Dix to seek court action. Her appeal was victorious. Conditions at the East Cambridge jailhouse improved. The facility was cleaned and the cells were heated for the prisoners.

Invigorated by her accomplishment, Dix investigated the conditions of mental patients and prisoners throughout Massachusetts. The former schoolteacher consulted with authorities and studied the available literature to learn the most advanced views on mental illness. The work of the Tukes in England and Pinel in France impressed Dix. Their enlightened techniques contrasted with the prevailing custodialism in most almshouses and jails.

During extensive travels throughout Massachusetts, Dix discovered that many facilities matched the appalling conditions she had encountered in the East Cambridge jailhouse.

Quarters in almshouses and jails were unfurnished, sanitation was neglected, heat was seldom provided, and diets were inadequate. Many mentally ill and "feebleminded" people roamed the countryside. In some respects, they may have been more fortunate than mental patients confined in asylums.

Conducting some of the earliest social research in America, Dix armed herself with data from her extensive investigations and prepared a "memorial" for the lawmakers of Massachusetts. With the help of powerful political figures such as Horace Mann, Senator Charles Sumner, and Dr. Samuel Gridley Howe, she convinced legislators that additional facilities and personnel were needed to provide for the care and treatment of the mentally ill. As a result of Dix's research and her memorial, funds were set aside for an expansion of the state hospital at Worcester. Instead of the one hospital at Worcester, Dix would have preferred an additional smaller hospital in a different location. Nevertheless, her memorial was successful and her career as a reformer was launched.

After the victory in Massachusetts, Dix continued her investigations in other states. Her reform activities followed a familiar pattern: extensive research into existing conditions, contact with key political figures, preparation of a memorial describing existing conditions, and requests for new or additional facilities. Dix didn't make public speeches; instead, she asked respected political figures to read her memorials to legislative bodies. Her forty years of reform work produced extensive accomplishments. She played a key role in the founding of thirty-two mental hospitals, several schools for those with cognitive deficits, training facilities for nurses, and improvements in prisons and mental institutions.

In part, her achievements were due to a prevailing mood that proved receptive to humanitarian reform. Dix was also well organized, energetic, and persuasive. Her extensive knowledge of psychopathology contributed to her success. Indeed, Dain (1964) contended that her knowledge compared favorably with leading authorities of her day. Her memorials (see Viney, 1996b; Viney & Bartsch, 1984) reveal an understanding of mental illness and acquaintance with the legal aspects of the subject. Her views on etiology recognized physiological, psychological, and social contributions. She believed the brain was the organ of the mind but mental illness was also *the offspring of civilization.* She was particularly impressed with the role of unemployment, loss of family or possessions, and abnormal religious excitement in the etiology of mental disorders. She believed that treatment should include good diet, exercise, amusement (including music, games, and reading), and meaningful occupation. Dix opposed custodialism, except for hopelessly incurable cases. Her memorials focused on treatment and curability. Accordingly, she raised money, not only for buildings but also for libraries, musical instruments, museums, and in one case, a bowling alley. She had a keen interest in anything that would facilitate therapeutic intervention.

Stevens and Gardner (1982) claimed that Dorothea Dix represented the conscience of early psychology. They argued that without Dix and other humanitarian reformers, psychology might have been restricted to laboratory investigations or might have stagnated altogether. Popular and practical concern created a friendly atmosphere for the development of a new discipline. Her ability to mobilize public opinion about psychological issues makes Dix's contributions greater than has been recognized.

During the American Civil War, Dix's reform activities were interrupted while she served as Superintendent of Union Army Nurses. Following the war, she returned to work as a reformer, but didn't enjoy the influence of her earlier years. This was partly due to the devastating economic effects of the Civil War. Funds for social projects such as the building of hospitals were no longer available. Interest in the needs of the mentally ill faded after her death in 1887. During the next decades, conditions in mental hospitals deteriorated. Unfortunately, many hospitals became almost as custodial as the jails and almshouses they had replaced.

Reform in the Care and Treatment of People with Cognitive Disabilities

Prior to the modern era, physical and mental disabilities were regarded as the work of demons or as evidence of the sins of the parents. For example, engaging in intercourse during menstruation was viewed as a sin that produced defective children. Ranke-Heinemann (1990) documented the teachings of numerous thirteenth-century theologians who attributed birth defects to the poisonous effects of menstrual blood on the male seed. Children born with disabilities were sometimes regarded as *changelings,* a term referring to a substituted infant. Some believed that an evil force replaced a legitimate and normal child with a defective one. Tragically, children branded as changelings were often neglected, abused, abandoned, or sacrificed.

More naturalistic approaches to people with mental deficiencies occurred alongside reforms in the care and treatment of people with mental illnesses. A pioneer in the study and training of mental deficiency was **Jean-Marc Gaspard Itard (1775–1838)**, a French physician and teacher of the deaf, who anchored his medical views on the primacy of the senses (Newman, 2006). An accidental discovery stimulated Itard's work on people with mental deficiencies. In 1799, three hunters found a naked boy covered in scars. He tried to escape but was captured. The boy, about ten years of age, had apparently been abandoned by his parents, but had somehow managed to survive in the wild near Aveyron in southern France. When he was first captured, he displayed characteristics of a wild animal and appeared unmanageable.

The "wild boy of Aveyron" aroused interest among scientists and the public. After considering his case, Philippe Pinel diagnosed the boy as an "incurable idiot" (Gaynor, 1973, p. 439). Itard disagreed.

He worked with the boy for approximately two years. Itard was not able to teach the boy to speak, but progress and desirable changes were made. The boy became affectionate and responsive. He learned to understand many words and could engage in useful tasks. Later commentators concluded that the boy was retarded and was unable to acquire language skills. Still, Itard's work was suggestive of what might be accomplished on a larger scale with other children with mental retardation.

Another Frenchman, **Édouard Séguin (1812–1880)**, developed a systematic approach for sensory training and self-care skills for individuals with cognitive disabilities (Toth & King, 2010). Séguin sought ways to assist individuals in developing their innate sensory and motor capacities so they could engage in useful skills. He worked first in France and later in the United States where his work attracted public attention. Soon, fund-raising efforts made by reformers such as Dorothea Dix resulted in training facilities for people with mental deficiency. Scholars realized the need for the systematic study of learning processes and the development of training techniques. Thus, another reform movement created a need for the systematic study of topics such as learning, sensory and motor processes, and motivation that were later to become standard content areas of psychology.

Women's Reform Movements

In Chapter 6, we discussed Mary Wollstonecraft's classic work *A Vindication of the Rights of Woman* and John Stuart Mill's work *The Subjection of Women.* These visionary writers were reacting to the long history of the subordination of women. Women, compared with men, were commonly regarded as less intelligent, less creative, more emotional, and relatively disinterested in commercial, political, economic, and philosophical questions. Gender stereotypes were used to justify restrictions on property rights, educational opportunities, voting privileges, and work opportunities for women. It was further argued that women were incapacitated once each month because of the menstrual cycle.

By the mid- to late nineteenth century, there was growing agitation for women's rights and a corresponding public interest in the abilities of women. Public interest was stimulated by

an outpouring of popular magazine articles on topics such as the education of women, the intelligence of women, gender differences in emotional expression, and voting rights for women. Many articles were written in defense of old stereotypes, but several challenged older ways of thinking. Such challenges, along with the demands of reformers in the women's movement, stimulated a climate conducive to impartial studies of gender differences. In fact, many of the sex stereotypes lent themselves to experimental investigation and some of the early psychological research delivered a deathblow to many of the old attitudes about women. For example, Leta Stetter Hollingworth (see Chapter 12) conducted research demonstrating that the menstrual cycle did not mentally or physically incapacitate women.

The women's reform movements grew out of a long and painful history with entrenched traditions regarded by many as sacred. Following the American Civil War, religious magazines presented an ongoing debate about whether women should be allowed to speak in church services (see Knowlton, 1867; Torrey, 1867). Disputes grew out of the interpretive difficulties of scriptures such as I Corinthians 14:34–35, which was used as a source of authority for those who forbid women to speak in church. If women could not speak in church, there was little possibility for them to assume positions of spiritual leadership. The undercutting of leadership roles for women in the religious arena was common in Western as well as Middle Eastern and Islamic traditions (Lippman, 1995, p. 96). It may be argued that the subordination of women in some religious traditions did not reflect true interpretations of those traditions, but as a practical fact, such subordination took place and continues to take place in some traditions. In many religious and cultural traditions, women were and are required to lower their eyes, cover their heads, veil their faces, avoid adorning themselves with jewelry, and cultivate habits of humility, obedience, submission, domesticity, and chastity. Only men could fill leadership roles in religious venues.

The late nineteenth century witnessed an unprecedented battle for a new orientation toward women and a new and informed appraisal of their intellectual abilities and personal and spiritual gifts. Such an appraisal, of course, would become grist for the work of psychologists. The battle itself was waged on many fronts (e.g., access to university education, new employment opportunities, property rights), but the most visible facet of the battle was in the arena of suffrage or the right of women to vote. American reformers such as Susan B. Anthony (1820–1906) and Elizabeth Cady Stanton (1815–1902) spearheaded the battle. The intensity of the battle is graphically illustrated in the film *Iron Jawed Angels* featuring the story of Alice Paul and other young activists who were jailed and force-fed when they went on a hunger strike (see Pilcher, 2004). Their story shocked the consciousness of lawmakers and the nation and played a significant role in the change of attitudes ultimately resulting in the passage of the Nineteenth Amendment. Even so, progress was slow as legislation was introduced in Congress each year for more than forty years before the Nineteenth Amendment to the U.S. Constitution was finally passed in 1920. Opponents of the legislation made radical claims that illustrate the depth of feelings and the fervor of the battle. In *The Ladies Home Journal*, then former president Grover Cleveland (1837–1908) argued that good conservative women (i.e., those described by Cleveland as "sensible women," p. 7) had no desire to vote and that they understood their divinely appointed subordinate roles (Cleveland, 1905).

MARGARET SANGER AND FAMILY LIMITATION   Another facet of the women's movement was as intense and controversial as suffrage and, in some quarters, remains controversial to the present day. The dynamics of family life and the effects of family structures on individual personality development would later become important areas for social and developmental psychologists, but early sensitivities to these topical areas are found in the work of reformers in the women's movement.

Margaret Sanger (1883–1966), as the sixth of eleven children, was convinced that the birthing

(all eleven children weighed more than ten pounds at birth) and rearing demands of a large family contributed to her mother's premature death at age forty-nine. Sanger observed critical differences between large and small families in her New York neighborhood, especially related to economic concerns. Large families were generally poor; smaller families were not. In her early years, she developed a concern with issues pertaining to the quality of life for children and women. Her mother remained a devout Catholic to her death while her father was best described as an intellectual, an impractical artist, a fiercely independent thinker, and an atheist. Sanger identified with the plight of her mother and with her father's intellectual independence. Her home life prepared her for a career as a reformer with its demands to fight for a cause while standing firm against critical attacks.

Educated as a nurse, Sanger was moved by the plight of poor women. Her work brought a renewed awareness of the poverty associated with large families. She also faced continuing inquiries from poor women about how to control conception. Women sometimes begged for the secrets of birth control, but Sanger had no satisfactory answers. Doctors often advised women simply to avoid sex, but the effectiveness of such advice assumed the cooperation of husbands. A turning point came when Sanger was called to the apartment of Sadie Sachs who fell ill after a self-induced abortion. Following her recovery, Sachs pleaded with her physician about information for avoiding another pregnancy. The doctor gave the usual unsatisfactory answer. Later, Sanger was called back to the apartment. This time, Sachs slipped into a coma and died from yet another self-induced abortion. As in earlier periods, such tragic events were common in the late nineteenth and into the mid-twentieth centuries. Sachs's death was pivotal and Sanger devoted herself to women's health issues. She focused on disseminating information on women's health and on safe and effective reproductive control.

Sanger believed that women's health and their social equality depended, in part, on birth control. In her campaign to improve public knowledge, she published pamphlets that

1950	*The Authoritarian Personality* by Theodor Adorno
	The Individual and His Religion by Gordon Allport
1952	First edition of the *Diagnostic and Statistical Manual of Mental Disorders (DSM)*
1954	Social scientists contribute to the case of *Brown v. Board of Education*
1958	*Psychotherapy by Reciprocal Inhibition* by Joseph Wolpe
1967	*Cognitive Psychology* by Ulric Neisser
1973	The last combat soldiers from the United States officially leave Vietnam
1979	*Eyewitness Testimony* by Elizabeth Loftus
1988	Founding of the American Psychological Society (APS)
1994	American Psychiatric Association publishes *DSM-IV*
2000	Scientists map human genome
2006	Final publications of *Psychological Abstracts;* the abstracts are replaced by an electronic guide to the world's literature in psychology known as PsycINFO
2013	American Psychiatric Association publishes *DSM-5*

10

■ ■ ■

Psychophysics and the Formal Founding of Psychology

I have proceeded on the conviction that law and order even if they are not fundamentally sound are better than contradictions and lawlessness.

—HERMANN VON HELMHOLTZ (1896)

As we have seen in previous chapters, many important intellectual forces contributed to a climate friendly to the birth and nourishment of psychology. The most direct influences, however, came from developments in physiology, pointing to the possibility that mental processes could be measured (Evans, 2000). This chapter examines selected scientific projects in physiology that led to the founding of the new discipline of psychology. The chapter then examines the formal founding of psychology and the first systematic approach to the discipline.

PSYCHOPHYSICS

The term **psychophysics** refers to the study of the relationships between physical properties of stimuli and the psychological or subjective impressions of those stimuli. Psychophysics began as informal speculation and wonder about the nature of the relationship between objects in the world and our perceptions of those objects. In Chapter 2, we reviewed theoretical positions regarding what we can claim to know about objects in the world. One extreme position is encountered in the solipsistic claim that we can know only our own private experience. Another extreme position, naïve realism, contends that we see external things as they are. In a limited and modest way, early studies in psychophysics challenged both extreme positions.

Psychophysics involves the study of the properties of stimuli as measured by a physical scale and psychological impressions of those stimuli. For example, we can measure a series of tones in terms of vibrations or frequencies. The term *hertz (Hz)* is used as the international unit equal to one cycle per second. With proper equipment, a graded series can be presented with known physical characteristics. One of the most obvious discoveries about any graded series is that there are values on the lower and upper extremes that do not register in experience. For tones, the average young person hears values from approximately 20 Hz to 20,000 Hz. In other words, there are lower and upper thresholds. The measurement of thresholds provides a small quantitative opening into the world of private experience. Part of the early work in psychophysics was directed at investigating *lower* and *upper thresholds* for varieties of stimuli in all sensory modalities. Such **thresholds** were defined operationally as that minimal or maximal stimulus intensity that is detected 50 percent of the time.

Another type of threshold that was investigated was called the **difference threshold**—the minimal stimulus difference that is detectable 50 percent of the time. For example, an experimenter may stimulate the surface of the skin of a research participant with two points of an adjustable compass known as an **aesthesiometer**. The participant, under certain conditions, may report the presence of a single sensation, even though both points of the aesthesiometer contact the skin. The task of the experimenter is to assess the two-point threshold (that distance where two points are experienced as two points instead of one point). It has been found that there are relatively insensitive areas (e.g., the back and thigh) where the two-point threshold may be well over 40 millimeters (mm) (over 1.5 inches). At the other extreme, the two-point threshold may be as small as 1 mm in a sensitive area (e.g., the tip of the tongue or the tips of the fingers).

Psychophysics contributed methods that permitted a quantitative assessment of certain mental processes. By assessing absolute thresholds, the limits of possible experiences within a single dimension could be established for each of the senses. Early psychophysics challenged naïve realism because it demonstrated measurable stimulus values below or above the threshold of awareness, and psychophysics as a field figures prominently in early psychology, even in the earliest plans for the first international congress (Nicolas & Söderlund, 2005). As illustrated with the aesthesiometer, there are stimulus differences that cannot be experienced by the unaided senses. In fact, some stimulus differences must be surprisingly large to be experienced. Studies in psychophysics also uncovered lawful relationships between stimulus differences according to a physical scale and experienced differences. Such lawful relationships showed promise for a science of the mind. The discovery of lawful relationships between physical values of stimuli and experience also challenged extreme solipsistic views. Such discoveries suggested that our experiences are tied to the physical world in lawful ways and that comparisons between individuals are meaningful.

The work of German physiologist **Ernst Heinrich Weber (1795–1878)** and physicist–philosopher Gustav T. Fechner (1801–1887) ushered in the formal beginnings of psychophysics.

Ernst Heinrich Weber

Ernst Heinrich Weber was born on June 24, 1795, the third of thirteen children. At age sixteen, Ernst enrolled at the University of Wittenberg. He later transferred to the University of Leipzig where he completed a thesis on the anatomy of the sympathetic nerves. Impressed with Weber's work, university officials offered him a faculty position. He accepted and stayed at Leipzig for the remainder of his career.

Weber worked in the fields of anatomy, physiology, physics, and biology. He collaborated with his brother, Eduard, on one of his most important contributions. They discovered the inhibition of heart action following stimulation of the peripheral end of the vagus nerve. Kruta (1976) noted that this discovery, together with subsequent research, "showed that inhibition is a common phenomenon in the central nervous system and that an adequate balance between excitation and inhibition is indispensable for its normal function" (p. 200). In 1826, Weber turned his attention to the skin and muscle senses. His pioneering work led to a book called *The Sense of Touch*, a classic in experimental psychology. Weber retained his chair in anatomy at Leipzig until 1871, just eight years before the university recognized Wilhelm Wundt's laboratory in psychology. Weber died on January 26, 1878.

Weber's Work on the Sense of Touch

Weber (1834/1978) employed the two-point threshold technique to systematically map the cutaneous sensitivity of the human body. As noted earlier, sensitivity varies depending on where we stimulate the body. Weber observed that we are less sensitive if the two points of the compass are applied longitudinally along the length of a limb than if they are laid transversely or in a crosswise direction to the axis of the limb. He noted that our sensitivity is greater when the two points of the compass contact contiguous body parts, such as the inside or red part of the lip and the outside skin adjacent to the inside lip. Weber showed that the two compass points appear to spread apart when moved over the surface of insensitive areas. By contrast, a convergence of the two points is experienced if the two points are moved over sensitive areas. The experience of the divergence of two points when moved over insensitive areas and the convergence of two points when moved over sensitive areas is known as **Weber's illusion**, which continues to be the focus of research (Longo & Haggard, 2011).

Weber also found less sensitivity when two points of the compass are presented simultaneously and greater when they are presented successively (one preceding the other). Similarly, perceived differences in the weights of objects are greater when such weights are presented successively. The same holds for perceived temperature differences.

Weber's work on two-point thresholds demonstrated that the world as experienced does

not directly correspond to the physical characteristics of the stimuli presented by the experimenter. In further explorations of the relationship between the physical and psychological worlds, Weber investigated just noticeable differences of weights of small containers filled with lead.

Imagine that a researcher asks you to lift a small jar weighing 50 grams. You pick it up and get a sense of about how much it weighs. Now how much weight could the researcher add to the jar before you could tell the difference between the original (standard) weight and the new (comparison) weight? The smallest detectable difference between the standard and the comparison is called the **just noticeable difference (jnd)**.

After conducting many experiments with many stimulus values, Weber observed a law-like relationship between standard and comparison stimuli. The amount that must be added in order to produce a jnd was a function of the amount of existing stimulation. For example, you might reliably detect a difference between a standard jar weighing 50 grams and a comparison jar weighing 1 gram more. But what would happen if you lift a jar weighing 100 grams? How much would the comparison jar have to weigh before you could detect a difference? The comparison jar would need to weigh about 102 grams. Again, the jnd is a function of the amount of existing stimulation. Based on this research, Weber created the first formula to bridge the physical and psychological worlds:

$$\frac{\Delta R}{R} = K$$

where R = the amount of existing stimulation
ΔR = the amount of stimulation that must be added to produce a jnd
K = a constant

Presumably, one could establish a fraction and then predict the jnd for any new stimulus value. As an example, for lifted weights, the fraction is about 1/50 (.02). Thus, for a 300-gram standard weight, the comparison should be about 306 grams.

Weber opened a door into an unexplored world. We cannot directly measure a psychological event, but we can quantify perceived differences in relation to scaled physical stimulus values. Psychological events, or jnds, can be studied in conjunction with measurable physical stimulus values. Although Immanuel Kant believed psychological processes could not be quantified, Weber demonstrated otherwise.

Weber's work inspired hundreds of early research projects investigating jnds for each of the sensory modalities. His work also triggered new and more rigorous methodologies for the study of thresholds. More than any other researcher, Gustav Fechner fulfilled Weber's vision of psychophysics.

Gustav Theodor Fechner

The relationship between mind and body captivated **Gustav Theodor Fechner (1801–1887)**. He devoted much of his career to studying relationships between the mental and the physical realms. Mind and body suggest a duality in nature, but Fechner was "a thoroughgoing monist, regarding body and soul as but a double manifestation of one and the same real thing" (Ward, 1876, p. 452). His psychophysics research represents a vital building block for the new discipline of experimental psychology.

Fechner's father was Samuel Fechner, a Lutheran pastor, and his mother was Johanna Dorothea Fischer Fechner. After completing his gymnasium studies, Fechner enrolled at the University of Leipzig. He completed an M.D. degree in 1822, but physics claimed his early scientific interests. He had established a reputation in physics by 1831. Three years later, he was appointed professor of physics at Leipzig.

The year 1839 posed an unfortunate turning point in Fechner's life. Haunted by a profound emotional disturbance, Fechner resigned from his university position. It seems that partial blindness may have initiated his mental collapse. Fechner had sustained visual problems while using improper lenses to gaze at the sun during his study of afterimages. Beginning in 1839, Fechner was

plagued by a persistent illness that forced him to resign his chair of physics the following year. Adler (1996) notes:

> It started with photophobia. Light hurt Fechner's eyes so much that he spent most of his days in a darkened room, venturing out only when he was wearing self-constructed metal cups over his eyes. He communicated with the family through a funnel-shaped opening in the door. His digestive system presented another problem. Fechner could not eat or drink and he was in danger of dying of starvation. Doctors tried animal magnetism, homeopathy, and moxibustion (the burning of herbs on the skin) without avail. About the only food he was able to keep down was a mixture of chopped raw ham with spices, soaked in Rhine wine and lemon juice. The recipe for this concoction had appeared to a lady acquaintance in a dream. Fechner's worst problem was his mind. He suffered from a flight of ideas; he was unable to concentrate, to speak coherently, or to tame his wild thoughts. (p. 5)

Throughout the process, Fechner kept detailed notes on his disorder. In October 1843, he began speaking again. Fechner gradually overcame his mystery illness, but did not resume his academic responsibilities, save for occasional public lectures.

Five years later, Fechner resumed work at the University of Leipzig, but now as a philosophy professor. In his new position, he explored both philosophical and scientific interests. On the philosophical side, Fechner profiled two opposite views of the universe. He viewed the basic stuff of the universe, including mental phenomena, as inert matter. He referred to this extreme materialistic position as the *night view*. A contrasting view would suggest that all things have a psychic component. Fechner argued that plants have a psychic life and that any organic whole has psychic qualities. He referred to his panpsychism as the *day view*. He created a pseudonym, *Dr. Mises,* to express his mystical beliefs in the day view.

In "Proof That the Moon Is Made of Iodine," his first paper as Mises, he satirized a popular medical notion that iodine was a panacea. For more than fifty years, the writings of Dr. Mises provided a whimsical outlet for Fechner's humanistic and aesthetic interests in art, music, dance, and poetry as well as more satirical topics (e.g., the comparative anatomy of humans and angels). Indeed, in 1851, Fechner first outlined his psychophysics program in a book on human immortality, the *Zend-Avesta,* or *Concerning Matters of Heaven and the Hereafter* (see Boring, 1963). He hoped his work in psychophysics would provide evidence for the day view.

In 1860, Fechner published his *Elements of Psychophysics,* a book widely recognized as the first major publication to demonstrate that experimental methods could fruitfully be applied to psychological phenomena (Robinson, 2010) and destined to become a classic in psychology. In 1876, he published *Vorschule der Aesthetic,* a seminal work in the experimental approach to aesthetic judgments. He continued work in psychophysics and experimental aesthetics until his death in November 1887. Angell (1913) called attention to Wundt's memorable words in his funeral oration for Fechner: "We shall not look upon his like again" (p. 49).

October 22, 1850, was a critical day in the life of Gustav Fechner. He commemorated it as the date when he realized there must be a discernible quantitative relationship between sensations and stimuli (Meischner-Metge, 2010). Unaware of Weber's research, Fechner believed there was not a one-to-one relationship between perceived increases in stimulus intensity and physical increases in stimulus values. Indeed, he concluded that perceived increases were related to the amount of existing physical stimulation. His conclusion is consistent with Weber's discovery.

Following this insight, Fechner discovered Weber's work and launched a vigorous experimental program. Fechner reported that "for several years I considered it a daily task to experiment about an hour for the purpose of testing Weber's Law and for elaborating new methods of research" (cited in Angell, 1913, p. 47).

Weber's formula provided the intellectual spadework for Fechner to develop a more ambitious formula for the measurement of sensation. By integrating Weber's formula, Fechner generated the new formula:

$$S = k \log R$$

where S is the mental sensation and R is the *Reiz* or stimulus magnitude. The formula specified that the strength of a mental sensation is a constant logarithmic function of the stimulus. It further specified that as a mental series increases arithmetically, the stimulus series must increase geometrically. Fechner's formula also predicted the observation that is familiar to anyone who has turned on a three-way light bulb, advancing it from 100 to 300 watts. Equal increments in a physical scale are experienced in terms of a diminishing series called **response compression**. The difference between 100 and 200 watts appears greater than the difference between 200 and 300 watts. Fechner, deferring to Weber's pioneering work, called his formula **Weber's law**. Today, we think of it as **Fechner's law** and the earlier simpler formula that inspired it as *Weber's law.*

In subsequent years, research on Weber's and Fechner's laws occupied a central place in early psychology laboratories. Investigations on these laws contributed to the construction of sensory scales, such as the decibel scale for dealing with the intensity of auditory stimuli. This research program also produced a greater understanding of the capacities of the sensory systems. Research confirmed that Weber's and Fechner's laws were accurate primarily for the middle ranges of sensory information. Predictions are less accurate for the lower and upper extremes of physical intensity.

Additionally, much of Fechner's classic 1860 work was devoted to inner psychophysics, and definitions of this term remain difficult (Billock & Tsou, 2011). Although Fechner argued that "Inner psychophysics [which] would go beyond the physics and physiology of stimuli, to the mind's interpretation of sensation" (Robinson, 2010, p. 425), was a more important field of study than external psychophysics, it did not become a research area for other scholars. For Fechner, inner psychophysics also included unconscious (or literally subliminal, i.e., below threshold) phenomena, but his robust body of scholarship on these topics remains largely unknown (Romand, 2012).

FECHNER'S METHODS Fechner's investigation of thresholds produced important methodological contributions, becoming an integral part of experimental psychology. In part, his methods were important because they were applicable to a variety of problems.

The Method of Limits Fechner referred to this method as the method of *just noticeable differences (jnd)*. A researcher named Delezenne had used it in tests of tonal intervals and Weber had as well in research on weights, touch, and vision (see Fechner, 1860/1966, p. 62). The **method of limits** consists of presenting a standard stimulus along with variable or comparison stimuli of greater and lesser value than the standard. The comparison stimuli are presented in ascending and descending series. For example, a standard weight of, say, 100 grams may be presented along with a comparison weight of 105 grams. As you can guess, it's easy to detect a difference between these two weights. In a descending series, subsequent comparison weights of 104, 103, 102, and 101 grams may be presented with the standard weight. Then, an ascending series may include comparisons of 100, 101, 102, 103, and 104 grams. In each series, the experimenter can assess the point at which a difference is no longer detected or the point at which the difference is first noticed. The average for several ascending and descending series defines the jnd.

This method also applies to absolute thresholds. In this case, single stimulus values are presented in ascending and descending series. For example, tones of 17, 18, 19, 20, and 21 Hz may be presented in an ascending series and the task is to report when the tone is first detected. In a descending series, starting above threshold (e.g., 25, 24, 23, and 22 Hz), the participant must specify the frequency at which the tone is no longer heard.

Fechner believed that the method of limits is the method of choice for preliminary studies but that other methods are superior for more rigorous studies (see Fechner, 1860/1966).

The Method of Constant Stimuli Fechner referred to this method as the *method of right and wrong cases*. In this method, comparison stimuli are coupled with the standard stimulus in a random fashion. The participant's task is to report whether the comparison stimulus is equal to, greater than, or weaker than the standard, or alternatively, detected or not detected. For absolute thresholds, single stimulus values above and below threshold are presented randomly. The participant simply reports whether the stimulus is detected. The **method of constant stimuli** avoids certain errors commonly associated with the method of limits. For example, errors of habituation (i.e., falling into the habit of saying that one stimulus is of greater or lesser value than the other) are easily established in a graded series. Such errors are eliminated when comparison values are randomized.

The Method of Average Error Sometimes called the *method of adjustment,* the **method of average error** permits the participant to manipulate a comparison stimulus until it appears to match a standard. Following the adjustment, the difference between the standard and the comparison stimuli can be measured. For example, a standard might consist of a light of a given brightness. The comparison could be a light source activated by a variable switch that permits the participant to adjust brightness. The brightness of the comparison stimulus can be adjusted until it appears to match the brightness of the standard. Normally, several ascending and descending series are employed and a mean is determined. Thus, in one series, the comparison starts at a higher or brighter value and is adjusted downward, and in a subsequent series, the comparison starts at a lower or dimmer value and is adjusted upward.

Although Fechner's methods generated criticism (Adler, 1998; Michell, 1999), his work had wide application and became standard in training experimental psychologists. Fechner raised issues more than a century ago that still resonate in modern psychophysics research and signal detection theory (Adler, 1998; Link, 1994; Murray, 1993). Contemporary psychologists use variations of Fechner's methods when investigating problems as divergent as perception of air quality to the discrimination capacity of a particular species. Although Fechner's dream of solving the mind–brain problem proved too ambitious, he did create the foundation for an experimental psychology. On occasion, in the history of science, a major research goal goes unrealized even as other fortunate benefits emerge through productive accident.

Rudolph Hermann Lotze

Rudolph Hermann Lotze (1817–1881) was born in Bautzen, Germany, on May 21, 1817. After completing school in Zittan, he enrolled at the University of Leipzig. Lotze studied anatomy and physiology under Weber and physics under Fechner. Both men had a profound influence on Lotze. After completing Ph.D. and M.D. degrees, he attempted medical practice. Within a year, he was back at Leipzig where he worked as a faculty member from 1839 to 1844. In 1844, he joined the faculty at Göttingen where he remained until 1881. Lotze then accepted the chair of philosophy at the University of Berlin, but died within weeks following his move.

Despite Lotze's broad interest in psychology, he did not produce a systematic approach to the field. An examination of his *Outlines of Psychology*, first published in 1881, reveals interests in memory, unconscious processes, psychopathology and treatment, and sensory processes. His theory of space perception influenced his successors.

E. G. Boring (1950) identified three reasons for Lotze's prominent place in the history of psychology. In 1852, he wrote *Medizinische Psychologie oder Physiologie der Seele,* considered to be the first book on physiological psychology. The second reason comes in Lotze's theory of space perception, a theory we'll discuss

later. The third reason for Lotze's prominence can be found in his influence on other researchers. He was enthusiastic about the new discipline of psychology and regularly taught courses on it at Göttingen.

Lotze accepted the Kantian notion that the mind can discern spatial relations in an a priori fashion. At the same time, he argued that the perception of spatial relations develops as a function of experience. Specifically, a nonspatial stimulus such as a particular light intensity may create a "local sign" or stimulated point in the eye. In the **theory of local signs**, an external object may consist of several colors, contours, surfaces, and projections, each resulting in a corresponding brightness intensity or local sign on the surface of the retina. The relationships between brightness intensity points from the object and corresponding points on the two-dimensional surface of the retina do not in themselves provide unambiguous cues to depth perception because slight movements of the eye or head result in a whole new distribution of points on the retina. But in time, relational discriminations are established such that the local sign in the retina for a given point on the object is discerned from the local sign for a different point on the object. Relational discriminations based on local signs become cues for the perception of depth.

Lotze also emphasized the role of the muscle sense in depth perception. Local signs for an outstretched arm are distinct from those for an unextended arm. Lotze (1881/1973) noted that people who are born blind construct an image of space by means of touch, but he doubted "whether the concept of space which the sense of touch affords a person born blind, is at all similar to that of one who sees" (p. 50). Later scholars challenged the assumption of such radical discontinuity between information from two sensory realms (see summary in Viney, 1991).

Gotesky (1967) pointed out that "Lotze's influence in Germany, France and England was considerable during his lifetime. Philosophers became more empirical-minded, less dogmatic" (p. 89). Though Lotze left no formal system of psychology, he influenced key figures in the new discipline such as Hermann von Helmholtz, Wilhelm Wundt, Franz Brentano, Carl Stumpf, Georg Elias Müller, and George Trumbull Ladd.

Hermann von Helmholtz

Psychology owes an immense intellectual debt to **Hermann Ludwig Ferdinand von Helmholtz (1821–1894)**, one of the most celebrated scientists and inventors of the nineteenth century. His original contributions in physics, physiology, and psychology mark him as one of the last scholars who could produce cutting-edge research in multiple scientific fields.

Born on August 31, 1821, Helmholtz was the first of four children of August Ferdinand Julius Helmholtz and Caroline Penne. Boring (1950) reported that Helmholtz was an undistinguished student, but his academic mediocrity may have contributed to his intellectual independence. At age seventeen, Helmholtz enrolled in a medical institute in Berlin. He obtained a government stipend that covered the costs of his medical education in exchange for eight years of military service following graduation. Helmholtz completed his dissertation under Johannes Müller and established close friendships with Müller's other students including Ernst Brücke, Emil DuBois-Reymond, and Karl Ludwig. In league with these men, Helmholtz was dedicated to a natural physicochemical approach to the study of life processes.

Helmholtz completed his M.D. in 1842 and served until 1848 as an army surgeon. He was released early from military duty to accept a faculty position in physiology at Königsberg. In 1855, he accepted a position in anatomy and physiology at the University of Bonn. One year after arriving at Bonn, he published Volume I of his classic *Handbook of Physiological Optics*. Kahl (1967) pointed out that this seminal work is "frequently called the *principia* in its field" (p. 469). The handbook established Helmholtz as one of Europe's most promising young scientists. By 1858, he accepted an appointment to the chair of physiology at the University of Heidelberg. He remained in that position for thirteen productive

years before accepting a position in 1871 as professor of physics at the University of Berlin. Turner (1972) stated, "By 1885 Helmholtz had become the patriarch of German science and the state's foremost advisor on scientific affairs" (p. 243). Helmholtz died on July 12, 1894.

As an interesting aside, Adler (2000) notes that a year before his death Helmholtz and his wife visited the United States and attended the World Columbian Exposition in Chicago. He met the American inventor Thomas Edison (1847–1931) and visited a number of cities including Boston, St. Louis, Denver, and Colorado Springs. He was deeply impressed with the promise of American civilization, but like so many European visitors, saddened by the gun violence and lawlessness described in daily newspaper accounts of robberies and murder.

HELMHOLTZ'S CONTRIBUTIONS Helmholtz rejected the idea that vital forces or mysterious energies influence physiological or psychological processes. He believed that all movements within the organism are, in principle, understandable in terms of physical laws (Turner, 1977). He demonstrated that a simple muscle contraction generates a slight increase in temperature. The total energy expended in a given unit of time is related to the way the organism metabolizes food. Helmholtz believed that the conservation of energy applies to living organisms just as it applies to physical phenomena. Furthermore, there are no mysterious forces or unknowable energies that activate the organism. The psychology that Helmholtz envisioned was grounded in physiology. Physiology, in turn, was grounded in physics and chemistry. Helmholtz's vision of the unity of the sciences was such that, according to Wertheimer (1991), "he hardly knew when he was doing psychology, physiology, or physics."

Visual Perception Although accomplished in many provinces of science, Helmholtz's most enduring contribution may have been in the study of sense perception (Wade, 1994). His masterpiece, *Handbook of Physiological Optics,* showcases the breadth of his interests in psychological, physiological, and physical problems. The physics and physiology of vision are covered in chapters on topics such as the physical characteristics of light, the crystalline lens, the cornea, refraction in the eye, mechanisms of accommodation, and the retina. His discussion on the retina includes detailed descriptions of rods and cones along with an analysis of their distributions. On psychological matters, the handbook contains chapters covering topics such as illusions (Gregory, 2007; Wade, 2005), the perception of depth, and color vision.

The handbook also covers methodological topics in optics. Helmholtz made a great methodological breakthrough when he invented the **ophthalmoscope**, an instrument for viewing the retina (Pearce, 2009). His genius is illustrated in the handbook as he discussed the theory of the ophthalmoscope (see Southall, 1962). Helmholtz noticed that light reaching the retina is partly absorbed and partly reflected, and he investigated the optical properties of the eye as though the eye were an optical instrument (Wade & Finger, 2001). His ophthalmoscope was an ingenious instrument that made it possible to intercept rays that are reflected. Thus, an observer could, for the first time, see images and anatomical details of the retina of another person's eye. If the senses are the windows of the mind, then Helmholtz's contributions made it possible to peer into those windows and to entertain the hope that science could forge ahead into another frontier.

Helmholtz's empirical approach to perception was set forth in an 1894 article titled "The Origin and Correct Interpretation of Our Sense Impressions" (see Kahl, 1971; Stromberg, 1989). He notes that a child hears sounds in the form of common names associated with objects in the world. Countless repetitions forge a connection between sounds (words) and objects in the world. Subtleties are slowly developed through connection of descriptive adjectives with nouns, allowing finer and finer discriminations. Helmholtz (1894/1971) pointed out that, in time, "we are able to follow the subtlest, most varied shadings of thought and feeling. If, however, we tried to say how we acquired this knowledge, we could

explain it only in the form of a general proposition: we always found certain words used in certain ways" (p. 502).

Helmholtz argued that something similar takes place with respect to sense impressions. For example, a baby gains different information when grasping a ball rather than a cube. At the same time, reaching and grasping are associated with visual cues. When connections are invariant, the baby gains a sense impression of a sphere and a cube. Helmholtz (1894/1971) concluded "from these facts that the meaning of some of the simplest, most important visual images for a human infant must be learned" (p. 506). Even if the baby were articulate, it could not specify how it gained sense impressions. As a result, Helmholtz emphasized "unconscious inferences" in perception that are built through countless repetitions of stimulus and response events.

Helmholtz employed this reasoning to explain depth perception. For example, we learn that object *A* is more distant than object *B* because of invariant connections between *A* and the feeling of the outstretched arm and *B* and the feeling of the arm when it is closer to the body. There are other connections (visual, proprioceptive, and perhaps verbal) that occur together and that gradually contribute to sense perceptions. It would be nearly impossible to specify all the cues that contribute to a given perception, but we do draw unconscious inferences that are exquisitely conditioned by our interaction with objects in the environment.

Helmholtz was particularly interested in depth perception including the study of monocular cues such as size, contours, shadows, and aerial perspective. He also discussed binocular cues, some of which could be demonstrated with the **stereoscope**, an instrument that produces a compelling three-dimensional effect by simultaneously presenting slightly different views of a visual scene to the left and right eyes. Much of Helmholtz's discussion of depth perception is still relevant today.

Color Vision   One of the first naturalistic theories of color was attributed to Aristotle, who apparently believed that all colors result from admixtures of lightness and darkness (see Barnes, 1984). Modern theories of color date from the work of Isaac Newton (1642–1727), whose classic work in optics described the properties of light. Newton demonstrated that a beam of sunlight passing through a prism is dispersed into a spectrum of colors. He also demonstrated that white light is attained again when the dispersed colors are recombined with a converging lens. Newton's demonstration was damaging to the then popular belief that white light was pure and devoid of color.

In time, it was understood that colors are associated with specific wavelengths. But how do we see in color? Do we have a specific structure for each discriminable wavelength? If so, the physiology of color vision would be complex because it is possible to split the visible spectrum into hundreds of different hues. A much simpler solution was proposed in 1802 by the physiologist **Thomas Young (1773–1829)**, who argued that all colors can be produced with various combinations of red, green, and blue (violet). Young suggested three types of specialized retinal structures, each sensitive to a specific primary color. Boring (1942) pointed out that by positing specialized nerves for color primaries, Young's theory "anticipated Johannes Müller's theory of specific nerve energies" (p. 112).

Interestingly, little experimental work was conducted on color vision in the two-hundred-year period from Newton to Helmholtz. Indeed, Young's studies on color vision, although provocative, were speculative in nature. By the middle of the nineteenth century, Helmholtz conducted experiments on color mixtures (Finger & Wade, 2002). As in other research on visual perception, Helmholtz held to the empiricist position, bringing him into conflict with the German physiologist Ewald Hering (1834–1918), who defended nativism in the study of color vision. In one of the most impassioned debates in modern science, Helmholtz clashed with Hering over issues such as space perception, color blindness, optical illusions, and the therapeutic practices of clinical ophthalmology (Turner, 1994). Helmholtz was

interested in discovering the minimum number of primaries from which one could obtain all colors of the spectrum. Initially, he argued against Young's belief in three primaries, opting instead for five: red, yellow, green, blue, and violet.

Scottish physicist **James Clerk Maxwell (1831–1879)** provided experimental work favoring Young's trichromatic theory (Finger & Wade, 2002). With sophisticated experimental techniques, Maxwell matched any spectral value with mixtures of red, green, and blue. Subsequently, Helmholtz embraced Young's trichromatic theory. Since that time, it has been known as the **Young–Helmholtz trichromatic theory**, although a more appropriate name might have been the Young–Maxwell–Helmholtz theory or even the Young–Maxwell theory. Helmholtz's contributions to color theory, however, should not be minimized. He tied Young's theory to possible physiological mechanisms and, in the words of Beck (1968), "extended the theory to account for color blindness, negative afterimages, and successive contrasts" (p. 347). The Young–Helmholtz theory remains an important theory in color science.

Acoustics and Hearing   Helmholtz's great breadth of interest in physics, physiology, and psychology is evident in his original work *On the Sensations of Tone*. His resonance theory of hearing, for example, identified possible physiological structures for pitch perception. Helmholtz observed that a string on a musical instrument such as a harp or piano is activated by an external sound source of the same frequency as the one to which it is tuned. Helmholtz speculated that fibers in the basilar membrane of the inner ear, like the strings of a piano or harp, may also resonate to specific frequencies. Thus, pitch discrimination is based on vibration of fibers in sympathy with external sources. In yet another extension of Müller's doctrine of specific energies, Helmholtz argued that each discriminable pitch activates separate specialized nerves, and his work was foundational for later psychologists, physiologists, and physicists who studied sound and audition (Palmieri, 2012).

He also accounted for the timbre or quality of sound. He reasoned that a specific pitch, say middle C, sounds different on different instruments because of the harmonics or overtones produced by the structural properties of the instrument.

Beck (1968) pointed out, "From the perspective of posterity. . .Helmholtz made his most significant contributions to the fields of sensory physiology and psychology. In particular, he laid the foundations for the experimental investigation of the sensory processes in audition and vision" (p. 345). These contributions, coupled with his measurement of the speed of the nervous impulse and his commitment to the doctrine of the conservation of energy, mark him as one of the most pivotal figures in the history of experimental psychology (Stumpf, 1895).

Wilhelm Wundt

WILHELM WUNDT

The formal beginnings of experimental psychology can be traced to 1879 when the University of Leipzig recognized Wilhelm Wundt's laboratory (Boring, 1950; Wade et al., 2007). Weber, Fechner, and Helmholtz had already established many conceptual and methodological tools for the new discipline. What remained was for someone with vision and knowledge, to tackle the risky business of agitating for institutional space and recognition. **Wilhelm Maximilian Wundt (1832–1920)** had the requisite vision, knowledge, and energy for such an undertaking. He faced an uphill battle because conservative university officials expressed only lukewarm interest in the new science. Some even voiced administrative concerns that Wundt's introspective methods might cause students to suffer mental breakdowns. To say the least, the outlook for the new laboratory was not optimistic.

Wundt's persistence produced monumental consequences. From a single room on the Leipzig campus, Wundt was the key player in launching a new discipline that would become international in scope. Who would have predicted that, within a century, a course in psychology would be required for many university majors or that psychology as a major subject would be among the most popular on university campuses? Of course, we can't credit Wundt with sole responsibility for psychology's popularity. But more than any other, he had the vision, talent, organizational skill, and enthusiasm for establishing psychology as a formal discipline. Accordingly, he occupies a singular place in psychology's history.

Wilhelm Wundt was born on August 16, 1832, in Neckarau, a small village located in a German principality close to the present city of Heidelberg. Wundt was the youngest of four children of Maximilian Wundt (1787–1868) and Marie Friederike née Arnold (1797–1868). Typical for the times, only two of the four children survived, Wilhelm and his older brother Ludwig (1824–1902).

Maximilian was a Protestant minister known for his moderate or even liberal theology. Marie was a competent, energetic, and thrifty individual who took a strong hand in the management of household economic matters. Both parents came from families of professionals including physicians and university professors. Diamond (1980) noted that "Wundt grew up in effect as an 'only child'" (p. 10). His brother Ludwig, who was eight years his senior, started work in the gymnasium at Heidelberg when Wilhelm was only two years old. Wundt's earliest years were marked by loneliness and poor health (he had a severe case of malaria in his first year). As a consequence of isolation from other children and loneliness, he reveled in his own fantasy world. Indeed, his habit of daydreaming interfered with his high school and early college studies.

In 1836, Maximilian received an appointment to a large parish in Heidelsheim, a rough town that did nothing to allay Wilhelm's shyness or his fear of other children. He had a single friend his own age, a gentle boy with apparent cognitive deficits and speech deficiencies. Wundt entered grammar school at age six, but the poorly socialized youngster struggled with his lesson materials. The school's oppressive atmosphere forced him to retreat deeper into his own thoughts. Wundt's personal difficulties were compounded at age eight when his father suffered a massive stroke. The resulting family hardship had a dramatic effect on Wundt's early education.

As a consequence of the stroke, Maximilian's young assistant, Friedrich Müller, assumed a large share of the parish responsibilities, and also took an interest in young Wilhelm. According to Bringmann, Bringmann, and Balance (1980), Müller "made his appearance when the boy must have been under considerable stress. His grandfather had just died, his brother remained away from home, and his mother's time was taken up with the care of her crippled husband" (p. 18).

Müller, who shared a room with Wilhelm in the parsonage, assumed the responsibilities of tutor. He assigned and graded lessons and often discussed the youngster's performance. Their bond was so intense that Wundt was overcome with grief when Müller was assigned to a church in Münzesheim. Wundt, then twelve years old, was allowed to go to Münzesheim to live with his tutor. Later, he enrolled in the gymnasium in Bruchsal. Again, the result was disastrous. Wundt enrolled in the equivalent of the first year of high school, and promptly failed. His teachers regarded him as lazy, inattentive, and poorly fitted for anything but an undemanding career. Wundt became all the more deeply embittered and withdrawn.

Wundt's academic prospects were dim, to say the least, following the disastrous year at Bruchsal. Within one year, however, a radical transformation had taken place. Diamond (1980) stated, "Wundt's family—which is to say, his Mother's family—saw to it that he was given another chance. At thirteen, he joined Ludwig in their aunt's home, to attend the Heidelberg gymnasium and do his studying in the same room with his industrious brother, with no daydreaming nonsense allowed" (p. 13). For whatever reasons (e.g., greater maturity, the presence of a good role model, new determination), Wundt's prospects improved. His attention was gradually directed outward, as evidenced by a newfound ability to make friends. His academic performance improved, but was still below expected standards.

Following graduation from the Heidelberg Lyceum in 1851, Wundt was still undecided about a career. However, he was accepted as a premedical student at the University of Tübingen where his uncle, Friedrich Arnold, taught anatomy. Following a year at Tübingen, Wundt was accepted for premedical studies at the University of Heidelberg. For the first time in his troubled academic career, Wundt surrendered himself to his studies. As a result, he completed the medical program in three years, obtaining his M.D. in 1855 with highest honors.

Wundt found he had little interest in the practice of medicine. As a consequence, in 1856, he sharpened his research skills in physiology in postdoctoral work at the University of Berlin under Johannes Müller and Emil DuBois-Reymond. Back at Heidelberg later in the year, he was hired as a docent with teaching and research opportunities. The monetary reward was meager, but Wundt at last found work suited to his interests. In 1858, Wundt published his first book, *The Doctrine of Muscular Movement.* In that same year, he applied for a position in Helmholtz's physiology laboratory. He was given the appointment and remained as Helmholtz's assistant for eight years. During this period, Wundt conducted research, instructed medical students, and offered his own courses. In 1862, he taught a course titled "Psychology as a Natural Science."

During this period, Wundt's research interests shifted from physiology to psychology. Two of his most important psychological contributions from the period include *Contributions to a Theory of Sensory Perception* (1862) and *Lectures on Human and Animal Psychology* (1863). The introduction to the book on sense perception announced the need for a new discipline of experimental psychology.

Wundt remained at Heidelberg for almost a decade after leaving Helmholtz's laboratory. The period from 1865 to 1874 was productive with the most noteworthy academic achievement coming from Wundt's 1873 publication of Volume I of *Principles of Physiological Psychology*. The second volume appeared the following year. Around the same time, Wundt married Sophie Mau in 1872 after several years of engagement.

In 1874, Wundt accepted an appointment as chair of inductive philosophy at Zurich, but in less than a year received a call to the larger, more prestigious University of Leipzig. Wundt's growing reputation in psychology prompted the call to Leipzig. According to Bringmann, Bringmann, and Ungerer (1980), the dean at Leipzig hoped Wundt would bring prestige and recognition to the university. In one letter, the dean wrote, "I hope that your call to the university will one day be viewed as [the beginning of] an epoch in the history of German philosophy, especially of psychology and epistemology" (p. 128). The dean's hopes were realized when the forty-two-year-old Wundt embarked on work that fulfilled the promise of a new science.

In his first four years at Leipzig, Wundt taught an average of two courses per semester, including psychology, anthropology, logic and methodology, history of modern philosophy, brain and nerve physiology, and cosmology. Wundt supervised dissertations and conducted his own research. He produced almost two publications a month, amounting to eighty-eight publications during the four-year period at Leipzig, including four books. Few scholars in any field or period of history can match Wundt's productivity.

In 1879, Wundt established the psychological laboratory at Leipzig. Much of the early equipment was provided by Wundt himself. By December, the first experiments were under way.

Wundt recognized the need for a scholarly journal to publish the numerous research papers emerging from his new laboratory. The new research didn't fit with established journals in physiology or philosophy. In 1881, Wundt published the first issue of *Psychological Studies*. Immediately, the title was changed to *Philosophical Studies* to avoid confusion with a parapsychology journal, published under the title *Psychological Studies*. Wundt's journal was primarily an outlet for research from the Leipzig laboratory.

Wundt's work stretched over the next four decades, and the high productivity in the first four years offered promise about coming research. In his years at Leipzig from 1875 to 1920, Wundt directed one hundred and eighty-six doctoral theses (see Tinker, 1980). Wundt revised his magnum opus, *Principles of Physiological Psychology*, through six editions, the last being issued in 1911. If all this were not enough, Wundt taught large classes. Indeed, Angell (1921) reported "that there was no lecture room in the university large enough to hold the audience that 'subscribed' to the lectures on psychology" (p. 164).

Wundt devoted much of his later years to his long-term interest in sociocultural psychology (*Völkerpsychologie*). The result was a ten-volume work covering areas in anthropology, psycholinguistics, forensic psychology, the psychology of religion, personality, and social psychology. In this massive work, he tackled issues that included the origin of belief in gods, the growth of complexity of rewards and punishments, the development of legal systems, marriage and family systems, the beginnings of language, and primitive societies. Part of *Völkerpsychologie* is available in English (see Wundt, 1916), and it remains understudied, likely from a combination of issues related to translation, cultural and scientific barriers across history, and the lack of a strong synthesis of ideas (Diriwächter, 2012). Criticisms of Wundt's *Völkerpsychologie* by Houston Stewart Chamberlain (who was a political but not a psychological figure) affected the trajectory of this research program; *Völkerpsychologie* became an applied area of research in ethnic differences, and Chamberlain and others expounded upon differences perceived as racial, particularly between Jews and others (Guski-Leinwand, 2009). This change resulted in a shift in public perception to include the idea that *Völkerpsychologie* has contributed to later totalitarian worldviews.

In view of his enormous productivity, one might conclude that Wundt was a social recluse, but such is not the case. He was active in politics twenty years before founding his psychology laboratory. In Heidelberg, he was elected to a parliamentary seat, which he held from 1866 to 1869. He was interested in social concerns of his day, such as improving education and working conditions. Wundt's adult personality is a matter of considerable interest, especially in view of his troubled and solitary childhood. Despite his dramatic turnaround and successful years in the M.D. program, the young scientist was still a misfit. Indeed, Titchener (1921) referred to his Heidelberg period as "seventeen years of depression" (p. 171).

Did Wundt's turbulent childhood and early adult years leave noticeable scars? The answer is not simple. Wundt did have difficulties with colleagues and was overly reactive to criticism (see Diamond, 1980). However, many positive personal qualities balanced negative traits. Wundt was patient and helpful with students and showed genuine concern about their progress and success. Although friendly and warm, he never allowed students to lose sight of the formal master–student relationship. He was generous in devoting time to student laboratory projects and theses. One student, Edward A. Pace (1921), celebrated Wundt's lack of ostentation even while students from around the world were flocking to his laboratory. Howard Warren (1921) and Walter Dill Scott (1921) commented on his encyclopedic knowledge and breadth of vision. A documented perspective on graduate study with Wundt was provided by Sokal (1980a).

Walter Dill Scott (1921) summed up Wundt's legacy as follows: "When he began his work psychology was thought of as a branch of

philosophy. His work changed it into an experimental science" (p. 183). Wundt's life and work mark a turning point in intellectual history. At the time of his death in 1920, the formal discipline he established was rooted in major universities around the world. By that time, psychology was both an experimental science and a fledgling professional discipline with branches extending into education, industry, the military, and the clinic.

General Characteristics of Wundt's Thought

Several general characteristics distinguish Wundt's philosophical and psychological vision. Although he changed positions on specific topics in psychology, many broader philosophical underpinnings remained stable.

MIND AND BODY In *Principles of Physiological Psychology*, Wundt speculated about the evolution of mental function. He rejected the extreme positions of **hylozoism** (the view that mind is manifested in all material movement— e.g., even the falling of a rock) and the dualistic Cartesian view that only humans have mental functions. Wundt believed that the lower limits of mental function are illustrated in movements that have a voluntary basis. He pointed out that voluntary movements, unlike simple reflexes or vegetative functions (like respiration), "are varied to suit varying conditions, and brought into connection with sense-impressions previously secured" (1910/1969b, p. 28). He gave an unlikely example: "The amoeba, which is regarded morphologically as a naked cell, will sometimes return after a short interval to the starch grains that it has come upon in the course of its wanderings" (p. 29). Wundt noted that such a phenomenon argues for continuity in mental processes. He believed that the origin of mental processes dated to the origin of life itself.

Wundt also speculated about the metaphysical or ontological status of mental processes. He recognized the popular assumption that mind is a substance or a real being, but argued that such an assumption is unnecessary. He noted that we do not treat virtue or honor as substances, yet that does not prevent our doing intelligent and logical work with these topics. In a similar manner, we may simply treat mind "as the logical subject of internal experience" (1910/1969b, p. 18).

In Wundt's psychology, experience is central. Mind is one meaningful subject of discourse and the physical system is another meaningful subject of discourse. Mental *and* physical processes are both known in experience, but psychology cannot, in its immaturity, specify the metaphysical basis of either process, and Wundt believed that the tools used to study the brain in his day could not provide a foundation for psychology (Wong, 2010). Wundt believed in the unity and interdependence of mental and physical processes. His perspective came closer to Spinoza's double-aspect monism than to a mind–body dualism.

BREADTH OF VISION   Wundt's philosophical and psychological vision offered enormous scope. In addition to teaching a wide range of courses, he published in diverse fields such as ethics, logic, sociocultural psychology, and physiology. Frank Angell (1921), one of Wundt's students, said, "For depth and range of learning, for capacity for generalization, for power of scientific imagination, he was the ablest man I ever met" (p. 166). Wundt's breadth of vision for the new psychology was illustrated in several ways. First, he employed a variety of methods. It is true that much of the work of the laboratory for which he is remembered was based on a rigorous form of what we often call introspection; however, he was quick to recognize other methods, including naturalistic observation such as in astronomy or field biology. He also recognized the historical methods employed in archeology and geology. In his laboratory work, Wundt emphasized precise measurements and the importance of being able to replicate findings. Although his laboratory work focused on sensory processes, perception, and reaction time, he nevertheless had the vision of a wider psychology that included social and cultural variables.

VOLUNTARISM   The name Wundt preferred for his system of thought was **voluntarism**. It is important to point out that voluntarism is *not* the same thing as free will. Wundt wrote in his *Ethics* (1892/1901) that "To be free, an action must be voluntary" (p. 38). It does not follow, however, that all voluntary acts are free. Wundt declared that volition was not a sufficient condition for freedom. Thus, "an insane person may balance motives one against another, and proceed with thoughtful circumspection, yet we do not call his decisions free" (p. 38). Wundt did, in fact, believe some people possess a free will, but free will is possible only when we attain a truly reflective self-consciousness. According to Wundt, true reflective self-consciousness is based on deep cognitions that are hard won through experience. Such a free will could hardly be expected to exist in children, people with mental illness, individuals with cognitive deficits, or those under unusual duress.

If voluntarism is not the same as free will, then what is it? A *voluntaristic psychology* is one that emphasizes psychological causality. For example, one may stand at the ice cream counter and choose chocolate over vanilla. Asked why, the individual may say, "Well, I love both, but it's been a long time since I've had chocolate. Plus, I caught a whiff of this wonderful fresh chocolate aroma." Wundt did not deny that there are underlying material and efficient physiological and biochemical causes for a choice. But, as psychologists, we study psychical motives, or in Wundt's (1892/1901) words, "ideas accompanying the voluntary act" (p. 52). Such ideas are the stuff of psychical causality. In one sense, Wundt's voluntarism affirms the legitimacy—even the primacy—of the world of experience and its causal forces.

WUNDT AND DARWIN   Wundt's emphasis on volition, with its obvious implications for adaptation, hints at the influence of Darwin. Such a conclusion, however, is unwarranted. Despite parallels between Darwinian theory and Wundt's system (see Richards, 1980), it's not clear that Wundt assimilated Darwinian ideas. References to Darwin in Wundt's major works are sparse and sometimes critical.

In his *Lectures on Human and Animal Psychology* (1894/1977), Wundt agreed with Darwin on the importance of the principle of adaptation. However, Wundt claimed his notion of voluntary action supplements and adds to Darwin's concept of adaptation. He pointed out that Darwinian adaptation is a passive concept not necessarily directed toward an object. Plants, for example, are altered by the interplay of environmental forces and adapt or die out. The same forces apply to animals, but in addition to passive adaptation, animals display a more active adaptation. In animals, volition has an object toward which it is directed and there is an "interaction of external stimulus with affective and voluntary response" (Wundt, 1863/1907, p. 409). Thus, the animal is not merely passive but acts on its world on the basis of affect and past associations. Acting on the world does not, of course, necessarily imply that animals have free will.

The Laboratory and the Broader Vision

Wundt's laboratory work was directed toward manageable, well-defined problems that lent themselves to available techniques and equipment. The goals of laboratory investigation were somewhat modest, but the basic canons of scientific research were not compromised. Wundt's broader vision included topics such as linguistics and social influences on behavior that did not lend themselves to his conception of laboratory research. Unfortunately, Wundt's larger view of psychology is often portrayed in terms of his laboratory work. The result is that his system has often been represented as narrow in terms of methodology and subject matter. There are numerous helpful criticisms of the stripped-down versions of Wundt presented in early history texts (see Blumenthal, 1975, 1998; Danziger, 1979; Farr, 1983; O'Neil, 1984). Wundt's experimental psychology is perhaps best illustrated with concrete examples of his research. Studies on the speed of reflexes, associations, and vision are

typical of experimental work that Wundt conducted or supervised during his years at Leipzig.

Before the formal founding of his laboratory, Wundt (1876) published an article in the journal *Mind* that presented research on the speed of different types of reflex action. During this time, the creation of scientific technology became a hallmark for the "new psychology of the laboratory" (Evans, 2000). Wundt contributed to this trend by conducting research on reflex action with the assistance of the *pendulum myograph,* an instrument that permitted precise measures of stimulus and response. In this case, the stimulus was an electric current and the response was reflex activity of a frog. Among the topics investigated, Wundt compared unilateral spinal conduction, transverse conduction, and longitudinal conduction. In unilateral conduction, excitation is from the sensory root to its corresponding motor root on the same side. Transverse conduction is from the sensory root on one side to the motor root on the opposite side. Longitudinal conduction follows the spinal axis from a lower sensory root to a higher motor root, or vice versa. Longitudinal conduction can follow unilateral or transverse paths. Wundt also studied the effects of temperature on the speed of reflexes. In addition, he examined the reflex process when adjacent nerves were receiving simultaneous stimulation.

Among the findings, Wundt reported that transverse and longitudinal reflexes were slower than unilateral reflexes. He also found that lowering body temperature increases the magnitude of the reflex, but the reflex is slower than that encountered when body temperature is normal. Wundt found that simultaneous stimulation of neighboring nerves had mixed effects on reflex activity. Simultaneous stimulation or compounding of stimulation may have excitatory or inhibitory effects.

This latter finding was important because it demonstrated the critical role of inhibitory processes in the nervous system. Wundt saw inhibition as an equal partner with excitation in lower and higher mental processes. For example, ordered voluntary behavior is based on a mix of inhibitory and excitatory processes. Wundt realized that the growth of inhibition is central to adaptive and voluntary behaviors. One of his abiding curiosities concerned the physiological and psychological nature of inhibition (see Diamond, Balvin, & Diamond, 1963, pp. 40–42, 159–164).

Wundt's laboratory research was focused on sensation, perception, and reaction time, and this narrow focus eventually led to perceptions of stagnation and a search in the United States for another foundation for psychological science; American functionalists emphasized Darwin rather than Wundt for these reasons (Green, 2009). Nevertheless, studies were conducted on topics such as attention, emotion, association, and dreams. Wundt also directed many dissertations in philosophy.

Some Key Concepts in Wundt's System

Certain terms occur again and again throughout Wundt's experimental work. Such terms represent themes in his thinking and provide keys to understanding his laboratory work. However, his laboratory work is but one phase of Wundt's larger psychological perspective. To use a metaphor once employed by Freud, it is as if Wundt recognized that the house has more than one floor. Insofar as the work of the laboratory was concerned, Wundt was content to remain on the lower floor. The constructs to which we now turn pertain to this lower floor.

DEFINITION OF PSYCHOLOGY   As far as the laboratory is concerned, Wundt defined *psychology* as a science that investigates "the facts of consciousness" (Wundt, 1912/1973, p. 1). He pointed out that psychology has two tasks: the first is to discover the elements of consciousness and the second is to discover the combinations that elements undergo and the laws that regulate combinations. He referred to a combination of elements as a *psychic compound* (see Wundt, 1912/1973, p. 44). Although Wundt agreed with his contemporaries, such as James, Freud, and Titchener, that psychology involves the study of consciousness, there was little agreement about definitions

of consciousness. The emphasis on consciousness in psychology would diminish in the early twentieth century and not return for over half a century (Ferrari & Pinard, 2006).

ELEMENTS   The term **element** in Wundt's thinking is a difficult abstraction that requires further comment. We normally think of an element as something simple, pure, and irreducible. Wundt believed that there are mental elements, or pure sensations such as the sensation of the beat of a metronome. However, he recognized that a single simple sensation on the psychological side—that is, a psychological element—is by no means simple on the physiological side. Nevertheless, we may treat simple sensations (e.g., blueness, redness, or sweetness) as elements.

SENSATIONS AND PERCEPTIONS   Wundt (1912/1973) defined **sensation** as an element of consciousness (p. 45). In addition to sensations, there are perceptions and ideas. He noted that the term *perception* generally refers to combinations of outward sense impressions (e.g., an object of a particular shape and color may be called an apple). An *idea,* by contrast, generally refers to combinations that may come from memory, previous associations, and so on. Wundt questioned the validity of the distinction between *idea* and *perception.* In both cases, we observe compounds or combinations and both can be equally lively as experienced phenomena.

ASSOCIATION AND APPERCEPTION   Wundt believed that compounds or combinations of elements may be passive or active. He described *passive combinations* as associations and *active combinations* as apperceptions. The distinction between *association* and *apperception* is important in Wundt's thought and carries implications for his larger psychological system.

Association and apperception are illustrated in the distinction between mere rote memory and memory with real awareness. Wundt (1912/1973) pointed out that in rote memory, separate words "are joined to each other by mere association. In the consciousness of the child they do not form a unified whole" (pp. 127–128). Association is manifested in the flight of ideas of a mental patient or in the immediate response to a simple stimulus. Wundt pointed out that a simple series of words such as *school, house, garden, build, stones, ground, hard, soft, long, see, harvest, rain, move,* and *pain* illustrate association. He then asked the reader, "Compare with this a context like the following out of the seventh book of Goethe's *Wilhelm Meister:* 'Spring had come in all its glory. A spring thunderstorm, that had been threatening the whole day long, passed angrily over the hills'" (pp. 124–125). What is the essential difference between these series? The first illustrates associations, but they are haphazard, aimless, not well connected, and only moderately intelligent. The second illustrates **apperception** marked by intelligent direction within a larger context. Apperception is characterized by activity with intelligent direction and inner unity—these are lacking in association. Wundt criticized British empiricism and associationism for failing to grasp the important distinction between association and apperception.

THE TRIDIMENSIONAL THEORY OF FEELING

In addition to studying cognitive concepts such as sensation, perception, ideas, associations, and apperceptions, Wundt was deeply interested in feelings. Wundt (1912/1973) warned that feelings must not be overlooked because they are tied to more complex psychological processes such as apperception, memory, imagination, perception, and cognition.

Through introspective studies, Wundt developed a **tridimensional theory of feeling** based on three dimensions: pleasure and pain, strain and relaxation, and excitation and quiescence. Certain sensations result in specific feelings. Thus, a bitter taste or a smell like ammonia is unpleasant almost to the point of pain, whereas sweetness is usually pleasurable. Wundt noted that red is exciting and blue is quieting. Colors, like music, may produce relaxation or strain.

Rarely are feelings isolated or partial with respect to the dimensions specified by Wundt. Instead, they combine to form a meaningful compound.

Thus, a given sensation may be pleasurable and exciting or pleasurable and relaxing. Varieties of combinations are possible. So-called emotions such as joy or hope represent pleasurable feelings tied to a particular cognitive content. Anger or fear may represent feelings of strain and unpleasantness tied also to a particular cognitive content.

THE PRINCIPLE OF CREATIVE SYNTHESIS

Whereas Wundt hoped to identify the elements of consciousness and to discover the laws that govern connections of elements, he nevertheless believed that there are inherent indeterminations in psychic compounds. In other words, there is real novelty and creativity in higher mental operations. Wundt's term for such novelty is the principle of **creative synthesis**. He wrote that this principle refers to "the fact that in all psychical combinations, the product is not a mere sum of the separate elements that compose such combinations, but it represents a new creation" (1912/1973, p. 164).

Wundt noted that one of the major manifestations of creative synthesis is illustrated in the principle of the **heterogony of ends**. This principle is exemplified in the emergence of new motives during the course of a chain of activities. Let's say you're invited to a friend's surprise birthday party. Your motives are to go, surprise your friend, and have a great time. But after surprising your friend, you meet someone you're attracted to at the party. Now a whole new set of motives emerge that exist alongside and in addition to the original motive (Should you ask the person out? Where would you go after the party?). The interplay of motives in our immediate experience defines our social behavior as well as our cognitive reaction to the world. Wundt also called attention to the changing motivational structure attached to the practice of ancient habits or customs. Original motives for a practice such as a religious rite or ceremony may be obscured or even be replaced by new motives that bear little relation to the original motives. For example, baptism in some Christian religions was once viewed as a way of casting out evil spirits; such motives for the practice are no longer encountered.

Wundt's Legacy

If there is one central dominating figure in the history of psychology, it is Wilhelm Wundt. Under his leadership, psychology gained status as a separate discipline in a major institution of learning. Undergraduates packed into classrooms and graduate students from around the world flocked to the Leipzig laboratory. Under Wundt's guidance, the new discipline was soon on a firm footing and the Leipzig experiment proved a viable model for other schools. Psychology gained recognition in other major universities.

There have been questions about the lasting effects of Wundt's substantive contributions (e.g., theories and laboratory findings). The fact is, however, that many laboratory findings were cited in early textbooks and some results held up remarkably well. For example, the finding, cited earlier, regarding the locus of retinal stimulation and perceived brightness is widely accepted. Blumenthal (1975) also called attention to additional lasting influences. For instance, factor analytic studies of feelings have yielded results that correspond closely to the predictions of Wundt's tridimensional theory. His work was also a central influence in the development of applied cognitive psychology (Hoffman & Deffenbacher, 1992). Unfortunately, his rigid view of memory as an imprecise and overly popular concept with little value for scientific psychology served to alienate some contemporaries (Danziger, 2001). Still, Wundt's substantive contributions to the new discipline cannot be dismissed. Indeed, additional historical work should be focused on the lasting effects and generalizability of Wundt's many substantive contributions.

Wundt's laboratory emphasis on sensory processes and reaction time was criticized for its narrowness. But, as noted by Wertheimer (1987), "This criticism may be somewhat inappropriate. After all, this was just the beginning of genuine experimental psychology. Wundt can hardly be blamed that there were no studies of learning in the early years at his laboratory; that kind of work was not yet in the Zeitgeist" (p. 69). Besides, as noted earlier, Wundt's larger vision did include a broader and encompassing psychology. It is perhaps no accident that many of Wundt's students helped implement his wider vision.

From the early 1970s, there has been an outpouring of scholarly work on Wundt's system of psychology (see Rieber & Robinson, 2003). Most of the scholarly projects have been designed to "correct misconceptions and distortions" (see Araujo, 2012, p. 33). As a pioneer in a new discipline marked by all kinds of uncertain boundaries, it is understandable that Wundt struggled with a host of substantive and methodological issues and that his ideas would evolve over the course of more than sixty years of his active work in psychology. There are clear discrepancies and different points of emphasis between many of his early and later works. Further, as noted by Araujo, Wundt, though not formally trained in philosophy, sought to establish a psychology consistently informed by a coherent philosophical framework (p. 45).

The Legacy of Wundt's Students in Applied Psychology

In his major works, Wundt (1897/1969a, 1863/1907) made numerous references to pathological psychology, so it is little wonder that some of his students pursued this area. Wundt (1863/1907) even argued that "pathological psychology has as good a claim to rank as an independent discipline beside normal psychology, as has the pathology of the body to be separated from its physiology" (p. 316).

The renowned psychiatrist **Emil Kraepelin (1856–1926)** learned experimental methodology from Wundt and, according to Blumenthal (1975), advanced a theory of schizophrenia derived specifically from Wundtian psychology. Kraepelin was awarded his M.D. at twenty-two, one year before Wundt established his laboratory at Leipzig. At twenty-seven, Kraepelin wrote a treatise on psychiatry that produced multiple editions (Boring, 1950). His early studies on the psychological effects of alcohol and morphine established Kraepelin as a pioneer in the field of psychopharmacology (Healy, 1993; Müller et al., 2006). He pioneered clinical observation and categorization of people with mental illnesses (deVries et al., 2008), and in 1883, he published an early taxonomy of psychiatric disorders that anticipated current classification systems. This work introduced enduring diagnostic terms such as *paranoia* and *manic-depressive psychosis*, a mood disorder later called bipolar disorder (Marneros, 2009). However, Kraepelin's clinical term *dementia praecox* (premature deterioration) was later, at an April 1908 meeting of the German Psychiatric Association (Kaplan, 2008), renamed *schizophrenia* (splitting of the mind) by Swiss psychiatrist Eugen Bleuler (1857–1939) (Palha & Esteves, 1997). Bleuler also broadened the nature of the definition and defined the disorder in a less pessimistic manner (Hoff, 2012). Kraepelin made a substantial impact on psychiatry and his ideas soon spread through Europe (Healy et al., 2008).

Kraepelin's interest in dementia led to pioneering studies on a disorder that would later be called *Alzheimer's disea*se (Cipriani et al., 2011). Prior to the definitive research of the German neurologist Alois Alzheimer (1864–1915), Kraepelin conducted early clinical work on presenile dementia (Weber, 1997). After Alzheimer published his classic description of the disorder in 1907, Kraepelin named it "Alzheimer's disease" in honor of his colleague.

Emil Kraepelin

As forensic research made an impact in Europe at the end of the nineteenth century (see Bartol & Bartol, 1999), Kraepelin played a crucial role in the development of criminal psychiatry. He was one of the first researchers to claim that criminal behavior should be considered a mental illness, and he became a vigorous opponent of the death penalty (Hoff, 1998). In a sentiment shared with modern clinicians, he urged the use of psychiatric treatment in rehabilitating prisoners. He envisioned a larger role for the psychiatrist in the courtroom and even suggested that clinicians have a voice in judicial decisions regarding the variety and length of imprisonment.

Born the same year as Sigmund Freud, Kraepelin was a staunch opponent of psychoanalysis, which he saw as art but not science. Instead, he believed the root of psychopathology to be organic and drew on his findings to educate the German public about the health dangers of alcoholism and syphilis (Engstrom, 1991). Kraepelin's medical work remains a source of ongoing interest to psychiatrists (Jablensky, Hugler, von Cranach, & Kalinov, 1993). Wundt's interests in pathological psychology were extended in the work of not only Kraepelin but also Lightner Witmer, the founder of clinical psychology.

Lightner Witmer (1867–1956) was born in Philadelphia. He earned a bachelor's degree from the University of Pennsylvania in 1888. Following a brief teaching career, he studied at the University of Pennsylvania, but later transferred to Leipzig where he earned a Ph.D. with Wundt in 1893. He returned to the University of Pennsylvania, where he worked until his retirement in 1937. He died at the age of eighty-nine in 1956.

Following his work at Leipzig, Witmer engaged in experimental work on topics such as the perception of pain and the special learning problems of children with mental disabilities (Wilkins & Matson, 2009). His work in this area held practical value for early school psychologists (Fagan, 1996). In March 1896, Witmer opened the world's first clinic headed by a psychologist. In its first year of operation, the clinic handled about two-dozen cases, primarily clients with learning disorders (McReynolds, 1996).

Later, the caseload increased and a greater diversity of clients was tested and treated (see Levine & Wishner, 1977). In 1907, Witmer founded a new journal, which he called *The Psychological Clinic*. McReynolds (1987) pointed out that "Witmer's opening article in the first issue of his new journal. . .called for a new profession and proposed that it be termed *clinical psychology*" (p. 852). Summarizing Witmer's contributions, McReynolds (1997) noted that he was the first to see that scientific psychology could serve as the basis for a helping professional discipline. In addition to founding the first clinic and clinical journal, Witmer showed by his own involvement in clinical activities how clinical professionals might function independent of the medical profession. He also believed that there should be close ties between scientific psychology and clinical psychology. Some have suggested that his work anticipated later developments in industrial/organizational and counseling psychology (McWhirter & McWhirter, 1997).

In subsequent chapters, we will encounter additional examples of how students from Wundt's laboratory extended the boundaries of psychology. If such students departed from the strict focus of the Leipzig laboratory, many nevertheless carved out areas of application consistent with their mentor's larger intellectual agenda.

Review Questions

1. Psychophysics explores the relationships between the properties of stimuli as measured by a physical scale and the psychological or subjective impressions of those stimuli. List and describe two extreme positions about the nature of the relationship of experience to objects in the world.
2. How did early psychophysics challenge the two extremes referred to in the previous question?
3. Define the term *threshold*.
4. List some of the findings that came out of Weber's work on difference thresholds.
5. Write both the Weber formula and the Fechner formula and explain their meanings.
6. Briefly describe three of Fechner's psychophysical methods.

7. Outline the reasons given by E. G. Boring for Rudolph Hermann Lotze's prominent place in the history of psychology.
8. Briefly explain Helmholtz's approach to the understanding of color vision and his approach to audition.
9. Outline four general characteristics of Wundt's thought.
10. Give two examples of representative research coming out of Wundt's laboratory.
11. How did Wundt define *psychology*?
12. How did Wundt distinguish between perception and apperception?
13. Briefly explain Wundt's tridimensional theory of feeling.
14. What did Wundt mean by *creative synthesis*?
15. What role did Emil Kraepelin play in the study of psychiatric disorders?
16. Briefly outline Lightner Witmer's contributions to the formal development of clinical psychology.

Glossary

aesthesiometer   A compasslike instrument used to measure tactile sensitivity. Two points can be stimulated simultaneously. The task of participants is to report whether they feel both points or only one.

apperception   In Wundt's psychology, an apperception is an active set of associations marked by intelligent direction within a larger context. A simple associative combination such as *sky* and *blue* would be counted simply as a perception. Apperception, by contrast, carries far more meaning. Thus, a statement such as "If the weather is clear in the morning, we will go sailing" denotes an intelligent direction within a context, an apperception.

creative synthesis   The principle advanced by Wundt that psychical combinations are not a mere sum of elements. Rather, a combination of associations includes new attributes not predictable from the sum of the elements.

difference threshold   The minimal stimulus difference that is detectable 50 percent of the time.

element   An abstraction referring to a simple irreducible sensation.

Fechner, Gustav Theodor (1801–1887) His *Elements of Psychophysics,* one of the great original classics in psychology, set forth a systematic approach to psychophysics. He proposed several early psychophysical methods and helped lay the conceptual and methodological foundations for the new discipline of psychology.

Fechner's law An integration of Weber's formula expressed as $S = k \log R,$ where S is a mental sensation and R is a stimulus magnitude. Thus, according to the law, a mental sensation is a logarithmic function of the stimulus multiplied by a constant.

Helmholtz, Hermann Ludwig Ferdinand von (1821–1894) One of the great scientists of the nineteenth century who, along with Thomas Young, advanced a trichromatic theory of color vision. He also advanced a theory of pitch perception and was the first to measure the speed of conduction of the nervous impulse.

heterogony of ends Wundt's position that an ongoing behavioral sequence must often be understood in terms of an ever-shifting pattern of primary and secondary goals. For example, a cat chasing a mouse may suddenly find it necessary to compete with a partner, overcome an unexpected barrier, or avoid a danger. Ends, goals, and purposes keep changing.

hylozoism The view that mind is manifested in all material movement.

just noticeable difference (jnd) The smallest detectable difference between a standard stimulus and a comparison stimulus.

Kraepelin, Emil (1856–1926) A student of Wundt. He created an influential classification system of psychiatric disorders and made numerous contributions to psychiatry and psychopharmacology.

Lotze, Rudolph Hermann (1817–1881) Wrote the first treatise on physiological psychology. He also advanced an early theory of space perception.

Maxwell, James Clerk (1831–1879) Scottish physicist who demonstrated that he could match any spectral value with various mixtures of red, green, or blue. He thus contributed directly to the Young–Helmholtz theory of color vision.

method of average error A psychophysical method that permits a participant to manipulate a variable stimulus until it appears to match a standard stimulus.

method of constant stimuli A psychophysical method in which comparison stimuli are judged against a standard stimulus. Various values of the comparison stimuli above and below the standard stimulus are presented on a random basis. The task of the participant is to specify whether each comparison stimulus is equal to, greater than, or less than the standard.

method of limits A psychophysical method whereby a standard stimulus is compared with various values of comparison stimuli presented in both ascending and descending series. The task of the participant is to specify when the standard and the variable appear to be the same. Also called the *method of limits* because it measured the quantitative limits of the variable stimulus values that appear to be greater than, less than, or equal to the standard stimulus.

ophthalmoscope An instrument designed by Hermann von Helmholtz for viewing the interior of the eye, especially the retina.

psychophysics The formal study of the relationship between the properties of stimuli as measured by a physical scale and the psychological impressions of those stimuli.

response compression In psychophysics, equal intervals on a physical scale may be experienced as a diminishing series. Illustrated in the experience of a diminishing series associated with a three-way light.

sensation According to Wundt, an element of consciousness referring to simple awareness of stimulation.

stereoscope An instrument that produces a three-dimensional effect by simultaneously presenting slightly different two-dimensional views to the left and right eyes.

theory of local signs A hypothetical sensory representation by means of which one can detect the position or locus of one part of a sensory surface relative to other points on that surface.

threshold   That stimulus intensity (or change in intensity) that is detected 50 percent of the time.

tridimensional theory of feeling   According to Wundt, a theory of feeling marked by three fundamental directions: pleasure and pain, strain and relaxation, and excitation and quiescence.

voluntarism   Technical term for the system of psychology advanced by Wilhelm Wundt. Voluntary behaviors are those that are varied to meet the demands of varying circumstances.

Weber, Ernst Heinrich (1795–1878)   Well-known nineteenth-century physiologist who was the first to establish a quantitative relationship between the physical properties of stimuli and the experience of those stimuli. Weber's book, *The Sense of Touch,* launched the field of psychophysics.

Weber's illusion   The perception that two points of a compass appear to move apart when the compass is moved over an insensitive area of the skin. By contrast, the two points appear to move together when the compass is moved over sensitive areas of the skin.

Weber's law   First quantitative law in psychology expressed as $\Delta R/R = K$, where $R =$ the amount of existing stimulation, $\Delta R =$ the amount of stimulation that must be added to produce a just noticeable difference, and $K = a$ constant.

Witmer, Lightner (1867–1956)   One of Wundt's students. Founded the first psychological clinic and coined the expression *clinical psychology.*

Wundt, Wilhelm Maximilian (1832–1920) The founder of the first psychology laboratory that functioned for a sustained period of time. Wundt also advanced the first systematic vision of psychology known as voluntarism. He is also the first person who, without qualification, can be thought of as a psychologist. His *Principles of Physiological Psychology* is one of the great classics in the discipline. More than any other, he can be viewed as the founder of modern psychology.

Young, Thomas (1773–1829)   English physiologist who formulated the trichromatic (red, green, and blue) model of color vision. He speculated that retinal structures must therefore be specialized for color primaries.

Young–Helmholtz trichromatic theory Young's theory that color vision is produced by separate receptor systems on the retina that are responsive to primary colors (red, green, and blue-violet). Maxwell and Helmholtz supported Young's theory in the nineteenth century.

11

■ ■ ■

Developments after the Founding

How many evils could be remedied. . .by knowledge of the laws according to which a mental state can be modified!

—Franz Brentano (1874/1973)

A rapid growth of interest followed the formal founding of psychology at Leipzig. Within a few years, a host of new lecture courses, laboratories, and degree programs emerged in Europe and the United States. In 1898, Edward Bradford Titchener, writing for the journal *Mind,* reminded readers, "It is now twenty years since Prof. Wundt instituted the first psychological laboratory in the University of Leipzig. A revolution, radical and far-reaching, was thus quietly inaugurated. . . . Laboratories have been established in most of the principal universities of Germany and in all the principal universities of the United States" (p. 311). Excitement about laboratories ran high as journals carried descriptions of research plans, announcements regarding the establishment of new laboratories, and descriptions of basic laboratory equipment. Titchener celebrated the fact that "to carry on the psychological work of a modern university the psychology professor must have acquired a body of what one may call 'technical' knowledge, knowledge of applied mechanics and applied electricity" (p. 311).

Wundt played a pivotal role in founding psychology, but not everyone agreed with him. Some appreciated his contributions but quarreled with Wundt's approach. In this spirit, European psychologists debated topics such as methodology, the appropriate subject matter of psychology, theoretical positions, definitions, and basic assumptions.

Before we consider alternatives to Wundt's psychology, let us explore the meaning of expressions such as *systematic thought* and *systems of psychology*. Courses in the history of psychology are sometimes called "History and Systems of Psychology." What do we mean by a system of psychology or, for that matter, a system of anything? The answer moves us into a rich intellectual arena that is relevant to the way people function in the world.

SYSTEMS

A **system** may be defined as an *organized way of envisioning the world or some aspect of the world.* There are integrated, all-encompassing systems that are nothing less than a "philosophy of life," or what German scholars call a *Weltanschauung* ("worldview"). More commonly, however, we encounter less-ambitious, single-domain systems that provide an organized way of envisioning a limited dimension of human experience. We have political systems, religious systems, economic systems, philosophical systems, and psychological systems. The remaining material will be more meaningful after we explore the characteristics of systems. We'll draw upon the discussion of Wilhelm Wundt in Chapter 10 to illustrate our mission here.

First, systems provide definitions. Wundt defined *psychology* as the "science that investigates the facts of consciousness." Of course, different systems offer different definitions of psychology. We can uncover countless terms in psychology that are defined in multiple ways depending on a given systematic position. For example, two notable learning theorists, Clark Hull and B. F. Skinner, defined the term *reinforcement* in different ways (see Chapter 14). Psychology is not alone with regard to such discrepancies; for years, physicists quarreled over the definition of a positron.

Second, systems include assumptions. Wundt thought that humans possess only a limited free will. By contrast, Sigmund Freud built his system of psychoanalysis on the deterministic assumption that all mental phenomena are caused. Systems of psychology vary with respect to assumptions about issues of nature and nurture, mind and brain, and free will and determinism. Assumptions are sometimes explicit and other times implicit. The behaviorist John B. Watson preferred to not waste time talking philosophy, but such assumptions are nevertheless evident in his system.

A third characteristic of systems is that they prescribe methodologies or ways to investigate their various subjects of interest. Most of us know about the different methods and assumed sources of truth in religious and political systems. The same is true in the sciences where a variety of methodologies are associated in different disciplinary areas. For example, historical sciences such as paleontology and geology employ different methods than meteorologists testing a weather model or wet lab chemists who are manipulating materials and instruments in a laboratory. Wundt's psychology emphasized controlled introspection, but his research team used additional methodologies in the laboratory. Introspection, naturalistic observation, and controlled laboratory experiments are among psychology's many methodological tools. Presumably, the methodologies employed by scientists result in observations that can be checked and replicated. Thus, the methods of science are associated with certain constraints and expectations that may not always be evident in nonscientific methods.

Fourth, systems also specify the subject matter of a disciplinary area. Among other things, Wundt was concerned with the discovery of the elements of consciousness and the way these elements combine. By contrast, Freud studied the unconscious mind and its influences, whereas the behavioral psychology of John B. Watson focused on observable behavior of humans and other animals. Humanistic psychology criticized these systems as narrow and insisted that joyfulness, peak experiences, and self-actualization are legitimate topics for study in psychology.

Fifth, a system may be construed as open or closed. An open system is responsive to new and multiple sources of information, whereas a closed system restricts or even censors the flow of ideas. Systems of thought also exist in a hierarchical arrangement. For example, one may embrace several single-domain systems, but one system is often dominant and serves as a filter for what is acceptable in other systems. Thus, a political or a religious system may serve as a filter for a scientific system or vice versa. A deep and critical awareness of the effects of such a hierarchy can be expected in a more open system of thought.

Sixth, systems of thought sometimes differ with respect to time. Some psychologists explore the past to understand the present. Psychoanalytic theory emphasizes the power of childhood trauma in coloring adult experiences and behavior. By contrast, behaviorism stresses the importance of present facts—new conditioning begins *now,* so there is not always a need to dwell on the past.

Seventh, systems of thought also vary along a liberal–conservative continuum. Conservative thought seeks to preserve stability by emphasizing traditions that have proved workable in the past. The term *liberal* means "worthy of a free person." Liberals do not reject tradition "out of hand," but they may argue that contemporary problems are not always solved by traditional methods. Systems tell us how to dress, what to eat, what to regard as primary or secondary, what to regard as relevant or irrelevant, and how to interact with others. Systems may also attach special significance to specific times, locations, and symbols. In many cases, our systems of thought even define, for better or worse, who we are.

EDWARD BRADFORD TITCHENER

Edwin G. Boring (1927) noted that "the best key to Titchener's life. . .lies in the fact that he emulated Wundt" (p. 504). One might conclude that **Edward Bradford Titchener (1867–1927)** had devoted years of study with the master. In fact, his studies in Leipzig were limited to the two-year period from 1890 to 1892. The relationship between the two men in that period could be described as businesslike and professional rather than intimate. Nevertheless, Titchener identified with Wundt's personal and professional style and with the elementary dimensions of his psychology. He did not admire Wundt's larger philosophical vision, especially his emphasis on social, cultural, and linguistic studies. Rather, he identified with the hard-core scientific work in Wundt's laboratory.

More than any other disciple, Titchener brought Wundt's experimental thought and work to the United States. Unfortunately, Titchener's psychology has often been mistaken as a close version of Wundt's psychology. Although similarities exist in their respective work, historical scholarship has clarified important differences between the two researchers (see Blumenthal, 1975, 1979; Leahey, 1981).

Edward Bradford Titchener was born in Chichester, England, on January 11, 1867, the son of John Titchener and Alice Field Habin. He studied at Malvern College in Worcestershire. Later, at Oxford University, he studied physiology, the classics, and philosophy. After graduating from Oxford in 1890, he attended Leipzig where he embarked on doctoral studies with Wundt. Following the completion of his Ph.D. program in 1892, Titchener returned to England. At that time, job opportunities in psychology were sparse. Despite its robust heritage with empiricism, England was one of the last European countries to recognize the new discipline of psychology. Unable to secure a British appointment, Titchener accepted a position at Cornell University in Ithaca, New York. He remained at Cornell until his death in 1927. For a time, Titchener was a powerful force in American psychology. His books were widely read and, like Wundt, he produced a large number of doctoral students. Even so, his system faded after his death.

Titchener thrived despite frustrations in setting up a new laboratory and establishing a new program. By 1895, he advanced to the position of full professor, an impressive accomplishment for a twenty-eight-year-old. He translated several of Wundt's works into English and produced a steady stream of his own books and articles. His first book was *An Outline of Psychology,* published in 1896. His *Primer of Psychology* followed in 1898; *Experimental Psychology* (4 vols) in 1901–1905; *Lectures on the Elementary Psychology of Feeling and Attention* in 1908; *Lectures on the Experimental Psychology of the Thought Processes* in 1909; *A Textbook of Psychology* in 1910; *A Beginner's Psychology* in 1915; and finally, a work that was never completed, *Systematic Psychology: Prolegomena* in 1929. In all, Titchener published eight books and over two hundred articles, in addition to his many translations.

Titchener also headed one of the most vigorous doctoral programs in the United States.

Boring (1927) listed fifty-six doctoral students who graduated from Cornell in the period from 1894 to 1927 (records before 1910 were incomplete, so the actual number of doctoral students may have been higher). Titchener's first graduate student, according to Boring, was Margaret Floy Washburn (1871–1939), later to establish a reputation for her work in comparative psychology. In all, nineteen of Titchener's fifty-six graduates were women. In the context of the times, this was a remarkable record. Evans (1991) reminds us that "Titchener took women into his graduate program at Cornell at a time when Harvard and Columbia would not. More women completed their Ph.D. degrees with him than with any other male psychologist of his generation" (p. 90).

Graduate education at Cornell resembled the classic German model with an emphasis on laboratory research and independent reading. If students wished, they could audit undergraduate courses provided such courses complemented their research interests. Graduate students also enrolled in selected seminars. Dallenbach (1967) noted that "many students were unable to survive this degree of freedom; they required the compulsion of a teacher. Those who did survive, who learned to depend upon their own initiative, were the productive scholars of the future" (p. 81). Research served as the major focus of the doctoral program.

Students who earned their degrees under Titchener came away with colorful anecdotes. Evans (1991) added, "Titchener's was an overpowering personality. He seemed bigger than life and often overwhelmed his students and colleagues by sheer strength of character" (p. 89). Boring (1961) remembered that "psychology at Cornell—at least the orthodox psychology that centered in the laboratory—revolved around and was almost bounded by the personality of E. B. Titchener" (pp. 22–23). He took a keen interest in the progress of his students and gave generous time to their research projects. Young (1972) told of "weekly conferences with Titchener in his home" (p. 334). Titchener conducted a small orchestra on Sunday evenings and students who could play an instrument were encouraged to participate. After the music, Sunday evenings were devoted to casual conversation, generally on topics other than psychology.

Titchener's erudition and brilliance are typical themes in the biographies of his students. Boring (1961) stated,

> He always seemed to me the nearest approach to genius of anyone with whom I have been closely associated. . . . He was competent with languages, and could ad lib in Latin when the occasion required it. If you had mushrooms, he would tell you at once how they should be cooked. If you were buying oak for a new floor, he would at once come forward with all the advantages of ash. If you were engaged to be married, he would have his certain and insistent advice about the most unexpected aspects of your problems, and if you were honeymooning, he would write to remind you, as he did me, on what day you ought to be back at work. (pp. 22–23)

Boring noted that Titchener, like Freud, demanded loyalty from his students. At Cornell, there was a strict European code on matters of decorum and conduct and those who violated the code could pay a severe penalty. Most students decided that the benefits of working with a man such as Titchener far outweighed the inconveniences brought about by his paternalistic nature. Titchener's closest relationships were with students rather than with colleagues. By temperament, he was not one who thrived in a rugged, democratic climate. Titchener also strongly promoted the new science. In 1904, in part due to his frustrations with the American Psychological Association, he and others created the Society of the Experimentalists, later named the Society of Experimental Psychologists, to reflect his narrower definition of laboratory psychology as discussed subsequently (Goodwin, 1985, 2005). Despite Titchener's acceptance and promotion of women as doctoral students, women were excluded from the Society of Experimental Psychologists until after his death; in 1929, his former student, Washburn, and another woman became charter members of the newly reorganized society.

After the first decade of the new century, the tide was turning against Titchener's systematic psychology. John B. Watson called for a radical new approach to psychology. The new Gestalt psychology from Germany issued devastating critiques that challenged Titchener's systematic vision. American functionalism provided an approach to psychology with broader appeal than his narrow approach to the discipline. Titchener died in 1927 and, though he produced many doctoral students, no one carried on his legacy. Accordingly, his systematic vision died with him. Some have speculated about how Titchener's system might have evolved had he lived a longer life (see Evans, 1972).

Titchener's Psychology

The technical term employed by Titchener for his system of psychology was **structuralism**. Like other systems, structuralism embraced a specific methodology, advanced definitions of the subject matter of psychology, and made assumptions regarding age-old philosophical problems. Titchener drew parallels between the physical sciences (especially physics and chemistry) and psychology. He hoped to establish the new discipline on the same conceptual footing that had proved so successful in the established sciences.

THE SUBJECT MATTER OF PSYCHOLOGY
Titchener (1910) argued that "all the sciences have the same sort of subject-matter; there can be no essential difference between the raw materials of physics and the raw materials of psychology" (p. 6). All science, according to Titchener, begins with experience. Without experience, there can be no cognition, no knowledge. Though all the sciences begin with experience, experience itself can be considered from different points of view. For example, we can consider a unit of time, say an hour, from the point of view of physics. The hour, from such a point of view, is a measured unit of time. The actual unit of measurement has

fixed qualities (e.g., 60 minutes or 3,600 seconds) that are independent of human judgment. But an hour, from the point of view of psychology, may be long or short, pleasant or unpleasant. The subject matter of psychology, thus, is experience, dependent on the experiencing person. Titchener (1910) stated that formal study from the first point of view (stated previously) "gives us facts and laws of physics; [the] second gives us facts and laws of psychology" (p. 8).

THE PROBLEM OF PSYCHOLOGY   Science, according to Titchener, always seeks to answer three sorts of questions: what, how, and why? *What* questions deal with the basic, most uncomplicated elements of the subject (e.g., what is water made of?). *How* questions deal with the appearances of things. For example, how do the basic elements that compose water combine with each other? Finally, Titchener (1910) stated that "science enquires, further, why a given set of phenomena occurs in just this given way, and not otherwise; and it answers the question 'why' by laying bare the cause of which the observed phenomena are the effect" (p. 37). The first problem for psychology is to identify the basic **elements** of experience, such as irreducible sensations or simple images. The second task is to assess the ways in which elements combine. The third is to determine causal relations in these phenomena. We shall return later to a more detailed consideration of these problems.

THE METHOD OF PSYCHOLOGY   The method of psychology, in Titchener's view, is really no different from the method employed by any other science. All scientific work begins with observation of the phenomena that have been designated as the subject matter of a particular science. The type of observation employed by the physicist is called *inspection,* whereas the type of observation employed by the psychologist is called **introspection**. Needless to say, special training is required for the unique observational tasks of any discipline. For an observation to be scientific, it is important that it be possible to isolate it, vary it experimentally, and repeat it. For example, the stimulation of a particular receptor site on the tongue with a particular substance may produce a specific response. Maybe a research participant declares that she or he experienced a taste of sweetness. Presumably, the site can be isolated, the substance can be varied many ways (e.g., with respect to quality or concentration), and the response for a particular isolated stimulus can be repeated. The observation, in this case, is a variety of introspection, but in Titchener's view, this need not be viewed as radically different from inspection.

THE SCOPE OF PSYCHOLOGY Because Titchener's method was limited to introspection, it might be argued that psychology, in his view, is limited in scope. For example, how can we ask a baby or nonhuman subject such as a cat or a dog to introspect? For that matter, how can we ask a mentally disturbed individual to introspect? It appears that Titchener's psychology is limited to the study of normal human beings. Further, it appears superficially, at least, that introspection reveals only the contents of the individual mind and that we are trapped in a kind of solipsism. Titchener was aware of the problem and took steps to ensure that his system did, in fact, have considerable scope. To argue that Titchener was interested only in the adult human mind is to caricaturize his system of thought.

Titchener believed that psychologists must make ample use of analogy. Although we have direct access only to our own experience, we have every reason to believe that a specific behavior (e.g., the expression of fear) in another is comparable to our own experience of fear. Such an argument provides the conceptual basis for social psychology and a similar line of argument provides the basis for comparative psychology. On this topic, Titchener (1910) wrote:

> If however, we attribute minds to other human beings, we have no right to deny them to the higher animals. These animals are provided with a nervous system of the same pattern as ours, and their conduct or behaviour, under circumstances that would arouse certain feelings in us, often seems to express, quite definitely, similar feelings in them. Surely we must grant that the highest vertebrates, mammals and birds, have minds. (p. 27)

In the same passage, Titchener argued that the range of mind seems to be as broad as the range of animal life. His view on the scope of psychology, then, was broader than what might be derived from an uncritical acceptance of his definition of psychology as human experience dependent on the experiencing individual. The architecture of the nervous system and analogies drawn from behavior provide the glue for the breadth of his vision. Titchener (1910) told his readers that there is

> a psychology of language, a psychology of myth, a psychology of custom, etc; [there is also] a differential psychology of the Latin mind, of the Anglo-Saxon mind, of the Oriental mind, etc.
>
> And this is not all: the scope of psychology extends, still further, from the normal to the abnormal mind. Life, as we know, need not be either complete or completely healthy life. The living organism may show defect, the lack of limb or of a sense-organ; and it may show disorder and disease, a. . . .lapse from health. So it is with mind. (pp. 28–29)

As Titchener's thought evolved, he realized the importance of the study of different types of consciousness. For example, he argued that studies of people with sensory impairment or with morbid fears are important in their own right. Furthermore, such studies may shed light on our understanding of normal conscious processes. In fact, the study of normal conscious processes commanded the most attention in Titchener's laboratory. In the words of Evans (1991), Titchener's "lasting contribution to American psychological thought was his championing of psychology as science and of the laboratory as the primary source of data for psychological research" (p. 102).

Titchener drew a distinction between science and technology, and although he did not oppose technology as such, he preferred that psychology identify—especially in its infancy—with laboratory science. We turn now to some of the major content areas explored by Titchener and his students.

ELEMENTARY MENTAL PROCESSES The first task of any science, according to Titchener, is to investigate the basic elements of its subject matter. His first concern was the nature and number of the elementary mental processes. Following the Leipzig tradition, Titchener focused on the senses as windows to the mind. His most immediate concern was to identify the basic elements associated with each of the senses. According to Titchener (1910), a true element "must remain unchanged, however persistent our attempt at analysis and however refined our method of investigation" (p. 46). The next task of the psychologist is to arrange "the mental elements precisely as the chemist classifies his elementary substances" (p. 49).

Though the senses occupied a central place in Titchener's system, he identified two additional elementary processes: images and affections. Sensations were regarded as elements of perceptions, whereas images were regarded as elements of ideas, memories, and thoughts. Affections were treated as the elementary processes of emotions. The relative emphasis of Titchener on these elementary processes is illustrated in the amount of page space devoted to each. For example, in *A Textbook of Psychology* (1910), Titchener devoted two hundred and ninety-three pages to sensation and perception, seventy pages to affection and emotion, and seventy-two pages to memory and thought. In that same book, twenty-one pages were devoted to association, thirty-seven pages to attention, and forty-one pages to a discussion of reactions and actions.

In addition to the identification and classification of elements, the psychologist, according to Titchener, must discover the **attributes of elementary mental processes**. For example, he found that all sensations, at a minimum, have four attributes: quality, intensity, clearness, and duration. *Quality* is the major identifying property of a sensation—its saltiness, sweetness, redness, coldness, and so on. *Intensity* simply refers to the fact that the sensation exists in some amount or strength. *Clearness* refers to the transparency or the distinctiveness of a sensation; a clear sensation is easily identified. *Duration,* of course, is a temporal attribute. As noted, all sensations share these four basic attributes, but some sensations have additional attributes. For example, certain solutions such as alcohol applied to the skin may have an attribute that could best be described as penetratingness. Such a solution stimulates the surface of the skin as well as areas below the surface.

Titchener also believed that the attributes of quality, intensity, clearness, and duration are associated with images. He found quality, intensity, and duration in association with affections, but clearness was not easily identified as an attribute of affection. Titchener and his students identified other attributes with specific elements. For example, he noted that "certain sensations have been credited with an attribute of insistence. They are self-assertive and aggressive; they monopolise consciousness. . . . We speak of the penetratingness of odours like camphor and naphthalene; of the urgency. . .of certain pains" (1910, p. 55).

One way to gain an appreciation for Titchener's system is to examine his position on some key issues of the day.

MIND AND BRAIN Titchener admitted that common sense tells us that we lose consciousness as a result of inhaling ether or that we run because of fear. In other words, the physical system influences the mental and vice versa. Titchener's position, however, was "that mind and body, the subject-matter of psychology and the subject-matter of physiology, are simply two aspects of the same world of experience. They cannot influence each other, because they are not separate and independent things" (1910, p. 13). Titchener referred to his position as *psychophysical parallelism,* but it is not completely clear that the label is accurate. Titchener could also be viewed as a double-aspect theorist because he declared that mind and body are but "two aspects of the same world of experience." A true psychophysical parallelist would posit the ontic status of both the physical and the mental but deny that the two interact.

Ambiguities are evident in Titchener's position. Heidbreder (1933) was correct when she declared that his "emotions were not involved in the problem for its own sake. . . . He is almost perfunctory in his discussion of the topic" (p. 127). At every turn, Titchener emphasized the primacy of experience. He studied experience in relation to the physical system and because he rejected commonsense interactionism. For all of these reasons, he is viewed as a psychophysical parallelist, just as he described himself. His psychophysical parallelism, however, may be of a pragmatic rather than a metaphysical variety. Psychophysical parallelism, for Titchener, is a useful assumption that helps the scientist get on with more important business at hand.

ATTENTION Like many early psychologists, Titchener was very interested in attention (Posner, Rueda, & Kanske, 2007). He distinguished between passive or involuntary attention and active or voluntary attention. He referred to involuntary attention as *primary* and to voluntary attention as *secondary*. Both represent types of consciousness that are identifiable at different stages of development. **Primary attention**, according to Titchener (1910), is "an attention that we are compelled to give and are powerless to prevent" (p. 268). It is brought about by strong stimuli, so the attribute of intensity is sufficient to activate it. Titchener believed that certain qualities are irresistible and observed that, in his own case, attention was commanded by stimuli such as the smell of musk, a bitter taste, or the sight of yellow. Examples of other factors that control involuntary attention include novelty and suddenness.

Secondary attention involves a focus on a subject that would not normally call attention to itself. For example, Titchener (1910) pointed out that "a problem in geometry does not appeal to us as a thunderclap does" (p. 271). Thus, "Secondary attention is attention under

difficulties, attention in the face of competitors, attention with distraction" (p. 272). Clearly, secondary attention is associated with a more advanced stage of development. The infant is capable of primary attention but may not yet be capable of secondary attention.

Titchener (1910) found still a third stage in attention, and that stage, he tells us, consists in nothing else than a relapse into primary attention. As we work our problem in geometry, we gradually become interested and absorbed; and presently the problem gains the same forcible hold over us as the thunderclap has from the moment of its appearance in consciousness. The difficulties have been overcome; the competitors have been vanquished; the distraction has disappeared. There could hardly be a stronger proof of the growth of secondary out of primary attention than this fact, of everyday experience, that secondary attention is continually reverting to the primary form (p. 273).

His laboratory investigated numerous topics such as the duration and effort of attention, the inertia of attention, and bodily conditions conducive to Titchener's attention. This area of scholarship remained robust until the 1920s, when the study of attention faded from the United States with the rise of behaviorism (Moray, 2007).

ASSOCIATION If Titchener's primary experimental focus was on sensory processes, he didn't neglect the importance of association. He acknowledged the debt of psychology to Aristotle and to British thinkers from Hobbes to Bain who emphasized the centrality of association. Furthermore, he quoted, with approval, the contention of David Hume that association is to the mental world as gravitation is to physics (see Titchener, 1910, p. 374).

Titchener recognized traditional attempts to establish laws of association but argued that all association can be reduced to the law of contiguity. He pointed out that even the so-called law of similarity really involves contiguity. In Titchener's (1910) treatment, association is characterized by the following statement: "Whenever a sensory or imaginal process occurs in consciousness, there are likely to appear with it (of course, in imaginal terms) all those sensory and imaginal processes which occurred together with it in any earlier conscious present. This we may term the law of association" (p. 378).

Titchener immediately recognized a possible objection to his law. What about affective processes? Feelings most assuredly play a role in associative processes. Titchener (1910) agreed but noted that feelings play a role in association only "by virtue of their sensory and imaginal components, and not in their affective character" (p. 378). However, he admitted that little is known about feeling and that his position was tentative.

THE EXPERIMENTAL STUDY OF ASSOCIATION   Titchener noted that, prior to the work of Hermann Ebbinghaus on memory, the experimental study of association was confounded because of the presence of previously acquired meanings. In a celebration of Ebbinghaus's contribution, Titchener (1910) offered the opinion that "it is not too much to say that the recourse to nonsense syllables, as means to the study of association, marks the most considerable advance, in this chapter of psychology, since the time of Aristotle" (p. 381). Nevertheless, according to Titchener, the nonsense syllable is not a complete panacea because we human beings find intrinsic meanings everywhere. Thus, even in a set of nonsense syllables, we may find that one has more meaning than another and the one with the greater meaning forms an impression. The impression then helps mediate associations. He argued that associations must be understood in the context of impressions that result from the fact that some stimuli, even some nonsense syllables, have a unique capacity to impress themselves on the brain. Accordingly, impression and associative processes supplement each other. In Titchener's view, the mere study of association without careful introspective analysis of what is taking place is inadequate. He also warned that our knowledge in this area will remain inadequate until such future time as we are able to devise means to study the physiology of association.

MEANING   According to Titchener (1910), "Meaning, psychologically, is always context" (p. 367). In Titchener's view of the **context theory of meaning**, meaning is understood as a function of the laws of attention in combination with the laws of the connection of sensations. An aggregate of sensations will also be supplemented by images that result from memories of previous encounters with the particular aggregate of sensations. The group of sensations and images, according to Titchener (1910), "has a fringe, a background, a context; and this context is the psychological equivalent of its logical meaning" (p. 371).

Titchener (1910) acknowledged that many psychologists would not accept such an associationistic approach to meaning:

> A square, they say, is more than four linear extensions, sensibly of the same length, and occupying certain relative positions in the visual field; a square is square; and squareness is a new character, common to all squares, but not to be explained by attention, or by the laws of sensory connection, or by those of imaginal supplementing. A melody, again, is more than rhythm and consonance and scale; a melody is melodic; we recognize its melodic character as such; the melodic character is something new and unique, common to all melodies, but not found elsewhere. (p. 372)

Titchener (1910) noted that he could not find this extra character in his own introspections. That is, he found no need for a new distinct mental content based on a combination or synthesis of the parts. He was nevertheless open to future research on the matter and added that it is "only right to say that the belief in a new mental content, or new mental character, peculiar to perception, is shared by many psychologists of standing" (p. 373).

EMOTION   The most widely discussed theory of emotion in Titchener's day was a rather paradoxical theory (see Chapter 12) advanced by William

James (1884b) and propounded independently by Carl Lange (1885/1922). Widely known as the **James–Lange theory of emotion**, the view stressed the dependence of emotions on the vasomotor system. According to the theory, we experience emotions such as fear, anger, or love because of bodily events (e.g., muscular arousal, discharge of adrenaline, and increase in heart rate) that interpose between one mental event and another. Thus, to use one of James's examples, we see a bear, we run, and we are afraid. The experience of emotion is a product of the running and the multitude of physical events that accompany it. We refer to the theory as paradoxical because it contradicts the commonsense idea that we see the bear, are afraid, and then run. The theory will be examined in more detail in Chapter 12, but it is sketched briefly here because it serves as a foil for Titchener's position.

Titchener noted that the so-called James–Lange theory was not really new. It had been anticipated, at least in part, by figures such as Malebranche, Descartes, Spinoza, Lotze, and Maudsley. The idea of an organic basis for emotions had been stirring for a long time. Despite its venerable history, Titchener found flaws in the theory.

The first problem, according to Titchener (1910), was that "the bodily changes to which James refers may appear identically in very different emotions. There are tears of joy and tears of rage, as well as tears of sorrow; we may strike in fear or in cruelty, as well as in anger; we may run as hard to overtake a friend as we run from a pursuing bear" (p. 477). In response to such criticisms, James modified his theory and admitted that stimuli themselves may produce responses with avoidance or approach characteristics (James, 1894).

Titchener also argued that mere sensations of organic conditions can hardly be identified with the richer, more complex experience of an emotion. Titchener did not deny the importance of organic correlates of emotion but argued for a much broader conception. He believed that in some cases instinctive tendencies are automatically toned with **affect**—a position James also

accepted. Such affect occurs in an environmental context and is also associated with organic conditions. Affect may also be associated with images or earlier memories. Thus, according to Titchener, the experience of emotion may have multiple causes.

Titchener discussed the difficulties of classifying emotions as well as emotional types. The major difficulty is that any classification scheme may serve only the convenience of the person doing the classifying and have nothing to do with the science of emotions. For example, he referred to the ancient typology advanced by Galen. Recall from Chapter 4 that Galen's temperamental types included the choleric, the sanguine, the melancholic, and the phlegmatic. Titchener (1910) referred to other possible classification schemes but noted that they are "of interest rather for an applied than for a general psychology" (p. 498).

Titchener (1910) pointed out that the sentiment "represents the last stage of mental development on the affective side, as thought represents the highest level of development on the side of sensation and image" (p. 499). A sentiment, according to Titchener, is more complex than emotion; it includes discrimination, a critical dimension, possible conflicting claims, and so on. For example, if patriotism counts as a sentiment, it includes emotions, but there are also tensions. What are the relationships between loyalty to state, to nation, or to humankind? What is substantive and what is mere symbol? Clearly, the sentiment involves emotion but is a much more complicated manifestation of the affective dimension.

AFFECT AND EMOTION   Earlier, we noted that Titchener identified three elementary mental processes: sensations, images, and affections. **Affections** were initially regarded as the elements of emotions. As Titchener's theory developed, the relationship between affect and emotion became troublesome. Titchener was suspicious that affections are really nothing more than sensations of pleasantness or unpleasantness (see Henle, 1986). The same suspicions had also been directed at the so-called images; perhaps they were but a species of sensation.

In the final years of his life, Titchener moved away from the concept of elements and thinking in terms of the dimensions or attributes of experience. As noted by Evans (1972), "As early as 1918 the system started out from 'the ultimate dimensions' of psychological subject matter" (p. 172). These ultimate dimensions consisted of what were earlier called attributes: quality, intensity, duration, and so on. Titchener's final approach to psychology was much closer to what we find naturally in experience. It could be argued that what is most immediate is a quality such as redness or sweetness or a sense of pleasantness or unpleasantness. Images, sensations, and feelings are not the ultimate elements or dimensions of experience but abstractions discovered through dissection or discrimination.

Though Titchener was moving toward a new organizational approach to psychology, there is no evidence that he would have changed his rigorously scientific approach. Indeed, though his original system did not survive, his rigorous scientific attitude enjoyed prominence among experimental psychologists. In his final years, Titchener celebrated the growing independence of psychology from physiology. The confidence betrayed in such celebration may have had salutary effects on psychologists who found security in the new discipline.

MARGARET FLOY WASHBURN: A BROADER PSYCHOLOGY

Titchener's first graduate student, **Margaret Floy Washburn (1871–1939)**, became a significant figure among a new generation of psychologists. Washburn had earned a bachelor's degree from Vassar in 1891. Science and philosophy dominated her academic interests, and she believed that the new field of experimental psychology joined her two interests in a near perfect union. Following graduation, she studied psychology at Columbia University under James McKeen Cattell. Columbia, at that time, accepted a few women as "hearers," but did not accept women

as degree candidates. Cattell recommended that Washburn transfer to Cornell University, where she would be permitted to work toward an advanced degree. She agreed and arrived in the fall of 1892 just as the twenty-five-year-old Titchener became a new faculty member. Washburn completed her degree with Titchener in 1894 and became the first woman in the United States to be awarded a Ph.D. in psychology. After brief academic and professional positions at Wells College, Cornell, and the University of Akron, Washburn accepted an appointment at Vassar, where she remained for the rest of her illustrious career.

Washburn accepted Titchener's emphasis on the central role of consciousness in psychology though she doubted that consciousness consisted of irreducible static elements. She was too much of an empiricist, in the classic sense of that word, to reject the mental world or consciousness as a legitimate topic in psychology. In spite of this, she could not accept Cartesian interactionism with its emphasis on a mental substance that can "go it alone" in the body. She accepted epiphenomenalism because it is friendly to both the mental and the physical worlds, but assumes that real causal force always works from the physical to the mental. Nevertheless, in her opinion, we learn about consciousness and its physical underpinnings by relying on introspection and other psychological techniques. Her willingness to seek harmony between conflicting systems of psychology was rare in her day (Viney & Burlingame-Lee, 2003).

In 1908, Washburn became a leader in comparative psychology with the publication of *The Animal Mind* (she authored substantial revisions in 1917, 1926, and 1936), and her scholarship was part of the growing trend toward animal research (Baker & Serdikoff, 2013). Her book provided a wealth of information on animal sensory systems, animal memory, intelligence, attention, behavior, and adaptation. The book's strong evolutionary thrust is evident in her speculations about the role of distance receptors such as the eye and the ear in the development of higher cognitive processes. Early species who had only contact receptors could never afford the luxury of the delay involved in our cognitive processes. Physical contact for such organisms demanded an immediate and appropriate response or else the organism would die or lose the chance to acquire food. By contrast, the development of distance receptors provided the luxury of delay because one may see or hear an enemy or prey at a great distance. With delay, adaptation is facilitated by the development of cognitive strategies, memory, discrimination, and plans. If she were alive today, Washburn would relish metaphors for intelligence that rely on visual and auditory imagery—expressions of cognition where we "gain insight," "see through," "truly hear," or develop a "visionary strategy."

As suggested in the title of her book, Washburn (1908) believed that animals possess consciousness that can be accessed via inference, the same way we study human consciousness. In her view, animal consciousness is an appropriate research topic for psychologists. Washburn always argued, however, for a rigorous methodology that challenges simplistic and anthropomorphic inferences. She recognized that facts may be distorted by people who attribute human qualities to animal consciousness. Washburn's *The Animal Mind* is a masterful work in comparative psychology as well as a primer in the evolutionary study of higher cognitive processes. In a review titled "*The Animal Mind at 100*," David Washburn (2010) (no relation) reminds us that the work remains remarkably relevant 100 years later "both as an introduction to animal psychology and as a marker of changes in the discipline that spanned the book's four editions" (p. 369).

Washburn (1916) is also well known for a book titled *Movement and Mental Imagery* that set forth a "motor theory of consciousness." According to the motor theory, mental activity has its origin in, and is supported by, subtle neurophysiological movement systems. An example is found in the work of Walter Samuel Hunter (1889–1954), who allowed a hungry but restrained dog to watch as meat was placed inside a goal box. As it stared hungrily at the goal box, the dog displayed what Washburn called "persistent tentative movements" in the direction of the box. We can assume that the dog "anticipates" food as it salivates and strains at the leash. The dog's behavior is "goal directed" and "purposive." If we release the dog, it will scramble toward the food and eat it. But if we introduce a delay, the dog will become distracted by other things and stop straining in the direction of the goal box. If released after losing its postural set, the dog no longer heads directly to the goal box. In other words, incipient muscular movements appear to support ongoing mental activity and purposive behavior has a motor or muscular component. If the movement system is broken up, the behavior (with respect to the goal) is changed. Consider a different example. Even without an instrument, a musician might practice moving her fingers as if playing a piece, engaging in incipient muscular movements that act as a kind of rehearsal for an actual performance. Washburn's motor theory of consciousness is sometimes regarded as counterintuitive, but it becomes more plausible the more it is studied (see Viney & Burlingame-Lee, 2003, for a more detailed explanation of the theory).

Margaret Floy Washburn was one of the leading American psychologists in the first three decades of the twentieth century. She served as president of the American Psychological Association (APA) in 1921, the second woman to hold that position. (Mary Whiton Calkins, the first female APA president, will be discussed in Chapter 12.) In 1931, Washburn was named to the National Academy of the Sciences, one of the highest honors for any scientist (the renowned anatomist Florence Sabin was the first woman named to the Academy). Washburn acted as president of the Psychology Section of the American Association for the Advancement of Science and served on the editorial boards of numerous journals. Scarborough (2000) claims that Washburn was regarded as the best lecturer at Vassar. She was a powerful force not only in the science of psychology but also for the full participation of women in the intellectual community.

FRANZ BRENTANO AND ACT PSYCHOLOGY

Franz Brentano (1838–1917) provided a striking alternative to Wundt's and Titchener's psychology. As early as 1874, his system, known as **act psychology**, rejected the exclusive alignment of scientific psychology with physiology. It also rejected older interpretations of empiricism that emphasized the content of experience and the building of experience through exclusive mechanical associations. According to Brentano, an authentic empirical psychology will find more in experience itself than mere contents or passive associations. A truly empirical psychology will discover that experience is forward looking, active, manipulative, and intentional. A psychology that does not recognize these dimensions of experience is not a true empirical psychology. According to Sussman (1962), Brentano insisted on the Aristotelian approach to empiricism, "reviving the concept of activity as the fundamental essence of empiricism. In this sense is the oft used quote from him: 'Experience alone influences me as a mistress'" (p. 504). Brentano's best-known psychological work is his book *Psychology from an Empirical Standpoint,* first published in 1874.

Standard biographies of Franz Brentano emphasize his family's impressive intellectual and cultural achievements. Franz's father, Christian Brentano, and his mother, Emilie Gegner, were both known for their contributions to Catholic religious literature. An uncle, Klemens (Clemens) Brentano, was a well-known poet and novelist, and an aunt, Bettina Brentano, was a famous German romantic writer. Lujo Brentano, Franz's younger brother, was a well-known economist who won the Nobel Prize in 1927 for his outspoken opposition to the growth of German militarism. Guests at the Brentano home included political as well as academic figures (Albertazzi, 2006).

Franz Brentano, born on January 16, 1838, was one of the five children of Christian and Emilie Brentano. Young Franz was educated in the Gymnasium at Aschaffenburg following private tutoring by a Catholic priest. Brentano excelled in language and mathematics but was also drawn to theological and philosophical studies. Rancurello (1968) noted that "the road to intellectual excellence took Brentano in succession to the universities of Munich (1856–57), Würzburg (1858) and Berlin (1858–59), to the Academy of Münster (1859–60), and to the University of Tübingen where in 1862 he was granted the degree in philosophy" (p. 4). After completing his Ph.D., Brentano studied for the priesthood and was ordained in 1864.

Brentano's career as a university professor included a seven-year period at Würzburg and a twenty-year period at the University of Vienna. Brentano enjoyed unusual success in inspiring students (Huemer & Landerer, 2010). His better-known students included Christian von Ehrenfels, later known for his holistic approach to sensation and perception; Edmund Husserl, a philosopher whose work in phenomenology had a profound influence in psychology; Alexius Meinong, the founder of the psychology laboratory at Graz; and Sigmund Freud, who took courses with Brentano at Vienna. Though scholars disagree about the extent of Brentano's influence on Freud, a case can be made (see Domenjo, 2000; Fancher, 1977) concerning similarities in their thought. Additionally, Brentano clearly influenced Carl Stumpf, who in turn influenced some of the later founders of Gestalt psychology.

Though Brentano was a brilliant teacher, his was by no means an untroubled career. Prior to the December 1867 meeting of Vatican Council I, debates raged in the church about the relative authority of the papacy versus church councils. Some scholars argued that, in selected spiritual matters, the word of the pope should be regarded as infallible. Catholics were deeply split on the issue, and Brentano sided with those who challenged the dogma of papal infallibility. Those opposed to the dogma of infallibility argued that popes had contradicted each other on spiritual matters and that the doctrine of infallibility was not necessary to the Catholic faith.

On July 18, 1870, the council voted 433 to 2 in favor of a doctrine of infallibility. Brentano's former teacher, Ignaz von Dollinger, also opposed the doctrine of infallibility and was excommunicated for his refusal to accept the council's decision. Brentano, like Dollinger, could not subordinate reason to faith, but neither could he suppress earlier theological doubts now exacerbated by Vatican I. As a consequence, Brentano resigned from the priesthood and separated from the church in 1873.

All of this was not irrelevant to Brentano's academic life. He had been appointed to his position on the Würzburg faculty as a priest. As noted by Puglisi (1924), he felt "morally bound to resign his chair" (p. 416). Brentano's former affiliation with the church haunted him in his subsequent position at the University of Vienna. In 1880, at age forty-two, he was engaged to marry Ida Lieben but, as pointed out by Puglisi (1924), she "as a Catholic could not contract in Austria a religious marriage with one who had formerly been an ecclesiastic. Brentano was therefore obliged to assume Saxon citizenship, and consequently to resign the title of *professor ordinarius* in the Austrian university. On September 16 of the same year, 1880, he was married in Leipzig to Miss Lieben" (p. 417). Brentano was allowed to work at the University of Vienna, but his status was reduced to that of lecturer. Brentano remained at Vienna until the death of his wife in 1894. In retirement years, he lived first in Florence and later in Zürich, where he died on March 17, 1917.

Brentano's Psychology

In *Psychology from an Empirical Standpoint,* Brentano (1874/1973) defined *psychology* as "the science of mental phenomena" (p. 100). In an elaboration of the meaning of *mental phenomena,* he referred to John Locke's famous experiment on the perception of coldness and warmth. Locke warmed one hand while simultaneously cooling the other. Then he placed both hands into a pan of lukewarm water, experiencing warmth in the hand that was previously cool and cool in the hand that was previously warm. Brentano argued that the experiment "proved that neither warmth nor cold really existed in the water" (p. 9).

Brentano provided other examples of the effects of context on experience and noted that the term *phenomenon* is close in meaning to the word *appearance*. In the example of the water basin, we experience the water as warm or cold, depending on the previous conditions to which the hands have been subjected. Brentano (1874/1973) believed that the succession of mental phenomena follows yet-to-be-discovered lawful patterns and that there is "a vast range of important problems for the psychologist" (p. 12). According to Brentano, mental phenomena are real. He rejected the idea that the only real things are those that exist in the outside world. We know all things through experience.

Brentano was optimistic about what a science of psychology could accomplish. He envisioned the development of a discipline broad in scope. For example, he asked, "How many evils could be remedied. . .by knowledge of the laws according to which a mental state can be modified!" (1874/1973, p. 22). He considered the enormous value of early diagnosis of aptitudes. Brentano argued that "for the individual and even more for the masses, where the imponderable circumstances which impede and promote progress balance each other out, psychological laws will afford a sure basis for action" (p. 24). Brentano saw psychology as the science of the future, a science both theoretical and practical. He repeatedly conveyed optimism about the potential applications of psychology and noted that "the practical tasks I assign to psychology are far from insignificant" (p. 22). Brentano's optimism is seldom appreciated, but in attitude and orientation, he must be considered as a forerunner of applied psychology.

On questions of method, Brentano advocated a pluralistic and developmental epistemology. He recognized that the history of science involves the adaptation of scientific method to ever more complex phenomena. Scientific method is not static and Brentano mentioned several psychological methods that could be valuable. Included are observations on the newborn, studies of primitive societies, studies of those with congenital disorders such as congenital blindness to assess the effects of sensory deprivation, animal research, and studies of diseased mental states.

In the study of normal phenomena, Brentano advocated a variety of methods such as the use of biographies and what he called *inner perception.* Brentano distinguished between *inner perception* and *inner observation.* The latter term he equated with introspection and declared it an impossibility. We can observe external objects, but it is pretentious to say we observe psychological phenomena in the same manner. We perceive inner events by focusing attention on the immediate past and on the flow of events. Thus, retrospection is involved in inner perception. Brentano noted that all sciences must consult memory in the course of their work, so psychology is not uniquely disadvantaged if it must trust memory to describe mental phenomena.

Brentano provided an example of inner perception by calling attention to the way we study our own anger. We do not observe it directly, but we can report our perception of the flow of events and their effects. We retrospect about those things that just took place, the things that preceded them, and the perceived consequences. We can know about the inner state of others through verbal reports and behavior. Indeed, he argued that behavior or practical conduct is often the most reliable guide to inner states (1874/1973, p. 39). He also recognized involuntary physical indices such as blushing as guides to the nature of inner states.

If the content of Brentano's psychology was broad in theory, it was nevertheless fairly focused in practice. His unique approach is still informative and provocative. Chances are that if Brentano were devising a curriculum in psychology, he would prefer that course titles, where possible, employ verb forms rather than noun forms. Rather than teaching a course titled "Sensation and Perception," we might better give the course a title such as "Sensing and Perceiving." The reason for Brentano's preference for the active verb form rather than the passive noun form is based on what he encountered in experience itself. Experience is an active, participatory, creative,

and constructive process. It does not consist simply of inert, static, or passive contents.

Fancher (1977) noted that, for Brentano, "physical phenomena are always objects such as sounds or colors, while mental phenomena are always *acts* that 'contain' *objects,* such as hearing a sound or admiring a color" (p. 208). Physical phenomena, such as the sounds of music over a stereo system, are mere facts in consciousness, but mental phenomena are much more. They may include admiration, reflections over the phrasing or rhythms of a passage, memories, comparisons, wishes, and so forth. The unique feature of the mental act is its intentionality, complexity, and involvement. It does not consist of mere awareness.

Brentano was interested in the classification of mental phenomena and provided an excellent overview and critique, beginning with Plato, of the history of classification schemes (1874/1973, pp. 173–193). His classification system divided mental phenomena into presentations, desires, and judgments. **Presentations** are basic because there could be no desires or judgments without them. A presentation is simply an event or a presence in experience. He pointed out that a presentation and a judgment "are two entirely different ways of being conscious of an object" (p. 201). **Judgment** clearly involves belief or disbelief and it helps define our relationship with a presentation. Similarly, **desire** further delineates our relationship to an object and is still another mode or dimension of consciousness. Presumably, one could desire an object in consciousness, such as an item of food, yet judge the food negatively in terms of its nutritional value. One might also encounter positive judgments or beliefs coupled with negative desires.

Brentano argued that the three types of mental phenomena are intertwined. Indeed, in *Psychology from an Empirical Standpoint,* he contended that "there is no mental act in which all three are not present. . .but it is conceivable without contradiction that there might be a form of mental life which is missing one or even two of these kinds of mental activities and lacks all capacity for them as well" (1874/1973, p. 265).

Later, Brentano changed his mind and expressed the belief that there are visual and even auditory sensations lacking in affect (see Rancurello, 1968).

Brentano, as much as any theorist in the history of psychology, struggled with the question of the unity of experience. Is experience, as we encounter it, a mosaic of bits and pieces that add together somehow to form the whole, or are all the parts intimate with each other? Brentano was a strong believer in the unity of consciousness and in the existence of a self in possession of experience. To deny such a self would reduce us to a kaleidoscope of sensations, much as we encounter in the philosophy of David Hume. The self, according to Brentano, is a reality that appropriates and integrates other realities. It ties past and present together, along with intentions about the future.

Brentano is a key figure in the history of psychology because he described an alternative approach that placed appropriate conceptual work in higher priority than experimental work. Brentano would have agreed with Descartes, who counseled that in any conflict between the results of an experiment and reason, we should embrace reason. Brentano did not oppose experimentation but believed that it should be preceded by appropriate conceptual homework.

Brentano's influence on the discipline of psychology is remarkable in view of the sparseness of his written work. He is remembered for his *Psychology from an Empirical Standpoint* and his lectures. Nevertheless, he had a direct and profound influence on phenomenological psychology and existential psychology (Gilbert, 1968). There are clear-cut intellectual affinities between his work and the psychology of William James, American functionalism, existentialism, Gestalt psychology, and, arguably, Freud's psychoanalytic thought. Although his ideas about mental phenomena did not always mesh with the positivistic temper of nineteenth-century psychology, Brentano has been rediscovered as a viable alternative to contemporary models of cognition (Macnamara, 1993).

CARL STUMPF

Born on Good Friday, 1848, to a distinguished family of scholars, **Carl Stumpf (1848–1936)** remarked that "the love of medicine and natural science was in my blood" (1930, p. 389). Despite a natural interest in science, his childhood passion was music. By seven, he learned to play the violin and, without formal instruction, had taught himself another five instruments. At ten, he composed the words and music for an oratorio. Stumpf's fascination with music proved to be an instrumental part of his professional career.

Stumpf studied law at the University of Würzburg because it was a career that would provide leisure time for his music. His interest shifted after Franz Brentano joined the faculty. Under Brentano's influence, Stumpf became a critical thinker devoted to the study of philosophy and psychology. Following his mentor's advice, Stumpf made scientific studies a priority and engaged in work on chemistry. Unfortunately, he made "some careless reaction" that nearly burned down the chemistry laboratory. Stumpf (1930) remembered that the blaze "might have spread over the whole building if the attendant had not come to the rescue" (p. 392).

Brentano encouraged Stumpf to study with Lotze at the University of Göttingen. In addition to research on physics and physiology, he pursued a long-standing interest in Plato as the basis for his 1868 dissertation. His fascination with Plato might have been fed partly by their common interest in music. A year following the completion of his dissertation, he entered an ecclesiastical seminary at Würzburg. Like Brentano, Stumpf lost faith in orthodox religion and left the ministry before his ordination. A chance encounter with Ernst Weber stirred his interest in psychophysics, as did an opportunity to serve as a subject in G. T. Fechner's studies on aesthetics.

After accepting a teaching position at Würzburg, Stumpf began pioneering work on acoustic psychology. He later accepted a position at Prague and published his classic book *Tonpsychologie* in 1883, followed by a second volume in 1890. This classic book in the psychology of music focused on topics such as the evolution of music, primitive instruments, and sound perception. In 1894, Stumpf moved to the University of Berlin and converted three modest rooms into an impressive Psychological Institute; in 1920, the Institute moved into twenty-five rooms in the former Imperial Castle. Although more than a decade younger than Wundt, Stumpf's tenacity helped establish Berlin as a dominant competitor to Leipzig for leadership in European psychology. By the time of Stumpf's retirement in 1921, the Berlin Institute was recognized as a preeminent center for psychological research. Stumpf died on Christmas Day in 1936.

As a disciple of Brentano, Stumpf made an impassioned protest against the artificial nature of reductionism and developed an approach to philosophy and psychology that placed emphasis on the value of holism. Stumpf shared Brentano's zeal for the study of mental events from an empirical standpoint, especially one that considered the rich, dynamic quality of human cognition. His work was founded on the holistic assumption that all aspects of consciousness are connected and perceivable as a unity. He was convinced that the attributes of any sensation—such as quality, brightness, or intensity—form a whole rather than a simple aggregate of the parts.

Stumpf made significant contributions to areas such as space and auditory perception, emotion, psychophysics, aesthetics, and phenomenology. However, music remained the central focus of his psychology. He wrote extensively on music, including its forms and origins (Stumpf, 1911/2012), and he became a leading figure in the emerging discipline of musicology.

In addition to the two-volume work on tone psychology, he founded an 1898 journal devoted to musicology, *Beiträge zur Akustik und Musikwissenschaft,* and amassed one of the world's leading ethnomusicological collections, housed at Berlin's Psychological Institute. Founded in 1900, the Phonograph Archives consisted of a large assembly of Edison cylinders containing the musical recordings of a vast number of cultures. Stumpf

provided the initial funding himself and named the young Berlin psychologist and musicologist Erich Moritz von Hornbostel (1877–1936) as director of the archives. Under the supervision of Stumpf and Hornbostel, the archives grew from a few wax cylinders to a collection of more than ten thousand gramophone recordings from all over the world (Lewin, 1937). The revolutionary phonographic technology became a popular resource for the psychological and anthropological study of native dialects and the musical culture of indigenous tribes. Stumpf also considered music to be an important tool in the holistic study of mental phenomena (see Ringer, 1969).

The American psychologist William James admired Stumpf's work on tone psychology. Although Stumpf proposed a cognitive-evaluative theory that opposed James's famous theory of emotion, the two scholars enjoyed an extensive correspondence (Reisenzein & Schonpflug, 1992). Like James, Stumpf was a strident critic of Wundt's research, especially his work on acoustics. Stumpf challenged the Leipzig school's assumption that a trained but nonmusical introspectionist could make more valid judgments about tone than a trained musician. For Stumpf, the sophisticated perceptual judgments of musical experts were far superior to those generated in laboratory studies of introspection. Wundt was upset by the critique and engaged Stumpf in a bitter and scathing debate. Decades later, Stumpf (1930) wrote that "Wundt's methods of procedure had been repellent to me even since his Heidelberg days, and continue to be so, although I admire his extraordinary breadth of vision and his literary productivity" (p. 401).

Beginning with studies of his own children, Stumpf devoted considerable time to research on the mental life of children. In 1897, he studied a four-year-old boy with exceptional memory and in 1900 helped found the Berlin Association for Child Psychology. In 1903, Stumpf combined his interest in music with developmental psychology when he began investigation of several musical child prodigies.

Like Brentano, Stumpf's psychology offered a holistic alternative to structuralism that inspired many European scholars, especially the Gestalt psychologists (Sprung & Sprung, 1996); Max Wertheimer, Wolfgang Köhler, and Kurt Lewin were graduate students of Stumpf (Bonacchi, 2009). Stumpf was a critical inspiration to Edmund Husserl (Fissette, 2009). Langfeld (1937) noted that Stumpf's death signaled that the "last important link with the early decades of experimental psychology, which produced Wundt, Müller and Ebbinghaus, was broken. It was a great period in which virgin soil was tilled and Stumpf had an important part in guiding the plow and sowing the seed from which our present day psychology has developed" (pp. 316–317).

GEORG ELIAS MÜLLER

There have always been diverse roads to greatness in any intellectual enterprise, but **Georg Elias Müller (1850–1934)**, by placing emphasis on extensive laboratory work, took the road less traveled. Many early psychologists were not strangers to the laboratory, but most were interested in providing encompassing systematic visions of the discipline. By contrast, Müller was content to focus on the rigorous experimental investigation of several important problem areas. As a result, some of the most productive work in the new experimental psychology came out of the University of Göttingen. Müller was head of the laboratory there for a fifty-year period from 1881 to 1931 and, according to Boring (1950), "As a power and an institution he was second only to Wundt" (p. 379). Boring also pointed out that Müller, unlike many of the other pioneers, "was little else than an experimental psychologist" (p. 379). His interests were directed almost entirely to problems of a psychological nature.

Müller, born on July 20, 1850, studied first at the University of Leipzig, and then at the University of Göttingen. He earned his Ph.D. under Hermann Lotze at Göttingen in 1873. In 1881, Lotze gave up his position at Göttingen to accept a position at the University of Berlin. He was succeeded by Müller, who remained at Göttingen for the remainder of his life. Müller retired in 1931 and died on December 23, 1934.

Müller, together with Friedrich Schumann and Alfons Pilzecker, was prolific in the areas of memory and association (McGaugh, 2000). Indeed, as noted by Diamond (1974b), the reports of the work on memory and association "run to over 2000 pages" (p. 271). Müller's early work on memory anticipated later work in the area of retroactive inhibition. For example, in an article published in 1900, Müller and Pilzecker reported studies of memory for an initial learning task along with memory for a second task. With the particular problems employed, memory was always better for the second task. Müller and Pilzecker noted that interpolated material may weaken or inhibit the associations necessary for the recall of the initial material. They went on to say, "For lack of any shorter expression we shall designate this type of inhibition as *retroactive inhibition*" (1900, p. 273).

Müller was also one of the first to conduct extensive studies on the problem of perseveration. He noted that some individuals shift easily from one task to another, whereas others tend to perseverate on an initial task. He even speculated about the practical consequences of differences in perseveration. Those who persevere on one task may be better fitted for some occupations, and those who shift quickly from task to task would be better fitted for different occupations. According to Diamond (1974b), Müller's work on perseveration provided "the first experimental breach in the theory that the 'train of thoughts' is determined solely by association, and it also points to the existence of a separate short-term memory process" (p. 271). Müller noticed that there was perseveration on materials presented to a subject, but there was also rapid decay in attention to the materials. His work is clearly an early precursor of later work in short-term memory.

Müller was one of the first to place strong emphasis on the importance of psychological variables in memorial and associative processes.

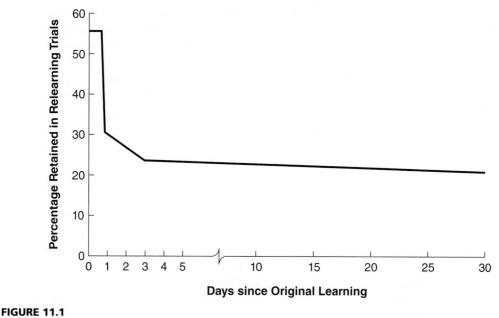

FIGURE 11.1

Ebbinghaus Curve Illustrating Retention as a Function of Time

new methodology and orientation he brought to the discipline (Danziger, 2001). Following Ebbinghaus, there was an exciting breadth of vision as to what could be included in the new discipline of psychology. Many psychologists might be tempted to agree with Titchener's (1910) opinion when he argued that Ebbinghaus's "recourse to nonsense syllables, as means to the study of association, marks the most considerable advance, in this chapter of psychology, since the time of Aristotle" (p. 381). There can be little question that he is a pivotal figure who changed the discipline.

WUNDT'S CONTEMPORARIES AND APPLIED PSYCHOLOGY

Titchener has seldom been regarded as a friend of applied psychology and it is true that his primary scientific interest was the adult normal mind. At the same time, as noted at the beginning of the chapter, Titchener recognized the importance of abnormal psychology, social psychology, animal psychology, and other subdisciplinary areas. He argued that all of these fields must be "cultivated,

if psychology is to progress" (1910, p. 29). He did not find time to include applied areas in his own research programs and placed the greatest value on pure scientific studies. At the same time, he was not closed to the future development of a psychology much broader in scope than he cultivated at Cornell University.

Wundt's other contemporaries also focused on basic scientific problems, but were open to a psychology larger in scope. Brentano was optimistic about the prospects of applied psychology. As noted, Ebbinghaus thought that the distinction between pure and applied studies is a function of context and not a basic or logical distinction. In one context, a problem could be regarded as basic or pure, but in another context, the same problem might be regarded as applied. With the study of a growing number of topical areas, it was inevitable that psychology, like the other sciences, would find it impossible to remain in the important but restricted environment of the laboratory. In Chapter 12, we will encounter a system that, from the beginning, advocated a psychology equally at home in the laboratory and in the world of daily life.

Review Questions

1. Contrast Titchener and Brentano with respect to methodology.
2. Give a typical example of a type of laboratory problem that might have been explored in Titchener's department at Cornell University.
3. Outline Titchener's distinction between primary and secondary attention. Do you regard the distinction as useful?
4. Briefly review Titchener's theory of meaning.
5. What were some of Titchener's criticisms of the James–Lange theory of emotion?
6. What was Washburn's "motor theory of consciousness" and how did her ideas about consciousness differ from Titchener's theory?
7. How did Brentano distinguish between inner perception and inner observation?
8. Outline Brentano's classification of mental phenomena.
9. Briefly describe Stumpf's contributions to the psychology of music. How did his work on tone psychology differ from Wundt's ideas?
10. Outline two of Georg Elias Müller's contributions to psychology.
11. Define *mental set* and show how it plays a role in problem solving.
12. Why was the work at the Würzburg school on imageless thought so crucial to the psychologies of Wundt and Titchener?
13. List five ways, as outlined by Postman, that Ebbinghaus influenced the field of psychology.
14. Briefly describe two important experimental findings coming out of Ebbinghaus's work on memory.

Glossary

act psychology   A system of psychological thought advanced by Franz Brentano emphasizing the forward-looking, intentional, planful character of experience. Brentano strongly rejected the simplistic characteristics of many of the early systems of psychological thought.

affect (affection)   According to Titchener's early theory, affections are the elementary mental processes associated with emotions. Later, he viewed affections primarily as sensations of pleasantness or unpleasantness.

attributes of elementary mental processes   According to Titchener, elementary processes such as sensations include four attributes: quality, intensity, clearness, and duration.

Brentano, Franz (1838–1917)   Founder of a system of psychological thought known as *act psychology*. Brentano emphasized a developmental and pluralistic methodology and the active, participatory, creative, and intentional characteristics of mental life.

context theory of meaning   According to Titchener, meaning depends on context or the association of a stimulus with other relevant surrounding stimuli.

desire   According to Brentano, a way of being conscious of an object marked by attraction or repulsion.

Ebbinghaus forgetting curve   A curve demonstrating that forgetting of nonsense material is rapid immediately after learning. After an initial rapid decline, the rate of forgetting slows down.

Ebbinghaus, Hermann (1850–1909)   One of the great pioneers in psychology, remembered for developing the nonsense syllable as a means of studying memory experimentally while minimizing past associations. Also developed an early form of a completion test and argued for the legitimacy of pure and applied psychology.

element   An abstraction referring to a simple irreducible sensation. *See also* Chapter 10 Glossary.

imageless thought   Belief that there are objective meanings in experience that are not associated with specific words, symbols, or signs.

introspection   A species of observation, but the subject to be observed is in experience itself. Thus, introspection is a kind of "looking in" to identify elements of experience and the way these elements combine, or the processes and adaptations of experience.

James–Lange theory of emotion   A theory of emotion advanced independently by William James and Carl Lange. The theory emphasizes the somatic substrate of emotional experiences and argues that the experience of emotion is the experience of the activity of the body—thus, the famous statement: We see a bear, we run, and we are afraid. James's later vision of emotion emphasizes constitutional determinants and the impossibility of separating cognition and emotion.

judgment   According to Brentano, consciousness of an object marked by belief or disbelief.

Külpe, Oswald (1862–1915)   Student of Wilhelm Wundt and well-known founder of an early psychological laboratory and school of thought at Würzburg. Külpe's experiments on imageless thought challenged the simplistic characteristics of other early systems.

mental set   Predisposition to respond in a given manner or tendency to organize an event in terms of an existing bias.

Müller, Georg Elias (1850–1934)   Prominent German psychologist remembered for his work in psychophysics, memory, learning, and vision. Numerous early psychologists studied with Müller at the University of Göttingen.

presentation   According to Brentano, consciousness of an object marked by simple awareness of the presence of the object.

primary attention   According to Titchener, primary attention is involuntary and typically activated by a sudden or strong stimulus.

secondary attention   According to Titchener, secondary attention is learned and persists under difficult conditions (e.g., staying alert while studying even under noisy circumstances).

structuralism   A system of psychological thought associated primarily with Edward Bradford Titchener, who attempted to model psychology after the more mature sciences, especially chemistry. Structuralism employed the method of introspection to search for the elements of consciousness and the rules by which elements combine.

Stumpf, Carl (1848–1936)   Student of Brentano and pioneer in the psychology of music. His holistic orientation focused on meaningful mental phenomena rather than arbitrary elements of consciousness.

system   An organized way of envisioning the world or some aspect of the world.

Titchener, Edward Bradford (1867–1927)   One of Wilhelm Wundt's best-known students and founder of a system of psychological thought known as structuralism. Titchener was a dominant force in U.S. psychology from the early 1890s until his death in 1927.

Washburn, Margaret Floy (1871–1939)   First woman to earn a doctorate in psychology and the second female president of the American Psychological Association. Washburn made significant contributions to the study of comparative psychology and was well known for her "motor theory of consciousness."

12

■ ■ ■

Functionalism

Nothing includes everything or dominates over everything. The word
"and" trails along after every sentence.

—WILLIAM JAMES (1909/1977)

In times of antiquity, process-oriented philosophers emphasized the fluid, changing, mutable, and dynamic nature of the world. The world of human experience is also a world of change, somewhat like a flowing stream. Psychologists in the functionalist tradition emphasized the developmental, adaptive, and dynamic features of experience. The result was a psychology radically different from structuralism. This chapter explores the loosely knit school of thought known as *functionalism*.

The term **functionalism** is difficult to define, but its meanings will unfold throughout the chapter. Whereas structuralism focused on *what* questions, functionalism explored *how* questions. The functionalists encouraged both basic and applied science and adopted a variety of methods. If there was one central focus, it was adaptation. Functionalism's most important figure was the American psychologist and philosopher William James.

WILLIAM JAMES AND HARVARD UNIVERSITY

Many Americans paid close attention to the birth and development of psychology in Germany. No one watched the emergence of the new science with a more careful eye than a brilliant young American named **William James (1842–1910)**. As early as 1875, James wrote articles for popular American magazines that informed the public about German psychology. In unsigned notices, he called attention to the publication of Wundt's *Principles of Physiological Psychology* (James, 1875) and to developments in applied psychology such as Franz Von Holtzendorff's work on the psychology of murder (James, 1876a).

James is difficult to characterize as a professional. His degree was in medicine, but he did not practice it. He trained in physiology, but spent little time teaching or researching it. He was not trained in psychology—indeed, the first lecture he heard on the subject was his own—nor was he trained in philosophy. Yet he held professorships in psychology and philosophy and

William James

enjoyed international acclaim in both disciplines. If American psychology had a favorite academic son, James would be the overwhelming choice. The philosopher Alfred North Whitehead (1938/1968) identified four great thinkers for "their achievements in philosophical assemblage. . . . These men were Plato, Aristotle, Leibniz and William James" (p. 2). The term *assemblage* refers to the sheer breadth of the contributions of these thinkers. As we will see, James delivers a psychology with enormous breadth in terms of both subject matter and methodologies, he stands at the headwaters of the psychology of religion with his classic book *The Varieties of Religious Experience*, and he was a pioneer in educational psychology. James was one of the founders of a new system of philosophy known as *pragmatism* and one of the first to understand that relations are as real as the things related. We will explore the rich meanings of this latter idea later, but it serves as a philosophical basis for the development of social psychology and affords new meanings for our concepts of science.

William James, the first of five children of Mary Robertson Walsh and Henry James Sr., was born in New York City on January 11, 1842. The other four children were Henry Jr., born in 1843 and destined to fame as a novelist and critic; Wilkinson, born in 1845; Robertson, born in 1846; and Alice, born in 1848. William was named after his grandfather William James of Albany, who migrated to the United States from Ireland around 1789. The perdurable elder William James, a staunch Calvinist, amassed an enormous fortune and fathered thirteen children by three wives. According to Allen (1967), the first wife died after giving birth to twin sons, and the second died after giving birth to a daughter. The third wife, Catherine Barber, the grandmother of William James, had seven sons and three daughters.

Henry James Sr., the fourth son of William and Catherine, was a lover of nature who found particular joy in hikes through fields and forests. The joy, however, was dampened by an ever-present Calvinistic conscience that produced guilt over any earthly pleasure. The tensions between the God of nature and the God of theology came to a head during a long convalescence from a tragic accident. Following a severe injury to his leg, Henry endured two amputations without benefit of anesthesia. The second amputation was necessary because of an infection that followed the first surgical procedure. The period of recovery marked the beginning of a life devoted to philosophy, religion, and introspection.

Though Henry completed a degree in theology and was ordained to preach, he never became a minister. Part of his reluctance was based on a conflict between orthodox Calvinism, with its emphasis on individual salvation, and his growing concern for the social gospel, with its emphasis on the salvation of the human lot. Brennan (1968) pointed out that Henry James's concern was for a truly caring and democratic society in which we seek not "individual salvation but universal salvation" (p. 17). Independently wealthy through a large inheritance from his father's estate, Henry James devoted most of his time to philosophical and religious interests. During the course of his life, he published fourteen books, which assured his niche in U.S. religion and philosophy.

In 1840, Mary Robertson Walsh and Henry James were married. It was a marriage that, according to Perry (1954), produced a tolerant, stimulating, and even indulgent environment including a great deal of travel, the stimulation of famous friends such as Ralph Waldo Emerson, and enrollment in the finest private schools in Europe and America. Perry goes on to note that the James children were "free not only from parental tyranny but through their parents, from the tyranny of the world. There was a general absence of institutional authority" (p. 42). As a result, according to Perry, "William James began to be William James at a very early age, and began to find and appropriate the food which his characteristic appetites required" (p. 44). When one of the James children spoke of a vocation, Henry James was concerned that it not be narrowing. In 1860, he reluctantly supported William's decision to study art, but William cut short his attempts to be a painter after deciding that the special genius required for that endeavor was missing.

Though evidence supports Perry's sunny vision of the James home, subsequent biographers are less sanguine about Henry's relations with his children. Simon (1998) describes an overly protective father involved in a consuming struggle to keep "his children isolated from a world that offered them choices, temptations, and satisfactions" (p. 63). She emphasized tense encounters between William and his father over the value of college. Henry was concerned about what he regarded as the stale university curricula coupled with the corruption and immorality of college students. Simon paints the picture of a controlling father who berated his children during occasional temper outbursts. Richardson (2006) called attention to the "intellectual chasms" between William and his father (pp. 83–84). Henry was a monist with God as the all-pervasive feature in the center of his universe, whereas William was a pluralist who took seriously the many things encountered in experience—a real God, a real moral life, a real material world, real evil, and so forth. For

Henry, individualism was an evil to be overcome, but William celebrated the individual and denigrated the social forces that undermine authentic selfhood (see Coon, 1996; James, 1899/1920b, p. 90). As noted in Perry's early biography, the James home was stimulating and offered enormous intellectual opportunities, but William's path to authentic selfhood was not uncomplicated as he worked through personal and philosophical differences with his father.

In the fall of 1861, William enrolled in the Lawrence Scientific School at Harvard University and studied the usual subjects: chemistry, biology, anatomy, and physiology. But, as noted by Perry (1954), "He was perpetually grazing and ruminating, wandering wherever the pasturage was good. . .[James's interests ranged] over the whole field of literature, history, science, and philosophy. They indicate a mind as energetic and acquisitive as it is voracious and incorrigibly vagrant" (p. 71). James's breadth of interest and extensive travel, including trips to Brazil and Europe, interfered with his medical training but helped refine his own vocational inclinations. He joined Louis Agassiz on a biological expedition to Brazil and discovered a profound distaste for mere collecting and classifying. In Europe, he became acquainted with leading figures such as Emil DuBois-Reymond, Wilhelm Wundt, and Hermann von Helmholtz. He also discovered a distaste for the rigors of routine laboratory work in physiology. James finally completed his M.D. in 1869, submitting a dissertation on the effects of coldness on the human body.

In 1870, James found himself in a state of intellectual and emotional turmoil, still uncertain about his vocational or personal prospects. During this period, he suffered intense anxiety and depression (brief summaries of James's symptoms and recovery are in McDermott, 1968, pp. 6–8). In 1872, James accepted an appointment as instructor of physiology at Harvard, but by 1873 he was expressing ambivalence about his career. Though a successful teacher, he knew that physiology was not his first love. In 1875, he offered a graduate course called the "Relations between Psychology and Physiology" and founded the psychology laboratory at Harvard. In 1876, James taught his first undergraduate course in psychology. Two years later, he signed a contract with Henry Holt and Company to write a psychology text. In 1878, James married Alice Howe Gibbens, a twenty-seven-year-old Boston schoolteacher.

Initial plans called for the text to be completed in two years, but James's classic *The Principles of Psychology* did not appear until 1890. The delay in publication was caused by the usual distractions of settling into a new career and James's wish to produce a significant work, not a mere collection of existing ideas and findings (King, 1992). His family obligations between 1878 and 1890 also colored the writing process. In that period, three sons and two daughters were born to William and Alice, and in 1885, their third child, Hermann, died of complications from whooping cough. Given such conditions, the gestation of *The Principles* was lengthy, but its success was nearly instantaneous. It became the leading text in the United States and was translated into many foreign languages. A briefer version of *The Principles*, published in 1892, was also a major success. *The Principles of Psychology* (1890) influenced generations of psychologists. Over seventy years after its publication, the historian of psychology Robert MacLeod (1969) said that it "is without question the most literate, the most provocative, and at the same time the most intelligible book on psychology that has ever appeared in English or in any other language" (p. iii).

More significant books followed in the wake of *The Principles,* including *The Will to Believe* (1897), *Talks to Teachers* (1899), and *The Varieties of Religious Experience* (1902). After 1900, James's publications were philosophical, though each one returned to specific psychological themes first discussed in *The Principles.* His key philosophical works include *Pragmatism* (1907), *A Pluralistic Universe* (1909), *The Meaning of Truth* (1909), and *Essays in Radical Empiricism,* published posthumously in 1912. The pattern of James's publications reveals the shift of his interest from psychology to philosophy. Even so, James the psychologist remained alive in James the philosopher. His acute mind returned to psychological topics time after time in his major philosophical works. As a philosopher, he remained interested in the welfare of the new discipline he helped found at Harvard University. James retired from Harvard in 1907 and died from a heart condition in 1910.

James embodied the Victorian ideal of a gentleman scholar. For his work and personality, appreciation has always outweighed criticism. He is eulogized for tolerance, industry, warmth, generosity, and intellectual conscience. The most common criticisms are directed at inconsistencies in James's system. Such criticisms are valid, but less so when James's psychology is understood in the context of his larger philosophical vision. We will now consider general characteristics of James's thought before focusing on his psychology.

General Characteristics of James's Thought

James's general philosophical orientation grew out of his sensitivity to people and their problems. Earle (1967) pointed out that "James addressed himself to the people. . .and he listened to the people to find out what life meant to them. He respected not so much their common sense as their common feelings and hopes" (p. 240). What emerged was a philosophy with face validity—a philosophy unique for its openness to differences and its willingness to experiment with methods. It is a philosophy that is integrated with the character of American thought. It is not pessimistic or optimistic—it is, above all, practical—but it leaves ample room for theoretical and nonutilitarian intellectual endeavor. Perhaps its major hallmark is its believability. Seldom is there anything in James that seems strained, narrow, superficial, or one sided, and his ideas are rich and complex and include apparent contradictions that have long inspired psychologists (Allport, 1943). James's psychology and philosophy are cut from the same cloth, so it is important to grasp the themes that run throughout all his writings.

INDIVIDUALISM A strong individualistic quality runs throughout James's writings. His emphasis on the importance of the individual was illustrated earlier in Chapter 1 in our discussion of the philosophy of history. James believed that a purely *Zeitgeist* theory of history causes us to go beyond scientific determinism into fatalism. He believed that circumstances shape individuals but, in turn, individuals act on the world and shape it in ways that would not happen without the unique contribution of the individual. Thus, individuals *and* circumstances make history.

James made extensive use of biographies and case studies to illustrate the importance of the individual. He believed that experience and reality are not easily separable. Indeed, we come down to reality, as such, in the experience of the individual. When we get away from individual experience, we study abstractions and are thus removed from what is most fundamental. James did not rule out normative analysis, but such analysis should itself be tested against experience; some view James as an early qualitative researcher (Carol & Owens, 2007).

Another strand of James's individualism arrives in his fierce denunciation of the impersonal and hollow forces found in large bureaucratic organizations. He has sometimes been portrayed as an insulated academic removed from the concerns of daily life. Coon (1996), however, documents James's active political involvement in the 1890s and his vigorous resistance to the growth of imperializing and dehumanizing forces in government, the military, and large corporations. One of his greatest concerns was with the failure of large institutions to recognize and honor traditional values of freedom, individuality, and pluralism.

MULTIPLE LEVELS OF ANALYSIS Trained in physiology and medicine, James was a strong believer in emphasizing the biological and physiological correlates of behavior. Nevertheless, he was not a reductionist. He understood, with equal vigor, the importance of the broad psychological world of experience along with the biological correlates. For James, there is a real sense in which experience cannot be reduced and cannot be explained by resorting to an alien biological substrate. His classic book *The Varieties of Religious Experience* illustrates this point. In James's day, it was popular to "explain" religious experiences in terms of neurological processes. James insisted that neurological processes are also applicable to atheistic beliefs. Even if one were to discover the biological basis of belief, that would not undermine its validity. He argued that the claims of theism and atheism must be adjudicated on other grounds. James affirmed multiple levels of analysis: molecular, biological, psychological, sociological, philosophical—all are legitimate and have their special value and application. For James, error begins when we believe that all things can be subsumed under any one rubric. This latter point leads to the next major characteristic of James's thought—his pluralism.

JAMESIAN PLURALISM In *Pragmatism,* James (1907/1975b) argued that the monism–pluralism issue is "the deepest and most pregnant question that our minds can frame" (p. 141). Although James was open to the possibility that there may be only one real thing and that all else is derived from that one reality (monism), he was nevertheless a pluralist and repeatedly referred to himself in that way (see 1909/1975a, pp. 124–125; 1909/1977, p. 26; 1912/1976, p. 133).

James's **pluralism** had implications for his psychology (Woody & Viney, 2009). The first implication is methodological. If we survey James's psychological and philosophical works, we discover a pragmatic pluralism in which methodology becomes subservient to vision. James embraced a variety of methods and was a methodological pluralist (see Viney, 1989). James's pluralism also had profound implications for the subject matter of psychology (see Viney, King, & King, 1992). Though experience is primary in his philosophy, there is no one content area (e.g., learning, sensing, and emotion) or worldview (Wiggins, 2009) that is foundational for all other areas; questions of pluralism or unification remain important in psychology (Sternberg, 2005). James's psychology had enormous scope, including basic and applied problems, the psychology of religion, and even paranormal phenomena (Sommer, 2012)—much to the dismay of his colleagues who believed psychic research was a pseudoscience that embarrassed the scientific integrity of psychology (Coon, 1992).

FREE WILL Few psychologists have struggled with free will and determinism with the intensity that James devoted to the issue. On one hand, he agreed that science, including psychology, may conduct business on the assumption of determinism. At the same time, James (1890/1981) insisted that science "must be constantly reminded that her purposes are not the only purposes, and that the order of uniform causation which she has use for, and is therefore right in postulating, may be enveloped in a wider order, on which she has no claims at all" (p. 1179). So James leaves room for a methodological determinism for psychology and science. But at the same time that psychology may proceed on the basis of a methodological determinism, James argued that we will probably never write a biography on an individual life in advance.

Although James reserved a place for methodological determinism in science, he rejected metaphysical determinism. In his early years, he was a determinist. During his period of depression and emotional crisis in the early 1870s, he abandoned metaphysical determinism with the declaration, "My first act of free will shall be to believe in free will" (1920a, p. 147). The idea for the affirmation of free will by an act of free will came to James through the philosopher Jules Lequier via Charles Renouvier (Viney, 1984, 1997).

James's best-known statement on the free will–determinism issue is in his article "The Dilemma of Determinism" (1884a, 1979a, pp. 114–140). For James, determinism is more consistent with monism, whereas belief in free will, even a limited free will, is more consistent with pluralism. James argued that the concept of causality, from a philosophical perspective, is as ambiguous as the concept of freedom. He believed there are ambiguities associated with the

future and real possibilities. He believed in regularities, so his was not an untrammeled free will. Indeed, he found that freedom is hard won and exercised only through effortful striving.

MORALISTIC PSYCHOLOGY AND PHILOSOPHY Rambo (1980) has pointed out that James's concern with what people *should* or *ought* to do influenced his writings. For example, James distinguishes between *easygoing* and *strenuous moods.* In the easygoing mood, we become perfunctory and lazy, but in the strenuous mood, we seize the opportunities for action and work with energy and enthusiasm. James believed we all have the capacity for the strenuous mood, but that capacity must be cultivated. In his famous chapter on habit in *The Principles,* he counseled, "Keep the faculty of effort alive in you by a little gratuitous exercise every day. . .do every day or two something for no other reason than that you would rather not do it, so that when the hour of dire need draws nigh, it may find you not unnerved and untrained to stand the test" (1890/1981, p. 130). James seldom lost an opportunity to apply psychology to human nature. He wanted a basic experimental psychology but one that made a useful difference in our daily lives as individuals and as cultures; he therefore wrote extensively about war and peace with emphasis on the prevention of armed conflict (Deutsch & Coleman, 2012).

RADICAL EMPIRICISM James lamented the misleading nature of brief names, but preferred that his philosophy be called *radical empiricism.* A fundamental postulate of **radical empiricism**, according to James (1909/1975a), is "that the only things that shall be debatable among philosophers shall be things definable in terms drawn from experience" (p. 6). The term *radical* means that things that are experienced must not be ignored. It also implies our right to exclude things that are not definable in terms drawn from experience. James was quick to admit, however, that there may be many real things that are not experienced. He was open to new possibilities and to borderline phenomena or to things that some people claim to experience and that others claim not to experience. Radical empiricism, for James, meant that we must find a place for everything that is a genuine part of experience. The term *radical* also implies that monism will be regarded as a hypothesis (James, 1897/1979b, p. 5). For James, any monism is a hypothesis open to the test of experience.

James did not believe, however, that monistic conceptions square with experience. He argued that monism, born in rationalism, tells us what to count and what not to count. Thus, if one is a materialistic monist, the whole mental realm is either not counted at all or rationalized. If one is an idealistic monist, the physical realm is intellectualized. James failed to find any monistic vantage point so encompassing that it could include everything—hence, his statement at the opening of this chapter: "Nothing includes everything" (1909/1977, p. 145). Monistic orientations whether they be inspired in political, religious, psychological, economic, philosophical, or scientific arenas are never sufficiently comprehensive or responsive to the ever-growing breadth and fullness of human experience in a changing and sometimes promiscuous world. According to James (1897/1979b), something "is still wrong and other and outside and unincluded, from *your* point of view, even though you be the greatest of philosophers" (p. 145).

Given James's view of process, it is questionable that he could ever believe in the adequacy of any monism. He truly believed that the world is in process, that creation was not an event but is an ongoing process, happening now as always; for better or worse, we are all participants. James once asked, "What has concluded, that we might conclude in regard to it?" (1910/1978, p. 190). Since the world is in process, there is no vantage point from which one can make the big claim for truth with a capital *T,* because our vantage points are themselves in constant flux. As a consequence, we must be content with provisional and practical truths that are subject to change. James's radical empiricism was nascent in *The Principles* (see Crosby & Viney, 1990) and is a key to understanding his system of psychology.

PRAGMATISM   The final general characteristic of James's worldview is his pragmatic philosophy. For James, **pragmatism** is a method, a theory of truth, and a way of thinking about the world. It opposes absolutistic schemes and contents itself with provisional (but workable) concepts and methodologies. James (1907/1975b) instructed his readers as follows: "If you follow the pragmatic method, you cannot look on any such word [e.g., *energy, reason,* and *God*] as closing your quest. You must bring out of each word its practical cash-value, [and view it] as a program for more work" (pp. 31–32). For James, words, theories, concepts, and the like are "instruments, not answers to enigmas."

The Varieties of Religious Experience illustrates the pragmatic method in which beliefs and practices are judged by the work they accomplish in the world. If good work is accomplished, then a belief or practice is vindicated. James (1907/1975b) rejected the idea that any belief or theory could make the claim to be "absolutely a transcript of reality" (p. 33).

James's pragmatism and pluralistic empiricism found a receptive intellectual climate in the United States. The commonsense nature of his philosophy, his unusual ability to communicate with both academics and the public, and the sheer charm of his personality combined to make him a force within psychology.

Jamesian Psychology

James (1890/1981) defined *psychology* as "the science of mental life, both of its phenomena and of their conditions" (p. 15). By *phenomena,* James meant feelings, cognitions, desires, and so on, and he centered psychology on personal consciousness (Taylor, 2010). By *conditions of mental life,* he meant bodily and social processes that influence mental processes. James defined *psychology* as the study of mental processes, but such processes take the psychologist into behavioral, physiological, and cultural dimensions.

HABIT   James believed that much of human life is understandable in terms of habits acquired through learning and education. He stressed the physical basis of habit by pointing out that stimulation follows the path of least resistance in living tissue. For example, a joint once sprained becomes more vulnerable to future stress. Similarly, a pathway once established in the nervous system is likely to be used again.

James discussed habit in functional terms, as essential to civilization and to the economy of individual action. Our lives follow habitual patterns in manner of dress, ways of greeting and departing, ways of getting to and performing work, and ways of eating and even sleeping. In a famous analogy, James suggested that habit does for the individual and for society what the flywheel does for an internal combustion engine. The flywheel smoothes the operation and keeps the engine running just as habit keeps us in our niche even when circumstances are difficult.

For James, the goal of education was instilling good habits. He believed that the individual's success or failure depended on achieving this goal. The commonsense quality of Jamesian psychology is best illustrated in his famous chapter on habit. We have, at every turn, an abundance of examples: the accomplished pianist who practices eight hours a day, the Olympic gold medal winner who tells of years of training, and the winner of a Nobel Prize who, for years, labors through eighty-four-hour workweeks.

James's chapter ends with practical suggestions for launching productive habits and breaking bad ones. He would counsel us to move toward a new habit with great initiative, enlist social support by making a public pledge, and never suffer an exception to occur. We should schedule activities, if possible, to decrease the expression of the old habit. Likewise, we should invite opportunities that promote the new habit.

THE STREAM OF THOUGHT James contended that psychologists abandon the empirical method when they dissected mental life into simple sensations. The reason for this contention is that, in our normal experience, we do not have simple sensations. Rather, according to James, continuities, relations, and complexities define consciousness. Psychology's starting point is not simple sensations but thinking itself. From such a starting point, James discussed five general characteristics of the **stream of thought**.

First, James found that thoughts are personal and *owned;* they are *our* thoughts. Such a contention runs headlong into difficulty. We are reluctant to own some dreams or intrusive thoughts and there are obvious cases of pathological dissociation that contradict James's belief in the personal nature of consciousness. James recognized the difficulty. His explanation illustrated an early recognition of unconscious processes. He argued that hysterical anesthesias, automatic writing, and multiple personalities are manifestations of what he called *secondary personal selves* that are sometimes out of touch with the normal self. But James believed that the various forms of dissociation do not constitute an exception to his position that thought tends to be part of a personal consciousness. He noted that within a so-called secondary personality there is some degree of organization and a sense of identity. He also argued that there is some limited communication between primary and secondary personalities.

A second characteristic of the stream of thought is that thoughts are constantly changing. James believed that the experience of constancy is an illusion that results from inattention. He was convinced that our state of mind is always in process; thus, a present state is not like a previous state. It may appear that we have the same view out a window each day, but *we* are a bit different each day, and the view itself is slightly different.

A third characteristic is that thought is characterized by continuity rather than division or separation. Again, difficulties arise with such a contention, but James anticipated the difficulties. A loud clap of thunder might appear as a separate and discrete event that breaks in on the continuity of thought. But James argued that what we hear "is not thunder *pure,* but thunder-breaking-upon-silence-and-contrasting-with-it" (1890/1981, p. 234). Time gaps such as we encounter in sleep would appear to contradict James's third characteristic, but he argued that consciousness following a time gap "belongs to" or is continuous with consciousness before it. It is the same thought that takes up the problem this morning that was put to rest last evening.

A fourth characteristic is that human thought conveys a sense of something other than itself. In other words, it is cognitive. The term *cognitive* is derived from a Latin verb *cognoscere*, which means "to know" or "to become acquainted with." James contended that the bridges we build between our past thoughts of an object and our present thought of the same object condition our belief in an outer reality.

The final characteristic of thought, according to James, is that selectivity, discrimination, choice, and shifting interests are in its very nature. James believed that selectivity is based on the nature and characteristics of the stimulus, aesthetics, and personal values. He argued that we find it quite impossible to be impartial in terms of how we direct our interest and attention.

THE SELF   For James, the *self* includes the totality of all things that belong to us: friends, children, a home, clothing, a pet, reputation, memory, perception, and a physical structure. He identified three constituents of the self: the material self, the social self, and the spiritual self. In addition to these, and in a class apart, was the pure ego.

The most intimate part of the material "me" is the body—and some parts are more "intimately me" than others. Clothing is also part of the **material self** (Watson, 2004), as well as family, furniture, collections, and other possessions. James argued that losing a possession is losing part of the self. So, we lose or gain with the ebb and flow of our possessions.

The **social self**, according to James, is not one but a variety of selves. He contended that we have a different social self for each person who recognizes us. He emphasized context and role-playing as determinants of social selves. Although a child may be shy or polite in the presence of parents or teachers, he or she may be "appropriately rude" or assertive in the presence of friends. For this reason, many descriptive adjectives assigned to us are names for a particular social self. We are honest, loyal, obedient, courageous,

competent, but not all at once and not in every social situation. A football player, brash and courageous on the field, may stand weak and inept in front of a speech class. All of us have experienced such duplicity or multiplicity, but James's theory of the self points to a way out of such experiences.

The material and social selves are outward manifestations, but the **spiritual self** is personal, subjective, and intimate. It is an inner citadel that sits in judgment on the other selves. Indeed, the other components of the self belong to the spiritual self and it is more permanent than the rest. In James's view, the spiritual self is a source of effort or will; it is a source of change and desire for change.

James believed that the selves engaged in tensions and rivalries. Tensions also flourish among potential selves. We might wish to be wealthy, athletic, scholarly, witty, philanthropic, adventurous, and beautiful. We cannot, however, appropriate the energy to be everything. We must be judicious and direct energy in ways that strike a balance between our ideals and reality.

James argued that our **self-esteem** is a function of the ratio of our success and our pretensions as follows:

$$\text{Self-esteem} = \frac{\text{Success}}{\text{Pretensions}}$$

James pointed out that the greatest burdens are lifted by adjusting pretensions downward. We may experience great release when we accept imperfection on some activity or when we realize we can drop the endeavor. James called attention to the different pretensions associated with the different selves. The material self may find esteem in wealth, the social self may find esteem in recognition, and the spiritual self may find esteem in purity or moral superiority.

Under the topic of pure ego, James contended that psychology encounters its most puzzling question: What is the nature of personal identity and the sense of continuity that runs through the present self and reaches backward and forward? Is there an arch-ego and, if so, what is its nature? James reviewed spiritualist theories of a substantive soul, transcendentalism, and associationism, finding difficulties in each. He concluded that psychology must content itself for the time with a mere functional approach to the self. Such an approach can do real work in the world and that is scientifically satisfying. For his part, James was open to the possibility that science has no special claims on dimensions of the self and other realities. James never demanded that any perspective, including science, provide totality.

THE EMOTIONS   James's original paper, titled "What Is an Emotion," published in 1884, inspired controversy. The reaction to the 1884 paper prompted James to publish another paper in 1894, titled "The Physical Basis of Emotion." The focus of the early papers was on the physiological correlates of emotion, but he explored some of the rich experiential dimensions of emotion in later works such as: *The Varieties of Religious Experience, The Will to Believe, Talks to Teachers,* and *Essays in Radical Empiricism.* In these later works, he examined topics such as the value of emotions, the control of emotions, paradoxical emotions, and what he called *the stream of feeling.* His larger view of emotion goes far beyond his physiological theory (see Viney, 1992).

A hallmark of Jamesian psychology is its commonsense appeal, but his physiological approach to emotion seems counterintuitive. The theory, advanced independently by Danish physiologist **Carl Georg Lange (1834–1900)**, has come to be called the **James–Lange theory of emotion**. James admitted that his theory departs from common sense. Let's say you are hiking in the woods when you encounter a bear. Common sense would say that you see the bear, become afraid, and then run. But the James–Lange theory insists that bodily changes precede the experience of emotion. In other words, you see the bear, run, and then experience fear. Or, as James tells us, "We feel sorry because we cry, angry because we strike, afraid because we tremble."

James could not imagine a disembodied emotion. If there were no activation, no arousal, how could there be an experience of emotion?

This problem puzzled him. In his article "The Physical Basis of Emotion," James (1894/1983) pointed out that his theory "assumes (what probably everyone assumes) that there must be a process of some sort in the nerve-centres for emotion" (p. 306). For James, the experience of emotion *is* the experience of the activity of the body. He never denied that stimuli evoke emotional behavior. We see a bear and run! The stimulus provokes emotional behavior. James did not deny the importance of context, either. If we see a bear in a zoo behind bars, or if we see a bear in the wilderness and we have a formidable weapon, we may not run. In James's view, a stimulus situation (a chance encounter with a bear in the woods or a view of a bear in a cage at the zoo) provokes an adaptive response. We may run or stand in admiration, depending on context.

We could see a bear and freeze in fright or we could see a bear and run. James would not deny that either reaction is possible but contend that the emotions associated with freezing are different from the emotions associated with running. The bodily conditions in the two circumstances are different and hence should be associated with different feelings.

James's physiological theory of emotion is still debated in the twenty-first century, and Papanicolaou (1989) has argued that there is still no evidence "indicating that the body is not a necessary condition of emotion. . . . Reports of affect, when detailed, are also reports of somatic sensations" (p. 127). James's vision of emotion, as set forth in *The Varieties* and in his philosophical works, recognized that some individuals are disposed to an optimistic outlook, whereas others are prone toward the darker side of things. James also found difficulty in separating emotion from cognition. The two, in his view, are interwoven.

INSTINCTS   James believed in instincts and was interested in events that play a role in their evolution within the individual. For example, habit and conditioning may gradually build on and replace instincts. The organism may become partial to the first stimulus to which it reacted. As an illustration, James cited Spalding (1873), who demonstrated that chicks born in the absence of a hen "will follow any moving object. And, when guided by sight alone, they seem to have no more disposition to follow a hen than to follow a duck or a human being. Unreflecting lookers-on, when they saw chickens a day old running after me. . . imagined that I must have some occult power over the creatures; whereas I had simply allowed them to follow me from the first" (p. 287).

James discussed the transiency of instincts. For example, the instinct to follow fades after a brief but critical period of time. Here again, he cited Spalding who placed hoods over chicks' heads and showed they would not follow after being hooded for a period of four days.

James believed that the principle of transiency is important in human and animal life. An instinct is ripe for only a brief period. The mode of expression first utilized is most likely to be followed or fixed and, according to James, there is an optimal moment for attaching an instinct to an appropriate stimulus and this optimal moment or moment of readiness has clear implications for educators. James believed instincts were important in early development and less important later. He believed that behaviors such as sucking, biting, clasping, crying, imitating, and certain fears are instinctive.

Dewsbury (1992) in a helpful overview traces the origins of James's interest in instincts, some of the details of James theory, and his influence on subsequent theorists. Dewsbury notes that while instincts are not at the center of Jamesian psychology, they are nevertheless present in the developmental core of the individual though they play changing roles as life proceeds.

MEMORY James opened his chapter on memory with a distinction between primary and secondary memory. **Primary memory**, according to James, is memory for the immediate past or the events that have most recently been in consciousness. He believed in a close connection between primary memory and afterimages—a topic of considerable interest in perception research. **Secondary memory**, for James, was memory proper. He defined it as knowledge of previous events that are not currently a part of thought or attention. James contended that the exercise of memory presupposes two things: first, the retention of a fact, and second, the demonstration of retention through reminiscence, recollection, reproduction, or recall.

James cited what he called the "heroic" work of Ebbinghaus on memory and concluded his chapter with a section on forgetting. He focused on the utility and the irregularities of forgetting. Under this latter subject, he included topics such as the difficulty of recall that sometimes occurs with strenuous effort and the subsequent ease with which the to-be-remembered material comes back when we relax. (Psychologists later described such forgetting as the "tip-of-the-tongue phenomenon.") James believed that memory is facilitated by quality of organization, interest, and active (as opposed to passive) repetition. He agreed with French psychologist Théodule Ribot that we have memories rather than memory. He believed that different individuals have different gifts for visual, auditory, tactile, verbal, and muscular memories.

In a lengthy footnote, James described his study on the transfer of learning. Briefly, he investigated whether learning lines from Victor Hugo's "Satyr" would shorten the time to learn lines from a different kind of material (Milton's *Paradise Lost*). He found that the learning of the first task did not facilitate the learning of the second task. This study foreshadowed later transfer of learning studies that proved embarrassing to the doctrine of formal discipline.

James's Legacy

James's leadership stimulated the expansion of the methodological, conceptual, and substantive boundaries of psychology. Some psychologists returned to a narrow, unified psychology after James. But in pluralistic America, such visions suffered at the hands of those infected with a Jamesian suspicion of grand, all-embracing schemes. James left us with a legacy that monism—any monism, be it spiritual, material, political, psychological, scientific, or religious—is but a hypothesis. The positive side of James's legacy is that he encouraged us to pursue alternatives. One of the greatest tributes to James is that his major works are in print a century after his death. He remains relevant!

James's continuing relevance is illustrated in scholarship on the ecological implications of radical empiricism, pluralism, and pragmatism (see Crosby, 1996; Heft, 2001). Though ecology, as a formal discipline, surfaced long after James's work, some scholars now argue for identifiable affinities between ecological perspectives and Jamesian metaphysics. James did call for the development of a deep and solemn sensitivity to the complexities of our relation to the world. For example, in a speech to a men's club at Harvard, he reminded his audience of the "innocent beasts [who] have had to suffer in cattle-cars and slaughter pens and lay down their lives that we might grow up, all fatted and clad, to sit together here in comfort and carry on this discourse" (1897/1979b, p. 47). James embraced the idea that human experience is not the highest or only type of experience extant in the universe. Neither are humans the only creatures with valuative types of experiences. Humans, he argued, "are tangents to the wider life of things" (1907/1975b, p. 144). James was not an ecologist and one can find isolated statements in his work that illustrate insensitivities to things we take for granted a century later. Nevertheless, his mature philosophy, with its strong emphasis on the importance of feelings, relations, particularity, diversity, perspective, and balance, provides a relevant metaphysical frame of reference for ecology.

HUGO MÜNSTERBERG

Though William James founded the first experimental laboratory in the United States, he was not suited to direct its activities or conduct experiments. Nevertheless, he wanted Harvard to maintain visible leadership in psychology at a time when competing universities established laboratories. A key to Harvard's leadership was to find an outstanding young scholar to direct the laboratory. James was impressed with the early career and promise of a feisty young psychologist

Hugo Münsterberg

named **Hugo Münsterberg (1863–1916)**, a former student of Wilhelm Wundt. James was aware that Münsterberg was critical of Wundt's work and also that his action theory of behavior was compatible with the James–Lange theory of emotion (Landy, 1992). Largely through James's efforts, Münsterberg was invited to join the Harvard faculty in 1892. He accepted and remained at Harvard until his death in 1916.

Münsterberg was born in Danzig, East Prussia (now Gdansk, Poland), on June 1, 1863. He received his Ph.D. under Wilhelm Wundt in 1885 at age twenty-two, and then earned an M.D. at the University of Heidelberg two years later. He moved to Harvard following a brief but productive assignment at Freiburg. His major assignment at Harvard was to run the laboratory but, like James, Münsterberg's interests were wide ranging. In fact, as discussed in Chapter 18, he is celebrated as a significant figure in the history of applied psychology (Landy, 1992).

Though Münsterberg established residence in the United States well before his thirtieth birthday, he never relinquished his strong German identity. As World War I approached,

Münsterberg's German sympathies became apparent to Americans. He had initially won favor in the United States, but fell into disfavor because of his public support for Germany (Spillmann & Spillmann, 1993). Münsterberg died of a stroke in 1916 at the age of fifty-three. His early death may well have been hastened because of the tensions he experienced over his divided loyalties and public rejection.

Münsterberg's Psychology

Though Münsterberg rejected the larger philosophical implications of James's pragmatism, he delivered a psychology that was tuned to the daily lives of people (Morawski, 1983). For example, Münsterberg (1916) wrote a book, *The Photoplay*, that analyzed "moving pictures," marking it as an early work on the psychology of film. Despite his early challenges to application of scientific psychology, he became a pioneer in several applied fields (Benjamin, 2006). His applications of psychology to daily life were often not grounded in solid experimental work, but they legitimized a broader vision of psychology. Münsterberg can be counted as a pioneer in educational psychology, industrial psychology, psychotherapy, and psychology and law. He argued that psychologists should acquaint themselves with the world of work, the school environment, and the courtroom before undertaking applied research.

Münsterberg's book *On the Witness Stand* (1908) is a classic in forensic psychology. The book explores problems associated with topics such as eyewitness testimony, methods of interrogation, suggestibility of witnesses in court, false confessions, and lie detection. On this latter topic, Münsterberg, like others dating back to Galen, was aware of the relationship between physiological arousal and emotional processes. He believed that the emotions associated with telling a lie might be detectable through physiological measures such as respiration and blood pressure. Münsterberg also believed that the day would come when psychological experts would be invited to the courtroom to testify, just like chemists, physicians, and other expert professional witnesses,

and he encouraged courts to consider findings from psychological research (Bornstein & Meissner, 2008). He anticipated later laboratory work on psychology and law (1913, pp. 292–293). Münsterberg's work in this area was a precursor of later efforts in the 1970s to establish formal scientific and professional organizations and educational programs in psychology and the law (see Packer & Borum, 2013).

In addition to legal psychology, Münsterberg was fascinated with clinical psychology. His text *Psychotherapy* (1909) is broad in scope with a discussion of the causes of emotional disorders along with treatment strategies and case histories. It also includes a discussion of the role of religion in treatment, the role of the physician, and the interest of the community. On treatment strategies, Münsterberg advised against a strict, systematic approach. He argued that the therapist should adjust the treatment to the special needs and abilities of the patient. Though hypnosis and suggestibility played strong roles in his therapy, he also recognized other techniques. For example, the patient experiencing depression might be asked to go through the motions of joyful expression. Münsterberg (1909) believed that such a process, though artificial, might open "the channels of motor discharge" (p. 218). He also noted that the confidence of the therapist, the capacity of the therapist for empathy, and the expectations of the patient all played crucial roles in psychotherapy.

In his final chapter on psychotherapy and the community, Münsterberg discussed the problems of prevention of emotional disorders. He noted the destructive effects of social and legal injustice and the problem, for the individual and for society, of finding a middle road between the extremes of inhibition and expression. Those extremes, also recognized by Pavlov and Freud, play pivotal roles in emotional disorders. Münsterberg contended that society should give due attention to processes that block emotional expression. On the other hand, he recognized that society is impossible without inhibition. In his view, the "middle way is again the real hygienic ideal" (1909, p. 397).

Münsterberg's *Psychology and Industrial Efficiency* (1913) is another classic in applied psychology (Landy, 1997). His aim, as stated at the outset, was "to sketch the outlines of a new science which is intermediate between the modern laboratory psychology and the problems of economics: the psychological experiment is systematically to be placed at the service of commerce and industry" (p. 3). The book covers content areas that would later comprise the subject matter of industrial and organizational (I-O) psychology. He explored topics such as vocational fitness, economy of movement, the problems of monotony and fatigue, job satisfaction, and advertisement, and he remains a pioneer in vocational counseling (Porfeli, 2009). He believed work can be one of the greatest sources of joy, pride, and satisfaction, but can also produce great depression and discouragement. Few things are as important as the systematic study of work, its conditions, and its relation to personality. The pioneering work of Hugo Münsterberg on industrial efficiency lives on around the world, and though I-O psychology has expanded and evolved in terms of content and methods, it thrives as one of the most vigorous topical areas in applied psychology (see Bryan & Vinchur, 2013).

Münsterberg is a giant in the history of applied psychology. His most original contributions were in forensic psychology and industrial psychology—two areas that gained momentum in the latter part of the twentieth century (Moskowitz, 1977). Though he did not identify with functionalism, his sympathies and contributions are more related to that tradition than to any other. Münsterberg had no wish to compromise experimental psychology; he simply had a larger vision of what counts as genuine experimental psychology.

G. STANLEY HALL AND CLARK UNIVERSITY

The functionalist spirit in psychology is nowhere better illustrated than in the work of **Granville Stanley Hall (1844–1924)** who, according to Averill (1990), explored "every human area and relationship: genetics, childhood, adolescence, family, education, aberration, and religious phenomena" (p. 125). No longer was psychology concerned solely with the dissection of consciousness. Expanding on the pluralistic and pragmatic tradition of his teacher William James, Hall challenged the conservative and stuffy psychology of his day. In a deliberate manner, he delivered a process-oriented evolutionary perspective. In his autobiography, Hall (1923) said, "As soon as I first heard it in my youth I think I must have been almost hypnotized by the word 'evolution,' which was music to my ear and seemed to fit my mouth better than any other" (p. 357). Because of the freshness of his evolutionary perspective and his breadth, organizational skills, energy, and enthusiasm, he was an enormous force in the new discipline.

Granville Stanley Hall was born on February 1, 1844, in his grandfather's house in Ashfield, Massachusetts. He was educated in the rural setting of western Massachusetts. At age sixteen, he was examined by a school committee and awarded a certificate of competence to teach in the public schools. He taught briefly in Chapel Falls, Massachusetts, before enrolling in college preparation studies at Williston Academy in Easthampton, Massachusetts. Hall later entered Williams College, where he studied Greek, Latin, and mathematics. He graduated from Williams in 1867 at age twenty-three and enrolled that fall in Union Theological Seminary in New York City.

The liberal climate of Union and the cosmopolitan setting combined to challenge his conservative and orthodox values. In her biography of Hall, Ross (1972) called attention to his "clandestine excursions" during the first two years of seminary (p. 32). He attended the theater, sampled a variety of religious services, and immersed himself in New York City's diverse cultural and intellectual opportunities. In 1869, Hall took a leave from the seminary to engage in philosophical studies in Germany. This period of personal and intellectual growth marked a shift from theology to natural philosophy. In 1870, Hall was back in New York to complete his final year at Union.

Following graduation, Hall's struggle to follow an academic career was beset with compromises between his real interests and practical financial necessities. Tall and imposing, Hall engaged in private tutoring and a four-year teaching assignment in the humanities at Antioch College in Yellow Springs, Ohio. With savings from his teaching assignment, Hall, at age thirty-two, enrolled in graduate studies at Harvard University. He did most of his work with William James but also studied physiology and psychopathology. Ross (1972) noted that his doctorate in 1878 was "the first in the field of psychology to be given in this country" (p. 79). Francis Bowen, William James, and Frederic H. Hedge signed Hall's handwritten dissertation on the muscular perception of space. Always strained, the relationship between Hall and James grew increasingly volatile over the years.

Following completion of his doctoral studies at Harvard, Hall returned to Germany where he worked with luminaries such as Emil DuBois-Reymond, Karl Ludwig, Hermann von Helmholtz, and Wilhelm Wundt. In 1881, Hall delivered a series of lectures at Johns Hopkins University, and these were followed by a full-time professorial appointment. Johns Hopkins offered space and money for a psychology laboratory that Hall (1923) described as the "largest and most productive laboratory of its kind in the country up to the time of my leaving" (p. 227). (Hall and James quarreled over priority in establishing the first American psychology laboratory.) At considerable personal expense, Hall founded *The American Journal of Psychology,* the first of its kind in English. The first volume was published in 1889 and he served as the journal's first editor.

Within a decade of completing the first Ph.D. in psychology, Hall was such a visible figure in the academic world that he received an invitation to become the first president of Clark University, founded in Worcester, Massachusetts, by Jonas Gilman Clark. As president of a new university, Hall was not hesitant to be chauvinistic for the new science, shaping the program at Clark into a dominant force in U.S. psychology.

Hogan (2003) observed, "For the most part, Hall's writings consider only two 'racial' minorities, Jews and Blacks" (p. 30), and Hall's biases clearly fit the existing prejudices of his times (Cravens, 2006). Despite racist themes that emerge in his writings (Youniss, 2006), his behavior revealed a complex individual who reached across the cultural divides he appeared to support. For example, in his journal, *Pedagogical Seminary*, he published an anonymous paper that challenged racist assumptions as well as the quality of the intelligence testing methods cited to support racist views (Anonymous, 1916; Ware, 2006). He also challenged prevailing stereotypes by providing opportunities to faculty and students who were underrepresented at universities. During a period of ripe anti-Semitism on college campuses, Hall invited three Jewish scholars to join the Clark faculty: anthropologist Franz Boas (1858–1942), physicist Albert A. Michelson (1852–1931), and chemist Morris Loeb (1863–1912). Additionally, as noted by Guthrie (2003), prior to his doctoral work Hall had sought to teach at Howard University, a historically black university in Washington, D.C., and Hall was one of the few psychologists to encourage African American students to enroll in graduate studies at other institutions as well. Under his direction, **Francis Sumner (1895–1954)** was awarded a Ph.D. from Clark University in 1920, making him the first African American to earn a doctorate in psychology in the United States.

Sumner's productive career resulted in more than forty-five publications on topics such as perception, advertising, and the psychology of religion. He proposed strategies for the higher education of African American youth, an issue he struggled with against the smothering backdrop of segregation (Sawyer, 2000). Sumner headed the psychology department at Howard University from 1930 until his death in 1954 (Guthrie, 2003). During Sumner's tenure, Howard was dubbed the "Black Harvard" and played a role in training influential psychologists such as Mamie Phipps Clark (1917–1983) and Kenneth B. Clark (1914–2005), later to become the first African American president of the American Psychological Association (Phillips, 2000). At Columbia University, Otto Klineberg supervised

Kenneth Clark's dissertation and encouraged the National Association for the Advancement of Colored People (NAACP) to cite Clark's research "as evidence of the harmful effects of school segregation" (Harris, 1999b, p. 793). After earning their Ph.D.s from Columbia, the Clarks continued to study prejudice and the impact of segregation on children, research that was cited in the 1954 Supreme Court case *Brown v. Board of Education* (Jackson, 2006). Only months before Sumner's death, the Supreme Court's ruling brought a legal end to segregated education in the United States. Although Hall died thirty years prior to the decision, he likely would have applauded the outcome.

Beginning with his status as the first to earn a doctorate in psychology, Hall was on the vanguard of several important developments in psychology. Wapner (1990) provided an overview of Hall's career in psychology during his thirty-one years as president of Clark University. Let's look at a few of his more noteworthy achievements:

1. Hall founded and often edited journals such as the *Pedagogical Seminary* (now the *Journal of Genetic Psychology*), the *Journal of Religious Psychology and Education*, and the *Journal of Applied Psychology*.
2. He founded and organized the American Psychological Association (APA) and served as its first president in 1892 and as its thirty-third president in 1924 (Sokal, 1992).
3. Hall brought Sigmund Freud and Carl Jung to the United States in 1909, introducing U.S. psychologists to psychoanalytic thinking.
4. His department at Clark University was a leader in producing many doctoral students in psychology.
5. His enormous scholarly output, consisting of a great many books, articles, and lectures, helped shape the direction of American psychological thought. We will examine this achievement in more detail as we turn to a consideration of Hall's viewpoint in psychology.

Hall retired from the presidency of Clark in 1920 but continued to work on personal and psychological projects. He completed *Senescence* in 1922 and his autobiography, *Life and Confessions of a Psychologist,* in 1923. He died of pneumonia on April 24, 1924. Ross (1972) noted, "At the small funeral in Worcester, the local minister caused a brief scandal by criticizing Hall for not having appreciated the importance of the institutional church, a scandal which Hall surely would have relished" (p. 436).

Though Hall's accomplishments were extensive, personal difficulties and tragedies tortured him. His first wife and an eight-year-old daughter were accidentally asphyxiated in 1890 (Hogan, 2003). Later, Hall's second wife was hospitalized with a severe mental disorder. Following the loss of his first wife, Hall lost himself in work and failed to develop a close relationship to his oldest child, Robert Granville Hall. Throughout his life, Hall was torn between passivity and aggression and between depression and stormy manic-like periods. He had an apparent need to surround himself with people who were dependent and accommodating. In an informative article, Sokal (1990) discussed this trait and its influence on the development of psychology at Clark. For all of his personal difficulties, Hall ranks as a key figure in U.S. psychology. We turn now to a further consideration of some of his contributions.

Hall's Psychology

Hall did not deliver a tightly reasoned system of psychology with clear-cut definitions and rigid methodological prescriptions. However, his published works and the experimental program he advocated had a definite thematic quality. In discussing Hall's laboratory at Johns Hopkins, Pauley (1986) noted that the major topics investigated were "binocular vision, perception of time, coordination of action between the two halves of the body and the relationship between psychological attention and muscular movement" (p. 28). Pauley pointed out that Hall envisioned a much wider experimental program, but most students, in fact, worked on these topics. Hall published in all these areas, but the focus of his early research was on the psychology of childhood (White, 1992). His long-term interest was life-span development.

In the preface to his classic *Adolescence,* Hall (1904) celebrated the "extension of evolution into the psychic field" (p. v). He argued that knowledge of the soul is dependent on knowledge of the history of the soul in the world. Thus, the study of the history of the individual should be complemented by studies of the history of the species. Hall (1904) repeatedly expressed the belief that "the child and the race are each keys to the other" (p. vii). He adopted the idea that ontogeny (the history of the individual) recapitulates phylogeny (the history of the species). Such a belief comes ready-made with methodological and substantive prescriptions. On the methodological side, Hall argued that, "animal, savage, and child-soul can never be studied by introspection" (p. vii). The methodology of psychology would have to be broader and more biological. On the substantive side, Hall declared, "We must go to school to learn the folk-soul, learn of criminals and defectives, animals, and in some sense go back to Aristotle in rebasing psychology on biology" (pp. vii–viii). Clearly, Hall's approach to psychology represents a radical departure from Titchener's psychology. Hall's developmental-evolutionary approach gives concrete expression to ideas that were included in the philosophy of William James, but not always translated into specific programs for action.

His vision for an experimental child psychology was set forth in a popular magazine article titled "A Children's Institute." In that article, Hall (1910) campaigned for institutes devoted to broad-based studies of children. Such institutes would have divisions or specializations on a host of topics such as growth norms, language development, special diseases of children, hygiene, juvenile crime, and educational techniques (Brooks-Gunn & Johnson, 2006). Much of Hall's personal research was designed to expand the public awareness of what children know and what they do. Thus, he published studies on topics such as what children know (e.g., vocabulary and number concepts), when they enter school (Hall, 1891), children's lies (Hall, 1890), showing off and bashfulness (Hall & Smith, 1903), and several works on children's concepts (Hall & Browne, 1903; Hall & Wallin, 1902). As noted by Arnett (2006), although many of Hall's ideas no longer have scholarly support, his discussions of delinquent behavior, sensation seeking, and vulnerability to peer and media influences in adolescence are particularly similar to current scholarship.

Hall's research work on children covered a variety of additional topics (e.g., fears, pets, curiosity, and companions), and he involved himself in the education of parents, particularly mothers, who in the 1920s were expected to provide almost all childcare (Brooks-Gunn & Johnson, 2006). His bibliography reveals a massive and programmatic effort to understand the mind and behavior of the child (see 1923, pp. 597–616). Hall's experimental and conceptual work on children apparently owed much to Theodate Louise Smith, who headed the Children's Institute at Clark. According to Sokal (1990), her interests "meshed effectively with Hall's. . .and contributed to some excellent science" (p. 121). The work of Hall, Smith, and others in the child study movement met a great public need and elevated the visibility and status of psychology. Hall's work contributed to the impression that psychology had something important to say about the real problems of living.

The child study movement was not restricted to the United States. Indeed, Hall had many counterparts in other countries. In Germany, Wilhelm Preyer (1841–1897) was an important pioneer in childhood studies. His book *The Mind of the Child* (1882) is one of the great classics in the field. In England, James Sully (1842–1923) wrote numerous books and articles on childhood. In France, Hippolyte Adolphe Taine (1828–1893) wrote an important early paper on lingual development in infancy. These early pioneers and others paved the way for the continuing emphasis on childhood later in the work of people such as Binet, Freud, and Piaget.

As noted earlier, Hall's larger interest was in life-span development from infancy to old age. His final book, *Senescence,* first published in 1922, is a classic work in the study of aging (Cole, 1993). Hall examined the treatment of the elderly in various cultures, along with literature by and on elderly people. He then turned to actuarial and mortality tables and pointed to the inevitable problems associated with the changing age demography, already evident in his day. He reviewed national old-age pension plans in other countries and stated, "The United States is the only nation that has no retirement system or provision for old age, even for its employees, save for soldiers and for judges of the Supreme Court" (1922, p. 180). On this matter, Hall was ahead of his time. It had been argued that a national retirement plan would undermine individual responsibility and that it ran counter to the best interests of a capitalistic society. Then, with the Great Depression, responsible families were devastated through no fault of their own. As a result of such widespread financial disaster, especially for the elderly, the Social Security Act of 1935 brought the United States into line with other nations. Hall would have approved because he was aware of countless elderly people in his day who were financially destitute.

Hall (1922) called for the creation of a kind of "senescent league of national dimensions" (p. 194) with educational, political, and social divisions that would serve an advocacy role for the elderly. The latter part of *Senescence* presents results of an attitude survey that Hall conducted on topics such as sources of pleasure, belief in an afterlife, death anxiety, beliefs about longevity, and recognition of the signs of aging.

Hall had many other interests, especially in education and pedagogy (Fagan, 1992), the history of psychology (Bringmann, Bringmann, & Early, 1992), and the psychology of religion (Vande Kemp, 1992). He was especially interested in the effects of religious education on youth. His book *Jesus the Christ, in the Light of Psychology* (1917) represents a kind of "working through" of tensions between his early Calvinistic background and his natural-science approach to psychology.

In terms of his influence on both the basic and the applied dimensions of psychology, his innovations, his selling of psychology to the public, and his specific developmental-evolutionary perspective and its subsequent influence, Hall must be counted as one of the great psychologists.

FUNCTIONALISM AND THE UNIVERSITY OF CHICAGO

In her classic book *Seven Psychologies,* Edna Heidbreder (1933) referred to the University of Chicago as "the capital of a new school" (p. 201). The term *capital* is appropriate because, whereas the functionalist perspective–dominated thought in many U.S. and European universities, it was nowhere more articulated than at the University of Chicago. The two elder leaders of the Chicago school, John Dewey and James Rowland Angell, studied respectively with G. Stanley Hall and William James. The third leader of the Chicago school, Harvey Carr, completed his degree under Angell at Chicago.

John Dewey

Regarded by many as America's most important philosopher of education, **John Dewey (1859–1952)** played a key role in launching functionalism. Dewey was born in Burlington, Vermont, on October 20, 1859. His early schooling was in Burlington and he graduated from the University of Vermont in 1879. Following a brief teaching career, he enrolled in the graduate program in philosophy at Johns Hopkins University. During that period, he studied with G. Stanley Hall and wrote a doctoral dissertation on the psychology of Immanuel Kant. He earned a Ph.D. from Johns Hopkins in 1884 and accepted a teaching assignment in psychology and philosophy at the University of Michigan. In 1894, he accepted an appointment as chair of psychology and philosophy at the University of Chicago. During his decade at Chicago, Dewey made his most visible contributions to psychology's functionalist viewpoint. In 1904, he moved from Chicago to Columbia University where he focused on the philosophy of education as well as a wide range of social, philosophical, and political topics (Cochran, 2010). Dewey's long and productive career came to an end in his ninety-second year, on June 1, 1952.

Dewey's classic article "The Reflex Arc Concept in Psychology," published in 1896, is so pivotal in the history of the functionalist school that Edwin G. Boring (1953) referred to it as "a declaration of independence for American functional psychology" (p. 146). In obvious celebration of Dewey's general philosophical and psychological orientation, William James wrote in 1903, "It rejoices me greatly that your school (I mean your philosophic school) at the University of Chicago is, after this long gestation, bringing its fruits to birth in a way that will demonstrate its great unity and vitality" (1903/1980, p. 204). What features of Dewey's thought warranted such praise?

Like James, Dewey believed that philosophy must begin with experience. Furthermore, experience must be understood in a naturalistic context. Dewey was critical of earlier idealistic philosophers whose concepts were not wedded to observable events in the world. As with James, Dewey was friendly to a pluralistic view that placed emphasis on the irreducible and unique features of the experiences of individual human beings. Dewey's article "The Reflex Arc Concept in Psychology" criticized attempts to dissect experience into artificial piecemeal units. Such dissection is inappropriate even for simple reflexes, let alone more complicated behaviors. Furthermore, such dissection violates what is found in experience and departs from an empirical approach to psychology.

Dewey asked his readers to consider the term *reflex*: Do we ever really consider the stimulus as a thing in itself or the response as a thing in itself? Such a distinction is unlikely except in a highly artificial laboratory situation. Dewey (1896) argued that a reflex is not "a patchwork of disjointed parts, a mechanical conjunction of unallied processes" (p. 358). Instead, what we encounter is "a continuously ordered sequence of acts, all adapted in themselves and in the order of their sequence, to

reach a certain objective end" (p. 366). The ends we seek, such as reproduction, safety, and locomotion, call attention to motivation and to observable behaviors associated with motivation. Shook (1995) has documented Wundt's influence on Dewey's earliest writings. However, Dewey found too much abstraction in the older psychologies and a failure to appreciate the special ends or functions of psychological processes.

Boring (1953) offered the opinion that "after Dewey went to Columbia in 1904 his mission to the new psychology was largely accomplished, like the mission of any parent when the child has grown up" (p. 147). Boring's statement is applicable to Dewey's mission to academic psychology; he continued, however, to have an influence on applied psychology, especially in educational circles (Jackson, 1998). Dewey's continued interest in the applied arena was fueled by a combination of interests in U.S. democracy, economics (Tilman & Knapp. 1999), schools, art (Jackson, 1998), the nature of learning, and his own six children.

According to Soltis (1971), Dewey believed that "democracy was more than a form of government; it was a way of living that went beyond politics, votes, and laws to pervade all aspects of society" (p. 84). Accordingly, Dewey believed that schools should afford firsthand opportunities for children to learn democracy and see it in action. Dewey's cardinal rule of education was that we learn by doing and by reflecting on what happened. So if we want to promote democracy, it should be learned in schools. Dewey believed that the educational system should respect individuality but at the same time should challenge our ethnocentrism. He opposed mere imitation, regimentation, and rote learning. Such learning, he felt, prepares us not for democracy but for totalitarianism. Dewey was a premier figure in the founding of functionalism and progressive education (Hilgard, 1996).

James Rowland Angell

Like Dewey, **James Rowland Angell (1869–1949)** was born in Burlington, Vermont. Angell's college work was at the University of Michigan, where he completed a B.A. in 1890 and an M.A. in 1891. Miles (1949) noted that a highlight in Angell's experience at Michigan was "a seminar with Dewey on William James' recently published *Principles of Psychology*" (p. 1). In fact, Angell declared that James's "book, more than any other, profoundly influenced his thinking for the next twenty years of his life" (p. 1). Following the completion of his work at Michigan, Angell enrolled at Harvard University where he worked with William James and the philosopher Josiah Royce (1855–1916). In his autobiography, Angell (1930/1961) reflected on studying Kant with Royce and abnormal psychology with James (p. 7).

Following his year at Harvard, Angell traveled to Germany where he enjoyed lectures from leading scholars in psychology, philosophy, and physiology. At the University of Halle, Angell submitted a dissertation on the meaning of freedom in Kant's philosophical work. His work was accepted, subject to revision. Rather than revising the dissertation, he accepted a position as instructor of philosophy and psychology at the University of Minnesota. Ironically, Angell received several honorary doctorates and was instrumental in granting many doctorates, but he never completed the formalities associated with his own Ph.D.

After one year at Minnesota, Angell joined the faculty at the University of Chicago where he and Dewey crossed paths again. Angell was discouraged because, in his words, "For seven years I received no promotion in rank and no advance in salary" (1930/1961, p. 13). He was finally promoted to associate professor in 1901 and to professor in 1904. Angell believed his promotion was granted because other universities such as Princeton had offered him faculty positions. In 1905, Angell became head of the psychology department at Chicago and then dean of the faculties in 1911. After that point in his career, Angell remained in administrative work. He served as dean at Chicago and then acting president. In World War I, he served with Walter Dill Scott on the Committee on Classification of Personnel. In 1921, Angell became president of Yale University where he served with distinction until his retirement in 1937. Following retirement, Angell worked as an educational counselor for the National Broadcasting Company. He died in New Haven, Connecticut, on March 4, 1949.

Angell's contributions to psychology are all the more remarkable in view of his enormous time commitments to administration (Dewsbury, 2003). His most visible contributions to psychology were produced during his tenure at the University of Chicago. In 1904, he published a text, *Psychology,* that went through four editions. In 1907, Angell published an article titled "The Province of Functional Psychology" based on his presidential address to the American Psychological Association. This work is regarded as a classic exposition of the functionalist school.

Although Dewey is often viewed as the founder of the Chicago school of functional psychology, Angell is recognized for making these views more systematic (Backe, 2001). Angell argued that functionalism was really not new: It had been around since Aristotle and, in modern times, since Spencer and Darwin. The first mark of the functionalist orientation, according to Angell (1930/1961), is that it involves "the identification and description of mental *operations,* rather than the mere *stuff* of mental experience" (p. 28). The second mark of functionalism is that it is concerned with the conditions or circumstances that evoke a mental state. A mental state does not exist in isolation; it must be understood in social and biological context. Finally, Angell argued that mental states or events must be understood in terms of how they contribute "to the furtherance of the sum total of organic activities, considered as adaptive" (1930/1961, p. 28). In other words, he asked, what contributions do mental events make to our adjustment to the world? These three marks of a functionalist psychology go a long way from a merely descriptive psychology of the stuff of consciousness. According to Angell, the functionalist approach is illustrated in studies of animal behavior, developmental psychology, and psychopathology. A functionalist psychology is inherently social and biological and emphasizes experience and behavior in the service of adaptation.

In his autobiography, Angell commented on other developments in his day. He found that psychoanalysis offered some sound contributions, but was troubled about parts that seemed romantic and unscientific. As for the testing movement, he was concerned about its premature application in industry and education, but saw potential if used properly.

Angell and Dewey were forces in U.S. psychology despite the fact that other activities outside psychology commanded their interests. They both served as presidents of the American Psychological Association (Dewey in 1899 and Angell in 1906). Also, both were named to the most prestigious scientific society in America—the National Academy of Sciences. According to Miles (1949), Angell, who was elected in 1920, was the sixth psychologist named to the academy. Others were James McKeen Cattell (1901), William James (1903), Josiah Royce (1906), John Dewey (1910), and G. Stanley Hall (1915).

Harvey A. Carr

The consolidation and extension of the functionalist position took place under the leadership of Angell's student, **Harvey A. Carr (1873–1954)**. Born in Indiana on April 30, 1873, Carr was educated at DePauw University and later at the University of Colorado at Boulder where he came under the influence of Arthur Allin, a disciple of G. Stanley Hall. After completing a master's degree at Colorado, Carr enrolled in the doctoral program at the University of Chicago. His dissertation, directed by Angell, was completed in 1905. Carr worked in a high school position in Texas and then at the Pratt Institute before returning to the University of Chicago in 1908. He remained at Chicago until 1938, chairing the department through much of that period. Under his leadership, Chicago became one of the leading schools in psychology.

Carr contended that psychology is concerned with mental activity. By *mental activity*, he referred to "the acquisition, fixation, retention, organization, and evaluation of experiences, and their subsequent utilization in the guidance of conduct" (1925, p. 1). Both experience and behavior (conduct) are central features of functionalism as interpreted by Carr. He argued, "The type of conduct that reflects mental activity may be termed adaptive or adjustive behavior" (p. 1). Adaptation or adjustment, according to Carr, involves a response that alters a situation so as to satisfy a motivating stimulus. A motivating stimulus may be a hunger pang, an itch, excessive temperature, pain, and so forth. Clearly, the subject of motivation is elevated in the functionalist system.

Carr accepted a variety of methods, including introspection and objective observation, and he investigated animal as well as human cognition (Dewsbury, 2000). He questioned whether the methods of all the sciences are really comparable. For example, he noted that "geology, astronomy, and mathematics are usually regarded as sciences, but are they experimental in the usual laboratory sense of the term?" (1930/1961, p. 80). Carr expressed doubt "that the experimental method—in the usual sense of that term—is the only scientific method" (p. 81). In his view, psychologists should not be doctrinaire about method, but attend, first and foremost, to the nature of the problem.

Carr, like Angell, believed in a psychology broad in scope, encompassing problems in learning, motivation, psychopathology, education, sensation, perception, and development. Like Angell, he believed all problems should be examined in terms of biological and social context.

The Chicago functionalists devoted little space to the metaphysical problems that occupied other psychologists. Carr, in his book *Psychology: The Study of Mental Activity,* discussed free will and determinism, but seemed most interested in the ways freedom might have meaning and utility. Such a position is consistent with the functionalist agenda. The metaphysical status of the two positions was not of great interest, but the meanings of the two positions—their utility, the work they accomplish, or the various meanings they convey—were important problems. Believing that freedom is acquired through knowledge, he quoted with approval the injunction, "Seek the truth and the truth shall make you free" (1925, p. 332).

PSYCHOLOGY AT COLUMBIA UNIVERSITY

We encounter another clear expression of functionalism in the early psychology at Columbia University. Nurtured and developed by James McKeen Cattell, the psychology department at Columbia became one of the most visible and productive in the United States.

James McKeen Cattell

One of psychology's more colorful and controversial figures, **James McKeen Cattell (1860–1944)** found his way to fame in his chosen discipline via an unusual route. His research program failed and, compared to others, he published few papers. Yet, for a time, he was one of the most visible and powerful figures in the discipline. He won his place in history through editorial and administrative skills. Through his editorial efforts, the experimental and conceptual work of psychologists was brought to the attention of other scientists and the public. The discipline of psychology enjoyed center-stage attention that might not have been possible without Cattell's unique contributions.

Cattell was born on May 25, 1860. He was a gifted student, graduating with honors from Lafayette College in Easton, Pennsylvania, in 1880. Following two years of travel and study in Europe, Cattell returned to the United States to enroll in philosophy at Johns Hopkins University. Despite excellent work in G. Stanley Hall's laboratory at Hopkins, his fellowship for the second year was not renewed. Reasons for the transfer of the fellowship from Cattell to John Dewey are not clear. Sokal (1980b) referred to Cattell's "continual bickering with Daniel Coit Gilman, the university president" (p. 43) and Ross (1972) implicated G. Stanley Hall in the decision (p. 145). For whatever reason, Cattell moved from Baltimore to Leipzig and, as noted by Sokal (1980b), "became the first American to earn a Ph.D. in experimental psychology from Wilhelm Wundt at Leipzig" (p. 43).

Following his work at Leipzig, Cattell went to England, where he worked with Francis Galton. Galton's obsession with the measurement of bodily and mental attributes had a profound influence on Cattell. On the philosophical side, he had earlier been influenced by the Baconian vision and by the enthusiasm of Rudolph Hermann Lotze for an empirical approach to the study of mental processes. Galton's work helped Cattell translate his philosophical biases into an experimental program.

Following work with Galton, Cattell returned to the United States in 1889 to accept an appointment at the University of Pennsylvania. In 1891, he accepted a position at Columbia University, which he held until 1917. Cattell's research programs at Pennsylvania and Columbia focused on the development of *mental tests,* a term he coined in 1890 (see Beins, 2010; Cattell, 1890). In Cattell's day, there were high expectations that mental abilities could be measured and that such measurements would have the most salutary consequences for schools and industry. The problem was to develop mental tests with demonstrated predictive efficiency. Cattell, following the lead of Galton, measured simple reaction times, complex reaction times, visual acuity, auditory acuity, strength of grip, and the like.

As noted by Sokal (1980b), Cattell's measurements "literally correlated with nothing. The result killed his career as a psychological tester and redirected his efforts away from experimental psychology" (p. 47). As we will see later, Binet, employing a different set of tasks, was able to develop tests with predictive efficiency. Though Cattell's research program failed, he established laboratories at the University of Pennsylvania and at Columbia University. Also, at Columbia, he helped promote one of the most active doctoral programs in psychology.

In 1894, Cattell embarked on work as an editor, a career that would span a half-century. One of his greatest accomplishments involved the journal *Science.* A New York journalist named John Michaels founded the interdisciplinary journal in 1880 with financial support from inventor Thomas Edison and later from Alexander Graham Bell. Despite such support, *Science* fell into serious financial difficulty. In 1894, Cattell purchased the journal for $500. *Science* provided an outlet for research in many fields, including physics, chemistry, biology, geology, and psychology. Cattell took over as editor of *Science* and established policies that rescued the journal and improved its visibility (see Sokal, 1980b). It was remarkable that a psychologist edited such an important outlet for all the sciences. As a result, psychology articles found their way into the prestigious journal alongside research from more established scientific disciplines.

In 1893, Cattell joined forces with James Mark Baldwin (1861–1934) to purchase G. Stanley Hall's *The American Journal of Psychology* (Sokal, 1997). When Hall refused to sell, Cattell and Baldwin founded the *Psychological Review* one year later, a journal that still occupies a central place in the discipline. In time, Cattell and Baldwin went on to found a family of successful journals including the *Psychological Index* and the *Psychological Monographs.* According to Johnson (2000), Hall's journals had a broader focus, whereas "the Baldwin and Cattell journals represented a narrower view of psychology, publishing more specialized experimental articles than general or theoretical articles and considerably fewer applied articles" (p. 1146). After years of feuding, Cattell and Baldwin dissolved their partnership in 1903 and the *Psychological Review* journals were sold to the American Psychological Association in 1925.

Cattell edited a variety of other journals. From 1900 to 1915, he served as editor of *Popular Science Monthly,* a magazine that informed the public about important developments in the sciences. Under Cattell's leadership, *Popular Science Monthly* included articles on psychology to satisfy an ever-growing public demand for information on topics such as child rearing, animal behavior, psychopathology, and mental testing. Cattell also served as editor of the *American*

Naturalist from 1907 to 1944 and *School and Society* from 1915 to 1939. Although not exhaustive, this list of his editorial responsibilities conveys the central role he occupied with respect to communication of scientific information. How did Cattell edit so many journals? He enlisted his graduate students and his wife and children to run his science publication machine. Most notably Cattell's wife, Josephine Owen Cattell, played a key role in the publication of *Science.*

In 1921, Cattell founded the Psychological Corporation as a "commercial firm designed to implement his 1904 call for an applied psychology" (Sokal, 2006, p. 32). The corporation made psychological services such as consulting and testing available in business and industrial settings. Cattell (1937/1992) predicted in the first volume of his *Journal of Consulting Psychology* that professional psychology would thrive in the twentieth century. His Psychological Corporation continues to prosper and, according to Garfield (1992), Cattell was correct in his predictions about the future of professional psychology. Another of Cattell's most noteworthy achievements was his work to recognize outstanding achievement in science. He founded the reference series *American Men of Science,* later to become *American Men and Women of Science,* and developed a rating system as a means of establishing eminence (Sokal, 1995). His system, however, was not always received with enthusiasm. For example, in 1903, Cattell asked William James to participate in an exercise to rank psychologists. James complied but expressed his suspicion about fine-tuned rankings. He also argued that the nature of the work of different individuals is not always homogeneous enough to warrant meaningful comparisons. In characteristic Jamesian honesty, he said, "Permit me to say that in my private breast *you* stand lower now than you did before I got this problem from you!" (1903/1986b, p. 313).

Many honors came to Cattell during his life. One of the original founders of the American Psychological Association, he served as its fourth president. As a powerful advocate for science and academic life, Cattell held strong opinions on many issues and did not hesitate to express them. Indeed, his stinging criticisms of key political and university officials ultimately led to his dismissal from Columbia University. There have been disagreements over the justifications for the firing of Cattell (see Gates, 1968; Sokal, 2009, 2011), but there can be little question that he made some important and unique contributions to the early development of psychology. Cattell died on January 20, 1944.

Robert Sessions Woodworth

One of the essential features of functionalism is that it broadened the scope of psychological inquiry. Both basic and applied problems were legitimate and there was an extension of research into areas such as learning and motivation. **Robert Sessions Woodworth (1869–1962)** became a key figure in the subject area of motivation.

Woodworth was born in Belchertown, Massachusetts, on October 17, 1869. Even as a youngster, Woodworth had broad-ranging academic interests that included music, philosophy, mathematics, and science. Initially, he planned to follow his father into a career in the ministry. On graduating from Amherst in 1891, he still considered the ministry as he taught science and mathematics classes to raise money for additional education.

Woodworth's experiences as a teacher caused him to reassess his vocational plans. Poffenberger (1962) claimed, "He entered Harvard in the autumn of 1895, fairly well committed to a teaching career in philosophy and psychology" (p. 678). Poffenberger pointed out that, while at Harvard, Woodworth worked with William James and developed friendships with fellow graduate students E. L. Thorndike and W. B. Cannon. He earned an M.A. degree from Harvard but then transferred to Columbia, where he graduated with a Ph.D. in psychology in 1899. Woodworth studied in Scotland and in England where he worked with the famous physiologist Sir Charles Sherrington. Woodworth held temporary instructorships before accepting a regular faculty position at Columbia in 1903. With the exception of the brief temporary assignments, Woodworth spent his entire academic career at Columbia University. Woodworth's lengthy career spanned six decades until his death at age ninety-two on July 4, 1962.

Woodworth is often categorized as a functionalist. However, he did not think of himself as a member of a school, but as an experimental psychologist seeking to understand cause–effect relationships in experience and behavior. Woodworth's published contributions to psychology extend over two hundred papers and ten books. Though he made substantive contributions in many areas, three areas are noteworthy.

First, as noted by Murphy (1963), under Woodworth's leadership, "the term *experimental* was extended to more and more kinds and fields of research endeavor" (p. 131). In 1938, he published *Experimental Psychology*, a book that was so influential it was known as the "Columbia Bible" (Winston, 1990). In the revised edition of this classic text, coauthored with Harold Schlosberg, Woodworth lauded research in multiple areas of scientific psychology. In the introduction, Woodworth and Schlosberg (1954) noted that the field of psychology started with a few scattered experiments conducted by scientists from several other disciplines. Reliable findings were demonstrated in experiments on the senses, but after years of hard work, experimental psychology encompassed the fields of learning, memory, thinking, attention, emotion, and motivation. Woodworth contributed to the growing breadth of perspective about the subject matter of experimental psychology. No longer was it restricted to the senses and to reaction times. Though Woodworth extended experimental psychology to a widening field of subjects, he narrowed the concept of what counts as an experiment. We will return to this topic later.

Woodworth's second contribution relates to the first but deserves special treatment. Specifically, in his work, we encounter a new and broader emphasis on the concept of motivation. Like the study of emotion, research on motivation had carried over from the last century as a popular topic for psychologists (Edwards, 1999). Woodworth took issue with an exclusively biogenic approach to motivation. He did not believe that all motives have their origin in instincts or in metabolic processes. He drew attention to learned drives and to the idea that there are "activities that have intrinsic incentive value" (Woodworth & Schlosberg, 1954, p. 685). Thus, play, manipulation, exploration, and even some forms of work may, in his words, "function autonomously" (p. 686).

The notion of **functional autonomy**, encountered later in the psychology of Gordon Allport (1937, 1955), refers to the idea that a means or mechanism for satisfying a motive may acquire drive properties. For example, a person may work at a bookstore as a means of earning a living. In time, however, he or she becomes acquainted with a good book and develops a strong drive to spend time each day reading. What started as a mere "means" has now become an acquired motive and is sustained because of its own intrinsic merits.

Woodworth's concept of motivation extended into the realm of the unconscious. Seward and Seward (1968), for example, pointed out that Woodworth "anticipated Freud in considering the dream to be the result of perseverating wishes; however, his theory rested on a broader base than Freud's, inasmuch as he believed that wishes underlying dreams might pertain to any area of interest" (p. 562). Thus, the wish behind a dream, according to Woodworth, need not be sexual; rather, it might be based on any strong human need such as a need for achievement, recognition, and security.

Woodworth called his approach *dynamic psychology*. The term *dynamic* refers to the importance of understanding the causes of behavior. Woodworth assumed that causes are not always reducible to a simple stimulus–response (S-R) formula. He was famous for arguing that the S-R concept should be replaced by a stimulus–organism–response (S-O-R) concept. The S-O-R formulation emphasizes the crucial role of the organism in the sequence. Examples of organismic variables, according to Woodworth, include learned motives, expectations, readiness to respond, and personal characteristics such as cautiousness or fearfulness.

A third contribution came through Woodworth's influential textbooks. His

introductory text titled *Psychology*, first published in 1921, was widely used, but the text that had the greatest influence on academic psychology was his *Experimental Psychology* (Winston, 2006). For over two decades, the book served as a standard reference for students preparing for graduate school. Noteworthy for its breadth, Woodworth's text reviewed classic studies and methodologies in a host of content areas including psychophysics, association, emotion, sensation, learning, motivation, memory, and problem solving.

Though Woodworth expanded sensitivity to the scope of experimental psychology, he also narrowed what counted as an experiment with a distinction between correlational and experimental research (Winston, 1990). Woodworth emphasized the importance of independent and dependent variables in true experimental research. An *independent variable* is one that the researcher systematically manipulates. Let us say we are studying the effects of coffee on anxiety. In this case, consumption of coffee is the variable controlled by the experimenter. Presumably, one group consumes no coffee, another may consume a placebo (e.g., a substance that passes for coffee but isn't), and another group actually consumes coffee. The presence or absence of coffee or the administration of a placebo would be counted as the independent variable. Anxiety, as measured by some test, is the *dependent variable.*

Winston (1990) noted that "nearly all textbooks, both introductory and experimental, adopted Woodworth's conceptualization of 'experiment' " (p. 397). Woodworth's definition of an *experiment* elevated the importance of "wet-lab" approaches to psychology and enhanced the scientific image of the discipline. In later years, however, the term *experiment* often has broader meanings. Thus, there are activities of astronomers that could possibly be viewed as experimental, even though variables are not manipulated in the usual sense. The discovery of a new planet, for example, may arise from hypothesis testing and controlled observation, but the procedure is not comparable to the typical experiment.

Woodworth made many additional contributions to the discipline of psychology. For example, he developed an early personality test to evaluate soldiers in World War I (Gibby & Zickar, 2008), but he may be best known for his famous studies with Edward Lee Thorndike on the transfer of training (discussed in Chapter 13). He did extensive editorial work for psychological journals and served as president of the American Psychological Association in 1914. In 1956, the American Psychological Foundation awarded Woodworth the Gold Medal for his outstanding contributions to the discipline.

MARY WHITON CALKINS

Shortly after 1900, functionalism gained momentum as the dominant orientation in numerous universities. However, some scholars sought to preserve the best in structuralism and functionalism. One such person was **Mary Whiton Calkins (1863–1930)**, the founder of an early psychology laboratory in the United States.

In the 1880s and 1890s, progressive colleges and universities encouraged the growth and development of psychology laboratories. Calkins, a young Greek and philosophy instructor at Wellesley College, was given the opportunity to establish a laboratory on the condition that she take time off and pursue advanced studies in psychology. She explored numerous options but encountered restrictions against women in most leading institutions in Europe and the United States. Initially rejected at Harvard, she was finally permitted to enroll on the condition that the courses would not count for a degree. She took a course with William James and later conducted research in Hugo Münsterberg's laboratory. Her work was of a distinguished quality and, in 1895, she presented a thesis and was given an unauthorized examination. The examining committee included distinguished faculty such as James, Münsterberg, and George Santayana (1863–1952). They affirmed that she met all doctoral requirements, but Harvard refused to grant the degree. Furumoto (1979) has outlined the details of her studies and the controversy over the degree.

Though she did not receive the Harvard doctorate, Calkins established the laboratory at Wellesley and became a productive scholar. In 1905, she was elected the fourteenth president of the American Psychological Association. She taught at Wellesley College until her retirement in 1929.

Calkins believed that *psychology* should be defined as the science of the conscious self. Although not a popular cause at the time, she was the most visible advocate of self-psychology for three decades. Wentworth (1999) concluded that Calkins's vigorous defense of the science of selves was, in part, rooted in her beliefs about ethics, religion, and morality. She viewed mind or consciousness as the ultimate reality and, in that sense, belonged to the idealist tradition and to a philosophical tradition known as *personalism*. Calkins argued that if the self is the focus of psychology, then there is room for reconciliation between structuralism and functionalism. Calkins believed that human consciousness is understood in terms of its environmental contexts. The functionalist engages in such explorations and thus makes valuable contributions. Consciousness must also be understood in its own terms as a reality unlike any lower reality from which it emerged. The structuralist is more likely to provide insights into the unique and irreducible dimensions of consciousness. She found a place for both functionalism and structuralism, a theme echoed in Calkins's presidential address before the American Psychological Association in 1905.

Calkins made additional contributions to psychology, including early development of the *paired associate method* as a means of studying retention. This method required research subjects to learn an association between a pair of stimulus–response terms such as *desk–moon* or *orange–hat*. When given the stimulus term *desk,* the subject would be expected to respond with the term *moon*. Calkins's short-term memory studies anticipated later developments in memory research (Madigan & O'Hara, 1992).

Calkins (1893) also conducted one of the first formal studies of dreams. She kept track of her dreams for fifty-five nights, waking herself up at various intervals to record dreams in a journal. Her colleague, Edmund Clark Sanford

(1859–1924), recorded his dreams for forty-six nights, and together they made several insightful findings. She accurately concluded that people dream every night, that four dreams are common in an average night, and that we can, to a degree, control our dreams. Several years later, Sigmund Freud acknowledged Calkins's seminal work in his book *The Interpretation of Dreams.* She is remembered appropriately as one of the pioneers who, in the words of Pratola (1974), demonstrated that "women have a rightful place in scientific and academic endeavors" (p. 780).

THE GROWTH OF APPLIED PSYCHOLOGY

Earlier we encountered Münsterberg's contention that psychological experiments should be placed in the service of practical day-to-day interests. Inspired by functionalism, many psychologists geared their research to problems and issues of daily living. Such research left its mark on public institutions and helped mold public and scientific attitudes about the practical value of psychology. An example of research that attacked and helped change public and scientific attitudes is visible in the work of Leta Stetter Hollingworth.

Leta Stetter Hollingworth

In the late nineteenth and early twentieth centuries, the so-called **variability hypothesis** was used as an explanation for the differential achievements of men and women in science, music, law, and so on. Briefly stated, the variability hypothesis held that men are physically and psychologically more variable than women. According to the hypothesis, women tended toward averages in all things, whereas men showed greater variety; men were thought to be more courageous but more cowardly, more virtuous but more corrupt, more intelligent but more stupid, and more violent but more peaceful. Superficial support for the variability hypothesis was found in the achievements of men compared to women and in the finding that more boys compared to

girls were diagnosed as intellectually deficient. Evidence against the variability hypothesis had been set forth in a classic study by Karl Pearson (1897). Pearson calculated means and measures of variability on literally thousands of boys and girls ages six through ten. Among other things, he examined height, weight, strength of grip, visual acuity, and numerous cranial measures. He found no reliable evidence for differential variability between boys and girls.

Leta Stetter Hollingworth (1886–1939) was aware of Pearson's work, but decided to test the contention that males are physically and psychologically more variable than females at birth (Shields, 1975). She conducted this study with the support of her advisor, Edward Lee Thorndike, despite Thorndike's support of the variability hypothesis (Shields, 1991). Hollingworth's study, unlike Pearson's studies, ruled out the possible effects of environmental influences on variability. It is altogether fitting that it would be a woman who would deliver the deathblow to the variability hypothesis. Born Leta A. Stetter, she was reared in Nebraska and earned her bachelor's degree at the University of Nebraska and her Ph.D. at Columbia University in 1916. Benjamin (1975) called attention to the fact that many early psychologists made claims for the inferiority of women. Such claims were sometimes derived from the predictions of the variability hypothesis.

As a means of investigating the variability hypothesis, Hollingworth compared male and female infants on a variety of physical characteristics such as height, birth weight, and cranial circumference. She found no differences in variability on any of the physical characteristics she explored. Male infants were slightly larger than females at birth, but were not more variable. Hollingworth acknowledged that more males than females were admitted to institutions for mentally disabled people, but in early-twentieth-century America, more was expected of males and hence a mental disability was more likely to be detected. She argued that greater male achievements are the result of unequal educational opportunities. Females had almost no vocational options; hence, achievement was next to impossible.

Hollingworth (1914) also conducted research that showed that the perceptual, motor, and mental abilities of women are not adversely affected during the menstrual cycle, a discovery that undercut another early-twentieth-century myth that women could never compete with men because of a monthly incapacity brought about by menstruation. Hollingworth's studies together with Pearson's studies now count as classics in the psychology of women and made important contributions to the reduction of prejudices that had prevented equal educational opportunities for women.

Following World War I, Hollingworth became active in clinical research on individual differences in intelligence, an area like the psychology of women that was "fraught with myth and misunderstanding" (Shields, 1991, p. 248). During the course of her prestigious career, Hollingworth (1920, 1942) focused on two extreme populations of children—"mentally disabled" children and gifted children with IQs above 180. Her work resulted in the celebrated book *The Psychology of the Adolescent* (1928) as well as a variety of conceptual issues that remain relevant for contemporary professionals (Klein, 2000).

Helen Wooley

Like Leta Hollingworth and Margaret Floy Washburn, **Helen Wooley (1874–1947)** was one of the first generation of women to receive a Ph.D. in experimental psychology (see Furumoto & Scarborough, 1986; Milar, 1999). After receiving her doctorate from the University of Chicago in 1900, Wooley became a pioneer in educational psychology and the study of gender differences.

As a backdrop to her work, child labor laws played a critical role in humanitarian reform movements during the time psychology emerged as a new discipline. In that tradition, Wooley served as the director of the Vocation Bureau in the public schools in Cincinnati, Ohio, from 1911 to 1921. As director, she worked on numerous problems such as the consequences of dropping out of school and how to best match educational programs with the intellectual and vocational abilities of children. Milar (1999) reviewed Wooley's work on a massive longitudinal study of students who remain in school compared with adolescents who drop out of school to enter the workforce. Because of measurement issues, her study did not yield clear-cut results and conclusions. Such a disappointing outcome comes as no surprise to those who follow scientific attempts to investigate problems of a much simpler nature (e.g., trials on the effects of drugs often do not yield unequivocal results).

Milar (1999) points out, however, that despite the disappointing results of the longitudinal study, Wooley was singled out for praise as a pioneer in childhood education and welfare. Further, "The Vocational Bureau [headed by Wooley] was one of the earliest psychological clinics in a public school and was used to support special education classes of various types and to consult with the juvenile courts" (Milar, 1999, p. 232). Wooley, as a part of the functionalist tradition, demonstrated strengths and limitations of psychology as a means of investigating practical social issues.

Binet and Intelligence Testing

Arguably, the measurement of intelligence became the most significant psychological research in terms of its lasting impact on public institutions. Earlier in the text, we referred to Galton's work on individual differences and to Cattell's unsuccessful attempts to measure intelligence. Shortly after 1901, the French experimental psychologist, Alfred Binet (1857–1911), declared his intention to measure intelligence by means of special tests. Early in his career, Binet flirted with research on physiognomy, the theory that physical appearance can reveal aspects of character (Collins, 1999). After numerous failures, Binet and his collaborator, Théodore Simon (1873–1961), constructed a scale generally regarded as the first successful intelligence test.

Binet is not associated with any of the dominant systems of psychology but, in her biography on Binet, Wolf (1973) argued that "he was in fact completely absorbed by the ideas of the functional viewpoints and terminology, by concerns about the nature of consciousness, and by the need for comparative and developmental studies" (p. 4). As an experimental psychologist, Binet's interests were wide ranging. In addition to work on intelligence, he conducted studies on topics such as hypnosis, attention, creativity, graphology, and eyewitness testimony. He helped found a laboratory for experimental approaches to education and assisted in the founding of the first French journal of psychology, *L' Année Psychologique.*

After considerable trial and error, Binet attempted to measure intelligence in a way that departed from the earlier approaches of Galton and Cattell. According to Wolf (1973), Binet realized that it might be possible to find differences "in complex superior processes rather than in elementary ones" (p. 146). Instead of studying simple reaction times, Binet looked at memory for numbers, ability to solve spatial or conceptual problems, and memory for designs. Test items were related to daily tasks. Binet also gathered normative data on types of problems that typical children in various age groups could solve. This approach yielded the first usable intelligence test, published in 1905 and revised in 1908 and again in 1911. The Binet–Simon scales, though ignored and even ridiculed in France, were translated into other languages and hailed as a major achievement (Schneider, 1992).

Unlike later theorists, Binet viewed a child's score on the test as simply a score on a particular test on a particular day (Gould, 1981). From Binet's point of view, a child's intelligence test score could change as after additional education. As discussed in Chapter 8, later thinkers, including Goddard, Terman, Yerkes, and others, reified IQ and viewed it as a genetic, unchangeable aspect of an individual, and this change had long-term consequences for both psychology and the larger culture.

Wolf (1973), quoting Simon, noted that educational psychologist and eugenicist Lewis Terman (1877–1956) purchased the rights to publish the first U.S. version of the Binet–Simon scale for $1. Terman translated the test, made adaptations, and standardized the test on a large group of American children. The first Terman adaptation was published in 1916 and was called the *Stanford–Binet Intelligence Scale.* (The name of

the test was based partly on Terman's affiliation with Stanford University.) Later editions of the Stanford–Binet were published in 1937 and 1960. Alternatives to the Stanford–Binet test quickly surfaced and often featured special conveniences or applications. For example, in World War I, a paper-and-pencil test designed for group testing and known as the *Army Alpha* was developed by Robert M. Yerkes (1876–1956) and his associates as a means of screening large numbers of service personnel. An alternative, known as the *Army Beta,* was designed for personnel who were illiterate. These tests were used as means of rejecting individuals for service and as an aid in making special assignments. Following the war, a steady growth in the use of intelligence tests led to a proliferation of different tests.

Though many theoretical and practical problems of measuring intelligence were solved early in the century, the social consequences of large-scale testing remain a concern. In his book *Even the Rat Was White,* Guthrie (2003) outlined the warnings of African American psychologists about the dangers of mental testing and the pitfalls of cultural biases in tests. In his book *The Mismeasure of Man,* Gould (1981) outlined the history and social consequences of conceiving intelligence as a single thing and of characterizing human beings in terms of an abstract number that serves as a symbol of merit. Numerous additional sources on the history of testing (DuBois, 1970; Sokal, 1987) are recommended reading.

INFLUENCE OF FUNCTIONALISM: AN EVALUATION

Functionalism grew out of a pluralistic, pragmatic, and radically empirical context and thus, as a philosophical psychology, was more inclined to open doors than to shut them. It entertained a host of interesting problems that affected the daily lives of people: the problems of child rearing, education, aging, the work environment, and emotional disorders. Furthermore, it refused to be restricted by narrow conceptions of the scientific method. Functionalism did not persist as an organized school or system of thought, but its values the impossibility of separating cognition and emotion.

Lange, Carl Georg (1834–1900) Danish physiologist remembered for a theory of emotion comparable to one proposed by William James and subsequently known as the James–Lange theory. See also *James–Lange theory of emotion.*

material self In James's theory, the material self is the body, friends, and possessions such as clothing, house, and automobile.

Münsterberg, Hugo (1863–1916) German American psychologist and a pioneer in applied psychology with his research on forensic, clinical, and industrial psychology.

pluralism A philosophical position that emphasizes the importance of alternative perspectives (methodological pluralism) and the existence of many realities (metaphysical pluralism).

pragmatism A U.S. philosophical movement associated with the work of Charles S. Pierce and William James. According to pragmatism, concepts must be judged in terms of their cash value or the practical work they do in the world. Thus, truth is judged by utility and the practical consequences achieved by an idea.

primary memory According to William James, primary memory is memory associated with nerve vibrations that have not yet ceased. It is memory associated with the specious present, what is immediately held in consciousness, and somewhat akin to an afterimage.

radical empiricism The name William James employed to characterize his larger philosophic vision. Radical empiricism emphasizes the primacy of experience and argues that things genuinely encountered in experience must not be excluded from philosophical and scientific inquiry. Radical empiricism treats various monisms as hypotheses.

secondary memory In James's psychology, secondary memory is memory proper or memory of past events that are not in present consciousness.

self-esteem A topic explored by William James and discussed in his work as a function of the ratio of success to pretensions.

social self In James's view, a dimension of selfhood born in various social contexts. Thus, the self in the presence of a parent may be different in some respects than the self in the presence of a friend.

spiritual self In James's view, the self that is "the home of interest" or that sits in judgment of other selves. The spiritual self, for James, is also the source of effortful striving.

stream of thought A concept advanced by William James that illustrates his view that consciousness is not composed of static elements. According to James, even a strong stimulus, such as a clap of thunder, is not pure; rather, it is "thunder-breaking-upon-silence-and-contrasting-with-it." James regarded consciousness as ever changing; each successive thought, even of the same object, changes by some degree.

Sumner, Francis (1895–1954) A pioneer in the study of black psychology and the first African American to earn a doctorate in psychology in the United States.

variability hypothesis A commonly held nineteenth-century belief that, in all things physical and mental, men are more variable than women. The research of Leta Stetter Hollingworth effectively dismantled the variability hypothesis.

Woodworth, Robert Sessions (1869–1962) A pioneer psychologist in the functionalist tradition who greatly extended the domain of experimental psychology. Woodworth was one of the first U.S. psychologists to emphasize the centrality of motivation. His text *Experimental Psychology* may be the most important classic in the field.

Wooley, Helen (1874–1947) American psychologist who emphasized practical social problems in her research on educational psychology.

13

■ ■ ■

Behaviorism

Psychology as the behaviorist views it is a purely objective experimental branch of natural science. Its theoretical goal is the prediction and control of behavior.

—JOHN B. WATSON (1913)

At its peak, behaviorism dominated American psychology and proved to be far more than a system of psychology. Like evolutionary theory, behaviorism captured public attention and sparked lively comment in popular magazines, editorials, books, and sermons. Behaviorism commanded intense loyalties and stirred harsh polemics. Titles such as "Men or Robots?" (McDougall, 1926b), "Does the Behaviorist Have a Mind?" (Johnson, 1927), "Behaviorism and Its Anti-Religious Implications" (Frick, 1928), and "Paradox of the Thinking Behaviorist" (Lovejoy, 1922) betray the alarm of critics and moralists. On the other hand, enthusiasts seized on the advantages of a more scientific psychology with assurances that behaviorism would not undermine moral and ethical interests. In an article on behaviorism and ethics, Weiss (1928) offered the optimistic opinion that "even the most advanced thinkers on social evolution have [failed] to foresee some of the possibilities of human achievement when scientific mechanism is taken as a fundamental postulate in human behavior" (p. 397).

Moving beyond psychology, the intellectual ferment over behaviorism spilled into literature, philosophy, political science, psychiatry, and sociology. For decades, behaviorism held a visible influence within these disciplines. In the twenty-first century, it continues to draw a substantial number of entries in major research databases. Behaviorism was also a subject heading, though with fewer entries, in other standard reference sources such as the *Humanities Index* and the *Sociological Abstracts*.

Though behaviorism revolutionized psychology and attracted widespread attention in other disciplines and in the popular press, its initial reception within psychology was cool or even grudging. American psychologist John B. Watson set forth the new system in a 1913 article titled "Psychology as the Behaviorist Views It." Later called "The Behaviorist Manifesto," his article is considered a pivotal and classic work in the history of psychology. At the time, older conservative psychologists greeted his work with criticism. Samelson (1985) documented behaviorism's chilly reception, but, quoting Watson, pointed out that "there was hope. 'The younger students. . .seem to be accepting behaviorism. The public is genuinely interested in it'" (p. 33). Watson made this statement fifteen years after the publication of his manifesto. A short time later, behaviorism dominated the American scene, securing Watson's place in the history of psychology.

ANTECEDENTS OF BEHAVIORISM

We can trace behaviorism's philosophical roots to ancient Greek atomic theory. In the work of Leucippus and Democritus, only the atoms and the void are real. The world, as it appears, is based on atomic combinations and the complex interplay of atoms creates psychological processes. Atomic theorists offer the first complete mechanistic and materialistic psychology. Over the centuries, various thinkers rediscovered, refined, and amplified the basic idea. In time, advances in neurophysiology reinforced behaviorism's modern philosophical foundation (see Chapter 8).

Although **behaviorism** is viewed as an American school of thought, Wertheimer (1987) pointed out that "its predecessors were Europeans rather than Americans" (p. 121). On many occasions, behaviorism assimilated key ideas from European thinkers. At every turn, we are reminded of materialists such as Condillac, Gassendi, Helvétius, and Hobbes; empiricists and associationists such as Locke and Hartley; and physician philosophers such as Cabanis and La Mettrie. According to Campbell (1967), the "Bible of all materialism" came from the pen of the German philosopher Paul Heinrich Dietrich d'Holbach (1723–1789). In d'Holbach's *System of Nature*, published under the pseudonym "Mirabaud," we find a thoroughgoing naturalism containing "the first behavioral analysis of mental concepts" (Campbell, 1967, p. 183). Although d'Holbach offered an early glimpse at a behavioral perspective, the Russian scientist, Ivan Pavlov, conducted research that moved it beyond theory into a testable model. Although Russian contributions remain systematically underrepresented (Aleksandrova-Howell et al., 2012), the roots of behaviorism extend into Russian physiology.

Ivan Mikhailovich Sechenov

Pavlov's immediate predecessor, **Ivan Mikhailovich Sechenov (1829–1905)**, is regarded as the founder of Russian physiology. Sechenov served as a military engineer in Kiev before embarking on medical studies at the University of Moscow. After completing a medical degree in 1856, Sechenov worked in an intense postgraduate program with luminaries in physiology such as Hermann von Helmholtz, Carl F. W. Ludwig, Johannes Müller, and Emil DuBois-Reymond.

Sechenov's academic work in Russia started with an appointment at the St. Petersburg Medico-Surgical Academy, where he influenced, among others, Ivane Tarchanoff, who would later discover the galvanic skin reflex and was a pioneer in the field of radiobiology (Tsagareli, 2012). After a decade, Sechenov resigned in disgust when the academy refused to hire the microbiologist

Ivan Sechenov

Ilya I. Mecnikov because he was a Jew. (Mecnikov was a pioneer in the study of immunology.) Sechenov returned to St. Petersburg after serving at the University of Odessa. His final academic appointment was at the University of Moscow.

Esper (1964) argued that Sechenov "wrote the first 'objective psychology' and became the first 'behaviorist' of modern times" (p. 324). The claim that Sechenov was a precursor of behaviorism is justified by his contention "that the psychical activity of man finds expression in external signs" (Frolov, 1938, p. 5). Sechenov argued for an objective psychology based on natural science in an 1863 essay titled *Reflexes of the Brain*. Brožek (1972) pointed out that "*Reflexes of the Brain* is the work of a young man who had just returned from postgraduate studies abroad. How modern, how daring it must have appeared, in 1863, 'an attempt to establish the physiological basis of psychological processes'!" (p. 18). Daring indeed—according to Frolov (1938), the government "imposed a prolonged ban on his book" (p. 4). Brožek (1972) reminded us that while *Reflexes of the Brain* anticipated the physiological approach to psychological processes, it did not "influence the development of the scientific study of behavior in the west" (p. 19). Indeed, *Reflexes of the Brain* was not published in English until 1965 and few English-speaking psychologists read the Russian edition.

Sechenov's psychological system relied on the philosophical assumption of materialistic monism. Sechenov, as quoted by Frolov (1938), noted that "the new psychology will have as its basis, in place of the philosophizings whispered by the deceitful voice of consciousness, positive facts or points of departure that can be verified at any time by experiment" (p. 6). Sechenov argued that the positive facts consist of measurable, observable movements or events and that the psychological and cerebral events are reducible to muscular movements.

The fundamental unit of study, according to Sechenov, is the reflex consisting of three parts: afferent activity, central connective processes, and efferent activity. Even so-called voluntary movements are best regarded as complicated reflex chains (see Kimble, 1996). This basic

idea was more attractive following Pavlov's later conditioning experiments. For Sechenov, the idea was promoted as a theoretical departure.

On the methodological side, Sechenov argued for a scientific psychology based on physiology. His article "Who Must Investigate the Problems of Psychology and How?" stresses that physiological methods provide the most promise for understanding psychological phenomena; he is known as "the father of Russian physiology" (Tsagareli, 2012, p. 394).

In summarizing Sechenov's psychological system, Razran (1968) emphasized "a radical environmentalism: the largest part of thoughts and ideas, 999 parts out of a 1000, as Sechenov would have it, derives from training, and only a minimal part is due to heredity" (p. 130). Such radical environmentalism held great appeal in the later Soviet system. American behaviorism under John B. Watson's leadership would also stress the priority of environmental influences.

Ivan Pavlov

Ivan Petrovich Pavlov (1849–1936) was born in Ryazan, Russia, on September 14, 1849. His

Ivan Pavlov

father was a poor village priest who cultivated vegetable gardens to feed his family. The Pavlov family endured more than its share of adversity and sorrow. Six of the eleven children did not survive childhood. Young Ivan sustained a severe head injury that delayed formal schooling until he was eleven. Fortunately, Pavlov's father, a lover of books, took a keen interest in the boy's education during this period, diminishing some detrimental effects of the injury.

In his autobiography, Pavlov (1955) stated that he received his "secondary education at the local theological seminary, which I recall with gratitude" (p. 41). In the seminary's liberal and stimulating atmosphere, a student who did not excel in one subject was encouraged in other areas. The seminary officials encouraged a vigorous exchange of ideas, permitting students to discover unique talents. At this time, Pavlov developed a love of argument, a passion that endured throughout his life. Drawing influence from Darwin and other Western scientists, Pavlov abandoned plans for the priesthood and dedicated himself to science (Windholz, 1997).

In 1870, Pavlov entered St. Petersburg University, where he pursued a degree in the natural sciences. After completing the degree in 1875, he enrolled in the Medico-Chirurgical Academy. He joined the academy "not for the purpose of becoming a physician, but with the idea that after getting the degree of doctor of medicine, I would qualify for a chair in physiology" (1955, p. 42). His doctoral thesis focused on the role of cardiac nerves in circulation. His medical degree was granted on December 19, 1879. He also won a gold medal and a scholarship for postgraduate studies.

In 1881, Pavlov married Serafina (Sara) Vassilievna Karchevskaya. Poverty and the death of two children marred their first nine years of marriage. During this time, Pavlov was in charge of S. P. Botkin's experimental laboratory at St. Petersburg. The laboratory afforded opportunities for Pavlov's early work in digestion that would later earn him a Nobel Prize. Unfortunately, the pay was meager. Sara Pavlov's difficulties were compounded when postgraduate

studies took her husband out of the country during a two-year period beginning in 1885.

Circumstances did not improve until 1890. At that time, Ivan was appointed chair of pharmacology at the Military-Medical Academy. Five years later, he was appointed chair of physiology. Pavlov could now devote himself to science without the distraction of nagging financial worries.

Pavlov's studies centered "on the physiology of circulation, digestion, and higher nervous activity" (Samoilov & Zayas, 2007, p. 75). In 1904, Pavlov won the Nobel Prize for his work on digestion (see Miyata, 2009). In his acceptance speech, he hinted at the conditioning research that would dominate his scientific life. Babkin (1949) pointed out that "the last thirty-four years of his life (from 1902 until 1936) Pavlov devoted almost exclusively to the study of the functions of the cerebral cortex by the method of conditioned reflexes" (p. 273).

Pavlov's popularity soared beyond his native Russia as he became one of science's most revered figures. Despite his international reputation, Pavlov seemed cursed with financial woes. He deposited the monetary award of his Nobel Prize into a St. Petersburg bank only to see it liquidated when the Bolsheviks came to power in the 1917 Revolution. He lost the entire sum of 73,000 gold rubles. Little wonder that Pavlov condemned the Revolution as the "greatest misfortune sustained by Russia" (Babkin, 1949, p. 161). Nonetheless, from Lenin to Stalin, the Soviet regime supported his research with funding and praise, even supporting a celebratory convention about Pavlov's work in 1951 (Academy of Sciences of the U.S.S.R., 1951). Pavlov was not appeased.

Disenchanted with communism, he flirted with the idea of moving his laboratory to either England or the United States. Recognizing his value, the Soviet government denied permission but allowed a visit to America. In July 1923, he attended a conference in New York City, where again financial hardship haunted him. After Pavlov and his son, Vladmir, boarded a train at Grand Central Station, two rough-looking men assaulted the seventy-four-year-old scientist while a third acted as a lookout. Later, Pavlov realized the men had taken his wallet, stealing as much as $2,000 in cash (Thomas, 1997).

Undeterred, Pavlov returned to the United States in 1929 and gave a rousing address before the International Congress of Psychology at Yale University. The spirited Pavlov spoke in Russian and then waited impatiently for a translator to share his words in English. Despite the language barrier, his audience was entranced. Edna Heidbreder, a young historian of psychology in the audience, recalled the animated talk delivered by the eighty-year-old physiologist:

> Pavlov seemed to be speaking with great enthusiasm, and the empathizing audience broke into enthusiastic applause without waiting for the translation. When the translation came the applauded passage proved to be a description of some apparatus used in Pavlov's laboratory. (Heidbreder, quoted in Duncan, 1980, p. 3)

While attending the 1929 Congress, Pavlov toured the Yale Primate Center with his host, Robert M. Yerkes (1876–1956), and a group of admiring comparative psychologists. During the visit, a chimpanzee singled out Pavlov and hurled its feces at him. The unflappable scientist glanced at the mortified group and realized he was the only one with facial hair. Turning to Yerkes, Pavlov joked, "How did you condition the chimpanzee only to throw at people with beards?" (Hothersall, 1995, p. 484).

Pavlov's biographers emphasized his fierce integrity, abundant energy, and complete devotion to science. Often, his obsession with research left little time for more practical matters. Sara Pavlov managed the money, bought her husband's clothes, and in general, tended to all family matters (Babkin, 1949). Sara's work was compounded not only by her impractical scientist-husband but by the four children born to the couple after the loss of the first two.

Gantt (1928) illustrated Pavlov's scientific devotion with a story of an assistant who arrived late for work one morning during the 1917 Russian Revolution. Pavlov confronted the young man about his tardiness. The assistant explained that it was difficult getting to work with all the fighting in the streets. Pavlov fumed, "What difference does a revolution make when you have work in the laboratory to do!" (p. 25). Pavlov could be blustery and demanding. Babkin (1949) admitted that "if he had been an ordinary man, he would be considered an egotist, for whom personal interests were of such paramount importance that everyone and everything had to serve them" (pp. 52–53). But then, Babkin added, Pavlov's "interests were not his personal interests in the strict sense of the word but lay outside him, so to speak" (p. 53). He was driven by a faith summed up in his classic *Lectures on Conditioned Reflexes*: "Only science, exact science about human nature itself, and the most sincere approach to it by the aid of the omnipotent scientific method, will deliver man from his present gloom, and will purge him from his contemporary shame in the sphere of interhuman relationships" (Pavlov, 1928, p. 41).

With the exception of a brief illness with gallstones in 1927, Pavlov remained vigorous and in good health until the spring of 1935, when he suffered from grippe complicated by pneumonia. Severely weakened, the eighty-five-year-old man had recurring bouts with flu-like symptoms until his death on February 26, 1936.

PAVLOV'S PSYCHOLOGICAL WORK   Pavlov's work on the gastric and salivary glands resulted in unexpected observations that led to work on "higher nervous activity." Pavlov and his colleagues measured the amount and quality of salivary and gastric secretion in relation to the nature of stimulus materials placed in a dog's mouth. Early on, there was evidence that secretions are "intelligent" in the sense that their amount and quality depend on the nature of stimulus materials. Edible materials stimulate thick and viscous saliva whereas materials high in acid or salt produce a more watery fluid. The fundamental fact, in Pavlov's words, was that "the kind of substances getting into the digestive canal from the external world, that is, whether edible or inedible, dry or liquid, as well as the different food substances, determined the onset of the work of the digestive glands, the peculiarities of their functioning in each case, the amount of reagents produced by them and their composition" (Pavlov, 1955, p. 131).

Pavlov observed another way in which salivary activity is "intelligent." In his Nobel speech, Pavlov (1955) noted that "it has long been known that the sight of tasty food makes the mouth of a hungry man water" (p. 139). He added that though such an observation is commonplace, its implications and mechanisms had never been investigated. Pavlov and his colleagues observed after multiple trials that dogs salivated at the mere sight of food used in gastric experiments. Furthermore, other stimuli such as containers and noises associated with food also produced salivation. Salivation produced in early trials, as a result of the direct action of the food, is understandable in terms of classic reflex theory. That is, food has a direct action on the receptor system and the response is understandable in terms of material and efficient causes. But salivation at the mere sight of the food or at the sight or sound of a stimulus associated with the food is a different matter. Pavlov referred to such salivation as **action at a distance** and in his early work also referred to it as a **psychical reflex**. Later, these terms were replaced with more exact terminology.

The concept of *action at a distance* was troublesome for Pavlov in the fields of physiology and psychology, just as the same term had been troublesome for other scientists such as Descartes and Newton in physics. The issue in physics centered on the action of magnets, gases, gravitational fields, and the transmission of light. How could such actions be explained in terms of direct action or efficient causes? (See Hess, 1967, pp. 9–15 for a brief but helpful discussion of the problem.) Action at a distance, at least from a superficial standpoint, appeared to challenge material and efficient causality, so central to science as Pavlov conceived it. Specifically, what was it that stimulated the salivary glands when the animal salivated at the mere sight of the food? The expression *psychical reflex* provided only a nominal solution. The term didn't really explain anything; it provided only a name for an observed relationship. Pavlov wanted to understand the mechanism responsible for the so-called psychical reflex.

Pavlov concluded that he was dealing with two kinds of reflexes. He regarded the physiological reflex as unconditioned. An external stimulus (food) stimulates an organism's nerves, acting on the effectors through connecting nerves. This simple reflex is understandable in terms of material and efficient causation. The second type of reflex also originates in external stimuli, but activates the eye, ear, or nose rather than receptors in the oral cavity. Pavlov (1955) observed that the new reflex "is permanently subject to fluctuation, and is, therefore, *conditioned*" (p. 144). Pavlov argued that conditioned reflexes, like the unconditioned reflexes, "can be easily conceived from the physiological point of view as a function of the nervous system" (p. 145). The task was then to discover the functional relations between the two types of reflexes.

Pavlov (1928) observed that "nervous activity consists in general of the phenomena of excitation and inhibition" and argued that either phenomenon can spread, or irradiate, over the cortex (p. 156). Such irradiation provides a conceptual basis for connections between stimulus events from various sensory modalities. Thus, through the spread of nervous activity over the cortex, visual, auditory, or other signals may be associated with the unconditioned reflex.

In time, Pavlov's basic paradigm was elaborated in terms of an **unconditioned stimulus (UCS)** that reliably produces an **unconditioned reflex (UCR)**. The unconditioned stimulus is a biologically adequate stimulus that has the capacity to automatically induce the reflex activity that terminates with the unconditioned reflex. The unconditioned, or unlearned, reflex has a high degree of automaticity. The **conditioned stimulus (CS)** was at one time a neutral stimulus, but after repeated pairings with the UCS, the CS produces a reflex similar to the UCR, the **conditioned reflex (CR)**. These findings would remain the topic of research into the present (Bitterman, 2006).

The temporal relations between the UCS and the CS resulted in findings that surprised

Pavlov and his coworkers. They discovered that conditioning was optimal when the CS precedes the UCS by a fraction of a second (see Figure 13.1A). This arrangement of the CS and the UCS is called *delayed conditioning*. Another temporal arrangement, much less efficient than delayed conditioning, is called *simultaneous conditioning* (Figure 13.1C). The most interesting discovery regarding the relationship of the CS and the UCS is called *trace conditioning*. In this arrangement, the CS and the UCS are initially paired, as in Figure 13.1A, but then the temporal interval between the two is increased so that the CS occurs prior to the UCS and is terminated before the UCS occurs (Figure 13.1B). As the temporal interval between termination of the CS and the onset of the UCS increased, Pavlov's dogs sometimes became drowsy or even fell asleep. Pavlov

argued that the CS may be associated with local cortical inhibition and that, in the absence of the excitatory UCS, the inhibition associated with the CS may irradiate over the surface of the cortex. Sleep resulted from the spread of inhibition.

Pavlov studied other topics that inspired learning research in the twentieth century. Some of the key areas are **extinction, spontaneous recovery, disinhibition, stimulus generalization,** and **discrimination**.

Extinction   When the CS is presented repeatedly in the absence of the UCS, Pavlov found that the CS loses its ability to produce salivary activity.

Spontaneous Recovery   As mentioned, the CS loses its ability to produce the CR if it is presented repeatedly in the absence of the UCS.

Type of Conditioning   **Temporal Relation of CS and UCS**

A. Delayed   CS   UCS

B. Trace   CS   UCS

C. Simultaneous   CS   UCS

Time

FIGURE 13.1
Temporal Relations between the CS and the UCS in Classical Conditioning

But, following a period of rest, the CS may again elicit the CR; Pavlov called this phenomenon spontaneous recovery. The CR, however, is extinguished if the CS is again presented several times without the UCS.

Disinhibition   An animal that has stopped salivating in the presence of the CS may salivate in the presence of a different, sudden, or unexpected stimulus. Pavlov assumed that the CS is associated with inhibition. An unexpected stimulus may release the inhibition and the animal will then salivate.

Stimulus Generalization   Stimuli similar to the original CS may also elicit the CR. Thus, if the original stimulus is a bell that produces a given pitch, then a bell that produces a similar pitch may also elicit the CR.

Discrimination   Pavlov observed that discriminations, sometimes even remarkably fine ones, can be conditioned. Thus, a circular shape may be reliably associated with food (the UCS), whereas an ellipse may never be associated with the UCS. The dog soon learns to salivate to a circle, but not to an ellipse. If the ellipse is gradually changed so that it looks more and more like the circle, the discrimination becomes difficult. Such a procedure tests the discriminatory capacity of the animal. It also serves as a major frustration, especially if it is important to make the discrimination, as it may well be for a hungry dog. The behavior of the dog in difficult discrimination tasks became a major curiosity for Pavlov and contributed to his interest in the problems of psychiatry (Wolpe & Plaud, 1997). Prior to elaborating on this topic, it is important to examine another dimension of Pavlov's theory.

Temperament   As noted earlier, Pavlov believed in two fundamental processes in the nervous system: inhibition and excitation. Both were distributed in different temperaments. He observed that some dogs, such as the terrier types, are nervous, excitable, quick, short tempered, and alert. Pavlov believed that such dogs have more excitation than inhibition. By contrast, other dogs are timid, hesitant, and shy. He believed that such

dogs (perhaps the collie) are dominated more by inhibition than excitation. Other dogs are warm, friendly, and affable. They represent a balanced temperament marked by an even mix of inhibition and excitation. Pavlov believed that Galen's classification of temperaments prove true for both humans and dogs. Pavlov's version of Galen's scheme is illustrated in Table 13.1.

In accepting the idea of temperamental differences, Pavlov departed from Sechenov's radical environmentalism. Pavlov concluded that temperamental differences interact with learning processes. More importantly, temperamental differences dictate how a dog will respond to laboratory-induced stress caused from difficult discrimination problems.

Experimental Neurosis   Beginning in the 1920s until his death in 1936, Pavlov's interests shifted to clinical problems (Windholz, 1990). Pavlov (1941) found that almost any assault on the nervous system might produce discernible consequences. Difficult discriminations or severe conflict, coupled with a rundown physical condition caused by periods of long work, lack of sleep, or physical illness, had an especially powerful effect. Resistance to stress was clearly a function of general health and temperament. Some dogs were naturally more resistant to stress than others.

Table 13.1 Galen's Classification of Temperaments

Temperamental General Type	Characteristics
Choleric	Excitable, touchy, quick tempered; marked by excess of excitation
Sanguine	Marked by warmth, balance of excitation and inhibition
Phlegmatic	Not easily excited, also balanced between excitation and inhibition
Melancholic	Tendency toward depressed moods, excess of inhibition

Pavlov found that severe stress-producing situations resulted in what he called ultraboundary or **ultramaximal inhibition**. The effects of such inhibition can be thought of as somewhat comparable to the effects of shock, which may also result from a severe biological insult. Just after a severe crash or life-threatening situation, an individual may show shock-like symptoms. Such symptoms may be marked by a vacant stare, unresponsiveness, or stereotyped responding. Pavlov believed that a powerful assault on the nervous system may convulse the brain in inhibition. If the entire cortex is in an inhibitory mode, then one could expect that the organism would be unresponsive. In the face of overwhelming threat, inhibition can be protective, at least in the sense that it may block the input of a still more threatening stimulation.

Laboratory studies revealed three different after effects of ultramaximal inhibition. First, some animals display the **equivalent phase**, whereby the dog responds with the same amount of saliva regardless of the strength of a stimulus. Sargant (1957) pointed out that "the observation is comparable to the frequent reports by normal people in periods of intense fatigue, that there is little difference between their emotional reactions to important or trivial experiences" (p. 64).

Following a more profound biological or psychological insult, the dog may display the **paradoxical phase**. In this phase, a strong stimulus produces a weak response (very little saliva) and a weak stimulus produces a strong response (much saliva). The paradoxical phase has counterparts in humans in stress situations. A whisper may produce an explosive outburst, whereas a shout may result in little more than an eyeblink. The paradoxical phase makes sense in terms of Pavlov's notion of ultramaximal inhibition. Perhaps there are circumstances in which a weak stimulus gets through the inhibitory barrier and is fully processed, whereas a strong stimulus does not get fully processed. If such were the case, then one might predict a weak response to a strong stimulus and a strong response to a weak stimulus.

Pavlov had the most interest in the **ultraparadoxical phase**. Following severe trauma, Pavlov observed a radical shift in the personality of the dog and its response system. In this phase, stimuli that previously produced a positive response now produced a negative response and vice versa. Sargant (1957) observed that in this phase the dog may "attach itself to a laboratory attendant whom it had previously disliked, and try to attack the master whom it has previously loved" (p. 65). The ultraparadoxical phase is all the more interesting in that its effects may be long lasting. In his book *Battle for the Mind*, Sargant (1957) showed how the ultraparadoxical phase may explain political and religious conversions, especially when such conversions follow an intense assault on the nervous system. Such an assault, at the human level, may include rhythmic chanting or singing, fatigue, and threats of damnation or death in an atmosphere that undermines individual adequacy and judgment. Sargant (1957) sought to use similar methods therapeutically to improve the condition of people with severe psychological illnesses, and he generated extensive controversy with his enthusiastic support of insulin and electric shock therapies, among others (Dally, 2004).

Pavlov became increasingly concerned that inhibition and excitation interact with temperament to produce a variety of psychiatric illnesses. He believed that choleric (predominantly excitatory) and melancholic (predominantly inhibitory) individuals are more vulnerable to breakdown, whereas sanguine and phlegmatic (balanced types) were more resistant to stress. However, any individual, subjected to sufficient stress, would likely break down. Pavlov's work in this area had a major impact on the field of neuroscience (Gray, 1999; Grimsley & Windholz, 2000; Pickenhain, 1999) as well as the development of behavioral therapy in Russia and abroad (Sukhodolsky, Tsytsarev, & Kassinove, 1995; Wolpe & Plaud, 1997).

Problem Solving In his final years, Pavlov became increasingly interested in the nature of problem solving. The Gestalt psychologist Wolfgang Köhler (see Chapter 15) had argued that higher primates do not solve problems in a mechanical stimulus–response fashion. Rather, in open situations, such as field settings, primates show evidence of true insight achieved not through mechanical means but through creative, novel, and flexible response modes. Such a holistic approach to problem solving represented a direct challenge to Pavlov's mechanistic and reductionistic system. As a consequence of Köhler's work, Pavlov initiated research in 1933 with two chimpanzees named Raphael and Rosa (see Windholz, 1984). During the last three years of his life, Pavlov replicated some of Köhler's experiments but offered his own explanations in terms of the mechanics of conditioning and trial and error.

Pavlov's conflict with the Gestalt psychologists was illustrated in polemical comments that came out of his Wednesday meetings with staff and colleagues. Pavlov's respect for and concern about Köhler's work is evident in a lecture from January 23, 1935:

> Now gentlemen, we shall pass from peaceful affairs, if we may say so, to matters of war, to Mr. Köhler. We are at war with him. This is a serious struggle against psychologists. Köhler is professor of psychology at Berlin University. A scientist of minor authority would hardly be elected to a chair in Berlin University; they respect hierarchy there. (Pavlov, 1955, p. 606)

Such a statement reflects Pavlov's tight systematic worldview and his sensitivity to storm clouds on the horizon that threatened his viewpoint. The tension between Pavlov's mechanistic view and Köhler's holistic psychology would dominate the intellectual agenda in psychology for years to come.

In his autobiography, Pavlov relished the happiness and success he found in science. "I devoted myself to the laboratory. I have renounced practicality in life with its cunning and not always

irreproachable ways, and I see no reason for regretting this; on the contrary, precisely in this I find now certain consolation" (Pavlov, 1955, p. 44). Pavlov did not live to witness the enormous worldwide influence of his system, but the later success of his work and its extensive heuristic value would doubtless have been a source of even greater satisfaction.

Other Russian Psychologies

There were concerted efforts in the former Soviet Union to impose intellectual constraints on all the sciences, including psychology. Scientific activities and theories were to be guided by, and consistent with, Marxist–Leninist ideology. As a result, there were topical areas such as research in genetics that were de-emphasized or even rejected altogether. Pavlov's psychology was viewed as congruent with many of the assumptions encountered in Marxist–Leninist thought though there is little evidence that he purposely set out to construct a system that fit in with the larger Soviet political ideology.

There were other systematic approaches to psychology in the early days of the Soviet Union that did not fare so well. For example, **Vladimir Mikhailovich Bekhterev (1857–1927)** advanced an objective psychology based on the idea that the reflex is the fundamental category of inquiry in psychology. His position, often referred to as **reflexology**, was practiced in the Bekhterev Psychoneural Institute, a research center dedicated to studies in pedagogy, law, criminology, medicine, and experimental psychology (Zhuravel, 1995). Though Bekhterev worked to reconcile his system with Marxist–Leninist thought, his work was gradually discredited for failure to comply with Soviet ideology (Misiak & Sexton, 1966, p. 267). Bekhterev may also have lost favor because he at one time had described the Soviet Communist dictator Joseph Stalin as "paranoic." Shereshevskii (1994) notes that Bekhterev's mysterious death prompted conspiracy theorists to speculate that the careless remarks about Stalin may have cost him his life.

Another attempt to construct a psychological system congruent with Marist–Leninist thought is encountered in the work of **Konstantin Nikolaevich Kornilov (1879–1957)**. Kornilov's system, known as **reactology**, stressed the importance of social and economic forces in shaping human reactions. In his treatment, psychology was not just a natural science; it was also a social science, and the behavior of the whole person in social context was emphasized.

Edward Lee Thorndike

In the United States, **Edward Lee Thorndike (1874–1949)** advanced a system of thought that was consistent with some of the major behavioristic viewpoints. Educated in the functionalist tradition, Thorndike remained sympathetic to the tolerant spirit of functionalism. Nevertheless, he favored a more objective psychology that focused on the observable actions of living organisms. He didn't care for the method of introspection and the study of people's minds (or inner states) as the appropriate subject matter for psychology. He believed that anything that exists, exists in some amount, and is thus quantifiable. Inspired by other sciences, he applied scientific methods to such a host of problems that he has been called "America's most productive psychologist" (Jonçich, 1968). From a broad philosophical standpoint, Thorndike can be considered a functionalist, but his practical work can be viewed as a precursor to behaviorism.

Thorndike was the second of the four children of Edward Roberts Thorndike and Abbie Brewster Ladd. His father abandoned law in favor of the Methodist ministry. The atmosphere of the Thorndike home was austere and serious, with emphasis on duty, industry, independence, discipline, honesty, and propriety. Many of the values of Thorndike's home were put to productive use in his adult years. Thorndike appropriated a moral code of his own that was more liberal than his family's, at least in matters of religion.

Thorndike entered Wesleyan University in Middletown, Connecticut, in 1891 and graduated from that institution in 1895. Later, he received a master's degree in psychology from Harvard, where he kindled a friendship with William James. Following his work at Harvard, Thorndike enrolled in the graduate program at Columbia, where he studied with James McKeen Cattell. He graduated with a Ph.D. from Columbia in 1898. After holding a brief faculty position at Western Reserve University, he accepted an appointment at Columbia, where he remained until his retirement in 1941. During his long and productive career, Thorndike was president of the American Psychological Association in 1912, was elected to the National Academy of Sciences, and won a gold medal award from Columbia for his distinguished research contributions to education. Thorndike died in Montrose, New York, on August 9, 1949.

THORNDIKE'S WORK   Thorndike's contributions ranged over a variety of problems in psychology and education (Hilgard, 1996). He was a pioneer in the experimental study of animal behavior and advanced an early learning theory. His work is best understood in the context of his views about human nature. Though Thorndike had one foot in the camp of associationists and empiricists such as David Hartley and John Locke, the other foot was planted in the camp of Francis Galton, who emphasized heredity. For Thorndike, simple social engineering of rewards and punishments cannot transmit all knowledge to humans. His research confirmed that heredity plays a powerful role in human life. He compared identical twins on various tasks (see Thorndike, 1905) and was struck by similarities in their performance. He also observed that correlations between identical twins were greater than correlations between other siblings. Jonçich (1968) noted that he believed in individual differences, but "Thorndike's individual is already armed, well or poorly, by. . .genes" (p. 333). The role of learning is critical to the individual and society, but learning alone will not achieve all things. In his view, genetic principles far outweigh learning and should not be neglected.

Thorndike's learning theory arose from early laboratory studies with cats (Baker &

Serdikoff, 2013; Chance, 1999). His doctoral dissertation at Columbia was published in 1898 under the title *Animal Intelligence*. In his dissertation, Thorndike rejected earlier anecdotal and anthropomorphic work on animal study in favor of groundbreaking methods that remain the basis for comparative psychology more than a century later (Galef, 1998). This work, now a classic in the psychology of learning, set forth the basics of a theory of learning known as **connectionism**.

In his doctoral research, Thorndike placed a cat in a "puzzle box" constructed of wooden slats and hardware cloth. He then positioned a fish outside the box as an incentive to escape. Once inside, the cat could open the door and escape by pressing a lever in one box or tugging on a wire loop in another. As the cats became "box wise," learning to escape from simpler boxes, Thorndike placed them in more challenging boxes. To escape "Box K" shown in Figure 13.2, a cat would need to depress a treadle, pull on a string, and push a bar up and down. While learning to escape from the fifteen different puzzle boxes, the cats exhibited behaviors that appeared random. (Thorndike

preferred to describe the learning process as "trial and accidental success" rather than "trial and error," but the latter became the more popular expression.) In time, irrelevant movements dropped out and a specific series of actions became associated with the desired consequence.

Similar to Pavlov, Thorndike sought to understand complex events (e.g., learning complex tasks) through more simple processes (e.g., building learned connections) (Donahoe & Vegas, 2011); therefore, he emphasized the connections or bonds between sense impressions and response patterns. Learning, in his view, involved the strengthening of bonds or connections, which he believed were grounded in physiology. This was one of the earliest and most influential of the stimulus–response or S–R psychologies. Thorndike formulated the **law of exercise**, which states that connections are strengthened through repetition or use and weakened through disuse. Stated in more simple terms, you use it or you lose it.

Thorndike also proposed a **law of effect** to explain that connections are strengthened or weakened as a result of their consequences. In its

FIGURE 13.2
Thorndike's "Box K"

early expression, the law of effect asserted that a connection is strengthened when followed by a "satisfying" state of affairs and weakened when followed by an "annoying" state of affairs. Thus, reward or reinforcement strengthens a connection and punishment weakens it. These two principal laws laid the foundation, in part, for his system of behavior analysis (Donahoe, 1999). Thorndike also recognized the importance of factors such as maturation or readiness to respond, the ability to generalize, and mental set or attitude.

Thorndike later modified both the law of exercise and the law of effect. He abandoned his law of exercise after determining that exercise alone (as mere blind repetition) does not strengthen a connection. Rather, exercise in conjunction with other conditions strengthens connections. For example, if information about the response's accuracy accompanies each repetition of a response then a connection might be strengthened. The modified law of effect, sometimes called the **truncated law of effect**, casts doubt on punishment as a means of weakening connections. According to the truncated law of effect, a satisfying state of affairs will strengthen the behavior that it follows. Thorndike's doubts about the efficacy of punishment arose from research in which participants matched one of five English words with a Spanish equivalent. When participants chose correctly, the experimenter rewarded them by saying *Right*. When participants chose incorrectly, the experimenter employed punishment by saying *Wrong*. It was found that punished connections did not tend to drop out, but rewarded connections tended to be retained. Thorndike explored the efficacy of punishment in other ways and concluded that it was not an effective means of weakening connections.

In other noteworthy research, Thorndike collaborated with Robert S. Woodworth on the transfer of training. Conventional wisdom held that knowledge of certain academic subjects improved intellectual ability in general. For example, studying Latin provided more than knowledge of the ancient language; it was thought to enhance logic and reasoning skills as well. The idea that

certain subjects held beneficial cognitive effects was called the **doctrine of formal discipline**. This doctrine assumes that the mind is somewhat like a muscle and that certain exercises can strengthen the "mental muscle."

The opposite view does not deny the importance of the exercise of intellectual functions, but holds that the transfer of abilities is more specific than assumed by the doctrine of formal discipline. This conflicting view, sometimes called the **identical elements transfer theory**, emphasizes the degree of identity between the first and second tasks. Thorndike and Woodworth (1901) demonstrated that the amount of transfer is a function of the similarities between two tasks. Transfer is sometimes small even when tasks are similar. For example, improvements in the accuracy of judgments of line lengths of 0.5 to 1.5 inches did not result in better subsequent judgments of line lengths of 6 to 12 inches.

Working with simple perceptual problems, Thorndike and Woodworth supported the identical elements transfer theory, but the concern remained that subjects such as Latin and geometry might have general transfer values in the real world. More than two decades after his work with Woodworth, Thorndike (1924) conducted a classic study on the transfer effects of specific high school courses. Using 8,564 high school students as subjects, Thorndike investigated the relative effects of a great variety of courses (e.g., algebra, physics, psychology, Latin, French, biology) on subsequent problem-solving ability. He found surprisingly small transfer effects of various subjects on later problem-solving ability. However, students in the upper levels of ability at the beginning of the study gained far more than students who entered the study with lower levels of ability. Thorndike's work had far-reaching implications for education.

Following Thorndike, educators emphasized the relationship between the content of a subject in school and the demands of daily life. The new educational rule was simple and practical: If you want to know English, study English; if you want to know algebra, study algebra; and so forth. Studies in the transfer of training remain an important area in the psychology of learning, and Thorndike is known as a pioneer of educational psychology (Beatty, 2005).

THORNDIKE'S OTHER INTERESTS   As noted, Thorndike had interests in a host of topics in psychology and education. His publications on the psychology of labor (Thorndike, 1922) and the psychology of the profit motive (Thorndike, 1936) are important early contributions to industrial psychology. On the subject of labor, Thorndike argued that work is not necessarily aversive and encouraged research on worker satisfaction and dissatisfaction. He was interested in ways to humanize capitalism. He believed in the value of the profit motive but thought psychology could address social problems associated with it.

Perhaps stemming from his early background, he found interest in the meaning of education in a scientific and technological age. Thorndike (1920) expressed concern about twentieth-century adherence to dogmatism and beliefs in magic as well as beliefs guided by emotion rather than intellect. He believed that our great task is to improve the quality of life. This belief fueled his mature work on the effects of social context on lifestyle. His books, *Human Nature and the Social Order* (1940), *Man and His Works* (1943), and *Your City* (1939), demonstrate his social–psychological interests and optimism about psychology's role in addressing problems of daily life. Thorndike was a "sane positivist" who believed that a science of values can guide moral assessment, social policy, and the betterment of humanity (Beatty, 1998; Dewsbury, 1998).

John B. Watson (1878–1958), the founder of American behaviorism, applauded Thorndike's work. As noted by Jonçich (1968), Watson seldom praised others, but he admired the way Thorndike conducted his investigations (p. 414). For his part, Thorndike appreciated Watson's behaviorist program, but in the Jamesian spirit, he worried that behaviorism could evolve into a "restrictive orthodoxy" (see Jonçich, 1968, p. 418).

FORMAL FOUNDING OF AMERICAN BEHAVIORISM

American behaviorism was rooted in familiar philosophical and scientific soil dating back to the early work of philosophical materialists (Leahey, 1992; O'Neil, 1995). Yet, when John B. Watson introduced his systematic vision in 1913, it seemed fresh and simple, even revolutionary. Behaviorism promised a radical break from the dominant psychologies of the day. Behaviorism held appeal because it offered a direct and unambiguous message. Watson promised a new and better way to do things—a way that offered hope for cutting through past complexities.

John B. Watson

We can find little in Watson's humble background to suggest he would become one of the most influential scientists of his age. John Broadus Watson was born in Travelers Rest near Greenville, South Carolina, on January 9, 1878. He was the youngest of four children of Pickens Butler Watson and Emma Roe. Watson's parents offer a study in contrast, and he was torn by ambivalent feelings about them. Pickens was a handsome man with powerful lusts for hard liquor and women. According to Brewer (1989), he ran a sawmill in Greenville but devoted weekends to indulging in his own pleasures. Unlike her roguish husband, Emma Watson was at home in the conservative atmosphere of Southern Baptist country. Her evangelical efforts influenced an older son but were lost on Pickens and John B. Watson.

In a candid autobiography, Watson (1961) described himself as a lazy and insubordinate youth. He seldom made above a passing grade in grammar and high school and was arrested twice, once for fighting and once for shooting a firearm in the city. In many respects, John was rowdy like Pickens but saw firsthand the consequences of his father's lack of responsibility. According to Buckley (1989), Emma Watson "singled out John Broadus Watson for a special destiny. Emma had named her son after John Albert Broadus, a prominent Baptist minister" (p. 4). Brewer (1989) noted that Emma once extracted a promise from John that he would enter the Baptist ministry. After Emma's death in 1900, however, Watson showed no interest in religion.

In the fall of 1894, Watson enrolled in Furman University. He worked his way through school and showed an improved but still undistinguished academic performance (Harris, 1999a). In his autobiography, he explained why he took five years and graduated with an A.M. instead of taking four years and graduating with an A.B. One of his professors declared that "if a man ever handed in a paper backwards, he would flunk him" (Watson, 1961, p. 272). Watson inadvertently handed his paper in backward, and the professor kept his word!

Watson's decision about where to pursue a Ph.D. was made partly on the basis of language requirements. He decided to attend the University of Chicago when he learned that Princeton still required reading knowledge of Greek and Latin. At Chicago, Watson studied with an all-star cast: John Dewey, the neurologist Henry Donaldson, and the well-known physiologist Jacques Loeb. However, James Rowland Angell had the most influence on Watson. Indeed, Angell became a father figure. Some years later, Watson discovered the pain of breaking intellectual ties with his mentor.

Watson developed rigorous work habits at Chicago that persevered his entire life. His work was so intense, however, that it may have contributed to a nervous breakdown in his third year at Chicago. He called it "a typical Angst," marked by sleeplessness and fear of the dark. Watson noted that his breakdown caused him "to accept a large part of Freud, when I first began to get really acquainted with him" (Watson, 1961, p. 274). He recovered, completed his dissertation, and graduated magna cum laude in 1903.

After graduation, Watson was appointed as a laboratory assistant at Chicago, a position he held for five years. The year 1903 was pivotal for Watson in another way. A young student named Mary Ickes had fallen in love with her handsome laboratory instructor. Watson's salary was hardly adequate to support a family, but emotion triumphed over practical considerations. The marriage was apparently successful for a number of years and brought forth two children, John and Polly.

In 1908, Watson accepted an offer as chair of psychology at Johns Hopkins University. He had achieved recognition for his research and was viewed as one of the country's most promising young psychologists. Despite his poor salary at Chicago, Watson had a difficult time leaving James Rowland Angell. Because Watson was departing from his teacher's brand of functional psychology, the separation had both a physical and an intellectual quality.

Watson developed the essentials of behaviorism during his early years at Hopkins. In the classroom, he "taught a modified James type of general psychology" (Watson, 1961, pp. 276–277), but his research focused on animal behavior. In his postdoctorate years, Watson carried on animated discussions with other psychologists such as Robert Yerkes, Knight Dunlap, and Karl Lashley. With these friends, he felt secure in exploring ideas that formed the later foundations of behaviorism (O'Donnell, 1985). Surprisingly, Watson remained friendly to Freud's work and even proclaimed in 1912 that "I believe thoroughly in the method of psychoanalysis" (cited in Rilling, 2000b, p. 304). Before long, though, his views on Freud hardened, leading him to predict in 1924 that "20 years from now an analyst using Freudian concepts and Freudian terminology will be placed in the same category as a phrenologist" (Watson, 1924a, p. 243).

Inspired by Pavlovian conditioning, Watson designed behaviorism as a new method to compete with Titchener's method of introspection and Freud's method of psychoanalysis (Rilling, 2000a). In 1913, the *Psychological Review* published Watson's classic article, "Psychology as the Behaviorist Views It." It was no easy matter for Watson to publish a paper that attacked the method of introspection and the old view that psychology is the study of consciousness. The reaction of his mentor, Angell, was predictable. According to Cohen (1979), Angell wrote to Titchener that "I shall be glad to see [Watson] properly spanked even though I cannot join the ceremony" (p. 79). Five years after Watson joined the Hopkins faculty, the die was cast. The new system was launched.

World War I interrupted Watson's work at Hopkins. He was inducted into military service and put in charge of aviation examining boards. A major task for such boards involved the selection of pilots for World War I fighter planes. He also worked on the use of homing pigeons in delivering military messages. Late in the war, he worked on a medical project on oxygen deprivation but ran into trouble with his supervisors. A superior recommended that he be "sent to the line," which conveyed, according to Watson's assessment, a wish on the part of his supervisors that he be killed! Fortunately, the war ended before the plan was put into action. He returned to civilian clothes as quickly as possible.

In his autobiography, Watson described his military work as a nightmare: "Never have I seen such incompetence, such extravagance, such a group of overbearing, inferior men" (Watson, 1961, p. 278). After his army experience, he claimed to understand how some officers fail to return from missions even when not engaged by enemy troops.

Back at Johns Hopkins, Watson's academic career came to an abrupt and dramatic halt following his affair with a new graduate student. Rosalie Rayner came from a respected Baltimore family and was a recent graduate of Vassar. Before long, whispered rumors about an affair between the renowned professor and the daughter of a distinguished family created a scandal in Baltimore. Community gossip hit a fever pitch when Watson and Rayner's love letters were discovered and published in local newspapers. University officials found no other recourse than to ask Watson to resign his position in 1920. After divorcing his first wife, the forty-two-year-old psychologist married Rosalie Rayner in 1921. The loss of his academic position embittered Watson. In his view, an affair between consenting adults should not constitute grounds for dismissal. University officials saw the matter from a different perspective. Rumors have endured

that Watson was fired not only for this affair, but also for inappropriately conducting research on physiological responses during sexual intercourse. Despite the persistence of these rumors, the allegations may not be true (see Benjamin, Whitaker, & Ramsey, 2007).

In his autobiography, Watson told of the hardships of the first few months after resigning from Hopkins: "I went to New York, stranded economically and to some extent emotionally. I lived the summer and fall out with William I. Thomas. What I should have done without his understanding counsel and his helpfulness on the economic side, I do not know. I was a product of schools and colleges. I knew nothing of life outside the walls of a university" (Watson, 1961, p. 279).

Similar to Watson, the sociologist William I. Thomas (1863–1947) had been dismissed from the University of Chicago following a career-threatening scandal. Thomas introduced his friend to Stanley Resor, president of the J. Walter Thompson Company, a prominent advertising firm. Watson was given a temporary assignment to study the rubber boot market. Soon he was ringing doorbells and canvassing the Mississippi River to determine boot preferences. Following this work, he was given a permanent position in charge of the sales of Yuban coffee and Pond's facial creams. Within a year, Watson reported that he had "found himself" and discovered it "just as thrilling to watch the growth of a sales curve of a new product as to watch the learning curve of animals or men" (Watson, 1961, p. 280). His behaviorism did not signal a revolution in advertising, though he rejected popular catchy slogans in favor of appeals to consumer attitudes about prestige and image (Coon, 1994). By 1924, Watson was vice president of the J. Walter Thompson Company. He was soon a wealthy man whose pioneering contributions to advertising and sales were as noteworthy in the business world as his contributions in psychology were to academia.

Watson and Rosalie Rayner had two children, William and James. Brewer (1989) suggested that the boy's first names were no accident, because Watson was a great admirer of

William James. Though Watson never returned to academia, he continued to write books and articles on psychology (Harris, 1999a). His writings after 1920, however, were geared for popular consumption. His later writings lacked discipline and were overly bold in their claims but gained public recognition for use of newspapers, popular magazines, and radio broadcasts to promote his message of behaviorism.

In 1936, Rosalie Rayner Watson died of dysentery. Now with the William K. Esty Company, Watson remained in advertising, but his creative spark had vanished with Rosalie's passing. After retiring in 1947, Watson withdrew more and more, though he attempted to be a good father for Billy and Jimmy, who were teenagers. He stayed in touch with a few academic colleagues, especially Karl Lashley (Dewsbury, 1993).

In an overview of the behaviorist's career, Bergmann (1956) declared that John B. Watson was second only to Freud as "the most important figure in the history of psychological thought during the first half of the century" (p. 265). Watson's contributions were substantial. First, of course, was the systematic objective approach to the discipline. His conceptual approach was also tied to important experimental work in comparative psychology, learning, and emotional conditioning in children (Morris & Todd, 1999). This latter work had a direct influence on the development of behavior therapy. All of this was accomplished in the relatively short span of Watson's academic career, from 1903 to 1920—a time interrupted by his service in World War I. Watson also influenced the world of advertising and, with his many popular articles, contributed to public awareness of psychology. His remarkable career came to an end when he died on September 25, 1958. Tragically, Watson burned his correspondence shortly before his death, depriving historians of invaluable insights into the man and his work.

WATSON'S PSYCHOLOGY   Behaviorism came to birth in a time when nearly all psychologies of the day—the psychologies of Angell, Dewey, James, Titchener, and Wundt—studied consciousness through the revered method of introspection. Watson (1924a) despaired that "literally hundreds of thousands of printed pages have been published on the minute analysis of this intangible something called 'consciousness'" (p. 5). No more. Behaviorism promised sweeping change. Watson (1924a) advised that "behaviorism is new wine and it will not go into old bottles. . .therefore. . .I am going to ask you to put away all of your old presuppositions" (p. 10).

Despite inconsistencies in his own work (see Salzinger, 1994), Watson's criticisms of the older psychologies were aggressive and unapologetic. We'll consider some of his concerns.

1. *The divisions of consciousness are arbitrary.* In his famous article "Psychology as the Behaviorist Views It," Watson (1913) asked the reader to consider "the question of the number of isolable sensations. Is there an extremely large number of color sensations—or only four, red, green, yellow and blue?" (p. 164). He argued that if we count each just noticeable difference, then "we are forced to admit that the number is so large and the conditions for attaining them so complex that the concept of sensation is unusable, either for the purpose of analysis or that of synthesis" (p. 164).

2. *Psychology is too human centered.* Another major criticism of the older psychology was that it had little use for observed facts outside of human consciousness. Animal behavior and comparative psychology were treated as embarrassments. In effect, the old psychology was too human centered; he argued that early biology faced the same dilemma. Watson (1913) discussed the predicament that arose when "the whole Darwinian movement was judged by the bearing it had upon the origin and development of the human race" (p. 162). When emphasis shifted to the experimental study of adaptation and descent, biology was rescued from anthropocentrism. By the same token, behaviorism promised to rescue psychology from the same intellectual danger.

3. *Introspection is unreliable and esoteric.* Watson (1913) noted that if one person cannot replicate another's results, it is assumed that the introspectionist was poorly trained. Thus, "the attack is made upon the experimental setting. In physics and chemistry the attack is made upon the experimental conditions. The apparatus was not sensitive enough, impure chemicals were used, etc. In these sciences a better technique will give reproducible results. Psychology is otherwise. If you can't observe 3–9 states of clearness in attention, your introspection is poor. If, on the other hand, a feeling seems reasonably clear to you, your introspection is again faulty. You are seeing too much. Feelings are never clear" (p. 163).

4. *Older psychologies are dualistic.* Watson (1913) claimed that the older psychologies were fed on the relative merits of parallelism and interactionism. He then declared, "I should like to bring my students up in the same ignorance of such hypotheses as one finds among the students of other branches of science" (p. 166). He believed that if behavior is the subject matter of psychology, then mind–brain positions should be of no greater interest to the psychologist than to the chemist or physicist.

With characteristic brashness, Watson (1913) attacked structuralists as well as functionalists. "I have done my best to understand the difference between functional psychology and structural psychology. Instead of clarity, confusion grows upon me. The terms sensation, perception, affection, emotion, volition are used as much by the functionalist as by the structuralist. The addition of the word 'process' . . . after each serves in some way to remove the corpse of 'content' and to leave 'function' in its stead" (p. 165). Ambiguity characterized both structural and functional psychologies. What was required, according to Watson, was a radical break with both.

Definition of Psychology Watson (1924a) argued that "the definition of any one science, physics, for example, would necessarily include the definition of all other sciences" (p. 11). Then we "mark a ring around that part of the whole of natural science that we claim particularly as our own" (p. 11). Just like the physicist, the psychologist studies reactions, adjustments, movements, activities, and behaviors. Watson promoted psychology as a behavioral science.

Relation to Other Sciences Watson (1913) declared in the opening of his manifesto that "psychology as the behaviorist views it is a purely objective experimental branch of natural science" (p. 158). In *Behaviorism*, Watson (1924a) pointed out that "its closest scientific companion is physiology. It is different from physiology only in the grouping of its problems, not in fundamentals or in central viewpoint" (p. 11). He acknowledged the importance of studying behavior in social and cultural context, thus recognizing that psychology is allied with social sciences.

Goals of Psychology Watson (1913) declared that, as in other sciences, psychology's "theoretical goal is the prediction and control of behavior" (p. 158). On the practical level, Watson (1924a) looked to a time when "we will have a behavioristic ethics, experimental in type, which will tell us whether it is advisable from the standpoint of present and future adjustments of the individual to have one wife or many wives; to have capital punishment or punishment of any kind; whether prohibition or no prohibition; easy divorce or no divorces" (p. 7).

Watson believed that prediction and control were best accomplished through environmental conditions. He was confident that environment shaped both human and animal behavior. During a Clark University address, Watson (1926) expounded on his radical environmentalism with the bold claim:

> I should like to go one step further tonight and say, "Give me a dozen healthy infants, well-formed, and my own specified world to bring them up in and I'll guarantee to take any one at random and train him to become any type of specialist I might select—a doctor, lawyer, artist, merchant-chief and, yes, even into beggarman and thief, regardless

of his talents, penchants, tendencies, abilities, vocations and race of his ancestors." I am going beyond my facts and I admit it, but so have the advocates of the contrary and they have been doing it for thousands of years. (p. 10)

Methods of the Psychologist

Unlike the structuralist method of introspection, Watson's behaviorism dovetailed with techno-scientific ideals in the United States that stressed quantification and standardization (Coon, 1993). Watson found no place for introspection, but he did acknowledge methods consistent with the behaviorist program. Like all sciences, the object is to gather facts, verify them, and subject them to logical and quantitative analysis. Watson recognized the legitimacy of Pavlov's conditioning techniques. He also accepted psychological tests so long as they are not called "mental" tests. "To the behaviorist tests mean merely devices for grading and sampling human performance" (Watson, 1924a, p. 35). He approved of a variety of tests and considered them important assessment tools. Watson also approved technical forms of social experimentation and naturalistic observation. His chapter "How to Study Human Behavior" in *Behaviorism* includes a rather broad methodological agenda. The acid test for methods is that they be truly public and lead to measurable results.

Scope of Psychology

Watson (1913) pointed out that the behaviorist "recognizes no dividing line between man and brute. The behavior of man, with all of its refinement and complexity, forms only a part of the behaviorist's total scheme of investigation" (p. 158). Psychology, then, according to Watson, has affinities with all the sciences and shares with biologists an interest in all life-forms.

Selected Content Areas

As noted by Samelson (1994), the focus of Watson's research interests shifted across several content areas during the course of his career. Habit and learning were the foundation areas for behaviorism, but other topical areas were also important.

Habit

The central concept of Watsonian behaviorism was habit. Watson (1924a) declared that at birth there is a stream of unlearned activities, but some of these activities begin to be "conditioned a few hours after birth" (p. 218). Ultimately, personality is a complex system of habits—and this applies to each arena of life. As an example, Watson asked what it means to say that a human being is religious. It may mean that the person attends church, reads religious literature, says grace at meals, and perhaps tries to convert others. "Let us put all of these separate activities together and call them the *religious habit system* of the individual. Now each of these separate activities making up this system has a dating back in the individual's past and a history" (p. 219). Watson went on to show how the child may have been taught to pray and may have been rewarded for memorizing Bible verses and attending church. Watson would not, of course, rule out sudden conditioning, perhaps through fear.

Watson argued that the so-called normal personality is based on a certain consistency of conditioning patterns. The person with the normal personality may have been fortunate enough to be reared in an environment free from excessive punishment and trauma. Weaknesses in personality or even illnesses result from habit conflicts. He quarreled with expressions such as *mental illness* or *mental disturbance*. Watson (1924a) pointed out that in many functional psychopathologies "there are no organic disturbances of sufficient gravity to account for personality disturbance. There may be no infections, no lesions anywhere, no absence of physiological reflexes (as there often is when there are organic diseases). And yet the individual has a sick personality" (p. 244). Watson argued that the expression *mental illness* raises the specter of interactionism. He preferred to emphasize conditioning in the acquisition and extinction of personality disturbances. His position is perhaps best illustrated in his infamous research on fear conditioning.

Fear Conditioning

Watson devoted extensive time to childrearing (Root, 2008) and to the study of children. His 1920 study with

Rosalie Rayner titled "Conditioned Emotional Reactions" counts as one of the most extensively cited studies in the history of psychology. Harris (1979) noted, "This work was the final published project of Watson's academic career, although he supervised a subsequent, related study of the deconditioning of young children's fears" (p. 152). Watson and Rayner conducted experimental work with an infant they identified as Albert B., whose mother was a wet nurse in a hospital environment. Watson and Rayner (1920) described Albert as "healthy from birth and one of the best developed youngsters ever brought to the hospital. . . . He was on the whole stolid and unemotional. His stability was one of the principal reasons for using him as a subject in this test" (p. 1). The claim that Albert was healthy has since been challenged. Fridlund et al. (2012) argue that Albert appears to have had hydrocephalus that led to evident impairment even during the study. Regardless of Albert's actual state of health, when he was about nine months of age, the researchers presented Albert with "a white rat, a rabbit, a dog, a monkey, with masks with and without hair, cotton, wool, burning newspapers, etc." (Watson & Rayner, 1920, p. 2). Albert showed no fear of any of these things. Also, at about nine months of age, Albert was tested to determine his reaction to a loud sound created by striking a four-foot-long suspended steel bar with a hammer. The sound characteristics (e.g., decibel level) were not specified, but sharp blows to the bar did result in a violent reaction, including crying and fear.

The stage was set to determine whether a conditioned emotional response could be established. Watson and Rayner hesitated for ethical reasons, but finally concluded that conditioned emotional responses occur in the world all the time. If such responses were to be understood, they must be subjected to experimentation. So, when Albert was eleven months and three days old, the white rat was presented to him. As Albert reached for the rat, the loud noise sounded. Albert jumped but did not cry. After seven repetitions, Albert displayed a conditioned emotional response to the rat. That is, when the rat

was presented alone, Albert cried and crawled away. Watson and Rayner found that Albert then avoided other objects such as a rabbit, a fur coat, and a dog. Despite methodological problems (see Harris, 1979) in the Watson and Rayner experiment, it was generally accepted as a demonstration of fear conditioning. The study also demonstrated the generalization of a fear response from the original conditioned stimulus.

Watson and Rayner chided the Freudians, who they guessed would analyze a twenty-year-old Albert's fear of a sealskin coat in terms of repressed memories from a time when he was scolded for attempting to play with his mother's pubic hair. They argued, "Emotional disturbances in adults cannot be traced back to sex alone" (Watson & Rayner, 1920, p. 14). The researchers did not attempt to decondition Albert or desensitize him. Beck et al. (2009, 2010) reported that they had discovered Little Albert's identity, although some have questioned their claims (Harris, 2011; Powell, 2010, 2011). Beck and colleagues contend he was Douglas Merritte, son of Arvilla Merritte, a wet nurse at the hospital where the research was conducted. The child died at age six of hydrocephalus, a condition linked to neurological difficulties.

Later, Watson supervised research by **Mary Cover Jones (1896–1987)** involving the experimental elimination of fear (Jones, 1924a). In her most famous study, she worked with a boy she described as "Albert grown a bit older" (Jones, 1924b, p. 309). Unlike Watson and Rayner's study with little Albert, Jones tried to remove fear rather than instill it. Three-year-old Peter had a profound fear of rabbits. After trying several methods, Jones used a "direct conditioning" approach with Peter. Through counter conditioning, she paired a pleasant stimulus (food) with a rabbit. In time, Peter's fear was extinguished. This study became the bedrock for later behavioral therapies (Beck et al., 2009). In the 1970s, Joseph Wolpe (see Chapter 18) described Mary Cover Jones as the "mother of behavior therapy" (Rutherford, 2006, p. 189). In later years, she made significant contributions to the study of child development.

Emotions   As we have seen, Watson believed that most emotional attachments occur through conditioning. Anxieties and phobias may result from unfortunate early conditioning experiences. The same may be said for positive attachments. Love for another person, objects, animals, and so on occurs through associations of pleasant circumstances with the loved object or person.

Watson quarreled with earlier psychologists on the unlearned beginnings of emotional reactions. He argued that there are only three responses—fear, rage, and love—that can be brought forth in the infant. He cautioned, however, that these terms must be stripped of their old connotations. Fear is brought forth naturally by sudden or unexpected stimuli such as a loud sound. Fear is also initiated by a sudden loss of support. Rage is observed when bodily movement is hampered or a goal-directed activity is blocked. He pointed out that stimuli that provoke "love responses" include "stroking of the skin, tickling, gentle rocking, patting" (Watson, 1924a, p. 123). In each of these cases—fear, rage, and love—Watson referred to broad undifferentiated response patterns. Such patterns are later differentiated in specific ways through conditioning. In their earliest expressions, they are somewhat diffuse yet distinguished from each other. For example, the cry of rage is easily distinguished from the cry of fear.

Instincts   Watson's position on the existence of instincts changed over the course of his career. In an early article on instinctive activity in animals, Watson (1912) argued, "There are at least three great divisions or classes into which we may provisionally throw the acts of animals: Instincts essentially perfect upon their first appearance; instincts which must be supplemented by habit; and finally, random activity of instinctive origin" (p. 377). Watson found evidence for the first type of instinct in his early field studies on noddy and sooty terns. He argued that the very young birds eat food in the same species-specific way with or without the parents as models. The same was true for other characteristic behaviors such as preening feathers. Watson also believed that fear responses, fighting, and nest cleaning are examples of congenital instincts. He argued that pecking is an example of the second class of instincts; it improves dramatically with practice. Examples of the third class are random responses to indefinite stimuli such as hunger, thirst, light, dark, warmth, and cold. More specifically, increased activity is normal when the organism is hungry. Random activity associated with hunger drops out when the right movements bring success.

Seven years after making these observations about instinct, Watson (1919) argued that "there is no sharp line of separation between emotion and instinct. Both are hereditary modes of action" (p. 231). In *Psychology from the Standpoint of a Behaviorist,* Watson (1919) defined *instinct* as "a hereditary pattern reaction, the separate elements of which are movements principally of the striped muscles" (p. 231). He contended that at the human level it is almost impossible to classify instincts, but meaningful classifications can be made at the animal level. Classification at the human level is difficult because habit dominates human actions.

Five years later, Watson devoted two chapters in *Behaviorism* to the topic of instincts. His chapter title "Are There Any Human Instincts?" betrays a new skepticism. Watson admitted that we inherit structures that interact with conditioning to determine what we can accomplish. He also admitted that there are unlearned responses such as hiccuping, crying, smiling, and grasping. He asked, however, whether there is any real utility in the concept of instinct. Smiling, for example, "begins at birth—aroused by intra-organic stimulation and by contact. Quickly it becomes conditioned, the sight of the mother calls it out, then vocal stimuli, finally pictures, then words and then life situations either viewed, told or read about" (Watson, 1924a, p. 104). He next raised the question of whether the whole concept of instinct is not meaningless. What is really important is conditioning and habit. Four years later, in *Psychological Care of Infant and Child*, Watson (1928) asserted, "There are no instincts" (p. 38). At least at the human level, he was embracing the

Lockean viewpoint when he declared that "we build in at an early age everything that is later to appear" (p. 38).

The 1920s and 1930s afforded a friendly climate for Watson's skepticism about the utility and scientific legitimacy of instinct. Anti-instinctivism flourished in the early part of the century and may have served as a corrective to psychologies that placed too heavy an explanatory burden on instincts, such as the work of William McDougall (1923, 1926a). The anti-instinct movement may also have flourished because of newfound optimism about the power of conditioning and the importance of the environment. For whatever reasons, the 1920s and 1930s witnessed an outpouring of argument against the concept of instinct. Representative works included Kuo's (1924) paper "A Psychology without Heredity" and Bernard's (1924) book *Instinct: A Study in Social Psychology*. Even at midcentury, questions remained about the usefulness of the concept of instinct (Beach, 1955). However, at the same time, behaviorists trained in zoology, often called *ethologists*, were marshaling powerful evidence for the role of instincts in animal behavior (Hess, 1962). For helpful overviews of the history of the concept of instinct, see Diamond (1971, 1974a).

Thinking and Speech   In his book *Behaviorism*, Watson (1924a) warned readers that they have been taught to believe "that thinking is something peculiarly uncorporeal, something very intangible, very evanescent, something peculiarly mental" (p. 191). He further warned that "there is always a strong inclination to attach a mystery to something you can't see" (p. 191). It appears, at least superficially, that thinking would present a problem to a psychology that denies the existence of mental events. Yet Watson argued that a natural science approach to thinking is both possible and productive. Watson (1924b) admitted that "thinking, with the behaviorist, is and must remain until the advent of experimentation partly a logical formulation" (p. 339). He was confident, however, that with the advancement of science, there would be "fewer and fewer

phenomena which cannot be observed" (p. 191). Accordingly, more and more scientific experimentation on thinking would be possible. What, then, was the behaviorist view of thinking?

In an article titled "The Unverbalized in Human Behavior," Watson (1924c) noted that a person "learning to play golf learns (usually) simultaneously to talk golf" (p. 273). Words can substitute for actions and objects. The utility of the substitutability or equivalence of words for actions or objects is obvious. Watson pointed out that as we develop, we soon have verbal organizations for every object or situation we have encountered. He compared verbal habits or organizations with the kinesthetic organization of playing a tune on the piano. Initially, one must look at each note on the score and find the corresponding key on the piano. Soon, however, the initial stimulus note may trigger a response chain. One may even take away the music or play in the dark. Watson (1924a) argued that "the same thing happens in word behavior" (p. 188). After a few repetitions, the first line of a poem or a fairy tale may trigger a repetition of the entire passage.

Watson believed that we learn muscular habits when we learn to speak. Speaking is not just a central process, it is also a peripheral process. We speak as a consequence of the interaction of the brain and the musculature. The primary muscle groups involved in speech are those associated with the larynx, but Watson (1924a) was aware that "removal of the larynx. . .does not destroy whispered speech" (p. 191). He believed that we really speak with our whole body—our hands, shoulders, tongue, facial muscles, throat, chest, and so on. The brain does not function in isolation from the rest of the physical system.

Another component in Watson's theory of speech grew out of his observations of children at play. When young children play alone, they typically talk to themselves. Watson (1924a) noted that even "deaf and dumb individuals who when talking use manual movements instead of words use the same manual responses they employ in talking, in their own thinking" (p. 193). In time, young children cease to talk aloud, but "talking" goes on nonetheless, behind the lips. "Behind these walls you can call the biggest bully the worst name you can think of without even smiling" (Watson, 1924a, p. 193). In an article titled "The Place of Kinesthetic, Visceral and Laryngeal Organization in Thinking," Watson (1924b) declared, "The behaviorist has preferred to call all verbalization that goes on behind the closed door of the lips 'thinking,' regardless of whether new verbal adjustments are effected or only old habits rehearsed" (p. 340). Thinking, then, as the behaviorist views it, is tied to speech. Indeed, thinking could be defined as subvocal speech.

Watson anticipated an important question about his theory: Do we think only in words? His answer was, "Yes, or in word substitutes, such as the shrug of the shoulders or other bodily response. . . . When the individual is thinking *the whole of his bodily organization is at work*—even though the final solution shall be a spoken, written or subvocally expressed verbal formulation" (Watson, 1924b, p. 341).

Under Watson's treatment, thinking and all other psychological processes are subject to investigation by the established methods of the natural sciences. By deemphasizing the role of central (brain) processes in thinking, he opened the door to the use of new response measures (e.g., throat movements, verbalization) in the study of thinking. Following Watson, there were many studies on the role of peripheral processes in thinking. He may have had a small impact on the literature on thinking, but his narrow approach to the topic had a truncating effect on the types of questions that were raised. In the end, a broader, more cognitive approach proved more productive. The broader approach made room for the investigation of topics such as the role of cognitive strategies in problem solving, the effects of the structure of a situation on problem solving, and problem solving as a function of the capacity to transform and rearrange parts or to see alternatives. The Watsonian approach to thinking was driven by the dictates of the larger behavioristic vision rather than by the special nature and requirements of the phenomenon in question.

BEHAVIORISM AND APPLIED PSYCHOLOGY

In his classic article "Psychology as the Behaviorist Views It," Watson (1913) declared, "One of the earliest conditions which made me dissatisfied with psychology was the feeling that there was no realm of application for the principles which were being worked out" (p. 169). In that same article, he pointed out that if psychology would follow his system, "the educator, the physician, the jurist and the business man could utilize our data in a practical way, as soon as we are able experimentally to obtain them" (p. 168). Watson lamented the sterility of the older psychology that explored such problems as the number of discriminable shades of gray. Watson (1913, p. 169) argued that he would rather explore problems such as the relative advantages of whole versus part learning, "the effect upon behavior of certain doses of caffeine. . .[and] the effects of recency upon the reliability of a witness's report." He stated boldly that "*behaviorism is the only consistent and logical functionalism*" (p. 166).

In terms of the systems examined in this book, behaviorism ranks high in its contributions to applied psychology. Both Pavlov and Watson were concerned with practical problems. Indeed, Pavlov's later career involved studies of clinical problems, and Watson supervised the earliest research on the counterconditioning of fear (Jones, 1924a, 1924b). Following Watson, there was an explosion of interest in behavior therapy techniques. Such interest was manifested in the founding of scholarly journals such as *Behavior Research and Therapy*, *Journal of Applied Behavior Analysis*, and *Behavior Therapy*. Numerous scientific and professional organizations were also founded as vehicles for the exchange of ideas on behavioral therapy. Such organizations include the Association for the Advancement of the Behavioral Therapies, the Association for the Behavioral Treatment of Sexual Abusers, the Association for Behavior Analysis, and the Society of Behavioral Medicine.

Watson's contributions to applied psychology extended into the field of advertising (see Larson, 1979). Watson understood that people buy products on the basis of needs and motives. In addition to the product itself, we buy ideas associated with the product. Hence, the successful advertising agency will show how a product can satisfy basic human needs such as security, adventure, and fame. The extent of Watson's contributions to the psychology of advertising and sales is still not sufficiently appreciated.

Behaviorism's interest in applied problems was inevitable because it was a science involved in what people actually do in the world. In contrast with psychologies that examined the mind, behaviorism was a matter-of-fact, rough-and-ready psychology that explored identifiable stimulus–response connections. It was a poor choice for anyone seeking philosophical subtleties and refinement. But if you were impatient to get on with a solution to practical problems, then behaviorism was a psychology deserving of loyalty.

Mental processes and experience as topical content areas in psychology were re-enfranchised with the advent of the so-called cognitive revolution in the late 1950s and 1960s. Psychologists who once focused largely on the study of mental processes via introspection moved to the study of behavior via more objective methodologies. The cognitive revolution did not exclude behavior as an important topic, but also included studies of the relations between behavior, neurological processes, and experience. Accommodations and tensions between behavioral psychologies and the new cognitivism and the historical accounts of their relations remain a relevant historiographic problem (see Watrin & Darwich, 2012).

Review Questions

1. Briefly outline some of the important intellectual antecedents of behaviorism.
2. Summarize Ivan Sechenov's approach to psychology.
3. Why was the concept of *action at a distance*, or *psychical reflex*, troublesome to Pavlov?
4. Define the terms *unconditioned stimulus, conditioned stimulus, unconditioned reflex,* and *conditioned reflex.*

5. Outline some of the possible temporal relations between the conditioned stimulus and the unconditioned stimulus.
6. What are the four temperament types included in Pavlov's system?
7. Define *extinction, spontaneous recovery, disinhibition, stimulus generalization,* and *discrimination.*
8. Discuss Pavlov's approach to experimental neurosis and specify the meaning of terms such as *ultramaximal inhibition, equivalence phase, paradoxical phase,* and *ultraparadoxical phase.*
9. Briefly outline the approaches to psychology in the works of Vladimir M. Bekhterev and Konstantin Kornilov.
10. How did John B. Watson define *psychology* and what methods did he advocate?
11. Outline Watson's critique of older systems of psychology.
12. Outline Watson and Rayner's classic work on fear conditioning.
13. Describe Watson's treatment of thinking. What criticisms can you offer of his approach?
14. Discuss the evolution of Watson's ideas on instinct.
15. Outline some of the contributions of behaviorism to applied psychology.
16. In what sense can Thorndike be considered a functionalist and in what sense can he be considered a behaviorist?
17. Distinguish between Thorndike's early law of effect and his later law of effect. Do you think he was correct in modifying the law of effect?

Glossary

action at a distance   Any apparent effect for which one cannot readily identify material and efficient causes.

behaviorism   A system of psychology founded by John B. Watson and marked by a strong commitment to the methods and values of the natural sciences. Watson saw psychology as a branch of the natural sciences and defined the discipline simply as the scientific study of behavior.

Bekhterev, Vladimir Mikhailovich (1857–1927) A contemporary of Ivan Pavlov who advanced an objective psychology in which the reflex served as the fundamental category of inquiry. Bekhterev's system was known as reflexology.

conditioned reflex (CR)   In classical conditioning, a learned reflex elicited by a conditioned stimulus. Also known as a conditioned response.

conditioned stimulus (CS)   In classical conditioning, any stimulus that is psychologically or biologically neutral prior to conditioning trials. Such a stimulus may be paired repeatedly with an unconditioned stimulus. After repeated pairings, the previously neutral conditioned stimulus will elicit a reflex similar to the unconditioned reflex elicited by the unconditioned stimulus.

connectionism   A formal term often applied to the theory of learning advanced by Edward Lee Thorndike. Thorndike believed that learning involved the development of connections or bonds between sense impressions and responses. Connectionism is one of the first S–R theories of learning.

discrimination   In classical conditioning, subjects may be conditioned to respond to one stimulus and to ignore or withhold a response to another stimulus. Discrimination is generally established through differential reinforcement.

disinhibition   In extinction trials a subject may have stopped responding to a given stimulus. However, a sudden new stimulus may trigger the old conditioned response.

doctrine of formal discipline   An early belief that the mind, like certain muscle groups, is developed most effectively by specific exercises such as the study of certain classics (e.g., Latin and geometry).

equivalent phase   A Pavlovian term referring to the tendency of a subject to respond in a highly stereotyped fashion to any stimulus. The equivalent phase may follow a biological insult that produces a shock-like reaction. In such circumstances, the subject may respond in the same way to all signals.

extinction   The weakening or elimination of a conditioned response. The major means of achieving extinction is to present repeatedly the conditioned stimulus in the absence of the unconditioned stimulus.

identical elements transfer theory   In contrast with the doctrine of formal discipline, the identical elements transfer theory holds that the learning of any new task will be facilitated most by experience with highly comparable previous tasks.

Jones, Mary Cover (1896–1987)   American psychologist famous for her work on counterconditioning fear responses in a boy named Peter. Her research in this area established her as a founding figure in behavior therapy.

Kornilov, Konstantin Nikolaevich (1879–1957)   Founder of a system of psychology in the former Soviet Union known as reactology. Kornilov was seeking a system of psychology completely consistent with Marxist–Leninist political thought. Kornilov's system was rejected by Soviet authorities because it neglected the activity of mind stressed by Lenin.

law of effect   Refers to Thorndike's early view that connections are strengthened when followed by a satisfying state of affairs and weakened when followed by an annoying state of affairs. Later, Thorndike dropped the second half of the law and argued that satisfiers strengthen associations, but annoyers do not weaken associations.

law of exercise   Refers to Thorndike's early belief that connections are strengthened through practice and weakened through disuse. Later, Thorndike denied that exercise alone controls the fate of connections.

paradoxical phase   According to Pavlov, a weak stimulus may sometimes produce a strong response and a strong stimulus may produce a weak response. The paradoxical phase sometimes follows shock induced by a biological insult.

Pavlov, Ivan Petrovich (1849–1936)   The most significant figure in the history of Russian psychology and pioneer in research in classical conditioning. His *Lectures on Conditioned Reflexes* is a classic work setting forth a psychology and psychiatry based on the principles of conditioning.

psychical reflex   An early term used briefly in Pavlov's laboratory to describe conditioned responses. See *action at a distance*.

reactology   A system of psychology set forth by Konstantin Kornilov. This system emphasized the importance of physiological and social forces in shaping human and animal behavior.

reflexology   A system of psychology set forth by Vladimir Bekhterev, a contemporary of Pavlov. According to this system, molar behavior must be understood in terms of its reflexive origins.

Sechenov, Ivan Mikailovich (1829–1905) Commonly regarded as the founder of Russian physiology. The author of *Reflexes of the Brain*, Sechenov argued for an objective psychology wedded to physiology and the principles of monistic materialism.

spontaneous recovery   Following extinction trials, a conditioned stimulus may lose its ability to produce a conditioned response. However, following a period of rest, the conditioned stimulus may once again elicit the conditioned response.

stimulus generalization   Stimuli similar to the original conditioned stimulus may also elicit a conditioned response.

Thorndike, Edward Lee (1874–1949)   U.S. psychologist who studied with James at Harvard and Cattell at Columbia. Thorndike was a pioneer in the experimental investigation of animal behavior and advanced one of the earliest and most influential learning theories. His practical work focused on behavior, and he can be considered a forerunner of behaviorism. Nevertheless, he believed that psychology might be best served by a variety of methods and viewpoints.

truncated law of effect   Thorndike's later theory that reward strengthens associations. In his later work, Thorndike raised doubts that punishment serves to weaken associations.

ultramaximal inhibition   Sometimes called *protective transmarginal inhibition*, refers to the effects of a severe biological or psychological insult. Such insults may produce a shock-like state that Pavlov regarded as protective. Massive inhibition, in this case, may serve a protective function by blocking out further stimulation. In shock-like states, subjects may feel no pain and be incapable of intelligent response.

ultraparadoxical phase   Following a severe shock, some subjects display an unusual reversal of values. Thus, a formerly positive or loved stimulus is regarded negatively or hated and a formerly negative or hated stimulus is regarded positively or loved. Such conversions may be relatively permanent.

unconditioned reflex (UCR)   Any naturally occurring reflex to a strong stimulus. Examples include salivation when hungry in the presence of food, withdrawal from a painful stimulus, or constriction of the pupil with increasing light. Also known as an unconditioned response.

unconditioned stimulus (UCS)   A stimulus that is biologically adequate to produce an unconditioned reflex.

Watson, John Broadus (1878–1958)   Founder of American behaviorism and twenty-fourth president of the American Psychological Association. Watson's system is remembered for its identity with the natural sciences and extreme emphasis on the environment in shaping behavior. With a strong belief in determinism and materialism, Watson argued that complete prediction and control of behavior could be achieved by a truly scientific psychology.

14

■ ■ ■

Other Behavioral Psychologies

The term existence *is only a synonym for movement.*

—PAUL WEISS (1924)

Shortly after publication of Watson's behaviorist manifesto, it seemed that psychology, after more than three decades, was finally becoming a coherent discipline (or in the words of Kuhn, a "paradigmatic science"). Optimism flourished, especially among the younger generation, as psychology seemed poised to achieve scientific status. The behaviorist perspective seemed to offer a methodology that better resembled other sciences. The subject matter was observable and quantifiable. Yet, after the founding, the behaviorist school appeared far from coherent. Even as it dominated American psychology (Mills, 1998), behaviorism was far from a unified system of thought. It was a house divided over numerous substantive and methodological issues. In spite of dissension, some harmony surfaced among behaviorists.

This chapter examines several behaviorist systems that represent alternatives to Watson's classic system. Before examining them, we'll explore threads of thought that are more or less common to behaviorist systems.

IMPORTANCE OF LEARNING

What do we know that we have not learned? This question reflects the central role of learning in human life. We are aware that we have learned a specific language and that skills such as swimming, riding a bicycle, and playing tennis are acquired through learning. It is also true that attitudes, fears, self-concepts, political orientations, and philosophical positions are subject to learning. The behaviorist psychologies regarded learning as foundational to psychology. The study of learning held extraordinary promise as a means of understanding and controlling behavior. For example, if an irrational fear of heights is conditioned, perhaps it could be as easily extinguished if we understand the processes behind it. If a prejudicial attitude is acquired, perhaps through learning principles we could find efficient ways to change it. Unlike earlier psychologies that concentrated on reaction time, sensation, perception, and attention, behaviorism focused on learning as the foundation for the science of psychology. Of course, determinism remained a cornerstone in the foundation of learning theory since its inception, giving rise to a variety of deterministic orientations in the behaviorist literature (Slife, Yanchar, & Williams, 1999).

IMPORTANCE OF PRECISION AND CLARITY

Behaviorists often disagreed with each other over exact meanings of essential terms such as *learning*, *reinforcement*, *discrimination*, and *extinction*. Nevertheless, there was agreement on the importance of linking such concepts to experimental procedures. If an expression such as *hunger drive* were employed, there was agreement that such an expression should be treated as if it had no trans-experimental meaning. Instead, the expression was tied to a specifiable metric employed in an experiment. *Hunger drive*, for example, might be defined in terms of hours of food deprivation. A group that had gone without food for twelve hours would, by definition, have more hunger drive than a group without food for six hours.

The importance of establishing empirical meanings for scientific terms is found in the work of Nobel laureate **Percy W. Bridgman (1882–1961)**. In his classic book *The Logic of Modern Physics*, Bridgman (1927) set forth the principles of operationism. As envisioned by Bridgman, **operationism** is a programmatic attempt to tie scientific terms to the measurements or operations of an experiment. For example, in physics, linear distance is linked to the procedures of measurement. Various measurement alternatives are usually available (e.g., use of a rigid rod to assess length, calculation of the speed of an echo from a sonic source). In psychology, one may measure a concept such as hunger drive in terms of hours of food deprivation, number of stomach contractions in a specified time period, blood chemistry changes, or number of approaches to a food container in a specified block of time.

Operationism, in its original form, challenged the idea of absolute meanings or intrinsic meanings. The assumption was that all meaning is relative. For example, Bridgman argued that there is no absolute time; rather, time is an arbitrary temporal interval marked off by the pointer readings on a clock. Bridgman also argued that the most meaningful references to topics such as energy, temperature, and light are cast in terms of the measures we employ. Many psychologists, most notably S. S. Stevens (1951), argued that the same must be true of psychological concepts.

Criticisms of operationism appeared after 1927 but were slow to capture the attention of psychologists. Indeed, operationism enjoyed considerable longevity in psychology (see Rogers, 1989). One criticism was that operationism described nothing new; it merely provided a label for a practice that had long been in use. Bridgman recognized the legitimacy of the criticism but contended that explicit clarification of scientific procedure is always useful.

A more damaging criticism was the intuitively appealing idea that measurement points to something beyond itself (see Henshaw, 2006). A major problem with operationism is that it leaves a truncated theory of meaning. Untrammeled operationism runs the risk of prescribing a rigid absolutist stance about the meaning of meaning. The difficulty is illustrated by the idea that one operational definition can be better than another. If "better than" implies something other than mere ease of administration or utility of procedure, then such a statement may reveal an implicit assumption that there is a relationship between a set of operations and a concept that is "other than" that set of operations. In fact, most scientists probably do not believe that concepts such as length, drive, intelligence, and so on are nothing but a set of operations. Operationism is beset with the problem of what Hodgson (1988) has called the "intransigence of evaluative concepts" (p. 321).

In a symposium on operationism nearly a quarter century after its founding, Bridgman (1954) agreed with critics who argued that scientists should pay more attention to "what it is that makes an operation 'good' for the purposes of the scientist" (p. 25). Such attention forces the scientist to go beyond operationism. At the same time, Bridgman found value in operationism and believed a sophisticated application does not restrict the scientist's intellectual freedom. Bridgman regretted the way operationism had sometimes become a dogma. In such cases, he compared it to a Frankenstein monster that had escaped from him. Debate continues about the success or failure of operationism in behaviorism as well as in later cognitive research (see Bickhard, 2001; Grace, 2001; Green, 2001b; Leahey, 2001).

The neobehaviorists were influenced by operationism and were largely in accord with a related movement in philosophy called **logical positivism**. Logical positivism, such as neobehaviorism, placed a strong emphasis on precision and clarity.

Logical positivism, sometimes called *critical empiricism* or *scientific empiricism*, grew out of a school of philosophy known as the Vienna Circle. It was a discussion group comprised of scientists and philosophers such as Moritz Schlick, Otto Neurath, Rudolf Carnap, Herbert Feigl, and Philipp Frank. The Vienna Circle promoted a unified science, devoid of ambiguous and meaningless metaphysical concepts. Such a science would be based on the finest empirical traditions and would insist first and foremost on clarity of expression in scientific work.

The logical positivists argued that many concepts are devoid of scientific meaning because they cannot be verified or confirmed. Such concepts are little more than collections of words without clear-cut references. The positivists were not referring to random collections of words as meaningless but to coherent statements that evoke feelings or trigger past associations. For example, a statement such as *The rat is happy* illustrates the point. The statement may be coherent and may evoke past associations, yet it is scientifically meaningless. Why? Because, according to the logical positivists, we cannot scientifically study an inner world devoid of clear and explicit references. We could, of course, operationalize *happiness* and study such behaviors as vigor of

response, amount of food consumed, or number of intromissions in a sexual episode. Each is measurable and confirmable by independent observers. By contrast, an expression such as *The rat is happy* calls for an assessment of the inner world of the rat. Such an expression cannot yield the same kind of quantitative, publicly verifiable data as, for instance, amount of food consumed.

Logical positivism's emphasis on publicly confirmable propositions and a suspicion of inner experience was consistent with behaviorism. Though logical positivism would later succumb to its critics, its consistency with behaviorism was remarkable.

IMPORTANCE OF EXPERIMENTATION

In general, neobehaviorists believed in experimental testing of major concepts and theories. It was agreed that theories and hypotheses must be subjected to vigorous experimental scrutiny. Neobehaviorism's reign in the 1930s, 1940s, and 1950s produced an unprecedented outpouring of research. At the same time, the rapid growth of new statistical procedures contributed to innovative design techniques.

Neobehaviorists were accused, however, of placing sophistication of design in higher priority than the significance of the problem. Scientists do sometimes employ powerful methodologies to explore trivial problems. Koch (1969) warned that it is a mistake to assume that the tools of scientific inquiry can "displace their human users" (p. 14). There was concern that neobehaviorists were guilty of studying problems that were relevant only in the context of their own rather insular and esoteric programs.

What was the reply to such a criticism? It is preferable to gain sure knowledge of simple events, even if such events seem trivial, than to have speculative knowledge of larger, more grandiose events. Basic experiments in the young science of physics (e.g., rolling balls down inclined planes or studying the movements of a pendulum) may have seemed trivial at the time but later proved valuable as the science progressed.

A priori assessments of what is relevant and what is trivial are not distinguished for their accuracy.

Though behaviorists agreed on the importance of experimentation, they did not agree on how experiments should be conducted. We encounter radically different approaches to experimentation in the literature of behaviorism from the hypothetico-deductive approach of Clark Hull to a more descriptive Baconian approach in the work of B. F. Skinner. Hull advanced a quasi-mathematical theory from which he derived hypotheses that were then tested in the laboratory. As we will see later in the chapter, Skinner denied that he tested hypotheses, and he eschewed grand formal theories and models. He simply strived for accurate descriptions of behavior as he encountered it.

Clearly, the behavioristic psychologists shared many beliefs but, as noted earlier, disagreed on numerous substantive issues. We turn now to a consideration of several behavioristic psychologies and issues that divided them.

EARLY BEHAVIORISTIC PSYCHOLOGIES

The call for a more objective psychology was present from the turn of the last century. Russian scientists such as Sechenov and Pavlov were among the first to emphasize the need for a more objective rigorous approach to the new discipline. In the United States, several psychologists preceded Watson in their call for an objective psychology. We will briefly review early behaviorally oriented psychologists before turning to neobehaviorists who were inspired directly or indirectly by Watson, but who modified his system.

William McDougall

In his *Outline of Psychology*, British psychologist **William McDougall (1871–1938)** described behaviorism as "a most misshapen and beggarly dwarf" (1923, p. ix). Nevertheless, he argued that the behavior of human beings is the major practical topic of interest for psychologists. Therefore, according to McDougall, "All psychology is

or should be behaviouristic" (1942, p. 16). The "misshapen and beggarly dwarf" in the previous quotation reflects his disdain for Watson's metaphysical behaviorism. In contrast, McDougall advocated a moderate pragmatic behaviorism marked by methodological and metaphysical openness.

McDougall was born in Chadderton, England, on June 22, 1871. His education at Manchester and Cambridge Universities was noteworthy for its breadth and quality. Prior to earning a medical degree, he was recognized for his meritorious work in biology. He held academic positions at Cambridge, London, Oxford, and Harvard University. Later, he became head of the psychology department at Duke University. During the last month of his life, McDougall kept a journal detailing his experiences with pain and the looming threat of death. Researchers have examined this work as a model of the dying process (Kastenbaum, 1995). McDougall died on November 28, 1938, leaving a legacy of prolific and diverse research, ranging over anthropology, psychology, and philosophy.

McDougall emphasized the centrality of activity, conduct, and behavior throughout his published works in psychology. Indeed, he preceded Watson in defining *psychology* as a positive science concerned with conduct (see McDougall, 1905, p. 1). McDougall argued, however, that the study of conduct or behavior need not blind us to what we encounter in common sense and common speech; namely, that there are mental activities that are part of a whole system of functions encountered in living organisms. Psychology should study both experience (mental activity) and behavior, especially in relation to social and physiological correlates. McDougall's early books, *Physiological Psychology* (1905) and *Introduction to Social Psychology* (1908), reflect his breadth of vision.

According to McDougall, goal seeking or purposeful striving is the central feature of mental activity and behavior. McDougall used the term **hormic**, from the Greek *horme* meaning "urge," to refer to this central feature of animal and human life. From the lowest organisms to humans, we encounter behavior directed toward objects in the environment that satisfy needs. He noted with regret that most psychologists ignored the hormic nature of organismic activity.

Whereas McDougall emphasized the purposeful nature of organismic activity, he did not neglect the importance of mechanistic explanations based on material and efficient causation. In his book *The Energies of Men*, McDougall (1942) argued for "the validity of both the mechanistic and the purposive principles of explanation, each in its own sphere" (p. 22). Thus, one might explore the correlates of experience considered from a purposive standpoint and neurological activity considered mechanistically. Uytman (1967) believed that McDougall's task was "to reconcile a presumably purposive mind with an apparently causally determined body" (p. 227). McDougall explored such a reconciliation through a kind of monadology found earlier in Leibniz's philosophy (see Chapter 7).

Because of its complex subject matter, psychology should employ all possible methods: laboratory methods, paper-and-pencil tests, introspection, free association, dream analysis, comparative methods, statistical methods, and field studies (see McDougall, 1942, p. 23). He was as pluralistic methodologically as William James and more explicit than James about the variety of methods psychology should employ. McDougall insisted that psychology not imitate other sciences; rather, psychology should have the courage to employ methods appropriate to its unique subject matter.

Unfortunately, McDougall was almost always out of step with the mainstream psychology of his day (see Innis, 2003). He faced criticism from colleagues such as Knight Dunlap (1875–1949), a behaviorist at Johns Hopkins University. At a time when most psychologists preferred mechanistic explanations, he advocated a purposive behaviorism. He emphasized the role of instincts in animal and human behavior during a time of radical environmentalism. He welcomed studies of paranormal phenomena such as mental telepathy and clairvoyance and helped establish Duke's parapsychology laboratory headed by J. B. Rhine

(1895–1980) (Asprem, 2010). He also embraced a Lamarckian approach to evolution and even conducted experiments designed to provide evidence for the inheritance of acquired characteristics.

If McDougall championed many unpopular causes, he was also one of the first to emphasize the importance of social psychology, and in 1908 he wrote what some consider one of the field's first textbooks (Gergen, 2008). In this context, he drew on the political climate of the early 1900s in reconciling "crowd psychology" with his views on democracy (see Allett, 1996). He also wrote an early text on abnormal psychology. Arguably, McDougall's most important influence was on neobehaviorist Edward Chace Tolman (discussed later in this chapter).

Edwin Bissell Holt

Edwin Bissell Holt (1873–1946) was born in Winchester, Massachusetts, on August 21, 1873. Though his father, a congregational minister, died when Holt was a young man, his mother encouraged him in his studies. In 1896, Holt received his bachelor's degree magna cum laude from Harvard. Five years later, he received his Ph.D. from the same institution.

Holt was deeply influenced by William James. Langfeld (1946) noted that Holt "was probably more like James than any other of James's disciples in the quality of his intellect, in his dislike of sham and outworn convention, in his independence of thought and criticism, in his brilliant conversation and originality of expression, and in his generosity in helping and encouraging little known but promising writers" (p. 251). Even if there were limits to Holt's understanding of James's radical empiricism (Taylor, 2011), Holt later mentored Edward Chase Tolman as well as J. J. Gibson, who would continue James's experiential legacy (Heft, 2001).

Holt was an assistant professor at Harvard, where he assisted Münsterberg with the psychological laboratory. Later in his career, Holt taught at Princeton, where his course in social psychology was one of the most highly regarded on campus. He died on January 25, 1946.

HOLT'S PSYCHOLOGY Holt agreed with Watson that psychologists should study behavior, and in that narrow sense he can be counted among the behaviorists. Holt's view of behavior, however, was broader and more philosophical than Watson's. Unlike Watson, Holt argued that organisms are goal directed and that movement toward goals is based on purposes, wishes, and plans.

Holt's emphasis on purposes and wishes may remove him from the behaviorist camp, but Holt denied this. He claimed that behavior is not random or without purpose or chaotic. Behavior is, above all else, purposive and goal directed. Unlike Watson, Holt did not deny the scientific legitimacy of consciousness and mental phenomena; instead, he attempted to provide a new interpretation of such phenomena. According to Holt, consciousness is inextricably linked with neurophysiological processes and with physical objects.

Holt's best-known book, published in 1931, was *Animal Drive and the Learning Process: An Essay Toward Radical Empiricism*. This book, plus other major works such as *The Concept of Consciousness* (1914) and *The Freudian Wish and Its Place in Ethics* (1915), delivers a philosophical and dynamic behaviorism that focuses on what organisms do in their environments. Holt's emphasis was on molar behavior. The term *molar* is distinguished from *molecular* and refers to large behavioral units, to things that organisms do such as building a nest, running a maze, driving a car, and so forth. The major characteristic of molar behavior is that it is purposive or goal directed. We will see later how this line of thought developed with Holt's student, Edward Chace Tolman.

Walter Samuel Hunter

Walter Samuel Hunter (1889–1954) could be counted with Holt as one of the liberals of the behaviorist movement. Although a behaviorist, Hunter avoided extreme positions marked by the use of terms such as *nothing but*, *all*, and *every*.

Walter Samuel Hunter was born in Decatur, Illinois, on March 22, 1889. He earned a bachelor's degree at the University of Texas in 1910 and was accepted for graduate work at the University of Chicago, where he earned a Ph.D. under the direction of Harvey Carr in 1912. Hunter's dissertation, titled "Delayed Reaction in Animals and Children" (1913), was regarded as an important work and was widely quoted in psychological literature. After completing his Ph.D., Hunter accepted a position at the University of Texas. His four years at Texas were productive and happy but were marred by the death of Hunter's wife in 1915. He was left with a daughter, born in 1914 (Hunt, 1956).

In 1916, Hunter accepted a position at the University of Kansas. In his autobiography, he remembered that James Angell, although supportive, expressed concern that Hunter "might be getting promoted too fast for [his] age" (Hunter, 1952, p. 169). At Kansas, Hunter enjoyed excellent laboratory facilities, remarried, and spent nine years as professor with sixteen months off for military duty in World War I.

In 1925, Hunter accepted a position at Clark University until 1936, when he became department head at Brown University. In 1930, Hunter served as president of the American Psychological Association. He was also one of those rare individuals honored with membership in the prestigious National Academy of Sciences. World War II interrupted his work at Brown. He served as a member of the Emergency Committee on Psychology and as chief of the Applied Psychology Panel of the National Defense Research Committee. In recognition of Hunter's efforts during World War II, President Truman honored him with the President's Medal of Merit. After the war, Hunter devoted his full attention to his academic career at Brown University until his death in 1954.

HUNTER'S WORK In the preface of his book *Human Behavior*, Hunter (1928) instructed the reader as follows: "The present discussion is written from what is generally called the behavioristic point of view, which I prefer to call the viewpoint of anthroponomy, the science of human behavior" (p. v). Hunter preferred the term *anthroponomy* to *psychology* because of the mentalistic connotations of psychology. The term **anthroponomy** comes from the Greek *anthropos*, meaning "man," and *nomos*, meaning "law." The term *anthroponomy* never caught on; years later, in his autobiography, Hunter (1952) said that he "was never under any delusion that the designation of the science would be changed to anthroponomy, but the path of our science would have been much smoother in its public relations had some nonpsychic term designated it" (p. 172). Many would agree with Hunter, but alternative designations such as anthroponomy or behavioral science never gained unanimous approval.

Although Hunter argued that the subject matter of psychology is behavior, he was open to a variety of methods such as field observation, clinical studies, and the experimental method. In short, he considered a broader range of problems than most behaviorists. Though he worked with animals, he was interested in human behavior. He emphasized the importance of basic studies, but also stressed applied studies that are relevant to education, the workplace, everyday adjustment, and the military.

Hunter's most famous research was on delayed reactions in animals and in children (Schlosberg, 1954). The work provided important information on representational processes in a variety of species. The delayed reaction experiment allows a subject to see a stimulus (a light) above one of three doors equidistant from a holding cage. The light signals the presence of food. The problem is that there is a delay between turning off the light and the release of the animal from the holding cage. Hunter found that rats and dogs tend to make the correct response (i.e., choose the correct door) if the delay was not so long that they lost their bodily orienting response. In other words, rats and dogs make the correct response if their muscular orientation remains intact. If the muscle orientation toward the correct door dissipates (during the delay period), the animal tends not to make the correct response. Hunter found that raccoons could handle much longer delays. The delayed reaction experiment was one way of testing cognitive or

representation processes in a variety of species. The approach has intuitive appeal because everyone can relate to trying to remember the location of an object after a delay.

In World War II, Hunter was called on to recommend psychologists who could conduct studies on human–machine systems. He was adamant that it was not just a war of machines. He pointed out that "men must operate machines and that their efficiency and morale are after all the fundamental factors" (Hunter, 1952, p. 182). Thus, he was one of the first to address human–machine questions.

Because of his breadth of vision and pluralistic approach to methodology, Hunter added to the vitality of the behavioristic movement (Plaud & Montgomery, 1993). His work contributed to the growing perception that behaviorism was not a sterile psychology restricted only to the laboratory or a single content area such as learning, but a psychology with a promising broad agenda.

Karl Spencer Lashley

Karl Spencer Lashley (1890–1958) was influenced by John B. Watson and was sympathetic with behaviorism. He did not, however, devote energy to the systematic or philosophical defense of behaviorism. Instead, he focused on specific problems in learning and their experimental investigation. His major interest was the cerebral localization of learning and discrimination. Although Lashley identified with behaviorism, his work on cerebral localization proved a better fit with Gestalt psychology.

Karl Lashley was born on June 7, 1890. His father was a successful businessman and his mother, a descendant from the American Calvinist theologian Jonathan Edwards, was a former schoolteacher. He studied zoology at the University of West Virginia. After graduation in 1910, he proceeded to the University of Pittsburgh, where he earned a master's degree in biology. In 1914 he received his Ph.D. in biology with an emphasis in genetics from Johns Hopkins University. Throughout his education, Lashley took only one formal course in psychology, but at

Hopkins he worked with John B. Watson and the psychiatrist Adolph Meyer. As a result, Lashley's interests turned more and more to psychological topics.

Lashley's academic career included a twenty-year appointment at Harvard University and a thirteen-year appointment at the Yerkes Laboratory of Primate Biology (Dewsbury, 2006). He served as president of the American Psychological Association in 1929 and received numerous honorary degrees and medals in recognition of his research. Bruce (1991) described Lashley as "the pre-eminent scientist of brain and behavior during the first half of the 20th century" (p. 307).

Few people in science could match Lashley in terms of diligence and integrity. Morgan (1968) noted that he "did all his own research, 'running' his animals, doing data analysis, making histological reconstructions, and writing his own papers" (p. 29). According to Morgan, Lashley was dismayed at the new funding trends for scientific research. He was fearful that ever larger dollar amounts would create pressures that would undermine scientific honesty and the integrity of the scientific process. Lashley was concerned that scientists would be tempted or even forced to become entrepreneurs focused excessively on details essentially tangential to the hard daily routine of careful scientific observation, data collection, and theory construction.

Lashley retired in 1955 and served as emeritus professor at the Yerkes Laboratories from 1955 to 1958. He died on August 7, 1958.

LASHLEY'S WORK Lashley conducted work on instinct and color vision, but his most influential research centered on the cortical basis of learning and discrimination. Following the completion of his Ph.D., Lashley engaged in postdoctoral studies with the physiological psychologist Shepherd Ivory Franz (1874–1933). Franz discovered that cats and monkeys as well as human participants could relearn habits that had been lost following brain injury. If brain injury had destroyed old pathways, then relearning must be based on establishment of new pathways laid down in a new cortical site. Franz's findings raised doubts about a precise cortical localization for behavioral functions.

After the turn of the last century, many scientists conceptualized brain functions in terms of strict point-for-point connections and found inspiration in the popular new telephone switchboard technology. The manual exchange switchboard featured endless rows of jacks allowing point-for-point connections, permitting callers to speak with one another. The telephone switchboard metaphor suggested a model of brain function. Lashley speculated that point-for-point connections should have a precise locus in the brain and that destruction of such connections should reveal important information about the neurophysiological underpinnings of learning and behavior.

Lashley taught an animal, typically a laboratory rat, to perform a specific task. For this phase of research, Lashley developed the jumping stand, an apparatus that now bears his name. The jumping stand consisted of an elevated platform situated in front of two stimulus cards. If the rat jumped to the correct stimulus card, the card fell over and the rat received a food reward. A jump to the wrong card resulted in a fall into a net situated beneath the cards. The rat had to establish a habit of jumping to the correct card (perhaps a black card as opposed to a white card). In a later phase of the experiment, the rat was tested for its ability to recall which card produced a reward.

After a habit was established, Lashley would lesion various sites in the cortex of the brain. In subsequent testing, he could determine the effects of the extirpation on retention of the previously acquired habit. Lashley's results, in experiment after experiment, came as a surprise to those who believed in a strict point-for-point connection between stimuli and responses. Though it is clear that some parts of the nervous system are "hardwired" in a point-for-point fashion, Lashley failed to find evidence of localization of function for most of the learning tasks.

Lashley found that his subjects retained previously acquired habits even when every conceivable pathway had been destroyed. To be sure, brain damage impaired performance, but Lashley's data suggested that a field theory approach to brain function characterized intelligent behavior more accurately than did a rigid point-for-point connectionism. By 1926, Lashley rejected the connectionist model because of its failure to account for the complexity of his findings (Bruce, 1998). Certain functions, especially sensory and motor functions, are localized, but Lashley's data suggested there is no so-called learning or intelligence center. His demonstrations of neural plasticity were important in their own right and influential on his longtime student, D. O. Hebb (Berlucchi & Buchtel, 2009).

Two principles that grew out of Lashley's work have been enduring. **Mass action** refers to the idea that the rate, efficiency, and accuracy of learning depend on the amount of cortex available. Thus, it is not so much the locus of an injury that is important; rather, the amount of cortex damaged is more critical to the resulting deficit in learned and intelligent behavior. **Equipotentiality** refers to the idea that one part of the cortex can take over the function of another part. Thus, some functions that are lost following brain damage can be restored through relearning using other regions of the brain.

During his career, Lashley was cautious about making any broad claim or sweeping generalization. He presented a measured and admirable approach to science.

NEOBEHAVIORISM

John B. Watson is commonly regarded as the founder of behaviorism, but as we have seen, behavioral approaches to psychology were in the air prior to the work of Watson. We now turn to four neobehaviorists who followed Watson and became dominant figures in American experimental psychology until the midpoint of the twentieth century.

Clark Leonard Hull

Clark Leonard Hull (1884–1952) was probably the leading figure in academic experimental psychology from about 1930 to 1950. According to Logan (1968), Hull earned this status because he

"presented his theoretical ideas with a degree of rigor and analytic detail then unfamiliar in psychology" (p. 535). Logan claimed that Hull's theory drew from dominant influences of the day—Watson, Pavlov, Darwin, Thorndike, and even Freud. According to Logan (1968), Freud's emphasis on "the central role of motivation in behavior [was] a position Hull increasingly adopted" (p. 535). We can characterize Hull's theoretical approach to learning and behavior as mathematical and deductive. His theory is set forth in terms of quasi-mathematical postulates and corollaries that lend themselves to experimental procedure.

Hull was born in rural New York close to Akron on May 24, 1884. As a youth, he had to overcome a severe case of typhoid fever and poliomyelitis, which left one leg paralyzed. Despite hardships, Hull graduated from the University of Michigan in 1913, where he studied with Walter B. Pillsbury (1872–1960). After teaching for a year, Hull enrolled at the University of Wisconsin, where he received his Ph.D. in 1918. Hull worked at the University of Wisconsin, focusing on aptitude testing. Later, his interests switched to suggestibility and hypnosis.

In 1929, James Rowland Angell hired Hull to work at the Institute of Human Relations at Yale University. During this time, he produced his monumental work in behavior theory. Hull was recognized with many honors during the course of his academic career, including election as president of the American Psychological Association in 1935.

Hull had a singular impact on experimental psychology and expanded the scope of stimulus–response (S–R) psychology (Rashotte & Amsel, 1999). One of Hull's best-known students, Kenneth W. Spence (1952), claimed that 70 percent of all experimental studies on learning and motivation "reported in the *Journal of Experimental Psychology* and the *Journal of Comparative and Physiological Psychology* during the decade 1941–1950 made reference to one or more of Hull's publications" (p. 641). Hull clearly enjoyed a position of leadership along with others, such as Pavlov and Watson, who also conceived of psychology as a natural science. Hull died of a heart condition on May 10, 1952.

HULL'S SYSTEM   As noted earlier, Hull had an early interest in the fields of aptitude testing and hypnosis. His books *Aptitude Testing* (1928) and *Hypnosis and Suggestibility* (1933) represent substantial contributions in these fields. In his autobiography, Hull (1952) noted that he became pessimistic about the future of aptitude testing, so he left the field. Despite such misgivings, he remained interested in mental testing and challenged Lashley's views on heredity and intelligence (Weidman, 1994). His departure from the experimental investigation of hypnosis was not completely voluntary. Hull worked in the field of hypnosis at Wisconsin for about ten years and his work, together with that of his students, resulted in thirty-two published papers. When he moved to Yale, however, members of the medical community opposed his work. Hull's students and collaborators at Wisconsin completed this work because in the Midwest, "the superstitious fear of hypnosis was not nearly so great" (Hull, 1952, p. 152). *Hypnosis and Suggestibility* was published four years after Hull joined the Yale faculty. In his words, "Despite its technical nature this book seems to have been read quite widely, not only by academic persons but by the general public as well" (p. 153). Hull's book is a classic in the field of hypnosis.

The intellectual background for Hull's general behavior theory was partly his love for quantitative predictions and his quest for scientific unity (see Mills, 1988). The theory is set forth in four books and a large number of scientific papers. His major books include *Mathematico-Deductive Theory of Rote Learning*, published in 1940, followed by the classic *Principles of Behavior* (1943), which became a powerful force in psychology into the mid-1960s (Kranz, 2005). Eight years later, *Essentials of Behavior* (1951) showed the maturity of Hull's system. Hull's final book, *A Behavior System* (1952), was published posthumously. According to Logan (1968), another book on "application to social and cultural

problems remained to be written at the time of Hull's death in 1952" (p. 536).

Hull was central in developing quantitative approaches to behavior. The anchoring events for the terms in his theory are stimuli and responses, but these are assumed to be bridged by intervening variables such as **drive**, **fatigue**, **habit strength**, and **incentive**. Hull established hypothetical quantitative connections between such intervening variables and observable stimulus and response events. An example is provided by the following formula:

$$_sE_R = {_sH_R} \times D \times V \times K$$

$_sE_R$ refers to action potential in a given situation; $_sH_R$ refers to habit strength or number of previous trials in the situation; D is drive strength (e.g., the number of hours of deprivation); and V refers to **stimulus intensity dynamism**. This last term recognizes that some stimuli have a stronger influence on behavior than others. For example, the rat, a nocturnal animal, might run more readily in a darkened runway than in a well-lighted runway. Thus, V would have a greater value in the darkened runway. Finally, K refers to incentive motivation. For example, a child might work harder for a marble than for a button. Presumably the marble would have more K, or incentive value.

Hull's formula indicates that reaction potential is a joint multiplicative function of habit strength, drive level, the nature of the stimulus, and incentive motivation. Thus, a rat might be expected to be vigorous in a familiar, slightly darkened runway working for a preferred food object under relatively high drive. The foregoing formula is somewhat simplified but provides a general sense of Hull's approach. Hullian formulas were suggestive and often made precise predictions about what subjects would do in specific situations.

Hull's work in psychology began with simple observations (e.g., performance improves with practice, we learn better under some circumstances than others, and under certain circumstances we quit engaging in what was once a well-established response). The terms Hull used as intervening variables (e.g., *drive*, *incentive*, and *habit strength*) all have intuitive appeal and are tied to observable behaviors and stimulus events. Let us now consider Hull's position on specific problems in behavior theory.

Reinforcement   Reinforcement played a key role in Hull's behavior system. He spoke of the law of reinforcement, which meant that stimuli that reduce drive stimuli are reinforcing. Thus, food reduces hunger stimuli produced by the depletion of solid material in the stomach, just as escape from shock reduces shock stimuli. Further, Hull recognized the crucial role of "secondary" reinforcement in the control of behavior: Any stimulus consistently associated with primary reinforcers takes on reinforcing properties. As noted earlier, Hull also recognized the role of incentive as an important dimension of reinforcement.

Experimental Extinction   Because of its theoretical and possible practical applications, the study of experimental extinction has been a topic of continuing interest from the time of Pavlov and Thorndike. The usual procedure is to establish a response through conditioning and then study the persistence of the response once reinforcement is terminated. The speed of extinction, the conditions that accelerate or retard it, and the explanations for why it occurs have occupied a prominent place in the literature of behavior theory.

Hull argued that each response generates some degree of inhibition. Such inhibition is an aftereffect of the response and akin to a negative drive, like fatigue or pain. Hull referred to the inhibitory potential associated with each response as I_R, or *reactive inhibition*. Hull assumed that I_R dissipates with the passage of time, so it is a temporary state of affairs that follows each response. When responses are massed close together or when responses require high effort, I_R should be increased.

A second component of Hull's theory of extinction is called *conditioned inhibition*, or $_sI_R$. Hull assumed that $_sI_R$ builds up during the

dissipation of I_R. To illustrate, assume that a rat during extinction has pressed an eighty-gram counterweighted bar several times. Such a bar would be fairly heavy for the typical laboratory rat. After such a response burst, the rat has presumably generated much I_R, or fatigue. Now the rat rests and the act of resting is reinforcing. In other words, the dissipation of I_R is reinforcing. So $_sI_R$, or conditioned inhibition, gets built up. Hull accounted for permanent extinction in terms of conditioned inhibition. Hull's predictions on the roles of effort and inhibition in extinction received support in the literature (see Capehart, Viney, & Hulicka, 1958; Fischer et al., 1968), but it is unlikely inhibition in its various forms is sufficiently robust to provide a complete account of extinction of responses.

The Role of Insight in Learning   Hull believed that learning proceeds in a continuous fashion and "the organism's own responses furnish the surrogates for ideas" (Hilgard & Bower, 1966, p. 183). Hull attempted to understand behavior mechanistically in terms of material, efficient, and formal causation. Although he did not deny that terms such as *purpose*, **insight**, and *intention* can be attributed to the behavior of organisms, his hope was to show that such terms are "secondary principles" that can be deduced "from more elementary objective primary principles" (Hull, 1943, p. 26).

How Does Learning Occur?   As noted earlier, Hull believed that reinforcement plays a crucial role in learning. Hilgard and Bower (1966), in summarizing Hull's position, pointed out that "mere contiguous repetition does nothing but generate inhibition; all improvement depends upon reinforcement. . .[and] the number of reinforcements is the basic variable in acquiring habit strength" (p. 182). Nevertheless, Hull's theory is by no means a single-factor theory. Reinforcement may be necessary for learning in Hull's system, but it is not sufficient, nor is any other element, such as contiguity, sufficient. Hull's theory accounts for learning in terms of a complex interaction of a variety of organismic and environmental variables.

APPRAISAL OF HULL'S THEORY Although a leading figure in neobehaviorism during his lifetime, Hull's visibility in the psychological literature diminished after his death (Webster & Coleman, 1992). A number of critics outlined potential concerns in Hull's system. However, Spence (1952) stated that "no account of Hull's point of view would be complete which failed to emphasize his appreciation of what it was necessary to do in order to develop a science of psychology" (p. 646). Hull has even been criticized for the very scientific qualities some psychologists count as virtues. The rigor of his approach, specifically his emphasis on substantive definitions, was both a strength and a weakness. Specifically, critics have argued that the approach is sterile, artificial, and irrelevant to real-life concerns. Spence (1952) replied to such criticism: "Hull fully realized that, just as the physicist found it necessary to introduce such unworldlike conditions as the vacuum and the biologist such unnatural situations as an isolated piece of tissue 'growing' in a test tube, so likewise the psychologist must not hesitate to observe behavior, whether animal or human, under controlled conditions, artificial or otherwise" (p. 646). The comparison with early physics and biology is provocative, but it is perhaps still too early to gauge its legitimacy.

Edwin Ray Guthrie

As Sheffield (1959, p. 643) pointed out, **Edwin Ray Guthrie (1886–1959)** "did not follow a conventional route to distinction in psychology," nor did he follow a conventional path to behaviorism. Guthrie came to psychology from mathematics, formal logic, and philosophy.

Edwin Ray Guthrie was born in Lincoln, Nebraska, on January 9, 1886, the eldest of the five children. From his early years, Guthrie showed scholarly promise. He remained in his home state to earn a bachelor's degree in mathematics and a master's in philosophy from the University of Nebraska. In 1912, Guthrie obtained his Ph.D. under E. A. Singer at the University of Pennsylvania.

Guthrie's first academic appointment was at the University of Washington in philosophy, but after five years he shifted to psychology. His academic career was interrupted by service in World War I and World War II. His final regular academic position at the University of Washington was as dean of the graduate school. He retired in 1956 and died in 1959. Guthrie, like Hull, received many honors during his academic career. He served as president of the American Psychological Association in 1945, and in 1958, the American Psychological Foundation awarded Guthrie the Gold Medal Award for his distinguished contributions to the science of learning.

GUTHRIE'S BEHAVIORISM Unlike Hull and Tolman, Guthrie avoided technical language and formal theory construction, even in his textbook, *The Psychology of Learning* (1935; Clark, 2005). Sheffield (1959) noted that Guthrie's "avoidance of formalized theory was apparently deliberate, motivated not only by a general skepticism of the ultimate validity of deductively proven 'truths' but also by a belief that construction of formalized scientific systems hampered the search for new knowledge" (p. 648). More than Hull, Guthrie was suspicious of intervening variables or hypothetical constructs. Perhaps more than any other behaviorist, he restricted himself to accounts of the actual behaviors of the organism in the world. He was wary of hypothetical central processes (e.g., inhibition, drive) even when such processes were tied to physiology. Let us take a look at Guthrie's position on some key behaviorist issues.

Reinforcement Guthrie believed that reinforcement per se has no direct logical or causal relationship to learning. Even reinforcement theorists must question possible causal relationships between a learned connection and, for example, the consumption of food. What possible physiological connections could there be between reinforcers and the establishment of neural connections involved in learning?

A major problem with reinforcement and drive-reduction theories, as noted by Voeks (1968), is that they may produce "an ever-lengthening list of motives (conscious and unconscious) or drives (primary, secondary, tertiary) or needs, in an attempt to account for seemingly dysfunctional learning" (p. 297). Consider the teenager who fails to hang up her coat when entering the house even though she has been reprimanded time and again. Drive-reduction explanations of such behavior could lead to questions about whether the teenager may have hidden motives (e.g., maybe she enjoys annoying her parents). Guthrie suggested an approach that did not rely on the concepts of reinforcement, drive reduction, or hidden motives.

The Law of Contiguity   Although the teenager in the previous example has been reprimanded for failing to hang up her coat, the reprimands have changed nothing. Guthrie suggested a different approach. A careful study of the sequence of events may reveal that closing the door is followed by a turn to the right in the direction of the sofa, instead of a turn to the left in the direction of the closet. The coat is then thrown on the sofa. Now the young woman is asked to put the coat back on, go back out, and go through the sequence of movements of coming into the house, but this time she is asked to close the door and turn to the left. Turning to the left brings her to the closet door, which she is now asked to open. She may now hang up her coat. Guthrie believed that such an approach to establishing a new habit or breaking an old one has remarkable effects. Why?

According to Guthrie, there is but one law of learning, and that is the *law of contiguity*. We learn connections when stimuli are arranged so that they can be effective cues for a desired response. **Contiguity** is a necessary and sufficient condition for learning based on close temporal or spatial conjunction. Reinforcement has nothing to do with learning per se, but a reinforcer, as a strong stimulus, may keep an organism in a situation so that the necessary cues are attached to the appropriate response.

Guthrie's position emphasized the importance of recency in learning situations. Thus, it is the last thing we do in one situation that sets

the stage for what is to come next. In the example of the teenager and the coat, what is important is that closing the door becomes the cue for a left turn instead of a right turn. Many athletes have an intuitive feel for Guthrie's emphasis on recency: Never end a practice session on a failure; rather, end on a success because we tend to repeat what we last did in a situation. If the last response ended in failure or fear, there is an increased likelihood that such failure or fear will become conditioned to the situation.

One-Trial Learning   Almost all learning theorists stressed the importance of practice effects and repetition. Guthrie offered a new interpretation of why practice or repetition appears to work. Learning, according to Guthrie, takes place in one trial. Thus, when there is appropriate conjunction between stimulus and response, a connection is immediately established. The idea that we learn in one trial is not completely counterintuitive because most of us have experienced what seems to be one-trial learning. At the same time, we experience the beneficial effects of practice and we observe trials when no apparent connections are made. So how are we to resolve the apparent discrepancies between Guthrie's idea that learning occurs in one trial and the obvious benefits of practice?

According to Guthrie, we simplify the meanings of the terms *stimulus* and *response*. What we call a *response* is actually many smaller responses consisting of a large number of postures and movements. Similarly, what we call a *stimulus* is usually a multifaceted affair. What we learn, according to Guthrie, is learned in one trial, but sometimes many small connections must be established to produce what we have designated to be the appropriate response. When all smaller connections are established (and each one, according to Guthrie, is established in one trial), then we may observe what we have designated to be the appropriate response.

How does Guthrie account for trials that seem fruitless or empty? Connections that are made in a single trial are not always visible. Guthrie also emphasizes the idea that we may make the wrong connections and thus retard progress. One of the most important functions of a teacher is to monitor learning and provide feedback when connections are not headed in the desired direction.

Extinction   According to Guthrie's theory, responses are not weakened by the mere passage of time. Furthermore, the withdrawal of reinforcement has no direct bearing on the extinction of a response. What we call **extinction** really amounts to new learning that results from the process of establishing new responses to old stimuli. Rearranging the stimulus situation brings back experimental extinction. Going back to our example about hanging up the coat, we could focus on how we have extinguished the habit of throwing down the coat. But old responses were replaced by new responses, so extinction cannot easily be separated from new learning. What is important for extinction is the same thing that is important for any learning: namely, contiguity of stimulus and response. Withholding reinforcement changes the stimulus complex and contributes to the probability that new responses will be learned. The withholding of reinforcement has only an indirect bearing on the extinction or new learning process.

Insight   Guthrie rejected mentalistic interpretations of insight but was impressed with experiments on insight conducted by the Gestalt psychologist Wolfgang Köhler. Working in open field situations, Köhler arranged stimuli to maximize the probability of a connection. Though Köhler and Guthrie would disagree on interpretations of so-called insightful learning, they would share interests in experimental and practical conditions that facilitate such learning.

APPRAISAL OF GUTHRIE'S THEORY   One appeal of Guthrie's theory is his use of illustrations from everyday life. He was interested in psychotherapy, the problems of habit breaking, and a host of educational problems. His anecdotes contributed to the impression that the theory is relevant to important issues of life. Such an impression is premature, however, until the theory demonstrates its mettle in rigorous experimental tests.

Although Guthrie had limited access to students who would develop and promote his ideas (Clark, 2005), some of his students and admirers (Estes, 1950; Voeks, 1950) formalized the theory so it could be subjected to experimental scrutiny. Voeks restated many of Guthrie's ideas in the form of testable theorems and postulates, whereas Estes advanced a formal statistical theory of learning.

Perhaps more than any behaviorist after Watson, with the exception of Skinner, Guthrie was concerned about the transitions from the laboratory to the world. Guthrie's practical interests are illustrated in his book *The Psychology of Human Conflict* (1938), an application of learning principles to psychopathology. His practical interests are further illustrated in his book *Educational Psychology* (1950), coauthored with Francis Powers, and his paper "Personality in Terms of Associative Learning" (Guthrie, 1944).

Guthrie's applications of learning foreshadowed developments in that same area in the 1960s. The weakness of the theory—namely, its anecdotal nature—may also have been a strength because the anecdotes, drawn as they were from real-life situations, contributed to the idea that learning does not have to be an insular and narrow subdiscipline of psychology. Indeed, in Guthrie's hands, learning is not just a sterile laboratory discipline. It is a vital and all-encompassing way of thinking about behavior in educational, clinical, industrial, and daily-life situations.

Edward Chace Tolman

Edward Chace Tolman (1886–1959) developed a "new formula for behaviorism" (see Tolman, 1922) that accepted behavior as the proper subject matter of psychology but rejected Watson's stark stimulus–response system. Tolman was influenced by Edwin B. Holt, his teacher at Harvard; William McDougall, with his emphasis on the role of purpose in living organisms; and Gestalt psychologists, particularly Kurt Koffka and Kurt Lewin. These influences are evident in Tolman's system of psychology, which focused on the role of cognition and purpose in animal and human life.

Tolman was born to an upper-middle-class family in Newton, Massachusetts, on April 14, 1886. He graduated from Massachusetts Institute of Technology and immediately enrolled in philosophy and psychology courses at Harvard, taught by Ralph Barton Perry and Robert M. Yerkes. Tolman thought he might want to be a philosopher, but after taking Perry's course, he (1952) declared, "I decided then and there that I did not have brains enough to become a philosopher (that was still the day of great metaphysical systems), but that psychology was nearer my capacities and interests" (p. 323). Instead, Tolman leaned toward the work of Yerkes, a pioneer in animal research and an early supporter of Pavlov's work (Wight, 1993). After his first year at Harvard, he spent part of a summer at Giessen with Kurt Koffka. That brief experience made Tolman receptive to Gestalt ideas. In 1923, Tolman went back to Giessen for more instruction in the Gestalt perspective.

Following graduation from Harvard, Tolman worked for three years at Northwestern University before taking a faculty position at Berkeley that he would hold the rest of his life. Tolman's life and work at Berkeley were rewarding until the early 1950s, when McCarthyism swept the country. It was a time when a paranoid fear of subversive activity resulted in the demand for loyalty oaths. Those who refused to sign were subjected to publicized personal attacks, intimidation, and threats. Normally a shy individual, Tolman assumed leadership in the fight for academic freedom (Carroll, 2012). In the words of Krech (1968), "It was Tolman (a member of the national board of the American Civil Liberties Union) who led the faculty in full battle against the university—a battle that saved academic freedom at the university" (p. 95).

Crutchfield (1961) pointed out that "Tolman's distinguished career as a creative scientist and as a leader in the academic and social community spanned four decades from 1918, when he came to the University of California in

Berkeley as an instructor in psychology, until his death in Berkeley on November 19, 1959" (p. 135). Like other prominent neobehaviorists, Tolman enjoyed many honors in his lifetime. He served as president of the American Psychological Association in 1937. Twenty years later, Tolman received the Distinguished Scientific Contribution Award from the American Psychological Association.

The citation for the Distinguished Scientific Contribution Award provides a fitting introduction to Tolman's work:

> For the creative and sustained pursuit of a theoretical integration of the multifaceted data of psychology, not just its more circumscribed and amenable aspects; for forcing theorizing out of the mechanical and peripheral into the center of psychology without the loss of objectivity and discipline; for returning [the human being] to psychology by insisting upon molar behavior purposely organized as the unit of analysis, most explicitly illustrated in his purposive-cognitive theory of learning. (*American Psychologist*, 1958, p. 155)

TOLMAN'S COGNITIVE BEHAVIORISM   A major complaint against Watsonian behaviorism was that it achieved scientific status at the expense of believability. Watson's system was hard to accept because cognition, belief, and goal directedness were either banished altogether or redefined in ways that defied common sense. In contrast, Tolman constructed an expansive psychology that retained the objectives of classical behaviorism, but with a greater sensitivity to events in our daily lives.

Tolman saw his system as a true behaviorism because the focus was on behavior rather than consciousness and on objective observation rather than introspection. He characterized his system as a *molar behaviorism* in contrast with Watson's molecular behaviorism. The term *molar* referred to large units or the kind of global behavior that we observe in the everyday world. Tolman believed that behavior is a legitimate scientific topic of inquiry in its own right. We gain no additional scientific respectability by correlating behavior with physiological processes. This theme was later amplified in B. F. Skinner's work.

Tolman also referred to his system as a **purposive behaviorism**. He understood that animals and humans are directed toward goals (Innis, 1999). Such goals have clear-cut observable qualities that can serve as objects of scientific analysis. We need not get lost in the philosophical subtleties of teleology to explain the goal-directed features of behavior.

According to Tolman, **molar behavior** has a purposive quality but it is also *cognitive* and *docile*. These two terms distinguish molar behavior from rigid, reflexive, path-bound mechanical behaviors. Molar behavior is not like a reflex. Molar behavior has a multitude of causes; it has an intelligent "teachable" quality, and it is not blind. The term *teachable* is close in meaning to Tolman's term *docile*. The term *cognitive* refers to abilities such as the capacity to discriminate, the sense of locations, a sense of what leads to what, and the capacity to form expectations.

Intervening Variables   Tolman believed we can identify meaningful psychological concepts that account for the behavior of living organisms. In other words, Tolman was not content to describe simple stimulus–response relationships. He believed psychological processes intervene between stimuli and responses. Such psychological processes are inferred from and tied to behavior. **Intervening variable** refers to psychological processes that direct behavior and mediate between stimuli and observable responses. For Tolman, examples of intervening variables include cognitions, expectancies, purposes, hypotheses, and appetite. To illustrate, consider the term *expectancy*. According to Tolman, an expectancy develops when a reward follows each successful response. Humans and animals develop expectancies anytime regular relationships occur between responses and environmental stimuli. Once developed, an expectancy is involved in directing and controlling behavior.

Many of Tolman's intervening variables had a mentalistic ring yet were always tied to observable events. We now turn to a consideration of Tolman's position on some key issues in learning.

Reinforcement   What we normally think of as a reinforcement (e.g., a food object) has nothing to do with learning as such, but reinforcements do regulate the performance of learned responses. Tolman, more than any theorist, drew a sharp distinction between learning and performance. Classic experiments on **latent learning** illustrate Tolman's position on the relationships among reinforcement, learning, and performance.

In a typical experiment (Tolman & Honzik, 1930), one group of rats is given a food reward following each successful run through a maze. Over the course of the experiment, the speed of running quickly increases and the number of errors decreases. Another group of subjects receives no food in the maze. After spending time in the maze each day, subjects in this group are removed and returned to their home cage. Speed of running and number of errors for this group does not improve significantly. At this point, one might conclude that the group that had been rewarded had learned while the group that had not been rewarded did not learn. Such an interpretation, however, is apparently incorrect. Perhaps the group that had not been fed had also learned the maze but had no reason to show that they knew it. So, on day eleven, Tolman and Honzik introduced food in the reward box for subjects that had not previously been rewarded. Their running speeds and error scores improved dramatically— so dramatically that it is reasonable to conclude that there was latent learning during the non-rewarded trials.

Tolman argued that rats learn spatial relationships or even develop a cognitive map of a maze by virtue of sheer exposure. Reinforcement influences motivation, and hence performance, but learning itself is an independent process. For practical purposes, he argued that we should still use reinforcement because of the important role it plays in motivation.

Experimental Extinction Extinction occurs largely because of changes in expectancies. Response strength remains high so long as conditioned stimuli continue, in a majority of cases, to serve as signs that food will be forthcoming. When stimuli no longer have value as signs, expectancies change and so do responses. One implication of Tolman's position is that extinction, in theory, can be a cognitive affair; that is, it could occur without responding. If one were in a position to see that a sign will no longer lead to a reinforcement, extinction could be accomplished without the necessity of responding. Experiments on latent extinction have provided evidence for cognitive interpretations of extinction.

In the typical experiment, subjects are repeatedly placed in an unbaited goal box that was once a place where they had obtained reinforcement. Subjects who are exposed to an unbaited goal box extinguish faster in subsequent extinction trials than do subjects who have had no such preextinction exposure to the unbaited goal box. Extinction, according to Tolman, results from changing cognitions that are influenced by sign stimuli in the environment. Such a position is in marked contrast with Hull's response-produced inhibition theory.

Cognitive Maps The emphasis in many early learning theories was on connections between stimuli and responses. Tolman accepted the idea that some learning involves stimulus–response connections, but he also emphasized stimulus–stimulus connections. Complicated stimulus–stimulus connections are vital components in Tolman's concept of the **cognitive map**.

Consider the complicated maze that the typical college student must run in order to get from a dorm room to a classroom. The maze may involve many left and right turns, some diagonal pathways, stairs, or even elevators. In animal laboratories, comparable situations are sometimes created for the white rat. When the maze is successfully traversed, we may ask ourselves what has been learned. Have we learned a complicated chain of stimulus–response connections?

According to Tolman, the answer is "no." In such a situation we learn a cognitive map.

For example, we do not learn that we must make three successive left turns, followed by two right turns, followed by a left turn, and so on. Instead, we develop a cognitive map that includes, at first, a vague sense of location and a sense of the layout of the situation, including many possible pathways connecting various locations. In other words, there is a rich and broad cognitive representation of the world in which we move (Nadel, 2013). We do not move about our world in a mechanical fashion; rather, we move in a flexible fashion, following first one pathway then another. Simpler organisms such as the rat do the same thing. Again, Tolman did not deny that some learning involves stimulus–response connections, but he insisted we learn stimulus–stimulus connections that are vital to the development of cognitive maps.

The Role of Insight in Learning Tolman accepted the idea that learning is often marked by radical discontinuities. Most learning is not of the blind trial-and-success variety discussed in Thorndike's work. Tolman believed in the "*capacity* for grasping field-relationships" (Tolman, 1932, p. 200). He referred to such a capacity as a *means–end capacity*. This expression refers to innate and acquired abilities to engage in intelligent commerce with pathways, routes, barriers, and various temporal and spatial characteristics of a field. Tolman spoke of the capacity for *inventive ideation*, which referred to "running back-and-forth, attempting alternatives, and making behavioral adjustments." Although Tolman avoided the term *insight* as used by Gestalt psychologists, he was friendly to the term's meaning. Along with the Gestalt psychologists, he rejected the idea that learning is a continuous, gradual, mechanical process.

APPRAISAL OF TOLMAN'S SYSTEM Tolman demonstrated that the desirable methodological rigor of classical behaviorism could be coupled with a richer, more believable psychology that recognizes the complexities and subtleties of human and animal life. His system provided the intellectual spadework that nurtured the cognitive movement in the 1950s. Hilgard and Bower (1966) noted that Tolman "gave a new cast to behaviorism by insisting that it be open to the problems created by cognitive processes, problem solving, and inventive ideation" (p. 228).

Finally, Tolman's work can be viewed as a springboard for developments in the 1950s and 1960s in such diverse areas as motivation (Festinger, 1962; Lawrence & Festinger, 1962), clinical psychology (Rotter, 1954), neuropsychology (Olds, 1954), and mathematical learning theory (Bower, 1962; MacCorquodale & Meehl, 1954). He was the first to publish research on selective breeding for maze-learning ability in rats, work that inspired his students such as Robert Choate Tryon (1901–1967) and influenced the field of behaviorial genetics (Innis, 1992). Tolman's work is one of the most important bridges between classical behaviorism and contemporary psychology (Goldman, 1999). Gleitman (1991) notes that Tolman was "clearly a forerunner of modern 'cognitive psychology'" and that he was well ahead of his times (p. 235). His achievements and influence persist in spite of the fact that he did not demand lockstep conformity from his students or set himself up as an intellectual cult leader. His writings are filled with good humor and a deep sense of the difficulties, blind spots, and uncertainties that beset scientific activity.

Burrhus Frederic Skinner

Hull, Guthrie, and Tolman were not neobehaviorism's sole champions. In the latter half of the twentieth century, B. F. Skinner not only dominated neobehaviorism, but also became one of psychology's most celebrated figures.

Burrhus Frederic Skinner (1904–1990) was born on March 20, 1904, in Susquehanna, Pennsylvania. He lived a pleasant childhood surrounded by a cordial family. However, occasional developmental events were instructive about the influence of aversive conditioning. Skinner (1967) recalled that he was never punished as a child but

B. F. Skinner

often heard lectures about the horrors of hell and the terrible consequences of antisocial behavior.

Skinner was a student of the humanities, though initially he was encouraged to pursue a career in law. In fact, Skinner's birth announcement in the local newspaper predicted succession to his father's legal practice: "The town has a new law firm: Wm. A. Skinner & Son" (Skinner, 1967, p. 394). Skinner, however, hoped to become an author and, though a careless student, studied literature at Hamilton College in New York. He decided against a writing career despite the poet Robert Frost's favorable appraisal of his work.

While at Hamilton, Skinner read Ivan Pavlov's *Conditioned Reflexes*, Bertrand Russell's *Philosophy*, and John B. Watson's *Behaviorism*. Though lacking an undergraduate course in psychology, he enrolled in the graduate program at Harvard University. Edwin G. Boring was the principal figure in an academic climate largely untouched by behaviorism; Walter Hunter traveled from Clark University as a guest lecturer and offered the only seminar on the subject (Plaud & Montgomery, 1993). Despite the minimal emphasis on behaviorism, the graduate program at Harvard allowed Skinner autonomy in developing research interests. He completed all requirements for his master's degree in 1930 and received his Ph.D. the following year. From 1933 to 1936, Skinner continued his research in the prestigious position of junior fellow of the Harvard Society of Fellows.

In 1936, Skinner joined the faculty of the University of Minnesota. His appointment proved productive in both laboratory and classroom activities. He contributed to wartime research while developing operant conditioning. He worked with exceptional students at Minnesota. Skinner (1983a) later recalled that over five percent of his students subsequently earned Ph.D. degrees in psychology. In 1945, he assumed the chair of the psychology department at Indiana University. After three years, he returned to Harvard University.

In 1958, the American Psychological Association honored Skinner with its Distinguished Scientific Contribution Award. In the same year, he was appointed to the prestigious Edgar Pierce Professorship, named in honor of the affluent Harvard alumnus who established the William James lecture series. Skinner, however, found little gratification in such veneration. Indeed, his style of life was self-effacing and uncomplicated. He answered his own phone, refused to display medals or trophies, and stored honorary degrees in a box in the basement of his home; he published with many faculty and student co-authors (McKerchar et al., 2011). When he allowed interviews or appearances on talk shows (such as a 1971 debate with the physicist Donald MacKay on the TV program *Firing Line*), it was not for self-aggrandizement but for the promotion of behaviorism (Washburn, 1997).

Skinner retired in 1974 to become Professor Emeritus of Psychology and Social Relations. In August 1990, the American Psychological Association presented Skinner with the unprecedented Citation for Outstanding Lifetime Contribution to Psychology. B. F. Skinner died from leukemia on August 18, 1990, a mere eight days after accepting the APA award.

For six decades Skinner was a prolific and animated defender of behaviorism. His experimental behavior analysis was set forth in numerous scientific and nontechnical books, including *The Behavior of Organisms* (1938), *Walden Two* (1948), *Science and Human Behavior* (1953), *Verbal Behavior* (1957), *The Technology of Teaching* (1968), *Beyond Freedom and Dignity* (1971), and *About Behaviorism* (1974). In addition, he published a three-volume autobiography *Particulars of My Life* (1976), *The Shaping of a Behaviorist* (1979), and *A Matter of Consequences* (1983a). Although his research was often marked with controversy and criticism (Rutherford, 2000), Skinner refused to answer his critics. His preference was to collect data and work out the details of his position.

PRECURSORS TO SKINNER'S BEHAVIORISM

Before considering Skinner's experimental behavior analysis, we should survey other scholars to whom he owed a conceptual debt.

Although Bacon, Sherrington, and La Mettrie comprise part of Skinner's intellectual history, five figures seem particularly prominent. Charles Darwin's insistence on the continuity of species reinforced the belief that data from animals were meaningful for all organisms. C. Lloyd Morgan's canon of parsimony counseled Skinner to neglect grandiose explanations in favor of simple, descriptive ones. Edward L. Thorndike's puzzle box research demonstrated that complex behavior could be studied in an objective manner without reliance on mentalism. Ivan Pavlov established the precedent for controlled laboratory investigations of lawful conditioning. Finally, John B. Watson's behaviorism inspired Skinner to adopt the scientific study of behavior as an alternative to the study of consciousness.

Although applauding the 1913 behaviorist manifesto, Skinner (1963) observed that Watson failed to support his position with a solid research program. Skinner was more successful than Watson in generating data for behaviorism. In an effort to promote research on behavior analysis, the *Journal of the Experimental Analysis of Behavior* was founded in 1958, the year of

Watson's death. The endurance of the journal is a singular tribute to Skinner's influence on the psychology of learning. His legacy is further reflected in professional organizations such as APA Division 25, a collective body of researchers interested in the experimental analysis of behavior (Lattal, 1992). For a better understanding of Skinner's work, it is important to examine the basic assumptions of his behavior analysis.

SKINNER'S PHILOSOPHY OF BEHAVIORISM
Skinner was a resolute positivist devoted to psychology as an objective natural science. According to Skinner (1963), behaviorism was more than the study of behavior; it was a philosophy of science. Like Watson, Skinner saw psychology as a natural science and, like Watson, was a thoroughgoing determinist. Skinner (1971) insisted that behavior is lawful and argued that the romantic notion of free will is counterproductive both to behavioral science and to society at large.

Though Skinner's writings gave the impression of hard determinism, his research on reinforcers that increase the probability of a future response suggests an interest in probabilistic lawfulness rather than strict determinism. Nevertheless, emphasis on prediction and control was central to Skinner's entire system of thought. Furthermore, his goal was to demonstrate the detrimental features of aversive control and the advantages of positive control. Skinner believed that individuals and societal institutions can progress through a "technology of behavior" drawn from the principles of behavior analysis.

Like most other neobehaviorists, Skinner was a student of behavior rather than of mental events. Although previous neobehaviorists adhered to methodological behaviorism (the emphasis on controlled, observable experimentation with falsifiable and replicable conclusions), Skinner went a step further as he complemented methodological behaviorism with a radical behaviorism—a philosophy supporting the *experimental analysis of behavior*. According to Skinner (1974), "The position can be stated as follows: what is felt or introspectively observed

is not some nonphysical world of consciousness, mind or mental life but the observer's own body" (p. 17). He claimed that three obstacles stand in the way of radical behaviorism: third-force psychology, psychotherapy, and cognitive psychology. Skinner (1987c) argued, "By their very nature, the antiscience stance of humanistic psychology, the practical exigencies of the helping professions, and the cognitive restoration of the royal House of Mind have worked against the definition of psychology as the science of behavior" (p. 784). Although he mourned the damage of these approaches, Skinner remained confident that radical behaviorism would deliver psychology from pseudoscientific factions. In his final article, completed the evening before his death, a resolute Skinner (1990) declared that a scientific psychology can only be an analysis of behavior, not a study of the mind.

Unlike Clark Hull, Skinner eschewed grandiose theory construction in favor of descriptive observations of behavior, and his bottom-up approach to the study of behavior has remained fruitful (Madden et al., 2013). More than any behaviorist, Skinner (1956) followed in Bacon's critical inductivist tradition. He denied that he constructed hypotheses or that he tested formal theorems or models. He assumed that behavior was lawful and understood the difficulty of discovering its laws. We turn now to a consideration of Skinner's specific contributions.

OPERANT CONDITIONING Skinner (1938) established experimental behavior analysis in his classic work *The Behavior of Organisms*. Based on his published research since 1930, this book presented a comprehensive system of methods for the **operant conditioning** of animals. Although some critics attacked Skinner for making no effort to tie his ideas to existing data and concepts, *The Behavior of Organisms* was hailed as a significant contribution to the psychology of learning (Knapp, 1995). As far back as 1932, Skinner had distinguished between two major types of conditioning, and five years later introduced the term *operant* in contrast with Pavlovian **respondent conditioning** (Coleman, 1981).

Pavlovian conditioning probed the correlations between unconditioned and conditioned stimuli, whereas Skinner stressed the relation of the response and reinforcement. Thus, Skinner referred to Pavlovian conditioning as *Type II* or *Type S* (reinforcement correlated with a stimulus) and operant conditioning as *Type I* or *Type R* (reinforcement correlated with a response). Type S encompassed conditioning of autonomic behavior, whereas Type R was conditioning of voluntary behavior.

From its genesis, operant conditioning involved modifying behavior as a consequence of reinforcement. Any consequence that increased the probability of a future response was deemed a reinforcer. A positive reinforcer (e.g., food, money) entails a stimulus that increases the likelihood of a future response. A negative reinforcer involves removal of an aversive stimulus to increase the probability of a future response (e.g., a termination of electrical shock or extreme heat). Operants comprise a class of behaviors strengthened by a class of consequences or reinforcers.

Because Skinner was not concerned with the antecedent association between stimulus and response, his work is not in the tradition of S–R psychology. Skinner denied this heritage: "I do not consider myself an S–R psychologist. The stimulus is only one among a lot of different variables. As it stands, I'm not sure that response is a very useful concept. Behavior is very fluid; it isn't made up of lots of little responses packed together. . . . It is a mistake to suppose that there are internal stimuli and to try to formulate everything as S–R psychology" (quoted in Evans, 1968, pp. 20–21).

You might note the similarity between the research of Skinner and of Edward L. Thorndike (Chance, 1999). In a letter to Thorndike, Skinner (1967) acknowledged that his work was an elaboration of the former's puzzle box research. As in Thorndike's revised law of effect, Skinner favored reinforcement over punishment in the strengthening of behavior. Intermittent punishment may produce unfortunate by-products and only short-term gains. Nevertheless, Skinner (1953) asserted that society had made progress in diminishing the aversive influence of punishment. He celebrated the demise of angry avenging gods and threats of hellfire that terrorized previous generations. He was also pleased that the "dunce cap" and birch rod in schools were replaced by more enlightened positive incentives to learn. Skinner verified reinforcement principles with data collected from various technological innovations. Indeed, his modification of ice chests into operant chambers revolutionized the study of animal behavior. The chamber allowed an animal subject to demonstrate a learned behavior (e.g., a bar press or pecking at a lit disk) that could be rewarded by a food dispenser. Interestingly, Clark Hull branded the operant chamber with the infamous title of "Modified Skinner Box," although in characteristic modesty, Skinner (1983a) protested usage of the eponym.

Skinner also constructed the cumulative recorder, a mechanical device that monitored patterns of operant behavior from a single animal subject. By the mid-1950s, operant instrumentation was manufactured by several companies. His experiences with operant technology led to new discoveries, such as the influence of different schedules of reinforcement on behavior (Crossman, 1991). Skinner (1956) reported that practical necessity motivated his early interest in schedules of reinforcement. One day it was clear that he was running out of food pellets, so he reinforced his subject once every minute. He saved his supply of pellets and observed a constant rate of responding. This serendipitous finding led to the study of fixed intervals and other schedules of reinforcement. Together with Charles Ferster, Skinner published a book containing over nine hundred figures on the specifications of these experimental reinforcement schedules (Ferster & Skinner, 1957).

Skinner's fundamental vision of operant conditioning did not radically change in the ensuing half-century (although ideas about drive and reflex were abandoned after the 1930s). However, Skinner's contribution extends beyond research on animal learning. In fact, the broad implications of his research on operant conditioning have served as the impetus for numerous applications.

SKINNER'S APPLIED RESEARCH One hallmark of B. F. Skinner's legacy is an effort to generalize his ideas from the domain of the laboratory to the complexity of the external world. Though initially he found little interest in the applications of operant conditioning (see Skinner, 1938, pp. 441–442), he later changed his position. Indeed, the 1968 debut of the *Journal of Applied Behavior Analysis* signaled one of many applications of the experimental principles of behavior analysis. Let's take a look at Skinner's more prominent applications.

Verbal Behavior One of Skinner's earliest applied efforts, started in 1935, was an analysis of verbal behavior. Although a disciple of Darwinian continuity, Skinner (1938) admitted, "The only differences I expect to see revealed between the behavior of rat and man (aside from enormous differences of complexity) lie in the field of verbal behavior" (p. 442). Skinner revealed his concept of language acquisition in his 1948 William James lectures, which were expanded into the controversial 1957 publication *Verbal Behavior*. He claimed that verbal behavior is learned and, like any operant behavior, is modified by ensuing consequences from a given community.

Critics, most notably psycholinguist Noam Chomsky, argued that Skinner's reinforcement explanation of linguistic development was simplistic and reductionistic. Chomsky (1959) believed that language was an abstract, rule-governed system. Chomsky's scathing review generated considerable attention while Skinner's work was largely neglected (Andresen, 1991). However, Skinner was convinced that Chomsky misunderstood the book and declined rebuttal to the psycholinguist's critique; these concerns persist (Palmer, 2006). Kenneth MacCorquodale (1970) later defended Skinner's verbal behavior perspective within the context of the nativism (Chomsky) versus environment (Skinner) debate. Despite criticism of the book, Skinner continued to support the reinforcement explanation of verbal behavior, and this explanation remains relevant in psychology (Schlinger, 2008).

Developmental and Educational Applications While at Indiana, Skinner gained notoriety for his invention of the aircrib, a large, well-lit chamber with proper temperature control for child rearing (Benjamin & Nielsen-Gammon, 1999). Originally called the "baby-tender," Skinner employed the chamber during the upbringing of Deborah, his second daughter. Contrary to rumors about trauma resulting from her upbringing, Skinner (1967) proudly noted that his daughter was a college graduate and an accomplished artist. Furthermore, Julie, his oldest daughter and an educational psychologist, raised Skinner's granddaughter in an aircrib.

Skinner also took an active interest in his children's education. After observing that education was often the product of inappropriate consequences, Skinner (1958, 1968) proposed a solution by way of programmed instruction. In the 1920s, Sidney L. Pressey (1888–1979) had constructed programmed machines for testing intelligence. Skinner revised Pressey's idea by designing programs that dispensed immediate feedback for each student response. Skinner's programmed instruction promoted sustained activity with self-paced mastery of the material. The idea generated a great deal of media attention (Rutherford, 2000). Although IBM and other companies were interested in marketing teaching machines, negotiations collapsed along with Skinner's dream of reforming American education (Bjork, 1993); nonetheless, Skinner anticipated computer-assisted instruction by several decades. His programmed instruction inspired other researchers to develop innovative educational methods. Most notably, Fred S. Keller formulated a Personalized System of Instruction (PSI), which emphasized the individual student's responsibility for mastering the material (Keller & Sherman, 1974). Despite such pedagogical innovations, Skinner (1984) remained dissatisfied with the direction of U.S. education.

Finally, Skinner explored the process of aging. Together with Margaret Vaughan, he published a nontechnical book titled *Enjoy Old Age* in 1983. This book contained practical suggestions and insights on gerontological concerns such as diet, exercise, retirement, forgetfulness, sensory deficiencies, and the fear of death. Ironically, Skinner (1983a) recalled the rigorous composition of the book: "We met a self-imposed deadline and finished it in three months, thereby violating, for me, one of its basic principles: avoid fatigue. I was scarcely enjoying old age when we finished the book, but I soon recovered" (p. 394).

Military Applications Perhaps Skinner's most unconventional idea was his so-called Project Pigeon research during World War II. With the assistance of several outstanding students from the University of Minnesota (including Keller and Marian Breland and William K. Estes), Skinner trained pigeons to navigate an armed glider named the "Pelican" (so named because like the bird, the glider had a large frontal store with a considerably smaller body). The enthusiastic researchers demonstrated the efficiency of their automated bombers to government officials but with disappointing results. Ironically, Skinner (1960) claimed that one military authority declared that the pigeons were more accurate than radar. Despite Skinner's certitude about the effectiveness of his "crackpot idea," the government rejected further support for the project. Despite initial funding by General Mills, the decision was made to discontinue funding in favor of other military projects.

However, the classified research did demonstrate the efficacy of operant conditioning. Skinner kept thirty pigeons and demonstrated immediate and accurate target strikes even after six years of inactivity. Franklin Taylor resurrected the research under the auspices of the Naval Research Laboratory in Washington, DC. A missile nose cone from Project Pigeon resides with a teaching machine in the Smithsonian Institution (Skinner, 1983b). Skinner's ideas were also implemented in an aerospace program that sent two bar-pressing chimpanzees into space (Rohles, 1992).

Walden Two: Another Behaviorist Utopia   In an essay titled "A Behaviorist's

Utopia," John B. Watson conceived of a society that controlled child care and social relationships from the time of birth to maturity (Buckley, 1989). Although far removed from Watson's utopia, Skinner proposed in detail an institution based on the use of behavioral principles of reinforcement to support well-being and social justice (Altus & Morris, 2009). In his 1948 novel *Walden Two*, he described life in a hypothetical experimental colony designed by behavioral engineering. The novel centered on Professor Burris, who is reacquainted with T. E. Frazier, a maverick colleague from their graduate school days. Frazier is the founder of Walden Two, a community maintained and established on positive reinforcement. Workers labor for four hours daily, have a credit system of payment, and enjoy numerous opportunities for creative relaxation. Through the observations of Burris and Frazier, the reader is allowed insight into Skinner's vision of a behaviorist utopia.

Written in a mere seven weeks, *Walden Two* became one of Skinner's most popular books, especially during the quest for alternative lifestyles in the 1960s. The controversial nature of a behaviorally designed community aroused curiosity among the general public, college students, movie studios, and even the Central Intelligence Agency (Skinner, 1983a). An experimental community based on *Walden Two* was established in 1967 in Twin Oaks, Virginia. The community proved only marginally successful (Kuhlmann, 2005), but led Skinner (1967) to reformulate the role of incentive, education, and sexuality in a behaviorist community. Although fictional, Skinner's *Walden Two* provides an intriguing glimpse into behavioral engineering for the collective good, an early step toward positive psychology (Adams, 2012).

Additional Applications   Skinner's experimental behavior analysis has also found application in psychotherapy. During the 1930s, he had an interest in employing operant techniques with psychotic patients but was prevented from doing so by a rigorous schedule. In 1948, he delivered a series of lectures at Worcester

State Hospital but was again unable to initiate a research program on psychotic behavior modification.

Finally in 1952, Skinner initiated a behavior therapy program at the Metropolitan State Hospital in Waltham, Massachusetts. Ogden Lindsley, one of Skinner's students, engaged in six hundred hours of successful behavior modification using candy, cigarettes, and pinup posters as reinforcers for people with psychoses (Skinner, 1983b). In November 1953, Skinner and his colleagues presented their research in the paper "Studies in Behavior Therapy," marking the first usage of the term *behavior therapy* (Reed & Luiselli, 2009). Today, Skinner is the "father of applied behavior analysis" (Morris et al., 2005, p. 99), and behavior therapy and modification remain an enterprising field of psychotherapy.

Skinner had two additional students who applied operant conditioning to animal training. While working with him on Project Pigeon, Keller Breland (1915–1965) and Marian Breland (1920–2001) recognized the commercial potential of operant conditioning. They decided against pursuing their doctoral degrees at Minnesota in favor of applying behavior analysis to train animals for commercial and entertainment purposes. Although Skinner tried to dissuade them, the Brelands formed Animal Behavior Enterprises (ABE) in 1943. Over the next few decades, ABE trainers trained more than one hundred and forty different species for advertising and public entertainment. After using operant conditioning to train dolphins, the Brelands wrote a 1955 manual that influenced later marine mammal training programs at Sea World (Bailey & Gillaspy, 2005). In the 1960s, they taught training skills to Navy dolphin trainers, allowing the Brelands to study dolphin communication, acoustics, and training methods. This venture brought them into partnership with Bob Bailey who became ABE's research director in 1965 and later its general manager.

The work of Breland and Breland stimulated interest in the media, exposing the public to operant conditioning. The popular press spotlighted their work in countless articles and the Brelands featured trained animals on *The Tonight Show with Johnny Carson* and the *Ed Sullivan Show*, among other television appearances (Bailey & Gillaspy, 2005). In 1961, they wrote "The Misbehavior of Organisms," a controversial article that challenged operant researchers to investigate instinctive behavior. Breland and Breland (1961) insisted that the "behavior of any species cannot be adequately understood, predicted, or controlled without knowledge of its instinctive patterns, evolutionary history, and ecological niche" (p. 684).

APPRAISAL OF SKINNER'S BEHAVIORISM

The praise for Skinner's work has been joined with dissension from both public and scientific sectors. Following the 1971 publication of *Beyond Freedom and Dignity*, Skinner reached the height of his public exposure and found himself embroiled in controversy that spilled into the *New York Times* among other media (Rutherford, 2000). His ideas usually provoked skeptical or condemnatory reaction and, at times, detractors perceived him as a sort of "scientific despot." A legion of critics from psychotherapist Carl Rogers to former Vice President Spiro Agnew damned Skinner's ideology. He was branded a fascist and a Nazi, protestors picketed his talks, and his image was hanged in effigy. His open criticism of the Vietnam conflict during the 1960s nearly jeopardized government funding of his research and made him the target of an FBI investigation (Skinner, 1983a; Wyatt, 2000).

Skinner also provoked criticism from colleagues within the scientific community. Critics such as Chomsky contended that Skinner's "simplistic explanations" appear sound in an artificial laboratory context but have little validity in the real world. Furthermore, behavior analysis has been accused of indifference toward topical areas such as the self, personality, cognition, feelings, purpose, creativity, and nativism. Skinner has also been blamed for advancing a mechanistic science that dehumanizes the individual. In addition, Mahoney (1989) charged that the radical behaviorist's intolerant opinion of contemporary psychology has jeopardized its future and called for a tempering of ideology if the discipline is to progress.

Rutherford (2003) provided a carefully researched study of the treatment of Skinnerian psychology in the popular press from the 1940s to the 1970s. It was clear that changing social contexts over the decades played a significant role in the reception of Skinner's work and often contributed to feelings of ambivalence among the public. Skinner's basic goals were often consistent with the goals of major social movements, but there were disagreements about how to achieve such goals. For example, Skinner opposed the Vietnam War, much like the counterculture of the 1960s, but he was a vocal critic of counterculture tactics. Skinner, like humanistic psychologists (see Chapter 17), promoted a societal and political system that was supportive and responsive to human needs and interests. The humanistic school of thought simply disagreed with Skinner about how to achieve such a society. Rutherford (2009) has also argued that a substantial part of Skinner's contribution comes from the technology of behavior change. If we move beyond the stereotype of Skinner as an unfeeling researcher, we can find good reason why he was named Humanist of the Year in 1972. Rutherford (2000) observed that in the 1980s there was a "shift in public opinion and a more philosophical evaluation of [Skinner's] impact on the popular culture of psychology" (p. 391). Following Skinner's death in 1990, scholarly studies are leading to a more nuanced view of his many innovations and connections between his ideas and other areas of psychology (Toates, 2009). At present, no adequate generalization does justice to Skinner's lasting influence, but there can be no denying his contributions to both experimental and clinical psychology (Goddard, 2012).

For his part, Skinner (1987a) was puzzled about the controversy surrounding his research. After all, anybody can go to the laboratory and check his results for themselves. That is the way science works! If there have been errors, they can be corrected through additional research.

FURTHER CONTRIBUTIONS TO APPLIED PSYCHOLOGY FROM NEOBEHAVIORISM

Classical behaviorism has always emphasized the applications of psychology to the problems of daily life. Indeed, one of Watson's criticisms of earlier psychologies was that they were too sterile—too far removed from the problems of law, business, education, medicine, and interpersonal relations. Watson embraced the part of functionalism that explored daily problems, but hoped to move beyond functionalism with a down-to-earth psychology that dealt with the tangible world. Other behaviorists shared Watson's interest in the problems of living. Though the bulk of the laboratory work of the behaviorist schools was devoted to the psychology of learning, representatives of those schools had unmistakable interests in a larger agenda.

Examples of the contributions of behaviorist psychologists to applied problems abound and are illustrated in Walter Samuel Hunter's studies of human–machine systems in World War II. Karl Lashley's work with brain-damaged subjects represents a pioneering effort to find ways to restore functions lost through injury and disease. Lashley's work foreshadowed the field of behavioral neuroscience with its emphasis on basic and applied problems associated with the structural and functional properties of the nervous system.

The neobehaviorists who followed in the tradition of John B. Watson also worked on practical problems. Though he was keenly aware of the problems of assessing human ability and potential, Hull's book *Aptitude Testing* (1928) is a classic in that area. His book *Hypnosis and Suggestibility* (1933) is also one of the most informed and substantial books on the topic of hypnosis.

As we have seen, Skinner was dedicated to the application of operant conditioning to a broad range of areas, including education, linguistics, development, and military and clinical psychology. Along with Skinner, Guthrie had the broadest range of interests in applied problems. Guthrie's major works are filled with practical anecdotes on how to apply his learning theory to daily problems. His book *Educational Psychology* (1950), published with Francis Powers, is an application of learning theory to the classroom. He also wrote on the topics of personality, psychotherapy, leadership, the evaluation of faculty performance, and the function of the state university. His interests were not restricted to learning theory. However, when Guthrie thought about the basic problems of learning, he seemed to be led irresistibly to place these problems in a larger practical context. His was truly a functional behaviorism.

Though most of Tolman's published works dealt with theoretical issues in learning, his cognitive emphasis brought new breadth to behaviorism. His was a more psychological behaviorism and his followers explored a larger range of problems while retaining the methodological rigor that characterized behaviorism. Tolman's book *Drives Toward War*, published in 1942, just after the United Stated entered World War II, illustrates his interest in the psychological sources of conflict. The book focuses on some of the psychogenic or learned needs that contribute to human conflict and war.

Behaviorism was the dominant force in U.S. psychology from the 1920s to the late 1950s. Though most behaviorists viewed learning as foundational to the field of psychology, their interests ranged broadly from the problems of psychopathology to the problems of social psychology. Even so, by the 1960s there was a growing consensus that their vision was too narrow, that both methodologically and substantively they had closed too many doors. Their many positive contributions, however, carried on in new, broader approaches to the discipline.

Review Questions

1. Briefly discuss three values that are more or less common to all behavioristic psychologies.
2. What is *operationism* and what are some of the common criticisms of it?
3. How did Edwin B. Holt's system differ from Watson's approach?

4. Outline two of Walter S. Hunter's contributions to psychology.
5. Define Lashley's concepts of equipotentiality and mass action.
6. Contrast Hull, Guthrie, Tolman, and Skinner with respect to their views on the subject of reinforcement.
7. What practical advice on the extinction of responses might come out of the theoretical work of Hull? Guthrie? Tolman?
8. Briefly explain the significance of the latent learning experiments.
9. What did Tolman mean by the expression *intervening variable*?
10. Briefly describe some of the applied interests of the psychologists covered in this chapter.
11. Contrast Skinner and Hull with respect to their views on the role of theory in science.
12. According to Skinner, what are the essential differences between Type S and Type R conditioning?
13. Discuss Skinner's philosophy of punishment and state why you think he is right or wrong on the issue.
14. Discuss three applications of Skinner's research.

Glossary

anthroponomy Because of the mentalistic implications of the term *psychology*, Walter Samuel Hunter suggested the term *anthroponomy*, meaning "the science of human behavior."

Bridgman, Percy W. (1882–1961) U.S. physicist and mathematician, known for his classic book *The Logic of Modern Physics* and for his emphasis on operationism, or the attempt to tie scientific terms to precise measurements.

cognitive maps A term employed by Edward Chace Tolman referring to "mental representations" of the environment that make it possible for an animal to grasp relationships and locations.

contiguity Refers to close temporal or spatial conjunction.

drive A term employed in different ways in different systems of psychology but generally referring to "inner stimulation" that results in action.

equipotentiality A term employed by Karl Lashley referring to the capacity of one part of the cortex to take over the function of another part.

extinction A term employed in different ways in the various learning theories but generally referring to the cessation of a response following changes in the circumstances that first supported the response.

fatigue In Hull's system, fatigue refers to theoretical position that each response generates some inhibition to is own reoccurence.

Guthrie, Edwin Ray (1886–1959) Well-known U.S. behaviorist and learning theorist remembered for a theory of learning based primarily on the law of contiguity. Guthrie served as the fifty-third president of the American Psychological Association in 1945.

habit strength A term employed by the learning theorist Clark Hull referring to number of reinforced trials in a situation that have contributed to strength of a connection between a stimulus and a response.

Holt, Edwin Bissell (1873–1946) Behavioristically oriented psychologist who argued that psychologists should study what organisms do in their environments, but that behavior should be regarded as purposive and goal directed.

hormic A term employed by McDougall from the Greek *horme* meaning "urge." A hormic psychology emphasizes the role of purpose in living systems.

Hull, Clark Leonard (1884–1952) One of the most famous neobehaviorists, known for a mathematical-deductive approach to animal and human behavior. Hull, a member of the National Academy of Sciences, served as the forty-fourth president of the American Psychological Association in 1935.

Hunter, Walter Samuel (1889–1954) Behavioristically oriented psychologist who argued for a variety of methods, including field, clinical, and laboratory experimental methods. A member of the National Academy of Sciences, Hunter served as the thirty-ninth president of the American Psychological Association in 1931.

incentive Generally refers to the attractive characteristics of reinforcement. For example, for a given subject, a piece of chocolate candy may have a higher incentive value than a dime.

insight Mental apprehension of relationships so that a problem is solved in an intelligent rather than a blind trial-and-error fashion.

intervening variable An unobserved process that accounts for connections between stimulus events and responses. For example, response rate may slow down under conditions of high effort. According to Clark Hull, response rate is slowed down because of reactive inhibition (I_R), a fatigue-like state. Fatigue, in this case, might be regarded as an intervening variable.

Lashley, Karl Spencer (1890–1958) Well-known and highly regarded biologist who collaborated with John B. Watson and who is remembered for classic studies on cerebral correlates of learning.

latent learning A term employed by Edward Chace Tolman referring to learning that has occurred but is not observed because environmental conditions have not been favorable to its display. When environmental conditions change appropriately, such learning, heretofore unobservable, may now show itself.

logical positivism Sometimes called *critical empiricism* or *scientific empiricism*, this school of thought contends that scientific concepts must be explicitly and operationally tied to observable events. Publicly confirmable propositions were to replace "inner experience" in all phases of scientific activity.

mass action A concept growing out of the work of Karl Lashley referring to the idea that the rate, efficiency, and accuracy of learning depend on the amount of cortex available, and that parts of the brain are interdependent and function as a whole.

McDougall, William (1871–1938) Pioneer psychologist with very broad-ranging interests in social psychology, abnormal psychology, and the philosophical problems of psychology. McDougall emphasized the study of purposive behavior and the role of instincts in human life.

molar behavior An expression employed by Tolman to designate the special domain of his psychology. Molar behavior is the behavior of the intact organism engaging in typical day-to-day activities. Molar behavior contrasts with molecular or isolated small units of behavior.

operant conditioning The term *operant* refers to behavior that is emitted. According to Skinner, operant conditioning occurs if reinforcement follows with a response that is emitted in a specific situation.

operationism A programmatic attempt to tie scientific terms to measurements or operations employed in experiments. Thus, abstract terms such as *anxiety* or *intelligence* are defined in terms of the measures or operations employed in research studies.

purposive behaviorism An orientation advanced by Tolman in which behavior is regarded as the proper subject matter of psychology, but behavior is construed as goal directed.

reinforcement A term highly subject to theoretical interpretation but generally referring to those objects or events that result, for whatever reason, in an increased probability of responding.

respondent conditioning Pavlovian conditioning that investigates correlations between unconditioned and conditioned stimuli.

Skinner, Burrhus Frederic (1904–1990) One of the foremost behaviorists of the twentieth century, who argued that scientific psychology must concern itself with the analysis of behavior rather than the study of the mind.

stimulus intensity dynamism A term employed by Clark Hull referring to the capacity of a stimulus to energize or direct behavior.

Tolman, Edward Chace (1886–1959) One of the leading behaviorists of the twentieth century, remembered for his attempts to combine features of behaviorism, Gestalt psychology, and McDougall's psychology. Tolman emphasized the purposive nature of behavior. He is properly regarded as one of the precursors of late twentieth-century cognitive psychology.

15

■ ■ ■

Gestalt Psychology

Is the human mind to be regarded as a domain of mere indifferent facts?
Or do intrinsic demands, fittingness, and its opposite, wrongness,
occur among the genuine characteristics of its contents?

—Wolfgang Köhler (1938/1966)

In 1910, a complex and radical psychology challenged the conventional psychologies of its day. Gestalt psychology promised a fresh perspective brimming with productive insights. The new school was the brainchild of **Max Wertheimer (1880–1943)** and his close associates **Wolfgang Köhler (1887–1967)** and **Kurt Koffka (1886–1941)**. Wertheimer, Köhler, and Koffka envisioned a broader psychology that disputed tired assumptions about human and animal psychology. At first, the Gestalt psychologists rebelled against the elementary dimensions of Wundt's psychology. As voluntarism and structuralism faded into history, the Gestalt school targeted American behaviorism.

We have no exact English counterpart for the German word **Gestalt** although *configuration, form, holistic, structure,* and *pattern* are offered as potential translations. We should avoid the trap of reliance on any one English word as an equivalent for the term *Gestalt*. For example, it can be misleading to translate the term *Gestalt* as "holistic." Michael Wertheimer (1983) noted that there have been many holistic psychologies, but most lack the precision and rigor that characterize Gestalt psychology.

We'll begin with a biographical review of the school's leaders before examining historical antecedents and major themes in the Gestalt system. The chapter closes with an estimate of the impact and continuing relevance of this important system.

MAX WERTHEIMER

Max Wertheimer was born in Prague, Austria-Hungary (later Czechoslovakia and still later the Czech Republic), on April 15, 1880, the second son of Wilhelm Wertheimer and Rosa (Zwicker) Wertheimer. Max's father was a prominent educator who pioneered a "kind of personalized

Max Wertheimer

The Nazi movement and subsequent losses of academic freedom (see Henle, 1978b) inspired a mass exodus of Germany's brightest scholars. Such notable intellectuals as Albert Einstein, John von Neumann, Edward Teller, and Max Delbrück were among the émigrés from Germany to the United States.

In his book *Hitler's Mistakes*, Lewin (1984) illustrated the loss to German science by pointing out that "five of those who transferred to the United States had already won the Nobel Prize and six were subsequently to do so" (p. 56). Fifty-three-year-old Max Wertheimer was among the German émigrés along with his wife, Anne, and their three children, Valentin, Michael, and Lise. Wertheimer accepted a professorial position in New York City at the New School for Social Research. He held this position from 1933 until his death in 1943 (King & Wertheimer, 2005). His decade in the United States was productive, resulting in papers that extended the Gestalt vision into humanistic concerns such as the meaning of truth (1934), ethics (1935), democracy (1937), and freedom (1940). We will see that Wertheimer's Gestalt vision is more than a system of psychology—it is a worldview with implications for other intellectual arenas such as philosophy, science, and education.

system of instruction, a tutorial approach for the teaching of business practice, typing, accounting, shorthand, and the like" (Wertheimer, 1980b, p. 6). Following high school, the young Wertheimer attended Charles University in Prague to study law, but he explored other fields such as philosophy, music, physiology, and psychology. Max's son, Michael Wertheimer (1980b), noted that "among his most important teachers at this time was the philosopher–psychologist Christian von Ehrenfels, from whom Max took several courses" (p. 9).

A career in law did not hold appeal for Wertheimer, although abstract ideas about justice, values, and ethics remained deep and lasting concerns. He shifted from law to philosophy, studying first at Prague, then later at Berlin, where he worked with notable figures such as Carl Stumpf; Friedrich Schumann, the codeveloper; with Georg Elias Müller of the memory drum; and Erich von Hornbostel, a musicologist. Following his time at Berlin, Wertheimer enrolled in the Ph.D. program at Würzburg, where he obtained his degree in 1904 with Oswald Külpe.

Wertheimer's academic career began at an institute in Frankfurt (later to become the University of Frankfurt). From 1916 to 1929, he worked at the Berlin Psychological Institute and, in 1929, returned to Frankfurt as a full professor.

WOLFGANG KÖHLER

Wolfgang Köhler (*KUR lur*) was born on January 21, 1887, in Reval, Estonia (Allik, 2007), but his early formal education was in Germany at the Gymnasium at Wolfenbüttel. He earned his Ph.D. in 1909 at the University of Berlin under Carl Stumpf. Following his doctoral work at Berlin, Köhler took a position as assistant in the psychology laboratory at the Frankfurt Academy, soon to become the University of Frankfurt. From 1913 to 1920, he was director of the Anthropoid Research Station on the Island of Tenerife located in the Canary Islands. His work on Tenerife resulted in one of the classic works in Gestalt psychology, *The Mentality of Apes*, first published in English in 1924, and his ongoing scholarship with animal

Wolfgang Köhler

models helped shape comparative psychology in Germany (Kressley, 2006).

Following work on Tenerife, Köhler returned to Germany to take a position as professor at the University of Göttingen. In 1922, he accepted a position as professor and director of the Psychological Institute at the University of Berlin, taking over the role of director from Carl Stumpf (Toccafondi, 2009). Henle (1978b) pointed out that the institute, under Köhler's direction, included an "all-star cast of characters." Faculty members present during all or part of Köhler's tenure included Max Wertheimer, Karl Duncker, Kurt Lewin, Otto von Lauenstein, and Hedwig von Restorff.

The 1920s and early 1930s at the Berlin Institute were productive years, but the delicate climate that encourages scientific creativity was shattered in 1933 when the Nazi regime came to power. Hitler immediately invoked changes that wreaked havoc in the German university system. Jewish professors and any professors who were unfriendly to National Socialism were dismissed. Scientific theories, methods, and problems were favored on the basis of their agreement with political authority (Ash, 1995). Professors found it difficult to obtain funds and the scientific enterprise was burdened with an unreliable bureaucratic structure marked by infighting and a continual breakdown of authority. Lewin (1984) remarked that as early as 1933, the great mathematician John von Neumann lamented that the Nazis would ruin German science for a generation. Psychology did not, however, disappear under National Socialism; in fact, professional psychology grew rapidly during the Third Reich (Geuter, 1984/1992).

In a thoughtful article titled "One Man Against the Nazis," Henle (1978b) called attention to Köhler's heroic struggles against the Nazis. Among many activities of resistance, Köhler wrote a powerful letter to protest the dismissal of Jewish professors. When the regime demanded that professors begin classes with a Nazi salute, Nazis and their supporters filled Köhler's class. He did a caricature of the salute followed by a passionate lecture on the importance of academic freedom. Köhler's comments were greeted with thunderous applause. The Nazi brownshirts in the crowd were undoubtedly not in agreement. Köhler's work at the Berlin Psychological Institute continued until 1935, but by that time conditions were all but unbearable. Finally, Köhler resigned his position and immigrated to the United States, where he accepted a position as professor of psychology at Swarthmore College.

Köhler was a prolific writer and advocate for the Gestalt movement. In 1929 he published *Gestalt Psychology*, a classic statement that opened with a trenchant attack on behaviorism. The book brings to focus the extent to which behaviorism is based on the atomism and mechanism of nineteenth-century physics. Köhler then set forth the Gestalt position that took its lead from the newer concepts of field physics. He published *The Place of Value in a World of Facts* in 1938 and *Dynamics in Psychology* in 1940.

Many honors came to Köhler. Among the most significant were his delivery of the William James lectures at Harvard University and his delivery of the Gifford lectures at Edinburgh in 1958. He was named research professor of philosophy and psychology at Swarthmore College in 1946 and was elected president of the American Psychological Association in 1958. A year before his APA election, he received the Distinguished Scientific Contribution award from the same association. The estimate of his biographers is noteworthy. Asch (1968) said, "There are few in any generation of his stature" (p. 119), and Henle (1978b), referring to Köhler's struggles with the Nazis, said, "It shows us once more what a human being can be" (p. 944).

Wolfgang Köhler made his home in Enfield, New Hampshire, following his formal retirement from Swarthmore. In his later years, he continued to write, give lectures, conduct research, and consult with interested students and colleagues. He died in Enfield on June 11, 1967.

KURT KOFFKA

Kurt Koffka was born on March 18, 1886, in Berlin, Germany. Koffka was expected to follow his father into the legal profession. Like Wertheimer, Koffka was drawn to more wide-ranging and theoretical interests. After beginning studies at the University of Berlin in 1903, he shifted from philosophy to psychology. Except for a year at Edinburgh, he stayed in Berlin, earning a Ph.D. in 1909 under Carl Stumpf. Afterward, he worked a year in the Freiburg laboratory of Johannes Von Kries and another year as assistant to Oswald Külpe at Würzburg. In 1910, Koffka discovered Gestalt psychology while working for three semesters at Frankfurt with Wertheimer and Köhler. In 1912, Koffka accepted a position at the University of Giessen in central Germany. After several visits to the United States in the mid-1920s and after holding visiting professorships, including at Wisconsin, where he had a politely contentious relationship with Clark Hull (Gengerelli, 1976), Koffka accepted a position at Smith College in 1927. He remained at Smith until his death in 1941.

In 1924, Koffka published *Growth of the Mind*, a creative and influential book that demonstrated the relevance of Gestalt principles to developmental psychology. In 1935, he published *Principles of Gestalt Psychology*, a major systematic treatise on Gestalt psychology. Koffka was the first to write on Gestalt psychology in English. His article, "Perception: An Introduction to the Gestalt-Theorie," was published in the *Psychological Bulletin* in 1922. Unfortunately, the article gave the impression that Gestalt theory was concerned only with perception. To the contrary, the first problem addressed by Gestalt psychologists was thinking. But, as discussed earlier, it is a system of psychology with a broad vision and an interest in a host of topics that extend beyond the borders of psychology.

INTELLECTUAL BACKGROUND OF GESTALT PSYCHOLOGY

Several intellectual forces shaped the Gestalt school, but there are unique features in the system that cannot be identified with any one antecedent influence. We will now consider traditions in philosophy, science, and psychology that left their mark on the Gestalt psychologists.

Philosophy

The philosopher Immanuel Kant (1724–1804) argued that our mental processes are organized in an a priori fashion. Meaningful experiences are not always the result of the mechanical laws of association. Instead, ordering principles such as intuitions of causality, time, and space interact with sense experience. Sensory experiences are not necessarily disjointed affairs that await an external connecting principle; rather, organization is a natural, ongoing process, and meanings are often given in experience itself.

Kant also believed that experience is the foundation on which knowledge is built. As noted in Chapter 7, he is regarded as a rationalist, but his emphasis on experience found him seeking a moderate position between the extremes of rationalism and empiricism.

Gestalt psychology is also often regarded as a system that is more akin to rationalism than empiricism. This is a mistaken assumption. Gestalt psychologists challenge us to adopt a more adequate empiricism based on those things that are most real in our experience. Gestalt psychologists would argue that an adequate empiricism would deny the conclusion that meaningful experiences are built from separate mechanical elements held together with the glue of association. The Gestalt position emphasizes conjunctions, meanings, and patterns that are given in the natural flow of experience. We will later examine the detailed arguments for this position. For the time being, we will note that the Gestalt school should not be placed in either of the philosophical extremes of rationalism or empiricism. The starting point for this school is experience, and thus Gestalt psychology is empirical, but proper attention to experience itself will confirm select claims of the rationalists.

Science

In the latter part of the nineteenth century and the early twentieth century, powerful new currents of thought in the scientific world influenced the Gestalt founders. Wolfgang Köhler had a rigorous background in the physical sciences and had studied with the theoretical physicist Max Planck (1858–1947). Planck and Köhler shared personal and intellectual similarities. On the personal side, they openly resisted the Nazi movement. Planck also resisted Hitler by demanding the release of German scientists imprisoned because of their political or religious beliefs. Because of his resistance, Planck was dismissed as president of the Berlin Physical Society. Later, the Nazi regime imposed a brutal penalty on the famous scientist by forcing him to attend the execution of his son, a member of the resistance movement against the Nazis.

Planck's approach to science, which included a critique of strict empiricism, also left its mark on Köhler. Planck argued that scientific progress is nurtured by creative theoretical work. An obsession with measurement for its own sake will interfere with scientific progress. Planck's emphasis was on the nature of the events and specific processes that underlie a measured effect. Like his teacher, Köhler was also critical of the premature elevation of measurement. His

position is illustrated in a scathing attack on operational definitions of intelligence defined as that which an intelligence test measures (see Köhler, 1929/1947, pp. 44–48).

Albert Einstein also influenced Gestalt psychology. As close friends, Einstein and Max Wertheimer spent long hours in conversation about the nature of science and creativity. Einstein once sought the company of Wertheimer and another friend, Max Born, to help him intervene in a dispute between the student council and the administration of the University of Berlin (see Clark, 1971, p. 198). The larger intellectual implications of Einstein's work in physics undoubtedly left their stamp on Wertheimer. Indeed, more than any other psychological system, Gestalt psychology is sensitive to the importance of the context of the observer or the so-called frame of reference. These concepts evolved from Einstein's work on electrodynamics of moving bodies. Wertheimer and Köhler were also influenced by the concept of field forces in the new physics. The concept can be illustrated with a magnetic field, as when small iron filings sprinkled on a sheet of paper are distributed into a definite configuration when a magnet is placed under the paper. The focus of the scientist is as much on the field or the pattern as on single elements within the field.

The work of physicist **Ernst Mach (1838–1916)** also influenced Gestalt psychologists. Although much in Mach's empiricism was disagreeable to Gestalt psychologists, his book *The Analysis of Sensations* (1886/1959) was a source of stimulation. Mach argued for space-form and time-form sensations that are essentially configural. An example of a time-form sensation is a melody, which is something different from its several elements. The elements, or individual notes, can all be changed, as when one transposes to a different key signature, and yet the melody remains. The melody is not just a collection of separate elements, but a pattern with a clear identity of its own. Similarly, a visual or space-form sensation maintains an identity independent of the elements. The form quality of a triangle persists regardless of one's spatial orientation to the triangle. Triangularity as a space form is thus something different from just lines that serve as the elements.

At the outset of the twentieth century there were developments in other scientific disciplines that challenged piecemeal, bit-by-bit, elementaristic approaches to the world. Field theory, along with a new emphasis on dynamic and evolving processes as opposed to an exclusive emphasis on static structures, was emerging in the philosophy of science.

Psychology

Christian von Ehrenfels (1859–1932), a philosopher–psychologist associated with the Austrian school of act psychology, elaborated on the concept of form qualities. Ehrenfels agreed with Mach that form qualities are different from the elements of which they are composed. In 1890, he published a pivotal paper "On Gestalt Qualities" (Kissinger, 2008) where Ehrenfels took the position that form qualities are given immediately in experience and may persist even when the elements change. Ehrenfels held a position at the University of Prague where the young Wertheimer took several courses from him from 1898 to 1901. Ehrenfels undoubtedly focused Wertheimer on the part–whole problem, though it would take over a decade later before Wertheimer proposed a solution that was radically different from the one embraced by his teacher. To look back an academic generation, both Ehrenfels and Stumpf (with whom Wertheimer, Köhler, and Koffka all studied) studied with Brentano, whose experiential perspectives are evident in Gestalt theory.

Ehrenfels, in accord with many holistic psychologists (Diriwächter & Valsiner, 2008), agreed that the whole is *more* than the sum of its parts, but the whole was still viewed as derivative or as another element. The unique feature of the Gestalt system, as noted by Michael Wertheimer (1983), is "the radical view that *the whole is psychologically, logically, epistemologically, and ontologically prior to its parts. A whole is not only more than the sum of its parts, it is entirely different from a sum of its parts: thinking in terms of a sum does violence to the very nature of the*

dynamics of genuine wholes" (p. 43, italics in original).

The relationship between the psychology of William James and Gestalt psychology calls for more detailed scholarly review than it has received to date (Woody, 2001). The leaders of the Gestalt movement quoted from James's psychological and philosophical works and not only found some points of agreement, but also found much with which to disagree.

James's powerful attacks on atomism mark a point of agreement. In particular, James's mature philosophical vision, especially his radical empiricism, reveals rich parallels with the Gestalt school. In a compelling analysis of common sympathies between the two approaches, Woody (2001) observed that "both Gestalt psychologists and William James begin investigations with experience, argue that science and other epistemological endeavors should be grounded in experience, experientially evaluate the truth of a given claim, emphasize the personal nature of experience, and embrace experienced relationships across many levels" (p. 40). And just as experience plays a critical role in epistemology, James and the Gestalt school agreed that methodological pluralism offers real promise for a robust science of psychology (Woody, 2001). The range of topical areas was clearly broader in these two systems than in many other systems.

As noted, the Gestalt psychologists found much in James's psychology to criticize. For example, Koffka (1924/1980, pp. 90–97) took issue with James's view of instincts as a series of chained reflexes. Köhler (1929/1947) criticized the Jamesian emphasis that boundaries in sensory experience have a pragmatic basis. James's interest in the boundaries of sensory experience also shows, however, that he was deeply interested in the part–whole problem. Köhler (1929/1947) recognized that James was sensitized to the same kinds of problems that concerned the Gestalt psychologists, but Köhler was critical of the Jamesian approach. Though James wrote extensively on the part–whole problem, the extent of his influence on Gestalt psychologists, if any, remains to be uncovered by further scholarship.

THE FUNDAMENTALS OF GESTALT PSYCHOLOGY

The formal founding of Gestalt psychology can be dated to 1910 when Max Wertheimer initiated experiments on the **phi phenomenon** (Wagemans et al., 2012a). The results of the experiments were published in Wertheimer's classic paper titled "Experimental Studies on the Perception of Movement" (1912). The phi phenomenon, or apparent movement, is illustrated in the simplest form by two discrete lights. If the lights are flashed onto two different locations on the retina and if one light succeeds the other by a brief time interval, then the participant sees movement. Though the lights are stationary and though they represent two discrete points, the participant sees a sweeping movement in a direction from the first flash to the second. In this case, the observer does not see two separate elements or two local events. What is seen is radically different from the elements. Indeed, one could study the elements separately but fail by such a procedure to provide an adequate understanding of the experience of movement. Max Wertheimer, working with Köhler and Koffka as research participants, collected data for the 1912 paper on the perception of movement. This work launched the Gestalt movement.

The standard explanation of the phi phenomenon was that movement is perceived because the eye itself moves in response to the successive flashes of light. The movement we experience is based on the kinesthetic feedback from the movement of the eye. But if a light is projected in the center of a field and if this light precedes two lights located on either side of it, the participant will see two movements simultaneously going in opposite directions. Such a finding proves embarrassing to the explanation based on eye movement. The eye could hardly move in two directions at the same time.

The phi phenomenon represents a particularly elegant demonstration that the quality of the whole is *different* from the sum of the parts. In this case, the parts are static elements, simply two stationary flashes of light. But given appropriate temporal and spatial relationships, we see something fundamentally and qualitatively different. Gestalt psychologists believed that the whole could never be understood by piecemeal examination of the isolated elements. Thus, a piecemeal approach from part to whole would prove inadequate to the understanding of experience.

By contrast, analysis that begins with what is given in experience will lead to a more adequate and believable psychology. The Gestalt psychologists took the position that the whole is prior to its parts, and thus, that part processes are governed by the nature of the whole. If this position seems untenable, consider the phi phenomenon again. What we see is movement; we do not see the isolated elements. In our immediate experience, the whole is quite literally prior to its parts. Starting with what is given in our experience, we may then proceed "from above" and discover the natural parts and their relations.

Consider another illustration. If a theoretician of music asked for an analysis of a melody, we would begin by focusing on the melody itself. The melody, like the phi phenomenon, has a clear identity in our experience. With that identity as a starting point, we may proceed with a meaningful analysis of the relative arrangement of the parts. According to Köhler (1929/1947), "One of the main tasks of Gestalt Psychology is that of indicating the genuine rather than any fictitious parts of wholes" (p. 168). We will now turn to an examination of Gestalt principles applied to various topics of psychology.

Principles of Perceptual Organization

In addition to the phi phenomenon, Wertheimer found Gestalt principles in many intellectual and sensory domains. Whether we are listening to a melody, perceiving movement, observing objects, or attempting to grasp an idea, we perceive our world in meaningful patterns or unified wholes. Organization is a given in our experience and not something to be added on by association to a collection of elements. The parts or elements are not what is most basic; what is most basic in our phenomenal world is the pattern or organization, and many scholars continue to view Gestalt phenomena as foundational in perceptual psychology (Pomerantz, 2006). In studying perceptual organization, the Gestalt psychologists discovered several principles that clarify the process, guided in part by Koffka's famous question "Why do things look as they do?" (Koffka, 1935, p. 75; van Leeuwen, 2007). Some of the most important Gestalt perceptual principles are as follows:

1. *Figure–ground.* The Danish psychologist Edgar Rubin (1886–1951) argued that there are two components in perception. There is that which stands out or that dominates or that has a "thingness" about it. Rubin referred to this component of perception as *figure*. Other things recede into the background and Rubin referred to these as *ground*. He observed that there are sometimes reversible **figure–ground** relations, as observed in Figure 15.1A. The Gestalt psychologists did not always agree with Rubin about some of the interpretations or the technical features of figure–ground phenomena, but the finding has persisted as a recognized principle of organization and has become a mainstay in psychological literature.

2. *Similarity.* One of the standard features of perceptual organization is that figures or *Gestalten* that are similar tend to be grouped together. **Similarity** is illustrated in Figure 15.1B.

3. *Proximity.* According to **proximity**, close temporal or spatial conjunction leads to a perception of togetherness. In Figure 15.1C, we tend to group *Gestalten* that are close together, so we tend to see three groups of three instead of nine squares.

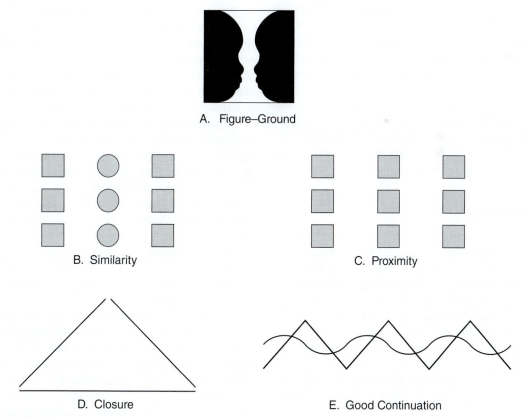

A. Figure–Ground

B. Similarity

C. Proximity

D. Closure

E. Good Continuation

FIGURE 15.1

Some Principles of Perception Emphasized in Gestalt Psychology

4. *Closure.* According to the principle of **closure**, we tend psychologically to complete that which is incomplete. In other words, we fill in the perceptual gaps. In Figure 15.1D, we tend to see a triangle rather than a series of disconnected lines.

5. *Good continuation.* In Figure 15.1E, it would be possible to see a series of broken lines if we transferred back and forth away from the wavy to the straight lines. However, we tend to see a **good continuation** of the wavy lines and a good continuation of angular lines.

Wertheimer's principles of organization contribute to what he called the **law of Prägnanz**. According to this law, perceptual organization tends to be as good as possible under prevailing conditions (Wagemans et al., 2012b). Thus, we see our world in as orderly, coherent, and economical a way as conditions permit.

It is important to emphasize that these principles of organization are givens in perceptual experience. Gestalt psychology does not deny that learning, association, and motivation influence perception, but it points to the importance of understanding what is given in experience. The Gestalt psychologists argued that the organization we find in psychological experience resembles physiological organizations. This topic will surface later in the discussion of the Gestalt treatment of the mind–brain problem.

Thinking

It is a common mistake to believe that Gestalt psychologists were interested first and foremost in perception. Michael Wertheimer (1980b) pointed out that the earliest Gestalt orientation of Max Wertheimer is found "in the psychology of thinking or in 'Völkerpsychologie' rather than in perception" (p. 13). Wertheimer's most extensive work on the psychology of thinking arrived in his classic book *Productive Thinking*, published posthumously in 1945. The book was reprinted in 1959 and again in 1982 to include fragments and additions found among Wertheimer's unpublished papers (King & Wertheimer, 2005).

Wertheimer was keenly interested in the distinction between **reproductive thinking** and **productive thinking**. The former is associated with mere repetition, conditioning, drills, habits, or the routine retracing of familiar intellectual territory. The latter, by contrast, results in new ideas, breakthroughs, or insights that make a difference (van Steenburgh et al., 2012). What really happens, asked Wertheimer, when productive thinking takes place? What are the conditions that foster it or that block it? How can we nurture it?

Wertheimer opened his book by reviewing traditional approaches to thinking. A widespread belief held that training in traditional logic nurtured thinking. Wertheimer encouraged such training because it stimulated rigor and a critical orientation, but he concluded that logic in and of itself does not give rise to productive thinking. One can be logical without being creative. He criticized associationist theories of thinking, pointing out that blind trials, drills, repetitions, and chance connections can hardly be construed as sensible thinking. He recognized the historical importance of Hegelian, Marxist, and functionalist approaches, but found that they do not offer satisfactory solutions to the problem of productive thinking.

Wertheimer declared that his approach to thinking would be understood in terms of field principles. He explored Albert Einstein's thinking that led to relativity theory and the thinking of Galileo that produced the law of inertia. His interest in the Gestalt process of discovery inspired his students. While directing the psychology department at Frankfurt, Germany, in 1932, Wertheimer challenged his students to write a paper on productive thinking and offered an award for the most outstanding work (Fromm, 1998). One student, Erika Fromm (then Erika Oppenheimer), wrote to one hundred prominent scientists and philosophers, inquiring about the productive thinking that led to their intellectual discoveries. Although she did not win the award, more than forty scholars responded to her survey, including Einstein and Freud. Einstein described his discovery process as "comparable with the attitude of somebody who wants to solve a puzzle or a chess problem, who is convinced that the solution exists, because the creator of the problem possesses the solution" (cited in Fromm, 1998, p. 1198).

In more common examples of productive thinking, Wertheimer explored such diverse problems as finding the areas of various geometric shapes to the thinking underlying the way we see ourselves in various social situations. *Productive Thinking* is filled with illustrations of alternative solutions to specific problems. For instance, the story is told of a teacher in the eighteenth century who presented this simple addition problem to a class of students:

$$1 + 2 + 3 + 4 + 5 + 6 + 7 + 8 + 9 + 10 = ?$$

Do you know the answer? Carl Friedrich Gauss (1777–1855), later to become a famous mathematician, but then only six years old, announced almost immediately that the answer is 55. Perplexed by his quick answer, the teacher asked young Gauss how he arrived at the solution. While other students added $1 + 2 + 3$, and so on, Gauss looked at the whole string of numbers and observed a pattern of five 11s. In Gauss's novel solution, he combined $1 + 10, 2 + 9, 3 + 8$, and so on. Gauss's solution illustrates Wertheimer's point that productive thinking results when we look for structural truths rather than piecemeal ones.

Wertheimer argued that productive thinking is based on the capacity to grasp structural features and to envision structural reorganization. In the preceding problem, Gauss broke out of the usual lockstep approach to addition. He looked first at the whole problem then structurally transposed it by looking at the two extremes and found the number 11. He then found that the number 11 repeated itself four more times.

Productive Thinking is filled with examples of problems that arise in human life. The book's continuing relevance is illustrated in a later emphasis on schemas, plans, and knowledge structures—all reminiscent of Wertheimer's approach to thinking (German & Defeyter, 2000).

Learning

As mentioned, Gestalt psychologists launched many attacks against behaviorism. They opposed the connectionism of Thorndike, the reflexological

emphasis of Pavlov, and the S–R psychology of Watson. Their opposition to these schools focused on learning theories that emphasized blind or mechanical connections as well as on artificial methodologies.

Working independently, Karl Lashley (1942) and Wolfgang Köhler (1929/1947) made an important contribution to the Gestalt model of learning. The study begins by training a research subject to select the darker of two shades of gray. Thus, as indicated in Figure 15.2, the subject is rewarded when it selects object 2, the darker of the two objects. The two objects are, of course, randomized with respect to position (left vs. right) so that the subject learns to respond to number 2 whether it appears on the left or the right. In phase 2, the formerly rewarded object is now paired with a new object 3 that is darker than number 2. The brightness interval between 2 and 3 is the same as the brightness interval between 1 and 2. Now confronted with 2 versus 3, subjects choose 3 in most cases.

Notice that number 3 has never been rewarded in the past, whereas number 2 has consistently been associated with reward. Yet the preference is for number 3. Such a finding is embarrassing to a strict connectionism or an S–R theory. In view of the reinforcement history with number 2, it should be the object that is firmly connected to the response. Yet the subject selects an object that has never been rewarded and ignores

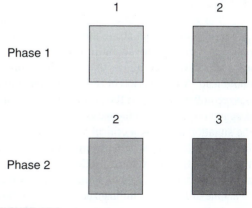

FIGURE 15.2
Discrimination Problem

the one that has always been rewarded. Köhler's (1938) interpretation is that in the total configuration, what is learned is the relational discrimination "darker than" rather than a response to an absolute stimulus value. If that is the case, then the stimulus is not what the behaviorist defines it to be. Furthermore, the established connection is not a hardwired connection between object 2 and the response. Instead, what is seen is the pattern of the relationship rather than an isolated element. If that perception of a relationship is established in the first problem, then the subject simply transposes from the first problem to the second one. In the transposition, it is "darker than" that wins. Although Spence (1937) provided an explanation of these findings with Hullian theory, the most parsimonious interpretation, according to Gestalt theory, is that relationships outweigh absolute stimulus values. The data suggest that what is learned is a cognitive structure rather than a response to an absolute stimulus value.

Insight: A Further Challenge to the S–R Formula

The best-known work on learning in the Gestalt literature is Köhler's classic book *The Mentality of Apes* (1925/1976). In his book, Köhler describes studies he conducted while on the Isle of Tenerife. These studies demonstrated that animals envision a whole situation and then restructure parts of the situation to attain a goal. Without such restructuring, the goal would be unattainable.

For example, Köhler suspended a banana by a string several feet above the head of a chimpanzee. Jumping proved futile because the banana was suspended higher than the chimpanzee could leap. After a period of reflection, the chimpanzee noticed boxes on the ground. If the chimp dragged boxes beneath the banana, it restructured the situation and took a critical step toward solving the problem. Though chimpanzees understand little of statics, they built crude and awkward structures that helped them achieve their objective. One of Köhler's chimpanzees named Grande even built a four-story structure of boxes. Köhler believed the restructuring of a field progresses

without any evidence of reinforcements for discrete responses.

The chimpanzees did not solve problems by blind trial and success or in a mechanical fashion where a reward follows every response. Given an open situation (the ability to see the relevant parts of the field), Köhler's chimpanzees demonstrated the ability to solve problems in inventive and insightful ways. Köhler's stated criterion for **insight** is "the appearance of a complete solution with reference to the whole layout of the field" (1925/1976, p. 190).

Köhler argued that behavioral studies are often structured to preclude the possibility that animals could see the layout of the whole field. In a typical maze, the possibilities of visualization are limited and there is little way to learn except by trial and error. A human in a maze would also learn by trial and error, but imagine how different that learning curve would be if the entire maze were viewed, even for a brief moment, from above (an *optically given situation* in Köhler's language). Most natural learning occurs in field situations in which there are possibilities for pattern recognition and restructuring. Artificial laboratory situations may lead to false conclusions about crucial questions such as what gets learned, what conditions facilitate learning, and what are the learner's capacities.

Developmental Concepts

Koffka's book *Growth of the Mind* provided a wider application of Gestalt principles by showing their operations and applications in developmental processes. The major emphasis of the book, in Koffka's words, is "upon the evolution of the child's mind" (1924/1980, Preface). He pointed out that without sound developmental and comparative psychologies, the psychology of normal adults will be defective. Koffka observed that the extreme positions of empiricism and nativism had undercut the study of development. Rather than attempting to understand the problems of mental growth as we find them, the empiricists and nativists searched for those things that fit their preconceptions.

METHODOLOGICAL CONSIDERATIONS IN DEVELOPMENTAL PSYCHOLOGY Koffka distinguished between the view *from without* and the view *from within*. The view from within is a descriptive concept (i.e., I know my toothache, my headache, or my feeling of elation; when someone else has a toothache, I cannot get out of my skin and know it directly.). But Koffka contended that if people weep, we may be assured they are sorrowful; if they laugh, we may feel that they are happy; and if they are animated, we may have certain confidences about their experience of energy and well-being. When we say that someone is animated or active, we are using behavioral concepts, but such concepts are also functional in that they refer to underlying experiences. Functional concepts assume an intimate relationship between observable behavior and experience. When we study infants and young children, we employ functional concepts, but with the assurance that if an infant smiles and coos, his or her behavior corresponds to experiences of well-being. We will now turn to some examples of Koffka's work in developmental psychology.

THE GROWTH OF LEARNING Kurt Koffka believed that much of early learning is what he called *sensorimotor learning*. An illustration of sensorimotor learning is found in the maxim, "The burnt child shuns the flame." Koffka (1924/1980) argued, "The withdrawal of the burned hand is naturally reflexive, but what is learned is not to withdraw the hand, but to avoid the fire in the future" (p. 302). What is learned is a configuration relating fire and pain, not a reflex that occurs naturally. If there were no attention, the child would not learn and then the experience would have to be repeated. So even in so-called sensorimotor learning, we do not learn mere connections; rather, what is learned is a constructive achievement with future adaptive significance.

IMITATION In addition to sensorimotor learning, Koffka argued that a great deal of learning occurs by imitation. Such learning occurs in natural settings but is less likely in artificial settings such as many laboratory experiments on learning.

Koffka contended that there is no need to explain imitation or its purposes; it simply occurs in the natural flow of events. What often is imitated is complex configurations, whether these be auditory or visual. We can observe children attempting to perfect their imitations. Koffka believed that the perceptual and motor systems are related so that configural recognition or transfer can go naturally from one to the other. Koffka was not talking about mere observational learning. Rather, for him, imitation implied a capacity to discern relevant relations.

IDEATIONAL LEARNING The highest type of learning in Koffka's developmental scheme is ideational learning, a type of learning that makes use of language. Koffka pointed out that it is a pivotal time in children's development when they grasp the idea that things have names. In early experience, the name is thought to inhere in the thing itself as an attribute. Koffka illustrated with a bit of humor that comes from an argument about the best language. One of the participants says, "The English language is the best, and I can prove it to you. Take the word *knife*; the French call it *couteau*; the Germans *Messer*, the Danes *kniv*, while the English say knife, and that's what it really is" (Koffka, 1924/1980, p. 324).

Following the naming stage, children enter a period marked by a new flexibility with respect to the application of language. A word, for example, that was originally associated with only one thing or event may now be applied to other things. Koffka related the case of Hilda Stern, who, after learning the word *nose*, applied it to the tips of her shoes. Such inventive manipulations are common in young children. Children also often generate words of their own in a playful manner. Michael Wertheimer's four-year-old daughter Karen preferred to describe a butterfly as a *flutterby*. Such a rearrangement illustrates verbal generation of ideational material that can play a role in learning. The new term *flutterby* is descriptive; it conveys an idea about the object that is not captured in the term *butterfly*. From a multitude of possible verbal rearrangements and new symbolic representations we have a powerful tool that extends our capacity to learn and to solve problems. We turn now from learning modes to one of Koffka's most speculative but interesting suggestions regarding developmental phenomena.

GESTALT PERSPECTIVES ON SCIENTIFIC METHOD

Gestalt psychology's approach to scientific methodology illustrates the thoroughness of its revolt against established psychology. In his book *Gestalt Psychology*, Köhler accused the established psychologies—particularly behaviorism and structuralism—of emulating physical sciences in their mature form. Such imitation, he argued, overemphasized quantitative methods per se while ignoring qualitative considerations that precede quantification. Köhler argued that psychologists should emulate physical sciences in early rather than later stages of development. Prior to sophisticated quantitative procedures, early physical scientists attended to the experiences of everyday life. As an example, Köhler discussed the work of Henry Cavendish (1731–1810) on electrical resistance. Prior to developing exact measures of resistance, Cavendish experienced shocks to his arm delivered through varying pieces of material inserted in an electrical circuit.

Köhler warned about the danger in copying the advanced quantitative form of established sciences without attending to the demands inherent in psychology's unique subject matter. A premature emphasis on measurement may compel us to overlook critical processes and phenomena. The net result is that we focus on things that lend themselves to measurement but neglect something of greater importance that cannot be quantified. Köhler (1929/1947) argued that "narrowness in observation protects narrowness in theory" (p. 54). Overvaluing quantitative techniques restricts the range of legitimate problems in the new discipline.

Köhler (1929/1947) was concerned that psychologists would conduct elegant but fruitless experiments. He found evidence in psychophysics where "thousands of quantitative psychophysical experiments were made almost in vain. No one knew precisely what he was measuring. Nobody had studied the mental processes upon which the whole procedure was built" (p. 44).

What, then, was the Gestalt solution to Köhler's methodological criticisms? First, according to Köhler (1929/1947), "a method is good if it is adapted to the given subject matter; and it is bad if it lacks regard for this material, or if it misdirects research" (p. 37). He warned that a successful methodological procedure in one science could prove useless in another discipline. Methodology should be adapted to the subject matter of a discipline rather than the other way around.

Köhler believed that Gestalt psychology occupied a central place among the natural sciences (Henle, 1993). Not surprisingly, we encounter a variety of scientific procedures within the Gestalt literature. For some problems, the Gestalt psychologists worked like astronomers or field biologists, employing naturalistic observation with minimum intrusion into their participants' ongoing activities. In other studies, Gestalt psychologists worked more like scientists in a wet-lab situation, manipulating and controlling variables.

Gestalt psychologists helped pioneer the phenomenological method, and they would likely be open to well-conceived questionnaire and interview techniques (so long as these methods are meaningfully tied to the problems under investigation). Their broad approach to methodology parallels William James's (Woody, 2001). As in Jamesian psychology, Gestalt science found inspiration in vision not method. In fact, the Gestalt psychologists argued for a greater metaconsciousness of science. They understood the dangers of losing critical perspective on methodology: We may restrict the range of legitimate problems or we could risk generating misinformation or even trivialize the scientific enterprise if we remove it from the flow of meaningful events.

The Gestalt concerns about methodology did not perpetuate differences between mission-oriented (applied) research and basic research. Indeed, the Gestalt school's philosophy of science might diminish the sharp dichotomy between applied and basic psychology. The dichotomy could disappear altogether because a truly basic science would yield sensible findings. Even if such findings are not immediately applicable, they would not strain credulity with respect to their eventual potential to make a difference somewhere in the world of our experience.

MIND AND BRAIN: ISOMORPHISM

The Gestalt perspective on the mind–brain problem has been called **isomorphism**. Köhler (1929/1947) defined the term as follows: "Experienced order in space is always structurally identical with a functional order in the distribution of underlying brain processes" (p. 61). Literally, the word *isomorphism* means having the same appearance or same form. In chemistry, two substances may be said to be isomorphic if they share similarities with respect to atomic structure. The term *isomorphism* in Gestalt psychology refers to the structural correspondence between experience and underlying brain processes. The ordered nature of an experience does not exist in isolation but corresponds to an ordered distribution of cortical events. If we experience an auditory temporal sequence (a rhythm), we may also expect a pattern of events in brain processes that are isomorphic with the experience.

Isomorphism is often misrepresented (see Henle, 1984). A common erroneous belief is that isomorphism means we have pictures in our heads that correspond to physical structures. Some critics have asked whether color in the external world is isomorphic with some part of the brain that matches that color (Gregory, 1974). What is missed in many misrepresentations of isomorphism is the importance of the word *functional*. Köhler (1938/1966) took pains to add that the *functional* cortical counterpart of a color would not have to be a color (p. 195). Likewise, the functional cortical counterpart of a sound of a violin would not need to replicate the physical features of such a sound. The "pictures in

the head" misrepresentation misses something even more fundamental. The Gestalt concept of isomorphism does not refer to a correspondence between physical events and brain processes. It is not a theory about the relationship of brain processes and physical events, but a theory about the relationship between experience and brain processes that Luccio (2010) connects to Spinoza's ideas. The position expresses faith in the fundamental structural similarity of two realms (experience and brain) that are vital to psychology.

THE INFLUENCE OF GESTALT PSYCHOLOGY

The 1920s proved to be a golden decade for Gestalt psychology. Wolfgang Köhler's Psychological Institute at the University of Berlin was the epicenter for the Gestalt revolution. Henle (1977) shared that "graduate students were coming to the Institute from a number of countries; the *Psychologische Forschung*, the journal of the Gestalt Psychologists, was founded, and work was progressing in many directions" (p. 3). During this time, the German school stretched to other cultures, including Italy and Japan (Sakuma, 1999; Verstegen, 2000). Köhler and Koffka attended the 1929 International Congress of Psychology at Yale University, giving the Gestalt school greater visibility in the United States. Despite fragile economic conditions in Germany's crumbling Weimar Republic, the 1930s promised another productive decade for Gestalt psychology.

And then Adolf Hitler came to power in 1933.

Not content to dominate politics and the military, Hitler imposed his will on cultural, artistic, and scientific works as well. It was his ambition to replace "Jewish science" with "Aryan science." Although Wertheimer was not a practicing Jew, he was among the first generation of professors forced into "retirement" by the new Nazi government (King & Wertheimer, 2005). Historians can only speculate about the outcome had the Berlin Psychological Institute prospered in a friendlier environment. A continuing research program and the production of doctoral students would have formed the core of a significant research force, something Gestalt psychology never enjoyed. In the devastating wake of the Nazi regime, the world could no longer look to Germany as a rich source of scientific ideas.

The small nucleus of Gestalt theorists separated and went to isolated colleges that did not offer major doctoral programs (Koffka at Smith College, Köhler at Swarthmore, and Wertheimer at The New School for Social Research). The Gestalt movement faced an uphill battle in another way. The major leaders, isolated from each other and from graduate students, labored on foreign soil in a country in the grip of behaviorism. The vicissitudes of Gestalt psychology in the United States are discussed in thoughtful articles by Sokal (1984) and Ash (1985).

Despite such obstacles, Gestalt research, argument, and theory had a telling influence. Its authority was felt in three important ways:

1. There were systematic approaches to sub-disciplinary areas such as motivation, personality, and social psychology inspired by Gestalt psychology, though not a part of the classic core of Gestalt thought.
2. Gestalt concepts and research discoveries found their way into textbooks that conveyed the mainstream of psychological knowledge.
3. Gestalt research findings served as a powerful stimulus for other systems, often forcing modifications in their positions.

We turn to an examination of an influential system that had roots and inspiration in Gestalt psychology.

KURT LEWIN AND FIELD THEORY

Wertheimer, Köhler, and Koffka made important contributions to the study of thinking, perception, learning, and development. As noted, however, the Gestalt vision is a worldview that reaches beyond the boundaries of psychology. In this tradition,**Kurt Lewin (1890–1947)** broadened the Gestalt perspective to include work on motivation, personality, social psychology, and conflict resolution.

Lewin was born in Mogilno, Prussia (later part of Poland), on September 9, 1890. When he was fifteen, his family moved to Berlin where Lewin completed his high school studies at the Kaiserin Augusta Gymnasium. After a semester at the University of Freiburg and another at the University of Munich, he enrolled at the University of Berlin where he completed the requirements for a Ph.D. in psychology under Carl Stumpf's direction. As with other Gestalt scholars, Stumpf's views affected Lewin substantially (Bonacchi, 2009).

Following graduate studies, Lewin enlisted in the German army and served through World War I. He was awarded the Iron Cross after being wounded in battle. Lewin's students (see Marrow, 1969, p. 11) have pointed out that his experiences in World War I served as a basis for his later field theory. Concepts such as *boundary*, *force*, and *zone* are as real on the battlefield as in ordinary human experience.

Upon completing his military tour of duty, Lewin took a position at the Psychological Institute at the University of Berlin, where he encountered Wertheimer and Köhler. Marrow (1969) pointed out that "Gestalt holism impressed Lewin. Though he was never a completely orthodox Gestalt psychologist, he did become a vital force in the new movement and contributed to it his own special insights" (p. 13). Lewin even was impressed with psychoanalysts because they worked with real-life problems, but he found flaws in their methods (Marrow, 1969). Lewin's work at the Berlin Institute continued with only minor interruptions until 1933. By that time, he had gained international visibility and an impressive publication record. Several articles brought widespread recognition, especially a paper contrasting Aristotelian and Galilean thought (Lewin, 1931).

At the outset of the Nazi movement, Lewin declared he could not continue to teach in a university where his children would not be welcome as students (see Marrow, 1969, p. 68). In 1933, he joined the exodus of German intellectuals and took a temporary position at Cornell University. Two years later, he accepted a position at the Child Welfare Research Station at the University of Iowa, a position he held until 1944. That same year, he was named director of the Research Center for Group Dynamics at Massachusetts Institute of Technology (MIT). He died of a heart attack at his home in Newtonville, Massachusetts, on February 12, 1947.

Like William James, Lewin was an intellectual democrat. He took ideas too seriously to demand intellectual conformity or loyalty. Many students were attracted to him and, as noted by Marrow (1969), they could move in and out of his circle without guilt or accusations of disloyalty. Lewin's openness could be characterized as a logical outgrowth of his philosophy of science. He was strongly committed to the idea that science must continually change. He insisted that "the idea of an eventual unification of all sciences is wishful thinking" (Marrow, 1969, p. 19).

Lewin's Field Theory

Lewin's psychology was a corrective for earlier systems that emphasized traits, inherited predispositions, learning, agencies, or other intrapsychic events or processes. In contrast with extreme individualistic approaches, Lewin's **field theory** emphasized the interdependence of the person *and* the environment. His most characteristic formula, $B = f(p,e)$, states that behavior is a function of person *and* environment. According to the formula, an adequate psychology of behaviors and mental states can be developed only by appreciating the full scope of forces that play a role in human life, including the biological and physical environment (Smith, 2009). Lewin believed that earlier psychologists had placed too large a burden on the explanatory role of association and other limited concepts. He also believed that earlier psychologies had neglected affect, motivation, and social forces.

One of the key concepts in Lewin's psychology is the **life space**, which refers to every psychological fact that is influential in the life of an individual at a given time. In any one slice of time, the life space consists of physical events (an impending storm, a new car, a cup of coffee, the aroma of cinnamon, a book), personal and biological facts (a toothache, a memory, fatigue, the exhilaration of a workout), and social facts (another person, membership in a group). It consists of the extensity of experience at a given moment. The life space of the child is limited both spatially and temporally, but with growth, the space expands. Lewin believed that the task of education is to extend the life space so that we can strive for goals that are further and further removed in time. Young children typically strive only for more concrete and visible things. With education and growth, the present can become more spacious, the future more pregnant with possibilities, and the past more enlarged. Lewin quoted with approval Goethe's famous statement, "Who cannot give an account of three thousand years remains in the darkness of inexperience, can live only from one day to another" (see Lewin, 1935, p. 173).

It is important to point out that the life space is not static. At a given time, its focal features may consist of a small group of people, a physical setting, food, and great conversation. In the midst of all that a phone call or email may bring salient information that changes the focus of attention, hence the life space.

Lewin referred to positive or negative features of objects in the life space as **valences**. A *positive valence* refers to the attractive or desirable qualities that reside in an object. In general, objects that satisfy a need possess positive valence and objects that frustrate or frighten have a negative valence. Valences fluctuate dynamically with needs. For example, a Pop Tart will have a higher positive valence for a hungry child. After consuming the snack, a favored toy may have a higher positive valence.

Lewin's emphasis on positive and negative valences led to some of the most productive work in the history of psychology on the nature of conflict. In the day-to-day world, we seldom encounter a simple pathway to a simple goal. Instead, we encounter complexities that require adjudication and choice. Lewin and his students called attention to common types of conflicts.

First, we may be caught between two objects with comparable positive valences. Though there may be considerable vacillation in such a circumstance, this type of conflict is usually regarded as fairly easy to resolve. Second, another type of conflict occurs when an object has positive *and* negative valences or when an object with a positive valence is surrounded by a physical or psychological barrier. The dynamics of conflict resolution in this type of situation are complex and depend on the relative weights of the positive and negative valences and the capacities of the individual. Lewin observed that individuals may attempt circuitous routes to the goal or, when the conflict is too intense, the individual may leave the field and search for an alternative goal. The third type of conflict surfaces when we are caught between two regions that both have negative valences. Lewin gave the example of the child who is required to perform an undesirable task and failure to do the task will result in punishment. This is a severe conflict, especially if escape from punishment is impossible and if the task is repugnant.

These types of conflict are easily recognized as part of the mainstream of psychological literature under the labels of **approach–approach conflict**, **approach–avoidance conflict**, and **avoidance–avoidance conflict**. Lewin's original work on conflict has inspired a great deal of research on simple conflict situations and on more complicated real-life situations in which there are multiple positive and negative valences associated with many regions.

Tension Systems and Recall

Lewin believed that needs are associated with tension systems and that the satisfaction of a need is associated with the dissipation of tension. Lewin's student Bluma Zeigarnik (1900–1988) tested one implication of his idea.

Under Lewin's direction, Zeigarnik gave her participants a series of simple tasks. At times, participants were interrupted before completing their task. In other instances, they were allowed to finish their work. Afterward, Zeigarnik tested her participants' memory about the various tasks. The researchers hypothesized that people would remember interrupted tasks better than completed work. The data supported their prediction. When we complete a task, tension dissipates. But tension persists for a longer period when we are not allowed to finish a job. The tension state produces a need for closure that begs for resolution. Someone who gets unexpectedly dumped might continue to mourn the broken relationship years after it ended. Or you might become addicted to a TV series or thriller novel because it leaves you hanging from one cliffhanger to the next. The tendency to recall uncompleted tasks better than completed tasks came to be known as the **Zeigarnik effect**.

One explanation for the Zeigarnik effect is that tension remaining from an uncompleted task may cause participants to persevere or rehearse the materials associated with that task. On the other hand, the completion of a task may free the individual to turn attention to other things. In other words, the uncompleted task serves as a barrier to interference. Regardless of why it works, the Zeigarnik effect suggests that a study unit might be ended most effectively with a question. A compelling question, by its very nature, means that something is not complete or that something is unanswered. A good question should result in a tension system that will keep the learner on task for a longer period of time than without the question. In 1931, Bluma Zeigarnik moved to the Soviet Union, where she continued her psychological work for more than fifty years (Zeigarnik, 2007), particularly in pathopsychology, the study of mental processes exhibited by people with mental disorders (Nikolaeva, 2011).

Group Dynamics

As mentioned, Lewin was named director of the Research Center for Group Dynamics at MIT in 1944. During this period, he focused on group dynamics, a term he coined and popularized (Carron & Brawley, 2008) and a problem of long-standing interest. The expression **group dynamics** is not easily defined, but in general it includes the study of the effects of groups on individuals and individuals on groups. Groups modify individual behaviors and perceptions, and individuals modify groups. Group dynamics also includes studies of the structures of groups with respect to leadership (e.g., democratic vs. authoritarian) and the effectiveness of leadership structures in various kinds of tasks and contexts.

Lewin's interests extended to wide varieties of groups, including industrial work groups, educational groups, and casual interest groups, and he was interested in destructive behaviors as well as prosocial actions (Wennberg & Hane, 2005). His 1939–1947 work with the Harwood Manufacturing Corporation helped bring group research from the lab to applied settings and was, among other things, an early study in organizational behavior (Burnes, 2007). He was also invested in community action programs where psychological theory could be tested in the day-to-day world; in this way he contributed to the history of community psychology (Dalton et al., 2013). Lewin inspired a representative experiment on integrated housing conducted by his students. A few years after Lewin's death, Deutsch and Collins (1951) studied housing projects in which blacks and whites were integrated in a random fashion. That is, houses were available on a first-come, first-served basis. In another condition, black and white participants were segregated in a block-type or checkerboard pattern. Results showed that integration resulted in more positive and accepting interracial attitudes. Segregated housing patterns resulted in increased resentment, prejudice, and a desire for greater segregation. Within integrated neighborhoods, people enjoyed more opportunities to build friendships and gain insight into the basic humanity of other ethnic members.

The Second Generation of Gestalt Psychologists

Aside from the contributions of Wertheimer, Koffka, Köhler, and Lewin, a legion of second-generation Gestalt psychologists enhanced the work of their mentors. Students of Gestalt psychology enjoyed a time of great productivity in Germany during the 1920s. Among the more influential students were **Karl Duncker (1903–1940)**, **Hedwig von Restorff (1906–1962)**, and **Solomon Asch (1907–1996)**.

KARL DUNCKER Karl Duncker was born on February 2, 1903, in Leipzig. Although his early training was in the German educational system, Duncker also studied in the United States and received his master's degree at Clark University in 1926. He returned to Germany and earned his doctorate in psychology at the University of Berlin in 1929. He stayed at Berlin as a research assistant for Wolfgang Köhler until 1935 when the Nazi government dismissed Duncker for political reasons (King, Cox, & Wertheimer, 1998). At that time, he immigrated to England and worked at Cambridge University with the eminent psychologist Frederick C. Bartlett (1886–1969). Beginning in the summer of 1937, he struggled with recurring bouts of depression, seeking treatment with the existential psychiatrist Ludwig Binswanger (1881–1966). In 1938, Duncker immigrated to the United States, where he joined the faculty at Swarthmore College. Tragically, Duncker committed suicide on February 23, 1940, twenty-one days after his thirty-seventh birthday.

Despite a brief career, he made several impressive contributions to the domain of Gestalt psychology. In early research, Duncker (1929/1950) found that people tend to perceive personal movement if their body is stationary but another object in their perceptual field is in motion. For example, standing at the middle of a bridge looking down at a passing stream may give the distinct impression that the perceiver, rather than the water, is in motion. Or maybe you've experienced that awkward moment when you're stopped at a red light and another car pulls up beside your vehicle. Even though your car isn't moving, you sense that it's rolling backward (the embarrassment comes when you slam on your brakes and the person in the next car laughs at you). This so-called *induced motion* was the basis of Duncker's research, proving an excellent addition to the Gestalt literature on perception.

Under Wertheimer's direction, Duncker also conducted an ingenious series of experiments on problem solving. Originally published in German in 1935, Duncker's research was translated a decade later into English (Duncker, 1935/1945). After conducting numerous experiments, Duncker found that many participants exhibited a **functional fixedness**, that is, an inability to find productive solutions to new problems (van Steenburgh et al., 2012). Duncker's research has continued to influence problem-solving research (German & Defeyter, 2000; Newell, 1985). According to Mandler and Mandler (1969), "Apart from the personal tragedy, there is reason to believe that [Duncker] was the most brilliant of the Gestalt group. . . . His main contribution has made a continuing impact on the psychology of thinking, both in the United States and elsewhere" (p. 393).

HEDWIG VON RESTORFF   After receiving her Ph.D. in psychology, Hedwig von Restorff (1906–1962) served as a research assistant for Köhler at the Psychological Institute in Berlin. Like Duncker, she was dismissed by the Nazis in 1933. In a classic experiment, Köhler and von Restorff found that isolated items are recalled better than a series of homogenous items. Participants in one of their experiments learned a list of nonsense syllables. However, when an individual three-digit item was presented with the nonsense syllables, participants recalled the three-digit number better than the nonsense syllables. According to Köhler and von Restorff (1935), the three digits acted as the figure to the ground of the homogeneous nonsense syllables. This phenomenon has been popularized with the eponym of the *Köhler–von Restorff effect* or the more inaccurate **von Restorff effect**. According to Baddeley (1990), the British Post Office even employed the research of Köhler and von Restorff in the design of its postcode. The von Restorff effect remains a viable research construct (Bireta & Neath, 2008; Kelley & Nairne, 2001).

It is an unfortunate circumstance that many of the heirs of Gestalt psychology were severely affected by the Nazi regime. Henle (1986) lamented, "By the end of World War II, the first generation of young Gestalt psychologists was essentially wiped out" (p. 119). Some were lost in the war, but most had moved to other countries. The Gestalt journal, *Psychologische Forschung*, resumed production after World War II. In the decades after the war, European researchers promoted Gestalt psychology in their work including Wolfgang Metzger (1889–1979), Edwin Rausch (1906–1994), Sarah Sliosberg (b. 1906), Paul Fraisse (1911–1996), Erna Hruschka (1912–1996), and Wolfgang Schönpflug (b. 1936). In the United States, Solomon Asch found great success in the incorporation of Gestalt theory into his research.

SOLOMON ASCH   During his career, Solomon Asch had the rare opportunity to work with both Max Wertheimer and Wolfgang Köhler. Asch's contributions to cognition, learning, personality theory, and perception all carry a Gestalt flavor (Gleitman, Rozin, & Sabini, 1997). Arguably, his most enduring work was in social psychology when he substituted "the dichotomy of individual and group with an integrated view of social interaction and its intrinsic dynamics" (Arnheim, 1986, p. 34). Asch's landmark research on group pressure and the judgment of line length is a classic in social psychology (Asch, 1955; Hewstone et al., 2007), and it has implications for destructive behavior (Roth, 2004). His work held great influence on later work on cognition and social psychology (Rock, 1990; Rozin, 2001). We'll discuss Solomon Asch's social psychology research in more detail in Chapter 18.

In a more indirect fashion, the work of other psychologists reflects the principal tenets of Gestalt psychology. Edward Chace Tolman, though a behaviorist, acknowledged that Gestalt psychology had been a major source of inspiration for his cognitive approach to learning. Muzafer Sherif's (*Sher-uhf*) conceptual approach to psychology, his experiments on the autokinetic effect, and his well-known boys' camp experiments (which incidentally inspired the novel *Lord of the Flies*) are best appreciated within a Gestalt orientation. Kurt Goldstein's organismic personality theory was directly influenced by Gestalt theory as was Andras Angyal's theory of personality. Other theorists such as Fritz Heider (1896–1988), Hans Wallach (1904–1998), and Herman Witkin (1916–1979) drew inspiration from the Gestalt school. Henle (1985) has also demonstrated that contemporary cognitive psychology owes a large and often unacknowledged debt to Gestalt psychology. Rock and Palmer (1990) have outlined additional influences.

COMMON MISUNDERSTANDINGS OF GESTALT PSYCHOLOGY

The Gestalt system perhaps offers greater complexity and subtlety than any other system we have covered. For this reason, a number of misunderstandings have arisen over the years. We'll summarize the most common misunderstandings.

Gestalt Psychology and Gestalt Therapy

Because of similarities in terminology, it would be reasonable to assume that Gestalt therapy, which had its origin in the work of Fritz Perls (1893–1970), is somehow related to Gestalt psychology. In an article titled "Gestalt Psychology and Gestalt Therapy" Mary Henle (1978a) examined **Gestalt therapy** and found it to be in marked contrast with the teachings of Gestalt psychology. Henle concluded that Perls borrowed terms from Gestalt psychology, stretching them beyond recognition. For her, the psychology advanced by Perls "is *not* Gestalt psychology" (Henle, 1978a, p. 31). In agreement with Henle, Michael Wertheimer (1987) found "*no* conceptual relationship between Perls' neoanalytic 'gestalt psychotherapy' and Gestalt psychology in the sense of the Wertheimer–Köhler–Koffka theory" (p. 139).

Gestalt Psychology and Scientific Analysis

Another common misunderstanding is that Gestalt psychology opposes analysis. This accusation is set forth in Pavlov's polemics against the Gestalt school (see Gibbons, n.d.). Earlier, we pointed out that Gestalt psychology should not be confused with holistic psychologies that do oppose analysis. Gestalt psychology has never rejected analysis of the natural units of the phenomenal field. Thus, if a unit is a genuine part of a whole, it is a legitimate task of the scientist to understand that unit. Köhler (1929/1947) said, "Analysis in terms of genuine parts is a perfectly legitimate and necessary procedure in Gestalt psychology" (pp. 168–169). From a Gestalt perspective, analysis starts with a phenomenal event, then proceeds to its natural parts and their relations.

Gestalt Psychology and Nativism

Another common misunderstanding is encountered in the belief that Gestalt theory is a nativistic psychology, meaning that it places heavier emphasis on heredity than on environment. In fact, Gestalt psychologists reject the nature–nurture dichotomy and argue that it is misleading to treat events in the psychological world as if they were *simply* inherited or learned. In his last book, Köhler (1969) declared it an error to treat "the terms 'learned' and 'inherited' as though these words indicated an 'either–or' alternative" (p. 89).

The Gestalt position goes back to a neglected feature of evolutionary theory—namely, that the physical–chemical forces of nature are applicable to living organisms. Thus, physical conditions (e.g., gravitational forces, pH values, ambient temperature) and principles (e.g., conservation of energy) all contribute to the dynamic distributions or possibilities. For example, at a relatively low ambient temperature, gelatin is a semisolid, but at a higher temperature, it is a liquid. The dynamic distribution and movement of particles is a function, among other things, of temperature. Temperature is associated with limits or constraints within which we observe invariant dynamics.

Köhler (1969) argued that "it is three factors (not two) by which events in organisms, and therefore also in nervous systems, are generally determined. First, the invariant principles and forces of general dynamics, secondly, anatomical constraints which evolution has established, and thirdly, learning" (p. 89). If we focus only on what is learned or inherited, we neglect attention to what Köhler called *invariant dynamics*, something we share with the inorganic world. Köhler (1969) asked whether "processes in our nervous system follow the laws of nature because some genes compel such processes to do so" (p. 69). The answer is clearly "no." The upshot of the Gestalt position is that it calls for a psychology informed by life sciences *and* physical sciences.

The Role of Past Experience

A final misunderstanding of Gestalt psychology is that it neglects past experience. Gestalt theory has been accused of neglecting history because it stands in sharp contrast with other systems that overemphasize the importance of the past. If thinking, learning, and perception work as the Gestalt theorists believe they do, then present facts are important, though the past is by no means unimportant. If the Gestalt position is correct, we may not be tied in a blind and mechanical way to our individual and collective histories because of insight and productive thinking. Both insight and productive thinking would be impossible without the ability to integrate the past into ongoing activities.

Recall that Lewin quoted with approval Goethe's statement, "Who cannot give an account of three thousand years remains lost in the darkness of inexperience." Gestalt concepts such as insight and productive thinking give a new intimacy with the past. We are hardly intimate with the past if its events dictate (either through conditioning or unconscious motivations) the present flow of events. In the Gestalt perspective, the present is elevated in importance, but the past and the future are not neglected. Indeed, time perspective may have greater breadth within a Gestalt framework than in any other system of psychology.

GESTALT PSYCHOLOGY AND APPLIED PSYCHOLOGY

Although focused on the study of perception, thinking, learning, development, and social psychology, Gestalt psychology was actively applied to topics such as the psychology of art, education, and psychotherapy. Behrens (1998) argued that the work of Cubist artists such as Pablo Picasso had an impact on Gestalt theory. Likewise, several illustrious artists including Paul Klee, Vassily Kandinsky, Josef Albers, and M. C. Escher found inspiration in the tenets of Gestalt theory (King, Wertheimer, Keller, & Crochetière, 1994). Like his mentor Max Wertheimer, Rudolf Arnheim (1943) saw the principles of Gestalt theory in the natural world, not only in the rigorous constraints of the laboratory. Born in 1904, Arnheim earned his Ph.D. from Wertheimer at the University of Berlin at age fourteen; his dissertation project involved handwriting analysis, which marked the beginning of a lifetime of studying perception, cognition, and meaning (Gardner, 2008). In 1932, due to his Jewish descent, he emigrated from Nazi Germany to Italy and later to the United States, where he held positions at Sarah Lawrence College, Harvard University, and the University of Michigan at Ann Arbor (Pariser, 2008).

Arnheim's greatest contribution involved his use of Gestalt theory to explore the psychology of art (Mandler & Mandler, 1969; Verstegen, 2005, 2007). His scholarly activities ranged from a molar study of architecture, music, film, radio, poetry, theater, and sculpture to a detailed Gestalt-inspired analysis of Picasso's creative thinking during the painting of his *Guernica* (Arnheim, 1962). Indeed, the majority of his books on the psychology of art bear the unmistakable stamp of Gestalt theory (Arnheim, 1966, 1974, 1986).

The Gestalt model also held important implications for education. The Gestalt perspective paralleled closely the functional ideology of progressive education as opposed to a more traditional approach based in repetition and rote memorization. Wertheimer's vision of a Gestalt theory of education had a profound influence on several students including George Katona.

Although he earned a Ph.D. under G. E. Müller at Göttingen, George Katona (1901–1981) came under the influence of Wertheimer and Köhler while studying in Berlin. In 1933, he immigrated to the United States and taught at the New School for Social Research from 1938 to 1942.

He later taught at the University of Michigan at Ann Arbor, where he joined the Institute of Social Research (Heukelom, 2010). Katona was a prolific researcher, particularly in the area of behavioral economics (Katona, 1959, 1979), in which he applied field theory to the study of economics in numerous books and articles.

Katona's most dynamic contribution to Gestalt psychology was a book on memory and education titled *Organizing and Memorizing* (1940). Like Duncker's research on problem solving, Katona's book complemented Wertheimer's work on productive thinking but with a greater application to educational psychology. Katona (1940) demonstrated that understanding of information based on insightful grouping (*meaningful* learning) would yield superior results to memorization of unorganized materials (*senseless* learning). Katona concluded that memorization would yield faster rates of forgetting than understanding and was less likely to transfer to learning of new tasks. He even challenged the utility of Ebbinghaus's retention curve by noting that the data were derived from nonsensical stimuli rather than meaningful material. Katona's work stands as an important precursor to research on organization in learning and memory (Baddeley, 1990).

The Gestalt contribution to psychotherapy is less evident than its applications to art and education. Although Wertheimer dismissed Freud's work as excessively associative and unscientific, several psychologists linked Gestalt theory with psychoanalysis and other psychotherapies. As with Fritz Perls's Gestalt therapy, most efforts bore no intellectual resemblance to the Gestalt theory of Wertheimer, Köhler, and Koffka (King et al., 1994). However, the Gestalt psychologists were not adverse to the application of their ideas to a clinical setting. Select passages in Wertheimer's *Productive Thinking* reveal an interest in psychopathology. In the 1920s, Wertheimer supervised a student named Heinrich Schulte on a Gestalt theory of paranoia (Schulte, 1938; Wertheimer, 1924/1986). According to Levy (1986), the Wertheimer–Schulte theory has relevance because it "claims to account for *all* forms of paranoid developments, regardless of whether they are exogenous or endogenous, psychogenic or somatogenic, and so offers a general theory which at present we do not seem to have" (p. 248). Furthermore, the work of Adhémar Gelb (1887–1936) and Kurt Goldstein (1878–1965) on brain injury and agnosia reflects the influence of Gestalt psychology, particularly in Goldstein's encouragement for psychologists to view humans as more than specific symptoms or test scores (Eling, 2012). Despite Gestalt therapy's mistaken identity, the Gestalt model can serve as a fruitful resource for the clinical psychologist (Crochetière, Vicker, Parker, King, & Wertheimer, 2001).

THE CONTINUING RELEVANCE OF GESTALT PSYCHOLOGY

In an address at a conference on the worldview of contemporary physics, the theoretical physicist Fritjof Capra (1988) contrasted the paradigm that has been dominant in the sciences and in society for the past several hundred years with an emerging new worldview. The old paradigm, according to Capra, included beliefs in a mechanical universe consisting of elementary building blocks, the human body as a machine, unlimited material progress through technological and economic growth, life as a competitive struggle, and the natural domination of the male over the female. Capra characterized the emerging new worldview under five points:

1. A shift from the part to the whole
2. A shift from structure to process
3. A shift from "objective science" to "epistemic science"
4. A shift in scientific metaphor from knowledge as a building block to knowledge as a network
5. A shift from truth to approximate description

Although there are many differences between Gestalt psychology and the new perspectives as outlined by Capra, there are also some important similarities. Long ago, Gestalt psychology rejected the view of the universe as a mechanical system consisting of elementary building blocks and the view of the human body as a machine. Gestalt psychologists could also offer a great deal of informed comment to all those who agree with Capra that there should be a shift of emphasis from the part to the whole, from structure to process, and from objective science to epistemic science.

The continuing relevance of Gestalt psychology is manifested in other later developments. Recall that one of the major positions of the Gestalt system is that there are internally determined organizations within physical forces. As stated by Henle (1985), "Physical interactions do not occur indiscriminately, but depend on the properties of the interacting events" (p. 105). In recent years there is increasing awareness of this very point and its implication that there is latent order within apparent disorder. For example, there are repeated orderly patterns in chaotic physical events such as shattered glass, a rising heat current, and the distribution of matter in an explosion. The Gestalt concept of free dynamics is applicable to these and other physical events. In some cases, computer-generated models of chaos (see Gleick, 1987) reveal striking repetitions of consistent and orderly patterns and shapes occurring on large and small scales, and further evidence of hard-to-see patterns comes from new statistical methods of data mining to reveal complex patterns in massive data sets.

Though psychologists today do not typically claim allegiance to the Gestalt school, there is much in this school that is consistent with the scientific orientations that prevailed at the outset of the twenty-first century. Indeed, Gestalt theory is more consistent with the scientific worldview of the twenty-first century than that of the 1940s. In an era marked by interest in ecological concerns and suspicion of reductionism, it would not be surprising if Gestalt theory continues to be rediscovered.

Review Questions

1. Trace some of the key influences on Gestalt theory coming out of science, philosophy, and psychology.

2. The standard explanation for the phi phenomenon was based on the idea that there was kinesthetic feedback from the movement of the eye. Describe a demonstration that proved embarrassing to the standard explanation. Why was the phi phenomenon so important to Wertheimer?

3. Distinguish between productive thinking and mere reproductive thinking.

4. What is the law of Prägnanz and how can it be illustrated?

5. Briefly review the evidence that learning is not based on strict point-for-point mechanical connections.

6. Outline three types of learning discussed in the work of Koffka.

7. Discuss the Gestalt approach to the scientific method. Contrast this approach to the behavioristic approach. Which do you believe to be more adequate? Explain your reasons.

8. Explain the Gestalt approach to the mind–brain problem. Why is the concept of "pictures in the head" a misrepresentation of isomorphism?

9. Explain Lewin's concept of the life space and why it was important to his overall conceptual approach to psychology.

10. What is the Zeigarnik effect and what are some of its practical implications?

11. Discuss Lewin's concept of motivation and its relationship to his approach to conflict.

12. Outline four common misunderstandings of Gestalt psychology.

Glossary

approach–approach conflict   A type of conflict marked by the presence of two attractive but mutually exclusive goals. Thus, the achievement of one goal precludes the possibility of attaining the other.

approach–avoidance conflict   A type of conflict in which a positive goal is associated with some unattractive or undesirable feature.

Asch, Solomon (1907–1996)   A second-generation Gestalt psychologist remembered for his work on social psychology, cognition, learning, perception, and personality theory.

avoidance–avoidance conflict   A type of conflict marked by the presence of two unattractive or undesirable alternatives.

closure The tendency psychologically to complete that which is incomplete, to fill in the gaps, or to see wholeness even when it is not present.

Duncker, Karl (1903–1940) Gestalt psychologist remembered for his work on the nature of problem solving and for work on the relativity of perceived movement.

field theory Generally associated with the psychology of Kurt Lewin. Field theory emphasizes the interdependence of the person and the environment. It may be viewed as a corrective to extreme individualistic psychologies that neglect the role of context.

figure–ground A principle of perception characterized by the tendency of the subject to see some things as standing out and other things as forming background.

functional fixedness The inability to find productive solutions to new problems. May also refer to the inability to see alternative uses for a particular tool or method.

Gestalt There is no exact English equivalent for this German term, but English words such as *whole* and *configuration* are close in meaning.

Gestalt therapy A form of therapy coming out of the work of Fritz Perls and having little or nothing in common with Gestalt psychology.

good continuation The perceptual tendency toward linearity, continuity, or coherence. Good continuation is manifested when a perceptual pattern is tracked even in the presence of irrelevant or competing cues.

group dynamics In Lewin's psychology, this expression refers broadly to the study of the effects of groups on individuals and the effects of individuals on groups. It also includes the study of group structures and their effect on work, productivity, and achievement of group goals.

insight The capacity to see a problem in a large context and perceptually to restructure relationships necessary to the solution of the problem.

isomorphism The Gestalt position on the mind–brain problem. Literally, this term refers to similarity of form. Isomorphism, in the context of the mind–brain problem, refers to an assumed functional relationship between experience and underlying brain processes.

Koffka, Kurt (1886–1941) Pioneering Gestalt psychologist remembered especially for introducing Gestalt psychology to the English-speaking world and for the extension of Gestalt theory into the field of developmental psychology.

Köhler, Wolfgang (1887–1967) Principal advocate of the Gestalt school. Köhler is remembered for his pioneering work on the role of insight in learning, for his treatment of value theory from a Gestalt perspective, and for his broad systematic approach to science and psychology.

law of Prägnanz The law of Prägnanz, according to Wertheimer, refers to the idea that perceptual organization tends to be as good as possible under prevailing conditions. Thus, perceptual organization is as orderly, coherent, and economical as possible under prevailing conditions.

Lewin, Kurt (1890–1947) Inspired by Wertheimer, Köhler, and Koffka, Lewin attempted to extend the Gestalt vision to other subdisciplinary branches of psychology, including motivation, personality, social psychology, and conflict resolution.

life space Key concept in Lewin's psychology referring to all the psychological facts that are influential in the life of an individual at a given point in time.

Mach, Ernst (1838–1916) Nineteenth-century physicist who argued that there are space-form and time-form sensations that are configural in their nature. Mach's analysis served as an inspiration for the early Gestalt psychologists who also argued that there are wholes that are grasped intuitively and that are more than a mere collection of elements.

phi phenomenon Apparent movement illustrated by successive activation of two stationary lights placed in close spatial conjunction. Phenomenally, what is seen is movement from the first to the second light.

productive thinking Wertheimer's term for a bold and radical centering of a problem that results in creative new ideas, breakthroughs, insights, or solutions. Einstein's revolutionary theory of relativity serves as a classic illustration of productive thinking.

proximity   The perceptual tendency to group figures or *Gestalten* that are close together in space or time.

reproductive thinking   Wertheimer's term for the routine reproduction of familiar solutions that result in blind conclusions with no sense of direction.

similarity   The perceptual tendency to group figures or *Gestalten* that are similar.

valence   According to Lewin, the positive or negative characteristics of objects in the life space.

von Ehrenfels, Christian (1859–1932)   One of the first to argue that form qualities are given immediately in experience. Although Ehrenfels believed that the whole is more than the sum of the parts, he still believed that it was derivative and thus acts simply like another part.

von Restorff, Hedwig (1906–1962)   A second generation Gestalt psychologist remembered for her study of memory with Wolfgang Köhler.

von Restorff effect   Refers to superiority of recall for isolated items in a list compared to more homogeneous items.

Wertheimer, Max (1880–1943)   Founder of the Gestalt school of thought and author of the influential book *Productive Thinking*.

Zeigarnik effect   Tendency to remember incompleted tasks better than completed ones.

16

Psychoanalysis

The ego is not master in its own house.

—SIGMUND FREUD (1917/1955)

Like behaviorism, psychoanalysis moved beyond a system of psychology to become an intellectual movement. Psychodynamic theory connected with many fields including literature, philosophy, art, religion, and history. And like behaviorism, psychoanalysis inspired both devotion and derision. Debate still rages about its true impact on psychology (see Crews, 1996; Horgan, 1996). Some scholars insist its influence is vanishing while others claim psychoanalysis is alive and robust. In terms of the number of professional organizations, journals, and books the evidence supports the latter claim. We begin with a biographical sketch of its founder, Sigmund Freud.

SIGMUND FREUD

Sigmund Freud (1856–1939) was born on May 6, 1856, in the small town of Freiberg, Moravia, now a historical region in the Czech Republic. His father, Jakob Freud, was a wool merchant who had two sons by a previous marriage. Sigmund was the first of the eight children of Jakob and Amalie Nathansohn. In 1860, Jakob and Amalie settled in Vienna, a city that became Freud's home for the next seventy-eight years. Anti-Semitism colored day-to-day life and narrowed vocational opportunities for Jewish citizens. Jones (1953) relayed the story of a thug who knocked Jakob Freud's new hat into a puddle of mud and then demanded, "Jew get off the pavement" (p. 22). Jewish citizens became common victims of hostile acts and demeaning humor. Such a climate had a profound effect on Sigmund Freud's thought and character (see Bakan, 1958; Miller, 1981; Roith, 1987).

Always a precocious student, Freud graduated from high school summa cum laude at age seventeen. He excelled in literature, history, and science. His facility with languages was evident in his competence in Latin, Greek, French, English, Italian, Spanish, and Hebrew. In 1873, Freud matriculated in the University of Vienna, where he pursued a degree in medicine. Like William James, his interests ranged over the entire curriculum. He attended Franz Brentano's courses in philosophy and psychology as well as a course on evolution taught by zoologist Carl Claus and

Sigmund Freud

a course on the physiology of voice and speech taught by **Ernst Brücke (1819–1892)**.

From 1876 to 1882, Freud worked in Brücke's laboratory, where he met a respected physiologist fourteen years his senior named **Joseph Breuer (1842–1925)**. In December 1880, Breuer began treating Bertha Pappenheim, a remarkable twenty-one-year-old woman who had developed hysteria while caring for her dying father. Breuer tried to determine the psychological cause for Pappenheim's headaches, loss of sensation, partial paralyses, and vivid hallucinations about skeletons and black snakes.

After Breuer hypnotized Pappenheim, she relived traumatic events that had escaped her conscious memory. During their sessions, she made dramatic progress after giving conscious expression to disturbing memories and emotions. Breuer referred to this process as catharsis while Pappenheim called it her *talking cure* or *chimney sweeping* (Gay, 1988). After several years of therapy and significant progress, Pappenheim announced she was pregnant with Breuer's child. Although the false pregnancy was another

symptom of her hysteria, Breuer stopped the therapy, leaving her in the care of a colleague. In time, she overcame the hysteria and became one of Germany's first feminists and a pioneer in the field of social work.

Breuer first described her to Freud in 1882. More than a decade later, they discussed Pappenheim's case in a classic book titled *Studies in Hysteria*. The authors used the pseudonym *Fräulein Anna O* rather than Pappenheim's real name. They also shrouded the details of her false pregnancy and actual recovery. In a previously unpublished letter discovered by Forrester and Cameron (1999), Freud described the case of Anna O as a "cure with a defect." Nonetheless, Anna O became the first case study in psychoanalysis and solidified Freud's early ideas about psychotherapy.

In his third year at the university, Freud received a grant that paid for two brief trips to Triste, where he studied marine biology. Afterward, his research interests centered on anatomy and physiology. Although he would have preferred work in Ernst Brücke's lab, dismal prospects for advancement as well as personal financial exigencies forced him into a medical career. He served as a resident in the Vienna General Hospital from 1882 to 1885 where he fell in love with a young woman named Martha Bernays. Not long after meeting her, Freud had flowers delivered every day to his "princess." He dreamed of marrying Martha, but the poverty-stricken student couldn't support her.

Around this time, Freud discovered a "magical substance" extracted from coca leaves. He noted that alkaloid cocaine gave him a sense of good cheer and energy, warding off depression and indigestion with "brilliant success." He initially denied its addictiveness (Cohen, 2012), and according to Jones (1953), Freud recommended the drug to "his friends and colleagues, both for themselves and their patients; he gave it to his sisters. In short, looked at from the vantage point of our present knowledge, he was rapidly becoming a public menace" (p. 81). In an awkward but enthusiastic letter to his fiancée, Freud raved about cocaine:

Woe to you, my Princess, when I come. I will kiss you quite red and feed you till you are plump. And if you are froward you shall see who is the stronger, a gentle little girl who doesn't eat enough or a big wild man who has cocaine in his body. In my last severe depression I took coca again and a small dose lifted me to the heights in a wonderful fashion. I am just now busy collecting the literature for a song of praise to this magical substance. (Jones, 1953, p. 84)

Freud hoped his research on the drug's medicinal benefits might establish his reputation (Markel, 2011) but soured on it after discovering cocaine's darker, more addictive side. After his disappointment, Freud impressively quit using cocaine. In addition, a friend named Karl Koller presented research on cocaine as a local anesthetic before Freud could deliver his "song of praise" (in a spurt of paranoia, he claimed Koller had first seen him use it on a patient, robbing Freud of the chance for scientific celebrity).

During his time at the Vienna General Hospital, Freud gained experience in surgery, internal medicine, dermatology, and ophthalmology, but found little joy in such pursuits. Everything changed when he discovered psychiatry. The turning point came when he worked in Theodore Meynert's psychiatric clinic and in Franz Schol's Department of Nervous Diseases.

In September of 1885, Freud was appointed *Privatdozent* (a lecturer paid only by student fees) in neuropathology. He worked five months in **Jean-Martin Charcot's (1825–1893)** neurology clinic at the Pitié-Salpêtrière Hospital in Paris. This opportunity sparked Freud's interest in hysteria and hypnosis. The experience was pivotal because the Paris School focused on the psychological nature of emotional problems, whereas the Vienna group advocated physical interpretations. Following his time in Paris, Freud returned to Vienna, where he launched a private practice on April 25, 1886. That same year, following a lengthy engagement, he married Martha Bernays.

Freud's system of psychotherapy did not develop suddenly. In fact, the term **psychoanalysis** did not debut until a full decade after Freud had established his clinical practice (Jones, 1953). During the earliest phases of his practice, he used electrotherapy (not to be confused with electroconvulsive therapy). Conventional wisdom held that deficiencies in circulation produced mental disorders. As a remedy, *electrotherapy* consisted of passing small currents of electricity through the skin and muscles of the head to improve circulation. Later, Freud used hypnotic suggestion before trying Breuer's cathartic method. His technique of free association evolved from a growing disillusionment with other therapeutic methods.

Freud's best-known book, *The Interpretation of Dreams*, appeared in November 1899 as *Die Traumdeutung* (the publisher postdated the book as 1900 to reflect a new way of thinking for a new century). Freud advanced his familiar position that dreams represent wish fulfillments in disguise. Now regarded as a classic in psychology, the book did not bring instant fame to its author (Fancher, 2000). Initial reaction was sharp and hostile, especially in Viennese circles. In time, the book attracted attention, granting renown for Freud within a decade after its publication.

Freud's bibliography following *The Interpretation of Dreams* reveals an impressive output of books, shorter papers, and case histories designed to elaborate and extend his system of psychological thought. So prolific were his writings that the collected works are now contained in twenty-three volumes with an additional volume devoted to indexes and bibliographies (see Strachey, 1953–1974).

In 1909, Freud accepted G. Stanley Hall's invitation to speak at Clark University. Gay (1988) observed that prior to his American lectures, psychoanalysts "represented a small, embattled minority in the psychiatric profession; Freud's ideas still remained the property of the few, and a scandal to most" (p. 206). The Clark visit enfranchised psychoanalysis in America, especially in the psychiatric community, and helped turn psychoanalysis into an international movement (see Burnham, 2013). The success of the American visit prompted Freud to regard the Clark University ceremony as the "first official

The 1909 Conference at Clark University played host to some of psychology's most influential pioneers. In the front row, Clark's president G. Stanley Hall (center, hat in hand) stands next to Sigmund Freud (hat and cane); Carl Jung stands to the right of Freud. E. B. Titchener stands in the front row, second from the left. To his right is William James (holding hat and coat) and J. M. Cattell appears behind and to the right of James.

recognition of our endeavors" (Jones, 1955, p. 57). William James was one of many luminaries who attended Freud's five lectures. The two men later met for a walk but were interrupted when James experienced pain from the aggravated heart condition that would claim his life nearly a year later. Inspired by James's stoicism, Freud (1924/1959a) later wrote, "I have always wished that I might be as fearless as he was in the face of approaching death" (p. 52); Freud would have the chance to find out.

Freud's biographers paint the picture of a brilliant thinker with a complex personality (Gelfand & Kerr, 1992). On one hand, he could appear shy almost to the point of lacking confidence, but the timidity was often only an appearance. Freud experienced brief periods of depression but could also be joyful, enthusiastic, or even jubilant. His creativity was often inconsistent as he suffered through periods when he seemed incapable of productive work. Such times were typically eclipsed by bursts of creative industry.

Freud had a strong devotion to his family. Although he worked unusually long hours, he nevertheless found time for Martha and their five children. His tastes in music were narrow,

but he had a great appreciation for art, especially sculpture. Besides cigars, his major indulgence was a collection of antiquities (mostly sculptures of ancient figures) that guarded his desk like battle-hardened sentries.

As with countless Jewish scholars, Freud's life and work faced upheaval with the rise of Adolf Hitler, and this upheaval for Freud and others in the growing psychoanalytic tradition had profound effects on the emergence of psychoanalysis (Gitre, 2011). On May 10, 1933, the Nazis burned Freud's books along with the works of other intellectuals in numerous public squares (Gay, 1988). After hearing news about the Nazi bonfire, Freud responded with characteristic gallows humor: "What progress we are making. In the Middle Ages they would have burnt me; nowadays they are content with burning my books" (Jones, 1957, p. 182). Tragically, the Holocaust would reveal that the Nazis conspired to destroy more than books.

In 1938, the Nazis invaded Austria. One day, a gang of Nazi authorities invaded Freud's home. His youngest daughter, Anna, escorted them to the family safe and opened it. The men took $840 (almost $14,000 in today's economy).

"Freud ruefully commented on hearing of it later that *he* had never been paid so much for a single visit" (Jones, 1957, p. 219). At first defiant, Freud finally agreed to leave Vienna at the urging of friends.

Stricken with cancer of the jaw, his last months were spent in exile in London. His affiliation with B'nai B'rith, as well as his theories, made him a prime target for Nazi hostilities. Had Freud been a gentile, perhaps his theory would have fared no better with Nazi ideology. Totalitarians such as Stalin and Hitler do not like to believe their intellectual constructions might have uncontrollable and unconscious psychological origins.

Freud's time in London was seldom pleasant. The shrill cry of air raid sirens announced night after night of Nazi assaults on the city. During much of it, he remained in bed, struggling to fight cancer. Despondent and in poor health, Freud convinced his friend and physician, Max Schur, to administer three centigrams of morphine on September 21, 1939 (Gay, 1988). Schur repeated the injection twice more the following day. After the final and fatal dose of morphine, Freud lapsed into a coma. He died on September 23 as a result of physician-assisted suicide.

General Characteristics of Freud's Thought

Though Sigmund Freud's psychology evolved over time, several philosophical assumptions guided his work. We'll review six defining characteristics of his theory and then consider details of his system.

DETERMINISM Freud was an unapologetic determinist. He argued for a methodology that assumes natural causes for all mental events (MacMillan, 1991). Gay (1988) wrote, "It is a crucial point in Freud's theory that there are no accidents in the universe of the mind" (p. 119). Sulloway (1979) noted that "Freud's entire life's work in science was characterized by an abiding faith in the notion that all vital phenomena, including psychical ones, are rigidly and lawfully

determined by the principle of cause and effect" (p. 94). Other scholars (Brown, 1964, p. 3; Jones, 1953, p. 304; Wisdom, 1943) have emphasized Freud's strong commitment to determinism. As we will see later, however, the issue of freedom surfaced in Freud's work.

BELIEF IN THE CONTINUITY OF THE ANIMAL KINGDOM In his autobiographical study, Freud (1924/1959a) basked in Darwinian theory because it suggested that knowledge of natural processes enhances our understanding of the world. In an open letter to Albert Einstein on the subject of war, Freud (1932/1964a) insisted that humans are not excluded from the animal kingdom. According to Jones (1953), Freud subscribed to the evolutionary position that "no spirits, essences, or entelechies, no superior plans or ultimate purposes are at work. The physical energies alone cause effects—somehow" (p. 42). Freud believed a naturalistic study of human nature offered distinct advantages.

ROLE OF UNCONSCIOUS INFLUENCES Freud's belief in the unconscious is a defining feature of his psychology. He believed that irrational unconscious motives influence rational conscious processes. It's a troubling idea that challenges our cherished belief in human rationality. Even more disturbing, he insisted that unconscious forces can sometimes marshal the authority to dominate the conscious mind. When this happens, according to Freud (1917/1955), "the ego is not master in its own house" (p. 143). Nevertheless, he believed human beings can escape the bondage of unconscious influences. As we will see later, Freud's goal of psychoanalysis returns the ego to "its mastery over lost provinces of. . .mental life" (Freud, 1938/1964b, p. 173).

DEVELOPMENTAL EMPHASIS Classic psychoanalytic theory stressed the importance of development and growth. Freud understood that needs and abilities vary as a function of age. According to his theory, early childhood events color later adjustment. At the same time, the child must negotiate critical developmental periods if she or he hopes to enjoy later psychological health and well-being.

EMPHASIS ON MOTIVATION   We often identify major systems of psychology with a preferred area of study. For example, we associate structuralism with the study of the senses and behaviorism with learning. In Freudian psychology, the study of human motivation is the privileged content area. What motivates us to do the things we do? Freud hoped to discover the answer. His discussion of patients and their clinical dilemmas are couched in the language of motivation. He did not deny the crucial roles that learning, perception, and social influence play in our lives, but clearly his emphasis was on motivation.

APPLIED PSYCHOLOGY   Freud's theoretical interests ran deep, but he hungered for a psychology that could speak to the daily problems of life. He dedicated a great deal of intellectual energy to problems of intervention and treatment. This applied emphasis is reflected in the term *psychoanalysis* because it refers simultaneously to a psychotherapy and a system of psychology.

FREUD'S SYSTEM OF PSYCHOLOGY

Psychoanalytic theory and practice evolved over the forty-three years of Freud's professional career. At first, he hoped to advance a psychology anchored in neurology and physiology, a psychology that would prove worthy as a natural science (Connors, 2000). Freud (1895/1950) expressed his early ambitions in a paper titled "Project for a Scientific Psychology." He soon realized it was premature to establish rigorous connections between physiology and the world of experience. After much debate, he abandoned his cherished project. Afterward, Freud showed some distrust of experimental attempts to validate his clinical model (Rosenzweig, 1997).

On numerous occasions, Freud pursued false leads that forced him to backtrack and start over. In terms of development, psychoanalysis did not travel a smooth linear progression of ideas. As we explore Freud's system, we'll begin with

his mature thought because it opens the broadest vista. We'll then work back to earlier ideas to fill in details of his psychology.

Life's Major Goal and Its Inevitable Frustration

In his book *Civilization and Its Discontents*, Freud (1930/1961a) outlined his belief that the **pleasure principle** dominates human nature. From the beginning of life, we seek pleasure and try to avoid pain. We seek pleasure by satisfying basic needs such as hunger and sexuality, but the world doesn't always cooperate with our hedonistic desires. Even our body betrays our best efforts to enjoy sustained pleasure. Freud observed that we know pleasure only through contrast, but we have a constitutional incapacity to experience contrast for sustained periods. Let's say you're shivering from a winter's chill, so you take a hot bath. You will experience pleasure as you submerge your body in the water's warmth, but such gratification is short-lived. The constancy of the bath would itself grow aversive if we remain in it too long. Freud (1930/1961a) reminded his readers of Goethe's warning that "nothing is harder to bear than a succession of fair days" (p. 76). In addition to constitutional constraints on happiness, Freud outlined three sources of suffering that oppose the pleasure we so highly prize.

The first source of suffering is our own body. As we age, it fails more and more to satisfy our appetite for pleasure. Although resilient, the body is doomed to deterioration, sending relentless warnings of its frailty and inevitable demise. The outer world constitutes the second source of suffering. Consider the threats it poses: earthquakes, flash floods, tornados, drought, avalanches, landslides, hurricanes, wildfires, famine, and bacterial and viral invasions. Our world rages against us with unrelenting insults. Even the grandest surroundings are beset with natural disasters that compromise happiness, replacing it with misery.

Freud saves the greatest source of suffering for last. Any idea what it is? Think about where you find the most anguish in your life. For Freud, the answer is simple: other people. As we live out our lives, other people bring chaos and pain and unhappiness to us. The sources of social suffering are great, arriving in the form of war, rape, theft, assault, prejudice, child and spousal abuse, daily insensitivities and hostilities, dishonesty, and authoritarian structures and attitudes. Given all the sources of unhappiness, Freud (1930/1961a) wondered if it was never intended that human beings should be happy.

So how do we cope with our foiled quest for pleasure? Freud suggested remedial actions that seek to preserve gratification (although most are flawed and temporary in their effects). One method is to withdraw from the world, savoring whatever satisfaction can be found in self-imposed isolation. Another approach—highly prized because it produces a small portion of happiness and independence from the world—is the method of intoxication. Despite his background with cocaine, Freud was not impressed with artificial intoxicants because they blur our sense of reality and require energy that could have been put to better use. Unafraid of controversy, Freud compared religion to intoxication, arguing that both involve an escape from reality. In his view, religion places us in a state of mental infantilism that depreciates the value of this world while promising the illusion of a better world to come.

The word *illusion* in Freud's writings does not refer to something that is false by definition. Freud (1927/1961c) noted, "An illusion is not the same thing as an error; nor is it necessarily an error" (p. 30). Rather, an illusion is a belief motivated by a powerful wish that is divorced from normal realistic expectations. Freud referred to alchemists who tried to transmutate base metals into gold. The motivation for wealth was a possible wishful underpinning for the beliefs that such a transmutation was possible. Perhaps such transmutation is possible, but it is doubtful. Freud believed that many religious beliefs are marked by blatantly obvious, but unrealistic wishes regarding the structure of reality and the fantastic acquisitions one might enjoy in an afterlife. He would find that it is no accident that many of the most cherished projected acquirements and fantasies

concerning an afterlife (wealth, leisure, beauty, and unimaginable sustained pleasures) are the very things we long for, but do not possess in this life. Neither would it be an accident that those who had sacrificed the most in this life would be the recipients of the greatest rewards. Pervasive wishes for justice and compensation in most belief systems are almost impossible to ignore. Freud's major critique of religion is outlined in his book *The Future of an Illusion* (1927/1961c).

We can create other methods for coping with the world. Freud included defenses such as loving and being loved, enjoyment of works of art, and the flight into mental illness. According to Freud, hard work and science offer the most admirable defense against the sources of suffering. Through both, we can make lasting contributions for the good of others (although Freud added that work is seldom valued by the masses).

Freud acknowledged that all strategies for attaining happiness and defending against suffering are incomplete. We are fighting a losing battle because the demands of the pleasure principle cannot be fulfilled. He believed that different alternatives must be judged in an equation sensitive to short-term and long-term interests and to individual and social interests. Difficulties, complexities, and ambiguities in the pursuit of happiness confront every person. Freud's views on the pleasure principle and its vicissitudes provide a backdrop for understanding human personality.

The Structure of Personality

Freud conceptualized the structure of human personality in terms of three interrelated systems called the *id*, *ego*, and *superego* (meaning, respectively, the *it*, *I*, and *over-I*). The three personality agents are embroiled in frequent battle, delivering conflict that we must conquer if we hope to adapt to the world. Our psychological adjustment depends on harmony among the three systems. If any of the three gains excessive control, severe consequences will follow. The three agencies offer differing strategies for coping with threats against the pleasure principle. Although Freud viewed the id, ego, and superego as hypothetical systems of personality, he often spoke of them as if they were real entities.

THE ID   In the beginning there is the **id**. It emerges as the first component of personality. Primitive and feral, it is driven by powerful biological needs necessary for physical survival. The needs of the id are common to all animal species and seek expression in the most biologically efficient manner. Society can claim no permanent hold on the id, but customs, morality, values, conventions, and ethics restrain it. Impulsively and reflexively, it is directed toward immediate gratification. According to Freud, the id operates on the pleasure principle.

The id is represented in impulsive and reflexive activity, but it also finds expression in **primary processes**, images, or memories of objects that satisfy needs. Let's say a person dreams about a sexual encounter. If the dream appears rich in imagery, then Freud would say it embodies primary processes. Such processes present themselves without the embellishment of polite social conventions and norms.

Freud employed the term *libido* to refer to the psychic energy that fuels our pursuit of need gratification. In our hunt for pleasure, libidinal energy is often directed toward beloved or desired objects in the world (*object libido*). However, the libido may attach itself to the ego. When this happens, an intense self-love called narcissism replaces object love.

THE EGO   The **ego** is the *I* or *me* of the personality (taken from the Latin first-person singular pronoun of *I*, *ego* is used in English translations for Freud's German term *Das Ich*). The ego is the center of organization and integration. Whereas the id is tied to the pleasure principle, the ego operates on the **reality principle**. The ego must serve as a mediator, balancing the demands of the id with the demands of social convention. Caught between such powerful forces, it learns to appropriate, compromise, substitute, and delay. The ego makes use of the **secondary process**, devising strategies through which the id's primary process can be satisfied in a socially acceptable

manner. Such techniques protect the individual and the social order by finding acceptable channels for the demands of the id. Often at odds, the demands of the id and society impose remarkable strain on the ego. To survive such aggressive and continuous conflict, it must be robust and stable. But this is not the complete story. In time, the ego must contend with still another force.

THE SUPEREGO   Every bit as irrational as the id, the **superego** consists of internalized social norms, ideals, and standards that are not grounded in reality. Rather than seeking pleasure, the superego is a kind of conscience with an inhibitory function. Over and above this, it pushes the ego to achieve higher values embraced by society. No more realistic than the id, the superego is an intolerant taskmaster, driving the ego to reach impossible standards of perfection.

Like Plato, Freud used the example of a charioteer struggling to reign in powerful steeds. Freud was consumed with documenting the conflicts among the id, ego, and superego. All three serve important roles and each must find legitimate and acceptable expression. The id represents dimensions of biological life that cannot be ignored. On the other hand, we must inhibit primal desires if we are to live with other people. If the id dominates the ego, antisocial behavior results and society must take action to correct such behavior. Likewise, an aggressive superego may block the expression of basic biological needs. Freud believed the repression of biological drives results in emotional difficulties common to civilized societies. (We'll return to this topic later.) According to Freud, the ego must have sufficient strength to deal with the complex and sometimes capricious demands of the external world while permitting the compromised expression of both id and superego. He believed the volatile interplay among the id, ego, and superego had far-reaching consequences for the mental health of his patients.

Motivation and Unconscious Processes

Orgel (1990) tells us that "the core idea of psychoanalysis begins with the assumption that in every human being there is an unconscious mind" (p. 1). Freud's early experiences with hypnosis had telling effects on his theoretical development. Before the July 1889 Congress on Hypnotism in Paris, Freud visited the clinic of Hippolyte Bernheim (1840–1919), a rival of Charcot. In a typical demonstration, Bernheim hypnotized patients and gave suggestions to be carried out after awakening from the trance. For example, a patient was instructed that the next time Bernheim and his assistants entered the room, the patient would open the physician's umbrella (conveniently placed in the corner) and hold it over Bernheim's head. The patient was brought out of hypnosis. When Bernheim and the assistants returned to the room, the patient greeted them and then opened the umbrella and hoisted it above the physician's head.

After the posthypnotic suggestion was carried out, Bernheim asked the patient why he had opened the umbrella. Embarrassed patients usually offered rationalizations. For example, a given patient might claim the weather forecast had called for rain and he or she needed to inspect the umbrella to make certain it didn't leak. In truth, patients couldn't account for their behavior because they could not consciously recall what had transpired during the hypnotic trance.

Commenting on such demonstrations, Freud said he "received the profoundest impression of the possibility that there could be powerful mental processes which nevertheless remained hidden from the consciousness of man" (cited in Jones, 1953, p. 238). The patients did not seem to understand the cause of their strange behavior. Bernheim's hypnosis demonstrations provided a graphic example of how unconscious forces can influence behavior. At the same time, conscious explanations of the behavior were superficial, even illusory, yet patients *believed* their fabricated explanations.

Freud described Bernheim's work with hypnosis as astonishing, and it had a clear influence on the development of psychoanalysis. No longer could consciousness be viewed as autonomous nor could we be certain we understood all that is in the mind. Freud viewed it as a mistake to equate mental processes with consciousness alone. To defend the powerful role of unconscious forces in human life, he drew from hypnotic phenomena, dreams, slips of the tongue, and everyday purposeful forgetting such as the forgetting of a dental appointment. No conscious event was sacrosanct, not even a religious experience. Freud provided an interesting case study to illustrate this latter point.

In the case study titled "A Religious Experience," Freud (1927/1961d) tells of a young physician who shared the story of his religious conversion in the hope of convincing Freud about the existence of God. In writing about his conversion, the doctor described seeing the corpse of an old woman as she was carted to the dissecting room. The sight inspired indignation over the apparent injustice of the woman's death. The man decided then and there to abandon his belief in God. But after reflecting on the matter, he reported that a voice "spoke to my soul that 'I should consider the step I was about to take'" (Freud, 1927/1961d, p. 169). Following that event, he was overcome with fear and remorse. In a dizzying moment of conversion, he accepted the Bible and the teachings of Jesus Christ.

In sharing his experience, the young doctor beseeched Freud to abandon his atheistic beliefs. He sent a polite reply to the doctor's letter and then proceeded to analyze the religious experience. Unable to accept the doctor's story at face value, Freud raised some important questions. Why had the young doctor been so outraged, and why had he renounced God at the sight of an old woman carried away for dissection? The questions are cogent because doctors see far more grisly sights than a corpse destined for autopsy. Why would this particular event initiate a renunciation of belief in God and a subsequent religious conversion? Wouldn't it prove a more stirring sight to witness the senseless death of a child or a young adult's heart attack after undergoing routine surgery?

But Freud reasoned that this particular event was well suited to initiate the doctor's conversion because it aroused unconscious motives. Freud insisted that the sight of the old woman triggered associations of the doctor's mother. In this case, the cruel fate of the mother is the work of God the father. In a cry of outrage, the doctor rebelled against the source of the indignity and injustice. He vowed to deny the existence of God. But why, then, was the doctor so quickly converted? Conversion, in this case, represents obvious fear and surrender to God the father. The reason for the conversion, according to Freud, is found in an unconscious conflict that most human beings experience at an earlier stage in their lives (although this conflict can reemerge symbolically in later life).

Freud believed that Sophocles's ancient Greek tragedy *Oedipus Rex* is characteristic of conflicts that young children experience. He claimed that in the course of development, a child develops a strong emotional attachment to its opposite-sex parent but finds conflict with the same-sex parent. For example, a boy with strong attachment to his mother may feel hostility toward his father because he is a usurper who robs the boy of exclusive rights to the mother. But hostility toward the father is fraught with danger. The boy is powerless while his father is formidable in comparison. How does the child resolve the Oedipus conflict? He might abandon his competitive stance and identify with the father. Identifying with power, even aggressive power, is a well-established psychological phenomenon. According to Freud, the Oedipus conflict may not be resolved in childhood and may rise again to haunt the person in adulthood.

Following Freud's analysis, it comes as little surprise that the young doctor could not sustain his anger at God. God was simply too powerful (the mere suggestion that the doctor should consider the step he was about to take led to fear followed by remorse for his childish rebellion). The doctor achieved resolution through an identification with God the father. Religious conversion was the end result. The case history illustrates Freud's beliefs about the possible weight of unconscious forces on mental processes. Critics, however, have raised understandable questions about Freud's approach to conversion (see Kovel, 1990; Meissner, 1984; Zilboorg, 1961).

The idea that reason serves unconscious motives comes as a blow to human pretensions. It is little wonder that Freud (1917/1955) claims that "the ego does not look favorably upon psychoanalysis and positively refuses to believe in it" (p. 143). Freud envisioned himself as a scientific champion like Copernicus and Darwin, challenging the frailties of human narcissism. With Copernican heliocentricity, our planet no longer occupied the center of the cosmos. With Darwin, we were no longer products of special creation. But Freud believed psychoanalysis posed the greatest challenge to collective human narcissism. Is there any more disturbing thought than the possibility that you are not in control of your own mind? Freud shattered our cherished belief that we are rational creatures with a free will that allows us to shape our destinies.

Though Freud stressed the influence of unconscious forces, his larger vision of human motivation was more complicated. We turn now to an important work titled "Instincts and Their Vicissitudes" (Freud, 1915/1957a). Unfortunately, the English term **instinct** is a poor equivalent for the German term *Trieb* used in Freud's original work. The term *drive*, as used in American psychology, comes closer in meaning to Freud's *Trieb*. Whatever the translation, Freud's concept of *Trieb* is an important key to his theory of motivation.

TRIEB   Freud argued that Trieb originates in a stimulus that persists until it finds satisfaction. He suggested that the term *need* best describes such a stimulus. We have a basic need to reduce powerful drives. Think about times when you've been hungry or dehydrated. How great did it feel when you finally had the chance to eat and drink? You can see how drive reduction can be pleasurable. But how many drives do we have? Freud (1915/1957a) claimed, "There is obviously a wide opportunity here for arbitrary choice" (p. 124). In addition to biological needs like thirst and hunger, drives are behind social actions ranging from play to aggression. Freud acknowledged that psychoanalysis, especially in its earliest development, focused largely on sexual drives.

He proposed four components associated with a drive or Trieb. The first component is the *source*. A drive has its source in a bodily stimulus. For example, mechanical and chemical changes in the body trigger hunger. The need for food will persist until the source is abolished. Satisfaction, however, is temporary because drives operate on a cyclical nature. Maybe you had a big breakfast and you're not hungry now, but you will be tonight.

A second characteristic, known as the *impetus*, refers to the amount of energy associated with the drive. He also used the expression *motor element* to define the term *impetus*. Presumably, the impetus grows as a function of the amount of time that has lapsed since the drive was last experienced. In other words, the impetus will grow more intense the longer you go without food.

The third characteristic of a drive is its *aim*. Satisfaction is the aim of every drive. Freud (1915/1957a) noted that drives always seek satisfaction through altering the stimulation that produced them in the first place. Though satisfaction is the aim, it may be attained in multiple ways. The ego plays a crucial role in achieving the aim by making compromises, temporary delays, substitutions, and so forth.

The final, and most interesting, component of a drive is its *object*. This is where the drive achieves its aim. Freud (1915/1957a) argued that the objects of drives are highly variable. Indeed, the object is the most flexible component of a drive. A single stimulus may serve more than one drive. And a given drive may become attached to a great variety of stimulus objects. A particularly strong attachment to a stimulus is called a **fixation**.

Freud observed that drives undergo many vicissitudes or changes. For example, drives may be sublimated, repressed, or even reversed into their opposites. He claimed that the vicissitudes of drives have far-reaching consequences for human adjustment and health.

Anxiety

In Freud's psychology, interplaying tensions confront every human being. Various components of personality may bring tension. So can competing drives and different sources of pain and suffering. Freud believed such tensions could produce anxiety.

OBJECTIVE ANXIETY   As noted, the outer world can rage against us. Our body is vulnerable to internal and external assaults. And most of all, other people can hurt us. Anxieties arise from such threats to our well-being, a process Freud called **objective anxiety**. It is part of the wear and tear of living in a world that can be hostile and forbidding. This brand of anxiety emerges when objective forces in the world threaten the ego. Its force is a function of the strength of the ego in relation to the perceived power of the threat. In a sense, this is healthy—even adaptive—anxiety. If you're hiking in the wilderness and you encounter a bear, it would seem abnormal if you don't experience at least a little anxiety.

NEUROTIC ANXIETY   Unlike objective anxiety, **neurotic anxiety** emerges from within our own personality and doesn't serve an adaptive or healthy purpose. Neurotic anxiety arises when the id dominates the ego. Because the source of threat arises from within, there is no obvious escape and no identifiable cause. Neurotic anxiety can have a mysterious quality because it can appear, for no apparent reason, at any time or place. Without noticeable cause, the individual may experience impending doom or a panicked feeling. Neurotic anxiety is more common when basic drives are thwarted or bottled up. During Freud's day, Victorian culture imposed rigid prohibitions on sexual expression. But if we stifle powerful drives at every turn, they will find expression in unwanted intrusions into the stream of experience.

MORAL ANXIETY   As a counterpart to neurotic anxiety, **moral anxiety** results when the superego dominates the ego. Here again the source of moral anxiety arises within the personality, so escape seems impossible. The original source of moral anxiety comes from caregivers and the outside world. Over time, the superego incorporates society's norms, values, customs, and prohibitions and is the source of internalized moral authority capable of meting out punishment. Moral anxiety appears when we feel guilt over real—even imagined—violations of internalized values. The more robust the superego, the greater the likelihood a person will experience moral anxiety. Sometimes the most virtuous and exemplary people experience the greatest moral anxiety. On the opposite extreme, some people almost never experience moral anxiety. Such individuals risk placing their own instinctual needs ahead of the rights of others. They may end up isolating themselves from others or, in some cases, being forcibly isolated from others by the criminal justice system. However, people ruled by excessive moral anxiety risk an existence that is colorless, overly controlled, and hollow.

The varieties of anxiety illustrate the importance of personality balance. Individual health and adjustment depends on a flow of channeled energy from the id and the superego. The ego must possess ample strength to deal with the harsh demands of the world and the nagging weight from its internal companions. But what happens when the id and the superego don't play nice? In those circumstances, the ego must resort to desperate measures to seize control over the irrational forces that challenge it.

Defense Mechanisms of the Ego

We mentioned that Freud believed work is the most admirable defense against pain and suffering. The capacity to work with vigor and joy is, in his view, a mark of good health. Freud believed the ego can employ admirable methods to cope with danger and anxiety. But everything may change if the id or superego overwhelms the ego, making it "no longer master in its own house." Moral and neurotic anxieties are hallmarks of neurosis (in psychosis, the id or superego may destroy the ego; Freud had no interest in treating psychotic patients because psychoanalysis cannot resurrect a dead ego). To reclaim the human psyche, the ego may engage in disguises, distortions, falsifications, denials, and misrepresentations of reality.

We'll now consider some of the ego's defensive strategies.

REPRESSION   Freud (1914/1957c) proclaimed that "the theory of repression is the cornerstone on which the whole structure of psychoanalysis rests. It is the most essential part of it" (p. 16). As a defense against irrational unconscious forces, **repression** involves forcing out dangerous or anxiety-provoking thoughts, memories or perceptions from consciousness into the unconscious realm. Gay (1988) compared the repressed unconscious mind to "a maximum-security prison holding antisocial inmates. . .[who are] heavily guarded, but barely kept under control and forever attempting to escape" (p. 128). For most of us, he believed, irrational thoughts and wishes escape from their unconscious lock-up before sneaking out to contaminate our dreams, slips of the tongue, and humor. Freud believed repression is involved to some degree in other defense mechanisms.

Whereas the ego makes use of repression, it may on occasion receive assistance from the superego. *Primal repression* refers to a class of ideas so painful and unthinkable they are barred from consciousness in the first place. Freud included ideas of incest and aggression against the same-sexed parent in this group.

PROJECTION   When personal motives or ideas are unacceptable or when they provoke anxiety, they may be repressed. In turn, the repressed materials may be ascribed to other people or events. **Projection** occurs when we attribute personal faults or weaknesses to other people, objects, or situations. For example, a husband tempted to have an affair with a coworker may instead accuse his wife of having unfaithful fantasies. Aggressive individuals or groups may claim that others are the real aggressors. Or people with repressed voyeuristic curiosities may fret about the moral decay of society and the prevalence of pornography. The ego finds safety in projection because it distances itself from motives and ideas that provoke anxiety. It's not a perfect refuge. A dramatic distortion of reality is the high price the ego pays for such protection.

REGRESSION   If the present proves too harrowing, the ego may find sanctuary in the past. **Regression** involves the retreat to an earlier stage of development, resulting in attitudes and behaviors that defined that period. Regressions may be brief and episodic or, in the face of overwhelming threats, may persist over months and years. Brief or episodic regression may be manifested in dreams or daydreams in which one returns to an earlier, more secure stage in life. Regression may be reflected in activities such as temper tantrums, easy submission to authority, masturbation, the need to be babied during an illness, or taking drugs as an escape from responsibility. The ego feels less accountable while operating in an earlier manner. In severe regression, the ego is removed from adult responsibility and is literally aided and assisted as in childhood.

REACTION FORMATION   In "Instincts and Their Vicissitudes," Freud (1915/1957a) talked about paradoxical situations in which a drive may undergo a reversal into its opposite. Because mental life is marked by polarities, reversals are always a possibility. Love may turn to hate, pleasure to pain, passivity to activity, and so forth. In the **reaction formation**, we encounter a defense in which the ego masks awareness of an anxiety-provoking motive by emphasizing its opposite. For example, a parent who harbors hostility toward a child may instead become overly indulgent and overprotective. A man troubled by latent homosexual fantasies may mask the threat by assaulting a gay man. In reaction formations, we find clear denials of certain motives. Such denials are made more plausible by engaging in activities that oppose the threatening motives. The idea that no one proclaims innocence louder than the guilty is a classic illustration of reaction formation. As with other defense mechanisms, this method can purchase the ego some degree of relief from anxiety, but the antagonistic extremes generate conflict of their own.

OTHER DEFENSES   The ego may practice a host of additional defensive strategies. Some involve less repression than those mentioned and may seem more realistic and adaptive. In **sublimation**, the ego takes a wish or thought that society deems improper and substitutes it with a more acceptable one. Many activities such as work, sporting events, art, and even philanthropic activities may involve a rechanneling of sexual energy into socially acceptable activities. Freud saw sublimation as important to the overall goals of civilization. Another defense, **rationalization**, involves the attempt to "explain away" personal shortcomings by providing logical but false reasons to excuse weaknesses or errors. Still another defense, **identification**, covers weaknesses by emulating significant or impressive role models. A teenager who admires a hip-hop artist may imitate his hero in everything from clothing, emcee style, and rap beats down to his loose-fingered wag while freestyle rapping. If the ego is not adequate in itself, it can at least borrow or steal from an idol. In cases of extreme psychopathology, the distinctions between self and model crumble until the person is lost in delusion, believing he or she is the object of identification.

In his work titled *The Ego and the Id*, Freud (1923/1961b) described the ego as "a poor creature owing service to three masters" (p. 56). Since those masters—the id, the superego, and the external world—are so powerful and uncompromising, the ego must amass a great psychological arsenal of its own. Yet it cannot make the necessary acquisitions without help. It must be nurtured and assisted in a supportive environment. Few psychologists have been as sensitive to the issues of development as Freud.

Stages of Psychosexual Development

Freud believed the quality of adult experience is connected to the quality of childhood experience. He is often accused of advancing a narrow view of psychology based on a narrow view of sexual motivation. Freud argued, however, that it is the common view of sexuality that is narrow. According to the common view, sex is limited to genital contact with a member of the opposite sex. Freud believed that all surfaces of the body, not just the genitals, are erotogenic. Some regions such as the lips are especially erogenous. He tied sexuality to the pleasure principle, viewing the subject in broad terms. Sexuality, for Freud, was not a single physical act. As discussed, he believed that the object is the most flexible characteristic of a drive. We turn now to Freud's stage theory of psychosexual development.

ORAL STAGE In the **oral stage**, a child's mouth offers him or her the initial interactions with the world. Powerful hunger and thirst drives are satisfied through sucking and needs are expressed through crying. In this early stage, the child learns a good deal: The world is either responsive or unresponsive to cries for help, the nursing situation is friendly or cold, and pleasure is derived through food and liquids. A bit later, the child experiments by shoving objects in her or his mouth. Freud assumed that neglect or overindulgence during this stage could produce negative consequences for later development. For example, overindulgence might result in unrealistic optimism whereas neglect might lead to a pessimistic or angry adult. Freud believed that later "oral characters" are based on fixations at early stages. Such fixations result from failures to meet basic needs during critical periods of development.

ANAL STAGE In the second and third years, the **anal stage**, the child finds new gratification in the relief of bowel and bladder tension. But this simple pleasure is fraught with difficulty because the external world imposes strict regulations concerning toilet training. Parent and child may clash during this stage. From the child's perspective, elimination is a source of pleasure; the feces are a curiosity and possibly even perceived as a part of one's self (the kid might wonder, "If my parents love me so much, why are they so eager to dispose of this part of me?"). DeMause (1974) illustrated the historical contempt for this stage with a quote from Martin Luther who protested that children "befoul the corners." DeMause then noted that "the Latin *merda*, excrement, was the source of the French *merdeux*, little child" (p. 39).

Freud's views on the anal stage are grounded in the historical context of toilet training. It is neither a pleasant nor an easy history to understand, especially in our time of disposable diapers, well-ventilated houses, indoor toilets, automatic washing machines, and hot and cold running water. In earlier centuries, proper toilet training was consequential to a well-ordered house. Children were forced to sit for long periods on training chairs, were subjected to enemas and purges, and were often the victims of whippings and beatings for failures to control bowel or bladder movements (see DeMause, 1974).

In this context, Freud was sensitive to the precarious balancing act confronting the small child. The newly discovered pleasures of elimination and the curiosity about feces must be steadied against the controlling demands of the world. Freud believed that this stage held consequences for later personality development. For example, if parents take a lenient and overly indulgent attitude and the child derives joy from releasing his feces, it might create an *anal-expulsive character*. In adulthood, he is prone to be reckless, messy, disorganized, and attracted to filth. Another child might find gratification in retaining her fecal matter. In an act of defiance, she might refuse to release her excrement, leading to traits associated with the *anal-retentive character*. As an adult, she is likely to be stingy, neat, meticulous, precise, and compulsive about rules and regulations.

PHALLIC STAGE From ages three to five, the **phallic stage**, child's interests shift to his or her sex organs and to the sex organs of the parents. In addition, the child begins to identify with the parent of the opposite sex. This identification involves positive sexual feeling of the boy for his mother and of the girl for her father. At the same time, the parent of the same sex is viewed as a threat and evokes hostile and rebellious actions. The affection for the parent of the opposite sex and the hostility toward the parent of the same sex is called the **Oedipus complex**. Freud found inspiration in Sophocles's (c. 470–399 BCE) Greek tragedy about a young man named Oedipus who unwittingly kills his father, Laius, and marries his mother, Jocasta. (Oedipus had been separated from both parents since birth.) After realizing he has murdered Laius, Oedipus blinds himself with Jocasta's brooch as an act of repentance.

As noted, when we discussed religious conversion, desire for the mother leads to anxiety born in a fear of the father. The boy would like to replace his father, but he recognizes that his father holds the threat of awesome retaliation. In Freud's theory, such retaliation includes the threat of castration. The father might castrate the boy, striking at the source of pleasure (in this case the genitals). Freud should not be taken literally with respect to the use of the word castration. Rather he seems to be referring to the sense of the overwhelming power and adequacy of the father to produce feelings of impotence or feelings of emasculation. Fearing the father's retaliatory power, the boy represses his feelings for his mother and then gradually identifies with the father. For the boy, repression and identification help resolve the Oedipal conflict.

According to Freud, this kind of crisis plays out in an entirely different way for girls. He believed that girls do not completely repress their striving for the father, nor do they thoroughly identify with the mother. Instead, the girl transfers her desire for the father to other men, making the father the prototype for her future husband. Freud insisted that the girl becomes envious of the protruding male sex organ and blames her mother for what she considers to be her castrated condition. Freud argued that so-called **penis envy** played an important role in the psychology of women. As with the male, the Oedipal situation (sometimes called the *Electra complex* for women) may never be completely resolved. As you can guess, his views on feminine sexuality remain a controversial facet of his theory (see Roith, 1987). We'll discuss criticisms of this perspective later in the chapter.

LATENCY PERIOD In the aftermath of the phallic stage, the child enters a phase of development in which erotic interest becomes latent or dormant. Signs of sexual interest are not explicit during this **latency period**. From age four or five until the beginning of puberty, children busy themselves with intense physical activity and strong interest in peer groups. Sexual attachments are present but less noticeable than at other periods of development.

GENITAL STAGE The **genital stage** of development begins as the person enters adolescence. Residue from earlier periods may be present, but if development is normal, the individual will forge emotional ties with members of the opposite sex. At this age, the genitals become the focus of sexual energy. During the genital stage, the individual is preoccupied with object choices relating to friends, social institutions, and vocations. The major goal of the genital stage is reproduction and ancillary activities (work, socialization) critical to the propagation of the species.

Psychoanalysis as a Therapeutic Technique

Freud believed that the unconscious mind is a kind of storehouse containing powerful drives along with repressed sentiments going back to childhood. Drives and repressed materials are not revealed in naked meanings but find expression in symbolic, mediated, or disguised forms. The conscious mind has only indirect access to the dangerous materials that reside in the unconscious. Freud posited a **preconscious** containing materials that are readily available to consciousness. Material that is not now in consciousness, but can be recalled with relative ease, is stored in the preconscious area. Freud believed that certain dangerous materials (drives, wishes, repressions) in the unconscious are not readily available to consciousness but may, nonetheless, play a crucial role in psychopathology.

As noted earlier, Freud found evidence for unconscious processes in hypnotic phenomena, slips of the tongue, forgotten appointments, and dreams. In each area, however, unconscious content is disguised. One who harbors hostility toward another person may forget an appointment with that person. Freud believed that dreams are the most important means for expression of unconscious wishes and drives. He argued that dreams have **manifest content** and

latent content. The former refers to the dream as described by the dreamer. It's the censored part of the dream that the ego wants you to remember. The latter refers to the specific way the dream expresses an unconscious wish or drive. The art of dream interpretation is the art of translating manifest content into latent content.

Freud believed that human emotional problems result from a buildup of repressed material. Excessive pressure in the unconscious may show itself in terms of a host of symptoms such as phobias, skin rashes, obsessive or compulsive behaviors, depression, or anxiety. Because repressed materials in the unconscious were thought to be responsible for many emotional problems, it was important to explore the origins of those materials. Freud assumed that the cautious uncovering of repressions might rob them of their energy. Such energy would no longer be available to feed the troublesome psychological symptoms that brought the patient to analysis in the first place.

In his book *An Outline of Psycho-Analysis*, Freud (1938/1964b) contended that a major goal of therapy is to return back to the ego "its mastery over lost provinces of. . .mental life" (p. 173). Freud (1932/1964a) wrote that the goal of psychoanalysis is "to strengthen the ego, to make it more independent of the super-ego, to widen its field of perception and enlarge its organization, so that it can appropriate fresh portions of the id: 'Where id was, there ego shall be'" (p. 80). In other words, the goal of psychoanalysis is to widen consciousness and to liberate the individual from destructive unconscious forces. How, then, was the goal of psychoanalysis to be carried out?

As noted earlier, Freud believed that dreams provide the most important avenue for the expression of unconscious forces. He also believed there was therapeutic value in sharing one's story with another person. In addition, he developed **free association**, the uninhibited verbal expression of whatever is central in consciousness during therapy. For the typical patient, free association is no easy task. It requires trust and a weakening of inhibitions and resistances. One's intimate psychic world is laid bare, leaving a sense of vulnerability.

Most normal conversation is guided by inhibition, convention, and a kind of meta-level awareness of what is appropriate to the situation. In free association, such defenses are suspended. Freud assumed that free association, such as the content of dreams, might provide a vehicle for the expression of unconscious processes. Patients in psychoanalytic therapy were encouraged to assume a comfortable position, often on a couch, and discuss their dreams and/or free associate.

In time, patients build trust in the analyst and share the content of their dreams and free associate. For their part, analysts listen and provide interpretations of dream materials and free associations. Such interpretations are offered with caution and only when patients are ready to confront the dark side of their mind. Freud found that patients often develop emotional attachments to their therapists, and that therapists may develop emotional attachments to their patients. He referred to the former as **transference** and the latter as **countertransference**. In successful therapy, the patient gradually works through the transference and develops an independence from the therapist. A major goal of psychoanalytic training is to teach therapists to learn how to cope with the issues of transference and countertransference.

Sometimes **resistance** slows or even halts the progress of psychoanalysis. There are presumably many symptoms of resistance: sustained inability to free associate; failure to talk about a dream because it is judged to be trivial, irrelevant, or simply humorous; out-of-hand rejection of the analysts' interpretations; or broken appointments. Freud found that resistance was weakened as patients gained trust.

In his brief essay titled "Family Romances," Freud (1908/1959b) remarked that one of the most painful and difficult tasks is to achieve liberation from parents or other significant authority figures. In successful psychoanalytic therapy, the individual is freed not only from the authority of the parents but also from the authority of the analyst. The influences of the id and the superego are also moderated as the ego grows in strength and authority. Ultimately, the goal is that the individual is able to enjoy loving and working and is an effective and contributing member within the human community. The balances necessary for the achievement of such a goal are hard-won because opposing forces from without and from within are powerful and ever-present. Freud's views on the difficulties facing the individual and humankind are set forth in his later works. As noted earlier, psychoanalysis is both a system of psychology and a therapy. We turn now to a consideration of his social psychological views.

Freud's Social Psychology

Although accused of neglecting social issues, Freud did tackle broad societal concerns in later works such as *Civilization and Its Discontents* (1930/1961a). The issue of war shaped his thinking, particularly after World War I and the detainment of one son in a prison camp at the end of the war (Fry, 2009). In 1932, Freud shared an open exchange with Albert Einstein titled *"Warum Krieg?"* ("Why War?"). At the time, Einstein recognized developments in physics that foreshadowed nuclear weapon systems. He was distressed that such weapons would soon be available to a species that had been unable to abolish war as a means of solving its difficulties. As a result, Einstein wrote an open letter to Freud.

Einstein's letter explored the problem of war and speculated about one possible solution. He proposed an international legislative and judicial body with the power to settle disputes among nation states. Einstein insisted that he was personally immune to nationalistic bias, but that underscores a problem with his proposed solution. Only a minority can identify on such a broad basis with the world community of human beings; clearly the Einsteins and Gandhis, of the world are few in number. The identities of great hosts of human beings are bounded by strict national, racial, religious, cultural, or even sexual lines of demarcation that set up rigid in-group and out-group distinctions.

Einstein noted other issues surrounding his solution to the problem of war. Namely, that in almost every nation there is a political minority "indifferent to social considerations and restraints [who] regard warfare, the manufacture and sale of arms, simply as an occasion to advance their personal interests and enlarge their personal authority" (Einstein, 1932/1964, p. 200). He questioned how a minority could work against the interests of the majority, excluding professional soldiers who believe they are working for the highest interest of their culture by choosing the military as their profession. He noted that the press, the churches, and the schools are also, in too many cases, under the control of the minority. Einstein also recognized a problem centering on the fact that some of history's greatest wars have been civil wars. Thus, he turned to Freud for a deeper analysis of the problem of war with its "collective psychosis" marked by a lust for violence, destruction, and hatred.

In a thoughtful reply, Freud agreed on the desirability of a world organization, but like Einstein, he was aware of the problems of instilling the broader base of identity humans need if they are to achieve such an ideal. In his mid-seventies at the time, Freud had witnessed the tribulation of the First World War along with countless examples of national and human interpersonal conflict. He described two antagonistic forces that seize human nature in a struggle for survival. *Eros* is a life-preserving drive that seeks to preserve and unite. *Thanatos* is an internal aggressive force that seeks to destroy or kill (Mills, 2006). Freud viewed both drives as essential and found they seldom work in isolation from each other. For example, he argued that "the instinct of self preservation is certainly of an erotic kind, but it must nevertheless have aggressiveness at its disposal if it is to fulfill its purpose" (Freud, 1932/1964a, p. 209). He believed motivation is always complicated; it is not a simple unidirectional matter. Freud claimed that events that run counter to eros can automatically reinforce opposite destructive instincts.

Unfortunately, civilization imposes constraints on eros. The price of civilization is that erotic gratifications must be delayed, drives must be sublimated, and the range of object choices must be restricted. Civilization becomes a valued acquisition but also a source of frustration that feeds destructive instincts. Certain repressive systems or governments foster despair, hopelessness, and a general devaluing of life. Unfortunately, when repressive systems strangle erotic instincts (including love of others, valuing of nature, and opportunities for expressing of self-actualizing motives), they are likely to trigger destructive thoughts and behaviors. The ensuing destructiveness may be directed at the self or at other people or at the self *and* others. Destructiveness aimed at the self is manifested in individual suicides or in collective suicides as in the Heaven's Gate group led by Marshall Applewhite, who convinced thirty-eight followers to commit suicide while the Hale-Bopp comet blazed across the skies in 1997. Destruction aimed at others is manifested in wars and massacres, including blind attacks or drive-by shootings of total strangers. Some of the most bizarre examples of the destructiveness that Freud identifies are marked by a general anger and devaluation of life when the self *and* others are targets as in the case of suicide bombers or in the all-too-common media accounts of murder–suicides.

Freud offers a complicated answer to Einstein's question. He agreed that an international government is a step in the right direction but pointed to conflicts of interest both within and between organizations. Freud argued that it is useless to attempt to rid ourselves of aggression because it is vital to our biological nature. However, social structures can be established to curb destructive instincts while permitting the expression of erotic instincts within reasonable constraints. Freud believed arbitrary religious and political authorities encroach on freedom of thought and work against world peace. In the end, he called for social structures sensitive to the intricacies of human nature that will not shut the door on reasonable interests.

Freud saw value in broadening identification by emphasizing common bonds and shared interests. He quoted with approval the golden rule, "Thou shalt love thy neighbor as thyself." Freud realized the difficulties in achieving such an ideal love and he doubted that this ideal could be realized through a simple command.

He believed, however, that we might achieve the ideal through the hard work of reason, education, and emotional and intellectual insight.

Appreciative Overview

Freud leaves us with a complicated legacy. Psychoanalysis opened intellectual vistas with far-reaching consequences for psychology and other disciplines. The appreciative commentary that follows reflects the expanded scope that Freud offered psychology. What then were his major contributions?

1. *Emphasis on development.* Freud was one of the first to recognize the importance of childhood and the special needs associated with stages of human development. It makes little difference if his stage theory does not hold up. His larger developmental perspective has had an enduring influence.

2. *Unconscious processes.* Though many do not value Freud's model of the unconscious, it has been a continuing influence in psychology along with repression and the ego defense mechanisms.

3. *Focus on motivation.* Freud was not the only psychologist to emphasize motivation, but he contributed to this content area so that it soon took its place alongside sensation, perception, and learning as a principle topic of inquiry.

4. *Psychotherapy.* Though we can find much to criticize in Freud's therapy, he nevertheless contributed to the notion that human problems originate in everyday life. Proper therapy for such problems is not simply medical but psychological. This idea ran counter to medical thought in Freud's Vienna, so it is little wonder he was not popular with his contemporaries. Still, many of his insights endured and now occupy a respected and undisputed place in clinical texts and reference sources.

5. *Interdisciplinary contributions.* As noted, Freud's thought had a widespread impact in diverse fields such as history, philosophy, religion, literature, and medicine. Although controversial, psychoanalysis forced psychology to be a less insular discipline. This in itself is a worthy achievement.

Critical Overview

A system as wide-ranging as psychoanalysis is bound to generate criticism, and reaction has ranged from thoughtful disapproval to sarcasm and mocking. We'll outline some of the better-known criticisms.

1. *Tendency to overgeneralize.* Freud often drew sweeping conclusions based on simple observation. Our earlier discussion of a young doctor's religious conversion is a case in point. If you wanted to draw conclusions about the psychology of conversion, wouldn't it make more sense to study many cases? Even then, generalizations should be cautious and couched in language that encourages experimental work. This last point leads to the next criticism.

2. *Empirical verification.* Despite experimental studies designed to test Freud's predictions, psychoanalysis does not lend itself to experimental verification. Part of the problem is that many of the terms of the theory (e.g., *libido, eros, primary process*) are not easily operationalized.

3. *Closedness.* Freud had an almost unmatched zeal in discovering new truths about the workings of the mental world. In time, however, he became dogmatic about his theory (Barratt, 2013; Rudnytsky, 2008). Freud's followers and associates were expected to be disciples dedicated to extending his theory. The range of acceptable ideas was truncated and any person who deviated too far from core concepts was viewed as disloyal. Unfortunately, loyalty and orthodoxy came to define classical psychoanalysis as an increasingly closed system.

4. *Sexual emphasis.* Freud is accused of advancing a monistic theory where all behavior is derived from a single motivation—namely, sex. This criticism calls for greater scrutiny. Freud did champion the sex motive, but his view of such motivation was broader than many critics acknowledge, and he explicitly recognized the existence of many drives.

5. *Psychoanalytic treatment.* Psychoanalysis has been criticized on several grounds. One harsh criticism suggests that practitioners are a closed club isolated from the meaningful correctives of critical and scientific research (see Masson, 1991). Treatment has also been criticized because it is expensive and time-consuming. Beyond its prohibitive cost, critics have questioned whether it accomplishes more than other therapies.

6. *Theory of female sexuality.* Freud's concept of penis envy and his views on female sexual conflict have faced withering criticism (see Horney, 1967; Sprengnether, 1990). Scholarly work has attempted to clarify the context of Freud's views (see Roith, 1987). Nevertheless, his notion that women are "incomplete men" must now be regarded as an error driven more by theory than sensitivity to the complexity of human sexuality. Freud did welcome women into the psychoanalytic movement. Here as in other institutions, however, they did not enjoy equality (see Roith, 1987, chap. 3; Wolberg, 1989). Perhaps most telling is Freud's confession that a baffling mystery for him is what motivates a woman. Gay (1988) reports that Freud "had, he thought, sincerely tried to understand the 'sexual life of the adult woman,' but it continued to intrigue and puzzle him. It was something of 'a *dark continent*'" (p. 501).

Future Perspectives

At some level, perhaps, psychology will never fully escape Freud's vision. As noted, many psychoanalytic journals continue to explore almost every facet of classical psychoanalysis along with modern reinterpretations of Freud's continually relevant work (Reppen, 2006). The larger Freudian vision continues to evolve and is by no means dead. Recent work (Gabbard, Litowitz, & William, 2012; Wallerstein, 1988/2006) celebrates the transition of psychoanalysis from its early narrow orthodoxy into an increasingly viable pluralistic discipline that welcomes conceptual and therapeutic innovations. Rudnytsky (2011) speaks of rescuing psychoanalysis from Freud as manifested by increasing diversity while retaining efforts to synthesize science and art.

Appraisals of psychoanalysis will increasingly need to be informed by careful assessments of recent developments.

NEOANALYTIC PSYCHOLOGIES

As with behaviorism, psychoanalysis became a house divided. Many who were influenced by Freud disagreed with his emphasis on sexuality. Deep divisions emerged over a host of topics, such as the nature of unconscious processes, the autonomy of the ego, the stages of development, and the nature of therapy.

ALFRED ADLER

In 1902, **Alfred Adler (1870–1937)** was welcomed into Sigmund Freud's Wednesday Psychological Society. Adler believed the discussion group would offer a broad intellectual agenda with open debate on psychiatric issues. He was mistaken. In time, Adler discovered that Freud held strong views and seldom tolerated contrasting opinions. Although respectful of each other at first, tensions between Adler and Freud deepened over the years. An irritated Freud interpreted the young man's challenges as an affront and a "hostile competition" (Gay, 1988, p. 224). In 1911, Adler escaped Freud's shadow to develop an alternative system of thought known as **individual psychology**. He was an original thinker who should not be remembered as a disloyal disciple (Ansbacher, 1994).

Adler was born near Vienna on February 7, 1870. His early years were marked by poor health aggravated by rickets. Adler graduated with an M.D. from the University of Vienna in 1895. After serving in the military during World War I, he opened Vienna's first child-guidance clinic. In 1926, he moved to the United States and joined the faculty at Columbia University and, later, the Long Island College of Medicine. Adler died after a heart attack on May 28, 1937, while on a lecture tour in Scotland. According to Gay (1988), "Freud was gratified to learn that he had outlived Alfred Adler. . . . He had hated Adler for

more than a quarter century, and Adler had hated him for just as long, and as vocally" (p. 615).

Adler's better-known books are *The Practice and Theory of Individual Psychology* (1964b), *Understanding Human Nature* (1957), and *Social Interest: A Challenge to Mankind* (1938). Ansbacher and Ansbacher (1956) provided an important secondary source titled *The Individual Psychology of Alfred Adler*. Scholarly work on Adlerian psychology is published in *Individual Psychology: The Journal of Adlerian Theory, Research and Practice*. A recent anthology titled *Alfred Adler Revisited* provides helpful overviews of Adler's positions on a variety of theoretical and practical issues (see Carlson & Maniacci, 2012). Additional scholarly journals and professional organizations promote the Adlerian viewpoint, including the North American Society of Adlerian Psychology.

Adler's System of Psychology

Adler's individual psychology is a study in contrast with Freud's classic psychoanalytic theory. In a paper devoted to these differences, Adler (1931/1964a) argued that "the Freudian view is that man, by nature [is] bad" (p. 210). By contrast, Adler insisted that we have a natural capacity to identify with the goals of society to achieve a common good. This **social interest** reflects a real concern for people and society. He also quarreled with Freud's use of pleasure as a regulative principle. According to Adler, happiness is a more important goal than pleasure, but more important yet is a striving for totality, unity, or wholeness. Another important difference is that Adler emphasized the centrality of goal setting in human life. His theory is teleological, whereas Freud's theory emphasized material, efficient, and formal causes. And, unlike Freud, Adler believed that human nature is logical, regardless of however bizarre or psychotic it may appear (Grey, 1998).

On the methodological side, Adler argued for a broader study of psychological phenomena than did Freud. Adler encouraged exploring old memories, but balanced this by studying plans or anticipations about the future. He also studied body language as manifested in postures and movements. He examined the role of birth order on personality. He studied dreams, interpreting them as forward-looking signs rather than pointing backward as in psychoanalysis.

His psychology contrasts with Freud's in additional ways. Adler's (1964a) article "The Differences between Individual Psychology and Psychoanalysis" provides a helpful overview on their differences concerning the Oedipus complex, the death wish, and dream interpretation among other issues. We turn now to key concepts in Adler's system.

GOALS AND THE STYLE OF LIFE   In his book *The Practice and Theory of Individual Psychology*, Adler (1964b) advances the proposition that "every psychic phenomenon, if it is to give us any understanding of a person, can be grasped and understood only if regarded as a preparation for some goal" (p. 4). Adler believed that psychological functions such as feeling and thinking are impossible unless they occur in the context of goals. In his radical stance on causality, he claimed that chaos would mark the psychological world if it resulted only from antecedent causes. In his view, an integration of psychological processes meant that past, present, and future interests are brought together. Without future considerations, ongoing present activities—considered only as results of material and efficient causes—are meaningless.

Adler believed our experiences and behaviors must be understood in terms of our goals. He used the expression **fictional final goals** to describe how our future plans aren't always grounded in reality. For example, a student may believe she has potential to become a great mathematician, even after struggling through an elementary algebra course. She may start living and behaving with the goal of becoming a great mathematician. Stone (2011) elaborates on potential self-deceptive characteristics of some fictional goals. Adler used the term **style of life** to refer to all the unique behaviors that characterize personality and that move us in the direction of specific goals. Adler's psychology emphasizes processes, strategies, and movements rather than structures. A style of life includes strategies, plans, short-term and long-term projects, designs, and behaviors that are in the service of life's goals. For Adler, a person who does not have social interest is living a "mistaken style of life" or a "life lie."

INFERIORITY AS A SOURCE OF MOTIVATION
In his book *The Science of Living* Adler (1929) suggested that "all persons feel inadequate in certain situations" (p. 60). This is especially true in childhood when we may feel inadequate or inferior in many situations. We may perceive a weakness in specific organs or functions that set the stage for special difficulties later on. Adler believed that the character and intensity of *organ inferiority* and other types of insecurities are keys to understanding personality. He described the **inferiority complex** as an intense or abnormal feeling of inferiority. Adler (1929) pointed out that an inferiority complex may shroud a complicated set of motives such as feelings of superiority (p. 79). In the same manner, people who act superior may be masking deep-seated feelings of inferiority with their *superiority complex.*

Feelings of inferiority are normal and widespread, setting the stage for important life goals as we struggle to overcome our perceived inferiorities (Overholser, 2010). Adler argued that many of our thoughts and activities are guided by compensation and overcompensation. With **compensation**, we overcome specific inferiorities by developing strengths in alternative areas. For example, a debilitating disease confined Stephen W. Hawking (b. 1942) to a lifetime in a wheelchair, but it did not prevent him from becoming an innovative thinker in theoretical astrophysics and cosmology. Sometimes there are *compensation ideals* in the form of other people such as Stephen Hawking who embody the traits we most desire. Such ideals become models, although extreme identity with such models is a form of pathology. **Overcompensation**, in Adler's view, involves attempts to develop strength in an area beset with difficulties. Despite a sickly childhood, the American president Theodore

Roosevelt (1858–1919) became the embodiment of William James's concept of the strenuous life. (Roosevelt had taken a class with James at Harvard.) Likewise, Demosthenes (384–322 BCE) overcame a speech impediment to become one of the great orators of antiquity. Finally, James Earl Jones (b. 1931) conquered childhood stuttering before honing his talent as an actor in movies and theater. His rich and booming baritone gave life to Darth Vader, making Jones one of the most recognizable voices in the world.

BIRTH ORDER In your family, are you the oldest child? The youngest? Or somewhere in the middle? Does it make a difference in personality development? Adler believed the family constellation played a critical role in forging personality. He believed that birth order influences the way we see our world and how we respond to it.

A first child enjoys a favored status in the family constellation until the fateful arrival of another sibling. Adler believed that the change can produce devastating or salutary consequences. First children can develop a caring attitude or can have difficulty overcoming the shock of being displaced. No longer the center of attention, the first-born child may view the new arrival as a usurper. In adulthood, they might exhibit a rigid and authoritarian personality. (Adler noted, with some satisfaction, that Sigmund Freud was a first-born child.) The second child may develop a competitive style while attempting to keep up with the older sister or brother. Not as pampered as his or her older sibling, the middle-born child cultivates a healthy sense of competition and has the best chance at positive development. (We'll let you decide if it was a coincidence that Adler was a middle child.) The youngest child grows up thinking that older siblings have more freedom and superior status in the family. This kid is typically more spoiled and protected than the other children. That's not a good thing. The youngest child may grow up believing she or he cannot conquer the world's demands. Despite apparent biases in his theory, Adler's birth-order model remains one of his most important contributions (Ekstein & Kaufman, 2012) and has had a continuing influence on research (see Ernst & Angst, 1983; Grey, 1998).

LIFE'S MAJOR PROBLEMS Adler argued that most human problems center around issues of work, interaction with others, and sexual intimacy. He viewed it as a mark of health when we pursue meaningful work-related goals. Adler also argued that life's problems must be understood in terms of social context and societal well-being (Ferguson, 2010). The prejudices, injustices, and preferences encountered in almost every society have devastating consequences for individual development. Adler thought all human beings strive for superiority in certain arenas both to overcome their own weaknesses and to overcome social barriers and injustices. He saw the capacity for sexual intimacy as a mark of one's larger relationship with humankind. Sexual intimacy may have a selfish and abusive component, or it may reflect social interest in true caring about the happiness and welfare of another person. A primary task of psychology, according to Adler, is to foster the development of social interest (Ansbacher, 1997). These facets of Adler's ideas continue to influence psychological practice (Carlson et al., 2006).

CARL GUSTAV JUNG

Though **Carl Gustav Jung (1875–1961)** was associated with Freud's psychoanalytic movement from 1907 to 1913, it is a mistake to view Jung as a disciple or as a defector. Many ideas in Jung's psychology were formulated before he met Freud. Despite some theoretical similarities between the two psychologies, Jung's system is far from derivative.

Jung was born in Keswil, Switzerland, on July 26, 1875. Later, the Jung family moved near Basel, where Jung received his formal education. In 1895, he enrolled at the University of Basel and received his medical degree five years later (at that time, five years from the date of initial enrollment in the university was normal for attaining the M.D.). After receiving the medical degree, Jung accepted an appointment at a psychiatric hospital in Zürich, where he studied with Eugen Bleuler (1857–1940), one of the premier authorities in psychiatry (Hayman, 2001). After two years with Bleuler, Jung took a brief leave to study with Pierre Janet (1859–1947) in Paris.

On his return to Zürich, Jung initiated experiments using Galton's word association tests. He put a spin on Francis Galton's concept, claiming that the speed and content of associations revealed pent-up unconscious dynamics. Let's say you administer the test, asking a male patient to offer an immediate response to your stimulus word. When you say "up," he says "down." When you say "far," he says "near." When you say "father," he says "murder." As embarrassment washes across his face, the man tries to convince you he meant to say "mother," not "murder." Jung believed that such responses, or failures to respond, may be diagnostic of conflict.

Jung proposed that word association could be used as a lie detection device, an idea that brought him into conflict with the Gestalt psychologist Max Wertheimer who had conducted similar forensic work (see Wertheimer, King, Peckler, Raney, & Schaef, 1992). Jung's work with the word association test was of interest to Freud, and Freud's classic *Interpretation of Dreams* had been of interest to Jung.

In 1907, Jung traveled to Vienna after a friendly exchange of letters with Freud. Their first meeting was legendary, lasting something like a marathon thirteen hours. Freud hoped to find a "crown prince of psychoanalysis" who would extend the range and application of his developing system of thought. Additionally, unlike Freud and other central figures of psychoanalysis, Jung identified with Protestant Christianity rather than Judaism. Like Adler, Jung was an original thinker and not well suited to discipleship. The friendly side of their relationship lasted only about five years. By 1912, strong theoretical differences had surfaced. In part, tensions developed when Jung shared his interest in mystical phenomena.

Since childhood, Jung believed he had competing sides to his personality. His "Number One" personality, as he called it, was grounded in logic and science. This side inspired Jung to become a man of science and the founder of a famous school of psychotherapy. His "Number Two" personality, by contrast, was drawn to mysticism and pagan spirituality. Like Jung's father, Sigmund Freud adored the Number One personality, but had little use for Number Two.

At first, Freud feigned interest in Jung's mysticism. In a 1909 letter, Freud wrote that he looked "forward to hearing more about your investigations of the spook-complex, my interest being the interest one has in a lovely delusion which one does not share oneself" (cited in Jung, 1961/1973, p. 363). Like Adler, Jung disagreed with Freud about the role of the sex motive in human nature. Ideology finally overshadowed personal bonds, dissolving their volatile relationship around 1914. Freud (1914/1957c) and Jung (1961/1973) published independent and sometimes conflicting reasons for their separation.

The conflict with Freud took its toll on Jung. In 1913, however, Jung had a series of revelations that transformed his life and career. Jung began practicing trancelike meditations he called "active imagination." During one dreamlike state, he encountered a wise old man named *Philemon*, a spiritual guide with a flowing white beard and held aloft by kingfisher wings. In his autobiography, Jung (1961/1973) wrote:

> Philemon represented a force which was not myself. In my fantasies I held conversations with him, and he said things which I had not consciously thought. . . . Psychologically, Philemon represented superior insight. He was a mysterious figure to me. At times he seemed to me quite real, as if he were a living personality. I went walking up and down the garden with him, and to me he was what the Indians call a guru. (p. 183)

In trancelike visions, Jung's eyes were opened to the power of the unconscious mind (see Shamdasani, 2009). After the break with Freud, he began recording inner visions and ideas that flooded from his unconscious during active imagination sessions. From around 1914 until 1930, Jung collected his illustrations and calligraphic text in a red leather-bound manuscript. Known as *The Red Book*, the manuscript remained private until his heirs allowed the Philemon Foundation to publish it in 2009. Inspired by his mystical journeys, Jung resolved to change the way people looked at the human mind and spirituality. As Jung aged, he plunged deeper into the mystical side of his Number Two personality.

In January 1923, Jung experienced a "frightening dream" involving the German god Wotan. In his nightmare, Wotan ordered a gigantic wolfhound to carry away a human soul. The next morning, Jung learned his mother had died. Two months after dreaming that Wotan had claimed his mother's soul, Jung began building a stone tower near the sleepy Swiss village of Bollingen. After three decades, he had built a sprawling complex of buildings beside the shallow upper end of Lake Zürich. Jung claimed that his Number One personality had built the first tower as a maternal structure, a tribute to his mother and his wife, Emma. In 1931, Jung began construction on a second tower, inspired by his Number Two personality. The second tower became Jung's "place of spiritual concentration." No one came in without his permission. Jung's spiritual retreat became known as "Bollingen Tower" or *Der Turm* (the Tower). The Bollingen facility was so important to Jung that he dedicated a chapter in his autobiography to *Der Turm* (Jung, 1961/1973).

In the decades after dissolving his relationship with Freud, Jung traveled throughout Africa, India, Europe, and the United States to gather ideas to bolster his theories. He received many honors, including honorary doctorates from leading institutions such as Harvard University, the University of Geneva, and the University of Zürich.

Jung's work is presented in the twenty-volume collection titled *The Collected Works of C. G. Jung* (Bollingen Series No. 20, Princeton University, 1953–1979). Many current journals such as the *Journal of Analytic Psychology*

publish scholarly research, theoretical papers, and book reviews on Jung's psychology, and many appreciative and critical biographies exist of Jung (Elms, 2005). In addition, a number of professional organizations and institutes are dedicated to the advancement of Jungian thought (Samuels, 1994). The best-known institute is the C. G. Jung Institute located in Zürich. Helpful secondary sources on Jung include books by Hall and Nordby (1973), Humbert (1988), Mattoon (1981), and Bishop (1999). Jung's later years were particularly productive, even after a heart attack in 1944. He died on June 6, 1961.

Jung's System of Thought

In terms of methodology and content, Jung's approach to science and psychology was broad. On the methodological side, he gained many insights from his patients, but also believed in the value of experimental work. Jung made use of the comparative method in his extensive travels. Specifically, he was interested in cross-cultural comparisons of symbols and their meanings. Jung might best be characterized as a methodological pluralist because he found legitimacy and value in a variety of approaches to knowledge.

Jung was suspicious of ideologies and theories that may limit our field of vision. He acknowledged the heuristic value of theories so long as they are used in a proper way. His concern was that human beings can be *used* by theories; the proper approach was that theory should enhance vision, but we should be ready at any turn to discard a theory. Jung (1910/1954b) once said, "Theories in psychology are the very devil" (p. 7). He was referring to situations where, in his words, "we have not even established the empirical extent of the psyche's phenomenology" (p. 7).

Jung's approach to content was as broad as his approach to methodology. His **analytic psychology** encompassed many things: the unconscious, an elaborate view of the structure of personality, psychotherapy, and even studies of paranormal phenomena. In terms of breadth of interest, he is almost without peer in psychology. Like Wundt, Freud, and James, he often journeyed outside the realm of psychology for inspiration. Jung drew insights from diverse areas including Gnosticism, literature, eastern religion, art, and pagan mythology. Past thinkers were critical in developing his theories, leading Jung (1961/1973) to declare that "without history there can be no psychology, and certainly no psychology of the unconscious" (pp. 205–206).

During his exhaustive studies, Jung (1944/1953, 1967) discovered the ancient practice of **alchemy**. Although often stereotyped as pseudoscientists bent on changing base metals like lead into gold, alchemists pursued more important challenges. Jung discovered that the alchemists were dedicated to spiritual values and psychological transformation. Another goal involved finding a universal cure for disease, an *elixir of life* that could transform a person and even grant immortality.

At first, Jung regarded alchemy as nonsense. After immersing himself in alchemical lore, he found himself "condemned to study alchemy" as he tried to decipher its riddles and mysteries. In time, Jung (1961/1973) realized that the "experiences of the alchemists were, in a sense, my experiences, and their world was my world. This was, of course, a momentous discovery: I had stumbled upon the historical counterpart of my psychology of the unconscious" (p. 205). He studied secret doctrines by Paracelsus and other alchemists, puzzling over their arcane concepts like *lapis, scintilla, radix ipsius, prima materia,* and *spiritus mercurii*. Jung (1961/1973) studied them as if he were "trying to solve the riddle of an unknown language" (p. 205). He discovered that alchemy "gave substance to my psychology," leading to a critical insight:

> Only after I had familiarized myself with alchemy did I realize that the unconscious is a *process*, and that the psyche is transformed or developed by the relationship of the ego to the contents of the unconscious. . . . Through understanding of alchemical symbolism I arrived at the central concept of my psychology: *the process of individuation.* (Jung, 1961/1973, p. 209)

For Jung, **individuation** is the process of becoming a psychological individual, a self-realization that signals a coming to selfhood. Let's turn now to an overview of Jung's key concepts in psychology.

THE STRUCTURE OF PERSONALITY   Jung used the term **psyche** to refer to the totality of human personality. Indeed, for Jung, *psyche* and *personality* are interchangeable terms referring to the compendium of what we are at both conscious and unconscious levels. Jung determined several interacting components in the psyche.

The Ego   The ego, according to Jung, is the *I* or *me* of the personality and, as such, is the center of consciousness. As in Freud's system, the ego negotiates with the outer world and has the task of forming an accurate picture of the world.

Unconscious Processes   Jung used the term **personal unconscious** to refer to the storehouse of repressed materials that are unavailable to consciousness as well as suppressed materials that can be called into consciousness. We might also find unimportant or irrelevant materials here. Like fingerprints, the personal unconscious is different for every person. Word-association methods can be used to document information in this realm of the unconscious. In contrast with the personal unconscious, Jung believed we all share in a **collective unconscious**, drawn from our common ancestors' biological past in the form of images and response predispositions. The collective unconscious ties us together with all other human beings.

The collective unconscious includes **archetypes**, a term similar to others such as *pattern, model, copy,* and *prototype*. Jung believed archetypes have their origin in the history of the experiences of humans and are present in each of us as potential modes or patterns of thought. For example, the species has had millions of years of experience with darkness, power, death, mothers, fathers, and so forth. It was inconceivable to Jung that collective experience is unrepresented in the life of the individual or in mythology. It is important to point out that an archetype is not initially a so-called picture in the head; rather, it is a primordial image or a kind of universal pattern or form that sets us to think or act in characteristic ways. As we will see, the archetypes in Jung's theory play an important role in the overall structure of the personality.

The Shadow   The **shadow** is an important component of the psyche that appears antagonistic to consciousness and to the goals of the ego. The shadow is not just the dark or evil side of the personality; it is the antagonist for whatever is publicly dominant in the personality. The shadow includes repressed materials from the personal unconscious and primitive materials from the collective unconscious that may provoke fear, awe, or anger. The shadow forces dialogue in consciousness by challenging conventional niceties and norms. Jung believed the shadow can be a doorway to reality and wholeness. It is not all evil because a negative quality in the shadow can be transposed into a positive quality in attitude and behavior. Thus, as noted by Mattoon (1981), "Anger can become assertiveness and. . .vulnerability can become sensitivity to the needs of others" (p. 27). Jung believed we can never achieve wholeness if we deny the positive lessons gained by confronting the dark and primal side of life. On the contrary, the failure to allow expression of darker images and motives may show up later in undesirable emotional explosions.

The Persona   Literally, the term **persona** refers to the playactor's mask, but psychologically, the term as used by Jung refers to the public image or the mask that we wear in front of others. Normally, the persona is the socially acceptable counterpart of the shadow. It is our public appearance, professional mannerisms, the roles we play, and our public profile. The persona is not just conditioned; indeed, it includes powerful unconscious components. The persona of an individual as a father is tied to the father archetype. The persona may become so dominant in personality that it attempts to murder the ego. In such cases, an individual can no longer discriminate social roles from other dimensions of his or her true self. When this happens, the persona appropriates and dominates everything and the individual is robbed of wholeness.

The Self   Sharing affinities with Jamesian psychology, Jung believed that the **self** is the great unifying principle in the psyche. He believed that *self-actualization* or self-realization is a major goal of life; those processes that direct us toward wholeness, integration, and assimilation are functions of the self. The self and the ego, in Jung's psychology, perform different functions but are interdependent. The ego is the *I* or *me*, the center of consciousness. Its immediate concerns are more pressing than the concerns of the self. The ego shows up early in personality development, but the self emerges later to integrate personality into the larger scheme of things. The claims of the ego may need to be subordinated to the claims of the self to achieve wholeness and unity. The self is symbolized by a **mandala**, "a magic circle" that represents a need to express selfhood such as in the Tibetan Wheel of Becoming.

The Anima and the Animus   Jung could not accept that male and female sexuality are bipolar opposites. Though there is a male consciousness and a female consciousness, each is complemented by its counterpart. Both males and females come out of a long history marked by both masculine and feminine awareness. Jung documented a feminine dimension in male consciousness and a male dimension in feminine consciousness. The **anima** is a female archetype in men and the **animus** is a male archetype in women. In his concern for wholeness, Jung saw it as important that the anima find expression in males, and that the animus find expression in females. Unfortunately, the persona and social conditioning may work against such awareness, locking the individual into a narrow consciousness with regard to sexuality. One may raise questions about the theoretical basis of the anima and animus as archetypes, but Jung was consistent with contemporary views when he challenged bipolar theories of sexuality. His work opens the door to further thoughtful and potentially productive questions about whether the subordination of women in many organizations and institutions interferes with the healthy development of the anima in males.

ATTITUDES AND FUNCTIONS   Jung is perhaps best known for his concepts of extroversion and introversion, which he thought of as **attitudes**. Both extroversion and introversion refer to the direction of psychic energy in our lives. **Extroversion** is marked by a concentration of interest in the external world. The extrovert usually has an active, outgoing preference for social company and a strong presence around others. If a person's energy flows outward, she or he is an extrovert. An extroverted person would "feel energized" in a large group of people at a club but might experience diminished energy when spending time alone. By contrast, **introversion** is marked by inwardness, withdrawal, shyness, and a preference for quiet time alone or with select company. A person whose energy flows inward is an introvert. An introvert might experience energy while reading a book or playing a videogame at home but notice decreased energy when interacting with a group. Jung believed that both introverts and extroverts have latent unconscious wishes for the opposite orientation. Most of us display both attitudes, but one is usually dominant.

Jung believed in four basic psychological **functions**: thinking, feeling, sensation, and intuition. All functions are prevalent in all people, but there are nevertheless strong preferences so that a given function may be clearly dominant in a given personality. A *thinking type* prefers rational discourse and problem solving whereas a *feeling type* tunes to the arousal of positive or negative emotions in every situation. Jung believed that the functions and the attitudes combine in various ways that give insight into the nature of an individual's conscious orientation. For example, an *introverted-thinking* type seeks seclusion and gets lost in a world of ideas that are enjoyed in their own right. By contrast, the sensation function combined with extroversion is illustrated in an individual who relishes company and the polite ceremony of a fine meal served in beautiful surroundings.

COMPLEXES   Jung claimed that a **complex** involves conscious materials accompanied by emotional or perceptual distortions. For example, an inferiority complex is based on perceptual distortions regarding personal adequacy. Jung used the word association test to identify complexes in his early work. When given stimulus terms such as *sex*, *God*, *father*, or *mother*, some subjects had difficulty finding an association. A complex, according to Jung, may result when the shadow fails to find expression in awareness. In his view, wisdom and dimensionality come with an awareness of the full spectrum of human nature, including both its light and dark side.

CAUSALITY   Jung believed that teleology, or final causation, complements the roles played by material, efficient, and formal causation in human life. He stressed the importance of plans, expectations, and meaning orientation and argued that psychology is incomplete without these concepts. Jung stressed causality from several sources, including those from the personal and the collective unconscious, but also argued that there "exist psychic contents which are produced or caused by an antecedent act of the will, and which must therefore be regarded as products of some intentional, purposive and conscious activity" (Jung, 1926/1954a, p. 91). Jung recognized the difficulties attending the problem of free will as he referred to the "popular illusion concerning the 'arbitrariness of psychic processes'" (p. 91). He thus rejected hard-core determinism and popular notions of free will based on arbitrariness. He was open to a kind of free will born in wholeness and expanded consciousness.

In addition to his beliefs in causality and teleology, Jung embraced the controversial concept of **synchronicity** where simultaneous events appear related, even though their occurrence cannot be explained by the usual principles of causality (Cambray, 2009). Two events may not be linked in a causal way, but they're meaningful nonetheless. For example, you might pick up the phone to call a friend at the very moment she's calling you. Or a person might dream about someone dying before learning the next day that the person had just passed away. We know synchronous events exist, but are they anything more than meaningful coincidence? Though Jung did not wish to apply the principle of synchronicity to paranormal phenomena such as clairvoyance or mental telepathy, he was interested in these areas because they are a part of human experience. Although controversial, synchronicity is a part of Jung's theory that cannot be dismissed.

PSYCHOTHERAPY As in alchemy, Jung believed the goal of psychotherapy was transformation. His approach to psychotherapy is less structured and standardized than Freud's psychoanalysis. Jung relied on standard Freudian approaches, but also analyzed dreams, used the word association test, asked the analysand to paint pictures of mandalas, or just engage the person in dialogue. Jung varied his approach as a function of the client's personality and problems. Because no one method fits all people in working toward wholeness, the analyst must be prepared to adjust to the needs and abilities the analysand brings to therapy. An extroverted-feeling type of client may require a different form of therapy than an introverted-thinking type.

Evaluation

Jung's concepts of introversion and extroversion have long been a part of mainstream psychology. An examination of PsycINFO will reveal that these concepts are often used as classification variables in research. Jung's early work on the word association test may also be counted as an important contribution with a continuing influence. Jung's approach to therapy also remains as a small but significant part of the work of mental health professionals. His great breadth with respect to content and methodology may also be viewed as a strength. As already noted, there are any number of controversial concepts in Jung's psychology that have been the subjects of severe

criticism: the collective unconscious, archetypes, the principle of synchronicity, and the vagueness of many terms in his theory. Jung's broad approach to science and his interest in the occult have also been sources of concern. Perhaps the cardinal weakness of Jung's psychology has been its failure to generate meaningful experimental studies.

KAREN DANIELSEN HORNEY

Like Adler and Jung, **Karen Danielsen Horney (1885–1952)** (*HORN eye*) initially found value in Freud's ideas but in time grew dissatisfied with the traditional assumptions of psychoanalysis. She challenged Freud's ideas about human sexuality, neurosis, and therapy. As a result, she incorporated a more sociocultural perspective into psychoanalytic thinking.

Karen Clementina Theodora Danielsen was born in Eilbek, Germany, on September 15, 1885. Although close to her mother, she felt alienated from her father, a captain of a steamship, who was often away at sea (Quinn, 1987). At an early age, she declared an interest in medicine. In 1901, she became one of the first women to attend the Hamburg Realgymnasium (an accelerated high school) and still later one of the first women in Germany to study medicine. She met Oskar Horney, a student of economics and political science, at the University of Freiburg. The young couple married in 1909 and moved to Berlin. She earned her medical degree in 1915 from the University of Berlin and delivered her first paper on psychoanalysis two years later. She underwent psychoanalysis with the renowned analyst Karl Abraham (1877–1925), who recognized her brilliance and wrote to Freud about her potential (Sayers, 1991). In time, she became the first female professor at the Berlin Psychoanalytic Institute, though her ideas were already at odds with traditional psychoanalysis.

In 1932, Horney immigrated to the United States, where she interacted with a diverse mix of scholars including Erich Fromm, Margaret Mead, Harry Stack Sullivan, and Max Wertheimer. In 1939, Karen and Oscar Horney were divorced after years of separation, and the ensuing period marked a time of great independence in her thinking. That same year, she published *New Ways in Psychoanalysis*. Her book took a critical stand against Freud, souring her relations with colleagues in the exclusive New York Psychoanalytic Society (Rubins, 1978). She resigned from the Society in 1941 and helped found the Association for the Advancement of Psychoanalysis (Sayers, 1991). She also served as a founder and dean of the American Institute for Psychoanalysis and founder and editor of the *American Journal of Psychoanalysis*. Karen Danielsen Horney died of cancer on December 4, 1952, in New York City.

Horney's System of Thought

Horney's powerful determination affected her approach to scholarship as well as her life (Eckardt, 2006). She was an innovative thinker and prolific critic of Freudian theory, as evidenced in her first book *The Neurotic Personality of Our Time* (1937). She revised and refined her personality theory in subsequent books including *Self-Analysis* (1942), *Our Inner Conflicts* (1945), and *Neurosis and Human Growth* (1950). Following emigration from Europe to the United States, Horney became attuned to sociocultural influences in the development of personality, especially in the shaping of neurosis. She believed that neurotic behavior did not develop from psychic tension between the ego and unconscious forces, but instead from conflict in interpersonal and social relationships. In her view, the *neurotic person of our times* was not the victim of sexual instincts, as suggested by traditional psychoanalysis, but rather a product of the sociocultural context of childhood.

BASIC ANXIETY AND NEUROSIS During the course of development, children naturally look to their caregivers for security and satisfaction. This process fosters the development of the **real self**, that "central inner force common to all humans and yet unique in each, which is a deep source of growth" (Horney, 1950, p. 17). Although children are born with a sense of

real self, some parents may undermine a child's security through excessive isolation, rejection, indifference, hostility, or ridicule. As a result, the child may experience a sense of **basic anxiety**, a "terrible feeling of being isolated and helpless in a potentially hostile world" (Horney, 1945, p. 39). Such debilitating anxiety is counterproductive to growth because it stifles and distorts a person's view of the real self.

Horney believed that basic anxiety was a universal aspect of childhood that could manifest itself in adult neurosis. In time, a person may develop certain **neurotic trends** or irrational strategies of coping against basic anxiety. Horney (1942) believed that her study of neurotic trends set her apart from other scholars in the psychodynamic school:

> Freud believed that the [neurotic] disturbances generate from a conflict between environmental factors and repressed instinctual impulses. Adler, more rationalistic and superficial than Freud, believes that they are created by the ways and means that people use to assert their superiority over others. Jung, more mystical than Freud, believes in collective unconscious fantasies which, though replete with creative possibilities, may work havoc because the unconscious strivings fed by them are the exact opposite of those in the conscious mind. My own answer is that in the center of psychic disturbances are unconscious strivings developed in order to cope with life despite fears, helplessness, and isolation. I have called them "neurotic trends." (p. 40)

During the course of neurotic trends, individuals may develop an insatiable need for affection, approval, power, perfection, social recognition, or prestige. Likewise, they may feel a need to exploit others, to restrict their life and goals to narrow borders, or to seek a partner who will assume control of their life. Although all people possess such needs to some degree, neurotic people adopt these trends as absolute needs that dominate their lives and relationships.

In *Our Inner Conflicts* (1945), Horney elaborated on three unconscious *movements* that neurotic individuals rely on to deal with basic anxiety. A **compliant type** of individual is motivated to reduce the anxiety of helplessness by *moving toward* other people in a style of interaction characterized by dependence and unassertiveness. According to Horney (1945), "This type needs to be liked, wanted, desired, loved; to feel accepted, welcomed, approved of, appreciated; to be needed, to be of importance to others, especially to one particular person; to be helped, protected, taken care of, guided" (p. 51). The **hostile type** is likely to use a more aggressive coping style of *moving against* people through exploitation and dominance. For the hostile type, any "situation or relationship is looked at from the standpoint of 'What can I get out of it?'—whether it has to do with money, prestige, contacts, or ideas" (Horney, 1945, p. 65). Finally, the **detached type** employs an interpersonal coping strategy based on withdrawal and detachment from society by *moving away* from people. Horney (1945) believed that this social resignation arises from an

> inner need to put emotional distance between themselves and others. More accurately, it is their conscious and unconscious determination not to get emotionally involved with others in any way, whether in love, fight, co-operation, or competition. They draw around themselves a kind of magic circle which no one may penetrate. (p. 75)

Unfortunately, such neurotic strategies further alienate the person from his or her real self and establish an **idealized self**, a fictitious view of neurotic selfhood that substitutes for the real self. Indeed, Horney noted that her patients often demonstrated a "neurotic search for glory," a powerful need to establish the idealized self even to the point of developing a "neurotic pride" about this false selfhood. To this end, a neurotic person may develop *blind spots* by denying any experiences that are inconsistent with the idealized self.

Horney (1945) illustrated this "refusal to see" with a case study:

> A patient, for example, who had all the characteristics of the compliant type and thought of himself as Christlike, told me quite casually that at staff meetings he would often shoot one colleague after another with a little flick of his thumb. True enough, the destructive craving that prompted these figurative killings was at that time unconscious; but the point here is that the shooting, which he dubbed "play," did not in the least disturb his Christlike image. (p. 132)

Blind spots and neurotic pride, together with cynicism, rationalization, and other neurotic *solutions*, have potentially destructive effects for healthy personality growth. Horney used the term *self-hatred* to describe the neurotic tendency to despise one's real self. This self-contempt was sometimes mixed with a relentless drive for perfection governed by an unrealistic *tyranny of the should*. For example, a neurotic woman may be driven by rigid and unrealistic expectations about how she *should* be a better student, *should* lose more weight, or *should* be more outgoing. Ultimately, such artificial harmony built around one's idealized self-image will foster neurotic pride and self-hatred but will also push the individual deeper into neurosis.

Horney provided a compelling alternative to psychoanalysis (Leslie, 1996). She believed that the goal of psychotherapy should be oriented around helping people resolve their inner conflicts by reestablishing the real self over the idealized self. In *Self-Analysis* (1942), she maintained that such *self-realization* decreases conflict and anxiety and helps individuals strive for truth, productivity, and harmony with others and themselves. Near the end of her life, Horney became interested in Zen Buddhism and tried to incorporate it with her ideas about psychoanalysis (DeMartino, 1991).

FEMININE PSYCHOLOGY   Between 1923 and 1936, Horney wrote a series of fourteen papers that constituted an aggressive counter to Freud's theory of female sexual development; the posthumous collection of essays appeared in 1967 under the title *Feminine Psychology*. Freud publicly condemned Horney's sociocultural theory, but she was undeterred by his criticism (O'Connell, 1990).

She took particular issue with Freud's belief that "anatomy is destiny." Horney concluded that culture, not anatomy, produces differences between women and men and found psychoanalysis to be excessively male oriented and phallocentric in matters of gender development (Gilman, 2001). For example, psychoanalysts discuss *penis envy* but disregard the possibility of *womb envy* despite evidence from several cultures and mythologies that men envy women's ability to bear and nurse children. Indeed, Horney (1967) asserted that the professional accomplishments of men may serve as compensation for an inability to bear children (Bayne, 2011). As her ideas about feminine psychology developed, she placed increasing emphasis on the cultural influences on female personality (Rubins, 1978).

For Horney, personality development and tensions between men and women were due to environmental, not biological, conditions. In particular, she believed that women's sense of inferiority is not constitutional but acquired from masculine society and psychology. Horney (1967) challenged society's "dread of women," which results in disparaging and hostile attitudes that define women as emotionally and intellectually inferior to men. To illustrate the prevalence of this patriarchal dread, she surveyed historical examples of female persecution ranging from biblical admonishments to the senseless slaughter of witches. She called for a new understanding of women but recognized the discouraging stereotypes of her day:

> Woman's efforts to achieve independence and enlargement of her field of activities are continually met with a skepticism which insists that such efforts should be made only in the face of economic necessity, and that they run counter to her inherent character and natural tendencies. Accordingly, all efforts of this sort are said to be without any vital significance for women, whose every thought should center upon the male or motherhood. (Horney, 1934, p. 605)

Taken as a whole, Horney's work represents an important step in advancing the psychological study of women, a field that gained momentum in the 1960s (Eckardt, 1991; Symonds, 1991). In addition, her ideas about psychotherapy and personality have influenced cognitive and rational-emotive therapy as well as the study of literature (O'Connell, 1990; Paris, 1991).

Unlike Adler and Jung, Horney did not replace psychoanalysis with a new theory of personality but rather challenged (Eckardt, 2005) and restructured the fundamental assumptions of the Freudian model to fit a different time and culture (Wallace, 1993). Her insightful work on cultural influences of personality and feminine psychology opened new frontiers and broadened the scope of psychoanalytic theory (Gilman, 2001; Ingram, 1985).

OTHER DEVELOPMENTS

Fine (1990) observed that psychoanalysis has been beset with "innumerable inner conflicts, so similar in many ways to the inner conflicts that psychoanalysts find in their patients" (p. 3). Psychoanalysts are divided on a variety of issues including the autonomy of the ego, female sexuality, and the role of social and cultural influences in experience and behavior (Bergmann, 2004).

One of the most important developments in psychoanalytic theory has been the attempt to "mate a new ego and an old id" (Klein, 1983, p. 505). Though he had recognized ego instincts or drives, Freud emphasized the id as the primary source of motivation. A major movement within the psychoanalytic tradition, known as ego psychology, has emphasized ego functions that are autonomous. This movement received its impetus from a seminal work by Heinz Hartmann (1894–1970) titled *Ego Psychology and the Problem of Adaptation* (1939). Since the publication of Hartmann's work, a great deal of work (see

Holt, 1967) has examined the relation of the ego to Freud's classic drive theory. Such work has led to the claim that there is much more room in Freud's expanded theory for a model of human freedom and rationality (see Macklin, 1976). The ego psychologists remind classical theorists of Freud's statement in the final chapter of *The Future of an Illusion* that "the voice of the intellect is a soft one, but it does not rest till it has gained a hearing" (Freud, 1927/1961c, p. 53). The importance of a stronger ego with independent functions is supported by another post-Freudian development that emphasizes social and cultural factors in human experience.

In addition to the neglect of ego functions, there has also been widespread agreement that classical psychoanalytic theory neglected social and cultural influences on personality. Freud's focus was on individual psychological processes and, as noted by Munroe (1955), he "profoundly distrusted environmentalist theories that attempt to explain 'everything' by social and economic causes" (p. 117). He was critical of the Soviet communist system, arguing that "the psychological premises on which it is based are an untenable illusion" (see Freud, 1930/1961a, pp. 112–113). Freud's distrust of all-pervasive environmentalist viewpoints may have contributed to his neglect of more moderate approaches. Post-Freudians such as Erich Fromm (1941, 1947), Harry Stack Sullivan (1953), and Erik H. Erikson (1963) have added the necessary correctives for the neglect of social influences.

Freud's daughter Anna became a prominent figure in the psychoanalytic community in her own right (Young-Bruehl, 2008), and she gained recognition for her work on ego defenses (Meerloo, 1956). In 1941, she opened the Hampstead War Nurseries for children orphaned by the war and then launched the Hampstead Child Therapy Course and Clinic in the late 1940s; this charitable institute was committed to study and care of children (Pretorius, 2012). She pioneered analysis of children based on extensive clinical research (Midgley, 2012), and she excelled as a teacher, trainer of analysts, and representative of psychoanalysis (Young-Bruehl, 2012).

As noted earlier in the chapter, Freud's views on female sexuality have also been subject to extensive criticism. He joined notable figures such as Friedrich Nietzsche and Charles Darwin, who, for all their important contributions, believed negative stereotypes in which women were regarded as inferior and subordinate to men.

Review Questions

1. The text outlined six general characteristics of Freud's thought. What kind of evidence might Freud have advanced for each characteristic?
2. Compare and contrast Freud and Jung with respect to their views on the structure of personality. Which view seems more adequate? Why?
3. Briefly review the posthypnotic phenomena that impressed Freud and that contributed to his view on the importance of unconscious processes.
4. Contrast Freud and Jung with respect to their positions on the unconscious.
5. Outline the four basic components of instincts according to Freud.
6. Distinguish between the three varieties of anxiety proposed by Freud.
7. Define *repression projection*, *reaction formation*, and *sublimation*. Why did Freud consider repression to be the most basic?
8. Critically evaluate Freud's stages of psychosexual development.
9. Distinguish between the manifest and latent content of dreams. Also briefly describe Freud's approach to psychotherapy, making sure you cover topics such as transference, free association, and countertransference.
10. Contrast Freud and Einstein with respect to their approaches to the causes of war.
11. Outline some of the new materials you encounter in the work of Freud that are not included in other systems of psychology.
12. Outline major criticisms of Freud's system of thought.
13. Contrast Jung and Freud with respect to their approaches to therapy.
14. What role did the ancient practice of alchemy play in shaping Jung's psychology?
15. Jung believed that the shadow can be a doorway to reality. What did he mean by this? He also believed that encounters with the materials in the shadow can lead to wisdom and wholeness. Do you agree with him? Why?

16. What did Jung mean by the term *archetype*? Give some examples. Briefly argue the pros and cons of the concept of archetypes.
17. Outline the four functions and two attitudes in Jung's psychology.
18. Discuss Jung's general approach to the problem of causality, including his position on teleology and a brief statement regarding his concept of synchronicity.
19. Outline some of the strengths and weaknesses encountered in Jung's system of thought.
20. Contrast Adler and Freud with respect to their approaches to motivation.
21. Contrast compensation and overcompensation in Adler's theory.
22. Briefly outline Adler's approach to the question of causation. Argue the pros and cons of Adler's teleological approach in contrast with an approach that places stronger emphasis on material and efficient causation.
23. Distinguish between the real self and the idealized self. What role does basic anxiety play in isolating the real self?
24. Briefly review Horney's ideas about the compliant, hostile, and detached neurotic types.
25. Compare and contrast Freud and Horney with respect to their position on feminine development.

Glossary

Adler, Alfred (1870–1937)   Founder of a system of psychological thought known as individual psychology, Adler emphasized the importance of overcoming early feelings of inferiority. He focused on the purposive or goal-directed nature of behavior and on the capacity of the individual to identify with the goals of society at large.

alchemy   The ancient practice of transformation. Jung found inspiration in alchemical practices, believing they gave substance to his psychology, spiritual values, and ideas about psychological transformation.

anal stage   According to Freud, in the second and third years of life, the child develops a deep awareness of the pleasures associated with relief of bowel and bladder tension. The expression of this pleasure may be in conflict with societal norms and thus create special difficulties that must be negotiated with care if the child is to develop normally.

analytic psychology   The name of the system of psychology advanced by Carl Gustav Jung.

anima   In Jung's theory, the female archetype in men.

animus   In Jung's theory, the male archetype in women.

archetype   According to Jung, archetypes exist in the collective unconscious. They are patterns or forms that help mold thinking about experiences with topics such as power, death, darkness, mothers, fathers, and so on. Jung assumed that the vast experiences of the entire species with such topics do not go unrepresented in the psychological apparatus of each individual.

attitudes   According to Jung, an attitude is a pervasive social orientation. Jung identified two attitudes: introversion and extroversion.

basic anxiety   An overwhelming feeling of helplessness and isolation in a threatening and hostile world.

Breuer, Joseph (1842–1925)   German physiologist and colleague of Sigmund Freud. Breuer's treatment of Bertha Pappenheim (*Anna O.*) played a central role in the early development of Freud's psychoanalysis.

Brücke, Ernst (1819–1892)   Famous physiologist who had a powerful influence on Sigmund Freud. Brücke emphasized the importance of a thorough-going, physical–chemical approach to the study of psychological topics.

Charcot, Jean-Martin (1825–1893)   French physician and neurologist who had a strong influence on the development of Freud's thought. Charcot emphasized the psychological basis of some physical symptoms.

collective unconscious   A controversial concept advanced by Carl Jung. He believed that the human mind includes unconscious memories from the biological past of topics such as darkness, death, and power. Most of what is in the collective unconscious is associated with topics that strongly influence survival.

compensation   In Adler's psychology, the normal attempts to overcome specific inferiorities by developing strengths in alternative areas (e.g., a person who is not athletic may excel in the classroom).

complex   A term employed by Jung to refer to conscious materials that are strongly associated with emotional or perceptual distortions. For example, in Jung's view, an inferiority complex results partly from perceptual distortions regarding personal adequacy.

compliant type   A neurotic attempt to reduce anxiety by *moving toward* people.

countertransference   In Freud's psychology, the emotional attachment of a therapist to a patient.

detached type   A neurotic attempt to reduce anxiety by *moving away from* people.

ego   In Freud's system, the ego is the *I* or *me* of the personality—the center of organization and integration that must adapt to the demands of reality. Jung uses the term to refer to a component of personality that is closely associated with conscious processes.

extroversion   In Jung's psychology, a quality of personality marked by love of other people and social interaction.

fictional final goals   According to Adler, fictions play major roles in the subjective world of the individual. Fictional final goals are those things that we wish to achieve. Such wishes are not necessarily grounded in realistic considerations.

fixation   A strong attachment to a specific stimulus in Freud's theory of instinct. For example, a childhood trauma may result in an oral fixation that might manifest itself in adulthood as a habit of smoking cigars.

free association   Therapeutic method developed by Sigmund Freud and marked by the uninhibited sharing of whatever happens to be in the center stage of consciousness at a given time.

Freud, Sigmund (1856–1939)   Founder of psychoanalysis, which is both a major system of psychology and a therapeutic technique.

function   According to Jung, a function is an expression of the psychic apparatus. He identified four functions: thinking, feeling, sensation, and intuition. He believed that, for many people, specific functions (e.g., thinking) are dominant features of the personality.

genital stage   According to Freud, this stage is associated with the adolescent years and is marked by the development of emotional ties with members of the opposite sex.

Horney, Karen Danielsen (1885–1952)
German American psychoanalyst who enlarged the domain of psychoanalysis with her study of sociocultural factors in neurosis and gender development.

hostile type   A neurotic attempt to reduce anxiety by *moving against* people.

id   In Freudian theory, the id is the most primitive component of the personality. It represents powerful biological needs and demands instant expression and immediate gratification.

idealized self   A fictitious view of neurotic selfhood that replaces the real self.

identification   In Freudian psychology, a defense mechanism of the ego marked by imitation of another person. The ego attempts to borrow from the success or adequacy of another individual.

individual psychology   The name of the system of psychology founded by Alfred Adler.

individuation   The name Carl Jung gave to describe the process of becoming a complete psychological individual, a self-realization that signals a coming to selfhood.

inferiority complex   According to Adler, children are inadequate or inferior with respect to most functions. Overcoming inferiority is a task for all people. An inferiority complex is an intense or unusually strong manifestation of feelings that all people experience.

instinct   This term is often used as the translation for Freud's term *Trieb*, which is close in meaning to the term *drive*. According to Freud, Trieb is an internal stimulus that persists until it finds satisfaction. It has a somatic source, a strength, an aim (its own satisfaction), and an object (that which will help it achieve its aim).

introversion   According to Jung, an attitude marked by preference for inwardness and for minimal or highly selected social contact.

Jung, Carl Gustav (1875–1961)   Founder of a system of psychology known as analytic psychology.

latency period   According to Freud, the period between the phallic stage and the genital stage. In the latency period there is no obvious localization of erotic interest.

latent content of a dream   According to Freud, the symbolic way a dream expresses an unconscious wish or drive.

mandala   According to Jung, a "magic circle" or symbol that expresses selfhood.

manifest content of a dream   According to Freud, the dream as described by the dreamer; the apparent content of a dream as censored by the ego.

moral anxiety   According to Freud, anxiety associated with the threat that the irrational demands of the superego might overcome the ego.

neurotic anxiety   According to Freud, this arises when the irrational demands of the id threaten to overwhelm the ego.

neurotic trends   Neurotic needs that form strategies of protection designed to counter basic anxiety.

objective anxiety   Objective threats from the world or from other people that threaten to overpower the ego.

Oedipus complex   A young boy's desire for his mother along with feelings of competition with his father. The term is used more generally to refer to strong emotional attachment to the parent of the opposite sex and feelings of competition with the parent of the same sex.

oral stage   In Freud's psychology, the first stage of psychosexual development. In this stage, the child's interactions with the world are primarily via the oral cavity and there is primitive learning about the responsiveness of the world to oral activities such as crying and sucking.

overcompensation   According to Adler, overcompensation involves attempts to develop great strength in the very area that is most beset with difficulties (e.g., a physically handicapped individual who becomes a great athlete).

penis envy   According to Freud, during the phallic period, the young girl is envious of the protruding sex organ of her father. Freud argued that the young girl holds her mother responsible for her own "castrated condition."

persona   Literally, the playactor's mask. In Jung's psychology, the persona is that part of the psychic structure that is most visible socially.

personal unconscious   Jung's term for the storehouse of materials based on each individual's experiences that are not immediately available to consciousness.

phallic stage   In Freud's psychology, that period from ages three to five when the child develops an interest in his or her sex organs and the sex organs of the parent. Freud believed that, at this time, the child begins to identify with the opposite-sexed parent.

pleasure principle   Freud argued that the pleasure principle is the dominant feature of the human mental apparatus. The pleasure principle calls for immediate release of tension and acquisition of those goals that fulfill needs.

preconscious   A feature of the mental apparatus, according to Freud, containing materials not now in consciousness but readily available to consciousness.

primary process   Freud's term for images and memories of objects that serve to satisfy needs. A dream rich in imagery is an example of primary process material.

projection   A defense mechanism of the ego manifested when personal faults or weaknesses are externalized or ascribed to objects, events, or other people. Thus, a married person tempted to be unfaithful may ascribe the wish to be unfaithful to the spouse.

psyche   According to Jung, the totality of a human personality.

psychoanalysis   The system of psychology and/or the treatment procedure set forth by Sigmund Freud. The term also has a broader meaning, referring sometimes to any group of psychologies that share some of the basic concepts associated with Freud's psychology.

rationalization   Defense mechanism of the ego marked by the practice of employing false but logical or even plausible explanations designed to excuse weaknesses or errors.

reaction formation   A defense in which the ego masks awareness of an anxiety-provoking motive by emphasizing its opposite. For example, a parent who harbors hostility toward a child, may become overly indulgent or overprotective.

reality principle   Social and environmental demands, constraints, or pressures that place limitations on alternative modes of action.

real self   In Horney's theory, the true source of healthy and positive growth in a human being.

regression   Return or retreat to an earlier stage of development and reinstatement of attitudes or behaviors characteristic of an earlier stage.

repression   An ego defense mechanism in which dangerous thoughts, memories, or perceptions are forced out of consciousness and into the unconscious realm.

resistance   Failure to cooperate with the therapist presumably because of the trauma of dealing with unconscious materials that are about to be brought to the surface.

secondary process   According to Freud, plans and strategies of the ego that provide compromised means for the expression of id impulses.

self   According to Jung, the self is the unifying component of the psychic apparatus. The self is that which seeks optimal development, integration, and wholeness.

shadow   According to Jung, the dark side of the personality that appears antagonistic to the social goals of the ego. Includes primitive materials from the collective unconscious; these materials may provoke negative emotions such as fear or anger.

social interest   The term employed by Adler referring to the capacity of the individual to identify with the larger social good and the altruistic goals of society.

style of life   Adler's term referring to unique personality qualities (including plans, strategies, and projects) designed to accomplish specific goals in life.

sublimation   According to Freud, any of a variety of socially acceptable activities such as work, play, or philanthropic activities that represent a rechanneling of sexual energy into socially acceptable forms. In general, sublimation involves the substitution of a higher, more socially acceptable activity for a less socially acceptable one.

superego   According to Freud, that part of the personality consisting of internalized social norms, values, and ideals. Like the id, the superego is not rational. It serves the goal of perfection and attempts to appropriate ego activities to serve its goal.

synchronicity   A term employed by Jung that describes unlikely simultaneous occurrences or events not easily explained by the usual principles of causality.

transference   According to Freud, this term refers to emotional attachments that patients may develop for their therapists.

17

■ ■ ■

Humanistic Psychologies

The darkness is habitable.

—MICHAEL NOVAK (1970)

Nicholas of Cusa (1401–1464), a legal scholar, mathematician, philosopher, and theologian, was remembered among other things for his doctrine of **learned ignorance** (Liddell, 1933). Nicholas applied the doctrine to theology in which it referred to the "discipline of clearly knowing how *not* to talk of God" (Marti, 1983). One way that learned ignorance might be helpful is illustrated in the compulsive behavior of a person with a psychological disorder who repeatedly made the sign of the cross after she walked every few steps. In the individual's view, the compulsion was a way of appeasing the anger of God and thus averting disaster. This patient needed the wisdom of Nicholas of Cusa, the wisdom of learned ignorance—the discipline of knowing how *not* to talk or think of God.

Those psychologists affiliated with the humanistic school share something in common with Nicholas of Cusa. Such psychologists believe human beings also need the art of knowing how *not* to think about themselves. As Nicholas found wisdom in negative theology, the humanistic psychologists find wisdom in challenging the models and metaphors associated with other systems of thought. Specifically, according to the humanistic position, it is misleading and even damaging to regard ourselves as information processors, black boxes, machines, or mere cultural products. Models such as the computer and the white rat can provide, at best, only partial perspectives; at worst, such models result in false leads and misinformation.

Humanistic psychologists have been vocal in their criticisms of behaviorism and psychoanalysis (DeCarvalho, 1992). The basic concepts (conditioning and unconscious processes) associated with these two systems are important but, according to humanistic psychologists, these concepts are overextended. The criticism is that behaviorists and psychoanalysts have been so enamored with their core concepts of conditioning and unconscious processes that they have lost sight of the primary subject of interest—human beings.

The criticism of behaviorism does not deny that conditioning plays an important role in human life, but it is argued that humans have the capacity to operate at a meta-level of awareness that makes it possible to overcome or reverse the effects of conditioning. The defiant capacity, the ability to neutralize or even transcend conditioning is, according to the humanistic psychologist, a unique feature of human nature.

A similar criticism is leveled at the psychoanalytic school. Unconscious forces may be at work, producing unexplained ideas or desires. Some individuals may act blindly on those ideas or desires, but most people are more conscious than unconscious. By overgeneralizing from a small sample of individuals with special kinds of illnesses, psychoanalysts advanced a distorted view of human beings—a view that fails to differentiate between normal human beings and emotionally disturbed individuals who provided data for Freud's theories.

The humanistic viewpoint gained momentum in the 1960s when behaviorism and psychoanalysis were dominant forces. After rapid growth, the humanistic viewpoint was hailed as the "third force" in psychology because it stood in contrast with the two older schools. Behaviorism and psychoanalysis were deterministic, whereas humanistic psychologists emphasized the capacity for free will (Barton, 1992). Behaviorism and psychoanalysis aped the methods of other sciences, whereas **third-force psychology** represented a broader epistemology adapted to the unique subject matter of interest. Thus, one might employ scientific, historical, philosophical, literary, or even artistic methods in studying human beings. Humanistic psychologists also argued for a broader concept of the subject matter of psychology. In addition to the traditional study of fear, aggression, learning, memory, and so on, it was argued that psychologists should study topics such as suffering, wisdom, growth, joy, meaning, authenticity, dignity, and peak experiences.

The humanistic psychologists asked nothing less of psychology than that it find ways to come to terms with human life, affectively, cognitively, and volitionally, and to recognize the variability and uniqueness of individual people (Ryback, 2012). The youthful discipline of psychology had been too narrow in terms of content, epistemology, and values; it had carved out too small a domain for itself. As a result, it lost contact with the fundamental issues of human nature and was in danger of becoming a sterile discipline.

INTELLECTUAL TRADITIONS

The intellectual background of humanistic psychology is encountered in the works of scholars who emphasized the importance of inner experience, the freedom of human beings to transcend their environmental circumstances, and the intentionality and activity of mind. In what follows, we review some of the dominant historical intellectual forces that influenced the development of third-force psychologies.

William James

The psychology and philosophy of **William James (1842–1910)** are important in the intellectual background of humanistic psychology for several reasons (Hoffman, 2010). First, the stream of experience played an important role in his philosophical vision. According to James, an adequate psychology cannot close the door on anything experienced. For all his background in physiology, medicine, and chemistry, James realized that experience deserves to be studied in its own right. We may find physiological and biochemical underpinnings and correlates of experience, but from a Jamesian viewpoint, experience, as it occurs, is a domain in itself with qualities that cannot be completely understood in terms of other underlying processes.

According to James, psychology ceases to be empirical when it strays too far from experience or attempts to explain away experience as nothing but the product of a more fundamental process. In the Jamesian view, classical behaviorism could not qualify as an empirical psychology because it denies the role of experience altogether. Ironically, the behaviorist uses experience to deny its role in psychology. The exclusion of experience as a proper subject matter is based on an intellectualist philosophy that tells us what to count and what not to count. James would view metaphysical behaviorism as faulty. Humanistic psychologists would agree.

James was a forerunner of humanistic psychology because he was a methodological pluralist. He was open about what counts as the subject matter of psychology. He hoped for psychology to make a real difference in the world. He was interested in the application of psychology to daily life, the problems of education, the world of work, and the problems of people suffering emotional distress. His interest in questions of value and meaning ran deep (Rathunde, 2001) and is illustrated in his major works.

James's psychology as an intellectual predecessor of humanistic psychology is illustrated in other ways. For example, one of the richest chapters in his classic two-volume *Principles of Psychology* is the chapter on the self, a topic of central interest in humanistic psychology. James's writings on human freedom and the significance of individuals also qualify him as a forerunner of humanistic psychology.

Existentialism

Humanistic psychology's ancestry is rooted in philosophers who devoted themselves to an understanding of the emotional, social, and intellectual issues of life. Such philosophers were concerned with the daily issues and concerns of human beings as they live their lives. **Existentialism** is a philosophical orientation marked by such concerns. The focus is on the individual and on the capacity of the individual to exercise freedom to rise above environmental and social constraints. Let us examine some teachings of selected existential philosophers.

MIGUEL DE UNAMUNO The Spanish philosopher and novelist **Miguel de Unamuno (1864–1936)** was born on September 29, 1864, in the Basque city of Bilbao. Reared in a strict Catholic tradition, he was educated at the University of Madrid. In 1884, Unamuno received a doctoral degree and, in 1891, he accepted a position at the University of Salamanca. On several occasions, he was removed from his university post for political reasons. From 1924 to 1930, he was deported because of his criticism of the Spanish dictator Primo de Rivera. Following the fall of Rivera, Unamuno returned to his post at the University of Salamanca. He died on December 31, 1936.

Unamuno had little interest in the abstract metaphysical problems of philosophy; however, he had great interest in what he called "the man of flesh and blood." Indeed, this expression is the title of the first chapter of Unamuno's classic book *The Tragic Sense of Life* (1913/1972). Sounding a theme consistent with the ideas of later humanistic psychologists, Unamuno lamented science and philosophy's failure to address the issues of human life. Science and philosophy fail, according to Unamuno, when specialization blocks the larger vision. In characteristic pejorative style, Unamuno reminded his reader that the specialist runs the danger of "murdering his humanity and burying it in the specialty" (Unamuno, 1913/1972, p. 36). Specialization breeds detachment, cold professionalism, and partial perspectives that do violence to human nature. The specialist can too easily treat another human being as an "it" rather than as a living "thou."

Science and philosophy also fail, according to Unamuno, when they place too great an emphasis on a purely cognitive intellectual analysis of human beings. He spoke with disdain for those who intellectualize; as he warned, "the people who think only with their brain turn into definition-mongers" (Unamuno, 1913/1972, p. 18). For Unamuno, cognition and thinking are not enough; we must also recognize the powerful role of emotion in human life. A philosophy or psychology that neglects the affective dimension is too quick to dismiss or reduce important dimensions of existence. Unamuno pleaded for a perspective that recognizes the role of feeling in human life. The expression "flesh and blood" refers, among other things, to those who think not just with their brains but "with their whole body and soul, with their blood, with the marrow of their bones, with their heart and lungs and viscera, with their whole life" (p. 18).

According to Koestenbaum (1967), Unamuno "extols the agony and the importance of the individual [and] the importance of personal integrity" (p. 183). Unamuno called for a new emphasis on emotional and intellectual honesty. Meaning orientation, truthfulness, practicality, and personhood are central themes in the works of Unamuno, just as they are in humanistic psychology.

SØREN AABYE KIERKEGAARD Søren Kierkegaard (1813–1855) is sometimes called the "Danish Socrates" and is regarded as a founder of existentialism. Kierkegaard was born in Copenhagen on May 5, 1813. A year after his first wife died, Michael Pedersen Kierkegaard married his servant, Anne Sørensdatter Lund. At the time of their marriage, Anne Lund was already five months pregnant with Søren. His parents' union helped cast a cloud of guilt and pessimism over the Kierkegaard home. A sense of despair also plagued Kierkegaard's father from his youth when he stood on a hill and cursed God. This single moment became a dominating feature in the long life of the elder Kierkegaard.

An orthodox Lutheran and a successful businessman, Kierkegaard's father viewed it as an irony that he prospered despite cursing God. His own tortured analysis was that God would punish him somehow through his wealth. He was convinced that he suffered the retributive anger of God through the misfortunes of several of his seven children. Two died in childhood, another died at age twenty-four, and two of his daughters died in early adulthood while giving birth. Young Kierkegaard labored under the stern tutelage of his domineering father who was bent on instilling a proper Christian perspective in the child. His mother, according to Lowrie (1970), "counted for little in the household. Whereas the father occupies so large a place in S. K.'s books and journals, not a single mention is made of his mother" (p. 24).

Søren Kierkegaard, though physically frail, showed early signs of brilliance. After attending a private school, he enrolled at the University of Copenhagen. He studied theology, philosophy, history, and language, but had difficulty focusing on any one topic. Indeed, he became something of a professional student and did not take his degree until 1840, two years after his father's death. He inherited a considerable sum of money from his father, making it possible to pursue the career of his choice—writing.

In 1840, the twenty-seven-year-old Kierkegaard was engaged to Regine Olsen, the seventeen-year-old daughter of a highly respected civil servant. The lengthy love story, worthy of a detailed review (see Lowrie, 1970), ended when Kierkegaard concluded that a great chasm existed between the young girl and the now middle-aged philosopher so burdened by the dark mysteries of the human mind. Over Olsen's strong and persistent protests, Kierkegaard broke off the engagement. The experience filled him with an anguish that had a profound effect on his thought and the content of the major philosophical works that came from his pen.

Following the termination of his relationship with Olsen, Kierkegaard turned to writing. Typically publishing under a pseudonym, he produced works that occupy a prominent place in twentieth-century existentialism. Among the many books were *Either/Or: A Fragment on Life* (1843/1987), *Fear and Trembling* (1843/1983), *Philosophical Fragments* (1844/1985), *Stages on Life's Way* (1845/1967), *Concluding Unscientific Postscript* (1846/1941), and *The Sickness Unto Death* (1849/1989).

In Kierkegaard's later years, he launched a bitter attack on the Danish Church, maintaining that church officials neglected the religion embraced by Jesus. Kierkegaard was more and more embittered and isolated by the counterattacks that followed. He died in 1855, leaving the simple but fitting epitaph, "That Individual."

Kierkegaard was ignored or ridiculed in his own time, but his work continues to enjoy prominence in the twenty-first century. His philosophical views have had enormous influence in philosophy, religion, psychology, and literature. In a comment on Kierkegaard's influence, Taylor (1987) noted that "the insights of this lonely Dane pervade contemporary thought and shape the way many people now understand their lives" (p. 300).

Kierkegaard is understood partly in terms of his rejection of rationalism. Systematic conceptual schemes are inadequate because experience is not yet finished. Furthermore, truths that are simply grasped by the intellect have little to do with the real issues of life. For such issues, we must freely and actively appropriate truth. If we fail to do this, we do not achieve real selfhood. Instead, we remain in the mode of the herd, marked by passive unexamined existence.

In his major works, Kierkegaard examined three modes of existence: the aesthetic, the ethical, and the religious. Each mode has a characteristic dominant goal as well as an ironic element that exposes certain absurdities. The **aesthetic mode of existence** is marked either by sensual goals or by rational–intellectual goals. The sensualist may be in love with love, but incapable of real loving commitment to another person. Instead, other individuals are used as means for the sensualist's erotic pleasures. Such an individual has no strong ties to the past or the future; it is only the temporary joy of the passing moment that counts.

In a similar manner, the rational–intellectualist is interested only in abstractions. Concrete individuals become lost in the vague generalizations of the intellect. As noted by Schrag (1982), "Just as for the sensualist every girl is a woman in general, so for the intellectualist all reality is dissolved into general categories. Speculative thought sees only the general movement of history, explained through the mediation of logical categories, but forgets the individuals who [apprehend themselves] within their particular and concrete history" (p. 1296). Both the sensualist and the intellectualist can be insulated from the pain of concrete real-life situations wherein individuals are faced with agonizing and vexing decisions. Both can remain aloof because of all-encompassing definitions and clean logical categories that efficiently and coldly dictate a course of action with no regard for the host of particularities confronting each individual. According to Kierkegaard, the aesthetic mode of existence breeds indifference, which may collapse into boredom. Such boredom results in a quest for new diversions, but when the excitement of a new diversion has run its course, one is confronted with emptiness, melancholy, and despair.

The **ethical mode of existence**, according to Kierkegaard, is marked by a deep concern for justice, universal good, and genuine moral commitment. Unlike those in the aesthetic mode, those in the ethical mode are reflective and oriented toward a careful evaluation of the future consequences of their actions. The ethical stage is characterized by the growth of individuation and

selfhood and a shouldering of responsibility. The ethicist recognizes the critical role of freedom in human life. Thus, the necessity and anxiety associated with choices have been confronted and accepted as one of the demands placed on a truly integrated self. Clearly, the ethicist is developmentally ahead of the aestheticist in the quest for selfhood.

Whereas aestheticism collapses into emptiness, melancholy, and despair, the ethical mode can lead to a profound sense of irony. The ethicist may become aware of moral complexities, of the difficulties of balancing conflicting claims, and of according proper weights to differing points of view. As a consequence, the ethicist may develop a deep sense of the many faces of irony in human life. Complete justice, balance, and equity—the primary goals of the ethical mode—are, in the end, impossible.

The **religious mode of existence**, according to Kierkegaard, is marked by sensitivity to one's contingency and complete dependence on God. In the religious mode, one is confronted with the crisis of the demands of faith versus human rational demands. Faith may require the impossible and the absurd, and one may collapse in terror at the prospect of faith flying in the face of reason. Authentic selfhood surfaces in the religious mode when one accepts responsibility for adjudicating between the claims of faith and those of reason.

Kierkegaard's modes are not necessarily stage-like or successive and rarely does one live exclusively in one mode. Rather, all of these modes operate in human life, and in the lives of most individuals one may see evidence of the operation of all three modes with one more dominant than another at a given time, but another more dominant later. Kierkegaard had a deep interest in the practical issues of life and in the ways human beings cope with their problems (Watkin, 1998), particularly the anxiety that appears fundamental for humans (Sharpless, 2012) and the ways in which people create meaning (Proulx, 2013). His work contains a kind of psychological philosophy much different from earlier philosophical systems in which the focus was on more rarefied problems such as the ultimate stuff of the universe, the existence of God, or the nature of truth.

MARTIN HEIDEGGER   Martin Heidegger (1889–1976) was one of the most important and original existentialists of the twentieth century. Following the work of Unamuno and Kierkegaard, he focused on questions that influenced philosophy, psychology, sociology, religion, and literature.

Heidegger was born on September 26, 1889, in Messkirch, Germany. Reared in a Catholic family, he developed interests in history and theology. For a brief period, he was a novitiate in the Jesuit Order but later pursued a Ph.D. in philosophy at Freiburg. He had had a long-standing interest in the psychology and philosophy of Franz Brentano. After completing his Ph.D. in 1915, he studied with Brentano's student, Edmund Husserl.

During the early 1930s, in the initial stages of his academic career, Heidegger's deep loyalty to Germany compelled him to favor National Socialism. For a time, he joined the Nazi party and even supported Hitler in speeches; these activities continue to raise questions about his ideas (Faye, 2009; O'Brien, 2010; Stolorow et al., 2010). Later, he changed his views, leading to tension with the Nazi government. As a consequence, he lost his university position and was forced into common labor. On more than one occasion, Heidegger experienced the difficulty of falling out of favor. Earlier, he had shifted his allegiance from orthodox Catholicism to a more liberal perspective. After the defeat of Hitler in World War II, Heidegger was restored to his professorial post at Freiburg, though his position was never secure because of his earlier affiliation with the Nazi movement. Heidegger's masterpiece is *Being and Time* (1927/1962), a classic book in existential metaphysics in twentieth-century philosophy. Heidegger died on May 26, 1976, in the town of his birth, Messkirch, Germany.

Heidegger's first concern was ontology or the nature of being. More specifically, he was concerned with the meaning of individual existence. He was also concerned with the practical questions of *how* we exist individually and collectively in this world. What is an authentic mode of being? How do we get trapped in unauthentic modes of being?

In his *Being and Time*, Heidegger employed the German term **Dasein**, which literally means "being there." We may find ourselves in a world not of our own choosing. Three hallmarks of this condition include factuality, existentiality, and fallenness. *Factuality* refers to the bare fact of our being in the world. *Existentiality* surfaces in the broader framework of time. Not only are we in the world, but we are directional creatures, always going somewhere with real possibilities. *Fallenness* refers to breakdowns in existentiality. We simply drift, filling time with vacuous or meaningless activities. Outside forces propel us, leaving us with no real sense that we appropriate things for our own ends.

To lead an authentic existence, we must recognize and confront our existence and our existentiality. More than anything else, we must come to grips with our own finitude—the fact that we are going to die. This sobering fact leaves many with anxiety and dread. Unfortunately, such emotions work against our efforts to lead an authentic existence.

Heidegger believed the challenge for every human being is to exercise freedom and accept responsibility for the future. Taking such a stand, unfortunately, will produce anxiety, a fundamental experience for Heidegger (Elkholy, 2008). But if we fail to assume responsibility, we will be haunted by lingering guilt (because we know that we should be striving to accept responsibility). Anxiety and guilt are not attractive or admirable, but that they can inspire the courage to accept and use whatever freedom we possess is the mark of an authentic life.

Heidegger used the term *Dasein*, or "being-in-the-world," to reflect his belief that the person and the world are inseparable. He analyzed the world in terms of regions that impose restrictions on our quest for authenticity. The **Umwelt** (the environment) refers to the surrounding world or the world of events and things. One person's world may be yielding or malleable, but for another it may be restrictive and uncompromising. Another region is the **Mitwelt** (the community) or our life with other people. The Mitwelt, like the Umwelt, may be yielding and responsive or rigid and constrictive. Dasein must be understood in the context of the Mitwelt and the Umwelt. Appropriation, movement, and authenticity must often be forged in difficult circumstances.

Heidegger recognized the powerful role of causal forces in human life. Circumstances in our life and environment may place restrictions on authenticity. He used the term **throwness** to refer to conditions, forces, or facts that do not easily yield to human effort. But according to Heidegger, the authentic individual who is aware of her or his own Dasein may produce real effects even when the Umwelt and Mitwelt seem almost overwhelming.

In addition to major impacts in philosophy (Emad, 2007), Heidegger's work has important implications for psychiatry (Bracken, 1999; Burston, 1998), especially his method of understanding being-in-the-world, known as *Daseinsanalysis*, which in turn inspired Ludwig Binswanger to develop an existential therapeutic perspective by that name (Holzhey-Kunz & Fazekas, 2012). Heidegger lamented that humans are so concerned with gadgets and technology that we fail to study the most important thing of all—our being-in-the-world.

Phenomenology

Scholars have used the term **phenomenology** in multiple ways (see Gavin, 1976; Schmitt, 1967), but as used here, it refers to a philosophical movement and to a way of studying or a method of approaching a subject. Literally, the term *phenomenon* means appearance, but it refers more specifically to that which is given in experience. The phenomenological method seeks to discover that which is given in experience as opposed to that which is dictated by the investigator's presuppositions or theories, and phenomenology has affected many areas of psychological science and practice (Ashworth & Chung, 2009). It may prove difficult to lay aside prejudices, theories, and assumptions that have

guided past inquiries, but phenomenological investigations demand the researcher make such an effort.

As an illustration of phenomenology, we can look to James and Freud for contrasting approaches to the issue of religious conversion. Freud (1927/1961c) reviewed a case study and then proceeded with an elaborate analysis showing how conversion was based on a resolution of the Oedipus complex. Following his review of the case, he raised the question of whether "by understanding this case we have thrown any light at all on the psychology of conversion in general" (p. 171).

In his classic book *The Varieties of Religious Experience* James provided careful descriptions of case after case of religious conversion. He studied the conversion experience based on individual descriptions. As a result, James's commentary remained close to the data. His study of religious conversion is more in keeping with phenomenological method than Freud's approach. With an emphasis on observation, description, and classification, James's softer methodology was more neutral than Freud's method. James's approach was comparable to the work of his contemporary, Edmund Husserl.

EDMUND HUSSERL   The German philosopher **Edmund Husserl (1859–1938)** is commonly regarded as the founder of phenomenology. He was born in Prossnitz, Moravia. Though trained in mathematics and science, Husserl shifted to philosophy after studying with Franz Brentano in Vienna. He taught at the University of Halle from 1887 to 1901, at Göttingen from 1901 to 1916, and at Freiburg from 1916 to 1929.

Like earlier philosophers such as Bacon and Descartes, Husserl was concerned about sources of error that interfere with knowledge. He argued for a deep epistemic awareness marked by a persistent quest for clarity. Nothing was taken for granted or accepted as truth without painstaking scrutiny. Husserl was critical of experimental psychology (Giorgi, 2010a), and he believed that our knowledge of the world and our knowledge of ourselves begins with an examination of human consciousness. Whatever is given, regardless of the nature of the inquiry, is given in consciousness. What is given in consciousness may be missed because of the narrowness of an investigation or the observer's prejudices. The phenomenological method calls for a different approach, one characterized as a kind of **disciplined naiveté** (see MacLeod, 1968b, p. 69). Husserl's ideal was to approach consciousness while suspending presuppositions so things can be captured in their givenness.

Husserl's phenomenology had numerous implications for psychology (Mays, 1998; Nissim-Sabat, 1999). First, it opposed any theory that restricts the range of human nature. Psychology from a phenomenological perspective should include the enormous varieties of consciousness. Another implication comes in the belief that the phenomena of consciousness cannot be compared with anything else. Theoretical models such as the computer model or animal models, at best, approximate human life. At worst, they dehumanize us. Phenomenological psychology also opposed reductionism (Giorgi, 2012). What is given in consciousness (such as a fear) is a legitimate subject for investigation in its own right. Nevertheless, phenomenologists encourage dialogue with those who work with models such as the computer (see Mruk, 1989).

Another implication for phenomenological psychology is methodological. Phenomenology calls for new kinds of *seeing*, a new way of exploring consciousness (see Natsoulas, 1990), and many methodological variations exist (Giorgi, 2010b). The method should not be confused with Titchener's introspection. MacLeod (1964) noted that, "there is no place in introspective analysis for meaning, except insofar as meanings can be reduced to elements and their attributes. For the phenomenologist, meaning is central and inescapable" (p. 54). The phenomenological method, unlike introspection, encourages the subject to report what is naturally there including the content, impressions, meanings, and associations.

In 1969, a journal titled *Journal of Phenomenological Psychology* was established to promote the discipline's appeal and research. In this journal one might encounter articles on methodological issues in the phenomenological framework or on topical areas such as "boredom" (Bargdill, 2000), "not belonging" (Clegg, 2006), or "the experience of spontaneous altruism" (Mastain, 2006). An examination of the journal reveals an emphasis on the daily world of lived experience. Though phenomenology does not represent a major school of psychology, it is influential. In the words of Mruk (1989) phenomenology reminds "psychology that it is foremost a human science, and can no more afford the stifling presence of intellectual monopolies than can any other genuinely scientific endeavor" (p. 37).

FRANZ BRENTANO Franz Brentano (1838–1917) had a profound influence on Husserl and phenomenological psychology. In Chapter 11, we saw that Brentano embraced numerous adaptations of scientific procedure. He viewed voluntary and involuntary behaviors such as blushing as practical guides to inner processes. Brentano talked about the importance of genetic studies (e.g., studies of the actions of infants) and comparative studies that make use of primitive societies. He spoke about the importance of applied psychology and stressed the proactive, intentional, or forward-looking aspects of human life. His emphasis on intentionality, the active and the central nature of experience, and on the unity of consciousness share affinities with humanistic psychology.

THE FORMAL EMERGENCE OF HUMANISTIC PSYCHOLOGIES

Following World War II, many psychologists were unhappy with behaviorism's pessimistic view of human nature (DeCarvalho, 1990). A number of psychologists advocated a broader methodology and expansion of topics along with a focus on healthy human beings rather than animals or poorly adjusted human beings. Founded in 1961, the *Journal of Humanistic Psychology* provided a formal support structure for the new orientation as did the American Association of Humanistic Psychology, later renamed the

Association of Humanistic Psychology. In the early 1970s, the American Psychological Association (APA) established Division 32, the Division of Humanistic Psychology. DeCarvalho (1990) noted, "Within the space of a decade, humanistic psychology has earned a small but official place within mainstream psychology" (p. 31). In the 1970s and 1980s, an increasing number of educational programs provided graduate courses and degrees with an emphasis on the humanistic orientation. In subsequent decades, the humanistic school flourished with support from institutes, correspondence courses, and seminars. We turn now to some of the founders of humanistic psychology.

Abraham Maslow

Abraham H. Maslow (1908–1970) was born on April 1, 1908. He became introverted and lonely during his time growing up in Brooklyn, New York. By his own account, his cold and domineering mother cast a shadow over his childhood. At times, Rose Maslow could be demeaning and even cruel. Hoffman (1988) shares a defining moment in Abraham Maslow's tragic relationship with his mother:

> As a youngster, he was walking alone one day, when he discovered two abandoned baby kittens on the street. He decided to take them home and care for them. Quietly he carried them into the house and down into the basement. That evening, Rose came home and heard the kittens' meows. She descended to the basement and found her son feeding the kittens from a dish of milk. Doubly enraged that he had brought stray cats into her house and then used her dishes to feed them, she seized the kittens. Before his horrified eyes, Rose smashed each one's head against the basement wall until it was dead. (p. 8)

Despite undergoing psychoanalysis later in his life, Maslow never overcame his bitter resentment toward his mother. He saw her only on sparse occasions after leaving home as a teenager.

Even in late middle age, Maslow's contempt was obvious in a personal journal entry:

> What I had reacted to and totally hated and rejected was not only her physical appearance, but also her values and world view, her stinginess, her total selfishness, her lack of love for anyone else in the world—even her own husband and children—her narcissism, her Negro prejudice, her exploitation of anyone, her assumption that anyone was wrong who disagreed with her, her lack of friends, her sloppiness and dirtiness, her lack of family feeling for her own parents and siblings, her primitive animal-like care for herself and her body alone.
>
> I've always wondered where my utopianism, ethical stress, humanism, stress on kindness, love, friendship, and all the rest came from. I knew certainly of the direct consequences of having no mother-love. But the whole thrust of my life-philosophy and all my research and theorizing also has its roots in a hatred for and revulsion against everything she stood for. (Cited in Hoffman, 1988, p. 9)

Maslow's father dreamed his son would become a lawyer, but Maslow was drawn to psychology. Around the same time, he married his cousin, Bertha Goodman. The shy young man attended the University of Wisconsin at Madison, where he became the first graduate student of Harry Harlow (1905–1981). Under Harlow's supervision, Maslow conducted research on primate dominance and sexuality. After earning his Ph.D. in 1934, he held positions at Columbia University, Brooklyn College, and Brandeis University. He had a remarkable education in psychology, working with notable figures such as Harlow, E. B. Titchener, Edward Thorndike, Erich Fromm, Karen Horney, and Max Wertheimer. Maslow served as APA president in 1968. Two years later, Maslow sustained a massive heart attack while jogging. He died on June 8, 1970.

Maslow's best-known books include *Motivation and Personality* (1954), *Toward a Psychology of Being* (1962), and *Religion, Values, and Peak Experiences* (1964). Throughout his major works, Maslow criticized the methodological and substantive narrowness of behaviorism and psychoanalysis. He set out to formulate a holistic system of psychology sensitive to the unique features of human experience. He designed a system of psychology that was *problem-centered* rather than *means-centered*. According to Maslow, a means-centered approach emphasizes methodology, techniques, apparatus, orthodoxy, an overemphasis on premature quantification, and a tendency to work on "safe problems" rather than significant ones. For Maslow, problems should be placed in higher priority than methods. He accepted the challenge of redrawing and expanding the discipline's boundaries into more humanistic territory without compromising scientific credibility (Nicholson, 2001).

As stated in his book *Motivation and Personality*, his goal was to create a perspective that was "holistic rather than atomistic, dynamic rather than static, dynamic rather than causal, purposive rather than simple-mechanical" (Maslow, 1954, p. 27). He disliked the idea that the fundamental unit in psychology is a reflex, simple sensation, muscle twitch, or unconscious memory. Instead, the fundamental datum in psychology is something larger, a whole rather than a part. He insisted that he was not attacking science, but an attitude toward science. He believed science could be approached from a holistic-analytic standpoint rather than from a reductive-analytic perspective. In the holistic-analytic orientation, the scientist studies part of a whole rather than the isolated part itself. Maslow did not oppose analysis as such; rather, he emphasized a global phenomenon (e.g., blushing, laughter, sense of self-esteem) and then the role of a given part in the organization and dynamics of the whole.

MOTIVATION   Maslow's focus on the dynamic and purposive dimensions of human life emerged in his well-known hierarchical theory of motivation. His motivation theory found its way into mainstream psychology and remains his best-known contribution. Although he saw his theory as consistent with both experimental and clinical psychology, Maslow disagreed with monistic theories of motivation that emphasize single or exclusive determinants of behavior. Instead he emphasized a pluralistic hierarchical approach.

Biological Needs   At the bottom of the hierarchy, we find basic *biological needs* such as hunger, thirst, and sleep that all creatures must meet to survive. Even at this level, needs are individually tailored by more basic biochemical conditions in the blood (e.g., fat content, acid level, calcium content). Thus, appetite is based on a great many influences, most of which are unconscious.

Safety Needs   The next step in Maslow's hierarchy is the safety needs: "If the physiological needs are relatively well gratified, there then emerges a new set of needs, which we may categorize roughly as the *safety needs*" (Maslow, 1954, p. 84). Safety needs cannot be a dominant force in life until physiological needs are gratified. A hungry or thirsty animal may be forced to forego safety to satisfy a physiological need. But once physiological needs are met, safety may become the dominant feature of life.

Psychological Needs   Following the gratification of biological and safety needs, the individual seeks to fulfill *psychological needs* for love, affection, and belonging. The search for authentic emotional ties with others may now become the dominant force in life. Maslow (1954) contended that the person "may even forget that once, when he was hungry, he sneered at love as unreal or unnecessary or unimportant" (p. 89). He believed that failure to gratify the needs for love and belonging is the most common force in human adjustment problems.

Esteem Needs   The fourth set of needs in Maslow's hierarchy includes needs for esteem and recognition. Here we find a need for feelings of worth, competence, recognition for achievement, and adequacy. Maslow claimed Adler recognized such needs even as Freud neglected them. Maslow contended that failure to satisfy these needs diminishes personality, leading to a sense of weakness, inferiority, and helplessness.

Self-Actualization In the early development of his work, Maslow conceived **self-actualization** as the pinnacle of his need hierarchy. The Gestalt psychologist Kurt Goldstein had coined the term and, as mentioned in Chapter 16, it occupied a place in Jung's psychology. According to Maslow, self-actualization refers to self-fulfillment that comes from realizing or accomplishing our individual potential. For one person, self-actualization may come from achievements in aesthetic activities (e.g., dancing, music, or art), whereas for another it may come about through achievements in cognitive activities (e.g., philosophy or science). Maslow suggested that self-actualization is delayed until other needs (i.e., physiological, safety, belonging, and self-esteem) have been satisfied.

As noted, in his early theory, Maslow placed self-actualization at the top of his need hierarchy. It has been argued, however (see Koltko-Rivera, 2006), that in his later work, Maslow intended that **self-transcendence** might occupy a still higher place in human need structures. Self-transcendence points to the capacity of an individual to examine her or his worldview and its limitations in relation to more comprehensive multicultural perspectives. Self-transcendence allows for the development of a kind of epistemic humility and a deeper understanding of the complexity of things. Such transcendence can be a source of wisdom, "peak experiences," and an innovative spirituality that rises above self-centered and culturally bound perspectives (Maslow, 1964).

Maslow's hierarchical theory of motivation represented a challenge to more monistic theories that emphasize the all-pervasive influence of one dominant motivational trend (e.g., sex, power, economic motivation). Not surprisingly, his hierarchical theory has drawn the attention of critics. Shaw and Colimore (1988), for example, argued that the theory is contradictory in that it "contains both democratic and elitist worldviews" (p. 51). They used it as an illustration of how socioeconomic and political contexts can condition psychological theory. Such a criticism may be valid, but it must also be disciplined. Einstein's physics was, on more than one occasion, accused of being

Jewish (see Gimbel, 2012). Cognitive work, even if conditioned by political or religious context, may nevertheless be applicable to a larger domain. If self-actualization is an innate need, as Maslow believed, then his theory could have considerable generality regardless of its origins.

A related criticism is that Maslow's theory is so individualistic that it leads to a kind of self-seeking and to a neglect of emphasis on the common good. In this context, Daniels (1988) claimed that "the central issue here is whether self-actualization is a goal to be sought directly or whether it emerges as a 'by-product' of living" (p. 21). The tensions between self-actualization and deep ecological and social awareness remain a central issue in motivation theory. Maslow found no necessary contradiction between being a self-actualized person and one with deep sensitivities to the larger good. Indeed, it is the person who is frustrated with respect to the gratification of lower-level needs who is a potential danger.

In his book *Toward a Psychology of Being*, Maslow (1962) contrasted the terms *being* and *deficiency* in relation to a variety of psychological functions such as love, motivation, and cognition. For example, *deficiency-love* and *being-love* (expressed by Maslow as D-love and B-love) are different. B-love is non-possessive, joyful, and less selfish and demanding. It takes pride in the being of another person and it shares in the achievements and accomplishments of the other person. D-love, by contrast, is more likely to be selfish, to use the other person for one's own need satisfaction. D-love is interested more in its own gratification than in the gratification of the needs of another person. It is more likely to include jealousy, possessiveness, and unrealistic expectations.

Maslow's application of the D and B concepts to motivation and cognition argues against the idea that his theory is overly individualistic. For example, as one grows in B-cognition, one is more likely to be ecologically and socially aware and insightful. By contrast, D-cognition is marked by a more truncated and selective approach to information, such that one is informed by only a single issue or a single system of thought. Under such conditions, information is often used as a means of reducing anxiety rather than for achieving true growth.

THE SELF-ACTUALIZING PERSON   During the 1930s, Maslow attended Max Wertheimer's lectures at the New School for Social Research and discovered a refreshing alternative to the molecular and mechanistic assumptions of behaviorism and psychoanalysis. Wertheimer promoted Maslow's interest in the role of values in human experience as well as the importance of studying healthy individuals. Around the same time, Maslow noticed that another mentor, Ruth Fulton Benedict (1887–1948), an eminent cultural anthropologist at Columbia University, shared remarkable characteristics with Wertheimer. Like Wertheimer, Benedict was a passionate champion of holism over reductionism. Both scholars offered a glimpse into a unique form of personality development. Secretly, Maslow examined Benedict and Wertheimer. He noted that these observations

> started out as the effort of a young intellectual to try to understand two of his teachers whom he loved, adored, and admired and who were very, very wonderful people. It was a kind of high-IQ devotion. I could not be content simply to adore, but sought to understand why these two people were so different from the run-of-the-mill people in the world. (Maslow, 1971, pp. 41–42)

Maslow realized his training in psychology could not put proper perspective on the bold and unusual character of his mentors (Frick, 2000). Maslow hosted a party and was delighted when both Wertheimer and Benedict attended. Following this stimulating evening at his home, he tried to find a common theme in their personalities:

> When I tried to understand them, think about them, and write about them in my journal and my notes, I realized in one wonderful moment that their two patterns could be generalized. I was talking about a kind of person, not about two noncomparable individuals. . . . I tried to see whether this pattern could be found elsewhere, and I did find it elsewhere, in one person after another. (Maslow, 1971, pp. 41–42)

Although crude and informal, Maslow's initial observations evolved into a disciplined undertaking that he recorded in a *GHB* (Good Human Being) notebook from 1945 through 1949 (Lowry, 1973). Maslow (1943) believed that his analysis of a life well lived was "in the functionalist tradition of James and Dewey, and is fused with the holism of Wertheimer, Goldstein, and Gestalt psychology, and with the dynamicism of Freud and Adler" (p. 371).

After rejecting terms such as *good human being*, *saintly person*, *self-fulfilling person*, or the unwieldy *almost ideally healthy human being*, Maslow seized on Kurt Goldstein's concept of *self-actualization* as a descriptor for his observations. Maslow read biographies and autobiographies of historically eminent women and men, searching for common characteristics of healthy-minded people. In developing his criteria of healthy people, Maslow (1954) was "fairly sure" he had discovered nine people who were *self-actualizing* individuals; Benedict and Wertheimer joined Thomas Jefferson and Abraham Lincoln on the list as well as several anonymous acquaintances of Maslow's. He also identified seven highly probable figures, including Jane Addams, Albert Einstein, Aldous Huxley, William James, Eleanor Roosevelt, Albert Schweitzer, and Benedict Spinoza. Finally, Maslow decided on thirty-seven potential cases of self-actualizing people that included Ralph Waldo Emerson, Johann Wolfgang Goethe, George Washington, and Walt Whitman.

Maslow believed that fifteen positive or favorable characteristics could be identified in self-actualizing people, including a realistic and problem-centered perception of the world, a refreshing sense of spontaneity and simplicity, and a genuine acceptance of one's self as well as others. He observed that such *good specimens* have a mature, unhostile sense of humor together with a quality of detachment and a fierce need for privacy and autonomy resulting in deep interpersonal relations with only a few friends. Nonetheless, Maslow believed that self-actualizing persons have a great need to identify with all of humanity, roughly analogous to Alfred Adler's concept of social interest (McFarland et al., 2012). Additionally, they have a strong ethical sense and belief in democratic values that fosters resistance to the stifling effects of enculturation and obedience. In this context, the Asian schools of Taoism and Zen Buddhism influenced Maslow's investigations of transcendent states of consciousness (Cleary & Shapiro, 1996). For example, the self-actualizing person's need for creative expression and continued freshness of appreciation and wonder about the world may manifest itself in periodic mystical or *peak experiences* (Maslow, 1964). Maslow observed many of these traits in Wertheimer, for example, as he would play on the floor with his children or leap onto a desk for emphasis during a lecture (Hoffman, 1988).

Despite the admirable personality characteristics of self-actualizing people, Maslow cautioned against the belief that anyone ever achieves perfection. Indeed, there are traits in self-actualized people that may be perceived in a less than favorable way by others. For example, in their quest for truth, such individuals may exhibit periodic absentmindedness, unexpected ruthlessness, and *surgical coldness*. They are not free of conflict, occasional self-doubt, mistakes, regrets, and the like. In balance, however, their lives are guided by a realistic, coherent, productive, healthy, and forward-looking perspective.

OTHER CHARACTERISTICS OF MASLOW'S PSYCHOLOGY Maslow believed there is more to be gained by studying healthy self-actualizing people than by studying sick people or nonhuman models. In his view, the study of healthy people will broaden the subject matter of psychology. New topical areas will, for example, include play, love, values, mystical experiences, humor, meanings of freedom, competence, and aesthetic needs. In other words, psychology should focus at least as much on the positive as on the negative

dimensions of life. One of the most important topics in Maslow's vision of the discipline is to understand *meta-level awareness*. Such awareness refers to a capacity for meaningful self-appraisal that fosters growth in the direction of meaningful and realistic personal goals. Above all, Maslow advocated a positive psychology, which he called Eupsychia (the *well-being of the psyche*, as Coon, 2006, shares it), as an alternative to the negative emphasis in other systems. His positive emphasis may account for the theory's enormous popularity. As noted by Coon (2006), Maslow had a significant influence in the field of psychology, but his impact on the business community, particularly on the field of consulting (O'Roark, 2007) and in the emergence of management ideas (Cooke et al., 2005), in educational circles, the women's movement, and the broader American culture was even greater. There has been a continuing belief that the motivation hierarchy has considerable theoretical and practical utility.

Gordon Allport

In the tradition of William James, **Gordon Allport (1897–1967)** maintained a belief in individual experience. He advocated a psychology consistent with democracy and freedom, and opposed any system that restrains us in methodological or substantive straightjackets. Although distinguished in several areas, the psychology of personality became the hallmark of Allport's career (see Nicholson, 1998, for insights about how Allport's personality work was grounded in the moral and cultural politics of his age).

Allport was born in Montezuma, Indiana, on November 11, 1897. He and his older brother, Floyd H. Allport (1890–1978), were raised in a hardworking Midwestern home. While Gordon completed undergraduate studies at Harvard, Floyd earned his Ph.D. in 1919 under E. B. Holt and Hugo Münsterberg. Floyd suggested that Gordon consider devoting his dissertation to the study of personality, an unorthodox subject in American psychology at the time (Nicholson, 2000). After completing his doctoral degree at Harvard in 1922, Gordon traveled to Europe,

Gordon Allport

where he had positive encounters with Carl Stumpf, Max Wertheimer, and Wolfgang Köhler among others. (Allport had met Sigmund Freud years before but came away unimpressed with the man and his depth psychology.) He returned from Europe and accepted a position at Harvard, where he worked for most of the next four decades.

During the early 1920s, the Allport brothers worked together on the classification and measurement of personality traits, culminating in their 1928 Ascendance-Submission (A-S) Scale. By 1924, however, their collaboration soured over theoretical differences as Floyd embraced a more objective behavioral approach and Gordon rejected it (Nicholson, 2000). In time, Gordon became the principal architect of American personality theory (Barenbaum & Winter, 2013) and Floyd assumed a significant role in founding social psychology (he wrote an early book in the area and directed America's first doctoral program in social psychology at Syracuse University). Gordon Allport served as APA president in 1939 and received the

Distinguished Scientific Contribution Award from that organization in 1964. He died at the age of seventy in 1967.

Allport's book *Personality: A Psychological Interpretation*, published in 1937, ranks as one of the important classics in that field (see Craik, Hogan, & Wolfe, 1993). His better-known works in personality include *Becoming: Basic Considerations for a Psychology of Personality* (1955) and *Pattern and Growth in Personality* (1961). He also published a work with P. E. Vernon and G. Lindzey titled *A Study of Values* (1951). Among his other works are the classics *The Nature of Prejudice* (1954) and *The Individual and His Religion* (1950).

In his book *Becoming*, Allport distinguished between the **Leibnizian tradition** and the **Lockean tradition** in psychology. The former emphasizes the proactive (purposive or goal-directed) nature of human life and the latter emphasizes the reactive (mechanistic) dimensions of life. Allport said that the Lockean tradition is evident in S-R behavioristic psychologies with their emphasis on animal models, machine theory, conditioning, and determinism. He preferred a Leibnizian tradition that argued for an active intellect, integrative self-actualizing capacities, and the important role of expectation or the forward-looking tendencies in human beings.

Allport also distinguished between **idiographic** and **nomothetic** orientations. The former places emphasis on individual experience (such as case studies) and the latter concentrates on statistical abstractions such as group norms, means, standard deviations, and the like. Allport did not deny the importance of the nomothetic orientation but was concerned that in the rush to be scientific, psychology might neglect the most important reality—namely, individual experience in all of its uniqueness and complexity. His emphasis on the nomothetic traditions is reflected in his enduring work on prejudice (Dovidio et al., 2005), particularly in the 1950s, when prejudice formed integral parts of the legal, constitutional, economic, and educational landscapes in the United States (Loewen, 2005). Although scholars had examined these ideas before Allport, he developed attitude measures and brought these ideas into the psychological mainstream (Webster et al., 2010). He examined social factors that decrease prejudice, including the conditions under which intergroup contact reduced prejudice (Tropp, 2006), and he also emphasized ideographic factors in prejudice, including the first proposal attempting to identify the nature of a prejudiced personality (Roets & Van Hiel, 2011).

Allport was interested in the subject of motivation. He believed biological drives, learned motives, and concepts of homeostasis and maintenance cannot do justice to the dynamic qualities of human motivation. He coined the term **functional autonomy** to mean that an activity is independent of its original source and is now motivating in its own right. He gave the example of a person who goes to sea to earn a living by fishing or transporting goods. In time, however, going to sea may be motivating in its own right so that the person enjoys being on the sea even after becoming financially independent. Allport believed that human motivation is not just a matter of maintaining equilibrium, nor just a matter of satisfying basic biological urges. On the contrary, it is often oriented toward growth, risk, novelty, and adventure.

Allport saw habit as an important early determiner of activity, but in time human beings make selections and live in terms of superordinate goals and motives. As we mature, we develop traits that provide stability to personality. In his book *Becoming* (1955) and in his classic contribution to the psychology of religion, *The Individual and His Religion* (1950), Allport discussed the conditions that contribute to radical personality changes. In *Becoming*, Allport (1955) wrote, "It sometimes happens that the very center of organization of personality shifts suddenly and apparently without warning. Some impetus coming perhaps from a bereavement, an illness, or a religious conversion, even from a teacher or a book, may lead to a reorientation" (p. 87). In *The Individual and His Religion*, Allport discussed the effects of battle experiences on such recentering. Allport proposed a broad system of psychology that challenged the behaviorist and

psychoanalytic traditions. He was a prominent figure in the founding of third-force or humanistic psychology.

Carl R. Rogers

The founder of a new approach to therapy (first called *nondirective*, then *client-centered*, and finally *person-centered therapy*), **Carl R. Rogers (1902–1987)** was an innovative almost revolutionary figure in the third-force movement. He received world acclaim for a new approach to psychology that influenced psychotherapy, education, and personality theory.

Rogers was born in Chicago on January 8, 1902. He was educated at the University of Wisconsin, at Union Theological Seminary in New York City, and at Columbia University, where he earned a Ph.D. in psychology in 1931. Rogers held positions at the Rochester Guidance Center, the Ohio State University, the University of Chicago, and the University of Wisconsin. From 1964 until his death in 1987, he worked in La Jolla, California, at the Center for the Study of the Person, an organization he helped found. In 1947, Rogers served as APA president. In 1956, he was among the first three (along with Wolfgang Köhler and Kenneth Spence) to receive the APA's Distinguished Scientific Contribution Award. Rogers's best-known books are *Client-Centered Therapy* (1951) and *On Becoming a Person* (1961). Rogers died on February 4, 1987.

Gendlin (1988) enumerated Rogers's contributions in terms of the ways he challenged established psychology. The first amounted to an assault on the mystery and secrecy of psychotherapy. Rogers was the first to insist on a wedding of psychotherapy with the objective techniques of experimental psychology. He recorded psychotherapy sessions (with the client's permission) and assessed improvement by employing tests before and after therapy and by comparing his clients to control groups (Cain, 2010). In the words of Gendlin (1988), it was nothing less than "war against monolithic authority" (p. 127). In the end, however, Rogers's experimental approach prevailed and contributed to substantial changes in the discipline (O'Hara, 1995). Indeed, following Rogers's work, research on the effects of psychotherapy became commonplace. No longer was psychotherapy a mysterious secret reserved for an elite priesthood. Behavior therapists, though theoretically at odds with Rogers, were also major contributors to the new, more open approach to psychotherapy (see Suinn & Weigel, 1975).

Gendlin suggested that another challenge to the profession came in Rogers's stance on diagnosis in the treatment of emotional problems. In the medical model of Rogers's day, diagnosis of a patient's illness precedes treatment, but Rogers was concerned about the negative effects of labeling, and he viewed his therapeutic work as empowering clients instead of diagnosing patients (Zucconi, 2008). As a consequence, he skipped diagnosis and proceeded to the business of listening to his clients. His emphasis on listening is reflected in his development of nondirective interviewing as a therapeutic technique (Lee, 2011).

Rogers's psychology focused on the **phenomenal field**, or what he referred to as the entire range of experiences that constitute a person's life. The phenomenal field consists of a differentiated and organized region called the *self*, which, according to Rogers, includes all the ways we evaluate ourselves, the ways we evaluate others, and the ways we relate to objects in the environment. The self, in Rogers's view, values the various dimensions of the phenomenal field. He pointed to the possible tensions between the self as it is and the self as one would like it to be, or the **ideal self**. The greater the congruence between the two, for most people, the greater the health. Exceptions occur, however, in people with severe pathology (Cole, Oetting, & Hinkle, 1967).

The valuing processes of the self develop in social context. Rogers outlined the difference between **unconditional positive regard** and the conditional love to which many children are subjected as well as the role of unconditional positive regard in therapy (Bozarth, 2007). Unconditional positive regard conveys a belief in the intrinsic worth of the child. It creates the feeling that the child is loved simply in his or her very existence.

The individual does not have to earn such love; it is a gratuity. Conditional love, by contrast, carries the connotation of "I will love you if…" (e.g., if you are a better student, conform, dress properly, develop the correct interests; only then you will be valued and loved). Rogers's core ideas, including person-centered therapy as well as the importance of empathy and unconditional positive regard continue to shape therapeutic practice in the United States (Kirschenbaum & Jourdan, 2005).

After noting that Rogers studied with Alfred Adler from 1927 to 1928, Watts (1998) drew a parallel between the Rogerian ideas of empathy and unconditional positive regard and the Adlerian concept of social interest. Although working from different perspectives, both men were dedicated to facilitating people's health and well being. Like Adler, Rogers's psychology is highly optimistic about basic human nature and potential. He believed in a drive toward self-actualization and that we have the capacity to choose and to appropriate things that contribute to our growth. The task of the therapist is to provide an accepting atmosphere marked by unconditional positive regard. Rogers believed that if the proper relationship could be established between client and therapist, the client would gain insight and freedom, and these would produce growth and the ability to assume responsibility for effecting desirable personal changes.

Rogers has had a continuing influence on the discipline of psychology manifested by an outpouring of scholarly articles referenced in recent years. His system has been extended beyond psychotherapy to other fields such as education and politics. In education, he advocated a student-centered rather than a teacher-centered pedagogy. He hoped to contribute to the humanization of political systems so often driven by rigid, uncompromising, self-serving ideologies as opposed to open and honest quests for truth in the service of the public good. A Rogerian approach to politics would call for leaders to listen and respond very carefully to the voices and needs of the public. He opposed shams and appearances and valued personal qualities such as authenticity, honesty, and openness. He was especially critical of institutional structures that undermine individuality and block the potential for growth.

Viktor Frankl

The Viennese psychiatrist **Viktor E. Frankl (1905–1997)** developed **logotherapy**, a system of thought that embodies a clear expression of third-force psychology. Frankl was born in Vienna, Austria, on March 26, 1905. He had a unique experience as a teenager; he sent a paper he had written to a famous scholar whom he revered. Sigmund Freud not only responded to the young man, but he also submitted Frankl's paper to the *International Journal of Psychoanalysis*. They agreed to publish Frankl's work in 1924 (Frankl, 1997). He received an M.D. and a Ph.D. from the University of Vienna and served as professor of neurology and psychiatry at the University of Vienna Medical School. As a young neurologist, Frankl was not afraid of debating respected figures such as Sigmund Freud and the man who would become his greatest mentor, Alfred Adler (Frankl, 1997). Early in his career, Frankl broke with Adler and founded his own school based on logotherapy. Following the schools of Freud and Adler, Frankl's theory became known as the "Third Viennese School of Psychotherapy" (Barnes, 2000; Längle, 2012). He enjoyed a prosperous career as a psychiatrist in Vienna. As with other Jewish intellectuals at the time, the rise of Adolf Hitler threatened not only Frankl's career but also his life.

Frankl was imprisoned in Nazi war camps from 1942 to 1945. During the Holocaust, the Nazi regime imprisoned several members of Frankl's family who did not survive. His experiences in four different camps contributed to his perspective on psychology. Frankl's best-known book, *Man's Search for Meaning* (1985), described his concentration-camp experiences and sketched the system that he developed in subsequent years. His book became an international bestseller. Following the war, Frankl held many positions, most notably as professor of logotherapy at the United States International University (San Diego). He also served as visiting professor

at numerous universities, including Harvard and Stanford. Frankl died in September 1997.

In the preface to *Man's Search for Meaning* (1985), Gordon Allport called attention to the fact that Frankl's "father, mother, brother, and his wife died in camps or were sent to the gas ovens" (p. 9). Allport asked how Frankl, in the face of such losses, in the expectation of his own death, and in the midst of barbarous indignities, could go on living. Allport offered the opinion that one who has survived such an ordeal is worthy of our attention. Although Frankl's ideas about meaning and life predated his Holocaust experience (Frankl, 1985; Pytell, 2007), his concentration camp experiences solidified his ideas.

Frankl referred to several polls that ask people to list priorities in their lives. In each case, the leading answer involved living a purposeful or meaningful existence. The human need for meaningful existence is a core concept in Frankl's system. It is a need that is easily frustrated, sometimes by the very psychological and philosophical systems designed to alleviate human suffering. Frankl argued that people experience despair and meaninglessness if taught that they are products of conditioning or little more than a battleground of unconscious forces. He believed that behaviorism and classical psychoanalysis exercise a dehumanizing influence.

Frankl did not deny the role of conditioning in human life or that some human problems originate in the frustration of instinctual drives such as sex. He argued, however, that many human problems have their origin in the failure to find a meaning or purpose in life. In addition to psychogenic neuroses (those that result from the frustration of basic drives), Frankl describes **noogenic neuroses** (the Greek word *noos* means "mind"). He uses the term *noogenic* to refer to neuroses resulting from existential distress and the failure to find a sense of personal worth. These neuroses often include anxieties that are physical and also metaphysical and spiritual (Costello, 2011).

Frankl's logotherapy was a therapeutic intervention system for treating noogenic neurosis. The Greek term *logos* refers to a reason or a controlling principle. Logotherapy seeks to assist the individual in discovering the logos of existence. It assumes that human beings have a unique capacity to work at a kind of meta-level above the ongoing events of life. Unlike the Freudian emphasis on past experiences, logotherapy seeks a balanced solution to human concerns in the moment (Frankl, 1997). We may get caught up in the monotony of an everyday routine, but we can adopt a positive attitude about our day-to-day lives. Our perspective—be it healthy or unhealthy—can have a powerful effect on the meaning of our daily lives and work. As humans, we have the responsibility and freedom to choose how a situation will affect us (Gerwood, 1998). We often have little choice about the routine of daily life. But Frankl discovered that even in concentration camps, certain people could find meaning in their suffering. Indeed, those who found meaning were more likely to survive the unspeakable trauma. We may find ourselves, as did Frankl, in overpowering circumstances. He argued, however, that there is an arena in which choice can be real. We can take a stance toward our suffering, we can see it in a larger context, or we can find some possible and meaningful goal that it may serve. As Leslie (1996) observed, Frankl was an unapologetic optimist "in spite of everything."

Frankl believed that humans have a capacity for what he called **paradoxical intention**. The expression refers to doing the very opposite of what we would like most to do. People who have an irrational fear may consciously engage in the very thing they fear. On several repetitions, the fear may subside. Frankl believed that the capacity for the defiant or even heroic stance lies dormant in all people. It counts as a unique feature of being human.

In logotherapy, Frankl worked on meaning orientation by helping his clients search for alternative perspectives. In one case, a client was unable to overcome the grief associated with his wife's death. Rejecting standard psychoanalytic interpretations, Frankl helped the elderly client find meaning in his loss. One day, Frankl asked the widower to discuss what might have happened

had he died before his wife. The man announced that this was a horrible thought because his wife would have had to endure the suffering he now experienced. Suddenly, the client saw the whole matter in a different light. By outliving his wife, she had been spared the suffering he now endured. Frankl (1985) noted that "suffering ceases to be suffering at the moment it finds a meaning" (p. 135). Logotherapy is designed to help clients explore the range of possible meanings relevant to their situation. Given this perspective, researchers have found logotherapy to be effective in many contexts including the treatment of nursing home residents (Seeber, 2000).

Frankl rejected the idea that one meaning orientation can be relevant to all people. Rather, all individuals must authentically explore the possible meanings in their particular situation. Imitation, secondhand interpretations, rationalizations, and so forth must be rejected in favor of a genuine quest. With his individual and experiential emphasis, Frankl's methods can provide foundations for *autoethnography*, a form of self-study that examines an individual's experiences (Esping, 2010).

Gordon Allport introduced Frankl to Rogers and Maslow, as well as other leaders in humanistic psychology, and, although Frankl debated questions of therapeutic technique, meaning, and self-actualization (Pytell, 2006), Frankl's system embodies many tenets of existential and third-force psychology. He opposed pandeterminism, reductionism, and all forms of what he called "nothingbutness." He emphasized those things that are uniquely human, including the capacity to take a stance toward the daily events of our lives. Michael Novak's quotation at the beginning of this chapter captures the defiant human spirit so central to Viktor Frankl's thinking. As one trained in neurology and pharmacology, Frankl did not underestimate the neurochemical basis of life. At the same time, he declared that the error begins when we believe human beings are "nothing but" neurochemical mechanisms. He elevated the role of psychology, mental processes, and values in the overall scheme of things. Frankl's psychology is not pessimistic nor is it naïvely optimistic (Leslie, 1996); instead, it offers a middle road of hope that, both individually and collectively, people can discover meaningful beliefs with survival value. Contemporary scholarly work on his system is encountered in numerous journals and specifically in the *International Forum for Logotherapy*, a journal as the name implies, that focuses on Frankl's continuing intellectual legacy.

Joseph F. Rychlak

As we will see later, a major criticism of humanistic or third-force psychologies is that they lack the rigor associated with scientific studies. Some members of the third-force movement would not deny the legitimacy of the criticism. They might argue, however, that theories meeting the test of scientific rigor have dealt with trivial phenomena that bear little relation to our lives. Their preference is for a psychology with ecological validity that speaks to issues confronting us here and now. In this spirit, **Joseph F. Rychlak (1928–2013)** argued for a psychology both rigorous *and* humanistic.

Rychlak received his Ph.D. in clinical psychology from the Ohio State University in 1957. Much of his career was devoted to the quest for a rigorous and humanistic psychology. His position is set forth in many papers and in major works such as *The Psychology of Rigorous Humanism* (1988) and *Artificial Intelligence and Human Reason: A Teleological Critique* (1991).

Rychlak believed that traditional psychologies, especially behaviorism, constructed a model of causality that is too narrow. The emphasis in such psychologies has always been on material and efficient causality (see Chapter 2). According to Rychlak, formal and final causes, as described long ago by Aristotle, cannot be dismissed if we are to have an adequate understanding of events in our world. Even in physical systems, the central role of formal causes is critical. Rychlak accepted it as axiomatic that human beings live on the basis of their plans, anticipations, and expectations; in short, we are telic creatures. An adequate psychology, according to Rychlak, will embrace a broad concept of causality, emphasizing material, efficient, formal, and final causes. The neglect of any of these, in his view, will result in conceptual blind spots as well as strained and unnatural explanations.

Rychlak also emphasized the human capacity for oppositional thinking. In his view, like that of William James, relations are as fundamentally real as the things related. Unipolar events are not joined by mechanical association; instead, relations are often given in the flow and logic of experience itself. Indeed, some unipolarities simply come with their opposites (e.g., the concept *up* implies its opposite *down*). Human beings, in Rychlak's view, are multipolar creatures in that we see alternatives and anticipate their consequences. We then act on the basis of anticipated consequences and are thus telic creatures rather than machines (Rychlak, 2005).

Rychlak found no reason why these views must be antithetical to science or to scientific understanding, nor did he think psychologists need to alter their methods as they proceed with scientific work. What is needed, according to Rychlak, is a radically new orientation regarding the assumptions we make about human behavior in both science and psychotherapy (Rychlak, 2000). In his view, psychologists can recognize the capacity for oppositional thinking, teleology (or *telosponsivity* as he calls it), and even some degree of free will without sacrificing their scientific integrity. He argued that the so-called hard sciences, such as physics, no longer operate in terms of the Newtonian assumption that every connection in the universe is complete. Psychology, like physics, can proceed with its scientific work, even if there are uncertainties and arenas of random or even chaotic events. According to Rychlak, human research data themselves do not contradict the assumptions of a rigorous humanistic psychology. There is always variance for which the psychologist cannot give an account. He also argued that psychologists providing expert testimony in the courtroom need not reject the assumption of the court that human beings have free will (see Rychlak & Rychlak, 1990).

OVERVIEW OF THIRD-FORCE PSYCHOLOGIES: MAJOR POSITIONS AND CRITICISMS

Third-force movements, methods, and topics of study have found a significant niche in psychology (Serlin, 2011). There are journals, professional organizations, institutes, training programs, and a sizable literature supporting the orientation. Though launched in protest against behaviorism and psychoanalysis, it has developed a positive motivation of its own. Members of the third-force movement share profound disagreements, but there are numerous points of agreement.

1. *Pluralistic methodology.* Third-force theorists believe psychologists should focus first and foremost on problems. Methods should be adapted to problems rather than vice versa. They might argue that science does not consist of a single well-defined method applicable in every situation. In the interest of understanding human beings, humanistic psychologists may also employ methods (e.g., literary or artistic methods) that are not in the scientific tradition.

2. *Opposition to reductionism.* Humanistic psychologists emphasize the uniqueness of human beings and argue against the adequacy of models and analogies. If we want to understand human nature, we should study humans.

3. *Emphasis on experience.* The primary subject matter for humanistic psychologists is not behavior, unconscious processes, a single dominant motive, learning, or the senses. Rather, the emphasis is on human experience in all its richness and variety. The humanistic psychologist does not leave out anything that is a demonstrable part of human experience. A psychology that omits or reduces anything that is experienced is, to that extent, not an empirical psychology. The strong emphasis on experience means that third-force psychologies embrace the mental realm.

4. *Contextualism.* Humanistic psychologists advocate holistic studies that give due attention to natural context. They are concerned that artificial situations may produce effects that cannot be replicated in the everyday world. Though they would admit that greater rigor is achieved in artificial situations, they emphasize testing findings in natural context.

5. *Free will.* Humanistic psychologists take the experience of free will at face value; however, they do not deny important and limiting biological and social constraints. Given such constraints, or what Heidegger called "throwness," they still argue for the human capacity to take a stance against opposition, misfortune, or constraint. Free will is tied to attitude or meaning orientation.

6. *Basic human nature.* Humanistic psychologists refuse the pessimistic assumption that human nature is nasty, brutish, and self-seeking. Instead, they believe people are growth-oriented and, in healthy circumstances, display goodness and altruism. Although the lack of discussion of evil by Maslow and Rogers was seen by Rollo May as a shortcoming that could lend credibility to claims that humanistic psychology is simplistic (Hoffman, 2009; Schmid, 2013), Rogers's view challenged both behaviorism and psychoanalysis.

7. *Emphasis on relevance.* Humanistic psychologists do not accept hard distinctions between basic and applied studies. They seek a problem-oriented discipline rooted in ecological validity. Their preference is for studies connected to real problems or at least having the promise of being connected to real problems. They do not promote abstract studies with little connection to daily life.

Despite such agreement, third-force psychology is not a coherent school. Many issues and points of disagreement emerge. For example, DeCarvalho (1990) outlined important distinctions between humanistic psychologists and dominant trends in European existentialism. The points outlined previously, however, summarize central themes in third-force psychology. We turn now to criticisms of humanistic psychology.

The third-force critique of behaviorism, psychoanalysis, and other psychologies did not go unanswered. Indeed, numerous counterarguments and criticisms surfaced in the literature (see Child, 1973; Wertheimer, 1978).

1. *What is humanistic psychology?* In a critique of humanistic psychology, Wertheimer (1978) called attention to contradictions and problems associated with the term *humanistic*. It is a term with multiple meanings from the time of the Renaissance. Further, there is the implication that behavioral or psychoanalytic traditions are not humane or humanistic. That problem was illustrated beautifully when the American Humanist Association named B. F. Skinner as their humanist of the year (see Skinner, 1972). Clearly, many psychologists and systems of psychology qualify as humanistic.

2. *Views of science.* From its inception, psychology cast its lot on the side of rigor and science. Psychologists have never denied other approaches (e.g., literary, artistic, philosophical) to the study of human beings. These approaches have existed for centuries, but a truly rigorous scientific approach is novel and recent. Such an approach may not tell the whole story but deserves a chance, among other approaches, to see what it can accomplish. It is premature to denigrate such an approach or to argue that psychology per se should complement its admittedly privileged perspective with other perspectives.

3. *Attitude toward basic scientific studies.* The history of science provides ample evidence for the value of basic studies and the importance of pursuing knowledge for its own sake. The demand for relevance can have a narrowing effect on the intellectual process and thus interfere with the discovery mission of science. Many studies in the history of science would have failed the test of relevance, yet such studies provided the foundations for later breakthrough studies. The insistence on relevance is, at best, anti-intellectual; at worst, it interferes with discovery.

4. *Antireductionistic position.* Many scientists might agree that the study of part processes, or the use of analogies or models, can never do justice to any global phenomenon of interest. At the same time, they might argue that science cannot neglect part processes. Indeed,

it is the very nature of science to begin with simple elements. Any topic of interest, from a mechanical conveyance such as an automobile to a complex biological event such as a disease, must be approached with due emphasis on all the working parts. A scientific approach to human beings is no different. Wertheimer (1978) argued that the holistic approach of the humanistic psychologists is not consistent with the more informed and scientific holism of Gestalt psychology.

5. *Free will.* The celebration of free will may, in fact, impede progress by blinding psychologists to real but subtle causes. Many traditional psychologists may suspend judgment on whether there is or is not free will, but when they function as scientists, they look for causes. Humanistic belief in free will runs the risk of offering glib accounts of complex events and, thus, of interfering with scientific analysis.

Critics have voiced numerous additional concerns about third-force psychologies. Wertheimer (1978) suggested that their therapeutic procedures are suspect in terms of effecting real change, and Child (1973) accused them of neglecting the hard work of systematic observation so essential in scientific work. In a friendly review of humanistic psychology, Smith (1990) commented on strands of this orientation that are affiliated with various countercultures and spiritual–mystical groups. Some might argue that such affiliations are natural consequences of the general philosophical orientation of this school of thought. In contrast, however, theorists such as Rychlak (1988, 1998) might argue that the best of the humanistic tradition will surface in a fairly rigorous psychology that still does justice to the richness and complexity of human experience and behavior.

Humanistic psychology has maintained a continuing presence in psychology. In contemporary work, a growing interest in the field of **positive psychology** reflects third-force thinking about our life journey. Sheldon and King (2001) describe positive psychology as the "scientific study of ordinary human strengths and virtues" while urging "psychologists to adopt a more open and appreciative perspective regarding human potentials, motives, and capacities" (p. 216). This perspective continues the legacy of the giants of the Golden Age of Greece and the Epicureans as well as Maimonides, Bentham, and the Mills along with James, Adler, Jung, and the humanistic psychologists. For Seligman and Csikszentmihalyi (2000), the positive movement is grounded in *positive subjective states* (invigorating thoughts and emotions such as confidence, bliss, and optimism), *positive individual traits* (such as courage, honesty, and persistence), and *positive institutions* (such as healthy families and work environments). Compton and Hoffman (2013) find promise in a science of optimal human functioning, one that explores a life well lived through creativity, wellness, loving relationships, gratitude, spirituality, positive coping, leisure, and happiness among other endeavors. As we will see in Chapter 18, mindfulness-based treatments also share an affinity with the existential-humanistic tradition.

Review Questions

1. In what sense does humanistic psychology follow the doctrine of *learned ignorance* advocated by Nicholas of Cusa?
2. Why was humanistic psychology referred to as a third force? What are some of the distinguishing features of third-force psychology?
3. Describe at least three features in the thought of William James that identify him as an intellectual forerunner of humanistic psychology.
4. What affinities can you find between third-force psychologies and the philosophy of Unamuno?
5. Identify Kierkegaard's three modes of existence and the specific ways that each one can collapse into an undesirable state.
6. Discuss the meaning of Heidegger's term *Dasein* and the significance of that term for psychology.
7. Define Heidegger's terms *throwness*, *Mitwelt*, and *Umwelt*.
8. Discuss the implications of Husserl's phenomenology for psychology.
9. Why is Franz Brentano included in the intellectual background of third-force psychologies?

10. Outline Maslow's hierarchical theory of motivation and discuss criticisms of the theory that you consider valid.
11. Discuss some of the defining characteristics of a self-actualizing person according to Maslow.
12. Define the concept of *functional autonomy* as employed by Allport. How might a behaviorist explain functional autonomy?
13. Some of Carl Rogers's major contributions to psychology were challenges to standard practices. Discuss two such contributions.
14. What did Rogers mean by *unconditional positive regard*?
15. Describe the major focus of Frankl's logotherapy and show how his concept of *paradoxical intention* might play a role in the treatment of a fear.
16. Advance arguments for or against Rychlak's contention that humanistic psychology can be rigorous.
17. Outline five major criticisms of humanistic psychologies.

Glossary

aesthetic mode of existence   According to Kierkegaard, the emphasis on sensual or intellectual pleasure. This mode breeds indifference and boredom and the collapse into melancholy and despair.

Allport, Gordon (1897–1967)   Well-known personality psychologist interested in the development of a psychology consistent with the principles of freedom and democracy. His individualistic psychology is consistent with many of the main themes of humanistic or third-force psychologies.

Brentano, Franz (1838–1917)   Founder of act psychology (see Chapter 11), which emphasizes intentionality, the unity of consciousness, a broad methodology, and the application of psychology. Brentano's system shares numerous affinities with humanistic psychology.

Dasein   Literally, the term refers to "being-in-the-world." The term was employed by Heidegger to refer to a kind of authentic self-awareness along with a deep awareness of the surrounding environment and one's role in that environment.

disciplined naiveté   The attempt to approach the phenomena of consciousness while suspending presuppositions so that such phenomena may be captured in their givenness.

ethical mode of existence   According to Kierkegaard, the ethical mode of existence is marked by deep concerns for justice, genuine and caring moral concerns, and a capacity to shoulder responsibility. In the face of moral complexities and absurdities, the ethical mode of existence may collapse into a profound sense of irony.

existentialism   A philosophical orientation typically traced to the work of Kierkegaard and Unamuno, marked by an emphasis on the centrality of experience, the role of freedom in human life, the irreducible uniqueness of each person, rejection of reductionism, and the quest for authenticity in the face of all of the absurdities and forces that threaten human dignity.

Frankl, Viktor E. (1905–1997)   Viennese psychiatrist and founder of a humanistic orientation known as logotherapy. Frankl emphasized the importance of the quest for meaning and the human capacity to construct alternative meaning orientations.

functional autonomy   A concept employed by Gordon Allport referring to the possibility that an activity may become independent of its original motivational source and may now become reinforcing in its own right. An example is the person who originally goes to sea to make a living but soon enjoys going to sea in its own right.

Heidegger, Martin (1889–1976)   German philosopher and one of the most important existentialists of the twentieth century. Heidegger's work focused on the theoretical meaning of existence and the practical questions of how we should exist individually and collectively in the world.

Husserl, Edmund (1859–1938)   German philosopher and founder of phenomenology. He emphasized the uniqueness of consciousness, the dangers of reductionism, and an approach to the study of consciousness that attempts to describe what is naturally there in terms of content, impressions, and meanings.

ideal self   According to Rogers, the self as one would like it to be.

idiographic   According to Gordon Allport, an approach to the study of personality that emphasizes individual experience. This approach makes use of techniques such as case studies, verbal reports, and interviews.

James, William (1842–1910)   American psychologist and philosopher (see Chapter 12) who emphasized the centrality of experience, individualism, a plurality of methods, and the dangers of reductionism. Some of the intellectual traditions in his work are reflected in the work of humanistic psychologists.

Kierkegaard, Søren (1813–1855)   Danish philosopher commonly regarded as one of the founders of existentialism. Kierkegaard rejected the concern of rationalist philosophy with the abstractions of the intellect and instead called attention to the daily practical issues that individuals encounter and the problems of coping with those issues in an authentic way.

learned ignorance   A concept coming out of the work of Nicholas of Cusa referring to learning how *not* to think of God. Applied to psychology, the term could refer to the discipline of learning how *not* to think of ourselves.

Leibnizian tradition   According to Allport, a tradition that emphasizes the proactive (purposive or goal-directed) nature of human life.

Lockean tradition   Allport's expression referring to deterministic and mechanistic approaches to psychology according to which human beings are regarded as primarily reactive or as mere products of social conditioning.

logotherapy   Viktor Frankl's approach to psychotherapy emphasizing meaning orientation and the capacity of the individual to appropriate alternative meanings for the events of life.

Maslow, Abraham (1908–1970)   One of the important founders and leaders of third-force psychology. Maslow is remembered, among other things, for his hierarchical theory of motivation, his studies on self-actualization, and his emphasis on studying healthy people as a means of building an appropriate database for an adequate psychology.

Mitwelt   Heidegger's term for the community or our life with other people.

Nicholas of Cusa (1401–1464)   Early legal scholar, mathematician, and philosopher remembered for his doctrine of learned ignorance, which refers to learning how *not* to think of God.

nomothetic   Allport's term for a research orientation that emphasizes statistical abstractions (e.g., means, standard deviations).

noogenic neuroses   Frankl's expression referring to the anxiety associated with loss of meaning or a feeling of worthlessness.

paradoxical intention   Frankl's expression referring to the capacity to do the very opposite of what one would most like to do. Thus, one who is fearful of flying might prefer to stay home but instead chooses to fly.

phenomenal field   An expression employed by Rogers to refer to the entire range of experiences that are part of a person's life.

phenomenology   A philosophical orientation and a method for approaching a subject of interest. The method seeks to discover what is given directly in experience itself in contrast to intellectualized content.

positive psychology   The scientific study of positive human functioning and fulfillment among individuals, families, and communities.

religious mode of existence   Kierkegaard's expression for an orientation to life marked by a deep sensitivity to one's contingency and dependence on God.

Rogers, Carl R. (1902–1987)   One of the most innovative figures in the tradition of humanistic psychology, remembered for his revolutionary attempts to wed psychotherapy with more traditional experimental psychology. His radical emphasis on the person represented a unique war against the authorities of institutions and systems.

Rychlak, Joseph F. (1928–2013)   A leader in the humanistic psychology tradition who argued for a rigorous humanistic psychology. He saw no necessary contradictions between humanistic psychology and rigorous scientific practices.

self-actualization   A term employed by psychologists such as Kurt Goldstein, Carl Gustav Jung, and Abraham Maslow. The term generally refers to fulfillment of positive potentials.

self-transcendence   The capacity of an individual to critically examine her or his worldview and its limitations in relations to more comprehensive and inclusive multicultural perspectives.

third-force psychology   A term commonly employed to refer to humanistic psychology viewed as an alternative to behaviorism and psychoanalysis.

throwness   Heidegger's term referring to those conditions, forces, or facts that do not easily yield to human effort.

Umwelt   Literally, *the world around*. Refers to the physical world or the environment.

Unamuno, Miguel de (1864–1936)   Spanish philosopher who was deeply concerned about the dangers of specialization and reductionism. Unamuno also stressed the importance of affect and warned against a purely cognitive or intellectual approach to the problems of psychology.

unconditional positive regard   Rogers's term for a belief in the intrinsic worth of another individual. Unconditioned positive regard contrasts with the kind of acceptance or love that comes with conditions.

18

■ ■ ■

The Rise of Contemporary Psychology

*Psychology is now characterized by a pluralism of conceptual and
methodic posit, and of research interest, so great as to suggest
a new humility before the actual complexities of the psychological
universe: problems are being addressed, rather than—as in the
past—evaded or liquidated by premanufactured explanations.*

—Sigmund Koch (1986)

The post–World War II era was an age of dynamic transformation in nearly every facet of Western civilization. Scientific, technological, economical, political, and religious enterprises all exhibited tremendous change during this period. Even more than before, psychology evolved at an extraordinary pace after the war and that development has continued into the present century. Membership in professional societies has blossomed, and a multitude of innovative instruments, techniques, and ideas have come forward. Major substantive advances have occurred in the content areas of basic experimental psychology and in the various branches of applied psychology. In what follows, we review some of the dominant contemporary developments in the discipline.

THE SYSTEMS OF PSYCHOLOGY IN RETROSPECT

The systems of psychology flourished from the time of Wundt until the mid-twentieth century. After that period, few psychologists identified themselves as members of the functionalist, structuralist, or Gestalt schools. There were, nevertheless, psychologists who continued to identify with various versions of psychoanalysis, neobehaviorism, and humanistic psychologies.

Psychoanalysis

Throughout his life, Sigmund Freud encountered both rejection and acceptance of his work. The political climate in Germany during the 1930s was not conducive to the advancement of psychoanalysis. Jahoda (1969) pointed out, "In October 1933 psychoanalysis was banned from the Congress of Psychology in Leipzig as a 'Jewish science'; soon after that psychoanalytic literature was burned, and the community of practicing psychoanalysts dispersed rapidly to save their lives and livelihoods" (p. 420). This unfortunate trend escalated after Freud's death in 1939 (Gitre, 2011). Eissler (1965) stated,

> In his autobiographical sketch, Freud records, with an implicit but justified pride, the fact that the first World War passed without damage to the psychoanalytic movement. Alas, the same cannot be said of World War II, from which psychoanalysis did not emerge without deep injuries. Totally excluded from cultural life in the vast area on the other side of the world, reduced to a precarious existence in the Catholic countries of the West, it flourishes almost solely in the English-speaking countries, and especially in North America. (p. 2)

Despite a troubled history, psychoanalysis achieved gains in Western psychology and remained a significant force in psychotherapy during the 1950s (Lazarus, 2000).

A proliferation of journals attests to the endurance of psychoanalysis in the West following World War II. In 1909, Sigmund Freud and Eugen Bleuler (1857–1939) established the first psychoanalytic periodical, the *Jahrbuch für Psychoanalytische und Psychopathologische Forschungen*. Later, psychoanalytic journals such as *Imago* (1912) and the *Internationale Zeitschrift für Psychoanalyse* (1913) struggled during Freud's lifetime. Additional psychoanalytic publications have flourished in English including the *Psychoanalytic Review* (1913), *American Imago* (1944), the *American Psychoanalytic Association*

Journal (1952), the *Journal of Analytic Psychology* (1955), *Contemporary Psychoanalysis* (1964), and *Modern Psychoanalysis* (1976). The *Encyclopedia of Associations* (see Burek, Koek, & Novallo, 1989, p. 2989) listed over forty national and international psychoanalytic societies, including the American Psychoanalytic Association, the American Academy of Psychoanalysis, and the International Psycho-Analytic Association. As noted in Chapter 16, psychoanalytic theory and practice evolved from the time of Freud and are now marked by increasingly pluralistic perspectives (see Gabbard et al., 2012; Rudnytsky, 2011).

Nevertheless, some scholars are skeptical about the future of psychoanalysis. Eissler (1965) warned that psychoanalysis was vulnerable to attacks from religion, government, biological and sociological perspectives, and especially medical orthodoxy. Recognizing the validity of such criticism, many psychoanalysts have worked to nullify such dangers (Kirsner, 2001). For example, the American Psychoanalytic Association established criteria during the 1930s that required psychoanalysts to attend medical school. However, in a landmark 1988 out-of-court decision against medical orthodoxy, psychoanalysts began recognizing the right of Ph.D.s to seek psychoanalytic training (Buie, 1988). Prominent psychoanalytic associations agreed to admit more psychologists to membership in professional societies and appointment at training facilities. This bold step broadened the base of psychoanalysis and helped ensure its future.

The advancement of psychodynamic theory may depend upon its unique contributions to research (Weinberger, Siegel, & Decamello, 2000). Gilgen (1982) claimed that psychoanalysis has made numerous contributions to the post–World War II study of developmental psychology, motivation, personality, and abnormal psychology. Silverman (1976) reported several psychoanalytic programs that have found scientific evidence for the relationship between psychopathology and unconscious wishes. Furthermore, Baars (1986) claimed that experimental psychologists have too often ignored psychodynamic theory, making it "the single greatest neglected topic in contemporary scientific psychology" (p. 412). Although the American fascination with psychoanalysis remains (Roth, 1998), its influence on psychotherapy has been diminished by the growth of humanistic psychology and behavior therapies.

Humanistic Psychology

In an overview of the history of humanistic psychologies, DeCarvalho (1990) noted that "Some psychologists during the 'golden age' of behaviorism of post World War II, discontented with behaviorism's view of human nature and method, drew on a long tradition linking psychology with humanities and in a rebellious manner institutionally founded humanistic psychology" (pp. 22–23). This rebellious manner began with an informal 1954 mailing list distributed by Abraham Maslow to one hundred and twenty-five psychologists who identified with the humanistic rejection of psychoanalysis and neobehaviorism.

As the list of followers grew, plans were made to establish an official humanistic psychology organization (DeCarvalho, 1992). The institutional support structure for the new orientation included the founding of the *Journal of Humanistic Psychology* in 1961 and the founding of the American Association of Humanistic Psychology (AAHP), later renamed the Association of Humanistic Psychology. James F. T. Bugental (1915–2008) was elected as the AAHP's first president. Over one hundred members attended the first national meeting, held in Philadelphia in 1963. In November 1964, the premiere figures in humanistic psychology attended a conference held in Old Saybrook, Connecticut. Abraham Maslow, James Bugental, Carl Rogers, Gordon Allport, Jacques Barzun, Charlotte Bühler, George Kelly, Rollo May, Gardner Murphy, and Henry Murray were among the participants (DeCarvalho, 1990). In the early 1970s, a coalition of over three hundred psychologists established Division 32 of the American Psychological Association (APA), titled the Division of Humanistic Psychology.

Although institutionalized by U.S. psychologists, humanistic psychology has broad appeal in other countries. DeCarvalho (1991) claimed that "Outside of the United States, primarily in South America, humanistic psychology has been as popular as behaviorism has been inside the United States" (p. 151). Indeed, recent decades have witnessed ambitious efforts to promote humanistic psychology at an international level; for example, in September 1983, one hundred and fifty North American psychologists visited the former Soviet Union as delegates for the Association of Humanistic Psychology (Hassard, 1990). In the following years, AHP and Soviet exchange conferences were held in Moscow, Leningrad, Tblisi, Vilnius, and Kiev. In 1986, Carl Rogers gave the keynote address to 2,000 North American and Soviet psychologists and educators at the USSR Academy of Pedagogical Science. Such multicultural projects have shared insights into practice and theory, fostered collaboration on mutual problems, and produced international recognition for humanistic psychology.

In the 1970s and 1980s, an increasing number of educational programs provided graduate courses and degrees with a humanistic orientation. Additional social support structures have emerged, including institutes, correspondence courses, and seminars. With this growth and the prompting of Rychlak (1988) and others, humanistic psychologists have considered adopting more rigorous and scientific methods (Cain, 2002; Schneider, Bugental, & Pierson, 2001; Sheldon & Kasser, 2001). In his presidential address to Division 32, M. Brewster Smith (1990) argued that the natural sciences play a complementary role in the development of humanistic psychology. At present, several prominent humanistic centers, such as the Saybrook Institute, have established research programs that offer challenging new directions for humanistic psychology in the twenty-first century.

Neobehaviorism and the Psychology of Learning

Despite the growth of psychoanalysis and humanistic psychology, neobehaviorism prospered as the dominant orientation in American psychology in the twentieth century (Mackintosh, 1997).

Neobehaviorism attained its apex of popularity under B. F. Skinner, possibly the most celebrated psychologist in the last half of the twentieth century. Gilgen (1982) reported that a random sampling of scholars in the history of psychology and members of the APA rated Skinner as both the most important person and the most important influence in U.S. psychology during the post–World War II period. During his most productive years, Skinner was regarded as one of America's most visible scientists (see "Visible Scientists," 1975). Rutherford (2009) shows how Skinner's laboratory work migrated to the public arena especially from the 1950s to the 1970s. Although never elected president of the APA, Skinner's experimental behavior analysis attracted countless researchers and practitioners. Based on careful observation, perseverance, and serendipity, Skinner compiled a corpus of work that revolutionized the study of learning and contributed to applied and clinical psychology (Gitre, 2011).

Aside from Skinner's ascendancy, other researchers have made substantial contributions to the psychology of learning, many with radically different orientations. The research of Harry Harlow offers an intriguing alternative to the neobehaviorism of Hull and Skinner.

HARRY FREDERICK HARLOW Born in Fairfield, Iowa, **Harry Frederick Harlow (1905–1981)** received an English degree at Stanford University and later was awarded his Ph.D. in experimental psychology in 1930. Although not Jewish, he was encouraged by a respected professor to change his name because anti-Semitism would prevent him from getting a job (LeRoy & Kimble, 2003). Harry Israel borrowed his father's middle name for a new surname. A short time later, Harlow was hired as an assistant professor at the University of Wisconsin at Madison, where he founded the Primate Laboratory and directed it until 1974 (Blum, 2011). During his distinguished career, Harlow worked long hours and maintained a quiet and unassuming demeanor despite his fame (LeRoy, 2008). He served as editor of the *Journal of Comparative and Physiological Psychology* from 1951 to 1963 and as president of the APA in 1958. He published numerous books and articles on topics such as learning, motivation, and social isolation.

Harlow devised the **Wisconsin General Test Apparatus** to test form discrimination in monkeys (Harlow, 1949), and the test became part of typical testing in clinical neuropsychology (Eling & Maes, 2008). The monkeys are confined in a cage while a variety of stimulus objects are presented on a horizontal tray. The objects are placed over small depressions that contain a desirable food reward. The monkey is trained to select a particular object; if the object shelters a food reward, the animal may remove the object and eat the food reward. A screen can also be lowered to allow the experimenter to create a new pattern of objects and stimuli. Although the task proved difficult at first, the monkey eventually made fewer errors in new discrimination tasks. According to Harlow, the primate had formed a **learning set**; the monkey's previous experience had facilitated the ability to discriminate among new stimuli.

Harlow's research on learning sets, or learning to learn, was a promising method for the study of learning ability in primates. Another enduring contribution was the study of attachment. In a seminal line of research, Harlow (1958) studied the effects of cloth and wire surrogate figures on the formation of affectional bonds (Vicedo, 2009). Harlow demonstrated that the tactile stimulation afforded by a cloth figure produced greater attachment for baby monkeys than the appetitive features of a wire figure. He also documented the detrimental effects of isolation on social interaction in young rhesus monkeys as well as the persistence of these effects into adulthood (Vicedo, 2010).

OTHER LEARNING THEORISTS In the 1960s, Albert Bandura (b. 1925) advanced a social learning theory focused on observational learning, especially the influence of symbolic models on aggression. As with Skinner, Bandura's ideas have found successful application in the clinical setting, particularly the notion of self-efficacy (Follette & Callaghan, 2011; Schunk, 2012). In the last three decades, several enterprising researchers have employed operant and Pavlovian conditioning principles to reveal intriguing new findings about learning. Martin E. P. Seligman (b. 1942) and his colleagues documented that laboratory animals may learn helplessness if the consequences of their behavior appear independent of that behavior. Seligman has applied his findings on learned helplessness to the study of depression, and he is a pioneer of positive psychology (Seligman & Csikszentmihalyi, 2000). The research of Robert A. Rescorla (b. 1940) on contingencies (learning relations among events) has expanded the fundamental principles of Pavlovian conditioning (Rescorla, 2002). Research with animals produced impressive advances in the understanding of learning and its neurophysiological underpinnings, but prohibitive costs, animal rights activism, and legitimate moral issues have increasingly challenged such research.

COGNITIVE PSYCHOLOGY

One of the most conspicuous trends in psychology since the 1950s has been the renewed interest in cognition (Gardner, 1985; Robins, Gosling, & Craik, 1999). Although many individuals have studied topics we now call cognitive (Bermúdez, 2010; Brook, 2006), the resurgence of cognition is evident in research on topics such as memory, pattern recognition, reasoning, child and adult development, and artificial intelligence. According to Neisser (1967), "The term 'cognition' refers to all the processes by which the sensory input is transformed, reduced, elaborated, stored, recovered, and used" (p. 4). **Cognitive psychology** offers a breadth of perspective with emphasis on higher mental operations such as sensation and perception, memory, learning, problem solving, and language. Lachman, Lachman, and Butterfield (1979) concluded that the "typical cognitive psychologist is, therefore, a scientist motivated to understand a natural system consisting of the human higher mental processes" (p. 6).

In what follows, we will consider some of the origins, dominant themes, substantive areas, and critiques of cognitive psychology. But first we will consider some of the influences that led to the founding of this orientation.

Intellectual Traditions

Whereas the investigation of mental events dates from the time of the pre-Socratic philosophers, the experimental analysis of cognition is a product of the nineteenth and twentieth centuries, especially a cognitive tradition that can be traced to the 1920s (Greenwood, 1999). The writings of Franz Brentano, William James, Wilhelm Wundt, John Dewey, and Sigmund Freud all exhibited a keen interest in mental events. Although approaching the study of cognition from diverse systems and perspectives, each thinker nurtured ideas that could find a role in contemporary representations of the mind. However, we will confine this discussion to a few specific forces that served to shape cognitive psychology.

HERMANN EBBINGHAUS Hermann Ebbinghaus's seminal research on memory remains a hallmark in the history of cognitive psychology. Like Fechner, Ebbinghaus applied a rigorous experimental method to the study of mental processes. Ebbinghaus's pioneering research contributed to the quantification of memory and inspired future generations of researchers to extend his methodology into new areas (see Eysenck, 1986; Gorfein & Hoffman, 1987). Although criticized for an overemphasis on associationism, artificiality, and reductionism (Kintsch, 1985), Ebbinghaus's research nevertheless contributed to a laboratory analysis of mental operations. Indeed, much of twentieth-century memory research can be traced back to Ebbinghaus's work (Wertheimer, 1986).

FREDERICK C. BARTLETT Another important pioneer in the study of cognitive processes was **Sir Frederick Charles Bartlett (1886–1969)**, who stressed the role of abstract representation in cognition. According to Bartlett, cognitive themes or *schemas* govern memory processes. These schemas exert a powerful influence on the retrieval and forgetting of information. Bartlett (1932) tested the role of schemas on story comprehension by methods such as *repeated reproduction* (present the participant with a picture and ask for repeated descriptions of the content)

and *serial reproduction* (present one participant with a complex and unfamiliar story such
as the Kwakiutl Indian folktale "The War of the
Ghosts"; the participant reproduces the story
from memory, and the reproduced story becomes
the stimulus for the second participant, whose reproduction of the story becomes the stimulus for
the third participant, etc.).

Bartlett's findings revealed a tendency
to replace esoteric terms and abstract concepts
with concrete and familiar ideas. He found that
as greater intervals of time passed, participants
made more errors in retrieval and substitution.
Far removed from associationist interpretations
of memory, Bartlett believed his results demonstrated thematic frameworks that modified
and organized new information. Consequently,
material unfamiliar to the schema would not be
recalled. Bartlett claimed that the world is re-
constructed in memory based on each person's
schematic pattern rather than on the basis of the
mechanical laws of association, and he recognized the influence of culture in cognition and
social behavior (Kashima, 2000). Some scholars
argue that Bartlett's investigations of illusions in
memory mark the beginning of the study of false
memories (Neuschatz et al., 2007).

Bartlett accepted the objective method of
the behaviorists but was critical of behaviorism, which he likened to a cult (Bartlett, 1923).
Although a prominent figure in early British
psychology (Collins, 2006), Bartlett was largely
ignored during the neobehaviorist era of the
1940s and 1950s because of his mentalistic orientation. However, cognitive researchers interested in schematic and reconstructive processes
in memory have rediscovered his ideas (Brewer,
2000; Iran-Nejad & Winsler, 2000; Neisser,
1982).

**JEAN PIAGET AND COGNITIVE DEVELOP-
MENT**   Born in Neuchâtel, Switzerland, **Jean
Piaget (1896–1980)** was a devoted student of
biology and zoology. By 1907, he had published
his first article, a brief comment on his observation
of an albino sparrow. The paper held a pragmatic
purpose: Piaget hoped the publication would win

him a job at the Neuchâtel Museum of Natural
Sciences (Piaget, 1952). By 1916, the twenty-year-
old scholar had produced a significant series of
publications, mostly in systematic zoology.

In 1918, Piaget was awarded a doctorate of
natural sciences from the University of Neuchâtel
for a thesis on mollusks. In the same year, he authored the essay "Biology and War," an angry
attack on instinctual explanations of war and on
individualism, in favor of socialism. His ideas
about war were influenced by the Soviet revolution of the Bolsheviks and by Piaget's membership in the liberal Protestant youth movement in
Switzerland, an affiliation that would impact his
later work (Vidal, 1987). Although his formal
training was in zoology, Piaget had studied some
psychology at the University of Neuchâtel. After
receiving his doctorate, he studied experimental psychology and psychopathology at Zürich
with Theodore Lipps, Eugen Bleuler, and Carl
Jung, and later with **Alfred Binet (1857–1911)**
at Paris from 1919 to 1920. Around this time,
Piaget studied the writings of Lucien Lévy-Bruhl
(1857–1939) on the cognitive abilities of "primitive" people. The young scholar found inspiration
in the French sociologist's thesis of "prelogical
mentality" and built it into his studies of children's cognitive abilities (Jahoda, 2000).

Piaget's interest in developmental psychology was evident in his first psychology article
titled "Relationship between Psychoanalysis and
Child Psychology," published in 1920. Two decades later, he had published six major books on
broad developmental topics such as language,
intelligence, moral judgment, reasoning, causality, and the construction of reality in children as
well as sociological perspectives on child development (Hsueh, 2004). Beginning with his early
research on intelligence, Piaget conducted extensive interviews with children rather than administer the tests in a standardized manner, and his
clinical methods developed as he worked (Mayer,
2005). According to Gruber and Vonèche (1977),
this unorthodox study of cognition proved to be
insightful: "What had been at the outset nothing
but a boring and annoying test situation became
a real dialogue with suggestions and counter

suggestions, an argument developed, a deepening of the child's thought, a new method of interrogating children was born" (p. 53).

Such methods led Piaget to develop a general theory of genetic epistemology that stressed the activation of schemas within serially progressive structural stages (Ferrari, Pinard, & Runions, 2001). He insisted that cognition develops in a sequence from sensory-motor coordination to abstract reasoning. In 1940, he continued studying the genesis of human knowledge as professor at the University of Geneva, where he ran a large and well-funded research program (Burman, 2012) until his appointment as professor emeritus in 1971. As Piaget (1952) remarked in his autobiographical sketch, "Instead of devoting five years to child psychology, as I had anticipated in 1921, I had spent about thirty on it; it was exciting work and I do not in the least regret it" (p. 255).

Although his contributions to developmental psychology are numerous (Beins, 2012), Piaget should be remembered as a genetic epistemologist. Whether studying the child's conception of number, physical quantity, space, or time, Piaget's research was guided by the quest for the psychogenesis of cognition. Indeed, one of his final publications was an epistemological account of the history of science (Piaget & Garcia, 1983/1989). Together with physicist and fellow epistemologist John Garcia, Piaget argued for a sequential order in history by investigating the development of science in the context of the psychogenesis of knowledge. This project had been initiated in the 1960s but was not completed until the day before Piaget contracted the illness that would claim his life. In many ways, this book represents an intriguing summary of Piaget's views on epistemology and psychology.

Although regarded for his contributions, Piaget was not the first psychologist to advance a cognitive theory of development. As we have seen, Charles Darwin, G. Stanley Hall, and Kurt Koffka also offered insight into the intellectual development of children. However, two names bear mentioning in this context. More than twenty-five years before Piaget's first

publication on cognitive child psychology, James Mark Baldwin (1861–1934) investigated developmental aspects of cognition (Obiols & Barrios, 2009) and described the processes of *accommodation* and *adaptation* in a three-stage theory of prelogical, logical, and hyperlogical cognition in his book *Mental Development in the Child and the Race* (Baldwin, 1895). In addition, Russian psychologist Lev Semenovich Vygotsky (1896–1934) expanded on Gestalt and Piagetian ideas by placing greater emphasis on the social nature of linguistic and psychological functions (Wertsch, 1985). Although once obscure, Vygotsky's work has commanded more attention from Western psychologists (Lloyd & Fernyhough, 1999).

GESTALT PSYCHOLOGY AND EDWARD TOLMAN Like Bartlett, the Gestalt psychologists rejected the rigid associationism encountered in behaviorism. Beginning with Max Wertheimer's analysis of the quantitative concept formation of tribal peoples (Wertheimer, 1912/1950), the Gestalt school introduced a dynamic approach to the study of mental events. The research of Wertheimer and Karl Duncker (mentioned in Chapter 15) continues to be cited in the cognitive literature on problem solving. Furthermore, George Katona's (1940) book *Organizing and Memorizing* has a distinctly cognitive orientation. As Baars (1986) noted, even the title of Katona's book sounds like a cognitive work.

The influences and similarities between Gestalt theory and cognitive psychology have not gone unnoticed. Indeed, Neisser credited the Gestalt psychologists with providing the early impetus for the study of cognition (see Baars, 1986, p. 274). Several research areas exhibit a Gestalt orientation including memory and cognition (German & Defeyter, 2000; Kelley & Nairne, 2001; Murray, 1995), human factors research (Foley & Moray, 1987), visual neuroscience (Wertheimer, 1999), evolutionary psychology (Murray & Farahmand, 1998), organizational theories of learning (Baddeley, 1990), artificial intelligence (Guberman & Wojtkowski, 2001), and perception (Chen, 2001; Kellman, 2000).

Edward Tolman, also influenced by the Gestalt tradition, was a key figure in the history of cognitive psychology. Tolman forged an uneasy alliance with neobehaviorism but did not acquiesce to popular explanations of psychology based on material and efficient causality. His concept of purpose presented a fresh theoretical alternative to neobehaviorism (Dewsbury, 2000). Indeed, Tolman's penchant for cognition is evident in concepts such as cognitive maps, sign expectancies, and means–end hierarchies (Innis, 1999; Tolman, 1932). His legacy is evident in later research in computer science and cognitive neuroscience (Goldman, 1999).

VERBAL LEARNING THEORY Following World War II, developments in information theory, human engineering, linguistics, and computer science created an intellectual climate conducive to a novel study of cognition. Ironically, several followers of neobehaviorism, the dominant force in psychology during the 1950s, provided the greatest impetus to the development of cognitive psychology.

In addition to the topics discussed in Chapter 14, a group of neobehaviorists studied memory under the banner of **verbal learning theory**, an approach that focused on "the acquisition, retention, and transfer of verbal units formed under controlled laboratory situations" (Jung, 1968, p. 3). The subject matter of verbal learning was vast, with a prominent research focus on the retention of verbal units (e.g., words, numbers, and nonsense syllables) and the distribution of errors in recall of those units (such as the serial position effect). Another popular research area centered on interference theory, the idea that competing sets of information can interfere with memories.

By the 1960s, verbal learning was at its zenith, culminating in the July 1962 founding of the *Journal of Verbal Learning and Verbal Behavior* (Cofer, 1978). Despite its popularity, several members became disenchanted with the restrictive, overly associationist assumptions of verbal learning theory. Researchers such as George A. Miller (1920–2012) and James J.

Jenkins (1923–2012) were considering a more cognitive orientation as a result of new findings that failed to conform to verbal learning explanations (Crowther-Heyck, 1999). Gardner (1985) marveled that "Seldom have amateur historians achieved such consensus. There has been nearly unanimous agreement among the surviving principals that cognitive science was officially recognized around 1956. The psychologist George A. Miller has even fixed the date, 11 September 1956" (p. 28). Miller's specific date refers to the Symposium on Information Theory sponsored by the Massachusetts Institute of Technology on September 10–12, 1956. Allen Newell and Herbert Simon delivered their revolutionary results on computer logic, Noam Chomsky laid the foundation for his theory of transformational grammar, and Miller presented his findings on the restricted capacity of short-term memory to roughly seven meaningful units. Other landmark events for cognitive psychology in the 1950s included contributions in the area of concept formation and perception (Bruner, Goodnow, & Austin, 1956) and Chomsky's (1959) critical review of B. F. Skinner's book on verbal behavior.

However, cognitive psychologists faced resistance and criticism from the more established discipline of neobehaviorism. George Miller remembers that during this time "'cognition' was a dirty word because cognitive psychologists were seen as fuzzy, handwaving, imprecise people who really never did anything that was testable" (cited in Baars, 1986, p. 254). Nonetheless, the *Zeitgeist* shifted to a more cognitive orientation in American psychology in the next decade. In 1967, Ulric Neisser (1928–2012) wrote *Cognitive Psychology*, an early attempt to present cognitive research in a coherent framework. Shortly thereafter, several scholarly resources were promoting the diverse literature of cognitive psychology. Beginning with the founding of *Cognitive Psychology* in 1969, more than fifteen journals featuring articles on basic and applied cognition were established in the next two decades. By 1985, the *Journal of Verbal Learning and Verbal Behavior* was rechristened the *Journal of Memory and Language*, a subtle victory for the so-called new perspective in psychology. We will consider the broad subject matter of cognitive psychology, but first a brief discussion of some general themes is in order.

Themes and Content Areas of Cognitive Psychology

Cognitive psychology can be distinguished by several dominant themes. The first involves the early influence of the **information-processing metaphor**, the idea that mental events operate in much the same way as a computer (Bower, 2000). More specifically, the organism is conceived as a sophisticated processor of information. For example, memory might entail the processing of information in successive stages or levels (such as sensory memory, working memory, and long-term memory) before the execution of a response. For this reason, cognitive psychology was sometimes referred to as *information-processing psychology*.

The information-processing approach enjoyed early support within the cognitive framework (Garnham, 2009). For example, cognitive psychologists depicted theoretical representations of cognition by using flowcharts, a method borrowed from computer science, which characterize the serial processing of information into various stages. The nomenclature of the cognitivists also exhibited a distinct computer flavor. The term *stimulus* was occasionally replaced with *cue* or *input*, and *response* was replaced by *output process*. The memory concepts of *encoding*, *storage*, and *retrieval* reflected the bond between cognitive psychology and computer science. According to Lachman and colleagues (1979), this new nomenclature was more than just substitution; the terms "are pointers to a conceptual infrastructure that defines an approach to a subject matter. . . . It implies different beliefs about the behavior's origin, its history, and its explanation" (p. 99).

A second theme in cognitive psychology concerns the role of the participant in cognitive experimentation. Many neobehaviorists conceptualized the individual as a passive receiver of information in whom associative bonds guide the organization of material in a linear fashion.

By contrast, the cognitive psychologists followed the Gestalt psychologists and Tolman by assigning a more dynamic role to the organism. The individual is viewed as an active organizer of information using hierarchical schemas or other processes.

Finally, it would be naïve to assume that cognitive psychology evolved without some residue of influence from verbal learning and neobehaviorism (Lachman et al., 1979). From these approaches, cognitive psychology inherited a robust empirical approach grounded in laboratory research, and it also inherited learning as a topic area but with renewed interest in cognitive phenomena and explanations (Leahey, 2013). In general, cognitive psychology has further adopted from its predecessors a nomothetic or general explanation of cognitive phenomena rather than an idiographic perspective.

From its inception, cognitive psychology has been characterized as one of the most pluralistic and interdisciplinary movements in the history of psychology. Indeed, cognitive research has spilled over and intertwined with growing cognitive interest in other areas so that on occasion the larger field has been called "cognitive science" to reflect its interdisciplinary orientation (Gardner, 1985). Cognitive science is an apt title because scholars in philosophy, anthropology, engineering, neuroscience, linguistics, artificial intelligence, and computer science have identified in one way or another with the study of cognitive processes (Gentner, 2010). Research on memory, attention, problem solving, judgment and decision making, concept formation, language, pattern recognition, artificial intelligence, and human development have all emerged as mainstream fields of cognitive science. Advances in methodology and technology, including new brain imaging techniques, allow greater interdisciplinary connections (Boden, 2006). Additionally, research in behavioral genetics and neuroscience holds great promise for the emerging field of cognitive neuroscience (Kolb, 1999). Likewise, information processing has become almost an addiction among some social psychologists who study social cognition (Schneider, 1991).

Critical Appraisal of Cognitive Psychology

Donald A. Norman (1980) wrote a perceptive article that outlined twelve issues that have been neglected by cognitive scientists. He argued that the science of cognition has neglected but should not ignore belief systems, consciousness, development, emotion, interaction, language, learning, memory, perception, performance, skill, and thought. Norman called for both a reconsideration of some popular research areas (e.g., memory, language, and perception) and a further examination of skill and interaction.

THE COMPUTER METAPHOR   As far back as the Victorian era, two British scholars played a critical role in the emergence of cognitive science (Green, 2001a). The Cambridge mathematician Charles Babbage (1792–1871) devoted years and a significant part of his fortune toward the invention of calculating machines. In 1834, he introduced his most ambitious invention, the Analytical Engine, which attracted the attention of Ada B. Lovelace (1815–1852). Although born the daughter of Lord Byron, Lovelace rejected poetry in favor of mathematics and science. In 1843, she wrote a paper about Babbage's Analytical Engine, which became the "first published example of what could be called a computer program—written over a century before the emergence of the technology needed to run it" (Woolley, 1999, pp. 1–2). Employing punched cards and memory elements, Babbage's calculating machine and Lovelace's program proved to be the forerunner to modern computer technology. (In 1980, the U.S. Department of Defense honored Lovelace by using "Ada" as the name for the standard programming language adopted for Department of Defense [DOD] military systems.) As Green (2001a) observed, the work of Babbage and Lovelace also introduced the possibility of a nineteenth-century cognitive science.

During the mid-twentieth century, the computer metaphor of mind liberated the new discipline of cognitive psychology from neobehaviorism. In this context, a computational cognitive science

provided a rigorous account of intentionality (Green, 2000) and addressed a growing frustration with the narrow disciplinary vision of neobehaviorism (Crowther-Heyck, 2000). From a more sympathetic orientation, Gardner (1985) outlined the radical differences between biological and mechanical systems, but saw promise in a synthesis of neurobiology and artificial intelligence. Roediger (1980) found value in the computer metaphor, but warned of other erratic trends in the history of psychology:

> The information processing approach has been an important source of models and ideas, but the fate of its predecessors should serve to keep us humble concerning its eventual success. In 30 years, the computer-based information processing approach that currently reigns may seem as invalid a metaphor to the human mind as the wax-tablet or telephone-switchboard models do today. Unless today's technology has somehow reached its ultimate development, and we can be certain it has not, then we have not reached the ultimate metaphor for the human mind, either. (p. 244)

MENTALISM   Among a number of critics (Uttal, 2000), B. F. Skinner was a resolute antagonist of the mentalistic foundation of cognitive psychology. Skinner (1963) voiced early concern about cognitive psychology's dependence on a mental rather than behavioral orientation. Troubled by the terminology of the cognitive psychologist, Skinner (1987c) argued against the faddish nature of mentalistic language:

> A curve showing the appearance of the word *cognitive* in the psychological literature would be interesting. A first rise could probably be seen around 1960; the subsequent acceleration would be exponential. Is there any field of psychology today in which something does not seem to be gained by adding that charming adjective to the occasional noun? (p. 783)

He further asserted that science should have a language, but one that is founded on objectively defined terminology. Skinner (1989) used etymological data to demonstrate that cognitive terms are not novel descriptors but merely reformulations of previous physical and behavioral nomenclature. Thus, words such as *mind, thinking, doing, waiting,* and *sensing* do not warrant inclusion in the psychologist's vocabulary.

Skinner (1977) believed that cognitive psychology was a threatening obstacle in the evolution of a scientific psychology. In his final publication, he found similarity in the tension between cognitive psychology and radical behaviorism and the older dissension between creationist explanations and evolutionary theory. Like Darwin, Skinner (1990) advanced a position that was plagued with opposition:

After almost a century and a half, evolution is still not widely understood. . . . A creation science has been proposed to be taught in its place. The role of variation and selection in the behavior of the individual suffers from the same opposition. Cognitive science is the creation science of psychology, as it struggles to maintain the position of mind. (p. 1209)

Meanwhile, Skinner (1987b) concluded, "Let us bring behaviorism back from the Devil's Island to which it was transported for a crime it never committed, and let psychology become once again a behavioral science" (p. 111).

ECOLOGICAL VALIDITY Although recognized as a founder of cognitive psychology, Ulric Neisser has voiced concern about the artificial nature of this orientation. After numerous discussions with J. J. Gibson (1904–1979), a leader in the field of perception, Neisser revised many early ideas in his landmark text on cognitive psychology. Borrowing from Gibson's approach, Neisser (1976) claimed that **ecological validity** is absent in cognitive psychology research. In other words, many cognitive experiments on mental events are artificial; they are hard to generalize

to real-world experience. Neisser (1976) declared that "The study of information processing. . .has not yet committed itself to any conception of human nature that could apply beyond the confines of the laboratory" (p. 6).

Neisser (1982) edited *Memory Observed: Remembering in Natural Contexts,* a volume of ecologically valid research on topics such as flashbulb memories (vivid memories of salient events such as John Kennedy's assassination or the 2001 terrorist attack on the World Trade Center), mnemonics (memory aids that promote efficient retrieval), memorists (people with exceptional memory), and eyewitness testimony. Neisser's plea for ecological soundness provides an intriguing challenge for cognitive psychologists.

Despite such criticism, cognitive psychology has made substantial contributions to psychology as a whole. Inventive methodologies and designs have been created to explore the impact of cognition in a variety of tasks. Currently, a broad cross section of subject matter is investigated under the guise of cognitive science and, as a result, psychology may be more interdisciplinary than in previous eras. But does cognitive psychology really signify a paradigm shift? Despite cognitive psychology's relatively short existence, historical treatises on the so-called cognitive revolution have been written (Baars, 1986; Gardner, 1985), but the idea of a revolution has been challenged by others (Leahey, 1992). An accurate evaluation of cognitive psychology must wait until a later date to be based on an adequate perspective.

CLINICAL PSYCHOLOGY

Clinical psychology is both a science of mental disorders (what they are, what causes them, and how they are to be treated) and a profession that treats mental disorders. As such, clinical psychology and related areas such as counseling, psychotherapy, positive psychology, and health psychology dominate contemporary psychology. At present, the largest two divisions of the APA are Divisions 42 (Division of Independent Practice) and 12 (Society of Clinical Psychology).

Close behind are divisions such as 40 (Clinical Neuropsychology), 29 (Psychotherapy), and 39 (Psychoanalysis). Psychologists demonstrate widespread interest in professional issues, but many practitioners in clinics, schools, hospitals, and private practice maintain interests in the basic science of psychology and some contribute through research and scholarly publications. As we have seen, the APA supports a number of divisions devoted to basic science. Psychology, like other disciplines such as biology and chemistry, has always had multiple identities involving the discovery mission (basic science), dissemination programs (the academic-educational arm), and practical outreach and healing endeavors.

Intellectual Traditions

Clinical psychology and related areas such as counseling and school psychology play a critical role in contemporary society. The historical material in preceding chapters is testimony to the continuing needs of humans to adjust to the daily problems of living. Activities now included under the rubric of clinical psychology have existed throughout history. For example, psychological therapy was present in early Aesculapian temples and in the works of physicians such as Hippocrates who provided a classification of mental disorders. Empedocles, who understood the critical role of homeostasis in adjustment, and Galen, who identified different temperamental types and speculated about physiological changes in relation to psychological processes, took significant steps to treat psychological disorders. We think of Plato as a philosopher whose first love was the abstract world of universal forms, but he could not resist turning attention to the problems of living (as noted in Chapter 3, he gave us the first conflict model of mental illness). In earlier chapters, we encountered tensions between supernatural and naturalistic accounts of mental anomalies, giving rise to witch-hunts of the sixteenth and seventeenth centuries. A powerful countermovement led by luminaries such as Baruch Spinoza, Johann Weyer, Philippe Pinel, Benjamin Rush, and Dorothea Linde Dix

stressed the natural origins of mental illness and the need for medical, psychological, and social intervention.

A history of psychological practice in the United States dates back to the early 1800s and before, when a variety of practitioners provided counseling and assessment, including phrenologists and spiritualists among others (Cautin et al., 2013). Near the century's end, abnormal psychology came of age during unprecedented reform in the United States. Known as *psychotherapeutics*, the clinical movement reflected the optimism and social activism of the Progressive Era (King, Niess, Maddi, & Perkins, in press). As the epicenter for psychotherapeutics, the Boston School of Abnormal Psychology became the foremost authority on scientific psychotherapy during the period (Taylor, 2000). Inspired by William James, the Boston School included scholars such as Henry Bowditch (1808–1892), Richard Cabot (1868–1939), Morton Prince (1854–1929), James Jackson Putnam (1846–1918), and Boris Sidis (1867–1923).

Developments in Europe, especially Sigmund Freud's founding of psychoanalysis, demonstrated a growing responsiveness to psychological problems of living. Despite Freud's medical training, he rejected the medical model he encountered in Meynert's clinic in Vienna. After the failure of his *Project for a Scientific Psychology*, Freud turned attention to a more psychological approach to issues encountered in his clinic.

Although Wilhelm Wundt's research focused on the senses as windows to the mind, his larger vision may have influenced his students and associates such as Emil Kraepelin and Lightner Witmer to theoretical and practical problems of adjustment. As noted in Chapter 10, the lead article in Witmer's journal, *The Psychological Clinic*, called for a new discipline to be named "clinical psychology" (see McReynolds, 1987, p. 852). Witmer envisioned a discipline that would involve both testing and treatment. In its earliest incarnation, however, clinical psychology was identified far more with testing than therapy in the formal sense.

Critical Developments

Psychological testing existed prior to 1914, but the testing movement didn't gain momentum until World War I. During that period, psychologists demonstrated the value of their skills in vital areas such as assessment, selection, research, and leadership. Subsequently, the applied branches of the discipline enjoyed strong positions in academic training programs and in the industrial world. In 1917, a handful of clinicians formed the American Association of Clinical Psychologists (AACP). The organization was short lived, but the AACP stimulated professional changes, leading to the creation of the Clinical Section of the APA in 1919. Despite clinical psychology's modest inroads in personality and intelligence testing, psychiatry continued to dominate the more prestigious therapeutic side of the helping professions.

During World War II, however, clinical psychology discovered a new momentum. With an escalating number of Allied troops suffering from "shell-shock," an earlier term for what is now called *posttraumatic stress disorder* (Monson et al., 2007), psychiatrists were forced to relinquish their stranglehold on the mental health field. Consequently, more and more psychologists were pressed into service to test *and* treat enlisted soldiers and veterans. In some cases, experimental psychologists with no clinical training contributed to the effort; many found the work so rewarding that it produced a "mass exodus" from the laboratory to the clinic (Hathaway, 1958).

In many respects, World War II provided a vital catalyst for the birth of clinical psychology in the modern sense (Street, 2006). As psychologists enjoyed greater responsibility as therapists, the area experienced a surge in interest. The Allied effort during the war enlisted the aid of around 1,500 psychologists, the majority coming from the academic or government sector. However, about three times as many psychologists worked in clinical settings in the postwar environment than in the years leading up to the war (Andrews & Dreese, 1948). Clinical psychology was experiencing growing pains.

In response to rising interest, the APA established accreditation standards and evaluations for graduate training programs. American psychologist **David Shakow (1901–1980)** became the principle architect of clinical training after World War II (Cautin, 2006). During a career that spanned six decades, Shakow developed methods for clinical research and contributed extensively to the literature on schizophrenia (Cautin, 2008). Additionally, Shakow (1942) envisioned a graduate curriculum in clinical psychology that included an internship in the third year. His wartime article also called for the establishment of a specialty board to certify clinical psychologists. (Following his lead, the APA later established the American Board of Examiners in Professional Psychology.) Impressed with his work, APA president Carl Rogers asked Shakow to chair a committee charged with defining educational and training standards for the emerging discipline of clinical psychology. Based on the committee's recommendations, the "Shakow Report" was presented at the 1947 APA convention and later adopted as APA policy.

Despite swelling interest in clinical psychology, many postwar Veterans Administration hospitals were understaffed and unprepared to meet the demand of treating veterans with psychiatric disorders. Cautin (2006) observed that the

> training of clinical psychologists thus became an immediate priority—and not just within the field of psychology. Governmental agencies such as the U.S. Public Health Service (USPHS) and the Veterans Administration also recognized this imperative; the former was primarily interested in developing a national mental health policy, and the latter in meeting the clinical needs of its clients. (p. 216)

The agencies took action, making a push to fund graduate programs in clinical psychology.

In 1949, David Shakow traveled to Colorado where he joined seventy colleagues for the two-week Boulder Conference on Graduate Education in Clinical Psychology (Petersen,

2007). Organized by the APA and subsidized by the USPHS, the conference goal was to determine training models and practices for clinical psychology. The "Shakow Report" set the agenda for the famous Boulder Conference (Baker & Benjamin, 2000). Hosted by University of Colorado psychologist Victor C. Raimy (1950), the conference addressed the pressing need to establish guidelines for clinical training in the postwar environment. In what became known as the **Boulder model**, it recommended that doctoral programs train clinical psychologists as research-practitioners (Petersen, 2007). The model's authors advised that students develop solid backgrounds in general and clinical psychology through classroom instruction, learn applied professional skills through extensive supervised experience, and acquire training in research. Within this view, clinical research and clinical practice are not separate fields but inform each other (Antony & Roemer, 2011).

In addition to solidifying clinical psychology's identity as separate from psychiatry, the Boulder model promoted professional clinicians who were solid researchers and could adapt their clinical work to emerging findings in a changing scientific field. In 1992, directors of 97.8 percent of ninety doctoral programs in clinical psychology claimed to follow the Boulder model (O'Sullivan & Quevillon, 1992), and enthusiasm for the model persists into the twenty-first century (Norcross, Karpiak, & Santoro, 2005).

In the wake of the Boulder Conference, ethical guidelines were established to direct practicing therapists. In 1953, the APA adopted a Code of Ethical Standards of Psychologists and, since that time, Handelsman, Gottlieb, and Knapp (2005) and others have emphasized the importance of teaching ethics to clinicians and other psychologists. Around the same time, a proliferation of journals occurred with titles such as the *American Journal of Psychiatry*, the *Journal of Clinical Psychology*, and the *Journal of Counseling Psychology*, among many others.

Despite its popularity, numerous critics have attacked the Boulder model. A persistent objection came from students who wanted a graduate education grounded more in practical clinical experience than in clinical research. Almost a quarter-century after the Boulder Conference, Colorado hosted another seminal conference when the National Conference on Levels and Patterns of Professional Training in Psychology met in Vail in July 1973. Unlike the Boulder Conference, the Vail conferees were not composed of clinical psychology's "establishment." In fact, the majority of the one hundred attendees were students, women, and minority-group members and their dissatisfaction with the Boulder model was palpable (Stricker, 1975). Although they recommended that the classic scientist–practitioner model continue in Ph.D. programs, the Vail Conference endorsed a new professional degree known as the Doctor of Psychology (Psy.D.). Whereas the Boulder Conference emphasized science in graduate clinical training, the Vail Conference stressed practice.

Another postwar development that influenced clinical psychology came in the establishment of norms for diagnostic psychiatric categories. In 1952, the American Psychiatric Association introduced the *Diagnostic and Statistical Manual of Mental Disorders* (*DSM*). The *DSM* was a categorical classification system designed to provide uniform assessment and diagnoses across the field of psychiatry, but it did not meet with universal favor (Berrios, 2006). Few psychologists contributed to the first two versions of the DSM (Gurley, 2009), and some critics charged that the first two versions of the *DSM* were vague (due in part to psychoanalytic concepts) and unreliable. Subsequent versions of the *DSM-III* in 1980 and *DSM-IV* in 1994 focused on symptoms rather than theory but faced ongoing criticisms about validity, reliability, and cultural bias. In 2000, the American Psychiatric Association published the text revision of the *DSM*'s fourth edition, the *DSM-IV-TR*. When the fifth edition was introduced in May 2013, the American Psychiatric Association dropped Roman numerals from the designated acronym, making it the *DSM-5*.

Critical directions in psychotherapy emerged in the last half of the twentieth century.

In addition to the schools of therapy mentioned in previous chapters, three distinct "waves" of psychotherapists emerged in modern clinical psychology. The first wave is *behavior therapy* based on learning principles from experimental psychology. *Cognitive therapy* (sometimes referred to as *cognitive-behavioral therapy* because it retained the central tenets of behavior therapy) is based, in part, on principles in cognitive psychology (Hollon & DiGiuseppe, 2011). The third wave consists of *mindfulness-based treatment* that builds on the first two waves while adding mindfulness practices and acceptance derived from Eastern traditions.

JOSEPH WOLPE One of clinical psychology's most influential figures, **Joseph Wolpe (1915–1997)**, was born on April 20, 1915, in Johannesburg, South Africa. An early interest in medicine compelled him to attend medical school at the University of Witwatersrand in Johannesburg. After earning his M.D. from "Wits," he joined the South African army as a medical officer during World War II. His psychiatric career began while he worked with patients at the Kimberely military hospital (Poppen, 1996). He studied South African soldiers struggling with combat-related anxiety. After noting that conventional therapies offered limited results, Wolpe resolved to find a more effective treatment. His research led to the development of systematic desensitization. In the tradition of his friend, Mary Cover Jones (discussed in Chapter 13), Wolpe was a pioneer in *behavior therapy*, a revolutionary approach that guided a first wave of modern psychotherapy.

After the war, Wolpe joined the faculty at the University of Witwatersrand before immigrating to the United States. After an appointment at the University of Virginia, he joined the faculty at the Temple University Medical School in Philadelphia in 1965 (Salkovskis, 1998). After more than two decades at Temple, he retired to California in 1988. During this time, he offered lectures at Pepperdine University. After battling lung cancer, he died on December 4, 1997.

Despite his training in psychoanalysis, Wolpe (1958) found inspiration in Pavlov's work on experimental neurosis. In an early experiment, the South African psychiatrist used electrical shock to condition cats to fear a cage. He extinguished the cat's anxiety through a series of steps that counterconditioned the cat's fear. Far away from the cage, he offered food to create a *dominant response* of eating that was incompatible with the cat's anxiety. Gradually, he moved the cat's feeding spot closer and closer to the cage, the source of the cat's anxiety. He found that after numerous pairings, the dominant response (eating) weakened and finally inhibited the anxiety response. Wolpe (1958) concluded, "If a response antagonistic to anxiety can be made to occur in the presence of anxiety-evoking stimuli so that it is accompanied by a complete or partial suppression of the anxiety responses, the bond between these stimuli and the anxiety responses will be weakened" (p. 71).

If anxiety could be learned, he realized, then it could also be unlearned. In 1958, Wolpe's landmark book *Psychotherapy by Reciprocal Inhibition* appeared in print, laying the groundwork for a behavioral therapy based on learning theory. Garfield and Bergin (1994) echoed the sentiment of many clinicians when they called his book the first to establish therapy in the formal sense.

Wolpe (1958) used the term *reciprocal inhibition* to describe the process of extinguishing learned neurotic reactions in anxiety-provoking situations. This work provided the genesis for his model of **systematic desensitization**. Let's say a client meets with a behavioral therapist to treat a phobia. After identifying the fear response, the therapist trains the client in relaxation methods as a coping strategy (in this case, the relaxed state becomes the dominant response that will compete with and weaken the anxiety response). After learning progressive-relaxation training, the therapist helps the client construct an *anxiety hierarchy*, a graduated sequence of anxiety-provoking situations (ranging from 0 for "comfortable and relaxed" to 100 for "extremely tense and anxious"). For example, a person with arachnophobia might rate hearing the word "spider" as a 5 and seeing a picture of a spider in a magazine as a 15, moving all the way up to the thought of venomous spiders crawling over one's face at the hierarchy's apex. While relaxed, the client imagines a series of anxiety-provoking situations, beginning with the least disturbing situation. After gradual exposure, the person learns to reach the highest point on the hierarchy without anxiety. In later years, Wolpe drew on his groundbreaking work to develop assertiveness training programs.

AARON T. BECK   The emergence of *cognitive therapy* stimulated a second wave of modern psychotherapy. The founder of cognitive therapy was the youngest child of Jewish immigrants from Russia who had settled in Providence, Rhode Island. Before **Aaron Temkin Beck's (b.1921)** birth, his family had lost an older sister to influenza. As a result, Beck's mother suffered severe depression but claimed his birth lifted her spirits (Weishaar, 1993). Later, he experienced a debilitating childhood illness that forced him to conquer his fears, a process that sparked his beliefs about cognitive therapy. After attending Brown University, he graduated with an M.D. from Yale Medical School in 1946. In the early 1960s, he broke with psychoanalysis and started the development of cognitive therapy (Rosner, 2012). He is the director of the Aaron T. Beck Psychopathology Research Center at the University of Pennsylvania. In 1994, he founded the nonprofit Beck Institute for Cognitive Behavior Therapy in suburban Philadelphia, where his daughter, psychologist Judith S. Beck, serves as the director.

A fundamental tenet of his work is that depression is the product of unrealistic negative views about our self, our world, and our future (Wills, 2009). Beck (1963) observed that his depressed patients were haunted by *automatic thoughts*, streams of spontaneous negative cognitions that fueled depression and other emotional difficulties. As he helped patients identify and correct cognitive distortions, they developed more realistic self-perceptions that inspired happiness and productivity.

Beck is viewed as the founder of cognitive therapy (Scott & Freeman, 2010), for which he was awarded the prestigious Albert Lasker Award for Clinical Medical Research in 2006. His method of psychotherapy has played a leading role in treating people with depression, anxiety disorders, personality disorders, and other conditions (Dobson, 2012). His *Beck Depression Inventory* (BDI) remains a popular self-report inventory designed to measure the severity of depression. First introduced in 1961, it has undergone a major revision, resulting in the BDI-II in 1996. Beck is the only psychiatrist to receive research awards from both the APA and the American Psychiatric Association. He has published over five hundred articles and authored or coauthored twenty-two books.

Although not as influential in academic clinical psychology as Beck, other theorists have contributed to a cognitive perspective that emphasizes the effects of cognition on behavior and emotional change (Keegan & Holas, 2010). Albert Ellis (1913–2007) developed **Rational Emotive Behavior Therapy (REBT)** as a comprehensive treatment that works to resolve irrational thoughts that lead to conflict and self-defeating thinking (Ellis, 2004). Scholars have found roots of REBT in Stoicism (Still & Dryden, 2012) and the ideas of Epicurus (Reiss, 2003).

MARSHA M. LINEHAN   Although not as closely tied to laboratory research as behavior and cognitive therapies, "mindfulness-based" treatments have claimed status as a third wave of influential psychotherapies. Born in Tulsa, Oklahoma, **Marsha M. Linehan (b.1943)** attended Loyola University for both her undergraduate and graduate education, culminating in her doctoral degree in 1971. After taking various academic positions at Loyola and the Catholic University of America, Linehan joined the faculty at the Psychiatry and Behavior Sciences Department at the University of Washington in 1977. She is the founder of the Marie Institute of Behavioral Technology, a nonprofit organization dedicated to advancing behavioral technologies and treatments. Along with numerous awards and honors, she was awarded the Career Achievement Award from the APA in 2005.

While treating clients with borderline personality disorder and suicidal tendencies, Linehan (1993) developed *Dialectical Behavior Therapy* (DBT), a blend of Eastern perspectives of healing with Western behavioral therapy (Neacsiu et al., 2012). Her treatment has its roots in contemporary behavioral science as well as the concept of *radical acceptance* (according to Linehan, 1993, p. 148, this is "acceptance from deep within") inspired from both Eastern meditative practices and Western contemplative spirituality. DBT draws on Zen practices to encourage people to foster compassion, wisdom, and *mindfulness*, the practice of observing thoughts without letting them entangle us (Linehan & Lungu, 2012). Essentially, mindfulness is a sense of being mindful in the present moment when we see reality and ourselves without delusion or judgment. The practice of mindfulness and radical acceptance form the core of DBT. Linehan and her colleagues have applied DBT models to treat depression, anxiety, suicidal behaviors, drug abuse, and borderline personality disorder as well as impulsive behaviors involving eating disorders, substance abuse, compulsive gambling, and overspending.

In the tradition of the mindfulness-practice movement, Zindel Segal, Mark Williams, and John Teasdale (2001) conducted seminal work on a mindful-based treatment of depression. DBT, along with Steven C. Hayes's related treatment known as *Acceptance and Commitment Therapy* (ACT), constitutes a third wave that has influenced psychotherapists perhaps more than academic clinical psychologists.

Future Developments

As with any intellectual enterprise, a number of debates have swirled around clinical psychology. In 1952, British psychologist Hans Jürgen Eysenck (1916–1997) published "The Effects of Psychotherapy: An Evaluation," an open challenge to the effectiveness of psychotherapy. Based on his controversial analysis of twenty-four studies, Eysenck determined that more than two-thirds of "severe neurotics" recovered through "spontaneous remission" without the aid of psychotherapy. His work sparked a firestorm of critical reaction and aggressive debate. These debates have extended through the present (Lambert, 2010; Routh, 2013), and the persistent gap between researchers and practitioners reflects these tensions (Cautin, 2011). The question of psychotherapy's efficacy underscores the need for clinicians to evaluate treatments with sound methodology. In his provocative book *The Great Psychotherapy Debate*, Wampold (2001) notes:

> There are over 250 distinct psychotherapeutic approaches, which are described, in one way or another, in over 10,000 books. Moreover, tens of thousands of books, book chapters, and journal articles have reported research conducted to understand psychotherapy and to test whether it works. It is no wonder that, faced with the literature on psychotherapy, confusion reigns, controversy flourishes, converging evidence is sparse, and recognition of psychotherapy as a science is tenuous. Any scientific endeavor will seem chaotic if the explanatory models are insufficient to explain the accumulation of facts. If one were to ask prominent researchers to list important psychotherapeutic principles that have been scientifically established and generally accepted by most psychotherapy researchers, the list would indeed be short. On the other hand, an enumeration of the results of psychotherapy studies would be voluminous. How is it that so much research has yielded so little knowledge? (p. 1)

Wampold insists that research findings are insightful, if clinical psychologists have the proper level of abstraction and skill to discover the scientific foundation of psychotherapy. He also argues that the common factors of treatment (such as empathy and warmth) are more important than the specific theoretically driven factors like systematic desensitization in behavior therapy or cognitive restructuring in cognitive therapy.

Another ongoing debate with historical roots is whether psychologists who are not physicians should have the ability to prescribe medication. In classical psychoanalytic traditions, each psychoanalyst had an M.D. and could therefore legally write prescriptions. In every state except New Mexico (where qualified psychologists have been able to prescribe medications since 2002), psychologists must refer clients to a psychiatrist who can prescribe drugs. Controversy remains; some doubt that psychologists can prescribe medications as safely as physicians whereas others argue a client should not have to make two mental health visits to receive the same services, particularly if the psychologist is most familiar with the client. There is also a debate on whether clinical psychologists should remain psychologists or enter into other levels of description or explanation such as the neurophysiological level. In addition to debate among clinicians, deliberation on this issue will continue at state and federal levels.

The continuing vibrancy of clinical and counseling psychology as a field is seen in the growing numbers of psychologists working in hospitals, academic departments, and private practice. The need for clinicians has not diminished. Despite Patricia Churchland's (1989) radical claim that clinical psychology will become an applied branch of neuroscience, it continues to grow and to incorporate perspectives from other fields including social psychology, educational psychology, psychology and the law, and cultural psychology.

BIOPSYCHOLOGY

As neuroscience came of age in the late eighteenth century, scholars speculated about the brain's role in cognition and behavior (Whitaker, Smith, & Finger, 2007). In time, biological psychology emerged as a formal discipline. With new methods and accelerating numbers of researchers and funding, this field of psychology has risen to prominence in basic and applied research fields and, particularly with the development of better psychopharmaceutical treatments, in clinical and counseling psychology as well.

The biological perspective in psychology was codified as Division 6 of the APA with the advent of divisions in 1944. The original name was Physiological Psychology and Comparative Psychology. Between 1949 and 1962, it was combined with Division 3 under the title Experimental Psychology; today, the division continues in similar topic areas under the name Behavioral Neuroscience and Comparative Psychology (Dewsbury, 1996). Past presidents include luminaries such as Harry Harlow, Donald O. Hebb, and William K. Estes. We'll explore some early figures who laid the groundwork for developments in neuroscience.

Intellectual Traditions and Critical Researchers

KARL LASHLEY   As mentioned in Chapter 14, Karl Lashley (1890–1958), embraced behaviorism early in his career, but he raised questions about the neurological underpinnings of Watson's claims. Lashley examined physiological linkages between stimuli and specific responses, and he could not justify claims that learning produced rigid stimulus–response connections in the brain. After extensive searches for the location of maze memory in rats' brains, Lashley (1950) reported that memories were distributed across the brain instead of localized in specific regions (Bruce, 1998). His findings challenged the claims of neurosurgeons such as Wilder Penfield (1891–1976). Penfield (1952) had conducted surgeries on conscious patients with epilepsy. He claimed that his patients recalled spontaneous and vivid memories in response to electrical stimulation. Penfield insisted that his work demonstrated that specific memories were stored in specific brain locations. Regrettably, he made no effort to evaluate patient memories for accuracy or external corroboration. Lashley's experimental work led to current perspectives of distributed memory storage.

DONALD O. HEBB   Canadian neuroscientist **Donald Olding Hebb (1904–1985)** pioneered investigations of the effects of learning on the brain and influenced much of current neuroscience (Cooper, 2005). At different points in his career, he studied with Wolfgang Köhler, Karl Lashley, and Wilder Penfield. Among his many productive research areas, Hebb was interested in the effects of learning on neural connections and on neural plasticity (Berlucchi & Buchtel, 2009). He argued that experience organizes networks of neurons into more efficient systems that he called *cell assemblies*. Hebb's notion of a cell assembly provided a neurological basis for learning simple and complex stimuli, and he argued that these assemblies were the foundation of complex cognitive ideas that could be activated by the environment or by the cognitive processes of the individual. These assemblies could form connections, called phase sequences and, in this way, Hebb (1959) provided a testable explanation of associationist learning. He applied these ideas in many ways, including pioneering work with rats raised in simple and complex environments. Hebb (1949) demonstrated the detrimental effects that simple environments had on the later abilities of rats.

ROGER W. SPERRY During the 1960s and 1970s, researchers drew on comparative research with animals to study the brains of patients with epilepsy. Less than two decades after completing postdoctoral research with Karl Lashley, **Roger W. Sperry (1913–1994)** and colleagues performed numerous studies on animals with surgically separated brains (Sperry, 1961). Additionally, Sperry and others did extensive research with humans who had surgery to lesion the corpus callosum to ease epileptic symptoms not otherwise treatable in the 1960s. This work led to increased understanding of the common and separate functions of right and left hemispheres of the brain (see Springer & Deutsch, 1985). In 1981, Sperry was awarded the Nobel Prize in Medicine for his split-brain research. Under Sperry's guidance, Michael S. Gazzaniga (b. 1939) played a critical role in this research and later became a founding figure in the discipline of *cognitive neuroscience*. He has written books for both the scientific community and general audiences, including a work based on his Gifford Lectures that offered a neuroscientific consideration of the issue of free will (Gazzaniga, 2011).

DONALD B. LINDSLEY Donald B. Lindsley (1907–2003) was an early cognitive and behavioral neuroscientist and a pioneer in the electrical study of the brain (Eason, 2004). He grew up in Ohio and attended Wittenberg College for his undergraduate studies before completing his doctorate at the University of Iowa in 1932 (Chalupa, 2005). In the late 1930s, the electroencephalogram was just emerging in psychology (see Kreezer, 1938), and Lindsley (1936) published groundbreaking results of his examinations of EEG patterns in children and adults in *Science*. He followed this work with many other applications of neurophysiological recording including in utero fetal EEG recordings (Lindsley, 1942), now a common procedure.

After holding teaching positions at several universities and a brief hiatus during World War II to select, train, and improve efficiency of radar operators for the military, Lindsley moved to the University of California, Los Angeles, in 1951 (Lindsley, 1995). Here, with many other innovative scholars, in 1959, he helped found the Brain Research Institute that continues to generate excellent scholarly research. Lindsley took a systems approach to the brain, a challenging position in the late 1950s and early 1960s. He employed both behavioral and neurological assessments of brain activity in his research, particularly in his investigations of the role of the brain stem in sleep, attention, and arousal.

ERIC R. KANDEL Eric Kandel (b. 1929) has led the movement toward reductionistic physiological and genetic approaches to the study of memory. Working with materials and subjects ranging from genes to individual neurons to the nervous systems of *Aplysia* (a giant marine snail), rats, mice, and other animals, Kandel's laboratory continues to push the boundaries of basic neurological knowledge of memory. Born to Jewish parents in Vienna, he was shaped by the violence that erupted when Hitler led Germany to annex Austria in 1938 (Kandel, 2001). His family immigrated to the United States in 1939, and Kandel attended medical school at New York University, intending to become a psychiatrist.

His developing interest in the biology of mental events compelled him to seek postgraduate training at Columbia, the National Institutes of Health, and Harvard Medical School (Kandel, 2001). Through several decades of productive work he demonstrated, among other findings, that memory functions are associated with changes in synaptic connections between neurons; that short-term and long-term memory formations are distinct processes; and that genetically modified animal models (e.g., mice) could better illustrate the roles of specific proteins and genes in the formation of memories. His long, illustrious, and ongoing career resulted in the 2000 Nobel Prize in Physiology or Medicine.

Technological Advances in Neuroscience

New methods continue to drive progress in biological psychology. The advent of single-neuron recording and stimulation opened the door to many research topics including visual and auditory processing and long-term potentiation in memory. Although researchers such as Lashley and Hebb studied larger functions of the brain, many neuroscientists moved toward single-cell recording. The movement prompted Wolfgang Köhler (1967/1971) to lament that "The microelectrode inserted in an individual cell seems to have abolished all interest in more molar functions of the nervous system" (p. 122). Single-cell research remains common, but despite these concerns, biological psychology has also moved forward with new methods that allow investigation into the brain as a whole.

Methods for recording electrical activity across the brain pushed the field forward. Austrian psychiatrist Hans Berger (1873–1941) had a long-standing interest in the mind–body problem and extrasensory phenomenon. His interests inspired an invention that could measure the electrical activity of the human brain (Borck, 2005). Experimenting with this new technology in the 1920s, Berger became the first to document different brain wave patterns (including the *alpha wave*, also known as *Berger's wave*). Berger

called the recording an *Electroenkephalogram* or electroencephalogram, better known as the EEG (Sourkes, 2006). Later advances involved the measurement of local brain electrical activity in response to specific events by recording event-related potentials (ERPs).

With the advent of structural and functional imaging, no area of psychology has benefited more from advances in technology than neuroscience. Developed in the late 1970s, computed tomography (CT) scans allowed researchers, neurologists, and other physicians to view the brain and potential brain injuries in live participants (Roberts, McGeorge, & Caird, 1978). Soon after, in the mid-1980s, magnetic resonance imaging (MRI) allowed observers to view the brain in higher levels of resolution than were possible with CT scans (DeWitt, 1985). By the end of the twentieth century, emerging functional imaging technology allowed neuroscientists to observe the brain in action in real time. For example, positron emission tomography (PET) scans permit the observation of blood flow during cognitive activities (Bunney, Garland, & Buchsbaum, 1983); in 1991, functional magnetic resonance imaging (fMRI) techniques provided researchers with high-resolution images of brains in action in real time (Bandettini, 2007). PET scans and fMRIs help scholars identify areas of the brain that are relatively active or inactive during specific operations. These results aid in the assessment and treatment of brain injuries in addition to serving research functions. The use of PET scans and fMRIs to describe the localization of brain functions has led some contemporary critics to argue that these approaches comprise "modern phrenology" (Raichle, 1999, p. 107). Many dispute these allegations (Frith, 2006), and the descriptive and predictive value of advanced imaging techniques is clear even if the ability to draw causal inferences remains in contention.

Psychopharmacology

Psychopharmacology, the study of the effects of drugs on thought and behavior, made significant advances based on research about how neurons communicate with one another. Between the twentieth century's world wars, many scholars investigated psychological drugs using methods from experimental psychology (Schmied et al., 2006). Questions about the nature of neural communication led to a debate that has been framed as the "war of the soups and the sparks" (Valenstein, 2005), one of the most central points of contention in the history of neuroscience (Todman, 2008). Neurophysiologists remained dedicated to their quest to demonstrate electrical communication between neurons ("the sparks"), whereas pharmacologists sought evidence for chemical transmission ("the soups").

The debate was largely resolved in 1936 when pharmacologist **Otto Loewi (1873–1961)** discovered the first neurotrasmitter while researching a frog's heart (the idea for his celebrated experiment had come to him during a dream). Loewi shared the Nobel Prize in Physiology or Medicine with English neuroscientist Sir Henry Hallett Dale (1875–1968) for the discovery of the neurotransmitter acetylcholine (Donnerer & Lembeck, 2006). (Loewi had called it *Vagusstoff*, but *acetylcholine* became the more popular term.) When Germany invaded Austria in 1938, the Nazis interrogated Loewi, despite his status as a Nobel laureate (Valenstein, 2005). Loewi's release was conditional on his willingness to relinquish his assets, including his Nobel Prize money, to Nazi control.

Since the discovery of acetylcholine, many scholars investigated its properties (Sourkes, 2009), and several other neurotransmitters (chemicals involved in synaptic transmission that are generated inside the body and have a mechanism for inactivation) have been identified. These discoveries have revolutionized our understanding of the brain and the rest of the nervous system as well as pharmacological treatments for people with mental illness. The discovery of monoamines—neurotransmitters including dopamine, serotonin, and norepinephrine—soon followed. By the late 1950s, despite some false starts related to the uses of hallucinogens as treatments for people with some psychological disorders, particularly schizophrenia (Mills, 2010), this basic research

knowledge had been translated into practice in the form of psychopharmacological treatments for mental illness (Kline & Saunders, 1959; Kuhn, 1958). In the late 1970s and early 1980s, neurotransmitter research expanded to include investigation of neuropeptides, peptides that communicate information between neurons (see Krivoy, Kroeger, & Zimmermann, 1977).

Drawing on discoveries from neurotransmitter research, clinical psychology benefited from advances in psychopharmacology. The use of medications to treat people with psychological disorders began in 1949 when Australian psychiatrist John Cade (1912–1980) used lithium salts to treat individuals with bipolar disorder (Mitchell, 1999; Schioldann, 2009). Despite its success, lithium did not enjoy widespread acceptance in psychiatry, particularly in the United States, until two decades after Cade's treatment (Shorter, 2009). (Two decades before Cade, lithium was used as an original ingredient in a soft drink called "Bib-Label Lithiated Lemon-Lime Soda"; in time, the unwieldy name was shortened to "7Up Lithiated Lemon Soda" before evolving into the more familiar "7Up.")

Following Cade's work, the field gained momentum with the development of tricyclics (Kuhn, 1958) and monoamine oxidase inhibitors (Kline & Saunders, 1959) to treat depression. Following a discovery by French physician Henri Laborit (1914–1995) that a specific group of antihistamine drugs calmed users, researchers developed a medication known as chlorpromazine. Marketed as Thorazine in the 1950s, it became the first antipsychotic drug, revolutionizing the prognosis and treatment of individuals with severe psychiatric disorders (López-Muñoz et al., 2005).

Since the 1980s, the field of psychopharmacology has exploded, and the range of available medications to treat people with mental disorders has rapidly expanded. With improved medications, many individuals with mental illnesses can function at higher levels and are more likely to adapt to life outside residential treatment. Increase in availability of psychopharmaceuticals influenced the general move away from institutionalization. This move brought success and independence to many people who formerly had debilitating mental illnesses. The unfortunate side of this trend, however, is that some patients did not adjust to life outside residential treatment; many become homeless or incarcerated (Gilligan, 2001). Important questions linger about medication, helping people continue their use of medication, and long-term responsibilities of caregivers, treatment centers, and government agencies. These issues continue to guide basic and applied biological research in psychology.

Behavioral Genetics

Behavioral genetics, the study of the role of genes in cognition and behavior, emerged from ethology and other biological fields before blending with existing work in psychology; Loehlin (2009) and others claim the field started with the textbook *Behavior Genetics* by Fuller and Thompson (1960). Scholars from biology and ethology such as Richard Dawkins (b. 1941) and E. O. Wilson (b. 1929) studied the role of genetics in insects and other animals (Dawkins, 2006; Wilson, 1975/2000). From this basis, they argue that human social behaviors, like the behaviors of other animals, have genetic roots that are adaptive for survival. For example, there exist strong cross-cultural norms for reciprocity and altruism. Dawkins (2006) suggests that human willingness to give back to others and to help others results from evolutionary selection of genes for these social traits. The work of Wilson and Dawkins, among others, led to the emergence of evolutionary psychology as a self-conscious discipline (Buss, 2005). Within this framework, researchers studied topics such as aggression (Buss & Duntley, 2006), jealousy (Buss, 2000), and gender differences (Geary, 1998).

Behavioral genetics also has deep roots in the history of psychology (Maxson, 2007). In his work *Hereditary Genius* (1869/2006), Francis Galton argued for the hereditary basis of intelligence. His perspective informed much of the early work in intelligence, and many early psychologists, including H. H. Goddard, Lewis Terman,

Robert M. Yerkes, and Catherine Cox Miles, argued that intelligence was entirely hereditary (see Gould, 1981). The emphasis on genetics was powerful and carried significant consequences. Let's say intelligence is completely genetic. If some are more economically or socially successful than others, it follows that successful people owe their success to hereditary superiority. According to this thinking, people who are not successful are limited by their genetics and cannot be educated to succeed. Unfortunately, such perspectives helped justify and perpetuate the existing racism and segregation in American society (see Winston, 2003).

Other early psychologists regarded the relative influence of nature and nurture as an open question, and this question persists today. For example, Barbara Stoddard Burks (1902–1943) evaluated the relative contributions of genetics and environment to an organism's traits through comparisons of the traits of children and the traits of their biological parents and foster parents (Burks, 1927, 1928; King, Montañez-Ramírez, & Wertheimer, 1996). To address these questions, Thomas J. Bouchard Jr. (b. 1937) evaluated the relative similarity of monozygotic and dizygotic twins raised together and apart (Bouchard, Lykken, McGue, Segal, & Tellegen, 1984). As director of the Minnesota Center for Twin and Adoption Research, his work continues to inspire replication, support, and criticism.

In recent decades, increasing power and availability of genetic manipulation techniques have allowed researchers to pursue important psychological questions in nonhuman species. The use of animal models allows researchers to investigate questions with more experimental control and more invasive procedures. For example, researchers investigate the role of genes in individual differences related to alcohol consumption (Rhodes et al., 2007), genetic influence on sex-specific courtship behaviors of fruit flies (Manoli, Meissner, & Baker, 2006), and genetic influences on the actions of psychotropic drugs (Duman, Schlesinger, Kodama, Russell, & Duman, 2007). Behavioral genetics also addresses psychopathology, with research on people with disorders such as schizophrenia and antisocial behavior (Carey, 2003).

Psychoneuroimmunology

Psychoneuroimmunology, the study of the interactions between the brain, behavior, the immune system, and the social and physical environments, emerged in the 1970s with the work of Robert Ader and colleagues. Ader and Cohen (1975) classically conditioned rat immune systems by pairing saccharine-flavored water with an immune system suppressant. They found that when the immune suppression agent was removed from the saccharine solution, rats still showed immune system suppression. Following this work, the field was formalized with the 1981 publication of *Psychoneuroimmunology*, now in its fourth edition (Ader, 2006).

The area has exploded with the recognition that social, behavioral, and neurological factors can influence the immune system and that the immune system communicates with neurons via cytokines and other chemicals. Additionally, stress, attitudes, and perceived control influence immune reactions, and immune responses affect and interact with much of human and animal behavior (Fleshner & Laudenslager, 2004). The discipline has offered insight into how organisms adapt to a variety of challenges with critical implications for real-world applications such as the control and prevention of chronic pain (Watkins & Maier, 2005). The journal *Brain, Behavior, and Immunity* was founded in 1986 to provide synthesis across the fields of psychology, neuroscience, and immunology. Central features include "the role of the brain and behavior in modulating immunity and the role of immune processes in the regulation of neural and endocrine functions and behavior" (Ader & Kelley, 2007, p. 20). Psychoneuroimmunology continues to grow, particularly as part of the interdisciplinary field of health psychology (Belar et al., 2013). Additionally, the field provides an additional example of the decreasing insularity in psychology; basic and applied psychologists are reaching into hospitals, recovery rooms, and long-term-care facilities, among other places, where people seek healing.

The future is wide open for the fields of psychoneuroimmunology, behavioral and cognitive neuroscience, and behavioral genetics. Although some scholars (Churchland, 1989) claim that biological approaches will eventually eclipse psychology, leading it to become a branch of applied neuroscience, others expect both fields to grow in unison. Researchers continue to develop new methodologies that expand potential knowledge in the field, and the overlap between psychology and other disciplines such as biology, neurology, and ethology will continue to stimulate new paradigms and knowledge.

SOCIAL PSYCHOLOGY

In an address celebrating the twenty-fifth anniversary of the APA, John Dewey (1917) argued that the development of social psychology was important to general psychology and to a more complete understanding of human experience and behavior. Early classics by scholars such as Baldwin (1911), Dewey (1922), Bartlett (1923), Dunlap (1925), and McDougall (1926) set the stage for what would later become one of the dominant subdisciplinary areas of psychology.

Intellectual Traditions

Scholars have long attempted to investigate social phenomena empirically (Jahoda, 2007; Kruglanski & Stroebe, 2012), and, as mentioned in Chapter 17, **Floyd H. Allport (1890–1971)** was a significant figure in the formal emergence of the discipline and is often regarded as the founder of experimental social psychology (Katz, 1979). At Harvard, Hugo Münsterberg had encouraged Allport to focus his doctoral research on the "behavior of individuals acting alone versus their action together in groups" (Allport, 1974, p. 3). Following Münsterberg's advice, Allport (1920) devoted his dissertation to the topic, marking it as one of the first studies on conformity. In 1924, he published a landmark book on social psychology that was important because it provided

"an objectively conceived and somewhat systematic presentation of the subject from the psychological rather than the sociological point of view;
and second, it suggested at least by implication
the possibility of a new experimental science of
social psychology" (Allport, 1974, p. 9). In later
years, he conducted research on social influence,
cultural change, political structures, Nazi propa-
ganda and persuasion, attitudes, and anti-Semitic
prejudice. Despite his interest in the latter area,
he couldn't always liberate himself from the biases of his day. In his social psychology textbook, Allport (1924) wrote, "The intelligence of
the white race is of a more versatile and complex
order than that of the black race. . . .[and] probably superior also to that of the red or yellow
races" (p. 386). Such biases pervade much of the
psychological study of groups and of individual
differences from this time period (Guthrie, 2003;
Winston, 2003).

Social psychology has centered on three
primary topical areas: within- and between-group
processes, attitudes and beliefs, and social- and
self-perception (Ross et al., 2010). In what follows, we will examine several pivotal studies in
social influence, a topic that has shaped the history of the field (Prislin & Crano, 2012). Social
influence is but one area of social psychology,
but it is an important part that reveals why social
psychology occupies such a prominent place in
contemporary psychology.

MUZAFER SHERIF AND THE AUTOKINETIC
EFFECT   **Muzafer Sherif (1908–1988)**, one of
the pioneers in the development of social psychology, was motivated by many life experiences, including the time he was held without
charge in solitary confinement in a Turkish prison
for his outspoken criticism of the Nazi movement
(Harvey, 1989). Problems concerning prejudice,
intergroup conflict, and destructive group influence fascinated Sherif. He earned B.A. and M.A.
degrees in his native Turkey and an M.A. degree
at Harvard followed by a Ph.D. at Columbia
under the direction of Gardner Murphy. He also
studied with Wolfgang Köhler in Berlin. (Gestalt
psychology's influence is evident in his mature

research and in his classroom teaching.) Sherif
is remembered for his text *An Outline of Social
Psychology*, originally published in 1948 and
revised in 1956 and 1969 with the help of his
wife Carolyn Wood Sherif (1922–1982), also a
social psychologist. Sherif's famous boys' camp
research in intergroup conflict and conflict reduction (Gaertner et al., 2000) was set forth in
Groups in Harmony and Tension, which he also
coauthored with Carolyn Sherif (see Sherif &
Sherif, 1953) when he was at Yale University,
and a follow-up book titled *Intergroup Conflict
and Cooperation: The Robbers Cave Experiment*
(see Sherif et al., 1961), which he published when
he was at the University of Oklahoma. Sherif was
also the recipient of many awards including the
Distinguished Scientific Contribution Award in
1968 from the APA (see Harvey, 1989).

Following Allport's work on conformity,
Sherif (1936) conducted early studies on a phenomenon known as the **autokinetic effect**, an illusion of apparent movement. Imagine you're in
a darkened room, staring at a stationary pinpoint
of light. Though stationary, the light appears to
move. Astronomers noted that if we focus on a
star or a planet on a dark night while blocking
other lights from the field of vision, the star in
focus will move in irregular or erratic ways. Such
apparent movement has been suggested as a possible explanation for flying saucer sightings.

Under the guise of a visual perception experiment, Sherif conducted systematic studies on
the autokinetic effect in individual and group settings. Alone in a darkened room, participants estimated the movement of a motionless pinpoint of
light. Later, they engaged in the same task while
participating in three-person groups. They initially diverged in their estimates, but after working together over many trials, they established a
group norm so that all reported about the same
amount of movement. This classic study demonstrated that a simple perception in an unstructured or ambiguous situation is conditioned or
shaped by group influence. If basic perceptions
are shaped in social context, how much more may
beliefs, attitudes, opinions, and the like be subject to social influences that might be below our

threshold of awareness? This question is pertinent when we think about the unstructured world of infants as they identify with their immediate surroundings.

SOLOMON ASCH AND CONFORMITY

Solomon Asch (1907–1996) was born in Warsaw, Poland. He immigrated with his family to the United States in 1920. Asch was an introverted child who mastered English after an intensive reading of Charles Dickens's novels. He flourished in his studies and earned his master's degree under Robert Sessions Woodworth at Columbia University. Asch received his Ph.D. from Columbia in 1932. He was captivated by the Gestalt orientation and became acquainted with Max Wertheimer shortly after his immigration to the United States. In the early 1940s, Asch joined Rudolf Arnheim in editing drafts of Wertheimer's *Productive Thinking*. When Wertheimer died in 1943, Asch replaced him as chair of psychology at the New School for Social Research (McCauley & Rozin, 2003). Two years later, Asch joined Wolfgang Köhler and Clara Mayer (Dean at the New School) in editing the first edition of *Productive Thinking* (Wertheimer, 1945/1982). Asch stayed at the New School until moving to Swarthmore College in 1947, where he established a strong relationship with Köhler. In 1966, he headed the Institute for Cognitive Studies at Rutgers University then moved to the University of Pennsylvania, where he retired in 1979. He died on February 20, 1996.

In a classic social influence study, Asch demonstrated group influences on individual behavior in a more structured situation than that employed in Sherif's autokinetic studies. In Asch's classic conformity studies, volunteer participants believed they were participating in an experiment on visual perception. The participant and several confederates inspected white cards displaying vertical lines. One card displayed a single vertical line (a standard) and the other displayed three lines of varying length to be compared with the standard. One of the comparison lines provided a clear "best fit" in terms of length with the standard line. In the typical experimental scenario, the volunteer

sat in a small room with six confederates. Though there were numerous variations in the experimental conditions, the central purpose of the study was to examine behaviors of the volunteer participant when the confederates, who had received prior instructions, made a wrong choice that flew in the face of direct visual evidence. What would the participant do when all the confederates, speaking one at a time, declared that the appropriate matching stimulus was a line that was longer or shorter than the standard? About three-quarters of Asch's participants conformed at least once; choosing the wrong line in the face of contradictory evidence caused less distress than publicly disagreeing with a group of strangers. Asch's findings have practical consequences in many areas such as marketing, crowd behavior, and jury decision making; people's willingness to conform to statements that are obviously false (as in Asch's line-length studies) justifies significant concerns about conformity in decisions involving more complex legal stimuli.

STANLEY MILGRAM AND DESTRUCTIVE OBEDIENCE

Born to Jewish immigrants in the Bronx, New York, **Stanley Milgram (1933–1984)** attended James Monroe High School with a classmate who was also destined to become a social psychologist, Phillip G. Zimbardo (b. 1933). Milgram studied political science at Queens College but never took a psychology course as an undergraduate (Blass, 2004). Harvard University rejected Milgram as a graduate candidate due to his insufficient background in psychology. After taking six courses in the area, he was finally accepted and earned his Ph.D. from Harvard in 1960. Milgram spent an influential postdoctoral year studying with Solomon Asch (McCauley & Rozin, 2003). Gordon Allport also played a critical role in shaping Milgram's psychological perspective. In 1967, Milgram conducted a "small world" experiment on social networks that inspired the popular notion of "six degrees of separation" among people. Although influential, his study was overshadowed by an experiment he had published four years before.

Milgram had joined the faculty at Yale University in the fall of 1960 and received a two-year National Science Foundation grant for a study on obedience the next year (Blass, 2004). He completed data collection during the 1960–1961 academic year, drawing on a participant pool from the New Haven, Connecticut area. His research was inspired in part by the destructive actions of Adolf Eichmann, the Gestapo chief of Jewish Affairs, who was responsible for mass deportation of Jewish citizens to ghettos and extermination camps in Nazi-occupied Eastern Europe. Eichmann was apprehended in Argentina. When Eichmann was placed on trial in Jerusalem in 1961, he insisted, in his own defense, that he was only following orders during his time as a high-ranking Nazi official (Cesarani, 2007). Eichman's words haunted the young Yale psychologist and, among other factors, inspired one of the most controversial experiments in the history of psychology (Blass, 2009).

The question Milgram raised was simple: How far would a person go to obey authority? The studies required extensive development and pretesting (Russell, 2011), and the answer was disturbing and complex. Acting as the "teacher," the participant worked with a forty-seven-year-old man with a heart condition who served as a "learner" (in reality, he was Milgram's accomplice). After the learner was strapped to a chair and rigged with electrodes, the teacher moved to an adjoining room to begin the experiment. Milgram (1963) promoted the study as an exploration of the role of punishment on forgetting, ordering the teacher to administer electrical shock to the learner for every mistake he made on the test. Given the power of the situation, many teachers felt social pressure to obey authority. But how many people would actually administer the maximum 450 volts? Despite violent protests from the learner, 65 percent of Milgram's participants gave what they believed were harmful shocks. Outcomes from a more recent and more ethical replication were consistent with Milgram's findings (Burger, 2009, 2011), and, tragically, history provides too many examples of destructive obedience (Navarick, 2012).

The repercussions were as staggering as the study itself. Critics blasted the research, demanding greater ethical standards in psychology research (Baumrind, 1964). Blass (2004) noted that when Milgram tried to join the APA, his application was put on hold pending an investigation into the ethics of his research (satisfied, the APA later allowed him to join). Undeterred, Milgram conducted a series of variations on his obedience experiments that stimulated other researchers.

In August 1971, Zimbardo created a "prison" in the basement of Stanford University's psychology building to study the psychology of authoritarian roles in prison life. Conceived as a two-week experiment, the Stanford Prison Experiment was cut short after only six days. During the simulation, participants who acted as "guards" became cruel and sadistic, while the "prisoners" grew demoralized and despondent. Like Milgram's research, Zimbardo's study produced devastating findings that too often mirror destructive social influence in the real world (Haney & Zimbardo, 1998), including the tragic abuses of detainees in the Iraqi prison Abu Ghraib (Drury et al., 2012; Zimbardo, 2007). The studies by Milgram and Zimbardo played significant roles in shaping public perceptions of psychology (De Vos, 2010).

Current Developments

Social Psychology gained ground in basic research departments with the work of Sherif, Asch, Milgram, Zimbardo, and others, and the field expanded to include questions related to attributions, attitudes, and culture. Today, the field explores many broad research areas including interpersonal attraction, social perception, prejudice, aggression, persuasion, and altruism among others.

Social psychology has also blended into other broad paradigms in psychology. For example, rather than separating social psychology from cognitive psychology, some researchers investigate *social cognition*, the ways people think about themselves and others in social situations (Fiske & Taylor, 1991; North & Fiske, 2012). Evolutionary psychologists generate hypotheses about adaptive human social interaction and then test these hypotheses with methods from social psychology (Buss, 2000). Although health psychology has its roots in psychodynamic and physiological approaches, some health psychologists today employ methods from social psychology to evaluate social and contextual effects on health behaviors (Belar, McIntyre, & Matarazzo, 2003). Additionally, some basic and applied fields of psychology emerged, in whole or in part, as subfields of social psychology. Parts of the broad fields of industrial-organizational psychology, with early roots in Münsterberg's *Psychology and Industrial Efficiency* (1913), apply social psychology to questions in the workplace. Environmental psychology, a field that formally emerged in the 1960s in response to increased concerns about questions of human population and degrading environmental health, uses some approaches from social psychology to evaluate the effects of built or natural environments on behavior and cognition (Richards, 2000). Some areas of psychology and the law, as discussed later, have roots in questions about the influence of eyewitnesses and other social factors.

At present, eight divisions of the APA are devoted in one way or another to the study of the effects of social influences on experience and behavior. Among the most prominent are the Society for Personality and Social Psychology (Division 8) and the Society for the Psychological Study of Social Issues (Division 9), whose social justice orientation reflects the moralistic roots that inspired much of early psychology (Morawski & Bayer, 2013). Other related divisions of the APA include Population and Environmental Psychology (Division 34); Society for the Study of Peace, Conflict, and Violence: Peace Psychology Division (Division 48); and Family Psychology (Division 43). Early studies on topics such as the senses, reaction times, individual differences, and the physiological underpinnings of behavior were important, but there is increasing awareness that social context determines much of who we are and what we do. All APA-accredited Ph.D. programs in clinical and counseling psychology require that students receive training in

the social forces that shape our lives. Moreover, social psychology is one of the more dominant areas for doctoral-level studies.

Social psychology continues to grow in basic fields as well as applied fields and in overlap between traditional social psychology and other areas of psychological science and practice.

INDUSTRIAL-ORGANIZATIONAL PSYCHOLOGY

Pioneers such as Sigmund Freud and Dorothea Lynde Dix agreed on the vital role that work plays in human adjustment. Dix (1845/1971) argued, "Of all the remedies for 'razing out the written troubles of the brain' none can compare with labor, wherein I include all useful employment" (p. 39). In her campaign to improve accommodations for people with mental illnesses, she repeatedly highlighted the therapeutic value of meaningful work. Freud (1930/1961a) noted that "No other technique for the conduct of life attaches the individual so firmly to reality as laying emphasis on work" (p. 27). He believed that the capacity to love and work are two of the most important indicators of mental health. The field of industrial-organizational psychology is the study of behavior, cognition, and experience in work settings. As such, this field touches many topics that are central to human happiness and well-being.

Intellectual Traditions

In Chapter 12, we discussed Hugo Münsterberg's critical role in establishing industrial-organizational psychology. His classic book *Psychology and Industrial Efficiency* (1913) helped launch the discipline and covered areas still vital to the industrial-organizational field, although the field has grown more complex and specialized since his seminal work (Bryan & Vinchur, 2013). Around the same time, American social worker **Mary Parker Follett (1868–1933)** conducted early work on political psychology that addressed issues relating to the human side of government and democracy, drawing the admiration of Theodore Roosevelt and other politicians. She also explored crowd psychology during two decades of civic work in Boston's immigrant neighborhoods.

In the 1920s, Follett focused on corporate issues, particularly adult learning to improve individual and corporate outcomes (Wheelock & Callahan, 2006). She was recognized as a leading management consultant, and she offered America's first executive development seminars in New York City (Tonn, 2003). In her writings, lectures, and seminars, she popularized phrases such as "conflict resolution," "power sharing," and the "task of leadership." Her legacy remains evident in discussions concerning worker empowerment, collaborative leadership, conflict resolution, and corporate social responsibility.

Walter Dill Scott

Several of Wilhelm Wundt's students, including **Walter Dill Scott (1869–1955)**, Lightner Witmer, and James McKeen Cattell, must be counted as pioneers in applied psychology (Landy, 1997). A pioneer in the world of business psychology (Vinchur & Koppes, 2007), Scott was critical in calling for managers to improve workers' attitudes and motivation in order to increase productivity.

After completing a doctorate with Wundt in 1900, Scott joined the faculty at Northwestern University, where he served as president from 1920 to 1939. He was founder and president of the Scott Company, the first personnel consulting firm and was elected president of the APA in 1919. Von Mayrhauser (1989) called attention to the similarities between Binet's and Scott's approaches to intelligence testing and to Scott's crucial role in developing successful group tests.

Strong (1955) argued that Scott "may properly be called the father of applied psychology for no one else applied psychology to such a variety of business problems as he did and at so early a date" (p. 682). If Scott had a favorite topical area in academic psychology, it was undoubtedly motivation, but his interest in theoretical problems in motivation was complemented by an interest

in practical motivational problems. Some of his earliest contributions in applied psychology were books and articles on advertising (Kuna, 1976). In an early popular article written for *Atlantic Monthly*, Scott (1904) reviewed the history and growth of advertising and argued that there was a significant role for psychologists in this field. He wrote about the roles of mental imagery, motivation, and suggestion in advertising and showed that psychologists, by virtue of their training, have relevant expertise for the field. Scott's other applied interests included the psychology of public speaking, the psychology of argument and persuasion, prediction of vocational interests and skills, methods of improving work efficiency, and management techniques.

Scott and Münsterberg were not alone in expressing enthusiasm for applied psychology. Despite occasional concerns about premature application, well-known scholars filled books and periodicals with suggestions on how psychology might be useful. For example, Royce (1898) pointed out that psychology might be useful to educators in finding ways to combat fatigue, boredom, and poor work habits. Seashore (1911), in a *Popular Science Monthly* article, offered the optimistic opinion that there was a need for consulting psychologists in a great range of human endeavors, including the arts, science, the professions, and industry. Others wrote on topics such as the value of humor (Kline, 1908), the importance of play and relaxation (Patrick, 1914), and the effects of strong emotions (Cannon, 1922). Psychology, almost from the beginning, had a promising potential that captured the attention and imagination of the public.

Lillian Gilbreth

Lillian Gilbreth (1878–1972) was born Lillian Evelyn Moller in Oakland, California. Undeterred by her family's bias against higher education for women, Gilbreth earned a master's degree in literature and was close to finishing a Ph.D. at the University of California at Berkeley. Following marriage to Frank Gilbreth in 1904, her graduate studies were delayed for the better part of a decade. After her husband's consulting firm relocated to Providence, Rhode Island, Gilbreth studied psychology at Brown University where she earned a Ph.D. in 1915.

Lillian and Frank Gilbreth were pioneers in the field of ergonomics, the study of how the workplace can be designed for maximum safety, productivity, and worker satisfaction. Their books on the topics of fatigue (Gilbreth & Gilbreth, 1916) and motion (Gilbreth & Gilbreth, 1917) addressed the problems of wasted time and effort in a variety of settings, and they were among the first to use film to study workers' motions (Hindmarsh, 2009). They sensitized the public and industrial leaders to the financial and psychological values of metalevel thinking about how work is and should be performed to maximize safety, productivity, and satisfaction. The results were salutary for both workers and employers and set the stage for the scientific and professional efforts of generations of industrial and organizational psychologists. The Gilbreths' work on fatigue represents their approach to other problems. They employed questionnaires and engaged in on-site inspections, examining effects of lighting, heating, ventilation, length of rest periods, arrangement of materials, seating arrangements, and type of clothing on worker fatigue. They argued that fatigue is a psychological and a physiological problem that accounts for enormous losses of time and money and a perennial waste of human energy.

In their book *Management in the Home*, Gilbreth, Thomas, and Clymer (1954/1962) provide fruitful discussions on topics such as how to eliminate unnecessary work, how to think about sequence of operations, how to simplify operations, and how to use tools with maximal efficiency. Many of their ideas for energy-saving kitchens are still in effect. According to Koppes (2000) two of Gilbreth's "most notable inventions were the shelves inside refrigerator doors and the foot-pedal trash can" (p. 499).

Gilbreth and Gilbreth were also interested in structural and procedural suggestions for homemakers and workers with disabilities. The creation of helpful and efficient settings, tools,

and procedures for disabled veterans and others were set forth in their book *Motion Study for the Handicapped* (Gilbreth & Gilbreth, 1920). In this context, they explored topics such as how an oral hygienist can work with one arm or with other disabilities. Additional topics included studies of typing with one hand, jobs that could be carried out effectively by people who are blind, and the need for reeducation programs for those who have acquired disabilities due to injuries or illness. After Frank Gilbreth died in 1924, Lillian Gilbreth continued with characteristic vigor and addressed the needs of workers and veterans with disabilities (see Yost & Gilbreth, 1944).

Given the visibility of her work, Gilbreth gained recognition as an early figure to publicly embrace a successful career and a successful marriage (Vasquez, 2007). She held appointments at Rutgers, Purdue University, and the Massachusetts Institute of Technology, where she was appointed lecturer when she was eighty-six years old. She once noted that for Frank, "time was always an opportunity" (Gilbreth, 1928/1951, p. 16), but the same was true for her. Gilbreth's contributions extend beyond industrial-organizational psychology to include diverse arenas such as military psychology, educational psychology, management, sports medicine, and engineering psychology. Her breadth and larger philosophic perspective mark her as a premiere example of a general psychologist (see Perloff & Naman, 1996). She received over a dozen honorary doctorates and, according to Koppes (2000), she served "on a number of committees appointed by Presidents Hoover, Roosevelt, Truman, Eisenhower, Kennedy, and Johnson" (p. 499). Books published by two of her twelve children, *Cheaper by the Dozen* (Gilbreth & Carey, 1948) and *Belles on Their Toes* (Gilbreth & Carey, 1950), celebrated life in the Gilbreth family. Their books inspired several successful Hollywood movies.

In early 1972, Lillian Moller Gilbreth died at the age of ninety-three. She was a unique and creative pioneer who extended the reach of psychology by exploring problems that gave the discipline a public face along with the promise of a productive dialogue with other disciplines such as mechanical engineering and business. Gilbreth is among the few psychologists who exemplify the empirical, pragmatic, and functionalist traditions set forth by William James, Hugo Münsterberg, John Dewey, and Walter Dill Scott.

Current Developments

As a subfield of psychology, industrial-organizational psychologists study topics such as fatigue, rest periods, leadership, motivation, performance appraisal, evaluation of job applicants, and all of the various dimensions of the workplace including lighting, motion studies, incentives, worker morale, job satisfaction, advertising, hiring, and compensation issues. Since the spread of graduate training following World War II (Lowman et al., 2007), there are now over sixty programs in the United States that offer doctorates in industrial-organizational psychology, far more programs offering master's level training in the area, and a national organization, Division 14 of the APA, Society for Industrial-Organizational Psychology (SIOP). Industrial-organizational psychologists are also some of the best-paid professionals in the United States, and they work in a great variety of settings including private consulting, universities, consulting firms, and large organizations that require assistance on topics such as employee training, selection, quality of work life, consumer issues, and efficiency issues associated with assembly lines and human–machine interactions. In an increasingly technological age, it is likely there will be increasing demand for workers who are skilled in this subdisciplinary area of psychology.

PSYCHOLOGY AND LAW

The intersection of psychological and legal themes played out long before the emergence of psychology as a formal discipline. For centuries, observers have speculated that human motives could contaminate legal outcomes. In the seventeenth century, Francis Bacon noted tensions between legal goals of justice and human drives for revenge. Hoping to separate vengeance from the legal system, he wrote that "Revenge is a kind of wild justice, which the more Man's nature runs to, the more ought the law to weed it out" (Bacon, 1625/1857, p. 46).

Intellectual Traditions

From the mid-1700s to modern times, legal systems in Western nations shifted from brutal to more lenient punishments with a greater role for extenuating factors such as the mental state of the defendant (Foucault, 1979). Early cases in English common law established distinct judgments for people with mental illnesses who may not recognize the difference between right and wrong (Brigham & Grisso, 2003). However, questions about mental illness and expert testimony came to the forefront of public perception in England with the trial of Daniel M'Naughton.

In 1843, M'Naughton tried to assassinate Sir Robert Peel, the Prime Minister of England, but due to an error, he shot and killed Edward Drummond, the prime minister's secretary (Rychlak & Rychlak, 1990). To aid the jury in its decision regarding M'Naughton's behavior and psychological state, the court invited nine medical professionals to address the court. After considering the recommendations of the experts, the jury found M'Naughton not guilty by reason of insanity. M'Naughton spent the remainder of his life institutionalized, first at Bethlem Royal Hospital and then at the Broadmoor. The landmark M'Naughton case established the role of expert psychological testimony in questions of mental illness.

Additional legal events shaped the relationship between psychology and law. Eight years before becoming a Supreme Court Justice, Louis D. Brandeis (1856–1941) brought social psychology into the legal system in a brief for a 1908 court case (Ogloff & Finkelman, 1999). In the early twentieth century, the state of Oregon, like much of the United States, regulated male and female labor differently. The state pressed criminal charges and convicted the owner of a laundry who mandated that his female workers had to spend more than ten hours a day on the job. The owner appealed to the U.S. Supreme Court, and

Brandeis, an eminent attorney who would later serve as a justice on the Supreme Court, wrote a lengthy brief in support of the state's position. The brief provided only a cursory review of legal arguments; a majority of Brandeis's materials presented data from social science to support the state's claims that long working hours were particularly detrimental to women. Brandeis based his arguments on claims of women's physical and psychological inferiority, and later scholars view the social science underlying Brandeis's work as rather poor in quality (Monahan & Walker, 1994). Despite these limitations, the Supreme Court upheld the laundry owner's conviction and the laws supporting gender differences in working hours. This case affected the legal system in important ways. First, the phrase "Brandeis brief" continues to describe any collection of scientific or other nonlegal materials submitted to support one side in a court case. Second, Brandeis paved the way for increasing contributions to legal decisions from social scientists.

The famous desegregation case, *Brown v. Board of Education* (1954), increased the prominence of psychology and motivated more interaction between psychologists and the legal system. In what Monahan and Walker (1994) referred to as "the best-known use of social science in any area of law" (p. 148), a group of thirty-five researchers in psychology, psychiatry, and other fields compiled and signed a Brandeis brief arguing that segregation causes consistent, significant, and preventable harm to children (Brigham & Grisso, 2003). With this case, psychologists anchored their continued involvement with the legal system.

In the late 1800s and early 1900s, psychologists initiated basic and applied research into legal issues, including well-known scholars such as Münsterberg, Jung, and Wertheimer as well as lesser-known scholars such as Arnold (1906, see Bornstein & Penrod, 2008). Carl Jung and Max Wertheimer engaged in an extended dispute over who should receive credit for pioneering the use of free association techniques to detect lies; Jung's paper was published first, but Wertheimer had submitted his work first (see King & Wertheimer, 2005). In the same year

as Brandeis's famous brief, Hugo Münsterberg (1908) opened the door to topics such as false confessions, including those that the false confessor believed to be true, and the role of hypnosis in memory and crime prevention. One of Münsterberg's most enduring legacies came in his work on eyewitness testimony.

Hugo Münsterberg

The accuracy of eyewitness testimony was an early interest for forensic investigators such as the German criminologist Franz von Liszt (1851–1919). As described by Münsterberg (1908), during class, von Liszt's students unexpectedly witnessed an intense argument culminating in an actual gunshot (the pistol had been loaded with a blank round). When von Liszt asked his students to describe the people and the events in question, students' reports varied and often proved inaccurate. Imagine being in the classroom for that demonstration! We can only wonder if the experience affected the students' hearing and emotional welfare along with their eyewitness memories.

In 1906, Münsterberg (1908) brought a similar demonstration to a scientific convention of "jurists, psychologists, and physicians, all, therefore, men well trained in careful observation" (p. 51). During Münsterberg's presentation, a commotion erupted as an individual in a brightly colored clown suit rushed into the meeting followed by a black man; there was a struggle and a gunshot before the confederates ran from the meeting. First, as Münsterberg stated, the attendees at the meeting were all men, and second, the black man was particularly distinctive because the audience, which included scholars who had attended universities that excluded applicants based on race, was composed of white men. After this unusual interruption, Münsterberg asked the attendees to write descriptions of the event. In the reports, he found extensive disagreement, errors, and missing details. In fact, many eyewitnesses had added false information to their testimony. Münsterberg's pioneering studies raised important legal questions about eyewitnesses as well as scientific questions about memory (Memon et al., 2008).

Münsterberg's success as a teacher, researcher, and writer in psychology and law helped the area gain popularity and inspired greater student enrollment in many fields of basic and applied psychology (Sporer, 2006). He was also a pioneer in encouraging courts to consider psychological research (Bornstein & Meissner, 2008). Unfortunately, the intrusion of social history lessened his impact on psychology, reducing scholarly interest in psychology and the law. Years before, Münsterberg had protested U.S. entry into World War I. Additionally, he never became a U.S. citizen and praised his native Germany, further straining his relations with some American citizens (Spillmann & Spillmann, 1993). Other influences also affected the viability of research in psychology and law; Münsterberg ended his career without graduate students, stifling subsequent research. At the same time, his critics gained favor in psychological and legal circles. The American jurist John Henry Wigmore (1863–1943) publicly assailed Münsterberg with a parody of his research. In his satire, Wigmore (1909) described a fictitious civil trial held on April Fool's Day. At this trial, Münsterberg and "Mr. X Perry Ment" were found liable for damaging the reputation of the legal profession and were assessed damages of $1 (see Sporer, 2006).

Elizabeth F. Loftus

Eyewitness testimony, along with other research topics in psychology and the law, faded to the background of psychology until **Elizabeth F. Loftus (b. 1944)** and other researchers led a "renaissance" in the 1970s (Sporer, 2006, p. i). Loftus's seminal work, *Eyewitness Testimony* (1979/1996), described the field at the time, provided testable hypotheses for future research, and, perhaps most importantly, inspired other researchers. Like Münsterberg, Loftus (1993) has faced cultural hostilities based on strong personal and scholarly resistance to her work, especially her investigations into repressed memories. Since the 1970s, the field of eyewitness testimony has grown through the systematic efforts of psychologists who have generated a well-developed body

of research on eyewitness testimony (Wells, Memon, & Penrod, 2006). Findings from this research have not remained insulated in psychology; psychologists who are experts in these areas formed an integral part of the working group that assisted the U.S. Department of Justice (1999) in writing guidelines for collecting evidence from eyewitnesses.

Current Developments

As in the M'Naughton case of old, contemporary forensic psychologists inherited the role of expert witnesses in the American legal system (Brigham & Grisso, 2003). Typically trained as clinicians, forensic psychologists work in the legal system to answer questions about defendants and other individuals interacting with the law (Nicholson, 1999) and address applied issues in criminal and civil trials. In contrast with researchers such as Loftus who apply psychological methods to legal questions, the professional activities of forensic psychologists vary and may include determining whether an individual is mentally ill, assessing the psychological harm of a crime or an injury, assessing a defendant's competency to stand trial, or evaluating a juvenile to determine whether he or she should be transferred to the adult court system (Grisso & Brigham, 2013). The growing role of forensic psychologists in the law, particularly since the 1970s (Packer & Borum, 2013), can be seen in the increasing number of active forensic psychologists and the growing number of training programs for forensic psychology, particularly joint law-and-psychology programs with forensic emphases (Bersoff, 1999).

Social and cognitive psychologists continue to investigate questions of legal importance. Basic and applied researchers study a wide range of topics including but not limited to eyewitness testimony (Wells et al., 2006), interrogation and confession (Kassin & Gudjonsson, 2004), pretrial publicity (Studebaker & Penrod, 1997), and civil and criminal jury decision making (Greene & Bornstein, 2003; Nietzel, McCarthy, & Kern, 1999).

The field of psychology and the law, including its research and clinical areas, received a major boost in 1969 when Eric Dreikurs and

Jay Ziskin gathered interested researchers, expert witnesses, and practitioners to form the American Psychology-Law Society (Pickren & Fowler, 2003). Since the late 1960s, psychology and the law has exploded into one of the fastest-growing and most diverse research and applied areas in psychology. The continued increase in the public and legal status of the field can be seen in the increasing number of psychological experts testifying in court, the growth of psychological consultants in the law, and the increasing citation of psychological research to justify legal decisions (Ogloff & Finkelman, 1999).

DIVERSITY AND PLURALISM IN MODERN PSYCHOLOGY

The expansion of contemporary psychology has produced a kind of *diaspora*, the Greek word for "scattering." As we have seen in this chapter, this diaspora is reflected in the pluralistic content of modern psychology in addition to the diversity of its professional organizations. The APA lists fifty-four divisions that reveal the growing interest in applied and professional psychology.

Psychologists have been involved in the application of psychology as a profession since the 1870s (Camfield, 1973). Applied psychology, particularly the expansion of clinical psychology, has proliferated since World War II (Gilgen, 1982). However, the rise of professionalism has produced tension within the discipline. The diversity of psychology is also manifested in the failure of psychologists to agree on a common core curriculum for doctoral programs (Benjamin, 2001).

Several professional societies were partly formed in protest against psychology's growing professionalism. A group of experimental psychologists founded the Psychonomic Society in the early 1960s, spawning several outstanding journals, including *Psychonomic Science* (founded in 1964 and changed to the *Bulletin of the Psychonomic Society* in 1973), *Perception and Psychophysics* (1967), *Behavior Research Methods, Instruments and Computers* (1969), and *Memory and Cognition* (1973). The American

Psychological Society (APS) also emerged from the strain between professional and scientific psychology. Following a decade of unsuccessful campaigns to reorganize the APA, the Assembly for Scientific and Applied Psychology formally elected to establish the APS in 1988. This national organization, devoted explicitly to scientific psychology, held the first APS convention in 1989. *Psychological Science*, the first APS journal, began publication the following year.

Does such diversity damage or promote a healthy psychology? Some psychologists have expressed concerns about the disunity of psychology (see Sternberg, 2005) including the claim that disunity undermines the status of psychology as a scientific discipline (Staats, 1999, 2005). Such concern is fueled by the belief that the more mature sciences are unified and coherent disciplines. For example, Staats (1989) has argued that "Each science undergoes a transition from early disunification to later unification" (p. 143). He noted that this transition has produced considerable consensus regarding theory, methodology, and philosophy in the natural sciences whereas the behavioral sciences are disunited and therefore "relatively backward" (p. 148).

However, in terms of administrative and organizational structures, psychology is as unified today as any of the sciences and more unified than some. Undergraduate programs are typically administered out of a single, usually large department. By contrast, it is not uncommon to encounter twenty or more separate departments in the various branches of the biological sciences, including botany, horticulture, range science, forestry, zoology, anatomy, animal science, microbiology, biophysics, and biochemistry. Perhaps psychologists overestimate the unity of other sciences; if so, such overestimation may result in an unfortunate devaluing of the scientific and professional status of psychology (see Viney, 1996a). Since the 1980s, a growing literature in the philosophy of science points to increased disunity and pluralism in all the sciences (see Dupré, 1993; Galison & Stump, 1996; Kellert, Longino, & Walters, 2006). Nevertheless, there is value in exploring various kinds of disciplinary unity (e.g., methodological unity, conceptual unity, unity of language, and unity of purpose). It remains problematic as to whether there is a grand unity that somehow brings together the great problems of epistemology and ontology. In the meantime, and in the spirit of William James, there may be value in celebrating the advantages that pluralism affords for psychology (Viney, 1989; Viney, King, & King, 1992). With a healthy respect for pluralism, Slife and Williams (1997) have suggested that theoretical consultants could be trained to educate psychologists about key theoretical issues and themes that influence applied and basic psychology.

Diversity and pluralism form the bedrock for psychology's unfolding expansion. As we have seen, the discipline has undergone unprecedented growth in the decades following World War II. Innovative ways of thinking have emerged while older perspectives have undergone reinterpretation for a new age. Dramatic technologies have opened fresh vistas while revealing the architecture and action of the brain. By design, psychology plays a role in the exploration and understanding of problems and issues that challenge us individually and collectively. Time after time, the ambitions of experimental and applied psychology have transformed how we look at ourselves as well as the world around us. As psychologists, we face a formidable test, as William James (1900/2010) said, "to get human life in its wild intensity" (p. 168). At its best, psychology exposes the trials and rich possibilities of existence, from suffering and pain to joy and fulfillment. Traveling deeper into the century, we anticipate a continuing fascination with a discipline that speaks so directly to the problems confronting the complicated world of human experience and behavior.

Review Questions

1. Outline some of the developments of psychoanalysis in the United States following World War II.
2. Identify major events in the institutionalization of humanistic psychology. What attempts have been made to increase the international and scientific appeal of humanistic psychology?

3. What were the main contributions of Harry Harlow's research? How is his work incongruent with the neobehaviorism of B. F. Skinner?
4. Describe specific developments that contributed to the advance of cognitive psychology.
5. Briefly discuss three major themes in cognitive psychology.
6. What are the main arguments for and against the computer metaphor?
7. In your opinion, does cognitive psychology represent a paradigm shift or revolution? What evidence would you employ in defending your position?
8. How is the diversity of psychology reflected in current psychological organizations? Would you be more likely to support a unified psychology or a pluralistic one?
9. Describe criticisms of cognitive psychology. Are these criticisms valid?
10. What are the historical roots of clinical psychology? What historical thinkers considered clinical questions before the advent of psychology as a formal discipline?
11. What were critical events in the emergence of clinical psychology as a subfield of psychology and a formal profession?
12. Describe the components of the Boulder model. Why do you think these factors were chosen?
13. Name three cognitive or cognitive-behavioral therapists. How are their views similar? How are their perspectives different?
14. Who are two reductionistic biological psychologists? Who are two biological psychologists who emphasize systems or wholistic approaches? What are methodological and topical differences between these perspectives?
15. Describe the major technological developments that have influenced biological psychology.
16. Is the use of fMRI and PET scan information to locate areas of the brain that correlate with specific cognitive functions the "new phrenology," or do these approaches provide valid methods to evaluate the relationship between cognition and neurology?
17. In what ways has biological psychology benefited from infusions of ideas and researchers from other disciplines?
18. What possible social and cultural problems can arise from the study of genes and behavior, specifically intelligence and genetics?
19. Describe similarities and differences in the methodologies and research topics of Muzafer Sherif, Solomon Asch, and Stanley Milgram.

20. Which early applied psychologist, in your opinion, provided the strongest foundation for early industrial and organizational psychology? How would you defend your choice?

21. How did early women in applied psychology successfully transcend the gender boundaries that existed in academia and the workplace in the early 1900s?

22. What famous legal cases led to the direct involvement of psychologists in the legal system, and how did psychologists contribute to each case?

23. What are some critical social and contextual differences that affected the successes and failures of Hugo Münsterberg and Elizabeth Loftus?

Glossary

Allport, Floyd H. (1890–1971) A founder of experimental social psychology, Allport pioneered research in conformity, social influence, and prejudice.

Asch, Solomon (1907–1996) A social psychologist in the Gestalt tradition, Asch performed classic conformity studies in which participants often conformed to strangers' mistaken perceptions of the length of a clearly visible line.

autokinetic effect The tendency of a fixed point of light to appear to move. Muzafer Sherif examined the ways that social norms influenced the perceived degree of movement.

Bartlett, Frederick Charles (1886–1969) British psychologist who stressed the role of representations or schemas in memory and cognition.

Beck, Aaron T. (1921–) An early cognitive therapist who helped clients reduce negative thoughts and more accurately perceive themselves. He developed the Beck Depression Inventory.

behavioral genetics The study of the role of genes in cognition and behavior.

Binet, Alfred (1857–1911) French psychologist and a major figure in the study of intelligence testing.

Boulder model The model for current clinical training that recommends doctoral programs

train clinical psychologists as research-practitioners with solid backgrounds in general and clinical psychology, extensive supervised experience, and research experience.

cognitive psychology A broad interdisciplinary effort to study the processing of information in memory, problem solving, judgment, and other forms of cognition. Also known as cognitive science or information-processing psychology.

computer metaphor The use of computers to model and study cognitive functions of humans and animals.

ecological validity The view that psychologists should study real-world, everyday events about the human condition. Cognitive psychology has been criticized for its lack of ecological validity.

Follett, Mary Parker (1868–1933) An early industrial-organizational psychologist who applied her background in political psychology to corporate issues and seminal executive development seminars.

Gilbreth, Lillian (1878–1972) Called the "Mother of Industrial and Organizational Psychology," she and her husband Frank Gilbreth helped launch the field of ergonomics. She studied many diverse topics including worker efficiency and effective management.

Harlow, Harry Frederick (1905–1981) American psychologist noted for his creative contributions to learning theory and the formation of attachment.

Hebb, Donald Olding (1904–1985) A pioneer in the neurobiology of learning, he provided a testable explanation of associationist learning and evaluated the effects of the environment on rats' neurological development.

information-processing metaphor The view that cognition involves the processing of information in a sophisticated manner or sequence. Also known as the computer metaphor.

Kandel, Eric (1929–) A biological psychologist taking reductionistic approaches to the physiological aspects of memory in animal models.

learning set Harlow's finding that previous experience can facilitate a primate's ability to discriminate among stimuli. Harlow also referred to this process as *learning to learn*.

Lindsley, Donald B. (1907–2003) An early cognitive and behavioral neuroscientist, he helped launch the electrical study of the brain, particularly with his application of the EEG to psychological research.

Linehan, Marsha M. (1943–) Developer of DBT, a blend of Western scientific approaches to behavior and Eastern mindfulness practices.

Loewi, Otto (1873–1961) He shared the Nobel Prize in Physiology for the discovery of the neurotransmitter acetylcholine. His work greatly increased understanding of the general processes of neural transmission.

Loftus, Elizabeth F. (1944–) She led the return to questions of eyewitness testimony that helped to revitalize the study of psychology and the law.

mentalism The use of words such as *mind*, *intention*, and *cognition* in the study of science. This aspect of cognitive psychology was challenged by B. F. Skinner.

Milgram, Stanley (1933–1984) A social psychologist who examined participants' willingness to obey an authority's orders to injure or even apparently kill another human.

Piaget, Jean (1896–1980) Swiss epistemologist who advanced a popular developmental theory of serially progressive stages of human cognition.

psychoneuroimmunology The study of the interactions between the brain, behavior, the immune system, and the social and physical environments. The field was launched by Robert Ader and colleagues in the 1970s and 1980s.

psychopharmacology The use of pharmaceuticals to treat individuals with psychological disorders.

Rational Emotive Behavior Therapy (REBT) An early form of cognitive-behavioral therapy developed by Albert Ellis. Initially called Rational Therapy, this system gained its formal name in 2004.

Scott, Walter Dill (1869–1955) American psychologist and a critical early figure in the study of applied and industrial psychology as well as the psychology of advertising.

Shakow, David (1901–1980) A prominent clinical psychologist who developed training models for clinical psychologists that included internship and certification standards. His "Shakow Report" formed the core of the Boulder model of clinical education.

Sherif, Muzafer (1908–1988) An early social psychologist in the Gestalt tradition. He studied social norms with the autokinetic effect, and he organized the famous boys' camp studies of prejudice.

Sperry, Roger W. (1913–1994) Biological researcher who studied the effects of split-brain operations on animals and humans with epilepsy.

systematic desensitization Joseph Wolpe's popular behavior therapy based on Pavlovian conditioning. Originally called *reciprocal inhibition*, the methodology involves progressive-relaxation techniques paired with an anxiety hierarchy.

verbal learning theory A branch of functionalism and neobehaviorism concerned with associationist explanations of memory and forgetting.

Wisconsin General Test Apparatus An apparatus designed by Harry Harlow to study form discrimination in primates.

Wolpe, Joseph (1915–1997) Psychiatrist and founding figure of behavior therapy. His work on systematic desensitization revolutionized therapy for anxiety disorders and placed him at the forefront of the "first wave" of psychotherapy.

REFERENCES

Aaen-Stockdale, C. (2008). Last but not least: Ibn Al-Haytham and psychophysics. *Perception, 37,* 636–638.

Academy of Sciences of the U.S.S.R. & Academy of Medical Sciences of the U.S.S.R. (1951). *Scientific session on the physiological teaching of academician I. P. Pavlov, June 28-July 4, 1950.* Moscow, U.S.S.R.: Foreign Languages Publishing House.

Adams, N. (2012). Skinner's Walden Two: An anticipation of positive psychology? *Review of General Psychology, 16,* 1–9.

Ader, R. (Ed.). (2006). *Psychoneuroimmunology* (4th ed.). Burlington, MA: Academic Press.

Ader, R., & Cohen, N. (1975). Behaviorally conditioned immunosuppression. *Psychosomatic Medicine, 37,* 333–340.

Ader, R., & Kelley, K. W. (2007). A global view of twenty years of Brain, Behavior, and Immunity. *Brain, Behavior, and Immunity, 21,* 20–22.

Adler, A. (1929). *The science of living.* Garden City, NY: Garden City Publishing.

Adler, A. (1938). *Social interest: A challenge to mankind* (J. Linton & R. Vaughan, Trans.). London: Faber and Faber.

Adler, A. (1957). *Understanding human nature* (W. B. Wolfe, Trans.). New York: Premier Books, Fawcett World Library.

Adler, A. (1964a). The differences between individual psychology and psychoanalysis. In H. L. Ansbacher & R. R. Ansbacher (Eds.), *Alfred Adler: Superiority and social interest* (pp. 205–218). Evanston, IL: Northwestern University Press. (Original work published 1931)

Adler, A. (1964b). *The practice and theory of individual psychology* (P. Radin, Trans.). London: Routledge & Kegan Paul.

Adler, H. E. (1996). Gustav Theodor Fechner: A German Gelehrter. In G. A. Kimble, C. A. Boneau, & M. Wertheimer (Eds.), *Portraits of pioneers in psychology* (Vol. 2, pp. 1–13). Washington, DC: American Psychological Association.

Adler, H. E. (1998). Vicissitudes of Fechnerian psychophysics in America. In R. W. Rieber & K. Salzinger (Eds.), *Psychology: Theoretical-historical perspectives* (2nd ed., pp. 3–14). Washington, DC: American Psychological Association.

Adler, H. E. (2000). Hermann Ludwig Ferdinand von Helmholtz: Physicist and psychologist. In G. A. Kimble & M. Wertheimer (Eds.), *Portraits of pioneers in psychology* (Vol. 4, pp. 15–31). Washington, DC: American Psychological Association.

Afnan, S. M. (1958). *Avicenna, his life and works.* London: Allen.

Aggarwal, N. (2011). Melancholia in Chahâr Maqâle, a 12th-century Persian text. *The British Journal of Psychiatry, 198,* 378.

Aiton, E. J. (1985). *Leibniz: A biography.* Boston: Adam Hilger.

Ajit, N. (2008). On the way to theory: A processual approach. *Organizational Studies, 29,* 173–190.

Alavi, H. R. (2007). Al-Ghazali on moral education. *Journal of Moral Education, 36,* 309–319.

Albertazzi, L. (2006). *Immanent realism: An introduction to Brentano.* Dordrecht, Netherlands: Springer.

Aleksandrova-Howell, M., Abramson, C. I., & Craig, D. (2012). Coverage of Russian psychological contributions in American psychology textbooks. *International Journal of Psychology, 47,* 76–87.

Alexander, F. G., & Selesnick, S. T. (1966). *The history of psychiatry.* New York: Harper & Row.

Al-Ghazali. (1963). *Al-Ghazali's Tahafut Al-Falasifah* [Incoherence of the philosophers] (Sabih Ahmad Kamali, Trans.). Lahore: Pakistan Philosophical Congress. (Original work published c. 1095)

Ali, S. H. (2012). Learning ecological ethics from Plato. *Science, 335,* 797–798.

Allen, G. (1878a). Hellas and civilization. *The Gentleman's Magazine, 245,* 156–170.

Allen, G. (1878b). Nation-making: A theory of national characters. *The Gentleman's Magazine, 245,* 580–591.

Allen, G. W. (1967). *William James: A biography.* New York: Viking.

Allett, J. (1996). Crowd psychology and the theory of democratic elitism: The contribution of William McDougall. *Political Psychology, 17,* 213–227.

Allik, J. (2007). History of experimental psychology from an Estonian perspective. *Psychological Research, 71,* 618–625.

Allport, F. H. (1920). The influence of the group upon association and thought. *Journal of Experimental Psychology, 3,* 159–182.

Allport, F. H. (1924). *Social psychology.* Boston: Houghton Mifflin.

Allport, F. H. (1974). Floyd H. Allport. In G. Lindzey (Ed.), *A history of psychology in autobiography* (Vol. 6, pp. 3–29). Englewood Cliffs, NJ: Prentice Hall.

Allport, G. W. (1937). *Personality: A psychological interpretation.* New York: Henry Holt.

Allport, G. W. (1943). The productive paradoxes of William James. *Psychological Review, 50,* 95–120.

Allport, G. W. (1950). *The individual and his religion.* New York: Macmillan.

Allport, G. W. (1954). *The nature of prejudice*. Cambridge, MA: Addison-Wesley.

Allport, G. W. (1955). *Becoming: Basic considerations for a psychology of personality*. New Haven, CT: Yale University Press.

Allport, G. W. (1961). *Pattern and growth in personality*. New York: Holt, Rinehart and Winston.

Allport, G. W. (1985). Preface. In V. E. Frankl (Author), *Man's search for meaning* (pp. 9–13). New York: Washington Square Press.

Allport, G. W., Vernon, P. E., & Lindzey, G. (1951). *A study of values* (Rev. ed.). Boston: Houghton Mifflin.

Alter, S. G. (2007). Race, language, and mental evolution in Darwin's *Descent* of man. *Journal of the History of the Behavioral Sciences, 43*, 239–255.

Altus, D. E., & Morris, E. K. (2009). B. F. Skinner's utopian vision: Behind and beyond Walden Two. *The Behavior Analyst, 32*, 319–335.

American Psychological Association. (1958). American Psychological Association distinguished scientific contribution awards: 1957. *American Psychologist, 13*, 155–158.

Anderson, F. H. (Ed.). (1960). *Francis Bacon: Baron of Verulam, Viscount St. Albans*. New York: Liberal Arts Press.

Andresen, J. (1991). Skinner and Chomsky 30 years later: The return of the repressed. *Behavior Analyst, 14*, 49–60.

Andrews, T. G., & Dreese, M. (1948). Military utilization of psychologists during World War II. *American Psychologist, 3*, 533–538.

Angell, F. (1913). Gustav Theodor Fechner. *Popular Science Monthly, 83*, 40–49.

Angell, F. (1921). Wilhelm Wundt. *American Journal of Psychology, 32*, 161–178.

Angell, J. R. (1909). The influence of Darwin on psychology. *Psychological Review, 16*, 152–169.

Angell, J. R. (1961). James Rowland Angell. In Carl Murchison (Ed.), *A history of psychology in autobiography* (Vol. 3, pp. 1–38). New York: Russell and Russell. (Original work published 1930)

Anonymous. (1916). Some suggestions relative to a study of the mental attitude of the Negro. *Pedagogical Seminary, 23*, 199–203.

Ansbacher, H. L. (1994). Was Adler a disciple of Freud? A reply. *Journal of Adlerian Theory, Research and Practice, 50*, 496–505.

Ansbacher, H. L., & Ansbacher, R. R. (Eds.). (1956). *The individual psychology of Alfred Adler*. New York: Basic Books.

Ansbacher, R. R. (1997). Alfred Adler, the man, seen by a student and friend. *Individual Psychology: Journal of Adlerian Theory, Research and Practice, 53*, 270–274.

Antony, M. M., & Roemer, L. (2011). History. In *Behavior therapy* (pp. 7–14). Washington, DC: American Psychological Association.

Araujo, S. F. (2012). Why did Wundt abandon his early theory of the unconscious? Towards a new interpretation of Wundt's psychological project. *History of Psychology, 15*, 33–49.

Aristotle. (1908). Nicomachean ethics. In W. D. Ross (Ed.), *The works of Aristotle* (Vol. 9). Oxford: Clarendon Press.

Aristotle. (1931a). De anima. In W. D. Ross (Ed.), *The works of Aristotle* (Vol. 3). Oxford: Clarendon Press.

Aristotle. (1931b). On dreams. In W. D. Ross (Ed.), *The works of Aristotle* (Vol. 3). Oxford: Clarendon Press.

Aristotle. (1931c). On memory and reminiscence. In W. D. Ross (Ed.), *The works of Aristotle* (Vol. 3). Oxford: Clarendon Press.

Aristotle. (1931d). On prophesying by dreams. In W. D. Ross (Ed.), *The works of Aristotle* (Vol. 3). Oxford: Clarendon Press.

Arnett, J. J. (2006). G. Stanley Hall's *Adolescence*: Brilliance and nonsense. *History of Psychology, 9*, 186–197.

Arnheim, R. (1943). Gestalt and art. *Journal of Aesthetics, 2*, 71–75.

Arnheim, R. (1962). *The genesis of a painting: Picasso's Guernica*. Berkeley & Los Angeles: University of California Press.

Arnheim, R. (1966). *Toward a psychology of art*. Berkeley & Los Angeles: University of California Press.

Arnheim, R. (1974). *Art and visual perception: A psychology of the creative eye*. Berkeley & Los Angeles: University of California Press.

Arnheim, R. (1986). *New essays on the psychology of art*. Berkeley & Los Angeles: University of California Press.

Arnold, G. F. (1906). *Psychology applied to legal evidence and other constructions of law*. Calcutta, India: Thacker, Spink & Co.

Asch, S. E. (1955). Opinions and social pressure. *Scientific American, 193*, 31–35.

Asch, S. E. (1968). Wolfgang Köhler: 1887-1967. *American Journal of Psychology, 81*, 110–119.

Ash, M. G. (1985). Gestalt psychology: Origins in Germany and reception in the United States. In C. E. Buxton (Ed.), *Points of view in the modern history of psychology* (pp. 295–344). New York: Academic Press.

Ash, M. G. (1995). *Gestalt psychology in German culture, 1890-1967: Holism and the quest for objectivity*. New York: Cambridge University Press.

Ash, M. G., & Woodward, W. R. (Eds.). (1987). *Psychology in twentieth-century thought and society*. New York: Cambridge University Press.

Ashworth, P., & Chung, M. C. (Eds.). (2009). *Phenomenology and psychological science: Historical and philosophical perspectives*. New York: Springer.

Asprem, E. (2010). A nice arrangement of heterodoxies: William McDougall and the professionalization of psychical research. *Journal of the History of the Behavioral Sciences, 46*, 123–143.

Augustine, A. (1955). *Augustine: Confessions and enchiridion* (A. C. Outler, Ed. and Trans.). Philadelphia: Westminster Press.

Austin, C. R. (1989). *Human embryos: The debate on assisted reproduction*. New York: Oxford University Press.

Averill, L. A. (1990). Recollections of Clark's G. Stanley Hall. *Journal of the History of the Behavioral Sciences, 26*, 107–113.

Averroës. (2008). *Tahafut Al-Tahafut* [The Incoherence of the Incoherence] (S. Van Den Bergh, Trans.). United Kingdom: Cambridge University Press. (Original work published c. 1180)

Baars, B. J. (1986). *The cognitive revolution in psychology*. New York: Guilford.

Babkin, B. P. (1949). *Pavlov: A biography*. Chicago: University of Chicago Press.

Backe, A. (2001). John Dewey and early Chicago functionalism. *History of Psychology, 4,* 323–340.

Bacon, F. (1857). Essay IV: Of revenge. In R. Whately (Ed.), *Bacon's essays: With annotations*. London: John W. Parker and Son. (Original work published 1625)

Bacon, F. (1960). *The new organon*. New York: Liberal Arts Press. (Original work published 1620)

Baddeley, A. (1990). *Human memory: Theory and practice*. Boston: Allyn & Bacon.

Baer, J., Kaufman, J. C. Y., & Baumeister, R. F. (Eds.). (2008). *Are we free? Psychology andf free will*. Oxford, United Kingdom: Oxford University Press.

Bailey, R. E., & Gillaspy, J. A., Jr. (2005). Operant psychology goes to the fair: Marian and Keller Breland in the popular press, 1947-1966. *The Behavior Analyst, 28,* 143–159.

Bakan, D. (1958). *Sigmund Freud and the Jewish mystical tradition*. Princeton, NJ: Van Nostrand.

Baker, D. B., & Benjamin, L. T., Jr. (2000). The affirmation of the scientist-practitioner: A look back at Boulder. *American Psychologist, 55,* 241–247.

Baker, S. C., & Serdikoff, S. L. (2013). Addressing the role of animal research in psychology. In D. S. Dunn, R. A. R. Gurung, K. Z. Naufel, & J. H. Wilson (Eds.), *Controversy in the psychology classroom: Using hot topics to foster critical thinking* (pp. 105–112). Washington, DC: American Psychological Association.

Bakewell, S. (2010). *How to live: Or a life of Montaigne in one question and twenty attempts at an answer*. New York: Other Press.

Baldwin, J. M. (1894). The origin of right-handedness. *Popular Science Monthly, 44,* 606–615.

Baldwin, J. M. (1895). *Mental development in the child and the race*. New York: Macmillan.

Baldwin, J. M. (1911). *The individual and society: Or, psychology and sociology*. Boston: Badger.

Baldwin, J. M. (1913). *History of psychology: A sketch and an interpretation* (2 vols.). New York: G. P. Putnam.

Ball, L. C. (2012). Genius without the "Great Man": New possibilities for the historian of psychology. *History of Psychology, 15,* 72–83.

Bandettini, P. (2007). Functional MRI today. *International Journal of Psychophysiology, 63,* 138–145.

Barenbaum, N. B., & Winter, D. G. (2013). Personality. In D. K. Freedheim & I. B. Weiner (Eds.), *Handbook of psychology, Vol. 1: History of psychology* (2nd ed., pp. 198–223). Hoboken, NJ: John Wiley & Sons Inc.

Bargdill, L. (2000). The study of life boredom. *Journal of Phenomenological Psychology, 31,* 188–219.

Barnes, J. (Ed.). (1984). *The complete works of Aristotle* (Vol. 1). Princeton, NJ: Princeton University Press.

Barnes, R. C. (2000). Viktor Frankl's logotherapy: Spirituality and meaning in the new millennium. *Texas Counseling Association, 28,* 24–31.

Barratt, B. B. (2013). *What is psychoanalysis? 100 years after Freud's "secret committee."* New York: Routledge/ Taylor & Francis Group.

Bartlett, F. C. (1923). *Psychology and primitive culture*. Cambridge, MA: Cambridge University Press.

Bartlett, F. C. (1932). *Remembering: A study in experimental and social psychology*. New York: Macmillan.

Bartol, C. R., & Bartol, A. M. (1999). History of forensic psychology. In A. K. Hess & I. B. Weiner (Eds.), *The handbook of forensic psychology* (pp. 3–23). New York: Wiley.

Barton, A. (1992). Humanistic contributions to the field of psychotherapy: Appreciating the human and liberating the therapist.*Humanistic Psychologist, 20,* 332–348.

Bayne, E. (2011). Womb envy: The cause of misogyny and even male achievement? *Women's Studies International Forum, 34,* 151–160.

Beach, F. A. (1955). The descent of instinct. *Psychological Review, 62,* 401–410.

Beatty, B. (1998). From laws of learning to a science of values: Efficiency and morality in Thorndike's educational psychology. *American Psychologist, 53,* 1145–1152.

Beatty, B. (2005). The rise of the American Nursery School: Laboratory for a science of child development. In D. V. Pillemer & S. H. White (Eds.), *Developmental psychology and social change: Research, history and policy* (pp. 264–287). New York: Cambridge University Press.

Beck, A. T. (1963). Thinking and depression: Idiosyncratic content and cognitive distortions. *Archives of General Psychiatry, 9,* 324–333.

Beck, H. P., Levinson, S., & Irons, G. (2009). Finding Little Albert: A journey to John B. Watson's infant laboratory. *American Psychologist, 64,* 605–614.

Beck, H. P., Levinson, S., & Irons, G. (2010). The evidence supports Douglas Merritte as Little Albert. *American Psychologist, 65,* 301–303.

Beck, J. (1968). Herman von Helmholtz. In D. L. Sills (Ed.), *International Encyclopedia of the Social Sciences* (Vol. 6, pp. 345–350). New York: Macmillan and Free Press.

Becker, C. L. (1932). *The heavenly city of the eighteenth-century philosophers*. New Haven, CT: Yale University Press.

Begley, S. (2007, March 19). Beyond stones & bones. *Newsweek*, 52–58.

Behrens, R. R. (1998). On Max Wertheimer and Pablo Picasso: Gestalt theory, cubism and camouflage. *Gestalt Theory, 20,* 111–118.

Beins, B. C. (2010). Teaching measurement through historical sources. *History of Psychology, 13,* 89–94.

Beins, B. C. (2012). Jean Piaget: Theorists of the child's mind. In W. Pickren, D. A. Dewsbury, & M. Wertheimer (Eds.), *Portraits of pioneers in developmental psychology* (pp. 89–108). New York: Psychology Press.

Belar, C. D., McIntyre, T. M., & Matarazzo, J. D. (2003). Health psychology. In I. B. Weiner (Series Ed.) & D. K. Freedheim (Vol. Ed.), *Handbook of psychology: Vol. 1. The history of psychology* (pp. 451–464). New York: Wiley.

Ben-Noun, L. (2004). Mental disorder that afflicted King David the great. *History of Psychiatry, 15,* 467–476.

Benjamin, L. T., Jr. (1974). Prominent psychologists: A selected bibliography of biographical sources. *Journal Supplement Abstract Service. Catalog of Selected Documents in Psychology, 4,* 1 (Ms. No. 535).

Benjamin, L. T., Jr. (1975). The pioneering work of Leta Hollingworth in the psychology of women. *Nebraska History, 56,* 493–505.

Benjamin, L. T., Jr. (1997). *A history of psychology: Original sources and contemporary research.* New York: McGraw-Hill.

Benjamin, L. T., Jr. (2001). American psychology's struggles with its curriculum; Should a thousand flowers bloom? *American Psychologist, 56,* 735–742.

Benjamin, L. T., Jr. (2006). Hugo Münsterberg's attack on the application of scientific psychology. *Journal of Applied Psychology, 91,* 414–425.

Benjamin, L. T., Jr., & Baker, D. B. (2009). Recapturing a context for psychology: The role of history. *Perspectives on Psychological Science, 4,* 97–98.

Benjamin, L. T., Jr., & Heider, K. L. (1976). History of psychology in biography: A bibliography. *Journal Supplement Abstract Service. Catalog of Selected Documents in Psychology, 6,* 61 (Ms. No. 1276).

Benjamin, L. T., Jr., & Nielsen-Gammon, E. (1999). B. F. Skinner and psychotechnology: The case of the heir conditioner. *Review of General Psychology, 3,* 155–167.

Benjamin, L. T., Jr., Pratt, R., Watlington, D., Aaron, L., Bonar, T., Fitzgerald, S., et al. (1989). *A history of American psychology in notes and news, 1883–1945: An index to journal sources.* Millwood, NY: Kraus International.

Benjamin, L. T., Jr., & VandenBos, G. R. (2006). The window on psychology's literature: A history of Psychological Abstracts. *American Psychologist, 61,* 941–954.

Benjamin, L. T., Jr., Whitaker, J. L., & Ramsey, R. M. (2007). John B. Watson's alleged sex research: An appraisal of the evidence. *American Psychologist, 62,* 131–139.

Benn, S. I. (1967). Punishment. In P. Edwards (Ed.), *The encyclopedia of philosophy* (Vol. 7, pp. 29–36). New York: Macmillan and Free Press.

Berenda, C. W. (1965). *World visions and the image of man: Cosmologies as reflections of man.* New York: Vantage Press.

Bergmann, G. (1956). The contribution of John B. Watson. *Psychological Review, 63,* 265–276.

Bergmann, M. S. (Ed.). (2004). *Understanding dissidence and controversy in the history of psychoanalysis.* New York: Other Press.

Bergsma, A., Poot, G., & Liefbroer, A. C. (2008). Happiness in the garden of Epicurus. *Journal of Happiness Studies, 9,* 397–423.

Berkeley, G. (1935). *Three dialogues between Hylas and Philonous.* Chicago: Open Court. (Original work published 1713)

Berkeley, G. (1948). An essay towards a new theory of vision. In A. A. Luce (Ed.), *The works of George Berkeley, Bishop of Cloyne* (Vol. 1, pp. 141–240). London: Thomas Nelson & Sons. (Original work published 1709)

Berkeley, G. (1957). *Treatise concerning the principles of human knowledge.* Indianapolis, IN: Bobbs II-Merrill. (Original work published 1710)

Berlucchi, G., & Buchtel, H. A. (2009). Neuronal plasticity: Historical roots and evolution of meaning. *Experimental Brain Research, 192,* 307–319.

Bermúdez, J. L. (2010). The prehistory of cognitive science. In *Cognitive science: An introduction* (pp. 4–27). Cambridge, England: Cambridge University Press.

Bernard, L. L. (1924). *Instinct: A study in social psychology.* New York: Henry Holt.

Bernard, W. (1972). Spinoza's influence on the rise of scientific psychology: A neglected chapter in the history of psychology. *Journal of the History of the Behavioral Sciences, 8,* 208–215.

Berrios, G. E. (2005). On the fantastic apparitions of vision by Johannes Müller [introduction]. *History of Psychiatry, 16,* 229–246.

Berrios, G. E. (2006). Classifying madness: A philosophical examination of the Diagnostic and Statistical Manual of Mental Disorders. *Social History of Medicine, 19,* 153–155.

Bersoff, D. N. (1999). Preparing for two cultures: Education and training in law and psychology. In R. Roesch, S. D. Hart, & J. R. P. Ogloff (Eds.), *Psychology and the law: The state of the discipline* (pp. 375–401). New York: Kluwer Academic/ Plenum.

Bettmann, O. L. (1974). *The good old days—They were terrible!* New York: Random House.

Bickhard, M. H. (2001). The tragedy of operationalism. *Theory and Psychology, 11,* 35–44.

Biddle, W. (1995). *A field guide to germs.* New York: Henry Holt.

Billock, V. A., & Tsou, B. H. (2011). To honor Fechner and obey Stevens: Relationships between psychophysical and neural nonlinearities.*Psychological Bulletin, 137,* 1–18.

Binet, A., & Féré, C. (1891). *Animal magnetism* (3rd ed.). London: Kegan Paul, Trench, Trubener. (Original work published 1887)

Binger, C. A. (1969). The dreams of Benjamin Rush. *American Journal of Psychiatry, 125,* 1653–1659.

Bireta, T. J., & Neath, I. (2008). Age-related differences in the von Restorff isolation effect. *The Quarterly Journal of Experimental Psychology, 61,* 345–352.

Bishop, P. (1999). *Jung in contexts: A reader.* Florence, KY: Taylor & Francis/Routledge.

Bitterman, M. E. (2006). Classical conditioning since Pavlov. *Review of General Psychology, 10,* 365–376.

Bjork, D. W. (1993). *B. F. Skinner: A life.* New York: Basic Books.

Bjornsson, A. S. (2004). *The foundations of the scientific revolution in ancient times and the Middle Ages*. Reykjavik: University of Iceland Press.

Blass, T. (2004). *The man who shocked the world: The life and legacy of Stanley Milgram*. New York: Basic Books.

Bloom, H. (Ed.). (1987). *Michel de Montaigne*. New York: Chelsea House.

Blum, D. (2011). *Love at Goon Park: Harry Harlow and the science of affection* (2nd ed.). New York: Perseus.

Blumenthal, A. L. (1975). A reappraisal of Wilhelm Wundt. *American Psychologist, 30,* 1081–1088.

Blumenthal, A. L. (1979). The founding father we never knew. *Contemporary Psychology, 24,* 547–550.

Blumenthal, A. L. (1998). Leipzig, Wilhelm Wundt, and psychology's gilded age. In G. A. Kimble & M. Wertheimer (Eds.), *Portraits of pioneers in psychology* (Vol. 3, pp. 31–48). Washington, DC: American Psychological Association.

Bochner, S. (1973). Mathematics in cultural history. In P. P. Wiener (Ed.), *Dictionary of the history of ideas* (Vol. 3, pp. 177–185). New York: Scribner.

Boden, M. (2006). *Mind as machine: A history of cognitive science* (Vols. 1 & 2). New York, NY: Oxford University Press.

Bohan, J. S. (1992a). *Re-placing women in psychology: Readings toward a more inclusive history*. Dubuque, IA: Kendall/Hunt.

Bohan, J. S. (1992b). *Seldom seen, rarely heard: Women's place in psychology*. Boulder, CO: Westview Press.

Bonacchi, S. (2009). Editorial. *Gestalt Theory, 31,* 100.

Boring, E. G. (1927). Edward Bradford Titchener. *American Journal of Psychology, 38,* 489–506.

Boring, E. G. (1942). *Sensation and perception in the history of experimental psychology*. New York: Appleton-Century-Crofts.

Boring, E. G. (1950). *A history of experimental psychology* (2nd ed.). Englewood Cliffs, NJ: Prentice Hall.

Boring, E. G. (1953). John Dewey: 1859-1952. *American Journal of Psychology, 66,* 145–147.

Boring, E. G. (1961). *Psychologist at large*. New York: Basic Books.

Boring, E. G. (1963). *History, psychology, and science: Selected papers*. New York: Wiley.

Boring, E. G. (1966). Introduction. In G. T. Fechner (Author), *Elements of psychophysics* (Vol. 1, H. E. Adler, Trans., D. H. Howes & E. G. Boring, Eds., pp. ix–xvii). New York: Hol, Rinehart & Winston.

Bornstein, B. H., & Meissner, C. A. (2008). Introduction: Basic and applied issues in eyewitness research: A Münsterberg centennial retrospective. *Applied Cognitive Psychology, 22,* 733–736.

Botting, E. H. (2006). Mary Wollstonecraft's enlightened legacy: The "modern social imaginary" of the egalitarian family. *American Behavioral Scientist, 49,* 687–701.

Bouchard, T. J., Jr., Lykken, D. T., McGue, M., Segal, N. L., & Tellegen, A. (1990). Sources of human psychological differences: The Minnesota study of twins reared apart. *Science, 250,* 223–228.

Boudewijnse, G. A., Murray, D. J., & Bandomir, C. A. (1999). Herbart's mathematical psychology. *History of Psychology, 2,* 163–193.

Boudewijnse, G. A., Murray, D. J., & Bandomir, C. A. (2001). The fate of Herbart's mathematical psychology. *History of Psychology, 4,* 107–132.

Bovaira, F., & Augustin, A. (Producers), Amenabar, A. (writer/Director), & Gil, M. (Writer). (2010). *Agora* [Motion Picture]. Santa Monica, CA: Lionsgate.

Bower, G. H. (1962). An association model for response and training variables in paired-associate learning. *Psychological Review, 69,* 347–353.

Bower, G. H. (2000). A brief history of memory research. In E. Tulving & F. I. M. Craik (Eds.), *The Oxford handbook of memory* (pp. 3–32). New York: Oxford University Press.

Bozarth, J. (2007). Unconditional positive regard. In M. Cooper, M. O'Hara, P. F. Schmid, & G. Wyatt (Eds.), *The handbook of person-centred psychotherapy and counseling* (pp. 182–193). New York: Palgrave Macmillan.

Bozeman, T. W. (1977). *Protestants in an age of science: The Baconian ideal and ante-bellum American religious thought*. Chapel Hill: University of North Carolina Press.

Braaten, E. B., & Viney, W. (2000). Some late nineteenth-century perspectives on sex and emotional expression. *Psychological Reports, 86,* 575–585.

Bracken, P. J. (1999). The importance of Heidegger for psychiatry. *Philosophy, Psychiatry and Psychology, 6,* 83–85.

Brackman, A. C. (1980). *A delicate arrangement: The strange case of Charles Darwin and Alfred Russel Wallace*. New York: Times Books.

Brailsford, H. N. (1963). Mary Wollstonecraft. In E. R. A. Seligman (Ed.), *Encyclopedia of the Social Sciences* (Vol. 15, pp. 436–437). New York: Macmillan.

Breland, K., & Breland, M. (1961). The misbehavior of organisms. *American Psychologist, 16,* 681–684.

Brennan, B. P. (1968). *William James*. New York: Twayne.

Brentano, F. (1973). *Psychology from an empirical standpoint*. (A. C. Rancurello, D. B. Terrell, & L. L. McAlister, Trans.). London: Routledge & Kegan Paul. (Original work published 1874)

Brett, G. S. (1965). *A history of psychology* (2nd rev. ed.) (Edited and abridged by R. S. Peters). Cambridge, MA: MIT Press. (Original work published 1912–1921)

Brewer, C. L. (Speaker). (1989). *Some observations on the life and times of John Watson* (cassette recording).

Brewer, W. F. (2000). Bartlett, functionalism, and modern schema theories. *Journal of Mind and Behavior, 21,* 37–44.

Brian, D. (1997). *Einstein: A life*. New York: Wiley.

Brickhouse, T. C., & Smith, N. D. (1990). What makes Socrates a good man? *Journal of the History of Philosophy, 28,* 169–179.

Bridges, J. H. (1976). *Life and work of Roger Bacon: An introduction to the Opus Majus*. Merrick, NY: Richwood.

Bridgman, P. W. (1927). *The logic of modern physics*. New York: Macmillan.

Bridgman, P. W. (1954). Remarks on the present state of operationism. *The Scientific Monthly, 79*, 224–226.

Bridgman, P. W. (1955). *Reflections of a physicist*. New York: Philosophical Library.

Brigham, J. C., & Grisso, J. T. (2003). Forensic psychology. In I. B. Weiner (Series Ed.) & D. K. Freedheim (Vol. Ed.), *Handbook of psychology: Vol. 1. The history of psychology* (pp. 391–411). New York: Wiley.

Bringmann, W. G., Bringmann, M. W., & Early, C. E. (1992). G. Stanley Hall and the history of psychology. *American Psychologist, 47*, 281–289.

Bringmann, W. G., Bringmann, N. J., & Balance, W. D. G. (1980). Wilhelm Maximilian Wundt 1832-1874: The formative years. In W. G. Bringmann & R. D. Tweney (Eds.), *Wundt studies: A centennial collection* (pp. 13–32). Toronto, Canada: C. J. Hogrefe.

Bringmann, W. G., Bringmann, N. J., & Ungerer, G. A. (1980). The establishment of Wundt's laboratory: An archival and documentary study. In W. G. Bringmann & R. D. Tweney (Eds.), *Wundt studies: A centennial collection* (pp. 123–157). Toronto, Canada: C. J. Hogrefe.

Brock, A. C. (2006). Rediscovering the history of psychology: Interview with Kurt Danziger. *History of Psychology, 9*(1), 1–16.

Bromberg, W. (1959). *The mind of man: A history of psychotherapy and psychoanalysis*. New York: Harper Torchbacks.

Brook, A. (Ed.). (2006). *The prehistory of cognitive science*. Basingstoke, Hampshire, UK: Palgrave Macmillan.

Brooks-Gunn, J., & Johnson, A. D. (2006). G. Stanley Hall's contribution to science, practice and policy: The child study, parent education, and child welfare movements. *History of Psychology, 9*, 247–258.

Brown, J. A. C. (1964). *Freud and the post-Freudians*. Baltimore: Penguin.

Brown, L. (1993). *The new shorter Oxford English Dictionary* (2 vols.). New York: Oxford University Press.

Brown-Sequard, C. E. (1890). Have we two brains or one? *Forum, 9*, 627–643.

Brown v. Board of Education, 347 U.S. 483 (1954).

Brožek, J. (1972). Russian contributions on brain and behavior. In J. Brozek & D. I. Slobin (Eds.), *Psychology in the USSR: An historical perspective*. White Plains, NY: International Arts and Sciences Press. Also published in (1966) Science, 152, 930–932.

Bruce, D. (1991). Integrations of Lashley. In G. A. Kimble, M. Wertheimer, & C. White (Eds.), *Portraits of pioneers in psychology* (pp. 307–323). Washington, DC: American Psychological Association.

Bruce, D. (1998). Lashley's rejection of connectionism. *History of Psychology, 1*, 160–164.

Bruner, J. S., Goodnow, J. J., & Austin, G. A. (1956). *A study of thinking*. New York: Wiley.

Brush, S. G. (1974a). The prayer test. *American Scientist, 62*, 561–563.

Brush, S. G. (1974b). Should the history of science be rated X? *Science, 183*, 1164–1172.

Bryan, L. K., & Vinchur, A. J. (2013). Industrial-organizational psychology. In D. K. Freedheim & I. B. Weiner (Eds.), *Handbook of psychology, Vol. 1: History of psychology* (2nd ed., pp. 407–428). Hoboken, NJ: John Wiley & Sons.

Bryan, M. L. M., Bair, B., & DeAngury, M. (Eds.). (2003). *The selected papers of Jane Addams: Preparing to lead, 1860-81* (Vol. 1). Champaign: University of Illinois Press.

Buckingham, H. W. (2006). The Marc Dax (1770–1837)/Paul Broca (1824–1880) controversy over priority in science: Left hemisphere specificity for seat of articulate language and for lesions that cause aphemia. *Clinical Linguistics & Phonetics, 20*, 613–619.

Buckingham, H. W., & Finger, S. (1997). David Hartley's psychobiological associationism and the legacy of Aristotle. *Journal of the History of the Neurosciences, 6*, 21–37.

Buckley, K. W. (1989). *Mechanical man: John Broadus Watson and the beginnings of behaviorism*. New York: Guilford.

Buckman, S. S. (1895). Babies and monkeys. *Popular Science Monthly, 46*, 371–388.

Buffon, C., de. (1977). *Selections from natural history general and particular* (Vol. 1). New York: Arno Press. (Original work published 1780–1785)

Buie, J. (1988, November). Psychoanalysis barriers tumble: Settlement opens doors to non-MDs. *American Psychological Association Monitor, 19*(11), 1, 15.

Bulkeley, K. (2008). *Dreaming in the world's religions: A comparative history*. New York: New York University Press.

Buncombe, M. (1995). *The substance of consciousness: An argument for interactionism*. Aldershot, England: Avebury.

Bunney, W. E., Garland, B., & Buchsbaum, M. S. (1983). Advances in the use of visual imaging: Techniques in mental illness. *Psychiatric Annals, 13*, 420–426.

Buranelli, V. (1975). *The wizard from Vienna: Franz Anton Mesmer*. New York: Coward, McCann & Geoghean.

Burek, D. M., Koek, K. E., & Novallo, A. (Eds.). (1989). *Encyclopedia of associations* (24th ed.). Detroit, MI: Gale Research.

Burger, J. M. (2009). Replicating Milgram: Would people still obey today? *American Psychologist, 64*, 1–11.

Burger, J. M. (2011). Alive and well after all these years. *The Psychologist, 24*, 654–657.

Burke, R. B. (Trans.). (1962). *The Opus Majus of Roger Bacon* (2 vols.). New York: Russell and Russell.

Burks, B. S. (1927). Foster parent-foster child comparisons as evidence upon the nature-nurture problem. *Proceedings of the National Academy of the Sciences of the United States of America, 13*, 846–848.

Burks, B. S. (1928). The relative influence of nature and nurture upon mental development: A comparative study of foster parent-foster child resemblance and true parent-true child resemblance. *27th Yearbook of the National Society for the Study of Education*, Part 1, 219–316.

Burman, J. T. (2012). Jean Piaget: Images of a life and his factory. *History of Psychology, 15,* 283–288.

Burnes, B. (2007). Kurt Lewin and the Harwood studies: The foundations of OD. *Journal of Applied Behavioral Science, 43,* 213–231.

Burnham, J. (Ed.). (2013). *After Freud left: A century of psychoanalysis in America.* Chicago: University of Chicago Press.

Burns, W. E. (2003). *Witch hunts in Europe and America: An encyclopedia.* Westport, CT: Greenwood Press.

Burston, D. (1998). Laing and Heidegger on alienation. *Journal of Humanistic Psychology, 38,* 80–93.

Burton, J. H. (1967). *Life and correspondence of David Hume* (Vol. 2). New York: Burt Franklin. (Original work published 1846)

Buss, A. R. (1977). In defense of a critical-presentist historiography: The fact-theory relationship and Marx's epistemology. *Journal of the History of the Behavioral Sciences, 13,* 252–260.

Buss, D. M. (2000). *The dangerous passion: Why jealousy is as necessary as love and sex.* New York: Free Press.

Buss, D. M. (2002). Human mate guarding. *Neuroendocrinology Letters, 23,* 23–29.

Buss, D. M. (Ed.). (2005). *The handbook of evolutionary psychology.* Hoboken, NJ: Wiley.

Buss, D. M. (2012). *Evolutionary psychology: The new science of the mind* (4th ed.). Boston, MA: Allyn & Bacon.

Buss, D. M. (2013). Seven tools for teaching evolutionary psychology. In D. S. Dunn, R. A. R. Gurung, K. Z. Naufel, & J. H. Wilson (Eds.), *Controversy in the psychology classroom: Using hot topics to promote critical thinking.* Washington, DC: American Psychological Association.

Buss, D. M., & Duntley, J. D. (2006). The evolution of aggression. In M. Schaller, J. A. Simpson, & D. T. Kenrick (Eds.), *Evolution and social psychology: Frontiers of social psychology.* Madison, CT: Psychosocial Press.

Buss, D. M., & Shackelford, T. K. (1997). From vigilance to violence: Mate retention strategies in married couples. *Journal of Personality and Social Psychology, 72,* 346–361.

Cadwallader, T. C. (1987). Origins and accomplishments of Joseph Jastrow's 1888—founded Chain of Comparative Psychology at the University of Wisconsin. *Journal of Comparative Psychology, 101,* 231–236.

Cain, D. J. (Ed.). (2002). *Humanistic psychotherapies: Handbook of research and practice.* Washington, DC: American Psychological Association.

Cain, D. J. (2010). *Person-centered psychotherapies.* Washington, DC: American Psychological Association.

Calder, R. (1970). *Leonardo and the age of the eye.* New York: Simon and Schuster.

Calkins, M. W. (1893). Statistics of dreams. *American Journal of Psychology, 5,* 311–343.

Cambray, J. (2009). *Synchronicity: Nature and psyche in an interconnected universe.* College Station, TX: Texas A & M University Press.

Camfield, T. M. (1973). The professionalization of American psychology, 1870–1917. *Journal of the History of the Behavioral Sciences, 9,* 67–68.

Campbell, K. (1967). Materialism. In P. Edwards (Ed.), *The encyclopedia of philosophy* (Vol. 5, pp. 179–188). New York: Macmillan and Free Press.

Cannon, W. B. (1922). What strong emotions do to us. *Harper's Magazine, 145,* 234–241.

Cantor, N. F. (2001). *In the wake of the plague: The Black Death and the world it made.* New York: Free Press.

Capehart, J., Viney, W., & Hulicka, I. M. (1958). The effect of effort upon extinction. *Journal of Comparative and Physiological Psychology, 53,* 79–82.

Capra, F. (1988). The role of physics in the current change of paradigms. In R. F. Kitchener (Ed.), *The world view of contemporary physics* (pp. 144–155). Albany: State University of New York Press.

Carey, G. (2003). *Human genetics for the social sciences.* Thousand Oaks, CA: Sage.

Carlson, E. T. (1977). Benjamin Rush and mental health. *Annals of the New York Academy of Sciences, 291,* 95–103.

Carlson, E. T. (1981). The history of multiple personality in the United States: I. The beginnings. *American Journal of Psychiatry, 138,* 666–668.

Carlson, E. T., & Simpson, M. M. (1964). The definition of mental illness: Benjamin Rush (1745–1813). *American Journal of Psychiatry, 121,* 209–214.

Carlson, E. T., Wollock, J. L., & Noel, P. S. (Eds.). (1981). *Benjamin Rush's lectures on the mind.* Philadelphia: American Philosophical Society.

Carlson, J., & Maniacci, M. P. (Eds.). (2012). *Alfred Adler revisited.* New York: Routledge.

Carlson, J., Watts, R. E., & Maniacci, M. (2006). *Adlerian therapy: Theory and practice.* Washington, DC: American Psychological Association.

Carol, M., & Owens, S. (2007). Qualitative research in psychology: Could William James get a job? *History of Psychology, 10,* 301–324.

Carr, H. A. (1925). *Psychology: A study of mental activity.* New York: Longmans, Green and Co.

Carr, H. A. (1961). Harvey A. Carr. In C. Murchison (Ed.), *A history of psychology in autobiography* (Vol. 3, pp. 69–82). New York: Russell and Russell. (Original work published 1930)

Carroll, D. W. (2012). The regents versus the professors: Edward Tolman's role in the California loyalty oath controversy. *Journal of the History of the Behavioral Sciences, 48,* 218–235.

Carron, A. V., & Brawley, L. R. (2008). Group dynamics in sport and physical activity. In T. S. Horn (Ed.), *Advances in sport psychology* (3rd ed., pp. 213–237, 452–455). Champaign, IL: Human Kinetics.

Cary, P. (2007). A brief history of the concept of free will: Issues that are and are not germane to legal reasoning. *Behavioral Sciences and the Law, 25,* 165–181.

Cassedy, S. (2008). A history of the concept of the stimulus and the role it played in the neurosciences. *Journal of the History of the Neurosciences, 17,* 405–432.

Cassirer, E. (1981). *Kant's life and thought* (J. Haden, Trans.). New Haven, CT: Yale University Press.

Castiglioni, A. (1941). *A history of medicine* (E. B. Krumbhaar, Ed. and Trans.). New York: Knopf.

Cattell, J. M. (1890). Mental tests and measurements. *Mind, 15,* 373–381.

Cattell, J. M. (1992). Retrospect: Psychology as a profession. *Journal of Consulting and Clinical Psychology, 60,* 7–8. (Original work published 1937)

Cautin, R. L. (2006). David Shakow. In D. A. Dewsbury, L. T. Benjamin, & M. Wertheimer (Eds.), *Portraits of pioneers in psychology* (Vol. 6, pp. 207–221). Washington, DC: American Psychological Association.

Cautin, R. L. (2008). David Shakow and schizophrenia research at Worcester State Hospital: The roots of the scientist-practitioner model. *Journal of the History of the Behavioral Sciences, 44,* 219–237.

Cautin, R. L. (2011). Invoking history to teach about the scientist-practitioner gap. *History of Psychology, 14,* 197–203.

Cautin, R. L., Freedheim, D. K., & DeLeon, P. H. (2013). Psychology as a profession. In D. K. Freedheim & I. B. Weiner (Eds.), *Handbook of psychology, Vol. 1: History of psychology* (2nd ed., pp. 32–54). Hoboken, NJ: John Wiley & Sons Inc.

Celesia, G. G. (2012). Alcmaeon of Croton's observations on health, brain, mind, and soul. *Journal of the History of the Neurosciences, 21,* 409–426.

Cesarani, D. (2007). *Becoming Eichmann: Rethinking the life, crimes, and trial of a "desk murderer."* Cambridge, MA: Da Capo Press.

Chalupa, L. M. (2005). Donald B. Lindsley. *American Psychologist, 60,* 193–194.

Chan, W. (1967). Confucius. In P. Edwards (Ed.), *Encyclopedia of philosophy* (Vol. 2, p. 189). New York: Macmillan and Free Press.

Chance, P. (1999). Thorndike's puzzle boxes and the origins of the experimental analysis of behavior. *Journal of the Experimental Analysis of Behavior, 72,* 433–440.

Chaplin, J. P., & Krawiec, T. S. (1979). *Systems and theories of psychology* (4th ed.). New York: Holt, Rinehart & Winston.

Charland, L. C. (2002). Tuke's healing discipline: Commentary on Erica Lilleleht's "progress and power: Exploring the disciplinary connections between moral treatment and psychiatric rehabilitation." *Philosophy, Psychiatry, & Psychology, 9,* 183–186.

Chen, L. (2001). Perceptual organization: To reverse back the inverted (upside-down) question of feature binding. *Visual Cognition, 8,* 287–303.

Child, I. L. (1973). *Humanistic psychology and the research tradition: Their several virtues.* New York: Wiley.

Chomsky, N. (1959). A review of Skinner's Verbal Behavior. *Language, 35,* 26–58.

Christen, D. (1984). *The genesis of misogynism and woman's subordination within the Christian church.* Unpublished senior honors thesis, Colorado State University Library.

Churchland, P. (2006). Do we have free will? *New Scientist, 192,* 42–45.

Churchland, P. S. (1989). *Neurophilosophy: Toward a unified science of mind-brain.* Cambridge, MA: MIT Press.

Cipriani, G., Dolciotti, C., Picchi, L., & Bonuccelli, U. (2011). Alzheimer and his disease: A brief history. *Neurological Sciences, 32,* 275–279.

Clanchy, M. T. (1997). *Abelard: A Medieval life.* Malden, MA: Blackwell.

Clark, D. O. (2005). From philosopher to psychologist: The early career of Edwin Ray Guthrie, Jr. *History of Psychology, 8,* 235–254.

Clark, E. (1972). Eduard Hitzig. In C. C. Gillispie (Ed.), *Dictionary of scientific biography* (Vol. 6, pp. 440–441). New York: Scribner.

Clark, R. W. (1971). *Einstein: The life and times.* New York: World.

Clarke, D. M. (1982). *Descartes' philosophy of science.* University Park: University of Pennsylvania Press.

Clarke, E., & O'Malley, C. D. (1968). *The human brain and spinal cord: A historical study illustrated by writings from antiquity to the twentieth century.* Berkeley & Los Angeles: University of California Press.

Clauser, B. E. (2007). The life and labors of Francis Galton: A review of four recent books about the father of behavioral statistics. *Journal of Educational and Behavioral Statistics, 32,* 440–444.

Cleary, T. S., & Shapiro, S. I. (1996). Abraham Maslow and Asian psychology. *Psychologia: An International Journal of Psychology in the Orient, 39,* 213–222.

Clegg, J. W. (2006). A phenomenological investigation of the experience of not belonging. *Journal of Phenomenological Psychology, 37,* 53–83.

Clements, R. D. (1967). Physiological-psychological thought in Juan Luis Vives. *Journal of the History of the Behavioral Sciences, 3,* 219–235.

Cleveland, G. (1905). Would woman suffrage be unwise? *The Ladies Home Journal, 22,* 7–8.

Clodd, E. (1972). *Pioneers of evolution from Thales to Huxley: With an intermediate chapter on the causes of the arrest of the movement.* New York: Books for Libraries Press. (Original work published 1897)

Cobb, M. (2006). *Generation: The seventeenth-century scientists who unraveled the secrets of sex, life, and growth.* New York: Bloomsbury.

Cochran, M. (Ed.). (2010). *The Cambridge companion to Dewey.* New York: Cambridge University Press.

Coe, G. A. (1900). *The spiritual life: Studies in the science of religion.* New York: Eaton & Mains.

Cofer, C. N. (1978). Origins of the Journal of Verbal Learning and Verbal Behavior. *Journal of Verbal Learning and Verbal Behavior, 17,* 113–126.

Cohen, D. (1979). *J. B. Watson: The founder of behaviorism.* London: Routledge & Kegan Paul.

Cohen, D. (2012). *Freud on coke.* London: Cutting Edge Press.

Cole, C. W., Oetting, E. R., & Hinkle, J. E. (1967). Nonlinearity of self-concept discrepancy: The value dimension. *Psychological Reports, 21,* 58–60.

Cole, T. R. (1993). The prophecy of "Senescence": G. Stanley Hall and the reconstruction of old age in twentieth-century America. In K. W. Schaie & W. A. Achenbaum (Eds.), *Societal impact on aging: Historical perspectives* (pp. 165–181). New York: Springer.

Coleman, S. R. (1981). Historical context and systematic functions of the concept of the operant. *Behaviorism, 9,* 207–226.

Collins, A. (2006). The embodiment of reconciliation: Order and change in the work of Frederic Bartlett. *History of Psychology, 9,* 290–312.

Collins, A. F. (1999). The enduring appeal of physiognomy: Physical appearance as a sign of temperament, character, and intelligence.*History of Psychology, 2,* 251–276.

Colp, R., Jr. (1986). Confessing a murder: Darwin's first revelations about transmutation. *Isis, 77,* 9–32.

Compton, W. C., & Hoffman, E. (2013). *Positive psychology.* Belmont, CA: Wadsworth.

Connors, C. (2000). Freud and the force of history: "The Project for a Scientific Psychology." In M. Rossington & A. Whitehead (Eds.), *Between the psyche and the polis: Refiguring history in literature and theory* (pp. 59–73). Aldershot, England: Ashgate.

Cooke, B., Mills, A. J., & Kelley, E. S. (2005). Situating Maslow in Cold War America: A recontextualization of management theory. *Group & Organization Management, 30,* 129–152.

Coon, D. J. (1992). Testing the limits of sense and science: American experimental psychologists combat spiritualism, 1880–1920. *American Psychologist, 47,* 143–151.

Coon, D. J. (1993). Standardizing the subject: Experimental psychologists, introspection, and the quest for a techno-scientific ideal. *Technology and Culture, 34,* 757–783.

Coon, D. J. (1994). "Not a creature of reason": The alleged impact of Watsonian behaviorism on advertising in the 1920s. In J. T. Todd & E. K. Morris (Eds.), *Modern perspectives on John B. Watson and classical behaviorism* (pp. 37–63). Westport, CT: Greenwood Press.

Coon, D. J. (1996). "One moment in the world's salvation": Anarchism and the radicalization of William James. *The Journal of American History, 83,* 70–99.

Coon, D. J. (2006). Abraham H. Maslow: Reconnaissance for Eupsychia. In D. A. Dewsbury, L. T. Benjamin, & M. Wertheimer (Eds.), *Portraits of pioneers in psychology* (Vol. 6, pp. 255–271). Washington, DC: American Psychological Association.

Cooper, S. J. (2005). Donald O. Hebb's synapse and learning rule: A history and commentary. *Neuroscience and Biobehavioral Reviews, 28,* 851–874.

Copleston, F. (1962). *A history of philosophy Vol. 2 Medieval Philosophy Part II.* New York: Image Books.

Coren, S. (2003). Sensation and perception. In I. B. Weiner (Series Ed.) & D. K. Freedheim (Vol. Ed.), *Handbook of psychology: Vol. 1. History of psychology* (pp. 85–108). New York: Wiley.

Costello, S. J. (2011). An existential analysis of anxiety: Frankl, Kierkegaard, Voegelin. *International Forum for Logotherapy, 34,* 65–71.

Cottingham, J. (1979). Varieties of retribution. *Philosophical Quarterly, 29,* 238–246.

Cottingham, J., Stoothoff, R., & Murdoch, D. (1984–1985). *The philosophical writings of Descartes* (2 vols.). Cambridge, MA: Cambridge University Press.

Craik, K. H., Hogan, R., & Wolfe, R. N. (Eds.). (1993). *Fifty years of personality psychology: Perspectives on individual differences.* New York: Plenum Press.

Cravens, H. (2006). The historical context of G. Stanley Hall's *Adolescence* (1904). *History of Psychology, 9,* 172–185.

Crawford, C., & Krebs, D. (Eds.). (2008). *Foundations of evolutionary psychology.* New York: Lawrence Erlbaum Associates.

Crews, F. (1996). The verdict on Freud. *Psychological Science, 7,* 63–68.

Crick, F. H. C. (1994). *The astonishing hypothesis: The scientific search for the soul.* New York: Scribner.

Crochetière, K., Vicker, N., Parker, J., King, D. B., & Wertheimer, M. (2001). Gestalt theory and psychopathology: Some early applications of Gestalt theory to clinical psychology and psychopathology. *Gestalt Theory, 23,* 144–154.

Crombie, A. C. (1961). *Augustine to Galileo* (2nd ed.). Cambridge, MA: Harvard University Press.

Crosby, D. A. (1996). Experience as reality: The ecological metaphysics of William James. In D. A. Crosby & C. D. Hardwick (Eds.), *Religious experience and ecological responsibility* (pp. 67–87). New York: Peter Lang.

Crosby, D. A., & Viney, W. (1990, August). *Toward a psychology that is radically empirical.* Paper presented at the annual meeting of the American Psychological Association, Boston.

Crossman, E. K. (1991). Schedules of reinforcement. In W. Ishaq (Ed.), *Human behavior in today's world* (pp. 133–138). New York: Praeger.

Crowther-Heyck, H. (1999). George A. Miller, language, and the computer metaphor and mind. *History of Psychology, 2,* 37–64.

Crowther-Heyck, H. (2000). Mystery and meaning: A reply to Green (2000). *History of Psychology, 3,* 67–70.

Crutchfield, R. S. (1961). Edward Chace Tolman: 1886–1959. *American Journal of Psychology, 74,* 135–141.

Cubelli, R., & De Bastiani, P. (2011). 150 years after Leborgne: Why is Paul Broca so important in the history of neuropsychology?*Cortex: A Journal Devoted to the Study of the Nervous System and Behavior, 47,* 146–147.

Curley, E. (Ed. & Trans.). (1985). *The collected works of Spinoza* (Vol. 1). Princeton, NJ: Princeton University Press.

Curry, O. (2006). Who's afraid of the naturalistic fallacy? *Evolutionary Psychology, 4,* 234–247.

Dain, N. (1964). *Concepts of insanity in the United States, 1789-1865.* New Brunswick, NJ: Rutgers University Press.

Dallenbach, K. M. (1967). Karl M. Dallenbach. In E. G. Boring & G. Lindzey (Eds.), *A history of psychology in autobiography* (Vol. 5, pp. 59–93). New York: Appleton-Century-Crofts.

Dally, A. (2004). Sargant, William Walters (1907–1988). In *Oxford Dictionary of National Biography*. Oxford University Press. Retrieved from http://0-www.oxforddnb.com.source.unco.edu/view/article/40195

Dalton, J. H., Hill, J., Thomas, E., & Kloos, B. (2013). Community psychology. In D. K. Freedheim & I. B. Weiner (Eds.), *Handbook of psychology, Vol. 1: History of psychology* (2nd ed., pp. 468–487). Hoboken, NJ: John Wiley & Sons Inc.

Daly, M. (1968). *The church and the second sex*. New York: Harper & Row.

Damasio, A. (2003). *Looking for Spinoza: Joy, sorrow, and the feeling brain*. New York: Harcourt.

Daniels, M. (1988). The myth of self-actualization. *Journal of Humanistic Psychology, 28*, 7–38.

Danziger, K. (1979). The positivist repudiation of Wundt. *Journal of the History of the Behavioral Sciences, 15*, 205–230.

Danziger, K. (2001). Sealing off the discipline: Wilhelm Wundt and the psychology of memory. In C. D. Green & M. Shore (Eds.), *The transformation of psychology: Influences of 19th-century philosophy, technology, and natural science* (pp. 45–62). Washington, DC: American Psychological Association.

Darwin, C. (1877). A biographical sketch of an infant. *Mind, 2*, 285–294.

Darwin, C. (1897). *Journal of researches into the natural history and geology of the countries visited during the voyage of the H. M. S. Beagle round the world under the command of Capt. Fitz Roy, R.N.* New York: D. Appleton & Co.

Darwin, C. (1958). *The autobiography of Charles Darwin 1809–1882* (N. Barlow, Ed.). London: Collins.

Darwin, C. (1998). *The expression of emotions in man and animals*. New York: Oxford University Press. (Original work published 1872)

Dawkins, R. (2006). *The selfish gene* (30th anniversary ed.). New York: Oxford University Press.

de Chardin, T. (1961). *The phenomenon of man* (B. Wall, Trans.). New York: Harper & Row.

Dear, P. (2005). What is the history of science the history of? Early modern roots of the ideology of modern science. *Isis, 96*, 390–406.

Deason, G. B. (1986). Reformation theology and the mechanistic conception of nature. In D. C. Lindberg & R. L. Numbers (Eds.), *God and nature: Historical essays on the encounter between Christianity and science* (pp. 167–191). Berkeley: University of California Press.

deBeer, G. (1964). *Charles Darwin: Evolution by natural selection*. New York: Doubleday.

DeCarvalho, R. J. (1990). A history of the "third force" in psychology. *Journal of Humanistic Psychology, 30*, 22–44.

DeCarvalho, R. J. (1991). *The founders of humanistic psychology*. New York: Praeger.

DeCarvalho, R. J. (1992). The institutionalization of humanistic psychology. *Humanistic Psychologist, 20*, 124–135.

Delahunty, R. J. (1985). *Spinoza*. Boston: Routledge & Kegan Paul.

Delaunay, P. (1958). Humanism and encyclopedism. In R. Taton (Ed.) & A. J. Pomerans (Trans.), *History of science: The beginnings of modern science*. New York: Basic Books.

DeMartino, R. J. (1991). Karen Horney, Daisetz T. Suzuki, and Zen Buddhism. *American Journal of Psychoanalysis, 51*, 267–283.

DeMause, L. (Ed.). (1974). *The history of childhood*. New York: Psychohistory Press.

Dennett, D. C. (1991). *Consciousness explained*. Boston: Little, Brown.

Dennis, M. (1985). William Preyer (1841-2897) and his neuropsychology of language of acquisition. *Developmental Neuropsychology, 1*, 287–315.

Dennis, W. (Ed.). (1948). *Readings in the history of psychology*. New York: Appleton-Century-Crofts.

DeRosa, P. (1988). *Vicars of Christ: The dark side of the papacy*. New York: Crown.

Descartes, R. (1985a). Discourse and essays (J. Cottingham, R. Stoothoff, & D. Murdoch, Trans.). *The philosophical writings of Descartes* (Vol. 1, pp. 109–175). Cambridge, MA: Cambridge University Press. (Original work published 1637)

Descartes, R. (1985b). The passions of the soul (J. Cottingham, R. Stoothoff, & D. Murdoch, Trans.). *The philosophical writings of Descartes* (Vol. 1, pp. 324–404). Cambridge, MA: Cambridge University Press. (Original work published 1649)

Descartes, R. (1985c). Treatise on man (J. Cottingham, R. Stoothoff, & D. Murdoch, Trans.). *The philosophical writings of Descartes* (Vol. 1, pp. 99–108). Cambridge, MA: Cambridge University Press. (Original work published 1664)

Deutsch, M., & Coleman, P. T. (2012). Psychological components of sustainable peace: An introduction. In P. T. Coleman & M. Deutsch (Eds.), *Psychological components of sustainable peace* (pp. 1–14). New York: Springer Science + Business Media.

Deutsch, M., & Collins, M. E. (1951). *Interracial housing: A psychological evaluation of a social experiment*. Minneapolis: University of Minnesota Press.

De Vos, J. (2010). From Milgram to Zimbardo: The double birth of postwar psychology/psychologization. *History of the Human Sciences, 23*, 156–175.

deVries, M. W., Müller, N., & Möller, H. (2008). Emil Kraepelin's legacy: Systematic clinical observation and the categorical classification of psychiatric diseases. *European Archives of Psychiatry and Clinical Neuroscience, 258*, 1–2.

Dewey, J. (1896). The reflex arc concept in psychology. *Psychological Review, 3*, 357–370.

Dewey, J. (1917). The need for social psychology. *Psychological Review, 24*, 266–277.

Dewey, J. (1922). *Human nature and human conduct: An introduction to social psychology*. New York: Henry Holt.

DeWitt, L. D. (1985). MRI and the study of aphasia. *Neurology, 35,* 861–865.

Dewsbury, D. A. (Ed.). (1989). *Studying animal behavior: Autobiographies of the founders.* Chicago: University of Chicago Press.

Dewsbury, D. A. (1990). Whither the introductory course in the history of psychology? *Journal of the History of the Behavioral Sciences, 26,* 371–379.

Dewsbury, D. A. (1992). William James and instinct theory revisited. In M. E. Donnelly (Ed.), *Reinterpreting the legacy of William James* (pp. 263–291). Washington, DC: American Psychological Association.

Dewsbury, D. A. (1993). The boys of summer at the end of summer: The Watson-Lashley correspondence of the 1950s. *Psychological Reports, 72,* 263–269.

Dewsbury, D. A. (1996). A history of Division 6 (behavioral science and comparative psychology): Now you see it. Now you don't. Now you see it. In D. A. Dewsbury (Ed.), *Unification through division* (Vol 1: Histories of the divisions of the American Psychological Association, pp. 41–65). Washington, DC: American Psychological Association.

Dewsbury, D. A. (1998). Celebrating E. L. Thorndike a century after "Animal Intelligence." *American Psychologist, 53,* 1121–1124.

Dewsbury, D. A. (2000). Comparative cognition in the 1930s. *Psychonomic Bulletin and Review, 7,* 267–283.

Dewsbury, D. A. (2003). James Rowland Angell: Born administrator. In G. A. Kimble & M. Wertheimer (Eds.), *Portraits of pioneers in psychology* (Vol. 5, pp. 55–71). Washington, DC: American Psychological Association.

Dewsbury, D. A. (2006). *Monkey farm: A history of the Yerkes Laboratories of Primate Biology, Orange Park, Florida, 1930-1965.* Cranbury, NJ: Bucknell University Press.

Diamond, S. (1971). Gestation of the instinct concept. *Journal of the History of the Behavioral Sciences, 7,* 323–336.

Diamond, S. (1974a). Four hundred years of instinct controversy. *Behavior Genetics, 4,* 237–252.

Diamond, S. (Ed.). (1974b). *The roots of psychology: A source book in the history of ideas.* New York: Basic Books.

Diamond, S. (1977). Francis Galton and American psychology. *Annals of the New York Academy of Sciences, 291,* 47–55.

Diamond, S. (1980). Wundt before Leipzig. In R. W. Rieber (Ed.), *Wilhelm Wundt and the making of a scientific psychology* (pp. 3–70). New York: Plenum Press.

Diamond, S., Balvin, R. S., & Diamond, F. R. (1963). *Inhibition and choice.* New York: Harper & Row.

Digby, A. (1983). Changes in the asylum: The case of York, 1777–1815. *The Economic History Review, 36,* 218–239.

Diriwächter, R. (2012). Völkerpsychologie. In J. Valsiner (Ed.), *The Oxford handbook of culture and psychology* (pp. 43–57). New York: Oxford University Press.

Diriwächter, R., & Valsiner, J. (Eds.). (2008). *Striving for the whole: Creating theoretical syntheses.* Piscataway, NJ: Transaction Publishers.

Dix, D. L. (1971). Memorial soliciting a state hospital for the insane submitted to the Legislature of New Jersey. In D. J. Rothman (Ed.), *Poverty U.S.A.: The historical record* (pp. 1–46). New York: Arno Press. (Original work published 1845)

Dobson, K. S. (2012). History. In *Cognitive therapy* (pp. 7–10). Washington, DC: American Psychological Association.

Dols, M. W. (2006). Medical madness. *Journal of Muslim Mental Health, 1,* 77–95.

Domenjo, B. A. (2000). Thoughts on the influences of Brentano and Comte on Freud's work. *Psychoanalysis & History, 2,* 110–118.

Donahoe, J. W. (1999). Edward L. Thorndike: The selectionist connectionist. *Journal of the Experimental Analysis of Behavior, 72,* 451–454.

Donahoe, J. W., & Vegas, R. (2011). Respondent (Pavlovian) conditioning. In W. W. Fisher, C. C. Piazza, & H. S. Roane (Eds.), *Handbook of applied behavior analysis* (pp. 17–33). New York: Guilford Press.

Dovidio, J. F., Glick, P., & Rudman, L. A. (Eds.). (2005). *On the nature of prejudice: Fifty years after Allport.* Malden, MA: Blackwell.

Drury, S., Hutchens, S. A., Shuttlesworth, D. E., & White, C. L. (2012). Philip G. Zimbardo on his career and the Stanford Prison Experiment's 40th anniversary. *History of Psychology, 15,* 161–170.

DuBois, P. H. (1970). *A history of psychological testing.* Boston: Allyn & Bacon.

Duman, C. H., Schlesinger, L., Kodama, M., Russell, D. S., & Duman, R. S. (2007). A role for MAP kinase signaling in behavioral models of depression and antidepressant treatment. *Biological Psychiatry, 61,* 661–670.

Dunlap, K. (1925). *Social psychology.* Baltimore: William & Wilkins.

Duncan, C. P. (1980). A note on the 1929 International Congress of Psychology. *Journal of the History of the Behavioral Sciences, 16,* 1–5.

Duncker, K. (1945). On problem solving. *Psychological Monographs, 58,* 1–113.

Duncker, K. (1950). Induced motion. In W. D. Ellis (Ed.), *A source book of Gestalt psychology* (pp. 161–172). New York: Humanities Press. (Original work published 1929)

Dupré, J. (1993). *The disorder of things: Metaphysical foundations of the disunity of science.* Cambridge, MA: Harvard University Press.

Durant, W. (1950). *The story of civilization: Part IV, The age of faith.* New York: Simon and Schuster.

Durant, W. (1954). *The story of civilization: Part I, Our Oriental heritage* (p. 259). New York: Simon and Schuster.

Durant, W., & Durant, A. (1961). *The story of civilization: Part VII, The age of reason begins.* New York: Simon and Schuster.

Durant, W., & Durant, A. (1967). *The story of civilization: Part X, Rousseau and revolution.* New York: Simon and Schuster.

Eacker, J. N. (1972). On some elementary philosophical problems in psychology. *American Psychologist, 27,* 553–565.

Eacker, J. N. (1975). *Problems of philosophy and psychology.* Chicago: Nelson-Hall.

Earle, W. J. (1967). William James. In P. Edwards (Ed.), *The encyclopedia of philosophy* (Vol. 4, pp. 240–249). New York: Macmillan and Free Press.

Eason, R. G. (2004). Donald Benjamin Lindsley. *American Journal of Psychology, 117,* 611–619.

Ebbinghaus, H. (1913). *Memory: A contribution to experimental psychology.* (H. A. Ruger & C. E. Bussenius, Trans.). New York: Teachers College Press, Columbia University. (Original work published 1885)

Eckardt, M. H. (1991). Feminine psychology revisited: A historical perspective. *American Journal of Psychoanalysis, 51,* 235–243.

Eckardt, M. H. (2005). Karen Horney: A portrait: The 120th Anniversary, Karen Horney, September 16, 1885. *The American Journal of Psychoanalysis, 65,* 95–101.

Eckardt, M. H. (2006). Karen Horney: A portrait. *The American Journal of Psychoanalysis, 66,* 105–108.

Edelman, G. (1992). *Bright air, brilliant fire: On the matter of the mind.* New York: Basic Books.

Edwards, D. C. (1999). *Motivation and emotion: Evolutionary, physiological, cognitive, and social influences.* Thousand Oaks, CA: Sage.

Ehrman, B. (2003). *Lost Christianities: The battles for scripture and the faiths we never knew.* New York: Oxford University Press.

Einstein, A. (1964). Why war? In J. Strachey (Ed.), *The standard edition of the complete psychological works of Sigmund Freud* (Vol. 22, pp. 199–202). London: Hogarth Press. (Original work published 1932)

Einstein, G. O., McDaniel, M. A., & Scullin, M. K. (2012). Prospective memory and aging: Understanding the variability. In M. Naveh-Benjamin & N. Ohta (Eds.), *Memory and aging: Current issues and future directions* (pp. 153–179). New York: Psychology Press.

Eiseley, L. C. (1957). Charles Darwin. In D. Flanagan (Ed.), *Lives in science.* New York: Simon and Schuster.

Eisenberg, L. (2007). Furor therapeuticus: Benjamin Rush and the Philadelphia yellow fever epidemic of 1793. *The American Journal of Psychiatry, 164,* 552–555.

Eissler, K. R. (1965). *Medical orthodoxy and the future of psychoanalysis.* New York: International Universities Press.

Ekstein, D., & Kaufman, J. A. (2012). The role of birth order in personality: An enduring intellectual legacy of Alfred Adler.*The Journal of Individual Psychology, 68,* 60–61.

Eling, P. (2012). Neurognostics answer. *Journal of the History of the Neurosciences, 21,* 119–125.

Eling, P., & Maes, R. (2008). On the historical and conceptual background of the Wisconsin Card Sorting Test. *Brain and Cognition, 67,* 247–253.

Elkholy, S. N. (2008). *Heidegger and a metaphysics of feeling.* London: Continuum.

Ellis, A. (2004). *The road to tolerance: The philosophy of rational emotive behavior therapy.* Amherst, NY: Prometheus Books.

Ellis, J. J. (1993). *Passionate sage: The character and legacy of John Adams.* New York: Norton.

Elmer-DeWitt, P. (1993, November 8). Cloning: Where do we draw the line? *Time,* pp. 64–70.

Elms, A. C. (2005). Jung's lives. *Journal of the History of the Behavioral Sciences, 41,* 331–346.

Emad, P. (2007). *On the way to Heidegger's contributions to philosophy.* Madison, WI: The University of Wisconsin Press.

Emerson, R. W. (1969). *Essays: Second series* (p. 264). Columbus, OH: Merrill. (Original work published 1841)

Emerson, R. W. (1981). Self reliance. In D. McQuade (Ed.), *Selected writings of Emerson* (pp. 129–153). New York: Modern Library. (Original work published 1841)

Engstrom, E. J. (1991). Emil Kraepelin: Psychiatry and public affairs in Wilhelmine Germany. *History of Psychiatry, 2,* 111–132.

Erikson, E. H. (1963). *Childhood and society* (2nd ed.). New York: Norton.

Ernst, C., & Angst, J. (1983). *Birth order: Its influence on personality.* Berlin: Springer-Verlag.

Esper, E. A. (1964). *A history of psychology.* Philadelphia: W. B. Saunders.

Esper, E. A. (1966). Max Meyer: The making of a scientific isolate. *Journal of the History of the Behavioral Sciences, 2,* 341–356.

Esping, A. (2010). Autoethnography and existentialism: The conceptual contributions of Viktor Frankl. *Journal of Phenomenological Psychology, 41,* 201–215.

Estes, W. K. (1950). Toward a statistical theory of learning. *Psychological Review, 57,* 94–107.

Evans, R. B. (1972). E. B. Titchener and his lost system. *Journal of the History of the Behavioral Sciences, 8,* 168–180.

Evans, R. B. (1991). E. B. Titchener on scientific psychology and technology. In G. A. Kimble, M. Wertheimer, & C. L. White (Eds.), *Portraits of pioneers in psychology* (pp. 89–103). Washington, DC: American Psychological Association.

Evans, R. B. (2000). Psychological instruments at the turn of the century. *American Psychologist, 55,* 322–325.

Evans, R. I. (1968). *B. F. Skinner: The man and his ideas.* New York: Dutton.

Eysenck, H. J. (1952). The effects of psychotherapy: An evaluation. *Journal of Consulting Psychology, 16,* 319–324.

Eysenck, M. W. (1986). Ebbinghaus: An evaluation. In F. Klix & H. Hagendorf (Eds.), *Human memory and cognitive capacities: Mechanisms and performances.* Amsterdam: Elsevier Science.

Fagan, T. K. (1992). Compulsory schooling, child study, clinical psychology, and special education: Origins of school psychology.*American Psychologist, 47,* 236–243.

Fagan, T. K. (1996). Witmer's contributions to school psychological services. *American Psychologist, 51,* 241–243.

Fancher, R. E. (1977). Brentano's psychology from an empirical standpoint and Freud's early metapsychology. *Journal of the History of the Behavioral Sciences, 13,* 207–227.

Fancher, R. E. (1996). *Pioneers of psychology* (3rd ed.). New York: Norton.

Fancher, R. E. (2000). Snapshots of Freud in America, 1899–1999. *American Psychologist, 55,* 1025–1028.

Fancher, R. E. (2009). Scientific cousins: The relationship between Charles Darwin and Francis Galton. *American Psychologist, 64,* 84–92.

Fancher, R. E., & Schmidt, H. (2003). Gottfried Wilhelm Leibniz: Underappreciated pioneer of psychology. In G. A. Kimble & M. Wertheimer (Eds.), *Portraits of pioneers in psychology* (Vol. 5, pp. 1–17). Washington, DC: American Psychological Association.

Farr, R. (1983). Wilhelm Wundt (1832–1920) and the origins of psychology as an experimental social science. *British Journal of Social Psychology, 22,* 289–301.

Faye, E. (2009). *Heidegger: The introduction of Nazism into philosophy* (M. B. Smith, Trans.). New Haven, CT: Yale University Press.

Fearing, F. (1970). *Reflex action: A study in the history of physiological psychology.* Cambridge, MA: MIT Press.

Fechner, G. (1966). *Elements of psychophysics* (H. E. Adler, Trans., D. H. Howes & E. G. Boring, Eds.). New York: Holt, Rinehart and Winston. (Original work published 1860)

Fellows, O. E., & Milliken, S. F. (1972). *Buffon.* New York: Twayne.

Ferguson, E. D. (2010). Adler's innovative contributions regarding the need to belong. *The Journal of Individual Psychology, 66,* 1–7.

Fernberger, S. W. (1935). Fundamental categories as determiners of psychological systems: An excursion into ancient Chinese psychologies. *Psychological Review, 42,* 544–554.

Ferrari, M., & Pinard, A. (2006). Death and resurrection of a disciplined science of consciousness. *Journal of Consciousness Studies, 13,* 75–96.

Ferrari, M., Pinard, A., & Runions, K. (2001). Piaget's framework for a scientific study of consciousness. *Human Development, 44,* 195–213.

Ferster, C. S., & Skinner, B. F. (1957). *Schedules of reinforcement.* New York: Appleton-Century-Crofts.

Festinger, L. (1962). *A theory of cognitive dissonance.* Stanford, CA: Stanford University Press.

Feyerabend, P. K. (1975). *Against method.* London: NLB.

Feyerabend, P. K. (1988). *Farewell to reason.* London: Verso.

Fine, R. (1990). *The history of psychoanalysis.* New York: Continuum.

Finger, S., & Wade, N. J. (2002). The neuroscience of Helmholtz and the theories of Johannes Müller: Part 2: Sensation and perception. *Journal of the History of the Neurosciences, 11,* 234–254.

Fischer, G., Viney, W., Knight, J., & Johnson, N. (1968). Response decrement as a function of effort. *Quarterly Journal of Experimental Psychology, 20,* 301–304.

Fisher, H. A. L. (1936). *A history of Europe.* Toronto: Longmans, Green & Co.

Fiske, S. T., & Taylor, S. E. (1991). *Social cognition* (2nd ed.). New York: McGraw-Hill.

Fissette, D. (2009). Stumpf and Husserl on phenomenology and descriptive psychology. *Gestalt Theory, 31,* 175–190.

Fleshner, M., & Laudenslager, M. L. (2004). Psychoneuroimmunology: Then and now. *Behavioral and Cognitive Neuroscience Reviews, 3,* 114–130.

Foley, P., & Moray, N. (1987). Sensation, perception, and systems design. In G. Salvendy (Ed.), *Handbook of human factors.* New York: Wiley.

Follette, W. C., & Callaghan, G. M. (2011). Behavior therapy: Functional-contextual approaches. In S. B. Messer & A. S. Gurman (Eds.), *Essential psychotherapies: Theory and practice* (3rd ed., pp. 1–37). New York: Guilford Press.

Ford, J. E. (1990). Systematic pluralism: Introduction to an issue. *The Monist, 73,* 335–349.

Forrest, D. W. (1974). *Francis Galton: The life and work of a Victorian genius.* New York: Taplinger.

Forrester, J., & Cameron, L. (1999). "A cure with a defect": A previously unpublished letter by Freud concerning "Anna O." *International Journal of Psycho-Analysis, 80,* 929–942.

Foucault, M. (1979). *Discipline and punish: The birth of the prison.* London: Vintage Books.

Frame, D. M. (Trans.). (1960). *The complete essays of Montaigne* (2 vols.). Garden City, NY: Anchor Books, Doubleday.

Frank, R. H. (2011). The strategic role of the emotions. *Emotion Review, 3,* 252–254.

Frankl, V. E. (1985). *Man's search for meaning* (Rev. ed.). New York: Washington Square Press.

Frankl, V. E. (1997). *Viktor Frankl recollections: An autobiography.* New York: Insight/Plenum Press.

Fraser, A. C. (Ed.). (1959). *An essay concerning human understanding.* New York: Dover.

Freud, S. (1950). Project for a scientific psychology. In J. Strachey (Ed.), *The standard edition of the complete psychological works of Sigmund Freud* (Vol. 1, pp. 283–397). London: Hogarth Press. (Original work published 1895)

Freud, S. (1955). A difficulty in the path of psychoanalysis. In J. Strachey (Ed.), *The standard edition of the complete psychological works of Sigmund Freud* (Vol. 17, pp. 136–144). London: Hogarth Press. (Original work published 1917)

Freud, S. (1957a). Instincts and their vicissitudes. In J. Strachey (Ed.), *The standard edition of the complete psychological works of Sigmund Freud* (Vol. 14, pp. 111–140). London: Hogarth Press. (Original work published 1915)

Freud, S. (1957b). Leonardo da Vinci and a memory of his childhood. In J. Strachey (Ed.), *The standard edition of the complete psychological works of Sigmund Freud* (Vol. 11, pp. 57–137). London: Hogarth Press. (Original work published 1910)

Freud, S. (1957c). On the history of the psycho-analytic movement. In J. Strachey (Ed.), *The standard edition of the complete psychological works of Sigmund Freud* (Vol. 14, pp. 3–66). London: Hogarth Press. (Original work published 1914)

Freud, S. (1959a). An autobiographical study. In J. Strachey (Ed.), *The standard edition of the complete psychological works of Sigmund Freud* (Vol. 20, pp. 7–70). London: Hogarth Press. (Original work published 1924)

Freud, S. (1959b). Family romances. In J. Strachey (Ed.), *The standard edition of the complete psychological works of Sigmund Freud* (Vol. 9, pp. 235–241). London: Hogarth Press. (Original work published 1908)

Freud, S. (1961a). Civilization and its discontents. In J. Strachey (Ed.), *The standard edition of the complete psychological works of Sigmund Freud* (Vol. 21, pp. 55–145). London: Hogarth Press. (Original work published 1930)

Freud, S. (1961b). The ego and the id. In J. Strachey (Ed.), *The standard edition of the complete psychological works of Sigmund Freud* (Vol. 19, pp. 1–66). London: Hogarth Press. (Original work published 1923)

Freud, S. (1961c). The future of an illusion. In J. Strachey (Ed.), *The standard edition of the complete psychological works of Sigmund Freud* (Vol. 21, pp. 3–56). London: Hogarth Press. (Original work published 1927)

Freud, S. (1961d). A religious experience. In J. Strachey (Ed.), *The standard edition of the complete psychological works of Sigmund Freud* (Vol. 21, pp. 167–172). London: Hogarth Press. (Original work published 1927)

Freud, S. (1964a). New introductory lectures on psycho-analysis. In J. Strachey (Ed.), *The standard edition of the complete psychological works of Sigmund Freud* (Vol. 22, pp. 3–182). London: Hogarth Press. (Original work published 1932)

Freud, S. (1964b). An outline of psycho-analysis. In J. Strachey (Ed.), *The standard edition of the complete psychological works of Sigmund Freud* (Vol. 23, pp. 141–207). London: Hogarth Press. (Original work published 1938)

Frick, P. L. (1928). Behaviorism and its anti-religious implications. *Methodist Review, 111*, 509–521.

Frick, W. B. (2000). Remembering Maslow: Reflections on a 1968 interview. *Journal of Humanistic Psychology, 40*, 128–147.

Fridlund, A. J., Beck, H. P., Goldie, W. D., & Irons, G. (2012). Little Albert: A neurologically impaired child. *History of Psychology, 15*, 302–327.

Friedrich, O. (1982). *The end of the world: A history*. New York: Fromm International.

Frith, C., & Rees, G. (2007). A brief history of the scientific approach to the study of consciousness. In M. Velmans & S. Schneider (Eds.), *The Blackwell companion to consciousness* (pp. 9–22). Malden, MA: Malden Blackwell Publishing.

Frith, C. D. (2006). The value of brain imaging in the study of development and its disorders. *Journal of Child Psychology and Psychiatry, 47*, 979–982.

Froese, T. (2009). Hume and the enactive approach to mind. *Phenomenology and the Cognitive Sciences, 8*, 95–133.

Frolov, Y. P. (1938). *Pavlov and his school*. London: Kegan Paul, Trench, Trubner.

Fromm, E. (1941). *Escape from freedom*. New York: Rinehart and Co.

Fromm, E. (1947). *Man for himself*. New York: Rinehart and Co.

Fromm, E. (1998). Lost and found half a century later: Letters by Freud and Einstein. *American Psychologist, 53*, 1195–1198.

Fry, H. (2009). *Freud's war*. Stroud, Gloucestershire, UK: The History Press.

Fuchs, A. H., & Viney, W. (2002). The course in the history of psychology: Present status and future concerns. *History of Psychology, 5*, 3–15.

Fuller, J. L., & Thompson, W. R. (1960). *Behavior genetics*. New York: John Wiley and Sons.

Furumoto, L. (1979). Mary Whiton Calkins (1863–1930) fourteenth president of the American Psychological Association. *Journal of the History of the Behavioral Sciences, 15*, 346–356.

Furumoto, L. (1989). The new history of psychology. In I. S. Cohen (Ed.), *The G. Stanley Hall lecture series* (Vol. 9, pp. 9–34). Washington, DC: American Psychological Association.

Furumoto, L., & Scarborough, E. (1986). Placing women in the history of psychology: The first American women psychologists. *American Psychologist, 41*, 35–42.

Gabbard, G. O., Litowitz, B. E., Bonnie, E., & Williams, P. (Eds.). (2012). *Textbook of psychoanalysis* (2nd ed.). Washington, DC: American Psychiatric Publishing.

Gaertner, S. L., Dovidio, J. F., Banker, B. S., Houlette, M., Johnson, K. M., & McGlynn, E. A. (2000). Reducing intergroup conflict: From superordinate goals to decategorization, recategorization, and mutual differentiation. *Group Dynamics: Theory, Research, and Practice, 4*, 98–114.

Gale, M. C., & Gale, H. (1902). Children's vocabularies. *Popular Science Monthly, 61*, 45–51.

Galef, B. G., Jr. (1998). Edward Thorndike: Revolutionary psychologist, ambiguous biologist. *American Psychologist, 53*, 1128–1134.

Galison, P., & Stump, D. J. (Eds.). (1996). *The disunity of science: Boundaries, context and power*. Stanford, CA: Stanford University Press.

Gallo, D. A., & Finger, S. (2000). The power of a musical instrument: Franklin, the Mozarts, Mesmer, and the glass armonica. *History of Psychology, 3*, 326–343.

Galton, F. (1872). Statistical inquiries into the efficacy of prayer. *Fortnightly Review, 12*, 125–135.

Galton, F. (1885, June 25). The measure of fidget. *Nature, 32*, 174–175.

Galton, F. (1907). *Inquiries into human faculty and its development*. New York: Dutton. (Original work published 1883)

Galton, F. (2006). *Hereditary genius: An inquiry into its laws and consequences*. Amherst, NY: Prometheus Books. (Original work published 1869)

Gantt, W. H. (1928). Ivan P. Pavlov: A biographical sketch. In W. H. Gantt (Ed.), *Lectures on conditioned reflexes* (Vol. 1 by Ivan P. Pavlov). New York: International.

García-Valdecasas, M. (2005). Psychology and mind in Acquinas. *History of Psychiatry, 16,* 291–310.

Gardner, H. (1985). *The mind's new science: A history of the cognitive revolution.* New York: Basic Books.

Gardner, H. (2008). Obituary for Rudolf Arnheim (1904-2007). *Psychology of Aesthetics, Creativity, and the Arts, 2,* 61–62.

Gardner-Thorpe, C. (2006). Erasmus Darwin (1731-1802): Neurologist. *Neurology, 66,* 1913–1916.

Garfield, S. L. (1992). Comments on "Retrospect: Psychology as a profession" by J. McKeen Cattell. *Journal of Consulting and Clinical Psychology, 60,* 9–15.

Garfield, S. L., & Bergin, A. E. (1994). Introduction and historical overview. In A. E. Bergin & S. L. Garfield (Eds.), *Handbook of psychotherapy and behavior change* (pp. 3–18). New York: Wiley.

Garforth, F. W. (Ed.). (1964). *John Locke: Some thoughts concerning education.* New York: Baron's Educational Series.

Garnham, A. (2009). Cognitivism. In J. Symons & P. Calvo (Eds.), *The Routledge companion to philosophy of psychology* (pp. 99–110). New York, NY: Routledge/Taylor & Francis Group.

Garraty, J. A., & Carnes, M. C. (1999). *American national biography* (Vol. 19). New York: Oxford University Press.

Gaukroger, S. (1997). *Descartes: An intellectual biography.* New York: Oxford University Press.

Gates, A. I. (1968). James McKeen Cattell. In D. L. Sills (Ed.), *International encyclopedia of the social sciences* (Vol. 2, pp. 344–347). New York: Macmillan and Free Press.

Gavin, E. A. (1976). What is phenomenological psychology? *Philosophical Psychologist, 10,* 1–4.

Gavin, E. A. (1987). Prominent women in psychology, determined by ratings of distinguished peers. *Psychotherapy in Private Practice, 5,* 53–68.

Gawronski, D. V. (1975). *History, meaning and method* (3rd ed.). Glenview, IL: Scott Foresman.

Gay, P. (1988). *Freud: A life for our time.* New York: Norton.

Gaynor, J. F. (1973). The "failure" of J. M. G. Itard. *Journal of Special Education, 7,* 439–445.

Gazzaniga, M. S. (2011). *Who's in charge? Free will and the science of the brain.* New York: Ecco.

Geary, D. C. (1998). *Male, female: The evolution of human sex differences.* Washington, DC: American Psychological Association.

Gelfand, T., & Kerr, J. (Eds.). (1992). *Freud and the history of psychoanalysis.* Hillsdale, NJ: Analytic Press.

Gendlin, E. T. (1988). Carl Rogers (1902–1987). *American Psychologist, 43,* 127–128.

Gendzel, G. (2011). What the progressives had in common. *The Journal of the Gilded Age and Progressive Era, 10,* 331–339.

Gengerelli, J. A. (1976). Graduate school reminiscences: Hull and Koffka. *American Psychologist, 31,* 685–688.

Gentner, D. (2010). Psychology in cognitive science: 1978-2038. *Topics in Cognitive Science, 2,* 328–344.

George, S. (Executive Producer), & Donner, C. (Director). (1988). *Stealing heaven* [Film]. Los Angeles: Virgin Vision.

Gerard, E. O. (1966). Medieval psychology: Dogmatic Aristotelianism or observational empiricism? *Journal of the History of the Behavioral Sciences, 2,* 315–329.

Gergen, K. J. (2008). On the very idea of social psychology. *Social Psychology Quarterly, 71,* 331–337.

German, T. P., & Defeyter, M. A. (2000). Immunity to functional fixedness in young children. *Psychonomic Bulletin & Review, 7,* 707–712.

Gerwood, J. B. (1998). The legacy of Viktor Frankl: An appreciation upon his death. *Psychological Reports, 82,* 673–674.

Gesundheit, B., Or, R., Gamliel, C., Rosner, F., & Steinberg, A. (2008). Treatment of depression by Maimonides (1138-1204): Rabbi, physician, and philosopher. *The American Journal of Psychiatry, 165,* 425–428.

Geuter, U. (1992). *The professionalization of psychology in Nazi Germany* (R. J. Holmes, Trans.). New York: Cambridge University Press. (Original work published 1984)

Gezundhajt, H. (2007). An evolution of the historical origins of hypnotism prior to the twentieth century: Between spirituality and subconscious. *Contemporary Hypnosis, 24,* 178–194.

Gibbons, J. (n.d.). *I. P. Pavlov: Selected works* (S. Belsky, Trans.). Moscow: Foreign Languages Publishing House.

Gibby, R. E., & Zickar, M. J. (2008). A history of the early days of personality testing in American industry: An obsession with adjustment. *History of Psychology, 11,* 164–184.

Gibson, E. J., & Walk, R. D. (1960). The "visual cliff." *Scientific American, 202,* 64–72.

Gilbert, A. R. (1968). Franz Brentano in the perspective of existential psychology. *Journal of the History of the Behavioral Sciences, 4,* 249–253.

Gilbert, F. (1967). Niccoló Machiavelli. In P. Edwards (Ed.), *The encyclopedia of philosophy* (Vol. 5, pp. 119–121). New York: Macmillan and Free Press.

Gilbreth, F. B., & Gilbreth, L. M. (1916). *Fatigue study: The elimination of humanity's greatest unnecessary waste.* New York: Sturgis & Walton.

Gilbreth, F. B., & Gilbreth, L. M. (1917). *Applied motion study: A collection of papers on the efficient method to industrial preparedness.* New York: Sturgis & Walton.

Gilbreth, F. B., & Gilbreth, L. M. (1920). *Motion study for the handicapped.* London: Routledge.

Gilbreth, F. B., Jr., & Carey, E. G. (1948). *Cheaper by the dozen.* New York: Grosset & Dunlap.

Gilbreth, F. B., Jr., & Carey, E. G. (1950). *Bells on their toes.* New York: Bantam.

Gilbreth, L. M. (1951). *Living with our children.* New York: Norton. (Original work published 1928)

Gilbreth, L. M., Thomas, O. M., & Clymer, E. (1962). *Management in the home.* Binghamton, NY: Dodd, Mead. (Original work published 1954)

Gilderhus, M. T. (1992). *History and historians: A historio-graphical introduction.* Englewood Cliffs, NJ: Prentice Hall.

Gilgen, A. R. (1982). *American psychology since World War II: A profile of the discipline.* Westport, CT: Greenwood Press.

Gilligan, J. (2001). The last mental hospital. *Psychiatric Quarterly, 72,* 45–61.

Gilman, S. L. (2001). Karen Horney, M. D., 1885–1952. *American Journal of Psychiatry, 158,* 1205.

Gimbel, S. (2012). *Einstein's Jewish science: Physics at the intersection of politics and religion.* Baltimore, MD: The Johns Hopkins University Press.

Ginn, S. R., & Lorusso, L. (2008). Brain, mind, and body: Interactions with art in Renaissance Italy. *Journal of the History of the Neurosciences, 17,* 295–313.

Giorgi, A. (2010a). Phenomenological psychology: A brief history and its challenges. *Journal of Phenomenological Psychology, 41,* 145–179.

Giorgi, A. (2010b). Phenomenology and the practice of science. *Existential Analysis, 21,* 3–22.

Giorgi, A. (2012). The descriptive phenomenological psychological method. *Journal of Phenomenological Psychology, 43,* 3–12.

Gitre, E. J. K. (2011). The great escape: World War II, Neo-Freudianism, and the origins of U.S. Psychocultural analysis. *Journal of the History of the Behavioral Sciences, 47,* 18–43.

Gleick, J. (1987). *Chaos: Making a new science.* New York: Viking.

Gleitman, H. (1991). Edward Chace Tolman: A life of scientific and social purpose. In G. A. Kimble, M. Wertheimer, & C. White (Eds.), *Portraits of pioneers in psychology* (pp. 227–241). Washington, DC: American Psychological Association.

Gleitman, H., Rozin, P., & Sabini, J. (1997). Solomon E. Asch (1907–1996): Obituary. *American Psychologist, 52,* 984–985.

Goddard, M. J. (2012). On certain similarities between mainstream psychology and the writings of B. F. Skinner. *The Psychological Record, 62,* 563–576.

Goldman, M. S. (1999). Expectancy operation: Cognitive-neural models and architectures. In I. Kirsch (Ed.), *How expectancies shape experience* (pp. 41–63). Washington, DC: American Psychological Association.

Goldstein, R. (2006). *Betraying Spinoza: The renegade Jew gave us modernity.* New York: Schocken Books.

Gollaher, D. (1995). *Voice for the mad: The life of Dorothea Dix.* New York: The Free Press.

Gondermann, T. (2007). Progression and retrogression: Herbert Spencer's explanations of social inequality. *History of the Human Sciences, 20,* 21–40.

Goodwin, C. G. (2005). Reorganizing the experimentalists: The origins of the Society of Experimental Psychologists. *History of Psychology, 8,* 347–361.

Goodwin, C. J. (1985). On the origins of Titchener's experimentalists. *Journal of the History of the Behavioral Sciences, 21,* 383–389.

Gordon, B. L. (1959). *Medieval and Renaissance medicine.* New York: Philosophical Library.

Gorfein, D., & Hoffman, R. R. (Eds.). (1987). *Learning and memory: The Ebbinghaus centennial conference.* Hillsdale, NJ: Erlbaum.

Goshen, C. E. (1967). *Documentary history of psychiatry.* New York: Philosophical Library.

Gotesky, R. (1967). Rudolf Hermann Lotze. In Paul Edwards (Ed.), *Encyclopedia of philosophy* (Vol. 5, pp. 87–89). New York: Macmillan and Free Press.

Goudge, T. A. (1973). Evolutionism. In P. P. Wiener (Ed.), *Dictionary of the history of ideas* (Vol. 2, pp. 174–189). New York: Scribner.

Gould, S. J. (1981). *The mismeasure of man.* New York: Norton.

Grace, R. C. (2001). On the failure of operationism. *Theory and Psychology, 11,* 5–33.

Gray, J. (1999). Ivan Petrovich Pavlov and the conditional reflex. *Brain Research Bulletin, 50,* 433.

Gray, P. H. (1967). The nature of man or man's place in nature? Bruno, Spinoza, and La Mettrie. *Journal of General Psychology, 76,* 183–192.

Grayling, A. C. (2005). *Descartes: The life and times of a genius.* New York: Walker.

Green, C. D. (1998). The thoroughly modern Aristotle: Was he really a functionalist? *History of Psychology, 1,* 8–20.

Green, C. D. (2000). Dispelling the "mystery" of computational cognitive science. *History of Psychology, 3,* 62–66.

Green, C. D. (2001a). Charles Babbage, the analytical engine, and the possibility of a 19th-century cognitive science. In C. D. Green & M. Shore (Eds.), *The transformation of psychology: Influences of 19th-century philosophy, technology, and natural science* (pp. 133–152). Washington, DC: American Psychological Association.

Green, C. D. (2001b). Operationism again: What did Bridgman say? What did Bridgman need? *Theory and Psychology, 11,* 45–51.

Green, C. D. (2003). Where did the ventricular localization of mental faculties come from? *Journal of the History of the Behavioral Sciences, 29,* 131–142.

Green, C. D. (2009). Darwinian theory, functionalism, and the first American psychological revolution. *American Psychologist, 64,* 75–83.

Green, C. D., & Groff, P. R. (2003). *Early psychological thought: Ancient accounts of the mind and soul.* Westport, CT: Praeger.

Green, M. (1985). *Descartes.* Minneapolis: University of Minnesota Press.

Greene, E., & Bornstein, B. (2003). *Determining damages: The psychology of jury awards.* Washington, DC: American Psychological Association.

Greenwood, J. D. (1999). Understanding the "cognitive revolution" in psychology. *Journal of the History of the Behavioral Sciences, 35,* 1–22.

Gregory, R. L. (1974). Choosing a paradigm for perception. In E. C. Carterette & M. P. Friedman (Eds.), *Handbook of perception* (Vol. 1, pp. 255–283). New York: Academic Press.

Gregory, R. L. (2007). Editorial essay: Helmholtz's principle. *Perception, 36,* 795–796.

Grendler, P. F. (1988). Printing and censorship. In C. B. Schmitt (Ed.), *The Cambridge history of Renaissance philosophy* (pp. 25–53). New York: Cambridge University Press.

Grey, L. (1998). *Alfred Adler, the forgotten prophet: A vision for the 21st century.* Westport, CT: Praeger Greenwood.

Gribben, J. (2006). *History of western science 1543-2001.* London: Folio Society.

Grimsley, D. L., & Windholz, G. (2000). The neurophysio-logical aspects of Pavlov's theory of higher nervous activity: In honor of the 150th anniversary of Pavlov's birth. *Journal of the History of the Neurosciences, 9,* 152–163.

Grisso, T., & Brigham, J. C. (2013). Forensic psychology. In D. K. Freedheim & I. B. Weiner (Eds.), *Handbook of psychology, Vol. 1: History of psychology* (2nd ed., pp. 429–447). Hoboken, NJ: John Wiley & Sons Inc.

Grmek, M. D. (1974). Francois Magendie. In C. C. Gillispi (Ed.), *Dictionary of scientific biography* (Vol. 9, pp. 7–11). New York: Scribner.

Groethuysen, B. (1963). Michel de Montaigne. In E. R. A. Seligman & A. Johnson (Eds.), *Encyclopedia of the social sciences* (Vol. 10, pp. 634–635). New York: Macmillan and Free Press.

Gross, C. G. (2007). The discovery of motor cortex and its background. *Journal of the History of the Neurosciences, 16,* 320–331.

Gruber, H. E., & Vonèche, J. J. (1977). *The essential Piaget.* New York: Basic Books.

Guberman, S., Wojtkowski, W. (2001). Reflections on Max Wertheimer's "Productive Thinking": Lessons for AI. *Gestalt Theory, 23,* 132–143.

Gullan-Whur, M. (1998). *Within Reason: A life of Spinoza.* New York: St. Martin's Press.

Gurley, J. R. (2009). A history of changes to the criminal personality in the DSM. *History of Psychology, 12,* 285–304.

Guski-Leinwand, S. (2009). Becoming a science: The loss of the scientific approach of Völkerpsychologie. *Zeitschrift für Psychologie / Journal of Psychology, 217,* 79–84.

Guthrie, E. R. (1935). *The psychology of learning.* New York: Harper & Brothers.

Guthrie, E. R. (1944). Personality in terms of associative learning. In J. M. Hunt (Ed.), *Personality and the behavioral disorders: A handbook based on experimental and clinical research* (Vol. 1, pp. 49–68). New York: Ronald Press.

Guthrie, R. V. (2003). *Even the rat was white: A historical view of psychology* (2nd ed.). Boston: Allyn & Bacon.

Guthrie, W. K. C. (1960). *The Greek philosophers from Thales to Aristotle.* New York: Harper & Row.

Gutmann, J. (Ed.). (1949). *Ethics; preceded by on the improvement of the understanding.* New York: Hafner.

Gutterman, S. S. (1970). *The Machiavellians.* Lincoln: University of Nebraska Press.

Haeckel, E. H. P. K. (1905). *The evolution of man* (5th ed., Vol. 1). (J. McCabe, Trans.). New York: G. P. Putnam.

Hagner, M. (2012). The electrical excitability of the brain: Toward the emergence of an experiment. *Journal of the History of the Neurosciences, 21,* 237–249.

Haight, A. L. (1978). *Banned books 387 B.C. to 1987 A.D.* (4th ed.). Updated and enlarged by C. B. Grannis. New York: Bowker.

Hall, C. S., & Nordby, V. J. (1973). *A primer of Jungian psychology.* New York: Taplinger.

Hall, G. S. (1890). Children's lies. *American Journal of Psychology, 3,* 59–70.

Hall, G. S. (1891). The contents of children's minds on entering school. *Pedagogical Seminary, 1,* 139–173.

Hall, G. S. (1904). *Adolescence.* New York: D. Appleton and Co.

Hall, G. S. (1910). A children's institute. *Harper's Magazine, 120,* 620–624.

Hall, G. S. (1922). *Senescence: The last half of life.* New York: D. Appleton and Co.

Hall, G. S. (1923). *Life and confessions of a psychologist.* New York: D. Appleton and Co.

Hall, G. S., & Browne, C. E. (1903). Children's ideas of fire, heat, frost and cold. *Pedagogical Seminary, 10,* 27–85.

Hall, G. S., & Smith, T. L. (1903). Showing off and bashfulness as phases of self-consciousness. *Pedagogical Seminary, 10,* 159–199.

Hall, G. S., & Wallin, J. E. W. (1902). How children and youth think and feel about clouds. *Pedagogical Seminary, 9,* 460–506.

Hall, V., Jr. (1950). Life of Julius Caesar Scaliger. *Transaction of the American Philosophical Society, 4,* 85–170.

Hallie, P. P. (1967). Stoicism. In P. Edwards (Ed.), *The encyclopedia of philosophy* (Vol. 8, pp. 19–22). New York: Macmillan.

Handelsman, M. M., Gottlieb, M. C., & Knapp, S. (2005). Training ethical psychologists: An acculturation model. *Professional Psychology: Research and Practice, 36,* 59–65.

Haney, C., & Zimbardo, P. G. (1998). The past and future of U.S. prison policy: Twenty-five years after the Stanford Prison Experiment. *American Psychologist, 53,* 709–727.

Hardcastle, J. (2009). Vygotsky's enlightenment precursors. *Educational Review, 61,* 181–195.

Harlow, H. F. (1949). The formation of learning sets. *Psychological Review, 56,* 51–65.

Harlow, H. F. (1958). The nature of love. *American Psychologist, 13,* 673–685.

Harms, E. (1967). *Origin of modern psychiatry.* Springfield, IL: Charles C. Thomas.

Harris, B. (1979). Whatever happened to little Albert? *American Psychologist, 34,* 151–160.

Harris, B. (1999a). John Broadus Watson. In *American National Biography* (pp. 795–797). New York: Oxford University Press.

Harris, B. (1999b). Otto Klineberg. *In American National Biography* (pp. 792–793). New York: Oxford University Press.

Harris, B. (2011). Letting go of Little Albert: Disciplinary memory, history, and the uses of myth. *Journal of the History of the Behavioral Sciences, 47,* 1–17.

Harris, M. (1974). *Cows, pigs, wars, and witches: The riddles of culture.* New York: Random House.

Harris, S. (2012). *Free Will.* New York: Free Press.

Harrison, E. (1987). Whigs, prigs, and historians of science. *Nature, 329,* 213–214.

Harrison, L. E. (2006). *The central liberal truth: How politics can change a culture and save it from itself.* New York: Oxford University Press.

Harrison, P. (2001). Curiosity, forbidden knowledge, and the reformation of natural philosophy in early modern England. *Isis, 92,* 265–290.

Hartley, D. (1966). *Observations on man, his frame, his duty and his expectations.* Demar, NY: Scholars' Facsimiles & Reprints. (Original work published 1749)

Hartmann, H. (1939). *Ego psychology and the problem of adaptation.* New York: International University Press.

Hartshorne, C. (1934). *The philosophy and psychology of sensation.* Port Washington, NY: Kennikat Press.

Harvey, O. J. (1989). Muzafer Sherif. *American Psychologist, 44,* 1325–1326.

Hassard, J. (1990). The AHP Soviet exchange project: 1983–1990 and beyond. *Journal of Humanistic Psychology, 30,* 6–51.

Hatfield, G. (2009). Rationalist roots of modern psychology. In J. Symons & P. Calvo (Eds.), *The Routledge companion to philosophy of psychology* (pp. 3–20). New York: Routledge.

Hathaway, S. R. (1958). A study of human behavior: The clinical psychologist. *American Psychologist, 13,* 257–265.

Haupt, E. J. (1998). Origins of American psychology in the work of G. E. Müller: Classical psychophysics and serial learning. In R. W. Rieber & K. Salzinger (Eds.), *Psychology: Theoretical-historical perspectives* (2nd ed., pp. 17–75). Washington, DC: American Psychological Association.

Hayman, R. (2001). *A life of Jung.* New York: Norton.

Häyry, M. (2005). The tension between self governance and absolute inner worth in Kant's moral philosophy. *Journal of Medical Ethics, 31,* 645–647.

Healy, D. (1993). One-hundred years of psychopharmacology. *Journal of Psychopharmacology, 7,* 207–214.

Healy, D., Harris, M., Farquhar, F., Tschinkel, S., & Le Noury, J. (2008). Historical overview: Kraepelin's impact on psychiatry. *European Archives of Psychiatry and Clinical Neuroscience, 258,* 18–24.

Hebb, D. O. (1949). *The organization of behavior: A neuropsychological theory.* New York: Wiley.

Hebb, D. O. (1959). A neuropsychological theory. In S. Koch (Ed.), *Psychology: A study of science* (Vol. 1, pp. 622–643). New York: McGraw-Hill.

Heft, H. (2001). *Ecological psychology in context: James Gibson, Roger Barker, and the legacy of William James's radical empiricism.* Mahwah, NJ: Erlbaum.

Heidbreder, E. (1933). *Seven psychologies.* New York: Appleton-Century-Crofts.

Heidegger, M. (1962). *Being and time* (J. Macquarrie & E. Robinson, Trans.). New York: Harper & Row. (Original work published 1927)

Helmholtz, H. L., von. (1896). *Handbuch der physiologischen Optik* (2nd ed.). Hamburg und Leipzig: L. Voss.

Helmholtz, H. L., von. (1971). The origin and correct interpretation of our sense impressions. In R. Kahl (Ed.), *Selected writings of Hermann Ludwig von Helmholtz* (pp. 501–512). Middletown, CT: Wesleyan University Press. (Original work published 1894)

Helson, H. (1972). What can we learn from the history of psychology? *Journal of the History of the Behavioral Sciences, 8,* 115–119.

Henle, M. (1976). Why study the history of psychology? *Annals of the New York Academy of Sciences, 270,* 14–20.

Henle, M. (1977). The influence of Gestalt psychology in America. *Annals of the New York Academy of Sciences, 291,* 3–12.

Henle, M. (1978a). Gestalt psychology and Gestalt therapy. *Journal of the History of the Behavioral Sciences, 14,* 23–32.

Henle, M. (1978b). One man against the Nazis—Wolfgang Köhler. *American Psychologist, 33,* 939–944.

Henle, M. (1984). Isomorphism: Setting the record straight. *Psychological Research, 46,* 317–327.

Henle, M. (1985). Rediscovering Gestalt psychology. In S. Koch & D. E. Leary (Eds.), *A century of psychology as science* (pp. 100–120). New York: McGraw-Hill.

Henle, M. (1986). The influence of Gestalt psychology in America. In M. Henle (Ed.), *1879 and all that: Essays in the theory and history of psychology* (pp. 118–137). New York: Columbia University Press. (Original work published 1977)

Henle, M. (1989). Two disciplines, one name? *Contemporary Psychology, 34,* 857–858.

Henle, M. (1993). Man's place in nature in the thinking of Wolfgang Köhler. *Journal of the History of the Behavioral Sciences, 29,* 3–7.

Henle, M., Jaynes, J., & Sullivan, J. J. (Eds.). (1973). *Historical conceptions of psychology.* New York: Springer.

Henley, T. B., & Thorne, B. M. (2005). The lost millennium: Psychology during the Middle Ages. *Psychological Record, 55,* 103–113.

Henshaw, J. M. (2006). *Does measurement measure up?* Baltimore: Johns Hopkins University Press.

Herbart, J. F. (1977). The science of education (H. M. Felkin & E. Felkin, Trans.). In D. N. Robinson (Ed.), *Significant contributions to the history of psychology* 1750–1920: Series B, Psychometrics and Educational Psychology (Vol. 1, pp. 57–268). Washington, DC: University Publications of America (from 1902 edition).

Herlihy, D. (1997). *The black death and the transformation of the West.* Cambridge, MA: Harvard University Press.

Herrmann, D. J., & Chaffin, R. (Eds.). (1988). *Memory in historical perspective: The literature before Ebbinghaus.* New York: Springer-Verlag.

Herrnstein, R. J., & Boring, E. G. (Eds.). (1966). *A source-book in the history of psychology*. Cambridge, MA: Harvard University Press.

Hess, E. H. (1962). Ethology: An approach toward the complete analysis of behavior. In R. Brown, E. Galanter, E. H. Hess, & G. Mandler (Eds.), *New directions in psychology* (pp. 157–266). New York: Holt, Rinehart and Winston.

Hess, M. (1967). Action at a distance and field theory. In P. Edwards (Ed.), *The encyclopedia of philosophy* (Vol. 1, pp. 9–15). New York: Macmillan.

Hesse, M. (1967). Models and analogy in science. In P. Edwards (Ed.), *The encyclopedia of philosophy* (Vol. 5, pp. 354–359). New York: Macmillan.

Heukelom, F. (2010). Measurement and decision making at the University of Michigan in the 1950s and 1960s. *Journal of the History of the Behavioral Sciences, 46,* 189–207.

Hewstone, M., Schut, H. A. W., De Wit, J. B. F., Van Den Bos, K., & Stroebe, M. S. (Eds.). (2007). *The scope of social psychology: Theory and applications*. New York: Psychology Press.

Hildebrand, J. H. (1957). *Science in the making*. New York: Columbia University Press.

Hilgard, E. R. (1996). History of educational psychology. In D. C. Berliner & R. C. Calfee (Eds.), *Handbook of educational psychology* (pp. 990–1004). New York: Macmillan Library Reference.

Hilgard, E. R., & Bower, G. H. (1966). *Theories of learning* (3rd ed.). New York: Appleton-Century-Crofts.

Hindmarsh, J. (2009). Work and the moving image: Past, present and future. *Sociology, 43,* 990–996.

Hiroshi, I. (Ed.). (2002). *Origin and development of scientific psychology in different parts of the world: Retrospect and prospect at the turn of the century*. New York: Psychology Press.

Hobbes, T. (1962a). Human nature. In W. Molesworth (Ed.), *The English works of Thomas Hobbes* (Vol. 4, pp. 1–76). London: Scientia Aalen. (Original work published 1650)

Hobbes, T. (1962b). Leviathan. In W. Molesworth (Ed.), *The English works of Thomas Hobbes* (Vol. 3, pp. 1–714). London: Scientia Aalen. (Original work published 1651)

Hodgson, B. (1988). Economic science and ethical neutrality II: The intransigence of evaluative concepts. *Journal of Business, 7,* 321–335.

Hoff, P. (1998). Emil Kraepelin and forensic psychiatry. *International Journal of Law and Psychiatry, 21,* 343–353.

Hoff, P. (2012). Eugen Bleuler's concept of schizophrenia and its relevance to present-day psychiatry. *Neuropsychobiology, 66,* 6–13.

Hoffeld, D. R. (1980). Mesmer's failure: Sex, politics, personality and the Zeitgeist. *Journal of the History of the Behavioral Sciences, 16,* 377–386.

Hoffman, E. (1988). *The right to be human: A biography of Abraham Maslow*. Los Angeles: Tarcher.

Hoffman, E. (2009). Rollo May on Maslow and Rogers: "No theory of evil." *Journal of Humanistic Psychology, 49,* 484–485.

Hoffman, E. (2010). Introduction to the William James memorial issue. *Journal of Humanistic Psychology, 50,* 407–409.

Hoffman, R. R., & Deffenbacher, K. A. (1992). A brief history of applied cognitive psychology. *Applied Cognitive Psychology, 6,* 1–48.

Hogan, J. D. (2003). G. Stanley Hall. In G. A. Kimble & M. Wertheimer (Eds.), *Portraits of pioneers in psychology* (Vol. 5, pp. 19–36). Washington, DC: American Psychological Association.

Hollingworth, L. S. (1914). *Functional periodicity: An experimental study of the mental and motor abilities of women during menstruation*. Contributions to Education (No. 69). New York: Teachers College Press, Columbia University.

Hollingworth, L. S. (1920). *The psychology of subnormal children*. New York: Macmillan.

Hollingworth, L. S. (1928). *The psychology of the adolescent*. New York: Appleton.

Hollingworth, L. S. (1942). *Children above 180 I.Q.* Yonkers, NY: World Book.

Hollon, S. D., & DiGiuseppe, R. (2011). Cognitive theories of psychotherapy. In J. C. Norcross, G. R. VandenBos, & D. K. Freedheim (Eds.), *History of psychotherapy: Continuity and change* (2nd ed., pp. 203–241). Washington, DC: American Psychological Association.

Holt, R. R. (1967). Ego autonomy re-evaluated. *International Journal of Psychiatry, 3,* 481–536.

Holzhey-Kunz, A., & Fazekas, T. (2012). Daseinsanalysis: A dialogue. In L. Barnett & G. Madison (Eds.), *Existential therapy: Legacy, vibrancy and dialogue* (pp. 35–51). New York: Routledge/Taylor & Francis Group.

Hooley, J. M., Maher, W. B., & Maher, B. A. (2013). Abnormal psychology. In D. K. Freedheim & I. B. Weiner (Eds.), *Handbook of psychology, Vol. 1: History of psychology* (2nd ed., pp. 340–376). Hoboken, NJ: John Wiley & Sons.

Horgan, J. (1996, December). Why Freud isn't dead. *Scientific American*, pp. 106–111.

Hornday, W. T. (1883). Mental capacity of the elephant. *Popular Science Monthly, 23,* 497–509.

Horney, K. (1934). The overvaluation of love: A study of a common present-day feminine type. *Psychoanalytic Quarterly, 3,* 605–638.

Horney, K. (1937). *The neurotic personality of our time*. New York: Norton.

Horney, K. (1939). *New ways in psychoanalysis*. New York: Norton.

Horney, K. (1942). *Self-analysis*. New York: Norton.

Horney, K. (1945). *Our inner conflicts*. New York: Norton.

Horney, K. (1950). *Neurosis and human growth*. New York: Norton.

Horney, K. (1967). *Feminine psychology*. New York: Norton.

Horton, J. O., & Horton, L. E. (2005). *Slavery and the making of America*. New York: Oxford University Press.

Hothersall, D. (1995). *History of psychology*. New York: McGraw-Hill.

Hsueh, Y. (2004). "He sees the development of children's concepts upon a background of sociology": Jean Piaget's honorary degree at Harvard University in 1936. *History of Psychology, 7,* 20–44.

Huarte, J. (1959). *The examination of men's wits* (M. Camillo & R. Carew, Trans.). Gainesville, FL: Scholars Facsimiles and Reprints. (Original work published 1594)

Huemer, W., & Landerer, C. (2010). Mathematics, experience and laboratories: Herbart's and Brentano's role in the rise of scientific psychology. *History of the Human Sciences, 23,* 72–94.

Hull, C. L. (1943). *Principles of behavior.* New York: D. Appleton-Century.

Hull, C. L. (1952). Clark L. Hull. In E. G. Boring, H. Werner, R. M. Yerkes, & H. S. Langfeld (Eds.), *A history of psychology in autobiography* (Vol. 4, pp. 143–162). New York: Russell and Russell.

Humbert, E. G. (1988). *C. G. Jung: The fundamentals of theory and practice* (R. G. Jalbert, Trans.). Wilmette, IL: Chiron.

Hume, D. (1978). *A treatise of human nature.* Oxford: Clarendon Press. (Original work published 1739–1740)

Humphrey, T. (1983). *Immanuel Kant—Perpetual peace and other essays on politics, history, and morals.* Indianapolis, IN: Hackett.

Hunt, J. M. (1956). Walter Samuel Hunter. *Psychological Review, 63,* 213–217.

Hunter, W. S. (1928). *Human behavior.* Chicago: University of Chicago Press.

Hunter, W. S. (1952). Walter S. Hunter. In E. G. Boring, H. Werner, R. M. Yerkes, & H. S. Langfeld (Eds.), *A history of psychology in autobiography* (Vol. 4, pp. 163–187). New York: Russell and Russell.

Huxley, T. H. (1874). Are animals automatons? *Popular Science Monthly, 5,* 724–734.

Huxley, T. H. (1898). *Hume with helps to the study of Berkeley.* New York: D. Appleton and Co.

Hyam, J. A., Paterson, D. J., Azoz, T. Z., & Green, A. L. (2011). Depiction of the neuroscientific principles of human motion 2 millenia ago by Lucretius. *Neurology, 77,* 1000–1004.

Ingram, D. H. (1985). Karen Horney at 100: Beyond the frontier. *American Journal of Psychoanalysis, 45,* 305–309.

Innis, N. K. (1992). Tolman and Tryon: Early research on the inheritance of the ability to learn. *American Psychologist, 47,* 190–197.

Innis, N. K. (1999). Edward C. Tolman's purposive behaviorism. In W. O'Donohue & R. Kitchener (Eds.), *Handbook of behaviorism* (pp. 97–117). San Diego, CA: Academic Press.

Innis, N. K. (2003). William McDougall: "A major tragedy?" In G. A. Kimble & M. Wertheimer (Eds.), *Portraits of pioneers in psychology* (Vol. 5, pp. 91–108). Washington, DC: American Psychological Association.

Iran-Nejad, A., & Winsler, A. (2000). Bartlett's schema theory and modern accounts of learning and remembering. *Journal of Mind & Behavior, 21,* 5–35.

Jablensky, A., Hugler, H., von Cranach, M., & Kalinov, K. (1993). Kraepelin revisited: A reassessment and statistical analysis of dementia praecox and manic-depressive insanity in 1908. *Psychological Medicine, 23,* 843–858.

Jackson, J. P., Jr. (2006). Kenneth B. Clark: The complexities of activist psychology. In D. A. Dewsbury, L. T. Benjamin, Jr., & M. Wertheimer (Eds.), *Portraits of pioneers in psychology* (Vol. 6, pp. 273–286). Washington, DC: American Psychological Association.

Jackson, P. W. (1998). *John Dewey and the lessons of art.* New Haven, CT: Yale University Press.

Jackson, S. W. (1969). Galen—On mental disorders. *Journal of the History of the Behavioral Sciences, 5,* 365–384.

Jacobi, J. (1958). *Paracelsus: Selected writings.* New York: Pantheon Books.

Jacobs, D. (2001). *Her own woman: The life of Mary Wollstonecraft.* New York: Simon and Schuster.

Jager, M., & VanHoorn, W. (1972). Aristotle's opinion on perception in general. *Journal of the History of the Behavioral Sciences, 8,* 321–327.

Jahoda, G. (1992). *Crossroads between culture and mind: Continuities and change in theories of human nature.* Cambridge, MA: Harvard University Press.

Jahoda, G. (2000). Piaget and Lévy-Bruhl. *History of Psychology, 3,* 218–238.

Jahoda, G. (2006). Johann Friedrich Herbart: Urvater of social psychology. *History of the Human Sciences, 19,* 19–38.

Jahoda, G. (2007). *A history of social psychology: From the eighteenth-century Enlightenment to the Second World War.* New York: Cambridge University Press.

Jahoda, G. (2009). The metaphysical mechanics of the mind. *The Psychologist, 22,* 558–559.

Jahoda, M. (1969). The migration of psychoanalysis. In D. Fleming & B. Bailyn (Eds.), *The intellectual migration: Europe and America, 1930–1960* (pp. 371–419). Cambridge, MA: Harvard University Press.

James, W. (unsigned). (1875). Notice of Wilhelm Wundt's principles of physiological psychology. *North American Review, 121,* 195–201.

James, W. (unsigned). (1876a). Notice of F. von Holtzendorff's psychology of murder. *Nation, 22,* 16.

James, W. (1876b, September 21). The teaching of philosophy in our colleges. *The Nation,* pp. 178–179.

James, W. (1880). Great men, great thoughts and the environment. *Atlantic Monthly, 46,* 441–459.

James, W. (1884a). The dilemma of determinism. *Unitarian Review, 22,* 193–224.

James, W. (1884b). What is an emotion? *Mind, 9,* 188–205.

James, W. (1890). *The principles of psychology* (Vol. 1). New York: Henry Holt.

James, W. (1894). The physical basis of emotion. *Psychological Review, 1,* 516–529.

James, W. (1911). The college bred. In *Memories and studies* (pp. 312–313). New York: Longman's Green & Co.

James, W. (1920a). Invalidism in Cambridge. In H. James (Ed.), *The letters of William James* (Vol. 1, pp. 140–164). Boston: Atlantic Monthly Press.

James, W. (1920b). Letter to Mrs. Henry Whitman. In H. James (Ed.), *The Letters of William James* (Vol. 2, p. 90). Boston: Atlantic Monthly Press. (Original letter written 1899)

James, W. (1975a). *The meaning of truth*. Cambridge, MA: Harvard University Press. (Original work published 1909)

James, W. (1975b). *Pragmatism*. Cambridge, MA: Harvard University Press. (Original work published 1907)

James, W. (1976). *Essays in radical empiricism*. Cambridge, MA: Harvard University Press. (Original work published 1912)

James, W. (1977). *A pluralistic universe*. Cambridge, MA: Harvard University Press. (Original work published 1909)

James, W. (1978). Pluralistic mystic. *Essays in philosophy* (pp. 172–190). Cambridge, MA: Harvard University Press. (Original work published 1910)

James, W. (1979a). The dilemma of determinism. In F. H. Burkhardt (Ed.), *The will to believe* (pp. 114–140). Cambridge, MA: Harvard University Press. (Original work published 1884)

James, W. (1979b). *The will to believe*. Cambridge, MA: Harvard University Press. (Original work published 1897)

James, W. (1980). Letter to John Dewey. In E. Hardwick (Ed.), *The selected letters of William James* (pp. 203–204). Boston: David R. Godine. (Original letter sent 1903)

James, W. (1981). *Principles of psychology*. Cambridge, MA: Harvard University Press. (Original work published 1890)

James, W. (1983). *The physical basis of emotion: Essays in psychology* (pp. 299–314). Cambridge, MA: Harvard University Press. (Original work published 1894)

James, W. (1985). *The varieties of religious experience*. Cambridge, MA: Harvard University Press. (Original work published 1902)

James, W. (1986a). Letter to Charles William Elliot. In F. J. D. Scott (Ed.), *William James: Selected unpublished correspondence 1885–1910* (pp. 151–153). Columbus: Ohio State University Press. (Original letter dated February 21, 1897)

James, W. (1986b). Letter to James McKeen Cattell. In F. J. D. Scott (Ed.), *William James: Selected unpublished correspondence 1885–1910* (pp. 312–313). Columbus: Ohio State University Press. (Original letter dated June 10, 1903)

James, W. (2010). What makes a life significant? In R. Richardson (Ed.), *The heart of William James* (pp. 164–182). Cambridge, MA: Harvard University Press. (Original work published 1900)

Jansz, J. (2004). Psychology and society: An overview. In J. Jansz & van Drunen (Eds.), *A social history of psychology* (pp. 12–44). Malden, MA: Blackwell.

Jastrow, J. (1903). Helen Keller: A psychological autobiography. *Popular Science Monthly, 63,* 71–83.

Jaynes, J. (1973a). Introduction: The study of the history of psychology. In M. Henle, J. Jaynes, & J. J. Sullivan (Eds.), *Historical conceptions of psychology*. New York: Springer.

Jaynes, J. (1973b). The problem of animate motion in the seventeenth century. In M. Henle, J. Jaynes, & J. J. Sullivan (Eds.), *Historical conceptions of psychology* (pp. 166–179). New York: Springer.

Jefferson, T. (1904). Notes on Virginia. In A. A. Lipscomb (Ed.), *The writings of Thomas Jefferson* (Vol. 2). Washington, DC: The Thomas Jefferson Memorial Association. (Original work published 1782)

Jeremias, J. (1975). *Jerusalem in the time of Jesus: An investigation into economic and social conditions during the New Testament period* (F. H. & C. H. Cave, Trans.). Philadelphia: Fortress Press.

Jesseph, D. M. (2004). Galileo, Hobbes, and the book of nature. *Perspectives on Science, 12,* 191–211.

Johannsen, D. E. (1971). Early history of perceptual illusions. *Journal of the History of the Behavioral Sciences, 7,* 127–140.

Johnson, D. F. (2000). Cultivating the field of psychology: Psychological journals at the turn of the century. *American Psychologist, 55,* 1144–1147.

Johnson, W. H. (1927). Does the behaviorist have a mind? *Princeton Theological Review, 25,* 40–58.

Jonçich, G. (1968). Edward L. Thorndike. In D. L. Sills (Ed.), *International encyclopedia of the social sciences* (Vol. 16, pp. 8–14). New York: Macmillan and Free Press.

Jonçich, G. (1988). *The sane positivist: A biography of Edward L. Thorndike*. Middletown, CT: Wesleyan University Press.

Jones, E. (1953). *The life and work of Sigmund Freud* (Vol. 1). New York: Basic Books.

Jones, E. (1955). *The life and work of Sigmund Freud* (Vol. 2). New York: Basic Books.

Jones, E. (1957). *The life and work of Sigmund Freud* (Vol. 3). New York: Basic Books.

Jones, M. C. (1924a). The elimination of children's fears. *Journal of Experimental Psychology, 7,* 383–390.

Jones, M. C. (1924b). A laboratory study of fear: The case of Peter. *Pedagogical Seminary, 31,* 308–315.

Juhasz, J. B. (1971). Greek theories of imagination. *Journal of the History of the Behavioral Sciences, 7,* 39–58.

Jung, C. G. (1953). Psychology and alchemy. In R. F. C. Hull (Trans.), *The collected works of C. G. Jung* (Vol. 12). New York: Pantheon. (Original work published 1944)

Jung, C. G. (1954a). Analytic psychology and education. In H. Read, M. Fordham, & G. Adler (Eds.), *The collected works of C. G. Jung* (Vol. 17, pp. 63–132). New York: Pantheon Books. (Original work published 1926)

Jung, C. G. (1954b). Psychic conflicts in a child. In H. Read, M. Fordham, & G. Adler (Eds.), *The collected works of C. G. Jung* (Vol. 17, pp. 1–35). New York: Pantheon Books. (Original work published 1910)

Jung, C. G. (1967). *Alchemical studies*. In H. Read, M. Fordham, & G. Adler (Series Eds.), *The collected works of C. G. Jung* (Vol. 13). Princeton, NJ: Princeton University Press.

Jung, C. G. (1973). *Memories, dreams, and reflections* (A. Jaffé Ed., R. Winston & C. Winston, Trans.). New York: Pantheon. (Original work published 1961)

Jung, J. (1968). *Verbal learning*. New York: Holt, Rinehart and Winston.

Kahl, R. (1967). Hermann von Helmholtz. In P. Edwards (Ed.), *The encyclopedia of philosophy* (Vol. 3, pp. 469–471). New York: Macmillan and Free Press.

Kahl, R. (Ed.). (1971). *Selected writings of Hermann von Helmholtz*. Middletown, CT: Wesleyan University Press.

Kandel, E. R. (2001). *Eric R. Kandel–Biographical*. Retrieved August 23, 2013, from http://www.nobelprize.org/nobel_prizes/medicine/laureates/2000/kandel-bio.html

Kant, I. (1952). *The critique of judgment* (J. C. Meridith, Trans.). Oxford: Oxford University Press. (Original work published 1790)

Kant, I. (1956). *Critique of practical reason* (L. W. Beck, Trans.). Indianapolis, IN: Bobbs-Merrill. (Original work published 1788)

Kant, I. (1960). *Religion within the limits of reason alone* (T. M. Greene & H. H. Hudson, Trans.). New York: Harper. (Original work published 1793)

Kant, I. (1965). *Critique of pure reason* (N. K. Smith, Trans.). New York: St. Martin's Press. (Original work published 1781)

Kaplan, K. J., Flicker, L., Wallrabenstein, I., Dodge, N., Laird, P., Theil, K., et al. (2007). Why does Zeno the Stoic hold his breath? "Zenoism" as a new variable for studying suicide. *Omega, 56,* 369–400.

Kaplan, R. M. (2008). Being Bleuler: The second century of schizophrenia. *Australian Psychiatry, 16,* 305–311.

Kashima, Y. (2000). Recovering Bartlett's social psychology of cultural dynamics. *European Journal of Social Psychology, 30,* 383–403.

Kassin, S. M., & Gudjonsson, G. H. (2004). The psychology of confessions: A review of the literature and issues. *Psychological Science in the Public Interest, 5,* 33–67.

Kastenbaum, R. (1995). "How far can an intellectual effort diminish pain?": William McDougall's journal as a model for facing death. *Omega: Journal of Death and Dying, 32,* 123–164.

Katona, G. (1940). *Organizing and memorizing: Studies in the psychology of learning and teaching*. New York: Columbia University Press.

Katona, G. (1959). The psychology of the recession. *American Psychologist, 14,* 135–143.

Katona, G. (1979). Toward a macropsychology. *American Psychologist, 34,* 118–126.

Katona, G. (2002). The evolution of the concept of psyche from Homer to Aristotle. *Journal of Theoretical and Philosophical Psychology, 22,* 29–44.

Katz, D. (1979). Floyd H. Allport (1890–1978). *American Psychologist, 34,* 351–353.

Keen, S. (1973). *Apology for wonder*. New York: Harper & Row.

Keegan, E., & Holas, P. (2010). Cognitive-behaviorial therapy: Theory and practice. In R. A. Carlstedt (Ed.), *Handbook of integrative clinical psychology, psychiatry, and behavioral medicine: Perspectives, practices, and research* (pp. 605–629). New York: Springer Publishing Co.

Keller, F. S., & Sherman, J. G. (1974). *The Keller plan handbook: Essays on a personalized system of instruction*. Menlo Park, CA: Benjamin.

Keller, M. (1943). The first American medical work on the effects of alcohol: Benjamin Rush's "An inquiry into the effects of ardent spirits upon the human body and mind." *Quarterly Journal of Studies on Alcohol, 4,* 321–341.

Kellert, S. H., Longino, H. E., & Waters, C. K. (2006). *Scientific pluralism: Minnesota studies n the philosophy of science XIX*. Minneapolis: University of Minnesota Press.

Kelley, M. R., & Nairne, J. S. (2001). Von Restorff revisited: Isolation, generation, and memory for order. *Journal of Experimental Psychology: Learning, Memory, and Cognition, 27,* 54–66.

Kellman, P. J. (2000). An update on Gestalt psychology. In B. Landau & J. Sabini (Eds.), *Perception, cognition, and language: Essays in honor of Henry and Lila Gleitman* (pp. 157–190). Cambridge, MA: MIT Press.

Kelly, J. (2005). *The great mortality: An intimate history of the black death, the most devastating plague of all time*. New York: HarperCollins.

Kelly-Gadol, J. (1977). Did women have a Renaissance? In R. Bridenthal & C. Koontz (Eds.), *Becoming visible: Women in European history* (pp. 139–164). Boston: Houghton Mifflin.

Kemp, S. (1990). *Medieval psychology*. Westport, CT: Greenwood Press.

Kemp, S. (1996). *Cognitive psychology in the Middle Ages*. Westport, CT: Greenwood Press.

Kemp, S. (1998). Medieval theories of mental representation. *History of Psychology, 1,* 275–288.

Kenny, A. (Ed. & Trans.). (1970). *Descartes' philosophical letters*. Oxford: Clarendon Press.

Kieckhefer, R. (1976). *European witch trials*. Berkeley: University of California Press.

Kierkegaard, S. (1941). *Concluding unscientific postscript* (D. F. Swenson & W. Lowrie, Trans.). Princeton, NJ: Princeton University Press. (Original work published 1846)

Kierkegaard, S. (1967). *Stages on life's way* (W. Lowrie, Trans.). New York: Schocken Books. (Original work published 1845)

Kierkegaard, S. (1983). *Fear and trembling* (H. V. Hong & E. H. Hong, Eds. & Trans.). Princeton, NJ: Princeton University Press. (Original work published 1843)

Kierkegaard, S. (1985). *Philosophical fragments* (H. V. Hong & E. H. Hong, Eds. & Trans.). Princeton, NJ: Princeton University Press. (Original work published 1844)

Kierkegaard, S. (1987). *Either/or: A fragment on life* (H. V. Hong & E. H. Hong, Eds. & Trans.). Princeton, NJ: Princeton University Press. (Original work published 1843)

Kierkegaard, S. (1989). *The sickness unto death* (A. Hannay, Trans.). London: Penguin Books. (Original work published 1849)

Kimble, G. A. (1996). Ivan Mikhailovich Sechenov: Pioneer in Russian reflexology. In G. A. Kimble, C. A. Boneau, & M. Wertheimer (Eds.), *Portraits of pioneers in psychology* (Vol. 2, pp. 33–45). Washington, DC: American Psychological Association.

King, D. B. (1992). Evolution and revision of the principles of psychology. In M. E. Donnelly (Ed.), *Reinterpreting the legacy of William James* (pp. 67–75). Washington, DC: American Psychological Association.

King, D. B. (2000). George Croom Robertson and Mind: The story of psychology's first editor. In G. A. Kimble & M. Wertheimer (Eds.), *Portraits of pioneers in psychology* (Vol. 4, pp. 33–48). Washington, DC: American Psychological Association.

King, D. B., Cox, M., & Wertheimer, M. (1998). Karl Duncker: Productive problems with beautiful solutions. In G. A. Kimble & M. Wertheimer (Eds.), *Portraits of pioneers in psychology* (Vol. 3, pp. 163–178). Washington, DC: American Psychological Association.

King, D. B., Montañez-Ramirez, L. M., & Wertheimer, M. (1996). Barbara Stoddard Burks: Pioneer behavioral geneticist and humanitarian. In G. A. Kimble, C. A. Boneau, & M. Wertheimer (Eds.), *Portraits of pioneers in psychology* (Vol. 2, pp. 213–225). Washington, DC: American Psychological Association.

King, D. B., Niess, A. B., Maddi, A. E., & Perkins, L. S. (in press). The rise of abnormal psychology during the progressive era: Reflections from an American scientific periodical. In T. G. Plante (Ed.), *Abnormal psychology through the ages*. Santa Barbara, CA: ABC-CLIO/Greenwood.

King, D. B., & Viney, W. (1992). Modern history of pragmatic and sentimental attitudes toward animals and the selling of comparative psychology. *Journal of Comparative Psychology, 106,* 190–195.

King, D. B., & Wertheimer, M. (2005). *Max Wertheimer & Gestalt theory.* New Brunswick, NJ: Transaction.

King, D. B., Wertheimer, M., Keller, H., & Crochetière, K. (1994). The legacy of Max Wertheimer and Gestalt psychology. *Social Research, 61,* 907–935.

Kintsch, W. (1985). Reflections on Ebbinghaus. *Journal of Experimental Psychology: Learning, Memory and Cognition, 11,* 461–463.

Kirk, G. S., & Raven, J. E. (1957). *The presocratic philosophers.* Cambridge, MA: Cambridge University Press.

Kirsch, I. (1978). Demonology and the rise of science: An example of the misperception of historical data. *Journal of the History of the Behavioral Sciences, 14,* 149–157.

Kirschenbaum, H., & Jourdan, A. (2005). The current status of Carl Rogers and the person-centered approach. *Psychotherapy: Theory, Research, Practice, Training, 42,* 37–51.

Kirsner, D. (2001). The future of psychoanalytic institutes. *Psychoanalytic Psychology, 18,* 195–212.

Kissinger, S. C. (2008). Christian von Ehrenfels. In R. Diriwächter & J. Valsiner (Eds.), *Striving for the whole: Creating theoretical syntheses* (pp. 13–20). Piscataway, NJ: Transaction Publishers.

Kitcher, P. (1982). *Abusing science.* Cambridge, MA: MIT Press.

Klein, A. G. (2000). Fitting the school to the child: The mission of Leta Stetter Hollingworth, founder of gifted education. *Roeper Review, 23,* 97–103.

Klein, M. I. (1983). Freud's drive theory and ego psychology: A critical evaluation of the Blancks. *Psychoanalytic Review, 70,* 505–517.

Klempe, S. H. (2011). The role of tone sensation and musical stimuli in early experimental psychology. *Journal of the History of the Behavioral Sciences, 47,* 187–199.

Kline, L. W. (1908). The nature, origin and function of humor. *Popular Science Monthly, 73,* 144–156.

Kline, N. S., & Saunders, J. C. (1959). Drugs for treatment of depression. *Neurology, 9,* 224–227.

Knapp, T. J. (1995). A natural history of the behavior of organisms. In J. T. Todd (Ed.), *Modern perspectives on B. F. Skinner and contemporary behaviorism* (pp. 7–23). Westport, CT: Greenwood Press.

Knowles, D. (1967). Anicius Manlius Severinus Boethius. In P. Edwards (Ed.), *The encyclopedia of philosophy* (Vol. 1, pp. 328–330). New York: Macmillan and Free Press.

Knowlton, S. (1867). The silence of women in the churches. *The Congregational Quarterly, 9,* 329–334.

Koch, S. (1969). Psychology cannot be a coherent science. *Psychology Today, 3*(14), 64–68.

Koch, S. (1986). Afterword. In S. Koch & D. E. Leary (Eds.), *A century of psychology as science* (pp. 928–950). New York: McGraw-Hill.

Koestenbaum, P. (1967). Miguel de Unamuno y Jugo. In P. Edwards (Ed.), *Encyclopedia of philosophy* (Vol. 8, pp. 182–185). New York: Macmillan.

Koffka, K. (1922). Perception: An introduction to the Gestalt-Theorie. *Psychological Bulletin, 19,* 531–585.

Koffka, K. (1935). *Principles of Gestalt psychology.* New York: Harcourt.

Koffka, K. (1980). *Growth of the mind.* New Brunswick, NJ: Transaction Books. (Original work published in 1924)

Köhler, W. (1938). Simple structural functions in the chimpanzee and in the chicken. In W. D. Ellis (Ed.), *A source book of Gestalt psychology* (pp. 217–227). London: Kegan Paul, Trench, Trubner & Company.

Köhler, W. (1940). *Dynamics in psychology.* New York: Liveright.

Köhler, W. (1947). *Gestalt psychology.* New York: Liveright. (Original work published 1929)

Köhler, W. (1966). *The place of value in a world of facts.* New York: Liveright. (Original work published 1938)

Köhler, W. (1969). *The task of Gestalt psychology.* Princeton, NJ: Princeton University Press.

Köhler, W. (1971). Gestalt psychology. In M. Henle (Ed.), *The selected papers of Wolfgang Köhler* (pp. 108–122). New York: Liveright. (Original work published 1967)

Köhler, W. (1976). *The mentality of apes.* New York: Liveright. (Original work published 1925)

Köhler, W., & Restorff, H., von. (1935). Analyse von Vorgangen in Spurenfeld. *Psychologische Forschung, 13,* 293–364.

Kohn, D. (Ed.). (1985). *The Darwinian heritage*. Princeton, NJ: Princeton University Press.

Kolb, B. (1999). The twentieth century belongs to neuropsychology. *Brain Research Bulletin, 50,* 409–410.

Koltko-Rivera, M. E. (2006). Rediscovering the later version of Maslow's hierarchy of needs: Self-transcendence and opportunities for theory, research, and unification. *Review of General Psychology, 10,* 302–317.

Kontantin, R. (1960). The problem of measurement in the psychology of the eighteenth century. *American Psychologist, 15,* 256–265.

Koppes, L. L. (2000). Lillian Gilbreth. In Alan E. Kaszdan (Ed.), *Encyclopedia of psychology* (Vol. 3, pp. 498–500). Washington, DC: American Psychological Association.

Korteweg, S. F. S., Van de Graf, R. C., & Werker, P. M. N. (2010). Sir Charles Bell was not affected by facial paralysis himself!*Arquivos de Neuro-Psiquiatria, 68,* 321–322.

Kovel, J. (1990). Beyond the future of an illusion: Further reflections on Freud and religion. *Psychoanalytic Review, 77,* 69–87.

Kramer, H., & Sprenger, J. (1971). *The malleus maleficarum* (Montague Summers, Trans.). New York: Dover. (Original work published 1486)

Kranz, D. L. (2005). Hull's *Principles of behavior* and psychology's unity. *PsycCRITIQUES, 50*(37).

Krech, D. (1968). Edward C. Tolman. In D. L. Sills (Ed.), *International encyclopedia of the social sciences* (Vol. 16, pp. 95–98). New York: Macmillan.

Kreezer, G. (1938). The electro-encephalogram and its use in psychology. *American Journal of Psychology, 51,* 737–759.

Kressley, R. A. (2006). Gestalt psychology: Its paradigm-shaping influence on animal psychology. *Gestalt Theory, 28,* 259–269.

Kristeller, P. O. (1967). Petrarch. In P. Edwards (Ed.), *The encyclopedia of philosophy* (Vol. 5, pp. 126–128). New York: Macmillan.

Krivoy, W. A., Kroeger, D. C., & Zimmermann, E. (1977). Neuropeptides: Influence of acute and chronic effects of opiates. *Psychoneuroendocrinology, 2,* 43–51.

Kruger, L., Otis, T. S., & Shtrahman, M. (2011). Golgi in retrospect: A historiographic examination of contextual influence in tracing the constructs of neuronal organization. *Brain Research Reviews, 66,* 68–74.

Kruglanski, A. W., & Stroebe, W. (Eds.). (2012). *Handbook of the history of social psychology*. New York: Psychology Press.

Kruta, V. (1976). Ernst Heinrich Weber. In C. C. Gillispie (Ed.), *Dictionary of scientific biography* (Vol. 14, pp. 199–202). New York: Scribner.

Kuhn, R. (1958). The treatment of depressive states with G-22355 (imipramine hydrochloride). *American Journal of Psychiatry, 115,* 459–464.

Kuhn, T. S. (1970). *The structure of scientific revolutions* (2nd ed.). Chicago: University of Chicago Press.

Kuhlmann, H. (2005). *Living Walden Two: B. F. Skinner's behaviorist utopia and experimental communities*. Champaign, IL: University of Illinois Press.

Kuhse, H., & Singer, P. (1993). Individuals, humans and persons: The issue of moral status. In P. Singer, H. Kuhse, S. Buckle, K. Dawson, & P. Kasimba (Eds.), *Embryo experimentation: Ethical, legal, and social issues* (pp. 65–75). Cambridge, MA: Cambridge University Press.

Külpe, O. (1973). *Outlines of psychology* (E. B. Titchener, Trans.). New York: Arno Press. (Original work published 1893)

Kumar, N. (2010). Karl Popper, psychology and philosophy. *Psychological Studies, 55,* 270–274.

Kuna, D. P. (1976). The concept of suggestion in the early history of advertising psychology. *Journal of the History of the Behavioral Sciences, 12,* 347–353.

Kuo, Z. Y. (1921). Giving up instincts in psychology. *Journal of Philosophy, 18,* 645–666.

Kuo, Z. Y. (1924). A psychology without heredity. *Psychological Review, 31,* 427–448.

Lachman, R., Lachman, J. L., & Butterfield, E. C. (1979). *Cognitive psychology and information processing: An introduction*. Hillsdale, NJ: Erlbaum.

La Mettrie, J. O. (1912). *Man a machine*. La Salle, IL: Open Court. (Original work published 1747)

Lambert, M. J. (2010). *Prevention of treatment failure: The use of measuring, monitoring, and feedback in clinical practice*. Washington, DC: American Psychological Association.

Landon, H. C. R. (1990). *The Mozart compendium: A guide to Mozart's life and music*. New York: Schirmer.

Landy, F. J. (1992). Hugo Münsterberg: Victim or visionary? *Journal of Applied Psychology, 77,* 787–802.

Landy, F. J. (1997). Early influences on the development of industrial and organizational psychology. *Journal of Applied Psychology, 82,* 467–477.

Lane, M. (2012). *Eco-Republic: What the ancients can teach us about ethics, virtue, and sustainable living*. Princeton, NJ: Princeton University Press.

Lange, C. G. (1922). *The emotions*. Baltimore: Williams & Wilkins. (Original work published 1885)

Langfeld, H. S. (1937). Carl Stumpf. *American Journal of Psychology, 49,* 316–320.

Langfeld, H. S. (1946). Edwin Bissell Holt: 1873–1946. *Psychological Review, 53,* 251–258.

Längle, A. (2012). The Viennese school of existential analysis: The search for meaning and affirmation of life. In L. Barnett & G. Madison (Eds.), *Existential therapy: Legacy, vibrancy and dialogue* (pp. 159–170). New York: Routledge/Taylor & Francis Group.

LaPointe, L. L. (2013). *Paul Broca and the origins of language in the brain*. San Diego, CA: Plural Publishing.

Larrimore, M. (2008). Antinomies of race: Diversity and destiny in Kant. *Patterns of Prejudice, 42,* 341–363.

Larson, C. A. (1979). Highlights of Dr. John B. Watson's career in advertising. *Journal of Industrial/Organizational Psychology, 16,* 3.

Lashley, K. (1942). An examination of the "continuity theory" as applied to discriminative learning. *Journal of General Psychology, 26,* 241–265.

Lashley, K. S. (1950). In search of the engram. *Symposia of the Society for Experimental Biology, 4,* 454–482.

Latham, R. E. (1959). Introduction. In R. E. Latham (Trans.), *Lucretius on the nature of the universe* (pp. ix–xxxii). Baltimore: Penguin.

Latham, R. E. (1967). Lucretius. In P. Edwards (Ed.), *The encyclopedia of philosophy* (Vol. 5, pp. 99–101). New York: Macmillan and Free Press.

Lattal, K. A. (1992). B. F. Skinner and psychology. *American Psychologist, 47,* 1269–1272.

Laver, A. B. (1972). Precursors of psychology in ancient Egypt. *Journal of the History of the Behavioral Sciences, 8,* 181–195.

Lawrence, D. H., & Festinger, L. (1962). *Deterrents and reinforcement. The psychology of insufficient reward.* Stanford, CA: Stanford University Press.

Lazarus, A. A. (2000). Will reason prevail? From classical psychoanalysis to New Age therapy. *American Journal of Psychotherapy, 54,* 152–155.

Lea, H. C. (Ed.). (1957). *Materials toward a history of witchcraft* (Vol. 3). New York: Thomas Yoseloff.

Leahey, T. H. (1981). The mistaken mirror: On Wundt's and Titchener's psychologies. *Journal of the History of the Behavioral Sciences, 17,* 273–282.

Leahey, T. H. (1992). The mythical revolutions of American psychology. *American Psychologist, 47,* 308–318.

Leahey, T. H. (2001). Back to Bridgman? *Theory and Psychology, 11,* 53–58.

Leahey, T. H. (2005). Mind as a scientific object: A historical philosophical exploration. In C. E. Erneling & D. M. Johnson (Eds.), *The mind as a scientific object: Between brain and culture.* New York: Oxford University Press.

Leahey, T. H. (2013). Cognition and learning. In D. K. Freedheim & I. B. Weiner (Eds.), *Handbook of psychology, Vol. 1: History of psychology* (2nd ed., pp. 129–154). Hoboken, NJ: John Wiley & Sons Inc.

Leary, D. E. (1980). The intentions and heritage of Descartes and Locke: Toward a recognition of the moral basis of modern psychology. *Journal of General Psychology, 102,* 283–310.

Lee, R. M. (2011). "The most important technique…": Carl Rogers, Hawthorne, and the rise and fall of nondirective interviewing in sociology. *Journal of the History of the Behavioral Sciences, 47,* 123–146.

Lehrer, K. (1989). *Thomas Reid.* New York: Routledge.

Leiber, J. (2011). Descartes: The smear and related misconstruals. *Journal for the Theory of Social Behaviour, 41,* 365–376.

Lequyer, J. (1998). The dialogue of the predestinate and the reprobate. In D. W. Viney (Ed. and Trans.), *Translation of works of Jules Lequyer* (pp. 51–156). Lewiston, NY: Edwin Mellen. (Original work published 1865)

Lerner, R. M. (2009). The scientific study of adolescent development: Historical and contemporary perspectives. In R. M. Lerner & L. Steinberg (Eds.), *Handbook of adolescent psychology (Vol. 1: Individual bases of adolescent development)* (3rd ed., pp. 3–14). Hoboken, NJ: John Wiley & Sons.

LeRoy, H. (2008). Harry Harlow: From the other side of the desk. *Integrative Psychological & Behavioral Science, 42,* 348–353.

LeRoy, H., & Kimble, G. A. (2003). Harry Frederick Harlow: And one thing led to another. . . . In G. A. Kimble & M. Wertheimer (Eds.), *Portraits of pioneers in psychology* (Vol. 5, pp. 279–297). Washington, DC: American Psychological Association.

Leslie, J. C. (2006). Herbert Spencer's contributions to behavior analysis: A retrospective review of Principles of Psychology. *Journal of the Experimental Analysis of Behavior, 86,* 123–129.

Leslie, R. C. (1996). Karen Horney and Viktor Frankl: Optimists in spite of everything. *International Forum for Logotherapy, 19,* 23–28.

Leuba, J. H. (1925). *The psychology of religious mysticism.* New York: Harcourt, Brace, & Company.

Leuba, J. H. (1928). Morality among the animals. *Harper's Magazine, 157,* 97–103.

Levine, H. G. (1978). The discovery of addiction: Changing conceptions of habitual drunkenness in America. *Journal of Studies on Alcohol, 39,* 143–174.

Levine, M., & Wishner, J. (1977). The case records of the Psychological Clinic at the University of Pennsylvania (1896–1961). *Journal of the History of the Behavioral Sciences, 13,* 59–66.

Levy, E. (1986). A Gestalt theory of paranoia. *Gestalt Theory, 8,* 230–255.

Lewin, K. (1931). The conflict between Aristotelian and Galileian modes of thought in contemporary psychology. *Journal of Genetic Psychology, 5,* 141–177.

Lewin, K. (1935). *A dynamic theory of personality: Selected papers* (D. K. Adams & K. E. Zener, Trans.). New York: McGraw-Hill.

Lewin, K. (1937). Carl Stumpf. *Psychological Review, 44,* 189–194.

Lewin, R. (1984). *Hitler's mistakes.* New York: William Morrow.

Lewis, P. (2012). In defense of Aristotle on character: Toward a synthesis of recent psychology, neuroscience and the thought of Michael Polanyi. *Journal of Moral Education, 41,* 155–170.

Libet, B. (1985). Unconscious cerebral initiative and the role of conscious will in voluntary action. *Behavioral and Brain Sciences, 8,* 529–566.

Liddell, A. F. (1933). Instructed ignorance: The philosophy of Nicholas of Cusa. *Psychological Bulletin, 30,* 606–607.

Lifton, R. J. (1968). *Revolutionary immortality. Mao Tse-Tung and the Chinese cultural revolution.* New York: Random House.

Lincoln, A. (1950). Letter to W. H. Herndon. In A. H. Shaw (Ed.), *The Lincoln encyclopedia* (p. 149). New York: Macmillan. (Original work published 1856)

Lincoln, M. R., & Ebers, G. C. (2012). Robert Whytt, Benjamin Franklin, and the first probable case of multiple sclerosis. *Annals of Neurology, 72,* 307–311.

Lindberg, D. C., & Numbers, R. L. (1986). *God and nature.* Berkeley: University of California Press.

Lindenfeld, D. (1978). Oswald Külpe and the Würzburg School. *Journal of the History of the Behavioral Sciences, 14,* 132–141.

Lindsley, D. B. (1936). Brain potentials in children and adults. *Science, 83,* 354.

Lindsley, D. B. (1942). Heart and brain potentials of human fetuses in utero. *American Journal of Psychology, 55,* 412–416.

Linehan, M. (1993). *Cognitive-behavioral treatment of borderline personality disorder.* New York: Guilford.

Linehan, M. M., & Lungu, A. (2012). Compassion, wisdom, and suicidal clients. In C. K. Germer & R. D. Siegel (Eds.), *Wisdom and compassion in psychotherapy: Deepening mindfulness in clinical practice* (pp. 205–220). New York: Guilford Press.

Link, S. W. (1994). Rediscovering the past: Gustav Fechner and signal detection theory. *Psychological Science, 5,* 335–340.

Lippman, T. W. (1995). *Understanding Islam: An introduction to the Muslim world.* New York: Meridian.

Ljungqvist, F. C. (2012). Female shame, male honor: The chastity code in Juan Luis Vives' de institutione feminae Christianae. *Journal of Family History, 37,* 139–154.

Lloyd, P., & Fernyhough, C. (Eds.). (1999). *Lev Vygotsky: Critical assessments: Vygotsky's theory.* Florence, KY: Taylor & Francis/Rutledge.

Locke, J. (1959). *An essay concerning human understanding* (A. C. Fraser, Ed.). New York: Dover. (Original work published 1690)

Locke, J. (1989). *Some thoughts concerning education* (J. W. Yolton & J. S. Yolton, Eds.). Oxford: Clarendon Press. (Original work published 1693)

Loehlin, J. C. (2009). History of behavior genetics. In Y.-K. Kim (Ed.), *Handbook of behavior genetics* (pp. 3–11). New York: Springer Science + Business Media.

Loewen, J. W. (2005). *Sundown Towns: A hidden dimension of American racism.* New York: Touchstone.

Loftus, E. (1993). The reality of repressed memories. *American Psychologist, 48,* 518–537.

Loftus, E. F. (1996). *Eyewitness testimony.* Cambridge, MA: Harvard University Press. (Original work published 1979)

Logan, F. A. (1968). Clark L. Hull. In D. L. Sills (Ed.), *International encyclopedia of the social sciences* (Vol. 6, pp. 535–539). New York: Macmillan.

Longo, M. R., & Haggard, P. (2011). Weber's illusion and body shape: Anisotropy of tactile size perception on the hand. *Journal of Experimental Psychology: Human Perception and Performance, 37,* 720–726.

López-Muñoz, F., Alamo, C., Cuenca, E., Shen, W. W., Clervoy, P., & Rubio, G. (2005). History of the discovery and clinical introduction of chlorpromazine. *Annals of Clinical Psychiatry, 17,* 113–135.

López-Muñoz, F., Boya, J., & Alamo, C. (2006). Neuron theory, the cornerstone of neuroscience, on the centenary of the Nobel Prize award to Santiago Ramón y Cajal. *Brain Research Bulletin, 70,* 391–405.

Lorch, M. (2011). Re-examining Paul Broca's initial presentation of M. Leborgne: Understanding the impetus for brain and language research. *Cortex: A Journal Devoted to the Study of the Nervous System and Behavior, 47,* 1228–1235.

Lorusso, L. (2008). Neurological caricatures since the 15th century. *Journal of the History of the Neurosciences, 17,* 314–334.

Lotze, H. (1973). *Outlines of psychology.* New York: Arno Press. (Original work published 1881)

Lovejoy, A. D. (1922). Paradox of the thinking behaviorist. *Philosophical Review, 31,* 135–147.

Lovett, B. J. (2006). The new history of psychology: A review and critique. *Journal of the History of Psychology, 9,* 17–37.

Lowman, R. L., Kantor, J., & Perloff, R. (2007). A History of I-O Psychology Educational Programs in the United States. In L. L. Koppes (Ed.), *Historical perspectives in industrial and organizational psychology* (pp. 111–137). Mahwah, NJ: Lawrence Erlbaum Associates Publishers.

Lowrie, W. (1970). *Kierkegaard* (Vol. 1). Gloucester, MA: Peter Smith.

Lowry, R. J. (1973). *A. H. Maslow: An intellectual portrait.* Monterey, CA: Brooks/Cole.

Luccio, R. (2010). Anent isomorphism and its ambiguities: From Wertheimer to Köhler and back to Spinoza. *Gestalt Theory, 32,* 219–262.

Lucretius. (1959). *On the nature of the universe* (R. E. Latham, Trans.). Baltimore: Penguin.

Lurie, A. T. (1979). The weeping Heraclitus by Hendrick Terbrugghen in the Cleveland Museum of Art. *The Burlington Magazine, 121,* 279–287.

Luther, M. (1967). Table talk. In H. T. Lehmann (Ed.), *Luther's works* (Vol. 54, pp. 358–359). Philadelphia: Fortress Press.

MacCormac, E. R. (1990). Metaphor and pluralism. *The Monist, 73,* 411–420.

MacCorquodale, K. C. (1970). On Chomsky's review of Skinner's Verbal Behavior. *Journal of the Experimental Analysis of Behavior, 13,* 83–100.

MacCorquodale, K. C., & Meehl, P. E. (1954). Edward C. Tolman. In W. K. Estes, S. Koch, K. MacCorquodale, P. E. Meehl, C. G. Muller, Jr., & W. N. Schoenfeld et al. (Eds.), *Modern learning theory* (pp. 177–266). New York: Appleton-Century-Crofts.

MacDonald, P. (2007). Francis Bacon's behavioral psychology. *Journal of the History of the Behavioral Sciences, 43,* 285–303.

Mach, E. (1959). *The analysis of sensations* (5th ed.). (C. M. Williams, Trans.). New York: Dover. (Original work published 1886; 5th ed. published 1905)

Machiavelli, N. (1977). *The prince* (R. M. Adams, Trans. & Ed.). New York: Norton. (Original work published 1532)

Mackintosh, N. J. (1997). Has the wheel turned full circle? Fifty years of learning theory, 1946–1996. *Quarterly Journal of Experimental Psychology, 50,* 879–898.

Mackler, B., & Hamilton, K. (1967). Benjamin Rush: A political and historical study of the "Father of American Psychiatry."*Psychological Reports, 20,* 1287–1306.

Macklin, R. (1976). A psychoanalytic model for human freedom and rationality. *Psychoanalytic Quarterly, 45,* 430–454.

MacLeod, R. B. (1964). Phenomenology: A challenge to experimental psychology. In T. W. Wann (Ed.), *Behaviorism and phenomenology: Contrasting bases for modern psychology* (pp. 47–73). Chicago: University of Chicago Press.

MacLeod, R. B. (1968a). Johannes Müller. In D. L. Sills (Ed.), *International encyclopedia of the social sciences* (Vol. 10, pp. 525–527). New York: Macmillan and Free Press.

MacLeod, R. B. (1968b). Phenomenology. In D. L. Sills (Ed.), *International encyclopedia of the social sciences* (Vol. 12, pp. 68–72). New York: Macmillan and Free Press.

MacLeod, R. B. (Ed.). (1969). *William James: Unfinished business.* Washington, DC: American Psychological Association.

MacLeod, R. B. (1975). *The persistent problems of psychology.* Pittsburgh, PA: Duquesne University Press.

MacMillan, M. (1991). *Freud evaluated: The completed arc.* Amsterdam: North-Holland.

Macnamara, J. (1993). Cognitive psychology and the rejection of Brentano. *Journal for the Theory of Social Behavior, 23,* 117–137.

Madden, G. J., Dube, W. V., Hackenberg, T. D., Hanley, G. P., & Lattal, K. A. (Eds.). (2012). *APA handbook of behavior analysis, Vol. 1: Methods and principles.* Washington, DC: American Psychological Association.

Madigan, S., & O'Hara, R. (1992). Short-term memory at the turn of the century: Mary Whiton Calkins's memory research. *American Psychologist, 47,* 170–174.

Magiorkinis, E., Sidiropoulou, K., & Diamantis, A. (2010). Hallmarks in the history of epilepsy: Epilepsy in antiquity. *Epilepsy & Behavior, 17,* 103–108.

Mahaffy, J. P. (1969). *Descartes.* Freeport, NY: Books for the Libraries Press. (Original work published 1902)

Maher, W. B., & Maher, B. A. (2003). Abnormal psychology. In I. B. Weiner (Series Ed.) & D. K. Friedheim (Vol. Ed.), *Handbook of psychology: Vol. 1. History of psychology* (pp. 303–336). New York: Wiley.

Mahoney, M. J. (1989). Scientific psychology and radical behaviorism: Important distinctions based in scientism and objectivism.*American Psychologist, 44,* 1372–1377.

Mak, G., & Waaldijk, B. (2009). Gender, history, and the politics of Florence Nightingale. In R. Buikema & I. van der Tuin (Eds.), *Doing gender in media, art and culture* (pp. 207–222). New York: Routledge.

Manchester, W. (1992). *A world lit only by fire: The Medieval mind and the Renaissance: Portrait of an age.* Boston: Little, Brown.

Mandler, G. (2003). Emotion. In I. B. Weiner (Series Ed.) & D. K. Freedheim (Vol. Ed.), *Handbook of psychology: Vol. 1. History of psychology* (pp. 157–175). New York: Wiley.

Mandler, J. M., & Mandler, G. (1969). The diaspora of experimental psychology: The Gestaltists and others. In D. Fleming & B. Bailyn (Eds.), *The intellectual migration: Europe and America, 1930–1960* (pp. 371–419). Cambridge, MA: Harvard University Press.

Manning, L., & Thomas-Antérion, C. (2011). Marc Dax and the discovery of the lateralisation of language in the left cerebral hemisphere. *Revue Neurologique, 167,* 868–872.

Manoli, D. D., Meissner, G. W., & Baker, B. S. (2006). Blueprints for behavior: Genetic specification of neural circuitry for innate behaviors. *Trends in Neurosciences, 29,* 444–451.

Markel, H. (2011). *An anatomy of addiction: Sigmund Freud, William Halsted, and the miracle drug cocaine.* New York: Pantheon Books.

Marneros, A. (2009). The history of bipolar disorders. In C. A. Zarate, Jr. & H. K. Manji (Eds.), *Bipolar depression: Molecular neurobiology, clinical diagnosis and pharmacotherapy* (pp. 3–16). Cambridge, MA: Birkhäuser.

Marrow, A. J. (1969). *The practical theorist: The life and work of Lewin.* New York: Basic Books.

Marti, F. (1983, April 1). *The social and political question of demythologizing.* Talk delivered before the Southern Society for Philosophy and Psychology, Atlanta, GA.

Martinez, J. L., Jr., & Mendoza, R. H. (1984). *Chicano psychology.* New York: Academic Press.

Martinich, A. P. (1999). *Hobbes: A biography.* Cambridge, MA: Cambridge University Press.

Maslow, A. H. (1943). A theory of human motivation. *Psychological Review, 50,* 370–396.

Maslow, A. H. (1954). *Motivation and personality.* New York: Harper and Brothers.

Maslow, A. H. (1962). *Toward a psychology of being.* Princeton, NJ: Van Nostrand.

Maslow, A. H. (1964). *Religion, values, and peak experiences.* New York: Viking.

Maslow, A. H. (1971). *The farther reaches of human nature.* New York: Viking.

Masson, J. M. (1991). *Final analysis: The making and unmaking of a psychoanalyst.* Reading, MA: Addison-Wesley.

Mastain, L. (2006). The lived experience of spontaneous altruism: A phenomenological study. *Journal of Phenomenological Psychology, 37,* 25–52.

Mathews, N. (1996). *Francis Bacon: The history of a character assassination.* New Haven, CT: Yale University Press.

Matson, W. I. (1982). De Corpore. In F. N. McGill (Ed.), *World Philosophy* (Vol. 2, pp. 851–856). Engelwood Cliffs, NJ: Salem Press.

Mattern, S. (2011). Galen and his patients. *The Lancet, 378,* 478–479.

Mattoon, M. A. (1981). *Jungian psychology in perspective*. New York: Free Press.

May, E. T. (2010). *America and the pill: A history of promise, peril, and liberation*. New York: Basic Books.

Mayer, S. J. (2005). The early evolution of Jean Piaget's clinical method. *History of Psychology, 8,* 362–382.

Mayrhauser, R. T., von. (1989). Making intelligence functional: Walter Dill Scott and applied psychological testing in World War I. *Journal of the History of the Behavioral Sciences, 25,* 60–72.

Mays, W. (1998). Genetic explanation in Husserl and Piaget. *New Ideas in Psychology, 16,* 1–10.

McCauley, C., & Rozin, P. (2003). Solomon Asch: Scientist and humanist. In G. A. Kimble & M. Wertheimer (Eds.), *Portraits of pioneers in psychology* (Vol. 5, pp. 249–261). Washington, DC: American Psychological Association.

McCool, G. A. (1990). Why St. Thomas stays alive. *International Philosophical Quarterly, 30,* 275–287.

McCullough, D. (2001). *John Adams*. New York: Simon and Schuster.

McDermott, J. J. (Ed.). (1968). *The writings of William James*. New York: Modern Library.

McDougall, W. (1905). *Physiological psychology*. London: J. M. Dent.

McDougall, W. (1908). *An introduction to social psychology*. Mineola, NY: Dover.

McDougall, W. (1923). *Outline of psychology*. Boston: Scribner.

McDougall, W. (1926a). *An introduction to social psychology*. Boston: Luce.

McDougall, W. (1926b). Men or robots? *Pedagogical Seminary, 33,* 71–102.

McDougall, W. (1942). *The energies of men*. London: Methuen.

McDougall, W. (1960). *An introduction to social psychology*. London: Methuen. (Original work published 1908).

McFarland, S., Webb, M., & Brown, D. (2012). All humanity is my ingroup: A measure and studies of identification with all humanity. *Journal of Personality and Social Psychology, 103,* 830–853.

McGaugh, J. L. (2000). Memory: A century of consolidation. *Science, 287,* 248–251.

McHenry, L. C. (1969). *Garrison's history of neurology*. Springfield, IL: Charles C. Thomas.

McInerny, R. (1990). *A first glance at St. Thomas Aquinas*. Notre Dame, IN: University of Notre Dame Press.

McKerchar, T. L., Morris, E. K., & Smith, N. G. (2011). A quantitative analysis and natural history of B. F. Skinner's coauthoring practices. *The Behavior Analyst, 34,* 75–91.

McReynolds, P. (1987). Lightner Witmer: Little known founder of clinical psychology. *American Psychologist, 42,* 849–858.

McReynolds, P. (1996). Lightner Witmer: A centennial tribute. *American Psychologist, 51,* 237–240.

McReynolds, P. (1997). *Lightner Witmer: His life and times*. Washington, DC: American Psychological Association.

McWhirter, P. T., & McWhirter, J. J. (1997). Lightner Witmer: Father and grandfather? *American Psychologist, 52,* 275.

Meade, M. (1979). *Stealing heaven: The love story of Heloise and Abelard*. New York: Soho Press.

Medawar, P. B. (1984). *The limits of science*. New York: Harper & Row.

Meehan, W. (2009). Partem totius naturae esse: Spinoza's alternative to the mutual incomprehension of physicalism and mentalism in psychology. *Journal of Theoretical and Philosophical Psychology, 29,* 47–59.

Meerloo, J. A. M. (1956). *Rape of the mind: The psychology of thought control, menticide, and brainwashing*. Cleveland, OH: World Publishing Company.

Meischner-Metge, A. (2010). Gustav Theodore Fechner: Life and work in the mirror of his diary. *History of Psychology, 13,* 411–423.

Meissner, W. W. (1984). *Psychoanalysis and religious experience*. New Haven, CT: Yale University Press.

Melville, H. (1976). *Moby-Dick, or the whale*. New York: Norton. (Original work published 1851)

Memon, A., Mastroberardino, S., & Fraser, J. (2008). Münsterberg's legacy: What does eyewitness research tell us about the reliability of eyewitness testimony? *Applied Cognitive Psychology, 22,* 841–851.

Mendelowitz, E. (2008). Meditations on dissociation: Kristina and the enigmatic self. In K. J. Schneider (Ed.), *Existential-integrative psychotherapy: Guideposts to the core of practice* (pp. 245–266). New York: Routledge.

Merchant, C. (1979). The vitalism of Anne Conway: Its impact on Leibniz's concept of the monad. *Journal of the History of Philosophy, 17,* 255–269.

Meredith, A. (1986). Later philosophy. In J. Boardman, J. Griffin, & O. Murray (Eds.), *The Oxford history of the classical world* (pp. 708–714). New York: Oxford University Press.

Merenda, P. F. (1987). Toward a four-factor theory of temperament and/or personality. *Journal of Personality Assessment, 51,* 367–374.

Merlan, P. (1967). Plotinus. In P. Edwards (Ed.), *The encyclopedia of philosophy* (Vol. 6, pp. 351–359). New York: Macmillan and Free Press.

Meymandi, A. (2010). Baruch Spinoza: The philosopher's philosopher. *Psychiatry, 7,* 47–50.

Michell, J. (1999). *Measurement in psychology: A critical history of a methodological concept*. New York: Cambridge University Press.

Michelmore, P. (1962). *Einstein, profile of the man*. New York: Dodd, Mead.

Midgley, N. (2012). Peter Heller's A Child Analysis with Anna Freud: The significance of the case for the history of child psychoanalysis. *Journal of the American Psychoanalytic Association, 60,* 45–70.

Milar, K. S. (1999). "A coarse and clumsy tool": Helen Thompson Wooley and the Cincinnati Vocation Bureau. *History of Psychology, 2,* 219–235.

Miles, W. (1949). James Rowland Angell, 1869–1949, Psychologist-educator. *Science, 110,* 1–4.

Milgram, S. (1963). Behavioral study of obedience. *The Journal of Abnormal and Social Psychology, 67,* 371–378.

Mill, J. S. (1969). *Autobiography* (J. Stillinger, Ed.). Boston: Houghton Mifflin. (Original work published 1873)

Mill, J. S. (1974). A system of logic ratiocinative and inductive. In J. M. Robson (Ed.), *Collected works of John Stuart Mill* (Vol. 8). Toronto, Canada: Routledge & Kegan Paul. (Original work published 1843)

Mill, J. S. (1988). *The subjection of women.* Indianapolis/Cambridge: Hackett. (Original work published 1869)

Miller, J. (1981). Interpretations of Freud's Jewishness, 1924–1974. *Journal of the History of the Behavioral Sciences, 17,* 357–374.

Mills, J. (2006). Reflections on the death drive. *Psychoanalytic Psychology, 23,* 373–382.

Mills, J. A. (1988). The genesis of Hull's Principles of Behavior. *Journal of the History of the Behavioral Sciences, 24,* 392–401.

Mills, J. A. (1998). *Control: A history of behavioral psychology.* New York: New York University Press.

Mills, J. A. (2010). Hallucinogens as hard science: The adrenochrome hypothesis for the biogenesis of schizophrenia. *History of Psychology, 13,* 178–195.

Mintz, S. I. (1962). *The hunting of Leviathan.* Cambridge, MA: Cambridge University Press.

Miranda, M., Slachevsky, A., & Garcia-Borreguero, D. (2010). Did Immanuel Kant have dementia with Lewy bodies and REM behavior disorder? *Sleep Medicine, 11,* 586–588.

Misiak, H. K., & Sexton, V. S. (1966). *History of psychology: An overview.* New York: Grune & Stratton.

Mitchell, P. B. (1999). On the 50th anniversary of John Cade's discovery of the anti-manic effect of lithium. *Australian and New Zealand Journal of Psychiatry, 33,* 623–628.

Miyata, Y. (2009). Pavlov's Nobel Prize in physiology or medicine. *Japanese Journal of Physiological Psychology and Psychophysiology, 27,* 225–234.

Molnár, Z., & Brown, R. E. (2010). Insights into the life and work of Sir Charles Sherrington. *Nature Reviews Neuroscience, 11,* 429–436.

Monahan, J., & Walker, L. (1994). *Social science in law: Cases and materials* (3rd ed.). Westbury, NY: Foundation Press.

Monson, C. M., Friedman, M. J., & La Bash, H. A. (2007). A psychological history of PTSD. In M. J. Friedman, T. M. Keane, & P. A. Resick (Eds.), *Handbook of PTSD: Science and practice* (pp. 37–52). New York: Guilford Press.

Montaigne, M. (1960). Apology for Raimond Sebond. In D. M. Frame (Trans.), *The complete essays of Montaigne* (Vol. 2, pp. 112–308). Garden City, NY: Doubleday.

Moore, J. (2005). Some historical and conceptual background to the development of B. F. Skinner's "Radical Behaviorism"—Part I. *Mind and Behavior, 26,* 65–94.

Moore, K. G. (1946). Theory of imagination in Plotinus. *Journal of Psychology, 22,* 41–51.

Morawski, J. G. (1983). Hugo Münsterberg on the possibilities for psychology and society. *American Psychologist, 38,* 1259–1260.

Morawski, J. G., & Bayer, B. M. (2013). Social psychology. In D. K. Freedheim & I. B. Weiner (Eds.), *Handbook of psychology, Vol. 1: History of psychology* (2nd ed., pp. 248–278). Hoboken, NJ: John Wiley & Sons Inc.

Moray, N. (2007). Attention: From history to application. In A. F. Kramer, D. A. Wiegmann, & A. Kirlik (Eds.), *Attention: From theory to practice* (pp. 3–15). New York: Oxford University Press.

Morens, D. M. (1999). Death of a president. *New England Journal of Medicine, 341,* 1845–1849.

Morgan, C. L. (1977). *Comparative psychology.* Washington, DC: University Publications of America. (Original work published in 1894)

Morgan, C. T. (1968). Karl S. Lashley. In D. L. Sills (Ed.), *International encyclopedia of the social sciences* (Vol. 9, pp. 27–30). New York: Macmillan.

Morris, D. (1967). *The naked ape.* New York: McGraw-Hill.

Morris, E. A., & Todd, J. T. (1999). Watsonian behaviorism. In W. O'Donohue & R. Kitchener (Eds.), *Handbook of behaviorism* (pp. 15–69). San Diego, CA: Academic Press.

Morris, E. K., Smith, N. G., & Altus, D. E. (2005). B. F. Skinner's contributions to applied behavior analysis. *The Behavior Analyst, 28,* 99–131.

Moskowitz, M. J. (1977). Hugo Münsterberg: A study in the history of applied psychology. *American Psychologist, 32,* 824–842.

Mozans (pseudonym for) Zahm, J. A. (1913). *Women in science.* New York: Appleton.

Mruk, C. J. (1989). Phenomenological psychology and the computer revolution: Friend, foe or opportunity? *Journal of Phenomenological Psychology, 20,* 20–39.

Muckle, J. T. (Trans.). (1992). *The story of Abelard's adversities.* Toronto, Canada: Pontifical Institute of Medieval Studies.

Müller, G. E., & Pilzecker, A. (1900). Experimental contributions to the theory of memory. In S. Diamond (Ed.), *The roots of psychology* (pp. 271–273). New York: Basic Books.

Müller, U., Fletcher, P. C., & Steinberg, H. (2006). The origin of pharmacopsychology: Emil Kraepelin's experiments in Leipzig, Dorpat and Heidelberg (1882-1892). *Psychopharmacology, 184,* 131–138.

Mumford, L. (1934). *Techniques and civilization.* New York: Harcourt Brace.

Munroe, R. L. (1955). *Schools of psychoanalytic thought.* New York: Holt, Rinehart and Winston.

Münsterberg, H. (1908). *On the witness stand: Essays on psychology and crime.* New York: Clark Boardman.

Münsterberg, H. (1909). *Psychotherapy.* New York: Moffat, Yard.

Münsterberg, H. (1913). *Psychology and industrial efficiency.* New York: Houghton Mifflin.

Münsterberg, H. (1916). *The photoplay: A psychological study.* New York: Appleton.

Murphy, C. (2012). *God's jury: The inquisition and the making of the modern world*. Boston, MA: Houghton Mifflin Harcourt.

Murphy, G. (1963). Robert Sessions Woodworth, 1869–1962. *American Psychologist, 18,* 131–133.

Murray, D. J. (1993). A perspective for viewing the history of psychophysics. *Behavioral and Brain Sciences, 16,* 115–186.

Murray, D. J. (1995). *Gestalt psychology and the cognitive revolution*. New York: Harvester Wheatsheaf.

Murray, D. J., & Farahmand, B. (1998). Gestalt theory and evolutionary psychology. In R. W. Rieber & K. Salzinger (Eds.),*Psychology: Theoretical-historical perspectives* (2nd ed., pp. 255–287). Washington, DC: American Psychological Association.

Nadel, L. (2013). Cognitive maps. In D. Waller & L. Nadel (Eds.), *Handbook of spatial cognition* (pp. 155–171). Washington, DC: American Psychological Association.

National Science Teachers Association. (2007). *The teaching of evolution*. Retrieved March 15, 2007, from www.nsta.org/159& psid=10

Natsoulas, T. (1990). Reflective seeing: An exploration in the company of Edmund Husserl and James J. Gibson. *Journal of Phenomenological Psychology, 21,* 1–31.

Neacsiu, A. D., Ward-Ciesielski, E. F., & Linehan, M. M. (2012). Emerging approaches to counseling intervention: Dialectical behavior therapy. *The Counseling Psychologist, 40,* 1003–1032.

Neary, F. (2001). A question of "peculiar importance": George Croom Robertson, *Mind* and the changing relationship between British psychology and philosophy. In G. C. Bunn, A. D. Lovie, & G. D. Richards (Eds.), *Psychology in Britain: Historical essays and personal reflections* (pp. 54–71). Leicester, England: The British Psychological Society.

Neider, C. (Ed.). (1959). *The autobiography of Mark Twain*. New York: Harper.

Neisser, U. (1967). *Cognitive psychology*. New York: Appleton-Century-Crofts.

Neisser, U. (1976). *Cognition and reality*. San Francisco: Freeman.

Neisser, U. (1982). *Memory observed: Remembering in natural contexts*. New York: Freeman.

Neuschatz, J. S., Lampinen, J. M., Toglia, M. P., Payne, D. G., & Cisneros, E. P. (2007). False memory research: History, theory, and applied implications. In M. P. Toglia, J. D. Read, D. F. Ross, & R. C. L. Lindsay (Eds.), *The handbook of eyewitness psychology (Vol. I): Memory for events* (pp. 239–260). Mahwah, NJ: Lawrence Erlbaum Associates Publishers.

Newell, A. (1985). Duncker on thinking: An inquiry into progress in cognition. In S. Koch & D. Leary (Eds.), *A century of psychology as science* (pp. 392–419). New York: McGraw-Hill.

Newman, S. (2006). "Study of several involuntary functions of the apparatus of movement, gripping, and voice" by Jean-Marc Gaspard Itard (1825). *History of Psychiatry, 17,* 333–339.

Nicholson, I. A. M. (1998). Gordon Allport, character, and the "culture of personality," 1897–1937. *History of Psychology, 1,* 52–68.

Nicholson, I. A. M. (2000). "A coherent datum of perception": Gordon Allport, Floyd Allport, and the politics of "personality." *Journal of the History of the Behavioral Sciences, 36,* 463–470.

Nicholson, I. A. M. (2001). "Giving up maleness": Abraham Maslow, masculinity, and the boundaries of psychology. *History of Psychology, 4,* 79–91.

Nicholson, R. A. (1999). Forensic assessment. In R. Roesch, S. D. Hart, & J. R. P. Ogloff (Eds.), *Psychology and the law: The state of the discipline* (pp. 121–173). New York: Kluwer Academic/Plenum.

Nicholson, S. (1995). The expression of emotional distress in Old English prose and verse. *Culture, Medicine and Psychiatry, 19,* 327–338.

Nicolas, S., & Söderlund, H. (2005). The project of an international congress of psychology by J. Ochorowicz (1881). *International Journal of Psychology, 40,* 395–406.

Nietzel, M. T., McCarthy, D. M., & Kern, M. J. (1999). Juries: The current state of the empirical literature. In R. Roesch, S. D. Hart, & J. R. P. Ogloff (Eds.), *Psychology and law: The state of the discipline* (pp. 23–52). New York: Kluwer Academic/Plenum.

Nightmare in Jonestown. (1978, December 4). *Time, 112*(23), 16–21.

Nikolaeva, V. V. (2011). B.W. Zeigarnik and pathopsychology. *Psychology in Russia: State of the Art, 4,* 176–192.

Nissim-Sabat, M. (1999). Phenomenology and mental disorders: Heidegger or Husserl? *Philosophy, Psychiatry, & Psychology, 6,* 100–104.

Noel, P. S., & Carlson, E. T. (1970). Origins of the word "phrenology." *American Journal of Psychiatry, 127,* 694–697.

Noel, P. S., & Carlson, E. T. (1973). The faculty psychology of Benjamin Rush. *Journal of the History of the Behavioral Sciences, 9,* 369–377.

Norcross, J. C., Karpiak, C. P., & Santoro, S. O. (2005). Clinical psychologists across the years: The division of clinical psychology from 1960 to 2003. *Journal of Clinical Psychology, 61,* 1467–1483.

Norena, C. G. (1970). *Juan Luis Vives*. The Hague: Nijhoff.

Norena, C. G. (1975). *Studies in Spanish Renaissance thought*. The Hague: Nijhoff.

Norman, D. A. (1980). Twelve issues for cognitive science. *Cognitive Science, 4,* 1–32.

North, M. S., & Fiske, S. T. (2012). A history of social cognition. In A. W. Kruglanski & W. Stroebe (Eds.), *Handbook of the history of social psychology* (pp. 81–99). New York: Psychology Press.

Novak, M. (1970). *The experience of nothingness*. New York: Harper & Row.

Nutton, V. (2006). The rise of medicine. In R. Porter (Ed.), *The Cambridge History of Medicine* (pp. 46–70). New York: Cambridge University Press.

Obiols, J. E., & Barrios, G. E. (2009). The historical roots of Theory of Mind: The work of James Mark Baldwin. *History of Psychiatry, 20,* 377–392.

O'Brien, M. (2010). Re-assessing the 'affair': The Heidegger controversy revisited. *The Social Science Journal, 47,* 1–20.

O'Connell, A. N. (1990). Karen Horney (1885–1952). In A. N. O'Connell & N. F. Russo (Eds.), *Women in psychology: A bio-bibliographic sourcebook* (pp. 184–196). New York: Greenwood Press.

O'Connell, A. N., & Russo, N. F. (Eds.). (1983). *Models of achievement: Reflections of eminent women in psychology.* New York: Columbia University Press.

O'Connell, A. N., & Russo, N. F. (Eds.). (1988). *Models of achievement: Reflections of eminent women in psychology* (Vol. 2). Hillsdale, NJ: Erlbaum.

O'Connell, A. N., & Russo, N. F. (Eds.). (1990). *Women in psychology: A bio-bibliograhic sourcebook.* New York: Greenwood Press.

O'Donnell, J. M. (1985). *The origins of behaviorism: American psychology, 1870–1920.* New York: New York University Press.

Ogden, R. M. (1951). Oswald Külpe and the Würzburg school. *American Journal of Psychology, 64,* 4–19.

Ogloff, J. P. R., & Finkelman, D. (1999). Psychology and the law: An overview. In R. Roesch, S. D. Hart, & J. R. P. Ogloff (Eds.), *Psychology and the law: The state of the discipline* (pp. 1–20). New York: Kluwer Academic/Plenum.

O'Hara, M. (1995). Carl Rogers: Scientist and mystic. *Journal of Humanistic Psychology, 35,* 40–53.

Okin, S. S. (Ed.). (1988). *The subjection of women.* Indianapolis/Cambridge: Hackett. (Original work published 1869)

Olds, J. (1954). A neural model for sign-gestalt theory. *Psychological Review, 61,* 59–72.

O'Neil, W. M. (1984). The Wundt's myths. *Australian Journal of Psychology, 36,* 285–289.

O'Neil, W. M. (1995). American behaviorism: A historical and critical analysis. *Theory and Psychology, 5,* 285–305.

Oon, Z. (2008). A critical presentation of the life and work of Franz Anton Mesmer MD and its influence on the development of hypnosis. *European Journal of Clinical Hypnosis, 8,* 32–40.

Ophuls, W. (2011). *Plato's revenge: Politics in the age of ecology.* Cambride, MA: MIT Press.

Orgel, S. (1990). The future of psychoanalysis. *Psychoanalytic Quarterly, 59,* 1–20.

O'Roark, A. M. (2007). The best of consulting psychology 1900-2000: Insider perspectives. *Consulting Psychology Journal: Practice and Research, 59,* 189–202.

O'Sullivan, J. J., & Quevillon, R. P. (1992). 40 years later: Is the Boulder model still alive? *American Psychologist, 47,* 67–70.

Otte, M. (2009). The analytic/synthetic distinction in Kant and Bolzano. In B. Sriraman & S. Goodchild (Eds.), *Relatively and philosophically earnest: Festschrift in honor of Paul Ernest's 65th birthday* (pp. 39–55). Charlotte, NC: Information Age Publishing.

Overholser, J. C. (2010). Psychotherapy that strives to encourage social interest: A simulated interview with Alfred Adler. *Journal of Psychotherapy Integration, 20,* 347–363.

Pace, E. A. (1921). In memory of Wilhelm Wundt. *Psychological Review, 28,* 159–162.

Packer, I. K., & Borum, R. (2013). Forensic training and practice. In R. K. Otto & I. B. Weiner (Eds.), *Handbook of psychology, Vol. 11: Forensic psychology* (2nd ed., pp. 16–36). Hoboken, NJ: John Wiley & Sons.

Pagels, E. (2003). *Beyond belief: The secret gospel of Thomas.* New York: Random House.

Palha, A. P., & Esteves, M. F. (1997). The origin of dementia praecox. *Schizophrenia Research, 28,* 99–103.

Palmer, D. C. (2006). On Chomsky's appraisal of Skinner's Verbal behavior: A half century of misunderstanding. *The Behavior Analyst, 29,* 253–267.

Palmieri, P. (2012). Signals, cochlear mechanics and pragmatism: A new vista on human hearing? *Journal of Experimental & Theoretical Artificial Intelligence, 24,* 527–545.

Panourias, I. G., Stranjalis, G., Stravrinou, L. C., & Sakas, D. E. (2011). The Hellenic and Hippocratic origins of the spinal terminology. *Journal of the History of the Neurosciences, 20,* 177–187.

Papanicolaou, A. C. (1989). *Emotion: A reconsideration of the somatic theory.* New York: Gordon and Breach.

Paris, B. J. (1991). A Horneyan approach to literature. *American Journal of Psychoanalysis, 51,* 319–337.

Pariser, D. A. (2008). Rudolf Julius Arnheim (1904-2007). *American Psychologist, 63,* 55.

Pastore, N. (1965). Samuel Bailey's critique of Berkeley's theory of vision. *Journal of the History of the Behavioral Sciences, 1,* 321–337.

Patrick, G. T. W. (1914). The psychology of relaxation. *Popular Science Monthly, 84,* 590–604.

Pauley, P. J. (1986). G. Stanley Hall and his successors: A history of the first half-century of psychology at Johns Hopkins. In S. H. Hulse & B. F. Green, Jr. (Eds.), *One hundred years of psychological research in America* (pp. 21–51). Baltimore: Johns Hopkins University Press.

Pavlov, I. P. (1928). *Lectures on conditioned reflexes* (Vol. 1) (W. H. Gantt, Trans. & Ed.). New York: International.

Pavlov, I. P. (1941). *Lectures on conditioned reflexes* (Vol. 2) (W. H. Gantt, Trans. & Ed.). New York: International.

Pavlov, I. P. (1955). *I. P. Pavlov: Selected works* (J. Gibbons, Ed., S. Belsky, Trans.). Moscow: Foreign Languages Publishing House.

Peach, B. (1982). Leviathan. In F. N. Magill (Ed.), *World philosophy* (Vol. 2, pp. 839–846). Englewood Cliffs, NJ: Salem Press.

Pearce, J. M. S. (2009). The ophthalmoscope: Helmholtz's augenspiegel. *European Neurology, 61,* 244–249.

Pearson, K. (1897). *The chances of death and other studies in evolution.* New York: Edward Arnold.

Pearson, K. (1914). *The life, letters, and labors of Francis Galton* (Vol. 1). London: Cambridge University Press.

Penfield, W. (1952). Memory mechanisms. *Archives of Neurology and Psychiatry, 67,* 178–198.

Perloff, R., & Naman, J. L. (1996). Lillian Gilbreth: Tireless advocate for a general psychology. In G. A. Kimble, C. A. Boneau, & M. Wertheimer (Eds.), *Portraits of pioneers in psychology* (Vol. 2, pp. 107–116). Washington, DC: American Psychological Association.

Perper, T. (2010). Will she or won't she: The dynamics of flirtation in Western philosophy. *Sexuality & Culture, 14,* 33–43.

Perry, R. B. (1954). *The thought and character of William James: Briefer version.* New York: George Braziller.

Peters, R. S. (Ed.). (1965). *Brett's history of psychology.* Cambridge, MA: MIT Press.

Petersen, C. A. (2007). A historical look at psychology and the scientist-practitioner model. *American Behavioral Scientist, 50,* 758–765.

Petzold, M. (1987). The social history of Chinese psychology. In M. G. Ash & W. R. Woodward (Eds.), *Psychology in twentieth-century thought and society* (pp. 213–231). Cambridge: Cambridge University Press.

Phillips, L. (2000). Recontextualizing Kenneth B. Clark: An Afrocentric perspective on the paradoxical legacy of a model psychologist-activist. *History of Psychology, 3,* 142–167.

Piaget, J. (1952). Jean Piaget. In E. G. Boring (Ed.), *A history of psychology in autobiography* (Vol. 4, pp. 237–256). New York: Russell and Russell.

Piaget, J., & Garcia, J. (1989). *Psychogenesis and the history of science* (H. Feider, Trans.). New York: Columbia University Press. (Original work published 1983)

Pickenhain, L. (1999). The importance of I. P. Pavlov for the development of neuroscience. *Integrative Physiological & Behavioral Science, 34,* 85–89.

Pickren, W. E. (2012). Internationalizing the history of psychology course in the USA. In F. T. L. Leong, W. E. Pickren, M. M. Leach, & A. J. Marsella (Eds.), *Internationalizing the psychology curriculum in the United States* (pp. 11–28). New York: Springer Science + Business Media.

Pickren, W. E., & Dewsbury, D. A. (2002). *Evolving perspectives on the history of psychology.* Washington, DC: American Psychological Association.

Pickren, W. E., & Fowler, R. D. (2003). Professional organizations. In I. B. Weiner (Series Ed.) & D. K. Freedheim (Vol. Ed.), *Handbook of psychology: Vol. 1. The history of psychology* (pp. 535–554). New York: Wiley.

Pilcher, L. D. (Executive Producer), & Garner, K. V. (Director). (2004). *Iron Jawed Angels* [Motion Picture]. New York: Home Box Office Inc.

Pinel, P. (1977). A treatise on insanity (D. D. Davis, Trans.). In D. N. Robinson (Ed.), *Significant contributions to the history of psychology, 1750–1920:* Series C. (Vol. III). Washington, DC: University Publications of America. (Original work published 1806)

Pivnicki, D. (1969). The beginnings of psychotherapy. *Journal of the History of the Behavioral Sciences, 5,* 238–247.

Plato. (1961a). Apology (H. Tredennick, Trans.). In E. Hamilton & H. Cairns (Eds.), *The collected dialogues of Plato including the letters* (pp. 3–26). Princeton, NJ: Princeton University Press.

Plato. (1961b). The Phaedo (H. Tredennick, trans.). In E. Hamilton & H. Cairns (Eds.), *Plato: The collected dialogues, including the letters* (pp. 40–98). Princeton, NJ: Princeton University Press.

Plaud, J. J., & Montgomery, R. W. (1993). On the influence of Walter S. Hunter in the shaping of modern behaviorism. *Psychological Record, 43,* 361–373.

Plekhanov, G. V. (1967). *Essays in the history of materialism.* New York: H. Fertig.

Plotinus. (1956). *The Enneads* (S. MacKenna, Trans.). London: Faber & Faber.

Plummer, B. L. (1970). Benjamin Rush and the Negro. *American Journal of Psychiatry, 127,* 793–798.

Poffenberger, A. T. (1962). Robert Sessions Woodworth: 1869–1962. *American Journal of Psychology, 75,* 677–689.

Poma, A. (2013). *The impossibility and necessity of theodicy: The "essais" of Leibniz.* Dordrecht: Springer.

Pomerantz, J. R. (2006). Colour as a Gestalt: Pop out with basic features and with conjunctions. *Visual Cognition, 14,* 619–628.

Popkin, R. H. (1967). Michel Eyquem de Montaigne. In P. Edwards (Ed.), *The encyclopedia of philosophy* (Vol. 5, pp. 366–368). New York: Macmillan.

Popkin, R. H. (1979). *The history of skepticism from Erasmus to Spinoza.* Berkeley: University of California Press.

Poppen, R. (1996). *Joseph Wolpe.* Thousand Oaks, CA: Sage.

Popper, K. R. (1959). *The logic of scientific discovery.* London: Hutchinson.

Popplestone, J. A. (1995). *Recent variations on a theme by Descartes.* Paper presented at the meeting of the American Psychological Association, New York.

Porfeli, E. J. (2009). Hugo Münsterberg and the origins of vocational guidance. *The Career Development Quarterly, 57,* 225–236.

Posner, M. I., Rueda, M. R., & Kanske, P. (2007). Probing the mechanisms of attention. In J. T. Cacioppo, L. G. Tassinary, & G. G. Berntson (Eds.), *Handbook of psychophysiology* (3rd ed., pp. 410–432). New York: Cambridge University Press.

Postman, L. (1973). Hermann Ebbinghaus. In M. Henle, J. Jaynes, & J. J. Sullivan (Eds.), *Historical conceptions of psychology* (pp. 220–229). New York: Springer. Also published in (1968) *American Psychologist, 23,* 149–157.

Powell, R. A. (2010). Little Albert still missing. *American Psychologist, 65,* 299–300.

Powell, R. A. (2011). Research notes: Little Albert, lost or found: Further difficulties with the Douglas Merritte hypothesis. *History of Psychology, 14,* 106–107.

Pratola, S. (1974). Up with our foremother. *American Psychologist, 29,* 780.

Pretorius, I.-M. (2012). From the Hampstead War Nurseries to the Anna Freud Centre. In N. T. Malberg & J. Rapael-Leff (Eds.), *The Anna Freud tradition: Lines of development—Evolution of theory and practice over the decades* (pp. 30–37). London, England: Karnac Books.

Preyer, W. (1888). The imitative faculty of infants. *Popular Science Monthly, 33,* 249–255.

Price, E. H. (2012). Do brains think? Comparative anatomy and the end of the Great Chain of Being in 19th-century Britain.*History of the Human Sciences, 25,* 32–50.

Prislin, R., & Crano, W. D. (2012). A history of social influence research. In A. W. Kruglanski & W. Stroebe (Eds.), *Handbook of the history of social psychology* (pp. 321–339). New York: Psychology Press.

Proulx, T. (2013). Beyond mortality and the self: Meaning makes a comeback. In K. D. Markman, T. Proulx, & M. J. Lindberg (Eds.), *The psychology of meaning* (pp. 71–87). Washington, DC: American Psychological Association.

Pubols, B. H., Jr. (1959). Jan Swammerdam and the history of reflex action. *American Journal of Psychology, 72,* 131–135.

Puglisi, M. (1924). Franz Brentano: A biographical sketch. *American Journal of Psychology, 35,* 414–419.

Pytell, T. (2006). Transcending the angel beast: Viktor Frankl and humanistic psychology. *Psychoanalytic Psychology, 23,* 490–503.

Pytell, T. (2007). Extreme experience, psychological insight, and Holocaust perception: Reflections on Bettelheim and Frankl.*Psychoanalytic Psychology, 24,* 641–657.

Quételet, J. A. (1968). *A treatise on man and the development of his faculties.* New York: B. Franklin. (Original work published 1842)

Quinn, S. (1987). *A mind of her own: The life of Karen Horney.* New York: Summit.

Radice, B. (1974). *The letters of Abelard and Héloise.* London: Penguin.

Raichle, M. E. (1999). Modern phrenology: Maps of human cortical function. In D. C. Grossman & H. Valtin (Eds.), *Great issues for medicine in the twenty-first century* (pp. 107–118). New York: New York Academy of Sciences.

Raimy, V. C. (Ed.). (1950). *Training in clinical psychology.* Englewood Cliffs, NJ: Prentice Hall.

Rambo, L. R. (1980). Ethics, evolution, and the psychology of William James. *Journal of the History of the Behavioral Sciences, 16,* 50–57.

Rancurello, A. C. (1968). *A study of Franz Brentano.* New York: Academic Press.

Rand, N. (2004). The hidden soul: The growth of the unconscious in philosophy, psychology, medicine, and literature, 1750–1900. *American Imago, 61,* 257–289.

Ranke-Heinemann, U. (1990). *Eunuchs for the kingdom of heaven* (P. Heinegg, Trans.). New York: Penguin.

Rapport, R. (2005). *Nerve endings: The discovery of the synapse.* New York: Norton.

Rashotte, M. E., & Amsel, A. (1999). Clark L. Hull's behaviorism. In W. O'Donohue & R. Kitchener (Eds.), *Handbook of behaviorism* (pp. 119–158). San Diego, CA: Academic Press.

Rathunde, K. (2001). Toward a psychology of optimal human functioning: What positive psychology can learn from the "experimental turns" of James, Dewey, and Maslow. *Journal of Humanistic Psychology, 41,* 135–153.

Rauch, J. (1993). *Kindly inquisitors: The new attacks on free thought.* Chicago: University of Chicago Press.

Ray, W. J. (2013). *Evolutionary psychology: Neuroscience perspectives concerning human behavior and experience.* Thousand Oaks, CA: Sage.

Razran, G. (1968). Ivan M. Sechenov. In D. L. Sills (Ed.), *International encyclopedia of the social sciences* (Vol. 14, pp. 129–130). New York: Macmillan and Free Press.

Reck, A. J. (1990). An historical sketch of pluralism. *The Monist, 73,* 367–387.

Reed, D. D., & Luiselli, J. K. (2009). Antecedents to a paradigm: Ogden Lindsley and B. F. Skinner's founding of "Behavior therapy." *The Behavior Therapist, 32,* 82–85.

Reid, T. (1786). *Essays on the intellectual powers of man.* Dublin: L. White.

Reid, T. (1790). *Essays on the active powers of man.* Dublin: P. Byrne and J. Milliken.

Reid, T. (1970). *An inquiry into the human mind* (T. Duggan, Ed.). Chicago: University of Chicago Press. (Original work published 1764)

Reik, M. M. (1977). *The golden lands of Thomas Hobbes.* Detroit, MI: Wayne State University Press.

Reisenzein, R., & Schonpflug, W. (1992). Stumpf's cognitive-evaluative theory of emotion. *American Psychologist, 47,* 34–45.

Reiss, S. (2003). Epicurus: The first rational-emotive therapist. *The Behavior Therapist, 26,* 405–406.

Reppen, J. (Ed.). (2006). Special issue: The relevance of Sigmund Freud for the 21st Century. *Psychoanalytic Psychology, 23*, 415–451.

Rescorla, R. A. (2001). Experimental extinction. In R. R. Mowrer & S. B. Klein (Eds.), *Handbook of contemporary learning theories* (pp. 119–154). Mahwah, NJ: Lawrence Erlbaum Associates Publishers.

Rescorla, R. A. (2002). Extinction. In L. Bäckman & C. von Hofsten (Eds.), *Psychology at the turn of the millennium, Vol. 1: Cognitive, biological, and health perspectives* (pp. 219–244). Hove, England: Psychology Press.

Resende, L. A. L., & Weber, S. A. T. (2010). "Sir Charles Bell was not affected by facial paralysis himself!": The authors reply. *Arquivos de Neuro-Psiquiatria, 68,* 322.

Rhodes, J. S., Ford, M. M., Yu, C. H., Brown, L. L., Finn, D. A., Garland, T., Jr., et al. (2007). Mouse inbred strain differences in ethanol drinking to intoxication. *Genes, Brain, and Behavior, 6,* 1–18.

Richards, G. (1987). Of what is history of psychology a history? *British Journal for the History of Science, 20,* 201–211.

Richards, J. M., Jr. (2000). A history of division 34 (population and environmental psychology). In D. A. Dewsbury (Ed.), *Unification through division: Histories of the divisions of the American Psychological Association* (Vol. 5, pp. 113–135). Washington, DC: American Psychological Association.

Richards, R. J. (1980). Wundt's early theories of unconscious inference and cognitive evolution in their relation to Darwinian biopsychology. In W. G. Bringmann & R. D. Tweney (Eds.), *Wundt studies: A centennial collection* (pp. 42–70). Toronto, Canada: C. J. Hogrefe.

Richards, R. J. (1987). *Darwin and the emergence of evolutionary theories of mind and behavior*. Chicago: University of Chicago Press.

Richardson, H. S. (1990). Measurement, pleasure, and the practical science in Plato's Protagoras. *Journal of the History of Philosophy, 28,* 7–32.

Richardson, R. D. (2006). *William James: In the maelstrom of American modernism*. Boston: Houghton Mifflin.

Richeson, A. W. (1940). Hypatia of Alexandria. *National Mathematics Magazine, 15,* 73–82.

Richter, J. P. (Ed.). (1970). *The literary works of Leonardo da Vinci* (3rd ed., 2 vols.). London: Phaidon.

Rieber, R. W., & Robinson, D. K. (Eds.). (2003). *Wilhelm Wundt in history: The making of a scientific psychology*. New York: Kluwer Academic/Plenum.

Riese, W. (1951). Philippe Pinel (1745–1826): His views on human nature and disease. His medical thought. *Journal of Nervous and Mental Disease, 114,* 313–323.

Riese, W. (1959). *A history of neurology*. New York: MD Publications.

Rilling, M. (2000a). How the challenge of explaining learning influenced the origins and development of John B. Watson's behaviorism. *American Journal of Psychology, 113,* 275–301.

Rilling, M. (2000b). John Watson's paradoxical struggle to explain Freud. *American Psychologist, 55,* 301–312.

Ringer, F. K. (1969). *The decline of the German mandarins: The German academic community, 1890–1933.* Cambridge, MA: Harvard University Press.

Roback, A. A. (1937). *Behaviorism at twenty-five.* Cambridge, MA: Sci-Art Publishers.

Roback, A. A., & Kiernan, T. (1969). *Pictorial history of psychology and psychiatry*. New York: Philosophical Library.

Roberts, M. A., McGeorge, A. P., & Caird, F. I. (1978). Electroencephalography and computerized tomography in vascular and non-vascular dementia in old age. *Journal of Neurology, Neurosurgery, and Psychiatry, 41,* 903–906.

Robins, R. W., Gosling, S. D., & Craik, K. H. (1999). An empirical analysis of trends in psychology. *American Psychologist, 54,* 117–128.

Robinson, D. N. (1977). *Significant contributions to the history of psychology, 1750–1920: Series C* (Vol. III). Washington, DC: University Publications of America.

Robinson, D. N. (1982). *Toward a science of human nature.* New York: Columbia University Press.

Robinson, D. N. (1989a). *Aristotle's psychology*. New York: Columbia University Press.

Robinson, D. N. (1989b). Thomas Reid and the Aberdeen years: Common sense at the Wise Club. *Journal of the History of the Behavioral Sciences, 29,* 154–162.

Robinson, D. K. (2010). Fechner's "inner psychophysics." *History of Psychology, 13,* 424–433.

Rocca, J. (2007). William Cullen (1710-1790) and Robert Whytt (1714-1766) on the nervous system. In H. Whitaker, C. U. M. Smith, & S. Finger (Eds.), *Brain, mind and medicine: Essays in eighteenth century neuroscience* (pp. 85–98). New York: Springer Science + Business Media.

Rock, I. (Ed.). (1990). *The legacy of Solomon Asch: Essays in cognition and social psychology*. Hillsdale, NJ: Erlbaum.

Rock, I., & Palmer, S. (1990). The legacy of Gestalt psychology. *Scientific American, 263,* 84–90.

Rodis-Lewis, G. (1999). *Descartes: His life and thought* (J. M. Todd, Trans.). Ithaca, New York: Cornell University Press.

Roediger, H. L. (1980). Memory metaphors in cognitive psychology. *Memory and Cognition, 8,* 231–246.

Roets, A., & Van Hiel, A. (2011). Allport's prejudiced personality today: Need for closure as the motivated cognitive basis of prejudice. *Current Directions in Psychological Science, 20,* 349–354.

Rogers, A. K. (1912). *A student's history of philosophy*. New York: Macmillan.

Rogers, C. (1959). *Introduction in the examination of men's wits by Juan Huarte* (M. C. Camilli & R. Carew, Trans.). Gainesville, FL: Scholars Facsimiles and Reprints. (Original work published 1594)

Rogers, C. R. (1951). *Client-centered therapy*. Boston: Houghton Mifflin.

Rogers, C. R. (1961). *On being a person: A therapist's view of psychotherapy*. Boston: Houghton Mifflin.

Rogers, E. M. (1960). *Physics for the inquiring mind.* Princeton, NJ: Princeton University Press.

Rogers, T. B. (1989). Operationism in psychology: A discussion of contextual antecedents and an historical interpretation of its longevity. *Journal of the History of the Behavioral Sciences, 25,* 139–153.

Rogow, A. A. (1986). *Thomas Hobbes: Radical in the service of reaction*. New York: Norton.

Rohles, F. H. (1992). Orbital bar pressing: A historical note on Skinner and the chimpanzees in space. *American Psychologist, 47,* 1531–1533.

Roith, E. (1987). New library of psychoanalysis: 4. In David Tuckett (General Ed.), *The riddle of Freud: Jewish influences on his theory of female sexuality*. New York: Tavistock.

Romand, D. (2012). Fechner as a pioneering theorist of unconscious cognition. *Consciousness and Cognition, 21,* 562–572.

Romanes, G. J. (1881). Intelligence of ants. *Popular Science Monthly, 19,* 495–510, 816–829.

Romanes, G. J. (1883). *Mental evolution in animals*. London: Kegan Paul, Trench & Co.

Ronan, C. A. (1982). *Science: Its history and development among the world's cultures*. New York: Facts on File.

Root, M. J. (2008). The evolution of psychologists' recommended childrearing practices in the United States. In D. G. Wiseman (Ed.), *The American family: Understanding its changing dynamics and place in society* (pp. 97–111). Springfield, IL: Charles C. Thomas.

Rose, F. C. (2009). Cerebral localization in antiquity. *Journal of the History of the Neurosciences, 18,* 239–247.

Rosenfield, L. C. (1968). *From beast-machine to man-machine: Animal soul in French letters from Descartes to La Mettrie.* New York: Octagon Books.

Rosenzweig, S. (1987). The final tribute of E. G. Boring to G. T Fechner: Concerning the date October 22, 1850. *American Psychologist, 42,* 787–790.

Rosenzweig, S. (1997). Letters by Freud on experimental psychodynamics. *American Psychologist, 52,* 571.

Rosner, R. I. (2012). Aaron T. Beck's drawings and the psychoanalytic origin story of cognitive therapy. *History of Psychology, 15,* 1–18.

Ross, D. (1972). *G. Stanley Hall: The psychologist as prophet.* Chicago: University of Chicago Press.

Ross, L., Lepper, M., & Ward, A. (2010). History of social Psychology: Insights, challenges, and contributions to theory and application. In S. T. Fiske, D. T. Gilbert, & G. Lindzey (Eds.), *Handbook of social psychology* (Vol. 1, pp. 3–50). Hoboken, NJ: John Wiley & Sons.

Rotenberg, M., & Diamond, B. L. (1971). The biblical conception of psychopathology: The law of the stubborn and rebellious son. *Journal of the History of the Behavioral Sciences, 7,* 29–38.

Roth, M. S. (1998). *Freud: Conflict and culture.* New York: Knopf.

Roth, P. A. (2004). Hearts of darkness: "Perpetrator history" and why there is no why. *History of the Human Sciences, 17,* 211–251.

Rotter, J. B. (1954). *Social learning and clinical psychology.* New York: Prentice Hall.

Routh, D. K. (2013). Clinical psychology. In D. K. Freedheim & I. B. Weiner (Eds.), *Handbook of psychology, Vol. 1: History of psychology* (2nd ed., pp. 377–396). Hoboken, NJ: John Wiley & Sons Inc.

Royce, J. (1898). The new psychology and the consulting psychologist. *Forum, 26,* 80–96.

Rozin, P. (2001). Social psychology and science: Some lessons from Solomon Asch. *Personality and Social Psychology Review, 5,* 2–14.

Rubenstein, J., & Slife, B. (1988). *Taking sides: Clashing views on controversial psychological issues* (5th ed.). Guilford, CT: Dushkin.

Rubenstein, R. E. (2003). *Aristotle's children: How Christians, Muslims, and Jews rediscovered ancient wisdom and illuminated the Dark Ages.* New York: Harcourt.

Rubins, J. L. (1978). *Karen Horney: Gentle rebel of psychoanalysis.* New York: Dial.

Rudnytsky, P. L. (2008). Inventing Freud. *The American Journal of Psychoanalysis, 68,* 117–127.

Rudnytsky, P. L. (2011). *Rescuing psychoanalysis from Freud and other essays in revision; the history of psychoanalysis series.* London: Kamac Books.

Ruggiero, G. (2007). *Machiavelli in love: Sex, self, and society in the Italian Renaissance.* Baltimore, MD: Johns Hopkins University Press.

Rush, B. (1806). *Essays, literary, moral, and philosophical* (2nd ed.). Philadelphia: Thomas and William Bradford.

Rush, B. (1818). *Medical inquiries and observations upon the diseases of the mind* (2nd ed.). Philadelphia: John Richardson. (Original work published 1812)

Russell, B. (1959). *Wisdom of the west.* New York: Crescent Books.

Russell, J. B. (1980). *A history of witchcraft.* London: Thames and Hudson.

Russell, N. J. C. (2011). Milgram's obedience to authority experiments: Origins and early evolution. *British Journal of Social Psychology, 50,* 140–162.

Rutherford, A. (2000). Radical behaviorism and psychology's public: B. F. Skinner in the popular press, 1934–1990. *History of Psychology, 3,* 371–395.

Rutherford, A. (2003). B. F. Skinner's technology of behavior in American life: From consumer culture to counterculture. *Journal of the History of the Behavioral Sciences, 29,* 1–23.

Rutherford, A. (2006). Mother of behavior therapy and beyond: Mary Cover Jones and the study of the "whole child." In D. A. Dewsbury, L. T. Benjamin, & M. Wertheimer (Eds.), *Portraits of pioneers in psychology* (Vol. 6, pp. 189–204). Washington, DC: American Psychological Association.

Rutherford, A. (2009). *Beyond the box: B. F. Skinner's technology of behavior from laboratory to life, 1950s-1970s.* Toronto: University of Toronto Press.

Ryback, D. (2012). Humanism and behaviorism. In L. L'Abate (Ed.), *Paradigms in theory construction* (pp. 297–315). New York: Springer Science + Business Media.

Rychlak, J. F. (1988). *The psychology of rigorous humanism* (2nd ed.). New York: New York University Press.

Rychlak, J. F. (1991). *Artificial intelligence and human reason: A teleological critique.* New York: Columbia University Press.

Rychlak, J. F. (1994). *Logical learning theory: A human teleology and its empirical support.* Lincoln: University of Nebraska Press.

Rychlak, J. F. (1998). How Boulder biases have limited possible theoretical contributions to psychotherapy. *Clinical Psychology: Science and Practice, 5,* 233–241.

Rychlak, J. F. (2000). A psychotherapist's lessons from the philosophy of science. *American Psychologist, 55,* 1126–1132.

Rychlak, J. F. (2005). In search and proof of human beings, not machines. *Journal of Personality Assessment, 85,* 239–256.

Rychlak, J. F., & Rychlak, R. J. (1990). The insanity defense and the question of human agency. *New Ideas in Psychology, 8,* 3–24.

Sahakian, W. S. (Ed.). (1968). *History of psychology: A sourcebook in systematic psychology.* Itasca, IL: F. E. Peacock.

Sahakian, W. S., & Sahakian, M. L. (1975). *John Locke.* Boston: Twayne.

Sajadi, M. M., Sajadi, M. M., & Tabatabaie, S. M. (2011). The history of facial palsy and spasm: Hippocrates to Razi. *Neurology, 77,* 174–178.

Sakuma, A. (1999). Gestalt psychology in Japan. *Japanese Psychological Review, 42,* 326–345.

Salkovskis, P. (1998). Changing the face of psycho-therapy and common sense: Joseph Wolpe, 20 April 1915–4 December 1997. *Behavioural and Cognitive Psychotherapy, 26,* 189–191.

Salzinger, K. (1994). On Watson. In J. T. Todd & E. K. Morris (Eds.), *Modern perspectives on John B. Watson and classical behaviorism* (pp. 151–158). Westport, CT: Greenwood Press.

Samelson, F. (1985). Organizing for the kingdom of behavior: Academic battles and organizational policies in the twenties. *Journal of the History of Behavioral Sciences, 21,* 33–47.

Samelson, F. (1994). John B. Watson in 1913: Rhetoric and practice. In J. T. Todd & E. K. Morris (Eds.), *Modern perspectives on John B. Watson and classical behaviorism* (pp. 3–18). Westport, CT: Greenwood Press.

Samoilov, V. O. (2007). Ivan Petrovich Pavlov (1849-1936) (V. Zayas, Trans.). *Journal of the History of the Neurosciences, 16,* 74–89.

Samuels, A. (1994). The professionalization of Carl G. Jung's analytical psychology clubs. *Journal of the History of the Behavioral Sciences, 30,* 138–147.

Sargant, W. (1957). *Battle for the mind.* New York: Harper & Row.

Sartre, J. P. (1965). Reply to Albert Camus. In J. P. Sartre (Ed.) & B. Eisler (Trans.), *Situations* (pp. 69–106). New York: George Braziller.

Sawyer, T. F. (2000). Francis Cecil Sumner: His views and influence on African American higher education. *History of Psychology, 3,* 122–141.

Sayers, J. (1991). *Mothers of psychoanalysis.* New York: Norton.

Scarborough, E. (2000). Margaret Floy Washburn. In A. Kazdin (Ed.), *Encyclopedia of psychology* (Vol. 8, pp. 230–232). Washington, DC: American Psychological Association, and New York: Oxford University Press.

Scarborough, E., & Furumoto, L. (1987). *Untold lives: The first generation of American women psychologists.* New York: Columbia University Press.

Scherer, L. B. (1975). *Slavery and the churches in early America: 1619–1819.* Grand Rapids, MI: Eerdmans.

Scherez, G. (1976). Niels Stensen also known as Nicolaus Steno. In C. Gillispie (Ed.), *Dictionary of scientific biography* (Vol. 13, pp. 30–35). New York: Scribner.

Schioldann, J. (2009). *History of the introduction of lithium into medicine and psychiatry: Birth of modern psychopharmacology 1949.* Adelaide: Adelaide Academic Press.

Schliemann, H. (1968). *Troy and its remains.* New York: Benjamin Blom. (Original work published 1875)

Schlinger, H. D. (2008). The long good-bye: Why B. F. Skinner's *Verbal Behavior* is alive and well on the 50th anniversary of its publication. *The Psychological Record, 58,* 329–337.

Schlosberg, H. (1954). Walter S. Hunter: Pioneer objectivist in psychology. *Science, 120,* 441–442.

Schlosser, M. E. (2012). Causally efficacious intentions and the sense of agency: In defense of real mental causation. *Journal of Theoretical and Philosophical Psychology, 32,* 135–160.

Schmid, P. F. (2013). Whence the evil? A personalistic and dialogic perspective. In A. C. Bohard, B. S. Held, E. Mendelowitz, & K. J. Schneider (Eds.), *Humanity's dark side: Evil, destructive experience, and psychotherapy* (pp. 35–55). Washington, DC: American Psychological Association.

Schmied, L. A., Steinberg, H., & Sykes, E. A. B. (2006). Psychopharmacology's debt to experimental psychology. *History of Psychology, 9,* 144–157.

Schmitt, R. (1967). Phenomenology. In P. Edwards (Ed.), *The encyclopedia of philosophy* (Vol. 6, pp. 135–151). New York: Macmillan and Free Press.

Schneck, J. M. (1978). Benjamin Rush and animal magnetism, 1789 and 1812. *International Journal of Clinical and Experimental Hypnosis, 26,* 9–14.

Schneider, D. J. (1991). Social cognition. *Annual Review of Psychology, 42,* 527–561.

Schneider, K. J., Bugental, J. F. T., & Pierson, J. F. (Eds.). (2001). *The handbook of humanistic psychology: Leading edges in theory, research, and practice.* Thousand Oaks, CA: Sage.

Schneider, W. H. (1992). After Binet: French intelligence testing, 1900–1950. *Journal of the History of the Behavioral Sciences, 28,* 111–132.

Schrag, C. O. (1982). Either/or. In F. N. Magill (Ed.), *World philosophy* (Vol. 3, pp. 1294–1306). Englewood Cliffs, NJ: Salem Press.

Schuchhardt, K. (1971). *Schliemann's excavations: An archaeological and historical study* (E. Sellers, Trans.). New York: Benjamin Blom. (Original work published 1891)

Schulte, H. (1938). An approach to a Gestalt theory of paranoic phenomena. In W. D. Ellis (Ed.), *A source book of Gestalt psychology* (pp. 362–369). London: Kegan Paul, Trench, Trubner & Company.

Schunk, D. H. (2012). Social cognitive theory. In K. R. Harris, S. Graham, T. Urdan, C. B. McCormick, G. M. Sinatra, & J. Sweller (Eds.), *APA educational psychology handbook, Vol 1: Theories, constructs, and critical issues* (pp. 101–123). Washington, DC: American Psychological Association.

Scobie, A., & Taylor, A. J. W. (1975). Perversions ancient and modern: 1. Agalmatophilia, the statue syndrome. *Journal of the History of the Behavioral Sciences, 11,* 49–54.

Scott, J., & Freeman, A. (2010). Beck's cognitive therapy. In N. Kazantzis, M. A. Reinecke, & A. Freeman (Eds.), *Cognitive and behavioral theories in clinical practice* (pp. 28–75). New York: Guilford Press.

Scott, W. D. (1904). The psychology of advertising. *Atlantic Monthly, 93,* 29–36.

Scott, W. D. (1921). In memory of Wilhelm Wundt. *Psychological Review, 28,* 183.

Searle, J. R. (1992). *The rediscovery of the mind.* Cambridge, MA: MIT Press.

Searle, J. R. (1995a, November 2). The mystery of consciousness. *New York Review*, pp. 60–66.

Searle, J. R. (1995b, November 16). The mystery of consciousness: Part II. *New York Review*, pp. 54–61.

Seashore, C. E. (1911). The consulting psychologist. *Popular Science Monthly, 78,* 283–290.

Seeber, J. J. (2000). Meaning in long-term care settings: Viktor Frankl's contribution to gerontology. *Journal of Religious Gerontology, 11,* 141–157.

Seeskin, K. (2008). Plato and the origin of mental health. *International Journal of Psychiatry and Law, 31,* 487–494.

Segal, Z. V., Williams, J. M. G., & Teasdale, J. D. (2001). *Mindfulness-based cognitive therapy for depression: A new approach to preventing relapse.* New York: Guilford.

Seidel, G. E., Jr., & Elsden, R. P. (1989). *Embryo transfer in dairy cattle.* Milwaukee, WI: Hoard & Sons.

Seligman, M. E. P., & Csikszentmihalyi, M. (2000). Positive psychology: An introduction. *American Psychologist, 55,* 5–14.

Serlin, I. (2011). The history and future of humanistic psychology. *Journal of Humanistic Psychology, 51,* 428–431.

Seward, G. H., & Seward, J. P. (1968). Robert S. Woodworth. In D. L. Sills (Ed.), *International encyclopedia of the social sciences* (Vol. 19, pp. 561–564). New York: Macmillan and Free Press.

Sexton, V. S., & Misiak, H. K. (Eds.). (1971). *Historical perspectives in psychology: Readings.* Monterey, CA: Brooks/Cole.

Sexton, V. S., & Misiak, H. K. (Eds.). (1976). *Psychology around the world.* Monterey, CA: Brooks/Cole.

Seymore, M. (2001). *Mary Shelley.* New York: Grove Press.

Shakespeare, W. (1964). *Measure for measure* (E. Leisi, Ed.). New York: Hafner. (Original work published 1604–1605)

Shakow, D. (1942). The training of the clinical psychologist. *Journal of Consulting Psychology, 6,* 277–288.

Shamdasani, S. (Ed.). (2009). *The red book: Liber novus.* New York: W. W. Norton.

Sharpless, B. (2012). Kierkegaard's Conception of Psychology. *Journal of Theoretical and Philosophical Psychology.* Advance online publication.

Shaw, R., & Colimore, K. (1988). Humanistic psychology as an ideology: An analysis of Maslow's contradictions. *Journal of Humanistic Psychology, 28,* 51–74.

Shea, W. R. (1986). Galileo and the church. In D. C. Lindberg & R. L. Numbers (Eds.), *God and nature: Historical essays on the encounter between Christianity and science* (pp. 114–135). Berkeley: University of California Press.

Sheffield, F. D. (1959). Edwin Ray Guthrie: 1886–1959. *American Journal of Psychology, 72,* 642–650.

Sheldon, K. M., & Kasser, T. (2001). Goals, congruence, and positive well-being: New empirical support for humanistic theories. *Journal of Humanistic Psychology, 41,* 30–50.

Sheldon, K. M., & King, L. (2001). Why positive psychology is necessary. *American Psychologist, 56,* 216–217.

Shereshevskii, A. M. (1994). The mystery of the death of V. M. Bekhterev. *Journal of Russian and East European Psychiatry, 27,* 103–113.

Sherif, M. (1936). *The psychology of social norms.* New York: Harper.

Sherif, M., Harvey, O. J., White, B. J., Hood, W. R., & Sherif, C. W. (1961). *Intergroup conflict and cooperation: The Robbers Cave experiment* (2nd ed.). Norman, OK: University Book Exchange.

Sherif, M., & Sherif, C. W. (1953). *Groups in harmony and tension: An integration of studies of intergroup relations.* Oxford: Harper & Brothers.

Shermer, M. (2002). *Why people believe weird things: Pseudoscience, superstition, and other confusions of our time.* New York: Henry Holt.

Shields, S. A. (1975). Ms. Pilgrim's progress: The contributions of Leta Stetter Hollingworth to the psychology of women. *American Psychologist, 30,* 852–857.

Shields, S. A. (1991). Leta Stetter Hollingworth: "Literature of opinion" and the study of individual differences. In G. A. Kimble, M. Wertheimer, & C. White (Eds.), *Portraits of pioneers in psychology* (Vol. 1, pp. 243–255). Washington, DC: American Psychological Association.

Shields, S. A., & Bhatia, S. (2009). Darwin on race, gender, and culture. *American Psychologist, 64,* 111–119.

Shoja, M. M., & Tubbs, R. S. (2007). The disorder of love in the canon of Avicenna (A.D. 980-1037). *The American Journal of Psychiatry, 164,* 228–229.

Shook, J. R. (1995). Wilhelm Wundt's contribution to John Dewey's functional psychology. *Journal of the History of the Behavioral Sciences, 31,* 347–369.

Shorter, E. (2009). The history of lithium therapy. *Bipolar Disorders, 11,* 4–9.

Shorto, R. (2008). *Descartes' Bones: A skeletal history of the conflict between faith and reason.* New York: Doubleday.

Silverman, L. H. (1976). Psychoanalytic theory: "The reports of my death are greatly exaggerated." *American Psychologist, 31,* 621–637.

Silverman, S. (2010). The death of Socrates: A holistic re-examination. *Omega, 6,* 71–84.

Simanek, D. E. (n.d.). *The dangers of analogies.* Retrieved December 14, 2006, from www. lhup. edu/~DSIMANEK/ scenario/analogy.htm

Simon, B. (1972). Models of mind and mental illness in ancient Greece: II. The Platonic Model. Section 1. *Journal of the History of the Behavioral Sciences, 8,* 389–404.

Simon, B., & Weiner, H. (1966). Models of mind and mental illness in ancient Greece: The Homeric model of mind. *Journal of the History of the Behavioral Sciences, 2,* 303–314.

Simon, L. (1998). *Genuine reality: A life of William James.* New York: Harcourt Brace.

Sizer, N., & Drayton, H. S. (1892). *Heads and faces and how to study them.* New York: Fowler & Wells.

Skinner, B. F. (1938). *The behavior of organisms: An experimental analysis.* New York: Appleton-Century.

Skinner, B. F. (1948). *Walden two.* New York: Macmillan.

Skinner, B. F. (1953). *Science and human behavior.* New York: Macmillan.

Skinner, B. F. (1956). A case study in scientific method. *American Psychologist, 11,* 221–233.

Skinner, B. F. (1957). *Verbal behavior.* New York: Appleton-Century-Crofts.

Skinner, B. F. (1958). Teaching machines. *Science, 128,* 969–977.

Skinner, B. F. (1960). Pigeons in a pelican. *American Psychologist, 15,* 28–37.

Skinner, B. F. (1963). Behaviorism at fifty. *Science, 140,* 951–958.

Skinner, B. F. (1967). B. F. Skinner. In E. G. Boring & G. Lindzey (Eds.), *A history of psychology in autobiography* (Vol. 5, pp. 387–413). New York: Appleton-Century-Crofts.

Skinner, B. F. (1968). *The technology of teaching.* Englewood Cliffs, NJ: Prentice Hall.

Skinner, B. F. (1971). *Beyond freedom and dignity.* New York: Knopf.

Skinner, B. F. (1972). Humanism and behaviorism. *The Humanist, 32*(4), 18–20.

Skinner, B. F. (1974). *About behaviorism.* New York: Knopf.

Skinner, B. F. (1976). *Particulars of my life.* New York: Knopf.

Skinner, B. F. (1977). Why I am not a cognitive psychologist. *Behaviorism, 5,* 1–10.

Skinner, B. F. (1979). *The shaping of a behaviorist.* New York: Knopf.

Skinner, B. F. (1983a). *A matter of consequences.* New York: Knopf.

Skinner, B. F. (1983b). Origins of a behaviorist. *Psychology Today, 17,* 22–23.

Skinner, B. F. (1984). The shame of American education. *American Psychologist, 39,* 947–954.

Skinner, B. F. (1987a). Controversy? In S. Modgil & C. Modgil (Eds.), *B. F. Skinner: Consensus and controversy* (pp. 15–18). New York: Falmer.

Skinner, B. F. (1987b). *Upon further reflection.* Englewood Cliffs, NJ: Prentice Hall.

Skinner, B. F. (1987c). Whatever happened to psychology as the science of behavior? *American Psychologist, 42,* 780–786.

Skinner, B. F. (1989). The origins of cognitive thought. *American Psychologist, 44,* 13–18.

Skinner, B. F. (1990). Can psychology be a science of mind? *American Psychologist, 45,* 1206–1210.

Skinner, B. F., & Vaughn, M. E. (1983). *Enjoy old age: Living fully in your later years.* New York: Warner.

Skolnick, M. (2008). On identity as multiple and basic assumption. In G. M. Saiger, S. Rubenfeld, & M. D. Dluhy (Eds.), *Windows into today's group therapy* (pp. 45–53). New York: Routledge.

Skues, R. (2012). Clark revisited: Reappraising Freud in America. In J. Burnham (Ed.), *After Freud left: A century of psychoanalysis in America* (pp. 49–84). Chicago, IL: University of Chicago Press.

Slife, B. D. (2005). The Kant of psychology: Joseph Rychlak and the bridge to postmodern psychology. *Journal of Constructivist Psychology, 18,* 297–306.

Slife, B. D., & Williams, R. N. (1997). Toward a theoretical psychology: Should a subdiscipline be formally recognized? *American Psychologist, 52,* 117–129.

Slife, B. D., Yanchar, S. C., & Williams, B. (1999). Concepts of determinism in radical behaviorism: A taxonomy. *Behavior & Philosophy, 27,* 75–96.

Smith, B. (2009). Toward a realistic science of environments. *Ecological Psychology, 21,* 121–130.

Smith, C. U. M. (1987). David Hartley's Newtonian neuropsychology. *Journal of the History of the Behavioral Sciences, 23,* 123–136.

Smith, C. U. M. (2010a). The triune brain in antiquity: Plato, Aristotle, Erasistratus. *Journal of the History of the Neurosciences, 19,* 1–14.

Smith, C. U. M. (2010b). Darwin's unsolved problem: The place of consciousness in an evolutionary world. *Journal of the History of the Neurosciences, 19,* 105–120.

Smith, M. B. (1990). Humanistic psychology. *Journal of Humanistic Psychology, 33,* 6–21.

Smith, N. W. (1971). Aristotle's dynamic approach to sensing and some current implications. *Journal of the History of the Behavioral Sciences, 7,* 375–377.

Smith, N. W. (1974). The ancient background to Greek psychology and some implications for today. *Psychological Record, 24,* 309–324.

Smith, R. (1988). Does the history of psychology have a subject? *History of the Human Sciences, 1,* 147–177.

Soble, A. (2009). A history of erotic philosophy. *Journal of Sex Research, 46,* 104–120.

Sokal, M. M. (1980a). Graduate study with Wundt: Two eyewitness accounts. In W. G. Bringmann & R. D. Tweney (Eds.), *Wundt studies: A centennial collection* (pp. 210–225). Toronto, Canada: C. J. Hogrefe.

Sokal, M. M. (1980b). Science and James McKeen Cattell, 1894–1945. *Science, 209,* 43–52.

Sokal, M. M. (1984). The Gestalt psychologists in behaviorist America. *American Historical Review, 89,* 1240–1263.

Sokal, M. M. (Ed.). (1987). *Psychological testing and American society: 1890–1930.* New Brunswick, NJ: Rutgers University Press.

Sokal, M. M. (1990). G. Stanley Hall and the institutional character of psychology at Clark, 1889–1920. *Journal of the History of the Behavioral Sciences, 26,* 114–124.

Sokal, M. M. (1992). Origins and early years of the American Psychological Association. *American Psychologist, 47,* 111–121.

Sokal, M. M. (1995). Stargazing: James McKeen Cattell, "American Men of Science," and the reward structure of the American scientific community, 1906–1944. In F. Kessel (Ed.), *Psychology, science, and human affairs: Essays in honor of William Bevan* (pp. 64–86). Boulder, CO: Westview Press.

Sokal, M. M. (1997). Baldwin, Cattell and the Psychological Review: A collaboration and its discontents. *History of the Human Sciences, 10,* 57–89.

Sokal, M. M. (2001). Practical phrenology as psychological counseling in the 19th-century United States. In C. D. Green & M. Shore (Eds.), *The transformation of psychology: Influences of 19th-century philosophy, technology, and natural science* (pp. 21–44). Washington, DC: American Psychological Association.

Sokal, M. M. (2006). James McKeen Cattell: Achievement and alienation. In D. A. Dewsbury, L. T. Benjamin, & M. Wertheimer (Eds.), *Portraits of pioneers in psychology* (Vol. 6, pp. 19–35). Washington, DC: American Psychological Association.

Sokal, M. M. (2009). James McKeen Cattell, Nicholas Murray Butler, and academic freedom at Columbian University 1902-1923. *History of Psychology, 12,* 87–122.

Sokal, M. M. (2011). Cattell, Columbia, and academic freedom: Rarely used sources enrich analyses of this significant episode.*History of Psychology, 14,* 100–104.

Sokal, M. M., & Rafail, P. A. (1982). *A guide to manuscript collections in the history of psychology and related areas.* Millwood, NY: Kraus International.

Soles, D. E. (1985). Locke's empiricism and the postulation of unobservables. *Journal of the History of Philosophy, 23,* 339–369.

Soltis, J. F. (1971). John Dewey. In L. C. Deighton (Ed.), *The encyclopedia of education* (Vol. 3, pp. 81–85). New York: Macmillan.

Sommer, A. (2012). Psychical research and the origins of American psychology: Hugo Münsterberg, William James and Eusapia Palladino. *History of the Human Sciences, 25,* 23–44.

Sourkes, T. L. (1998). An element of thought: Phosphorus and mental philosophy in the nineteenth century. *Journal of the History of the Neurosciences, 7,* 108–124.

Southall, J. P. C. (Ed.). (1962). *Helmholtz's treatise on physiological optics.* New York: Dover.

Southard, M. M. (1927). *The attitude of Jesus toward women.* New York: George H. Doran.

Spalding, D. A. (1873, February). Instinct. With original observations on young animals. *Macmillan's Magazine, 27,* 282–293.

Spence, K. W. (1937). The differential response in animals to stimuli varying within a single dimension. *Psychological Review, 44,* 430–444.

Spence, K. W. (1952). Clark Leonard Hull: 1884–1952. *American Journal of Psychology, 65,* 639–646.

Spencer, H. (1873). *Study of sociology.* New York: D. Appleton & Co.

Sperry, R. W. (1961). Cerebral organization and behavior. *Science, 133,* 1749–1757.

Spillmann, J., & Spillmann, L. (1993). The rise and fall of Hugo Münsterberg. *Journal of the History of the Behavioral Sciences, 29,* 322–338.

Sporer, S. L. (2006). The science of eyewitness testimony has come of age. *Psychological Science in the Public Interest, 7,* i–ii.

Sprengnether, M. (1990). *The spectral mother: Freud, feminism, and psychoanalysis.* Ithaca, NY: Cornell University Press.

Springer, S. P., & Deutsch, G. (1985). *Left brain, right brain* (Rev. ed.). New York: Freeman.

Sprung, H., & Sprung, L. (1996). Carl Stumpf (1848–1936), a general psychologist and methodologist, and a case study of a cross-cultural scientific transition process. In W. Battmann & S. Dutke (Eds.), *Processes of the molar regulation of behavior* (pp. 327–342). Lengerich, Germany: Pabst Science Publishers.

Sprung, L., & Sprung, H. (2000). George Elias Müller and the beginnings of modern psychology. In G. A. Kimble & M. Wertheimer (Eds.), *Portraits of pioneers in psychology* (Vol. 4, pp. 71–91). Washington, DC: American Psychological Association.

Staats, A. W. (1989). Unificationism: Philosophy for the modern disunited science of psychology. *Philosophical Psychology, 2,* 143–164.

Staats, A. W. (1999). Unifying psychology requires new infrastructure, theory, method, and a research agenda. *Review of General Psychology, 3,* 3–13.

Staats, A. W. (2005). A road to and philosophy of unification. In R. J. Sternberg (Ed.), *Unity in psychology: Possibility or pipedream?* (pp. 159–178). Washington, DC: American Psychological Associaiton.

Stace, W. T. (1962). *A critical history of Greek philosophy.* New York: St. Martin's Press.

Stahnisch, F. W. (2008). Instrument transfer as knowledge transfer in neurophysiology: François Magendie's (1783-1855) early attempts to measure cerebrospinal fluid pressure. *Journal of the History of the Neurosciences, 17,* 72–99.

Steiner, G. (2006). Descartes, Christianity, and contemporary speciesism. In P. Waldau & K. Patton (Eds.), *A communion of subjects: Animals in religion, science, and ethics* (pp. 117–131). New York: Columbia University Press.

Stephen, L. (1993). Mrs. Mary Wollstonecraft Godwin. In L. Stephen & S. Lee (Eds.), *The dictionary of national biography* (Vol. 8, pp. 60–62). New York: Oxford University Press.

Stephen, L., & Lee, S. (Eds.). (1960). *Dictionary of national biography* (Vol. 9). London: Oxford University Press.

Stephens, J. (1975). *Francis Bacon and the style of science.* Chicago: University of Chicago Press.

Stern, C. (1949). *Children discover arithmetic: An introduction to structural arithmetic.* New York: Harper.

Sternberg, R. J. (Ed.). (2005). *Unity in psychology: Possibility or pipedream?* Washington, DC: American Psychological Associaiton.

Steudel, J. (1974). Johannes Peter Müller. In C. C. Gillispie (Ed.), *Dictionary of scientific biography* (Vol. 9, pp. 567–584). New York: Scribner.

Stevens, G., & Gardner, S. (Eds.). (1982). *The women of psychology: Pioneers and innovators.* Cambridge, MA: Schenkman.

Stevens, S. S. (1951). Mathematics, measurement, and psychophysics. In S. S. Stevens (Ed.), *Handbook of experimental psychology* (pp. 1–49). New York: Wiley.

Stewart, D. (1802). *Elements of the philosophy of the human mind.* London: T. Cadell Jun. and W. Davies in the Strand, and W. Creech in Edinburgh. (Original work published 1792)

Stewart, M. (2007). *The courtier and the heretic: Leibniz, Spinoza, and the fate of God in the modern world*. New York: Norton.

Still, A., & Dryden, W. (2012). *The historical and philosophical context of rational psychotherapy: The legacy of Epictetus*. London, England: Karnac Books.

Stocking, G. W. (1965). On the limits of "presentism" and "historicism" in the historiography of the behavioral sciences [editorial]. *Journal of the History of the Behavioral Sciences, 1*, 211–218.

Stolorow, R. D., Atwood, G. E., & Orange, D. M. (2010). Heidegger's Nazism and the hypostatization of being. *International Journal of Psychoanalytic Self Psychology, 5*, 429–450.

Stone, M. H. (2011). The meaning of life and Adler's use of fictions. *The Journal of Individual Psychology, 67*, 13–30.

Strachey, J. (Ed.). (1953–1974). *The standard edition of the complete psychological works of Sigmund Freud*. London: Hogarth Press.

Strandh, S. (1979). *A history of the machine*. New York: A. W. Publishers.

Stratton, G. M. (1917). *Theophrastus and the Greek physiological psychology before Aristotle*. New York: Macmillan.

Street, W. R. (2006). Foundations of National Security Psychology. In A. D. Mangelsdorff (Ed.), *Psychology in the service of national security* (pp. 29–40). Washington, DC: American Psychological Association.

Stricker, G. (1975). On professional schools and professional degrees. *American Psychologist, 30*, 1062–1066.

Stromberg, W. H. (1989). Helmholtz and Zoellner: Nineteenth century empiricism, spiritism, and the theory of space perception. *Journal of the History of the Behavioral Sciences, 25*, 371–383.

Strong, E. K. (1955). Walter Dill Scott: 1869–1955. *American Journal of Psychology, 68*, 682–683.

Studebaker, C. A., & Penrod, S. D. (1997). Pretrial publicity: The media, the law, and common sense. *Psychology, Public Policy, and the Law, 2–3*, 428–460.

Stumpf, C. (1895). Herman von Helmholtz and the new psychology. *Psychological Review, 2*, 1–12.

Stumpf, C. (1930). Carl Stumpf. In C. Murchison (Ed.), *A history of psychology in autobiography* (Vol. 1, pp. 389–441). Worchester, MA: Clark University Press.

Stumpf, C. (2012). *The origins of music* (D. Trippett, Trans.). New York: Oxford University Press. (Original work published 1911)

Suibhne, S. M. (2009). "Wrestle to be the man philosophy wished to make you": Marcus Aurelius, reflective practitioner. *Reflective Practice, 10*, 429–436.

Suinn, R. M., & Weigel, R. G. (1975). *The innovative psychological therapies: Critical and creative contributions*. New York: Harper & Row.

Sukhodolsky, D. G., Tsytsarev, S. V., & Kassinove, H. (1995). Behavior therapy in Russia. *Journal of Behavior Therapy and Experimental Psychiatry, 26*, 83–91.

Sullivan, H. S. (1953). *The interpersonal theory of psychiatry*. New York: Norton.

Sulloway, F. J. (1979). *Freud, biologist of the mind: Beyond psychoanalytic legend*. New York: Basic Books.

Sully, J. (1886). Development of the moral faculty. *Popular Science Monthly, 29*, 23–33.

Sully, J. (1894, 1895, 1896). Studies of childhood. *Popular Science Monthly, 45*, 323–330, 577–588, 733–742; *46*, 186–197, 348–363, 433–446, 781–792; *47*, 1–11, 340–353, 648–664, 808–817; *48*, 105–113, 166–180, 381–395.

Summers, M. (1965). *The geography of witchcraft*. New York: University Books.

Summers, M. (Trans.). (1971). *The malleus maleficarum of Heinrich Kramer & Jacob Sprenger*. New York: Dover.

Sussman, E. J. (1962). Franz Brentano—Much alive, though dead. *American Psychologist, 17*, 504–506.

Swammerdam, J. (1758). *The book of nature* (T. Flloyd, Trans.). London: C. G. Seyffert.

Swazey, J. P. (1975). Charles Scott Sherrington. In C. C. Gillispi (Ed.), *Dictionary of scientific biography* (Vol. 12, pp. 395–403). New York: Scribner.

Symonds, A. (1991). Gender issues and Horney theory. *American Journal of Psychoanalysis, 51*, 301–312.

Taine, H. A. (1876). Lingual development in babyhood. *Popular Science Monthly, 9*, 129–137.

Taylor, B. (2003). *Mary Wollstonecraft and the feminist imagination*. New York: Cambridge University Press.

Taylor, E. (2000). Psychotherapeutics and the problematic origins of clinical psychology in America. *American Psychologist, 55*, 1029–1033.

Taylor, E. (2010). William James on a phenomenological psychology of immediate experience: The true foundation for a science of consciousness? *History of the Human Sciences, 23*, 119–130.

Taylor, E. (2011). William James's radical empiricism: Did E. B. Holt get it right? In E. P. Charles (Ed.), *A new look at New Realism: The psychology and philosophy of E. B. Holt* (pp. 105–126). Piscataway, NJ: Transaction Publishers.

Taylor, G. R. (1983). *The great evolution mystery*. New York: Harper & Row.

Taylor, M. C. (1987). Søren Kierkegaard. In M. Eliade (Ed.), *The encyclopedia of religion* (Vol. 8, pp. 298–301). New York: Macmillan.

Taylor, R. (1967a). Causation. In P. Edwards (Ed.), *The encyclopedia of philosophy* (pp. 56–66). New York: Macmillan.

Taylor, R. (1967b). Determinism. In P. Edwards (Ed.), *The encyclopedia of philosophy* (pp. 359–373). New York: Macmillan.

Teilhard de Chardin. (1961). *The phenomenon of man* (B. Wall, Trans.). New York: Harper & Row.

Terman, L. M. (1917). The intelligence quotient of Francis Galton in childhood. *American Journal of Psychology, 28*, 209–215.

Thielman, S. B., & Melges, F. T. (1986). Julia Rush's diary: Coping with loss in the early nineteenth century. *American Journal of Psychiatry, 143*, 1144–1148.

Thomas, R. K. (1997). Correcting some Pavloviana regarding "Pavlov's bell" and Pavlov's "mugging." *American Journal of Psychology, 110*, 115–125.

Thomas, R. K. (2001). *Lloyd Morgan's canon: A history of misinterpretation.* Retrieved March 24, 2007, from http://htpprints.yorku.ca/archive/00000017/00/MCWeb. htm

Thorndike, E. L. (1905). Measurements of twins. *Archives of Philosophy, Psychology, and Scientific Method, 1,* 1–64.

Thorndike, E. L. (1920). The psychology of the half-educated man. *Harper's Magazine, 140,* 666–670.

Thorndike, E. L. (1922). The psychology of labor. *Harper's Magazine, 144,* 799–806.

Thorndike, E. L. (1924). Mental discipline in high schools. *Journal of Educational Psychology, 15,* 1–22, 83–98.

Thorndike, E. L. (1936). The psychology of the profit motive. *Harper's Magazine, 173,* 431–437.

Thorndike, E. L., & Woodworth, R. S. (1901). The influence of improvement in one mental function upon the efficiency of other functions. *Psychological Review, 8,* 247–261, 384–395, 553–564.

Thorne, J. O. (Ed.). (1969). *Chambers' biographical dictionary.* New York: St. Martin's Press.

Thornhill, R., & Adcock, J. (1983). *The evolution of insect mating systems.* Cambridge, MA: Harvard University Press.

Thurston, H. (1994). *Early astronomy.* New York: Springer-Verlag.

Tigiripalli, K. K., & Kadarla, L. K. (2009). Religion and human rights: A historical and contemporary assessment. In A. Sharma (Ed.), *The world's religions after September 11, Vol 2: Religion and human rights* (pp. 27–35). Westport, CT: Praeger Publishers.

Tilman, R., & Knapp, T. (1999). John Dewey's unknown critique of marginal utility doctrine: Instrumentalism, motivation, and values. *Journal of the History of the Behavioral Sciences, 35,* 391–408.

Tinker, M. A. (1980). Wundt's doctorate students and their theses, 1875–1920. In W. G. Bringmann & R. D. Tweney (Eds.), *Wundt studies. A centennial collection* (pp. 269–272). Toronto, Canada: C. J. Hogrefe.

Titchener, E. B. (1892). The Leipsig school of experimental psychology. *Mind, 1* (new series), 206–234.

Titchener, E. B. (1896). *An outline of psychology.* New York: Macmillan.

Titchener, E. B. (1898). A psychology laboratory. *Mind, 7,* 311–331.

Titchener, E. B. (1910). *A textbook of psychology.* New York: Macmillan.

Titchener, E. B. (1921). Wilhelm Wundt. *American Journal of Psychology, 32,* 61–177.

Toates, F. (2009). *Burrhus F. Skinner: Shaper of behaviour.* London: Palgrave Macmillan.

Toccafondi, F. (2009). Stumpf and Gestalt psychology: Relations and differences. *Gestalt Theory, 31,* 191–211.

Todman, D. (2008). Epilepsy in the Graeco-Roman world: Hippocratic medicine and Asklepian Temple medicine compared. *Journal of the History of the Neurosciences, 17,* 435–441.

Tolman, E. C. (1922). A new formula for behaviorism. *Psychological Review, 22,* 44–53.

Tolman, E. C. (1932). *Purposive behavior in animals and men.* New York: Century.

Tolman, E. C. (1952). Edward Chace Tolman. In E. G. Boring, H. Werner, H. S. Langfeld, & R. M. Yerkes (Eds.), *A history of psychology in autobiography* (Vol. 4, pp. 323–339). New York: Russell and Russell.

Tolman, E. C., & Honzik, C. H. (1930). Introduction and removal of reward and maze performance in rats. *University of California Publications in Psychology, 4,* 257–273.

Tomlinson, S. (2005). *Head masters: Phrenology, secular education, and nineteenth-century social thought.* Tuscaloosa: University of Alabama Press.

Tong, B. R. (2003). Taoist mind–body resources for psychological health and healing. In S. G. Mijares (Ed.), *Modern psychology and ancient wisdom: Psychological healing practices from the world's religious traditions.* New York: Haworth Integrative Healing Press.

Tonn, J. C. (2003). *Mary P. Follett: Creating democracy, transforming management.* New Haven, CT: Yale University Press.

Torrey, C. W. (1867). Women's sphere in the church. *The Congregational Quarterly, 9,* 163–171.

Toth, K., & King, B. H. (2010). Intellectual disability (mental retardation). In M. K. Dulcan (Ed.), *Dulcan's textbook of child and adolescent psychiatry* (pp. 151–171). Arlington, VA: American Psychiatric Publishing.

Toulmin, S. (1972). *Human understanding* (Vol. 1). Princeton, NJ: Princeton University Press.

Tropp, L. R. (2006). Stigma and intergroup contact among members of minority and majority status groups. In S. Levin & C. van Laar (Eds.), *Stigma and group inequality: Social psychological perspectives* (pp. 171–191). Mahwah, NJ: Lawrence Erlbaum Associates Publishers.

Tsagareli, M. B. (2012). Ivane Tarkhnishvili (Tarchanoff): A major Georgian figure from the Russian physiological school. *Journal of the History of the Neurosciences, 21,* 393–408.

Tsanoff, R. A. (1964). *The great philosophers* (2nd ed.). New York: Harper & Row.

Tuke, D. H. (1872). *Illustrations of the influence of the mind upon the body in health and disease.* Philadelphia: Lindsay and Blakiston.

Tuke, D. H. (1878). *Insanity in ancient and modern life, with chapters on its prevention.* London: Macmillan.

Tuke, D. H. (1892). *A dictionary of psychological medicine.* London: J. & A. Churchill.

Turgeon, Y., & Whitaker, H. A. (2000). Pierre Jean Georges Cabanis (1757-1808): An early nineteenth century source for the concept of nervous energy in European behavioral neurosciences. *Brain and Cognition, 43,* 412–417.

Turner, R. S. (1972). Hermann von Helmholtz. In C. C. Gillispie (Ed.), *Dictionary of scientific biography* (Vol. 6, pp. 241–253). New York: Scribner.

Turner, R. S. (1977). Hermann von Helmholtz and the empiricist vision. *Journal of the History of the Behavioral Sciences, 13,* 48–58.

Turner, R. S. (1994). *In the eye's mind: Vision and the Helmholtz-Hering controversy*. Princeton, NJ: Princeton University Press.

Tye, M. (1995). *Ten problems of consciousness: A representational theory of the phenomenal mind*. Cambridge, MA: MIT Press.

Tylor, E. B. (1872). Quételet on the science of man. *Popular Science Monthly, 1*, 45–55.

Unamuno, M. (1972). *The tragic sense of life* (A. Kerrigan, Trans.). Princeton, NJ: Princeton University Press. (Original work published 1913)

U.S. Department of Justice. (1999). *Eyewitness evidence: A guide for law enforcement*. Washington, DC: Author.

Uttal, W. R. (2000). *The war between mentalism and behaviorism: On the accessibility of mental processes*. Mahwah, NJ: Erlbaum.

Uytman, J. D. (1967). William McDougall. In P. Edwards (Ed.), *The encyclopedia of philosophy* (Vol. 5, pp. 226–227). New York: Macmillan and Free Press.

Valenstein, E. S. (2005). *The war of the soups and the sparks: The discovery of neurotransmitters and the dispute over how nerves communicate*. New York: Columbia University Press.

Valsiner, J. (2007). Returning to the future of psychology: Cultural psychology and the study of mental self-regulatory processes.*Intellectica, 46–47*, 251–268.

Vande Kemp, H. (1992). G. Stanley Hall and the Clark School of Religious Psychology. *American Psychologist, 47*, 290–298.

van Drunen, P., & Jansz, J. (2004). Child-rearing and education. In J. Jansz & P. van Drunen (Eds.), *A social history of psychology* (pp. 45–92). Malden, MA: Blackwell.

van Leeuwen, C. (2007). Towards an interdisciplinary science of visual Gestalten. *Gestalt Theory, 29*, 213–222.

van Steenburgh, J. J., Fleck, J. I., Beeman, M., & Kounios, J. (2012). Insight. In K. J. Holyoak & R. G. Morrison (Eds.), *The Oxford handbook of thinking and reasoning* (pp. 475–491). New York: Oxford University Press.

Vartanian, A. (1967). Julien Offray de La Mettrie. In P. Edwards (Ed.), *The encyclopedia of philosophy* (Vol. 4, pp. 379–382). New York: Macmillan.

Vasquez, M. J. T. (2007). Lillian Evelyn Moller Gilbreth: The woman who "had it all." In E. A. Gavin, A. Clamar, & M. A. Siderits (Eds.), *Women of vision: Their psychology, circumstances, and success* (pp. 45–60). New York: Springer Publishing Co.

Vedral, V. (2006). Is the universe deterministic? *New Scientist, 192*, 52–55.

Veehoven, R. (2011). Can we get happier than we are? In I. Brdar (Ed.), *The human pursuit of well-being: A cultural approach* (pp. 3–14). New York: Springer Science + Business Media.

Verstegen, I. (2000). Gestalt psychology in Italy. *Journal of History of the Behavioral Sciences, 36*, 31–42.

Verstegen, I. (2005). *Arnheim, Gestalt and art: A psychological theory*. Vienna, Austria: Springer-Verlag, Vienna.

Verstegen, I. (2007). Rudolf Arnheim's contribution to Gestalt psychology. *Psychology of Aesthetics, Creativity, and the Arts, 1*, 8–15.

Vicedo, M. (2009). Mothers, machines, and morals: Harry Harlow's work on primate love from lab to legend. *Journal of the History of the Behavioral Sciences, 45*, 193–218.

Vicedo, M. (2010). The evolution of Harry Harlow: From the nature to the nurture of love. *History of Psychiatry, 21*, 190–205.

Vidal, F. (1987). Jean Piaget and the liberal protestant tradition. In M. G. Ash & W. R. Woodward (Eds.), *Psychology in twentieth-century thought and society* (pp. 271–294). Cambridge, MA: Cambridge University Press.

Vinchur, A. J., & Koppes, L. L. (2007). Early Contributors to the Science and Practice of Industrial Psychology. In L. L. Koppes (Ed.), *Historical perspectives in industrial and organizational psychology* (pp. 37–58). Mahwah, NJ: Lawrence Erlbaum Associates Publishers.

Viney, D. W. (1984). William James on free will and determinism. *The Journal of Mind and Behavior, 7*, 555–556.

Viney, D. W. (1997). William James on free will: The French connection. *History of Philosophy Quarterly, 14*, 29–52.

Viney, W. (1989). The cyclops and the twelve-eyed toad: William James and the unity–disunity problem in psychology. *American Psychologist, 44*, 1261–1265.

Viney, W. (1990). The tempering effect of determinism in the legal system: A response to Rychlak and Rychlak. *New Ideas in Psychology, 8*, 31–42.

Viney, W. (1991). Charles Hartshorne's philosophy and the psychology of sensation. In L. E. Hahn (Ed.), *The philosophy of Charles Hartshorne. The library of living philosophers* (Vol. 20, pp. 91–112). LaSalle, IL: Open Court.

Viney, W. (1992). A study of emotion in the context of radical empiricism. In M. E. Donnelly (Ed.), *Reinterpreting the legacy of William James* (pp. 243–250). Washington DC: American Psychological Association.

Viney, W. (1996a). Disunity in psychology and other sciences: The network or the block universe? *The Journal of Mind and Behavior, 17*, 31–43.

Viney, W. (1996b). Dorothea Dix: An intellectual conscience for psychology. In G. A. Kimble, C. A. Boneau, & M. Wertheimer (Eds.), *Portraits of pioneers in psychology* (Vol. 2, pp. 15–31). Washington, DC: American Psychological Association.

Viney, W. (2001). The radical empiricism of William James and philosophy of history. *History of Psychology, 4*, 211–227.

Viney, W. (2010, April). *The adaptive festures of historical consciousness*. Paper presented at the Rocky Mountain Psychological Association, Denver, CO.

Viney, W., & Bartsch, K. (1984). Dorothea Lynde Dix: Positive or negative influence on the development of treatment for the mentally ill. *The Social Science Journal, 21*, 71–82.

Viney, W., & Burlingame-Lee, L. (2003). Margaret Floy Washburn: A quest for the harmonies in the context of a rigorous scientific framework. In G. A. Kimble & M. Wertheimer (Eds.), *Portraits of pioneers in psychology* (Vol. 5, pp. 73–88). Washington, DC: American Psychological Association.

Viney, W., King, C. L., & King, D. B. (1992). William James on the advantages of a pluralistic psychology. In M. E. Donnelly (Ed.), *Reinterpreting the legacy of William James* (pp. 91–100). Washington, DC: American Psychological Association.

Viney, W., King, D. B., & Berndt, J. (1990). Animal research in psychology: Declining or thriving? *Journal of Comparative Psychology, 104,* 322–325.

Viney, W., Wertheimer, M., & Wertheimer, M. L. (1979). *History of psychology: A guide to information sources.* Detroit, MI: Gale Research.

Viney, W., & Woody, W. D. (1995). Psychogeny: A neglected dimension in teaching the mind–brain problem. *Teaching of Psychology, 22,* 173–177.

Virués-Ortega, J., Buela-Casal, G., Carrasco-Lazareno, M. T., Rivero-Dávila, P. D., & Quevedo-Blasco, R. (2011). A systematic archival inquiry on Juan Huarte de San Juan (1529-88). *History of the Human Sciences, 24,* 21–47.

Visible scientists. (1975, May). *Time, 105,* 44.

Vlastos, G. (1967). Zeno of Elea. In P. Edwards (Ed.), *Encyclopedia of philosophy* (Vol. 8, pp. 369–379). New York: Macmillan and Free Press.

Voeks, V. (1950). Formalization and clarification of a theory of learning. *Journal of Psychology, 30,* 341–362.

Voeks, V. (1968). Edwin R. Guthrie. In D. L. Sills (Ed.), *International encyclopedia of the social sciences* (Vol. 6, pp. 296–302). New York: Macmillan.

Voltaire. (1991). *Candide, or optimism* (2nd ed.). (R. M. Adams, Ed. & Trans.). New York: Norton. (Original work published 1759)

Voltaire, F. M. (1980). *Letters on England* (L. Tancock, Trans.). Harmondsworth, Middlesex, England: Penguin. (Original work published 1733)

Vrooman, J. R. (1970). *René Descartes: A biography.* New York: G. P. Putnam.

Wade, N. J. (1994). Hermann von Helmholtz (1821–1894). *Perception, 23,* 981–989.

Wade, N. J. (2000). Editorial: An upright man. *Perception, 29,* 253–257.

Wade, N. J. (2005). *Perception and illusion: Historical perspectives.* New York: Springer.

Wade, N. J. (2008). Guest editorial essay: Natural historians. *Perception, 37,* 479–482.

Wade, N. J. (2009). Guest editorial essay: Berkeley's essay. *Perception, 38,* 317–320.

Wade, N. J. (2010a). The Darwins and Wells: From revolution to evolution. *Journal of the History of the Neurosciences, 19,* 85–104.

Wade, N. J. (2010b). Guest editorial essay: Reid on perception. *Perception, 39,* 443–446.

Wade, N. J., & Finger, S. (2001). The eye as an optical instrument. From camera obscura to Helmholtz's perspective. *Perception, 30,* 1157–1177.

Wade, N. J., Sakurai, K., & Kyoba, J. (2007). Guest editorial essay: Whither Wundt? *Perception, 36,* 163–166.

Wagemans, J., Elder, J. H., Kubovy, M., Palmer, S. E., Peterson, M. A., Singh, M., et al. (2012a). A century of Gestalt psychology in visual perception: I. Perceptual grouping and figure-ground organization. *Psychological Bulletin, 138,* 1172–1217.

Wagemans, J., Feldman, J., Gepshtein, S., Kimchi, R., Pomerantz, J. R., van der Helm, P. A., et al. (2012b). A century of Gestalt psychology in visual perception: II. Conceptual and theoretical foundations. *Psychological Bulletin, 138,* 1218–1252.

Wagner, E. J. (2006). *The science of Sherlock Holmes. From Baskerville Hall to the valley of fear, the real forensics behind the great detective's greatest cases.* Hoboken, NJ: John Wiley & Sons, Inc.

Waithe, M. E. (1987a). Arete, Asclepigenia, Axiothea, Cleobulina, Hipparchia, and Lasthenia. In M. E. Waithe (Ed.), *A history of women philosophers* (pp. 197–209). Boston: Martinus Nijhoff.

Waithe, M. E. (1987b). Early Pythagoreans: Themistoclea, Theana, Arignote, Myia, and Damo. In M. E. Waithe (Ed.), *A history of women philosophers* (pp. 11–18). Boston: Martinus Nijhoff.

Waithe, M. E. (1989). Heloise. In M. E. Waithe (Ed.), *A history of women philosophers. Vol. II Medieval, Renaissance and Enlightment women philosophers A.D. 500–1600* (pp. 67–83). Boston: Kluwer Academic.

Walker, P. N. (1973). *Punishment: An illustrated history.* New York: Arco.

Wallace, W. A. (1993). *Theories of personality.* Boston: Allyn & Bacon.

Wallerstein, R. S. (2006). One Psychoanalysis or Many? In A. M. Cooper (Ed.), *Contemporary psychoanalysis in America: Leading analysts present their work* (pp. 691–720). Arlington, VA: American Psychiatric Publishing, Inc. (original work published 1988)

Wampold, B. E. (2001). *The great psychotherapy debate: Models, methods, and findings.* Mahwah, NJ: Erlbaum.

Wapner, S. (1990). Introduction [to a series of papers on psychology at Clark University]. *Journal of the History of the Behavioral Sciences, 26,* 107–109.

Warburton, N. (2011). *A little history of philosophy.* New Haven, CT: Yale University Press.

Ward, J. (1876). An attempt to interpret Fechner's law. *Mind, old series 1,* 452–466.

Ward, L. (2010). *John Locke and modern life.* New York: Cambridge University Press.

Ware, M. E. (2006, November). *Oral Presentation,* Joint Nebraska Psychological Society/Association for Psychological and Educational Research in Kansas Teaching Conference, Fort Hays, KS.

Warren, H. (1921). In memory of Wilhelm Wundt. *Psychological Review, 28,* 166–169.

Washburn, D. A. (1997). The MacKay–Skinner debate: A case for "nothing buttery." *Philosophical Psychology, 10,* 473–479.

Washburn, D. A. (2010). The animal mind at 100. *The Psychological Record, 60,* 369–376.

Washburn, M. F. (1908). *The animal mind: A textbook of comparative psychology.* New York: Macmillan.

Washburn, M. F. (1916). *Movement and mental imagery.* New York: Houghton Mifflin.

Wasserman, E. A. (2013). Comparative cognition. In R. J. Nelson, S. J. Y. Mizumori, & I. B. Weiner (Eds.), *Handbook of psychology, Vol. 3: Behavioral neuroscience* (2nd ed., pp. 480–508). New York: John Wiley & Sons.

Watkin, J. (1998). Søren Kierkegaard's psychology of the self. *Journal of Psychology and Christianity, 17,* 362–373.

Watkins, J. W. N. (1965). *Hobbes's system of ideas.* London: Hutchinson University Library.

Watkins, L. R., & Maier, S. F. (2005). Glia and pain: Past, present, and future. In H. Merskey, J. D. Loeser, & R. Dubner (Eds.), *The paths of pain 1975–2005* (pp. 165–177). Seattle, WA: International Association for the Study of Pain Press.

Watrin, J. P., & Darwich, R. (2012). On behaviorism in the cognitive revolution: Myth and reactions. *Review of General Psychology, 16,* 269–282.

Watson, C. A. (2004). The Sartorial self: William James's philosophy of dress. *History of Psychology, 7,* 211–224.

Watson, F. (1915). The father of modern psychology. *Psychological Review, 22,* 333–353.

Watson, J. B. (1912, February). Instinctive activity in animals. *Harper's Magazine, 124,* 376–382.

Watson, J. B. (1913). Psychology as the behaviorist views it. *Psychological Review, 20,* 158–177.

Watson, J. B. (1919). *Psychology from the standpoint of a behaviorist.* Philadelphia: Lippincott.

Watson, J. B. (1924a). *Behaviorism.* New York: Norton.

Watson, J. B. (1924b). The place of kinesthetic, visceral and laryngeal organization in thinking. *Psychological Review, 31,* 339–347.

Watson, J. B. (1924c). The unverbalized in human behavior. *Psychological Review, 31,* 273–280.

Watson, J. B. (1926). What the nursery has to say about instincts. In C. Murchison (Ed.), *Psychologies of 1925* (pp. 1–34). Worcester, MA: Clark University Press.

Watson, J. B. (1928). *Psychological care of infant and child.* New York: Norton.

Watson, J. B. (1961). John Broadus Watson. In C. Murchison (Ed.), *A history of psychology in autobiography* (Vol. 3, pp. 271–281). New York: Russell and Russell.

Watson, J. B., & Rayner, R. (1920). Conditioned emotional reactions. *Journal of Experimental Psychology, 3,* 1–14.

Watson, J. D. (1968). *The double helix.* New York: New American Library.

Watson, R. I., Sr. (1966). The role and use of history in the psychology curriculum. *Journal of the History of the Behavioral Sciences, 2,* 64–69.

Watson, R. I. (Ed.). (1974/1976). *Eminent contributors to psychology* (2 vols.). New York: Springer.

Watson, R. I. (1978). *The history of psychology and the behavioral sciences: A bibliographic guide.* New York: Springer.

Watson, R. I., & Evans, R. B. (1991). *The great psychologists: A history of psychological thought* (5th ed.). New York: HarperCollins.

Watt, W. M. (1965). Al-Ghazali. In B. Lewis, Ch. Pellat, & J. Schacht (Eds.), *Encyclopedia of Islam* (Vol. 2, pp. 1038–1041). London: Luzac.

Watts, R. E. (1998). The remarkable parallel between Roger's core conditions and Adler's social interest. *Journal of Individual Psychology, 54,* 4–9.

Weber, E. H. (1978). *The sense of touch* (H. E. Ross, Trans.). New York: Academic Press. (Original work published 1834)

Weber, M. M. (1997). Alois Alzheimer, a coworker of Emil Kraepelin. *Journal of Psychiatric Research, 31,* 635–643.

Webster, R. J., Saucier, D. A., & Harris, R. J. (2010). Before the measurement of prejudice: Early psychological and sociological papers on prejudice. *Journal of the History of the Behavioral Sciences, 46,* 300–313.

Webster, S., & Coleman, S. R. (1992). Hull and his critics: The reception of Clark L. Hull's behavior theory. *Psychological Reports, 70,* 1063–1071.

Wegner, D. M. (2002). *The illusion of conscious will.* Cambridge, MA: MIT Press.

Weidman, N. (1994). Mental testing and machine intelligence: The Lashley-Hull debate. *Journal of the History of the Behavioral Sciences, 30,* 162–180.

Weinberger, J., Siegel, P., & Decamello, A. (2000). On integrating psychoanalysis and cognitive science. *Psychoanalysis & Contemporary Thought, 23,* 147–175.

Weiner, D. B. (1992). Philippe Pinel's "memoir on madness" of December 11, 1794: A fundamental text of modern psychiatry. *American Journal of Psychiatry, 149,* 725–732.

Weinstein, C. E., & Way, P. J. (2003). Educational psychology. In I. B. Weiner (Series Ed.) & D. K. Freedheim (Vol. Ed.), *Handbook of psychology: Vol. 1. History of psychology* (pp. 269–277). New York: Wiley.

Weishaar, M. E. (1993). *Aaron T. Beck.* Thousand Oaks, CA: Sage.

Weiss, A. P. (1924). Behaviorism and behavior I. *Psychological Review, 31,* 32–50.

Weiss, A. P. (1928). Behaviorism and ethics. *Journal of Abnormal and Social Psychology, 22,* 388–397.

Weiss, K. J. (2012). Classics in psychiatry and the law: Francis Wharton on involuntary confessions. *Journal of the American Academy of Psychiatry and Law, 40,* 67–80.

Weiss, R. (1989). The hedonic calculus in the Protagoras and the Phaedo. *Journal of the History of Philosophy, 27,* 511–529.

Welles, S. (Ed.). (1957). *The world's great religions.* New York: Time.

Wells, G. L., Memon, A., & Penrod, S. D. (2006). Eyewitness evidence: Improving its probative value. *Psychological Science in the Public Interest, 7,* 45–75.

Wennberg, B.-A., & Hane, M. (2005). Kurt Lewin's heritage: A possible breakthrough? *Gestalt Review, 9,* 245–270.

Wentworth, P. A. (1999). The moral of her story: Exploring the philosophical and religious commitments in Mary Whiton Calkins' self-psychology. *History of Psychology, 2,* 119–131.

Wertheimer, M. (Max). (1912). Experimentelle studien über das Sehen von Bewegung. *Zeitschrift für Psychologie, 61,* 161–265.

Wertheimer, M. (1934). On truth. *Social Research, 1,* 135–146.

Wertheimer, M. (1935). Some problems in the theory of ethics. *Social Research, 2,* 353–367.

Wertheimer, M. (1937). On the concept of democracy. In M. Ascoli & F. Lehmann (Eds.), *Political and economic democracy* (pp. 271–283). New York: Norton.

Wertheimer, M. (1940). A story of three days. In R. N. Anshen (Ed.), *Freedom: Its meaning* (pp. 555–569). New York: Harcourt Brace.

Wertheimer, M. (1950). Numbers and numerical concepts in primitive peoples. In W. D. Ellis (Ed.), *A source book of Gestalt psychology* (pp. 265–273). New York: Humanities Press. (Original work published 1912)

Wertheimer, M. (1982).*Productive thinking* (M. Wertheimer, Ed.). Chicago: University of Chicago Press. (Original work published 1945)

Wertheimer, M. (Michael). (1961). Psychomotor coordination of auditory and visual space at birth. *Science, 134,* 1962.

Wertheimer, M. (1972). *Fundamental issues in psychology.* New York: Holt, Rinehart and Winston.

Wertheimer, M. (1978). Humanistic psychology and the humane but tough minded psychologist. *American Psychologist, 33,* 739–745.

Wertheimer, M. (1980a). Historical research—why? In J. Brozek & L. J. Pongratz (Eds.), *Historiography of modern psychology* (pp. 3–23). Toronto, Canada: C. J. Hogrefe.

Wertheimer, M. (1980b). Max Wertheimer, Gestalt prophet. *Gestalt Theory, 2,* 3–17.

Wertheimer, M. (1983). Gestalt theory, holistic psychologies and Max Wertheimer. *Personale Psychologie, 5,* 32–49.

Wertheimer, M. (1985). A Gestalt perspective on computer simulations of cognitive processes. *Computers in Human Behavior, 1,* 19–33.

Wertheimer, M. (1986). The annals of the house that Ebbinghaus built. In F. Klix & H. Hagendorf (Eds.), *Human memory and cognitive capacities: Mechanisms and performance.* Amsterdam: Elsevier Science.

Wertheimer, M. (1987). *A brief history of psychology* (3rd ed.). New York: Holt, Rinehart and Winston.

Wertheimer, M., King, D. B., Peckler, M. A., Raney, S., & Schaef, R. W. (1992). Carl Jung and Max Wertheimer on a priority issue. *Journal of the History of the Behavioral Sciences, 28,* 45–56.

Wertheimer, M., & Schulte, H. (Trans.). (1986). An attempt at a theory of the paranoid ideas of reference and delusion formation.*Gestalt Theory, 8,* 231–255. (Original work published 1924)

Wertsch, J. V. (1985). *Vygotsky and the social formation of mind.* Cambridge, MA: Harvard University Press.

Westheimer, G. (1999). Gestalt theory reconfigured: Max Wertheimer's anticipation of recent developments in visual neuroscience.*Perception, 28,* 5–15.

Westman, R. S. (1986). The Copernicans and the churches. In D. C. Lindberg & R. L. Numbers (Eds.), *God and nature: Historical essays on the encounter between Christianity and science* (pp. 76–113). Berkeley: University of California Press.

Wheeler, W. M. (1906). The queen ant as a psychological study. *Popular Science Monthly, 68,* 291–299.

Wheelock, L. D., & Callahan, J. L. (2006). Mary Parker Follett: A rediscovered voice informing the field of human resource development. *Human Resource Development Review, 5,* 258-273.

Whitaker, H., Smith, C. U. M., & Finger, S. (Eds.). (2007). *Brain, mind, and medicine.* New York: Springer.

White, A. D. (1910). *A history of the warfare of science with theology in Christendom* (2 vols.). New York: D. Appleton and Co. (Original work published 1896)

White, A. D. (1978). *A history of the warfare of science with theology in Christendom* (2 vols.). Gloucester, MA: Peter Smith. (Original work published 1896)

White, S. H. (1992). G. Stanley Hall: From philosophy to developmental psychology. *Developmental Psychology, 28,* 25–34.

Whitehead, A. N. (1968). *Modes of thought.* New York: The Free Press. (Original work published 1938)

Whitehead, A. N. (1971). *The concept of nature.* New York: Cambridge University Press. (Original work published 1920)

Whitehead, A. N. (1979). *Process and reality.* New York: Free Press.

Wichler, G. (1961). *Charles Darwin, the founder of the theory of evolution and natural selection.* New York: Pergamon Press.

Wiggins, B. J. (2009). William James and methodological pluralism: Bridging the qualitative and quantitative divide. *Mind and Behavior, 30,* 165–184.

Wight, R. D. (1993). The Pavlov-Yerkes connection: What was its origin? *Psychological Record, 43,* 351–359.

Wigmore, J. H. (1909). Professor Münsterberg and the psychology of testimony. *Illinois Law Review, 3,* 399–445.

Wilkins, J., & Matson, J. L. (2009). History of treatment in children with developmental disabilities and psychopathology. In J. L. Matson, F. Andrasik, & M. L. Matson (Eds.), *Treating childhood psychopathology and developmental disabilities* (pp. 3–28). New York: Springer Science + Business Media.

Wills, F. (2009). *Beck's cognitive therapy: Distinctive features.* New York: Routledge/Taylor & Francis Group.

Wilson, A. N. (1997). *Paul: The mind of the apostle.* New York: Norton.

Wilson, E. O. (2000). *Sociobiology: The new synthesis* (25th anniversary ed.). Cambridge, MA: Belknap Press. (Original work published 1975)

Windholz, G. (1984). Pavlov vs. Köhler: Pavlov's little known primate research. *Pavlovian Journal of Biological Science, 19,* 23–31.

Windholz, G. (1990). Pavlov, psychoanalysis, and neurosis. *Pavlovian Journal of Biological Science, 25,* 48–53.

Windholz, G. (1997). Ivan P. Pavlov: An overview of his life and psychological work. *American Psychologist, 52,* 941–946.

Winston, A. S. (1990). Robert Sessions Woodworth and the "Columbia Bible": How the psychological experiment was redefined. *American Journal of Psychology, 103,* 391–401.

Winston, A. S. (2003). *Defining difference: Race and racism in the history of psychology.* Washington, DC: American Psychological Association.

Winston, A. S. (2006). Robert S. Woodworth and the creation of an eclectic psychology. In D. A. Dewsbury, L. T. Benjamin, & M. Wertheimer (Eds.), *Portraits of pioneers in psychology* (Vol. 6, pp. 51–66). Washington, DC: American Psychological Association.

Winter, I. J. (1976). *Montaigne's self-portrait and its influence in France, 1580–1630.* Lexington, KY: French Forum.

Wisdom, J. O. (1943). Determinism and psychoanalysis. *International Journal of Psychoanalysis, 24,* 140–147.

Wolberg, A. (1989). Pilgrim's process through the psychoanalytic maze. *Psychoanalysis and Psychotherapy, 7,* 18–26.

Wolf, T. H. (1973). *Alfred Binet.* Chicago: University of Chicago Press.

Wollstonecraft, M. (1929). *Mary Wollstonecraft's the rights of woman/John Stuart Mill the subjection of women.* New York: Dutton. (Original work published 1792)

Wolpe, J. (1958). *Psychotherapy by reciprocal inhibition.* Stanford, CA: Stanford University Press.

Wolpe, J., & Plaud, J. J. (1997). Pavlov's contributions to behavior therapy: The obvious and the not so obvious. *American Psychologist, 52,* 966–972.

Wong, W. (2010). Retracing the footsteps of Wilhelm Wundt: Explorations in the disciplinary frontiers of psychology and in Völkerpsychologie. *History of Psychology, 12,* 229–265.

Wood, N. (1968). Niccolò Machiavelli. In D. Sills (Ed.), *International encyclopedia of the social sciences* (Vol. 9, pp. 505–511). New York: Macmillan and Free Press.

Woodworth, R. S., & Schlosberg, H. (1954). *Experimental psychology* (Rev. ed.). New York: Henry Holt.

Woody, W. D. (2001). Gestalt psychology and William James. In F. Columbus (Ed.), *Advances in psychology research* (Vol. 4, pp. 33–48). Huntington, NY: Nova Science.

Woody, W. D., & Viney, W. (2009). A pluralistic universe: An overview and implications for psychology. *Mind and Behavior, 30,* 107–120.

Woolley, B. (1999). *The bride of science: Romance, reason, and Byron's daughter.* New York: McGraw-Hill.

Worburton, N. (2011). *A little history of philosophy.* New Haven, CT: Yale University Press.

Workman, L., & Reader, W. (2008). *Evolutionary psychology: An introduction.* New York: Cambridge University Press.

Wright, P. (2005). George Combe—phrenologist, philosopher, psychologist (1788-1858). *Cortex: A Journal Devoted to the Study of the Nervous System and Behavior, 41,* 447–451.

Wundt, W. (1876). Central innervation of consciousness. *Mind, old series 1,* 161–178.

Wundt, W. (1901). *Ethics* (E. B. Titchener, J. H. Guilliver, & M. F. Washburn, Trans.). New York: Macmillan. (Original work published 1892)

Wundt, W. (1907). *Lectures on human and animal psychology* (J. Creighton & E. B. Titchener, Trans.). New York: Macmillan. (Original work published 1863)

Wundt, W. (1916). *Elements of folk psychology* (E. L. Schaub, Trans.). New York: Macmillan.

Wundt, W. (1969a). *Outlines of psychology* (C. H. Judd, Trans.). St. Clair Shores, MI: Scholarly Press. (Original work published 1897)

Wundt, W. (1969b). *Principles of physiological psychology* (5th ed., Vol. 1). (E. B. Titchener, Trans.). New York: Kraus Reprint Co. (Original work published 1873; 5th ed. published 1910)

Wundt, W. (1973). *An introduction to psychology.* New York: Arno Press. (Original work published 1912)

Wundt, W. (1977). Lectures on human and animal psychology. In D. N. Robinson (Ed.), *Significant contributions to the history of psychology 1750–1920: Series D: Comparative psychology* (Vol. 1). Washington, DC: University Publications. (Original work published 1894)

Wyatt, W. J. (2000). Behaviorial science in the crosshairs: The FBI file on B. F. Skinner. *Behavioral and Social Issues, 10,* 101–109.

Yerkes, R. M. (1900). The formation of habits in the turtle. *Popular Science Monthly, 58,* 519–525.

York, G. K., III. (2011). Comment: Lucretius the Epicurian neurologist. *Neurology, 77*(10), 1003.

Yost, E., & Gilbreth, L. M. (1944). *Normal lives for the disabled.* New York: Macmillan.

Young, P. T. (1972). An eclectic in psychology. In T. S. Krawiec (Ed.), *The psychologists* (Vol. 1, pp. 325–355). New York: Oxford University Press.

Young, R. M. (1966). Scholarship and the history of the behavioral sciences. In A. C. Crombie & M. A. Hoskin (Eds.), *History of science* (Vol. 5). Cambridge: W. Heffner & Sons.

Young-Bruehl, E. (2008). *Anna Freud: A biography* (2nd ed.). New Haven, CT: Yale University Press.

Young-Bruehl, E. (2012). Anna Freud: The teacher, the clinician, the person. In N. T. Malberg & J. Rapael-Leff (Eds.), *The Anna Freud tradition: Lines of development—Evolution of theory and practice over the decades* (pp. 10–13). London, England: Karnac Books.

Youniss, J. (2006). G. Stanley Hall and his times: Too much so, yet not enough. *History of Psychology, 9,* 224–235.

Zagorin, P. (1968). Thomas Hobbes. In D. L. Sills (Ed.), *International encyclopedia of the social sciences* (Vol. 6, pp. 481–487). New York: Macmillan.

Zargaran, A., Mehdizadeh, A., Yarmohammadi, H., & Mohagheghzadeh, A. (2012). Zoroastrian priests: Ancient Persian psychiatrists. *The American Journal of Psychiatry, 169,* 255.

Zeigarnik, A. Z. (2007). Bluma Zeigarnik: A memoir. *Gestalt Theory, 29,* 256–268.

Zhuravel, V. A. (1995). From the history of the Bekhterev Psychoneurological Institute. *Journal of Russian and East European Psychiatry, 27,* 115–129.

Ziegler, P. (1991). *The black death.* Great Britain: Bath Press. (Original work published 1969)

Zilboorg, G. (1941). *A history of medical psychology.* New York: Norton.

Zilboorg, G. (1961). *Freud and religion.* Westminster, MD: Westminster Press.

Zimbardo, P. G. (2007). *The Lucifer effect: Understanding how good people turn evil.* New York: Random House.

Zitzlsperger, U. (2006). Women's identity and authoritarian force: Women pamphleteers of the German reformation. In H. Chambers (Ed.), *Violence, culture and identity: Essays on German and Austrian literature, politics and society* (Vol. 1, pp. 65–83). New York: Peter Lang Publishing.

Zubov, V. P. (1968). *Leonardo da Vinci* (D. H. Kraus, Trans.). Cambridge, MA: Harvard University Press.

Zucconi, A. (2008). From illness to health, well-being and empowerment: The person-centered paradigm shift from patient to client. In B. E. Levitt (Ed.), *Reflections on human potential: Bridging the person-centered approach and positive psychology* (pp. 131–146). Ross-on-Wye, England: PCCS Books.

Zusne, L. (1975). *Names in the history of psychology: A biographical sourcebook.* New York: Wiley.

Zusne, L. (1984). *Biographical dictionary of psychology.* Westport, CT: Greenwood Press.

PHOTO CREDITS

NAME INDEX

Page numbers in *italics* refer to reference section.

SUBJECT INDEX